CW00551861

THE SOPRANO:
A CULTURAL HISTORY

MATTHEW BOYDEN

Ragueneau
PUBLISHING THE ARTS

Also by Matthew Boyden

The Rough Guide to Classical Music

The Rough Guide to Opera

Opera: 100 Essential CDs

Classical Music: 100 Essential CDs

Icons of Opera

Richard Strauss

Beethoven and the Gothic

The Tenor: A Cultural History

For Rachel

Glück, das mir verblieb,
rück zu mir, mein treues Lieb.
Abend sinkt im Hag
bist mir Licht und Tag.

And for the other women in my life

Lucia, Amelie and Octavia

O süsser Heiland mein,
einst werd ich um dich sein.
In deiner Liebe Hut
werd ruhen ich so gut.

Ragueneau Press
7 Friars Mill
Bath Lane
Leicester
LE3 5BJ

hello@ragueneaupress.com
www.ragueneaupress.com

The Soprano: A Cultural History

Matthew Boyden

First Published 2023

Jacket Design by Lee Haynes © Ragueneau Press 2023

Typeset in Garamond Pro by Jill Sweet

Front Cover: Maria Callas performing as Norma, in 1964, at the Paris Opéra.

Back Cover: Portrait of Maria Jeritza as Brünnhilde, in *Die Walküre*, taken in Vienna, circa 1930, by Atelier Setzer.

ISBN: 978-1-3999-6040-3

Printed and Bound in the United Kingdom

Contents

Author's Note

This is the second in a series of five books on the human singing voice.[1] It is the most ambitious project of its kind, ever. It was originally to have been four volumes. During the writing of the present book, however, it became obvious that castrati, countertenors and the male soprano would require a volume of their own. It has been decided, in consequence, to end the series with *The Male Soprano: A Cultural History*, in around 2030 – at which time concepts of gender, and the legal, social and political status of gender-diverse people, might have moved beyond the present entrenchments. My editor asked early on why there was not going to be a separate volume on the mezzo-soprano and the contralto. My answer, then and now, is that the blurring of the voices and the repertoire is so great among female singers that any distinguishing between them would result in confusion and repetition. The same is *not* true of the baritone and the bass voices (although there is some overlapping), because there is a distinct and culturally significant resonance in the emergence (and codification) of the bass voice, particularly east of Vienna.

The general analytical criteria set out in the Author's Note for *The Tenor* apply equally to *The Soprano*. The same is not true conversely. There have been many books on sopranos. None of them – at least in English, French, Italian and German – has looked beyond the confines of the sung voice to the wider cultural issues effecting sopranos as women. This explains, in part, why *The Soprano* is considerably longer than *The Tenor*. Whereas a single chapter in the earlier book addressed gender and gender identity directly – as it relates to Russian culture and high male voices[2] – almost the entirety of this volume attaches to the history of sopranos within the ambit of what would now be considered the study of gender. It might be thought problematic for a man to be writing about women in the 21ˢᵗ century – although it's plainly fine for men to review the work of female composers and performers. A more subtle dilemma arises from the need for any serious history of the soprano to address the complex of circumstances in which women performed when reduced for most of history as inferior to men.

That polarity is made more complicated still by the pre-eminence of the male hegemony where it concerns repertoire. It's routine for scholars, critics and writers to re-invent the status of female composers prior to the latter years of the 20ᵗʰ century; the facts as they are recorded in libraries and archives across Europe and the

---

1   Boyden, Matthew (2021). *The Tenor: A Cultural History*. Ragueneau Press.
2   The politics of gender and voicing in Russia are more revealing where they concern the patriarchy. The issues concerning female singers in Russian (and Eastern European) culture as they have been defined by the masculine hegemony will be addressed in *The Bass: A Cultural History*.

United States are clear that the number of performances of works by women of music published prior to WWII would run to fewer than one tenth of a single per cent of everything performed. Conversely, there are *actual* anomalies in the traditional narrative where the history of composition is concerned. Bach's music, for example, plays almost no part in the book because little is known of the women who created it; the same is true of singers who might have warranted whole chapters, obviously Rosa Ponselle.

In any event, this book is about the culture of the soprano voice and the women who mastered it – not the people who composed for them. It is not a miscellany of anecdotes or record reviews, or an anthology of tributes to the "best" and most beloved singers. It concerns the music they sang only insofar as it furthers the subject and the narrative. Around twice as many singers are featured here than in the preceding volume; there have always been many more gifted sopranos than tenors. It is for this reason that there is no "View from the Pit," as closes *The Tenor*.

There are thousands of books on composers and their works; many others have been devoted to individual performers – particularly Maria Callas, whose centenary this book has been timed to commemorate. For singers active during the 20th century, there is only limited equivalence between those whose work warrants detailed consideration, their contemporary achievements and their lasting popularity. This is a *cultural* history, so each chapter's sum reaches further than its parts. Anyone keen to know more of the life and work of Elisabeth Schwarzkopf, for example, can read Alan Jefferson's biography in English, or a variety of alternatives in German. This book is about the soprano, not sopranos. It's important also to emphasise that it's part of a series; there is a lot of cross-referencing to *The Tenor* that preceded it, therefore – as there will be throughout the volumes to follow. Every tenor mentioned during the course of this book is featured in its predecessor. It is a function of the project's encyclopaedic ambition that, when complete, it will serve as the most comprehensive single-collection of its kind ever published. The cycle has been carefully planned to avoid repetition, therefore. For example, the peculiar nature of the French-language singing voice during the 20 years either side of 1900 is considered in detail in *The Tenor*, but not in *The Soprano* – because it is a constant across all voice-types. *The Tenor* features a detailed consideration of Manuel Patricio Rodríguez García – as a teacher, and a singer – so this volume does not need to. Conversely, body image occupies *The Soprano* only. The one sub-culture to which this book makes no substantive reference (beyond a limited consideration of silent film in Italy), is the soprano and the cinema.[3]

Unlike the tenor – for whom the relative limits of register, fach and repertoire are definitive – the soprano voice spans a much wider range of pitch and voice type. Within the broad family of "sopranos" there are four established vocal sub-families, all of them defined by trait, technique and training: the soprano, the mezzo-soprano, and the contralto. As the highest of the four primary fachs, the soprano register is commonly between C4 (as middle C) and C6 (the "high C" for sopranos), with some

---

3   While it was possible to add a chapter on film to *The Tenor*, the subject is simply too huge as it concerns sopranos and female voices in a single-volume history. It needs (and warrants) a substantial book of its own.

coloratura voices being able to reach as high as F7. Mezzo-sopranos are required to sing from A3 (as A below middle C) to B5, while contraltos, as the lowest of the female voices, have a range from F3 (as F below middle C) to F5. Within these broad categories there are a variety of sub-divisions, all of them defined by repertoire. Because the world's most famous soprano at the time of publishing is a fictional character called Tony, it's probably useful to set out a framework of term and title, as well as a metric for valuing individual voices, to ensure that repeating references make sense for readers not accustomed to the taxonomy of register and repertoire.

This book is *not* about opera singers – although opera plays a major part in the narrative; it is likely to assist readers to understand the analytical context by reference to operatic roles, however – the primary sources for which are Richard Boldrey's monumental *Guide to Operatic Roles & Arias* (which identifies more than 3,500 parts in 1,000 operas) and Rudolph Kloiber's *Handbuch der Oper*. While it is unnecessary for the reader to be able to read music, it will be useful to know that a number placed after a note (written as a capital letter) is the expression of (American) Standard Pitch Notation or International Pitch Notation, a method of specifying pitch through the combination of (1) a musical note and (2) a number identifying the octave.

The generic title "soprano" will, for the majority, identify anyone singing the core lyric repertoire, from Mozart's Donna Anna (*Don Giovanni*) to the title role in Puccini's *Manon Lescaut*. For modern audiences, a classic exemplar would be Mirella Freni, whose voice was easy, beautiful and focussed – though not especially large; it was better suited to roles that valued tone, line and diction above acrobatics and amplitude. The clouds are occupied by coloratura sopranos – specialists in singing music that sits high above the stave. Coloratura means "colouring" in Italian; as such, it is misapplied to a style of singing defined absolutely by the largely technical virtues of dexterity, ornamentation and elevation.[4] The coloratura repertoire reaches back to the 17th century, but its bella epoca spanned from the late 18th century, and the work of Vivaldi, Handel, Mozart (famously the Queen of the Night's aria "*Der Hölle Rache kocht in meinem Herzen*"[5]), and Gluck to the transformative operas of the bel canto era, and a generation of increasingly dramatic masterpieces by Rossini, Bellini and Donizetti. The taste for florid writing for high sopranos lapsed after the 1850s, but the 20th century saw periodic returns to fashion, memorably so in the form of Zerbinetta, a character in Richard Strauss's *Ariadne aux Naxos*. Other notable coloratura roles from after 1900 appear in Stravinsky's *Le Rossignol*,[6] Martinů's *Ariane*, Braunfels' *Die Vögel*,[7] Szymanowski's *Król Roger*[8] (Roxana), Ligeti's *Le Grand Macabre* (Venus, and Gepopo) and Bernstein's *Candide* (Cunégonde). Since 2000, Thomas Adès' *The Tempest* (Ariel) and *The Exterminating Angel* (Leticia Meynar) have stood out as masterpieces as well as voice-vehicles. It's important to remember that even though coloratura singing is associated with high notes, there are numerous mezzo, contralto and tenor roles that necessitate dexterity as well as reach. As an

---

4   The origins of the term, and the repertoire, are considered further below.
5   From *Die Zauberflöte*.
6   'The Nightingale.'
7   'The Birds.'
8   'King Roger'.

exemplar, the American Reri Grist[9] was an exceptional talent, who sailed through the lighter Italian, French and German coloratura repertoire with equal measures of personality, fluency and discipline – which extended to flawless diction. As an actress, Grist's talent separated her from many other relatively one-dimensional songbirds; she perceived her art as theatre as well as (and frequently as more than) *mere* singing.

Sopranos with the brightness and sweetness of timbre associated with coloratura, but without the high notes or the virtuosity are often referred to as soubrettes, with a range extending approximately from C4 to C6. The soubrette's tessitura sits lower than the lyric soprano and spinto[10] soprano and is commonly lighter in weight and tone. If Isolde and Turandot can be said to occupy one end of the spectrum, then Mozart's Susanna (*Le nozze di Figaro*), Despina (*Così fan tutte*) and Zerlina (*Don Giovanni*) occupy the other. One of the most popular and renowned soubrettes of the 20th century was Graziella Sciutti, who was able to project as an actress as well as a singer, and whose word-use remains a model of its kind.

The spinto (or lirico-spinto) soprano shares the same ground as the spinto tenor, with a sensibility that calls for a darker timbre as well as brightness and a ready extension. Obvious examples in the Italian repertoire include Leonora (in *Il trovatore*) Aida, Madelena de Coigny (*Andrea Chénier*), and Tosca; among German works, Beethoven's Leonore (*Fidelio*) Elsa (*Lohengrin*) and Elisabeth (*Tannhäuser*) are typical. Among German singers, Lotte Lehmann and Elisabeth Grümmer represented the ideal; for Italian opera, Renata Tebaldi and Leontyne Price were exceptional by any standards. These singers had powerful voices, but they used them with care, refusing to force (or risk harming) instruments that were naturally of a size that abjured distension and shouting. The most powerful of the soprano voices is set commonly in opposition with the largest orchestras, and the densest of orchestrations. It's unusual for dramatic sopranos to be asked to sing anything higher than a B6, and their vocal tone will need to be darker and more resonant in the centre of its tessitura. The father of the dramatic soprano was Wagner, whose Sieglinde (*Die Walküre*), Brünnhilde (*Siegfried, Die Walküre* and *Götterdämmerung*), Isolde (*Tristan und Isolde*) and Kundry (*Parsifal*) cast the die that climaxed with the work of the Swedish soprano, Birgit Nilsson. She was acclaimed also in Strauss' more stentorian operas (*Elektra, Salome*, and *Die Frau ohne Schatten*) as well as Puccini's Minnie in *La fanciulla del West* and, most famously of all, *Turandot*.

There is inevitably some cross-over as between these voice types. Maria Callas sang Norma and Anna Bolena, as well as Isolde and Tosca; Price sang in operas by Monteverdi and Handel, Ravel, Poluenc and Barber – as well as "bread and butter" work by Verdi and Puccini. Birgit Nilsson recorded the role of Donna Anna *twice*. A certain amount of sfumato has always characterised the work of mezzo-sopranos and contraltos, for whom there is neither rule nor regulation when it comes to range and repertoire. The dramatic mezzo-soprano was primary for Rossini, who composed many of his finest characters for mezzos (including Angelina in *La Cenerentola*, and Rosina in *Il barbieri di Siviglia*); the mezzo was *en vogue* for almost every significant French composer for most of the 19th century, spanning *Carmen* (Bizet), *Béatrice*

---

9   29 February, 1932 –

10   Meaning "pushed" – to describe a more dramatic and powerful lyric voice.

et Bénédict, *La damnation de Faust*, and *Les Troyens* (Berlioz), *Charles VI* (Halévy), *Mignon* (Thomas), *Samson et Dalila* (Camille Saint-Saëns), *Don Quichotte*, and *Werther* (Massenet). The versatility of certain mezzo-sopranos has enabled them to sing a much wider range of repertoire than pure sopranos – such as Christa Ludwig, who was able to perform Mahler's *Das Liede von der Erde*, Kundry, and lengthy excerpts as Isolde and Brünnhilde with the same security, intensity and colour that characterised her stage and studio performances as Cherubino (*Le nozze di Figaro*), Despina and Zerlina. Contraltos are a shade darker still, and stand in range beside (or in competition with) counter-tenors and male sopranos – even if their repertoires rarely, if ever, overlap. Handel, Rossini and Donizetti wrote numerous excellent roles for contralto, and even if it was unusual for contraltos to be given the lead (at least on stage), almost every major composer of opera and song wrote splendidly for the lowest of the female voices. Some, like Mahler and Britten, attached themselves to individual performers, including Kathleen Ferrier, for whom Britten composed *The Rape of Lucretia*.

Hundreds of sopranos are considered during the course of this book; many of them will be unknown even to serious devotees and collectors; some will complain that a cherished artist has been left out. As was true of *The Tenor*, it has not been possible within a single volume to consider more than those about whom something meaningful can be said; mere quality alone (or favoured status) has not been sufficient to admit a large number of singers who made recordings or gave celebrated performances. Everyone has been included for a reason; whether the reader agrees with the resulting *dramatis personae* is a construction of taste and prejudice – as it has been for the author. Again, record labels and disc numbers have not been included because there are excellent catalogues and databases available digitally and in print. The same is true of recordings, the majority of which can be heard online through a variety of (mostly) free-to-use services. Opera titles (and the title of any published work) are in italics and capitalised. Title roles are in plain text, as is any regularly used non-English descriptor (such as vibrato, bel canto, portamento, verismo *etc.*). References to localised institutions and venues (such as the Wiener Staatsoper or La Scala, Milan) are in English as well as their original to allow for syntactical variety. All translations into English are by the author, unless otherwise indicated.

16 April, 2023
Palazzo Negri, Verona

Preface – Anatomy of a Muse

In August, 1975, Carolee Schneemann presented a series of "happenings" in East Hampton, New York, at the *Women Here and Now* exhibition to audiences consisting primarily of women artists. Schneemann's "performance" began when she approached a long table carrying a book and two bed sheets. Having undressed, and wrapped herself in one of the sheets, Schneemann climbed onto the table and announced that she would be reading from her book, *Cézanne, She was a Great Painter*. Schneemann proceeded to disrobe, and after applying dark paint to her face and body she adopted a series of "action poses".[1] While standing naked, and with her legs apart, she drew from her vagina a scroll of paper onto which she had written a rambling text, taken from *Kitch's Last Meal*, a Super-8 film Schneemann had begun in 1973. It was later confirmed that Schneemann was attempting to distinguish female intuition and appearance from traditionally "male" notions of order and rationality, a narrative that operated in the absence of male archetypes and, of course, men. Schneemann's "performance" was over the moment it was finished. It was an event that could not be transcribed or repeated since it attached absolutely and inextricably to Ms Schneemann and *her* vagina.

190 years earlier, Mozart and Da Ponte set out to create in *Le nozze di Figaro* a similarly purposed commentary on the male and the female, through cyphers as real and as identifiable as Schneemann's were abstruse, detached and transitory. Marcellina's Act 4 lament that male and female sheep and goats were able to get along while "rational" humans were not[2] echoed throughout a work that revealed more of the feminine and the female than any number of women pulling any number of things from their vaginas. The differences between men and women as Mozart and Da Ponte saw them in their presumed superiority as totems of a patriarchal society are as resolute today as they were for Beaumarchais. Their translation of the ways, means, virtues and vices of human nature to a work of theatre was at no point undermined by their unavoidable maleness; indeed, Mozart's score reveals infinite shades of grey through music of kaleidoscopic, gender-less vibrancy. It speaks to the petty and the mean (Marcellina and Susanna's duet "*Via Resti Servita*") as well as the humble and the profound (the Count's plea to the Countess "*Contessa Perdono…*"), and it forms a three-dimensional space through which a million generations might better learn what it is to be human.[3]

---

1 Schneemann, Carolee (1997). *More Than Meat Joy: Performance Works and Selected Writings*. McPherson, p. 235.

2 "*Il capro e la capretta*" ['The goat and the nanny'].

3 See generally Andrews, Richard (2001). *From Beaumarchais to Da Ponte: A New View of the Sexual Politics of "Figaro"*. Music & Letters, Vol. 82, No. 2 (May). pp. 214–233.

For Schneemann, Mozart's formalist celebration of a gendered dynamic was problematic. Her films *Fuses 1964–7* (based on footage of Schneemann and her partner making love) were typical of her conviction, and her insistence, that the body was explicitly sexual and primary as a means of communication. It's accepted that the 1970s' identification of the body as a source of knowledge and experience (and as a vehicle for the tracing of lost and forgotten cultures) was meaningful for the emerging women's movement. The 'vulvic space', as Schneemann called it, resonated:

> as a translucent chamber of which the serpent was an outward model: enlivened by its passage from the visible to the invisible, a spiralled coil ringed with the shape of desire and generative mysteries, attributes of both female and male sexual powers. This source of 'interior knowledge' would be symbolized as the primary index unifying spirit and flesh […] the source of conceptualising, of interacting with materials, of imagining the world and composing its images.[4]

There is a great deal one might say of this; most of it is better left unsaid. But for writing as she did, anyone seeing (or reading about) Schneemann's performance would have struggled to discern her intentions when reciting vulvic doggerel in her birthday suit. In the alternative, Mozart's scandalous transformation of the chaste admiration of a 13-year-old boy for the sentimental affections of his godmother into a study in erotic obsession was more radical still than *La folle journée* because it used music to sweeten pills that many refused flatly to swallow. The vocalising of contemporary tensions between gender and class enabled women in particular to transcend the barriers (and, in Cherubino's case, the corsets) with which the majority struggled in 18th century Europe. The soprano, in particular, was one of the few professional roles and occupations in which a woman might stand inviolate, even with men willing to castrate their children to keep some skin in the game.

The story of the soprano reaches considerably further than singing, therefore, just as a history of women equates to more than a flipbook of vaginas. The reduction of the female to sound and appearance is damaging and misrepresentative, even if the soprano is, at its simplest, a coterminous construction of singing and, when heard in the theatre, acting. Unlike male voices and singers, sopranos continue to be the subject of complex social, psychological and memetic influences that owe nothing to the art and profession of singing. Tenors, baritones and basses occupy a narrower emotional and intellectual space than sopranos because male voices resonate with centuries of unthinking patronage. Every significant composer of opera was male; not until 2019 did a female composer (Olga Neuwirth) see her work performed on the stage of the Vienna Staatsoper.[5] So too has every notable librettist and every important conductor of opera been a man. Until some years into the 20th century most

---

4   Schneemann, Carolee (1997). *More Than Meat Joy: Performance Works and Selected Writings.* McPherson, p. 234.

5   Depressingly for some, it was a setting of Virginia Woolf's 1928 novel *Orlando*. A number of critics had hoped that the first opera by a woman at the Staatsoper might have confronted something other than themes of gender fluidity and duality.

teachers of singing were men. Zaha Hadid was the first woman to be commissioned to design a major opera house, in Guangzhou, China – in 2010.[6] Even the artists engaged to paint, photograph and film singers were male until relatively late into the 20th century.

Ezra Pound held that music decays when it moves too far from the dance, and that poetry decays when it neglects to sing; it may be said by context that painting decays when it fails to speak. Purposive inarticulacy was an integral feature of the representation of sopranos as individuals for most of their history. The first to be captured by a significant portraitist was Barbara Strozzi,[7] one of only two women to be recognised during the seventeenth-century in Italy as a composer.[8] She was the daughter of the celebrated poet Giulio, whose final will, written in 1650, recognised "*Barbara di Santa Sofia, mia figliuola elettiva, e per chiamata comunemente la Strozzi*".[9] This designation alluded to Barbara's illegitimacy at birth,[10] a status her father disregarded from as early as 1634, when he invited her to sing informally at his home in Venice for the elite among local writers, musicians and travellers. Giulio was himself born illegitimate, and his achievements as an imported member of the ancient Florentine Strozzi family were prodigious. He composed libretti for Claudio Monteverdi, Francesco Cavalli, Francesco Manelli, and Francesco Sacrati, and his friendship with dramatists and poets produced a number of commissions for Barbara – as a composer as well as a singer. Nicolò Fontei, for example, was inspired by Strozzi to compose two volumes of songs (his *Bizzarrie poetiche* of 1635 and 1636) to words by her father.[11]

In 1637, Giulio recognised Barbara's talent publicly when establishing the *Accademia degli Unisoni*, through which he presented his daughter to a membership that featured almost everyone associated with the evolving art of the libretto in Venice during the 1640s – the decade when opera was finally established as a repeating, seasonal event. The Academy's motto was *Ignoto Deo*,[12] a loaded nod to a necessarily genderless platform that collided head-on with an Academy publication, *Le Veglie de' Signori Unisoni*,[13] which was dedicated to Barbara. By adding the word "Signori" to *Unisoni*, the Academy employed sledgehammer wit when referencing the circumscribed gender of its membership while coincidentally attaching to the radicalism of a programme that advocated the entitlement of women to perform in equivalence with men – more than 160 years before the publication of Mary Wollstonecraft's

---

6 The House opened on 9 May, 2010.

7 6 August, 1619 – 11 November, 1677.

8 The other was Strozzi's contemporary, Francesca Caccini (18 September, 1587 – [a date after] 1641). Her *La liberazione di Ruggiero* (her only surviving stage work) is the earliest known opera by a woman composer.

9 'Barbara of Santa Sofia, my elective daughter, and commonly known as Strozzi.'

10 She was baptised 'Barbara Valle'. Strozzi appears not to have used her surname until 1638, when previously she was merely "*la virtuosissima cantatrice*".

11 See generally Rosand, Ellen (1978). *Barbara Strozzi, "virtuosissima cantatrice": The Composer's Voice*. Journal of the American Musicological Society, Vol. 31, No. 2, pp. 241–281.

12 'The unknown god' ("Agnostos Theos"). This originates with the Apostle Paul's speech in Athens, as it was recorded in Acts 17:23. Paul is said to have seen an altar with an inscription dedicated to the Unknown god, and because the Jewish God could not be named, Paul's audience considered his deity to be "the unknown god above all others."

13 'The Vigils of Men United' (1638).

A Vindication of the Rights of Woman. Proto-feminism was fashionable at the time in Venice, and it suited what Ellen Rosand has identified as the Academy's "*brand of salacious iconoclasm*."[14] The Academy's motto appears on the title page of Gian Francesco Loredano's almost pornographic *Sei dubbi amorosi*[15] as an inscription on the base of a veiled statue which Loredano identifies as the *unknown woman* seeking answers to questions no-one other than a man would dare ask in print. Barbara Strozzi was plainly alive to the erotic, and a number of anonymous satires lampooned her elevated status by correlating the art of music when made by women with the arts of love when sold to men. The *Satire e altre raccolte per l'Academia de gl'Unisoni in casa di Giulio Strozzi*[16] contains the slanderous "*Bella cosa donare i fiori dopo aver dispensati i frutti*"[17] and the even less subtle "*è come educata in libertà passarvi il tempo con qualche amore ella nondimeno impiega tutte le sue affettioni in un castrato*"[18]

When being painted during the 1630s by her distant relative, Bernardo Strozzi (known as *il Cappuccino*[19] and *il Prete Genovese*[20]), Barbara was no more than 21 years of age. By modern standards she appears much older. Her cheeks have been rouged, either by the painter or when she was preparing to sit; either way, her blushes are presumed to have been well-earned. She is seen holding an instrument with which she was presumably expert,[21] while leaning next to an open folio of sheet-music, below which sits a viola da braccio.[22] The music is a duet, suggesting that Strozzi is waiting for (and unable to perform without) someone else.[23] She is wearing a flamboyant red-silk dress, with a lace blouse; she has a ring on her right hand and jewelled bracelets on both wrists. Most strikingly, the left of her ample breasts is exposed almost entirely. The right is partially covered, with the nipple fully visible. The parsing of her breasts with silk, and the addition of flowers to her hair cast Strozzi

---

14   Rosand, Ellen (1978). *Barbara Strozzi, "virtuosissima cantatrice": The Composer's Voice*. Journal of the American Musicological Society, Vol. 31, No. 2, pp. 241–281; p. 248.

15   'You are your amorous doubts' (1647). Loredano was plainly aware of Pietro Aretino's *Dubbi amorosi* from 1526, in which the poet engaged in erotic reflections using rhyming rhetoric. See Rosand, Ellen (1978). *Barbara Strozzi, "virtuosissima cantatrice": The Composer's Voice*. Journal of the American Musicological Society, Vol. 31, No. 2, pp. 248–249. In 2007, the composer Michael Nyman set some of Aretino's *Sonetti lussuriosi* to music, as *8 Lust Songs*. Aretino's texts were still sufficiently "obscene" in 2008 for concert programs created for a performance of Nyman's settings at the Cadogan Hall in London to be withdrawn by the promoters.

16   'Satire, and other collections for the *Accademia degli Unisoni* in the house of Giulio Strozzi' (1637).

17   'It is a fine thing to distribute the flowers after having already surrendered the fruit.'

18   'It is like being educated by someone who could pass the time with some lover while concentrating all of her affections on a castrato.'

19   It's worth noting that his nickname had nothing to do with coffee. The etymology of cappuccino is the Latin "Caputium", the diminutive form of *cappuccio* in Italian, which means "hood" or something covering the head (a "small capuchin", therefore). The origin of the word in its application to the drink is now attributed to the Capuchin friar, Marco d'Aviano – who was born fifty years after Strozzi.

20   'The Genoese Priest'. Strozzi also painted Barbara's father, Giulio, as well as Monteverdi and numerous other members of the *Accademia degli*.

21   Artemisia Gentileschi painted only two female musicians – one of them a self-portrait (*Self-Portrait as a Lute Player* (1616–1618); the other significant painting by Gentileschi of a musician was *Saint Cecilia* (1620), whom she portrayed (again) as a lutenist; neither is seen to be a singer, and neither is shown to play the instrument with which they are associated.

22   An early member of the violin family corresponding most obviously with the modern viola.

23   Braccio means "arm" in Italian, so that she is further seen waiting for the arms of another.

as the mythical Flora – the Roman goddess of springtime.[24] There is considerable precedent for this. Titian's *Flora* from 1515 employs posies and silk; it also reveals the model's left breast, leading some commentators to identify the sitter as a courtesan. Others have isolated marriage as thematic. Bartolomeo Veneto's *Idealized Portrait of a Courtesan as Flora* from 1520 (again with a single breast exposed) heightens the notion of love commercialised, while Francesco Melzi's allegory (also from 1520) balances the subject's partial nudity with the jasmine in her right hand, which was symbolic at the time of purity. Bernardo's painting of Barbara conveys a range of possible meanings.[25] It might simply have been intended as a figuration of music, or it could have been a product of the contemporary Venetian taste for *belle donne* for the sake of it. Whatever the objective, Barbara was not identified as its subject. The painting has been known for the longest time as *Suonatrice di viola da gamba*,[26] and while recent detective work[27] has established that it *is* a painting of Barbara Strozzi, the fact remains that Barbara – as the most highly regarded soprano in Venice at the time – was painted as something other than the finest soprano in Venice at the time.[28] Even her femininity is symbolic, so while it represents a facsimile of her facial features, it was not *actually* Barbara Strozzi. Even as one of the most celebrated women in Italy, her painting by a (distant) family member, when paid for by her father and with the presumed patronage of the *Unisoni*, adhered more generally to the role of women in contemporary Italian society. The idealisation of Strozzi reached beyond recognition, therefore, to ensure that the modification and enhancement of her features flattered the sitter while ensuring that her outward appearance reflected her inner beauty and allegorical worth. Of course, there had been progress; even if Strozzi's presentation as wealthy and talented was designed to extol Giulio before it did anything for Barbara, her portrait captured significant shifts in perception and status from a century earlier, when women had been represented routinely in profile as coinage.

45 years after Strozzi's death in 1677, Marie Pélissier[29] performed for the first time at the Paris Opéra. In 1726, she created the role of Thisbé in *Pirame et Thisbé*, by François Francoeur and François Rebel, after which she emerged as one of France's three most popular sopranos (her rivals being Catherine-Nicole Lemaure and Marie Le Rochois). For Jean-Philippe Rameau she created the roles of Aricia in *Hippolyte et*

---

24 The fullness of the red silk below her breasts might suggest that Strozzi was pregnant at the time; this would certainly reinforce the adoption of the mythical Flora and springtime as thematic.

25 Research from the 1990s revealed considerable detail of her financial dealings and her four children, three of whom were fathered by Giovanni Paolo Vidman, a colleague of Giulio and a supporter of early opera. See Glixon, Beth L. (1997). *"New light on the life and career of Barbara Strozzi"*. The Musical Quarterly 81(2); pp. 311–335; and Glixon, Beth L. (1999). *"More on the life and death of Barbara Strozzi"*. The Musical Quarterly 83(1); pp. 134–141.

26 'Player of the viola da gamba' (1635 – 1639).

27 See generally Rosand, David and Rosand, Ellen (1981). *"Barbara di Santa Sofia" and "Il Prete Genovese": on the Identity of a Portrait by Bernardo Strozzi*. The Art Bulletin, Vol. 63, No. 2; pp. 249–258.

28 For an overview of the portraiture of women in Italy (rather than of sopranos, of which there were essentially none) from a century earlier, see generally Christiansen, Keith; Weppelmann, Stefan and Rubin, Patricia Lee (2011). *The Renaissance Portrait: From Donatello to Bellini*. Metropolitan Museum of Art. In particular, the essays "Florence", "Some Thoughts on Likeness in Italian Early Renaissance Portraits", and "Understanding Renaissance Portraiture" provide excellent insights.

29 1706 / 1707 – 21 March, 1749.

Aricie (1733), Emilie in *Les Indes galantes* (1735), Telaira in *Castor et Pollux* (1737), and Iphise in both *Les fêtes d'Hébé, ou Les talents lyriques*[30] (1739) and *Dardanus* (1739). During the early 1730s she sat for François-Hubert Drouais, who painted her as Flora, with flowers in her hair, and a garland held between her hands. If her breasts are not actually exposed, then there is a considerable *décolletage*. Pélissier's reddened cheeks and enigmatic smile speak to the usual tropes. To one printing of an engraving of Pélissier, based on Drouais' painting, was added the words "[…] you give to the lyrical scene. Without you the opera are only concerts". There is no sign of a dramatic artist in either representation.[31]

Whenever female singers were painted during the decades and centuries that followed they were robbed of their art, their individuality and femininity. Matilde Juva Branca, an amateur soprano admired by Rossini, and known through her husband to Verdi, was painted by Francesco Hayez in 1851. The Venetian-born Hayez was a close associate of Verdi and Manzoni, and when accepting Giovanni Juva's commission he was well-aware of his client's literary circle, and of the famed beauty of his younger wife. For all its technical skill, which is formidable, the painting was widely condemned when it was first shown because of the entirely chilling image it presented. Matilde was a musician, albeit not employed as such; there is nothing lyrical in the face that stares back at the viewer. If Juva had wanted to present his wife to the salon, or record her beauty for posterity, then Hayez misunderstood his instructions. Matilde's expression is severe and unsmiling; her hands suggest she is relaxed; her lowered eyelids and hard-lined mouth speak to something other than happiness. She leans against a heavy ermine coat, which celebrates without ambiguity the power and influence of her husband. The dark silk dress and yet darker hair frame the appearance of someone in mourning, an effect which may well have resonated for a musician defined by an unhappy marriage.

Hayez was kinder to himself and to others – his self-portraits, his paintings of Rossini and Cavour, his Odalisques and, most famously, *The Kiss*, evidence a more sensitive eye and a gentler brush. There are a hundred different reasons for why his life-size portrayal of Matilde was numbing; whatever their formulation, the outcome was characteristic of an approach to the feminine when personified rather than imagined. The states occupied by Juliet, Bathsheba and Mary Magdelene drew warmth and expression from the infamously romantic Hayez, but Matilde is presented as a woman who appears never to have opened her mouth, whether to sing or to do anything else.

Hayez's Dutch-French contemporary, Ary Scheffer, was close friends with the husband of legendary mezzo-soprano Pauline Viardot. He became closer to Pauline with time, and she later remembered him as one of her most trusted confidants. He was part of the circles in which Viardot mixed with Sand, Chopin, Rossini, Gounod, Bertin, Berlioz and Liszt during the 1840s and '50s. Scheffer was particularly close to Liszt, who sent his son to the painter for training in 1855. He sat for Scheffer in

---

30 'The Festivities of Hebe, or The Lyric Talents'.

31 There were exceptions – inevitably. Rosalba Carriera's beautiful pastel portrait of Francesca Cuzzoni from the 1720s is outstanding. The otherwise dominant place of etchings as records of fact presumed that whatever happened on stage or in the salon was never likely to be referenced anywhere else.

1837, and it is one of the finest paintings of the composer-pianist.[32] The portrait captures the intensity and beauty of its subject, using almost precisely the same palette of colours employed by Hayez for Branca. The portrait enhances the elemental romanticism of Liszt and his era; it raises and celebrates the man's Promethean talent, and then with only four of his fingers on reluctant display. Scheffer's portrait of his friend Viardot is another matter entirely. She is rendered matronly and constrained, having been stitched into an unyielding black dress with a high white-lace neckline. Her hands are folded in front of her, and her hair is pulled harshly to her head. It was first shown more than a year after her legendary debut in London as Rossini's Desdemona, but the image is devoid of the erotic energy that colours Hayez's tribute to Liszt's transcendental sexuality – despite Viardot being considered one of the most exciting and passionate stage performers of the 19th century. She was equally admired as a pianist, with independent accounts from Liszt, Moscheles, Saint-Saëns and her teacher Anton Reicha[33] acclaiming her to be as talented as any of her male peers. Even if an observer didn't know anything about Liszt it would be reasonable to conclude from Scheffer's portrait that the subject was someone *like* Liszt. One would presume from his representation of Viardot that she was definitively a wife, a daughter or a mother. This was consistent, of course, with her status as "Madame Viardot", a formulation achieved at the age of 18 when she entered strategically into marriage with a man just months from his 40th birthday.[34]

Scheffer's portrait of Viardot was not typical of his paintings of women more generally,[35] which were sensual whenever the feminine was theoretical or fictional. He completed around a dozen versions of Dante's Francesca da Rimini, for example, the finest of which[36] is positively salacious – but since his model for Francesca is not identified other than through Dante her naked appearance as an ideal was acceptable to the moral minority. When thirty years later Thomas Dewing started to paint female "musicians" and "singers" he did so at a cultural and socially respectable distance, never painting an *actual* musician; instead, he pictured women holding or sitting next to instruments they are never seen to play. Ilya Repin's 1883 portrait of Alexandra Molas, a mezzo-soprano, presents a smiling, double-chinned, peasant-caricature with ruthless, aseptic efficiency. The only clue to Molas being anything to do with music or singing or the stage is the manuscript she is seen holding in her right hand. First shown in 1885, Henry Lerolle's *Organ Rehearsal* is wonderfully

---

32   Brody, Elaine (1985). *All in The Family: Liszt, Daniel and Ary Scheffer*. Nineteenth-Century French Studies. Vol. 13, No. 4. University of Nebraska Press, pp. 238–243.

33   One of Beethoven's best friends.

34   Viardot's marital status secured her respectability when the majority of husbands in Europe, Russia and the United States were at liberty to forbid their wives from performing in public. This common feature of 19th century life was employed by Sand for her *La Prima Donna* (1831), in which a soprano is forced by her husband to retire from the stage. Because Louis Viardot was an impresario, Pauline was assured absolute freedom to perform professionally. Indeed, it was Louis who abandoned his career as a theatre director to focus on managing his wife's career.

35   A painting of Viardot's sister, Maria Malibran, held by the museum of La Scala, Milan, fails to capture something of the younger woman's celebrated glamour. It is anonymous, probably at the request of the painter.

36   First shown in 1855 as *The Shades of Francesca da Rimini and Paolo Malatesta Appear to Dante and Virgil*. Now part of the collection at the Louvre.

stylised and well executed; so too is the singer's femininity. She appears to hover in a dress that must have made breathing, far less singing, extraordinarily difficult.[37] In 1897, John Singer Sargent was one of the first important portraitists to embrace the scandal of showing an identified woman with her mouth open[38] when he painted the amateur mezzo-soprano and socialite Mabel Batten in "performance." Considering Batten's reputation, it was probably more accurate than many appreciated at the time.

Just ten years later, Picasso presented *Les Demoiselles d'Avignon* as a shocking dissertation on women being paid to do something for which Batten didn't need the money. Of course, by 1907, Marie Wittich had more than once refused to kiss the mouth of the decapitated Jochanaan for Richard Strauss, so public sensibilities were evolving as rapidly as music and taste, even with "decency" blasting its trumpets against the gathering regiments. Wittich never sat for Egon Schiele and had she done so she would have kept her clothes on and her knees together. In June, 1903, the same year that Strauss completed *Salome*, the 23-year-old Viennese philosopher Otto Weininger caused a sensation with the publication of his misogynistic, Jewish-self-hating *Sex and Character*.[39] Ford Madox Ford wrote at the time of how

> one began to hear in the men's clubs of England and in the cafés of France and Germany – one began to hear singular mutterings among men. Even in the United States where men never talk about women, certain whispers might be heard. The idea was that a new gospel had appeared.[40]

Weininger's new gospel correlated the probable success and progress of Mankind with the necessary disavowal of womankind. Women – like Jews, to whom Weininger attached parallel status – were material beings corrupted by sensuousness, simple-mindedness, animalism and amorality. They could act only in accordance with a *"universalised, generalised instinct."*[41] Weininger's construction of the pre-eminence of the male over the female was brutally and hatefully expressed; it was also the prevailing point of view for the majority of men, who had little reason to overturn

---

37 It is conceded that corsets have been prized by *some* as an asset for the securing of the diaphragm.

38 Men and women painted male characters with their mouths open routinely, and for a host of reasons that spanned real-world, religious and mythological scenarios. A handful of women were painted and sculpted with their mouths open, as history or in allegory only. An obvious renaissance example is Titian's *The Penitent Magdalene* (1565); Baroque examples include Gentileschi's *Cleopatra* (1633–3) and her three versions of *Susanna and the Elders* (1610, 1622 and 1652), and Bernini's *The Ecstasy of Saint Theresa* (1645–52). Two hundred and fifty years later, Jean-Léon Gérôme was sufficiently disgusted by "L'affaire Dreyfus" to paint *La Vérité sortant du puits armée de son martinet pour châtier l'humanité* ['Truth coming from the well, armed with her whip to chastise mankind'], in which a woman (naked in truth) is seen emerging from the darkness gripped by rage (1896). For the curious, Raphael's *Saint Margaret and the Dragon* (1518) and Rubens' *The Hippopotamus and Crocodile Hunt* (1615–1616) contain open mouths of a different kind entirely.

39 Weininger, Otto (1903). *Geschlecht und Charakter: Eine prinzipielle Untersuchung.* Wilhelm Braumüller.

40 Ford Madox Ford (1918). *"Women and Men"*. The Little Review, 4, pp. 40–1; cited in Dijkstra, Bram (1986). *Idols of Perversity: Fantasies of Feminine Evil in Fin-de-Siecle Culture*, p. 218.

41 Kramer, Lawrence (1993). *"Fin-de-siècle Fantasies: 'Elektra', Degeneration and Sexual Science."* Cambridge Opera Journal, Vol. 5, No. 2; pp. 141–165.

the presumption that sustained their "natural" superiority. It's difficult to know how Weininger reconciled his hatred of women to his adoration of Beethoven, whose *Fidelio* came closer to operating as a feminist paeon than almost any other opera of the 19th century. On 3 October, 1903, Weininger rented a room at Schwarzspanierstrasse 15 in Vienna – the house in which Beethoven died in 1827. The following evening, Weininger committed suicide by shooting himself in the chest. His revulsion at the female was exacerbated by the direction in which contemporary art and music appeared to be headed. Although Richard Strauss was sympathetic to some of the philosopher's prejudices,[42] Weininger is unlikely to have approved of Strauss erotic veneration of the female through opera and song, and certainly not in the forms of Salome and Elektra. In any event, between 1806 (when the soprano Angelica Catalani was painted as a naif by Elisabeth-Louise Vigée Le Brun) and 1906[43] (when Henri Gervex painted Nellie Melba as an infant, flower-decked Ophelia), sopranos were subjected routinely by painters to sterilisation as artists, performers and women.

Things have moved on considerably – academically and socially – since the publication of Catherine Clément's ground-breaking *Opera, or the undoing of Women*[44], in which the author went to great and expressive pains to coruscate composers, poets and dramatists for their cruelties to women

> who die poisoned, gently; those who are choked; those who fold in on themselves peacefully. Violent deaths, lyrical deaths, gentle deaths, talkative or silent deaths [...] there is always that constant: death by a man.[45]

Clément's assertion that the "*result is fatal* [...] *just like real life*" was warranted in the 1970s; she erred, however, when drawing an analogy between the lyric stage and the realities it served to imitate. The 100 most popular works in the repertoire contain 131 named characters whose destiny it is to die;[46] 71 (54%) of them are male, 60 (46%) are female. Mozart, Verdi and Richard Strauss all created remarkable dramas around the fulcrum of patricide, with the murders of the Commendatore (*Don Giovanni*), the Marquis of Calatrava (*La forza del destino*), and Agamemnon (*Elektra*) leading directly to the deaths of Mozart's Don Juan, Verdi's Carlo, and Strauss' Aegisthus. Alvaro is redeemed only when Leonora dies, and Strauss kills Klytemnestra (off-stage) as well as her daughter through music that writhes and dances with black-hearted glee. The cliché that opera's narrative appetites have subsisted on femicide is less warranted than most presume, however. The actual picture is more complicated. In *Aida* and *Andrea Chénier*, for example, the eponymous lovers die alongside their paramours, and even the Guignol theatre of high romanticism and verismo involves at least as much cruelty being meted out to men as to women. In Massenet's *Werther*, it is the hero who dies, by his own hand, and even in that most purple of operas,

---

42 See (and hear) Strauss' portrayal of the Five Jews in *Salome*.
43 The precise date is uncertain. It is generally held to be "between 1906 and 1910".
44 First published in France, as "L'opéra ou la défaite des femmes", in 1979.
45 Clément, Catherine (1988). *Opera, or the undoing of Women*, trans. Betsy Wing. University of Minnesota Press. p. 47.
46 Not including named characters who die off stage, like Don José's mother and Nemorino's uncle, or those who are already dead, like Buoso Donati in *Gianni Schicchi*.

Pagliacci, Canio's murder of Nedda is attendant to his stabbing of Silvio. At the very least, it's a draw. In *Cavalleria rusticana*, the only character to die (off stage) is the tenor lead, Turiddu. Clément did not linger on Tosca's murder of Scarpia with a table knife because her actions operated as self-defence and contrary to Clément's narrative. Indeed, Tosca's decision to take her own life in the final scene is shocking only in its animation of Puccini's sadism. The composer believed profoundly in the axiom from *Il Tabarro* "*Chi ha vissuto per amore, per amore si mori.*"[47] Women die in nine of his twelve operas; four of them feature women committing suicide.[48] The only composer of opera whose oeuvre can be said to have hinged more completely on the predation of women was Alban Berg because he completed just two works, *Wozzeck* and *Lulu*, and both hinge on femicide.[49]

Excepting Puccini and Berg, the cliché that opera is built on a mound of female corpses is unfounded; it's undeniable, however, that the narrative impulse for many of its better-known exemplars have attached in a variety of ways to female suffering. Of the eight most frequently performed operas on the modern stage, six conclude with the death of the heroine: *La traviata*, *Carmen*, *La bohème*, *Tosca*, *Madama Butterfly* and *Rigoletto*.[50] On the other hand, not one of these dramas originated with its composer. Verdi, Bizet and Puccini relied in each case on established and popular novels and plays, whose authors were renowned for romanticising and fetishising violence against beautiful young women long before any of it was set to music.[51] The portrayal of women in some kind of pain or fear or subjugation has been consistent with the experiences of many throughout the lifetime of the art. Even so, the effect of operatic narratives in isolation was less damaging over time than the insidious manner in which sopranos were represented when not being strangled, suffocated, frozen and stabbed for art.

Roberta Montemorra Marvin's analysis of the portrayal of female singers in the *Illustrated London News* demonstrates the extent to which women were defined and determined by the manner in which men chose to portray them.[52] The *ILN* was pivotal, in particular, to the navigation for Victorian England of the unsteady dance between art, class and probity, with sopranos using their voices and bodies autonomously – in the service of exclusively male composers. Professional singers, particularly those specialising in opera, were transgressive in their defiance of status and station. The conjoining of applause and approbation as between the genders when a woman

---

47 'He who has lived for love, has died for love.' From the *scena* in which The Song Seller sings: "*Primavera, primavera, non cercare più i due amanti. là fra l'ombre della sera. Chi ha vissuto per amore, per amore si mori…*".

48 *Tosca, Madama Butterfly, Suor Angelica* and *Turandot*.

49 He did not, of course, complete *Lulu*, which remained unfinished at his death.

50 It's worth remembering that Verdi's Violetta and Puccini's Mimi both die from tuberculosis, as distinguished from acts of violence.

51 In order of popularity: *La Dame aux camélias* (1852), a play adapted by Alexandre Dumas *fils* from his novel of the same name (1848); *Carmen*, a novella by Prosper Mérimée (1845); *Scènes de la vie de bohème*, a "novel" by Henri Murger (1851); *La Tosca*, a play by Victorien Sardou (1887); *Madame Butterfly: A Tragedy of Japan*, a one-act play by David Belasco (1900); and *Le roi s'amuse*, a play by Victor Hugo (1832).

52 Marvin, Roberta Montemorra (2012). "Idealizing the Prima Donna in Mid-Victorian London". In *The Arts of the Prima Donna in the Long Nineteenth Century*. Ed. Cowgill, Rachel, and Poriss, Hilary. Oxford University Press, pp. 21–41.

was celebrated in a theatre for her successful appearance as the morally-objectionable Violetta undermined the established socio-economic prescriptions of what qualified as good and decent. The fantastical element attaching to singing (as opposed to speaking) generated valuable distance for men appalled and intimidated by the threat of female emancipation. That sense of unreality was exacerbated by the use of foreign languages, which only the educated and liberally-inclined were able to appreciate. A woman singing of her feelings in Italian was tolerable for the British because British-born men did not, as a rule, converse with their wives in Italian, and never as concerning their feelings.

Appearances mattered as a function of control. One Victorian commentator observed that by reason of a woman's

> habitual delicacy of mind and reserve of manner, dress becomes a sort of symbolic language – a kind of personal glossary – a species of body phrenology. [For anyone] proficient in the science, every woman walks about with a placard on by which her leading qualities are advertised.[53]

The pages of the *ILN* were filled with engravings of sopranos rendered either in costume (as "character" portraits) or as exemplars of polite and civilised society. The use of the former aided the offended and the fearful when distinguishing a woman from her purpose as a singer. The latter were designed to ensure a positive equivalence between the best of their kind and the worst as it was embodied by women judged for their "crimes" on stage. By way of summary, Marvin notes how:

> In these images visual and verbal portrayals exemplify the significance of physical traits and apparel as markers of character, virtue and ethnicity. During much of the Victorian era, conventional thinking suggested that a woman's moral and mental condition was reflected in her outward appearance. Facial features, bodily form and bearing, and clothing were coded in various ways, as attested by published manuals and journal articles in broadly distributed sources [...]. With regard to the role of morality in these ideas, facial features were understood to be manifestations of levels of normalcy and or deviancy or restraint or excess.[54]

For these reasons and many others, the life-story of the soprano records the experiences of musicians over centuries subjected culturally and socially to the prescriptions, whims and largesse of men. This continued beyond the decades during which Carolee Schneemann did her bit to fight back, and it will doubtless survive by adaptation beyond the date of this book's publishing. Of course, it is to be expected that Tucker Carlson and his Tuckermites would squeal and spume at the idea of art being reduced to the social mechanics of "woke" culture but since before the soprano

---

53 "The Art of Dress" (1852). *Quarterly Review*. John Murray, pp. 68–69.
54 Marvin, Roberta Montemorra (2012). "Idealizing the Prima Donna in Mid-Victorian London". In *The Arts of the Prima Donna in the Long Nineteenth Century*. Ed. Cowgill, Rachel, and Poriss, Hilary. Oxford University Press, p. 28.

was first coined as a word the experience of women as singers has supported no other conclusion than that gender has been definitive. The sexual and sensual ambiguities promulgated by the work of a tenor like Giacomo Lauri-Volpi or the baritone Ezio Pinza can be isolated only after the fact, and in the near-total ignorance of dubiety on the part of both men. The soprano's status as a woman has operated as a constant for the extraordinary journey from St. Paul's injunction that women be "silent" in the churches to the temple-felling wonder that was Birgit Nilsson. Anyone seeking a history of the soprano that ignores the female discourse as it has evolved since the 17th century should read elsewhere.

The complexity of what it is to "be" a soprano is amplified by the convolution of female identities either side of the proscenium arch. Only rarely are tenors called upon to play fathers; most perform as characters driven by variations on relatively one-dimensional themes of love, desire and revenge. Basses are required commonly to perform as fathers, and patrician figures of a certain age and authority. The soprano, on the other hand, is tasked with persuading as a village ingenue, a demi-god, a nun, a witch, a queen, a cowgirl and a priestess before she is recognisably a woman. A soprano is a grandmother, mother, daughter, sibling or wife before any consideration is given to her identity by name, nature and circumstance. During a routine career, an operatic soprano will travel across seasons navigating shades of chastity and sin, violence and sacrifice, cowardice and heroism, servitude and autocracy, compassion and revenge, despair and jubilation. She must appear on a Monday as a 13-year-old Capulet and on a Thursday as a French prostitute or a Gaulish druid, or as a young man with a penis. Verdi's middle-period operas – from *Luisa Miller* (1849) to *Simon Boccanegra* (1857) – speak to the composer's developing obsession with fathers' relationships with their daughters, and mothers with their sons. Whatever can be said of Manrico in *Il trovatore* as an heroic cypher, or as Leonora's lover, is less interesting than what flows from his relationship with Azucena. Something similar can be said of Violetta and Germont in *La traviata,* while *Rigoletto* is, of course, a study in paternal-filial dynamics that concludes with the father commissioning the murder of his child. A soprano performing as Gilda or as Violetta has to sing music as a daughter or a daughter-in-law with a father or a father-in-law that is equally as passionate as anything either woman sings when sharing the stage with anyone else. The romantic is subsumed to a complex of instincts that challenge a soprano to manoeuvre emotional and cultural intricacies while co-existing as a daughter, a lover, a wife, and a mother – states of being that trigger fractals of female experience spanning prejudice, activism, history, sexuality, religion, biology, politics and economics. The tenor performing as Alfredo, the Duke or Manrico will be a son; he might also be a brother, a lover and a father, but he will exist without choice in a culture that has for millennia perpetuated the primacy of men through admixtures of masculine certainty, cultural security, and social authority.

The place and resonance of the feminine and the female – in its transmission through the work of sopranos born as women – is manifest from the different vernaculars that continue to distinguish the genders when performing. It's to state the obvious that no-one has much cared how a man is dressed when he sings in concert or, for that matter, on stage. Men have always been forgiven their physical appearance because the male voice has operated as absolution. A miscellany of tenors of note who might objectively be considered handsome or beautiful would not fill a school bus, and yet women continue to be judged by their physical and sartorial appearance as adjuncts to their talent and art. The casting of a morbidly obese tenor, baritone or bass when appearing as a bohemian poet or painter starving in a French garret has never challenged the credulity of an audience. Even in the 21ˢᵗ century it is routine to hear ticket-holders (albeit never critics or professionals, of course) commenting on the size of the soprano singing the role of Puccini's Mimi, whose death from cold and consumption precludes her from being anything more than a size zero – presumably because opera is a construction of verisimilitude and naturalism.

A cursory glance at how sopranos have been presented by their record companies since the year 2000 cannot but provoke cynicism. Beauty sells, and it now absolves many footlight singers of weaknesses in tone, technique and talent that would not have been forgiven 40 years ago. It is a value-system that measures the worth of a book by its cover alone. The media's routine reporting that beauty is no longer homogenised has been greatly exaggerated, therefore. Even with Lizzo blowing her own flute for women refusing to conform to expectation, fat continues to be as much a feminist issue as the questionable authenticity of women submitting themselves to trowels and hawks before risking the scrutiny of appearance or publication. At a time when the world's most celebrated Jenner is a social media and reality-TV celebrity, rather than the scientist responsible for creating vaccines, the scale of the challenge facing women choosing to live their lives for art resists exaggeration.[55]

The same is true of the unequal manner in which women have for centuries been judged as hysterical or petulant while their male counterparts have engaged in behaviour that has gone largely unnoticed and unbridled. For every anecdote in which a tenor has been dismissed from the stage during rehearsals or in performance[56] there are many more concerning the rejection of women for doing nothing more than asserting their equivalence or, worse still, some measure of entitlement. The attachment of unreasonableness to the words and actions of sopranos pursuing independence (on the stage and off it) generated the cliché of the *prima donna*, by reference to which Maria Callas was denounced for actions that paled beside the psychotic insecurities of Di Stefano, Björling, Lanza, Corelli and Bonisolli. The "eccentricities" of tenors have been accepted as congenital and self-regulated; only rarely have they been contained by the sensibilities of colleagues, principles and market forces. Certainly, what happened to Kathleen Battle at the Met could never have happened to a man. Aesthetics and politics coincided most recently when the "Me-Too" movement prompted a slow-dawning realisation that the worlds of opera and classical music had been as tolerant of impropriety as every other. Vitorrio Grigolo's public scolding in September, 2019, was unlikely to have been an accident of timing;[57] either way, it

---

55   Edward Jenner (17 May, 1749 – 26 January, 1823) pioneered the concept of vaccines and created the world's first vaccine, for smallpox. Jenner is frequently identified as "the father of immunology", and his work is said to have saved more lives than the work of any other human being, not least during the Covid-19 crisis.

56   Obvious examples include Antonio Arámburo, Franco Bonisolli and Roberto Alagna.

57   In the light of compelling allegations of inappropriate behaviour, Grigolo was dismissed by the Royal Opera House, Covent Garden, while the company was touring Japan. The tenor's contract with the Metropolitan Opera in New York was cancelled shortly after.

has since become more difficult for anyone to conduct themselves other than in the company of *Il grillo parlante*. Time will tell whether the lurch towards transparency has achieved more than the meeting of obligations.

The soprano voice, and the experience of women singing as sopranos, has been equally problematic where issues of race and ethnicity are concerned. The number of black sopranos with careers on the world stage continues to represent a serious and challenging dilemma while noting that allegations of institutional prejudice among opera companies and promoters globally have begun to wear thin. The vast majority of those in positions of responsibility, including commentators, educators and singing professionals, have recognised the wider problem of cultural access for communities not aware of (or prevented from having access to) the sort of cultural diversity that is likely to generate positive change. Because most young black women in the United States are introduced by their families to music of black origin only (or primarily), and because music is not taught at all in American public schools, the onus is now on the guardians of singing as an art form (as distinct from the business of music when created and performed for profit in isolation) to ensure that minority communities are introduced to the soprano voice when distinguished from the "female artist." It is uncontroversial to assert that Lady Gaga is not a soprano – even if her register might warrant the attribution. She is a singer – and a jolly good one according to the Grammy's.

In 2020, Lady Gaga won the "Best Pop Duo / Group Performance" for her duet with Ariana Grande, "Rain On Me." This was her 11th Grammy – and her 29th nomination. She did not win Best Pop Vocal Album for *Chromatica* (an honour that went to Dua Lipa, for *Future Nostalgia*); neither did she win "Best Female Artist" because the Grammy's no longer distinguish between male and female. Women are now set in competition with men, so that "Record of the Year" in 2020 was adjudged to be "Everything I Wanted" by Billie Eilish, albeit for undisclosed reasons. Indeed, there are no published criteria for the 350 or so "Academy voting members" who decide which singer wins which prize. The membership is characterised as a body formed of

> experts in various fields [who] ensure that entered recordings meet specific qualifications and have been placed in appropriate fields.

There is a category for "Best Solo Artist", which is emphatically gender-neutral. There are categories for Best Traditional Pop Vocal Album, Best Pop Vocal Album, Best Rock Performance, Best Rock Song, Best Rock Album, Best Alternative Music Album, and a similar tranche of "bests" for R&B, Rap, Latin, Country, New Age, Jazz, Gospel, Christian Music, Blues, Roots, Folk, Reggae, Global, Children's Music, Spoken Word, Comedy, Musical Theatre and Classical. There is even an award for Best Album Liner Notes. Not one of these categories admits gender as meaningful – not even the nomination for Best Classical Solo Vocal Album – whereas the Music of Black Origin (MOBO) awards distinguish between Best Male Act and Best Female Act. The decision to abandon gender was taken in 2011. Five years later, Taylor Swift defied house rules by openly encouraging other female artists when she acknowledged her own milestone achievement as the first woman to win Album of the Year at the Grammys twice:

> I want to say to all the young women out there: there are going to be people along the way who will try to undercut your success or take credit for your accomplishments or your fame, but if you just focus on the work and you don't let those people sidetrack you, someday when you get where you are going, you'll look around and you will know that it was you and the people who love you who put you there, and that will be the greatest feeling in the world.[58]

These comments provoked many others across social media by consumers concerned with issues of privilege, gender and race. The last of these intersections proved more tendentious still in 2014, when Iggy Azalea's four nominations fostered widespread accusations of cultural appropriation. Some dared even suggest that Azalea's album, *The New Classic*, was unworthy of nomination for Best Rap Album. An analysis in 2015 of two generations of albums and records "of the year," and best new artist winners (according to race, gender, and age), revealed the extent to which white men had dominated the music industry since inception. It was an irony lost on many that categorisation by gender had been introduced in the first place to combat sexism in the music industry. The Recording Academy's Vice President of Awards, Bill Freimuth, told BuzzFeed News that:

> In the early days of the awards, it was a very different time in the music business, a time in which women on the whole had a much more difficult time, not only as producers and engineers, but as artists, getting their recordings played on the radio, getting noticed; but the Grammys didn't fold categories like Best Male Country Vocal Performance and Best Female Country Vocal Performance into a single, genderless category because sexism has been eradicated: they did so in order to give solo awards and nominations more weight, as part of a larger initiative to make the Grammys more competitive overall.[59]

The Recording Academy was concerned that categorisation by gender would create instability and unevenness in sectors where women were not traditionally well-represented. Their fears were misdirected. Between 2011 and 2016 (when "male" and "female" were replaced by "solo"), only 38% of the songs *nominated* for Best Country Solo Performance were written and performed by women; 60% of the *nominations* for best R&B solo performance were by a female artist, a female-male duet or a female-fronted group.[60] It is telling that between 1991 and 2002, and from 2005 until 2011, only 11% of the total nominees for Best Rap performer / song / album were women. It's self-evident, therefore, that the replacement of gender with "solo" as a criterion for a Rap performance award was engineered to disguise the low volume of entries by female artists. All rappers now compete on a putatively level playing field that nonetheless prevents anyone from knowing what proportion of

---

58 www.buzzfeednews.com/article/katiehasty/gender-race-grammy-awards.
59 *Ibid.*
60 *Ibid.*

men and women are nominated. The outcome, is that the currency of "equality" as it is being promoted (ostensibly at least) by the Grammy's can no longer be evidenced or tested statistically.

For an aspiring African-American soprano, the pressure to exist as something other than a black performer in a near-exclusively white world has been compounded by the corresponding dilemma of women working in an environment dominated by men. The threat of sophistry replacing enquiry and debate has become more onerous still because the presumption that Gershwin's Bess can only ever be black collides unavoidably with the truism that Otello almost never is. The pressure on women as sopranos is worse, therefore, than at any time previously when registering the cross-cultural drive to ensure equality, the socio-demographic improbability of women of colour becoming classically trained, and the concomitant objectification of beauty by consensus. These nightmarish interactions have been complicated by the de-sexualisation of artists whose job it is to seduce. Is the Marschallin meant to persuade as a woman to whom Octavian might regularly be making love? Did Strauss intend for his music to convey the same? Did Puccini wish for Tosca to sound and appear as a temptress capable of inspiring Cavaradossi to paint her, and Scarpia to rape her? Did Bizet design Carmen to provoke Don José into calling her a devil, and to stab her having only 60 minutes earlier declared the eternity of his love? Such rhetoric deflects the enormous problems facing a singer required to perform as a harlot or a goddess when in costume (depending, of course, on matters of opinion and perspective), and as merely beautiful when appearing in concert (or in a record company advert) swathed in $15,000 of silk and chiffon. It is unlikely any soprano will ever again disrobe for the pleasure of Herod when dancing her veils off, not because she might fail as a sex-object but because the threat of being perceived as such by colleagues, agents, Board members and media commentators overreaches any dramatic value that might be achieved by the alleged scandal of nudity. If Ms Wittich wouldn't remove her costume then why should anyone else?

Women have been contending with these issues as sopranos for hundreds of years; the tensions, burdens and struggles they represent run as a thread through what qualifies as a great deal more than the history of a voice. Even if the idealisation and objectification of sound and image have been divisible since the invention of recording, the need for a woman to persuade as something more than an instrument, even when performing in concert or on record, carries with it volumes of entanglements that cannot be reduced or understood in isolation. The most graphic embodiment of these tensions was captured in the life and work of the woman whose centenary this book has been published, in part, to commemorate.

Maria Callas is acclaimed by many to be the finest singing actress of the 20th century – if not every other. As a performer, a fashion icon, a celebrity, a wife and a woman of paradigmatic intelligence, beauty and glamour, she embodied many of those contradictions and complexities that characterise the history of the soprano as more than an assemblage of personalities and voices. For a number of years, Callas was the world's most photographed woman; she remained its most famous opera singer even after retiring. More books have been written about La divina than any other female singer, including Billie Holiday, Barbra Streisand and Madonna. Callas established and idealised so many of the tropes that attach to the modern conception of the *diva* that it is impossible for anyone to train or perform as a soprano without being cognisant of her example, on and off the stage. What Callas represents, more than anything else, is the *idea* of the soprano as a character capable of meeting her reputation, with a talent greater than her personality. Her memetic resonance continued to occupy artists long after her death in 1977. In 1982, Julian Schnabel painted a series of four large[61] abstract portraits in which he captured something of the singer's high-strung intensity and vocal opulence. More than one critic at the time read them as Schnabel thumbing his nose at his patrons, with the unambiguous references to the expressionist mannerisms of Jackson Pollock and Franz Kline operating as commentaries on celebrity and wealth. The use of purple velvet was something of a give-away for those seeking to isolate satire and self-aggrandisement. Some years later, however, Schnabel provided Sotheby's with a commentary on his portrait from 1987 of Joe Glasco, in which he wrote how:

> from Joe's studio you couldn't see outside because the floor-to-ceiling red velvet curtains were only partially open…Joe was in his kitchen, sitting in the dark in a Metropolitan Opera Egyptian-style black velvet chair. He was listening to Maria Callas […] isolated in the dark, far away from everybody…

The kitsch and social commentary on which the critics agreed was distinguished by that sense of separation and relocation engendered by Callas when performing, and also by the manner in which she lived her life – fleeing the attention to which she was otherwise addicted as an artist. Callas' tragic decline in retirement and her semi-calculated retreat into the spotlight of fading achievements provoked in Schnabel both empathy and admiration, his acknowledgment of which celebrated the voice and the singer without having to relocate her to Sunset Boulevard. Callas was as much a woman for Schnabel as she had been for Onassis, Di Stefano and the audiences who dared not breath while she sang. She survives her passing as a construction of influences, stimuli and effects that crystalise as they do because of, and not despite, her gender. The same could never have been written of a tenor.

Callas' status as an *imprimatur* was most recently in evidence during 2020, when the performance artist Marina Abramović used her unwarranted celebrity to create *7 Deaths of Maria Callas: an Opera Project by Marina Abramović*. This monstrous folly was summarised by Abramović in the following terms:

> For thirty-one years, I have wanted to make a work dedicated to the life and art of Maria Callas. I have read all of her biographies, listened to her extraordinary voice and watched her on film. A sagittarius, like me, I have always been fascinated by her personality, her life — and her death. Like so many of the characters she created on stage, she died for love. She died from a broken heart. Most operas end with the woman dying and more often than not, it is because of love. She will leap from precipices, burn, be strangulated stabbed or simply go mad. I want to

---

61   Each 9 feet by 13 feet.

reenact the death scenes from seven operas — seven deaths that Maria Callas has died before me.

There is much from which to recoil in this comically stupid statement. Notwithstanding the questionable relevance of Callas being "a Sagittarius," it is well-established (not least in the biographies that Abramović claimed to have read)[62] that the soprano did not die for love, or from "a broken heart". Neither did Callas assert a lien over her characters' stage deaths – or, at least, over and above the Renatas Tebaldi and Scotto, or any other of the leading dramatic sopranos specialising in Italian opera written between 1820 and 1920. Even worse than the tumefaction of her vanity was Abramović's delusion when claiming that having read about Callas' life, and having listened to her sing and having watched her on film, she was equipped in consequence to "star" as Callas on stage. In episodes of toe-curling horror, Abramović invoked her heroine through a series of arias and short films, which included her miming to recordings of Callas singing. The conceit of it all was inflamed by Abramović's conviction (which she stated without qualification in an interview with the *New York Times*) that she had been haunted throughout her life by her shared experiences with Callas – the sum of which appeared to reach little further than toxic relationships with their mothers and proximate birthdates. What she did not share with Callas was talent. As much was obvious from her reliance on Marko Nikodijevic for original music, and (in Munich) Adela Zaharia and Rosa Feola for live performances of "*Il dolce suono mi colpì di sua voce!*" from Donizetti's *Lucia di Lammermoor*. Abramović can neither compose, nor sing, nor paint, and her reliance on banal imagery (which included the ever-captivating but presumably retired Willem Defoe wrapping a huge snake around the *auteur*) suggested a crippling lack of imagination as well as absent talent. Many in the audience had cause to lament that Callas was not around to write "Marina Abramović has died before me."

The dominant impression formed by this calamitous extravagance was that Marina Abramović had thought considerably more about herself than she had about Maria Callas. Any insights to be found slinking at the bottom of the barrel concerned the arias rather than the woman singing them – which isolated the definitive issue faced by anyone seeking to approach the life and work of Maria Callas, or sopranos more generally: that no soprano has ever been *just* a soprano. It was not without a sense of irony that this was demonstrated beyond peradventure by a woman.

---

62   If Abramović read even one of the many books on Callas, it can presumed to have been Stassinopoulos Huffington's biography, which cast the singer as a victim of her own instincts and impulses, and a gallery of ghoulish, domineering men.

CHAPTER ONE

Engendered Slavery

"If woman had no existence save in the fiction written by men, one would imagine her a person of the utmost importance; very various; heroic and mean; splendid and sordid; infinitely beautiful and hideous in the extreme; as great as a man, some think even greater. But this is woman in fiction. In fact, as Professor Trevelyan points out, she was locked up, beaten and flung about the room."

Virginia Woolf, *A Room of One's Own* (1929)[1]

In 2010 the British comedians David Mitchell and Robert Webb wrote and performed a memorably funny and insightful sketch for British television[2] in which Caesar's aide announced that "henceforth you are to refer to yourself only in the third person... Instead of saying 'I am listening,' you say 'Caesar is listening'." Caesar grasps neither the value nor the mechanics of identifying himself other than "I" and "me"; there follows a sublime exchange in which the aide has eventually to blow into a reed whenever Caesar gets it wrong, which is most of the time. A messenger arrives and becomes even more confused than the Emperor, at which point the authors' writing sails close to perfection before it resolves in a paradigmatically English joke about Caesar being advised not to look down Cleopatra's blouse. In the decade since, pronouns have become hugely controversial in their application to forms of address and gender. There are currently more than 60 different terms in English to describe identity across what is now categorised as the gender spectrum. The traditional binary definitions of "man" and "woman" are, for now, a thing of the past. It is remarkable how many "normal" people become splenetic with rage over an issue that cannot possibly affect them, other than that they (as the unwittingly cis-gendered) are required to employ neutral pronouns as a function of respect for individuals whom plainly they hold in contempt. Examples include "they" / "them," and "theirs"; "ze," "hir," and "hirs"; "ze," "zir," and "zirs" and "xe," "xem" and "xyrs." Without having openly to discount the vaguely hateful dialectic promoted by Jordan Peterson and his followers, it can be agreed that the wished-for ossification of language as it relates to "he" and "she" fails to take account of the profound effects of linguistic hierarchies on anyone affected by a nebulous or conflicted sense of gender. This splintering of meanings and values has degenerated into a social and psychological land-grab, for the politically agenda'd.

---

1   Woolf, Virginia (2001). *A Room of One's Own*. Broadview Press, pp. 52–53.
2   *That Mitchell and Webb Look* (2010). Season 4, episode 1. BBC 2 Television.

Advocates of a binary narrative tend commonly to overlook (or care nothing for) the serious consequences suffered by those enduring or willingly embracing significant changes in mind and body. These issues have become complicated for men choosing in the 21st century to castrate themselves for reasons unconnected with gender re-alignment or body dysmorphia. The irritation experienced by those who see the world at its simplest cannot, perhaps, conceive of the sort of complexities that would lead a man of sound mind and articulate reason to remove his own testicles when encountering no conflict of identity by gender. The ubiquity of *orchiectomy*[3] has compelled urgent medical, psychological and psychiatric research; there are now hundreds of articles published in journals seeking better to understand what is happening, and why.

In 2014, "The hidden world of self-castration and testicular self-injury," by Thomas W. Johnson, and Michael S. Irwig, was published, with the following Abstract:

Eunuchs are biological males who have undergone voluntary castration for reasons other than male-to-female transsexualism. The term 'eunuch wannabe' refers to individuals who desire, or are planning, voluntary castration. Out of fear of embarrassment or rejection, many eunuch wannabes do not consult medical professionals regarding their desire for voluntary castration. Instead, they commonly resort to self-castration, castration by nonmedical professionals, or self-inflicted testicular damage via injections of toxic substances. Urologists should be aware of the growing popularity of these procedures. In particular, intratesticular injection of toxins is performed so that urologists will remove the damaged testicles.[4]

Other titles published between 2004 and 2021 include "Eunuchs in contemporary society: characterizing men who are voluntarily castrated (Part I),"[5] "New age eunuchs: motivation and rationale for voluntary castration,"[6] "Eunuchs in contemporary society: expectations, consequences, and adjustments to castration (part II),"[7] "Management of self-inflicted orchiectomy in psychiatric patient. Case report and non-systematic review of the literature,"[8] "Gender Preference in the Sexual Attractions, Fantasies, and Relationships of Voluntarily Castrated Men,"[9], "Differences in the Psychological, Sexual, and Childhood Experiences Among Men

---

3   The surgical procedure whereby one or both of a patient's testicles are removed.
4   Johnson, T.W. and Irwig, Michael S. (2014). *Nature Reviews Urology*. 11(5), pp. 297–300.
5   Johnson, T.W., Brett, M.A., Roberts, L.F., Wassersug, R.J. (2007). *Journal of Sexual Medicine* (Pt 1), pp. 930–45.
6   Wassersug, R.J., Zelenietz, S.A., Squire, G.F. (2004). *Archives of Sexual Behaviour*. 33(5), pp. 433–42.
7   Brett, M.A., Roberts, L.F., Johnson, T.W., Wassersug, R.J. (2007). *Journal of Sexual Medicine* (Pt II), pp. 1946–55.
8   Garofalo, M., Colella, A., Sadini, P., Bianchi, L., Saraceni, G., Brunocilla, E., Gentile, G., Colombo, F. (2018) *Archivio Italiano di Urologia e Andrologia*. 30:90(3), pp. 220–223.
9   Handy, A.B., Jackowich, R.A., Wibowo, E., Johnson, T.W., Wassersug, R.J. (2016). *Sex Medicine*, 4(1), pp. 51–9.

with Extreme Interests in Voluntary Castration,"[10] and "Voluntary genital ablations: contrasting the cutters and their clients."[11]

The scale of the "problem" is exacerbated by the agnosticism of the literature, which cannot approach volition as problematic. Numerous on-line forums exist for the sharing of fantasies and real-world experiences, in which men either talk of wanting to be castrated or of how they have undergone the process by their own hands. Much of it is troubling to read because the outcomes being discussed are irreversible, and because the hundreds of those courageous enough to share their feelings do so knowing that, for all the putative openness of contemporary western society, there are taboos even for the liberal. The issue is complicated further by the constantly evolving interactions between identity, sexuality and desire, with many relishing an imagined "final" sexual encounter during (or immediately following) their emasculation *sine qua non*. The scenario is less difficult to understand, perhaps, when imagined by women, the most celebrated example of which featured in Nancy Friday's anthology of female fantasies, *My Secret Garden*.[12]

How is a society so inured to dialectics of freedom to interact, process and, police such extremes of self-harm? In 2021, the Legislature of the State of Texas in the United States of America passed (as one of a bundle[13] of new Bills) "An Act relating to abortion, including abortions after detection of an unborn child's heartbeat – authorizing a private civil right of action." "The Texas Heartbeat Act" was enabled by people unable to prove they could detect one among themselves. The inevitable consequences of this medieval genuflection to extremism is twofold; firstly, women in Texas are now certain to suffer as a result, even after being raped by a family member;[14] secondly, the fine people of Texas are now authorised as vigilantes to inform on each other after the manner (and without apparently being aware) of the Nazi government's defining malfeasance.

Texas represents an outlier by the standards of allegedly developed societies; it is otherwise normal almost everywhere for mothers to pierce the ears of their children for the sake of beauty and for fathers to circumcise their sons as a votive to religion. In the Jewish faith, it is now possible to have a woman carry out the act of "*bris*".[15] An article published in the *New York Times*[16] on 28 February, 2020, reported how:

---

10 Wong, S.T.S., Wassersug, R.J., Johnson, T.W., Wibowo, E. (2021) *Archives of Sexual Behaviour*, 50(3), pp. 1167–1182.

11 Jackowich, R.A., Vale, R., Vale, K., Wassersug, R.J., Johnson, T.W. (2014). *Sex Medicine*. 2(3). pp. 121–32.

12 Friday, Nancy (1973). *My Secret Garden: Women's Sexual Fantasies*. Simon & Schuster

13 Not without irony, this bundle was comprised of 666 different pieces of legislation.

14 In 2018, there were 197,023 reported incidents of family violence in Texas. Of these, 1.5% were incidences of rape of a woman by a man – approximately 3,000. It's worth noting additionally that 238 women resident in Texas were murdered by a man during 2018. The population of Texas in 2018 was 28.6 million. Also in 2018, approximately 840 women (three and a half times as many) were murdered by men across the European Union, a collective of 28 member-state countries with a population of approximately 513 million – more than 18 times as populous as Texas (https://www.statista.com/statistics/1096116/femicide-in-europe-in-2018/).

15 The *brit milah* (or *bris*) is the formal "circumcision ceremony", to be performed on an 8-day-old Jewish boy.

16 By Alyson Krueger.

> When Dr. Amy Brown, a pediatric pulmonologist who lives in Irvington, New York, and is Jewish, found out she was expecting a son, she started asking friends and family about mohels…

Dr. Brown did not, apparently, ask whether her son should be circumcised *at all.* Instead, she considered the options available to her, all of which were "less than appealing":

> I learned about one man who had a license plate that said, 'SNIP IT,' and I was like, 'No.'" A month before her due date and still without a mohel, Dr. Brown read an article about Dr. Dania Rumbak, a pediatrician and a mohel, and felt huge relief, she said, thinking that Dr. Rumbak, as a woman, would bring empathy to a procedure that so often is rote. "Men have this tone of, 'This is how it has been done,'" she said. For centuries, the role of mohel was dominated by male religious leaders. As most rabbis and cantors have been male in the past — the Rabbinical Assembly, a Conservative Jewish association didn't let women become rabbis until 1985 — men have performed most of the rituals involved in Jewish life.

Even with cold wisdom waiting on superfluous folly, there is nothing to correlate between circumcision and castration, at least culturally; both involve a process of physical intervention that changes irrevocably the appearance (and experience) of a human being.[17] These changes affect the self-conception of the person changed as well as the perception of those interacting with them – individually and collectively. It is necessary, therefore, to consider the effect of the castrated on those who are (for want of a better word) "whole."[18] This emergent process of social identity[19] is hugely complicated, and then for a host of cultural-psychological reasons. Even if a man does not appear to be missing a primal feature of his person and identity, his knowledge of this difference will have a profound effect on his relationship with everyone and pretty much everything around him. The modern sense of what it is to be a "male" for gay and straight men standing within the routine parameters of the gender spectrum is so fundamentally attuned to the presence and function of testicles that anyone deviating from that norm cannot avoid becoming alien and alienated.

This social construction is forced for someone who has suffered or welcomed the loss of his testicles by the warranted suspicion that the majority will laugh or cry

---

17   Irrevocability might yet prove less certain than it used to be. Foregen is a company, with offices in Chicago and Rome, that claims to be "the first and only foreskin regeneration company in the world. Our goal is to apply regenerative medicine and tissue engineering techniques to regenerate the male foreskin and restore its biological functions and benefits. To date, this research has consisted of preliminary tests on animal foreskin tissue to prove our decellularization method, and successful testing of this method on human foreskin tissue. This will be followed by the animal trials phase, which is in progress, to recellularize the tissue, and ultimately a human clinical trial."

18   It is important to understand the clear distinction between men who are undergoing re-assignment treatment or surgery, and men who are neither experiencing nor undergoing hormonal therapies who, nonetheless, have sought (or are fantasising about) their own castration.

19   As a manifestation of Social Identity Theory, as it was formulated during the 1970s and 1980s by psychologists Henri Tajfel and John Turner.

before anyone thinks to listen. The abiding theme for forums on-line is fear – of ridicule, isolation and cruelty. At a time when difference is allegedly the oxygen of all progress it is disheartening to reflect that there are currently thousands of straight and heterosexual men globally whose identity is deemed unacceptable even within outlier communities. There are numerous reasons for this – many of them flowing from the shame fostered by religion, the shadows of Victorian prudery, macho notions of masculinity, and a general ignorance across every society of human form and function. Even now, the majority of those with college and university educations are unable to identify the major organs and bones in their own bodies. That ignorance grows more dangerous with the encroaching sterilisation and separation fostered by providers of healthcare and, worse still, by those dealing with what are now called "end of life" scenarios. The majority cope with death in the same way they relate to castration – by dissemblance and with humour.

The British enjoy a good euphemism more than most; the Rosetta-stone is "the dog's bollocks" and its affiliate "the mutt's nuts" – both signifiers of something excellent. On the other hand, "bollocks" in and of themselves indicate nonsense. Depending on whether the testicles in question are canine or more generically mammalian, therefore, many British people characterise something as positive or negative by reference to a scrotum. For those looking beyond the obvious, there are more than 1,250 alternative synonyms in use for testicles in the English language. Some are more tenuous than others. At least half are racist, sexist, offensive or insensitive; in certain cases they qualify as all four. The British obsession with testicles as a conduit for shame, suffering and humiliation does not equate with the depressingly literal analogy in the United States between virility and masculinity. "Balls" in America are commonly a symbol of pride, a short-hand for courage and determination – and little else. As anyone who has read a novel by Tom Sharpe or Terry Pratchett will know, however, the causing of damage to a man's plummage is a near-infinite source of belly-laughter. Of course, the British didn't invent puerility, although some believe they mastered it; the origins of violence to (or the loss of) testicles can be traced to Chaucer's *Pardoner's Tale*, the medieval *Reynard the Fox* (in which a cat called Tybald brings a Roman Catholic priest to his knees), and literally dozens of euphemisms in Shakespeare's sonnets and plays[20] (famously, "Let's to billiards come" in *Antony and Cleopatra*).[21] More recent assays in the talking of bollocks include Laurence Sterne's *Tristram Shandy* (featuring an exhaustively described scene in which a burning chestnut falls into the open trousers of one poor unfortunate) and the peculiar fixation among authors of James Bond novels, including Ian Fleming (who delighted in testicular torture in *Casino Royale*), Kingsley Amis (whose Colonel Sun observes that genital mutilation is "too ordinary" a device for causing pain), and John Gardner (in whose *Licence Renewed*, 007 punches low, and more than once, during a wrestling match). The British delight in gonadal-cruelty has been adopted, to a lesser extent, in the USA – memorably so on film, as evidenced by *Something About Mary* and the *Jackass* series. Obvious literary exemplars include *To Kill a Mockingbird*, in which Scout kicks a man in the groin when acting to protect Jem, Joseph Wambaugh's *The*

---

20   See generally Webb, J. Barry (1989). *Shakespeare's Erotic Word Usage*. Cornwallis Press.
21   Act II, Scene V.

Choirboys, which features an episode described as "The Night My Balls Blew Up," and almost the entire oeuvre of Stephen King, for whom the cracking of nuts has been something of a pre-occupation.[22]

It follows that the scrotum – in its place and, on occasion, its ruin and relocation – has been a source of entertainment for as long as men have been slipping on ice and falling from trees. As organs with multiple manuals, however, testicles have always served more than a singular purpose. They are inherently symbolic and operate as both a source of power and a necessary vulnerability for those inclined to wave them figuratively and literally. If they are valuable as identifiers for men then they are equally important for the majority of heterosexual women – for whom procreation is not quite yet a table for one. The traditional reliance on testicles in their operation is trite, but there was a time when their removal served professionally and institutionally to deny women their voices in tandem with their common experience of a perennially male-dominated society. Indeed, the determination among men to keep women silent was sufficiently manic for tens of thousands of sons to authorise the castration of their own and other men's children for nothing more than money, power and, at a dim remove, art.

There are numerous books devoted to castrati. Each deals primarily or uniquely with the issue of voice – of the "creation," sound, technique and repertoire of the male soprano in isolation. A handful recognise the probable ramifications of castration psychologically for the boy and for the man; none of them acknowledges the context as it related to women. It is easily forgotten that the only reason boys were turned into sopranos in the first place (at least initially) is because of the Christian Church's concern for its own security as an institution for those with testicles. They took their lead from the bug-eyed, woman-hating Paul who, in I Corinthians, 14:34, instructed the devoted to

> Let your women keep silence in the churches: for it is not permitted
> unto them to speak; but they are commanded to be under obedience as
> also saith the law.

The history of the castrato is well-known and much rehearsed. The Vatican was happier for the little children to suffer[23] than risk the consequences of allowing their mothers to sing in church, as plainly they could. Everyone remembers the rank misogyny of Corinthians 14:34 (as do many Christian sects in 2023), but the Bible features numerous other aphorisms that would challenge the most egalitarian of Christians.[24] Titus 2:4, for example, commands all men to "train the young women to love their husbands and children," which suggests, if nothing else, Paul's exposure to an imperfect childhood or an unhappy marriage, while Titus 2:3 lunges further in

---

22   There are distressingly memorable episodes in *Gerald's Game*, *The Dark Half*, *The Body*, *Needful Things*, *Chattery Teeth*, *IT*, *The Stand*, *Wolves of the Calla*, *Rose Madder*, *My Pretty Pony*, and *The Cat From Hell*.

23   Jesus is said to have used these words when rebuking his disciples for preventing a group of children from approach him. Of course, "suffer" in this context equated to "allow." See Matthew 19:14.

24   Certain well-intentioned readers of the Bible sought an equivalence where none exists – as "*Christian Egalitarianism*."). Not to be confused with *Complementarianism*, which is, if anything, worse even than the text it seeks to legitimise.

its advocacy that "Older women likewise are to be reverent in behaviour, not slanderers or slaves to much wine. They are to teach what is good." It might be difficult for some to separate "what is good" from "much wine", even noting the suspicion that the drinking of it caused difficulties for Paul when in the company of women.[25] It is equally certain that the Bible's authors sought more generally to prevent women from making music – long before Paul extinguished any lingering ambiguity. The only verse in either book to encourage the raising of the female voice in song is 2 Chronicles 35:25, which reports how

> Jeremiah lamented for Josiah: and all the singing men and the singing women spake of Josiah in their lamentations to this day, and made them an ordinance in Israel: and, behold, they are written in the lamentations.

The Pauline epistles' repeating dread of female seduction, and the converse appetite for repressing women, operated in tandem with Deuteronomy's disgust for a man with damaged or detached testicles: "No one who has been emasculated by crushing or cutting may enter the assembly of the Lord."[26] This injunction failed to distinguish between volition and misadventure, so that a man was rejected of God whether or not he was the author of his own undoing. The callousness of this judgment can be defended only by the indefensible,[27] and in necessary ignorance of Deuteronomy's further mandate (at 25:11–12) that:

> When men strive together one with another, and the wife of the one draweth near for to deliver her husband out of the hand of him that smiteth him, and putteth forth her hand, and taketh him by the secrets: Then thou shalt cut off her hand, thine eye shall not pity her.

This compelled that a woman defending herself against a rapist should (then and now, presumably) expect to have her hand amputated for grabbing an assailant by

---

25 The Ancient Hebrew word "*yayin*", one of many used for 'wine,' appears 140 times in the Old Testament alone. Noah's priority after reaching dry land was to plant a vineyard from which he was able to become intoxicated without apparently having to attend on the process of fermentation: "And Noah began to be an husbandman, and he planted a vineyard: And he drank of the wine, and was drunken; and he was uncovered within his tent…" Genesis 9: 20–21.

26 Deuteronomy 23:1.

27 Natalie Regoli has had a crack at it: "A large portion of the law of Moses is what is called ceremonial law […] ceremonial law was temporary, and the whole thing was intended as an illustration from God about his holiness and perfection. The world today looks at the ceremonial laws, like the injunction against cross-breeding cattle, or against mixing fabrics in clothing, as a reason to ignore the moral laws of the Bible. This is simply dishonest. The ceremonial law included the sacrificial system for the atonement for sin. The message was that God is holy, and the fallen world is not. An emasculated person was loved by God, but in the age of the ceremonial law, when God used the law to teach the differences to his people and the watching world between clean and unclean, perfect and imperfect, holy and profane, the one who was thus imperfect could not be let in, though provision was always made for the outcast, even in the Old Testament. The glorious Good News is that Jesus came to fulfill the ceremonial law and has put an end to the practices which God intended to be temporary. Even a crushed or emasculated person is made clean and holy by the blood of Jesus if they turn to him in repentance for everlasting life." (https://connectusfund.org).

his "secrets." Deuteronomy appears to have been composed in Jerusalem during the reign of King Josiah (641 and 609 BCE). 1,600 years later, the state and play of a man's scrotum remained capital in value. Peter Abelard, a medieval French philosopher, theologian, poet and musician, was well-equipped to experience love at its most complex; during the first half of the 12th century he was consumed by a Tristanesque obsession for Héloïse d'Argenteuil, a celebrated French philosopher, writer, scholar and the "most educated woman in France." For the usual reasons, their relationship was condemned, on this occasion by Héloïse's uncle, Fulbert, who arranged for Abelard to be assaulted in his home and castrated. Fulbert was a canon, and he weathered his resulting censure; Abelard retired permanently to the monastery of St. Denis, near Paris. Unfairly, perhaps, Abelard insisted that Héloïse take vows as a nun, which she did under force of law. The couple continued to write to each other, regardless, and their correspondence is memorable for its modernity, and because of the survival of their love platonically.

A few years after Abelard's death in 1142, Wolfram von Eschenbach wrote his legendary epic *Parzival*, in which the King of Sicily goes the whole hog when exacting the ultimate revenge against his wife's lover, Clingschor:

> Clingschor the Duke was in the mouths of all, both men and women, until he fell into disgrace. Sicily had a noble king called Ibert, and Iblis was his wife, the loveliest woman ever weaned from a mother's breast. Clinschor served her until she rewarded him with love. For this the king robbed him of his honour. If I am to tell you his secret, I must ask your forgiveness, for it is unseemly for me to say such things. One cut of the knife, and Clinschor became a eunuch." Gawan burst out laughing. Then she told him still more, "In the famous castle of Kalot Enbolot he became the mock of the world. The king found Clinschor with his wife, sleeping in her arms. If he found a warm bed there, he had to pay the heavy price that by the hand of the king he was made smooth between his legs. The king thought that was his right. He clipped him in such a way that he can never more give pleasure to any woman.[28]

The Dark Ages remained so for many years, and with good cause. On 30 March, 1282, for example, the War of the Sicilian Vespers was launched in Palermo with a battle, at the end of which more than 2,000 of Charles I's soldiers and sympathisers were castrated by Sicilian rebels. Trophies of the most gruesome kind were displayed throughout the city until being consumed as carrion. The abuse of male genitalia politically and punitively played no part in the prevention of women from speaking – and singing – in public. The dozens of authors who have since written about castration in Renaissance Italy have reached no further than the proposition that boys were castrated to preserve the purity of their voices. Few have attempted to account for why this might have been necessary, or in any way useful to the art – and how castrati and female singers came to co-exist. The English Tudor tradition,

---

28   Eschenbach, Wolfram von (1961). *Parzival*. Trans. Helen M. Mustard and Charles E. Passage. Vintage Books, pp. 345.

for example, managed perfectly well with unmutilated boys and counter-tenors, and most other corners of the Christian world operated without resorting to the commission of atrocities against the pre-pubescent. In Italy, and almost singularly, the Catholic Church was adamant that Paul was onto something when demanding that women hold their peace and during the 16th century incidences of castration became sufficiently common for Pope Sixtus V to publish the Bull *Cum pro nostro pastorali munere*.[29] This edict determined that the choir of St Peter's, as the Capella Sistina, should include four castrati, who were to replace boys and the increasingly unsatisfactory *falsettisti* as the treble line in the standard SATB formulation.[30] If it seems incredible that the Church might have thought to ratify the mutilation of young boys simply to prevent women from singing then it should be noted that at least one modern Catholic teaching institution is able to think of something worse. On 19 December, 2018 (while preparing to celebrate the birth of their saviour), the editors of a website[31] operated by the *Faith & Reason Institute,*[32] published an article by Anthony Esolen, a professor employed by Magdalen College of the Liberal Arts, in New Hampshire,[33] with the title "Some Men Are Born Eunuchs":[34]

> Far be it from me to say anything exculpatory about the filthy priests whose vices warped the lives of many boys and young men and reduced many a parish and diocese to penury. But when those wicked men were done fondling the family jewels, they were at least still attached to the kid. He might still grow up to be a husband and father. That is not the case when the boy "transitions," that is, when he undergoes surgery to make it seem as if he is a girl when he is not and never can be. The boy who decided to be mutilated did so to secure something that was in itself good. It is good, not evil, to have a beautiful voice. It is good to be the solo in Allegri's Miserere. […] [The castrated boy] was not rejecting his sex. He was not seized by the madness of believing that he was really a girl. He had not been taught in school that his sex was responsible for all the evil in the world. He would not have grown up in a divorce, with a mother infected with feminist fantasies, of a world bleached clean of the masculine. […] However sick it was to [castrate back] then, it is far sicker to do what we do now.[35]

---

29   'As for our pastoral responsibility'; on 27 September, 1589.

30   Non-native castrati arrived in Italy earlier, during the middle of the century, but the Church did not act to regulate the practice of castration until the publishing of *Cum pro nostro pastorali munere*.

31   https://www.thecatholicthing.org.

32   A Washington think-tank, supported by, and popular among, right-leaning conservatives.

33   Recognised as a Catholic college by the Diocese of Manchester, New England.

34   A quotation from Matthew 19:12: "For there are some eunuchs, which were so born from their mother's womb: and there are some eunuchs, which were made eunuchs of men: and there be eunuchs, which have made themselves eunuchs for the kingdom of heaven's sake. He that is able to receive it, let him receive it."

35   https://www.thecatholicthing.org/2018/12/19/some-men-are-born-eunuchs.

This excerpt cannot hope to convey the rabid malevolence that characterises the remainder of what Professor Esolen was encouraged by an allegedly Christian institution to write about matters of which he was plainly ignorant. Anyone spinning a silver lining for paedophilia while extending choice to the victims of castration should probably not be teaching anything to anyone.

On the other hand, if an "educated" Catholic can hold and articulate such horrifying views in the 21st century then it is not difficult to understand how readily the Church in the 16th century abandoned the values of its totem when elevating self-interest as primary. Of course, the Vatican took little formal note of secular developments within and as between the private houses of the nobility, and it is unsurprising that the growing regiment of humanists then establishing itself behind closed doors did not do as commanded when commissioning the first operas.

Emasculation of the innocent was considered to be a price worth paying by the Church. Even so, the emergence of the castrati as an island of male superiority did not operate to silence women for secular audiences at Court, who had for the longest time been hearing (and encouraging) women to sing – albeit only in private. On 2 May, 1589, the Florentine Famiglia de' Medici threw their considerable resources at the wedding of Ferdinando de' Medici and Cristina de Lorraine.[36] The wildly extravagant celebrations continued for a month, with mock battles, parades, jousting and a game of football.[37]

The opulence peaked with a staging at the recently completed Teatro Mediceo degli Uffizi[38] of *La Pellegrina* – a *commedia dell'Arte* by Girolamo Bargagli.[39] The comedy was subsumed to a series of musical and scenic *intermedi*, directed by the wildly polymathic Emilio de' Cavalieri, with contributions from many of the city's most gifted composers, including Cristofano Malvezzi, Antonio Archilei, Giulio Caccini, Luca Marenzio and Jacopo Peri.[40] Strikingly, considering the publication in the same year of the *Cum pro nostro pastorali munere*, the vocal performances were divided equally between women and men – none of whom had been castrated.

---

36   Potter, John, and Sorrell, Neil (2012). *A History of Singing*. Cambridge University Press, pp. 85–86.

37   The sport at that time was called Calcio Fiorentino and played by men between the ages of 18 and 45 – grouped in teams of 27 players, called *calcianti* ('kickers'). Each match lasted 50 minutes and, like football today, entailed the scoring of goals (*caccia*).

38   The theatre was huge by contemporary standards. It had a 20-metre stage and the 55 metre-deep auditorium seated 1,500. The once double-height space is now occupied by the "Primitives" and the vast "Cabinet of Drawings and Prints" at the Gallerie Degli Uffizi.

39   Pasqui, Teresa (2010). *Book of Accounts of the Comedy: the theatrical tailoring of Ferdinando I De 'Medici in 1589*. Nicomp Editorial Laboratory.

40   The *Intermedi* were composed as follows: Intermedio I: The Harmony of the Spheres (Cristofano Malvezzi). Intermedio.II: The context of the Pierides and the Muses; and Intermedio III: The combat of Apollo with the serpent Python (Luca Marenzio). Intermedio IV: Heavenly spirits announce the advent of a new Golden Age (Giulio Caccini, Cristofano Malvezzi and Giovanni de' Bardi). Intermedio V: Arion and the dolphin (Cristofano Malvezzi and Jacopo Peri). Intermedio VI: Jupiter appears in the sky with the council of the gods (Cristofano Malvezzi and Emilio de' Cavalieri).

The brightest of the stars to descend from *il paradiso degli Uffizi*[41] for Ferdinando (as "Strong Hercules") and Cristina (as "New Minerva") was Vittoria Archilei.[42] Known by the sobriquet "Romania," Vittoria was the second most venerated soprano of the 16th century. First among the unequal was Isabella d'Este,[43] Marchioness of Mantua and the most influential woman of the Renaissance. Isabella was not, of course, a professional singer, but she was a talented musician, renowned for her instrumental and vocal abilities. She excelled in a manner that set her apart for her times, and she came to represent an ideal to which many aspired long after her death:

> Isabella herself forms rather a paragon of women's musical talents and tastes than a typical example. Her abilities, if contemporaneous accounts are to be believed, were outstanding not in the simple fact that she was a moderately proficient amateur musician, but rather in the degree of her accomplishments and in the central role music took in her life. Her own letters and those of others show plainly that music rapidly became for her an *idée fixe*, and, as she mastered the art, an essential part of her self-image. Such a statement does not alter the fact that Isabella's deliberate undertaking is indicative of a larger trend of women making music. In a world that severely limited a woman's possibilities to excel – to achieve that personal fame that was so central a part of the thought of Renaissance men – Isabella chose music as a culturally permissible avenue toward wide celebrity and distinction.[44]

On 11 February, 1490, a decade after being promised to the Gonzaga family by her father, Ercole I, Duke of Ferrara, the 15-year-old Isabella married Francesco II, Marquess of Mantua.[45] Six months later, on 30 August, she wrote to her "most illustrious father":

---

41   "Heaven" was the name given casually to the backstage area containing the stagecraft, the flyloft in which was contained the flats and mechanics necessary for the illusion of "flying" – a popular stage effect from the first among Italian aristocracy. Because early theatre structures were temporary, architectures were rarely strong enough to support the complicated and sophisticated flying machines. Once theatres began to be seen as more-permanent assets, designers employed increasingly massive convolutions of rope, wood, wire, iron and lead to support the often considerable weight of singers *en masse*. Another method utilised a vertical track mounted to a horizontal beam, which lifted a platform on which performers could stand.

42   *circa* 1550 – 1618. She married the composer Antonio Archilei in 1578.

43   19 May, 1474 – 13 February, 1539.

44   Prizer, William F. (1999). "Una Virtù Molto Conveniente A Madonne": Isabella D'este as a Musician. *The Journal of Musicology* (Winter, Vol. 17, No. 1), pp. 10–49; pp. 11.

45   When starting work on *Rigoletto*, Verdi wanted to keep the drama in Paris, and the court of Francis I, where it was located by Victor Hugo for *Le roi s'amuse*. Because the censors would not have allowed this, the composer and his librettist, Piave, transferred the opera's events, and the evil Duke, to the Duchy of Mantua. The Gonzaga Family was extinct before the beginning of the 18th Century so there was nobody left to take offence. Within days of the triumphant premiere, at La Fenice on 11 March, 1851, the people of Mantua began to identify (and invite tourists to visit) the buildings and sites that "appeared" in the opera. The rectory of the Cathedral, located in front of the Ducal Palace (at Piazza Sordello 23), was soon enough renamed "Casa di Rigoletto," with neither cause nor justification. In 1978, a statue of Rigoletto by Aldo Falchi was installed in the rectory garden. If the attachment of the mythical jester to Mantua was unwarranted, then the gratuitous execration of the Gonzaga family's reputation by Verdi was more tragic even than the death of Gilda.

I would like to learn how to sing, and because there is no-one who sat-isfies me as much as Johannes Martini, who is known to me and who has taught me previously, I beg of your Lordship that if you would like to loan him to me for two or three weeks, you could do me no greater favour.[46]

Isabella acquired her love of music and art from her father, whose influence as a patron was unprecedented in Italy. He supported his daughter's training as a soprano and a lutenist and encouraged her to perform at court. Her correspondence evinces regular requests for sheet music as well as [...] Isabella did not compose or engage in impro-vised settings of poetry; she nonetheless retained a stable of composers, while poets from across Europe submitted their verses to the Gonzaga Court, inviting publicity as well as patronage. Isabella's sensitivity to her gender when studying and performing as a musician within a traditionally male arena of attainment filters throughout her correspondence. She utilised her authority when urging other women to sing, defy-ing ecclesiastical law and institutional misogyny. On 8 May, 1512, Isabella wrote to the Abbot of San Benedetto Po:

Reverend in Christ, Dear Father. You will remember when last we spoke you were asked to arrange for the venerable nuns of San Giovanni to be able to learn singing and psalmody, because it is a great shame that such a venerable and exemplary college of women should not have reason and order in this way, as they do in others. And so, we ask you again that that your chapter comes to terms with those reverend fathers [to whom the nuns answered locally] and provide practised and discreet persons who know how to teach them. This will honour Religion and the greater glory of Our Lord God, but we shall be very satisfied also because when we go to the said monastery and feel such discord, our ears are greatly offended and little consoled.[47]

It's reasonable to presume that anyone submitting an opinion of a performance by Isabella to writing, in public or in private, was cognisant of the risks attendant to a bad review. What survives is largely anodyne and sycophantic, therefore; it is useful, regardless, when trying to establish what Isabella sang, and how she might have sung it. The earliest report is from February, 1502, and a banquet hosted by Isabella for an impressive table of guests to celebrate the marriage of Alfonso I, d'Este, to Lucrezia Borgia, in Ferrara. This was a very different dining experience to the "Banquet of the Chesnuts," attended by Lucrezia four months earlier in Rome.[48] This infamous throwback to the good old days of Caligula and Nero was hosted by Lucrezia's brother, the former Cardinal, Cesare Borgia – one of the many illegitimate children fathered by Pope Alexander VI. The Master of Ceremonies, Johann Burchard, recorded in his diary:[49]

---

46 Archivio di Stato di Mantova, Archivio Gonzaga, busta 2904, libro 136, folio 5(iv).
47 *Ibid.*, busta 2996, libro 30, folio 15.
48 On 30 October, 1501.
49 The veracity of Burchard's account has been challenged.

On the evening of the last day of October, 1501, Cesare Borgia arranged a banquet in his chambers in the Vatican with "fifty honest prostitutes," called courtesans, who danced after dinner with the attendants and others who were present, at first in their garments, then naked. After dinner the candelabra with the burning candles were taken from the tables and placed on the floor, and chestnuts were strewn around, which the naked courtesans picked up, creeping on hands and knees between the chandeliers, while the Pope, Cesare, and his sister Lucretia looked on. Finally, prizes were announced for those who could perform the act most often with the courtesans, such as tunics of silk, shoes, barrets,[50] and other things.[51]

Isabella's dinners provided less *outré* entertainment. In February, 1502, she asked the singer-composer, Marchetto Cara, to perform songs set to verses by her favourite poets. She was even persuaded to perform herself: "After dinner, we danced the hat dance. After this was done, so many requests and demands were made of me that I had to demonstrate my singing to the lute."[52] One of the guests, the Marchesa di Crotone, went further when recalling how "after dinner, and because of the requests of these lords, [Isabella] sang two sonnets and a capitolo, and they were as delighted as it is possible to be."[53] D'Este's pre-occupation with music and poetry was lifelong, and it brought her into the company of just about every contemporary composer and poet of renown, just as her love of painting made her an obvious focus of attention for Da Vinci, Bellini, Raphael and Titian. In April, 1503, she was sent three new verses by the poet, literary scholar and theologian, Pietro Bembo. Three months later, Bembo wrote that he was

> sending your most excellent Ladyship and my most illustrious Patroness ten sonnets and two strambotti[54] that break the rules somewhat, not because they merit coming into your hands, but because I too desire that some of my verses be recited and sung by your Ladyship, remembering with what sweetness and gentleness you sang [the verses of] others that happy evening and esteeming no other favour for my verses than this. Some of the sonnets are not yet known here, and none of the strambotti have been seen by anyone. It displeases me if by chance they neither live up to your Ladyship's expectations nor to my wishes, but I am comforted that if they are to be sung by you, then they can be called most fortunate and will have need of nothing more, because they will please the listeners

---

50   A small cap.

51   *Johann Burchard, Pope Alexander VI and His Court: Extracts from the Latin Diary of Johannes Burchardus* (1921). Ed. F.L. Glaser. N.L. Brown, pp. 154–155.

52   Letter to Francesco Gonzaga, 6 February, 1502. Archivio di Stato di Mantova, Archivio Gonzaga, busta 1238. See also Prizer, William F. (1985) "Isabella D'Este and Lucrezia Borgia as Patrons of Music: The Frottola at Mantua and Ferrara," *Journal of American Musicology*. XXXVIII, pp. 1–33.

53   Letter of 6 February, 1502, to Francesco Gonzaga in Mantua. Archivio di Stato di Mantova, Archivio Gonzaga, busta 1238, pp. 359–60.

54   An eight-line satirical verse.

and will be welcome in that they come from the lovely and delicate hand
and the pure and sweet voice of your most illustrious Ladyship.[55]

While it is difficult to know anything certain of Isabella's voice or the manner of
her singing, there is, at least, good evidence for what she sang. In May, 1514, the
Marchesa sent Francesco Aquaviva, the Marchese of Bitonto, a book of new songs
by Marchetto Cara. In his reply of thanks, dated 27 December, Aquaviva wrote "you
have forgotten to send me the song that begins 'Cantai,' as you promised me; I am
very fond of it, principally as a souvenir of that evening in Pozuolo."[56] Two months
later, Isabella duly sent a copy of Cara's setting of Baldassar Castiglione's "*Cantai
mentre nel core fioria.*"[57] The composer's delicate treatment of Castiglione's Petrarchan
four-verse poem is cut precisely to the dimensions of a noblewoman performing in
her own court. The music begins on an A4 and never moves beyond a seventh; the
pacing is stately, with only two crotchets (in the penultimate bar). It's reasonable to
suppose that Isabella would have added a moderate number of ornaments, but there
is nothing in the song to strain the least capable of singers. It's clear, in fact, that the
primary challenge presented by Cara was the colouring of Castiglione's words. In the
case of "Cantai," these are archetypically wistful, with the performer's heart becoming
the "poisoned home of bitterness." The music is extremely light, adhering largely to
the prevailing syllabic formula (*i.e.*, one note to a syllable); it rewards a chambered
softness that would have required little or no vocal technique – at least as it is understood today. There would have been no need for projection because the lutes played
by Isabella and her peers produced an ethereal tone. The rooms in which she is likely
to have performed all featured high ceilings and hard-finished walls, with significant
resonance. A little will have gone a long way.

Did Isabella perform other than at intimate dinners, and for private guests? It's
almost certain she didn't. In 1518, the courtier Andrea Cossa wrote by way of confession that "Madonna Laura has let us hear her sing secretly, not without bringing
to mind your Ladyship and your singing in the Castello of Milan." William F. Prizer
has argued, with some force, that the phrase "*cantare secretamente*" speaks to a culture
of gendered roles, routines and covenants that not even Isabella D'Este was able to
undo. So while she was gifted, and a seismic influence, her contribution to sung art
adhered to the courtly confines of decorum and probity – affecting little or no change
on what was written during her lifetime. She was one of the hardest working women
of the century, drawn and quartered between responsibilities that merely included
motherhood to eight children.[58]

Isabella's influence was much evidenced in Ferrara, where her appetite for *Intermedi*
– tableaux-precursors to what would become opera – distinguished the prevailing
taste for *commedia*, productions of which the Marchesa dismissed as "boring" – "a

---

55 Prizer, William F. (1999). "Una Virtù Molto Conveniente A Madonne": Isabella D'Este as a Musician.
The Journal of Musicology (Winter, Vol. 17, No. 1), pp. 10–49; pp. 11.
56 Archivio di Stato di Mantova, Archivio Gonzaga, busta 809.
57 'I sang while my joyful heart blossomed.' Printed in 1513, in Antico's third book of *frottole* – an early
species of madrigal.
58 Six of whom survived infancy.

remark destined to be often repeated."[59] The aristocracy's cultivation of *intermedi* was pivotal to the modernisation of singing and monody. In particular, Ferrara's renowned *concerto delle donne* presented fertile soil for court rivalry, with small groups of female singers trained in the teeth of competition; soloists emerged by default in consequence of developing values, chiefly the art of improvisation.[60] It was as an improviser that Vittoria Archilei was distinguished from her peers when being lowered, *deus ex machina*,[61] at the first performance of *La Pellegrina*.[62] Peri described Vittoria as the "euterpe of our age,"[63] and her primacy among her peers was amplified by the decision to gift her two solos (placed, with meaning, in the first and fifth *intermedi*) as well as two ensemble numbers in which her part was made express. Her performance at the beginning of the first *intermedio*, "*Dalle più alti sfere*,"[64] secured her reputation as the leading female singer of her generation, thanks to her flair for semi-improvised *foriture* – a talent revered by her contemporaries, including Jacopo Peri, who wrote that

> Archilei is the singer who has always made my music worthy of her singing, by adorning it not only with those gruppi and those long windings of the voice, both simple and double, that her liveliness of invention can devise at any time – more to obey the usage of our time than because she regards the beauty and force of our singing to rely upon them – but also with those pleasantries and beauties that cannot be written down, and even if written, cannot be learnt from written [examples].[65]

Improvised embellishments were common for secular singers in Italy during Isabella d'Este's lifetime, particularly among Roman-Neapolitan circles[66] – within which Vittoria spent her formative years – but they were never complicated or florid. Vittoria, was characterised by Vincenzo Giustiniani[67] as the extemporiser against whom all others were to be measured – which suggests she was the "leading exponent

---

59   Shearman, John (1967). *Mannerism*. Pelican, p. 105.

60   See Newcomb, Anthony (1980). *The Madrigal at Ferrara, 1579–1597*, 2 vols. Princeton; and Newcomb, Anthony (1986). "Courtesans, Muses, or Musicians? Professional Women Musicians in Sixteenth-Century Italy", in *Women Making Music: The Western Art Tradition, 1150–1950*, Eds. Jane Bowers and Judith Tick. Urbana and Chicago, pp. 90–115.

61   'Dorian Harmony.'

62   There was a second performance, on 15 May.

63   Potter, John, and Sorrell, Neil (2012). *A History of Singing*. Cambridge University Press, p. 86.

64   'From the highest spheres.' Composed ostensibly by Vittoria's husband, Antonio Archilei; however, the aria has also been attributed to Emilio de' Cavalieri – and also to Vittoria herself. See Treadwell, Nina (2004). "She Descended on a Cloud 'From the Highest Spheres': Florentine Monody 'alla Romanina'". *Cambridge Opera Journal*, Vol. 16, No.1 (March), pp. 1–22.

65   Treadwell, Nina (2004). "She Descended on a Cloud 'From the Highest Spheres': Florentine Monody 'alla Romanina'". *Cambridge Opera Journal*, Vol. 16, No.1 (March), p. 10.

66   See Hill, John Walter, (1997). *Roman Monody, Cantata and Opera from the Circles Around Cardinal Montalto*, 2 vols. Oxford University Press.

67   In his *Discorso sopra la musica, a* "letter" of instruction for young noblemen, written in 1628 and published only in 1878.

of a style that only later found its way into written form."[68] When sat atop her tremulant cloud[69] as the *Armonia Doria*, Vittoria's performance of "*Dalle più alti sfere*" had to be audible in a performance space that dwarfed the intimate rooms in which she had mastered her art. She had also to soar above an "orchestra" formed of her own bass lute[70] (tuned in D),[71] and two chittarone,[72] a six-foot extended lute famed for its resonance.[73] She was unaffected by the band of 41 instrumentalists formed beneath her[74] because solos were accompanied by plucked instruments alone. Vittoria had to accommodate a huge audience of men and women, the majority of whom (like the stage) were draped in the richest, most acoustically absorbent fabrics. The theatre's acoustic might be expected to have dried out. Remarkably, however, the double-cube design ensured the music and the voices bloomed within the space to so great an extent that "echo" effects (real and simulated) were employed, not least by Vittoria. One audience member, Giuseppe Pavoni, reported that:

> There were two cloths covering the front of the stage. The first one which went down was red; the perspective remained but was also covered by another cloth which was blue, in the middle of which a woman seated on a cloud with a lute began to play and sing a madrigal very sweetly. And thus playing and singing she came, being lowered down little by little, hiding herself among certain rocks, and finishing the madrigal among those rocks with an echo so wonderful that it seemed like its reflection was a good mile away.[75]

Two years after the wedding, the Medici family commissioned a commemorative print of *La Pellegrina*, a responsibility delegated to Malvezzi, who documented solos either as madrigals (in partbooks, as was typical in 1591) or in score, with embellishments captured as they were performed. "*Dalle piu alte sfere*" was printed in score rather than as a partbook, with a simplified version of Vittoria's vocal part in the upper voice (without the text). It's widely accepted that Malvezzi's notations of the *passaggi* as they were sung by Vittoria are inaccurate, if not fabricated, because the singer's "liveliness of invention"[76] exceeded the snap of Malvezzi's quill and the fidelity of his memory.

---

68   Treadwell, Nina (2004). "She Descended on a Cloud 'From the Highest Spheres': Florentine Monody 'alla Romanina'". *Cambridge Opera Journal*, Vol. 16, No.1 (March), p. 11.

69   It was reported to shake badly during rehearsals. *Ibid,* p. 11. Five hundred years later, Robert Lepage's staging of Wagner's *Der Ring der Nibelungen* at the Metropolitan Opera in New York did away with clouds entirely, and suspended his Reinemaidens from wires and harnesses.

70   In Bernardo Buontalenti's drawings of the costume designs, Vittoria is portrayed carrying a harp.

71   Some commentators have suggested Vittoria was tasked with playing a six-foot chitarrone. Considering the difficulties of floating her atop a cloud, this is highly unlikely.

72   Also known as the theorbo.

73   They were played backstage, one of them by Vittoria's husband.

74   Instrumentalists were placed around the theatre because there was insufficient space in front of the stage.

75   Treadwell, Nina (2004). "She Descended on a Cloud 'From the Highest Spheres': Florentine Monody 'alla Romanina'". *Cambridge Opera Journal*, Vol. 16, No.1 (March), p. 13.

76   The word "*ingegno*" translates as imagination, inventiveness or wit. All seem appropriate. See Treadwell, Nina (2004). "She Descended on a Cloud 'From the Highest Spheres': Florentine Monody 'alla Romanina'". *Cambridge Opera Journal*, Vol. 16, No.1 (March), p. 9.

More reliable are Bernardo Buontalenti's drawings of the stage and costume designs.[77] His cartoon of Vittoria's outfit for "*Dalle piu alte sfere*" records a heavy velvet dress, with numerous layers, a formed corset and an elaborate headdress.

As any modern recording of *La Pellegrina* demonstrates, Vittoria's gifts were considerable. Isabella D'Este and her peers could not have sung this music. The high-lying melody and melismatic architecture cry out for ornamentation; if done well – or exceptionally[78] – the runs, skips, leaps, echoed-phrases and *staccato* enunciation are within the reach of only the most technically accomplished professionals. During the three decades preceding *La Pellegrina*, voice training had become something of an obsession for the court of Mantua, where the grandson of Isabella D'Este, Guglielmo Gonzaga, indulged his ancestor's passion for the arts when training as a composer,[79] and by spending money he didn't have on musicians he couldn't afford.[80] Guglielmo had hoped to challenge the glories of Ferrara; rather than promote the voices of women, however, he allowed his contempt for the *concerto delle donne* to drive him into the arms of Italy's *ultima moda*: the castrati.

Misogyny was *mise en scene* pretty much everywhere in the 16th century; for all its diversity, Italy was no exception. The clichés attaching to female subjugation have not gone unchallenged;[81] for all the attempts at retrograde empowerment, the quotidian female experience was unequal. Women in their gender were cherished if the same proved useful and necessary to men – as emblems of Catholic morality, as mothers, and as domestic matriarchs. This did little to redraft an educational and cultural cadence that prioritised obedience and devotion above independence and influence. The lives lived by Lucrezia Borgia and Isabella D'Este were exceptional even by the standards of the aristocracy, such that the less privileged were denigrated and prescribed, even if directed practically towards the preservation and management of their husbands' property. The pursuit of knowledge for aesthetic and intellectual purposes was problematic outside confinement, where young women were disposed of according to their dowries and treated badly if there were no dowries to give. The well-rehearsed tradition that every Italian man loves his mother did not translate to every Italian man loving women. Guglielmo Gonzaga's apparent loathing of his grandmother's gender was frothy even for the time; on 15 May, 1581, for example, his reaction to a concert by "three ladies" was recorded by the Florentine ambassador:

> Having presented with great ceremony to His Excellency [Guglielmo] the music of these ladies, while he [Duke Alfonso II] was waiting for him to praise them to the skies [Guglielmo] interrupted, saying in a loud voice that could be heard by the ladies and the duchesses who were

---

77   Of which there were 286 in total.

78   Emma Kirkby's recording with Andrew Parrott and the Taverner Players is peerless (Erato/Warner Classics; 1988).

79   Sherr, Richard (1978). "The Publications of Guglielmo Gonzaga." *Journal of the American Musicological Society*, 31, pp. 118–125.

80   Sherr, Richard (1980). *Gugliemo Gonzaga and the Castrati*. Renaissance Quarterly, Vol. 33, No. 1, pp. 33–56.

81   See, for example, Dialeti, Androniki (2011). "Defending Women, Negotiating Masculinity in Early Modern Italy." *The Historical Journal*. Vol. 54, No. 1 (March), pp. 1–23.

present, "Ladies are a big deal; actually I would rather be an ass than a lady," and with this he rose, and forced everyone else to rise so that the singing would come to an end.[82]

Guglielmo was born with a twisted spine; it is tempting to align his self-image with Shakespeare's construction of disability as articulated by Richard III in his rage at "Edward's wife, that monstrous witch" – "behold mine arm […] that by their witch-craft thus have marked me".[83] The temptation becomes greater still when reflecting, as did Guglielmo that his wife, the Archduchess Eleanor of Austria, was thought to be the ugliest princess not to have remained a frog.[84] The Duke's enthusiasm for the emasculated began to crystalise shortly after his wedding on 26 April, 1561, when work began on the Basilica Palatina di Santa Barbara, the Palatine Chapel of the House of Gonzaga. In early 1565, Guglielmo instructed his agent, Girolamo Negri, to scout for castrati in Spain. Negri confirmed in May that Phillip II's own music master didn't believe there were more than six "excellent" male sopranos in the entire country. He proposed instead, and with gallows humour, that Guglielmo should "make his own."[85] With the demand for castrati in Mantua outstripping supply,[86] the Duke was informed by his *maestro di cappella*, Giulio Bruschi, that he had chanced upon three newly-unemployed castrati as they were passing through Mantua.[87] He invited them to an audition, and pressed the most gifted of their number, a 28-year-old Spanish priest, into ducal service. It's apparent from the resulting correspondence that the Duke's priorities for his castrati were easy high notes and an aptitude for improvisation ("*contrapunto*"). The young priest was soon commended for both,[88] but so too were many of the more readily available singers to have been born without testicles. The Duke's preferences were well-established, however; on 14 July, 1565, he wrote to inform Negri that Gonzaga had only three castrati, to whom he was paying a salary of three ducats a month. Any newly-retained castrati would have to be satisfied with the same desultory emolument. The Duke's retinue of voices was charged, for the most part, to sing only church music (with Bruschi pioneering polyphony for the Basilica's liturgy)[89] and during the 1560s and '70s Mantua was the first Italian court

---

82 Newcomb, Anthony (1970). *The Musica Secreta of Ferrara in the 1580s.* Ph.D. Dissertation; Princeton. p. 404.

83 *Richard III.* Act III, Scene IV.

84 Of the various portraits to survive, the most unfortunate was painted by Jakob Seisenegger when Eleanor was five and suffering from a fever that caused her extremities to swell – including her head and face. Quite why her parents (Ferdinand I, the Holy Roman Emperor, and Anna of Bohemia and Hungary) thought it a time in their daughter's life worth fixing in oil is anyone's guess. It has been suggested, unkindly but with some justification, that the question of what to do with the "ugly one" (as the eighth of fifteen children, and the sixth daughter) made Guglielmo an obvious solution.

85 Sherr, Richard (1980). *Gugliemo Gonzaga and the Castrati.* Renaissance Quarterly, Vol. 33, No. 1, p. 36.

86 One of his last castrati retired with a ducal pension in August, 1565, in which month Gugliemlo wrote to ducal officials requesting a pension for "Guglielmo Fordos castrato Francese." *Ibid.*

87 The Cardinal of Augsburg had recently dissolved his Chapel.

88 Guglielmo received an enthusiastic report of the singer's talent on 27 June, 1565. Sherr, Richard (1980). *Gugliemo Gonzaga and the Castrati.* Renaissance Quarterly, Vol. 33, No. 1, pp. 33–56.

89 Fenlon, Iain (1980). *Music and Patronage in Sixteenth-Century Mantua, Volume 1.* Cambridge University Press, pp. 105–106.

to promote the use of castrati in place of women. It would be simplistic to attribute the elevation of male sopranos to cultural and institutional misogyny, but the facts speak to the prejudices of a hunchback with an ugly wife preferring the company of the "un'semniar'd"[90] to the inseminated.

The Duke's enthusiasms peaked during the 1580s, after the majority of castrati in Mantua, and Italy more generally, were imported from France, Flanders and Spain. His prescriptions were also secular, as is evident from a letter he wrote to his agent in Paris on 4 May, 1583, outlining what he was seeking:

> Principally [they need to] be good Catholics and modest youths so that we can hope for long and happy service from them. They should sing in a secure manner and have good voices. And if they know contrapunto and how to accompany themselves on the lute, they will be appreciated all the more.[91]

The lute was a chamber instrument, and Guglielmo's tastes were evolving in tandem with courtly appetites for *commedia dell'arte* and *intermedi*, when Vincenzo Giustiniani identified in his *Discorso sopra la Musica* a "new" florid type of solo singing in Naples, Rome and Florence. It follows that the emergence of the castrato as a voice in competition with the female soprano at the end of the 16th century was animated less by religious prescription than by the technical requirements of an evolving musical typography. According to Richard Sherr:

> It may have been that Guglielmo and others recognized the aptness of the castrato voice for such performance, and became more occupied with musica da camera. In fact, castrati may have entered the Church in force rather late; the earliest we can now find them in the papal chapel, for instance, is the 1580s. It seems to me then that Guglielmo Gonzaga in his later constant search for castrati was in fact motivated by the same considerations that caused Alfonso d'Este to establish the "three ladies": a wish to be entertained by high virtuoso solo voices. His use of castrati can be seen finally not as an aspect of sacred music as much as a response to the changing style of secular music with its increased emphasis on the solo singer.[92]

The Duke died in August, 1587, less than two years before the publication of *Cum pro nostro pastorali munere*, and the wedding of Ferdinando and Cristina in Florence. Appearing alongside Vittoria Archilei at the Uffizi were three castrati: Pierino Palibotri, Niccolò Bartolini and Onofrio Gualfreducci. The last of this trio, and the most celebrated Italian castrato of the time, left Rome in 1584, where he had been

90 *Antony and Cleopatra*, Act I, Scene V. Part of Cleopatra's pun-riddled characterisation of the eunuch Mardian.

91 Sherr, Richard (1980). *Gugliemo Gonzaga and the Castrati*. Renaissance Quarterly, Vol. 33, No.1, p. 38.

92 *Ibid*, p. 46.

one of the leading voices of the Sistine choir. After completing his contract for the Medici – one of his first secular engagements – Gualfreducci returned to Rome in service to his former patron, Cardinal Montalto, who was now Pope Sixtus V.[93] He lived into the age of opera while contributing nothing to it. For *La Pellegrina*, Gualfreducci performed Cavalieri's monody "*Godi turba mortal*" in the sixth *intermedio*. The song is brief, at around a minute in length, and it spans only a ninth, with quavers notated in place of improvised semi-quavers; it is less challenging technically than "*Dalle piu alte sfere*," but neither Vittoria nor Gualfreducci would have struggled to sing either song. At the same time, castrati were recognised universally to produce more clarion high notes, and greater tone, breath management and ornamental dexterity. The necessity for castrati, such as it was, can be said in consequence to have emerged from an admixture of cultural, social and liturgical prejudices, all bolstered by a genuine predilection for male sopranos being capable of things that were not routinely within the armoury of contemporary women. It was not, as many have suggested, a construction of the male misappropriation of the feminine; rather, it facilitated a simpler, more pragmatic displacement that enabled the Church and the aristocracy to take advantage of a disgrace that cultivated an instrument not otherwise commonly available.[94]

It is equally certain that obsidian misogyny contributed to the bifurcation of the soprano voice between genders, as a function of complex psychological aberrations that preferred mutilated men to unmarried women at risk of pregnancy. Sixtus V died shortly after Guglielmo Gonzaga, to be replaced 13 months (and three Popes) later[95] by Clement VIII – who inherited the bounteous advantages of the Catholic Church's legalisation of castration. Nine years later, the first opera, Peri's *La Dafne*,[96] was premiered during the 1598 Carnival,[97] at the Palazzo Corsi Salviatti in Via Tornabuoni in Florence.[98] For the next two centuries, the soprano voice would belong to men as well as women in what, with hindsight, can be characterised as the most extreme, perverse and gratuitous expression of male cultural prejudice in human history. That is not to condemn castrati – all of whom were victims as children of morally-criminal

---

93   The Cardinal was promoted on 24 April, 1585. It follows that Gualfreducci was known to (and singing for) the Pope when he authorised the publication of *Cum pro nostro pastorali munere*.

94   King, Thomas A. (2006). "The Castrato's Castratian", in *Studies in English Literature, 1500–1900.* Restoration and Eighteenth Century. Vol. 46, No. 3, pp. 563–583; p. 575.

95   In a series of Conclavic mishaps, Sixtus V was followed by Urban VII, who lived for 12 days, Gregory XIV, who lived for 315 days, and Innocent IX, who lived for 62 days. Clement VIII was more robust and reigned for 13 years and 32 days.

96   The ensemble is known to have featured just five instrumental parts. In real terms, *Dafne* was a more developed form of *intermedio*, distinguished by a more defined narrative and the interaction of characters whose theatrical purpose reached further than the prescribed functionality of symbolism, metaphor and allegory.

97   Carnival is a Christian festive season that occurs before the liturgical season of Lent. The main events typically occur during February or early March, during the period known historically as Shrovetide. The most famous Carnival is, of course, celebrated in Venice.

98   The room in which *La Dafne* was first performed is now the "Brunelleschi Suite", a 175 sqm one-bedroom apartment on the second floor of the former Palace that is now rented out for travellers as part of the Palazzo Tournabuoni, a wildly-expensive residence-club operated by Four Seasons and Hotels (https://palazzotornabuoni.com).

violence.[99] Rather, it is to isolate the comically absurd circumstances in which female singers after 1600 were separated from (and challenged when using) their voices. It was a farcical conceit that operated in tandem with the unfolding history of the soprano – best summarised by an apologetic misquotation from Virginia Woolf's *Orlando*: "As long as he sings like a woman, nobody objects to a woman singing also."[100]

---

99 Castration was all but outlawed during the middle 19th century. Unsurprisingly, perhaps, it remained unlawful until the 1930s, when the NSDAP embraced the procedure as part of its statutory sterilisation programme. 400,000 men were castrated between 1933 and 1945. See Giles, Geoffrey J. (1992). "'The Most Unkindest Cut of All': Castration, Homosexuality and Nazi Justice. *Journal of Contemporary History*, Vol. 27, No. 1, pp. 41–61.

100 "Love, the poet has said, is woman's whole existence. And if we look for a moment at Orlando writing at her table, we must admit that never was there a woman more fitted for that calling. Surely, since she is a woman, and a beautiful woman, and a woman in the prime of life, she will soon give over this pretence of writing and thinking and begin at least to think of a gamekeeper (and as long as she thinks of a man, nobody objects to a woman thinking)." Woolf, Virginia (2006). *Orlando, a Biography*. Houghton Mifflin Harcourt, p. 198.

CHAPTER TWO

Origin of the Species

Among the many exhibitionist feats of literary modernism that characterised the *avant garde* during the first third of the 20th century, Ezra Pound's *The Cantos* takes the biscuit as well as the tin in which it was served. It dwarfs both Eliot's *The Waste Land* (which Pound helped to edit) and Joyce's *Ulysses* in its appetite for the obscurantist and the byzantine. Even with an atlas and a university library to hand, Pound's abstruse reliance on remote points of reference, telescopic allusion and languages other than English – which extended to Greek (in which Pound was far from fluent) and Mandarin (which he was unable to read or write at all)[1] – make digestion of *The Cantos* impossible for anyone not blessed with infinite patience and an encyclopaedic primer.

One of Pound's pre-occupations throughout the poem's 116 parts[2] is a Venice-centred nostalgia for the Florentine *Accademia* for which Pound considered himself to be uniquely well-suited. His lurching romantic affection for the imagined intellectual purity of a culture untainted by Jews – amplified by his flinty revulsion for profit and usury – lingered on Gemistos Plethon,[3] a charismatic Greek scholar and philosopher who pioneered the revival, preservation and propagation of Greek cultural patrimony in Western Europe. Plethon exercised a Rasputin-like influence over Cosimo de' Medici, whose seduction by Plethon's wished-for revival of the Hellenic gods inspired him in 1439 to establish with Marsilio Ficino the Accademia Platonica in Florence. Based on what they had understood of Plethon's lectures,[4] the Platonica set about translating all of Plato's works, the *Enneads* of Plotinus and numerous other Neo-platonist manuscripts, into Latin, feats of brilliance that operated to launch a three-century fashion in Italy for (mostly-humanist) Academies.[5] With Cosimo's influence waning during the 1450s, dozens of Academies sprang into existence in overt competition, mainly across northern Italy, but in Rome also. A century after Cosimo's death, in 1563, his namesake, Cosimo I, founded the Medici Accademia delle Arti del Disegno, which operated as the country's first formally organised art

---

1   Pound's arch delight in Mandarin was first evidenced by *Cathay* (1915), a collection of classical Chinese poetry which he "translated" using Ernest Fenollosa's notes on Mandarin characters, acquired by Pound in 1913.
2   The *Cantos* extends to almost 800 pages in modern print.
3   *circa* 1355 – *circa* 1453.
4   It has been argued that Cosimo will have understood very little of Plethon's talks. Hankins, James (2003). *Humanism and Platonism in the Italian Renaissance*, Volume 1, "Humanism." Edizione di Storia e Letteratura, p. 207.
5   The birth of the Italian Academies is commonly dated to in 1525, and the establishment of the Accademia degli Intronati and the Congrega dei Rozzi – both in Siena.

academy. In 1573, the Camerata de' Bardi (or Florentine Camerata) was established to promote the study, creation and performance of music as art – albeit only for men.[6]

Unremarkably for the time, the founders and operators of Academies were patrician, with women invited to attend as performers (when need and opportunity collided) and less often as (silent) guests. Though routine, and absolute among the lower classes, the institutional isolation of women was problematic throughout the second half of the 15th century for the majority of the educated in Italy. It was thanks to the Academies that the female voice began slowly to become audible among the elite.[7] Though not formally an Academy, Domenico Venier's salon in Campo Santa Maria Formosa[8] gathered just about every male literary and political figure of note in Venice to his door, including Girolamo Molino, Federico Badoer, Sperone Speroni, Fortunio Spira, Lodovico Dolce, Bernardo Cappello, Girolamo Mutio, Girolamo Parabosco and Pietro Aretino. Venier frequently added Venetian female poets to his guest list, notably Gaspara Stampa and Veronica Franco (whose portrait was painted by Tintoretto). Venier was also among the first to make a habit of bringing female singers and musicians to his home, notably Polissena Perocina, Polissena Frigera and Franceschina Bellamano. To the last of these composer-performers he wrote the following heartfelt poetic tribute:

> *Con varie voci or questa, or quella corda*
> *Tocca da bella man sul cavo legno*
> *Mirabilmente il canto si al suon accorda.*[9]

Any honorarium was better than none, even if it was patronising, self-serving and double-edged. Alessandro Piccolomini (then a member of the Academy of the Infiammati di Padua) famously presented a sonnet that defended women in terms that were condescending even for the time,[10] while the chess player and writer Annibale Romei's most celebrated *Discorsi*,[11] from 1586, struggled to challenge the *status quo* when accounting unequally for female and male voices at the Court of Don Alfonso da Este.[12] For all his chivalric panegyrics, Romei's female characters are still required to do little more than ask questions, perform music and keep the men happy and

---

6   There were exceptions, inevitably. See below Veronica Gambara and the Academy of Sonnacchiosi.

7   See, generally, Dialeti, Androniki (2004). *The Debate About Women and its Socio-Cultural Background in Early Modern Venice*. PhD thesis. University of Glasgow, and Dialeti, Androniki (2011) "Defending Women, Negotiating Masculinity In Early Modern Italy." *The Historical Journal* Vol. 54, No. 1, pp. 1–23.

8   A city square 600 meters north of St. Mark's.

9   'With various words, now this, now that string; Does the lovely hand touch on the hollow wood; Miraculously tuning her song to its sound.' No. 68, vv. 9–11. Feldman, Martha (1995). *City Culture and the Madrigal at Venice*. University of California Press, pp. 103–104.

10   *Dialogo della bella creanza delle donne* (1540). See, generally, *The Italian Academies 1525–1700: Networks of Culture, Innovation and Dissent* (2016). Eds. Jane E. Everson, Denis V Reidy, Lisa Sampson. Legenda.

11   *Discorsi del conte Annibale Romei divisi in sette giornate, nelle quale tra Dame e Cavaglieri ragionando...* ('Discourses by Count Annibale Romei divided into seven days, between myself and a knight of reason.' (Venice, 1619).

12   Don Alfonso (Duke of Ferrara) had died fifty years earlier, in 1535.

cheerful. Thomaso Pellegrini's lecture extolling women to the Academia di Occulti,[13] in Brescia, was more bullish in its advocacy of the virtue of women in parity with the best interests of the Academicians. In the preface to their *Rime degli Academici Occulti* (1568), they employed a Silenus[14] to symbolise the value of the secret as something beautiful for hiding beneath something rough and rustic.[15] The Bolognese Accedemia di Sonnacchiosi directed a number of lectures towards the interests of women, and it subsequently became the first Academy to invite a woman to join, although this progressive genuflection was not inherently virtuous because Veronica Gambara was a politician as well as a poet, and the ruler of Corregio for more than three decades.[16] When Scipion Bargagli delivered his *Oratione* to the Academy of Accesi in Siena, he identified as a condition precedent for all Academies

> the divine grace and celestial favour that always pours down from the beautiful, lovable and courageous women; they always keep the virtuous young men cheerful and fit, and lead them to pleasant and honourable undertakings.[17]

Piccolomini aimed higher when criticising the Sienese Academy of the Intronati for their improper attitude towards women; Cristofano Bronzini openly damned Giuseppe Passi, a fellow-member of the Accademia degli Informi in Ravenna, for his infamous treatise *I donneschi Difetti*.[18] Passi's breathless disparaging of the "natural inferiority" of women was welcomed by many in private, but his cataloguing of female vice was enough for the Informi (most of whom were either married or a father to a daughter) to submit the controversy to the arena of proto-feminist debate. Women in the right quarters were soon sufficiently confident to speak, learn and, even, write for themselves. The prominent courtesan, Tullia d'Aragona, was skilled in languages and letters; in her will she left thirty-five Latin and Italian volumes on a variety of subjects, including thirteen books of music – all of which she is presumed to have performed in private, if not also for those Academies she was known to frequent. D'Aragona was educated at home, under the primary care of her mother. Her relative privilege was typical of many with parents inclined to break with tradition and convention. In 1574, Stefano Guazzo wrote in *La civil conversazione* to praise fathers who wished their daughters "to be instructed in reading, writing, poetry, music and painting," rather than "nothing but spinning and the management of the household."[19] Tutors for girls and female teachers were retained with increasing frequency during the second half of the 16th century, with moral guidance, literacy, needlework,

---

13   In its use by the Academy, "*occulti*" was understood to mean 'hidden.' It was not intended to allude to the English-language concept of the 'occult.'
14   Creatures of the wild – part man, part beast.
15   The Academy's motto was "*intus non extra*" ('Within, not without').
16   1518 – 1550.
17   *The Italian Academies 1525–1700: Networks of Culture, Innovation and Dissent* (2016). Eds. Jane E. Everson, Denis V Reidy, Lisa Sampson. Legenda, p. 166.
18   'The Defects of Women' (1598).
19   Dialeti, Androniki (2004). *The Debate About Women and its Socio-Cultural Background in Early Modern Venice*. PhD thesis. University of Glasgow, pp. 72–73.

arithmetic, singing and the playing of instruments providing the primary skills by which a daughter might become attractive to a man, and a family worth joining.

Lucrezia Marinella blew a memorably stentorian raspberry at Giuseppe Passi when writing "*La nobilità, et l'eccellenza delle donne,*"[20] in which she steered the political issue of gender towards a patriotic celebration of pride in Venice and an archly Venetian (and imagined) digression on the glories of the Fourth Crusade. Marinella later distanced herself from her dialectical ferocity with *Amoro Innamorato et Impazzato*[21] – a poem in which she applauded the domestication of women and the dangers of intellectual study[22] – but her courage and learning contributed much to the escalation of the *Querelle des femmes*, a centuries-long divergence that can be considered ongoing if not eternal. The majority of Academies preferred not to dig in, one way or another, but the discourse as between the genders was entrenched by 1600, when Moderata Fonte's[23] posthumous dialogues *Giustizia delle Donne*[24] and *Il Merito delle Donne*[25] were published with the subtitle *Le nobiltà, et eccellenze delle donne: et i diffetti, e mancamenti de gli huomini.*[26]

The *Merito delle Donne* frustrates convention through a dialogue between seven Venetian women in a house overlooking the Grand Canal: Adriana, an elderly widow; Virginia, Adriana's unmarried daughter; Leonora, a young widow; Lucretia, an older married woman; Cornelia and Corinna, young unmarried women, and Helena, a young woman, recently married. The discussion focusses on the status of women and the function of marriage. Under the worldly supervision of Adriana, the party divides between Leonora, Corrina and Cornelia (who condemn the prevailing order and the rules and structures subverting women as naturally secondary) and Helena, Virginia and Lucretia (who are painted as victims or, at the very least, conspirators in the gender war). Fonte attributes economic duress, maltreatment and sequestration to husbands and the men among their relatives. Women pushed back by looking up, and yet the promotion of female rights, and the political and cultural application of "voice" to the understanding of the female perspective as meaningful, did not equate to progress. Sienna, for example, had evolved sufficiently to promote the intellectual rights of aristocratic women. Before the end of the century the progressive climate chilled to a point whereby Scipione Bargagli could reflect in *Dell' imprese*:[27]

> in the happy days of their youth [the Accademia degli Intronati] used to mix more often and with greater freedom with the beautiful and virtuous women of Siena than happens in these present wretched and corrupt times.[28]

---

20   'The Nobility and the Excellence of Women.'

21   'Love Enamoured and Driven Mad.' Published in 1618.

22   A retrograde construction which she nonetheless dedicated to the Duchess of Mantua, Catherine de' Medici.

23   The pseudonym of Modesta di Pozzo di Forzi.

24   'Women's Justice.'

25   'The Worth of Women.'

26   'The nobility and excellence of women: and the defects and failings of men.'

27   'Of business.'

28   Published in 1594. Fahy, Conor (2000). "Women and Italian Cinquecento Literary Academies." In

If "Promethean fire" (as a shorthand for improvement) was not self-evident in "the academes that show, contain, and nourish all the world" then in "women's eyes"[29] change was manifest in the music being written for them, and by them. Before 1600, the repertoire performed by female singers in Italian courts, academies and salons was simple, song-form and improvised. The solo madrigal, frottola, villanella and other short-settings of isolated verse operated as vernacular. *Intermedi* only rarely promoted a narrative, with most of them attaching to a human emotion, experience or virtue – necessarily in praise of the family or individual picking up the bill. What story there was to tell was almost always presented in the guise of a mythological allegory. Theatrical spectacles were just that; even when performed by more than one singer, the music was in every case brief, piecemeal and "closed."

On 6 October, 1600, the female voice underwent a paradigm shift. Only a handful of people were aware of it at the time, and none of them could agree on what to call it.[30] The first performance of *Euridice* was given as part of Marie de' Medici and Henry IV's wedding celebrations.[31] Jacopo Peri is remembered as the work's creator, but Giulio Caccini made a number of significant contributions; the uneasy hierarchy between the composers degenerated into petty squabbles, the most childish of which saw Caccini refusing to allow "his" singers to perform Peri's music.[32] Among the guests was the Duke of Mantua, Vincenzo Gonzaga, who attended with his court composer, Claudio Monteverdi. Although the expressive palette of *Euridice's* score is limited in range and theatricality, the vocal writing makes novel use of solos, ensembles and choruses, with character and tension created and released by words and music in an evolving proximity that idealised dramatic speech after the fashion of the Greek dramas venerated by the Florentine Camerata. Peri's structural innovations gave rise to the definitive mechanism of aria and recitative – which, for *Euridice*, was serviced across twelve roles, eleven of them scored for male-born singers. In addition to four parts for tenor (including Orfeo, which was sung by the composer at the premiere), two are for bass, four for castrati and one for a "boy." The only role scored for a woman – the first for a soprano to survive – was Euridice, personified by Vittoria Archilei. Peri's *Euridice* was followed by Emilio de' Cavalieri's *Rappresentatione di anima, et di corpo*[33] (1600), Giulio Caccini's *Il rapimento di Cefalo*[34] (1600) and *Euridice* (1602), Agazzari's *Eumelio* (1606) and Marco da Gagliano's *Dafne* (1608). The various prefaces written by the composers Peri, Caccini and Cavalieri, and the librettists Striggio, Rinuccini and Chiabrera, leave no doubt that everyone jostling for recognition was conscious of their part in the creation of a new genre, with the price of patronage being publication and the printing of dedications. Without a patron

Panizza, Letizia (2000). *Women in Italian Renaissance Culture and Society, Women in Italian Renaissance Culture and Society.* Oxford University Press, p. 440.

29   *Love's Labour's Lost*, Act 4, Scene 3.

30   The first reported use of the word "opera" dates to 1639.

31   *Euridice* is the first opera score to have survived to the present day.

32   Carter, Tim (1980). *Jacopo Peri.* Music & Letters, Vol. 61, No. 2, pp. 121–135; p. 126.

33   'Portrayal of the Soul and the Body.'

34   'The Abduction of Cephalus.' Caccini's opera was premiered just three days after Peri's *Euridice* – as part of the Medici wedding celebrations. It was staged in the Sala delle Commedie of the Palazzo Uffizi, rather than the Palazzo Pitti. The audience at the Uffizi was formed of 3,000 men and 800 women.

there was no hope of a performance – since there were no theatres suitable for opera outside the palaces of the aristocracy,[35] and no public to hear them.

Female sopranos were retained by every self-respecting court, but it was to castrati that the earliest composers of opera turned for their leads. The first and most celebrated exception to that rule was Caccini's *Il rapimento di Cefalo*. This five-hour extravaganza cost the Medici family 60,000 scudi, a mind-boggling sum of money for a single performance that generated no revenue.[36] Among the singers were Melchior Palantrotti, Jacopo Peri, Francesco Rasi and five members of the composer's own family.[37] Caccini's infamous ambition suggests a working knowledge of Princes in writing as well as in person, but it is equally certain that his nepotism was overreached by the legitimacy of his family's abilities. Tim Carter has proposed that the cast for the premiere of *Il rapimento di Cefalo* included Caccini's second wife (Margherita di Agostino Benevoli della Scala), his sister-in-law by his first wife (Margherita Gagnolanti), his son Pompeo and Ginevra Mazziere detta l'Azzurina.[38] The star of the show was undoubtedly his second youngest daughter, Francesca,[39] a truth evidenced by Michelangelo Buonarotti *il giovane*,[40] who published a detailed account of *Il rapimento's* first production and the performers' "angelic voices."[41] Years later, Pietro della Valle recalled how

> Signora Francesca Caccini, daughter of our Romano, called in Tuscan La Cecchina,[42] has been greatly admired for many years in Florence, where I heard her in my youth, both for her musical abilities in singing, and in composing and for her poetry not only in Latin but also in Tuscan.[43]

---

35 Peri's *Euridice*, for example, was premiered at the Palazzo Pitti, a gargantuan building of more than 30,000 square metres, acquired by the Medici in 1549. It is now the largest museum space in Italy.

36 Converting the value of the scudo in 1600 into modern currency is hideously difficult, if not impossible. However, 80,000 to 100,000 scudi equated in 1600 to the average annual income of a respectable provincial town with a population of around 5,000, with twice as many peasants in the environs. It follows that the Medici family committed almost the equivalent of the annual income of the city of Ivrea (population in 1600: 4,200; in 2022: 25,000) to a single theatre performance.

37 Carter, Tim (2003). "Rediscovering Il rapimento di Cefalo." *The Journal of Seventeenth-Century Music*. Vol 9, No. 1.

38 According to Tim Carter, Ginevra Mazziere detta l'Azzurina, was seduced, raped, or made pregnant by Pompeo Caccini. They may eventually have married.

39 18 September, 1587 – *circa* 1641 / 42. Caccini's youngest daughter, Settimia (born, 6 October 1591) was only nine (and 3 days) at the time and although she too was a singer of talent, it is unlikely she would have been expected (or required) to take part.

40 'The Younger.' His grand-uncle was the painter-sculptor, Michelangelo. *Il giovane* and Francesca went on to become close friends, and they collaborated often as librettist-composer.

41 Michelangelo Buonarotti, "Descrizione delle felicissime nozze ... della Cristianissima Maestà di Madama Maria Medici, Regina di Francia e di Navarra". Giorgio Marescotti (1600); in *Opere varie in versi ed in prosa*, (1894). Ed. Pietro Fanfani. Le Monnier, pp. 403–54. See also Carter, Tim (2003). "Rediscovering Il rapimento di Cefalo." *The Journal of Seventeenth-Century Music*. Vol. 9, No. 1.

42 It's worth noting that "Cecchina" in Tuscan meant "songbird." In modern Italian, it means "sniper," as in "*È stata uccisa da un cecchino...*" ('She was killed by a sniper...'). It's worth noting that Caccini and Cecchina sounded the same when spoken – but for the suffix vowel.

43 Silbert, Doris (1946). "Francesca Caccini: La Cecchina." *The Musical Quarterly*, Vol. 32, No.1, pp. 50–62; p. 51.

In the history of musical art there have been few debuts so fantastic. Had Francesca needed at any time to write a *curriculum vitae*, she could have recorded her first public performance at the age of 13[44] as the lead in the second opera ever published, in front of 4,000 of the closest friends and admirers of King Henry IV of France to celebrate his wedding to one of the most influential women in history. Francesca was a manifestly impressive woman; she more than lived up to the burden of her youth. Until reaching her maturity, she sang routinely in the company of her family in an ensemble identified as *le donne di Giulio Romano*.[45] When touring to France in 1604 with Rinuccini to perform for Henry IV and Queen Marie, the King remarked that Francesca sings "better than anyone in France." He implored the Grand Duke to allow her to join the French court, but Ferdinando I held fast[46] and Francesca remained with the Medici as a singer, teacher and composer of chamber and stage music for more than two decades, until early 1627. In 1614, when Francesca was the Court's highest paid musician,[47] the Caccini family travelled with the Court to Pisa, as they did every year for Lent. During Holy Week, on 26 March, the Medici's chronicler, Cesare Bastiano Tinghi, recorded how

> There was music by four choirs, consisting of the musicians who had come expressly for this purpose from Florence, there were two choirs in the church and two in the gallery [leading into the church][48]; one including Vittoria Archilei and Antonio Naldi and the other, Francesca, daughter of Giulio Romano, Giulio himself, his wife, and the husband of the aforementioned Francesca.[49]

It is coincidentally extraordinary and depressing that the two most celebrated sopranos of the early 17th century were joined in art and worship in what equated to the tradesmen's entrance for the church. They were united also in oppression, despite the Medici court being dominated at the time by the influence of women (a *status quo* remembered by Bronzini in his *Della dignità e nobiltà delle donne*[50] as being "politically necessary to the health of the state,") and Archilei and Caccini appear not to have competed. The 19th century theatrical historian, Alessandro Ademollo, characterised Vittoria as a "good natured and very tranquil virtuosa [...] content to let others live in peace."[51] He described Caccini as "proud and restless"[52] because of

---

44   She had celebrated her birthday only three weeks earlier.

45   Her father's sometime stage name.

46   He did, however, offer up Settimia, Francesca's sister, in her place.

47   In 1623, she earned 240 scudi. Cunningham, Caroline (1996). *Women Composers: Music Through the Ages*. Eds. Schleifer, Martha Furman; Glickman, Sylvia. G.K. Hill, p. 226.

48   The women were not, of course, welcome to sing *inside* the church. They could be heard, but neither seen nor admitted.

49   Silbert, Doris (1946). "Francesca Caccini: La Cecchina." The Musical Quarterly, Vol. 32, No.1, pp. 50–62; p. 51.

50   'On the dignity and nobility of women Dialogue.' (1628).

51   Cusick, Suzanne G. (1993) "Thinking from Women's Lives: Francesca Caccini after 1627." *The Musical Quarterly*, Vol. 77, No. 3, pp. 484–507; p. 484.

52   *Ibid.* See Ademollo, Alessandro (1888). *La bell'Adriana ed altre virtuose del suo tempo alla corte di Mantova*. Citta di Castello.

her infamous feud with the librettist Andrea Salvadori, a disquiet inflamed by her public ridiculing of Salvadori's private entanglements with the Court's female singers. More accurately, and with less prejudice perhaps, Caccini's contemporary, Bronzini, recalled the singer as

> friendly and admirable, never tiresome or resentful but merry and charming [...] and whether playing, singing, or pleasantly talking, she worked such stunning effects in the minds of her listeners that she changed them from what they had been.[53]

It's easy to appreciate why Francesca's abilities as a singer were eclipsed by her appetites as a composer. She created a considerable body of music, most of it lost, so her legacy vests with a collection of monodies, *Il primo libro delle musiche*,[54] and the comic opera-ballet *La liberazione di Ruggiero dall'isola d'Alcina*.[55] With a libretto by Ferdinando Saracinelli,[56] based on Ludovico Ariosto's *Orlando Furioso*, Caccini's sole surviving stage work was premiered on 3 February, 1625, at the Villa di Poggio Imperiale in Florence. It is thought to be the first opera composed by a woman. The score contains some fine music, with the part-writing featuring a large number of *ritornelli*, the purpose of which is made obvious by the growing complexity of a vocal score that is rich with chromaticism, ornamentation and melismas – much of it notated. Caccini's creativity is routine and uninspired; it adheres to the Monteverdian juxtaposition of set pieces and recitative, with flat-keys employed for the female characters (Alcina and Sirena) and sharp-keys for the men (Ruggiero and Pastore). Francesca reserves C major for the genderless sorceress, Melissa. It seems likely that Francesca wrote the role of Sirena for herself; it certainly contains the most technically challenging music, with numerous semi-quaver runs calling on secure breath control and dexterity. The fact that Caccini wrote out many (though not all) of the vocal ornaments ensures that any modern performance adhering to the music as written will provide a reliable approximation of the qualities needed for performances of music in "public" during the first quarter of the century. For all her talent, it would be absurd to suggest that Caccini's compositions were of the first rank. Her defining achievement was to prevail. Indeed, the changes to which her modest success as a composer alluded were far from contiguous; the exceptional talent of her only child, Maria, was insufficient to prevent her being sent to the convent of San Girolamo in Florence, where she took the name "*Suor Placida*." Severo Bonini, a composer and writer on music (and a student of Francesca's father) heard Maria at San Girolamo, and reported that she had become

> so polished and brilliant in the profession of singing that everyone raced to hear her, admiring her smooth voice almost like resonant silver pipes,

---

53   Beer, Ann (2017). *Sounds and Sweet Airs: The Forgotten Women of Classical Music.* Oneworld Publications, p. 38.
54   'The First Book of Songs.'
55   'Liberation of Ruggiero from the island of Alcina.'
56   The libretto was to have been written by Salvadori, who refused to do anything to help Caccini.

full of trills and articulated ornaments accompanied with miraculous and feeling-filled dyna§mic shadings.[57]

No paintings survive of Francesca Caccini – although a medallion was forged during her thirties, on which was inscribed the legend "*Cechine pulchritudinis immortalitati.*"[58] There are three paintings of Adriana Basile – all by the same painter.[59] Born in Posillipo, on the Neapolitan coast, Basile moved with her brothers, Giambattista (a poet) and Lelio (a composer), and her sisters, Margherita and Vittoria (both singers), to the Gonzaga court in 1610. Although he didn't cast her in any of his operas, Monteverdi acclaimed Basile more talented even than Francesca Caccini – with whom she engaged in at least one public competition, in November, 1623. Her status, and the growing prominence of female singers, was captured in three Caravaggesque paintings by Antiveduto Gramatica of *St Cecilia and Two Angels,*[60] each featuring a triptych of musicians, with Basile at their centre. The work from 1613 features a halo'd Cecilia singing from a manuscript, with a male harpist to her right and a female lutenist to her left. But for the wings, the image is from life. Even if Gramatica did not expressly identify Basile as his model, the ornate gilded harp features the singer's coat of arms.[61] As between the three versions of the painting, the one constant is the representation of Cecilia. She is refined, feminine and focussed; her lips are barely parted and her gaze is fixed on the score as the source of her art, rather than on the viewer. It is unusual to see a singer from this time performing *a libro* – without holding an instrument. Basile was, of course, a skilled lutenist, so Gramatica's focus on her talent as a singer is striking. There is a clear precedent in Raphael's Bolognese *Cecilia* for the saint's separation from the material world,[62] with Raphael scattering broken, unstrung and useless instruments at the foot of his painting to symbolise the abandonment of earthly pleasures and the personification of music as a path to God. Gramatica's composition features a table on which sits a violin and a chitarrino, both in perfect working-order and ready-strung for playing. The isolation of Basile from her instruments alludes in consequence to the music of the spheres – to the timeless realm of the heavenly, a consensus that attaches Gramatica's imagery to a genre of 17th century painting known as *vanitus vanitatum* – a school that utilised still-life to evoke mortality and the perils of the material. The addition to the painting's composition of walnuts, apples, pears, roses, anemones, tulips and carnations signifies the beauty of nature while reminding the viewer that each of these divine "gifts" has been severed from its source. The juxtaposition of Basile as Cecilia singing *a libro* was, in effect, an acknowledgment by the Duke that the singer's art was eternal even if she wasn't.[63]

---

57   It says much of life in a 17th century Florentine convent that performances of this kind and variety were not only tolerated, but appreciated.

58   Silbert, Doris (1946). "Francesca Caccini: La Cecchina." *The Musical Quarterly*, Vol. 32, No.1, pp. 50–62; p. 62.

59   *circa* 1580 – *circa* 1640.

60   The painting is not the same as that on display at the Kunsthistorisches Museum, Vienna – which is similar, but features a different harpist, and is absent the castle on the horizon.

61   It also features Gonzaga's coat of arms, in case anyone failed to remember who was paying the artist.

62   Completed a century earlier, in 1515.

63   Vincenzo Gonzaga and his sons so admired Adriana that she was gifted an estate and a title in modern-day Montferrat, Piedmont.

Caccini and Basile were "beautiful songbirds." It was as singers rather than as composers that they made their living. The same was true for every other early 17th century female musician, with singing and teaching providing the only reliable mechanisms for employment and advancement. Such a narrow, prescriptive and prejudicial environment can be viewed only with hindsight, an imperfect vantagepoint from which to appreciate the extraordinary good fortune that singing, and being able to sing well, afforded young women in the absence of schools and academies, and with *very* few appetising alternatives to a life of poverty, parenthood or prostitution.[64] Few of those who lived with, and through, the Covid-19 pandemic will have fond memories of lockdowns, masks and vaccinations. For the majority, however, the worst that was experienced was boredom – with the internet at hand to ensure that isolation was never truly isolating. Hard though it is to remember a time when vaccinations were considered universally to be a blessing, it was once the case that diseases were fatal for everyone, all of the time. For Italians at the turn of the 17th century, a life at Court, or in service to the Church, was a life less ordinary because it afforded a measure of protection against the commonality of death and disease. Some diseases were worse than others.

On the third Sunday of every July, and until Covid threw a *chiave inglese* into the works, Venice has for centuries hosted the *Festa del Redentore*[65] – now marked routinely by fireworks. It was inaugurated as a feast of thanks following the ruinous plague of 1575–8, which killed more than 50,000 Venetians,[66] around a third of the city's population.[67] Among the victims was Tiziano Vecellio (Titian), although considering his age his death was other than premature.[68] The Doge Alvise I Mocenigo undertook to build a church on the Island of Giudecca[69] once the plague was over, for which Andrea Palladio was sent the commission.[70] The cornerstone was laid by the Patriarch of Venice, Giovanni Trevisano, on 3 May, 1577, as part of an elaborate series of ceremonial events that included religious services, outdoor musical performances and parades. The church was consecrated in 1592 as Chiesa del Santissimo Redentore[71] – twelve years after Palladio's death. The city breathed a sigh of relief, only to see the return of *I dottori della peste* in 1630. In less than 18 months, 46,000 people, more than a third of the already much-depleted population of 140,000, were dead.[72] At the height of the pandemic, on 26 October, 1630, the Doge Nicolo Contarini announced his endowment of another church of redemption, to be built

---

64   It was more commonly the case that all three states were enjoyed coincidentally.

65   'Festival of the Redeemer.'

66   By way of comparison, the 1575–1578 plague killed 17,329 in Milan and 17,396 in Brescia (almost half the population).

67   448 years later, the population of Venice is not much larger, at approximately 255,000.

68   He was almost 90.

69   A small island to the south of the sestiere Dorsoduro, to which it is joined administratively.

70   The cornerstone was laid by the Patriarch of Venice, Giovanni Trevisano, on 3 May, 1577. It is today as it appeared when consecrated in 1592. The *Redentore* was one of Canaletto's favourite churches; he painted it many times.

71   'Church of the Most Holy Redeemer.'

72   Between 1629 and 1631, northern and central Italy suffered somewhere between 300,000 and 1,000,000 deaths from a plague that is now thought to have heralded the end to Venice's fortunes commercially and politically.

on Dorsoduro.[73] Pursuant to a competition in 1631, the 26-year-old Baldassarre Longhena was awarded the honour of designing the Santa Maria della Salute, which became Venice's largest church after St. Mark's Basilica when it was finished in 1681. The vast, imposing Baroque masterpiece, with its octagonal rotunda and paired domes and bell-towers,[74] was built on a platform formed of a million wooden piles, all of which remain in place to this day. Long before the church's consecration, the building was decorated, appropriately enough, with 12 paintings by Titian, including "The Descent of the Holy Ghost," "St. Mark Enthroned with Saints Cosmas, Damian, Sebastian and Roch,"[75] and several ceiling paintings.[76] With the plague declared over, numerous other votives were commissioned to celebrate Venice's deliverance from suffering, chief among them a Solemn Mass for the Feast of Sancta Maria from the city's leading composer, Claudio Monteverdi. The plague was terrible for many, and Monteverdi was no exception. His younger brother, Giulio Cesare, his friend and librettist Alessandro Striggio, and his assistant as *maestro di cappella* of San Marco, Alessandro Grandi, were all killed by the disease. So too were many of the singers of St. Mark's – with the ladies of the choir being decimated. After the plague, Monteverdi auditioned dozens of singers from outside the city, settling on eight sopranos, for each of whom he took personal responsibility – as had become his habit after moving to Mantua to work for the son and heir of Guglielmo Gonzaga, Vincenzo, Duke of Mantua.

Vincenzo's devotion to the arts was greater, even, than his father's. He appointed Monteverdi *maestro di capella* in 1602 (shortly after retaining Rubens and Tasso)[77] – around a decade after he first joined the Mantuan court. Monteverdi and the Duke endured a fractious relationship; one of the few things on which they appeared to agree was the need to develop a strong female presence among the Court's voices. Unlike his father, Vincenzo was not especially enamoured of castrati, so Monteverdi and his colleagues were tasked to ensure that the Court's increasingly renowned musical standards benefitted from the sound of women. Monteverdi was required to care for them accordingly, as evidenced by a shopping list of items he ordered for sending to the most important among the cortege:

> To Signora Lucia Pelizzari 2 measures of veal, 2 of fish, 35 lire 17s 11d[78] in money; to Signora Isabella Pelizzari, the same; to Signora Lucretia Urbana 2 measures of veal, 2 of fish, 4 of salt, 2 of oil and 2 candles, 3 measures of cheese and 120 lire in money; to Signora Catarina Romana

---

73 'Saint Mary of Health.'
74 He was fortunate to be so young. The building took 50 years to complete; it was consecrated in 1681, shortly before the architect's death at the age of 81.
75 An altarpiece painted originally for the church of Santo Spirito in Isola; it was Titian's first independent commission, dating from 1508–9.
76 "David and Goliath," "Abraham and Isaac," "Cain and Abel," and eight *tondi* (a circular work of art) of the eight Doctors of the Church and the Evangelists.
77 Tasso eventually settled eventually at the Este Court in Ferrara.
78 The article was published in England, in October, 1970. Decimalisation came into effect four months later, on 15 February, 1971.

6 measures of veal, 4 of fish, one of salt, 7 of oil and 7 candles, 120 lire in money.[79]

Shortly before the young composer's arrival in Mantua, the Duke travelled to Ferrara with "four ladies from Vicenza who sing very well and play the cornetto and other instruments."[80] Contemporary pay records identify three of these sopranos as Europa Rossi, and the sisters Lucia and Isabella Pelizzari – to whom the composer had sent meat, fish and money.[81] Though not identified expressly, the fourth singer to travel was Claudia Cattaneo,[82] who became Monteverdi's wife in 1599. These *concerto delle donne* were valued primarily as ensemble performers (in which tradition the Pelizzari sisters were raised within a family of musicians, for whom Monteverdi composed many five-part madrigals), but Mantua encouraged the emergence of solo-celebrity, a shift in perspective rooted in the work of Europa Rossi.[83] "Madama Europa," as she was known after her triumph in Giovanni Giacomo Gastoldi's *Il ratto di Europa*[84] (an *intermedi*, with a libretto by Chiabrera, first performed during the celebrations held to mark the wedding of Francesco Gonzaga in 1608),[85] was the first Jewish singer to achieve widespread fame outside the Jewish community.[86] She appears to have been an artist of unusual expressive power, with one observer recalling how

> she sang to the listeners' great delight and their greater wonder, in a most delicate and sweet-sounding voice [...] delightfully modulating her mournful tones that caused the listeners to shed tears of compassion.[87]

Rossi's prominence failed to protect her when Mantua's Jewish ghetto was put to the sword by the Holy Roman Empire's largely Austrian army in 1630. In Mantua, she was rivalled only by Cattaneo (who died young, leaving Monteverdi with two

---

79 Arnold, Denis (1970). "Monteverdi's Singers." *The Musical Times*. Vol. 111, No. 1532, pp. 982–985.

80 Document from 14 April, 1589. Archivio di Stato, Firenze; Archivio Mediceo, f. 2905, No. 86. Quoted in Newcomb, Anthony (1980). *The Madrigal at Ferrara, 1579–1597*, Vol. 1. Princeton University Press, pp. 98–99.

81 Gibbons, William James (2006). *Issues of Voice Range and Transposition in Monteverdi's Mantuan Madrigals*. Master' Thesis. Chapel Hill.

82 [Unknown] – 10 September, 1607.

83 1570 – 1630.

84 Her most famous role; 'The Rape of Europa.'

85 See, generally, Harrán, Don (1995). "Madama Europa, Jewish Singer in Late Renaissance Mantua." In *Festa Musicologica: Essays in Honour of George J. Buelow*. Thomas J. Mathiesen and Benito V. Rivera, Eds. (Pendragon Press), pp. 197–231.

86 Jewish women were not allowed to worship communally in 16th century Italy – which meant they were forbidden from singing at synagogue. Most Italian temples maintained a separate area for women where they could worship – assuming they had been allowed to learn Hebrew. The primary contribution of Italian women to a religious service during the 16th and 17th centuries was to disrupt it. In a delightful synthesis of socio-cultural clichés, Italian-Jewish women were renowned for yelling curses at the men by whom they had invariably been disappointed.

87 Harrán, Don (1999). *Salamone Rossi, Jewish Musician in Late Renaissance Mantua* (Oxford University Press), p. 37.

small children to care for)[88] and Caterina Martinelli.[89] The latter arrived in Mantua from Rome in 1603 – at the age of thirteen – to train with Monteverdi, whose ambitions as a composer had been much influenced by events in Florence and Rome. Martinelli lived with Monteverdi and his family for three years, during which time the composer began work on a commission from Vincenzo and the Accademia degli Invaghiti,[90] a musical society founded in Mantua in 1562 by Cesare I Gonzaga. The Duke wanted a musical drama after the fashion of Peri's *Euridice* for presenting at the annual Carnival season in Mantua in 1607. Monteverdi and his librettist, Striggio *il giovane*, created *L'Orfeo*, a *"favola in musica,"*[91] the premiere of which on 24 February, 1607, marked the first maturity of opera as an art form.

From letters between the Duke's sons, Prince Francesco and his younger brother, Prince Ferdinando, it's obvious that Monteverdi was in dire need of castrati. On 5 January, 1607, Francesco wrote to announce that he had

> decided to have a play in music performed at carnival this year, but as we have very few sopranos here, and not very good ones, I should be grateful if Your Excellency would be kind enough to tell me if those castratos I heard when I was in Tuscany are still there. I mean the ones in the grand Duke's service, whom I so much enjoyed hearing during my visit. My intention is to borrow one of them (whichever Your Excellency thinks the best as long you agree that the grand Duke will not refuse to lend them.[92]

Giovanni Gualberto Magli – a student of Giulio Caccini – was duly "borrowed" from the Medici to portray La Musica and Proserpina, and possibly one other part. On 5 February, 1607 – less than three weeks before the first performance – Prince Ferdinando wrote a letter of introduction for Magli, in which he anticipated Joseph II's imagined put-down of Mozart:

> You will hear from his own lips of the difficulty he has had in learning the part which was given to him; so far he has managed to commit only the prologue to memory, but not yet the rest because it contains too many notes.[93]

Something of the power enjoyed by castrati when being dragged from chapels into theatres can be discerned from Francesco's reply to his brother's letter of introduction:

---

88   Two sons. A third child, a daughter, died shortly after birth, in 1603.

89   *circa* 1590 – 7 March, 1608.

90   'Academy of the Lovestruck.'

91   'Story in music.'

92   Harrán, Don (1999). *Salamone Rossi, Jewish Musician in Late Renaissance Mantua* (Oxford University Press), p. 37.

93   Carter, Tim (1999). "Singing *Orfeo*: on the performers of Monteverdi's first opera." *Recercare*. Vol. 11, pp. 75–118; p. 106.

The castrato arrived yesterday [...] he knows only the prologue, such that although he has no doubt that he will not have time to learn the other part before this carnival – in which case I shall have no choice but to postpone the performance of the play until this Easter – nevertheless this morning he began to study not only the music but the words as well. And yet if he had learned the part, for all that it might contain too many notes, as Your Excellency says, he would at least know the melody, and the music would be altered to fit him, and we would not waste so much time in having him learn it by heart.[94]

Noting the speed with which women – and even girls – were expected to learn and memorise newly-written parts, the patience extended to Magli articulated common prejudices and preferences. The role of Orfeo was mastered and performed to the highest standard by the tenor, Francesco Rasi. The rest of the cast was formed of four "sopranos," three castrati, three tenors and three other male singers. The distinction between "sopranos" and castrati is moot because it appears that none of the Court's prized collection of female soloists contributed to the first night, with the certain exception of Lucrezia Urbana (a beneficiary of veal, fish, salt, oil, candles, cheese and money), who played the harp in the orchestra. According to Tim Carter, the use of castrati reflected

Duke Vincenzo's noted reluctance to display his singing ladies in public (a point made by Federico Follino in his account [...] and it squares with the likely all-male environment of the first performance before the members of the Accademia degli Invaghiti.[95]

The range of Monteverdi's writing favoured castrati; the virtuosity is contained, adhering as it does to an "economy of means in the context of a small-scale performance;"[96] depending on the tempi adopted *in situ*, the long-spun lines of song would have gained from a male pair of lungs in 1607, particularly considering the shift in instrumental forces from *La Pellegrina's* pair of Chittaroni in 1589 to *Orfeo's* two harpsichords, two contrabassi de viole, ten viole de brazzo, two violini piccolo alla francese, two chitarroni, two organi de legno, three bassi da gamba, five trombones, two cornets, one regal, one flautino alla vigesimaseconda, one clarino,[97] and a double harp. From among his small coterie of castrati – and without knowing whether parts were doubled – Monteverdi cast Giovanni Sacchi, Giuli Cardi and Isacchino della Profeta, all of whom are recorded as being available. Profeta was long in the tooth, having been in service since 1580; he was also Jewish, a condition tolerated in 1607 just as it would be endured by Ezra Pound three centuries later. Profeta did not sing at the premiere of *L'Orfeo*, but he appears to have played one or more of the orchestral instruments and, as a dancing master, he may have contributed to the choreography

---

94 *Ibid*, p. 106.
95 *Ibid*, p. 107.
96 *Ibid*, p. 91.
97 A portable organ.

also. Either way, his part in proceedings ensured that on 2 April, 1607, the Court felt it appropriate to exempt him from wearing his customary yellow star.[98] The Duke is known to have been searching for another castrato during the spring of 1606, from which a number of conclusions can be drawn. Monteverdi almost certainly composed *L'Orfeo* for castrati, absent a ready supply of male sopranos in Mantua. It follows that it was preferable for all concerned to rely on overweight and dramaturgically improbable men for soprano voices[99] than to ascribe the female and the feminine to neoteric and capable women.[100] With the applause for *L'Orfeo* ringing in his ears, Monteverdi turned to *L'Arianna*,[101] which the Duke requested for the celebrations of the marriage of his elder son, Francesco, to Margaret of Savoy. He composed the title role for the now-18-year-old Caterina Martinelli, whom he trained and rehearsed at home with his family – a unit decimated by the death of Monteverdi's wife on 7 September, 1607. The composer later commented that the burden of writing his second opera nearly killed him, and the loss of his wife added inevitably to his devastation. He was doubtless comforted by Caterina Martinelli, at least until 9 March, 1608, when she died during rehearsals for *L'Arianna*, days after performing the role of Venus in Marco da Gagliano's *Dafne*.[102]

Martinelli must have been supremely talented. As much is obvious from the affection and trust of the greatest composer of the early 17th century, and by the effect her death had on the Duke, who ordered that her remains be interred in the church of the Carmine in Mantua. Inscribed on the marble tomb, in Latin, is the legend:

> Look, read and weep! Caterina Martinelli of Rome, who by the tunefulness and flexibility of her voice easily excelled the songs of the Sirens and the melody of the heavenly spheres, dear above all to Vincenzo,

---

98 Readers may not be aware that the Nazis were merely reviving one of the many hateful customs employed by the Catholic Church to humiliate and torture Jewish people. In 1215, the inappropriately-named Pope Innocent III ruled as part of the Canons of the Fourth Lateran Council that Jews and Muslims had to be marked as such. Canon 68 reads: "In some provinces a difference in dress distinguishes the Jews or Saracens from the Christians, but in certain others such a confusion has grown up that they cannot be distinguished by any difference. Thus it happens at times that through error Christians have relations with the women of Jews or Saracens, and Jews and Saracens with Christian women [...] we decree that such Jews and Saracens of both sexes in every Christian province and at all times shall be marked off in the eyes of the public from other peoples through the character of their dress. Particularly, since it may be read in the writings of Moses [Numbers 15:37–41], that this very law has been enjoined upon them." *Readings in Medieval History*, Edited by Patrick J. Geary. University of Toronto Press, p. 452.

99 This description is fine for Profeta. On the other hand, Magli pulled a coniglio from the hat. Francesco wrote to his brother on the day before the premiere: "Not only has he thoroughly learned the whole of his part, he delivers it with much grace and a pleasing effect." *Ibid*, p. 107.

100 As evidence for the obvious, the opera begins with a prologue by La musica, a figure designed to represent the art and philosophy of music. In the Italian language, La musica is feminine. The word can be traced to the similarly feminised Greek work mousikē (tekhnē) which corresponds to the nominative feminine singular of the adjective "mousikos." Greek word(s) relating to music are feminine for an obvious reason: mousike was supervised and mastered by a set of goddesses, the Muses.

101 'Ariadne.'

102 In the preface to *Dafne's* published score, Gagliano praised Martinelli's performance as being so beautiful as "to fill the whole theatre with delight and wonder." Strainchamps, Edmond (1985). "The Life and Death of Caterina Martinelli: New Light on Monteverdi's 'Arianna,'" *Early Music History*, Vol. 5, pp. 155–186; p. 164.

Serene Duke of Mantua, for that famous excellence, the sweetness of her manner, her beauty, her grace and charm, snatched away, alas, by bitter death, rests for eternity in this tomb, commanded by a most generous prince who still grieves at this sudden blow. Let her name live in the world, and her soul with God. She died in the eighteenth year of her youth, the ninth of March, 1608.[103]

Five weeks later, the Duke ordered that Mantua's Carmelite priests celebrate Masses and Offices for Caterina's soul for 12 months, commencing on the first anniversary of her death. This was unheard of at a time when the distinctions between classes and genders were normative; it speaks to the profound impact of a teenager on a court with thousands of personnel. The calamity for Monteverdi was practical as well as emotional. Instead of calling on one of the various castrati to whom the composer had access, however, he turned initially to a Florentine soprano, Margherita Romana, and thereafter to a Neapolitan singer-guitarist, Ippolita Recupita; neither proved suitable. He was directed to the singing-actress, Virginia Andreini (*née* Canali), who was already in the Duke's service and admired for her performances of the lament from the *intermedio La Florinda*.[104] Virginia and her husband, Giambattista Andreini, had worked as actors in *I Gelosi*,[105] a *commedia dell'arte* company managed by the Andreini family, and later in her own troupe, *I Fedeli*.[106] Virginia performed as the *prima donna inamorata*[107] and managed the company which, in 1605, entered the service of Vincenzo Gonzaga. For the wedding celebrations, Virginia and the *Fedeli* were commissioned to present *La idropica*,[108] an unpublished prose comedy by the "father of the *librettisti*," Giovanni Battista Guarini. The staging was presented as a prologue and four *intermedi*, with music by Monteverdi and Salamone Rossi. The juxtaposition of *intermedi* and an opera, and the casting of a singing actress in the title role of a work that was composed for a "professional" soprano, emphasises the blurring of the boundaries between the *commedia dell'arte* and the "modern art" of recitative and aria.[109]

---

103 *Ibid*, p. 171.

104 *circa* 1562 – *circa* 1630. "*La Florinda*" became her stage name. See, generally, Andrews, Richard (2005). "Isabella Andreini and Others: Women on Stage in the Late Cinquecento." In *Women in Italian Renaissance Culture and Society*. Ed. Letizia Panizza. Legenda, p. 316.

105 'The Jealous.'

106 'The Faithful.'

107 *Innamorati* ('the lovers') were stock-characters in the *Commedia dell'arte*, personified by Clarice / Silvio and Beatrice / Florindo[a]. They are always in love, but their proximity was complicated (or thwarted, more commonly) by circumstances. *Innamorati* narratives were driven commonly by separation and reunion.

108 'Dropsy.' Written in 1584. In modern parlance, dropsy is edema, the increase of interstitial fluid in one or more organs.

109 The wedding celebrations continued into the summer – with Adriana performing on 4 June, 1608, in the premiere of another "blurring" invention by Monteverdi, his *Il ballo delle ingrate* ('The Ballet of the Ungrateful'). The score was published in 1638 as part of Monteverdi's Eighth Book of Madrigals (*Madrigali guerrieri, et amorosi*). See, generally, Wilbourne, Emily (2007). "'Isabella ringiovinita': Virginia Ramponi Andreini before Arianna." *Recercare*, Vol. 19, No. 1/2, pp. 47–71.

Andreini's casting reached considerably further than the Gonzaga's temporary theatre. In 1601 she was inducted into the Accademia degli Intenti[110] of Pavia – in recognition of her poetry and her philosophical writings – at a time when women performing in the *commedia dell'arte* were demonised as immoral. Even before her creation of the role of Arianna, Andreini's compelling admixture of talents was realised in her pastoral, *La Mirtilla*,[111] the first play by a woman to be published.[112] Andreini was admired publicly by Tasso, whose misogynist conception of the female operated officially and subconsciously to legitimise the portrayal of women as debauched, weak, corrupt and immoral.[113] *La Mirtilla*'s proto-feminist denunciation of Original Sin was based on Tasso's *Aminta*,[114] and painted women as accommodating of decorum. They were also intelligent, talented and able to make choices on their own and for themselves. Filli, Mirtilla and Ardelia are imagined characters, but their capacity for love and choice codified desire and rationality as mutually inclusive, with neither delaminating the other. The gifting of Arianna to one of the most progressive women of the new century operated as a resonant defence of opera by Monteverdi, and the Duke. Andreini's radicalism was met at every turn by her talent. Rehearsals were conducted over many weeks, with a courtier, Antonio Costantini, reporting that Virginia had memorised her role in just six days – including the celebrated "*Lamento d'Arianna*"[115] – written for her by Monteverdi. She sang "with such grace and manner of affect that all present were amazed."[116] The Duke created a vast temporary opera house for the two and a half hour production, which the Court's chronicler, Federico Follino, claimed to have contained an audience of 6,000, with many crowding the doors from outside the theatre.

The absurdly lavish production was typical of the lunatic demonstrations of wealth and talent with which Italian families waged war during the 16th and 17th centuries. 300 men were required to operate the stage machinery alone, with waves and clouds seen to be in constant motion. Follino's wild enthusiasm for the event, though a necessary feature of his duties as the family's minister for propaganda, was consistent with the common view (as it was articulated by the composer, Marco da Gagliano), that Monteverdi's score had "moved the entire audience to tears."[117] The ambassador for the House of Este reported that Andreini's singing of the "Lament" "made many weep,"[118] while Follino wrote that "there was not one lady who failed to shed a tear."[119] The poet Giambattista Marino immortalised the singer's performance in Canto VII

110　'Academy of Intent.'

111　Andreini, Isabella (1995). *La Mirtilla*. Ed. Maria Luisa Doglio. M. Pacini Fazzi.

112　Together with Maddalena Campiglia's *Flori*. *La Mirtilla* was published in 1588 (nine editions). It was almost immediately translated into French. At the first staging, Isabella Andreini played the role of Filli. The title role was played by Vittoria Piissimi. Mirtilla is the main character, but Filli is more dramatic and substantial.

113　See, generally, Riverso, Nicla (2007). *La Mirtilla: Shaping a New Role for Women*. Modern Language Notes, Vol. 132, 1, pp. 21–46.

114　1581. Andreini first played the male lead in *Aminta* at the age of 11.

115　'Ariadne's Lament.'

116　Carter, Tim (2002). *Monteverdi's Musical Theatre*. Yale University Press, p. 204.

117　Redlich, Hans (1952). *Claudio Monteverdi*. Oxford University Press, pp. 101–103.

118　Fabbri, Paolo (1994). *Monteverdi*. Trans. by Tim Carter. Cambridge University Press, p. 92.

119　*Ibid*.

(the 'Delights') of his epic *L'Adone*.[120] Having compared her beauty and quality of voice to Adriana Basile, Marino wrote:

> You heard Florinda, O Mantua,
> There in the theatres beneath your royal roofs,
> Recite the bitter torments of Arianna,
> And draw from a thousand hearts a thousand sighs.[121]

The Lament is the only part of the score to survive intact.[122] The composer acknowledged its significance on 20 March, 1620, writing that it was "*La più essential parte dell'opera.*"[123] He took the unusual step of distributing handwritten copies of the aria, but didn't publish it until 1614, when he produced a five-voice madrigal arrangement.[124] Nine years later he published the Lament as a monody; two years before his death, he re-composed it as a sacred hymn, "*Lamento della Madonna.*" It's obvious the music meant a great deal to Monteverdi; indeed, more than four centuries after it was first performed by Virginia Andreini, it can be appreciated as the first important operatic aria written for a female soprano.[125] According to Suzanne Cusick:

> Monteverdi's fame and historical status rested for centuries on the universal appreciation of his achievement in the celebrated lament [which] was among the most emulated, and therefore influential, works of the early 17th century, virtually creating the lament as a recognizable genre of vocal chamber music and as a standard scene in opera – a scene-type that would become crucial, almost genre-defining, to the full-scale public operas of 17th-century Venice.[126]

The scene is emotionally and psychologically heterogenous, with the luxuriant proximity between happiness and suffering resonating in Theseus' actions and the attendant discovery by Bacchus of the weeping Ariadne. Structurally, the Lament operates as an extended recitative with more than 70 lines of verse, formed as five sections with a chorus-led commentary. Some of the poetry is prefigured in the preceding scene, in which the First Envoy characterises Arianna's plight. Monteverdi's anguished music

---

120   'The Adonis.'

121   The full verse reads: "*Tal forse intenerir col dolce canto / suol la bella Adriana i duri affetti / e con la voce e con la vista intanto / gir per due strade a saettare i petti; e'n tal guisa Florinda udisti, o Manto / là ne' teatri de' tuoi regi tetti / d'Arianna spiegar gli aspri martiri / e trar da mille cor mille sospir.*"

122   According to Claudio Gallico, the Lament was accompanied by violins and violas at the premiere, and it seems likely from the surviving libretto that was performed with an interjecting chorus. Gallico, Claudio (1967). *I due pianti d'Arianna di Claudio Monteverdi*. Chigiana XXIV, p. 30.

123   'The most essential part of the work.' Leopold, Silke (1993). *Claudio Monteverdi und seine Zeit*. Laaber, p. 164.

124   The five-voice adaptation was included in the composer's Sixth Book of Madrigals.

125   The importance of the Lament to the development of 17th-century opera is considered in detail in Rosand, Ellen (2007). *Opera in seventeenth century Venice: the creation of a genre*. University of California Press, pp. 361–86.

126   Cusick, Suzanne (1994). "'There Was Not a Lady Who Failed to Shed a Tear.' Arianna's Lament and the Construction of Modern Womanhood." *Early Music*. 22(1), pp. 21–43; p. 21.

employs a *chiaroscuro* palette to paint the fear, anger, desolation, self-pity and futility provoked by her abandonment. The scene begins with the words "You let me die":

> *Lasciatemi morire!*
> *E che volete voi,*
> *che mi conforte in cosi dura sorte,*
> *in cosi gran martire?*
> *Lasciatemi morire!*"[127]

Even without knowing anything of the dramatic-narrative context, it's easy to attach the pain and melancholy mined by the poet and the composer to the circumstances of the Lament's creation. Martinelli died on 9 March, 1608; Virginia Andreini was not cast until the end of the month, at which point Rinuccini wrote his words and Monteverdi his music. The suffering as it has been captured cannot be separated from the pain experienced by a community that only days earlier gathered for the burial of the Court's muse. Monteverdi commonly cited *L'Arianna* rather than *L'Orfeo* as his first great achievement in the new medium;[128] he later claimed to have been inspired by his ability to identify with Arianna "because she was a woman [and] Orfeo because he was a man [...] Arianna brought me to a true lament, as Orfeo did to a true prayer."[129] It's equally true that Martinelli's death resonated in Arianna's desertion by Teseo – a proto-feminist trope for artists, poets and composers throughout the 17th century – and Monteverdi's feelings of loss at the death of "his" singer. The breaking of all that she promised echoes throughout the Lament. Even if she was unable to sing his music, Martinelli appears nonetheless to have become Arianna in the mind of its composer.

The first two note-syllables of the first "*Lasciatemi*" are scored as a brittle, rising semi-tone (A4 – B flat4), with the repeated words accompanied by a dominant seventh chord of landmark significance. What follows covers as much ground as a soliloquy by Shakespeare, with the musical language tracing Arianna's unfolding emotions with unprecedented expressive resonance and lucidity. The fluctuations between extremes of indignation and vulnerability resolve in a concluding "*O Teseo*"[130] that marks the point at which opera and the vernacular of lyric theatre took on a form and adhered to principles that have remain unchanged ever since. This was widely recognised at the time – not least by Duke Vincenzo, whose reverence for Virginia Andreini and her immortalisation of Arianna's Lament resulted in a commission for Domenico Fetti to produce *Arianna e Bacco nell'isola di Nasso.*[131] Completed between 1611 and 1613, the painting depicts the singer in full theatrical gesture, looking down and away from Bacchus, with her right arm extended and her left covering her breasts.

---

127 'Let me die! And what do you want / when you comfort me in my destiny / And who do you think can comfort me in my harsh fate / in such great martyrdom? Leave me to die!'

128 McClary, Susan (1989). Constructions of Gender in Monteverdi's Dramatic Music. *Cambridge Opera Journal*. Vol. 1, No. 3, pp. 203–223; p. 217.

129 Cusick, Suzanne (1994). "'There Was Not a Lady Who Failed to Shed a Tear.' Arianna's Lament and the Construction of Modern Womanhood." *Early Music*. 22(1), pp. 21–43; p. 21.

130 'O Theseus.'

131 'Ariadne and Bacchus on the Island of Naxos.'

Bacchus looks on, and up, with his right hand touching his heart, his left turned open in supplication. After the fashion of the time, and as it was memorialised in *Il Corago* (the first and most influential guide to the staging of musical theatre during the first quarter of the 17th century),[132] the figures' exaggerated dynamism is cast from life as it was seen on stage, with every gesture cueing an emotional or psychological state.[133] At Arianna's feet lie the shells of oysters, long-established symbols of erotic intent from which it is plain that Andreini was admired for more than her voice and art in isolation.[134] The status of the Lament as the origin-envoicing[135] of the feelings of a woman for performance by a woman remains one of the most consequential events in the history of the soprano voice. Its revolutionary effect was recognised immediately, not only by the circle surrounding Caterina Martinelli, but also by everyone who came to hear or perform this music during the 20 years after Arianna's creation by Virginia Andreini. As Suzanne Cusick put it in her landmark study of the Lament:[136]

> The death caused by 'Lasciatemi' is the death of Arianna's passionate self, a self that leaves her as gradually as Teseo's physical self leaves her sight, as he sails beyond the horizon. Her pious wifely self survives, oxymoronically, precisely because this passionate, independent self dies. The 'morire' motive that initially stands for her fate comes eventually to be a musical space that is verbally filled with Teseo, with her father, with the triumph of her soul over her body, and with her own delivery of the Orloggian moralizing conclusion 'Cosi va chi tropp'ama e troppo crede' ('So it goes with those who love and trust too much') – all signalling her willingness to surrender herself to patriarchal control.

There is something startlingly romantic about the origins of the soprano, as the first female voice to be audible above the patriarchy, being attributable to the grief experienced by a man when losing the voice of a woman. Caterina Martinelli is all but forgotten, but the truth of her legacy was carved into something more lasting than

---

132 It is believed that "*Il Corago*" was written by Pier-Francesco Rinuccini, the son of *L'Arianna's* librettist. See, generally, Savage, Roger and Sansone, Matteo (1989). "*Il Corago*" and the Staging of Early Opera: Four Chapters from an Anonymous Treatise circa 1630." *Early Music*. Vol. 17, No. 4, *The Baroque Stage*, pp. 494–511.

133 There are strong parallels between the apparent minimalism of movement in Japanese *Noh*, which serves a similarly structural, narrative function for the achievement of *kurai*, and overarching expressive quality of the play.

134 In 1613, Virginia and the Fedeli began the first of several tours outside Italy. During the troupe's second visit to France scandal broke out when Giambattista's rival, Pier Maria Cecchini ("*Fritellino*") and his wife Orsola ("Flaminia") revealed publicly that Giambattista was having an affair with another actress in the troupe, Virginia Rotari. Virginia either knew about it or didn't care. Either way, they lived and performed *ménage à trois* for the remainder of Virginia's life; shortly after her death, Giambattista married Rotari. Emerson, Isabelle Putnam (2005). *Five Centuries of Women Singers*. Greenwood Publishing Group, p. 13.

135 See, generally, "Opera, or The Envoicing of Women" in *Musicology and Difference: Gender and Sexuality in Music Scholarship* (1993). Ed. R.A. Solie. Berkeley, pp. 225–58.

136 Cusick, Suzanne (1994). "'There Was Not a Lady Who Failed to Shed a Tear.' Arianna's Lament and the Construction of Modern Womanhood." *Early Music*. 22(1), pp. 21–43; p. 26.

marble. As Ezra Pound wrote in *Cantos XX*: "God what a woman! My God what a woman."[137]

---

137 Pound's allusion to the 12th century epic poem, "*El Cantar de mio Cid*" ('The Song of my lord), celebrates the king's physical acknowledgment of the beauty and power of the nameless "woman" ("[...] *telo rigido*"). This is undone the moment he discovers she is his sister.

CHAPTER THREE

So Potent Art

Between 2005 and 2017, the creation,[1] loss and discovery of *Salvator Mundi*[2] – the "missing"[3] Da Vinci – brought a rare and largely unwelcome spotlight to the business of art. A rogue's gallery of characters, spanning dealers, brokers, restorers, experts, and the artist himself, formed a stark and unromantic profile in which money, power and the tension between public and private conceptions of genius and creativity produced an impression best locked in an unseen attic. Even now, with the painting appearing for some reason to be lost again, there is no consensus that it's the work of Da Vinci. The scale of the restoration equated for many to an interpretation. It was not as invasive as Elías García Martínez's infamous re-working of *Ecce homo* in Zaragoza's Santuario de la Misericordia; there is nonetheless sufficient intervention to cause doubt in the mind of the viewer. That uncertainty was exacerbated by the grubbiness of some of the people involved in the painting's ultimate relocation to Saudi Arabia, and the questionable ethics and absent morality that characterised the painting's journey from a 2005 auction house catalogue[4] to its sale by Christie's in New York, on 15 November, 2017.

The application of morality to art – in its creation, presentation and evaluation – need not crystallise in extreme exemplars like Wagner's *Die Meistersinger von Nürnberg*,[5] Aleksandr Gerasimov's *Stalin and Voroshilov in the Kremlin*[6] or Gustav Klimt's *Rosebushes under the Trees*.[7] In March, 2022, the refusal by Valerie Gergiev to denounce the Russian Federation's invasion of Ukraine all but ended his career in the West.[8] The ethics of requiring a conductor to take a political stand were ideated by Richard Strauss' decision to replace the threatened Bruno Walter in Berlin, on 20 March, 1933. It cannot be agreed that the articulation of democratic sentiments by

---

1 Between 1499 and 1507 – to a commission very probably from the noted amateur soprano Isabella d'Este.

2 'Saviour of the World.'

3 The jury is, of course, out as to whether the painting sold to the Saudi Arabian prince Badr bin Abdullah, for $450.3 million, is by Da Vinci. See Lewis, Ben (2019). *The Last Leonardo: The Secret Lives of the World's Most Expensive Painting*. Ballantine Books.

4 In which it was listed as "After Leonardo da Vinci" and estimated to be worth between $1,200 and $1,800.

5 The most overtly anti-Semitic opera to remain in repertoire.

6 Gerasimov was chairman of the infamous Orgkomitet of the Union of Soviet Artists between 939 and 1954, and the first president of the USSR's Academy of Arts in 1947. His hostility for innovation led directly to the death of artists like Gustav Klucis, and to the starvation or ruin of many more.

7 Returned by the Musée d'Orsay to its rightful owners more than 80 years after it was stolen from a Jewish family in Austria in 1938 by the Nazi government.

8 See also Netrebko, Anna, in Chapter 19.

the undemocratic operates to anyone's clear advantage, particularly as it concerns the private thoughts of a conductor whose "public" voice is heard speaking through music by (mostly) dead composers. Art is amoral until someone says it isn't. The personal beliefs and values of the creator are presumed to code with those of the viewer, which is fine and dandy for anyone reading *120 Days of Sodom*[9] under the covers with a flashlight, and problematic when staging Halévy's *La Juive* in Israel.[10]

Controversy is unavoidable and healthy when artistic freedoms and the purpose and function of art are challenged. The relationship between the artist and society are subject always to analysis, never more so than when art and ethics collide. The subjectivity of art translates uneasily to estimations of decency, as anyone who has had to walk a retrospective of Francis Bacon will attest; the vulnerability of art in its function has always traduced the ethical unless that was the stated intention of the artist. History generates context, sufficient for aesthetics to fall in-line with fashion and conscience. The absence of a framework does not render ethical judgments wrong or irrational, however; instead, a work appreciated despite (or because of) its disconnection from the world in which it was created can be appreciated with alacrity unless someone asserts that its creator was a pedophile or a supporter of Vladimir Putin.

The issue becomes complicated if the adoption of a subject is presumed to align the artist with its meaning. No-one in the 17th century believed a painting of the Death of Holofernes implied that the artist wanted to decapitate a man – even if painted by Artemisia Gentileschi – and only conspiracists would hold that Walter Sickert was a serial killer simply because he created a quartet of paintings in 1908 under the title *The Camden Town Murder*.[11] Sickert's thoughts and sensibilities are meaningful because of who he is alleged to have been; his art did not service the needs of those who wanted it to speak to more than itself, resolving a species of acculturated transubstantiation wherein the art was valuable only because of the identity of the person creating it. The *Salvator Mundi's* equivalent metamorphosis from an interior dialogue between a man and a woodworm-infested marouflage panel[12] to the gaudy and trivial scrutiny of lesser men equated to a similar process, wherein the private and the public operated in perennial antinomy.

This unease resolved early on for composers, whose work was defined necessarily by intervention. Monteverdi was able to play his own music at the harpsichord and the organ; for everything else he was at the mercy of the collegium, and the talents, tastes and personalities of musicians over whom he had limited influence. His affections for Martinelli were formed as a tutor; he was willing to take on the burden of another child at home because it gave him an opportunity to achieve by training something that chance alone could not. His investment in a young girl just

---

9 '*Les 120 Journées de Sodome ou l'école du libertinage*,' a novel by Donatien Alphonse François, Marquis de Sade, written in 1785 and first published in 1904.

10 *La Juive* has been staged in Israel. Tel Aviv imported David Poutney's production in 2010, with great success.

11 The novelist Patricia Cornwell proposed that Walter Sickert was "Jack the Ripper," and that the *Camden Murders* were in some way, and for some reason, redolent of events from 20 years earlier that appeared wholly unlike anything represented in the paintings.

12 The *Salvator Mundi* is painted on a cheap (and knotty) piece of wood, which fact has caused the unpersuaded to argue that the painting cannot be by Leonardo da Vinci.

as castrati were becoming fashionable amplified the politicisation of the performance of music at the turn of the 17th century, when gender was merely one aspect of a cultural landscape that was unfathomably semiotic. The presentation of art music has evolved through generations of vernaculars wherein symbolism and meaning were codified through almost every feature of a work's content and presentation. Beethoven's premiere of his *Eroica* Variations, in 1802, at the home of its dedicatee, Karl Lichnowsky, spoke openly to the interactions between art, class and patronage for everyone *except* the Prince and his guests; had the composer conducted his *Eroica* Symphony for Napoleon Bonaparte in Paris two years later then the work (absent its dedication) would have resonated then, and ever since as an essay in appeasement. Certainly, whenever Furtwängler conducted the same composer's Ninth Symphony for the Nazi administration the entire experience, for the musicians and the audience alike, collapsed under a weight of Swiftian irony.

The language of music cannot protect composers even as performers of their own music, a truth evidenced by some of the memorably disappointing recordings conducted by Stravinsky and Vaughan-Williams. For the earliest authors of opera, this private-public dilemma was muted because there was no public to hear what was, in every case, a private performance. During the first forty years of opera's existence, literally everything was staged for the family that had paid for it to be written; it was heard only by the invited. Until a score was published, sufficient for others to remove it from the confines of patronage and originalism, a work existed only during its first (and commonly last) appearance. The *status quo* was undone on 6 March, 1637, by the Tron family, who opened their Teatro di San Cassiano to the purchasers of tickets for a production of Francesco Manelli's *L'Andromeda*.[13] This first "public" staging of an opera, directed by an impresario with a palette for popular taste, relocated performers and liberated composers by enabling a market that was now irreversibly commercial. The audience that gathered for this landmark event had limited expectations of what an opera was supposed to sound like, particularly in a permanent theatre.[14] The Cassiano was small, seating only 405 (with 153 boxes, over five tiers), and the acoustics differed from the domestic spaces and the churches in which the majority had heard singing at its finest. Cesare Crivellati summarised the common view when writing "in churches you sing differently from music-rooms; in churches you sing with a loud voice; in music-rooms with a subdued voice."[15] The need for projection in a "dry" space with a (modest) orchestra presented challenges for which the ensemble and the audience were equally unprepared.

The innovations of Peri, Caccini and Monteverdi were tailored to a female discourse idealised by Ovid's *Heroides*, in which the Euripidean totems Phaedra and Medea idealised monody as an interior voice made audible. Before these dramatic tropes became established[16] the monody and the madrigal were the primary vehicle

---

13 With a libretto by Benedetto Ferrari.

14 The Cassiano was built in 1607, to replace an earlier theatre that was opened in (or before) 1581. The original theatre was constructed for the performance of spoken drama only – primarily comedy – with boxes available for noble families to rent at enormous cost. This was not "public" theatre, therefore, but rather opportunity for the aristocracy to compete with itself.

15 *Discorsi musicali* (1624).

16 See generally Holford-Strevens, Leofranc (1999). "Her eyes became two spouts: Classical Antecedents

for secular musical discourse. The singing voice was transformed into a soliloquean force for expressing secret feelings which consolidated the common association between the lament and the female voice, acoustically and semiotically. Plato invoked that association by describing tragic laments as womanly;[17] as Blair Hoxby observed:

> When Lucian was attending tragedies in Rome, he found it tolerable to hear Andromache and Hecuba 'melodising' their 'calamities' on stage, even though he found it risible to hear Heracles burst into song. Not coincidentally, the vast majority of monodic laments published in the first decades of the seventeenth century were written for female characters portrayed by the soprano voice. But the association of abandoned women with song is just one of many that Euripides naturalised through sheer repetition. Although he may not have been the first to think of setting a recognition scene as a sung duet (the uncertain date of Sophocles's Electra leaves the question open), there is no doubt that he left the most numerous examples of such duets in his late tragedies. In the Ion, Iphigenia in Tauris and Helen, he showed how lyric dialogue could be turned into a theatrical expression of intellectual discovery, spontaneous joy and mutual feeling as parent and child, brother and sister, or husband and wife are reunited. His example paved the way for the sudden, expansive lyricism of Penelope when she at last recognises her husband in Giacomo Badoaro and Monteverdi's Il ritorno d'Ulisse."[18]

More than 200 books of monodies were published in Italy during the first 40 years of the 17th century,[19] with 90 per cent of the music being scored for a high voice, and with predominantly soprano clefs. None of these books distinguished specifically between male and female singers; however, Giovanni Battista Doni,[20] the leading musicologist of his day, was contemptuous of the castrati, whom he dismissed as "unnatural and too feminine."[21] The composer and poet Bellerofonte Castaldi went further still, writing in the preface to his collection, *Primo mazzetto*, that it is

> laughable that a man with the voice of a woman should set about proposing to his mistress and demanding pity of her in the voice of a falsetto.[22]

of Renaissance Laments." *Early Music*, Vol.27, pp. 379–405.

17   Plato (1961). *The Republic*, in *The Collected dialogues of Plato*. Eds., Edith Hamilton and Huntington Cairns. Princeton, p. 831.

18   Hoxby, Blair (2005). "The doleful airs of Euripides: The origins of opera and the spirit of tragedy reconsidered." *Cambridge Opera Journal*, Vol. 17, 3, pp. 253–269.

19   Fortune, Nigel (1954). "Italian 17th Century Singing." *Music & Letters*. Vol. 35, No. 3, pp. 206–219; p. 206.

20   Doni was a prominent member of Florence's Accademia della Crusca, which published the first Italian-language dictionary in 1612 – 133 years before Samuel Johnson published his Dictionary of the English Language. Between 1640 to 1647, Doni occupied the gloriously titled "Chair of Eloquence" at the University of Florence.

21   *Ibid*, p. 208.

22   *Ibid*, p. 207.

The Church was all out of pity where "mistresses" were concerned, and the castrati remained *primogenitura* for an institution that abjured women being seen on stage with the same vitriol that banned them from being heard at church. The Pope's authority was more limited than the Vatican might have wished. For all the moral indignation provoked by women appearing in the *commedia dell'arte*,[23] the dangers represented by females performing as women for the purposes of entertainment was tolerable only with an *obligato* of gnashing teeth. In his *Actores et spectatores comoediarum nostri temporis paraenesis*,[24] published in 1621, Father Francesco Maria del Monaco foamed:

> The honest performances are those in which absolutely no woman appears [...] No woman, I say, because wherever a woman is present, especially if she is very graceful and pretty (as are most of those who act in theatres), there is always a temptation to lust, and she shows her power in corrupting moral customs.[25]

The Church consoled itself by providing regular employment for castrated men, a caste that was able during the first decade of the 17th century to choose between a life of liturgical service and the increasingly handsome fees being offered by a new species of Italian businessman, the impresario. Doni and Castaldi were not alone in their condemnation of *any* man singing secular music using the voice of a woman, and their disdain encouraged the instruction of women in an art form that was just beginning to toy with theatrical verisimilitude. The first operatic stages were shared by female and male sopranos, therefore, even if castrati proved to be less controversial and more tolerably exotic. As many noted of Archilei, Caccini and Andreini, female singers were better suited to the theatre than castrati because women had in most cases performed on stage as girls, in spoken as well as sung repertoire. Male sopranos, on the other hand, were made for the Church rather than God-given, and until the emergence of traditions and tutoring tailored specifically for the opera house, the majority of castrati had to transition from the sacred to the secular out of necessity. A beautiful voice did not presuppose an equivalent talent for acting.

We can know something of what late 16th century castrati sounded like from the early 20th century recordings made by "the last castrato," Alessandro Moreschi.[26] The first of his two sessions for the Gramophone & Typewriter Company was produced by brothers Will and Fred Gaisberg in April, 1902. Seventeen usable sides of performances by members of the Sistine Chapel Choir were captured on wax, four of them featuring solos by Moreschi.[27] The second set of recordings was produced, again in

---

23   Riverso, Nicla (2016). "Fighting Eve: Women on the Stage in Early Modern Italy." *Quaderni d'Italianistica* 37, 2, pp. 23–47; p. 25.

24   'Actors and spectators of the comedies of our time.'

25   Fortune, Nigel (1954). "Italian 17th Century Singing." *Music & Letters*. Vol. 35, No. 3, pp. 206–219; p. 206.

26   11 November, 1858 – 21 April, 1922. It is believed Moreschi suffered castration as a "cure for a hernia" when he was 12 (in 1870). He joined the Sistine Chapel Choir in the 1870s as First Soprano, having auditioned in front of an entire gathering of every sitting member. Moreschi remained First Soprano until his position was rendered obsolete 30 years later by Pope Innocent XI.

27   For a more detailed consideration of Moreschi, his culture, his recordings and his performance style

Rome, two years later, under the direction of W. Sinkler Darby – a year after the newly ascended Pius X effectively banned *castrati* from the Vatican.[28] Moreschi can tell us much about the quality of vocal tone produced by male sopranos during the 1600s. He can reveal nothing of matters of style and technique because his approach was so emphatically of the 19th century that it would be absurd to attach his sobbing, effect-laden lamentations to the work of his forbears. In the alternative, much can be concluded of female sopranos from the many detailed accounts left by contemporaries. It can be asserted with confidence that human anatomy has not changed since 1600, a truism that narrows the range of sounds available to a soprano. This doesn't mean that the placement of a female voice as it was trained and heard by Monteverdi equates to what might now be expected of a soprano specialising in the performance of Baroque music; neither does it exclude the possibility that Caccini and Archilei sounded like Maria Callas or, for that matter, Mariah Carey.[29] If the question of tone is irresolvable then there is considerable evidence for the emerging portfolio of operatic expression around the turn of the century. Caccini advocated that a singer should "save" the breath "to give greater spirit to the increasing and diminishing of the voice, to exclamations and other passions"[30] – a catechism that prized tone above volume while venerating extreme dynamic contrasts and the primacy of dramatic vocal gestures. Doni raged perennially against the ubiquity of "graces and divisions," a technical box-of-tricks that operated broadly as the separation of a melodic line into shorter, faster-moving runs of notes that gained from trills, turns, leaps, *cambiamenti* and arpeggios. These effects sustained the art of improvisation – a *zevah* for Monteverdi's contemporaries that idealised the use of effects as fundamental to a singer's expressive palette. Giulio Caccini described "divisions" as

> those long windings and turnings of the voice which have been invented, not because they are necessary unto a good fashion of singing, but rather for a certain tickling of the ears of those who do not well understand what it is to sing passionately; for if they did, undoubtedly divisions would have been abhorred, there being nothing more contrary to passion than they are.[31]

The frequency, complexity and dramatic merit of "divisions" resolved as a consecration for some, as a curse for others. Almost from the outset, the singing of opera formed into entrenched positions, with the once natural concordance between word, melody and ornament calcifying into philosophical agendas from which melody and floridity emerged in opposition. One of the fathers of the lyric tradition, Giovanni

see Boyden, Matthew (2021). *The Tenor: a Cultural History*. Ragueneau Press, pp. 5–11.

28   "Effectively" only since the 1903 *motu proprio* doesn't prohibit *castrati*; rather, it provides that "*the high voices of the sopranos and contraltos [...] must be taken by boys*".

29   Without wishing to cause offence to admirers of both singers, neither outcome is likely. See Chapters 18 and 20 respectively.

30   Fortune, Nigel (1954). "Italian 17th Century Singing." *Music & Letters*. Vol. 35, No. 3, pp. 206–219; p. 206.

31   *Ibid*, p. 212.

de' Bardi, nailed his colours to all things "*soave*," "*leggiadro*," "*dolce*," and "*angelico*" – values he distinguished from the "*appassionato*" and the "*energico*":

> the nice singer will endeavour to deliver his song with all the suavity and sweetness in his power, rejecting the notion that music must be sung boldly, for a man of this mind seems among other singers like a plum among oranges.[32]

The politics of ornament were especially controversial where female sopranos were concerned, primarily because they were better at it. Audiences hung on every note, and appetites increased by what they fed on; even the hallowed Vittoria Archilei came in for criticism, with Della Valle writing that "she ornamented the written monody with long flourishes and turns which disfigured it but were very popular."[33] Composers were inevitably quick to decry the arts of improvisation once the developing business of publishing made permanent what had once been transitory. Doni railed against "the stupid adulation of the ignorant mob, who often applaud things which deserve only cat-calls."[34] The values of the elevated were promoted in opposition to the low tastes of the cheap seats, a feature of western philosophical debate likely to remain in near-constant application. The vacuous notion that elitism facilitates disparity has become quintessentially political in the 21st century;[35] for the early 17th century, however, these issues were debated by people who could not wait for barbarians of whom they were in ignorance. The "cheap seats" could be occupied only by the wealthy and the privileged; the "ignorant mob" disdained by Doni numbered among the world's most educated. The cognoscenti might not like to know it, but the tensions between the sublimity of art and the vulgarity of the theatre were hard-wired to opera from the start.

Della Valle spoke for many when directing his angriest criticism at the tenor, Giuseppe Cenci, of whose performances he wrote that he commonly

> inserted divisions where they were inappropriate. You never could tell whether his singing was supposed to be sad or gay, since it always sounded the same; or rather, it was always gay because he always sang so many notes and sang them so fast. And I am sure he did not know himself what notes they were.[36]

Most of what was written at this time about female voices falls neatly within what would now be known as bel canto, and applied most commonly to music from the 19th and 20th centuries. The presumption that improvised coloratura[37] – as ornamentation – was invented by Rossini and Bellini and mastered by Donizetti and Verdi

---

32   "*Discorso mandato* […] *a Giulio Caccini detto Romano sopra la musica antica e'l cantar bene.*" (1580).
33   *Ibid.*
34   *Ibid.*
35   That is, for anyone who has never had to send their child into surgery. Egalitarianism is a wonderful idea made dangerous by the hypocrisy of the desperate.
36   *Ibid.*
37   The Italian word "coloratura" means literally 'colouring.'

is unsupported by the evidence. It is equally certain that the clichés and prejudices attaching during the 19th century to Italian vocalism (particularly by French critics) can be traced to the first two decades of opera's existence. The racist French polymath, Marin Mersenne, took obvious delight in drawing a distinction between French and Italian singing when writing that Italian singers

> represent for all they are worth the passions and affections of the mind and the soul, for example, anger, fury, rage, spite, swooning and several other passions, and they do this with incredible violence [...] whereas our French composers are content to tickle the ear and to use all the time in their songs a sweetness which is inimical to strength.

The weight of criticism from within France cannot be dismissed as nationalist cant; the "violence" of which French composers and writers complained was fomented expression as well as ornament. Although it's impossible to know what this meant for Monteverdi and his peers, there is a useful exemplar in the first recording made of *L'Orfeo*,[38] in November, 1939, by EMI/Angel, in Milan, conducted by the Argentinian-born Ferruccio Calusio. This was the only Italian-voice recording of the opera until 1996;[39] for all its flaws (most of them discernible only because of subsequent historical research and training), the performance is revealing. The role of La musica is sung by Ginevra Vivante[40] – a specialist (for the time, at least) in early music. She sings with a quick, strong and unrelenting vibrato; her tone is extremely full, and she employs portamento in a manner that would be unforgivable even 30 years later. The performance is Permessus by way of Castel Sant'Angelo. The most striking feature of Vivante's singing of the Prologue is the complete absence of ornamentation and her apparent disregard for the meaning of the words she is singing. Striggio went to the bother of creating disparate allusions for Monteverdi to characterise in music, which he does with almost orthopedic. In the second verse, for example, La musica sings "*Et hor di nobil'ira, et hor d'amore.*"[41] The proximity between anger and love is scored (without dynamic or expressive markings) as semi-quavers, repeating on an F4, low in the voice. The word "*hor*" and the second syllable of "*d'amore*" are scored as quavers – rising to a D4 dotted minum for "*poss'in[...]*"[42] (as the phrase "*[...] infiammar le più gelate menti*").[43] The potential for expressive licence in this music is considerable – overlooked entirely by Vivante. The use of juxtaposition is even more acute in the final verse, when La musica sings "*Hor mentre i canti alterno hor lieti, hor mesti.*"[44] The words "*hor lieti*" are written as crotchets (D4 to C4), but

---

38   This was the first *complete* recording. The earliest voice recordings of Monteverdi's music (two excerpts from *L'Orfeo* by the American baritone Reinald Werrenrath) were recorded for Victor's educational series in 1914.

39   Sergio Vartolo conducted the Capella Musicale di San Petronio di Bologna and an Italian voice-cast ensemble for Naxos.

40   24 June,1902 – 12 January, 1996.

41   'And so with noble anger, and so with love.'

42   'Can I [...].'

43   'Can I inflame the coldest minds.'

44   'While I vary my songs, now happy, now sad.'

"*mesti*" is scored as two minims (B flat 4 to A4) – with a plainly intended *fermata* over the singer's petition to sadness. Vivante again ignores this expressive adjacency, and ploughs on in noisy acknowledgment of the recording technology and the Milanese bus timetable.

Fewer than fifty years later,[45] John Eliot Gardiner conducted an *echt* period-performance recording with Lynne Dawson singing the role of La musica. Her voice is antithetical to that of Vivante; her tone is *very* light, with almost no consonants at all, and she employs vibrato only where a word invites it musically; she too overlooks the authors' allusions, save for the application of a welcome but anomalous *fermata* to the phrase "*poss'in infiammar.*" Dawson makes judicious use of embellishments; her performance is elegant and sensual, at least when considered purely as song. From what was written by those who heard *L'Orfeo* at its first performance, however, that is not what was expected of female sopranos at the time.

In July, 1602, five years before *L'Orfeo's* premiere, Giulio Caccini published clear guidance in the preface to his *Le Nuove Musiche*,[46] a collection of madrigals and songs for high voice and basso continuo. It is valuable because of what Caccini wrote of the use of ornaments – which should "in every case" be used only to colour and characterise a precise emotion – and because of his repudiation of effects for their own sake. Caccini was adamant that a singer should use "exclamations" as "the principal means of moving the emotions; by reference to his own song, "*Cor mio, deh, non languire,*" he illustrated how the word "*deh*"[47] warranted more passionate emphasis than "*cor mio.*"[48] Exclamations were said to be valuable to all "passionate" music, particularly minims and crotchets dotted (as with La musica's "*poss'inp[…]*") and for shifts to a lower note (as with "*hor lieti, hor mesti.*"). Semibreves were reserved for the extreme expansion and contraction of tone, with "*messa di voce*" advocated as a mechanism by which a singer might

> sweetly increase his voice in liveliness but not in tone; then he should gradually quieten it and make it smooth until it can scarcely be heard and seems to be coming from the depths of a cavern.[49]

Caccini encouraged the use of "*sprezzatura,*" a then newly-minted word that first appeared in Baldassare Castiglione's influential *Il Libro del Cortegiano*,[50] where it was used to signify "a certain nonchalance, so as to conceal all art and make whatever one does or says appear to be without effort and almost without any thought about it."[51]

---

45   Recorded in 1985; released on LP in 1986, by Archiv. This performance is one of the miracles of the recording age for the playing of The English Baroque Soloists and His Majesties Sagbutts and Cornetts, and for the invention of John Eliot Gardiner. Anyone inclined to take a swing at period performance should listen to this recording, and then the production conducted by Ferruccio Calusio. They do not compare, at least not favourably for the ensemble in 1939.

46   'The New Music.'

47   'Alas.'

48   'My heart.'

49   Fortune, Nigel (1954). "Italian 17th Century Singing." *Music & Letters*. Vol. 35, No. 3, pp. 206–219; p. 218.

50   'The Book of the Courtier.' First published in 1528.

51   Castiglione, Baldesar (2002). Ed. Javitch, Daniel, *The Book of the Courtier: The Singleton Translation*.

It has been translated into English as "studied carelessness,"[52] although in modern Italian the word signifies "contempt."[53] Caccini's use of *sprezzatura* equates in musical terms to *rubato*, or *ad libitum*.[54] In the Preface to his *Nuove Musiche e nuova maniera di scriverle*,[55] published in 1614, Caccini defined *sprezzatura* as

> that gracefulness in singing which, if applied in the right place (as it might be during a sequence of quavers or semiquavers passing through various harmonies), takes away from the singing a certain constricting stiffness and dryness and makes it pleasing, free and airy; just as in ordinary speech an eloquent delivery makes the things one says sweet and agreeable.

The keeping of time was *alla moda* in Italy during the early 1600s;[56] it appears not to have mattered much to composers, however. Ignazio Donati, for example, held that "you should never beat time at all;" he advocated by way of preference "singing in the broadest possible manner." Others attached fear and anxiety to a rigid beat (typified for modern ears by the work of Arturo Toscanini), and it was agreed universally that accompanists should adapt in every case to the needs and instincts of a singer. Tempo markings first emerged in 1611 – with generalised references, such as *adagio* and *presto*. The arbiter of time for early 17th century singers was neither musical nor scientific, however. Pulse and expression were determined in every case by poetry, and the priority of ensuring that every word was enunciated and audible.[57] Neither Vivante nor Dawson met any of these originalist expectations when singing the Prologue to *L'Orfeo*. This is not to criticise either singer; instead, it presents a correlate for observing that sopranos at the beginning of the 17th century were trading in an expressive currency that made more of extremes of contrast and dramatic emphasis than anything known to modern times, and certainly since the invention of recording.

To appreciate some of the idiosyncrasies of performances by sopranos during Monteverdi's lifetime, and the probably hyper-exaggerated attention to word use, there is more to gain from listening to actors than to singers. In 1911, Ellen Terry,[58] the most respected British-born actress of her generation, recorded "The Quality of

---

Translated by Charles S. Singleton. W.W. Norton, p. 32.

52   Oxford English Dictionary: "(noun) Studied carelessness, especially as a characteristic quality or style of art or literature."

53   It has become a common point of reference for students of Renaissance painting.

54   To be distinguished in any event from *tempo rubato*.

55   'New music and a new way of writing it.'

56   The watch was created in Italy around 1500. In 1541, the scholar Giglio Giraldi wrote that he had "often seen a watch, which admirably, showed the hours, placed in the handle of an eyeglass of Pope Leo X [r. 1513–21] of which he availed himself while hunting and traveling." Watch manufacturing became an industry after 1600.

57   The proximity between acting and singing – personified by the work of Andreini – resulted in a model that reached its apogee with the work of Richard Wagner, who obsessed over the clarity of his words, and the diction of his singers, to such a degree that he pinned a note to a wall backstage of his theatre in Bayreuth before the premiere of *Der Ring der Nibelungen* that read "The big notes will take care of themselves; the little ones and the text are the chief things." See Chapter 14.

58   27 February, 1847 – 21 July, 1928.

Mercy" from *The Merchant of Venice* for the Edison company.[59] Terry's parents were born in 1817 and 1819 respectively; her grandfather, whom she knew as a child, was born in the 1780s, during the reign of George III, who was himself born in 1738 – only 122 years after the death of Shakespeare. Terry made her first stage appearance at the age of nine, in 1856, as Mamillius in *The Winter's Tale*. She learned the role with Charles Kean, who appeared alongside her as Leontes. Kean was born in 1811 – a century before Terry recorded for Edison. Charles trained for the theatre with his father, Edmund, the greatest Shakespearean of his day, who was born in 1787. Edmund's grandfather was the celebrated poet, dramatist and songwriter, Henry Carey, born in 1687 – just 17 years after the death of Shakespeare's grand-daughter, Elizabeth.[60] It follows that we can hear a recording by an actress who trained with an actor whose great-grandfather could have asked Shakespeare's grand-daughter to remember the author of *Hamlet*.

The significance of this timeline amplifies the relative proximity of Ellen Terry to the 17th century as well as to the 21st, a fact that makes her declaiming of "The Quality of Mercy" useful for anyone wanting to appreciate the differences between performances of the Prologue to *L'Orfeo* in 1623 and 2023. Terry's voicing of Portia's words is deliberate, and heavy with consequence. She comes close to singing the verse, with vibrato and portamento employed discreetly and with pre-meditation. There is a symmetry and purpose to her elongation of certain words, and the emphasis she brings to word-endings highlights meaning above rhyme and metre. The words "crown," "awe," "kings," "above," "God himself," "salvation," "prays" and the "deeds of mercy," are drawn out or emphasised to develop the playwright's construction of the divinity of justice. Terry does not labour Portia's metaphors; instead, she traces a less obvious, more persuasive line of reasoning that operates almost subliminally when steering Shylock towards clemency. For Polly Findlay's 2015 production of *The Merchant of Venice* for the RSC, Patsy Ferran delivered the same words without gravity, and in open defiance (or complete ignorance) of the oratorical traditions to which Terry was introduced by Charles Kean. Ferran's delivery of the speech is disinterested, such that Portia appears to care nothing for the outcome she is seeking to avert. Of course, she was speaking as a modern woman to a modern audience ill-disposed to oratory; had Ferran attempted to vocalise like Terry she would not have been cast by Findlay. The differences between the two styles of acting are vast and irreconcilable, therefore, a divergence that compels pause for thought when imagining what Richard Burbage and all The King's Men must have sounded like traversing the Globe.

Shakespeare's river-side theatre was built in 1599 and destroyed by fire in 1613; the first Teatro San Cassiano opened in 1581 and burned to ash in 1633. The success of the second Teatro San Cassiano inspired in quick succession the construction of three more large theatres in Venice, where Monteverdi had been maestro di capella at the Basilica di San Marco since August, 1613.[61] The success of Manelli's *L'Andromeda*

---

59   Act IV, Scene 1.

60   Elizabeth was born in 1608, and knew (and later remembered) her grandfather. She was 8-years-old at the time of his death.

61   The 50 ducats provided for his expenses were robbed from him at knife-point by highwaymen during his journey from Mantua. Any reader having a bad day should reach for even a half-decent biography of Monteverdi. The man's sufferings throughout his long life would have made Job forget his own.

proved an inspiration for the almost 70-year-old composer, who was largely (but not entirely) distracted from the stage by his commitments to the Church. For the 1640 carnival, Monteverdi and Benedetto Ferrari[62] oversaw a revival of *L'Arianna* at the Teatro San Moisè, a tiny prose-theatre that allowed for no stagecraft and a small ensemble only. Monteverdi was persuaded to write another opera, the aptly named *il ritorno d'Ulisse in patria,*[63] he did so on the understanding that the venue was capable of satisfying his ambitions. The Teatro Santi Giovanni e Paolo was Venice's third purpose-built opera house; it was formed of wood and stone and designed to seat an audience of 900. The space behind the proscenium arch was larger even than the auditorium, which allowed for unparalleled stagecraft and a novel range and variety of mechanics and acrobatics. The SS Giovanni e Paolo opened on 20 January, 1639, with the first performance of Francesco Manelli's *Delia ossia La sera sposa del sole.*[64] The libretto was written by Giulio Strozzi, the father of a young and rising soprano named Barbara.[65] With Francesco Manelli making a habit of opening opera houses and winning plaudits as a composer, singer and impresario, Monteverdi returned to the theatre in a spirit of collaboration rather than competition. In fact, the premiere of *il ritorno d'Ulisse in patria* during the Carnival of 1640 was staged by Manelli's company with Benedetto Ferrari. Manelli's value to Monteverdi extended to his creation of the bass role of Nettuno, while his wife Maddalena sang the role of Minerva; their son, Costantino, played the role of L'Amore. Such was the work's success that it received ten performances during the season as well as a touring production to Bologna (again managed by Manelli). The work was revived in Venice for the 1641 Carnival, an honour without compare during the 17th century.

The composer's triumph energised him to write another opera for the following season, *Le nozze d'Enea in Lavinia*[66] (again staged at the SS Giovanni e Paulo),[67] and in 1642 he composed his last stage work, *L'incoronazione di Poppea,*[68] with help from a younger generation of composers, including Francesco Cavalli. The libretto by Giovanni Francesco Busenello[69] transformed an episode of Roman history into a sorceress myth, with Poppea introduced in a prologue that established virtues absent triumph. Poppea is portrayed as cynical, manipulative and murderous, even when compared to the Emperor Nero; her schemes resolve in success because of her unchecked immorality. The opera was first performed on 26 December, 1642, with 28 characters played by two female sopranos, five castrati, two tenors and two basses. Even though *il ritorno d'Ulisse in patria* was grander, with a larger cast (of thirty) and ten roles for women,[70] *Poppea* represented the female operatic soprano's first full

---

62   Ferrari dedicated a sonnet at the head of the published libretto, "*Al Signor Claudio Monteverdi oracolo della Musica.*"

63   'The Return of Ulysses to his Homeland.'

64   'Delia or the evening bride of the sun.'

65   See the Preface to this book.

66   'The marriage of Aeneas to Lavinia.'

67   Tragically, the score was lost soon after the first run.

68   'The Coronation of Poppea.'

69   A member of several literary academies, notably the Umoristi, and the Accademia degli Incogniti.

70   In the surviving manuscript, the role of Eumete changes halfway through Act II from a tenor to a soprano castrato.

maturity.[71] Appropriately enough, the only cast member whose name survived from the premiere was the originator of the role of Ottavia, Anna Renzi.[72]

Some commentators have taken to identifying Renzi as the first *prima donna* or, more foolishly, the first *diva*. While overlooking (for now) the slim value of both terms of reference, neither Renzi's birthdate nor the date of her death are known, a testament to the uncertain quality of stardom for women during the 17th century. Renzi died childless and unmarried, which meant her commitment to her art was re-membered only by those who experienced it. Almost four centuries after she worked for Monteverdi, her defining achievement was to thrive independently as the first operatic soprano whose social status superseded the limiting cultural imperative to marry a man, or Christ Himself.[73]

Renzi was born in Rome – where she made her debut as a child, in 1630, as Lucinda/Armido – a cross-dressing role in *Chi soffre speri*,[74] an operatic "*comedia*" by Marco Marazzoli and Virgilio Mazzochi. Women were forbidden from appearing on stage in Rome, and the rules were broken for Renzi only because the performance was given at the French Embassy. She appeared in her first "full" opera ten years later, at the same venue[75] and as another Lucinda, in *Il favorito del principe*,[76] a new opera by Filiberto Laurenzi.[77] Misogyny was less regulated in Venice, where Renzi relocated at the end of 1640. The experience for anyone new to the city during the 1640s can best be appreciated through the eyes of the English diarist, John Evelyn, whose remarkably detailed account of his stay in Venice in 1645 included a night at the Teatro Novissimo to hear Renzi perform in Giovanni Rovetta's *Ercole in Lidia*:[78]

> It was now Ascension-week, and the great mart, or fair, of the whole year was kept, everybody at liberty and jolly; the noblemen stalking with their ladies on [...] high-heeled shoes, particularly affected by these proud dames, or, as some say, invented to keep them at home, it being very difficult to walk with them; whence, one being asked how he liked the Venetian dames, replied, they were "mezzo carne, mezzo legno," half

---

71   The title role is much larger than Ottavia, although little is known about the soprano who created it, Anna di Valerio. On 29 November, 1642, the owner of the the the SS Giovanni e Paolo, Giovanni Grimani, wrote to the Ferrarese Marquess Cornelio Bentivoglio discuss the size of di Valerio's roles in Poppea (the "second opera"): "As for the part of Signora Anna [di Valerio], it has been looked over, and [Strozzi] has already set about composing additions. And I think it is certain, as for the second [opera], that it will be appropriate for her to be entitled to choose what she wants, although Signor Busenello has destined the role of Poppea for her as being larger and more appropriate [than her role in the first opera]. The "first opera" was *La finta savia* ('The Pretend Wise-Woman'), by Filiberto Laurenzi and Giulio Strozzi. It was a sequel to *La finta pazza*. Schneider, Magnus Tessing (2012). Seeing the Empress Again: On Doubling in "L'incoronazione di Poppea." *Cambridge Opera Journal*, Vol. 24, No. 3, pp. 249–291; p. 260.

72   c. 1620 – after 1661. It is likely that she also created the roles of La Virtù and Drusilla.

73   Nuns were not required to take a vow of celibacy because it was believed, and understood, that they were married to Christ.

74   'Those who suffer hope.'

75   In the presence of the king-maker and patron of the arts, Cardinal Richelieu.

76   'The Favourite Prince.'

77   Laurenzi was one of Renzi's tutors, and he followed her to Venice, where he worked with Monteverdi when contributing to *L'incoronazione di Poppea*.

78   'Hercules in Lydia.' The score is now lost.

flesh, half wood, and he would have none of them. The truth is, their garb is very odd, as seeming always in masquerade; their other habits also totally different from all nations. They wear very long, crisp hair, of several streaks and colours [...] In their tire, they set silk flowers and sparkling stones, their petticoats coming from their very arm-pits, so that they are near three quarters and a half apron; their sleeves are made exceedingly wide, under which their shift-sleeves as wide, and commonly tucked up to the shoulder, showing their naked arms, through false sleeves of tiffany, girt with a bracelet or two, with knots of point richly tagged about their shoulders and other places of their body, which they usually cover with a kind of yellow veil of lawn, very transparent. [...] I have never seen pearls for colour and bigness comparable to what the ladies wear, most of the noble families being very rich in jewels, especially pearls, which are always left to the son, or brother who is destined to marry; which the eldest seldom do. The Doge's vest is of crimson velvet, the Procurator's, etc. of damask, very stately. Nor was I less surprised with the strange variety of the several nations seen every day in the streets and piazzas; Jews, Turks, Armenians, Persians, Moors, Greeks, Sclavonians, some with their targets and bucklers, and all in their native fashions, negotiating in this famous Emporium, which is always crowded with strangers.

This night, having with my Lord Bruce taken our places before we went to the Opera, where comedies and other plays are represented in recitative music, by the most excellent musicians, vocal and instrumental, with variety of scenes painted and contrived with no less art of perspective, and machines for flying in the air, and other wonderful notions; taken together, it is one of the most magnificent and expensive diversions the wit of man can invent. The history was, Hercules in Lydia; the scenes changed thirteen times. The famous voices, Anna Rencia, a Roman, and reputed the best treble of women; but there was an eunuch who, in my opinion, surpassed her; also a Genoese that sung an incomparable bass. This held us by the eyes and ears till two in the morning, when we went to the Chetto de san Felice, to see the noblemen and their ladies at basset, a game at cards which is much used; but they play not in public, and all that have inclination to it are in masquerade, without speaking one word, and so they come in, play, lose or gain, and go away as they please.[79]

Renzi's relocation to Venice had been scheduled to coincide with the opening of the Novissimo on 14 January, 1641.[80] Though made of wood, and being only half the

---

79 Evelyn, John (1819). *The Memoires of John Evelyn*. Ed. by W. Bray, Vol. 1, p. 191.

80 Planned, paid for and operated by the Accademia degli Incogniti. The history of this short-lived theatre is engagingly bonkers. On 30 May 1640, a consortium of Incogniti entered into a contract with the Dominican friars of Santi Giovanni e Paolo to construct and operate a theatre on land adjacent to the monastery that was then occupied by a large shed. The contract stipulated that the theatre would allow for the performance of "heroic" operas only, and never comedies. Ticket sales were unable to cover

size of the SS Giovanni e Paolo, the Accademia degli Incogniti spared no expense designing the opening night, which featured Renzi as Deidamia in the premiere of Giulio Strozzi and Francisco Sacrati's *La finta pazza*[81] – only the tenth opera to be staged in Venice. The event was captured in a detailed account published by the Incognito historian and librettist Maiolino Bisaccioni in 1641.[82] He described Renzi's appearance opposite a "young castrato from Rome,"[83] who presented on stage as Achilles wearing a silver-embroidered dress of green that made him appear like "an Amazon" in whom were joined "the warrior spirits with feminine delicacies".[84] At one fabulous point in the drama, Giulio Strozzi has Achilles soliloquise:

> Sweet change of nature, Woman into man transformed, Man in Woman changed, Change of name and figure. I am no longer beautiful Phyllis, But return today as Achilles: How many envy my state, To play the man, and the damsel?[85]

There is a lot to unpack here. The convolutions of gender fluidity overreach the ambition of this single-volume history, but much can be concluded of a librettist requiring a man without testicles to self-identify as one of fiction's greatest male heroes while wearing a dress and singing (with the voice of a woman) about his enforced duality as "*un travestito travestito*."[86] There was nothing transgressive in any of this for audiences used to navigating the semiotic and metatextual complexities of gender and sexuality. On the other hand, Renzi's status within a society that advocated the silence of women was provocative for those who assessed female sensuality as a value for private consumption rather than public exhibition. She prevailed on stage because of her "virtuosic verbal, physical, and sonic feats in cross-dressed roles [that] called a new social subject into being,"[87] and because audiences delighted in her dynamic, expressive and dramatic sensibilities. As Ottavia in *Poppea*, Renzi was celebrated by Strozzi for "the temperament of her chest and throat, for which [...] much warmth is needed to expand the passages and enough humidity to soften it and make it tender."[88] In 1644 he described:

---

the on-going expenditure, and with debts continuing to mount, the friars demanded the return of their land. In 1645, several investors, and four singers (including Anna Renzi) sued for fees and wages, and the following year the friars re-possessed the theatre and knocked it down, in October, 1647. The following year, the Friars leased the site to the operator of an equestrian school and stables.

81   'The pretend madwoman.'

82   *Il Cannocchiale della Finta Pazza* ('The Spyglass of La Finta Pazza').

83   Wier, Claudia Rene (2020). *Animating Performance: Tracing Venice's Resonant Diva Attraverso Il Palco e La Soglia*. York University, Toronto, p. 128.

84   *Ibid.*

85   *Ibid.*

86   'A transvestite disguised.' The Italian language makes no distinction between the dual use of the word, despite the different contemporary meanings attaching to it.

87   Wier, Claudia Rene (2020). *Animating Performance: Tracing Venice's Resonant Diva Attraverso Il Palco E La Soglia*. York University, Toronto, p. 221.

88   Gordon, Bonnie (2004). *Monteverdi's Unruly Women: The Power of Song in Early Modern Italy*. Cambridge University Press, p. 22.

the action that gives soul, spirit, and existence to things must be governed by the movements of the body, by gestures, by the face and by the voice, now raising it, now lowering it, becoming enraged and immediately becoming calm again; at times speaking hurriedly, at others slowly, moving the body now in one, now in another direction, drawing in the arms, and extending them, laughing and crying, now with little, now with much agitation of the hands. Our Signora Anna is endowed with such lifelike expression that her responses and speeches seem not memorized but born at the very moment. In sum, she transforms herself completely into the person she represents, and seems now a Thalia full of comic gaiety, now a Melpomene rich in tragic majesty. I call her the fourth Grace...[89]

Renzi's triumph outside the theatre was as a celebrity and an entrepreneur.[90] These socially allusive roles transcended the confines of gender, and enabled Renzi to achieve an unprecedented measure of independence while accommodating patrician control and condescension. In essence, the public's concern for codes and mores collided with its appetites for talent, passion and fantasy. Even if Renzi remained perpetually in service to men (and a predominantly male audience) she was sufficiently resourceful and determined to manage her own contracts and finances; her coincident navigation of the complex morays that defined social and professional hierarchies was nothing short of subversive. According to Claudia Wier

she accomplished this at least momentarily by virtue of the spell she cast on listeners inducing them to forget what she should or should not be doing. The anonymous poet of the Abozzo featured in the last chapter affirms that "by magical enchantment, she was transformed, with pretended disdain." Hence, Renzi's sound and vision performed an extra-lingual authority within the "institutional conditions" of the theatre and the public square that worked as a magical force to influence changes in paternalistic attitudes. All this is not to say that there was immediate social change for all women. It is more to say that Renzi and the other divas affected incremental, generational changes and impressions – as new models of independent agency – within their social environs that forged links in the long-term project of women's liberation.[91]

The primary difference between Renzi's skill as the foremost soprano of her day, (at least in Venice), and that of her forebears is that she was the first woman to sing in

---

89 Rosand, Ellen (1991). *Opera in Seventeenth-Century Venice: The Creation of a Genre*. University of California Press, p. 232.

90 It is accepted that this word would not have been used in Italy at the time. Or anywhere else. It was first coined in 1800 by the French-Irish economist Jean-Baptiste Say.

91 Wier, Claudia Rene (2020). *Animating Performance: Tracing Venice's Resonant Diva Attraverso Il Palco e La Soglia*. York University, Toronto, p. 128. See also Belgrano, Elisabeth (2011). *Lasciatemi Morire o Faro La Finta Pazza. Embodying Vocal Nothingness on Stage in Italian and French 17th century operatic Laments and Mad Scenes*. University of Gothenburg, p. 36.

a truly public space for a subjectively egalitarian audience. What had once been a private alchemy, for the consumption of the 00000.1%, was now available to anyone with *some* money, a decent outfit and a ticket. This made popular something that had been distinguished previously by its concealment – with the voicing of women operating as a dark art for the heretical and equitable pleasure of an audience of "people," as distinct from a family gathering to celebrate a private wedding. Renzi's battery of *passaggi*, sighs and flourishes engendered women as artists, therefore – empowering a *vox feminae* for a *populi* that had not had access to a *circus* since 692CE.[92] The public presentation of womanhood was problematic, of course, for those who considered everything done in a theatre to qualify as improperly erotic or debauched. The paradigmatically soft was expected to cause men to harden, albeit not in public. Renzi's use of her body for the pubic entertainment of the people compelled the subjugation of the male; their submission to a woman in a theatre ensured she was protected from scorn, condemnation and violence by the use of a proscenium arch and an admixture of appreciation and lust. This populist embodiment of the composer's potent art operated to recover Prospero's drowned book, using a heavenly music to wake the sleeping from their graves. Like Shakespeare's magus, the composer was refashioned as a public magician, in consequence of which the first operas, and the resulting flurry of theatre construction, set in motion four centuries of still-continuing concert-hall and opera house design.

For the Renaissance, the fulfilment of the magical (as occultism) necessitated a fusion of three essential qualities: isolation (as a function of absolute devotion), elitism (as the attainment of excellence) and pride (whereby God's secrets were revealed only to the ambitious, brilliant and vain). The same was true for any composer of opera, and anyone singing it. Although there was cross-cultural parity in Christianity's conflation of blasphemy and women singers, the contemporary English obsession with the occult and secret societies was processed very differently in Italy,[93] where Academies indulged their status as publishers. It was here that the fantastic and opera shared in another significant development. The entire premise of Renaissance magic hinged on the presence of an instruction manual.[94] Soon after the first operas were staged, they were printed also; when submitting their work to the relative immortality of publishing, composers revolutionised the art for anyone wanting to perform it. Different singers were now at liberty to play the same role for the same audience, or a different audience in a different city on the same night. The effect of publishing was transformative on sopranos in particular, for whom the creation of a forum in which to be heard as an individual did much to change the lives of all women, whether or not they were able to sing.

---

92 The last of the "Roman" entertainments (associated with the amphitheatre) was banned officially by the Trullan Council in 692CE.

93 The only "secret" Academy in Italy, the *Academia Secretorum Naturae* ('Academy of Secrets'), was founded in Naples in 1560 by the scientist and philosopher Giovanni Battista Della Porta. Members were uninterested in the occult; in fact, candidates were obligated to present a novel natural scientific fact as a pre-condition of membership. The *Secretorum* is considered to be the first scientific academy in Europe. Members referred to themselves as the *otiosi* ('men of leisure').

94 At a time when the library of the University of Cambridge contained fewer than 500 books and manuscripts, the library of the occultist John Dee contained more than 4,000.

CHAPTER FOUR

Sweet Madness[1]

First published anonymously in 1849, *The Maiden and Married Life of Mary Powell, afterwards Mistress Milton* is one of the whackier endowments of Victorian literature. Anne Manning's[2] epistolary novel painted a Holbeinsian portrait of the second wife of John Milton, telling her story through imagined diaries and letters, and recasting her as a Victorian lady and an ideal wife, devoted in service to her husband. It is the most fantastically awful thing written about Milton, which did nothing to prevent it from becoming a huge success among women pining for men of genius with substantial private incomes. Tellingly, the author is without compassion for Mary, whom she blames entirely for her troubled relationship with Milton. Manning relied heavily on Anna Brownell Jameson's *The Memoirs of the Loves of the Poets*,[3] which attributed the writing of *Paradise Lost* to Milton's third wife, Elizabeth Mynshull, and the "peace and comfort she brought to his heart and home [...] what a debt immense of endless gratitude is due to the memory of this unobtrusive and amiable woman." Manning asked of the part played by Milton's wives:[4]

> What but the most reverential and lofty feeling of the graces and virtues proper to our sex, could have embodied such an exquisite vision as the Lady in Comus?[5] Or created his delightful Eve?[6]

Manning's sentimental casting of Milton ignored the author of the *divorce tracts*[7] and formed instead an idealised impression that preferred soft-soap to scandal. Milton did not marry for the first time until May, 1642 (when he was 33-years-old), at which point he was deemed an appropriate subject for novelisation by an English woman. His life while single was off limits, to which end his *Ad Leonoram Romae canentem*[8] speaks to one of the suppressed passions of his youth. This trio of Latin epigraphs was

---

1 "Scylla wept, And chid her barking waves into attention, And fell Charybdis murmured soft applause. Yet they in pleasing slumber lulled the sense, And in sweet madness robbed it of itself." John Milton: *Comus, a Masque*. Scene I (Lines 257–261).
2 17 February, 1807 – 14 September, 1879.
3 1829.
4 Manning was acknowledging Powell for *Comus* and Mynshull for *Paradise Lost*.
5 *Comus*; a masque in honour of chastity (1634). This was his longest work to date, which his friend, Henry Lawes, set to music.
6 *Paradise Lost* (1667).
7 Milton's four polemical pamphlets (*The Doctrine and Discipline of Divorce*, *The Judgment of Martin Bucer, Tetrachordon*, and *Colasterion*; 1643–1645) sought to legitimise divorce on the grounds of spousal incompatibility.
8 'To Leonora Singing in Rome.'

dedicated to, and inspired by, the soprano Leonora Baroni[9] – the daughter of Adriana Basile, star of the Gonzaga court, and muse to Antiveduto Gramatica. Written during the late 1630s, these heavily paradoxical verses were written by arguably the most educated man of the second millennium for an audience that probably numbered fewer than 2,000 at the time of their publication in the *Poemata* of 1645. The first begins "An angel protects each person…":

> *Angelus unicuique suus (sic crédité gentes)*
> *Obtigit aethereis ales ab ordinibus.*
> *Quid mirum? Leonora tibi si gloria major,*
> *Nam tua praesentem vox sonat ipsa Deum.*
> *Aut Deus, aut vacui certè mens tertia coeli*
> *Per tua secretô guttura serpit agens;*
> *Serpit agens, facilisque docet mortalia corda*
> *Sensim immortali assuescere posse sono.*
> *Quöd si cuncta quidem Deus est, per cunctaque fusus,*
> *In te unâ loquitur, caetera mutus habet.*[10]

Milton's allusions to Baroni align her with the angelic, with dualist references to the mind and will of God, humanity's articulation of the divine, and music as a path to immortality disguising the poet's manifest delight in Baroni's more corporeal attainments. The second epigram employs references to one of the sirens (Parthenope), Virgil's resting place in Pausilipo and her magical effect on both "Gods and Men." Milton's tribute to Baroni looms large because he identifies the object of his passions by name and in consequence of direct experience, while in Venice. His identification of an actual singer in preference to an ideal reveals the force of the young poet's admiration and attraction. Even if his verses tell us nothing about her singing, it's clear that Baroni inspired him to attach heavenly value to her earth-bound talents. Milton's praise survived Baroni's reputation, which does not appear to have been typical of every non-Italian observer. One French commentator, Maugers, was almost indifferent when describing her

> fine parts, and a happy judgement in distinguishing good from bad music: she understands it perfectly well, and even composes, which makes her absolute mistress of what she sings, and gives her the most exact pronunciation and expression of the sense of the words [...] She sings with an air of confident and liberal modesty, and with a pleasing gravity. Her voice reaches a large compass of notes, is just, clear, and

---

9   December, 1611 – 6 April, 1670.

10   'An angel protects each person (believe it, ye peoples) / Heavenly winged from the celestial orders. / What wonder, Leonora, if to you comes greater glory / Your voice itself expresses God among us. / God, or at least a third mind leaving heaven / Steals on his own through your throat and works his way; / Works his way, gently leading mortal hearts / Sensibly to grow used to immortal sounds. / But if God is really all, and infused through all, / In you alone he speaks, and keeps the rest in silence.' McColley, Diane Kelsey (1984). "Tongues of Men and Angels: Ad Leonoram Romae Canentem." In *Milton Studies*, Vol. 19, *Urbane Milton: The Latin Poetry*, pp. 127–148; p. 128.

> melodious; and she softens or raises it without constraint or grimace
> [...]; her looks have nothing impudent, nor do her gestures betray any-
> thing beyond the reserve of a modest girl.[11]

That Milton was willing to personify Baroni by the use of her name in the body of
the verse as well as the title, and that he identified her in all three epigrams as angelic
or *as of heaven*, speaks to the growing capacity of female singers to cultivate celebrity
whether or not they were performing in an opera house. By the middle of the 17th
century, sopranos born, raised and trained in Italy were a commodity, disseminated
throughout Europe for increasingly appreciable sums of money. In early 1644, for
example, Baroni relocated to the French court of Anne of Austria, whose husband,
Louis XIII, died in May the previous year. The appointment proved to be a disaster
because Baroni sang as an Italian, with more frills and filigree than was tolerable for
jejune French tastes. Predilections were forming regionally across Europe within three
decades of the first Italian operas. Milton's puritanical certainties appear not to have
collided with his bilaterally Catholic and humanist hosts during his time in Italy. As
he recalled of his two-month stay in Florence:

> I at once became the friend of many gentlemen eminent in rank and
> learning, whose private academies I frequented—a Florentine institu-
> tion which deserves great praise not only for promoting humane studies
> but also for encouraging friendly discourse. Time will never destroy
> my recollection – ever welcome and delightful – of you, Jacopo Gaddi,
> Carlo Dati, Frescobaldi, Coltellini, Buonmattei, Chimentelli, Francini,
> and many others.[12]

Milton attended a number of operas, including a performance of Monteverdi's
L'Arianna in Venice, in 1639. When returning to England he travelled with a "chest
or two of choice Musick-books of the best Masters flourishing about that time in
Italy,"[13] and soon after began to draft his own staged tragedies on religious themes.[14]
The effect of the new art on Milton was absolute – as it was on just about everyone
else who travelled to Italy during opera's adolescence. The burgeoning popularity
of the "Grand Tour" (the origins of which date back to Thomas Coryat's eccentric
travelogue, *Crudities: Hastily gobled up in Five Moneth's Travels*)[15] was escalated by
the Peace of Münster in 1648. After Richard Lassels' *Voyage of Italy* was published
in Paris, in 1670, the appetite for European tourism caused the demand for public
entertainment to explode. As with all great art, it was money rather than manners
that madeth Man.

---

11   *Ibid*, p. 130.
12   *John Milton Prose: Major Writings on Liberty, Politics, Religion, and Education*, Ed. David Loewenstein.
Wiley-Blackwell, p. 347.
13   Lewalski, Barbara K. (2003). *The Life of John Milton: A Critical Biography*. Blackwell Publishing,
p. 106.
14   *Adam Unparadiz'd* and *Paradise Lost* both made extensive use of a chorus, with one memorable
instruction reading "Chorus of angels sing a hymme of the creation."
15   First published in 1611.

The influence of opera on the growing resonance of women's voices was European before the first performances of Staden's *Seelewig*[16] in Germany in 1644, Calderón de la Barca's *El laurel de Apolo*[17] in Spain in 1657, Lully's *Cadmus et Hermione*[18] in France in 1673, and John Blow's *Venus and Adonis* in England, in 1683.[19] Outside Italy, music for sopranos *ad interim* was in song-form. John Dowland's *First Booke of Songes or Ayres* was published in London in 1597 (with a dedication to Elizabeth Spencer, Baroness Hunsdon).[20] His last work, *A Pilgrimes Solace*, published in 1612, revealed the extent to which Dowland had been influenced by Italian monody. The same was true of John Attey's *First Booke of Ayres of Foure Parts, with Tableture for the Lute*, published in 1622, which was one of the last English collections of lute songs. Attey's *Booke* was dedicated to the Countess Frances of Bridgewater who, like Lady Hunsdon, was likely the first to perform them. In Germany, the Church was ubiquitous. In 1609, Dowland printed a translation of a 16th century treatise by the German composer and theorist Andreas Vogelsang (under his *nom de plume* "Andrew Ornithoparcus"). This insightful, often witty volume painted a grim portrait of the contemporary art of singing in Germany:

> they howl like wolves and bellow and bray in church [...] and his in-
> structions are very straightforward: know the music, present it properly,
> sing in time and in tune and do not distort the words (as in *aremus* – let
> us plough – for *oremus* – let us pray). Do not bray like an ass (God is not
> deaf) and do not make mad faces.[21]

The primacy of text in England and Germany was no less acute than in Italy, and yet the writing and performance of music in English and German until the emergence of native operatic traditions was distinguished by the studied absence of virtuosity. Sopranos trained outside Italy were culturally and technically averse to self-indulgence, with any natural inclination to vanity subsumed to the restraint of their composers and the fun-crushing sensibilities of Protestantism. The acquiescence of composers and singers to the prelacy of the poet was a product of contemporary social architecture, therefore, but it was a function of linguistics also. The open

---

16   The first opera to be composed and performed in Germany. The full title is *Das geistliche Waldgedicht oder Freudenspiel genant Seelewig* ('The Sacred Forest Poem or Play of Rejoicing called Seelewig'). Many claim Heinrich Schütz's *Dafne* as the first opera in Germany. It was not an opera, however, but rather a work of prose theatre with music and dance interpolated. The drama was first performed in the (still operating) banquet hall of Hartenfels Castle near Torgau, Saxony, in celebration of the marriage of Princess Sophia Eleonore of Saxony and George II of Hesse-Darmstadt on 13 April, 1627. As an inappropriate gesture towards Teutonic clichés, Schütz's work was eclipsed by less elevated entertainments on 9 April (a wolf hunt), and on 7 and 10 April (bear fights).

17   'Apollo's Laurel.' The first opera to be composed and performed in Spain. The dramatist's full name was Pedro Calderón de la Barca y Barreda González de Henao Ruiz de Blasco y Riaño.

18   The first opera to be composed and performed in France.

19   The first opera to be composed and performed in England by an English composer. The first performance of any opera in England was recorded by John Evelyn in his diary on 5 January, 1674, when he wrote "I saw an Italian opera in music, the first that had been in England of this kind."

20   One of England's most important patrons of the arts, and a scholar of rare invention and wit.

21   Potter, John, and Sorrell, Neil (2012). *A History of Singing*. Cambridge University Press, p. 81.

vowel sounds of the Italian language reward the natural acoustics of human vocal mechanics, something that cannot be said of most other European languages, with the tyranny of the consonant making the fluency of sung-speech more challenging for a composer and a singer operating in service to a poet. Singers performing works in English have to wrestle with dipthongs; the German language trades in guttural consonants to the point of caricature. The mid-17th century fashion for Italian music presented huge advantages and opportunities for singers raised on an oats-and-water diet of northern European asceticism; the impact of Italian music and singing was generally positive and constructively-received. The same could not have been said of the French.

Catherine and Marie de Medici, and Louis XIII and his wife, Anne of Austria, had all welcomed Italian musicians to Paris – most notably (and controversially) Leonora Baroni. Louis XIII died on 14 May, 1643. Five months before his death, Louis appointed Cardinal Jules Mazarin as Chief Minister to the king – in which post he remained when Louis XIV inherited the throne, four months before his fifth birthday. Mazarin advocated the importing of Italian musicians to Paris, for whom he developed an insatiable appetite while posted to Rome as a Papal envoy. In 1640, a new opera by Filberto Laurenzi, *Il favorito del principe*, was staged at the French embassy, starring a young soprano called Anna Renzi. The opera was novel for the Romans for more than the scandal of a woman singing in it. Ottaviano Castelli's libretto bypassed gods and allegories for a tempestuous tale of love, intrigue and desperation – features of modern life for Mazarin and his diplomatically-inclined peers. On 7 February, 1640, Castelli wrote to Mazarin:

> I don't want to omit telling you how I'm getting on with my great idea that I mentioned to Your Most Illustrious Lordship, which is working out so well that I have hopes of great marvels, because, beyond the beauty of the human events which take place, the views and machines are so novel that the world, I swear, has never seen anything like it, not excluding the Greeks or the Romans [...] and soon it will appear with music, so Your Most Illustrious Lordship does not want to fail to come, because everyone is dying to do it. More so, because we have right now three works nearly learned, that is, the big one for this Carnival in which these lady virtuosos have done so well [...] having stupefied all the nobility of Rome.[22]

These "lady virtuosos" were women, and Italian. Castelli continued:

> the Lord Marshal is so satisfied with them, that he is thinking of giving them – rather, he commanded me, as graciously as I am able, to try and see if they would come, if necessary, to France. And I feel so much agreement that each one of them is dying to do so; in such a way that seeing the applause for these women, the other honest virtuosos have called me

---

22   Murata, Margaret (1995). "Why the First Opera Given in Paris Wasn't Roman." *Cambridge Opera Journal*. Vol. 7, No. 2, pp. 87–105; p. 95.

on their own, with gifts from themselves. And they are angelic voices, My Most Illustrious Monsignore, and what matters most, they are obedient. And believe me […] because not only have they gained applause in the theatre, but also all the Prelatura – not only the Chambers of the Rota and the Segnatura – have favoured their cause with most splendid evening favours and grand gifts, because they do not have displeasing faces in addition to beauty of voice.[23]

It is for the reader to conclude what was meant by "most splendid evening favours and grand gifts," particularly when noting the common application of the title *cortigiana* to women whose capabilities reached beyond the bedroom. Revisionist commentary has sought to designate the word "courtesan" as knowing slander (particularly where Barbara Strozzi is concerned), but Castelli's characterisation of Rome's "lady virtuosos" amplifies the extent to which aspirationally professional women were drawn to the *chaise longue* by circumstances over which they had no control. This was particularly true where powerful men were concerned; there were few more powerful than Mazarin. In 1639, he left Rome and returned to Paris where, six years later, he recruited the scenery designer Giacomo Torelli[24] to oversee the first production, in France, of *La finta pazza*. A further six operas were presented, including a lavish staging in 1647 of Luigi Rossi's *Orfeo*.[25] In 1653 Mazarin appointed Nicholas Fouquet as Superintendent of Finances, in which role he achieved conspicuous personal success, sufficient for him to build Château de Vaux-le-Vicomte, the largest private house in France prior to Versailles.[26]

When Mazarin died in March, 1661, Louis was advised by those with silver spoons to collect that Fouquet was a threat to the power of the throne and a drain on the country's finances. With Machiavellian calculation, Jean-Baptiste Colbert, the new First Minister of State,[27] proposed a series of celebrations in Louis' honour. Fouquet was tasked with managing the project, for which he turned to Molière, who was invited to present a play and, (separately) a ballet, for the amusement of a monarch renowned for his love of dancing. Molière opted to combine the two art forms; the premiere of *Les fâcheux*[28] at Vaux-le-Vicomte on 17 August, 1661, marked the creation of the *comédie-ballet*[29] and the coincident ruin of Nicholas Fouquet. The production was extravagant even by the standards of the French royal family; vast sums were spent on stage machinery, costumes and performers. Despite believing *Les fâcheux* to be the best thing since sliced brioche,[30] Louis allowed Jean-Baptiste

---

23 *Ibid*, p. 96.
24 One of the most brilliant and inventive designers in the history of theatre.
25 The first Italian opera to be premiered in France.
26 The same design team was retained for Versailles: Louis Le Vau (architect), Charles Le Brun (painter), and André le Nôtre (garden designer).
27 Colbert secured the King's favour, and his promotion, by revealing the location of some of Mazarin's hidden assets. Nests of vipers are known to have employed "the French court" as a metaphor.
28 'The Bores.'
29 The work was subtitled *Comédie faite pour les divertissements du Roi Les fâcheux* ('A comedy for the King's amusements').
30 So great was the King's pleasure that he commissioned twelve more *comédies-ballets* from Molière.

Colbert to order his arch rival's arrest on charges of *peculation* (the maladministration of State funds) and *lèse-majesté* (actions harmful to the well-being of the monarch). Lasting more than three years, Fouquet's trial was held before a "special" court with a bench formed of 22 judges handpicked by Colbert. Fouquet was renowned as an orator, and forbidden in consequence from speaking at court; he was required to prosecute his defence in writing. Thirteen of the judges ruled for banishment; nine opted for execution. Louis "commuted" Fouquet's sentence to life in prison,[31] where he spent his remaining 19 years. Louis confiscated Château de Vaux-le-Vicomte[32] while gifting Alexandre Dumas a plot for "The Man in the Iron Mask."[33]

Torelli was caught up in the storm caused by *Les fâcheux*, which flung him and most other Italian musicians at court back to Italy. His influence in France was profound, however – especially among dramatists. the same machines that Torelli had created for Rossi's Orfeo, but the grinding gears and creaking ropes compelled Corneille to turn to Charles d'Assoucy for incidental music, airs, duets, and choruses. This did not create a species of opera; indeed, Corneille considered music a necessary evil for disguising noisy stagecraft.

> I have been most careful not to have anything sung which might be necessary to the understanding of the play, since ordinarily those words which are sung are not understood by the audience [...]. I have introduced music only to charm the ears while the eyes are engaged in watching the descent or ascent of the machines or are occupied with something else which would prevent attention being given to what the actors might be saying.[34]

The significance of these events on the life of the soprano in France is located in the often preposterous politicisation of art, design, music, literature and theatre during the 17th century – and the priority above all else of comprehension. Meaning and inference were written, painted, carved, stitched, and moulded into just about everything, resolving an aristocratic vernacular that operated in mutuality with a precipitate increase in nationalism following the Peace of Münster. Louis XIV had welcomed Italian opera into France. With the emergence of populist nativism, however, he came to prefer (and did much to promote) a culture for France that disavowed every other – an ambition prompted in part by his father's failure to attend to the Chapel Royale, in particular, and music more generally, during his reign. In 1666, the last of Paris' semi-resident opera companies was sent back to Italy. None would

---

31 At a fort in modern-day Pinerolo, Piemonte.

32 Before the reader reaches for a handkerchief, it is worth noting that Fouquet's plan for Vaux-le-Vicomte necessitated a work force of 18,000 and the demolishing of three villages. He then "retained" the now-displaced villagers to maintain the gardens that were laid over their former homes.

33 Dumas' novel *Le Vicomte de Bragelonne, ou Dix ans plus tard* was the third and last of the d'Artagnan Romances, following "The Three Musketeers" and "Twenty Years After." It was first published in serial form between 1847 and 1850. In its English translation, Dumas' novel was separated commonly into three parts: The Vicomte de Bragelonne, Louise de la Valliere, and The Man in the Iron Mask.

34 Grout, Donald Jay (1941). "Some Forerunners of the Lully Opera." *Music & Letters*, Vol. 22, No. 1, pp. 1–25; p. 10

return until the middle of the eighteenth century. Throughout this period the French government published *l'Etat de la France*,[35] a handbook for foreign and domestic reference that detailed the operation of the French royal court in all its complexities.[36] Music was pivotal to private and public activities, and the *L'Etat* reveals the extent to which everything was proscribed and denoted. There were three different forums for the performance of music at court, *La Chapelle, La Chambre* and *L'Ecurie*.[37]

In 1661, the Chapel required eight *chapelains* and five *clercs* for High Mass, with two *sous-maitres*, an organist, and other (unspecified) musicians. In 1669, there were four *sous-maitres* and a composer. Three years later, two composers and four organists were considered necessary, and in 1692 the Chapel's forces spanned *chapelains*, *clercs*, *sous-maitres*, organists, composers, a full-time instrumental and vocal ensemble comprising four violins, three players to double the inner voices, three string basses, two serpents, two flutes, two bassoons, and a crumhorn, nine sopranos, six boys, 13 *haute-contres*, 18 *haute-tailles*, 26 *basse-tailles*, and eight basses. Each performer and their salary was recorded in the *L'Etat*. By 1665 (when Jean-Baptiste Lully's name appeared for the first time), the coterie of musicians needed for the *Chambre du Roi*[38] was symphonic in number. The "French soprano" during these years of transition was characterised primarily by being *other than* Italian, and identified as "*dessus*," "*premier dessus*" or "*haute dessus*." The hostile reaction to Baroni can be considered typical of the xenophobic construction of "great art" as local; unsurprisingly, the first female singer to achieve celebrity in France did so because she was French.

Anne Chabanceau de la Barre[39] was the daughter of Pierre Chabanceau de La Barre, an organist of the *chapelle royale* at Notre-Dame. She made her stage debut in Torelli's production of Rossi's *Orfeo* in 1647, which led to her being invited to sing at the court of Queen Christina of Sweden in Stockholm, where she was awarded the title of *kammarsångerska*. De la Barre relocated to the royal court in Denmark and at the end of 1655 she returned to Paris to perform the sung-verses in a series of *ballets de cour* by Lully, notably *La Galanterie du temps*,[40] *Ballet royal d'Alcidiane*,[41] and the *Ballet de la Raillerie*.[42] Lully and Molière then collaborated for a series of *comédie-ballets*, in which de la Barre starred as the *premier dessus*. In 1661 she was honoured with the

---

35   First published in 1649, but on a much grander scale from 1661. For a list of English translations of *l'Etat* see The British Library General Catalogue of Printed Books to 1975, Vol. 114.

36   See generally Cohen, Albert (1992) "L'Etat de la France: One Hundred Years of Music at the French Court." *Notes*; Second Series, Vol. 48, No. 3, pp. 767–805.

37   The Stable. Established in 1657, the Music of l'Ecurie covered a lot of bases. It provided the wind, brass, percussion, and mixed-ensemble music necessary for celebrations in the chapel and the chamber, as well as open-air entertainments, parades, and mounted festivities (thus "the stable,"). L'Ecurie also provided the musical signals and calls of the military and royal bodyguards. Cohen, Albert (1992) "L'Etat de la France: One Hundred Years of Music at the French Court." *Notes*; Second Series, Vol. 48, No. 3, pp. 767–805; p. 773.

38   The musicians of the Chambre performed at dinner, evening entertainments, court festivities and bed-time.

39   1628 (baptised on 3 July) – 1688.

40   'The gallantry of time,' premiered on 14 February, 1656 – the first of the French ballets, written for – and danced by – Louis XIV.

41   14 February, 1658.

42   19 February, 1659.

title "*Fille ordinaire de la musique de la Chambre*" (a title she retained until her death). On 7 February, 1662, during Cavalli's residency at the French court, de la Barre created the role of *La bellezza* in a bastardised version of *Ercole amante*;[43] she was one of only three French singers in an otherwise Italian cast of 19.[44] In May, 1664, four plays by Molière were staged at Versailles as part of Louis XIV's *divertissement royal*, to which was given the title *Les Plaisirs de l'Île enchantée*.[45] In addition to new stagings of *Les Fâcheux* and *Le Mariage force*,[46] Molière presented two new works: *Tartuffe*[47] and *La Princesse d'Élide*.[48] Neither was an opera, but rather a play with musical interludes sung by de la Barre and others. Three years later, she retired after marrying Antoine Coquerel. Tiberio Fiorelli, the most celebrated Scaramouche for the *commedia dell'arte* (a role he performed for Molière's *Le Bourgeois gentilhomme*) described de la Barre as "This girl, who with her voice charms queens and kings [is] wise, amiable and beautiful, with many abundant gifts, of excellent golden vermeil [...];"[49] the diarist Jean Loret[50] recorded how her "voice is so clear and so rare [that it] surpasses in sweetness a nightingale's trills on a rose-bush."[51]

The clarity identified by Loret venerated language over lyricism; words when sung were more important than music. The ambition of French composers at the time, and of Lully primarily, was to "move the listener with sweet sighs, painful cries and tones that represented a range of passions," an ordinance of values that distinguished the French idealisation of meaning and expression from Italian voices given to "trilling." The lyrical and the dramatic were indistinguishable from a singer's response to music as an adjunct to the truth and beauty of poetry at its purest. Jean Loret dedicated one of his poems to de La Barre:

> I say farewell to you a thousand times!
> I believe that in the waters of Neptune
> You would face no danger
> For if the winds or mutinous waves
> Wanted to tease you there
> Your songs, your charms, your face
> Would soon have calmed the storm.[52]

---

43 'Hercules in Love.'
44 One of the other two singers was another lauded soprano, Hylaire Dupuis, about whom almost nothing is known.
45 'The Pleasures of the Enchanted Island.'
46 'The Forced Marriage.'
47 12 May, 1664.
48 'The Princess of Elis.' Premiered on 8 May, 1664.
49 Paradoxically, a silver-gilt.
50 Jean Loret (1600 – 1665), a poet and diarist considered by Charles Dickens to be "one of the best." Not to be confused with Jean-Marie Loret (25 March, 1918 – 14 February, 1985), a French railway worker believed by many to have been an illegitimate son of Adolf Hitler.
51 Loret, Jean (1857). *La Muze Historique ou Recueil des Lettres en Vers contenent les Nouvelles du Temps, écrits a son Altesse Mademoizelle de Longueville, depuis Duchesse de Nemours, 1650–1665.* Vol. 1–4.
52 *Je te dis mille fois adieu! / Je croy qu'aux climats de Neptune / Tu ne courras nulle fortune, / Car, si les vents ou flots mutins / Vouloient faire ille les badins / Tes chants, tes apas, ton vizage, / Auroient bien-tôt calmé l'orage.* Belgrano, Elisabeth (2011). *"Lasciatemi Morire" O Farò "La Finta Pazza." Embodying Vocal Nothingness*

Loret was a better diarist than a poet, and if his doggerel reveals nothing of the manner of de la Barre's singing then his reference to *les vents ou flots mutins* speaks unambiguously to the rivalries and treacheries that defined life at court. Between 1644 and 1664, Lully composed or contributed to twelve *ballets de cour* (spanning *Le Libraire du PontNeuf, ou les romans*[53] and *Les Amours déguisés: Ballet du roy*[54]) in which a variety of *recites* and *aires* were performed either by de la Barre or by Anna Bergerotti,[55] her Italian rival for the affections of the French court. Bergerotti first arrived in Paris in 1654 for the premiere of Carlo Caproli's *Le Nozze di Peleo e di Theti*,[56] an opera commissioned by Cardinal Mazarin, who co-wrote the libretto – in Italian. The premiere on 14 April, 1654, was staged in the Salon of the Théâtre du Petit-Bourbon, with designs by Torelli[57] and *ballet intermèdes* with texts by Isaac de Benserade and music by a variety of uncredited composers. The precocious 15-year-old Louis XIV appeared in no fewer than six choreographed roles. Bergerotti was admired by Lully (whose talents she promoted at court) and Constantijn Huygens. Anna of Austria and Mazarin were sufficiently enamoured to provide her with an apartment near the royal residence and a substantial court salary of 3,600 *livres*. More remarkably, Bergerotti was one of the last of those artists who survived the Italian exodus following the death of Mazarin and the *Scandale Fouquet*.[58]

With Bergerotti's departure from Paris, the French Court set about extinguishing the influence of Italian music and musicians from *L'Etat*, a cull that accounted for style as well as voice, spanning men, women and the reviled castrati. The flamboyance of Italian music-drama was antithetical to the classical priorities of Corneille and Racine, for whom the concept of *Règlement*[59] was "*la gloire de la France d'avoir achevé de regler tous les beaux Arts.*"[60] According to Donald Jay Grout, French music dramas before the first official opera

> [were] characterised by objectivity, repose, simplicity, massiveness and nobility of proportions, and by a clearness of outline which the frequent ornamentations were never allowed to obscure. These qualities may be observed in such diverse examples as the architecture of the Louvre, the gardens of Versailles, the tragedies of Racine and the operas of Lully.

---

on Stage in Italian and French 17th Century Operatic Laments and Mad Scenes. A Music Research Drama Thesis in a Prologue and 3 Acts. University of Gothenburg, Sweden, p. 92.

53   'The Bookseller of the Pontneuf, or the Novel.'
54   'Disguised Loves; the King's ballet.'
55   1630 – 1700.
56   'The Marriage of Thetis and Peleus.' The same title was used previously by Cavalli for an opera that was first performed at the Teatro San Cassiano on 24 January, 1639.
57   The dimensions of the hall were tiny by modern standards but considerable for the time. The entire floor space was 15 meters wide and 35 meters long, with an apse at one end adding 13.5 meters for occupation by the king and his court. The "general public" was accommodated in two tiers of balconies positioned on the walls.
58   She remained at Court until marrying in 1669.
59   The bringing of practical order to the philosophy of reason. Grout, Donald Jay (1941). "Some Forerunners of the Lully Opera." *Music & Letters*, Vol. 22, No. 1, pp. 1–25; p. 3.
60   According to the royal courtier Claude-François Ménestrier, in 1682. 'It is the glory of France to have finished regulating fine art.'

An opera in France had to be something different from what it was in Italy. The confused plots of the Italian works; the overwhelming number of irrelevant details and secondary characters; the implausibility of the dramatic situations; the meaningless repetitions of the texts; the florid embellishment of the vocal lines; even the frequently chromatic and dissonant harmonies – all these things produced on the French an impression of intolerable artistic anarchy. Order and clarity were wanted.[61]

To understand why the French regarded early Italian opera and singing with such suspicion it's useful to turn to an Italian opera that was known to the French Court during Mazarin's administration. Cavalli's *La Calisto* was staged in Paris, and detested by the anti-Italian faction, for whom French art was definitive by reason of origin. In Act I, Scene 4, Calisto sings the recitative "*Sien mortali o divini*,"[62] which is followed by the aria "*Non è maggior piacere che*":

> *Non è maggior piacere che,*
> *seguendo le fere*
> *fuggir de l'uomo i lusinghieri inviti:*
> *tirannie de' mariti*
> *son troppo gravi e troppo è il giogo amaro.*
> *Viver in libertade è il dolce, il caro.*
> *Di fiori ricamato*
> *morbido letto ho il prato,*
> *m'è grato cibo il mel, bevanda il fiume.*
> *Da le canore piume*
> *a formar melodie tra i boschi imparo.*
> *Viver in libertade è il dolce, il caro.*[63]

Cavalli's sprightly treatment of Giovanni Faustini's pastoral reverie adds little to Calisto's sentiments; it is far from clear what emotion she is supposed to be feeling when revelling in her freedom from the male of the species. It could be relief, anger, despair or exhaustion; she might simply be venting at having to subsist on honey and water while having to sleep in a field with only birds for company – the sort of empty sincerity of which Molière was so devastatingly critical in *Le Bourgeois gentilhomme*. In answer to the *new money* Jourdain's question, "Why is it always the shepherds?" the Music Master replies:

> When we have characters that are to speak in music, it's necessary, for believability, to make them pastoral. Singing has always been assigned to

---

61 *Ibid*, p. 4.
62 'Mortal or Divine.'
63 'There is no greater pleasure than to flee amidst the herds of wild animals the flattering requests of men: the tyranny of husbands is too heavy and their yoke too cruel. To live in freedom is sweet and dear. For my bed I have the downy meadow carpeted with flowers, I feed on honey and I drink water from the river. The birds teach me their melodies in the woods. To live in freedom is sweet and dear.'

shepherds; and it is scarcely natural dialogue for princes or merchants to sing their passions.

Cavalli repeats numerous words and phrases – notably *"troppo gravi e troppo è il giogo amaro;"* he indulges *"libertade"* in the repeated phrase *"Viver in libertade,"* with both iterations unfolding over dozens of notes that require immense technical ability on the part of the soprano and, for contemporary French audiences, absent considerable patience. Suspicion yielded to scorn for those who considered Faustini's poetry vacuous and Cavalli's settings frivolous. The serious business of language was a ubiquitous obsession for the French court, with significant intellectual and financial capital invested by Louis XIV in one of his father's more durable legacies, the Académie Française. The *Académie* was first established in 1634; on 22 February, 1635, at Cardinal Richelieu's urging, letters patent were issued, and two years later the *Parlement de Paris* formalised the Council's primary function as

> *de travailler avec tout le soin et toute la diligence possibles à donner des règles certaines à notre langue et à la rendre pure, éloquente et capable de traiter les arts et les sciences.*[64]

These founding men of letters were alive to the paradox of being loved and raised by mothers whose voices were inaudible outside the home, and of whom silence was expected other than when singing *briefly* in the theatre.[65] The first occupant of the Académie's seat number four, Jean Desmarets, was no misogynist, but he did little to promote the female voice when otherwise preoccupied by self-advancement at Court. Having succeeded early on as a dramatist, Desmarets was appointed *"Conseiller du roi, contrôleur-général de l'extraordinaire des guerres,"* and Secretary-General of the fleet of the Levant. Desmarets' abandoned his success in the theatre for epic religious poetry, notably his proto-Miltonian *Clovis.*[66] Navigating the corridors of power was a secondary priority for his young pretender, Pierre Corneille,[67] whose challenges to the Académie formed primarily as attacks on the unities, expressed as *"une peinture de la conversation des honnêtes gens."*[68] Corneille and Desmarets were academicians in every sense of the word – for whom women prevailed as object or observer. Far less respectful (and at no time a seat-holder) was Molière, who committed habitually to the satirising of the Académie's formalistic ambitions – initially with *Les*

---

64 'To work with all possible care and diligence to give certain rules to our language and to make it pure, eloquent and capable of dealing with the arts and sciences." Article XXIV, published 10 July, 1637. The *Académie Française* has continued to regulate French grammar, spelling, and literature. In 2017, the Academy claimed that the French language was in *"danger mortel"* because of the increasingly common use of non-standard, gender-inclusive language. Post-Brexit, English is already be replaced as the primary "working language" of the European Union by French and German. Louis XIII would be proud, and it would be difficult to blame him for being so.

65 The Académie consists of 39 members, who are known as *immortels*. In its almost four hundred year history, it has elected 718 members, of whom only six have been women. Marguerite Yourcenar (8 June, 1903 – 17 December, 1987) was the first woman to be elected – to seat number three.

66 1657.

67 1606 – 1684.

68 'A painting of the conversation of the gentry.'

Précieuses Ridicules. He was equally scornful of French misogyny, typified by Jacques Olivier's infamous anti-feminist pamphlet, *Alphabet de l'imperfection et malice des femmes*.[69] Molière recoiled from the dangers of keeping girls and women isolated from the world, particularly during their formative years; he took to proselytising his proto-feminist values through the satires *L'Ecole des Maris* and *L'Ecole des Femmes*. With *Les Femmes Savantes*, his penultimate stage play, Molière questioned whether women could demand education without coincidentally disrupting the established domestic order. His answer is one of the funniest plays in any language.

L'école des femmes was first staged at the Théâtre du Palais-Royal on 26 December, 1662.[70] This near-perfect comedy revolves around the sorrows of Arnolphe, a man so intimidated by the feminine that he determines to marry his young, ward – whom he has been raising since the age of four.[71] The play was controversial at the time, and it would be difficult to stage in the 2020s. Notwithstanding the problematic narrative, the purpose of Arnolphe's curriculum is to ensure the ignorance of his reluctant pupil rather than her enlightenment. Molière's preoccupation with the growing significance of the value of education for women filtered in some shape or form throughout each of his major works, the majority of which were driven by his loathing for didacticism, which he equated to the monologic speech-giving employed by the church and the town hall when acting in opposition to the multiplicity of dialects and linguistic codes for which la mère de Marianne was notable. It is regrettable that France thought to formalise its language at court with so many dialects persisting outside it, particularly along the country's borders. Until the second half of the 19th century, for example, Italian was the dominant language in and around Nice; among the elites of the Italian Kingdom of Piemonte, French was spoken with a pronounced dialect and, even today, the linguistic boundaries between Occitan and Italo-Romance are sufficiently diaphanous for Ligurian dialects to be spoken in the French towns of Saorge, Breil-sur-Roya, Fontan, Brigue and Tende. 17th century "French" was determined by where, as well as by whom, it was being spoken.

"Voice" was a conceptual as well as a pragmatic concern for most women. Other than at court, they were seen commonly as a household mechanism for succession and domestic order, a balance of priorities that motivated Molière to promote the education of girls through comedy. He was not alone in confronting the issue. In 1673, François Poullain de la Barre published his treatise on the equality of the sexes, *De l'Égalité des deux sexes, discours physique et moral où l'on voit l'importance de se défaire des préjugez*,[72] which inspired the abbot and historian Claude Fleury to publish his *Traité du choix et de la méthode des études,* in 1685,[73] followed two years later by the

---

69 'The School for Wives.' First published in 1617 and reprinted at least eighteen times by 1650. The work's relevance and popularity survived Molière by at least a decade, having been re-printed in 1683 – ten years after the writer's death.

70 Theatre in the east wing of the Palais-Royal, on the Rue Saint-Honoré, which opened on 14 January, 1641, with a performance of Desmarets' tragicomedy *Mirame*.

71 In June, 1663, Molière responded boldly to the uproar with *La Critique de L'École des femmes*.

72 'On the Equality of the Two Sexes: A Physical and Moral Discourse, Which Shows That it is Important to Rid Oneself of Prejudice.'

73 'Treatise on the choice and method of study.' The essence of his treatise was that "the mind has no sex." It should probably be noted that both Venus and Mars were observed reliably for the first time more than 60 years earlier, by Galileo.

theologian Fénelon's *Traité de l'éducation des filles*,[74] a thesis formed around the noble principle that "*rien n'est plus négligé que l'éducation des filles*,"[75] the virtue of which he qualified when observing unhelpfully that "the weaker they are, the more important it is to strengthen them." The female voice in France was advantaged by a small number of women who were allowed either to write or sing. A *demi-société* of literary Madames – de Sévigné, de Grignan, de La Fayette, de La Sablière and Dacier – produced a stunning, still relevant body of work, which Molière and his peers ridiculed as *literature précieuse*. Molière was less critical of the primacy of women in the theatre – not least since he was married to an actress. The leading sopranos to sing Molière's *comedies-ballets* at court (Anne de La Barre, Anna Bergerotti and Anne Fonteaux de Cercamanan) were relocated from the *Chapelle* and the *Chambre*. La première voix belonged to Hilaire Dupuy,[76] whose voice was of such beauty that it earned her the sobriquet "the human crystal." Dupuy may be considered the first "operatic" soprano in France, although she remained throughout her career in the shadow of Armande-Grésinde-Claire-Élisabeth Béjart,[77] better known as Mademoiselle Molière. Béjart was revered as an actress, whose talents included singing. One contemporary praised her "extremely pretty voice," which she used in "French and Italian with great taste,"[78] but Béjart was overlooked by Lully – even though the libretto had been written by her husband. This fact speaks clearly to the growing separations between lyric and spoken theatre in France.

In 1671, Molière, Corneille, Philippe Quinault and Lully collaborated for *Psyché* – a five-act *tragicomédie et ballet* that served as a portal to the writing two years later of the first opera by Lully, *Cadmus et Hermione*. It's unlikely the singing equated to the crystalline precision of a modern performance. Lully was not a trained singer; he still opted to sing in his own operas, and there was clearly a willingness among audiences to accept an imperfect technique where words and theatrical substance were prioritised. *Le Sicilien*, for example, features a love-song with an *alla Turca* refrain, "*D'un caur ardent*."[79] This was performed at the premiere by a skilled voice-artist, Jean Gaye. When Molière published *Le Sicilien* in 1668, he assigned the song to a different character, Hali – a role performed customarily by the comic-buffo actor "La Thorilliere." The distinction between *farceurs* and *chanteurs* was left vague by Molière, who used trained singers as foils for comic performers. In *La Princesse d'Elide*, the character Moron attempts to seduce a shepherdess (yes, more shepherds) by taking singing lessons from a satyr. At the court premiere, Moron was played by Molière; the satyr by a virtuoso-bass, Guillaume d'Estival.

---

74 'Treatise on Girls' Education.'

75 'Nothing is more neglected than the education of girls.'

76 1625 – 1709.

77 1645 – 30 November, 1700.

78 It needs to be admitted that the same commentator proceeded in the same sentence to observe, without irony, that "no one knew how to show off her face better by the arrangement of her hairstyle, and more nobly by the adjustment of her dress." A rather better description of Béjart is by Molière in Act 3, Scene 9 of *Le Bourgeois gentilhomme*, in which Cléonte characterises the "treacherous" Nicole's many virtues.

79 'With an ardent heart.'

Operatic art in France took on fully-professional form with the first performance of Lully's *Alceste* at the Théâtre du Palais-Royal on 19 January, 1674. Staged in celebration of Louis XIV's victory against Franche-Comté, the work was a triumph.[80] Five of the leading roles were scored for sopranos: the Nymph of the Seine (Mlle de Saint-Christophe), La Gloire (Mlle de La Garde), the Nymph of the Tuileries (Mlle Rebel), and the Nymph of the Marne (Mlle Ferdinand). The title role was created by Mlle de Saint-Christophe, for whom the composer wrote music of exceptional elegance, even if it spans only a ninth (D3 – F4). Thanks to Lully's bizarre fecundity, the appetite in Paris for opera after 1680 fostered a generation of French sopranos whose reputations were inseparable from the roles they created. Marie Le Rochois[81] joined the Paris Opéra in 1678, where she was idolised by Lully, Desmarets, Marc-Antoine Charpentier and André Campra. She is best remembered for her creation of the title role of *Armide*, on 15 February, 1686, in the presence of the Grand Dauphin – but not the King, who excused himself in consequence of the composer's scandalous affair with a young page boy, Brunet.[82] *Armide* was the first opera to succeed nationally, being revived on seven occasions in Paris before 1764, and with a variety of productions between 1686 and 1751 in Marseilles, Brussels, Lyon, Lunéville and Metz. It even made its way to Den Haag, Berlin and Rome.

For Lully, La Rochois created roles in *Proserpine* (1680), *Persée* (1682), *Amadis* (1684), *Roland* (1684), *Acis et Galatée* (1686), and *Achille et Polyxène*[83] (1687). She was also the originator of roles for Desmarets, Charpentier (most famously *Médée*; 1693), Marais, Destouches and Campra. La Rochois lived a quiet and respectable life, which resolved in a long career as a teacher of singing. The same could not be said of Julie d'Aubigny[84] – better known as Mademoiselle Maupin. Théophile Gautier relied (loosely) on d'Aubigny for the title character of his novel *Mademoiselle de Maupin*,[85] although he was unable to characterise many of the more *outré* elements of her life story. d'Aubigny was the only child of a secretary to Count d'Armagnac, Louis XIV's *Grand Écuyer*.[86] She spent much of her childhood in the Palais des Tuileries in Paris and relocated to Versailles' newly-constructed Grande Écurie in 1682. In addition to

---

80 So much so that it was revived at Court twice in 1677 and again in 1678.

81 1658 – 8 October, 1728. Also known as "La Rochois."

82 Much has been made of the King's disapproval of Lully's bisexuality – a controversy that caused him less difficulty than his did fall-out with Molière. Indeed, while homosexuality was a capital offence, Philippe d'Orléans, the King's brother, was gay; Louis turned a blind eye to France's prevalent gay culture, even if this meant not being able to hear his favourite composer's music.

83 First performed on 7 November, 1687 – eight months after Lully died (on 22 March, 1687) after refusing to have a gangrenous toe amputated. Lully had caused his own injury when stabbing himself with a wooden staff, which he was using to conduct by "banging" time. To add irony to injury, he was directing a performance of his own *Te Deum*, which he had prepared in celebration of Louis XIV's recovery from surgery. This entailed substantial dental work, that resulted in the accidental removal of part of the King's jaw. For those with an interest in French dental history, and the strongest of stomachs, there is nothing to compare with the death of Maximilien Robespierre in 1794.

84 1670 / 1673 – 1707.

85 1835. The epistolary novel is not about an opera singer. Instead, Gautier tells the life of Madeleine, a noble girl, who runs away from home disguised as a soldier and travels the world under the name of Theodore. The poet D'Albert, who suspects the truth, falls in love with Madeleine. D'Albert's previous mistress, Rosetta, also loves with Madeleine / Teodoro. The drama resolves, fittingly, in a duel...

86 Effectively "Master of the King's horses" for the wealthiest horse-owning family on Earth.

being a superb equestrian, d'Aubigny was celebrated for her swordsmanship, a talent that resulted in her being educated in classrooms of boys, in whose clothes she was required to dress to avoid discovery. Her romantic spirit materialised in almost every context as rebellion.

Her father encouraged his daughter's pugnacity, and he could do little about it after she began to sleep with the boss as a 14-year-old. In 1687, d'Armagnac directed d'Aubigny's marriage to Sieur de Maupin, of Saint-Germain-en-Laye. Even before the confetti had settled, the teenaged D'Aubigny entered into an affair with her fencing master, Sérannes. When the Maréchaussée attempted to apprehend Sérannes for killing a man in an illegal duel, the pair fled to Marseille, where d'Aubigny made her living performing in fencing demonstrations at public fairs, an abstraction that did nothing to diminish her reputation as a duellist. d'Aubigny viewed Louis XIV's increasingly strict prohibitions against duelling with the same contempt in which she held the courts' mandates against homosexuality.[87] Her affairs (in parallel with her slaying of at least ten men in sword fights) were transgressive of laws that applied only to men; it was on this basis that d'Aubigny secured at least two royal pardons.

Louis XIV fathered approximately 22 children, of whom six were legitimate. His three daughters were required to abide by rules and codes of behaviour for which d'Aubigny cared nothing, and the King either tolerated or encouraged her behaviour on the basis that it made for entertaining gossip at court. One of the wildest tales revolved around d'Aubigny's seduction of a merchant's daughter, whose resulting shame led to her sequestration at a convent. When discovering that one of the sisterhood had passed away only days earlier, d'Aubigny engineered a plan to steal the dead woman's body, which she delivered to her lover's room – before burning the convent to the ground. The pair eloped in the resulting chaos, only to be discovered and arrested a short time later. D'Aubigny was charged with arson, kidnapping and body-snatching. Appropriately enough for a bisexual pyromaniac, she was sentenced to death by fire. Uncaring of the court's judgment, d'Aubigny entered into an affair with Gabriel-Vincent Thévenard, a much-admired baritone at the Opéra. Motivated by infatuation, he persuaded the court to allow its prodigal daughter to audition. It transpired that d'Aubigny was as gifted at singing as everything else and Louis granted yet another pardon. The King's affections for opera were fickle; it was nonetheless agreed that d'Aubigny's talent was worth snatching from the flames. She joined the Opéra in 1690 – at the age of 17 – and made her debut in Lully's *Cadmus et Hermione*. She became the darling of a public that relished the fantasies of her life off-stage as well as her artistry on it. But for a handful of roles,[88] she specialised in revivals.[89]

During his account of a performance by d'Aubigny of *Omphale* by André Destouches at the Trianon in Versailles, the Marquis de Dangeau described her voice as "the most beautiful in the world." The following year, in 1702, Campra composed

---

87   Punishable by "death by burning." Quite how this was seen to be a "punishment" is anyone's guess. The authors of the Bible had been content previously with the "abomination" of homosexual love warranting nothing more specific than that "they shall surely be put to death." (Chapter 20, verse 13).
88   Notably the Magician in Desmarets' *Didon* (1693), Clorinde in Campra's *Tancrède* (1702), Diana and Thétis in Campra's *Iphigénie en Tauride* (1704) and Mélanie and Vénus in Campra's *Alcine* (1705).
89   In contrast, Gabriel-Vincent Thévenard created more than sixty roles.

the role of Clorinde in *Tancrède* for her *bas-dessus* (contralto) range; three years later she appeared for the last time in the first production of *La Vénitienne* by Michel de la Barre. D'Aubigny retired from the Opéra in 1705 and, for probably ambiguous reasons, entered a convent in Provence, where she is believed to have died in 1707, presumably from exhaustion. She was 33-years-old, and "destroyed by an inclination to do evil in the sight of her God."[90] Her body was said to have been "cast upon the rubbish heap."[91]

D'Aubigny makes for great story-telling, and her Cyrano-esque bravura must have been intoxicating. She was nonetheless despised by many who considered her antics "typical" of women in the theatre, and of Opéra as an institution; she was, as such, the unnatural consequence of unchecked female decadence. The moralist Charles Denis de Saint-Évremond anticipated the inevitability of d'Aubigny in his 1676 play, *Les Opéra,* in which a teenaged woman goes mad after hearing works by Lully and Quinault. Nicolas Boileau-Despréaux may well have been thinking directly of d'Aubigny when writing his *Contre les femmes* in 1694, in which he cautions husbands to be minded that the degeneration of women can be traced directly to the Opéra, and to songs of love. For its critics, musical theatre was a hive of infidelity, immorality and madness, and to be avoided at all costs.[92] This was problematic for women being introduced to "society," with attendance at the Opéra considered as much a part of the gallant world as any other feature of life at court.

d'Aubigny was both a propagator and a product of operatic corruption, therefore. Her critics overlooked the talent and the commitment necessary for performing on stage because any recognition of ability was indistinguishable from a tacit acknowledgement of parity with men. d'Aubigny was not trained professionally, although she was clearly gifted with a technique sufficient to allow her to meet the demands of repertoire and regimen. What is known of her life as a singer suggests discipline and conformity; even so, tales of her recklessness fed the gossip machine for the rest of her short life. She entertained an on-off affair with the Dauphin, sharing his bed with her sister, and it was claimed she threatened to shoot (among others) the Duchess of Luxembourg. She is known to have been sued for attacking one of her many landlords, and during a brief stint as a lady in waiting to the popular Countess Marino, d'Aubigny threaded the back of her hair with radishes shortly before her Ladyship entered the salon of a grand ball. One of her lovers, the Elector of Bavaria, found her to be insufferably intense; after d'Aubigny stabbed herself with an actual knife during a performance at the Opéra (and with the Elector in the audience) he offered her 40,000 francs to end their relationship. She spurned his money and disappeared to Spain for 12 months. Both of her final love affairs resolved in tragedy. She lived for two years with Madame la Marquise de Florensac, the "most beautiful woman in France," who died of a fever in 1705 – leaving d'Aubigny heartbroken for the first time. She was driven subsequently to attempt suicide after being rejected by another of the Dauphin's lovers, Françoise "Fanchon" Moreau.[93]

90 Gilbert, Oscar, Paul (1932). *Women In Men's Guise*. John Lane, p. 176.
91 *Ibid.*
92 Cowart (1994). "Of Women, Sex and Folly: Opera under the Old Regime Georgia Cowart." *Cambridge Opera Journal*, pp. 206–207.
93 1668 – after 1743.

Moreau was another soprano at the Opéra, a stage she shared with her older sister, Louison.[94] Both were admired for their singing, but Françoise was the greater beauty, and it appears that Louison was embarrassed during her introduction to the Dauphin, who had heard much of "Moreau's beauty." Approximately three years older than her sister, Louison made her debut at the Opéra in 1680, shortly after which date she was dismissed for being pregnant. She was reinstated when Françoise joined the company, in 1683, and she remained until 1692, during which time she created the role of Amasie in *Orontée* by Jean-Louis Lully – Jean-Baptiste's son. Nothing is known of her life after 1692, and it is presumed she died young. Fanchon's life and career were much longer. She made her debut at the Opéra as Astrée in the first performance of Lully's *Phaëton* in January, 1683 – the first opera to be staged at Versailles – and during almost two decades with the company she performed in dozens of new works for Lully (including Astrée in *Phaëton*, 1683; Oriane in *Amadis*, 1684; Sidonie in *Armide*, 1686), Desmarets (including Anne in *Didon*, 1693); Charpentier (including Créuse in *Médée*, 1693), Destouches (including Doris in *Issé*, 1697), and Campra (including Olympia in *L'Europe galante*, 1697; and the title role in *Hésione*, 1700).

The most lasting impression by any of the Opéra's founding sopranos was achieved in her absence by Marie-Louise Desmâtins.[95] She too worked closely with Lully during preparations for performances of new works[96] – including *Persée* (1682) and *Armide* (1686) – and she was instrumental in promoting his legacy with numerous revivals, memorably of *Thésée* (1698), *Isis* (1704), *Roland* (1705), *Bellérophon* (1705), and *Alceste* (1706). Her career was long by the standards of the day, and her status sufficiently exalted to warrant a painting by Robert Tournières, in around 1700. The canvas presents a woman with a fuller figure and no obvious beauty, who is portrayed holding sheet music and pointing with her right hand to some unseen object. Little more is known of Desmâtins but for what emerges in *La musique du Diable*, a novel by Robert le Turc,[97] published in 1711, in which the soprano (whom the author describes as a "known debauchee") is sent to Hell with Lully. No singer ever received a worse review.

Le Turc published his novel, "*À Paris: Chez Robert le Turc, rüe d'Enfer,*" an address that was either diabolically coincidental or a product of the author's sledgeham- mer wit. The novel recounts the events leading up to the soprano's death, and it is singu- larly less kind than Tournières who, though renowned for the accuracy of his por- traits, removed a large amount of weight from a woman whom Le Turc characterised as morbidly obese. He took grim delight in recounting how, prior to Desmâtins' damnation, she retained the finest butcher in Paris to remove her fat – which she then used to prepare a lavish dinner party:

---

94   1668 – after 1692.
95   1670 – 1708.
96   She created the role of Briséis in the first performance of *Achille et Polyxène*, which was staged a few months after Lully's death in 1687. She shared the stage with Fanchon Moreau (as Andromaque), and Marie le Rochois (as Polixène).
97   'The Devil's Music.' The novel's full title is *La musique du diable, ou Le Mercure galant devalisé* ('The Devil's Music, or The Gallant Mercury Robbed').

> She had prepared fine saveloys, puddings, sausages, and andouilles wherein she [...] presented them to anyone that her fancy picked, not sparing even her dear Royal treasurer nor her most devoted lovers, in one word to anyone who upon eating them would unanimously agree that they had never come across pieces so tasty in their lives.[98]

After dinner, Le Turc feeds Desmâtins her just desserts:

> At the moment she would begin to walk in her chamber, and dressmakers and tailors would work day and night to make models and new garments appropriate for the beauty & delicacy of her new body, death ruthlessly sent her to these grounds, where she presently enjoys a happiness, which she had not experienced and had not hoped for.[99]

The soprano is welcomed to Hell with the highest of honours and the most scandalous of indictments, spanning her prostitution for money (rather than status), ruining a registry-book of marriages, driving respectable merchants to bankruptcy, transmitting venereal diseases to politicians (an allegation that Le Turc plainly intended as a compliment), causing acid to be thrown into the face of a rival, contemplating the assassination of the director of the Académie Française, and poisoning two prelates and numerous fellow singers – including Marie Le Rochois, who was alive and well at the time of publication. In addition, Desmâtins is said to have worn her theatre costumes at home and behaved "like a princess." To add spice to the punch, Le Turc asserted that Desmâtins had four abortions and neglected confession for twenty-two years. These charges were meant to be read together. Desmâtins' response is the funniest thing in the book:

> I have done nothing that an opera girl as tolerably pretty as I should not have done [...] interrogate [the Devil] and punish him, because as far as I am concerned, I am sweetness itself and the most innocent creature that has existed on earth.[100]

She is saved by Pluto, who has her transferred to his palace, on the basis that her behaviour was

> regulated only by our orders, and so long as she stayed on earth, it was only for the glory and spread of our empire.[101]

Pluto in this context is Louis XIV; the empire is France. Desmâtins' sins were exaggerated by Le Turc, who admitted:

---

98 Chrissochoidis, Ilias (2007). "La Musique du Diable (1711). An obscure specimen of fantastic literature throws light on the elusive opera diva Marie-Louise Desmatins." *Society for Eighteenth Century Music*. Issue No. 11, pp. 7–9; p. 8.

99 *Ibid.*

100 *Ibid.*

101 *Ibid.*

All that they are going to see about this so well-known, famous actress is only a lesson we give to those who by their natural constitution, the inclination they have towards women of the stage, the little comparison they make between vice and virtue & the unhappy chains that their conduct with this kind of creatures leads them, stray furiously from the divine path.

The operatic soprano first came into life in the form of a woman, Leonora Baroni, whose "happy judgement [and] liberal modesty" inspired Milton to portray her as "an angel [...] Heavenly winged from the celestial orders." Within fewer than 70 years, the art and business of opera warranted the publishing of a portrait of a female singer as emblematically cruel, selfish, vulgar, greedy, vain, lascivious, corrupted, psychopathic and amoral – deserving of a life infernal. Pursuant to this shift in perception, women were able finally to be heard in equivalence with men, even if only on stage and exclusively in France. It is correspondingly certain that Le Turc's literary assassination of Desmâtins was in no way misogynistic. He did not pick on the soprano because of her gender, and much of the novel is plainly affectionate of a singer whom Le Turc saw often at the Opéra. His brutal take-down of a woman whose death prevented her from defending herself memorialised a kind and variety of equality that admitted ridicule and satire as well as praise and respect. While progress for women at the end of the 17th century can be traced to an increase in the freedoms afforded by musical theatre, it is manifest also in the publishing of an evisceration that was designed to undermine, excoriate and humiliate an individual rather than women across their sex. It's an odd route to parity, of which Desmâtins is certain to have approved.

CHAPTER FIVE

Counterintuitively Speaking

The love-lives of female singers have been a source of fascination for centuries. A once frivolous and puritanical curiosity in the genuinely private yielded during the 1980s to a trashy obsession among consumers with the grotesqueries of clinically-managed relationships – as real as the talents of most of those doing the singing. Taylor Swift has made a career out of writing songs about her ex-boyfriends – all but one of whom has been a singer or an actor with their own careers to promote. Adele's 2021 album *30* committed overtly to her divorce from Simon Konecki, with numerous songs alluding to a "secret" relationship about which she was happy to sing for the millions who bought the album during the year of its release. Adele's skill as a composer-performer is greater than those retained to direct it, but the fact that all of her studio albums have been autobiographical, and concerned in no uncertain terms with her personal life, suggests the public taste for narcissism is unlikely to fade any time soon.

Arguably the first soprano to live her life in public was Arabella Hunt.[1] A child prodigy, whose skill as a lutenist and a singer brought her to the attention of the court of St James where she participated in 1675 as a 13-year-old in John Crowne's masque, *Calisto, or the Chaste Nymph*. Celebrity among the wider public came via her marriage as an 18-year-old to "James Howard" on 12 September, 1680 – at St. Marylebone Parish Church, London. Because Hunt was independently wealthy, having inherited a sizable estate in Upton, Buckinghamshire, after her father and both of her siblings died before her 18th birthday,[2] her reasons for marrying are open to scrutiny. The reasons for her divorce are less opaque: Hunt sued her "husband" in London's Consistory Court[3] for being other than a man – specifically because "he" was an hermaphrodite.[4]

This remarkable case was not as novel as posterity might suppose. In 1718, Jacob Giles, a writer on common law, published his *Treatise of Hermaphrodites*, in which he described these "wonderful secrets of nature" as "curious discoveries," and advocated their inclusion in society, sufficient to inherit property and engage in other legal actions. To do so they had to opt, to be male or female – there being nothing in between, at the time. They were otherwise as "normal" as men and women in their binary certainties.[5] Hunt's designation of her husband's natural status was mislead-

---

1   27 February, 1662 – 26 December, 1705.
2   She was survived by her mother, Elizabeth, who was the sole beneficiary of her will.
3   An ecclesiastical court, operated by and within the Church of England. Each diocese has a consistory court, although they fell into abeyance in the 19th century.
4   See generally Sudai, Maayan (2011). *Sex Ambiguity in Early Modern Common Law (1629–1787).* Cambridge University Press.
5   Anyone who thinks progress has been made in recent years where transgender issues are concerned should read Giles' work, and decide for themselves.

ing, however, since "Mr. Howard" was, in fact, a woman called Amy Poulter (née Gomeldon); at the time of their wedding "she" was already married to a man called Arthur Poulter.

Arabella was first introduced to Howard "disguised" as a "young heir, not yet of age." Other than in Hunt's company, she was said to have gone about her day as Amy / Mrs Poulter. It's unclear why it took Hunt six months to discover that her husband "went under the suspicion of one of a double gender,"[6] but when seeking an annulment it was to her husband's genitals that she directed the court's attention. Hunt demanded that Amy be examined to prove the truth of her sex.[7] No fewer than five midwives were appointed by the court to act as a jury, which concluded that she was, indeed, a "perfect woman in all her parts."[8]

Hunt had married a woman, and while this remains problematic for many in the 21st century, 17th century England was moderately relaxed about such matters, with lesbianism in particular being an issue only if it suited a third party's malfeasant interests. Hunt's marriage to Howard was annulled without either of them being criticised or censured by the court – which found on 15 December, 1682, that two women could not legally marry each other. According to Valerie Traub, the ecclesiastical court in *Hunt v Poulter*

> was concerned with the legal status of their marriage, not their personal motivations. These texts do not tell us, however, about some of the conditions under which women's erotic activities with other women were construed as a social problem. Such a construal, it is important to note, was not inevitable. Female-female eroticism was not universally or uniformly scandalous, or even criminal.[9]

For all the tacit controversy, Hunt's unlawful marriage was unexceptional, and it provoked neither scandal nor malice. While nothing can be presumed of an 18-year-old woman's expectations of her wedding night, it's striking that Hunt waited six months

---

6   Traub, Valerie (2002). *The Renaissance of Lesbianism in Early Modern England*. Cambridge University Press, p. 49.

7   The case is reminiscent of Ruskin's (annulled) marriage to his wife, Effie. As she later recalled, Ruskin "had imagined women were quite different to what he saw I was, and that the reason he did not make me his Wife was because he was disgusted with my person the first evening." It was presumed that Ruskin's understanding of the appearance of a woman was formed by the smoothness of classical statues, in whose company he spent most of his life prior to his wedding night. The long and short of it is that Ruskin was horrified to discover that his wife had pubic hair; he fled the bedroom in consequence. The actual events, and their context, are rather different, and examined splendidly in Brownell, Robert (2013) *Marriage of Inconvenience. Euphemia Chalmers Gray and John Ruskin: the Secret History of the Most Notorious Marital Failure of the Victorian Era.* Pallas Athene.

8   More than three centuries later, in 2015, Gayle Newland was sentenced to eight years in prison for duping a female friend into having sex (while wearing a blindfold) when pretending to be a man. This charade continued for two years without Newland's friend realising the deception. Newland disguised her appearance and her voice and was discovered to be a woman only after having had sex on ten occasions, when Newland's friend removed her mask and saw her lover wearing a prosthetic penis. Newland's conviction was overturned on appeal, on the grounds that the judge at first instance had sided with the prosecution. The case has since become meaningful for Transgender debate and activism.

9   *Ibid*, p. 50.

to issue her suit. The failure of her marriage can be better attributed to a collapse in their relationship, therefore, rather than her putatively shocking discovery that Mr. Howard was, in fact, Mrs Poulter.[10] Amy took her own life within a month of the annulment,[11] and Hunt neither married again nor bore any children. This was as unusual for women at the time as was bachelorhood for men, but Hunt's sexuality appears to have had no bearing on her career, or her success. Indeed, her passing notoriety did nothing to diminish her celebrity; it is believed she had affairs *inter alia* with the playwright Aphra Behn[12] and Charles II's mistress, Nell Gwyn. Hunt's popularity with Queen Mary[13] led to her appointment as a teacher of singing and lute to Princess (later Queen) Anne – for which she was rewarded by Mary with an annual pension of £100. Her performances at court brought her to the attention of most of the leading contemporary poets, painters and composers of the day. She was painted by Godfrey Kneller, wrapped in red satin and sat behind a lute; during the early years of the 18th century, William Congreve published *On Mrs. Arabella Hunt Singing*, the second verse of which proclaims:[14]

> Come all ye Love-sick Maids and wounded Swains,
> And listen to her Healing Strains.
> A wond'rous Balm, between her Lips she wears,
> Of Sov'reign Force to soften Cares;
> 'Tis piercing as your Thoughts, and melting as your Tears:
> And this, through ev'ry Ear she does impart,
> (By tuneful Breath diffus'd,) to ev'ry Heart.
> Swiftly the gentle Charmer flies,
> And to the tender Grief soft Air applies,
> Which, warbling Mystick Sounds,
> Cements the bleeding Panter's Wounds.
> But ah! beware of clam'rous Moan:
> let no unpleasing Murmur or harsh Groan,
> Your slighted Loves declare:
> Your very tend'rest moving Sighs forbear,
> For even they will be too boist'rous here.
> Hither let nought but Sacred Silence come,
> And let all sawcy Praise be dumb.

---

10   She is said to have claimed at the time that her marriage to Hunt was a prank. This is not persuasive.

11   The tragic Poulter is buried still in the cemetery of St. John the Baptist Church in Cottered, Hertfordshire.

12   In 1682 Behn's play, *The False Count*, alluded to Hunt and Poulter: an elderly husband is troubled by his wife's relationship with a maid ("I have known as much danger hid under a Petticoat, as a pair of Breeches. I have heard of two Women that married each other – oh abominable, as if there were so prodigious a scarcity of Christian Mans Flesh.")

13   Some have commented (by way of Mary's fairly unambiguous correspondence with the royal courtier Lady Frances Aspley) that Mary favoured Hunt because of the singer's equally unequivocal sexuality.

14   Congreve was clearly smitten. When Hunt died in 1705, he produced an *Epigram Written after the Decease of Mrs. Arabella Hunt*: "Were there on Earth another Voice like thine, Another Hand so blest with Skill Divine! The late afflicted World some Hopes might have, And Harmony retrieve thee from the Grave."

John Blow, who wrote a number of songs for Hunt, declared that she "reigns alone, as Queen of music by the people's choice." Her most famous collaboration was with Henry Purcell. William's court was derided by Dryden as a "stupid Military State,"[15] and Purcell appears to have laboured under the yoke of Mary's questionable taste in music – even with his muse, Arabella Hunt, a ready source of support and inspiration. The best known story of the composer and the soprano in concert was told by the bass John Gostling:[16]

> The tune "Cold and Raw" was greatly admired by Queen Mary [...] Having a mind one afternoon to be entertained with music she sent to Mr. Gosling to Henry Purcell and Mrs. Arabella Hunt, who had a very fine voice, and an admirable hand on the lute, with a request to attend her [...] Mr. Gosling and Mrs. Hunt sang several compositions of Purcell, who accompanied them on the harpsichord. At length, the queen beginning to grow tired, asked Mrs. Hunt if she could not sing the old Scots ballad "Cold and Raw." Mrs. Hunt answered yes, and sang it to her lute. Purcell was all the while sitting at the harpsichord unemployed, and not a little nettled at the queen's preference of a vulgar ballad to his music. But seeing her majesty delighted with the tune, he determined that she should hear it upon another occasion, and accordingly in the next birthday song – that for the year 1692 – he composed an air to the words "May her bright example chase Vice in troops out of the land," the bass whereof is the tune "Cold and Raw."[17]

It has been argued by Curtis Price that Purcell's awkward harmonic treatment of "Cold and Raw" was designed deliberately to comment not only on the Queen's judgment, but also the political tensions fomented by Mary after being left so often to rule on her own:

> Purcell's mostly homophonic setting strides with tonic-dominant pomp and glitter, the staggered entries of the second strain obscuring only the penultimate line of the verses quote above. But near the end of the forthright chorus is a truly awkward progression that apparently cannot be explained by faulty manuscripts or Purcell's love of quirky harmonies.[18]

Hunt was a court singer, and neither required nor expected to appear on stage. It was easy in consequence for court singers to remain feminine, and tolerable within the

---

15   When writing his *Epistles and Complimentary Addresses To Sir Godfrey Kneller, principal Painter to His Majesty*, Dryden wrote: *"Then all the Muses in one ruin lye / And Rhyme began t'enervate Poetry. Thus in a stupid military state / The pen, and pencil find an equal fate."*

16   See generally Hawkins, Sir John (2010). *General History of the Science and Practice of Music*. Gale ECCO.

17   The work was performed on the Queen's birthday, 30 April, 1692. By Purcell's standards, it's a little forced harmonically, although the string *ritornello* is more than efficient.

18   Winn, James A. (2010). "Confronting Art with Art: The Dryden-Purcell Collaboration in King Arthur." In *Restoration: Studies in English Literary Culture, 1660–1700*, Vol. 34, No. 1/2, pp. 33–53.

boundaries of social decorum. The acoustics of small rooms required little projection and nothing of the diaphragm. Theatres were a different matter entirely. When Purcell was casting the role of Cupid for the first performance of *King Arthur* in 1691 he bypassed Hunt for the singing actress Charlotte Butler. Considering her popularity, and the number of productions in which she was a prominent feature, it is bizarre that there is no certain record of Butler's dates of birth and death. She appears to have made her stage debut in 1680, in the first performance of Aphra Behn's comedy, *The Revenge; Or, A Match in Newgate* – in a production by the Duke's Company at the Dorset Garden Theatre in London. More than half a century later, Colley Cibber remembered Butler as "the Daughter of a decay'd Knight," whose

> Christian Name of Charlotte [had been] given her by King Charles
> [...and who] had the Honour of that Prince's Recommendation to the
> Theatre; a provident Restitution, giving to the Stage in kind, what he
> had sometimes taken from it: The Publick, at least, was oblig'd by it; for
> she prov'd not only a good Actress, but was allow'd, in those Days, to sing
> and dance to great Perfection. In the Dramatick Opera's of Dioclesian,
> and that of King Arthur, she was a capital, and admired Performer.

The "King Arthur" to which Cibber was referring was Purcell's "dramatick opera"[19] in five acts, to a libretto by Dryden. First performed at the Queen's Theatre in 1691, the work is notable for its "Frost Scene," in which the bass playing the Cold Genius sings "What power art thou who from below" to an accompaniment of tremulous strings (in homage to the "shivering" chorus, *L'hiver qui nous tourmente,* from Act IV of Lully's *Isis*). Cupid's responses to the Genius' chattering plea, "Let me, let me freeze again to death," were written for Butler, whose singing at the first performance was acknowledged to be one of the highlights in a work formed of little else. Butler's modest birth and circumstances entitled her to perform in public, where the appearance of a woman singing was less consequential than it would have been in court circles. The writer and lawyer, Roger North, described her performance as "beyond anything I ever heard upon the stage" – a distinction arising from the "liberty she had of concealing her face, which she could not endure should be so contorted as is necessary to sound well, before her gallants, or at least her envious sex."[20] In choosing to "turne her face to the scean, and her back to the theatre,"[21] Butler was ignoring stage convention while challenging the presumptions of English audiences, who expected female performers to be inhibited and restrained – even when vanquishing the more demanding acoustics of a theatre. North considered that

> The English have generally voices good enough, tho' not up to the pitch
> of warmer countreys. But come into the theatre or musick-meeting, and

---

19 Dryden's preferred term.
20 Baldwin, Olive and Wilson, Thelma (1982). "Purcell's Sopranos." *The Musical Times*, Vol. 123, No. 1675, pp. 602–603; p. 603.
21 Parrott, Andrew (2015). *Composers' Intentions?: Lost Traditions of Musical Performance.* The Boydell Press, p. 280.

you shall have a woman sing like a mouse in a cheese, scarce to be heard, and for the most part her teeth shut.[22]

The root of North's criticisms attached to the manner in which singing was being taught, with teachers focussing "on tunes, whereas they should begin with pronunciation."[23] If it seems improbable that English audiences raised on Shakespeare should not have been concerned with the clarity and audibility of language in the theatre then it's important to remember that singing wasn't taught in England as it was on the continent. Butler was an actress who sang; she was not an opera singer – if only because the short supply of operas was met with a comparably limited demand. Colley Cibber described Butler's manner on stage as "blending her assuasive Softness, even with the Gay, the Lively, and the Alluring,"[24] the last of which catalogue of virtues contributed to her success as well as her reputation as a harlot. Whatever the substance of this notoriety, it appears to have been exacerbated by her commitment as a performer, and the success it brought her. Most of her critics were excessively unkind, with many preferring personal attacks to digressions on art and craft. In *Satyr on the Players*,[25] for example, the splenetic authors fumed that

> Fam'd Butler's Wiles are now so common grown
> That by each Feather'd Cully, she is known
> So that at last to save her Tottering Fame
> At Musick Club , She strives to her a Name
> But mony is the Syren's chiefest Aym.[26]

A *Satyr* from 1683 was nastier still:

> Harwood whom Butler clap'd & made a Chouse,[27]
> To save his Stake Married & Clapt his Spouse.

Purcell cared nothing for such jibes. From 1688, when he pledged himself for the first time to the theatre, Butler was his preferred "soprano," and the only female singer to be identified prior to the first performance of *The Fairy Queen* in 1692. Before turning to his "semi-opera," Purcell tailored three songs to Butler's rare talent for engaging with an audience: "For Iris I sigh," "Hang this whining way of wooing" and "No, no, poor suff'ring heart."[28] These short works have more than an element of music hall

---

22 *Ibid.*

23 *Ibid.*

24 Baldwin, Olive and Wilson, Thelma (1982). "Purcell's Sopranos." *The Musical Times*, Vol.123, No.1675, pp. 602–603; p. 603.

25 *Circa* 1682.

26 *Ibid*, p. 602.

27 A deceiver and a fraudster.

28 "No, no, poor suff'ring heart" was Purcell's sole contribution to the music for the first production, in 1692, of Dryden's *Cleomenes, the Spartan Heroe: A Tragedy*. The original Theatre Royal, Drury Lane, cast included Thomas Betterton as Cleomenes, Anthony Leigh as Cleonidas, John Verbruggen as Ptolomy, Samuel Sandford as Sosybius, William Mountfort as Cleanthes, Edward Kynaston as Pantheus, John Hodgson as Coenus, Mary Betterton as Cratisiclea, Anne Bracegirdle as Cleora and Elizabeth Barry as Cassandra.

about them;[29] they are designed to profit the poet and the singer before they do service to the composer. The same is true of the courtship dialogues, written for Butler to sing with the bass, John Bowman: "No more Sir," "Fair Iris and her swain" and "Why, my Daphne?" More than anything else, these songs project Purcell's affection for his leading lady through word settings that bounce off the page. The extraordinary energy of much of Purcell's music, even steeped in shadow, was subsumed over time to a vernacular of studied proportionality and good taste. This is nowhere more in evidence than in recordings of "Strike the Viol," a song composed by Purcell as one of a series of six odes formed as *Come, Ye Sons of Art*, to commemorate the birthday of Queen Mary in April, 1694. The words (by Nahum Tate) are:

> Strike the viol, touch the lute,
> Wake the harp, inspire the flute.
> Sing your patroness's praise,
> In cheerful and harmonious lays.

As the last of a cycle written to celebrate the monarch's birthday, it can be presumed that Purcell determined to inspire, and accompany dancing. The purposefully repetitious drive of the setting amplifies the power of the words "strike," "wake," "inspire," "praise," and "cheerful." When recording the song for L'Oiseau-Lyre in 1953, the counter-tenor Alfred Deller and his Consort performed the song as if in anticipation of Purcell's *Music for the Funeral of Queen Mary*, composed eight months later. The tempo is somnambulant and absent theatre; there is no rhythmic bite, and it would be impossible to dance to the performance, other than in slow-motion. This tradition remains intact for the 21st century. A recording by Sally Sanford exemplifies the bleaching of music that ripples with spirit on the page. The counter-tenors Andreas Scholl and Carlos Mena, have reached further, but they still fall short of capturing the music's vibrancy. The closest anyone has come to doing justice to the music recently is the Belgian soprano, Céline Scheen,[30] whose performances with L'Arpeggiata of an arrangement by Christina Pluhar[31] have bucked expectations in a number of ways, chiefly Scheen's energy, easy tone, crystalline diction, and the vivid addition of an electric organ and jazz obligatos. The performance is presented as "an improvisation," and it is extremely fine, speaking as it does to the vitality of music that gains from less reverence than has become routine among the British.

Purcell based *The Fairy Queen* loosely on *A Midsummer Night's Dream*; his cast duly included a chorus of fairies and attendants and at least 20 solo voices[32] – around half of whom were scored as sopranos. He gave the short but memorable role of the Nymph to Butler, whose final words are unlikely to have been coincidental: "I'll be as false and inconstant as he." It may be imagined that Purcell's attachment to one of his favourite singers allowed him to look beyond the prejudice and gossip to which

---

29   This quality leaps off the page when it is read; modern performances are singularly too elegant, and burdened with good taste and technical finesse. They fail to capture either the music's biting rhythmic energy or the wit of the poetry.

30   1976 –

31   Performed in numerous theatres, commonly with a large dance company; also recorded by Erato.

32   It's not known whether there was any doubling between named characters / voices.

she had been born as a woman; it's equally probable that the scene's resolving chorus was directed to Butler herself:

> A Thousand Thousand ways we'll find
> To Entertain the Hours;
> No Two shall e're be known so kind,
> No Life so Blest as ours.

The Fairy Queen is wildly inventive, with a catalogue of memorable scenes, among which Juno's "O let me weep" is a characteristically Purcellian study in melancholy that anticipates the heart-rending "When I am laid in Earth," from Act III of *Dido and Aeneas*.[33] Nothing is known of the girl for whom it was composed and by whom it was first performed;[34] her privilege in being tasked with its creation is infinite even if her identity is not. *Dido* was first performed in 1688 (three years before *The Fairy Queen*) by a company of school girls. Unsurprisingly, therefore, seven of the nine roles was written for a female voice. This was significant for a number of reasons. As England's foremost composer,[35] Purcell's access to resources was near-limitless. His stage works all made considerable use of women's voices because he had access to the finest singing actresses in London – and he needed women to reach where altos and countertenors could not. Arabella Hunt, for example, was said to have a voice "like the pipe of a bullfinch," a compliment intended to acknowledge her range rather than her power, which explains why Purcell had cause to rely on singers of both genders.

The composer was able to draw on an equally abundant reserve of counter-tenors and male altos.[36] The distinction between these kinds of singer may be reduced to differences in technique – with male altos employing falsetto and countertenors moving between the tenor and soprano registers.[37] Andrew Parritt has argued that the first unequivocal reference to a male alto (as distinct from a countertenor) dates to 1673.[38] Purcell certainly made use of both – frequently for the same performance of the same work; his scores feature roles described as being written for countertenor although they are tailored more obviously to a tenor register. It was routine also for men to play

---

33 It carries great power in arrangement also. A television recording exists of Stokowski conducting his arrangement, which proves not only his genius as a conductor, but the capacity of Dido's Lament to cleave the soul in almost any guise.

34 The first performance of *Dido and Aeneas* was given at Josias Priest's School for Girls in Chelsea, London, in the summer of 1688. The first performance may have taken place earlier, on 1 December 1687, and there is evidence to suggest it was performed at the school again in 1689. Some have argued that the opera was composed for the English court, for Charles II (or as early, even, as 1684 for James II) but the absence of any contemporary records or references makes this unlikely.

35 Purcell was not at any time Master of the Queen's Music, however. For most of his professional life that post was occupied by the infinitely less talented Nicholas Staggins, who held the post from 1674 until his death in 1700.

36 Purcell was himself a countertenor, and it's likely he fell within the range of what was known in France as an haute-contre. See generally Boyden, Matthew (2021). *The Tenor: a Cultural History*. Ragueneau Press.

37 See DeMarco, Laura E. (2002). "The Fact of the Castrato and the Myth of the Countertenor." *The Musical Quarterly*, Vol. 86, No. 1; pp. 174–185.

38 Parritt, Andrew (1995). "Performing Purcell," in *The Purcell Companion*. Ed. Michael Burden. Faber & Faber, pp. 417–18; p. 442.

as women, and women as men, with both singing into the soprano range. English musical theatre in the 17th century relied heavily on trouser-roles, with Charlotte Butler being cast on many occasions as a man; Purcell saw the interchangeability of voice and gender as uncontroversial because he was given to changing his mind whenever the circumstances merited it. The role of Mopsa in *The Fairy Queen*, for example, was written for and first performed by a soprano. On revising the work, Purcell proposed it should be played by "Mr. Pate in woman's habit," re-casting the refrain "No, no, no, no, no; no kissing at all" in Corydon and Mopsa's dialogue as inherently comic. John Pate was one of two of the most celebrated countertenors of the day (the other being John Freeman); he appears to have trained in Italy, almost certainly with castrati.[39] On 30 May, 1698, the diarist John Evelyn recorded:

> I dined at Mr. Pepyss, where I heard that rare Voice, Mr. Pate, who was lately come from Italy, reputed the most excellent singer, ever England had: He sang indeede many rare Italian Recitatives, etc.; and severall compositions of the last Mr. Pursal, esteemed the best composer of any Englishman hitherto.[40]

Purcell's common reliance on male altos and countertenors was analogous to the contemporary Italian dependency on castrati – a presumptively Catholic phenomenon reviled in Protestant England. Hunt and Butler were exceptional as sopranos performing on English stages at the end of the 17th century because women were defined by institutionally misogynistic political and social norms. They had to transcend their gender to be deemed acceptable, even when doing things that could not otherwise be done within the confines of nature. The unwillingness of English parents, surgeons and barbers to separate young boys from their testicles, whether in the name of art or for the love of money, ensured that men continued to sing as women on English stages until the beginning of the 18th century. Purcell's use of male altos and countertenors was soon enough anachronistic, in consequence of the emerging taste for Italian opera in London, which fed off the importing of foreign and exotic singers whose pre-existing conditions liberated the English from having to get their hands dirty. Purcell's brief but incandescent career as a composer of opera threw brilliant light onto the art of male altos and countertenors; both voices nonetheless died with the composer. Purcell's operas were the first and the last to be composed for a countertenor for more than two centuries. Ultimately, Hunt, Butler and Pate were unusual as well as extraordinary because they represented the last native form

---

39 Pate led an interesting life, although little is known about it. In 1700, Narcissus Luttrell recorded in his diary: "Letters from France say that Mr. Pate, who belonged to the playhouse here and sung so fine, is committed to the Bastile at Paris for killing a man, and that he is condemned to be broke on the wheel." He was pardoned, or escaped, for he appeared three years later in London to give a concert in Drury Lane, which was advertised on the basis that "Mr. Pate (having recover'd his Voice) will perform several songs in Italian and English." He died shortly after, and was buried in Hampstead Churchyard on 14 January, 1704. The burial register records him as "belonging to ye old Playhouse." Baldwin, Olive and Wilson, Thelma (1969). "Alfred Deller, John Freeman and Mr. Pate." *Music & Letters*, Vol. 50, No. 1, pp. 103–110; p. 107.

40 *Ibid*, p. 107.

of musical theatre in England prior to the 20th century.[41] Within 25 years of Purcell's death, the fully male soprano, like the English composer, would be silenced by George Frederic Handel. His arrival in London transformed the art and performance of opera by treating castrati and sopranos as rivals in what was finally, and for the first time, a fair fight.

---

41 Purcell's tragically young death (at the age of 36), and the sudden decline in English opera, did nothing to damage the composer's reputation. Writing over half a century later, Charles Burney noted that Purcell "is as much the pride of an Englishman in Music, as Shakespeare in productions for the stage, Milton in epic poetry, Locke in metaphysics, or Sir Isaac Newton in philosophy and mathematics," an opinion that has survived without qualification ever since. Burney, Dr. Charles (1957). *A General History of Music: From the Earliest Ages to the Present Period (1776–89)*. Ed. Frank Mercer. Dover Publications, p. 380.

CHAPTER SIX

Faster Pussycat![1]

Many readers have attended the performance of an opera in a theatre.[2] Many more are likely to have enjoyed a concert with a singer, accompanied by an orchestra or a piano. It is certain in every case that the singers, whether male or female, adhered to a range of behaviours that the majority will have taken for granted. Whether for staged or concert performances, its commencement is anticipated by the dimming of the lights and the descent of the audience into hushed reverence. Those inclined to speak, cough or indulge bags of plastic-wrapped confectionary will have endured the bourgeois terrorism of tutting and levelled gazes. Serial offenders are likely to have been asked to "be quiet please," while anyone using a phone will have been punched in the throat, and dragged from the theatre to an unmarked van, never to be seen again.[3] A singer's entrance is met with silence or encouraging applause. The lights when dimmed presume the tacit agreement of everyone in the theatre to respect the company of players, singers and stage-hands, whose months of preparation, rehearsal and personal investment will have conspired sub-consciously to justify the astronomical ticket prices.

It is different at a pop concert, where performers routinely invite fans to "make some noise," on the proviso that whatever volume they are able to generate will be swamped by the banks of amplifiers and speakers arraigned before them. The volume generated by a modern rock concert would have reduced Jericho to dust. Within the ambit of the law, there is nothing a stadium audience can do to disturb or curtail a performance.

These "norms" have evolved in tandem with the moderating influence of western manners. While Rostand could imagine Cyrano interrupting Montfleury's performance of Barro's *La Clorise* in 1640, the reality for the real de Bergerac would have compelled him to take a number, and join his voice to the hundreds of others shouting at the stage or each other. An appropriate 21st century comparator for an opera house in the early 18th century would be a boxing match. Each aria (or round) would have submitted singers to violent competition, with rival groups of fans willing their idols to victory pursuant to adversarial displays of physical and aesthetic virtuosity.[4] Opera houses operated as venues for social interaction, with commercial and

---

1   See Russ Meyer.
2   As opposed to the Albert Hall, or the Bregenzer Festspiele theatre on Lake Constance – both of which employ amplification for singers and chorus alike.
3   This may be wishful thinking on the part of the author.
4   The author's points of reference are Sugar Ray Robinson, Muhammad Ali and Teófilo Stevenson, rather than Rocky Marciano, Joe Frazier and Mike Tyson.

romantic affairs being conducted in the relative gloom of a building lit by candle; the outfits worn by an audience mattered more than the costumes being presented on stage. Boxes were owned and leased by the wealthy, with food and wine served on china and glass by hundreds of servants moving between the balconies, staircases and improvised kitchens.

The parterre[5] was for standing-room only, and employed commonly as a space for meeting, drinking, gambling and gossip. Audiences were more interested in their own voices; a night at the opera was frequently an opportunity to engage in conversation without being overheard. Indeed, it is difficult to appreciate the extent to which the 18th century auditory landscape was dominated by human speech. Discretion and privacy were a privilege of extreme wealth; even for the aristocracy there was little to hide behind the rattling of a spinet. Matters improved with time, albeit slowly. After a visit to La Scala in 1770, Charles Burney complained that the "abominable noise and inattention" of his fellow patrons had rendered all but a few passages of music inaudible. Twelve years later, when Pierre Choderlos de Laclos published his *Les Liaisons dangereuses*,[6] it's clear that talking throughout an opera was reasonable, routine and preferable to whatever was happening behind the proscenium. In Letter 29 of *Les Liaisons*, Cecilia Volanges writes to Sophia Carnay:

> She has asked Mother's permission to take me to the opera, to her own box, the day after tomorrow; she told me we should be by ourselves, and would chat all the while, without danger of being overheard. I like that a great deal better than the opera. My marriage will be, in part, the subject of our conversation, I hope: because she told me that it was very true that I was going to marry.[7]

Composers would take eventually to crafting *aria di sorbetto*,[8] incidental passages that gave time and opportunity to audiences wanting to buy food or drink without fear of missing anything significant.[9] The chaos of opera was bizarre and unfamiliar for the English until the early 1700s.[10] Works were presented initially at the Queen's (or King's) Theatre (putatively The Opera House), and the playhouses of Drury Lane and Covent Garden – all of which operated with patents awarded after the Restoration in 1660. Because royal patronage signified more than it occasioned (compelling the art to function as a business), the majority of operas during the ten years either side of 1700 were performed in English. Only with the arrival in London of the castrati

---

5 The "Stalls," in English.
6 The same year that Mozart's *Die Entführung aus dem Serail* was first performed.
7 *"Elle a demandé aussi à maman de me mener après-demain à l'Opéra, dans sa loge; elle m'a dit que nous y serions toutes seules, & nous causerons tout le temps, sans craindre qu'on nous entende; j'aime bien mieux cela que l'opéra. Nous causerons aussi de mon marriage…"*
8 'Sherbet Aria.'
9 Rossini mastered this particularly talent, like every other.
10 The first native opera to be performed in England was *The Siege of Rhodes*. It was staged in 1656 by William Davenant at Rutland House, his home in Aldersgate Street, London. The work is remarkable also for its score having been written by no fewer than five composers: Henry Lawes, Matthew Locke, Henry Cooke, Charles Coleman and George Hudson.

Valentino "Valentini" Urbani[11] and Nicolò "Nicolini" Grimaldi[12] did Italian become *vox populi*. Between 1707 and 1709, Valentini and Nicolini starred in a variety of works by Pepusch, Haym and Conti, all of which were delivered with bilingual libretti. Colley Cibber wrote of Grimaldi that "no Singer, since his Time, has so justly, and gracefully acquitted himself, in whatever Character he appear'd."[13] Even the polemicist Joseph Addison was persuaded:

> [Grimaldi] sets off the Character he bears in an Opera, by his Action, as much as he does the Words of it, by his Voice; every Limb, and Finger, contributes to the Part he acts, insomuch that a deaf Man might go along with him in the Sense of it – He performs the most ordinary Action, in a manner suitable to the Greatness of his Character.[14]

The Italian onslaught heightened opera's exotic qualities for audiences encouraged to treat the foreign as alien. It was easy for nativists to categorise a different and uncompromising culture as threatening. The actual circumstances, as far as immigration was concerned, were more complicated. England had only recently begun to welcome an influx of French-speaking Calvinists. During the last decade of the 17th century, hundreds of boats discharged thousands of Huguenots, with conservative estimates suggesting as many as 50,000 refugees fleeing persecution and martyrdom[15] during the reign of Louis XIV.[16] The majority were urbanites, and trained as artisans in sewing, weaving, metalwork and watchmaking; a greater number still of clergy, doctors, merchants soldiers, teachers and lesser nobility ensured the majority were able to contribute more than labour on arrival. Anti-Popery was at its height in England, and the common desire to protect fellow Protestants ensured a smooth transition for anyone seeking to join with the country's established systems, conventions and values. The majority spoke English, and they spoke it well. This was sufficient to dissipate the nascent domestic hatred of the French; it served equally to justify hostility for Italian culture – even though thousands of English had, like Milton, committed to Grand Tours, with prolonged stays in Italy. With dozens more Italian singers following in the wake of Valentini and Grimaldi, the prevailing view was summarised by Addison in 1711:

> There is no question but our great grand-children will be very curious to know the reason why their fore-fathers used to sit together like an

---

11   1690 – 1722.

12   1673 – 1732.

13   Cibber, Colley (1968). *An Apology for the Life of Colley Cibber: With an Historical View of the Stage During His Own Time*. Edited by B.R.S. Fone. University of Michigan Press, p. 210.

14   Addison, Joseph (1854). *The Works of Joseph Addison*. Ed. by George Washington Greene. G.P. Putnam & Co., pp. 61–62.

15   Huguenots did not relish the prospect of relocating to another Catholic territory, which explains the great attraction of England after 1688, when the Glorious Revolution replaced James II with William and Mary.

16   At a time when the population of England numbered approximately five and a half million. Louis reigned for 72 years – the longest ever.

audience of foreigners in their own country, and to hear whole plays acted before them in a tongue which they did not understand.[17]

The English playwright John Dennis was less sardonic; in 1706 he penned "An Essay on the Opera's [sic] After the Italian Manner, Which are About to be Establish'd on the English Stage: With Some Reflections on the Damage Which They May Bring to the Publick." Dennis claimed that opera made women lose their "original Innocence [to] those Heroes with luxurious Voices;" he continued that

> [opposing] a popular and prevailing Caprice, and to defend the English Stage, which together with our English Liberties has descended to us from our Ancestors; to defend it against that Deluge of mortal Foes, which have come pouring in from the Continent, to drive out the Muses, its old Inhabitants, and seat themselves in their stead; that while the English Arms are every where Victorious abroad, the English Arts may not be vanquish'd and oppress'd at home by the Invasion of Foreign Luxury.

Addison resorted to describing his personal experience:

> At length the audience grew tired of understanding half the opera; and therefore to ease themselves entirely of the fatigue of thinking, have so ordered it at present, that the whole opera is performed in an unknown tongue. We no longer understand the language of our own stage. I cannot forbear thinking how naturally an historian who writes two or three hundred years hence...will make the following reflection: 'In the beginning of the eighteenth century, the Italian tongue was so well understood in England, that operas were acted on the public stage in that language.

Others recognised the advantages of hearing Italian voices singing "Italian" music in Italian, whether or not it was composed by someone from Italy. In 1709, an English translation of *Parallèle des Italiens et des Français en ce qui regarde la musique et les opèras*[18] was published in London, in which a French physician, François Raguenet, compared the pros and cons of French and Italian music. The primary virtue for Italian opera was recognised to be the Italian language, which Raguenet considered better suited to singing, even, than his native French.[19] He was certain that Italian

---

17   The article was published in *The Spectator*, a magazine launched in 1711 by Addison and John Steele. It's worth noting that Addison's *second* Grand Tour in 1700 took him to Savona, Genoa, Milan, Venice, San Marino, Rome, Naples, Capri, Ostia and Florence. He reached Genoa in 1701. After a few stops in Vienna, Hamburg and Holland he returned to England for good, in 1703. The account of his trip to Italy was published by Jacob Tonson in 1705 as *Remarks on several parts of Italy, & c. in the years 1701, 1702, 1703.*

18   Published as (2010) *A Comparison Between the French and Italian Musick and Opera.* Gale ECCO.

19   This argument raged for centuries, and only rarely entailed a French person conceding Italian superiority in this regard, or any other.

vocalists were the finest in Europe because they had learned to "sing from their cra-dles."[20] Fifty years later, Burney would confirm the consistency of this prejudice:

> It is universally allowed that the Italian tongue is more sonorous, more sweet, and of more easy utterance, than any other modern language; and that the Music of Italy, particularly the vocal, perhaps for that reason, has been more successfully cultivated than any other in Europe. Now the vocal Music of Italy can only be heard in perfection when sung to its own language and by its own natives, who give both the language and Music their true accents and expression. There is as much reason for wishing to hear Italian Music performed in this genuine manner, as for the lovers of painting to prefer an original picture of Raphael to a copy.[21]

English audiences were not conversant with Italian;[22] as such, the preference for Italian voices was formed uniquely by the sound made by singers articulating open vowel sounds, using techniques that were unknown (and unavailable) to native per-formers. Audiences were soon criticised for attending performances only to hear the singers, without caring either for the drama or the meaning of the words. Burney summarised the issue when holding that

> the poetry of an Italian opera in England is wholly out of the question; nor has the Music much to do with its success; it is generally upon the singing that its favour entirely depends. Great and favourite singers only can save an Italian musical drama of any kind in this country.[23]

Differences of opinion were more in evidence where matters of gender were con-cerned. The novelty and thrill of the castrato for most of Europe is difficult to overstate;[24] for the only recently Puritan English, the hosting of an emblematically Catholic aberration generated a *recherché frisson* that titillated audiences whose "las-civious Mirth and Levity" had only recently provoked the closure of most of London's theatres.[25] According to Raguenet, castrati were unrivalled in

> the power, grace, and beauty in all of music: No Man or Woman in the World can boast of a Voice like Theirs, they are clear, they are moving, and affect the Soul it self [sic] a Voice the most clear, and at the same time equally soft, pierces the Symphony, and tops all the instruments with an

---

20   Kinder, Kaylyn (2013). *Eighteenth-century reception of Italian opera in London*. Electronic Theses and Dissertations, 753. University of Louisville, p. 21.

21   Burney, Dr. Charles (1957). *A General History of Music: From the Earliest Ages to the Present Period (1776–89)*. Ed. Frank Mercer. Dover Publications, p. 528.

22   On the other hand, many in the emerging middle class, and the entire aristocracy, spoke French natively.

23   *Ibid*, pp. 680–681.

24   France was the only country to reject castrati (all but) absolutely.

25   This condemnatory language was adopted by the Long Parliament that repressed and later closed the vast majority of London's theatres and theatre companies between 1642 and 1648.

agreeableness which they that hear it may conceive, but will never be able to describe. What can be more affecting than the Expressions of their Sufferings in such tender passionate Notes.[26]

Although castrati were not welcome in France, the rest of Europe was thrilled by the novelty of it all, and novelty was necessary in an environment in which many opera singers were as indifferent as their audiences. The satirist Benedetto Marcello[27] observed of life before the castrato:

> The director will see that all the best songs go to the prima donna, and if it becomes necessary to shorten the opera he will never allow her arias to be cut, but rather other entire scenes. [If a singer] has a scene with another actor, whom he is supposed to address when singing an air, he will take care to pay no attention to him, but will bow to the spectators in the loges, smile at the orchestra and the other players [...] All the while the ritornello of his air is being played the singer should walk about the stage, take snuff, complain to his friends that he is bad voice, that he has a cold, etc., and while singing his aria he shall take care to remember that at the cadence he may pause as long as he pleases, and make decorations, and ornaments according to his fancy; during which time the leader of the orchestra shall leave his place at the harpsichord, take a pinch of snuff, and wait until it shall please the singer to finish.[28]

The fact that every castrato was Italian fostered a cultural bias that led to Italian singers being considered superior to any other. This doesn't mean that every Italian singer was a castrato, of course; neither does it mean that English-born sopranos were not established prior to the *grande migrazione*. Indeed, during the years immediately preceding Valentini's debut, the most celebrated soprano in England was English. Catherine Tofts[29] was the first native singer to perform Italian opera in England successfully. She sang primarily in her mother tongue, under contract with Drury Lane, and was sufficiently well-established in 1705 to complain to the Lord Chamberlain of her treatment by the Theatre's infamously brutish manager, Christopher Rich,[30] who had

> Tooke all the Opportunitys he could be Revenged on her: which was in calling on her to sing oftener than she was Able to performe... Through his ill Nature he called on [Tofts] to sing on a Tuesday, Thursday, and Saturday in the same week, not ion hopes of getting audiences (I being

---

26 Kinder, Kaylyn (2013). *Eighteenth-century reception of Italian opera in London*. Electronic Theses and Dissertations, 753. University of Louisville, p. 22.

27 See generally Pauly, Reinhard G. (1948). "Benedetto Marcello's Satire on Early 18th-Century Opera." *The Musical Quarterly* Vol. 34, No. 2. pp. 222–233.

28 Marek, George (1969). *Beethoven: Biography of Genius*. William Kimber, p. 15.

29 Also "Katherine" (1685 – 1756).

30 This was the most public of their many disputes concerning money. Tofts had received a fee for work outside Drury Lane of £60, to half of which Rich considered himself entitled.

Midsumer the Weather Excessive hot and the Towne very Empty) but only to shew his ill will.[31]

Tofts won her case, because she was something of a national heroine, having represented almost single-handedly the English soprano in England since 1703 – albeit only in proto-operas and songs. On 29 January, 1704, she was confronted for the first time with competition, in the form of Margherita de l'Épine, an Italian soprano whose contract with Drury Lane joined her to a rivalry she had not invited. As an Italian, de l'Épine was used to a certain combativeness in the theatre; little can have prepared her for the behaviour of the audience at her second performance at Drury Lane, on 5 February – the first having been witnessed by Tofts. Oranges and insults were hurled in tandem with hissing, booing and stamping. The Watchmen were called and an arrest was made. The culprit turned out to be one of Toft's servants. Such was the coincidence that Tofts was compelled to write to the Manager of the theatre – a letter published shortly afterwards in the *Daily Courant*:

> Sir, I was very much surpriz'd when I was informed that Ann Barwick, who was lately my servant, had committed a rudeness when Mrs l'Épine the Italian gentlewoman sang. I hope no one can think that it was in the least with my privity, as I assure you it was not. I abhor such practises and I hope you will cause her to be prosecut'd, that she may be punish'd as she deserves. I am, Sir, your humble servant.[32]

One feels for the unfortunate Ms Barwick, who had plainly acted on instructions. It's inconceivable that a servant would have had a suitable outfit, or the funds necessary to purchase a ticket. Tofts was able to accommodate both, as well as the ensuing embarrassment and the loss of a servant.[33] Tofts and l'Épine were paid the same fees. The latter had the better voice; the former was more beautiful, which goes some way to explaining Marco Ricci's painting of the sopranos at a "Rehearsal of an Opera" in 1709. Ricci was a talented painter of landscapes, but his series of six rehearsal scenes are Hogarthian cartoons,[34] more interesting for their content than their execution. His painting of Tofts and l'Épine is entertaining for presenting the sopranos with their backs to each other when preparing for a performance of Scarlatti's *Pirro e Demetrio*. l'Épine is seen with her hands buried inside a bright red muff; this may have been intended as a joke by Ricci, on the basis that Tofts, rather than the Italian L'Epine, was known to complain routinely of the English climate. In any event, Ricci's presumed loyalty to his compatriots did not extend to misrepresentation. Tofts was tall, classically handsome and thin; l'Épine was short, unattractive and

31   Highfill, Philip H., Burnim, Kalman A., Langhans, Edward A. (1993). *A Biographical Dictionary of Actors, Actresses and Musicians and other stage personnel in London, 1660–1800*. Vol. 15, Viking, p. 12.
32   Christiansen, Rupert (1984). *Prima Donna: a History*. Viking, p. 17.
33   Her annual salary at Drury Lane alone was £400, sufficient to keep a skilled labourer in full-time employment for 12 years.
34   One of the series is committed primarily to Nicolini, who can be seen singing in lavish attire and heavily bewigged, with his right hand outstretched, and sheet music in his left.

fat.[35] Rivalries made for good sport, and the singers and their antagonism provoked profitable gossip and sensation. Even Alexander Pope was more exercised by the English soprano's fees than her talent, sufficient for him to pour scorn "On Mrs Tofts:"

> So bright is thy beauty, so charming thy song,
> As had drawn both the beasts and their Orpheus along:
> But such is thy av'rice, and such is thy pride.
> That the beasts must have starv'd, and the poets have died.

John Hughes was concerned that members of the ruling class appeared to favour a foreigner:

> Music has learn'd the discords of the state, And concerts jar with Whig and Tory hate;
> There fam'd L'Epine does equal skill employ, While list'ning peers croud to th'ecstatic joy:
> Bedford to hear her song his dice forsakes, And Nottingham is raptur'd when she shakes:
> Lull'd statesmen melt away their drowsy cares
> Of England's safety, in Italian airs.

It may seem outlandish that Italian opera was considered a threat to national security, but the rapid emergence of opera, and the male and female soprano in conjunction, coincided with the popularity of newspapers, for whom content was no less titillating and inflammatory then than now. The first "sheet," *The Daily Courant*, was launched in London in 1702, followed soon after by *Lloyd's News* and Daniel Defoe's *The Review*, both of which were printed three times a week. *The Tatler* followed in 1709 and *The Spectator* two years later. In 1710, *The Examiner* was published to disseminate Conservative political propaganda – with Jonathan Swift editing 33 issues between November, 1710, and June, 1711. By the 1720s, there were twelve newspapers in London, and 24 in the provinces.

The correlation between issues of "voice" in its written form and when sung and heard on stage was a driver for a host of contemporary shifts in the conception and navigation of gender and sexuality. It's easy to forget that women were not allowed to perform in an English theatre until after the Restoration; opera's rootedness in English life collided with the emancipation of women as public figures – if only by individuation. This signal moment in the history of British and European gender politics was undermined simultaneously by the importing of castrati. Coincident to the liberation of women to appear as women on stage, an assembly-line of taller, stronger and better-trained men divided the candle-light, turfing an instantly par-adoxical but relatively level playing-field on which the identity of singers and roles

---

35   Her character and nature were much admired, but L'Epine's appearance was not. Even her husband, the composer Pepusch, gifted her the nickname "Hecate," after the goddess of magic and spells. A witch, therefore.

was subsumed to a trans-gendered reality that caused fewer problems in 1700 than in 2023.[36] The ordering of voices and role-casting in relation to gender provoked little disturbance for audiences raised (within living memory) on the appearance of men playing women on stage; many commentators baulked regardless at the "effeminacy" of the Italian nation. From atop his tower of soap-boxes, the populist John Dennis held that

> An Englishman is deservedly scorned by Englishmen, when he descends so far beneath himself, as to Sing or to Dance in publick, because by doing so he practices Arts which Nature has bestow'd upon effeminate Nations, but denied to him, as below the Dignity of his Country, and the Majesty of the British Genius.[37]

According to Veronica T. Faust:

> By labeling both Italian opera and the country in which it was born the 'feminine Other,' Dennis forged masculine British military and republican identity in relation to the debauched and effeminate monarchies of France and Italy. Dennis was part of the eighteenth-century cultural effort to stabilize the uncertain category of gender and lock the two sexes in difference. Rejecting the older notion of gender as imperfect variations on a single sex, writers constructed gender as fixed and immutable difference grounded in nature. For Dennis, then, castrati singers threatened the strict opposition of the sexes with their unnatural and ambiguous sexual identity. On one hand, British writers labeled the castrati as effeminate as the music they sang and the nation they came from. On the other hand, the castrati's reported sexual prowess with women, and their identification as the ultimate British-woman pleaser,

---

36   Movies and television programmes after the fashion of *Mrs Doubtfire* and Tyler Perry's *Madea* films are unremarkable for 21st century audiences because (1) they are comedies, (2) the actors are known to be heterosexual and cis-gender, and (3) the context is purposefully farcical – analogous to the appearance by male actors as "The Widow Twanky" in Christmas pantomimes across the United Kingdom. Movies like *Albert Nobbs* and *The Danish Girl* are problematic because they address serious issues of gender-identity in a real-world context; they require insight, compassion and understanding, as well as narrative-engagement. Such films are deemed commonly to be "art-house," and unlikely to draw audiences who consider Robin Williams and Tyler Perry to be hilarious. The actual experience of men and women being other than the sex as which they were born is still too much for those who find the idea of gender uncertainty and adjustment inconceivable and, worse, dangerous. In the USA, at the time of publication, Florida has passed legislation making it illegal for "Widow Twanky" to perform in a pantomime. Or for the actor playing "her" to read a nursey rhyme to children. It's worth remembering, on point, that many cultures around the world continue to feel the same about homosexuality. The same groups continue to be fearful also of women in authority (the Catholic Church), consensual sex between men and women (the Catholic Church), mixed marriage (Islam and Judaism), electricity and technology (the Amish), and cameras (the Mennonites). It's presumed, in the teeth of hope, that the passage of time will see the "abnormal" becoming acceptable to the judgmental, just as it has become normal for women to be afforded the *principle* of equality, even if the *practice* of that ambition fails routinely to meet expectations.
37   Faust, Veronica T. (2006). "'Music has learn'd the discords of the state': The Cultural Politics of British Opposition to Italian Opera, 1706–1711." Masters Thesis. Haverford College, p. 22.

threatened British masculinity. Attacks against castrati, then, embodied a compelling paradox, revealing the British discomfort with the contingent nature of gender and sexuality that the castrati exposed.[38]

Castrati reinforced their ambiguous sexual identity by attracting and pleasuring men as well as women. Because sex with a castrato ensured (different measures of) satisfaction without risk of insemination, many women were quick to take advantage of what qualified, in real terms, as an organic sex toy. Castrati were outsiders, so it was inconceivable that any woman recognisable to society would have considered courtship or marriage. What passed in the night remained there, even though gossip was habitual. In 1749, for example, William Rufus Chetwood self-published his (mostly reliable) *A general history of the stage*, in which he recalled "a Lady, of some Quality," who "fell desperately in Love with Nicolini; which occasioned the following Lines, that were pinn'd to Nicolini's Coat in a Chocolate house":

> Soft thrilling Notes, swell'd out with Art,
> May wound, alas! the fair one's Heart;
> Yet these Italians will not feel;
> The Wounds they give, they cannot heal.[39]

The popularity of castrati among the aristocracy, male and female, extended their careers after they had left the stage. Dennis may have had his own fill, such was the fervour of his conviction (and judgment) that castrati *must* be homosexual. He repeated the trite (and misplaced) presumption that a man without testicles could feel nothing for a woman. He was more certain still that women were at risk of being abandoned by men in consequence of opera's more generically malign influence:

> The Ladies, with humblest Submission, seem to mistake their Interest a
> little in encouraging Opera's; for the more the Men are enervated and
> emasculated by the Softness of the Italian Musick, the less will they care
> for them, and the more for one another […] if our Subscriptions go on,
> at the frantick rate that they have done, I make no doubt but we shall
> come to see one Beau take another for Better for Worse.[40]

The onset of the "frantick rate" of subscriptions can be dated to the first performance in 1705 of *Arsinoe, Queen of Cyprus*, by Thomas Clayton – the first through-sung opera to be performed in England. The title role was created by Catherine Tofts, whose casting was pivotal to Rich's decision to stage the work.[41] Tofts was no less key to its success. *Arsinoe* was performed twenty-four times during its first season; eleven the following year. Tofts' triumph cemented her authority as well as her celebrity.

---

38 *Ibid.*

39 Chetwood, W. R. (2018). *A general history of the stage: from its origin in Greece down to the present time*. Forgotten Books, p. 142.

40 Faust, Veronica T. (2006). "Music has learn'd the discords of the state': The Cultural Politics of British Opposition to Italian Opera, 1706–1711." Masters Thesis. Haverford College, p. 23.

41 The leading male role (Ormondo) was performed by the countertenor, Francis Hughes.

Indeed, anyone tracing the origins of the "prima donna" need look no further than Tofts' re-negotiation of her contract with Drury Lane in 1706. She required a shade under £17 a performance, which had on every occasion to be paid in advance.[42] Under no circumstances would she sing more than once a day. A harpsichordist had to be on hand whenever necessary, as well as a room in which to practice. Two people were to be provided to dress her, with bottles of wine for "the Gentlemen that practice with her." Finally, she demanded "jewels." This last condition precedent may not have been entirely serious. One of Tofts' routine complaints attached to the losses she suffered when paying for her own costumes;[43] it's clear she was requesting stage gems rather than precious stones, therefore. The point was well made, since it was normal at the time for singers to furnish their own outfits, irrespective of an opera's setting. Plainly, Tofts was not the easiest of colleagues, but she appears to have been worth every guinea. Colley Cibber remembered her with affection and respect:

> Mrs Tofts, who took her first Ground of Musick here in her own Country, before the Italian Taste had so highly prevail'd, was then not an Adept at it: Yet whatever Defect the fashionably Skilful might find in her manner, she had, in the general Sense of her Spectators, Charms that few of the most Learned Singers ever arrive at. The Beauty of her fine proportion'd Figure, and exquisitely sweet, silver Tone of her Voice, with that peculiar, rapid Swiftness of her Throat, were Perfections not to be imitated by Art or Labour.[44]

Notwithstanding the questionable merits of her repertoire, Tofts' career blossomed. She sang Queen Elinor in *Rosamond* (March, 1707), Cleora in *Thomyris* (April, 1707), Licisca in *Love's Triumph* (February, 1708), Deidamia in *Pirro e Demetrio* (December, 1708), and Isabella in *Clotilda* (March, 1709) – all of them forgettable. She could not have known or anticipated the infirmity of her timing, but only months before Handel arrived in London, Tofts emigrated to Italy. It has been suggested she was ousted in tandem with her nemesis, Christopher Rich, who was fired from Drury Lane towards the end of the 1708 / 09 season, another (unidentified) source asserted she was suffering from mental exhaustion. Whatever the reason for her departure, Tofts performed for the last time in London in May, 1709. Little is known about the rest of her life; the last substantive reference to her career as a singer was published on 25 April, 1712, in *The Daily Courant*, whose Venetian correspondent reported that

> An English Gentlewoman named Mrs. Tofts hath been much applauded here for her fine singing, wherein she hath succeeded all the excellent voices on the stage of Venice. This lady hath sung in all the great

42 This is reminiscent of Franco Corelli's sometime demand, when appearing at the Met in New York, that his fees be paid in cash, and delivered in carrier bags by the Intendant, Rudolf Bing, before the curtain went up.
43 It would be churlish not to observe that everything "demanded" of Rich by the "difficult" Tofts was standard practice a century later.
44 Highfill, Philip H., Burnim, Kalman A., Langhans, Edward A. (1993). *A Biographical Dictionary of Actors, Actresses and Musicians and other stage personnel in London, 1660–1800*. Vol.15. Viking, p. 12.

Assemblies that were held at the Electoral Prince of Saxony's and Signor Grimani[45] hath endeavoured by all means to prevail upon her to remain here to sing in the Theatre of Chrysostome,[46] but it is believed she will rather chuse to return to her own Country[47] […] seeing the Opera's at London are better served than any in Europe.[48]

Tofts did not return to England; neither was she favoured by Handel and Grimani after her arrival in Venice during the summer of 1709. The title role of *Agrippina* was offered to the Crisostomo's new *prima donna*, Margherita Durastanti,[49] whom Handel had known since he nominated her for the first performance of his oratorio, *La resurrezione*, in 1708. She would eventually follow Handel to London, in 1720, a transfer that caused the librettist Rolli to declare "Oh! What a bad choice for England! I shall not enter into her singing merits, but she really is an Elephant!" The Dresden court poet, Steffan Pallavicini, was less inclined to judge a book by its cover when confirming that

> You will find my recommendation not only trustworthy, but even superfluous, because this worthy virtuosa will recommend herself, for she is among the most excellent actresses who have appeared in the theatre here in recent years.

Tofts and Durastanti's careers at the Crisostomo overlapped; it appears that Durastanti disliked the competition, for she left Venice in 1712, just as Tofts was hitting her stride. She didn't maintain it for long. In 1716, Joseph Smith,[50] England's Consul

---

45   Vincenzo Grimani was an Italian cardinal, diplomat, and librettist. He and his family owned the Teatro San Giovanni Crisostomo in Venice, among many others. Grimani's only successful libretto was written for Handel. *Agrippina* was first performed on 26 December, 1709 – nine months to the day before Grimani's death.

46   The Teatro San Giovanni Crisostomo opened in 1678. It was the largest, most beautiful and most abundantly subsidised theatre in Venice. It was later renamed the Teatro Malibran, after the soprano who created the title role for Bellini's *La sonnambula* in 1835. When Malibran arrived for the first rehearsals, she was so horrified by the building's condition that she refused her fee, and told the impresario to keep it on condition he spent it on restoration works.

47   Tofts did not return to England. In fact, she appears to have taken forcibly against England. In 1712, the Spectator published a letter from the Soprano, in which she wrote *inter alia* "I little thought in the green Years of my life that I should ever call it an Happiness to be out of dear England; but as I grew to Woman, I found myself less acceptable in Proportion to the increase of my Merit. Their Ears in Italy are so differently formed from the Make of yours in England that I never come upon the Stage, but a general Satisfaction appears in every Countenance of the whole People […] The Humour of Hissing, which you have among you, I do not know any thing of […] the whole City of Venice is still when I am singing, as this polite Hearer was to Mrs. Hunt. But when they break that Silence, did you know the Pleasure I am in, when every Man utters his Applause, by calling me aloud the *Dear Creature*, the *Angel*, the *Venus* […]. I am very much in Ease here, that I know nothing but Joy; and I will not return, but leave you in England to all Merit of your own Growth off the Stage […]. P.S. I am ten times better dress'd than ever I was in *England*." *Ibid*, p. 15.

48   *Ibid*.

49   Active *circa* 1700 – *circa* 1730. Durastanti's dates of birth and death are not known.

50   Tofts died in 1756. She is buried in the Protestant cemetery of San Nicolo del Lido. Her tombstone reads "*Catherine Tofts / uxori incomparapibili / de se bene merenti / quae obit anno MDCCLVI / diutino vexata*

in Venice, took her as his wife, at which point Tofts retired from performing.[51] The singer was felled subsequently by a degenerative mental illness, resulting from the death of her only child in infancy. According to Sir John Hawkins, in his *A General History of the Science and Practice of Music*, Tofts spent the rest of her long life

> sequestered from the world, in a remote part of the house,[52] and had a large garden to range in, in which she would frequently walk, singing and giving way to the innocent frenzy which had seized her in the earlier part of her life.[53]

For her final performance in London, on 21 May, 1709, Tofts returned to Bononcini's *Camilla*,[54] which she had created (in English) for Drury Lane three years earlier. The evolution of *Camilla's* casting is revealing. Having reigned supreme at the premiere, Tofts yielded the title role to de l'Épine for the fourth performance. Six months later, de l'Épine was cast as Prenesto, and from 7 February, 1708, the role of Metius, which was owned by its creator, the English baritone, Lewis Ramondon, was handed (in transposition) to the castrato Giuseppe Cassani. After Tofts' departure for Italy, the title role passed without contest to de l'Épine, and Cassani was replaced by Nicolini. Their requited triumph inspired wild enthusiasm, and managed finally to persuade audiences of the virtue of an all-Italian singing culture in London. This barometric shift was made absolute by the arrival in the city of a German musician, whose genius as a composer of Italian opera achieved nothing less than the ontogenesis of the modern soprano, while nurturing a culture of competition that would reach its apogee with the careers of Maria Callas and Renata Tebaldi.

Four years before he disembarked at Dover in 1710, George Frederic Handel travelled extensively throughout Italy, with prolonged stops in Florence, Rome, Naples and Venice. He attended numerous operas, and came to know dozens of singers, performers and composers, including Corelli, Alessandro and Domenico Scarlatti, and Agostino Steffani. Handel's titanic abilities extended to his osmotic absorption of Italian style, which revealed itself in a flawless capacity for setting Italian verse,

---

morbo / Nec unquam displicuit nisi erepti / Joseph Smith Consul Britannicus / morens fecit." ('Catherine Toft / his incomparable wife / well deserved / who died in 1756 / afflicted by a long illness / placed here by her husband, the British Consul.') Joseph Smith remarried in 1757; he died four years before his hundredth birthday, on 6 November, 1770.

51   Smith was an interesting man, who continues to be remembered for his skill and insight as a patron of art and artists in Venice. He is notable in particular for his patronage of Canaletto – with whom he worked closely for many years. Smith spent his own considerable wealth (generated through private banking) on collecting prints, drawings and paintings. In 1762, he sold the majority of his collection – which included books, gems and coins – to the young George III, for £20,000. Three years later, George launched his own library by purchasing Smith's, for £10,000. Smith's books form the nucleus of what is now known as the King's Library (transferred later from the British Museum to the British Library). The Royal Collection contains many other treasures sourced from Smith.

52   This is unlikely to be the Palazzo Balbi (on the Grand Canal in Dorsoduro), which Smith purchased on 20 April, 1740 or his "other" Palazzo, Mangilli Valmarana – since neither palace had a garden. The premises to which Hawkins was referring was almost certainly Smith's summer villa in Mogliano Veneto, 17km north of Venice. Unlike his palaces, this property was destroyed after Smith's death.

53   Hawkins, Sir John (2010). *General History of the Science and Practice of Music*. Gale ECCO.

54   In Haym's adaptation.

spanning declamation, recitative and, of course, sung melody. The success of his second Italian opera, *Agrippina*, added considerably to the anticipation that preceded his arrival in London in late 1710 to write an Italian opera after Tasso's epic *Gerusalemme liberate* for Aaron Hill, manager of the Queen's Theatre.[55] Handel is said to have composed *Rinaldo* in 14 days,[56] in part because he was able to use pre-existing music for an audience that could not have known it. Even though Rossi's libretto is something of a mess, Handel's music elevates Armida's joy-killing separation of the earnest Christian hero, Rinaldo, from his lover, Almirena.

Because male sopranos were unwelcome in German-speaking territories, it's unclear how much contact Handel had with castrati prior to *Agrippina*;[57] he was happy, regardless, to accommodate London's newly *recherché* appetites when scoring the role of *Rinaldo* for the local hero, Nicolini, and Eustazio for Valentini.[58] He gave the female *travesti* role of Goffredo to the Bolognese contralto, Francesca Vanini-Boschi[59] (the first Otho in *Agrippina*) and he drew on friendship as well as memory when offering the role of Armida to Elisabetta Pilotti-Schiavonetti.[60] Handel had known the soprano and her husband, Giovanni, since their time in service at the court of Sophia Dorothea of Hanover;[61] it was no coincidence that the composer and his favourite singer should be invited to Britain by Sophia's brother, George.[62]

If most of Handel's cast was Italian then not all of his singers were new to England. For the role of Almirena he turned to Isabella Girardeau,[63] a soprano who had been performing in London as "La Isabella" since December, 1709. Girardeau's contract with the theatre identified her as "Mad Girardo," a signifier for "Mademoiselle" that attested no less accurately to her personality, which appears to have picked up where Tofts left off. Girardeau enjoyed her status, and she took immediately against the more talented Pilotti-Schiavonetti; their rivalry generated as much commentary as their singing. Hill and Handel were disinclined to supress tensions that generated gossip and publicity. *Rinaldo*'s triumph at the premiere was enormous. The invention and beauty of Handel's music, the extravagance of the staging, and the excellence of the singing united critics, cynics and converts.[64] Hawkins reported that the applause "was greater than had been given to any musical performance in this kingdom: in a

---

55   After George I's accession in 1714, the "Queen's" became necessarily the "King's."

56   The first Italian opera to be written for performance (and premiered) in England.

57   Handel composed the role of Nero for Valeriano Pellegrini (*circa* 1663–18 January, 1746), a castrato renowned for his supreme technique, who followed Handel to London in 1712. He later performed numerous roles for Handel, including among Mirtillo in *Il pastor fido* (1712), the title role in *Teseo* (1713), and Lepidus in *Silla* (1713). After retiring from the stage in 1728, Pellegrini joined the priesthood.

58   Though his career was in the decline, Valentini was chosen subsequently by Handel to create the roles of Silvio in *Il pastor fido*, and Egeo in *Teseo*.

59   – 1744.

60   *Circa* 1680 – 5 May, 1742.

61   A widely admired Venetian-born oboist, cellist, and harpsichordist.

62   George I, from 1714.

63   c. 1680 – 5 May, 1742.

64   The usual suspects were damning of Hill's extravagance. Addison's bitterness was informed by the failure of his own ambitions as a librettist and promoter. Steele, writing for *The Spectator*, called the production a "Punch and Judy show," a judgment of which Hogarth noted that Steele's attacks "seem to have had little effect in turning people from the entertainment."

word, it established Mr. Handel's character on a firm and solid basis."[65] Burney hailed the work as "superior in composition to any opera of that period which had ever been performed in England [...] its great success does honour to our nation."[66] The first performance, at the Queen's Theatre, prompted the scheduling of another 14; even though Handel churned out new works almost annually, *Rinaldo* remained in repertoire until the end of the 1717 season, at which point it had been performed 47 times. Girardeau could not compete; she left London – and the stage – in 1712, leaving Pilotti-Schiavonetti to reign supreme. Her achievement was attributable as much to graft as to talent – a work ethic evidenced by her being the only member of *Rinaldo's* original cast to appear in each of the initial 47 performances. Pilotti-Schiavonetti's art was a continuing inspiration for Handel, who composed another four roles for her (Amarilli in *Il pastor fido*,[67] Metella in *Silla*,[68] Medea in *Teseo*, and Melissa in *Amadigi di Gaula*[69]); she retired from the stage in 1716, when entering the service of Caroline of Ansbach, Princess of Wales (and Queen from 1714).[70] Replacing the irreplaceable proved to be a realistic strategy. Thanks to the city's immense wealth, and because of Britain's power as a pre-eminent trading nation, vast sums of money were available for spending on music and musicians. The most expensive commodity was the soprano, and London paid more for its leading ladies than anywhere else. It was inevitable that singers would become famous for more than their talent and attainments.

The word celebrity is an eighteenth-century neologism; it was employed to denote fame when ascribed, and it emerged as a value in the wake of mass printing and publishing. The common obsession with personality collided with the commodification of British public life, which in turn transformed the aristocracy, politicians, lawyers, painters, writers, musicians and stage performers into heroes and villains, as constructs of identity and signifiers of ambition conspiring to distract and entertain a society in which 74% of the populace died before the age of five.[71] London's appetite for fame was fuelled by the emerging business of portraiture, a nascent middle-class, and an exponential increase in printing technologies, print shops and publishers. The emergence of managers and agents, necessary for negotiating performers' fees, duties, scheduling and repertoire, threw petrol onto a bonfire of vanities that transformed opera into a public and aggressively commercial enterprise. Though unconnected other than by title with the royal court, opera's need for musicians encouraged George I to patronise The Royal Academy of Music in 1719, with Handel appointed its inaugural director.[72] By the turn of the 1720s, opera was established as art and entertainment, with literally thousands of men and women contributing annually to the creation of a musical-theatrical culture in London that was unrivalled during the

---

65   Hawkins, Sir John (2010). *General History of the Science and Practice of Music.* Gale ECCO, p. 814.
66   Burney, Dr. Charles (1957). *A General History of Music: From the Earliest Ages to the Present Period (1776–89).* Ed. Frank Mercer. Dover Publications, p. 675.
67   1712.
68   1713.
69   1715.
70   The Royal family's close association with female sopranos extended to George I and the Princess Royal serving as godparents in 1721 to Margherita Durastanti's daughter.
71   For the years 1730 to 1749.
72   The composer remained in the post until his death in 1759.

first 50 years of the century. The number of sopranos being presented audiences new to opera in England ensured that no one singer was more entitled to hallowed status than another. Until, that is, England became home to two of the most gifted ever.

CHAPTER SEVEN

First Ladies

During the first third of the 18th century there was a flurry of theatre-building. The largest were built in London: the Queen's/King's, Haymarket; the Theatre Royal, Covent Garden; the Little/New Theatre, Haymarket; the Theatre Royal, Lincoln's Inn Fields; the Theatre Royal, Drury Lane; the New Theatre, Lincoln's Inn Fields; and the Dorset Garden Theatre.[1] It has been demonstrated that between 1688 and 1801, no more than about 3% of the families in England and Wales had sufficient income to purchase more than a bare minimum of "cultural" products,"[2] among which tickets to the opera were the most expensive. With 20 shillings in a pound, it's clear that a first-rank singer's fee of £30 for an evening's performance necessitated the sale of most of the shilling-seats in the dress circle and first tier-gallery, and all of the more costly seats in the pit and the boxes. Few theatres were ever full, however,[3] a commercial pressure that forced the emergence of the modern business of event marketing.

Promoters in early 18th century London relied on four primary tools: personal sales, public relations, direct promotions (including free gifts, such as libretto-sheets) and advertising.[4] The use of "puffs" became essential to the anticipated virtue of a new singer or performer, with the salivation "coming soon" justifying audiences saving for an event or compelling the purchase of subscription tickets for an entire season. In 1704/5, the number of newspapers printed ranged from around 2,000 on Wednesdays and Fridays, to 14,000 on a Thursday. There were twenty times as many readers as papers.[5] A subset of newspapers carried adverts for operas and concerts, with copy for events trebling between the 1680s and the 1740s. In 1759, Samuel Johnson cautioned that "Advertisements are now so numerous that they are very negligently perused."[6] Opera and concert promoters were quick to realise that bills had to appeal to differently formed enthusiasms and interests. The common use of the phrase "At the desire of several Ladies of Quality…," was designed to remind men of women's expectations when courting; an interest in the opera was a sure route to

---

1 Also known as the Duke of York's, it was built in 1691 and demolished in 1709.

2 Hume, R. D. (2014). "The Value of Money in Eighteenth-Century England: Incomes, Prices, Buying Power—and Some Problems in Cultural Economics", *Huntington Library Quarterly*, Vol. 77, No. 4, pp. 373–416.

3 Harbor, Catherine (2020). "The Marketing of Concerts in London 1672–1749." *Journal of Historical Research in Marketing*. Vol. 12, Issue 4, p. 19.

4 Colbert, F. (2007). *Marketing Culture and the Arts*, HEC, Montréal, p. 227.

5 Harbor, Catherine (2020). "The Marketing of Concerts in London 1672–1749." *Journal of Historical Research in Marketing*. Vol. 12, Issue 4. *Ibid*, p. 20.

6 *Ibid.*

being thought educated, open-minded and sensitive. The "desire of ladies of quality" was no less certain to encourage women to attend the theatre when hoping to catch the eyes of suitors. With opera functioning as an adjunct to the emerging construction of "lifestyle," the increasingly fluid operation of social mobility enabled people of low birth to become attractive to the high-born. A night at the opera amplified the levelling effect of talent, the appearance of which on stage was, in every case, the province of "ordinary" people made exotic by reason of origin and ability. Even when a performer was native to Britain, the promotion of foreign novelty was a sinecure to curiosity. One typical advert from 1713 asserted:

> At the Desire of Several Ladies of Quality [...] On Friday being the 21st Day of April, will be perform'd A Consort of Vocal and Instrumental Musick by the best Masters. Several New Cantata's [sic], with other songs and Italian pieces, lately brought from Italy will be sung by Mrs. Hemmings ad [sic], and she will also Accompany to her own Voice on the Harpsechord, being the first time of appearing in Publick.

Women embraced life in public with understandable zeal. The social reformer, Elizabeth Montagu, admitted to "raking in town" (a reference to Hogarth's celebrated series of eight paintings),[7] which she characterised as being primarily for the opera, where women were advantaged by "seeing and being seen" midst a crowd of "Spectators [who] came to hear." Female spectators defied long-established gender roles that had for centuries been prescribed by politeness and propriety. Opera was a direct challenge to the casual certainties of patriarchal authority. Samuel Richardson, for example, denigrated Anne Donnellan, the daughter of an Irish peer and a prominent member of London society, when writing to Mary Delany that unmarried women like Donnellan were "Playing with Public and Private" sensibilities by behaving in an "intolerably independent manner." Women were liberated by the appearance of women on stage, and then in circumstances (and as characters in scenarios) that would have been illegal a few years earlier. Unsurprisingly, men were happy for foreigners to tread the boards, so that the encroaching of sensualist ways could be dismissed legitimately as alien to the domestic probity of which Italians, in particular, were alleged to be ignorant.

As the world's foremost composer of opera, and with England proving a fertile city for ambitious singers, Handel's position in London assured him the best of everything: a royal post, unfettered access to a world-class opera house, the pick of the finest singers and instrumentalists anywhere, and a budget for productions that ensured not only his own financial security, but also the security of an art form that was productively controversial. Handel's influence was enhanced in February, 1719, when he joined a group of wealthy aristocrats in founding The Royal Academy of Music – a company established for the staging of *opera seria* in London. The Academy was inaugurated in April, 1719, with an orchestra comprised of seventeen violins, two violas, four cellos, two double basses, four oboes, three bassoons, a theorbo and a trumpet. The first productions were of Giovanni Porta's *Numitore*, Handel's *Radamisto*

---

7   *Rake's Progress* (1732–1734).

and Domenico Scarlatti's *Narciso*. In May, and by reason of necessity, Handel was ordered by the Lord Chamberlain (and governor of the new Academy), to locate new singers on account of Nicolini and Valentini having returned to Italy. Handel didn't look locally; he travelled instead to Dresden and the city's newly-built opera house (where most of the singers were Italian). The *primo uomo* was a Sienese-born castrato, "Senesino,"[8] whose talent as a 13-year-old treble in the choir of Siena Cathedral led to castration only a few months before his fourteenth birthday. Handel is certain to have made an attractive offer, but Senesino didn't join the Academy until the end of 1720, after an alleged dispute with Dresden's court composer, Heinichen (concerning an aria in his opera, *Flavio Crispo*), which resulted in his dismissal. The incident was engineered by Senesino, who made his first appearance in London in a revival of *Radamisto* on 28 December, 1720.

From Dresden, Handel made his way to Italy, where he met Gaetano Berenstadt[9] and heard Francesca Cuzzoni,[10] a 24-year-old soprano reputed to be the finest in Germany.[11] She made her debut as an 18-year-old, in September, 1714, after being trained by her musician father, and by Francesco Lanzi, a Neapolitan church organist and trumpet player. Cuzzoni studied with Lanzi only briefly before appearing on stage for the first time; within three years, she was appointed *virtuosa da camera*[12] to the court of Violante Beatrice, Grand Princess of Tuscany. She was engaged to sing in Florence, Siena, Genoa, Mantua, and Reggio Emilia, in operas by Vivaldi and the now-forgotten Bassani, Buini, Gasparini, Orlandini and Pollarolo. Between 1719 and 1722, she triumphed in Milan, Turin, Padua and Venice, where she performed in five operas, including a revival of Monteverdi's *Poppea*.

Although it's probable Handel attempted to retain Cuzzoni in 1719, the Academy delayed entering into formal negotiations until after the composer returned to London. By the time the parties agreed terms, Senesino[13] had made his Academy debut (in September, 1720). Cuzzoni demanded to be paid at least as much as the theatre's *primo uomo*. The Academy agreed, and the singers received the same salary, initially. In October, 1722, the *London Journal* reported with great excitement that "Mrs. Cotsona [sic], an extraordinary Italian Lady [...] is expected daily," with a "much finer Voice and more accurate Judgment, than any of her Country Women who have performed on the English stage."[14] Cuzzoni was unable to keep the *Journal's* promise until December, 1723, when she attended at the King's Theatre to rehearse

8   *né* Francesco Bernardi, 2 April / 31 October, 1686 – 27 November, 1758.

9   7 June, 1687 – (buried) 9 December, 1734. An Italian alto-castrato who visited London in 1717 to perform the role of Argante in a revival of *Rinaldo*.

10   2 April, 1696 – 19 June, 1778. For readers of Italian, the most authoritative study of Cuzzoni's life is Franco, Paola Lunetta (2001). *Francesca Cuzzoni (1696–1778): Lo Stile antico nella musica moderna*. University of Pavia. See also Kettledon, Lisabeth M. (2017). *A Lyric Soprano in Handel's London: A Vocal Portrait of Francesca Cuzzoni*. Doctoral Thesis. University of Connecticut.

11   In performances of Antonio Lotti's *Giove in Argo* ('Jupiter in Argos'), and *Teofane*.

12   'Chamber virtuoso.'

13   Cuzzoni had known Senesino personally and professionally since Dresden, where they worked together for Lotti.

14   *George Frideric Handel: Collected Documents, Vol. 1, 1609–1725*. (2013). Burrows, Donald; Coffey, Helen; Greenacombe, John; and Hicks, Anthony, Eds. Cambridge University Press, p. 7.

the premiere staging of Handel's *Ottone*.[15] The role of Teofane had not been written for Cuzzoni, and rehearsals were fratious. When she refused initially to sing her first aria, "*Falsa imagine*,"[16] Handel is said by John Manwairing to have replied[17]

> "Oh! Madame I know well that you are a real she-devil, but I hereby give you notice, me, that I am Beelzebub, the Chief of Devils." With this, he took her up by the waist, and, if she made any more words, swore that he would fling her out of the window. It is to be noted that this was formerly one of the methods of executing criminals in some parts of the Germany, a process not unlike that of the Tarpeian rock,[18] and probably derived from it.[19]

The first performance of *Ottone* on 12 January, 1723, caused a sensation. Burney reported that Cuzzoni's singing "fixed her reputation as an expressive and pathetic singer,"[20] and her performance in particular of "*Falsa Imagine*" made her famous, quite literally overnight. Scored for soprano and a melting 'cello *obbligato*, Handel's music is languid and lachrymose; it presents no great difficulties technically. It is nonetheless demanding of breath, phrasing and diction; indeed, it is a *tour de force* for any soprano capable of isolating the emotional and musical shape of Teofane's disillusion when realising that Ottone, her husband-to-be, looks nothing like the portrait she has been carrying in a locket around her neck.[21] Cuzzoni's success was total; it was not singular. Berenstadt's triumph as Adelberto[22] – notwithstanding his "huge unwieldy figure"[23] – and Senesino's creation of the title role compounded their reputations as the finest castrato of his generation. His talents as a singer distinguished his abilities as an actor. After seeing him perform in Lotti's *Teofane*,[24] Johann Quantz was generous when observing that

---

15 Cuzzoni arrived in London only a few weeks earlier, in December, 1722.

16 'False image.'

17 The wildly curious might want to seek out a hilarious documentary featuring the American soprano, Joyce DiDonato, playing Cuzzoni in a splendidly flattering dress, with "Handel" at the harpsichord. di Donato acts out the scene described by Manwairing, and is heard to rehearse a song from Handel's *Serse*, an opera written for the *alto* castrato, Caffarelli – long after the *soprano* Cuzzoni had left the stage. So much for period performance.

18 A reference by Manwairing to the site in Rome where murderers, traitors, perjurors, and larcenous slaves were thrown to their deaths onto rocks eighty feet below the cliff-edge.

19 Manwairing published the words exchanged by the composer and the singer in French, being that Italian was still not known to the majority of English readers. Manwairing, John (1760). *Memoirs of the Life of the Late George Frederic Handel*. R. & J. Dodsley, p. 110.

20 Burney, Dr. Charles (1957). *A General History of Music: From the Earliest Ages to the Present Period (1776–89)*. Ed. Frank Mercer. Dover Publications.

21 In true operatic form, this is because Adelberto is pretending to be Ottone when attending on Teofane.

22 The only role by Handel to be performed by Farinelli.

23 Burney, Dr. Charles (1957). *A General History of Music: From the Earliest Ages to the Present Period (1776–89)*. Ed. Frank Mercer. Dover Publications.

24 In Dresden, in September, 1719.

His countenance was well adapted to the stage, and his action was natural and noble. To these qualities he joined a majestic figure; but his
aspect and deportment were more suited to the part of a hero than of a
lover.

Senesino's deportment was legendary for its limits. Upon entering the stage, he
would strut to the footlights wearing a heavily-brocaded frock-coat, crowned at one
end by a vast powdered wig and booted at the other in platform-heals that caused
him to tower over everyone else on stage – especially the "short, squat and doughy"
Cuzzoni.[25] Senesino's appearance rendered interaction with fellow cast-members
physically impossible, even when directed. Having indulged his welcome, Senesino
headed to his mark, where he would remain for the duration – exiting and entering
according to the limited prescriptions of the score. His "acting" was confined to
hand and arm movements, with the left subordinate commonly to the right. Count
Francesco Zambeccari, an impresario, lamented of one performance in Naples how

Senesino continues to comport himself badly enough; he stands like a
statue, and when occasionally he does make a gesture, he makes one
directly the opposite of what is wanted.

The limited dramaturgy framed opera as oratorio,[26] a theatrical paradox for which
Senesino's singing was deemed to be satisfactory compensation. Quantz heralded his

powerful, clear, equal and sweet contralto voice, with a perfect intonation and an excellent shake. His manner of singing was masterly and his
elocution unrivalled […] he sang allegros with great fire, and marked
rapid divisions, from the chest, in an articulate and pleasing manner.

---

25   Charles Burney's description was written after he saw her on stage at the end of her career. He added
that Cuzzoni was "not a good actress; dressed ill; and was silly and fantastical." A more accurate account
of her appearance, and then from her youth, is captured in a pastel portrait by Rosalba Carriera, one of
the most gifted female artists of the 18th century. Created during the decade 1720–1730, the portrait
reveals a beautiful and slim woman, with blond hair, a long neck and piercing eyes. She wears flowers in
her hair and pearl earrings; her white and blue dress is worn on a single shoulder only; it is an alluring, but
modest image, made striking by the artists' dramatic use of *sfumato*. Carriera created at least two portraits
of Faustina Bordoni; the first dates to 1724 (shortly before her arrival in London), and reveals a woman
with classically Italian features, dark brown hair, heavy eyebrows and, remarkably for the time, an exposed
breast. The image created a decade later suggests Bordoni indulged her wealth and success with alacrity.
26   This palpably absurd denial of the stage as theatre has returned to fashion. In 2019, the German
director Ulrich Rasche designed and "directed" a production of *Elektra* in Munich (which transferred
to Geneva three years later) in which the stage was dominated by a huge metal tower, formed of
clockwise-revolving cages constructed from 12 tonnes of steel. As the cages turned (which they did for the
duration of the performance), the cast was required to walk counter-clockwise, so as to remain visible to
the audience. They were roped to the tower's central core, to protect against the risk of health and safety
violations; this regulatory conformity undermined the production's solitary, laboured metaphor. Nothing
happened during a performance – which was not even semi-staged; there was no interaction between any
of the performers, and in Geneva the mechanism was sufficiently noisy to be audible to anyone within 20
metres of the proscenium arch, including the author. But for the cage turning, the staging was, in essence,
static and devoid of narrative impulse and dramatic incident. Senesino would have loved it.

Senesino's annual income from opera performances was reported variously to be as much as 3,000 guineas[27] – a vast sum, sufficient to keep 100 skilled labourers fully-employed for a year. His income from other sources, primarily private concerts, was five times as much again; it was thanks to these purse-bursting fees that Senesino remained in London for sixteen years. Berenstadt (who left London in 1724) was paid less,[28] as was Cuzzoni, whose fees at the Haymarket in 1724–25 were £2,000, with private engagements generating at least three times as much. *Ottone's* success warranted the salaries, with half-guinea seats being sold at eight times their face value. Two months later, tickets for Cuzzoni's benefit concert in London were selling for fifty guineas. Many were jealous of *Ottone's* brilliance; many more resented its popularity, which threatened to suffocate everything around it. John Gay, for example, complained to Jonathan Swift:

> As for the reigning amusements of the town, it is entirely music [...] there is nobody allowed to say "I sing" but a eunuch or an Italian woman. Everybody is grown now as great a judge of music as they were in your time of poetry, and folks that could not distinguish one tune from another now daily dispute about the different styles of Handel. People have now forgot Homer, and Virgil, and Caesar, or at least, they have lost their ranks; for, in London and Westminster, in all polite conversations, Senesino is daily voted to be the greatest man that ever lived.[29]

The scandal prompted by singers' fees, the price of tickets and the generally low repute of the opera in London was exacerbated by the Haymarket's mounting of masquerades, an "immoral" fad promoted by another foreigner, John J. Heidegger, an (alleged) Swiss Count whose work as an impresario made him extravagantly wealthy. The tensions provoked by opera and masquerades were played out in the press between rival camps and political factions for whom the new theatre operated as a forum for social, philosophical and cultural antagonism, underpinned by the common fear that "legitimate" theatre was at risk of suffocation and eradication. In February, 1724, Hogarth produced a one-sheet satire to which he gave the title "The bad taste of the town." To the right of the etching, a theatre presenting Marlowe's *Dr Faustus* draws a crowd of respectable men and women. To the left Heidegger can be seen leaning out a window of the King's Theatre (identified in the faintest of wording as "Handel's,") to which has been attached a huge sign featuring caricatures of Senesino, Berenstadt and Cuzzoni. The Devil is seen steering the crowd into the King's Theatre while, to his right, a woman tows a cart containing the "waste paper" of Ben Johnson, Shakespeare, Dryden, Congreve and others. Masquerades and operas offended the moral rectitude of a minority who considered the majority ill-equipped to resist imagined episodes of sexual danger and mystery being acted out on stage,

---

27   A guinea was 21 shillings – one more shilling than a pound.
28   For Handel, Berenstadt created the roles of Tolomeo in *Giulio Cesare*, the title role in *Flavio*, and the role of *Adelberto* in Ottone. He left London in 1724, and returned permanently to Italy.
29   Burrows, Donald (2012). *Handel*. Oxford University Press, p. 113.

while failing coincidentally to complain of the presence of *actual* prostitutes, male and female, among the audience.

By 1725, Handel's standing as a composer of opera in London was unrivalled, an achievement for which he was appropriately grateful to his *primi uomini e donne* – all of whom were paid more than the composer for their efforts. Although his sopranos guaranteed a measure of adulation that overreached the value and merit of whatever they were singing, everyone knew that Handel had composed his operas for the singers who created them. Between 1723 and 1729, he composed nine operas[30] and 73 arias for Cuzzoni – a body of work that makes their relationship one of the most important in the history of music.[31]

If it was recognised that Handel's music was difficult to perform, then he was sufficiently cognisant of the challenges to travel Europe to locate the best singers. If he needed to find vocalists to meet his expectations, then he had to meet theirs in turn. The hesitancy of star singers to relocate to cities hundreds of miles from home and family was not informed by money alone; they needed to be reassured by theatres and composers that the roles they would be creating were suited to them vocally, dramatically and, even, psychologically. It's important to remember that none of Handel's singers knew what they would be singing before they arrived in London because he had yet to write it; for this reason, the relationship between composers and singers was closer during the early 18th century than at any time subsequently.

In 1720, the composer Benedetto Marcello noted how "before he actually starts to write the music, the composer should pay calls to all the female singers in the company and offer to include anything they would care to have [in the opera]."[32] While this sardonic *nota bene* was warranted, it failed to account for the sympathies and sensibilities of individual actresses. Neither did Marcello recognise the social and psychological pressures to which women were subjected when off the stage. The compositional process was not, as it would later become, a simple matter of finding a singer capable of managing the technical and tonal demands of larger orchestras and theatres;[33] instead, composers had to navigate social morays and codes of conduct that dissuaded "decent" women from being seen to behave other than "decently." There is no surviving correspondence between Cuzzoni and Handel, but one of the soprano's colleagues at the Royal Academy, the British contralto Anastasia Robinson, wrote two letters to the diplomat Giuseppe Riva asking him to petition Handel to make changes to her role in *Ottone*:

---

30 *Ottone* [Teofane] (1723); *Flavio* [Emilia] (1723); *Giulo Cesare* [Cleopatra] (1724); *Tamerlano* [Asteria] (1724); *Rodelinda* (1725); *Scipione* [Berenice] (1726); *Alessandro* [Lisaura] (1726); *Admeto* [Antigona] (1726); *Riccardo Primo* [Costanza] (1727); *Siroe* [Laodice] (1728); and *Tolomeo* [Seleuce] (1728).

31 Apart from Handel's less consequential (albeit productive) relationship with Anna Maria Strada, it is difficult to think of any other between a composer and a soprano that generated more music of the first rank – with the single exception of Rossini and Isabella Colbran (see Chapter 9).

32 LaRue, C. Steven (1995). *Handel and His Singers: The Creation of the Royal Academy Operas, 1720–1728*. Oxford University Press. p. 14.

33 The problem of managing a singer's personality when casting a new work would not become problematic again until after 1900, when Richard Strauss's *Salome* and *Elektra*, and Berg's *Wozzeck* and *Lulu*, required women to do things that polite society deemed inappropriate.

Not knowing how to ask you to give your self the trouble of coming here, and the necessity obliging me to beg a favour of you, I must do it by writing. I am very sensible the Musick of my Part is exstreamly [sic] fine, but am as sure the Caracter causes it to be of that kind, which no way suits my Capacity; those Songs that require fury and passion to express them, can never be performed by me according to the intention of the Composer, and consequently must loose [sic] their Beauty. Nature design'd me a peacable Creature, and it is as true as strange, that I am a Woman and can- not Scold.[34]

Cuzzoni was not a "peacable Creature," but neither was she pre-eminent as an actress – with Quantz finding her "somewhat cold." Her only title role was *Rodelinda*, and in every other case she was junior to Senesino, the *primo uomo*, or equal to her rival, Bordoni. Handel went to great pains to ensure that his leads were distinguished from each other; he recognised Cuzzoni's flair for playing *ingénue* characters in disastrous situations wrestling with consequences beyond their control – for whom the ideal species of musical expression was slow and, in most cases, melancholy.[35] Faustina Bordoni was better equipped for faster-tempo coloratura singing than Cuzzoni. The castrato and pedagogue, Pier Francesco Tosi, characterised their

merit superior to all praise; who with equal force, in a different style, help to keep up the tottering profession from immediately falling into ruin. The one [Faustina] is inimitable for a privileged gift of singing and for enchanting the world with a prodigious felicity in executing and with singular brilliancy (I know not whether from nature or art), which pleases to excess. The delightful, soothing cantabile of the other, joined with the sweetness of a fine voice, a perfect intonation, strictness of time, and the rarest productions of a genius are qualifications as particular and uncommon as they are difficult to be imitated. The *pathetic* of the one and the *allegro* of the other are the qualities the most to be admired respectively in each of them. What beautiful mixture would it be if the excellence of these two angelic creatures could be united in one person.

At a time when thousands of women are now capable of performing Handel's music without (apparent) difficulty, it is well to remember that the Academy's company of singers were the first to be able to do so to the composer's satisfaction. Their abilities were rarely, if ever, called into question, therefore – at least during the prime of their careers. It was this pre-eminence of voice as art-in-isolation that gave rise to the first flowering of the soprano as virtuoso – a cultural meme that coincided with the emergence of what would become known as bel canto. The adumbration of Baroque sensibilities – attendant to the science of dexterity, articulation and floridity – was

---

34 LaRue, C. Steven (1995). *Handel and His Singers: The Creation of the Royal Academy Operas, 1720–1728*. Oxford University Press, p. 126.

35 The one consistent exception to this rule was *Giulio Cesare*, in which Handel overreaches Cuzzoni's essential lyricism by writing five out of her eight arias with fast tempos.

fused to a capacity for languid, spun melody that pre-empted the work of Rossini, Bellini and Donizetti by more than a century. It was striking also that Senesino and Cuzzoni were performing works in revivals that only 50 years earlier would have been lost to the march of novelty. The re-staging of a work ten years after its premiere was as unusual then as it is now, and in most cases the only reason for reaching into the library was the prospect of hearing a fading masterpiece revitalised by a favoured singer.

The growing power of women's voices when heard in the theatre was diminished only when they were turned against each other. This was a lesson learned by Handel after he retained Faustina Bordoni,[36] the third of his triumvirate of soprano-totems, to create the role of Rossane in the first production of *Alessandro*, for the launching of the 1725/1726 season. When Bordoni failed to arrive as anticipated, Handel substituted his own *Scipione* in March and April, leaving the mezzo-soprano only a few weeks in which to prepare for her debut on 5 May, 1726. She did not disappoint. One of the most reliable accounts of Bordoni as a performer was given to Charles Burney by Johann Quantz:

> Faustina had a mezzo-soprano voice, that was less clear than penetrating. Her compass now was only from B flat to G in alt; but after this time she extended its limits downward. She possessed what the Italians call un cantar granito; her execution was articulate and brilliant. She had a fluent tongue for pronouncing words rapidly and distinctly, and a flexible throat for divisions, with so beautiful a shake that she put it in motion upon short notice, just when she would. The passages might be smooth, or by leaps, or consisting of iterations of the same note; their execution was equally easy to her as to any instrument whatever. She was, doubtless, the first who introduced with success a swift repetition of the same note. She sang adagios with great passion and expression, but was not equally successful if such deep sorrow were to be impressed on the hearer as might require dragging, sliding, or notes of syncopation and tempo rubato. She had a very happy memory in arbitrary changes and embellishments, and a clear and quick judgment in giving to words their full value and expression. In her action she was very happy; and as her performance possessed that flexibility of muscles and face-play which constitute expression, she succeeded equally well in furious, tender, and amorous parts. In short, she was born for singing and acting. Burney himself remarked on the strength of the note E (E5) in her voice, and it is worth noting that half of the arias written for her by Handel are in E or A (minor or major), keys which could give this note particular prominence.

Bordoni worked with Cuzzoni in Venice, in 1719 and 1720; this prior experience did nothing to dissuade her from travelling to London for her British début during

---

36   30 March, 1697 – 4 November, 1781. Bordoni was known (and identified routinely) by her first name.

the spring of 1726. Even before she arrived, the press was fomenting *animus* between the singers' supporters, provoking a rivalry that didn't exist before journalists and promoters whipped it into existence. John Hawkins recorded how

> the town no sooner became sensible of the perfections which each was possessed of, than they began to compare them in their own minds, and endeavour to determine to whom of the two the greatest tribute of theatrical applause was due. Some ladies of the first quality entered very deeply into the merits of this competition; a numerous party engaged to support Cuzzoni, and another not less formidable associated on the side of Faustina. Thus encouraged, the behaviour of the rivals to each other was attended with all the circumstances of malevolence that jealousy, hatred, and malice could suggest; private slander and public abuse were deemed weapons too innoxious in this warfare, blows were made use of in the prosecution of it, and, shame to tell![37]

Handel was being knowingly provocative when he nominated *Alessandro* for Bordoni and Cuzzoni's London debut. Ortensio Mauro's *La superbia d'Alessandro* was well-known to London audiences thanks to Nathaniel Lee's *The Rival Queens, or the Death of Alexander the Great*, a frequently-revived play from 1677. The drama's central conflict concerns two women, Lisaura (Cuzzoni) and Rossane (Bordoni), competing for the attentions of Alessandro (Senesino); the public did not struggle to isolate parallels between the drama's protagonists and the composer and his female leads, a symmetry that led inevitably to a wave of supposition, conjecture and gossip. One of Bordoni's agents in London, Owen Swiny,[38] was sufficiently concerned to warn the Academy

> never to consent to any thing that can put the Academy into disorder, as it must, certainly, if what I hear […] is put in Execution: I mean the opera of Alexander the great; where there is to be a Struggle between the Rival Queen's, for a Superiority.

Swiny's advice was informed by his experience of the cat-fighting for which Tofts–de l'Épine, and Girardeau–Pilotti-Schiavonetti were remembered; whether by design or good fortune, Cuzzoni and Bordoni stooped to a hissing, spitting antagonism that inspired an audience largely uninterested in opera to rally for the lowest common

---

37   Hawkins, Sir John (2010). *General History of the Science and Practice of Music*. Gale ECCO, p. 873.

38   Swiny was one of the first of what would become known as "artist agents." In 1708 he was responsible for the London debut of Nicolini, for whose performance of Scarlatti's *Pyrrhus and Demetrius* Swiny translated the singer's Italian words into English. Scarlatti's opera opened at the Queen's Theatre on 14 December, 1708, with Nicolini appearing as Pyrrhus – a role he created in 1694 in Naples. The English premiere also featured Valentini (as Demetrius), Lewis Ramondon as Cleartes, Margherita de L'Epine as Marius, and Catherine Tofts as Climene. After a decade of court intrigues and commercial politics, Swiny settling in Venice in 1721 as an agent signing Italian performers of opera for the London stage, while also commissioning paintings from Italian artists for collectors in England, notably Canaletto. Swiny was close friends with Joseph Smith, the Venetian Consul.

denominator. Rumours of enmity were exacerbated and manipulated by the Academy – whose managers understood the value of antagonism where artists' reputations were concerned – and by the press, which delighted in claques and factions. Even though *Alessandro*'s initial run passed without event, matters boiled over during rehearsals for *Admeto*, first performed at the King's Theatre on 31 January, 1727, with Senesino in the title role, Bordoni as Alceste, and Cuzzoni suited ideally to Antigona. All hell broke out during rehearsals, in a manner that generated significant commentary – and black-hearted amusement – at a time when the effect of feminism was being felt across western society, even if no-one knew what to call it at the time.[39]

Audiences were not troubled by the appearance of an Italian man playing the role of a Macedonian king from the 4th century BCE, singing as a mezzo-soprano, wearing a huge powdered wig,[40] tights and an elaborate feminised costume. It might seem odd, bizarre even, that male sopranos should have been preferred as leads when in the company of the world's finest female singers, but castrati were perceived as male, even when sounding female. On the other hand, it remained unusual for women to be seen and heard empowered on stage as agents of influence competing for the attentions of men without testicles. This shift in perception and status was made all the more radical because Handel's stage was populated routinely by men and women who sounded more than similar – a transformative dialectic that reframed the male as female. The tradition of the *travesti* – according to which women would pretend to be men – was upended by the operatic stage, which saw masculinity conform by appearance, vocal range and projection to an emerging female heuristic. Having appeared for centuries on stage as men, women were rendered paradigmatically feminine by opera; male leads were played on every occasion by a castrato, whose virtuosity testified to his character's superiority when having to distinguish between the sonic equivalent of female voices. Alessandro's power for Handel flowed from skill rather than sound, a transcendence that no-one confused with realism. Opera's formulaic reliance on mythology, fantasy and symbolism abandoned verisimilitude long before a man performed on stage in imitation of his mother. Because the discrepancy between pitch and gender was acknowledged to be as improbable as the gods, distinctions between the genders were resolved as pure tone, a simulacrum made palatable by the application of technique, wherein sopranos of both sexes were required to perform music of unprecedented virtuosity and difficulty that admitted neither disparity nor tension as between the genders. Even if Handel's music for his castrati was more difficult than his music for women, audiences would not have been able to isolate those differences ontologically. The fascism of craft as it now occupies modern voice academies and conservatoires has recast art as competition. Every year, and in every country with a western musical tradition, panels of singers, instrumentalists and conductors isolate the first, second and third among barely distinguishable equals. For the singers of Handel's Academy, the battles were between class, culture and gender, with the 21st century's anodyne reduction of merit to accuracy conspicuous by its absence. Very

---

39   The word was used for the first time, in 1837, in France (as "*féminisme*") by the socialist Charles Fourier – who employed it positively to describe a utopian ideology.

40   It's important to note that women did not wear full wigs in the 18th century. Rather, they wore a "*coiffure*" supplemented by externally-sourced hair. Even on stage, women wore their own hair, powdered.

little of the critical assessment of Handel's first team of performers isolated an adherence to pitch, or any semblance of precision, as valuable. Technique was the equal of expression. Giambattista Mancini recorded how Cuzzoni

> possessed sufficient agility, the art of leading the voice, of sustaining it, clarifying it, and drawing it back, all with such attention to perfection, and to that degree which made her deserve the title "professor." If she sang a cantabile aria, she did not fail in fitting places to vitalize the singing with rubato, mixing proportionately with mordents, gruppetti, volatinas, and perfect trills without marring the melody; now blending, with passages executed in varied styles, now legato, now vibrant with trills and mordents; now staccato, now held back, now filled with redoubled volatinas; now with a few leaps tied from the low to the high; and finally by perfect execution she gave perfect attention to everything she undertook; all was done with surprising finish; all of this together produced admiration and delight.[41]

Singers "marring the melody" was a defining concern for audiences, for whom a heightened expressive palette mattered more than "mere" acrobatics.[42] The latter became known as *disposizione*,[43] and were formed routinely of mordents, *gruppetti*, *volatinas* and "shakes" (trills) – and it's clear from the arias written for her by Handel that Cuzzoni was less comfortable with virtuosity than Bordoni. This can be attributed to a number of factors, the most obvious being her training, or lack of it. Modern singers have been fed through a "method" with its origins in the teachings of Manuel García the younger's *Traité complet de l'art du chant*,[44] published in Paris in 1840 and reworked subsequently in English in 1847. García was a product of the master-apprentice system as it had been taught by his father, Manuel the elder, a famed early 19th-century tenor and pedagogue. Cuzzoni's father and Lanzi, her only teacher, were instrumentalists; neither was a vocalist, so it is unlikely they were able to do more than direct Cuzzoni's training as a generalist musician and improviser. She was, moreover, 18 when she first performed in a theatre – which means that Lanzi had months, at best, in which to steer the natural talents of a woman already working as a professional singer. García would have spat his teeth out at the idea of anyone creating new repertoire without having committed years to training. There was little training for women, from which it follows that Cuzzoni was all but self-taught. It would not be possible in the 21st century for a soprano to attempt a performance of an opera by Handel with two weeks' of rehearsals and no formal tuition. It can be presumed in consequence that Cuzzoni's technical facility – as a construction of tone and technique – was *very* different from what we know of recordings and contemporary live performances. Bordoni will have sounded nothing like Joyce DiDonato.

---

41   Mancini, Giambattista (1777). *Pensieri e riflessioni pratiche sopra il canto figurato* [Practical Reflections on Figured Singing]. Trans. and Ed. by Edward Foreman. *Masterworks on Singing*, Vol. VII. Pro Musica Press, p. 60.
42   See also Chapter 20.
43   'Disposition, or skill.'
44   'A complete treatise on the art of singing.'

Cuzzoni's particular talent was for the "pathetic." Her focus was on line, colour and dynamics – cardinal virtues when considering the small scale of most 18th century theatres, and also her slight timbre.[45] Rather than firing off fusillades of demi-semi-quavers, as was standard for Senesino, Cuzzoni employed an expressive vernacular made glorious by her storied *messa di voce*,[46] a technique that allowed for extreme variations in tone.[47] This trick of her trade was rarely a product of nature; indeed it necessitated exceptional diaphragm and breath control, particularly if a sustained half-voice resolved in a trill or rapid passage-work articulated in the throat. Her first aria in *Tamerlano*, for example, "*Se non mi vuol amar*,"[48] is a slow-moving *siciliana* with a simple, homophonic accompaniment. The sung line employs repeating notes that invite the singer to focus on the lachrymose sentiments of Nicola Haym's verse:[49]

> *S'ei non mi vuol amar*
> *Almeno il traditor,*
> *Perfido ingannator,*
> *Il cor mi renda.*
> *Se poi lo serba ancor,*
> *Che non lo sprezzi almen,*
> *O nell'amarlo il sen*
> *Poi non l'offenda.*[50]

When wrestling with the thorny question of what Cuzzoni might have sounded like, there is much to gain from performances of Handel's music by sopranos trained during the 19th century. In 1920, for example, Anna Case,[51] recorded the aria,[52] "O sleep, why dost thou leave me?" from Act II of Handel's English-language[53] "musical drama," *Semele*.[54] The American-born Case studied with Augusta Öhrström-Renard[55] (a muse to Gounod, Massenet and Widor), who was taught by Fredrika Stenhammar,[56] a

---

45   For anyone who has attended a production of a Handel opera at a large theatre, like the Met in New York, or La Scala, Milan, or the Coliseum in London, it will be obvious that amplitude is a necessity that would not have existed during the 18th century.

46   'Placing the voice.'

47   At its simplest, the swelling of a note from soft to loud, and back again.

48   'If he doesn't want to love me.'

49   There exists a particularly fine, if not peerless, performance of the aria by Mata Katsuli, produced on the back of a production in Athens by the Greek National Opera in 2007, conducted by George Petrou. The soprano's range of colour, her expressive diction, and her judicious use of ornament are a model of their kind. Katsuli's treatment of the aria's cadenza alluded to the best of which Cuzzoni may have been capable.

50   'If he does not wish to love me, At least that traitor, That wicked deceiver, Can give me back my heart. If he still keeps it, May he at least not despise it, Or if he loves it, May he cease to wound it.'

51   29 October, 1887 – 7 January, 1984.

52   For Thomas Edison.

53   The libretto was written by William Congreve.

54   The title role was written for Élisabeth Duparc ("La Francesina"), a French soprano greatly admired by the composer.

55   16 February, 1856 – 4 November, 1921.

56   19 September, 1836 – 7 October, 1880. Stenhammar joined Vienna's Theater am Kärntnertor in 1859, where she worked with von Suppé, Flotow and Meyerbeer.

pupil of "Rossini's tenor," Gilbert Duprez. Case is best remembered for her recordings, and for having created the role of Sophie at the first performance in the United States of *Der Rosenkavalier* in 1913.[57] It's obvious she didn't specialise in early music, because no-one did during the 1920s, and her singing of the aria would now be considered anachronistic, if not something worse.[58] Even so, the performance is a revelation, regardless.

The aria is written in E major,[59] but Case sings it in F – whereas René Fleming (on record) and Cecilia Bartoli (on stage) transposed the aria down only a semi-tone down, to E flat. Following a brief orchestral introduction, dated by the players' unapologetic use of portamento, Case frames her waking phrase, "O sleep," between barely audible pianissimos, to allow her to swell a richly placed F4, followed by a technically perfect trill. Her diction is peerless, and she employs variegated vibrato and seamless portamento to colour her lament, "why dost thou leave me?" The melancholy is judged perfectly; when repeating the phrase "O sleep," beginning on an exposed F4, Case robs the note of vibrato and colours it instead with a crescendo (as an example of *messa di voce*), the stark effect of which brings greater expression to the portamento she uses for the ensuing descending fourth. Handel's rising and falling treatment of the words "wand'ring love," is made haunting by Case's speech-like articulation; she brings a similar effect to the words "again deceive me," which she conveys in a manner that suggests Semele has yet to wake from her dream. Her vibrato is either light or absent, assigning her characterisation of emotional vulnerability to an effortless cantabile made heavy by grief and resignation. Even if Case's pitching of the final "restore" would now result in censure, the bleached tone on the high A4 amplifies by context the impossible beauty of the resolving phrase, "my wand'ring love." Case's singing of these five cadential notes is a masterclass in expression, and one of the wonders of the recorded age.

It cannot be suggested that Case and Cuzzoni were similar, which admits nothing of either singer. The human larynx hasn't changed over thousands of years, so the diversity of intonation of which women are capable challenges the presumption that the 18th century "sounded" like the 20th. As much is obvious from the span of contemporary female voices across the superabundance of World Music, typified by the incomparability of Tuvan-Mongolian throat-singing (the most extreme example of what is possible), Bulgarian folk-song, Japanese Noh theatre, and Congolese Baka yodelling. The ubiquity of western aesthetics and the relative constancy of what is perceived to be an "operatic" voice risks the reduction of tone to constancy – a supposition undermined by the accents and voices as they were recorded by the linguist Wilhelm Doegen during the First World War,[60] and by what is known of boys singing within the English Tudor tradition. The former prove beyond doubt how the human voice, whether sung or spoken, is in a state of perpetual cultural flux; the latter demonstrates the unchanging quality of boys' voices within Anglican practice.[61]

---

57   At the New York Metropolitan Opera, where Case was a company member between 1909 and 1916.
58   Case re-recorded the aria eight years later, electrically. The singing remains magnificent, although it is
59   In Robert Carsen's 2009 production for Opernhaus Zurich, conducted by William Christie.
60   These priceless recordings span German, French, Hindi, Bengali, Punjabi, Welsh, Scots and Irish voices.
61   The boys' choir as it was recorded in October, 1911, singing "*Gloria in Excelcis Deo*" (under the

Of course, children sing without art; phrasing, articulation and placement are determined by the untutored operation of prepubescent laryngeal mechanics. Music when sung is produced by vocal cords, which are pulled apart by the muscles of the larynx. The laryngeal structures are supported by cartilage that attaches, in turn, to muscles, all of which change with time and maturity, as does a singer's awareness of technique, style and expression. Education and training are transformative – when they are available, and capable of effecting modification. The Tudor tradition, for example, continues to flourish after more than five centuries of immutable continuity; the emerging conventions of opera embodied by Cuzzoni, Bordoni and Senesino were only a few decades old when they first sang for Handel; sopranos, in particular, were making it up as they went along.

The continuum as it is evidenced by an English cathedral choir played no part in the ways and manners in which women sang over the same period – as evidenced by what we know of "*Casta Diva*" when performed on record by Adelina Patti in 1906, Maria Callas in 1954, and Sonya Yoncheva in 2017. In consequence, it is well to remember that the vocal techniques employed by sopranos in 1720 were nascent, because Cuzzoni, Bordoni and their peers represented the origins of a school of singing with a narrow precedent, no academies, and only limited access to skilled tutoring. Sopranos routinely made their debuts shortly after their 18th birthdays, some years before a woman's diaphragm and musculature are fixed in maturity. The only singers whom ingénues were able to know (and from whom they could learn) had to be known and heard in person. Just as a young soprano would today be unable to sing like Cecilia Bartoli after seeing her perform even a hundred times in the theatre, Bordoni and Cuzzoni were original in every sense of the word. They will have been able to study the work of fewer than twenty world-class sopranos (at a time when the "world" extended to five or six countries) before being invited to create new roles and music for Handel and his peers. A soprano graduating from a music academy in 2023 can listen to at least 100 different live and studio recordings of Bellini's *Norma*, on a mobile phone; she can watch any number of the dozens of filmed performances available on Youtube, before thinking to study the role in print. The USA has 4,200 registered singing coaches, not including the tens of thousands of teachers working in private and public schools,[62] all of whom are products of a western tradition that originated with Cuzzoni and Bordoni.[63]

Singers during the first quarter of the 18th century were not exposed to any of these disadvantages; neither were they provided with potions to give them skills unattainable other than by genetic and sociological chance.[64] For every woman capable

---

direction of the Abbey's organist Sir Frederick Bridge) is identical to the choir that sings the same music more than 110 years later. The sceptical should listen to the recording of the Abbey Choir singing Parry's "I was glad" at the Coronation of George VI on 12 May, 1937, and again for Queen Elizabeth II's Coronation in 1953, and again when Prince William and Kate Middleton married, in the same building, on 29 April, 2011. The boys are indistinguishable across the recordings. When the anthem was performed at the Coronation of King Charles III, it sounded as it did when it was first performed at the Coronation of Edward VII in 1902.

62 The USA has more than 130,000 schools.

63 Few women at the time had access to training by castrati.

64 There are, of course, exceptions to the rule that qualify in the nicest possible way as freakish. Rosa Ponselle and Cecilia Bartoli are merely the most obvious.

of singing a major role in a Handel opera in her early 20s, there have been tens of thousands for whom it was physically and technically impossible. Part of the difficulty where Handel's music is concerned, and one of the obstacles to understanding anything of how Cuzzoni and Bordoni sang it, vests with the intractable problem of ornamentation and improvisation.

There are two kinds of embellishment: standard (spanning trills, appoggiaturas, slides, mordents, and turns) and free (entailing the expansion of melodic lines).[65] Handel rarely notated ornaments, preferring to leave them to the discretion of his singers. He expected soloists to nominate their own tempi and dynamics, while making any interpolations they considered appropriate to the narrative and the character. What qualified as appropriate was a question of taste and judgment; it is here, in the improvisatory, that the difference between the good and the legendary crystallised. Handel's gift to his singers was to repeat his texts, using the *da capo* aria, a tertiary form in which the first part ends in the tonic, and the second part employs modulations and evolving textures of mood and tempo. The third part was marked "*da capo*"[66] – which invited singers to do whatever they liked with a repeat of the first part. These repetitions allowed for melodic and rhythmic variation. Most singers approached the form as a vehicle for exponential expression, with the number of ornaments increasing cyclically. Handel and his librettists wrote between three and seven solos for each main character, which afforded ample opportunity for extravagant displays of plumage. Embellishments that distorted (or obliterated) a composer's melody were likely to win favour with no-one except a soloist and their claque.[67] For the early 18th century, ornaments were more than mere decoration, however; they served a specific expressive purpose, allowing for the enhancement of a character's text-determined emotional state and condition.[68]

There are a handful of autographs featuring Handel's vocal ornaments, notably Teofane's five arias in *Ottone* and one aria from *Floridante*. Winton Dean's estimations of the composer's intentions are far from conclusive; moreover, it's clear from 130 years of recording how approaches to ornament and improvisation have changed since the end of the 19th century alone.[69] Cuzzoni may, in 1723, have had the technical armoury necessary to persuade as a soprano auditioning in 2023. Then again, Charlie Chaplin came 20th in a Chaplin-impersonation competition.[70] Expectations

---

65   Donington, Robert (1982). *Baroque Music: Style and performance.* W.W. Norton & Company, p. 107.
66   Literally 'from the head.'
67   For a simple analogy, one might look to the more absurd examples of Paganini's inclination for self-harm. His exceptional talent for melody was subjected more often than it should have been to a tool-box of technical wizardry. This entertained and delighted the cheap seats, of course, but his peers, in almost every case, isolated the violinist's legato as his defining achievement. That Paganini could leap about his fret board as he did was not considered, by composers and critics at least, to be insufficient justification for doing so.
68   See, generally, Donington, Robert (1982). *Baroque Music: Style and performance.* W.W. Norton & Company.
69   See Lee, Junghyun (2020). *An Understanding of Style and of Baroque Ornamentation In Handel's Operatic Arias: A Study of Selected Recordings (1950s – 2010s).* PhD. Thessis. University of Kenucky.
70   According to an article in *The Straits Times of Singapore* in August, 1920, it was reported ("How Charlie Chaplin Failed,") that "Lord Desborough, presiding at a dinner of the Anglo-Saxon club told a story which will have an enduring life. It comes from Miss Mary Pickford who told it to Lady Desborough,

are formed by experience, such that a trill can be said to have been well-executed until someone does it better. As much is apparent from the ignorance of modern audiences and the coincidental popularity of Andrea Bocelli – a world-class tenor for those who haven't heard Tito Schipa, Franco Corelli, Carlo Bergonzi or any of the hundreds of other artists whose talents and abilities dwarf his own.[71]

To better appreciate Cuzzoni and Bordoni's pre-eminence, and to understand how ornaments and improvisation were capable of "marring" a melody, there is exemplar evidence in modern recordings of what are claimed to be historically-informed performances. One of Handel's best known arias, "*Lascia ch'io pianga*,"[72] has a tempo marking of *Largo*. As far as the composer was concerned, that was the sum of his instructions. In the first edition, published by John Walsh, the orchestration is unspecified, with the solo line supported only by an unfigured bass. "Violins" are identified at bar 23, where the soprano breaks.[73] The aria is performed by Almirena when responding to a declaration of love by her captor, Argante, Jerusalem's Saracen king. Giacomo Rossi's words are:

> *Lascia ch'io pianga mia cruda sorte,*
> *e che sospiri la libertà.*
> *Il duolo infranga queste ritorte,*
> *De' miei martiri sol per pietà.*[74]

Handel's setting is famed for its insular beauty, and for his use of a halting melodic line that exploits rests and dotted minims to enhance Rossi's verse in its characterisation of Almirena's unfolding grief. In 1994, the American early music specialist, Julianne Baird,[75] recorded the aria for Newport Classics, with the Brewer Chamber Orchestra, conducted by Rudolph Palmer. Baird's tone is light, effortless and absent artifice. For the aria's first part, she keeps things simple, adding an isolated trill at bar 7, and two unwritten quavers at bar 10. Music and words are enhanced by her unfussy concentration on the essence of Almirena's feelings. It's reasonable to believe that Handel's equivalent treatment of the second verse left the door open for a degree of improvisation. Whether Baird takes matters too far is a question of taste and prejudice. The introspective stillness that colours Baird's performance of the first complete verse is subsumed in the second to a significant number of unwritten notes, which consume and occlude the emotional space created by Handel's leading use of minims and rests. Trills, semi, and demi-semi-quavers allude to fear and anxiety, although

---

'Charlie Chaplin was one day at a fair in the United States, where a principal attraction was a competition as to who could best imitate the Charlie Chaplin walk. The real Charlie Chaplin thought there might be a chance for him so he entered for the performance, minus his celebrated moustache and his boots. He was a frightful failure and came in twentieth.'

71   It is equally certain that the *vox populae* has not been able to appreciate Bocelli's contemporaries Jonas Kaufmann and Juan Diego Flórez because neither has "crossed-over," whereas Bocelli has only ever really been a popular singer, after the fashion (but not the talent) of Mario Lanza.

72   'Let me weep,' from *Rinaldo*.

73   In most modern editions, there is an 8-bar introduction, which means the singer breaks at bar 31.

74   'Let me cry my cruel fate, and what sighs freedom / May sorrow shatter these chains, of my torments out of pity alone.'

75   10 December, 1952 –

not, perhaps, in the way imagined by the composer and the librettist. Baird employs passing and double appoggiaturas to lacquer the words "*Il duolo infranga,*"[76] which she does beautifully. "*Martiri*"[77] and "*pieta,*"[78] however, are diffracted by embellishments that border on the ugly. For the final da capo section, Baird adheres to the rests as marked, and the basic structure just about survive, but so much auxiliary notation is introduced, melodically and rhythmically, that the score, as written, is lost to scales, appoggiaturas, mordents and turns. Bars 17 to 20 of the score contain 14 notes for the singer; Baird adds a further 20. None of them contributes anything significant to the words, the music or the character's emotions.

Is this what was imagined by Handel? Does it approximate the singing of Cuzzoni and Bordoni in form and function? It's possible that this is exactly what every soprano was doing at the time; it's equally possible that singers did less than Baird. And yet, Handel is known not to have relished hearing his work distended. Accepting that improvisation as a form of creative licence was a value for every singer until the second half of the 19th century, Cuzzoni and Bordoni were required to extemporise – to a point. It is probable, however, that what made Cuzzoni special was her judgment. Tosi isolated her "exotic production of genius, [a] merit particular [and] difficult to imitate,"[79] while Mancini observed her "gift of a creative mind, and accurate discernment in making choices; by reason of these her singing was sublime and rare."[80] The Baroque is not remembered for less being more; even so, the art of singing as it was invented by Handel, and for every composer writing for voices who followed, fed primarily from a singer's willingness to communicate emotion and sentiment at cost to their vanity and brilliance.

This doesn't mean that Cuzzoni and Bordoni were uncaring of their social and cultural standing as prima donnas. Had they not been affected by pride and jealousy then they would not have taken to punching each other in the face during an Academy performance in 1727. The events leading up to this illustrious episode are well-known. One of the composer's closest female friends,[81] Mary Pendarves[82] attended the first rehearsal of *Admeto*[83] on 25 January, 1727, with a friend who (so she told her sister in a letter) was "driven out of her senses" by Senesino, Cuzzoni and Bordoni. Charles Burney was "told by persons who heard this opera performed when it first came out, that Senesino never sung or acted better, or more to the satisfaction of the public, than in the opening scene," which fact was lost to the growing tensions between the claques forming around Cuzzoni and Bordoni.

---

76 'Shatter.'
77 'Sufferings.'
78 'Pity.'
79 Kettledon, Lisabeth M. (2017). *A Lyric Soprano in Handel's London: A Vocal Portrait of Francesca Cuzzoni.* Doctoral Thesis. University of Connecticut, p. 61.
80 *Ibid*, p. 57.
81 And his neighbour in London.
82 *née* Delany. An artist in her own write, Delany's botanical *decoupage* (all of it at the British museum) is the most beautiful of its kind.
83 The last performance of *Admeto* prior to the 20th century was on 6 April 1754. This turned out to be the last performance attended by Handel of one of his own operas.

> Cuzzoni had been publicly told [...] she was to be hissed off the stage on Tuesday; she was in such concern at this, that she had a great mind not to sing, but I [...] positively ordered her not to quit the stage, but let them do what they would [...] and she owns now that if she had not had that order she would have quitted the stage when they cat-called her to such a degree in one song, that she was not heard one note, which provoked the people that liked her so much, that they were not able to get the better of their resentment, but would not suffer the Faustina to speak afterwards.[84]

The disturbances continued. In June, during a performance of Bononcini's *Astianatte* – patronised by the Princess of Wales[85] – Cuzzoni and Bordoni were onstage together when the audience interjected whenever one or other of the sopranos began to sing. On this occasion, agitation exploded into violence, silencing Cuzzoni, Bordoni and the pit. While waiting for the brawling to subside, one of the sopranos said something the other didn't like, and they began to trade their own insults, in Italian. Inspired by the punches being thrown in the auditorium, Cuzzoni and Bordoni exchanged their own blows before resorting to tearing at each other's hair. They were separated, and the performance was abandoned. The resulting scandal was exacerbated by the newspapers, all of which reported events with black-hearted glee. Twenty years earlier, Jeremy Collier published a pamphlet with the self-explanatory title *A Short view of the profaneness and Immorality of the English stage*. Collier's rejection of Restoration theatre (itself a response to the puritanism of Cromwell's Protectorate) voiced the disdain of the middle-class for the perceived profanity, blasphemy and indecency of a culture propagated uniquely by the low-hanging denominator of popular taste.

Augustan drama celebrated a sensibility in which pathos, delicacy and refinement superimposed the moral and the didactic. To counter the sympathetic depiction of vice, writers promoted a value system that memorialised the principle of *quae sursum sunt quaerite*.[86] Richard Steele summarised his ambition when vowing "to banish out of conversation all entertainment which does not proceed from simplicity of mind, good nature, friendship and honour." Cibber, Centilivre, Kelly, Lillo, Cumberland and a host of other playwrights employed sentimentalism to force a moral outcome for characters guilty of licentious behaviour; the reformation of drama, with virtue triumphing over sin, occluded the more complex brilliance of Congreve and Etherege, and as with any other regime of moral prohibition the outcome was disappointing. Augustan tragedy was near universally terrible, which explains in part the popularity of Handel's *opera seria*. When London's critics and commentators had cause to turn on the Royal Academy, however, they did so with ruthless uniformity. The most successful rejoinder was *The Beggar's Opera*, by John Gay (with music

---

84   *The London Journal*, No. 410, Reported on Saturday, 10 June, 1727.

85   Caroline of Ansbach, who was crowned five months later alongside her husband, George II, on 11 October, 1727.

86   The aphorism was drawn from Colossians 3: "*Quae sursum sunt quaerite, ubi Christus est in dextera Dei sedens; quae sursum sunt sapite, non quae super terram.*" ['Seek those things that are above, where Christ is sitting at the right hand of God; taste the things that are above, not the things that are upon the earth.'

arranged by Johann Christoph Pepusch[87] – the husband of Margherita de l'Epine). This English-language satire employed barely disguised metaphors to skewer contemporary politics, class and culture. It was more successful than anything by Handel, or anyone else – an outcome that delighted Pepusch, in particular, who was unable to compete with his more successful German colleague. Gay began *The Beggar's Opera* shortly after Cuzzoni and Bordoni's humiliation in the press; it was first performed seven months later, at Lincoln's Inn Fields Theatre, on 29 January, 1728, where it ran for 62 consecutive performances – to that time the longest run of anything in English theatrical history, and the second-longest anywhere else.[88]

Gay's anti-opera was aimed directly at Italian music and the English public's enthusiasm for the Academy. He made use of popular tunes – some of them by Handel – and presented characters recognisable to everyone. Where the Academy celebrated mythology, wealth and privilege, Gay's story attacked corruption across the span of English society, targeting politics, poverty and injustice while aggrandising murderers, prostitutes and conmen. He based the leading female characters, Lucy Lockit and Polly Peachum, on Cuzzoni and Bordoni. The former is the daughter of the jail keeper, and the business partner of a well-known criminal, Peachum. Lockit's love of profit above all else was an obvious swipe at capitalism's emerging metric; it swung also at Cuzzoni's infamous greed. When Macheath is captured and sent down, his various wives emerge from the crowd – but it is Polly/Bordoni, the daughter of a rival gang leader, whom he chooses as his partner for life. Polly is naïve and innocent, feminine and modest in appearance despite working as a prostitute. *The Beggar's Opera* is fantastically misogynistic, and typical of the attitude towards male and female sopranos as it was represented in "Epistles," a sub-genre of verse-publishing that drove satire into a dark and hateful corner of the gender battlefield. Written in Latin, English and, on occasion, Italian, these vitriolic poems were intended to demean the institution of Italian opera and the world that patronised it. Broadsides were aimed at singers as well as their admirers, therefore.[89] In the course of his examination of the Epistles, Thomas McGeary noted how

> the epistles amplify the sexual danger of Italian opera. As a genre, these epistles on opera singers share the wider context of Restoration misogynist satire. [...] Above all, woman is portrayed as possessing an insatiable lust and deviant carnal desire that is satisfied by resorting to adultery, bestiality, lap-dogs, dildoes, servants, and eunuchs. It is the carnality of the granddaughter of Eve that tempt and corrupts men. The key text in this tradition is Juvenal's Sixth Satire against the lusts of Roman

---

87   After the Theatre's Manager, John Rich, decided that *a capella* wouldn't work, Pepusch was allowed a week in which to arrange the 69 songs chosen, adapted or written by Gay. He had also to write an Overture. Rich's judgment was sound. On 3 February 1728, shortly after the premiere, *The Craftsman* reported, "This Week a Dramatick Entertainment has been exhibited at the Theatre in Lincoln's-Inn-Fields, entitled *The Beggar's Opera*, which has met with a general Applause, insomuch that the Waggs say it has made Rich very Gay, and probably will make Gay very Rich."

88   Robert Cambert's pastoral opera, *Pomone*, ran for 146 performances in Paris in 1671.

89   See generally McGeary, Thomas (2000). "Verse Epistles on Italian Opera Singers, 1724–1736." *Royal Musical Association Research Chronicle*. No. 33, pp. 29–88.

matrons, "a Common-place", according to John Dryden, who translated him, "from whence all the Moderns have notoriously stollen their sharpest Raileries."[90]

The characterisation of sexual desire as corrupt, debauched and merchantable amplified the male fear of the feminine and the effeminate. Women singers and castrati were easy and obvious targets for misogynists, with sopranos of both genders portrayed as lascivious and illicit. Women were said to disseminate disease and immorality, while castrati challenged normative conceptions of masculinity. The author of *A General Satyr on Woman* was not exaggerating when asserting that "To be damn'd is to be effeminate."[91] The Epistles highlighted a defining paradox, wherein Italian opera could be stigmatised as ruinous while being revered coincidentally for its glamour, exoticism and aesthetics. They were also anonymous. The author of *The Beggar's Opera* was out and proud, however, and he delighted in his success, which he shared with Lavinia Fenton,[92] the first Polly. Fenton's status as *prima donna della capitale* led to prints of her portrait outselling those of every other singer; she became the focus of near-constant attention in the press and among publishers. Fenton remained a celebrity even after her last appearance as Polly, on 19 April, 1728, at which point she eloped with her married lover, Charles Powlett, 3rd Duke of Bolton. Powlett was 23 years older than Fenton, and the father of Fenton's three illegitimate children. After the death of the Duke's wife in 1751, Fenton became the second Mrs Powlett, and the Duchess of Bolton.

The scandal of the duelling sopranos, and the sensational success of *The Beggar's Opera*, had a disastrous effect on the Royal Academy of Music, which collapsed at the end of the 1728–29 season. The company's backers were unwilling to fund Cuzzoni and Bordoni's exorbitant fees while suffering coincident embarrassment and ridicule. Cuzzoni left London for Vienna, and concerts for Sir Robert Walpole, the British Prime Minister. She travelled with her husband, the composer Giuseppe Sandoni, who joined with her in living beyond their means. Even at the height of her fame, during her first two seasons with the Academy, Cuzzoni was renowned for improvidence and a destructive gambling habit. Anastasia Robinson and Gaetano Berenstadt both wrote letters to the Academy undermining their (then new) colleague. The former claimed that shopping for clothes was "more dear to her," than her husband;[93] the latter punched lower still when writing that Cuzzoni was "mad and unpredictable," while suggesting that if her "behaviour were as good as her singing, she would be a divine thing."[94] Of Sandoni he admitted no quality: "lavishness, finery, jewellery,

---

90   *Ibid*, pp. 29–30.
91   In 1679, four satiric poems were published under the title *Female Excellence, Or, A Woman Display'd*: A General Satyr on Woman; A Satyr upon Woman's Usurpation; A Satyr on Woman's Lust; In Praise of a Deformed, but Virtuous Lady, Or A Satyr on Beauty. The author was identified as a "Person of Quality." He was, in fact, John Wilmont, the 2nd Earl of Rochester, whose "quality" manifested itself primarily in virulent STDs, alcoholism, and an appetite for excess that resulted in his death at the age of 33.
92   1708 – 24 January, 1760.
93   Kettledon, Lisabeth M. (2017). *A Lyric Soprano in Handel's London: A Vocal Portrait of Francesca Cuzzoni*. Doctoral Thesis. University of Connecticut, p. 19.
94   *Ibid*.

eating, drinking, bastards, debts, [and] love affairs are the delights of this wretched madman."[95]

Cuzzoni's character does seem to have been less admirable than her talent. When, in 1729, Handel established a new Royal Academy, he became joint manager of the King's Theatre with John J. Heidegger, who funded another trip by the composer to Italy to search for new singers. Cuzzoni was not invited to return by Handel, which made her attractive to a rival company, the Opera of the Nobility, established by a group of aristocrats known to be hostile to George II.[96] Owen Swiny was retained as the talent scout, and Nicola Porpora became the first music director; they were able to agree terms with Cuzzoni and Senesino[97] in 1733. Cuzzoni returned to London in April the following year;[98] she was joined shortly after by the castrato Carlo Maria Michelangelo Nicola Broschi – better known as Farinelli.[99] When the Opera of the Nobility went bankrupt in 1737, Cuzzoni left London and spent the next 13 years touring Europe. In 1741, she was accused of poisoning her husband; she later served time in prison for failing to clear her gambling debts. Cuzzoni's career ended in humiliation. In 1750, having been unable to earn money anywhere else, the 64-year-old soprano gave concerts in London, where she was heard by Charles Burney, who wrote of "her third arrival in this country" that

> she was grown old, poor, and almost deprived of voice, by age and infirmities […] Poor Cuzzoni returned to the Continent after this unprofitable concert, more miserable than she came.[100]

Exactly one year later, Cuzzoni gave her last performance, in London. Before doing so, she appealed directly to the public for support when writing to the *General Advertiser*:

> I am so extremely sensible of the many Obligations I have already received from the Nobility and Gentry of this Kingdom (for which I sincerely return my most humble Thanks) that nothing but extreme Necessity, and a Desire of doing Justice, could induce me to trouble them again, but being unhappily involved in a few Debts, am extremely desirous of attempting every Thing in my Power to pay them, before I quit England; therefore take the Liberty, most humbly to intreat them, once more to repeat their well-known Generosity and Goodness, and to honour me with their Presence at this Benefit, which shall be the last I will ever trouble them with, and is made solely to pay my Creditors; and

---

95 *Ibid*, pp. 19–20.

96 Patronised by George's eldest son, Frederick, Prince of Wales, who animosity for his father was legendary while both lived.

97 Who had fallen out with Handel and was also available.

98 Sandoni survived the episode, and lived on for another seven years until his death in London in 1748.

99 24 January, 1705 – 16 September, 1782.

100 Kettledon, Lisabeth M. (2017). *A Lyric Soprano in Handel's London: A Vocal Portrait of Francesca Cuzzoni*. Doctoral Thesis. University of Connecticut, p. 115.

to convince the World of my Sincerity herein, I have prevailed on Mr. Hickford to receive the money, and to pay it to them.[101]

Cuzzoni was cursed with a long life. It is said she died while working in a button factory in Bologna. Despite this inglorious ending, she was, for almost a decade, the most celebrated female musician in history – adored by crowds and composers alike for her voice and artistry. Although she created only a single title role for Handel, her achievement was to have provided one of history's most gifted composers of opera with access to an instrument for whom he could write what he wanted, in the manner in which he wished to write it. If Cuzzoni was not exactly a muse – at least in the sense that Maria Jeritza would be for Richard Strauss – then she was nonetheless an artist for whom Handel was moved to compose music like "*Se pietà di me non senti*,"[102] Cleopatra's haunting plea to Giulio Cesare, in F sharp minor with bassoons in unison, that speaks powerfully to the character's feelings, as well as her own crystalline fragility. As legacies go, it's a good one.

Cuzzoni made her debut in London in January, 1723; later the same year, Tosi published his *Opinioni de' cantori antichi e moderni*, which summarised the basic elements of vocal training. His method became the standard for the teaching of singing until the 19th century. If Handel's first generation of sopranos was left largely to its own devices then the second wave was able to rely to some extent on Tosi, whose teachings enabled them to cultivate tone and art systematically. Rather than striving for unity between the registers, Tosi's aim was to allow for the differentiation between chest and falsetto/head voices, which an artist learned to disguise through training and technique.

The market for singers equipped with the technical resources necessary for performances of Handel's music remained a constant because he kept writing it. Between 2 December, 1729 (*Lotario*), and 10 January, 1741 (*Deidamia*), he composed 17 original operas;[103] 13 of them contained roles for Anna Maria Strada, whom Handel appears to have trained prior to her debut as Adelaide in *Lotario* on 2 December, 1729. Because of opera's dramatic decline in popularity in London after 1730, almost nothing is known about Strada's life, save for what can be adduced from Handel's affections. He was grateful also, since she was the only singer in the composer's company not to defect to the Opera of the Nobility in 1733, in consequence of which Handel presented her with two title roles, *Partenope* and *Atalanta*.[104] One of the composer's librettists, Paolo Rolli, described Strada as "a copy of Faustina, with a better voice and better intonation, but without her charm and brio." He reported elsewhere that she

sings better than the two who have left us, because one of them (Faustina) never pleased him at all and he would like to forget the other (Cuzzoni).

101 Deutsch, Otto (1974). *Handel: A Documentary Biography*. Da Capo Press, p. 709.
102 'If you don't feel sorry for me.'
103 Not including *pasticcio* works, formed of music drawn from earlier works.
104 Known also by her married name, del Pò. Her husband, Aurelio, was a theatre manager and librettist. It was claimed that Strada married her husband in settlement of debts.

The truth is that she has a penetrating thread of a soprano voice which delights the ear, but oh how far removed from Cuzzona [sic].

If Strada's voice was admired then her appearance was not. Burney was unkind when reporting that

> A singer formed by [Handel], and modelled on his own melodies. She came hither a coarse and awkward singer with improvable talents, and he at last polished her into reputation and favour [...] Strada's personal charms did not assist her much in conciliating parties, or disposing the eye to augment the pleasures of the ear; for she had so little of a Venus in her appearance, that she was usually called the Pig. However, by degrees she subdued all their prejudices, and sung herself into favour.

Elsewhere, Handel drew periodically on the talents of three other sopranos, all of them born outside Britain:[105] Margherita Chimenti,[106] Celeste Gismondi,[107] and Élisabeth Duparc.[108] His last significant relationship with a soprano encompassed opera and oratorio. Handel first met Cecilia Young[109] after hearing her sing in concert; he was sufficiently impressed to cast her as Dalinda in *Ariodante*, which was first performed at Covent Garden on 8 January, 1735. She went on to create the role of Morgana in *Alcina* (1735) and she sang the soprano roles in the first performances of the oratorios *Alexander's Feast* (1736) and *Saul* (1739). On 15 March, 1737, she married a young composer called Thomas Arne, whose Op. 1, *Rosamund* (an *opera seria*), was premiered at Lincoln's Inn Fields Theatre in 1733. Thirty years later, Arne produced *Artaxerxes*, the only known attempt by an English composer to write a Metastasian *opera seria* in the English language.[110] The work was a triumph in Britain, Ireland and the United States. It didn't travel well, and neither did it sustain an appetite for opera in Britain. After Handel's death in 1759, and with *Artaxerxes* representing the end of the British operatic tradition for nearly two centuries, the art and craft of the soprano returned to Europe, where it was picked up by a young man who later recalled with respect and affection having attended a performance of *Artaxerxes* when visiting London as an 8-year-old boy in 1764. Britain may have ruled the waves, but the future of opera, and the soprano voice, belonged to Wolfgang Amadeus Mozart.

---

105 As far as it is possible to know. Of the five singers, only Chimenti's year of birth is known.
106 1734–1746.
107 – 11 March, 1735.
108 – 1778.
109 January, 1712 – 6 October, 1789.
110 Using recitative rather than spoken dialogue.

CHAPTER EIGHT

Donne d'ogni grado,
d'ogni forma, d'ogni età[1]

In July, 2006, the world gasped in wonder as one of history's most remarkable photographs came up for sale. The copy of a *daguerreotype*, said to have been taken in October, 1840, showed the Swiss composer Max Keller seated between two women, one of whom, to his right, was alleged to be Mozart's widow, Constanze, *née* Weber.[2] It was entirely possible that a photograph had been taken of Constanze, and the British newspaper, *The Guardian*, was typical of most when reporting the discovery without challenging its authenticity:

> Her hair severely parted, Constanze Weber Mozart looks unsmilingly away from the camera. She appears to be staring at her feet. Next to her is Max Keller, a Swiss composer and old family friend, surrounded by his daughters and the rest of his family. In the background is a cottage with two garden-facing windows. The newly discovered black and white image is the only photograph ever taken of Constanze Mozart, the widow of the Austrian composer and genius Wolfgang Amadeus Mozart. The previously unknown print was discovered in archives in the southern German town of Altötting, local authorities said on Friday, and has now been authenticated as including Mrs Mozart, on the far left. The long-lost photograph was taken in October 1840, when Constanze Weber was 78-years-old, at Max Keller's home. The Altötting state archive said it was the only time in her life that she was photographed. The picture is one of the earliest examples of photography in Bavaria, it said. Daguerrotype photography was first practised in the southern German state around that time.[3]

Although the photograph was incontestably of Max Keller (who was born the same year as Beethoven),[4] it was not taken in 1840.[5] Neither can it have featured Constanze,

---

1 'Women of all levels, of all shapes, of all ages.' From "*Madamina, il catalogo è questo*" (the "Catalogue" aria), Act I, Scene 2 of *Don Giovanni*.

2 5 January, 1762 – 6 March, 1842.

3 *The Guardian*, London. 7 July, 2006.

4 1770.

5 The first surviving photograph of a human being was captured by Louis Daguerre in 1838, in Paris, as *View of the Boulevard du Temple*. Because the image required an exposure time of as much as 12 minutes, the busy street appears all but empty. At the lower right, however, a man can be seen having his

who had not visited Keller in Switzerland since 1826. She remained capable despite her years, but Constanze was two months from her 79th birthday in October, 1840, and at least two decades older than the woman seated to Keller's right. Had it been alleged that the woman on his left was Mozart's widow then there might have been a case to make;[6] unfortunately, this was known to be Keller's wife. Every other fact as it was asserted by *The Guardian* was equally amiss. The photograph was produced in around 1850 – when Keller was 70. The four standing individuals were Keller's two daughters (to the right), his brother-in-law, Phillip Lattner (leaning to the composer's left) and the family cook. It has not been possible to name the misidentified woman, although various sources claim her to have been "somebody's aunt," which is statistically credible. The first German *daguerreotypes* date to May, 1842 – two months after Constanze's death on 6 March.[7] The possibility that there was a photo of the wife of history's most revered composer – whom she had married almost 60 years earlier – was sufficient to suspend cynicism, if not disbelief. The grubby truth revealed the whole episode to have been a hoax, perpetuated by Keller's grandson.

If the photo's back-story was interesting, then its reporting was alarming. European and American press coverage in 2006 was united in referring uniquely to Constanze as a wife. She was "Frau Mozart," an appendage to the quasi-mythical composer whose children she bore and whose legacy she protected. Journalists and cultural commentators were happy to reduce Constanze to her conjoined status as a spouse and a mother, denying and subverting her for a readership that was presumed to care for the achievements of women when not attending to the needs of their husbands and children. This salutary reminder that the 21st century was less enlightened than it might have been served to discount the obvious, namely that had Constanze Weber not married Mozart on 4 August, 1782, she would have been remembered as the soprano who sang the first performance in 1783 of one of the most perfect of the composer's more than 600 compositions. Although it stands apart as an apogee of western art, the Mass in C minor is less well-known than the Requiem on which Mozart was working at the time of his death in 1791. Both scores were left unfinished. The latter is dark, frightening and in keeping with the mood and circumstances of a man who he was dying; the former is, as far as a mass can be, a burst of uninterrupted sunlight, and as filled with joy as anything to which Mozart gave his name. The Mass' inspiration was Constanze, an achievement in and of itself that should have assured her the same recognition as Teresa Brambilla, whose sole legacy attaches to her creation of

---

boots polished, which means that at least one of the two first people to be photographed was a probably illiterate bootblack. Also *visible* is a young girl looking out of a window towards Daguerre. In 1839, the American Robert Cornelius took the first successful portrait (of himself, using the *Daguerreotype* system; the following year Hippolyte Bayard took the first European portrait (again of himself) in the pose of "A Drowned Man." It follows that Constanze could have been photographed, as could Paganini (who died in 1840; his alleged photo is an obvious fake), Cherubini (who died in 1842), Stendhal (who died in 1842) and Hölderlin (who died in 1843). It transpired that the only Mozart to be photographed was the elder of the composer's two surviving sons: Karl Thomas Mozart (1784–1858).

6   Or possibly his mother, judging by appearances. She is almost comically wizened.

7   These were produced by Hermann Biow, who photographed Hamburg after its destruction by fire. One of the earliest German-made portraits was of Alexander von Humboldt, in 1847 – an image taken indoors, like every other portrait until Joseph Petzval's innovations in lens design.

the role of Gilda for Verdi.[8] Mozart began the score after Constanze was taken by a life-threatening illness. On 4 January, 1783, he wrote to his father:[9]

> I meant what I said about morality – it was not without intention that it flowed from my pen. I really promised in my heart to keep my promise. My wife was still single when I made it, but as I was firmly resolved to marry her soon after her recovery it was easy for me.[10]

Mozart's protean faith was rejuvenated by Constanze's brush with death, and it's clear he pledged to compose a "Great" Mass in celebration of Christ's sacrifice, should she recover and become his wife. His prayers were answered; however, like many who make promises when falling to their knees, Mozart didn't keep to his side of the bargain:

> Time and circumstances frustrated our journey, however, as you yourself know. Let the score of half a Mass, which lies there hopeful of conclusion, serve as proof that my promise was real.[11]

The conviction of his feelings was inarguable; the truth of what he wrote to his father was not. Wolfgang's letter was designed to manage Leopold's impatient demands that he leave Vienna for Salzburg; decades later, Constanze told her second husband, Georg Nissen, and also Vincent and Mary Novello, that the Mass had been written to commemorate her emergence from "confinement." This is supported by the chronology, since their first child, Raimund, was born on 17 June, 1783 – five weeks before the Mozarts left Vienna. They arrived in Salzburg on 29 July – leaving Raimund with a wet-nurse. The composer worked on the Mass while at home with his father, as preparation for which he wrote out the wordless "*Solfeggio,*" K.393, No. 2, "*per la mia cara Costanza*"[12] – which he later used for the opening of the *Christe eleison*. Mozart may well have assisted with the writing of parts in advance of the premiere, which was given in St. Peter's Abbey (rather than the Cathedral) on 26 October, 1783.[13] Although it's unclear why Mozart was willing to submit an unfinished work to public scrutiny, it's more than probable that he and Constanze anticipated her status as a

---

8   In *Rigoletto*. Equally singular, and comparable for other reasons with Constanze, was the soprano Giuseppina Strepponi, who created only a single role for Verdi, Abigaille in *Nabucco*. She too is better remembered as a wife, to Giuseppe Verdi.

9   All letters by any of the Mozarts are drawn from *Wolfgang Amadeus Mozart, My Dearest Father* (2015). Trans. Stewart Spencer, Penguin Books.

10   Krister, Konrad (1996). "A Promise Kept? The C Minor Mass, K. 427" in *Mozart: A Musical Biography*, trans. Mary Whittall. Clarendon Press, p. 153.

11   *Ibid.*

12   'For my dear Constanze.'

13   The Mass was held at St. Peter's Abbey, rather than Salzburg Cathedral, for a couple of reasons. Firstly, Mozart had for almost two years been *persona non grata* with the Archbishop, and secondly because women were still not allowed to take part in musical performances for church worship. Abbeys were "exempt religious," and answerable directly to the Pope rather than to any secondary power, even that of an Archbishop. The rules were less strictly applied by St. Peter's, therefore.

mother ending her career as a singer, as was common at the time;[14] it was almost certainly the last opportunity they would have to perform in public together, therefore. On 19 August, Raimund died. His parents were not made aware of the boys death until their return to Vienna on 27 October. The Mass remained unfinished; Mozart abandoned the "*Credo*" immediately after composing the "*Incarnatus*," which is also incomplete, with only the vocal solo, the bass and three *obbligatos* for flute, oboe, and bassoon being fit for performance. Of the string parts, the opening and closing *ritornelli* were alone in being written out.[15] Mozart never explained his failure to complete what was recognised at the time to be a masterpiece. It can be surmised, however, that revisiting a work with which he had been occupied while his son was dying in his absence was never likely to become a priority. The premiere proved to be the work's only performance during Mozart's lifetime. Even if the C minor Mass was not composed "for Constanze," at least in isolation, its musical and structural summit, and among the most sublime works by anyone for the female voice, immortalised the intensity of the composer's feelings for mother and child. "*Et incarnatus est*" is nothing less than a divine benediction; the repeating words are

> *Et incarnatus est de Spiritu Sancto*
> *ex Maria Virgine Et homo factus est.*[16]

The music is in F major, and scored for four solo voices – soprano, flute, oboe and bassoon – with a string and *continuo* accompaniment. The aria's substance is self-evident from the words and, more obviously still, their setting. Mozart's pre-occupation with the divinity of incarnation added metaphysically to the music he was writing for his unborn son; he approached the challenge of writing for his wife as a singer through a filter of *Idomeneo's* "*Se il padre perdei*"[17] – which Mozart is known to have relished hearing Constanze perform – as well as the recently premiered *Die Entführung aus dem Serail*,[18] into which Mozart had thrown the kitchen-sink when writing "*Martern aller Arten*."[19] Enervated by his immersion in Handel's Italian operas, this nearly-10-minute coloratura aria joined Mozart's unique gift for melody to an almost absurdist virtuosity, the scale of which continues to intimidate even the most capable of singers. It's no coincidence that both "*Martern*" and "*Incarntus*" feature obbligato woodwind. Although the music for his wife is less flamboyant than for *Entführung's* Konstanze, it was sufficiently technical to impress her miserablist father-in-law at their first meeting in Salzburg, in July, 1783.

---

14   The same was not the case for Constanze's sister, Aloysia, who continued to sing throughout her (unhappy) marriage to Joseph Lange, an actor and amateur painter. Lange's portrait of Mozart was said by Constanze to be the most accurate likeness.

15   It has been suggested that, for the first performance, Mozart improvised an accompaniment from the organ.

16   'And was made flesh by the Holy Ghost; from the Virgin Mary, and was made human.'

17   'If I have lost my father.' This short but taxing aria from Act II, Scene 4, also features *obbligato* parts for flute, oboe, horn, and bassoon.

18   'The Abduction from the Seraglio.'

19   'Tortures of every kind.' From Act II, Scene 8.

The "*Incarnatus*" is an imposing but intimate characterisation of applied love; the quartet of "soprano" voices unfolds as a contrapuntal fabric by which the orchestral bass is silenced, in a conscious act of separating the music and its ambition from the human and the earthly. The long cadenza is drafted, and bare of virtuosity, comparable in the mastery of its part-writing to the *Sinfonia Concertante*, K.364; it is prognostic also of the Quintet for Piano and Wind Instruments, K. 452 – written a year after the C minor Mass, which Mozart identified in a letter to his father as "the best I've ever written in my life."[20] Constanze's talent as a singer is evidenced by the span of *Incarnatus'* intervals, the unforgiving demands of a near-infinite melody, some brutally exposed *trills* and a C5 that continues to terrify many and defeat most. She was plainly an exceptional soprano, if not, perhaps, the equal of her better-known sister, Aloysia.[21]

Aloysia and Constanze Weber were two of four siblings, all of them acclaimed for their talents as singers. In 1777, Aloysia was introduced to the 21-year-old Mozart, whose training as a boy treble by the castrato, Giovanni Manzuoli, had equipped him to give Aloysia singing lessons. The following year, Aloysia made her debut at the Munich Opera, and in 1779 she relocated to Vienna, where she remained for the next two decades as one of the city's most beloved prima donnas. Mozart focussed on her coloratura, which he considered weak, and at the end of his training he presented her with a fearsome concert recitative and aria, "*Alcandro, lo confesso; Non sò, d'onde viene*," K.294,[22] which Aloysia mastered at Mozartian speed.[23] As he wrote to his father:

> When I had it ready, I said to Mlle Weber: learn the aria yourself, sing it as you wish; then let me hear it and I will tell you honestly what I like and what I don't like. After two days, I came and she sang it to me, accompanying herself. Then I was obliged to admit that she had sung it exactly as I had wanted it and as I would have taught it to her myself. That is now the best aria she has; with it she certainly brings credit on herself wherever she goes.[24]

The Danish actor and musician, Joachim Preisler, was sent by the Royal Theatre in Copenhagen to study opera production across mainland Europe; while in Vienna he heard Aloysia sing.[25] Preisler wrote in his diary:

---

20   10 April, 1784.

21   Maria Aloysia Antonia Weber [Lange] (*circa* 1760 – 8 June, 1839).

22   'Alcandro, I confess; I don't know where it comes from.'

23   Mozart later wrote a number of other works for Aloysia, including the infamous recitative and aria "Popoli di Tessaglia!" ('People of Thessaly!'), K.316/300b, which reaches a G6, the highest prescribed note in the established classical repertoire. In 2017, Audrey Luna outdid Aloysia when singing an A6 during a performance of Thomas Adès's *The Exterminating Angel*.

24   Mahling, Christoph-Hellmut (1996). "Junia's aria in Lucio Silla." In Stanley Sadie (Ed.). *Wolfgang Amadè Mozart: Essays on His Life and Music.* Clarendon Press, pp. 389–390.

25   She was pregnant at the time, and on leave.

The voice is something exceptional! but ... not by a long way as good as our Müller;[26] yet her high range and her delicacy, her execution, taste and theoretical knowledge cannot fail to be admired by any impartial critic. [...] She can sing the longest and most difficult parts incomparably better than the [Italian] songstresses who are here pampered by the "Viennese nobility."[27]

In a development befitting a rom-com, the master fell in love with the student – who didn't reciprocate. When two years later Mozart moved to Vienna he stayed for a time with the Weber's – a household that included Constanza, with whom Mozart also fell in love. The father, Fridolin, had died in 1779, compelling his widow, Cäcilia, to open the family home to lodgers. Mozart's relationship with Cäcilia was fractious initially – mirroring the tensions that coloured her relationship with Constanze – but with time, money and children, matters improved. In 1825, Sophie recalled how

Mozart became fonder and fonder of our dear departed mother and she of him. Indeed he often came running along in great haste to the Wieden (where she and I were lodging at the Golden Plough), carrying under his arm a little bag containing coffee and sugar, which he would hand to our good mother, saying "Here, mother dear, now you can have a little Jause."[28] She used to be delighted as a child. He did this very often.[29]

Mozart's best friend throughout his life was his sister, Nannerl. He was close also to his aunt, Sophie, and his cousin, Maria Anna.[30] He was attached by gossip to dozens of women while still a teenager, and between the ages of 17 and 26 his romantic affairs were the subject of perennial gossip. When, for example, he relocated from the Webers' home to his first apartment in Vienna, he is said to have promised himself to one of his pupils, Josefa Auernhammer. Mozart was quick to correct the rumour in a letter to his father on 22 August, 1781, in terms that do nothing for the composer's reputation:[31]

If a painter wanted to portray the devil to the life, he would have to choose her face. She is as far as a farm-wench, perspires so that you feel inclined to vomit, and goes about so scantily clad that really you can read as plain as print: "Pray, do look here." True, there is enough to see, in fact quite enough to strike one blind; but – one is thoroughly punished for

---

26   Caterine Möller, a *prima donna* at the Royal Theatre in Copenhagen.

27   Deutsch, Erich Otto (1965). *Mozart: A Documentary Biography*. Stanford University Press, p. 324.

28   A snack (usually coffee and cake), to be served between meals, commonly during the afternoon.

29   Solomon, Maynard (1995). *Mozart: A Life*. Harper Perennial, p. 274.

30   Known as "Bäsle."

31   A charitable interpretation of the letter's contents can be sustained by a neutral consideration of the pressure felt by Wolfgang to address the interminable gossip that made its way to Salzburg. Putting a story to bed, as he did on numerous other occasions where women were concerned (including Constanze) is a perennial feature of his correspondence with Leopold.

the rest of the day if one is unlucky enough to let one's eyes wander in that direction – tartar is the only remedy![32]

Wolfgang and Auernhammer later became life-long friends,[33] as was true of almost every woman with whom Mozart came into professional and personal contact after 3 July, 1778, when his mother, Maria Anna, died in Paris, at the age of 58.[34] This was a predictably monumental event, but the consequences of his loss exceeded the ordinary. Mozart's relationship with his mother had been definitively loving and un-usual for the composer because mother and child shared little through music. He adored and trusted her in contradistinction to his father, whose personality was cruel, indifferent and manipulative.[35] Leopold's bitter, selfish and petty nature, sustained by serried inadequacies, populate his correspondence with his wife and children; his worst excesses were reserved for his son. The most shocking evidence for the psychological effects of seeing the only male figure in his life terrorise his mother, sister, wife and everyone else who threatened Leopold's power over his son is the letter Mozart wrote to his father while his mother lay dead in the room next door. Having warned that his mother was "very ill," he proceeded to describe in detail the rehearsals and first performance of his latest symphony[36] his prospects at the Paris Opéra, and a raft of professional issues that Mozart knew his father would consider either more important than, or a distraction from, Maria Anna's illness. A few hours later, Wolfgang wrote to confirm that his mother had died; his father's reply suggested his son was to blame.

Leopold was an oppressive and controlling agency until his death, in 1787. Wolfgang remained dutiful and respectful throughout, a code of conduct on which he relied psychologically when engineering the physical distance after relocating per-manently to Vienna in 1781. Although the journey between Salzburg and Vienna was less than 400km – an overnight coach trip of around 12 hours' duration – Leopold made only a single visit to the capital of the Austro-Hungarian Empire, in 1785. It proved to be his last. Much has been written of the complicated alliance between father and son, the majority of it pivoting on Wolfgang's deference to a man without whose investments and sacrifices he would not have become history's most celebrated musician. Their unusual and probably unique experience as parent and child was

---

32   Glover, Jane (2005). *Mozart's Women*. Harper Collins, p.112. The common construction of this letter is that he was seeking to distract his father from his proximity to the Weber family.
33   He dedicated his Op. 2 set of Violin Sonatas to her, K.296 and K.376–80, and Francesca joined him when he gave the first performance of his Sonata for Two Pianos, K.448.
34   She was accompanying her son on tour, for the first time on their own (from 23 March, 1778, until (for Mozart) 26 September, 1778). Maria Anna died in the company of her son, and a nurse provided by friends of the family.
35   Probably the best-known example of Leopold guilt-tripping his son was the letter he sent on 5 February, 1778, in which he wrote 'I must be clear as noonday to you that the future of your old parents and of your good sister who loves you with all her heart, is entirely in your hands. When you were children, I gave up all my time to you and in the hope that noy only would you be able to provide later on for yourselves, but that also I might enjoy a comfortable old age, be able to give an account to God of the education of my children, be free from anxiety, devote myself to the welfare of my soul and thus be able to meet my death in peace.'
36   On 18 June, 1778.

the only male relationship of any significance to which Mozart could refer as a man. Throughout the last decade of his life, Constanze's influence as a woman was singular;[37] both of their surviving children were male.

The effect of this imbalance cannot be countered by his habitually masculine delight in scatological humour[38] (something in which he was joined by Nannerl, and various other female friends), or the absolute dominance of men at court, and his navigation of Vienna's administrative corridors, or his love of male company in the cups of rich living, or as a member of the Masonic temple. The evidence suggests that Mozart's nature adhered to what would now be considered a feminine archetype. His infamous sensitivity was emotional as well as physical,[39] redolent of the autistic spectrum as it is studied in the 21st century. The delicacy of his senses and sensibilities as someone who breathed the "air of other planets" was legendary,[40] and it would be facile to overlook the effect of his experiences on a predisposition for the company and art of women. This evolved as a construction of philosophical and political reflection, counteractively to his father's authority as someone who enjoyed the unearned privileges of a zealously patriarchal society. Leopold's fascistic conception of women as secondary, inferior and, even, dangerous prescribed his sacking of Maria Anna and, to a lesser extent, Nannerl. Leopold had to tread more carefully with his daughter since the siblings' affection was insular and sustained by righteous pride. The brother encouraged, supported and praised his sister, whose gender contributed nothing to the substance of Wolfgang's letters. Leopold, on the other hand, was preternaturally concerned by the fact of his wife and daughter *being* women; his prolonged absences only rarely made him fonder. On 29 January, 1778, he urged that his son "refrain from all familiarity with young Frenchmen," and "even more so with the women, who run after people of talent in an astonishing way in order to get at their money, draw them into their net, or even land them as husbands." He was quick to remind Maria Anna of all he had done for her and their six named children (four of whom were buried in infancy); his undermining of his wife as a woman fed the misogyny to which he turned with alacrity whenever warning his son of the evils of the female. On 5 February, 1778, for example, he wrote to Wolfgang:

> You're a young man of 22; and so you don't have the earnestness of old age that could deter a young lad of whatever social class, be he an adventurer, a joker or fraud and be he young or old, from seeking out your acquaintance and friendship and drawing you into his company and then gradually into his plans. One is drawn imperceptibly into this and cannot then escape. I shan't even mention women,[41] for here one needs the greatest restraint and reason, as nature herself is our enemy, and

---

37   His first daughter died within six months (Theresia; 27 December, 1787 – 29 June, 1788). His second, Anna Maria, died soon after birth (16 November, 1789).

38   For the truly curious, see Simkin, Benjamin (1992). "Mozart's Scatological Disorder." *British Medical Journal*, Vol. 305, No. 6868, pp. 1563–1567.

39   As a child he would fall to the ground whenever he heard a trumpet, for example.

40   Stefan George's poem, "*Entrückung*," begins with the line "*Ich fühle Luft von anderem Planeten*" ('I feel air from another planets'). See Chapter 16.

41   Plainly, he does.

the man who does not apply his whole reason and show the necessary restraint will later do so in vain in his attempt to escape the labyrinth, a misfortune that mostly ends only in death.[42]

It is no small irony that Mozart's primary philosophical concern for much of his life (insofar as it can be discerned from what he wrote in words and music) was death. He understood mortality to operate as the driver, if not also the purpose, for existence.[43] Although his father chose not to educate him in philosophy, Wolfgang's mind was of such astonishing elasticity and compass (evidenced by his ability to learn languages in a matter of weeks),[44] that it is probable he was well-acquainted with the rudiments of philosophical reasoning without also being especially well-read. The only book of philosophy in his possession at the time of his death was *Phaedon*. Published in 1767, and a best-seller within its first year, Moses Mendelssohn's widely admired defence of immortality was foundational for Immanuel Kant (who removed its wings when producing the *Critique of Pure Reason*).[45] Mendelssohn's submission that eternity was the product of unending moral progress resonated for the composer; it enhanced his cultivation of values that resolved in the ultimate expression of his conviction that the union of men and women was paradigmatic for society as a whole. The words sung by the devoted and enlightened Pamina and Papageno in *Die Zauberflöte* summarise not only Mozart's feelings for Constanze, therefore, but the "exalted goal of Nature":

Ihr hoher Zweck zeigt deutlich an:
nichts Edler's sei, als Weib und Mann.
Mann und Weib, und Weib und Mann,
reichen an die Gottheit an.[46]

The uncharacteristic use of the first person speaks for Mozart as well as the lovers, with the intersection between Christian and Masonic thought assimilating the composer's humanism as it was idealised by Kant's assertion that

The highest moral good cannot be achieved merely by the exertions of the single individual towards his own moral perfection, but requires a union of such individuals into a whole towards the same goal.[47]

---

42 p. 44.

43 In one of his last letters to his father, Mozart wrote "Since death is the true final purpose of our lives, I have, over the past few years, made myself familiar with this true, best friend of humanity, so that its image is no longer frightening to me, instead it is very much calming and comforting to me! And I thank the Lord that he let me have the opportunity to get to know death as the key to true happiness." (April 1787).

44 He was fluent in Latin, German, French, Italian, English and various dialects, including Swabian.

45 Published in 1781. It's worth noting that Mendelssohn won first prize in the Berlin Academy competition of 1763. Kant secured an honourable mention.

46 'Its exalted goal is manifest: Nothing is more noble than man and wife. Man and wife, and wife and man, reach out to the deity.' Mozart once signed a letter to his father using a similar phrase. For her 2007 translation, Amanda Holden preferred the depressingly materialist: "When we aspire to heaven in life, nothing competes with man and wife; man and wife and wife and man, that's how human life began."

47 Engstrom, Stephen (1992). "The Concept of the Highest Good in Kant's Moral Theory." *Philosophy and Phenomenological Research*. Vol. 52, No.4, pp. 747–780; p. 749.

It's a short step from Sarastro's sun and stars to Kant's "heavens above,"[48] by way of Mozart's belief in a "moral law within" for the benefit of a "union of individuals."[49] On 14 December, 1784, Mozart was admitted to *Zur Wohltätigkeit*,[50] – one of Vienna's eight lodges of Freemasonry. His predisposition for the enlightened, rationalist and avowedly humanist views promoted by Jean-Jacques Rousseau and Denis Diderot steered him away from the provincial anachronisms of Salzburg towards a less divided, more liberated society, in which equivalences might be pursued in anticipation of equality. After the death of his mother, Mozart moved for two months to the home of his protector in Paris, Baron Friedrich Melchior Grimm, whose close friendship with Jean le Rond d'Alembert, Baron d'Holbach, Diderot and, for a time, Rousseau equipped him to explore contemporary principles of theoretical emancipation with Mozart – to which the Masons were open, even if their doors were not.[51] Mozart's feminine sensibilities were attuned to Rousseau's conviction that art had to imitate nature – and its human variant in particular – as a means of advancing a community spirit in defiance of a community of saints. In the words of Alfred Schutz:

> Mozart's main topic is […] the metaphysical mystery of the existence of a human universe of pure sociality, the exploration of the manifold forms in which man meets his fellowman and acquires knowledge of him. The encounter of man with man within the human world is Mozart's main concern. This explains the perfect humanity of his art. His world remains the human world even if the transcendental irrupts into it. The sacred realm of *The Magic Flute* or the supernatural occurrences in *Don Giovanni* belong themselves to the human world. They reveal man's place in the universe as experienced in human terms.[52]

Mozart's perfection of melody as an agent of unity enabled him to articulate the ages; his genius for music drama brought him into conflict with a dilemma, born of the irreconcilability of a truly moral law to the casual and inveterate subjugation of women. He had to be able to write for women as people before he could care for their abilities as singers. He was the first to do so. To appreciate the scale and effect of his achievement as a composer for the operatic soprano, it's necessary to understand something of the context in which audiences as well as singers responded to the miraculous beauty and invention of *Die Entführung aus dem Serail, Le nozze di Figaro*,[53] *Don Giovanni, Così fan Tutte*,[54] and *Die Zauberflöte*. Mozart's revolution was

---

48 Kant's tombstone near the cathedral of Kaliningrad (formerly Königsberg) contains a passage from his *Critique of Practical Reason* (in German): "Two things fill the mind with ever new and increasing admiration and awe, the more often and steadily we reflect upon them: the starry heavens above me and the moral law within me."

49 As 'Temple Initiates.'

50 'At Beneficence.'

51 While Mozart was staying with Grimm, Márton Heinzeli, the head of a lodge in Budapest, initiated three women as Freemasons. This pre-empted calls for the establishment of a separate lodge for women – a move that was forbidden expressly by Heinzeli's Viennese superiors.

52 Schutz, Alfred (1956). "Mozart and the Philosophers." *Social Research*. Vol. 23, No. 2, pp. 219–242.

53 'The Marriage of Figaro.'

54 'Women Are Like That.'

preceded by Gluck's reforms, in which he was supported by a company whose female singers are little remembered beyond their names. The first performance of *Orfeo ed Euridice*, on 5 October, 1762, at the Burgtheater in Vienna, was notable for its castrato (Gaetano Guadagni), while the premiere of *Alceste*, on 26 December, 1767, was striking for its "reforms," which included[55] the dilution of recitative (which was to be accompanied, rather than *secco*), simpler melodic lines, and more intelligible, less repetitive word-settings. As far as singers were concerned, *da capo* arias, vocal improvisation and ornaments were *verboten*, a controversial development that Mozart addressed when replacing stolen thunder with divine lightning. Gluck's works were pre-eminent in a market populated by (mostly) Italian composers of opera, whose names have been forgotten, other than by academics and musicians specialising in period-performance: Alessandri, Anfossi, Bertoni, Bianchi, Borghi, Cafaro, Colla, Ferradini, Fischietti, Galuppi, Guglielmi, Jommelli, Latilla, Mysliveček, Paisiello, Pampani, Piazza, Piccinni, Ponzo, Pugnani, Sacchini, and Traetta produced dozens of operas, few of which were performed more than once. Hundreds of works were staged without a composer even being identified, while others utilised the same libretti. In the majority of cases, audiences attended the opera to hear their favourite singers.

To meet the public's appetite for new work, academies and conservatoires sprang up across Europe, with every major city from Palermo to Stockholm teaching singing to boys and girls for whom the ever-growing number of theatres promised fame and fortune.[56] The reach of Farinelli's reputation nailed ubiquitous value to supernatural feats of virtuosity and, until the end of the century, sopranos were trained routinely in coloratura. Few could resist the allure of the money and the applause earned by virtuosi; for those with the most wind, caution was rarely a priority. Lucrezia Aguiari[57] was renowned for her capacity, with a voice of more than three and a half octaves and technical and musical faculties that enabled her to master new roles in a matter of hours. In a letter dated 24 March, 1770, Leopold Mozart described hearing Aguiari perform a C7 at the Ducal opera in Parma:[58] "I could not believe that she was able to

---

55   These "rules" were set out in the Preface to the published score.

56   For example, the Conservatorio dell'Ospedaletto was founded in 1777 within a hospital that was serving as an orphanage, for children up to the age of 12. When not in classes, the boys were taught woodworking; girls studied singing. Concerts and church performances generated significant income for the orphanage and conservatoire.

57   1743 – 18 May, 1783.

58   Aldous Huxley refers to Aguiari's singing in *Brave New World*. In Chapter 11, after the "sense-organ" has finished playing a "Herbal Capriccio," Huxley describes a "synthetic music machine" performing a "trio for hyper-violin, super-'cello and oboe-surrogate that now filled the air with its agreeable languor. Thirty or forty bars – and then, against this instrumental background, a much more than human voice began to warble; now throaty, now from the head, now hollow as a flute, now charged with yearning harmonics, it effortlessly passed from Gaspard Forster's low record on the very frontiers of musical tone to a trilled bat-note high above the highest C to which (in 1770, at the Ducal opera of Parma, and to the astonishment of Mozart) Lucrezia Ajugari, alone of all the singers in history, once piercingly gave utterance." Huxley's historical references were in error. "Forster's" name was Kaspar Förster, the "Mozart" who commented on the C7 was Leopold (not Wolfgang), he misspelled Aguiari's name, and Erna Sack was renowned for being able to sing a C7 at least 5 years before *Brave New World* was published in 1932. Huxley's laboured point – that machines cannot exceed human capacities where the production of pitch is concerned – was demonstrable nonsense at the time.

reach [it] but my ears convinced me."[59] The Belgian composer André Grétry was less easily impressed; he decried the murderous cult of improvisation as "absurd," and an inadequate surrogate for simple, true feeling.[60] Having winced through yet another exhausting performance of an opera by Gluck, Grétry asked why singers insisted on presuming their art superior to that of the composer: "the more genuine an air, the less [should] embellishment [be] permitted."[61] After a concert performance of one of his most sombre duets, Gluck was confronted by a member of the audience from England, who "asked me for what comic opera I had written [it]."[62]

Aguiari studied with the composer Brizio Petrucci in Ferrara; she was further educated at a convent in Florence, under the supervision of a priest, Abbé Lambertini. After a period as a court singer in Parma, she travelled to Naples for the premiere of Paisiello's *Le nozze di Peleo e Tetide*, in 1768 – staged as part of the festivities commemorating the wedding of King Ferdinand IV of Naples and the Archduchess Maria Carolina of Austria. Aguiari married the composer Giuseppe Colla in 1780, and retired from the stage two years later in consequence of ill health – said, by rumour, to have been caused by a rival poisoning her food. Aguiari died of tuberculosis in 1783, at the age of 40. She is interesting to posterity because of the amazing number of works in her repertoire. The records are incomplete, but Aguiari is known to have created at least 60 roles. Other singers may have bested this record; none did so before reaching the age of 41. Colla was succeeded as *prima donna d'europa* by Brigida Banti[63] who, between 1782 and 1803, also created a huge number of roles – albeit for composers whose work was forgotten while they lived. Banti's father was a street mandolin player, with whom she performed often as a child; she also worked *in duetto* with the legendary double-bassist and sometime guitarist, Domenico Dragonetti – who was appointed principal at the Opera Buffa in Venice at the age of 13.[64] Banti completed numerous seasons in Paris and London before making her way to Vienna in 1780. Had she remained in the city, it's certain she would have come to the attention of Mozart; instead, she returned to Italy and a decade of near-constant triumphs that culminated in her being invited to take part in the inauguration of La Fenice in 1792.

A lot of nonsense has been written about Banti, much of it more revealing of the authors than the singer. Even now, it's claimed she never learned to read music, and that she had by necessity to memorise parts by ear. Even a cursory study of her roles, and the composers for whom she created them, demonstrates the absurdity of a prejudice for which there is no evidence. For example, Haydn composed a *Scena di Berenice*[65] for Banti to perform at his final benefit concert in London, on 4 May,

---

59 For anyone interested in hearing this pointless note, there are recordings of it being "sung" by Mado Robin and Yma Sumac.
60 Jerold, Beverly (2008). "How Composers Viewed Performers' Additions." *Early Music*. Vol. 36, No. 1, pp. 95–109; p. 104.
61 *Ibid.*
62 *Ibid.*
63 1757 – 1806.
64 Palmer, Fiona M. (1997). *Domenico Dragonetti in England, 1794–1846.* Oxford University Press. p.10.
65 Using text taken from Act III, scene ix of Metastasio's libretto, *Antigono*.

1795.[66] The extensive double-recitative and aria (the first, an Adagio beginning "*non partir bell'idol mio*,"[67] the second, an Allegro beginning "*perché se tanti siete che delirar mi fate*"),[68] is almost a quarter of an hour in length, and dramatically intense in its characterisation of the emotional turmoil suffered by the abandoned Berenice. Haydn's writing is remarkably theatrical for a composer who hadn't written an opera in more than a decade;[69] it reveals much of what he must have known and heard of the soprano for whom he wrote it. Banti was approaching the end of her career, and the music's range is that of a mezzo – dropping to a low B3, and rising only rarely above the stave, with a single C6, scored as a crotchet. Despite the general absence of notated acrobatics,[70] there are hints at what must have been, including a passage of nine frightening *in tempo* triplets towards the scene's conclusion. On the only surviving handbill, an anonymous commentator wrote: "Banti has a clear, sweet, equable voice, her low & high notes equally good, her recitative admirably expressive." The suggestion that Haydn entrusted his music to a woman who couldn't read it is laughable; it's probable, therefore, that the rumour originated with the poverty of Banti's origins or the jealousy of rivals. It was perpetuated in print, and into the 21st century, by someone who claimed to have known her. Richard, the 2nd Earl of Mount Edgcumbe, was a peer and amateur musician; he wrote his memoirs of musical life during the last quarter of the 18th century, some 30 years into the 19th.[71] After decades' listening to many of the world's finest singers, his Lordship declared his favourite soprano to be Banti, of whom he wrote:

> She had begun the world as a *cantante di piazza*,[72] and as such, having attracted notice by her fine voice, she had been taken from her humble calling, taught and brought out as a singer in concerts, first at Paris, and then in England, as before mentioned, at the Pantheon, under the name of Giorgi. But though she had the best masters, she was an idle scholar, and never would apply to the drudgery of her profession: but in her, genius supplied the place of science, and the most correct ear, with the most exquisite taste, enabled her to sing with more effect, more expression, and more apparent knowledge of her art, than many much better professors. She never was a good musician, nor could sing at sight with ease: but having once learnt a song, and made herself mistress of its character, she threw into all she sung more pathos and true feeling than any of her competitors. Her natural powers were over the finest description: her voice sweet and beautiful throughout, had not a fault in any part of its unusually extensive compass. Its lower notes, which reached below

---

66   The programme also featured Haydn's recently composed 'Military' and 'London' Symphonies (No.'s 100 and 104), as well as concertos by Viotti and Ferlandis and songs by Paisiello and Rovedino.

67   'Do not leave, my beautiful idol.'

68   'Why, if you who overwhelm me are so numerous.'

69   His last, *Armida*, was premiered in 1784.

70   Haydn is clearly resigned to the inevitability of Banti's predilection for improvision.

71   The falsehood continues to be promulgated throughout British, French, Italian, German and American sources.

72   'A square singer,' literally; better translated as a 'busker.'

ordinary sopranos, were rich and mellow; the middle, full and powerful; and the very high, totally devoid of shrillness: the whole was even and regular, one of those rich *voci di petto*, which can alone completely please and satisfy the ear. In her youth it extended to the highest pitch, and was capable of such agility, that she practised and excelled in the bravura style, in which she had no superior; but losing a few of her upper notes, and acquiring a taste for the *cantabile*, she gave herself up almost entirely to the latter in which she had no equal.[73]

Edgcumbe's memoir was a popular success, and it continues to be relied upon even though its author's judgments are questionable, at best. He makes not a single reference to Beethoven, and of Rossini he opined that he "will not long have ceased to write before he will cease to be remembered."[74] His love of Banti appears to have been informed by her willingness to sing an opera by Richard Edgcumbe. It is not explained how she was able to do this "by ear," even if Edgcumbe's choice of words clarifies that she was unable to "sing at sight *with ease*." The same was no less true of Marie Wittich[75] and Annie Krull.[76] Between 1794 and 1802, Banti was engaged as prima donna at the King's Theatre by its manager, William Taylor, with whom she was said, by Lorenzo Da Ponte, to be having an affair. Da Ponte also characterised her as vulgar, dissolute, ignorant and foolish – qualities that Haydn chose presumably to overlook. There is a clue to the basis for Da Ponte's loathing of the soprano in his use of two further descriptors: impudent and insolent. Banti had clearly not shown the requisite deference to the now-famous librettist. She survived his conceit, and continued to sing into the 19th century, until shortly before her death in 1806. The scale of her voice was so unusual that medical science subjected her corpse to an autopsy, so as to better understand how she sang as she did. To no-one's surprise, she was discovered to be in possession of a larynx and lungs, the latter being unusually large. Both the story, and its findings, are inane, but they allude to the direction in which singing, and composition for voices, was headed after 1800.

Although she was born three decades earlier, Regina Mingotti[77] outlived Banti by two years. Charles Burney acclaimed her the "perfect mistress of her art," and equal in "musical intelligence" to any composer known to him, an opinion written after he had made the soprano's personal acquaintance. Mingotti was tutored by the church (while resident, by her father's order, in a convent) and in Dresden by the most respected singing teacher of the 18th century, Nicola Porpora. In 1747, Mingotti created the title role of Ercole in Gluck's *Le nozze d'Ercole e d'Ebe* – one of many gifted to her during her long career. During the seasons 1751 to 1753, she was resident in Madrid, appearing in operas under the direction of Farinelli, and during the ensuing decade she was lionised in Paris and London for her virtuosity and furious temper, both of which brought her into conflict with the long-suffering Faustina Bordoni.

---

73 Edgcumbe, Richard; Earl of Mount Edgcumbe (1834). *Musical Reminiscences, containing an account of the Italian Opera in England, from 1773*. John Andrews & F. H. Wall, pp. 78–80.

74 *Ibid*, p. 142.

75 The soprano who created the title role of Strauss' *Salome*. See Chapter 16.

76 The soprano who created the title role of Strauss' *Elektra*. See Chapter 16.

77 16 February, 1722 – 1 October, 1808.

Charles Burney's portrait of Caterina Gabrielli[78] was characteristically partisan; even so, his view that she was "the most intelligent and best-bred virtuosa"[79] was typical. Gabrielli was the daughter of a chef in service to a Cardinal, whose name she took when travelling to Venice to study with Porpora. After appearing regionally throughout Italy, and having created a number of roles for Galuppi and Jommelli in Venice (where she was known as "*La cochetta*"),[80] Gabrielli was hired by the imperial court in Vienna, where she excelled between May, 1755, and December, 1756 – an *annus mirabilis* during which she premiered two large-scale sacred works for Georg Wagenseil (*Gioas re ti Giuda*[81] and *Il roveto di Mosè*),[82] and no fewer than four operas for Gluck: *La danza*,[83] *Le cinesi*,[84] *L'innocenza giustificata*,[85] and *Il re pastore*.[86] Gabrielli was clearly homesick, and she spent the rest of the decade in Italy. In 1760, she returned to Vienna for the premieres of Gluck's *Tetide* Giuseppe Scarlatti's *L'Issipile*, and Johann Hasse's *Alciade al Bivio*.[87] After another stellar decade in Italy, Gabrielli relocated in 1772 to the imperial court in Saint Petersburg, accompanied by her sister, Francesca. Three years later, it transpired that her paymasters in Russia wouldn't meet her fees, so she relocated to London.

Gabrielli's career was unusual for its longevity, a record to that time; it culminated in a curious mix of glory and ignominy, when she opened Milan's carnival season of 1780 with the first performance, at La Scala, of Mysliveček's *Armida*, on 26 December, 1779. The work was a spectacular failure. Many of the composer's arias had to be substituted with music by Giuseppe Sarti and Francesco Bianchi,[88] and Gabrielli was forced to withdraw from the first (and only) run in order to give birth. She did so a month and a half after celebrating her 50th birthday – and with the unacknowledged father rumoured to be Mysliveček.[89] Milanese audiences were

---

78   12 November, 1730 – 16 February or 16 April, 1796.

79   Burney, Dr. Charles (1957). *A General History of Music: From the Earliest Ages to the Present Period (1776–89)*. Ed. Frank Mercer. Dover Publications.

80   'Little cook.' This was a significant improvement on Lucrezia Aguiari's *nome cantato*, "*La Bastardina*" (or "*La Bastardella*"). Her nickname reached no higher than confirming the (presumed) truth of her illegitimacy.

81   'Joash, King of Judah.' (1755).

82   'The Bush of Moses' (1756).

83   'Dance' (1755). Not performed again until 1987, in Bologna.

84   'The Chinese Women' (1755).

85   'Innocence justified' (1755).

86   'The Shepherd King' (1756). Mozart's opera of the same name was based also on Metastasio's libretto; however, Mozart (and his father) were inspired not by Gluck's opera, but rather a performance of a setting by Felice Giardini.

87   'Alciade at the crossroads.'

88   The work's first (semi-staged) revival was given in Lisbon, on 22 May, 2015, by the Lisbon Metropolitan Orchestra.

89   It has been suggested that the father was the composer Tommaso Traetta, who invited Gabrielli to Saint Petersburg in 1772. It's unlikely Traetta was the father since he married a woman from Russian-Finland, Elizabeth Sund, in 1776. Their son Filippo, was born in Venice, on 8 January, 1777. He moved with his mother to the United States in 1800, where he became a fairly successful composer. As for Tommaso, he died on 6 April, 1779, also in Venice – a little over nine months before the first performance of *Armida*. He is interesting for a another reason, tangential to more recent events concerning the Russian Federation. When he left Saint Petersburg in 1775, it's claimed he did so having been threatened with assassination by Catherine the Great. She was provoked into an apparent rage by the happy resolution with which he ended

less admiring of her character, resolve and talent than they should have been, and she was subjected to abuse and denigration, in person and in print. Gabrielli retired to Bologna, where she died in 1796. It has been suggested that she should have performed for Mozart, considering the reach of her fame and the scale of her talent. Mozart certainly knew her voice, but his preferences (and loyalties) lay elsewhere. On 19 February, 1778, during the course of an unusually rancorous series of letters with his father, Wolfgang wrote:

> By my advice, Herr [Fridolin] Weber has engaged Madlle. Toscani (an actress) to give his daughter [Aloysia] lessons in acting. All you write of Madlle. Weber is true, except, that she sings like a Gabrielli, for I should not at all like her to sing in that style. Those who have heard Gabrielli say, and must say, that she was only an adept in runs and roulades; but as she adopted so uncommon a reading, she gained admiration, which, however, did not last longer than hearing her four times. She could not please in the long run, for roulades soon become very tiresome, and she had the misfortune of not being able to sing. She was not capable of sustaining a breve properly, and having no messa di voce, she could not dwell on her notes; in short, she sang with skill, but devoid of intelligence. Madlle. Weber's singing, on the contrary, goes to the heart, and she prefers a cantabile. I have lately made her practise the passages in the Grand Aria, because, if she goes to Italy, it is necessary that she should sing bravuras. The cantabile she certainly will never forget, being her natural bent. Raaff (who is no flatterer), when asked to give his sincere opinion, said, "She does not sing like a scholar, but like a professor."

The distinctions isolated by Mozart between Aloysia Weber and Caterina Gabrielli flowed from a prejudice that owed nothing to singing. Mozart's judgment was in no way corrupted by his emotions, however; indeed, it was humanity that made the man and the music so extraordinary. His sensitivity to the rights as well as the virtues of women as performers originated with his moral conviction that the success of a dramatic narrative depended equally on the presence of believable female characters and the fecundity of their voices. Central to this evolving conception of theatrical truth was Mozart's mature preference for female sopranos over male. For all their manifest unreality, he had made routine and custom use of castrati for his earlier operas;[90] because the "*evirati*" were in every case Italian, Mozart was doubtless generalising in his descriptions of Gabrielli's differentiators as an inability to "sustain a breve," or achieve a "*messa di voce*" – elements of vocal technique subsumed to the populist ploughshare of the "roulade."[91] The composer's swingeing dismissal of Gabrielli as "devoid

---

his opera *Antigona*, to which he had added music associated commonly with Polish independence. While he made it out in time, his librettist did not. He died in Russia, having been poisoned.

90   Mozart created leading castrato roles for *Mitridate, re di Ponto*, K.87 (1770), *Ascanio in Alba*, K.111 (1771), *Lucio Silla*, K.135 (1772), *Idomeneo, re di Creta*, K.366 (1781) and *La finta giardiniera*, K.196 (1774). Mozart did not write another role for castrato for almost seventeen years (thirteen operatic projects later), when composing *La clemenza di Tito*, K.621, in 1791.

91   A common word to describe exaggerated vocal ornaments.

of intelligence" impugned the merits of her judgment (and the judgment of Italian note-spinners of both genders) rather than the quality of her mind – which is why Aloysia's singing was preferable for its *cantabile*. Mozart conceded that Aloysia would need to master "bravuras" should she travel to Italy, and this tension between the substance of pure melody and the artifice of its interpretation pumped the heart of Mozart's revolution when writing for the women who first performed *Die Entführung aus dem Serail*, *Le nozze di Figaro*, *Don Giovanni*, *Così fan Tutte*, and *Die Zauberflöte*.

Fundamental to the reach of Mozart's insights in his writing for character and voice is an Oz-like duality that employs brilliance as dissimulation. The composer's near-infinite compassion germinates despite (rather than because of) his unprecedented technical mastery of form and expression; if he preferred Aloysia Weber's singing to Gabrielli's then he did so because Weber was willing to accommodate Mozart's aversion to vocal improvisation. Particularly as a composer for female voices, he revealed a freakish ability for capturing subtleties, sensibilities and inferences that eclipsed the finest of which everyone else was capable because it could not be improved upon in performance. Mozart's rejoinder to Josef II's alleged gripe after the premiere of *Die Entführung* – that it had "just the right number of notes" – may have been a fiction, but it captured incontrovertible truth. Franz Niemetschek, a friend of Mozart's, attended the first performances of *Die Entführung* and *Figaro*. He attributed the composer's apotheosis of natural sentiment to his daring "to oppose the Italian singers and banish all those useless, nondescript warblings, flourishes, and passages!"[92] – an intransigence that was said by Niemetschek to explain the alleged aversion of Italian singers to his operas. In his biography of the composer, von Nissen noted how Mozart's songs and their accompaniments are so closely connected that they cannot be separated or amended without causing harm to both:

> By the essence of his style, therefore, Mozart is an irreconcilable foe of warblings and trimmings-in short, all the lavishness of embellishment disfiguring the musical phrase and crippling the expression [...] To touch the heart, arias such as "*Voi che sapete*" need neither trills nor leaps, neither jaw contortions nor even those chromatic so-called runs up and down.[93]

The Viennese conductor Ignaz Franz von Mosel reported that Mozart responded badly to any meddling by performers:

> One could not offend the sublime Mozart more deeply than by adding ornaments to his compositions. Incensed, he always said: "I certainly would have written it that way if I had wanted it."[94]

The implacability of the composer's expectations was a clear challenge at a time when a soprano's identity was inseparable from her virtuosity. Mozart compromised by

---

92 Jerold, Beverly (2008). "How Composers Viewed Performers' Additions." *Early Music*. Vol. 36, No. 1, pp. 95–109; p. 104.
93 *Ibid.*
94 Neumann, F. (1986). *Ornamentation and improvisation in Mozart*. Princeton University Press, p. 238.

writing out the floridity on which his singers' reputations depended, a discipline he exploited for "inside" jokes that required coloratura sopranos to hold onto high notes without being able to improvise, interject, colour – or breathe[95] – while simultaneously indulging the virtuosity of the orchestra. The Queen of the Night's two window-rattling arias in *Die Zauberflöte* are fixed in form and function, with neither allowing for improvisation or its discernment. There is neither room nor permission for a soprano to add anything to *"Der Hölle Rache kocht in meinem Herzen,"*[96] which has a range of two octaves, from F4 to F6, with a challenging tessitura of A4 to C6. The Queen's fearsome nature, and her self-perception as the dramatic heroine, are inextricable from the detail and force of Mozart's music. This pivot from ornament to substance was tailored to the character as whom he was speaking and the exacting depth of expression that this required of each of his singers. These fundamentals of dramatic truth overreached his prejudice for Italian musical culture, which explains his non-sectarian approach to casting during his final decade.[97] For *Die Entführung*, for example, he chose the Austrian born sopranos Caterina Cavalieri[98] (as Konstanze) and Theresia Teyber[99] (as Blonde). For *Figaro*, he cast Nancy Storace,[100] an English singer, as Susanna, Luisa Laschi[101] as the Countess Rosina Almaviva, and Dorotea Bussani[102] as Cherubino. The first performance of *Don Giovanni* in 1787 featured Teresa Saporiti[103] as Donna Anna – a role he gave the following year to Aloysia Weber for the Viennese premiere. For *Così fan tutte*, he presented Dorabella to a French-born and trained soprano, Louise Villeneuve, and Fiordiligi to an Italian, Adriana Ferrarese. *Die Zauberflöte* was notable at the time for being first performed by an entirely German-born cast. Anna Gottlieb sang as Pamina[104] and Barbara Gerl as Papagena. Mozart cast another sister-in-law, Josepha Weber, as the Queen of the Night.[105]

The "modernity" of Mozart's sopranos was forced upon them. For all their obvious brilliance (demonstrable pursuant to their casting by arguably the most complete musician in history) most had to re-learn their craft as theatrical singers when sublimating the self to Mozart. The only soprano not to return to school was

---

95 Most memorably, perhaps, the uninterrupted (and static) four bars of semi-breves (pitched as a G4), and the three bars of semi-breves (as C5s, running, without pause, into a further two and a half bars of unbroken G4s) towards the end of *"Martern aller arten."*

96 'Hell's vengeance boils in my heart.' From Act II, Scene 2.

97 The exception to this rule, and a number of others, is *La clemenza di Tito*, an *opera seria* commissioned by the impresario Domenico Guardasoni at the invitation of the Estates of Bohemia, who wanted a new work to celebrate the coronation of Leopold II, Holy Roman Emperor, as King of Bohemia. The entire cast at the first performance on 6 September, 1791 (a day under three months before his death) was Italian: Maria Marchetti-Fantozzi (Vitellia), Domenico Bedini (Sesto), Carolina Perini (Annio), and Antonina Campi (Servilia).

98 11 March, 1755 – 30 June, 1801. Born Katharina Magdalena Josepha Cavalier.

99 15 October, 1760 – 15 April, 1830.

100 27 October, 1765 – 24 August, 1817.

101 *Circa* 1760 – *circa* 1790.

102 1763 – after 1810. .

103 1763 – 17 March, 1869.

104 29 April, 1774 – 4 February, 1856.

105 1758 – 1819. At the time of the premiere, Josepha was married, and known professionally as Josepha Hofer.

Dorotea Bussani, because she made her professional debut, at the age of 23, as the first Cherubino.[106] In 1790, a correspondent for the *Grundsätze zur Theaterkritik* acclaimed Bussani for her "beautiful and charming chest voice," which she used with "humour and so mischievously."[107] In his memoirs, the petty and mean-spirited Da Ponte described her as[108]

> a vulgar woman of little merit, had purely by means of pulling faces and silly clowning, and perhaps by methods more theatrical still, built up a great following among cooks, ostlers, waiters, lackeys, and wig makers [...] and in consequence, was thought a gem.[109]

In his setting of the trousered Cherubino to music, and with Bussani in mind, Mozart painted a sympathetic portrait of a pageboy moving easily among servants and nobility, whose initial reticence yields to a confidence and sexual ambition that equip him to move on Susanna, the Countess and, eventually, Barbarina. In Act I, Scene 5, Cherubino sings "*Non so più cosa son, cosa faccio*,"[110] a patter-aria that compels crystalline diction, polar extremes of vocal colour and a steel-riveted technique. After being caught with the gardener's daughter (Barbarina), and having been banned by the Count from his home, Cherubino sees a ribbon belonging to the Countess, in exchange for which he presents Susanna with a song in homage to women, infatuation and love itself. The aria is "*agitate*," with a range from E flat 4 to G5. It begins with offbeat quavers in the strings, with muted violins (*con sordino*) that anticipate the breathlessness of Cherubino's feelings. Mozart's halting melody repeats the word "*desio*,"[111] using step-wise pitching to indicate the character's psychological and physical fluctuations ("*or di foco, ora sono di ghiaccio*").[112] The volatility is settled by the first-beat discipline of the second section, beginning "*Solo ai nomi d'amor, di diletto, mi si turba, mi s'altera il petto*."[113] Without varying the tempo, Mozart depicts Cherubino engaging with his feelings for "*ogni donna*,"[114] while utilising wide leaps in vocal registration to colour the character's newly-pubescent vivacity, as well as the range of Bussani's chest register.[115] Mozart achieves a perfected symmetry between singer, narrative, personality and emotion – a three-minute homage to newly-minted adolescence that is among the opera's most demanding arias for soprano.[116] Cherubino descends to poetics that employ banal, albeit sincere allusions to nature, after the

---

106   Her husband, the *basso buffo* Francesco Bussani joined her in the roles of Dr. Bartolo and Antonio.

107   Gonzalez, Erin (2019). *"Mozart's Mezzos": A Comparative Study Between Castrato and Female Roles in Mozart's Operas*. Ph.D thesis, Chapman University, p. 29.

108   Mozart disagreed. Four years after *Figaro*, he cast Bussani as Despina in *Così fan tutte*.

109   Bolt, Rodney (2006). *The Librettist of Venice*. Bloomsbury, p. 193.

110   'I don't know any longer what I am, what I'm doing.'

111   'Desire.'

112   'Now I'm burning, now I'm made of ice.'

113   'At the very word love or beloved, my heart leaps and pound.'

114   'Every woman.'

115   Cherubino is considered a mezzo-soprano role. Bussani later sang the role of Susanna also – although Mozart was not admiring of her interpretation. It appears, in any event, that Bussani's range reached further than that of a mezzo.

116   For those in doubt, it is this aria, more than any other, that is failed by singers in live performance.

satirical fashion of *Romeo and Juliet*; following a brief but surgically-accomplished lament that he is without an audience, the aria ends with an *allegro vivace* in which he confronts his isolation by deciding to talk of love to himself; in front of an audience. This wildly clever resolution employs a single bar of music to paint Cherubino as petulant as well as earnest, rounding a spectrum of instinct and feeling for which there was simply no model.

Mozart's engagement with authentic emotion, to which everyone could relate, transformed opera as well as the soprano. The women with whom he worked were collaborators, not personnel, and through the voices he created, on and off the stage, he became the unrecognised hero of a social revolution that was anticipated a century earlier by John Locke in his 1689 *Essay Concerning Human Understanding* and his 1693 treatise *Some Thoughts Concerning Education*. Mozart's mature operas glorified women as strong and virtuous, funny and clever, independent and powerful. They were the women who raised him, the women he loved, and the women without whom his voice would otherwise have remained inaudible. Just as Mozart's characters transcended the objectification of beauty and capacity as commodities of sexual and reproductive ordinance, so his singers were freed as women to challenge the prevailing social order, wherein women occupied a passive focus for the unfolding of events over which they had neither agency nor control. Mozart's women were not enlightened by education; rather, they abjured the stereotypes of patience, docility, and reasonableness for complex human sentiments that, in their embodiment, memorialised the capricious, the determined and the independent.

The first Viennese Donna Elvira,[117] Caterina Cavalieri, was trained (and seduced) by Antonio Salieri, who helped elevate her to the first rank of coloraturas. This brought her into direct competition with Aloysia Weber. Although Mozart sought to curry favour with Salieri when inviting Cavalieri to sing Konstanze in *Die Entführung*, her nomination as the Countess for the *Figaro* revival of 1789 reflected his genuine admiration – on which he acted when writing "*Dove sono*"[118] especially for her.[119] If there was any tension between Aloysia and Cavalieri then Mozart deflected it on 7 February, 1786 – three months before the premiere of *Figaro* on 1 May – when he cast the sopranos as rivals in a short, very funny comedy,[120] *Der Schauspieldirektor*.[121] The libretto was written by Mozart's poet for *Die Entführung*, Gottlieb Stephanie, an actual impresario who relied on personal experience when collaborating with Mozart in the creation of a satire on the staging of an opera.

The circumstances of *Schauspieldirektor's* origins read as if created by Tom Stoppard. Mozart and Stephanie submitted their work as an entry to a competition patronised by Joseph II, which pitted a singspiel (for presenting at one end of a room in the

---

117   *Don Giovanni.*

118   'Where am I?' from Act III, Scene 11.

119   Cavalieri is a nonspeaking role in Peter Shaffer's play *Amadeus*. When writing the script for Milos Forman's 1984 Oscar-winning film of the play, Shaffer included Cavalieri as a speaking role (played by Christine Ebersole, with Suzanne Murphy performing the sung music). The film suggests that Cavalieri and Mozart had an affair during rehearsals for *Die Entführung aus dem Serail*. There is no evidence for this dalliance, any more than there is evidence to support the suggestion by Alfred Einstein, in his 1945 book, *Mozart: His Character, His Work*, that Mozart had an affair with Nancy Storace.

120   Singspiel.

121   'The Impresario.'

Schönbrunn Palace) against an Italian opera buffa by Salieri (for presenting at the other end). Salieri's submission, *Prima la musica e poi le parole*,[122] is a masterpiece of its own, and 156 years later, Clemens Krauss and Richard Strauss created *Capriccio*, the most perfect art-musical comedy of the 20th century, in homage to Mozart and Salieri's reflections on music drama and the collaborative-creative process. The private premieres (for a dining audience of 80) were followed by three public performances, four days later, at the Kärntnertor in Vienna.

Der Schauspieldirektor is a parody of opera sopranos and their vanity – as evidenced by arguments over status and pay – that was completed in just two weeks for Vienna's leading prima donnas, both of whom were known to argue over status and pay. It is a testament to Mozart's charisma, talent and influence that he was able to persuade the Austro-Hungarian Empire's pre-eminent sopranos to commit to a work that might, in other hands, have resulted in humiliation. There are only four vocal solos, and the musical content accounts for half of the hour's running time; the sight and sound of sopranos singing of the nobility of art while trying to outdo each other with ever higher notes is an unadulterated joy, to which Strauss turned his own genius for the "nonsense" duet "*Addio, mia vita addio*" in *Capriccio*.[123]

Mozart's sensitivity to voice, and to singers, equipped him to tailor every role to its creator. Having gifted Aloysia Weber the Countess, he presented Cavalieri with Donna Elvira in *Don Giovanni* – a role that is considered to be less complicated than Rosina because she is seen (and played routinely) as deranged – in accordance with the Don's opinion in Act I that she is "*la povera ragazza, e pazza* [...]".[124] Her "madness" is rooted in her pursuit of Giovanni even after she discovers the truth of his wickedness as an adulterer, murderer and rapist.[125] In forming the untenable belief that he can be saved by true love, she is categorised as delusional or weak, even though her position is palpably more complicated. Elvira is an aristocrat, raised by a family with expectations to meet, and values to uphold. Her feelings of humiliation by the Don's seduction carry with them social and psychological baggage that cannot remain unpacked, save that her sense of self submits to the bromides of tolerance and tradition. Instead, Elvira vows revenge in her ferocious aria, "*Ah, chi mi dice mai*,"[126] after which she confronts the Don with the consequences of his actions. Her motives form less as vengeance than determination to bring him to honour through marriage to her. Mozart's subtle fostering of Elvira's motives posits ambiguities that leave audiences uncertain as to whether she is acting to protect women more vulnerable than herself, or to preserve him as her own. Her apparent delusion is informed by pride as well as faith, therefore – not in God, but in her own capacity to make good something that nature and nurture made bad. Mozart's music for Elvira can

---

122 'First the Music, then the Words.'
123 'Farewell life, farewell.'
124 '[...] the poor girl, and crazy [...].'
125 In his defence, he is (as far as the *libretto* allows) an *attempted* rapist only.
126 'Ah, who could ever tell me.' From Act I, Scene 6a. It is not always as ferocious as it might be. For example, when Lisa Della Casa sang the role for Furtwängler in Salzburg in 1954, the tempo adopted by the conductor is so slow that she might be taking names for a roll call. Della Casa makes a beautiful noise, as always, and her *legato* is beyond compare, but the aria drags horribly.

appear angular and clamorous, particularly *"Mi tradì quell'alma ingrata,"*[127] a rondo, in which her betrayal forms as abandonment, misery and a kind of hope – in the heroic (and Masonic) key of E flat – with a fugal orchestral accompaniment that Mozart varies with each of the aria's three parts. The perceived harshness of Elvira's music is a common fault of performers unable to reveal vulnerabilities to which etiquette and status prevent her from submitting. She is a survivor rather than a victim – a woman whose ultimate decision to "retreat" is her own.[128] Mozart venerates choice as emblematic of freedom, so that it's no coincidence Elvira's music as she sings *"Io men vado in un ritiro a finir la vita mia,"*[129] is the same as Zerlina's for the phrase *"Noi, Masetto, a casa andiamo, a cenar in compagnia!"*[130]

Mozart was raised by a mother who also loved her husband, notwithstanding an obsession with station and reputation that ensured there was no sacrifice not worth making by his wife. Based on their correspondence alone, it's obvious that Wolfgang learned from Leopold and Maria Anna that appearances mattered to those whose love was presumed to survive the privately experienced exigencies of weakness and fallibility. Men and women in the 21st century succumb no less often to violent and oppressive relationships, even if their social media accounts promote a rosier picture.[131] Mozart's portrayal of Elvira as an independent, proud but ultimately generic symbol for a woman's experience of fear in a patriarchal society speaks to the ages, whatever the online status. His sense of a "moral law within" represented all women – as *"donne d'ogni grado, d'ogni forma, d'ogni età."*

It is a bitter injustice that Mozart should be remembered as an artisan bound by servitude while Beethoven continues to be lionised for his dissent. It was Mozart's operas that first challenged the inviolability of social rank among musicians by the raising as narrative currency of spirit, character and ambition. In Mozart's philosophy, the poor and the female (as substrates of social and natural "inadequacy") could be noble in spirit, just as the noble-born could be mean, unkind and sadistic. The experience of love was transcendent for Mozart because it could be given and received without restraint, censure or boundary – a language, in and of itself, for which music could do nothing more than serve as an accompaniment. The ultimate expression of this article of faith was *Le nozze di Figaro*, in which Mozart's proto-feminism was developed not only for female characters, but also the male. Beyond the simple fact of the low-born Figaro triumphing as the hero, and with the Count's boorish behaviour causing his undoing, the most remarkable episode in this celebration of womanhood, the feminine, and the soprano begins with a man begging for forgiveness.

The facts require little rehearsal. Count Almaviva has lost his way, and fallen in lust with Susanna, his wife's chambermaid. Susanna is to be married to the Count's manservant, Figaro. Even though the Count has recently abolished the feudal *ius*

---

127 'That ungrateful soul betrayed me.' From Act II, Scene 13.

128 In another wretched (but accepted) translation, *"ritiro"* is presumed synonymous with a "convent" – and presented as such.

129 'I shall retreat, so to end my days.' From the Epilogue, Act II.

130 'We, Masetto, will go home to dine with friends!' *Ibid.*

131 Merely the best-known example of this contemporary appetite for dissembling and deceit is the murder of Gabby Petito by Brian Laundrie. They were online darlings until he strangled her to death and dumped her body before killing himself in a Floridian swamp in 2021.

primae noctis,[132] he wants Susanna for himself on her wedding night. His intentions are frustrated by the Countess, in collusion with Susanna. At her wedding dinner, Susanna passes a note to the Count, inviting him to a rendezvous – not realising that Susanna and the Countess have swapped clothes. The Count unwittingly sets about seducing his own wife. Now dressed as the Countess, Susanna pretends to be overcome by passion for Figaro – in earshot of the Count, whose rage draws the ensemble to the scene. As the Count curses his wife's perceived adultery, and as she begs (as Susanna) for forgiveness, the Countess reveals her identity – exposing her husband's deceit, and creating a heart-stopping moment in which the stage and the audience freeze while the Count considers his options.

What happens next is miraculous. The silence is interrupted by the Count, who sings "*Contessa, perdono! Perdono, perdono!*"[133] Mozart frames his petition as an ascending sixth, in a slowly rising gesture that mirrors the Count's dropping to his knees in enlightened supplication. When this physical gesture proves inadequate, Mozart has the Count repeat himself, twice more – forming an entreaty that extends the first syllable of "*perdono*" as a seventh, amplifying the force and sincerity of the Count's submission. The final rising shift, as between the second and third syllables, occupies a semitone, from A sharp to B natural, and then tails away into silence. It is a gesture in music that represents the choking of a voice that can say nothing more. The Countess also pauses before speaking; when finally she replies, "*Più docile sono, e dico di sì,*"[134] her phrasing is almost identical to that of her husband, save that the Countess begins on a G and rises a perfect fifth – evoking love, order and no small measure of control. This is her situation to manage, and she does it with Christ-like compassion, sufficient to soften the hardest of hearts. Again, Mozart has the Countess imitate her husband's repetition of "*perdono*" by having her repeat "*e dico di sì,*" using a downward slide from D to C, as if she is extending her hand to help lift her husband to his feet. First and second violins introduce a G-major chord, using a descending step-wise figure that heralds every member of the cast joining with the Countess' act of love, by repeating her melody and the words "*Ah, tutti saremo così.*"[135] Most English translations opt for something like 'all will be happy,' but that is not how the words read if treated literally. More accurate is "we will be like that," an ambition for a future in which men and women treat each other with respect and decency, no matter their origins or the foolishness of their behaviour. If Mozart was not actually envisioning a life beyond death, and the "heavens above," then his repetition of the words "*Saremo, saremo così*" operate as an appeal to humanity for the cultivation of a "moral law within," sufficient to ensure that love prevails in defiance of gender, class and culture. The scene survives as the most perfect in opera, an opinion shared by everyone from Beethoven, Schumann and Mendelssohn, to Wagner, Strauss and Schoenberg. It resonates for men and women in equivalence and as equals, and it

---

132   'Right of the first night.' Also known as *droit du seigneur* – although the French wording is applied improperly. Voltaire wrote a five-act comedy, *Le droit du seigneur or L'écueil du sage*, in 1762. It was first performed posthumously seven years before *Figaro*, in 1779.
133   'Countess, forgive me, forgive me, forgive me.' From Act IV, Scene 15c.
134   'I am kinder, and I say yes.' The Italian word "docile" is translated in numerous ways, but "docile" (as the English word) is a poor substitute.
135   'Ah, all is happy; we will be like that.'

captures the essence of Mozart's astonishing approach to the female voice and the place of women in music as well as society.

Even as he lay dying, the composer's ineffable, perfect mind turned at its last to the sound of a soprano. As Ignaz von Seyfried recalled in a letter written in 1840, Mozart whispered to Constanze:

> Quiet, quiet! Hofer is just taking her top F – now my sister-in-law is singing her second aria, "Der Hölle Rache;" how strongly she strikes and holds the B-flat: "Hört! hört! hört! der Mutter Schwur!"[136]

---

136 'Listen! listen! listen! The mother's oath!' Deutsch, Otto Erich (1965). *Mozart: A Documentary Biography*. Stanford University Press, p. 556.

CHAPTER NINE

Colouring by Numbers

The building of the Teatro di San Carlo in Naples is a tale of two Italies. The first was revealed during the theatre's inauguration on 4 November, 1737, when it was represented to be the world's most beautiful opera house. The architect, Giovanni Medrano, and the designer of the interior, Angelo Carasale, were lauded by the nobility, critics and audiences for the beauty of the building, and the clarity of its acoustics. In Chapter 4 of Book 1 of Alexandre Dumas' *Les Bourbons de Naples*,[1] he repeated the apocryphal story that Charles III was so impressed by the theatre that, shortly before a performance of *Achille in Sciro* by Domenico Sarro,[2] he presented Carasale to the audience in person. Having listed the theatre's many virtues, he lamented that the only thing missing was a private passageway connecting to the Royal Palace next door. After the performance, Carasale approached the king and announced that the passageway had been completed. The second slice of *Italiana* was served four years later, when Medrano and Carasale were discovered to have been defrauding the kingdom of large amounts of money set aside for the constuction of the opera house.[3] Both men were convicted and imprisoned in Sant' Elmo Castle on charges of embezzlement.[4]

The San Carlo was very large – and larger still after it was rebuilt in 1816.[5] The first theatre's stage was 28.6 meters deep, and 22.5 meters wide. The walls held 184 boxes, arranged in six orders, together with a royal box capable of accommodating up to ten guests. With standing-room included, it was possible to accommodate an audience of more than 3,500. Considering the repertoire of works and composers available in 1737, the San Carlo's size is incongruous today and wholly inexplicable for the time. By way of analogy, the Drottningholm Palace Theatre in Stockholm, which opened 17 years later, had few boxes and a seating capacity of only 400.[6] The proscenium arch measured only 8.2m, although the depth (at 17.4m) was enormous, for the purposes of creating visual illusions rather than an improving acoustic. Drottningholm's repertoire during the 1750s was dominated by the tastes of Sweden's Gustav III, who favoured Molière, Lully, Voltaire and Beaumarchais.[7] Although

---

1 Published in 7 volumes by Dumas' Italian newspaper, *L'Indipendente*.
2 The role of Achilles was created by Vittoria Tesi, "La Moretta".
3 The project's published budget was 75,000 ducats.
4 The records are unclear on whether Carasale considered another tunnel while resident in the castle.
5 It was destroyed by fire shortly after Rossini's arrival.
6 The building's dimensions were preserved when it was rebuilt after being burned down in 1762.
7 Gustav III saw Beaumarchais' *Figaro* twice during his visit to Paris in 1784. He loved the play and instructed that it be performed by the French troupe in Drottningholm. When Gustav learned that Da Ponte's libretto was in Italian, he understood why the Emperor Joseph had allowed it to be performed in

Drottningholm is now associated commonly with Mozart (thanks in part to Ingmar Bergman's 1975 film version of *Die Zauberflöte*),[8] the King's operatic preferences were limited exclusively to Gluck.

The majority of opera houses built during the 18th century aligned more obviously with Drottningholm than Naples. In Italy, theatre construction was a competitive art form, and the rivalry between cities and regions became positively medieval in its escalating vanities. Three years after the San Carlo cemented Naples' status as the capital of Italian opera, Turin established the Teatro Regio – with a stage 20m wide and 25m deep. In 1767, Mantua constructed the Teatro Bibiena (with a stage 17m by 25m); Milan followed suit in 1778 with La Scala – the stage of which (when first used) was larger, even, than San Carlo's, at 26m by 30m. Bergamo opened the Teatro Grande in 1791 (with seating for fewer than 1,500 and a comparatively small stage), and Venice erected the first of its Fenici a year later. The size of most of these theatres was counter-intuitive when considering the scale of the work being performed and the amplitude of all but a few of the voices performing it. By contrast, the Estates Theatre in Prague, which opened in 1783, was designed to accommodate 1,000 patrons, making it ideal for the first production of *Don Giovanni* in 1787 – with an orchestra numbering fewer than 40. Mozart's opera is frequently performed at the New York Metropolitan, which seats an audience of almost 4,000, with a stage 24m wide and 30m deep. The pit of the Metropolitan seats up to 110 players, using modern instruments, with metal strings, wide-bore brass, metal flutes and a significantly expanded percussion section.[9] When James Levine conducted Mozart's late works at the Met, his orchestra featured routinely as many as 80 players; Fritz Reiner's orchestra fielded 90. For the premiere of *Lohengrin* in Weimar, on the other hand, Liszt conducted an orchestra with 21 strings.[10]

Northern and central European tastes during the second half of the 18th century did not favour large orchestras. The availability of exceptional wind players from east of Vienna, and the evolving tradition of wind and brass playing throughout France, Germany and what would become the Austro-Hungarian Empire, allowed for a richer, more varied tone than was common throughout Italy, where violins and basses were preferred – particularly when accompanying voices. Differences in the approach to orchestra size and timbre were amplified during Haydn's concerts in London. For the Salomon series in 1791–3, he conducted an orchestra of around 40; four years later, when he wrote for (and accompanied) Brigida Banti, the composer was provided with an orchestra of more than 60. The common view, among critics and public alike, judged the ensemble in the later concerts to be ragged and heavy-handed; Haydn admitted to his diary that the "orchestra is larger this year, but just as mechanical as it was before, and indiscreet in its accompaniments."[11] These

---

Vienna. He was nonetheless advised that he'd not like the opera, delaying the arrival of Mozart's music by decades.

8   None of his operas was staged there until some years into the 19th century.

9   Chiefly for works by Wagner, Strauss, Puccini *etc.*

10   Brown, Clive (1992). "Performing Practice." In *Wagner in Performance*. Eds. Millington, Barry, and Spencer, Stewart. Yale University Press, p.100.

11   It's notable also that Anton Schindler wrote in Beethoven's Conversation Book, in 1824, that "Lichnowsky says that a smaller orchestra in the hall of the Theater an der Wein is more effective than a large one in the Redoutensaal."

were intimate events, necessarily so considering the size of the hall in the Hanover Rooms where, 15 years earlier, in April, 1776, Edward Piggot attended a concert performed by Carl Friedrich Abel, Johann Christian Bach and various guest artists, of whom he wrote in his diary:[12]

> [...] the others were Giardini, who plays on the Violin suprising [sic] well is Cramer; Crosdill on the Violoncello plays exceeding well, Fischer on the hautboy the same, all Capital performers, Savoi, Grassi & several others sang; Signora [sic] Grassi has a supprising [sic] voice being a tenor, which is very singular and I think disagreeable. In all about 22 musicians; this concert [hall] is reckoned the best in the world, every thing executed with the greatest taste and exactness; a very fine room 115 feet long 40 broad; it was almost full, every body Dressed; very elegantly painted; between the acts they go in another room underneath where you have tea; it is by subscription; it begins at 8 and ends at 10; every thing is elegant.[13]

It follows that around 20 musicians performed for 500 people in a room 35m by 12m[14] – a space *half* the size of San Carlo's *stage* after it was rebuilt in 1816.[15] The theatre's new proscenium arch spanned 33.5m by 30m,[16] and reached back a cavernous 34.5m. At 1,122 meters squared, this colossal footprint equated to a size greater than four tennis courts joined together – outspanning, even, the new Metropolitan Opera exactly 150 years later.[17] To add to the acoustical challenges, the San Carlo (like every other theatre or concert hall prior to 1783)[18] was lit by candles. This created problems for anyone seated or standing close to the stage – with already hampered visibility being made worse by smoke. The idealised impression created by Degas when he painted (from memory) a ballet scene from a production of *Robert*

---

12 The youngest of Johann Sebastien's eleven children.

13 Woodfield, Ian (2003). *Salomon and the Burneys: Private Patronage and a Public Career*. Ashgate Publishing. p.10.

14 The Hanover Rooms compare most obviously with the modern Wigmore Hall, also in London. This miraculous double-cube also seats around 500, and is the same width. It is 12m shorter, however, with a very small stage, suitable (comfortably) for a maximum of 10 musicians.

15 Because of evolving fire regulations, the San Carlo now seats around 1,500 people.

16 Again, for context, this is almost twice the size of the first Burgtheater (1741), which Joseph II identified as the "Deutsche Nationaltheater" in 1776. Mozart's *Die Entführung, Figaro* and *Così fan tutte* were all premiered at the Burgtheater. From 1794, the theatre was renamed the K. K. Hoftheater nächst der Burg. Beethoven's 1st Symphony was first performed there on 2 April, 1800. The theatre was relocated (and greatly expanded in scale) in 1888.

17 Built as part of the Lincoln Centre, and inaugurated in 1966.

18 This transformed opera during the 1850s by allowing the expansion in dramaturgical invention and stagecraft. Of course, the use of oil was unpopular with singers, because of the unpleasant smells, smoke and green-tinted light. The biggest change to stage lighting occurred in 1803, when Henry Drummond invented the limelight – a directional spotlight formed by the heating of a piece of lime by an oxygen and hydrogen flame. This device was popular at the Paris Opéra before (eventually) it made its way to Italy and the rest of Europe. Gas lighting emerged after 1830, most famously for an 1831 production (again in Paris) of Meyerbeer's *Robert Le Diable*.

Le Diable[19] would have been inconceivable to an audience from a century earlier.[20] The heat and the smell from the stalls was enough to cause the price of boxes to rise dramatically during the second half of the 18th century, at around the same time, conversely, that the work of *parfumiers* became affordable.[21] The limited visual field – for performers and audiences alike – was eclipsed by auditory demands that rendered many singers voiceless for all but the best seats in the house. Modern studies of the "formant" – a prominent spectrum-envelope (peaking near 3 kHz) common to singers of art music – has demonstrated the benefits of training, at least as far as amplitude, reach and "volume"[22] are concerned. The results of one recent study evidenced the startling difference in power and projection between singers performing popular song without training, and long-tutored singers specialising in opera.[23] Of course, conservatoire-voices in the 21st century have benefitted from more than 150 years of post-Wagnerian learning, and there is simply nothing to compare between voices at the turn of the 19th century and what would now be considered "an opera singer." Had Birgit Nilsson performed anything from the role of Donna Anna for Mozart prior to the premiere of *Don Giovanni* in 1787, he would likely have fled his rooms at Domgasse 5 with his hands over his ears.[24]

At a time when the tenor voice was some years distant from maturing as an instrument and a dramatic trope, female sopranos competed uniquely with castrati, baritones and, on rare occasions, basses. Albert Nouritt's celebrated spitting of his vocal cords – a landmark event, of consequence for sopranos as well as tenors[25] – had neither precedent nor comparator among sopranos, for whom technique was individuated and indistinguishable from speech, at least for students without access to a standardised method for study and performance. Some female singers were inevitably less vociferous than others; when having to account for the gallery, this shift in perspective resolved a criteria for value and analysis that owed little to art. The rebuilt San Carlo opened on 12 January, 1817, with a performance of Simon Mayr's *Il sogno di Partenope*. Stendhal attended the second night, of which he wrote: "There is nothing in all Europe, I won't say comparable to this theatre, but which gives the

---

19   1876. On display at the Victoria & Albert Museum, London.

20   See, generally, Cruz, Gabriela (2020). *Grand Illusion: Phantasmagoria in Nineteenth-century Opera.* Oxford University Press.

21   Thanks in no small part to the resurgence of the whaling industry. 17th and 18th century perfumes fell into two general categories: floral and musky. Floral scents of the time were made from flower oils or waters distilled from blooms, such as roses, orange flowers, and jasmine. Musks were base notes, animal-based and favoured by both sexes. Until some years into the 19th century, there was very little to distinguish between male and female perfumes. The contribution of the sperm whale industry to women's fashions (see, further, Chapter 10) also increased the availability of ambergris, a substance found inside the stomach of a whale that many identify (erroneously) as "whale vomit". It is nothing of the sort. Apart from anything else, it is expelled from the other end of the animal.

22   This is a largely meaningless term for singers. Some "big-voiced" sopranos are far less clear in their reach and projection than "light-voiced" singers; volume – in the sense that it might be controlled by a dial on an amplifier – is a lazy concept where acoustics are concerned.

23   Hunter, Eric J., Švec, Jan G., and Titze, Ingo R. (2006). "Comparison of the Produced and Perceived Voice Range Profiles in Untrained and Trained Classical Singers." *Journal of Voice.* 20(4), pp.513–526.

24   She recorded the role twice: in 1959 (with Leinsdorf, for RCA), and again in 1967 (with Böhm, for DG). Her success when singing Mozart is a matter of taste as well as judgment. See Chapter 14.

25   See Boyden, Matthew (2021). *The Tenor: a Cultural History.* Ragueneau Press, pp.48–70.

slightest idea of what it is like [...] it dazzles the eyes, it enraptures the soul..."[26] It was plainly also a nightmare for singers as well as audiences wanting to hear them. On 15 February, 1817, Louis Spohr held that

> there is no better place for ballet and pantomime. Military movements of infantry and cavalry, battles, and storms at sea can be represented here without falling into the ludicrous. But for opera, itself, the house is too large. Although the singers, Signora Isabella Colbran, and the Signori Nozzari, Benedetti, etc., have very strong voices, only their highest and most stentorian tones could be heard. Any kind of tender utterance was lost.

Many others visiting the rebuilt San Carlo were dismayed by the size of the stage and the auditorium; it's clear that similar sentiments formed among composers and performers. Haydn's frustration with "indiscreet accompaniments" coincided with Stendhal's regret for the loss of "tender utterances" – opinions best summarised as critical of an unwelcome increase in amplitude. Whether by necessity (as in the largest theatres) or because of changes in taste (as it was evolving in Paris after 1805), the effect on voices, and the voices of women in particular, was transformative. In Naples, San Carlo's scale compelled sopranos to push themselves in repertoire that gained nothing from it. Paisiello wrote almost 100 operas,[27] none of them for the San Carlo – even if that was the venue for their first performance.[28] His lightly-orchestrated work was better suited to Naples' chamber theatres, like the dei Fiorentini, the Bellini, the Nuovo – and Vienna's Burgtheater, where *Il re Teodoro in Venezia*[29] was premiered in 1784. They are tuneful, infrequently inventive, and written for singers whose voices could not have filled a theatre with 3,500 patrons. This was as true for Anna Davia de Bernucci,[30] (creator of Rosina for Paisiello's *Il barbiere di Siviglia*)[31] as for those castrati to whom Paisiello remained loyal throughout his career[32] (chiefly Gasparo Pacchierotti).[33]

As the most popular Italian composer during the last 20 years of the century, Paisiello fed and enabled a culture of vocal celebrity that was antithetical to the

---

26 See generally Maffei, Luigi; Iannace, Gino; Ianniello, Carmine; Romano, Rosario (1998). The Acoustics of the Italian Opera House "Teatro di San Carlo" in Naples, Italy. *Acoustical Society of America*.

27 Many are still unpublished.

28 The following operas were premiered at the San Carlo: *Antigono* (1785), *Olimpiade* (1785), *Pirro* (1787), *Giunone e Lucina* (1787), *Fedra* (1788), *Catone in Utica* (1789), *Zenobia in Palmira* (1790), *Elfrida* (1792) *Elvira* (1794), *Didone abbandonata* ('Dido Abandoned') (1794), *Andromaca* (1797), *Elisa* (1807), and *I pittagorici* (1808).

29 'King Theodore in Venice.'

30 16 October, 1743 – 1810.

31 'The Barber of Seville' (1782). There were many settings of Beaumarchais' *Le Barbier de Séville* prior to Rossini's; Paisiello's version remained the most popular for a number of years, even after the tumultuous premiere of Rossini's opera in 1816.

32 Other operas by Paisiello with leading roles for castrati are *Catone in Utica, Antigono* and *Demetrio*.

33 21 May, 1740 – 28 October, 1821. On 16 May, 1792, Pacchierotti created the leading role of Alceo in Paisiello's *I giuochi d'Agrigento* ('The Games of Agrigento'), alongside Brigida Banti for the inauguration of La Fenice in Venice.

ambition of his contemporary Mozart.[34] Paisiello's aria, "*Destrier che all'armi usato*,"[35] from *Alessandro nell'Indie*,[36] is the sum of its parts, all of them adhering to a series of roulades formed around an unchanging retracted vowel,[37] through which not even the finest soprano would be able to reveal feeling or incident. It is an empty vessel for singers more interested in the sound of their own voices than anything attendant to the psychological penetration to which Mozart was aspiring with Da Ponte. Mozart also diverged with Paisiello through his aversion to (and eventual abandonment of) the castrati – an instinct that aligned with his distaste for self-serving virtuosity.[38] A putatively Lutheran[39] predilection for vocal restraint prevented Mozart's operas from traversing the Alps, at least initially;[40] there were other reasons for his slow progress in Italy. *Die Entführung aus dem Serail* had threatened to undermine the Italian school in northern Europe, a suspicion confirmed by *Figaro*, which was Italian only in the language of its libretto. It might now seem like sacrilege, but when finally Mozart's operas were staged in Italy they were subjected to a range of abuses that included the addition of arias from other works – by Mozart and others. In 1824, for example., the *Rivista teatrale* complained that a recent performance at the Teatro Nuovo in Naples had mutilated *Don Giovanni* because of the number of interpolations – all of them designed to advantage the "art" of the singers.[41]

Nationalist prejudice was amplified by the complexity of Mozart's musical and dramatic language; the physical demands of his orchestrations were as challenging as the restrictions he placed on his singers. This left Italy in happy service to an

---

34   Mozart and Paisiello first met in Naples in May or June, 1770, and again in Turin in January the following year. 14 years later, they were reintroduced in Vienna – where Paisiello was preparing the premiere of *Il re Teodoro in Venezia*. On 9 June, 1784, Mozart wrote to his father: "Tomorrow Herr Ployer, the agent, is giving a concert in the country at Döbling, where Fräulein Babette [Ployer] is playing her new concerto in G [K453] and I am performing the quintet [K452]; we are then playing together the grand sonata for two pianos [K448]. I am fetching Paisiello in my carriage, as I want him to hear both my pupil and my compositions."

35   'Destrier who weapons used.'

36   'Alexander in the Indies.'

37   In this case, "ah."

38   The coloratura in *Die Zauberflöte* is for comic as well as dramatic effect; because Mozart wrote out every note it's obvious his indulgence of display was a nod towards his sister-in-law rather than a concession to popular taste. an inclination appreciated by Beethoven, whose admiration for *Figaro* and *Don Giovanni* as pure music was levelled by his dismissal of the plots and the libretti as frivolous and debauched. On the other hand, when asked to name his favourite of his own operas, Rossini's stock answer was "Don Giovanni."

39   Insofar as restraint and self-rule was a direct legacy of Luther's intellectual declaration of independence from the Catholic Church.

40   La Scala secured the Italian premiere of *Don Giovanni* in 1814, and *Figaro* in 1815 – almost 25 years after Mozart's death.

41   In his *Mémoires*, Berlioz recalled these dark ages and castigated those "charming monsters" who enabled Mozart's "bastard works" and the "gradual degradation of style, the destruction of all sense of expression, the neglect of dramatic proprieties, the contempt for the true, the grand and the beautiful, and the cynicism and decrepitude of art." Berlioz, Hector (1966). *Memoirs of Hector Berlioz*. Trans. and Annotated by Newman, Ernest Newman (1966), Dover Publications. p. 372. On the subject of interpolations, see Poriss, Hilary (2001). "Making Their Way Through the World: Italian One-Hit Wonders." *19th-century Music*, 24, pp. 197–224, and the same author's (2001) "A Madwoman's Choice: Aria Substitution in Lucia di Lammermoor," *Cambridge Opera Journal*, 13, pp. 1–28.

operatic caste system that favoured and rewarded singers as superior to composers. No-one remembers the stage works of Anfossi, Sacchini, Curcio, Borghi, Insanguine, Bertoni, Tozzi, Fischetti, Rauzzini or Bianchi; they were nonetheless among the first rank during the final third of the 18th century. Even Paisiello's popularity overreached his influence, and it fell briefly to a German to become Italy's foremost musician – albeit for reasons unconnected with his many stage works. Johannes (Simone) Mayr is buried in Bergamo's idiotically vulgar Santa Maria Maggiore, alongside his most celebrated pupil, and one of Italy's supreme composers of opera, Gaetano Donizetti. Mayr was responsible also for introducing Beethoven's music to Italian audiences during the composer's lifetime, and while his own work is now forgotten, Mayr's greatest success, *Medea in Corinto*,[42] remains notable because of its libretto by a then-unknown writer, Felice Romani,[43] and for Mayr's gifting of the title role to a local soprano,[44] Isabella Colbran,[45] and because of the effect the Act I aria, "*Sommi dei, che I giuramenti*,"[46] had on a young composer from Pesaro called Gioachino[47] Rossini.

This *spumoni napoletano*,[48] of librettist, composer and soprano, was managed, manipulated and monopolised by the impresario and creator of the *Barbaiata*,[49] Domenico Barbaja.[50] Musical theatre had always been expensive, and never profitable; it was an indulgence savoured by monarchies, the aristocracy and family enterprises. The cost, hassle and difficulty of maintaining a major venue for regular productions of opera became a problem only when it needed to be funded by ticket sales, or some other source of revenue. Barbaja knew nothing of music, caring little for the noise it made; he had a rare talent for making money, however. When his aptitude for the pecuniary collided with Rossini's genius for melody, their partnership turned opera into a business that, in turn, transformed the art as well as the voices that sang it.

---

42   'Medea in Corinth' (1813).

43   The most important and influential Italian librettist between Metastasio and Boito, he worked closely with Rossini (*Il turco in Italia*, *Bianca e Falliero*, and *Aureliano in Palmira*), Bellini (*Il pirata*, *La straniera*, *Zaira*, *I Capuleti e i Montecchi*, *La sonnambula*, *Norma* and *Beatrice di Tenda*), and Donizetti (*Anna Bolena* and *L'elisir d'amore*).

44   It's probable Colbran would now be defined a mezzo-soprano with an unusually high extension, to a high F.

45   2 February, 1785 – 7 October, 1845.

46   Act I, Scene 7. 'Sum of the oaths.'

47   The Italian variant of 'Joachim.'

48   The likely origins of "Neapolitan" ice-cream, a trio of flavours and colours formed as a "*tricolore*" in (ultimate) homage to the Italian flag, the origins of which date to 7 January, 1797, when the first red, white and green national flag of a sovereign Italian state was adopted by the Fourteenth Parliament of the Cispadane Republic. See Palmer, R. R. (2014). *The Age of the Democratic Revolution: a Political History of Europe and America, 1760–1800*. Princeton Classics.

49   Having begun his working life as a waiter in Milan, Barbaja made his name as the operator of a café, where he was the first (or so he claimed) to serve a rich hot chocolate drink topped with whipped cream – the *Barbaiata* (also "*Barbajada*"). Purists consider the *Barbaiata* to be chocolate and cream, in isolation. Many others claim the *Barbaiata* to be a form of *Bicerin*, with coffee included. It is also claimed that the *Barbaiata* was nothing more than a *cappuccino* – a coffee mixed with frothy milk. See Eisenbeiss, Philip (2013). Bel Canto *Bully: The Life of the Legendary Opera Impresario Domenico Barbaja*. Haus Publishing, p.14.

50   Also "Barbaia."

Barbaja's achievement over three-decades, as the *sine qua non* of *impresari*, involved him promoting a different kind of house to a different kind of audience. The San Carlo was subsidised to a limited extent by the Bourbons, but the running costs were punishing even for a royal family, which is why the majority of opera houses in Italy traded coincidentally as casinos. Unlike the Protestant Church,[51] the Catholic view of gambling was accommodating – except when the indulgence was deemed inconsistent with duty. Barbaja was not a mobster, at least *avant la letter*; even so, he adhered by nature and through his business practices to what would become synonymous with the *Camorra* of Naples and the Mafia of New Orleans, New York and Las Vegas. The first recorded use of the word "*camorra*" dates from 1735, when a royal decree authorised the establishment of eight gambling houses in Naples.[52] The earliest official mention of the *Camorra* as an organisation dates from 1820, in a police file referencing the organisation's first written statute, the *frieno*. Barbaja was in the right place at the right time for his value to be considered useful. He was renowned for his success during the first five years of the 19th century when operating the gambling concession at La Scala, where he was the first to introduce roulette. When relocating to Naples in 1806 (without his wife and children), Barbaja made a substantial contribution to the *Camorra's* provision of stability after the Parthenopean Republic was established in 1799, in the wake of the French Revolution and the Bourbon Restoration. Nature abhors a vacuum, and Barbaja and the *Camorra* counteracted the temporary loss of order in a city long-renowned for its challenging conditions. According to Pasquale Peluso, Naples was

> infamous for its utter disorder, images of extreme poverty, merry making and filth. Street vendors hawked a variety of merchandise. Street urchins in rags roamed about, specializing in the theft of handkerchiefs. All Neapolitan people competed in an atmosphere of the unwashed. It was among this multitude that the "Bella Società Riformata" found its opportunities. The streets of Naples contained men who invited gullible passers-by from the provinces to try their hand at games of chance. By tradition, these open-air gambling operations were "protected" by the Camorristi. They took their twenty-percent off the top. The gamblers had cheerful demeanors; they accepted without complaint paying the price to remain in business and not be hassled by anyone.[53]

---

51 Protestant churches forbidding or condemning gambling do so without being able to cite anything *en point* from scripture. The routine scraping of the Bible for arguments against gambling include generic assaults on covetousness and greed ("which is idolatry" according to Colossians 3:5) and a neck-snapping reliance on the 1st, 2nd and 10th commandments. Many refer to Matthew 6:24, a casuistic injunction by Christ that condemns every church's bank and accountancy firm in tandem with the more obvious sins perpetuated by mafia-operated casinos.

52 The word is likely a portmanteau of "*capo*" ('boss' or 'head') and the name of an ancient Italian street game, "*morra.*" The game of *morra* dates back thousands of years to ancient Roman. Each player simultaneously reveals their hand, extending any number of fingers, and calls out a number. Any player who guesses correctly the total number of fingers revealed by all players combined scores a point. Morra was used to decide issues, equivalent to the tossing of a coin.

53 Peluso, Pasquale (2013). "The Roots of the Organized Criminal Underworld in Campania. *Sociology and Anthropology*, pp.118–134; p.120.

Whether Barbaja was formally a member of the *Camorra* matters less than that he could not have rebuilt the San Carlo in under a year[54] or operated casinos in Naples without their active support. The *Camorristi* generated a barbarous kind of order during the political upheaval, which was confronted administratively by the introduction of the *Code Napoléon* – an extraordinary innovation that forced radical social and economic changes on a community that had operated feudally for more than a millennium. This should have qualified as bad timing for the *Camorra* and the casino operators; Gioachino Murat[55] was a practical man, however, and his promotion of Napoléon's social contract did nothing to impede the common pursuit of money, by almost any means. Reform was controversial and messy, but the institution of a civil service based on merit, that allowed modest citizens to advance and to profit no matter their origins, fostered an economic middle-class while introducing a host of changes for women that recognised an unprecedented compass of rights, notwithstanding the Code's otherwise predictable adherence to Rousseau's conviction that women were inferior to men. Feminism was still without a name; the rights of women were acknowledged to be consequential, however, across a panoply of institutions and structures. If Barbaja was no feminist then he was sufficiently pragmatic to understand that an opera house's provision of popular entertainment required new work as well as women able to sing it. Barbaja invited Rossini to serve as musical director and composer for the theatres of Naples while allowing him the option of writing simultaneously for other houses in Italy. Rossini was being presented in his twenties with security, prestige and unprecedented resources, the sum of which provided him with the chance to experiment and innovate as a composer while gaining coincidentally from a guaranteed percentage of profits from the casinos.

Barbaja acquired the management of the San Carlo in 1809, three years after he first took control of the gaming tables. By the time he invited Rossini to become Naples' resident composer, in 1815, Barbaja was already extravagantly wealthy. His private collection of paintings included works by Dürer, Caravaggio and Titian, some of which he kept at a house on the island of Ischia and a grand beach-front villa in the village of Mergellina; his primary residence was a vast palazzo in Naples (now named Palazzo Barbaja) on via Toledo, which is today identified as having been "*residenza di Giachino Rossini 1815 -22.*" Rossini secured Barbaja's future by creating operas that spoke to the people on whose money gaming businesses were dependent. In precisely the same way that hotels and casinos in Las Vegas now provide musical and theatrical spectacles to entice casual gamblers, the San Carlo operated as a novelty for patrons uninterested in mythological *opera seria* featuring gods and goddesses trading in encomiums for the classically educated. If opera was to succeed as an adjunct to the roulette wheel then Barbaja had to be certain that the house would never lose. It is for this reason that his offer to Rossini of a seven season contract, obligating the composer to produce two operas a year, was almost diabolically prescient. As things

---

54   He achieved this in less than ten months. As anyone who has lived in Italy for any length of time will testify, getting anything done in ten months or less, excepting the birth of a child, necessitates divine intervention or organised crime.

55   Born Joachim Murat. He was Napoleon's brother-in-law, the 1st Prince Murat, Grand Duke of Berg, and King of Naples (as Joachim-Napoleon), from 1808 to 1815.

turned out, Rossini ended up completing ten works (nine of them serious, one of them comic), over a period of eight years:[56]

Elisabetta regina d'Inghilterra;[57]
La gazetta;[58]
Otello;[59]
Armida;[60]
Mose in Egitto;[61]
Ricciardo e Zoraide;[62]
Ermione;[63]
La donna del lago;[64]
Maometto II;[65]
Zelmira.[66]

In addition, and during the same time-period, Rossini composed:

Torvaldo e Dorliska;[67]
Il barbiere di Siviglia;[68]
La Cenerentola;[69]
La gazza ladra;[70]
Adelaide di Borgogna;[71]
Eduardo e Cristina;[72]
Bianca e Falliero;[73]
Mathilde de Shabran;[74]
Semiramide.[75]

At least seven of these 19 operas number among the finest in the repertoire – without accounting for the three masterpieces Rossini produced before his relocation to

---

56 All premieres at the Teatro San Carlo, unless otherwise stated.
57 'Elizabeth, Queen of England.' First performed on 4 October, 1815.
58 First performed on 26 September, 1816, at the Teatro de Fiorentini, Naples.
59 First performed on 4 December, 1816, at the Teatro del Fondo, Naples.
60 First performed on 11 November, 1817.
61 'Moses in Egypt.' First performed on 5 March, 1818.
62 First performed on 3 December, 1818.
63 First performed on 27 March, 1819.
64 'The Lady of the Lake.' First performed on 24 October, 1819.
65 First performed on 3 December, 1820.
66 First performed on 16 February, 1822.
67 First performed on 26 December, 1815, in Rome
68 'The Barber of Seville.' First performed on 20 February, 1816, in Rome.
69 'Cinderella.' First performed on 25 January, 1817, in Rome.
70 'The Silken Ladder.' First performed on 31 May, 1817, in Milan.
71 First performed on 27 December, 1817, in Rome.
72 First performed on 24 April, 1819, in Venice.
73 First performed on 26 December, 1819 at La Scala, Milan.
74 First performed on 24 February, 1821, in Rome.
75 First performed on 3 February, 1823, in Venice. This was Rossini's last opera for an Italian theatre.

Naples: *Tancredi*,[76] *L'italiana in Algeri*[77] and *Il turco in Italia*.[78] Of the ten Neapolitan operas, all but one of them was written for the same soprano: Isabella Colbran. Born in Madrid, to a family of musicians, Colbran studied as a teenager in Paris with the castrato Girolamo Crescentini. His predictably gruelling regime equipped her to begin performing at an absurdly young age, so that she was able to make her theatrical debut in Paris in 1801 – when she was 16 years of age. She was famous before her 21st birthday.

Colbran was only 22 when Rossini met her for the first time, as a newly-pubescent 15-year-old student, after hearing her city-debut in Bologna in 1807. Rossini was happy to take advantage of her celebrity, beauty and talent when presenting her with *Elisabetta regina d'Inghilterra*, his Neapolitan premiere – and the prototype of Italian "history" opera. Rossini's first work for the San Carlo proved to be his last, at least for the original theatre, which burned to the ground on 13 February, 1816, while he was in Rome overseeing the premiere (seven days later) of *Il barbiere di Siviglia*.[79] Just as Barbaja re-used the façade and the walls of the old opera house when building its replacement, so Rossini recycled some of Elisabetta's music for *Il barbiere*, notably Rosina's aria "*Una voce poco fa.*"[80] On returning to Naples, Rossini discovered he had no theatre in which to present his latest work, *La gazzetta, ossia Il matrimonio per concorso*,[81] which was staged instead at the dei Fiorentini. Rossini's second Neapolitan opera was much anticipated by the newly crowned Ferdinand IV, and by a fledgling media wrestling with the impositions of Robespierre's paranoid conception of journalism as "the heart of the discord that [...] engulfed the revolutionary movement."[82] Post-revolutionary thinking was less rabid in France; in Naples, the press was condemned officially as perfidious and invasive; impotent and frivolous. Robespierre's shadow was long and suffocating:[83]

> What is our aim? It is the use of the Constitution for the benefit of the people. Who is likely to oppose us? The rich and the corrupt. What methods will they employ? Slander and hypocrisy. What factors will encourage the use of such means? The ignorance of the sans-culottes. The people must therefore be instructed. What are the obstacles to their

---

76 First performed on 6 February, 1813, in Venice.

77 First performed on 22 May, 1813, in Venice.

78 First performed on 14 August, 1814, in Venice.

79 At the Teatro Argentina.

80 'A voice a while ago…'

81 'The Newspaper, or The Marriage Competition.'

82 Pettegree, Andrew (2014). *The Invention of News: How the World Came to Know About Itself*. Yale University Press, pp.339–340.

83 It is nonetheless *du jour* for post-Trump America, where many will recognise the "public accuser's" invitation to the Committee of Public Safety to punish "treacherous journalists who are the most dangerous enemies of liberty:" The United States was not especially enlightened, even after breaking with the tyranny of the English. John Adams forced through the Sedition Act, which made it a crime for American citizens to "print, utter, or publish [...] any false, scandalous, and malicious writing" about the Federal government. This was allowed to lapse by Thomas Jefferson, who paid for it when the interested parties that had backed Adams employed their First Amendment rights as press barons, editors and journalists to assault the President's reputation on a daily basis.

enlightenment? The paid journalists who mislead the people every day by shameless distortions. What conclusion follows? That we ought to proscribe these writers as the most dangerous enemies of the country, and to circulate an abundance of good literature.[84]

When summarising the 20-year-old Rossini's *La pietra del paragone*[85] for his *Vie de Rossini*,[86] first published in 1824, Stendhal delighted in railing against the Italian press:

> Among the swarm of parasites and flatterers of all sorts and species who swarm and buzz about the count's domain, the librettist has given place of honour to one don Marforio, the local journalist. In France, there are no finer intellects in all the land than those upon whom devolves the daily responsibility of addressing us through the newspapers; but in Italy, the case is very different […]. The absurdity of such characters, whose existence would be almost inconceivable in France, thanks to the comparative (if limited) freedom of the press which we enjoy, is common enough to meet with in Italy, where newspapers are subjected to a censorship of intolerable severity, and where governments think nothing of flinging into gaol a dozen or more poor gossips, whose only crime was to have sat in a coffee-house bandying about some insignificant snippet of local news — nor of keeping them there indefinitely, until one by one they choose to confess the source of their criminal information, which, more often than not, is nothing but the dullest item of libellous invention.[87]

Rossini's *La gazzetta* was tolerated as a comedy – his only *opera buffa* for Naples, and alone among his works for the city in not being written for Colbran, whose nature, instincts and stature were better suited to drama. Giuseppe Palomba's libretto, after Goldoni's *Il matrimonio per concorso*, is a biting and extremely funny satire on the influence of newspapers, which were as riddled with gossip, intrigue and scandal as the lives of the rich and famous on whom they fixated. By 1816, this included Rossini and Colbran *in flagrante privato*,[88] which made the text a fitting subject for Rossini – who created the score using almost 50% recycled material. Colbran's allure was a fixation for journalists in the city, and no-one begrudged the composer falling in love with the prima donna – not even Barbaja, who conceded his loss without complaint because it threatened no harm to his earnings. The impresario's priorities were pragmatic and financial, and he used the press in whatever way best served his commercial interests – a broad church that included, where necessary, the emerging praxis of

---

84 *Ibid.*
85 'The Touchstone' (1812).
86 'Life of Rossini' (1824).
87 Stendhal (1824). *Life of Rossini.* Trans, and Annotated by Coe, Richard N. (1985). John Calder, p.87.
88 They married on 15 March, 1822 – after Rossini had broken with Barbaja, and while they were *en route* to Vienna.

Italian nationalism. Although Rossini would be late to this particular party,[89] submitting fully to the *Risorgimento* only in 1829,[90] and then from his mansion in Paris, the same was true of many others given to fearing censorship. It was true of immigrants and visitors as well as natives. Orest Kiprensky's 1829–30 painting, "Newspaper readers in Naples," portrayed four young men in close proximity, one of whom is reading to the others. It has been suggested that Kiprensky was commenting on the state and condition of life for Polish immigrants in Italy; the background to the painting shows an active Vesuvius, however, the meaning of which speaks more directly to the native shift in local dynamics.[91] The grouping of the image owes a pronounced debt to Caravaggio's *The Incredulity of Saint Thomas*, in which the apostles Peter and John observe "the way, the truth, and the life"[92] being tested through Thomas' physical interaction with the risen Christ. The parallels are obvious, insofar as the press was perceived to be as revolutionary and life-changing as Jesus' resurrection. The audience painted by Kiprensky is neutral, at best, but the focus of concentration is sufficient to allow for the metaphorical alignment between religion and journalism as comparable forces for change.

Most of the serious printed commentary on Rossini during his years in Naples attached itself to matters of style and genre. This had been a theme of the earliest critical evaluations of his work in the north of the country. After the 1812 premiere of *La pietra del paragone*, for example, the *Corriere delle dame* asserted that

> close observers find that this work contains a few pieces that exhibit too
> much gravity, passion, and seriousness; which, they say, is unsuitable for
> a comic opera […] if the play is a comedy, and if in a comedy it is not
> inappropriate to insert pathetic and heartfelt expressions and sublime
> language in between humorous scenes, it should not be out of place for
> a librettist to do the same in a comic opera: therefore, the composer will
> have to try and match his music to the spirit of the words."

In his essay "On the Differences and Moral Characters of Styles and on Musical Language,"[93] published by *Antologia*, Giuseppe Carpani complained that "Rossini's music belongs to no genre," and that his operas "being always the same in […] accompaniments […] are similar in both the serious and the comic." The composer was attacked for making "indistinct use of the same colours, of the same phrases, and of exactly identical moves and steps and modes in every manner of composition, confusing genres and styles."[94] Carpani questioned Rossini's ability to express precise concepts and ideas, as a critic who had almost certainly been advantaged by gaining

---

89 It is conceded that some of his works dance around the handbag of nationalism, notably *L'Italiana in Algeri*, the final aria of which, "*Pensa alla Patria*," is a peon to country that would later become an anthem for the *Risorgimenti*. See further below.

90 With the first performance of *Guillaume Tell*.

91 Vesuvius was active around this time only in 1822 and 1834 – some years before and after Kiprensky completed his painting.

92 John 14:6.

93 *Ibid.*

94 *Ibid.*

access to Mozart's scores. Much of the initial hostility among local critics was the product of a sense of duty to defend long-established composers in Naples from the onslaught of a definitively northern influence. When finally Rossini's talent won the day it did so after the premiere of *Ricciardo e Zoraide* in 1818, after the *Giornale delle due Sicilie*,[95] Naples' official daily newspaper, published a letter from Cimarosa extolling Rossini as the saviour of Italian opera.[96] This landmark event made its way across Europe, and eventually to Britain, where "The Quarterly Musical Magazine and Review" reported "On the actual state of music in Naples" that:

> It was then that the famous epistle of Cimarosa appeared, posted from the Elysian fields, which elevated Rossini's music to the skies, and ranked him amongst the greatest geniuses that Italy could boast. The interpreter of love, Paisiello, the tender and impassioned Piccini, exclaimed with delight on seeing this work, and applauded it before the Gods.[97]

Ricciardo e Zoraide is a simple work, which Rossini composed primarily for three of Naples' star tenors, Andrea Nozzari, Giovanni David and Giuseppe Ciccimarra; Colbran's performance as Zoraide was cheered to the gods, however, as was the opera – in stark contrast to the choleric backlash earned the following year by *La donna del lago*. Rossini settled on Walter Scott's narrative poem, The Lady of the Lake, after Spontini withdrew from a commitment to write two works for the San Carlo. Inspired by his rival's embarrassment,[98] Rossini created a complex,[99] inventive and thrilling work, for which he threw the kitchen into the pit, prescribing two flutes, two oboes, two clarinets, two bassoons, two trumpets, two horns, three trombones, harp, timpani, bass drum, a large string orchestra and a chorus. The premiere in September, 1819, was avowedly Neapolitan, with Colbran as Elena, Benedetta Pisaroni[100] in the *travesti* role of Malcolm, and Giovanni David as Uberto. In the royal court's absence, the gallery aimed low and with agrarian malice. Booing, whistling and jeering were directed at the composer and his cast throughout both acts – even during and after the finale of Act 1, which is among the most exhilarating of any of his operas. Only with Colbran's spectacular rondo finale, "*Tanti affetti*,"[101] did the audience concede the genius of all concerned. In a typically bi-polar reversal of fortune, Colbran was called onto stage more than two dozen times, which led to Rossini being summoned

---

95   'The Paper of the Two Sicilies.'

96   Jacobshagen, Arnold (2022). "Reimagining Rossini" in *Obituaries as Transnational Narratives of Italian Opera*. Edited by Körner, Axel and Kühl, Paulo M. Cambridge University Press, pp.147–166.

97   Volume XXXVII. p.40.

98   The rivalry was Spontini's, who detested the younger composer's success. According to Heine, after a statue of Rossini was unveiled at the Paris Opéra, Spontini purposefully "bumped himself against it. Our Meyerbeer is much more wary: invariably he takes the precaution to avoid encountering this statue, or tries to avert his eyes, just as the Jews of Rome, even if they are in a hurry, always take a long detour so as not to pass near the Arch of Titus, erected in memory of the destruction of Jerusalem." Weinstock, Herbert (1968). *Rossini*. Oxford University Press, p.146.

99   The plot is absurdly complicated; some might say muddled, which explained (in part) the audience's animosity.

100   6 May, 1793 – 6 August, 1872.

101   'Many affections.'

in tandem; he didn't appear because he had already left Naples for Milan. The hostility of the press was countered by its reverence for Colbran's artistry, and this led to the opera becoming a fixture of the San Carlo's diary. It was soon after performed in Paris, Berlin and London (in February, 1823), New Orleans and New York.[102]

Colbran remained in Naples, but her reputation as the "mother" of Rossini's operas travelled with his work; as such, she can be considered the first soprano to become known internationally while remaining a localised phenomenon. It's hard to imagine what performances of Rossini's eternally challenging character-coloratura must have sounded like when performed by sopranos not raised on his music. Although Rossini rarely notated his vocal embellishments, at least at this stage in his career, one can easily conjure the reaction of neophytic sopranos when having to acclimatise to a score like *La donna del lago*, with numerous scenes as long as Mozart's "*Martern aller arten*," an entirely novel range of colour and character, and a much larger orchestra and chorus with which to compete. The admiration earned globally by Colbran as her husband's muse dissipated abruptly in Naples between the premieres of *Maometto II* and *Zelmira*, when it appears the cost of meeting Rossini's demands was paid for with her voice.

Stendhal's biography was published two years into Rossini and Colbran's marriage; there is much in it with which its subject will have been pleased – chiefly the prominent sense that Rossini was the "new Mozart"[103] and otherwise beyond comparison with anyone else.[104] Subsequent biographers have, of course, deviated with many of the facts and much of the commentary; in general terms; the book is nonetheless accepted broadly to be "truthful." It is difficult in consequence to read Stendhal's hateful observations of Isabella Colbran, to whom he committed a single substantive paragraph.[105] It's worth repeating (almost) in full:[106]

> Signorina Colbran [...] amused herself by making a fool of him all day long, and consequently had him exactly where she wanted him. Signorina Colbran, who is to-day Signora Rossini was between 1806 and 1815 one of the most celebrated sopranos in all Europe. In 1815, however, she began to "suffer from a strained voice," an affliction which, in singers of lesser distinction, would have been vulgarly termed singing off key. From 1816 to 1822, Signorina Colbran revealed a marked tendency to sing either above or below the required pitch, and her singing became what (in inferior mortals) would certainly have been termed execrable; but God forbid that one should have suggested anything of the kind in Naples! In spite of this minor indisposition, however, Signorina Colbran retained her position as prima donna at the San-Carlo theatre, and was invariably

---

102   In many cases, Rossini's operas made their way around the globe in a matter of months, where Mozart's were delayed commonly for decades.

103   An opinion he felt entitled, having written his *Life of Mozart* ten years earlier.

104   Rossini was born on 29 February, 1792 (a leap year) – 91 days after Mozart died. Beethoven is hardly mentioned in Stendhal's book; what few references there are adhere to contemporary cliché and prejudice – with Stendhal's criticisms of Rossini's music hinging on it being too German!

105   In the French original, the soprano's name is spelled throughout as "Colbrand."

106   Any redaction is for purely syntactical purposes.

applauded whenever she appeared on the stage. This, to my mind, represents one of the most flattering victories ever achieved by rank despotism; for, if there is one passion which outstrips all others in the breasts of the inhabitants of Naples – the most emotional, irrepressible people on earth! – it is incontrovertibly their passion for music. And yet, for five whole years, from 1816 to 1821, this unquenchable race was obliged to endure the most excruciating and tyrannical oppression, directed specifically at those activities to which it was accustomed to look for its most fervent and coveted pleasures! But Barbaja was under the thumb of his mistress; and she was the protectress of Rossini. Barbaja, sitting at the King's right hand, held the purse-strings; and if he paid anyone, it was only "them as had earned it"(as they used to say vulgarly in Naples at the time) ; he basked in his sovereign's favour, and he put up as best he could with his mistress. If I have sat once in the San-Carlo theatre, I have sat a score of times, and listened to Signorina Colbran embark upon an aria, which after the first few bars, would tail off into the most excruciating, the most insupportable cacophony; and one by one I have watched my neighbours creep out of their seats, shaking, neurotic, their patience frayed and their endurance exhausted – yet all in dead silence, without a word! And after that, let anyone deny that terror be the principle of despotic government – if anyone dare deny that, as a principle of any government, it can work miracles! When it can compel silence upon a crowd of furious Neapolitans! On those occasions, I used to accompany my neighbours outside the theatre, and together we would take a stroll around the Largo di Castello; and then, some twenty minutes or so later, we would return sheepishly to our seats, just in case we might happen to hit on some odd duet, some forgotten ensemble, which the fatal protégé of the King and of Signor Barbaja was not, for once, devastating and laying waste with the noble ruin of her voice. During the ephemeral rule of the constitutional government of 1821, Signorina Colbran never once dared show her face upon the stage without first sending on a prologue to grovel in abject apology; and the audience, to show their opinion of her, found especial amusement in building up a tremendous reputation for a certain Mademoiselle Chaumel (known in Naples as la Comelli), who was well known to be her detested rival in every respect.[107]

An instant interpretation of this unfettered character assassination is that Colbran and Stendhal detested each other – even though they appear not to have been acquainted, at least not to the extent necessary for revulsion to germinate. The composer neither authorised nor contributed to the writing of the biography,[108] which fact explains

---

107   Stendhal (1824). *Life of Rossini*. Trans. and Annotated by Coe, Richard N. (1985). John Calder, pp.149–151.

108   It's edifying to note that the first edition of the book in English – which appeared while Rossini was living in Britain – was admitted by the publisher, Hookham, to have been rushed to press. It was titled inaccurately as *Memoirs of Rossini by the Author of the Lives of Haydn and Mozart*. In the Preface, the translator refused to identify himself with the passages cited here concerning Colbran, and he admitted

some of the author's less than charitable judgments; they were not collaborators, therefore, despite appearing to meet in Paris after Rossini's relocation to the city. Stendhal was an epicurean, famed for his advocacy of a life well-lived through pleasure, but he considered Rossini and Colbran antediluvian, with his construction of Colbran pivoting on an addiction to gambling being the least awful of her many habits.[109] Stendhal was also a republican, who likely resented Colbran's popularity with Murat and Ferdinand, and a canonical European racist, a complexion that resolved neatly with his comprehensive dismissal of France's southern neighbours:[110]

> In Spain or in Italy, every man has the profoundest contempt for his neighbour, and savagely delights in the pride of his own opinions. This, of course, is the reason why no really "fashionable" person could ever endure to live in either country.[111]

In his slim defence, Stendhal praised Colbran's ability in its prime, which he dated to 1815, and her creation of the role of Elisabetta:

> In all the huge arena of the San-Carlo, there can scarcely have been a man who had not, at that moment, thought death an insignificant price to pay for a glance from so beautiful a Queen. Signorina Colbran, as Elizabeth, used no gestures, did nothing melodramatic, never descended to what are vulgarly called tragedy-queen poses. The immensity of her royal authority, the vastness of events which a single word from her lips could call into being, all this lived in the Spanish beauty of her eyes, which at times could be so terrible. Her glance was that of a queen whose fury is restrained only by a last rag of pride; her whole presence was that of a woman who still has beauty, and who for years has grown accustomed to beholding her first hint of a whim followed by the swiftest obedience.[112]

---

openly to having removed many sections concerning Stendhal's views on religion, politics, Italian manners and morals.

109   It's a question of perspective. Others may be more sympathetic to Rossini's displeasure with Colbran's "accursed dogs," which, according to Rossini, "have ruined sofas, rugs and everything beautiful we have in this city." Colbran admitted to her addiction, and its cost. As she wrote to a friend: "When fortune is remote from you, everything conspires against you. I must tell you that my health is always bad, that my affairs go from bad to worse, and in order to distract myself I have turned to gambling, with such disaster that I cannot take a card that doesn't become a victim." Christiansen, Rupert (1985). *Prima Donna: A History*. Viking, p.62.

110   It's worth remembering also that Stendhal's biography was first published in French for a primarily Parisian audience enraptured by the residency of its subject whenever he was in Paris, as an *émigré*. In Italy, the book was much sought after despite its huge cost. The composer's admirers baulked at Stendhal's criticism; his detractors were surprised that anyone should have taken him seriously. It was a considerable success, regardless.

111   *Ibid*, p. 299.

112   *Ibid*.

Stendhal was no less aware of Colbran's celebrated beauty, of which he wrote with characteristic elegance and passing generosity:[113]

> never before or since did she possess greater beauty than at that time. It was a beauty in the most queenly tradition: noble features, which, on the stage, radiated majesty; an eye like that of a Circassian maiden, darting fire; and to crown it all, a true and deep instinct for tragedy. Off-stage, she possessed about as much dignity as the average milliner's-assistant; but the moment she stepped on to the boards, her brow encircled with a royal diadem, she inspired involuntary respect, even among those who, a minute or two earlier, had been chatting intimately with her in the foyer of the theatre.[114]

During the writing of his *Life of Rossini*, Stendhal failed to live up to the manner and ambition of Boswell's *Life of Johnson* – which evolved in the extended company of its subject. Like his novels, his biography is beautifully written and occasionally hilarious, but it must be read as the work of a fan rather than a student of music or a detached observer. His approach to Rossini is laboriously political, wildly opinionated, and uninformed by musical training of any kind.[115] He promotes nothing to validate his denigration of Colbran's work "from 1816." Indeed, his praise is more consistent with the tone and content of the prevailing view to 1820–21, at which point the soprano's voice does appear to have failed.[116] Colbran was, regardless, the first soprano of the romantic age – a muse whose influence informed a body of work that remains among the most important in the history of music. She was the first working soprano to feature in the written life of a composer,[117] and the first to occupy the press for reasons unconnected with her performances on stage. Her contribution to Rossini's reforms and the emergence of romantic opera more generally cannot be overstated. While it's true she was sleeping with the composer throughout much of their collaboration, that intimacy makes Colbran's impact all the more significant because it filters through some of the most perfect operas ever published – whether or not she contributed to their premieres.

Colbran's fame originated with her three octave range, but her talent reached considerably further than acrobatics. This is best illustrated by the third act of Otello,

---

113   A number of paintings of Colbran survive in public circulation (it is rumoured that the now late Silvio Berlusconi held one captive in a bathroom in one of his many houses), including a portrait by Johann Heinrich Schmidt. Far more impressive is Johann Reiter's painting, completed in 1835, when the artist was only 23 years of age. The Ingres-like depth of colour, at its most astonishing in the folds of her silk dress, amplify her striking jet-black hair, styled *à la mode espagnole*, and an almost diffident expression that conveys a mannish, defiant confidence, more compelling than her *jejune* attachment to the piano beside which she sits.

114   *Ibid.*

115   He was unable to read a score.

116   Being that Colbran made her debut in 1801, albeit too early not to have risked causing harm and damage, she still managed a career lasting two decades.

117   Georg Nissen (the second husband of Mozart's wife, Constanze) never completed his biography of Mozart. He died in 1826, having only written a small portion of the work. It was completed in 1828 by others.

in which Desdemona almost completely dominates the narrative and the score. In particular, her *Willow Song*[118] punctuates an opera exemplified by bravura (most of it gifted to the numerous tenor roles) with a scene of mesmerising emotional intensity that marked a turning point in Italian opera, as well as the art of the soprano. Beginning "*Assisa a' piè d'un salice*," and ending with the short scena, "*Deh calma, o ciel, nel sonno*," this glorious oasis created and defined the archetype of the romantic soliloquy. Its importance as a genre-defining episode is sustained by the beauty and intimacy of the music, which operates at a psychological frequency audible previously only to Mozart. It is among the most affecting scenes in the musico-dramatic canon, and for any reader unpersuaded by Rossini's seismic consequence, the scene is as compelling as it is timeless. It could have been the work by Bellini, Donizetti or, even, a young Verdi – who admired (and referred more than once to) Rossini's *Otello* when writing his own. The source episode from Act 4, Scene 3 requires little rehearsal. Desdemona is preparing for bed, fearful of Othello's unwarranted anger; she sings "*canzone del salice*,"[119] a mournful ballad in which a nameless woman laments the passing of love. Desdemona is able to sing only two verses before she is interrupted by her maid, Emilia.[120] Shakespeare changes the victim in the song from a man to a woman, making it more relevant to Desdemona's circumstances. The first of Berio di Salsa's three verses begins:

> *Assisa a' piè d'un salice,*
> *immersa nel dolore,*
> *gemea traffita Isaura*[121]
> *dal più crudele amore*[122]

Rossini's setting introduces Desdemona with a virtuoso solo for harp, creating a spellbinding atmosphere that resonates with femininity and intimations of the supernatural. While the song is simple enough, it employs a vast expressive range, even noting the atypically limited vocal span of C3 to F4; there are two conjoined A flats in the aria's final bar (which Rossini scores as a semi-quaver and a quaver) for the second of the two repeated uses of the word "*l'ingrato*"[123] – excepting which the melody never leaves the stave. The first verse begins with a simple rising theme in quavers, formed as a statement that addresses the subject of the song being seated; the identification of the willow ("*salice*") is scored as a double-dotted D4 quaver descending, like the

---

118   Act III, Scene 8. The author considers it the equal of, if not superior to, Verdi's version of the same scene.
119   Willow Song.
120   The earliest record of "The Willow Song" is in a book of lute music from 1583 – with eight verses. It concerned a man who dies because of his beloved's cruelty and betrayal.
121   For a fascinating reading of the Willow Song's context racially for Rossini and his audiences in the 1820s see Abdullah, Paul (2020). "Rossini's Willow Song: Shakespeare Reception and Race in Restoration Paris." *Bollettino del Centro Rossiniano di Studi*, pp.127–159: "Note that in Berio's text, Desdemona learned the Willow Song from Isaura, the same invented name (Isaure) employed by Ducis (replacing Shakespeare's Barbary)…" p.137. A character called Isaura appeared previously in *Tancredi* (1813).
122   'Sitting at the foot of a willow, immersed in grief, moans pierced Isaura from the cruellest love.'
123   'The ungrateful.'

branches of the tree it describes, to the song's "ground," an oft-repeating G3.[124] From this point on, Rossini employs a large number of accidentals for the solo voice, most of them descending,[125] to emphasise the falling of the subject's "*ruscelletti limpidi*"[126] and the shuddering that accompanies them. The aria's chromaticism was radical for the time; it required exceptional vocal discipline from Colbran, particularly when accounting for the incremental ornaments written by Rossini into the first verse (for the leading words "*dolore*," "*crudele*," and "*ripeteva*"), and the more elaborate, overtly pictorial second verse, which characterises the murmuring river by the use of winding chromatic demi-semi-quavers. The final stanza is unusual in being the least involved, despite the use of repeating triplets – triggered by Berio's reference to "*l'afflitta vergine*."[127] For the phrase "*flebile ne ripeteva il suon*,"[128] a clarinet and then a flute repeat Desdemona's resolving motif, which, again, conveys the physical effects and sounds of weeping.[129] Depending on the accents applied by a singer to the words (*e.g.*, "*mea traffitta* […]"; "*il mormorio* […]," and "*di mie sciagure* […]"), the emotional impact of this tumbling pattern is as acute as it is poetic; it challenges even the most capable of singers because there is nowhere to hide, with words and music in idealised, mutually-sustaining equivalence. Berio's text ignores Shakespeare's characterisation of the subject of the song being in the foetal position ("Her hand on her bosom, her head on her knee"); it's clear, however, that Rossini knew the source material because the power of his setting is contained in its subject's isolation and confinement, the intimacy of which can cause an audience to submit by instinct to voyeurism. That sense of invasiveness is developed by Rossini in the scene immediately following, which qualifies for many as the opera's highlight:

> *Deh calma, o ciel, nel sonno*
> *per poco le mie pene,*
> *fa', che l'amato bene*
> *mi venga a consolar.*
> *Se poi son vani i prieghi,*
> *di mia brev'urna in seno*
> *venga di pianto almeno [si si]*
> *il cenere a bagnar.*[130]

This remarkable invention established the lyric-melancholic form as it would be mastered by Rossini's successors, most obviously Bellini. "*Deh calma*" is a petition of rare, Mozartian intensity that is absent contrasting or melismatic development, and chastening of the relationship between text and music to the point of folk-song.

---

124   The aria begins on a D3, to which note it returns only once, for the opening of the final verse.

125   Notably the falling line D, C sharp, C, B flat, A flat.

126   'Limpid streams.'

127   'Afflicted virgin.'

128   '[a breeze through the] mournful branches repeats the sound.'

129   The "weeping willow" was known in Italy as "*salice piagente*" from early in the 18th century.

130   'Oh, calm, ye heavens, in slumber For a while at least, my sorrows; Grant that the beloved of my heart May come to console me. But, if my prayers are in vain, Let him shortly come at least to bathe with his tears The ashes within my urn.'

It might be thought uncomplicated for a trained singer, but it is among the most difficult episodes technically in all of Rossini's operas because it conjoins the soprano voice to a small wind band, all performing *piano*, that prioritises sensibility and fragility over decoration and effect. Even if only briefly, Rossini liberates Desdemona of ornament and artifice, subsuming the art of the singer to the emotions of the character she is playing.[131] By aligning service to words and music in equivalence, Rossini met the challenge presented by Colbran's talent wherein projection was preferable to tone and technique. That Colbran could be heard singing this music from the stage of the San Carlo is a testament to abilities that exceeded every other virtue for which she was admired during her prime. Her final role for Rossini was *Semiramide*, which she created in February, 1823, at La Fenice. The following year she joined her husband when he travelled to London. Following a series of increasingly disastrous performances, Colbran retired, in 1827. Her marriage survived officially for another thirteen years;[132] in 1836, however, Rossini secured a legal separation so he could formalise his long-running relationship with the retired courtesan, Olympe Pélissier, to whom he remained married until his death in 1868.[133] Colbran continued to live with Rossini's father until his death in 1839.[134] After she died six years later,[135] Rossini married Pélissier, in Bologna.[136]

Colbran's legacy as *the* Rossini *cantante originale* is unique; no other soprano played such a productive role in the evolution of Rossini's creative identity when consecrating the fantasy of bel canto coloratura.[137] His only other platonic collaboration of note with a soprano was Benedetta Pisaroni, for whom he composed three important roles, Zomira (*Ricciardo e Zoraide*), Andromaca (*Ermione*) and Malcolm (*La donna del lago*); thanks to a nasty bout of smallpox early in her career, her voice darkened and she reinvented herself as a mezzo / contralto – those lower female voices whose particular vocal qualities Rossini was the first internationally-performed composer to exploit.[138] He had written for lower female voices prior to moving to Naples,

---

131   On record, it has been done no more better than by Frederica von Stade, whose performance for Jesús López Cobos' recording for Philips (1979) sets a standard that threatens the inimitable.

132   Rossini was habitually adulterous. Among the many things he gave his wife, the least welcome were chlamydia and gonorrhea.

133   A fascinating woman, Pélissier was the lover of a raft of European intellectuals, including Alfred d'Orsay, Bellini, and Balzac, who described her (on separate occasions) as "an evil courtesan" and the "most beautiful woman in Paris." The latter opinion is open to challenge, when considering the photo-realistic portrait completed in 1831 by another of her lovers, Horace Vernet. Tastes change, of course, and there is no objectivity where beauty is concerned. As a 32-year-old woman in the prime of her life, however, she was subjectively something of a "tug boat," and clearly capable in ways that a painting was unable to communicate.

134   It cannot have been an easy co-habitation. On one occasion he wrote to his son that his wife was "a spendthrift who looks only for ways to show spite, and that because one doesn't want to kowtow to her grandeurs and insanities." Christiansen, Rupert (1985). *Prima Donna: A History*. Viking, p.62.

135   She was buried alongside her parents in the Cimitero Monumentale della Certosa di Bologna. The tomb is well-maintained to date.

136   In August, 1846.

137   The word coloratura was not used at the time. Singers were simply expected to be able to sing coloratura because that was the nature of the repertoire at the time of its writing.

138   Handel's operas were not performed internationally until the 20th century. It is important to note, also, that Rossini's conception of voice types was extremely fluid. For example, he wrote Ninetta, the

in circumstances in which his predilection for the *alto* timbre and range qualified as infidelity. Castrati remained a circus attraction into the 1820s, with Giovanni Battista Velluti becoming the last of his kind to create a role in a major opera – Armando in Meyerbeer's *Il crociato in Egitto*.[139] Rossini had composed for Velluti in 1813, when casting him as Arsace in *Aureliano in Palmira*;[140] many years later he acknowledged all that he had learned from the castrati:

> I have never forgotten them. The purity, the miraculous flexibility of those voices and, above all, their profoundly penetrating accent – all that moved and fascinated me more than I can tell.[141]

It is no accident that Rossini's work with Velluti on *Aureliano in Palmira* was succeeded by *Tancredi*,[142] in which the male protagonist, an heroic warrior, was written for a contralto, Adelaide Malanotte.[143] Neither was it chance when, during the first run of *Aureliano*, Rossini started writing the role of Isabella in *L'italiana in Algeri* for another woman, Marietta Marcolini,[144] the first and most prominent of "his" contraltos. Marcolini appears to have made her debut in Venice, in 1800, where her work brought her to the attention of predominantly minor composers, including Guglielmi, Tritto, and Bigatti. In 1811, she appears to have begun an affair with Rossini, which fact is frequently trotted out with misogynistic delight as justification for his gifting of five roles to Marcolini, between 1811 and 1814 (all of them operating within the mezzo-contralto register): Ernestina in *L'equivoco stravagante*[145] (Bologna), *Ciro in Babilonia* (Ferrara), Clarice in *La pietra del paragone* (Milan), Isabella in *L'italiana in Algeri* and *Sigismondo* (Venice). Marcolini's brilliance was admired by many who were not also sleeping with her, including Stendhal, who remembered with unfettered admiration and respect her "ravishing contralto voice and for her magnificent gifts as a comic actress":[146]

> It may well be imagined that, in a land such as Venice, Rossini's glory as a composer was easily equalled by his triumphs as a man. It was not long before la Marcolini, a delightful cantatrice buffa, and, at the same time, a woman in the fullest flower of her youth and talent, swept him away from the great ladies who had been his first protectresses. The gossips whispered of base ingratitude; and there were many tears shed [...][147]

soprano lead in *La gazza ladra*, for Maria Teresa Belloc-Giorgi (2 July, 1784 – 13 May, 1855), an Italian contralto famed for her performances of Rossini's contralto roles. It's reasonable to assume that her voice darkened with time, but she was only 32 when appearing in the premiere of *La gazza ladra* – as a soprano.
139   'The Crusader in Egypt.' First performed on 7 March, 1824, at La Fenice.
140   First performed on 26 December, 1813.
141   Osborne, Richard (2007). *Rossini*. Oxford University Press, p.13.
142   Premiered just two months later.
143   1785 – 31 December, 1832.
144   *circa* 1780 – 26 December, 1855.
145   'The Curious Misunderstanding.'
146   Stendhal (1824). *Life of Rossini*. Trans, and annotated by Coe, Richard N. (1985). John Calder, p. 66.
147   *Ibid.*

There is a wealth of evidence in the score for *Algeri* to prove Marcolini's abilities, including "*Per lui che adoro*,"[148] a patter song emblematic of Rossini's flair for absurdist word-play, and "*Pensa alla patria*," Isabella's final scene, for which a soprano is required to draw on cetacean breath control, a seamless *cantabile*, some sparkling *staccato*, and judicial enunciation.[149] Isabella is significant for other reasons unconnected with technique. Firstly, and *contra* Mozart's preference for individuated cunning and manipulation, Rossini's heroine is a virago, whose power, confidence and self-belief determine outcomes that reach beyond her needs and preferences. This *aperçu* tribute to feminine and female equality is amplified by a contralto's lower registration, which comes closer to the sound of the (then emerging) tenor voice, and articulates a measure of warmth and social inclusion that, through its projection, approximates the timbre of speech, particularly when employed for oratory and persuasion. In Isabella's vocal form, feminine authority and heroism ("*Già so per pratica*")[150] are ritualised as a means for defeating male stupidity and vanity ("*Ai capricci della sorte*");[151] it is Isabella's wit, intelligence and sensuality – rather than the societal norms and customs into which she has been born as of right – that serve others as well as the self. Rossini's authority when promoting a woman dramatically and theatrically, as fiction, was given force and effect by his transformation of women vocally, as artists. It was one thing to represent an ideal by way of aspiration; it was another entirely to compel the embodiment of that objective through the training, technique, charisma and talent of women born hundreds of years after his death, and without which Isabella could be nothing more than fantasy and abstraction. As such, *Algeri* can be heard as the first blast for that monstrous regiment of women[152] whose subjugation as songbirds was no less a cage than the millennia of discrimination to which they had been subjected since Adam first gave Eve "His flesh, his bone [...] Out of my side to thee, nearest my heart."[153]

The finest of Rossini's coloratura for women was reserved for his outright comedies,[154] *Il Barbiere di Siviglia* and *La Cenerentola*. These miraculous works were created during Rossini's *annus mirabilis*,[155] and they contain some of the most joyful

---

148 'For him who I adore.'

149 Shortly after *Algeri's* premiere, Rossini was accused of having plagiarised an earlier setting of Angelo Anelli's libretto, by Luigi Mosca, first performed in 1808 at La Scala, Milan. Without telling Rossini of her plans, Marcolini agreed with the orchestra to replace Rossini's "*Pensa alla patria*" with the version by Mosca. Half-way through the aria, the audience made it clear whose music they preferred. This was the second time a member of the Mosca family was said to have been the victim of theft by Rossini. Luigi's older brother, Giuseppe, was the composer of an opera, *I pretendenti delusi* ['The Disappointed Suitors'] from which Rossini allegedly stole the "Rossini" crescendo (immortalised by the closing scene of Act I of *Cenerentola*). For the sake of completeness: Rossini stole only from himself. Liberally, and without apology.

150 'I know from experience.'

151 'To the whims of fate.'

152 The traditions against which Rossini was pushing are captured with grim clarity by John Knox's polemic, of 1558, *The First Blast of the Trumpet Against the Monstruous Regiment of Women*.

153 John Milton, Book IV, *Paradise Lost*.

154 The role of Fiorella in *Il turco in Italia* was created by a soprano, Francesca Maffei Festa (1778 – 21 November, 1835); it has more recently fallen within the compass of mezzo-sopranos, including Cecilia Bartoli, who can be seen in a video-recording of a performance from a production at the Zürich Opera in 2002.

155 Between 20 February, 1816 and 25 January, 1817 he composed, and oversaw the first productions

music written for a female voice. The highlights, "*Una voce poco fa,*"[156] and "*Nacqui all'affanno* [...] *Non più mesta,*"[157] require no commentary. Neither does the talent of Geltrude Righetti,[158] the mezzo-soprano for whom Rossini composed the roles of Rosina and Angelina. Born into aristocracy, Righetti made her debut at the age of 19; after achieving immortality in 1817 she married and never performed again – other than as an amateur at her own much-vaunted salon in Bologna.[159] These roles crystalise the essence of Rossini's achievement as a composer for women. He was first and last a man of the theatre, whose understanding of the whims and predilections of the crowd anticipated the work of Gustave Le Bon by more than 80 years.[160] His mutually profitable relationship with the female voice was as modern as it was vampiric, with each gaining equally from an arrangement without which both would have remained silent – then and now. Opera singers before Rossini's ascendence were artisans, audible only when singing for their supper. Their autonomy was prescribed and ordained by the arbiters of entertainment for appreciation locally and in person, as ciphers for a violently patrician culture that regarded women as essential for little more than sex and procreation. Rossini gave his sopranos agency, as characters and as singers, which he nurtured by ending many of his operas with solo show-pieces. He also enabled their respectability as professionals, to whom the press and publishers could turn for opinions, insights, memories and sales. Thanks to Rossini, sopranos evolved as musicians, actresses and personalities, capable of separating themselves from their denigrating synonymy with mechanical Turks and music boxes. Rossini was opera's first international celebrity, and he was sufficiently decent and sensible to recognise the value of this emerging culture for the women on whom he depended for his success. After his ultimate departure from Naples, female singers were able to determine their careers and identities on the basis of ability alone; they could provide or withdraw their services in accordance with the same market forces that had transformed opera into a business at the San Carlo. Talent and celebrity were now a currency to compare with money, and the broader social acceptance of women as artists occupied a space left empty by the now-absent castrati and the still-forming cult of the tenor. The modern soprano, mezzo and contralto are a construction of financial as well as artistic values, and it was these competing forces that would determine the long 19th century for female singers as well as the composers writing for them.

---

of, *Il Barbiere di Siviglia*, *Otello* and *La Cenerentola*, very probably the three finest of his Italian operas.

156 *Il Barbiere di Siviglia*, Act I, Scene II. 'A voice just now.'

157 *La Cenerentola*, Act I, Scene 2. 'I was born out of breath [...] No longer sad.'

158 1793 – 1862. Also known as Righetti-Giorgi, her married name. Stendhal asserts her first name to be Maria.

159 She was a huge value to posterity also as a writer. In 1823, in response to an article written by Stendhal, Righetti wrote a memoir entitled "*Cenni di una donna già cantante sopra il Maestro Rossini,*" ('Notes from a woman who sang with Maestro Rossini.') which contains the only reliable account of the première of *Il Barbieri*.

160 See *Psychologie des Foules* (literally 'Psychology of Crowds'), first published in 1895. Le Bon, Gustave (2002). *The Crowd: A Study of the Popular Mind*. Dover Publications.

CHAPTER TEN

The Incredibles

In 1934, a group of concerned American Catholics established the National Legion of Decency, a "think" tank dedicated to rating the suitability for Catholics of motion pictures, to which it assigned codes A to C, with C representing a film the Legion wothy of "condemnation."[1] In April the previous year,[2] the Reichstag passed dozens of laws restricting the lives of Jewish people throughout Germany, a campaign policy that was supported by the Catholic Church's most prominent voice in the USA, Father Charles Coughlin. Although the Legion was far from alone in considering the content of films more important than the lives of Jewish people, the reach of the Legion's values was sufficient to determine a film's success or failure whenever the letters B and C were stamped to a can. In 1938, the Legion requested that members take an annual Pledge of Decency, on 8 December – the Feast of the Immaculate Conception:

> I condemn all indecent and immoral motion pictures, and those which glorify crime or criminals. I promise to do all that I can to strengthen public opinion against the production of indecent and immoral films, and to unite with all who protest against them. I acknowledge my ob-ligation to form a right conscience about pictures that are dangerous to my moral life. I pledge myself to remain away from them. I promise, further, to stay away altogether from places of amusement which show them as a matter of policy.

In 1948, the Legion condemned *The Genius and the Nightingale*,[3] the American release of *Maria Malibran*, an Italian, Cinecittà-produced biography,[4] first released in 1943. They might have condemned the director, Guido Brignone, for serving

---

1   Charles Laughton's 1955 film, *Night of the Hunter*, was branded "B," with the singular comment "suggestive sequences; tends to degrade the dignity of marriage." It follows that the Legion chose not to condemn a film in which a religious fanatic and serial killer (Rev. Harry Powell, played by Robert Mitchum) terrorises women and brutalises children. Pope Francis finally condemned paedophilia in 2018, although he has not allowed women to serve as priests – because the clergy is supposed (without biblical authority) to represent the likeness of Christ.

2   In September, a speech by Joseph Goebbels' to the German nation, delivered in Nürnberg, was published in the United States, in English. Among the less racist and genocidal of his observations was his lengthy assertion, beginning "One cannot make sense of this situation without understanding the significance of the racial or Jewish Question [...]." https://research.calvin.edu/german-propaganda-archive/goeb41.htm.

3   Also, 'The Life and Loves of Maria Malibran.'

4   24 March, 1808 – 23 September, 1836.

Mussolini's administration as a proselytiser,[5] or Thea Gabriele von Harbou,[6] one of the film's writers, for her commitment to Nazi ideology, or the cast of fascist collaborators[7] which included the Viennese Gustav Diessl, who had starred in one of the Nazis' final propaganda movies, the historical epic *Kolberg*. The title role of *Malibran* was played by Diessl's husband, Maria Cebotari, one of the most gifted sopranos of the 20th century. Her status as a Nazi collaborator is remembered less often than her reputation as an exceptional Salome.[8] The Legion led the way in moral and ethical obloquy when overlooking the filmmakers' crimes in preference to the "disgrace" of a (largely fictional) account of the life of a woman persecuted by a presumably decent Christian man.

In its 1959 list of unsuitable movies for Catholics, the Legion summarised its objection to *Malibran* on the basis that the "story it tells condones and glorifies illicit actions."[9] The Legion was less bothered by the more-shocking *Johnny Belinda* (1948) and *Outrage* (1950).[10] The narrative trades in the usual fluff and nonsense that typifies the majority of biographical films portraying the lives of artists and performers. The most famous scene involves Malibran "duelling" with her legendary rival, Henrietta Sontag,[11] when the sopranos "share" a performance of "*Non più mesta*," accompanied by Rossini, grinning like a shot fox. The scene is known to be fiction because Rossini failed to persuade the sopranos to perform together in public; they did so finally at a private house, singing apart, for a small audience.[12] The film dances around Malibran's miserable experience of marriage[13] and dwells instead on its settings, the singing and the procession of corsets and crinolines.[14] None of the women's outfits features bones or stays.

Corsets served as undergarments throughout the 16th and 17th centuries, with two and as many as three or four additional layers of clothing being laid over. One of the few surviving prints of the soprano Caterina Cavalieri shows her performing on stage wearing a waist-shrinking bodice, a puffed-skirt and hoisted breasts – a creature whose appearance was indistinguishable from the majority of the women in the audience or what would become known as the red light district. The use of

---

5   Roberto Vezzani (2018). "Fascist Indirect Propaganda in 1930s America: The Distribution and Exhibition of Italian Fiction Films," *The Italianist*, Vol. 38, pp. 156–173.

6   von Harbou was a German screenwriter, novelist, film director, and actress. Born in 1888, she is remembered as the screenwriter of *Metropolis* (1927), and for the 1925 novel on which it was based. Harbou collaborated frequently as a screenwriter with *Metropolis'* director, Fritz Lang, her husband since 1922. Lang divorced von Harbou in 1933, before leaving Germany for France and, in 1936, Hollywood.

7   Rossano Brazzi as "Carlo de Beriot" (Charles de Bériot), Loris Gizzi as Rossini, Roberto Bruni as Bellini and Renato Cialente as "Ernesto Malibran."

8   See further Chapter 16.

9   Motion Pictures Classified by National Legion of Decency (1959). Legion of Decency. The Legion considered adultery and childbirth out of wedlock more worthy of condemnation than the Holocaust, World War II and the attempted eradication of the "*entartet*" ['degenerate'].

10   US films that addressed the effect of rape on young women.

11   Played by Silvia de Bettini.

12   Fitzlyon, April (1987). *Maria Malibran*. Souvenir Press, p. 74.

13   Her first, see further below.

14   Crinoline is a stiff fabric, made of horsehair and cotton or linen, used throughout the 19th century to make women's underskirts and dress linings. A stiffened or structured petticoat using crinoline was designed to widen skirts so as to achieve the illusion of a smaller waist.

quotidian clothing on stage ensured the corset's durability, which became as axiomatic of femininity as the skirt; its fall from popularity after 1700 was uninfluenced by fashion. The whaling industry expanded aggressively during the first half of the 18th century, pursuant to the effects of the Seven Years' War[15] and the American Revolutionary War,[16] which caused the price of sperm whale oil to collapse. Market contraction impacted the corset industry's access to baleen, and by 1788 British and Dutch whaling had halved in scale and capacity. Two years later, only eleven British ports remained in operation as centres of whaling. Further harm was caused by the French revolution and Napoleonic wars, in consequence of which the price of oil and bone fluctuated between £30 and £40 a ton.

Cavalieri died in 1801, at which time the absence of baleen forced the hands of designers and tailors towards a dress style that spurned the corset. Women's clothing softened into what would become known as the "neoclassical" or "Empire line," typified by Ingres' 1806 portrait of Caroline Rivière, and by Maria Callas' costume when performing as Tosca for Franco Zeffirelli at Covent Garden in 1964. The "columnar" silhouette raised a woman's waistline to immediately below her breasts, which were supported by fabric in the absence of a bra.[17] Comfort overreached containment during the first 15 years of the 19th century, therefore, with Napoleon's court setting the pace for what would become au moderne for the entire of Europe.[18] The lead was taken initially by *Les Incroyables*[19] and their female counterparts, *Les Merveilleuses* – an aristocratic Parisian subculture that celebrated the virtues of luxury, decadence and the absurd.[20] By attending society balls as little more than mannequins, their exaggerated and affected outfits – all without corsets – procured fame and notoriety *a propos ne rien*.

After the market for whaling was stabilised by the Congress of Vienna, the boned corset returned to popularity during the 1820s – because neoclassical fashion was useless in cold weather, and because the columnar did nothing for women having to account for female chauvinism as well as male proclivity.[21] Whatever Rubens' intentions might have been, the hourglass figure (according to which cliché a woman's waist is most attractive to a man when her hips are 30 per cent wider)[22] did not fall from grace; the most efficient means of achieving this golden ratio was the whale bone corset.[23] By 1830, the ideal silhouette was a wide open triangle beneath which

---

15 1756 – 1763. The effect of war for Britain's whaling fleet is recorded. In 1759, there were 83 vessels committed to whaling. In 1763 there were 40.

16 1775 – 1783.

17 Bras were not available until the end of the century.

18 See, for example, Jacques-Louis David's painting *Coronation of Emperor Napoleon I and Coronation of the Empress Josephine in Notre-Dame de Paris, December 2, 1804.*

19 'The Incredibles.'

20 See Cage, E.C. (2009). "The Sartorial Self: Neoclassical Fashion and Gender Identity in France, 1797–1804." *Eighteenth-Century Studies.* 42, 2, pp. 193–215.

21 Kościński, Krzysztof (2014). Assessment of Waist-to-Hip Ratio Attractiveness in Women: An Anthropometric Analysis of Digital Silhouettes. *Archives of Sexual Behavior.* Vol. 43, pp. 989–997.

22 Traditional male preferences are evolutionary rather than products of cultural norms.

23 Unlike the conical stays of the eighteenth century, early nineteenth-century stays were long and compressed the hips in furtherance of the columnar line, and they introduced gussets underneath the breasts in order to support them above the high waistline.

floated a bell-shaped skirt; the disparity between a woman's waist, her bust and her hips was made greater still by sleeve supports, formed of down or cotton and shaped with more bone, to create what became known as "leg o'mutton" or "*gigot*" sleeves.

Later iterations involved bustles, the addition of padding to the hips and the bust, petticoats, *chemisettes* and dropped shoulder lines – all to amplify the illusion of a small waist.[24] Corsets were held together by stays, made of baleen; these were sufficiently rigid to carry the weight of the skirt while simultaneously forcing a woman's bosom north of Venus. The achievement of a well-fitted corset was hailed by men and women to be a wonder of the modern age, a function of industrial evolution for which women were alone, in paying the price.

Initially, at least, corsets were held together by buttons – which made the process of assembly difficult, even with two or three women in attendance. This led to the practice of tight-lacing, which employed cords to pull the bones closer and tighter, forcing an hourglass figure on a woman's ribs, abdomen, lungs and pretty much every other useful organ.[25] By 1830, the effect of corsetry on women across Europe and the United States was sufficient to cause serious concerns for health and safety. Corsets were blamed for breathing difficulties, collapsed lungs, bruised and fractured ribs, stunted growth, dizziness and fainting, blood clots, the distortion of the spine, chronic gastrointestinal problems, and damage to (and the displacement of) internal organs. In 1830, in Salem, Massachusetts, a public lecture by two concerned men, R.H. Mack, and T.S. Lambert, was advertised with the title "THE LUNGS":

> These delicate and beautiful Organs will be the subject of THIS EVENING'S Lecture, when by taking the Lungs and Heart from the MANIKIN, and also by inflating a pair of Lights, we shall endeavour to show in the kindest, yet most undeniable manner, the evil effects of the COMPRESSING THE CHEST, and would therefore invite the attention of LADIES, especially YOUNG LADIES, that you may see how often LIFE IS CUT SHORT by this injurious practice; and that if you desire all that beauty of form and complexion [...] you must use all your influence to eradicate this pernicious custom from society.[26]

"Young men" were warned that the risks of disease for women submitting to corsets was sufficient to urge "our own comfort and profit in the selection of partners [that] we must necessarily adopt the motto 'NATURAL WAISTS OR NO WIVES.'" Industrialisation facilitated the "metal eyelet" – necessary to protect against the tearing of a corset's fabric – which resulted eventually in mass production. This meant that corsets had no longer to be hand-sewn or properly fitted. Like the modern business of bra-sizing, corsets during the 1830s were made for women to squeeze

---

24 While some corsets have been measured to 18 inches, the common dimensions were between 22 and 26 inches.

25 It's worth remembering what is contained within a woman's abdomen: stomach, small intestine (jejunum and ileum), large intestine (colon), liver, spleen, gallbladder, pancreas, uterus, fallopian tubes, ovaries, kidneys, ureters, bladder, and many blood vessels (arteries and veins).

26 New York Historical Society Museum & Library.

themselves into, a practice of which the *Dublin Weekly Herald* complained in 1844 when announcing that

> Corset lacing, as practised in Europe and America, is in truth no other than an impious, murderous, suicidal fashion. Impious, because it undertakes to give the female a better shape than the Lord intended her [...] Murderous, because parents are often the cause of the fatal disease of the children. Suicidal, because vast numbers continue to wear corsets after they know; they materially injure them.[27]

Deaths from corsetry were common throughout the first three decades of the 19th century; lacing continued to kill women into the 20th. In 1844, 22-year-old Jane Goodwin died during a church service in England; her demise was attributed to tight-lacing. [28] Six years later, the death of another woman of the same age was said by the Coroner to have been "caused, or at least much accelerated, by the pernicious practice of tight-lacing [...] the compression of the stomach and viscera [...] caused idiopathic asphyxia."[29] In 1860, E.Y. Robbins, a doctor in New York, alleged publicly that "10,195 females died [the previous year] of consumption to 5,640 males, [the] difference owing mainly to tight-lacing."[30] Across Europe and the United States, scores of women were killed by organ failure, internal bleeding, pneumonia and suffocation; autopsies regularly identified livers with calcified indentations caused by whalebone.

Sopranos were especially effected because they were prevented from breathing as required, and for other, more personal consequences arising from the operation of female anatomy. It transpired that the crushing of a woman's torso behind bone and lace was not conducive to bladder control; women who had given birth were known to suffer vaginal prolapses while on stage. A woman's pelvic diaphragm is formed of a complex musculature, located between the coccyx and the pubic bone, within the architecture of the pelvis; it operates to support a woman's bowel, bladder, uterus and vagina. The power of a soprano's abdominal muscles can be compared to those of an athlete; even so, many during the latter years of the 19th century took to wearing corsets to help combat the passage of time and to buttress their voices, using medically prescribed elastic fabrics.

During the 1820s and '30s, singers wore corsets routinely, as evidenced by the mass of portraiture from the time. In 2002, H. Colin Slim was gifted a painting of an unnamed soprano by Joseph Weber, dated 1839; his remarkable detective work led him to conclude that its subject[31] was the German soprano, Wilhelmine Schröder-Devrient.[32] She is dressed in a wine-coloured velvet bodice, cut low across

---

27 *Dublin Weekly Herald* (15 August, 1840). "Tight Lacing," p. 4.
28 *The Baltimore Sun* (11 June, 1860). "Corsets and Consumption," p. 1.
29 *Ibid.*
30 *The Observer* (17 March, 1851). "Death from Tight Lacing," p. 7.
31 Slim, H. Colin (2006). "Joseph Weber's Diva, Pinxit 1839: Visual, Musical, Societal Considerations. Music in Art; Iconography as a Source for Music History, Volume II. *Music in Art*, Vol. 31, No. 1/2, pp. 5–49.
32 See Chapter 11 below.

her shoulders; a brutally tight-laced whalebone corset narrows her waist to a point that suggests her kidneys were as close to her heart as her lungs. She is holding a scroll of sheet music, on which is written the title "*Iphigenia*," and the words, "*O lasst mich Tiefgebeugte weinen,*"[33] from Act II of Gluck's opera. As painted, Schröder-Devrient is not a slim woman; her double-chin and thick neck are highlighted by an awful (albeit fashionable) hairstyle that frames her oval face in a way that causes her waistline to appear ridiculous and unnatural. It is hard to know how she can have survived such an outfit.[34] In 1900, the American soprano, Emma Thursby,[35] described in a letter to a friend the difficulties and risks faced by singers wearing too-tight a corset:

> I ordered the Doctor's Corset from Modica's place. Wore it two days and was nearly killed. It upset all my internal arrangements and made me sick at my stomach. Dr. Fisher says I should never wear them, so I have had to order another from somewhere else. Rather dear expensive – 80 francs worth. Mrs Walden treated me four times & said my liver was cured.[36]

Women began to push back during the 1870s. In 1873, the fearless American feminist, Elizabeth Ward, declared:

> Burn up the corsets! […] No, nor do you save the whalebones, you will never need whalebones again. Make a bonfire of the cruel steels that have lorded it over your thorax and abdomens for so many years and heave a sigh of relief, for your emancipation I assure you, from this moment has begun.[37]

The corset was a ready metaphor for activists. The restriction of a woman's ability to breath resonated across many areas of life, wherein keeping men happy was indistinguishable from obedience.[38] Although the strain of societal expectation is worse in the 21st century than at any time previously, few are now killed by it.[39] If those freedoms have done little to mitigate the now-pervasive culture of sexual objectification then it

---

33 'O let me bow down.'

34 She did not survive it for long. She was dead at the age of 54.

35 21 February, 1845 – 4 July, 1931.

36 *Ibid.*

37 Phelps, Elizabeth (1873). *What to Wear*. Osgood, p. 79.

38 It would be a mistake to assume that every advocate of women's rights opposed corsets. One author, Lydia Becker, wrote in the "Women's Suffrage Journal" that women should "stick to your stays," while Emily Thornwell's *The Lady's Guide to Perfect Gentility* (1856, Derby & Jackson) survives as a depressing but often hilarious insight into the battles faced by women when challenging the traditions into which they had been born. The subtitle to Thornwell's book reads "Manners, dress, and conversation in the family, in company, at the pianoforte, the table, in the street, and in gentlemen's society."

Then again, millions of American women in 2023 continue to believe that women should not hold political office. A disturbingly large number of women in the United States remain opposed to suffrage.

39 Emily Dickinson's allegorical poem "I Died for Beauty" (written in 1862; first published 1890) is a terse evocation of the Platonic correlation of Truth and Beauty, rather than a disquisition on fashion and the cosmetics industry.

is, at least, possible for a woman in the developed world to determine her appearance socially and professionally. Middle and upper-class ladies during the 19th century dressed at home as they did for work, assuming they were able (and at liberty) to secure employment. This was true even for singers, for whom corsets were a curse long before they became a symbol.[40] Almost every painting, etching and sketch of a working soprano prior to 1800 and after 1825 shows them corseted. The first soprano of African descent to succeed in Europe, Vittoria Tesi,[41] was recorded in caricature with her embonpoint joined to her chin.[42] The Grisi sisters, Giulia and Giuditta, alternated between columnar and corset,[43] but Malibran and Sontag were represented without variation as victims of something proximate to medieval torture. The burden of performing as a woman in costume was preceded by the physiological realities of womanhood; menstruation was either not discussed or reserved to discreet medical reporting. Euphemisms[44] proved fruitful for anyone needing to be "indisposed," or suffering from "the sickness," or having to "plead the woman." In France, periods were endured as "*les règles*,"[45] and "*les cours*;"[46] in Germany, women were said to be in the company of "*der rote König*,"[47] while in Italy, ovulation was experienced with "*il marchese*,"[48] or on "*la strada rossa*."[49] The United States preferred floral imagery for a time, with menstruating women said to be with their "flowers," or "budding" or "in bloom."[50]

Enduring the vicissitudes of life as professionals working for men with little or no understanding of women's "problems" compelled sopranos to learn, rehearse and create new repertoire while suffering from menstrual *dysmenorrhea* – an intense pain concentrated in the lower abdomen and pelvis.[51] Because performance schedules

---

40 The suffocation of women as witches is trite; it's less well-known that women not accused of witchcraft were tortured similarly by the use of *strappado*, a vile practice wherein the victim was suspended by the wrists, with their arms behind their backs. Much like crucifixion, this ghastly abuse made breathing extremely difficult, and immensely painful. For a modern neo-romantic, eroticised take on the practice, see Nikolay Bessonov's painting *Inquisition* (1992).

41 Tesi's surname was Tramontini, but she was known by her middle name, and also as "*La Tesi*," "*La Fiorentina*" [the 'Florentine'] and "*La Moretta*" ['The Moorish Girl'] (13 February, 1701 – 9 May, 1775).

42 Of the various sketches and caricatures by Antonio Maria Zanetti, the drawing from November, 1741, is the most "flattering."

43 This is commonly because certain roles required the character they were playing to appear virginal, *i.e.*, Desdemona.

44 Joffe, Natalie F. (1948). "The Vernacular of Menstruation," *WORD* (International Linguistic Association) 4:3, pp. 181–186.

45 'The rules.'

46 'The courts.'

47 'The red king.'

48 'The marquis.'

49 'The red road.'

50 The floral tradition dated back centuries. In his 1651 *Directory for Midwives*, Nicholas Culpeper wrote "They are called by some Flowers, because they go before Conception, as flowers do before fruit." See Thulesius, O. (1994). "Nicholas Culpeper, father of English midwifery." *Journal of the Royal Society of Medicine*. 87 (9), pp. 552–556.

51 This requires an explanation only because a disturbing number of men in the developed world still have no understanding of *dysmenorrhea*, its causes, effects and consequences. See Rajak, Ishwari (2015). "She Got Her Period: Men's Knowledge and Knowledge and Perspectives on Menstruation." PhD thesis. Minnesota State University (Mankato).

changed routinely, singers were unable to make plans to accommodate their cycles; it was inevitable that anyone unable to appear on stage in consequence of excruciating pain was condemned at some point as unprofessional. This was in addition to having to contend routinely with disease, childbirth, abortion and domestic violence, as well as the habitual threat of rape, enforced sectioning, psychological torture, economic sequestration, social isolation and public humiliation.[52] On the other hand, corsets gave women a rare measure of autonomy that allowed them to contain, preserve and utilise their sexuality – a paradox that transformed constraint into an aesthetic as well as gendered value. This was embodied by a new generation of sopranos whose attainments and resulting celebrity were defined by the work of two composers, Vincenzo Bellini and Gaetano Donizetti. Like Rossini, they were commercial animals, as sensitive to market forces as to the voices of their singers. Artistic authenticity reformed as a construction of box office reality,[53] in accordance with the credo that music could exist as art only when it was performed. Bellini judged ticket sales to be "the real thermometer of pleasure,"[54] while Donizetti would pass

> details of his triumphs to his correspondents, at least his most intimate ones, including their total box-office receipts, which in his colorful language he called "*denari a bizzeffe*" (gobs of money). Composers, and nearly everyone else, described public reactions – especially extreme ones-with a standard theatrical terminology that seems analogous in its uniformity, strangely enough, to that used to describe performances or musical forms. Spectacles that failed to please were *fiasco* – the worst cases being "*fiaschissimo*" (big fiascos), which is the term that Donizetti employed for his Maria Padilla in Venice. Donizetti, who was a lover of linguistic deformation, referred to great successes ironically as "*fiasco coi-fiocchi*" (first-rate fiascos). Less frequently, disasters earned the "disgust" (disgust) of the public or its "*noja*" (boredom); these terms were popular but never canonized. Positive reactions generated furore (enthusiasm), if not its colorful superlatives "*furorone*" (as Bellini described the reception of *I puritani*) or "*furorissimo*" (Donizetti on Marino Faliero).[55]

Bellini and Donizetti were discerning of their status as demigods in an increasingly self-aggrandising age; they were the first to exploit the alignment of those factors on which fame was dependent – an objective for which a team of managers, press agents, artists, writers, publishers, investors and impresarios was obligatory. The opera machine's appetite was at its most Grendelian when chewing through sopranos, of which there were literally thousands operating across hundreds of opera houses by 1830. It was now routine for singers to perform a new work outside its city of origin,

---

52 The burdens to which women were subjected across class and culture until at least 1900 is considerably more expansive.
53 Huebner, Steven (1989). *Opera Audiences in Paris 1830–1870*. Music & Letters, Vol. 70, No. 2, pp. 206–225.
54 Sorba, Carlotta (2006). *To Please the Public: Composers and Audiences in Nineteenth-Century Italy*. The Journal of Interdisciplinary History, Vol. 36, No. 4, Opera and Society: Part II, pp. 595–614; p. 605.
55 *Ibid.*

in defiance of the perception as between Italian states of neighbours as adversaries. After *Norma* had "amazed the people of Bergamo," for example, Bellini delighted in the opera's success, even with "all the foreigners in the theatre from Brescia, Verona, and Milan."[56] Having replaced Rossini for Barbaja in Naples, Donizetti adopted a commercial philosophy of creating roles for singers who would then travel Europe and the United States as ambassadors. Motivated by the priority of dissemination, and believing publicity to be as meaningful as talent, he collaborated with hundreds of individual singers in the creation, staging and revival of more than 60 operas over a period of 27 years.[57] His instincts resolved a somewhat ruthless philosophy. He was asked on one occasion how best to promote two young singers, to which he replied that they should be presented "in the cafés, in the piazzas, in the homes, in the hovels *etc.*"[58]

Bellini, on the other hand, was the last to attach himself to a small corps of singers. Over a life's work of just eleven operas,[59] he composed for only four sopranos – two of whom created seven roles between them. The bar was set by a French teenage sensation, Henriette Méric-Lalande,[60] who made her stage debut at the age of 17 in Nantes, before being introduced by Castil-Blaze to the vocal demagogue (and father of Maria Malibran), Manuel García, in 1823. With García's assistance, she was cast in 1824 by Meyerbeer alongside the castrato Velluti for the first production of *Il crociato in Egitto*. Two years later Bellini invited Méric-Lalande to create one of the title roles in *Bianca e Gernando* at the San Carlo; the other was given to the tenor, Giovanni Rubini. They were joined by the bass-baritone,[61] Luigi Lablache, whom Bellini replaced with Antonio Tamburini for the opera's second premiere, as *Bianca e Fernando*. These singers made up three quarters of what would become known as the "Bellini Quartet."[62] They also came to define modern operatic singing, in part because of their celebrity but also because they were working for a composer whose transformative approach to musical theatre redefined singing, and the soprano voice. It's difficult to overstate Bellini's impact, or the role played by reciprocity in his

---

56   *Ibid.* p. 600. Bergamo is 43 miles from Brescia, 70 miles from Verona, and 33 miles from Milan.

57   Between 1818 and 1845. Despite completing 65 operas, Donizetti created only three roles for Eugenia Tadolini (1809 – 11 July, 1872), of whom he wrote, "She is a singer, she is an actress, she is everything." Ashbrook, William (1983). *Donizetti and His Operas*. Cambridge University Press, p. 498. He also created three roles for Adelaide Tosi (c. 1800 – 27 March 1859): Argelia in *L'esule di Roma* (1828), *Neala in Il paria* (1829), and Elisabetta in *Il castello di Kenilworth* (1829). On 7 April, 1828, she portrayed Bianca in the first production of Bellini's *Bianca e Fernando*.

58   Sorba, Carlotta (2006). *To Please the Public: Composers and Audiences in Nineteenth-Century Italy.* The Journal of Interdisciplinary History, Vol. 36, No. 4, Opera and Society: Part II, pp. 595–614; p. 600.

59   *Adelson e Salvini* (1825), *Bianca e Gernando* (1826) / *Bianca e Fernando* (1828) , *Il pirata* (1827), *La straniera* (1829), *Zaira* (1829), *I Capuleti e i Montecchi* (1830), *La sonnambula* (1831), *Norma* (1831), *Beatrice di Tenda* (1833), *I puritani* (1835). It was, of course, a very short life: Bellini died at the age of 33, two months before his 34th birthday.

60   1798 – 7 September, 1867.

61   Lablache was a bass, although the registration of voices was more fluid at the time than it is now. The role of Filippo is performed by a baritone in the 21st century.

62   The "Bellini Quartet" was a promotional gimmick that reached its ultimate iteration in 1835, with the premiere of *I puritani*, which featured Giulia Grisi, Giovanni Rubini, Antonio Tamburini and Luigi Lablache. They became known thereafter as the "I Puritani Quartet," although the title was never formalised.

success as the first great romantic of Italian music history. The list of admirers probably begins with Wagner, who wrote at length of his affection and respect for Bellini's
use of melody and word-setting; just about everyone who followed, including the
20th century's tutelary melodists, Puccini and Strauss, acknowledged Bellini's alchemy
when spinning gold from lead.[63] The essence of his art as a composer for the human
voice can be reduced to his divesting of what he inherited from Rossini. He stripped
out ornament and improvisation, making interpolation impossible; he attached his
melodies directly to the rhythms of the Italian language as spoken. It was less a case
of bel canto, therefore, than *canto declamato*, because the vitality of Bellini's word-use
was rooted in settings that attached a single syllable to a single note. It was a departure
from tradition that turned singers into actors. Whether in free *arioso* or lyrical solos,
no-one performing his music was able to rely on technique alone; there was no hiding
behind floridity and showmanship, and through his binding of a character's emotion
to a singer's ability to communicate it he abjured the symbolic, the metaphorical and
the artificial for a vernacular that spoke to everyone.

It's clear that Méric-Lalande was able to meet Bellini's expectations during the
1820s because he kept writing for her, specifically Imogene in *Il pirata*, Alaide in
La straniera[64] and the title role in *Zaira*. Her voice declined rapidly at the end of the
decade – an assessment confirmed by Henry Chorley, who later recalled her defining "wobble." Vibrato was used sparingly as colour by Bellini's singers, and not as
an inveterate and unchanging construction of training and technique, as is routine
for the 21st century. Chorley's most coruscating attack on ubiquitous vibrato was
published in 1862 – almost thirty years after Bellini's death, when he called it "that
vice of young Italy, bad schooling, and false notions of effect."[65] Rossini deplored it,
and since he is known to have admired the singing of Adelina Patti, whose voice was
recorded on good quality '78s, her avoidance of vibrato during the early years of the
20th century can, at the very least, be deemed evidence for its disavowal by singers
70 years earlier. It follows that Méric-Lalande didn't employ vibrato until she had to,
at which point she was past her best.[66] The same was true for her peers, all of whom
had to navigate Bellini's vast spans of exposed melody with nothing to protect them
from discovery. Poor phrasing, febrile breathing and imperfect diction were revealed
like Blanche Dubois by Bellini's luminous writing, which explains why the finest lyric
sopranos have always relished it, and why so many others have not. The new style was
recognised for what it represented. In 1829, one reviewer wrote for *L'eco*, an Italian
journal devoted to the arts, that:

> We do not really know whether it should be called sung declamation or
> declamatory singing […] The goal of this method seems to be to reunite
> the force of declamation with the gentleness of singing.[67]

---

63   Although it's a subject for a different book, it can be stated without fear of too much argument that
Bellini's libretti were less deserving than their composer.

64   'The Foreign Woman,'

65   Potter, John (1998). *Vocal Authority: Singing Style and Ideology*. Cambridge University Press, p. 57.

66   This fact did nothing to dissuade Donizetti from casting Méric-Lalande as the first *Lucrezia Borgia* in
1833, when the soprano was more famous than the composer.

67   Esse, Melina (2009). "Speaking and Sighing: Bellini's *canto declamato* and the Poetics of Restraint."

The changes in singing forced by Bellini's early operas matured with three roles, *La sonnambula*,[68] *Norma*, and *Beatrice di Tenda* – all of which were created by the last Italian soprano of note to be born in the 18th century, Giuditta Pasta.[69] Even before she sang his music, this remarkable woman would have occupied a mythical place in history for having been Bellini's inspiration when writing it. Almost two centuries after the premiere of *Norma*, it's easy to forget the extent to which composers of opera relied on their singers to prescribe what they could not do for themselves. Paganini, Liszt and Chopin were independent as composer-performers, but opera was collaborative to the point of dependency. Sopranos were more than muses, therefore, since whatever they inspired they had also to sing. Notwithstanding the routine diminishing of the female muse as passive and voiceless – after the destructive fashion of Edie Sedgwick's undoing by Andy Warhol – the cursory utility of women as models for painting and photography is counteracted by the mutualised alliances of Auguste Rodin and Camille Claudel, Dante Rossetti and Elizabeth Siddal, Gustav Klimt and Emilie Flöge, and Man Ray and Kiki de Montparnasse – among many others. Unusually for such relationships, Pasta appears not to have been seduced by Bellini, an independence that adds dignity to her status as one of history's most significant and influential singers.

Pasta was the first *cantante di recitazione*,[70] a category of performer precluded pre-viously by the nature of the repertoire and the manner of its presentation. This is not to suggest that Cavalieri and Colbran *et al.* operated as recitalists when appearing in works by Mozart and Rossini, but the heavily stylised nature of operatic production and stage movement prior to the Bellinian revolution tolerated interpolation and encouraged vanity before it pursued anything approximating dramatic truth. Bellini's pure strain of through-composed theatre lived and died according to the ambit and amplitude of its performers' submission to the characters they were playing – an ambition as often frustrated by an audience's conversation as by the episodic and piecemeal architecture of recitative and aria. At the time Pasta exited the stage in 1818, to give birth, she had been singing on it for only three years; no-one noticed or cared much for her absence. On her return, however, it appeared to many that she had signed a contract in blood. Stendhal recalled in his *Life of Rossini*:

> The temptation to sketch a musical portrait of Madame Pasta is too strong to be resisted. It may be averred that there was never a more difficult undertaking; the language of musical description is ungrateful and outlandish; I shall find myself constantly baulked by inadequacies of vocabulary; and even on those occasions when I am lucky enough to light upon the exact word required to convey my thought, the chances are that it will awaken none but the vaguest associations in the reader's mind. Furthermore, there can scarcely be one single music-lover in all Paris who has not already invented his own epithets in praise of Madame

---

Current Musicology, No. 87, p. 7.

68 'The Sleepwalker.'
69 26 October, 1797 – 1 April, 1865.
70 'Acting singer.'

Pasta; none, therefore, will escape the disappointment of failing to find his own thought reflected here; and even the most favourably-disposed of readers, in the heat of devotion which this great singer so deservedly inspires among her admirers, is bound to find any portrait of her from another hand flat, insipid, and a thousand times less wondrous than he had a right to expect.[71]

Stendhal was no disinterested observer. He wrote his *Life of Rossini* in an apartment immediately above Pasta's salon in Paris, on Rue de Richelieu – 800 metres from the Palais Garnier.[72] So frequently did he visit her rooms that many presumed they were engaged in an affair; while adultery was unbelievable of Pasta, whose marriage was stable and life-long, Stendhal was given to grand, unrequited passions. His classic *De L'Amour*[73] in which he characterises the "birth of love" as a trip from Bologna (*qua* indifference) to Rome (*qua* absorption), was published in 1822, at the same time as Pasta's reputation first began to travel. She was renowned initially for performing male as well as female roles, an enforced travesty for a woman predictably alive to contemporary sensibilities.[74] As she complained to Lady Morgan "I came out as Télémaque. I was so ashamed at showing my legs! Instead of minding my singing, I was always trying to hide my legs. I failed!"[75] *Post-partum*, Pasta evolved as a *soprano sfogato*, with a range that spanned a contralto and a high soprano – although these distinctions were as immaterial at the time as the designation "coloratura." What mattered most was her extension, which spanned two and a half octaves from an A3 to a D6, and her line, which, though subject inevitably to the vagueries of language, was applauded routinely for its power, evenness across the registers, and effulgent tone. Stendhal spoke for the majority in his celebration of the richness of Pasta's voice, and the "kind of resonant and magnetic vibration, which, through some still unexplained combination of physical phenomena," exercised "an instantaneous and hypnotic effect on the soul of the spectator."[76] Stendhal's descriptions of her voice remain the most reliable because he saw her play the roles for which she became famous at the time of their first performance:

> Pasta's incredible mastery of technique is revealed in the amazing facility with which she alternates head-notes with chest-notes; she possesses to a superlative degree the art of producing an immense variety of charming and thrilling effects from the use of both voices. To heighten the tonal

---

71 Stendhal (1824). *Life of Rossini*. Trans, and Annotated by Coe, Richard N. (1985). John Calder, p. 361.
72 For the true fan, it is now possible to rent rooms in Pasta's former home Lake Como, at Blevio, Lombardia, Italy – where Donizetti wrote most of *Anna Bolena*.
73 'On Love.'
74 William Hazlitt admired her "very handsome legs" when describing her appearance in Cimarosa's *Penelope* in 1817. Pasta didn't need the praise. Lady Morgan, Sydney Owenson (1863). *Lady Morgan's Memoirs: Autobiography, Diaries and Correspondence*, 2 vols. William H. Allen, p. 361.
75 *Ibid.*
76 Stendhal (1824). *Life of Rossini*. Trans, and Annotated by Coe, Richard N. (1985). John Calder, pp. 366–367.

colouring of a melodic phrase, or to pass in a flash from one ambiance to another infinitely removed from it, she is accustomed to use and falsetto technique covering notes right down to the middle of her normal range; or else she may unconcernedly alternate falsetto notes with ordinary chest-notes. In all such displays of virtuosity, she apparently finds as little difficulty in securing a smooth transition between the two voices when she is employing notes in the middle of her normal chest-range, as she does when she is using the highest notes which she can produce. The characteristics of Madame Pasta's head-notes are almost diametrically opposed to the characteristics of her chest-notes; her falsetto is brilliant, rapid, pure, fluent and enchantingly light. As she approaches the lower part of this falsetto register, she can *smorzare il canto*[77] to a point where the very fact of the existence of sound becomes uncertain. Without such a palette of breath-taking colour deep within her own being, and without such an extraordinary and compelling natural gift, Madame Pasta could never have achieved the over mastering force of natural expression which we have learnt to associate with her — a miracle of emotional revelation, which is always true to nature, and, although tempered by the intrinsic laws of ideal Beauty, always alive with that unmistakable, burning energy, that extraordinary dynamism which can electrify an entire theatre. But think how much pure artistry, and how much discipline and training has been necessary before this enthralling singer learned to harness the restive secrets of weaving such divine enchantments out of two different and utterly contrasting voices. Her art appears to be infinitely perfectible; its miracles grow daily more astonishing, and nothing can henceforth stop its power over the audience from growing progressively more binding. Madame Pasta long ago overcame the last of the physical obstacles which stood in the way of the realization of pure musical enjoyment.[78]

It's impossible to draw a detailed comparison, but Stendhal's characterisation of Pasta's singing would apply without adaptation to the voice of Maria Callas, an artist famed for the unusual vibration of her timbre, steel-bright chest notes, tonal range and kaleidoscopic colour which made her the most recognisable and cliquish female singer after the invention of recording. Any performance by Callas of "*Casta diva,*"[79] captured live or in the studio, is enough to ensure that even those new to the art of the soprano will be able to distinguish anything else by Callas after the passage of a single interval. Her power was never purely vocal, of course; not even the "best"[80] of her recordings can do more than paint a veiled, half-lit portrait of her art as a dramatician. It was the joining of Callas' skill as a singer to her instincts as an actress

---

77 'Diminish her tone.'
78 *Ibid.*
79 'Chaste goddess.'
80 It is the author's contention that all recordings are "bad," even if they can be of exceptional utility, and a source of shameful pleasure.

that resolved the creation of a character on stage, and that admixture of vocal and physio-psychological complexity appears, at the very least, to have circumscribed Pasta's achievement as the first of her kind. When Lady Morgan raised the issue of dramatic character with Pasta, she was careful to ask whether she pursued immersion (to discount, presumably, the possibility that it all came naturally, without process and calculation), rather than *how* she achieved it:

> "Do you transport yourself into your part?" [to which Pasta] replied *"oui, après les première lignes. Je commence toujours en Giudetta (mon nom), mais je finis toujours en Medea en Norma!"*[81]

It would be churlish to rehearse the malignance of recording – a science that has, for more than a century, separated opera singers from the art and its aspiration. The disembodying of a voice cannot, however, avoid denuding a singing-actress of her potential in the guise of someone other than herself. If it is enough, as it was for Berlioz when writing *La damnation de Faust*, for singers to submit to the idiosyncrasy of a composer's voice *in absentia* of stagecraft, then opera companies can – and probably should – spare their sponsors the ruinous cost of presenting works that warrant being seen by sound alone. Opera is theatre of the greatest complexity; it is best performed by singers able to pick up the gauntlet that Pasta hammered into existence during the 1830s. Susan Rutherford has gone further than most in her dissection of Pasta's corporeality as an actress,[82] isolating the extent to which she achieved the melodramatic without stooping to the histrionic, a metric supported by a vast body of contemporary criticism and commentary. Rutherford relies on the insight and perception of Carlo Ritorni, who dubbed Pasta *"cantante delle passioni,"* because of the originality of her approach to gesture and body:

> The principal talent of Pasta is in having invented with shrewd intelligence the proper dramatic action and expression of melodramma, and of that kind of anti-dramatic opera that she found on the stage when she began her career, to which she not only adapted her sublime histrionic gifts (learnt in France) by honing them more finely, but directed them towards hiding its defects.[83]

In 1826, London's *Quarterly Musical Magazine* reviewed a performance by Pasta of Mayr's *Medea in Corinto*, during which the author dwelled on Jason's question *"Che sperar posso? Che mi resta?"*[84] and Pasta's two-syllable reply: *"Io"*:

---

81   'Yes, after the first lines. I always start as Giudetta (my name) but end always as Medea and Norma.' Lady Morgan, Sydney Owenson (1863). *Lady Morgan's Memoirs: Autobiography, Diaries and Correspondence*, 2 vols. William H. Allen, p. 361.

82   Rutherford, Susan (2007). "'La cantante delle passioni': Giuditta Pasta and the Idea of Operatic Performance. *Cambridge Opera Journal*, Vol. 19, No. 2, pp. 107–138.

83   *Ibid*, p. 112.

84   'What can I hope for? what remains for me?'

It is impossible to convey the dignity with which Madame Pasta invested these two notes. She gave them with the whole power of her voice, at the same instant flung wide her arms above her head, and her whole figure seemed to dilate with a passionate majesty that can only be understood when seen.[85]

In Susan Rutherford's conception:

A conventional "mimed" approach to such a moment of self-identification might have seen the right arm bent across the chest, with the hand placed on the heart, and the head slightly inclined. But Pasta found a gesture that did not merely express the literal meaning of text, but rather supremely embodied both character and underlying dramatic action, and was thus symbolic both of Medea's sense of self-worth and of the risk she takes in offering herself again to Jason. In so doing, she made visually explicit (in a kind of 'piercing' of dramatic substance, to borrow a concept from Peter Brooks) a crucial pivot in the plot: rejection of such a highly valued prize, and one offered with such imperious grandeur, can only bring ruin to all. It is important to note too that the critic both saw and heard this gesture – that it was an accent of vocality as much as of physicality, and that it produced a visceral response beyond translation into words.[86]

Pasta was revered in particular for her creativity as a performer, an impulse towards imagination and invention that manifested itself in a refusal (or an inability, perhaps) to adhere to a single "reading" or interpretation. As between two performances of the same role during the same run she would isolate details, effects, and qualities previously unseen and unheard, so that by her intonation of a phrase, or her shaping of a line, or her physical ideation of a feeling, she was able to reveal more of the character as whom she was appearing than had been imagined even by its composer. This mutability was never artificial, as it can be for performers submitting to the sometimes malignant influence of a conductor or a director; instead, and as Stendhal observed, Pasta

may indeed sing the same note in two different scenes; but, if the spiritual context is different, it will not be the same sound. These are the sub-limest heights to which the art of singing can attain. I have seen perhaps thirty performances of Tancredi; but Madame Pasta's musical intonation is always moulded so closely upon the momentary inspirations of her heart, that I may claim to have heard the aria: "Tremar Tancredi,"[87] for instance, sung on some occasions with an inflexion of gentle irony; on

85   Russo, Paolo (2002). "Giuditta Pasta: cantante pantomimica." *Musica e storia*, 10, p. 517.
86   Rutherford, Susan (2007). "'La cantante delle passioni': Giuditta Pasta and the Idea of Operatic Performance. *Cambridge Opera Journal*, Vol. 19, No. 2, p. 114.
87   'Tremble Trancredi.'

others, with a manly intonation of courage, with the intrepid accents of a hero assuring his followers that there is nothing to fear, and strengthening the uncertain heart of timidity; on other occasions still, with an air of disagreeable surprise already tinged with resentment [...] and then, suddenly, Tancredi remembers that it is his beloved Amenaida who is speaking, and the first growlings of the storm of anger vanish into the smiling sunlight of reconciliation. Ah! Who can gaze into her face, and not burn with love?

Pasta created the role of Amina in *La sonnambula* on 6 March, 1831; she sang the first Norma nine months later, on 26 December. Her achievement as the inspiration for these extraordinary inventions was complemented by her fulfilment of the composer's expectations. Public and critics aligned in their reverence for the works and their performers, with Pasta being identified as the progenitor of the bel canto soprano. Her genius was not a local phenomenon, however; indeed, it travelled well and without dissent. One critic in Vienna held that

> In the modern musical world, madame Pasta becomes an extraordinary phenomenon: a phenomenon so powerful and of such a distinct kind that a minute exposition of her merits is a duty of the critic [...] One cannot here speak of her in passing, as we sometimes allow ourselves to with the usual productions: what madame Pasta does is like a work of art so particular for itself, and so important with respect both to its time and to art in general, that it must be regarded as a very worthy topic for the most profound and zealous reflections of every scrutineer of the arts.[88]

One of the most revealing exemplars of the creative value of Bellini and Pasta's collaboration is the "mad" scene of *La sonnambula*, "*Oh! se una volta sola* [...] *Ah! non credea mirarti.*"[89] This is not, of course a traditional "mad" scene, since Amina does not "lose her mind," as does Lucia for Donizetti. As a sleep-walker, she is not "in her mind" so as to lose it; Bellini's music during the opera's psychological and dramatic climax creates a sense of dislocation and unease without debilitating what is unquestionably one of the most sublime melodies in all of music.[90] Bellini employs high notes on weak-beats, and interrupted, halting phrases to communicate the instability of Amina's reason, as well as the insecurity of her step. The score is littered with fragments of memories, notably the duet, "*Prendi l'anel ti dono,*"[91] to convey the wandering of her mind; most compellingly, Bellini's writing for the soprano amplifies

---

88 *Ibid*, p. 121.

89 The first four bars (and words) of "*Non credea*" are carved into Bellini's tombstone in Catania. They are apt: "*Ah! non credea mirarti, sì presto estinto, o fiore*" ('That I could I see him again, dear flower, perished so soon.').

90 Somnambulism / Sleepwalking is a form of *parasomnia*. The most significant and influential artistic interpretation of the condition is the sleepwalking scene in Act V, Scene 1, of *Macbeth* (1606). "*Non credea*" was not Bellini's first such scene. Act II, Scene 3 of *Il Pirata* features Imogene singing "*Col sorriso d'innocenza,*" ('With the smile of innocence').

91 'Take the ring I give you.'

her febrility when inviting the most elastic *rubato* – an effect that can be hypnotic if a conductor adheres to the fixed string cantilena as it is written.[92] It's obvious that Pasta was able to push against the bar-lines without breaking them – as is routine in most modern performances; even if liberties are reasonable (particularly during the plastic languidity of Amina's duet with solo cello), it's worth remembering that the body of "*credea*" is marked with a single *fermata*, on the word "*pianto*," during the first stanza's repeat. There are two further *fermatas* in the concluding melisma, which is otherwise scored without rests. It's here that Pasta's technical resources are most clearly evidenced. The aria's final four bars, set to the words "*passasti al par d'amore*,"[93] begin on a G4 quaver, and lead after a semi-quaver rest to a run of some 30 semi-quavers, spanning a ninth – all of them indicated to be sung *lento* – without any further rests being indicated, save for a single comma after the first "*d'amor*." That comma does not admit any interruption in the sung line, however, because Bellini slurs the crotchet-semi-quaver G3 on the penultimate "[…] *mor*" – confirming without ambiguity that the final three and half bars are to be completed in a single breath. The challenge is stupendous; anyone meeting it qualifies as superhuman.

It's accepted that many singers developed exceptional techniques before Pasta; Farinelli's apparent capacity for circular breathing remains the stuff of definitive legend. However, no-one before her was able to imbue coloratura with such intense emotional and psychological focus. It is here – in the art of the singing actor – that Pasta remodelled the theatrical soprano. She achieved this revolution across Europe, over a period of more than two decades, spanning sixty-three roles – the most famous of which, Norma, she performed on 108 occasions. Her influence was no less acute behind the curtain, where she exercised an authority without precedent. Even before her creation of Amina, her contracts established through the sharpest of clauses that she was in charge. Article 6 of her contract for the 1826 season at the King's Theatre, Haymarket, provided:

> In all the operas in which Madame Pasta will perform, she alone will have the choice of the actors and the distribution of the roles, the absolute direction for all that regards the rehearsals and all else concerning the *mise en scéne* of the said operas. No one will have the right to intervene in rehearsals, nor to meddle in anything concerning the performance of those operas.[94]

On 26 December, 1830, Pasta created *Anna Bolena* at the Teatro Carcano, Milan – the same theatre in which *La sonnambula* would be premiered a few months later.[95] She played a major part in the work's success, which secured Donizetti's status as

---

92   Inevitably, most do not.

93   'You died as did our love.'

94   Rutherford, Susan (2007). "'La cantante delle passioni': Giuditta Pasta and the Idea of Operatic Performance. *Cambridge Opera Journal*, Vol. 19, No. 2, p. 111.

95   The Carcano is substantially smaller than La Scala, with a stage around half the size and seating for only 1,500. The modern interior of the theatre has been modernised and cannot now stage opera. The refit removed the original interior, the pit and the acoustics; the house now presents popular music and theatre productions, exclusively with amplification.

one of the country's most important composers. It's clear from Karl Bryullov's portrait of Pasta in the role of Boleyn, which he completed around the time of the first performance,[96] that the soprano had gained a lot of weight during the preceding six or seven years. The painting shows Pasta strapped into a fearsome corset, rather than the columnar dress in which she had been painted by Gioachino Serangeli in 1821, or the nightdress she wore for most of *La sonnambula*, or the priestess robes in which she appeared as Norma. A change in diet and body shape may have affected her singing negatively, although the critics were sufficiently respectful not to say as much after her voice began to fail during the 1830s. Henry Chorley dated Pasta's decline to 1833 – less than two years after the premiere of *Norma* – which seems improbable, for the simple reason that Pasta created the role of Beatrice in March of that year, a production in which she was said to be the only successful performer. It is no less true, however, that Norma is a fearsomely demanding role, a fact to which Pasta was the first to admit during rehearsals at La Scala when objecting that "*Casta diva*," in particular, was unsuited to her voice. Bellini did not agree, and persuaded the soprano to persevere. A few hours before the first night, Pasta sent the composer a parchment lampshade, hand-decorated by the singer with fabric petals, together with a note, which read:

> Allow me to offer you something that was some solace to me for the immense fear that persecuted me when I found myself little suited to performing your sublime harmonies, this lamp by night and these flowers by day witnessed my studies of *Norma* and the desire I cherish to be ever more worthy of your esteem.[97]

The widely-reported indifference of the first night audience was attributable to fatigue and a hostile faction operating on instructions from the Contessa Giulia Samoyloff, the mistress of the composer Giovanni Pacini. Bellini's genius survived the intrigue; *Norma* was performed 34 times during its first season at La Scala, with a further 174 performances before the century's end. The composer told one of his librettists that *Norma* navigates "the human soul in slow motion," and the title role more than lives up to that ambition in being one of the most difficult in the operatic repertoire.[98] The vocal and dramatic challenges begin for the soprano in the second scene of the first act, with "*Casta Diva*." Bellini's most popular aria is in F major, and very slow moving (with a meter of 12/8); it occupies a vocal span of an octave and a half (from F3 to B flat 4). By the use of a lachrymose melody that is objectively human in its convulsive anguish, the music transmits faith and a confidence formed of religion that can be shocking in its revelation of Norma's fears for her future during the aria's two climaxes. There is nothing tranquil in the repeating A4s that colour the words

---

96 It was certainly completed *before* 1833, when Bryullov completed his *magnum opus, The Last Day of Pompeii* – after which he left Rome and returned to Russia.

97 Christiansen, Rupert (1985). *Prima Donna: a History*. Viking, p. 67.

98 Littlejohn, David (1992). *The Ultimate Art: Essays Around and About Opera*. University of California Press, pp. 156–171.

"*sembiante*,"[99] and, for the second verse, "*pace*"[100] – which are scored *piano* while being marked with accents as they herald the two resolving B flats, which Bellini coloured *fortissimo* and without a *crescendo* in anticipation.[101]

Pasta's skill was formidable; by 1837, however, her voice was acknowledged to be a remembrance of things past, as Chorley noted in his spiteful review of her final appearance in Britain:[102]

> Nothing more inadvised could have been dreamed of. Madame Pasta had long ago thrown off the stage and all its belongings [...] Her voice, which, at its best had required ceaseless watching and practice, had long ago been given up by her. Its state of ruin on the night in question passes description.[103]

Chorley did not flinch from describing it, adopting for his more generous adjectives "broken, hoarse and destroyed."[104] Pasta was in her fortieth year at the time, and approaching the last of her 1,240 operatic performances and 860 recitals.[105] She retired at an age when most sopranos in the 21st century are beginning to hit their stride. Whether it was too much work,[106] or the work she was singing, is impossible to know for certain,[107] but for his next, and last, opera – *I puritani*[108] – Bellini turned to Giulia Grisi, a soprano thirteen years younger than Pasta, whose sister, Giuditta, he had earlier cast as the first Adalgisa in *Norma*, and Romeo (a travesti role) for the first production of *I Capuleti e i Montecchi*.

The Grisi sisters stepped happily into Pasta's dimming candle. Giuditta[109] was a mezzo-soprano; her sister Giulia[110] was a high soprano; their cousin, Carlotta, was among the most influential ballerinas in the history of dance.[111] The sisters' aunt, Giuseppina Grassini,[112] was a noted contralto, beloved of Cimarosa, Mayr, Méhul

---

99   Strictly 'Semblance,' but 'face' is the routine translation.

100   'Peace.'

101   Almost no-one has sung these features of the aria as they are written, at least on record.

102   In the audience on this occasion was a much younger soprano, Pauline Viardot, who commented, "you are right! It is like the *Cenacolo* of Da Vinci (*The Last Supper*) – a wreck of a picture, but the picture is the greatest picture in the world." Chorley, Henry (1862). *Thirty Years' Musical Recollections*, 2 vols. Hurst and Blackett, I, p. 138.

103   *Ibid*, p. 137.

104   *Ibid*, p. 138.

105   For context, Callas gave approximately 500 performances in staged opera, of which 89 were as Norma.

106   If hazarding a guess, it would be the volume of work that did for her, being that she performed routinely as often as three times a week.

107   When equated across the span of her career, Pasta performed between 90 and 150 times a year. A soprano in the 21st century will perform less, giving between 50 and 75 performances a year. Of course, Pasta had to travel between theatres by horse-drawn coach. She had also to rehearse and perform new repertoire in theatres where companies had to learn everything from scratch.

108   'The puritans.'

109   28 July, 1805 – 1 May, 1840.

110   22 May, 1811 – 29 November, 1869.

111   She created Adolphe Adam's *Giselle* in 1841.

112   8 April, 1773 – 3 January, 1850.

and Cherubini, although she is better known for having had affairs with Napoleon *and* the Duke of Wellington. Unlike Pasta, the Grisis were the focus for popular infatuation, as a talented and relevant prototype for the innocuous Kardashians. Their lives were lived almost entirely in the public eye, albeit not always for the right reasons. Before being discovered by Bellini, Giuditta specialised in the music of Rossini; she also created several roles for Persiani, Coccia and Pacini, the strain of which exacerbated a premature vocal crisis that was resolved only by her death at the wretched age of 34. Giulia survived her sister by almost quarter of a century, a life-span into which she crammed more than most. Her first marriage to Count Gérard de Melcy, an insufferable bully, was a disaster. Within weeks of the wedding in 1836, Grisi was making stentorian requests for a separation – all of them refused. After de Melcy discovered a love letter from Frederick Stewart, the 4th Marquess of Londonderry,[113] and having insisted on satisfaction, the love-rivals engaged in a duel on 16 June, 1838, at which the Marquess was wounded by the Count. It has been suggested that Grisi's decision to leave her husband soon after was motivated by his superior aim, but this is incorrect. She was, in fact, five months pregnant when pistols were drawn. Stewart's son, George Frederick Ormsby, was born in November, 1838. After Grisi's relationship with the Marquess failed, she was swept from her feet by "Mario" Giovanni de Candia – a fascinating, profoundly romantic and, for a time, stupendously popular tenor.[114] After a tumultuous and widely-reported battle in the courts, Grisi obtained her divorce from de Melcy, and married Mario in 1844, in London's Hannover Square. George was adopted as George-Frederick de Candia Ormsby, and the family divided its time between a mansion in London, the magnificent *Villa Salviati* in Florence,[115] and a "cottage" in Bordighera. Of their six children, all of them daughters, three died in infancy; the longest living was Cecilia Maria de Candia, a writer and her father's biographer, who survived to 1926.

Having already shared the stage with Giuditta Pasta for the premiere of *Norma* – an event that would be sufficient for most *curriculum vitae* – Grisi was invited by Bellini to create the role of Elvira in *I puritani*. The premiere, on 24 January, 1835, was staged at the Théâtre-Italien in Paris,[116] where Grisi was joined by the tenor Giovanni Rubini as Arturo, the baritone Antonio Tamburini as Riccardo, and Luigi Lablache as Giorgio. The first night was recognised at the time to be the most

---

113   After his father succeeded to the marquessate of Londonderry in 1822, Frederick Stewart became known by the courtesy title Viscount Castlereagh.

114   See Boyden, Matthew (2021). *The Tenor: A Cultural History*. Ragueneau Press, pp. 95–101.

115   The Villa is now a boutique hotel – renamed the *Villa Salviatino*. Even before Grisi and Mario made it their home, it had a remarkable history. Located between Florence and San Gimignano, the Villa is named after Francesco Salviati, an extravagantly wealthy priest who purchased it in 1475, being his elevation as Archbishop of Florence. Like the good Christian he must have been, Salviati was essential to the Pazzi family's plotting when planning their invasion of the city for which Salviati sat as Archbishop. When the Pazzi conspiracy failed, in 1478, Salviati fled to his Villa, having swapped his archbishop's robes with an unfortunate, and clearly uninformed local man, who was then hanged in his place. As a conspirator, Salviati was fundamental also to the assassination of Giuliano de' Medici – who was stabbed 19 times during Mass, at the sounding of the (Eucharistic) Elevation. Jesus would be proud. The Villa is meaningful also for admirers of the computer game, *Assassin's Creed: Embers*, for which the Villa was used as a model.

116   The opera was commissioned by the theatre.

spectacular in the history of opera, transporting Bellini's "Quartet" to the pantheon of the gods of singing. Even the dress rehearsal on 20 January, 1835, was attended by "all of high society, all the great artists, and everyone most distinguished in Paris."[117] Their reaction was described by Bellini in a letter to his friend, Francesco Florimo:

> The French have all gone mad; there were such noise and such shouts that they themselves were astonished at being so carried away [...] In a word, my dear Florimo, it was an unheard of thing, and since Saturday, Paris has spoken of it in amazement [...] I showed myself to the audience, which shouted as if insane [...] How satisfied I am! [...] Lablache sang like a god, Grisi like a little angel, Rubini and Tamburini the same."

During rehearsals for the opera's first performance in London, on 21 May, 1835 – less than three months after the world premiere – François Bouchot painted Grisi and Lablache in costume, waiting in the wings of Her Majesty's Theatre to appear as Elvira and Giorgio. Bouchot was a gifted portraitist;[118] his painting is grossly out of proportion, however. Lablache is reproduced as a giant, with a head as large as Michelangelo's *David*, while Grisi appears to have sat for Bouchot at the wrong end of a telescope, with what seems to be a broken neck – as would have been necessary for her to turn as she does to the viewer. It is interesting only for its presentiment of atmosphere, and the sense of acute anticipation experienced by performers before meeting an audience. The incandescence seen bursting through the parted curtain was powered by gas,[119] the source of which Bouchot should probably have considered before throwing indiscriminate light onto Grisi and her silk dress.[120] The project was presumably rushed, in consequence of the proximity of the English and Italian premieres and because Bouchot was "courting" one of Lablache's thirteen children at the time. Whatever the reason, the painter was more capable than this awful painting suggests,[121] a talent to which he testified in 1840 when producing an excellent neo-classical three-quarter portrait of Giulia Grisi,[122] with the soprano seated on a balcony, dressed in white lace, and wearing black half-gloves. The latter symbolised Grisi's status and wealth, while revealing her openness to the intimacy and love she was experiencing indiscreetly in Paris with Mario.[123] Four months after *I puritani's*

---

117 Letter from Bellini to Francesco Florimo, in Weinstock, Herbert (1971). *Bellini: His Life and His Operas*. Knopf, p. 184.

118 A year after Bouchot's death in 1842, Francesca married the pianist and composer Sigismond Thalberg. For those who can remember him, the American actor Stewart Granger was Lablache's great-great-grandson. Lablache was close friends with Niccolò Paganini, as whom Granger starred in the atrocious 1946 biopic, *The Magic Bow*.

119 An innovation that transformed opera production during the 1830s.

120 Fixing, and accounting for, a source of light is key to the success of any narrative portrait and / or scene, as Caravaggio established two centuries' earlier.

121 A few weeks after Bouchot returned to Paris in 1835, Louis Philippe I's government presented him with the Legion d'Honneur, which had been restored five years earlier by the July Monarchy.

122 He had already created a fine portrait of Maria Malibran (see further below).

123 Gloves were exchanged as courtship gifts into the 20th century, a tradition to which Shakespeare referred in Act IV, Scene 4 of *A Winter's Tale*, when the shepherdess Mopsa addresses her sweetheart: "Come, you promised me a tawdry lace and a pair of sweet gloves."

triumph in London, Lablache was called upon to sing Mozart's *Requiem* at Bellini's funeral.[124] Although his relationship with Romani had been tested by the librettist's Catholic work ethic, his tribute to the composer was the most touching and appropriate:

> Perhaps no composers other than ours, know as well as Bellini the necessity for a close union of music with poetry, dramatic truth, the language of emotions, the proof of expression. [...] I sweated for fifteen years to find a Bellini! A single day took him from me!"

Exactly one year, to the day, after the death of Bellini, Maria Malibran died[125] in Room 9 of the Mosley Arms, in Manchester[126] – having collapsed a week earlier on stage[127] from injuries sustained after being thrown from her horse. She was 28-years-old, and pregnant.[128] A death mask was taken, and copied subsequently for sale; it captures an extraordinary face, of huge dimensions for a woman born in the 18th century. The shape of the mouth, jawline and lips are pronounced and remarkably full; they are the features of a woman with proximate African heritage. It is more than a little bizarre that only two of the many paintings of Malibran completed during her lifetime look anything like the woman whose face was recorded in gypsum three hours after her death. Although the mask's authenticity has been debated, Malibran's friend Edmond Cottinet exclaimed on seeing it for the first time:

> It is she! [...] It is she with her slightly African type, containing perhaps a little negro blood [...].[129]

---

124   Lablache also sang at Beethoven's funeral (for which he was also one of the thirty-two torchbearers surrounding the coffin) and he would later perform as one of the soloists in Mozart's Requiem at Chopin's funeral, in 1849.

125   On 17 March, 1837, La Scala presented the first performance of *In morte di Maria Malibran de Bériot*, a cantata in memory of Malibran composed by Gaetano Donizetti, Giovanni Pacini, Saverio Mercadante, Nicola Vaccai, and Pietro Antonio Coppola. Among the soloists performers was the contralto, Maria ("Marietta") Brambilla (6 June, 1807 – 6 November, 1875), who created Maffio Orsini in Donizetti's *Lucrezia Borgia* on 26 December, 1833, and Pierotto in Donizetti's *Linda di Chamounix* on 19 May, 1842. Her younger sisters, Teresa, and Giuseppina, were sopranos, and greatly admired by Verdi and Ponchielli.

126   This profound tragedy should not be confused with Werner Schroeter's tragically awful 1972 film *Der Tod der Maria Malibran* ('The Death of Maria Malibran'). Starring Magdalena Montezuma as Malibran, with contributions from Warhols' muse, Candy Darling, the film is a series of tableau set to absurdly inappropriate (and butchered) excerpts from musical works written many years after Malibran died, including Brahms' *Alto Rhapsody* and Puccini's *Tosca*. His earlier homages to Maria Callas are less terrible in being considerably shorter: *Maria Callas Porträt* (1968), *Callas Walking Lucia* (1968) and *Callas-Text mit Doppelbeleuchtung* (1968).

127   While performing at the Theatre Royal on Fountain Street on Wednesday, 14 September, with Rosalbina Caradori-Allan (1800 – 1865) – who is remembered for performing the soprano solo in the British premiere of Beethoven's 9th Symphony on 21 March, 1825. After performing a duet from Handel's *Tamerlano*, the audience petitioned an encore. After that final performance, and during the applause, Malibran fainted, and never fully recovered.

128   Her former husband, Eugène, died just over two weeks later, on 12 October, at the age of 53.

129   Fitzlyon, April (1987). *Maria Malibran: Diva of the Romantic Age*. Souvenir Press, p. 230.

Keats' death mask from 1821 is identical to the portrait painted of the poet by Joseph Severn in 1819. The death masks of Wagner and Liszt record the same faces as appeared in dozens of photographs from the 1870s and 80s. The best of Malibran's portraits is one of the finest of any singer from the 19th century. Henri Decaisne painted her in 1830 as Rossini's Desdemona,[130] as evidence for which the bottom left hand corner of the portrait features a small impression of the Lion of Venice – the ancient bronze winged sculpture mounted on a column in the Piazza San Marco. Malibran was 23-years-old at the time, and already an international celebrity, but neither this impression, nor the more romantic portrait created by François Bouchot in 1831, bears any likeness to the death mask. Indeed, Decaisne's portrait renders her skin and appearance as stereotypically angelic, consistent with Desdemona's Caucasian purity when appreciated beside the dark, brooding, eternally foreign Otello. He shows her looking up, and away from her travails, to the empty space at the left hand of God. Decaisne and Bouchot came closer than anyone else to representing what can be *presumed* of Malibran's ethnicity. Nothing can be *known* about it definitively because there are no records, and her family tree on her father's side began with her father, the legendary tenor, Manuel del Pópulo Vicente García.[131] Having never known his own father, and in the absence of better information, García claimed him to be a gypsy – the then tolerable face of immigration in southern Europe.

The issue of Maria García [Malibran]'s race has been largely overlooked.[132] However, just as Caruso's febrile, hirsute and unfettered Italian masculinity would be diminished or overtly attacked by American critics and commentators with strong views on immigration,[133] so too was Malibran's "darkness" re-positioned throughout European and American society as Mediterranean[134] or, more commonly, "exotic." The poet Wayne Koestenbaum writes in his monologue, *The Queen's Throat*, how

> opera culture used images of darkness to demonize the diva […]. Roles like Carmen rely on the notion of the diva's "Latin blood." When divas have been made up to appear Asian or African for such roles as Aida, Selika, Cio-Cio San, and Iris, they were expressing opera's insistence on the dark nature of the diva, as well as underscoring, in a problematic masquerade, the white diva's separation from the women of colour she portrays.[135]

Malibran was not the first soprano with presumptively African roots, but the fine line between *black* and *exotic* (as constructions by white people determining cultural, societal and spiritual merit) was consequential in Europe, and fatal in the United States, where an institutionally racist dialectic manifested itself shortly after Malibran's return

---

130 The portrait is on display at the Musée Carnavalet, Paris.
131 See Boyden, Matthew (2021). *The Tenor: A Cultural History*. Ragueneau Press.
132 As it was in Germany at much the same time, whenever Caroline Branchu was portrayed. See Chapter 11 below.
133 *Ibid*, pp. 162–188.
134 Guarracino, Serena (2010). "An Ethiopian Princess' Journey: Verdi's *Aida* across the Mediterranean (and beyond)." *California Italian Studies*, 1(1).
135 Koestenbaum, Wayne (1993). *The Queen's Throat*. GMP Publishers, p. 106.

to Europe in the burlesques and comic *entr'actes* of the Minstrel shows. Koestenbaum asserts (without evidence or citation) that it was speculated during her lifetime that Malibran was not anatomically a woman; she was, rather, claimed to be "*an andro-gyne or hermaphrodite.*" If this seems unlikely then it's worth remembering how often the same thing has been written of black women by white men in the 21ˢᵗ century, with the most obvious victim of abuse being Michele Obama. Malibran's critics and observers did not enjoy absolute freedom of expression, particularly in the United States, which is why she was subjected routinely to a prism of evasion and innuendo. The repeating themes of the critical appreciation of Malibran's unusually passionate style of singing hinged on the consensus that she went "too far," as a woman as well as a soprano. This was a common refrain in Britain, where one reviewer articulated the prevailing opinion that Malibran's singing adhered to a "vehemence too entrenched in frenzy to be true."

Early 19ᵗʰ century formulations of normalcy, and the evolving status of gender and sexuality, were profoundly disrupted by the imagining of character and its re-creation by women on the operatic stage. The lingering dissonance created by the castrati was resolved by the concomitance of Malibran and Velluti as performers of music by the same composers on the same stages – which caused the levelling of a field invaded soon after by the ultimate romantic icon, the tenor. The achievement of Rossini's bari-tenors, particularly Domenico Donzelli, led to the triumphant vocal and nar-rative masculinity of Donizetti's heroes, Albert Nourrit and Gilbert Duprez – whose resonance bypassed the feminised elegance of Rubini and Mario.[136] It's tempting to deny the striking coincidence of the romantic tenor's emergence when sopranos were excelling socially and culturally, but the fact remains that women were still consid-ered inferior by a majority less interested in Mary Wollstonecraft's *Rights of Woman* than her daughter's *Frankenstein*. It's obvious that the promotion of "natural" female inferiority was made harder by seeing Malibran or one of her peers and successors triumph as Desdemona and Norma. The substitution of the travesti hero as the *sec-onda donna* of Romantic opera forced the reconstruction of characters and voices as "singing bodies" – a function of sexualisation and, inevitably, of race, education and status that subverted formalised notions of femininity. There was something inher-ently dangerous in the sight of a woman sweating in her nightdress while admitting to the experience of nocturnally-articulated passions which she could express only in the most intimate way by the use of her entire body. The eroticised components of performance were catalogued routinely, and with trembling, ill-contained rage. In 1839, for example, a Dr. Michael Ryan lamented:

> Who has not seen actresses appear in […] dresses as white as marble, and fitting so tightly that the shape of their bodies could not be more apparent, had they come forward on the stage in a state of nature? Again, the opera dancers appear nightly before crowded moral audiences, in dresses made for the express purpose of exposing their […] figure, while the style of dancing is such as to excite the most wanton thoughts and lascivious desires. The attitudes and personal exposure of these females

---

136   See Boyden, Matthew (2021). *The Tenor: A Cultural History*. Ragueneau Press.

are most disgusting to every really modest mind, and more suited to an improper house than to a public exhibition [...] were the scenes and figures depicted in prints and drawings [instead of on the stage], and offered for sale, they would be considered outrages on public morals.[137]

The historically pervasive sequestration of women evolved into a more strategic campaign of denigration and judgment. Comparing opera singers to prostitutes was a grubby but effective line of attack, analogous to the once-tyrannous judgment of the church, the family and the courts. Western society was at its most polite in its denial of the reality of independent employment, sexual emancipation and miscegenation; just as women had to be contained in their clothing in order to be considered decent, so too were women of mixed race lightened by paint, damned when employed, and displaced by description. The controlling of women in their appearance was challenged by an emerging scientific and social discourse sustained by "medical" diagnoses of women's biological and psychological inferiority. Menstruation was merely the least discussed "evidence" for an imperfection established by the shadows of original sin. The writing and performance of Italian opera (rather than opera in Italy) advanced the established gender narrative and its accompanying codes of conduct, with gender, body and identity being normalised by their rigidity – for which, again, the corset was an ideal metaphor. Maria Malibran was wearing a corset when thrown from her horse in July, 1836.[138] A woman riding without one in the 1830s in London would equate in the 21st century to a woman travelling as Lady Godiva. Across the UK, Europe and the United States, the advertising of women's clothing for horse-riding during the first half of the 19th century promoted corsets and tight-laced waistcoats for women to wear in public.[139] That Malibran's injuries were exacerbated by her corset is probable – if only because it allowed her considerably less freedom to move and adapt as she fell. It was routine for contemporary newspapers to report serious and fatal accidents by women falling from their horses; broken necks were less common than serious injuries resulting from corsets, with external and internal damage being caused by the snapping and shattering of bones and stays. Across Europe and America, thousands of women were harmed or killed by horses in incidents that would have produced fewer casualties but for the corset.

---

137 Davis, Tracy C. (1989). "The Actress in Victorian Pornography." *Theatre Journal*. Vol. 41, No. 3, pp. 294–315.

138 The incident was remembered by one of her companions, Lord William Lennox: "On setting off at a canter, she plied her light riding-whip too severely upon the horse's neck. The animal, usually quiet, got his mettle up, and suddenly increased his pace. A clatter of some horses behind added to his excitement, and in a few seconds the rider had lost all control over her steed. I was a few paces in the rear, and called upon Mr and Mrs Clayton to check their speed at once. Bounding round the inner circle of Regent's Park at an awful pace, Malibran, feeling herself lost, shouted for help, when a policeman rushed forward and seized the horse by the bridle. Unprepared for this sudden movement, the rider was precipitated against the wooden paling, and fell exhausted to the ground." Lord William Pitt Lennox (1863). *Fifty Years' Biographical Reminiscences*, 2 vols. Hurst and Blackett, 2, pp. 207–9.

139 See Dorré, Gina M. (2006). "Three Horses and Corsets: Black Beauty, Dress Reform, and the Fashioning of the Victorian Woman." In *Victorian Fiction and the Cult of the Horse*. Routledge. Also in *Victorian Literature and Culture* (2002). Vol. 30, No. 1, pp. 157–178.

The physical constraint resulting from tight-lacing was dualistic in its fostering of the contradictory rhetorics of respectability and scandal.[140] Malibran's containment as a woman of probable mixed-race began with her family, and her father in particular – who defined the cliché of the violently pushy parent. He was Maria's first teacher, so it's possible to know something of her practices and routines as they were prescribed by García's *Exercises and Method* from 1824 – which required the mastery of slow *mesa di voce* exercises (gradual *crescendo* and *decrescendo* on long held notes), followed by increasingly florid exercises using scales and arpeggios, and improvisation and embellishment – essential for performing operas by Rossini and his predecessors. García helped focus his daughter's chest register – pushing her towards what would now be called a mezzo-soprano, and helping her master a *tessitura* spanning B flat 4 to E flat 5. Malibran gave her London premiere performing "*Nacqui all'affanno* [...] *Non più mesta*," from *La Cenerentola*, in a concert at Almack's Rooms[141] on 9 June, 1824. She was 16-years-old. It's hard to credit that anyone can have sung this music effectively at so young an age; the following year, however, *The Times*' correspondent wrote of Malibran's theatrical debut on 11 June, 1825, as Rosina, that she was

> a very agreeable young lady. Her figure is good – her features rather expressive than handsome – her action free yet modest. Her voice is very pleasing, but it is not of extensive power. She, however, manages it with infinite skill. Her opening air ["*una voce poco fà*"], a composition of great difficulty, was beautifully sung, and was rapturously encored. She here displayed all the florid, yet delicate execution, for which her father is so remarkable.[142]

She repeated her success in the same role for the first Italian-language production of *Il barbiere di Siviglia* in the United States,[143] on 29 November 1825 – during which (for the lesson scene) she played a canny hand when accompanying herself at the piano singing "Home Sweet Home."[144] She made a sensational debut in Paris in the title role of *Semiramide* on 14 January, 1828, of which François-Joseph Fétis wrote that "The audience was conquered, and passed from the most disdainful coldness to the most immoderate enthusiasm."[145] She went on to a series of unqualified triumphs singing the operas of Rossini, who described her as:

---

140   See, generally, Craik, Jennifer (1994). *The Face of Fashion: Cultural Studies in Fashion*. Routledge.

141   A large assembly room on King's Street. These were frequently used for concerts from the 1820s. On 7 April, 1848, Berlioz conducted an orchestra for the Amateur Musical Society of his "Hungarian March" from *La damnation de Faust*, among numerous other works.

142   Radomski, James (2000). *Manuel García: Chronicle of the Life of a* bel canto *Tenor at the Dawn of Romanticism*. Oxford University Press, p. 183.

143   It was not the first US performance, as many claim. *Il barbiere* received its American premiere on 3 May, 1819 – in English – at the Park Theatre in New York. It was first performed in French at the Théâtre d'Orléans in New Orleans on 4 March, 1823.

144   In the audience was Joseph Bonaparte (brother of Napoleon, and the former King of Spain), James Fenimore Cooper (author of *The Last of the Mohicans*), the actor Edmund Kean, and Lorenzo Da Ponte (Mozart's librettist).

145   *Revue et gazette musicale, II*, 1827–8, p. 589. Quoted in Fitzlyon, April (1987). *Maria Malibran*. Souvenir Press, p. 70.

> That wonderful creature! With her disconcerting musical genius she sur-
> passed all who sought to emulate her, and with her superior mind, her
> breadth of knowledge and unimaginable fieriness of temperament she
> outshone all other women I have known.

Malibran was greatly admired by Bellini in *Norma*, *La Sonnambula*, and *I Capuleti e i Montecchi*, and he undertook to create a revision of *I puritani* for her mezzo-soprano register. Donizetti acclaimed her a phenomenon, and while in London she was tri-umphant as Leonora in an English-language production of *Fidelio*. Some considered her "extreme passions" to be primitive and ill-disciplined – as adjuncts to the preju-dices attaching to her miscegenation. Eugène Delacroix, for example, was critical of her absent refinement, and recoiled from her sensitivity "to the masses who have no artistic taste." Conversely, Castil-Blaze remembered Malibran's voice as

> vibrant, full of brightness and vigor. Without ever losing her flattering
> timbre, this velvet tone that has given her so much seduction in tender
> and passionate arias. [...] Vivacity, accuracy, ascending chromatics runs,
> arpeggios, vocal lines dazzling with strength, grace or coquetry, she pos-
> sessed all that the art can acquire.[146]

The majority of her contemporaries were similarly admiring of her intensity – in-cluding Chopin, Mendelssohn and Liszt. Numerous other composers paid tribute through instrumental pastiches. On hearing of her death, Moscheles composed an *Hommage Caractéristique à la Mémoire de Madame Malibran de Bériot, en forme de Fantaisie*, Op.94b,[147] which subsumed the soprano's palette of *legato*, portamento, vibrato, declamation, inflection and word placement to the mechanics of a piano. Curiously, she created only a single major role for Donizetti, *Maria Stuarda*, in 1835,[148] the opening night of which was a rare disaster for the composer. Malibran had been ill at the beginning of December, and this appears to have affected her mood as well as her voice. The crowd and the censors were both ill-pleased – with Malibran reintroducing texts that had been declared unacceptable. Like the other prima donnas whose oxygen she shared during the 1830s, Malibran's private life was a source of tawdry fascination. Her widely rumoured and oft-reported travails began in 1827, with the collapse of her first marriage to Eugène Malibran, followed by her controversial extra-marital relationship from 1829 with the Belgian violinist Charles de Bériot. Her pursuit of a divorce from the eternally impecunious Eugène was ex-pensive, humiliating and time-consuming. What should have been a simple matter of a petition required six years and "*va te faire foutre*" money. It was this passing feature of Malibran's life – that she was sufficiently unhappy in her marriage to engage in an affair, and pursue the legal and financial independence necessary for her to marry the man she loved – that the National Legion of Decency judged objectionable in 1948.

---

146 Saint Bris, Gonzague (2009). *La Malibran*. Belfond.
147 'Characteristic tribute to the memory of Madame Malibran de Bériot, in the form of a fantasy.' He previously composed a similar tribute to Giuditta Pasta: *Gems a la Pasta, Fantasia Dramatique*, Op.71a.
148 She also gave the premiere of Michael Balfe's *The Maid of Artois* in 1836.

But for her wealth and influence, Malibran would have lived out her years in a miserable, violent and destructive relationship – which is, presumably, what the Legion thought Jesus would have wanted. Only by reason of her status as "La Malibran" was she able finally to extricate herself, in February, 1835; a few weeks later, on 29 March, 1836, she married de Bériot – three months before dying in Manchester. Her only surviving child, Charles-Wilfrid de Bériot, was two years old.[149]

The press was predictably shocked and horrified, with tributes published globally in studied dismay. The irony of this predominantly sensationalist reporting (which included a significant number of French newspapers blaming England for her death) was that acres of print had been given during her lifetime to gossip and conjecture, with editors fomenting antagonisms where none existed. The Italian press, was famed for setting supporters of Pasta (the "*Patisti*") against the Malibran faction (the "*Malibrandisti*"), a manufactured rivalry that

> revisited issues common throughout operatic history: the artificial positioning of one singer against another; the challenge to an established artist by a new arrival. The language and imagery used by the critics also resonate with more modern constructions of stardom, and the blurring of boundaries between star-persona, role and performer. Battaglia's homage to Pasta's unexpected triumph (described by some as a star that had set, she now 'rises again in all the fullness of her genius to belie such calumny') evokes unconsciously the role of Norma as a metaphor for the singer's own situation: the public as a faithless Pollione, whose affections had momentarily transferred to the younger, more winning Malibran/Adalgisa, but who were now once again transfixed by the full bloom of Pasta's artistry.[150]

Stendhal had long been frustrated by the fickle nature of the crowd, whose variable support for singers was cultivated by changes in taste, nurtured by absent tensions. In his *Life of Rossini*, he told

> The tale [...] of a Neapolitan dilettante who, referring to two fair singers, one of whom was idolised like the morning star by her audiences, while the other was scarcely tolerated on the stage, stood up in the middle of the San Carlo, seized by one of those mighty paroxysms of indignation and passionate anger which are not infrequently met with in that city, and cried aloud: "In three years' time, you will be trampling your idol underfoot; in three years' time, you will be worshipping the goddess whom you now reject!" Scarcely eighteen months had rolled by before the prophecy was accomplished, for the cantatrice who had sung with

---

149   Born out of wedlock on 12 February, 1833, Charles-Wilfrid grew into a much-respected pianist, teacher and composer. He was the dedicatee of Ravel's *Rapsodie espagnole* (1907 and 1908). He died on 22 October, 1914.

150   Rutherford, Susan (2007). "'La cantante delle passioni': Giuditta Pasta and the Idea of Operatic Performance. *Cambridge Opera Journal*, Vol. 19, No. 2, p. 126.

expression had utterly supplanted the sometime *prima donna* whom nature had gifted with an infinitely finer voice.[151]

More remarkable for the time, but less interesting to newspaper and magazine editors, was the achievement collectively of a tiny group of operatic sopranos whose transcendence as professional women, determined on deciding if (and when) they would perform and for how much, changed the lives of every other woman to follow. Malibran, the Grisi sisters and Pasta were transformative because they took aggressive advantage of their influence and indispensability. It was not a simple matter of continuing to work *after* marriage – as a function of bloody-minded defiance – but rather their will and determination as decision-makers that would have been impossible even a decade earlier. Malibran, for example, was implacable in her promotion of de Bériot – whom she made pivotal to her contract negotiations: if de Bériot wasn't booked to play then Malibran wouldn't turn up. Grisi protected her position using tactics that would have made Machiavelli flinch; she was as formidable off the stage as she was compelling on it, and anyone who didn't do as she demanded suffered for it financially. In January, 1843, for example, she was invited by Donizetti to play Norina in the first production of *Don Pasquale* at the Théâtre-Italien; her co-operation was leveraged against the casting of Mario, rather than Rubini, in the role of Ernesto.[152] A few years later, the manager of the King's Theatre in London stood his ground over another detail of casting, provoking Grisi into presenting her ultimatum, and acting on her threats after decamping to Covent Garden with her husband and half a dozen of the Company's leading virtuosi.

These fearless and ferocious women generated vast fortunes from huge fees that enabled them to live in singular luxury. They performed their parts and played the game – "wearing the corset" as a compromise that facilitated their right to become indispensable for something other than sex and procreation. "Opera soprano" became the first aspirational job title to which women were entitled since humans first walked the planet;[153] this power and independence forced changes that everyone was compelled to accept as irreversible if they wanted to hear a woman sing on stage as a woman, with a woman's voice, in a woman's body, wearing a woman's clothing. In 2004, Pixar's allegedly "feminist" *The Incredibles* begins with a flashback to Mr. Incredible and his fiancé, Elastagirl, fighting crime as equals; Elastagirl establishes her independence by observing "Get married, me? Sit at home and let the men save the world? Are you serious?" Two decades later, Elastagirl is married as Mrs (sub?) Parr and living as the economic dependent of a selfish husband who considers himself entitled to ignore his family because he works an eight-hour shift outside the home. The retrograde ambition of a 21st century construction of a society in which "everyone is special because no-one is"[154] would have caused revulsion for the incredible

---

151 Stendhal (1824). *Life of Rossini*. Trans. and Ann. by Coe, Richard N. (1985). John Calder, p. 360.
152 Tamburini played Malatesta and Lablache created the title role.
153 No-one had previously to label women as "mothers" since that "job" was recognised to be fundamental to the species, and unavoidably a woman's sole source of absolute power.
154 A sentiment articulated by their son, Dash, when demanding that he be allowed to exist as himself in an argument with his parents concerning his ability to run faster than everyone else in his school. Or anywhere.

women whose talent, courage and conviction dug, laid and paved the 19th century's arduous path to enfranchisement. The necessity for their struggles and achievements was grimly memorialised in 1869, after Giulia Grisi died at the age of 58, following an accident suffered while travelling by train in the company of her family to Saint Petersburg. When her husband, Mario de Candia, delivered her body to Paris for internment at Père Lachaise, he instructed that the tombstone be inscribed uniquely with the name "Juliette de Candia."[155]

---

155 Malibran's husband did the same thing when wording the inscription on the brass plaque for attaching to her coffin. It was the first time in her life since marrying Eugène that she was identified publicly as someone other than Maria Malibran.

CHAPTER ELEVEN

The Road to Bayreuth

Given its infamous diversity, it would be unfair and reductive to table the character-istics of German pornography; it's reasonable, regardless, to assert that Germany has a reputation for *nische* erotica. The world's first sex shop opened in West Germany, in Flensburg, in 1962, while the oldest representation of sexual behaviour to be dated reliably was unearthed in Zschernitz in 2005.[1] The archaeologists who dis-covered two 7,000-year-old figurines depicting a heterosexual couple engaging in intercourse asserted in consequence that sex had been other than taboo for Teutonic stone-agers. Germany was not recognised as libertine until after the Weimar Republic took root in 1919; the German-speaking[2] people nonetheless developed a hearty appetite for print-erotica during the middle decades of the 18th century, which was satisfied primarily by lithographers producing *verboten* images with chastened men and women peeping through doors and windows. Literary *erotica* was less prevalent, but in 1815, a novel attributed to the writer, composer, critic and gothic icon E.T.A. Hoffmann was published with the snappy title *Schwester Monika erzählt und erfährt. Eine erotisch-psychisch-philantropisch-philantropinische Urkunde des säkularisierten Klosters X.*[3]

'Sister Monica' is a Bildungsroman,[4] a literary genre in which the psychological, physical and moral progress of a child is depicted on its journey towards maturity. The novel's flamboyance, and the author's numerous digressions on Shakespeare, Voltaire, Kant, Schiller and Schopenhauer give it an Hoffmannesque panache; it is more entertaining and worthwhile than a routine work of smut, therefore. Whoever wrote it was under the influence of de Sade's *Justine, ou Les Malheurs de la Vertu,*[5] a novel saturated in scandalised convents and sacrilegious nuns. The narrative features a zoetrope of romantic clichés, including monks, bandits, knights, priapic Frenchmen,

---

1   They are now a permanent exhibit at the Staatliches Museum für Archäologie Chemnitz (The State Museum for Archaeology, Chemnitz).
2   References in this chapter to "Germany," and variations of the same, are references to German-speaking territories.
3   'The Experiences and Confessions of Sister Monika: an erotic-psychic-physical-philanthropic document from the secularized monastery X.' The novel was published anonymously. The cultural historian Gustav Gugitz was the first to investigate Hoffmann's authorship; the critic Rudolf Frank later provided more compelling reasoning, and for the purposes of this book, it is accepted that Hoffmann was the author. See Boyden, Matthew (2018). *Beethoven and the Gothic*. Verba et musica.
4   Literally, a portmanteau of the German words "*bildung*" (meaning 'education' or 'forming') and "*roman*" (meaning 'novel'). The best-known example of a *Bildungsroman* at the time was Goethe's *Wilhelm Meisters Lehrjahre*, ('Wilhelm Meister's Apprenticeship') first published in 1796.
5   'Justine, or The Misfortunes of Virtue' (1791).

virgins, villains and villainesses. A child-bride and an eccentric aristocrat[6] deliver barmy monologues littered with hilarious invective.

Hoffmann's novel is literary erotica, and its preoccupations reach further than the protagonist's sexuality. As Foucault recognised, the book's defining pre-occupation is with the heroine's body in its objective state and condition, rather than as a subjective portrait for the servicing of a reader's lust. Some of what Monica endures was common at the time, including being drugged and raped;[7] this sense of what qualifies as normal colours the many descriptions of her appearance, which is represented to be proper and decent until Monica compares her reflection with a sculpture of Aphrodite, the standard for female beauty at the time. For all her comparative "perfection," Monica's experiences are universal in their resonance for every girl transitioning to womanhood; they are descriptive also of the status and treatment of German women during the early 19th century, insofar as her sexual and psychological journey from discipline and containment to freedom and (a form of) self-fulfilment are transcendent of the social and cultural structures that kept the majority of women in bondage.[8]

Monica's allegorical relocation from her family home to a series of schools, convents and monasteries is the transfer of authority over her body by her parents to a succession of pedagogues and institutions, which includes a health resort where the inmates are controlled according to instructions and codes of behaviour deemed medically and socially necessary. Some of the events to which Monica submits are forced upon her; mind and body are remade by suffering, but it is not the kind or species of cruelty that amused de Sade. Instead, Monica's endurance of a developing knowledge of self forms as a narrative for what it is to be a woman – a process that causes her to be transfigured for the reader as well as those falling into her orbit. The novel ends with Monica changing her name, withdrawing from society and retiring to a life of devotion in a convent where she is at liberty to pursue her own pleasures because sequestration has allowed her to "forget about the existence of the stronger sex."

Hoffmann's insights were remarkable at a time when women were still treated as objects d'art and utensils. *A Vindication of the Rights of Woman* was first translated into German in 1794, as *Rettung der Rechte des Weibes*,[9] it has been demonstrated how the substance of Wollstonecraft's radical thinking was reshaped by its passage into German.[10] Not until Henriette Herz's edition appeared in 1832[11] were the rights

---

6 Modelled on de Sade, in a wittier less violent form.

7 As it is for many in the 21st century. According to a British "YouGov" survey in 2021, one in nine (11%) of every woman in the United Kingdom believes they have had a drink spiked with drugs.

8 Not de Sade's kind of bondage.

9 Literally 'Saving the rights of women,' by Christian Salzmann and Georg Weissenborn.

10 Kirkley, Laura (2022). "Mary Wollstonecraft's Translational Afterlife: French and German Rewritings of A Vindication of the Rights of Woman in the Revolutionary Era." *European Romantic Review*, 33:1, pp. 1–24. See generally Simon, Sherry (1996). *Gender in Translation Cultural identity and the politics of transmission*. Routledge. It's interesting to note Wollstonecraft's own expertise as a translator. She completed English versions of Jacques Necker's *On the Importance of Religious Opinions* in 1788, and Madame de Cambon's *Young Grandison* in 1790. While writing *The Rights of Woman*, she translated *Christian* Salzmann's *Elements of Morality for the Use of Children*.

11 Another important translation of The Rights of Woman was completed in 1899 by Bertha

of German women represented finally as Wollstencraft articulated them in English. Herz's influence was confined largely to a circle of prominent Jewish émigrés, who met at her salon in Berlin. In addition to scientists like Wilhelm von Humboldt, her meetings were frequented by writers and poets, notably Jean Paul, Heinrich Heine and the Friedrich's Rückert, Schlegel and Schiller. More influential still was Amalie Beer's salon, on Berlin's Tiergartenstraße, where Germany's leading composers gathered to discuss contemporary developments in music and theatre. The list of patrons suggests these events during the 1820s and '30s must have been among the most stimulating in western history. Weber, Clementi, Hummel, Moscheles, Spohr, Paganini, Schumann and Mendelssohn were regular attendees – in certain cases as teenagers;[12] five or six languages were spoken routinely at the same time. Beer was Jewish, and her marriage to the sugar magnate, Jacob Herz Beer, gave her the resources with which to encourage and advocate changing the prevailing attitudes to race, religion and gender. It is difficult to credit the charisma, intelligence and brilliance of a woman who was able to secure the respect and patronage of Frederick William III of Prussia and his son, Prince Wilhelm, as well as a group of artists for whom the only common denominator outside music was an invitation to Beer's salon. Amalie's seismic relevance was compounded by her achievements as a mother to Michael, a poet and playwright; Wilhelm, an astronomer;[13] and Jacob,[14] a composer, who later changed his surname to Meyerbeer.[15] Beer's astonishing list of invitees included few women because women were not free to practice or hear what was otherwise preached in Germany's abundant miscellany of academies, conservatoires and universities. It is unsurprising, therefore, that the two who attended Beer's salon most frequently were the most celebrated German-born women at the time: Henriette Sontag[16] and Wilhelmine Schröder-Devrient. These legendary sopranos had been made famous by Beethoven.

Sontag was chosen to sing the soprano part at the premiere on 7 May, 1824, of the Ninth Symphony, the merciless tessitura of which borders on the misogynistic. The adversity is exacerbated by the setting of Schiller's words, the meaning of which

---

Pappenheim, the leading Jewish feminist and social reformer, and the "Anna O" analysed by Breuer and discussed by Freud. See Chapter 16.

12 Psujek, Jenifer Lauren (2010). *The Intersection Of Gender, Religion, and Culture in Nineteenth-Century Germanic Salons*. Masters thesis. Bowling Green State University.

13 In 1830, Heinrich Beer and Johann Mädler created the first globe of Mars; ten years later they calculated the planet's rotation to be 24 hours, 37 minutes and 22.7 seconds. Their calculations were 0.1 seconds different from the rotational period as it has been established using satellites in the 21st century.

14 Giacomo Meyerbeer's birthname was Jacob Liebmann Beer. He took the surname Meyerbeer on the death of his grandfather, Liebmann Meyer Wulff, in 1811. He italianised his first name while studying in Italy in 1817.

15 Giacomo's success was, of course, something of a double-edged sword, insofar as his colossal achievements as a composer of opera brought him celebrity as well as jealousy and loathing from the less successful, who conveyed their hatred as virulent anti-Semitism.

16 *née* Gertrude Walpurgis Sontag; after her marriage she was entitled Henriette, Countess Rossi (3 January, 1806 – 17 June, 1854). Sontag's unusual middle name is difficult to explain. She was neither conceived nor born on (or close to) Walpurgis Night, the German celebration of witches and witchcraft that falls on the night of 30 April and the day of 1 May. December 6th for Germans is *Nikolaustag* – or St. Nicholas' Day – when children leave out an empty boot for filling either with a gift, or a stick – depending on how they have behaved during the previous year.

are more than usually significant for the soloist as well as the audience. Sontag was 18-years-old at the time of the Symphony's first performance; her colleague, the contralto, Caroline Unger, was 20.[17] Beethoven's hearing was almost entirely gone by this stage in his life, and the nomination of singers was made by the Kapellmeister of the Theater am Kärntnertor, Michael Umlauf. During the Autumn of 1822 – when Sontag was 16-years-old – she was invited to attend on the composer with Unger, an event which he described in a letter to a friend:

> Two women singers called on us today and as they absolutely insisted on being allowed to kiss my hands and as they were decidedly pretty, I preferred to offer them my mouth to kiss.[18]

To add to the creepy atmosphere, Beethoven plied both women with wine, which left Sontag the worse for wear. Two days later, a friend reported to the composer that she

> vomited fifteen times the night before [...] with Unger the effect was in the opposite direction. What a pair of heroines! [...] Both beauties send you their regards and ask for a better and more wholesome wine in future.[19]

The first performance of the new symphony was one of the most significant events of the year. The pressure of anticipation did not resolve the casting of an experienced soprano, however. Because the writing necessitated a coloratura, even in the absence of *fioratura* and ornament, youth had much to recommend it. Sontag was only three months past her 18th birthday at the time, and little more than 12 months into her professional career; she had proven herself in performances of roles by Rossini, and as Agathe in a production of *Der Freischütz* in Leipzig. The latter must have been something wondrous, because it inspired Weber to gift Sontag the title role in the premiere of *Euryanthe* in December, 1823. It is impossible in the 21st century to imagine how a teenager might have been able to satisfy the requirements of music that continues to be among the most challenging technically, particularly considering the lack of adequate rehearsal time. Much has been written about the premiere of the Ninth, some of it evidenced.[20] What is certain is that it must have been acutely stressful for an 18-year-old singer to prepare for a premiere by the world's most original and oddest composer. According to Alexander Thayer:[21]

---

17 28 October, 1803 – 23 March, 1877.

18 Sachs, Harvey (2010). *The Ninth: Beethoven and the World in 1824*. Random House, p. 20.

19 Swafford, Jan (2014). *Beethoven: Anguish and Triumph*. Faber & Faber, p. 762.

20 For the most extensive account of the circumstances of the premieres of the Ninth and the *Missa Solemnis*, see Levy, David Benjamin (1979). *Early Performances of Beethoven's Ninth Symphony: A Documentary Study of Five Major Cities*. PhD Thesis. University of Rochester, pp. 43–107.

21 Jan Swafford attributes Unger's comments to the rehearsals for the first performance of three of the movements from the *Missa Solemnis* (the *Kyrie*, *Credo*, and *Agnus Dei*) – three days after the Ninth, on 7 May, 1824.

the principal singers found it difficult to assimilate the Beethovenian manner. [...] They pleaded with the composer for changes which would lighten their labors, but he was adamant. Unger called him "a tyrant over all the vocal organs' to his face," but when he still refused to grant her petitions she turned to Sontag and said: "Well, then we must go on torturing ourselves in the name of God!"[22]

Umlauf urged everyone to ignore Beethoven during the performance, even though he remained on stage throughout; it was advocated, instead, that the musicians focus on the conductor, Louis Duport. Joseph Böhm, a violinist in the Kärntnertor orchestra, described why this was necessary:

Beethoven himself conducted, that is, he stood in front of a conductor's stand and threw himself back and forth like a madman. At one moment he stretched to his full height, at the next he crouched down to the floor, he flailed about with his hands and feet as though he wanted to play all the instruments and sing all the chorus parts – the actual direction was in Duport's hands; we musicians followed his baton only.[23]

The first, still-remarkable review of the premiere, and three further performances[24] – together with the premiere of movements from the *Missa Solemnis*, for which Sontag was again the solo soprano – was written by Friedrich Kanne, and published by the *Allgemeine musikalische Zeitung* (AMZ). Kanne's account makes no reference to the composer's lunatic gesticulations, but it does speak to the pathos of the concert and the culture-war then raging in Vienna:

What feeling person, who was present at both performance days and saw the transfigured master at the side of the directing Kapellmeister Umlauf, reading along in the score, feeling doubly every small nuance and gradation of delivery and almost indicating them — what person who loves musical art in general will not wish from the heart that the reward for his exertions, whose size and value is unfortunately determined during the artist's lifetime by such unartistic occasions, causes, and motivations, and which is often endangered by completely unexpected external influences – might cheer the master and lift him beyond troublesome circumstances! The extent of the enthusiasm of the nation's most educated people puts in perspective the judgment of those who do not perceive in art anything more than a means of heightening sensual pleasure – and who were absent.[25]

---

22 *Thayer's Life of Beethoven*. Ed. Forbes, Elliot. Princeton University Press, Vol. 1, p. 907.
23 Cook, Nicholas (1993). *Beethoven: Symphony No. 9*. Cambridge University Press, p. 22.
24 5 June, 9 June, 16 June, 1824.
25 *The Critical Reception of Beethoven's Compositions by His German Contemporaries, Op. 125*. Trans. and Ed. by Wallace, Robin. Boston University, p.8.

The demands of the Symphony's soprano part became a theme of most of the criticism and commentary published after the Symphony began to be performed more widely. On 29 June, 1825, the *AMZ* published "News from the Lower Rhine," which reported of the Ninth that

> The whole is lacking in just proportion and practicability. The singing voices, namely soprano and bass, lie almost without interruption in their highest possible range, and the bass drum with triangle and piccolo, and likewise the contrabassoon and contrabass, are treated in a very obligato manner, and lay claim to more than is rightly theirs.[26]

Beethoven's rough treatment of sopranos, and of Sontag and Unger in particular, dates back two decades to *Fidelio*, the composer's only opera, which was first performed at the Theatre an der Wien on 20 November, 1805. The title refers to a character played within the drama by Leonore, the wife of the imprisoned Florestan. He-she was plainly an inspiration, or a point of reference at least, for the mysterious figure of Fredegunde/Camille – the young man disguised as a woman in Hoffmann's *Schwester Monika* – although the prudish Beethoven wouldn't have welcomed the parallels.[27] Significantly, however, and *contra* Mozart's Cherubino, "Fidelio" is a transvestite rather than *travesti*; Leonore is disguised as a man, who has to appear and behave *as* a man without revealing the truth of her gender. She is required to suspend the disbelief of Pizarro and her husband's persecutors, rather than the audience facing the stage. It does not require a leap of reasoning to appreciate how this narrative might have resonated for women living in a world determined by men. Of course, Beethoven's aspirations for marital bliss, as extolled by *Fidelio*, were undimmed by his emerging deafness, a contrary personality and, most problematically of all, a self-destructive apperception of class. That's not to suggest that Beethoven approached *Fidelio* as a feminist; his opera was concerned first and foremost with societal freedom – as it is apostrophised by Florestan in his cell when singing "*Zur Freiheit, zur Freiheit!*" Liberation from the abuses of the State (domestic and foreign) was a lifelong pre-occupation for the composer;[28] he was sensitive also to a range of surrogate iterations of confinement, attaching to his disability, his catastrophic nephew, the privations forced upon him by his publishers and, even, the actions of his friends. The much-revised opera (which he allowed to rest only in 1814) passed through the hands of three consecutive librettists, Joseph Sonnleithner, Stephan von Breuning and Georg Treitschke – each of whom emphasised the work's political resonance above its abrogation of normative gender roles. Beethoven was political in the same way he was a humanist – he loved humanity but detested people; his attitude to the French Revolution was as theoretical as his conception of women, therefore. Beethoven enjoyed female friendships; women enjoyed his company during his

---

26 *Ibid*, p. 27.

27 Beethoven and Hoffmann did not know each other, but the composer appreciated his writings on music, especially his landmark essay on the Fifth Symphony.

28 On 2 August, 1794, for example, Beethoven observed in a letter to Nikolaus Simrock that "no one dares to speak aloud, for fear of arrest by the police." In *Thayer's Life of Beethoven*. Ed. Forbes, Elliot. Princeton University Press, p. 170.

(relative) youth, and after the first performance of *Fidelio* he was subjected to what appears to have been an unforgettable evening during which he was besieged by his inner circle to revise the opera.[29] At two in the morning, Princess Lichnowsky was sent in to bat; she alone was able to persuade him to change his mind by beseeching:

> "It must be! Give in! Do it in memory of your mother! Do it for me, who am only your best friend!"[30]

Beethoven's reaction to the Reign of Terror was complicated. He was for the proletariat as long as they were for him, a self-dooming dialectic for someone unable to sustain an intimate relationship with a woman. It's clear from his dreadful conflict with his brother's widow that he was a conservative – a characteristic that can be traced to his studies with Christian Neefe, one of whose published articles averred with emblematic certainty, "They don't think much, the female souls [...] To think is virile!"[31] Beethoven was never *not* interested in female company; he raged over pennies when visiting brothels, but he also welcomed the attentions of women drawn to his talent and celebrity. His friend, Ferdinand Ries, remembered how the composer

> very much enjoyed looking at women; lovely, youthful faces particularly pleased him. When we passed a girl who could boast her share of charms, he would turn around, look at her sharply through his glass, then laugh or grin when he realised I was watching him. He was very frequently in love, but usually only for a short time.[32]

Beethoven did not oppose emancipation as it was assured by *The Declaration of the Rights of Man and of the Citizen*,[33] Article 1 of which declared that "Men are born and remain free and equal in rights." Viennese society was happy to accommodate enfranchisement, although the granting of equality in matters of inheritance did not extend to political freedom. The negative reaction among German states to the anonymous publication of "*Über die bürgerliche Verbesserung der Weiber*,"[34] a fiercely argued pamphlet in support of female rights,[35] adhered to the common view that Napoleon's Civil Code was an excellent model for the French. Even after the Congress of Vienna enabled a raft of theoretically Europe-wide reforms, the experience of most women

---

29 This remarkable evening saw Beethoven harangued in his apartment for four hours by Prince and Princess Lichnowsky; his brother Carl; Stephan von Breuning; two of Mozart's brothers-in-law, Joseph Lange and Friedrich Meyer; the playwrights Heinrich von Colin and Georg Treitschke; the violinist Franz Clement, and the tenor August Röckel – who sang through the opera for Beethoven while Prince Lichnowsky played the piano from Beethoven's original full-score, in illustration of the changes everyone wanted to see. Röckel was later rewarded for his efforts when Beethoven honoured him with the creation of the second Herr Florestan. Swafford, Jan (2014). *Beethoven: Anguish and Triumph.* Faber & Faber, p. 418.
30 *Ibid*, p. 419.
31 *Ibid*.
32 *Ibid*, pp. 391–392.
33 26 August, 1789.
34 'On Improving the Status of Women.'
35 By Theodor G. von Hippel, The Mayor of Königsberg.

was unchanging, with Austrian and German territories forbidding any activity of a political nature.

For this reason, Beethoven's decision to turn Bouilly's *Leonore* into an opera was bold because its most compelling feature – the transformation of the leading "man" into a "damsel in distress" – celebrated female empowerment and autonomy at a time when the majority of women in Europe could speak only if spoken to. Notwithstanding the novelty of his tenorial bravado, Florestan is an archetype of traditionally feminine vulnerability, as it was memorialised by a graveyard of gothic writers during the twenty years either side of 1800. Ann Radcliffe's *The Mysteries of Udolpho*, Matthew Lewis' *The Monk* and E.T.A. Hoffmann's *Die Elixiere des Teufels*,[36] are classically-ordered exemplars of narratives in which vulnerable women are saved by heroic men.[37] Leonore's courage as a scion of privilege submitting to the risk of violence and death for seducing Marzelline (the jailor's daughter), or for courting the working-class Jaquino, or for saving Florestan from certain death, is the beatification of *l'amour conjugale*.[38] Impressive though this is, the audience in 1805 was in no doubt that Leonore and Florestan's relationship after the final chorus would be defined thereafter by la loi conjugale.[39] The power of the patriarchal state over women as prisoners of conscience was such that, for all his gratitude, Florestan would have presumed married life to continue in accordance with *his* expectations once the dust had settled.

Leonore's transcendence of this depressing outcome is sanctified in her defiance of the certainty of her adversaries' cruelty and violence, which Pizarro embodies as virility. As they square off in the dungeon, their exchanges codify the pretext for fear as between the genders – with Pizarro contemptuous of any man trembling before a woman. It is in the opera's subsequent modelling of female "perfection" that *Fidelio's* dissection of virulent masculinity is at its most insightful. After Leonore protects Florestan by throwing herself in front of Pizarro with the words "*Töt´ erst sein Weib!*"[40] even Pizarro concedes (as an aside) the bravery of Leonore's deceit. His attitude changes when she draws a pistol and points it at his head; as she utters the words, "*Noch einem Laut und du bist todt,*"[41] a trumpet sounds, announcing the arrival of Fernando. This *deus ex machina* does not save Florestan; it spares Pizarro. Leonore is preserved coincidentally from the shame and ignominy of living as a murderer, so while order is restored, and the *status quo* preserved, it is the heroine's anomalous, Christ-like purity that prevails against the abuses of a modern world given "naturally" to violence and persecution.[42]

Leonore was the most demanding role for a soprano at the time; it may be considered the first "dramatic" part for any woman in opera – in any language and by

---

36 'The Devil's Elixirs.'
37 See Boyden, Matthew (2018). *Beethoven and the Gothic*. Verba et musica.
38 The sub-title of the source for *Fidelio's* libretto, by Jean-Nicolas Bouilly.
39 'Marital law.'
40 'Kill his wife first!'
41 'Another word, and you are dead!'
42 See, generally, Buch, Esteban (2021). "Fidelio or the Musical Prison: A Dark Essay on Freedom, Gender, and the State." *Music & Practice*, Vol. 8.

any composer.[43] Beethoven's orchestra was large for the time, requiring a piccolo, two flutes, two oboes, two clarinets, two bassoons, contrabassoon, four horns, two trumpets, two trombones, timpani, and a string band of around 20 (with two or three double-basses, four or five cellos, and between ten and 15 violins).[44] The vocal part requires considerable stamina, with wide intervals that present onerous technical challenges for a singer – none of them are virtuosic. In its embrace of the range of a soprano and a mezzo,[45] much of the writing is placed awkwardly and Beethoven's approach to text and mood is avant-garde in its expressive reach; Leonore's tentpole solo in Act I evidences his divergence with the theatre of Gluck and Mozart. In the lengthy scene beginning "*Abscheulicher!*"[46] Leonore responds to what she has learned of Pizarro's evil scheme:

> *Wo eilst du hin?*
> *Was hast du vor in wildem Grimme?*
> *Des Mitleids Ruf, der Menschheit Stimme*
> *Rührt nichts mehr deinen Tigersinn?*[47]

The most striking feature of Beethoven's settings of these words is their tendency to-wards the ugly – at least when compared to what was being written by his contempo-raries. The leading interval for the word "*Abscheulicher*," for example, is a descending minor seventh (E4 – to F sharp 3) that clashes dissonantly with the second violins and violas playing an A, and the first violins a C an octave above; the basses play an F sharp to sustain the soprano in the use of her chest voice. Even if the effect is not as shocking as Florestan's Act II lamentation, "*Gott! Welch Dunkel hier,*"[48] the ambition is identical. Beethoven composed music for words that are neither benign nor passive; he was cutting his cloth with exacting psychological precision, therefore. Mozart did the same, but without compromising the primacy of beauty or the capacities of his singers. Beethoven was uninterested in the needs of anyone performing his music, and he cared nothing for beauty *in absentia*. While much of *Fidelio* is lyrical – un-forgettably so during the Act I quartet, "*Mir ist so wunderbar*"[49] – its composer's obsession with aesthetic-philosophical truth was uncompromising; indeed, it's worth remembering that the man who wrote *Fidelio* would go on to compose the Late Quartets and the Piano Sonatas Op.109, Op.110 and Op. 111. Leonore's dramatic intensity can shock, even now, as evidenced by his setting of the nine syllables in the words, "*Der blickt so still, so friedlich nieder,*" which unfold over five bars with

---

43   References to the *Fidelio* are references to the final edition, in two acts.

44   For context, when in 1843 Berlioz attended a performance of *les Huguenots* in Berlin (see further below) he noted in passing the orchestra having 28 violins – which means at the very least 14 first violins and, in all probability, ten violas, eight 'cellos, and six double-basses, a total string band of around 50. It's routine in the 21st century for any orchestra performing *Fidelio* (other than as a "period" ensemble) to feature as many as 80 players.

45   It continues to be performed by both voices.

46   'You Monster.'

47   'Where will you go? What have you planned in cruel fury? The call of pity, the voice of mankind – Will nothing move your tiger's wrath?'

48   'God, what darkness here.'

49   'A feeling never known.'

eighteen notes formed of only three repeating, contiguous pitches (G3, F sharp 3 and F natural). Beethoven assumed that whoever was singing the role would be able to act out the sentiments, as a *Schauspielsängerin* to rival any *attrice cantante* as yet unimagined by Bellini.

For the transition from recitative to aria ("*Komm, Hoffnung, lass den letzten Stern*"[50]), Beethoven employs three horns but the first bassoon to colour the shift in tone towards Leonore's newly-minted feelings of hope; the ensuing quintet, for soprano, horns and bassoon is wondrous and technically arduous. The obstacles come thick and fast during the *Allegro con brio*, beginning "*Ich folg' dem innern Triebe.*"[51] Beethoven requires a soprano to sing consecutive notes spanning almost two octaves, as well as a metrically complex *parlando* that places her in competition with the horns, bassoon and strings. The wide variations in pitch, rhythm and tempo are closer to speech than any composer had attempted previously; it's impossible not to marvel at his invention when conveying Leonore's transformation from rage to faithfulness and love.[52] Much of Beethoven's vocal score is syllabic – with one syllable to a note; for the phrase "*Die Liebe, sie wird's erreichen,*"[53] he treats "*erreichen*" literally, scoring it in its repetition as two melismatic runs, the second of which begins on an F3 and climaxes with a soaring B4 that descends stepwise by seven notes to a low B3 – a two-octave span. This intransigent disregard for the performer is compounded by the cadence at the end of the second of the two runs, which Beethoven delays by the use of a fermata on the final F sharp; the concluding phrase is otherwise absent pauses or rests, and impossible for most to complete without at least one corset-stretching breath.

Nothing in *Fidelio* is designed to feed a soprano's vanity; every note and every word is joined in service to the dramatic moment and the narrative impulse. Singers raised on Italian opera at the turn of the century must have been horrified to see what was being asked of them,[54] which is why Pauline Anna Milder[55] warrants recognition as the inceptive German soprano of the 19th century. In addition to navigating the manic and abrasive Beethoven, Milder had to commit to rehearsals with 15,000 French troops marching into Vienna. The markets were closed, accommodation was appropriated, and the streets emptied. Baron Braun decreed that the theatres should remain open, unless there were bombardments, a detail that can have generated little reassurance for a company attempting to stage the most "difficult" opera in the city's history. The premiere was given just seven days after Vienna's occupation, to a largely empty house, in which the acoustics must have been more than usually generous to the singers. It is impossible to frame the intensity of the emotion that greeted the

---

50 'Come hope, let not the last bright star.'

51 'I shall follow my impulses.'

52 "*Der treuen Gattenliebe.*"

53 'Through love I shall reach it.'

54 For German audiences at the turn of the century, the majority of singers, like the majority of composers, were from Italy and singing in Italian. Opportunities for German-speaking singers increased during the last fifteen years of the 18th century, thanks to the work of a small number of influential non-Italian artists, notably Gertrud Elisabeth Mara (23 February, 1749 – 20 January, 1833) and the Portuguese-born Luísa Rosa de Aguiar Todi (9 January, 1753 – 1 October, 1833), whose wildly successful tour of Germany in 1790 led to her performing for Beethoven privately.

55 After marriage, she performed as Milder-Hauptmann (13 December, 1785 – 29 May, 1838).

supreme episode towards the opera's end, when Leonore is passed the keys to her husband's chains and invited to remove them while the chorus sings of their "inexpressible happiness." It's a difficult scene to survive without a handkerchief in the 21st century; it must have been overwhelming in 1805.

Milder was 20-years-old at the premiere. As with Sontag, age was not an issue; it must be questioned, however, whether a woman only recently a teenager can have performed Beethoven's music to his satisfaction. The rushing of young girls onto stage was primarily etiological; "woman hath but a short time to live, and is full of misery" was only slightly less true in 1805 than it had been for Margarete Cranmer when her husband wrote the *Book of Common Prayer* in 1549. A large number of sopranos born in the late 18th and early 19th centuries never lived to see 40, which predicated against "students" committing more than a year or two to a privilege that now entails a decade's uninterrupted training. If a woman of 20 could not hope to do more than get through "*Abscheulicher*" in the 21st century, far less a complete performance as Leonore in costume, then it's reasonable to ask why Beethoven invited Milder to create all three premieres of *Fidelio* over a span of nine years[56] – particularly in the light of his decision to cast a different Florestan on each occasion.[57]

What can Milder have sounded like? The earliest useful recording of "*Abscheulicher*" was made in 1907, by Lilli Lehmann. Born in 1848, her mother was the soprano Maria Theresia Löw,[58] a childhood friend of Richard Wagner, who worked closely with Marschner and Spohr. She trained Lilli and her sister, Marie, who created two roles for Wagner at the first staging of *Der Ring des Nibelungen*[59] at Bayreuth, Wellgunde (a Rhinemaiden) and Waltraute (a Valkyrie). Lilli made her debut in 1865, and nine years later she also created two roles for the first *Ring*: Woglinde (a Rhinemaiden) and Helmwige (a Valkyrie). She was 58-years-old when she recorded "*Abscheulicher*."[60] Her pitching is inconsistent, and it's clear she has to "find" any note above an F4. The abundant portamento is used as a shield as well as a sword; she employs an expressive (and perfectly clear) diction that adds considerably to the drama of the interpretation. Her tone is full, and consistent with Lehmann's reputation as the greatest Wagner soprano of the late 19th century; her languorous phrasing of "*Liebe wird's erreichen*," touches on greatness – an impression blunted by the car-crash that is her singing of the (admittedly onerous) passage of quavers, "*Mich stärkt die Pflicht der treuen Gatten liebe*."[61] She employs limited vibrato, for colour only, which exposes her phrasing to ungenerous scrutiny. It is an often lumpen performance by a woman who was known to overwork, which might be sufficient to explain the

---

56 They must have become friends, after a fashion; their relationship survived her refusal to perform Beethoven's concert aria, "*Ah! Perfido*." ('Oh Deceiver'), Op. 65, after Beethoven insulted Milder's fiancé during a rehearsal. Her place was taken by Josefine Killitzky (1790–1880) – the sister-in-law of Ignaz Schuppanzigh, the leader of "Beethoven's" Quartet.

57 See Boyden, Matthew (2021). *The Tenor: A Cultural History*. Ragueneau Press, pp. 119–122.

58 27 March, 1809 – 30 December, 1885.

59 'The Ring of the Nibelung.'

60 Consider, by contrast, the longevity of Christa Ludwig's career, and the consistency of her voice into her 70s.

61 'My duty strengthens me, the truth of my marital love.'

prominent sense of effort that colours the performance – an impression made worse by Lehmann's tendency to "squawk"[62] mid-phrase.

Contextually, Renée Fleming was in her 59th year when Decca released her recording of Lieder by Brahms, Schumann, and Mahler, which included a performance of "*Er, der Herrlichste von allen*,"[63] from *Frauenliebe und leben*,[64] Op. 42. It is an unfair comparison – and not because of the differences in recording technology.[65] The flexibility and expression of Fleming's voice when singing what is recognised to be one of Schumann's most difficult songs is incomparable to Lehmann's effortful performance of "*Abscheulicher.*" In matters of technique in isolation, the American soprano's voice is transcendent in its pitching, line and word-use. Portamento is used to facilitate the architecture of the song's phrasing, rather than as a mechanism for disguising weaknesses in placement. It might be concluded either that Lehmann was past her best at the time, or that her sound and sensibilities were within reach of the ideal in 1907. Since Lehmann continued to sing seasons in Vienna and Salzburg post-1910, and given that she delayed her retirement as a lieder singer until the 1920s, the former explanation is distinguished. It follows that what Lehmann was doing in 1907 – little more than seventy years after Milder gave her last performance as Leonore – comes closer to the standard of the time at the premiere. Lehmann was, of course, much changed by her experience of working with Richard and Cosima Wagner, a fact to which she admitted. Her bad habits, as evidenced in 1907, must have been hard-wired to her voice at her debut, aged 17. That voice, at least by modern standards, was unschooled.

The same thing was observed of Milder. On 20 May, 1806, the *Zeitung für die elegante Welt* published a short review, in which it observed that she "had a lovely though little-trained voice."[66] Many other opinions construed her limitations as an absence of dramatic ability. On 8 January, 1806, the AMZ published its "News. Vienna, Mid-December of the *Previous Year*," in which it recorded:

> The most noteworthy among the musical products of the previous month was the long-awaited Beethoven opera: *Fidelio* or *Conjugal Love*. It was given for the first time on 20 November, but was very coldly received. I will speak somewhat more extensively about this. [...] The performance also was not first-rate. Miss Milder has, despite her beautiful voice, too little passion and life for the role of Fidelio, and Demmer[67] sang almost continually flat. All of this taken together, along, in part,

---

62   'Snatching' would be a more commonly applied technical term to characterise voices suffering from technical insecurity.

63   'A Woman's Love and Life.'

64   'He, the noblest of all.'

65   Lehmann does not force her voice during the recording, and she makes some use of dynamic contrast, just not very much.

66   Senner, Wayne M., Wallace, Robin, Meredith, William (2001). *The Critical Reception of Beethoven's Compositions by his German Contemporaries, Vol. 2.* University of Nebraska Press, No.240, p. 180.

67   See Boyden, Matthew (2021). *The Tenor: A Cultural History.* Ragueneau Press, p. 119.

with the present circumstances, explains why the opera could only be given three times.[68]

What emerges from the AMZ's reviews during the first quarter of the century is that opera singers – and sopranos in particular – were perceived as *acting* singers. The 20th century's obsession with recording isolated voice from body, suffocating one half of an artist's dramatic vernacular. There are few reviews of performances from before 1900 that do not address a singer's acting abilities in equivalence with their voices, and many weak singers were forgiven the worst of their sins because they managed to persuade by other means. Lilli Lehmann, for example, was as renowned for her skill as an actress as she was worshipped for her talent as a singer. That does not explain how women as young as 16 were able to do either proficiently.

This is not a fallacy of progress. A woman's cranial physiognomy does not "fix" until she is in her middle to late twenties, at which point it continues to change with the years. The cheekbones withdraw as the forehead moves forward; the facial bones become more pronounced with time, causing a woman's sound to change in tandem with her appearance. The human voice is a construction of complex physiological interactions that co-ordinate when facilitating the vibrations produced by phonation. In simple terms, the human head is comprised of a neurocranium (the part of the skull that houses the brain) and a visceral cranium – the outer structure and the bones in the face. The neurocranium grows rapidly during a child's early development and is fully-formed by the age of three or four; the visceral cranium grows more slowly, and never stops doing so – insofar as the bones are shifting constantly until death. There is an optimal period, spanning from around 25 to 45 during which a woman's head-shape aligns with the rest of her anatomy, wherein the security of the abdominal muscles, the diaphragm and the lungs coincide with practice, experience and insight. It is not now, nor has it ever been, possible for a teenager to project as can a fully-grown woman in her middle thirties. Since 1900, there have been exceptional cases of women achieving physical and artistic maturity at a young age; Rosa Ponselle, Alexia Cousin and Cecilia Bartoli[69] are obvious outliers. Premature mastery of tone, amplitude and line has been sufficiently rare, however, to exclude the possibility that German-language sopranos during the first quarter of the 19th century were capable during their teens of doing justice to a character like Leonore. It's reasonable to conclude what Milder and her peers did *not* sound like, therefore.

The common immaturity of sopranos in Vienna was evidenced by Beethoven's casting of the 21-year-old Louise Müller[70] as Marzelline for the first production of

---

68 Senner, Wayne M., Wallace, Robin, Meredith, William (2001). *The Critical Reception of Beethoven's Compositions by his German Contemporaries, Vol. 2.* University of Nebraska Press. No.240, p. 174.

69 1979 – . Though little known and mostly forgotten, this English-French polyglot soprano was a phenomenon in her very early twenties. On 3 March, 2005, she chose without explanation to retire from all performance at the age of 25. In a press release she explained, "*J'ai pris la décision de mettre un terme à ma carrière artistique. C'est la passion et l'intégrité profonde avec lesquelles j'ai toujours chanté qui orientent aujourd'hui ma vie vers d'autres activités.*" ('I made the decision to put an end to my artistic career. It is the passion and deep integrity with which I have always sung that now orients my life towards other activities.').

70 *née* Ludovika Müller (1784 – after 1837).

Fidelio.[71] He stuck with Müller for the second; she may have been too old for the composer in 1814, because he turned for the third version of the opera to a 16-year-old, Anna "Nanette" Bondra.[72] The AMZ's review on 5 June, 1814, noted only that "Miss Bondra the younger (Marzelline) contributed especially to the success."[73] She had little career afterwards, and died at the age of 38 from Scarlet Fever. The AMZ during Beethoven's lifetime is littered with the names of hundreds of female singers whose careers began in their teens and who either died young or were forgotten while alive. With European intendants preferring youth and exuberance to age and treachery, French theatres were the first to delay the submission of female singers to the grinder of theatrical avarice. On 3 August, 1795, the government combined the École Royale with the Institut National de Musique to create the Conservatoire de Musique. One of the first to enrol, in October, 1796, was Thimoléone-Rose-Caroline Chevalier Lavit – who performed under her married name, Caroline Branchu.[74]

Branchu is remembered for having been taken as a mistress by Napoleon in 1802,[75] an attainment that added buttery irony to her creation five years later for Spontini of the title role of *La vestale*.[76] She was 27 at the time, and better equipped than her teenage rivals to compete with the opera's sizable orchestra, which included two flutes, two oboes, two clarinets, two bassoons, four horns, two trumpets and three trombones. *La Vestale* travelled northern Europe at furious speed, and it had a puissant effect on Carl Maria von Weber's approach to voice and orchestra when composing his defining romantic operas, *Der Freischütz*[77] and *Euryanthe*. This fact was overlooked by Spontini, who railed against both operas, as well as the very concept of indigenous German music theatre.[78] Weber was an accomplished kapellmeister; as

---

71   As much was evidenced for the author's grandfather, who played the trumpet in a performance of *Parsifal* at Covent Garden in 1939, conducted by Felix Weingartner (1863 – 1942). Frank Boyden's second son, the author's father, was then a small boy, but he happened to attend rehearsals with his mother, who was asked to introduce the child to the conductor. Having shaken his hand, Weingartner leaned forward and announced, "young man, you will one day wish to remember that I was friends many years ago with a woman who sang in the first performance of Beethoven's Ninth Symphony…" Weingartner was friends also with Liszt, who invited him to Weimar and later introduced him, as a 19-year-old, to Wagner at the first performance of *Parsifal* in 1882. The chorus member who sang at the premiere of the Ninth was 20-years-old at the time; she was 80 when Weingartner came to know her as a 20-year-old himself, in 1883/4. It should be noted that if anything was conveyed to Weingartner of the Ninth's premiere by the aged soprano then it resolved little of value for the conductor when recording the Symphony in 1935 with the Vienna Philharmonic. It is a dull, clinical and clichéd performance. The only reason for seeking out the recording is the magnificent singing of the soprano, Luise Helletsgruber (30 May, 1901 – 5 January, 1967).
72   21 March, 1798 – 11 July, 1836. Should not be confused with her elder sister, also a soprano, Therese Bondra (1794 – 1816).
73   *Ibid*, p. 182.
74   Also known as Alexandrine-Caroline Branchu. Born mixed race at Cap-Français in Santo Domingo, now Haiti (2 November, 1780 – 14 October, 1850).
75   She became Napoleon's mistress in early 1802, after he saw Branchu perform as Gluck's *Iphigenia*. In a probably unconnected event, Bonaparte decided to restore slavery in Santo Domingo during, or very shortly after, the affair came to an end. Like many others, Branchu's mixed-race was either ignored or negated by portraitists.
76   'The Vestal Virgin.'
77   'The Free Shot.'
78   He did so from his offices in Berlin, where he was Kapellmeister and chief conductor of the Königliches Opernhaus.

the son of an operatic soprano he favoured experience over youth when inviting the geriatric 31-year-old Caroline Seidler[79] to create the role of Agathe. Seidler's father, Karl, was among the most respected violinists of his day; he was instrumental to his daughter's training and, as a friend of Beethoven's, her appointment to Prince Lobkowitz's theatre in Vienna. Seidler was a teenager at the time of her debut. In 1815, she triumphed as *Die Vestalin*, and from 1816 she made regular appearances in Leipzig, Dresden, Hanover, Breslau, Pest and Prague – where Weber was transfixed by her portrayal of Leonore. Considering the reputed size of her voice, Seidler's casting as Rosina in the first Berlin production of *Der Barbier von Sevilla* at the Hofoper might seem like an anomaly,[80] but she was typical in being expected to perform a wide range of repertoire, little of it in German, even if that was the language in which it was written. Italian bel canto was an established ingression, against which the only substantive resistance during the first two decades of the century was Beethoven's *Fidelio*. Everything changed on 18 June, 1821, with the premiere of *Der Freischütz* in Berlin.[81]

As an expression of romanticised nationalism, and in its ideation of linguistic identity (which the German people were alone in being "able" to appreciate), Weber's gothic masterpiece triumphed as the first symptomatically German opera. The score's nativism was at its most resonant in the writing for orchestra, which was more virtuosic than anything in the vocal parts.[82] In the *Journal des Débats*, on 23 June, 1835, Berlioz recognised how Weber's orchestrations were "as far from Beethoven's as from that of Rossini." Again for the *Débats*, Berlioz wrote on 8 September, 1857, that Weber was

> as great in Freischütz as in Oberon. But the poetry of the former is full of movement, passion, and contrasts. The supernatural leads to strange and violent effects. The melodic style, harmony, and rhythm have in combination a thunderous and incandescent power; everything conspires to arrest attention. The characters are also taken from everyday experience and have widespread appeal. The depiction of their feelings and daily lives calls for a less elevated style, which is enhanced by exquisite workmanship. This gives the work irresistible charm, even for those minds who disdain musical amusements, and to the general public it comes across in this form as the pinnacle of art and a miracle of inventiveness. [...] The language [...] derives its main charm from harmony, its melodic language is capriciously vague, its rhythms are unpredictable and veiled, and thus often difficult to grasp. It is a language that is all the

---

79 She became Seidler-Wranitzky after her marriage to Berlin's Royal Concertmaster, Karl Seidler – a respected German violinist.

80 Seidler-Wranitzky remained at the Hofoper, as one of the city's two leading *prima donnas*. The other was Pauline Milder.

81 At the Schauspielhaus, which shortly after became the Theater am Gendarmenmarkt und Komödie. It is now the Konzerthaus.

82 The immense care taken by Weber required singers to confront an orchestral fabric that was unprecedented in its colour, contrast and density compelled clarity, not volume. This is not the case, however, for Agathe's best known aria, beginning "*Leise leise fromme Weise*" ('Softly, softly, and devoutly').

more difficult for the general public to follow as its subtleties cannot be experienced, even by musicians, without extremely close attention combined with a lively imagination.[83]

The work's constitutional teutonism was discernible in its valuing of word and gesture above *pure* tone and technique – a prejudice that brought Weber into alignment with E.T.A. Hoffmann, with whom he worked closely in Bamberg. Weber's success as a "uniquely" German composer for the stage was decisive because it actualised a partisan obsession with word-projection – an ambition developed further still by *Euryanthe*,[84] the first "through-composed" opera by a German composer. Nine months earlier, on 9 November, 1822, a performance of *Fidelio* in Vienna added tectonically to this accretion of Germanic cultural traits when a 17-year-old soprano, Wilhelmine Schröder-Devrient,[85] engendered the "*singende Schauspielerin*"[86] and her coincident immortality as the most consequential woman in the history of German opera.

The revelation of Schröder-Devrient's performance as Leonore followed rehearsals in the presence of the composer, whom the soprano remembered for his

Bewildered face and unearthly inspired eyes, waving his baton back and forth with violent motions, he stood in the midst of the performing musicians and didn't hear a note [...] with each number, our courage dwindled further, and I felt as though I were watching one of [E.T.A.] Hoffmann's fantastic figures appear before me.[87]

The point at which everyone other than Beethoven realised something unusual was happening on stage occurred during Leonore's exclamation, "*Töt´ erst sein Weib!*" According to the singer's biographer, Claire von Glümer,[88] Schröder-Devrient approached this scene in a state of exhaustion, leaned backwards "and put her hands to her forehead, involuntarily emitting that famous, unmusical cry which later interpreters of the role have sought to emulate, with such poor results." Although the soprano was a known commodity in Vienna, even as a teenager, the audience's reaction to her performance marked a watershed moment in the history of German music theatre that led within five decades to the writing of *Lohengrin*, *Tannhäuser*, *Tristan*

---

83 *Thayer's Life of Beethoven*. Ed. Forbes, Elliot. Princeton University Press, Vol. 2, pp. 811–812.

84 First performed on 25 October 1823, at the Theater am Kärntnertor, Vienna.

85 *née* Wilhelmine Schröder (6 December, 1804 – 26 January, 1860). Even though she did not marry until 1823, references to the singer use her married name – as she would have expected.

86 'Actor-singer.'

87 The whole thing fell to pieces, and Michael Umlauf was required to take over. Beethoven attended each performance, sitting behind the conductor with his score on his lap.

88 *Erinnerungen an Wilhelmine Schröder-Devrient* (1862) remains in print. It's important to note that Glümer was not present at this mythical performance. She was born in 1825 (and died 81 years later, in 1906). She became sufficiently close to her subject for the finished work to be uncertain if not, in some respects, entirely unreliable. Alfred von Wolzogen (father of Wagner's friend, Hans) characterized the biography as "*Dichtung und Wahrheit*" ('fact and fiction'). He developed this thesis in his own study of the singer's life and work, *Wilhelmine Schröder-Devrient: ein Beitrag zur Geschichte des musikalischen Dramas* (1863).

und Isolde, Der Ring des Nibelungen, and the building of the Bayreuther Festpiehaus. In its "Diary of the Viennese Stage," for November, 1822, the *Wiener allgemeine Theaterzeitung* reported:

> Beethoven's masterwork in the area of opera, unfortunately his only creation of this type, has once again appeared upon the scene, been studied with exertion and diligence, performed with the greatest success, and received with lively pleasure. [...] The part of Fidelio was portrayed by Miss Schröder with such diligence, such exertion, such fire, that although we are accustomed to only the most vital and brilliant performances from her, she nevertheless surprised us. This young talent is on her best way to becoming a completely outstanding declamatory singer. Her voice increases daily in power, her delivery in accuracy and effect. It only remains for her, in order not to be hindered in any way from the perfect delivery of every declamatory vocal part, primarily to establish a uniform delivery of all her sounds and a similarly clear sounding of all her intervals, even in the faster notes. It cannot be said too much that Miss Schröder as Fidelio surpassed not only herself, but all the expectations of the public. The repetition of the duet gave proof of the power and endurance of the young singer in that she sang up to the last note extemporaneously with Mr. Haizinger, despite the monstrous exertion of the preceding quartet. Miss Schröder was unanimously called out at the end of the opera.

Of the same performance, the AMZ held that

> The role of Fidelio was given with a degree of skill that was certainly not unexpected from Miss Schröder, but that, in regard to the difficult role, was truly astonishing. For she not only performed this role, which is distinguished by much difficult intonation and rich figurations of the most noble style, with a beautiful, exuberant voice and exceptional precision, but she also knew how to impart to her acting such a degree of life that acting and singing seemed to be melted together into a beautiful unity, and the not easy task of portraying this character was solved by her in a truly satisfying way.[89]

The effect of Schröder-Devrient's innovation would be felt across the compass of German theatre, poetry, literature and politics. Glümer, Wolzogen, Wagner and every subsequent German nationalist isolated her achievement in 1822 as the point at which German musical art separated itself from every other. The proclaimed virtue of "declamatory" voicing, and the instant of Schröder-Devrient's "unmusical cry," encapsulated the essence of the Germanic cultural rejection of "mere singing"[90] and

---

89 Senner, Wayne M., Wallace, Robin, Meredith, William (2001). *The Critical Reception of Beethoven's Compositions by his German Contemporaries, Vol. 2.* University of Nebraska Press. No.240, pp. 233–234.
90 See generally Nakhutsrishvili, Luka. (2018). "The promising ruins of the German prima donna:

mythologised an event that compared in its significance to the tenor Gilbert Duprez's creation of the "do di petto" high C sung from the chest.[91]

The genius of Schröder-Devrient's performance as Leonore would not have surprised her family. Her mother, the actress Sophie Schröder,[92] was considered to be "the German Siddons;" her father was a tenor, Friedrich Schröder, who died in 1818. Her second cousin was Goethe. A few months after her landmark appearance as Florestan's wife, she married into Germany's leading family of actors and singers. Karl Devrient was seven years older than Wilhemine; before turning to acting in 1819, he served as a cavalry officer with the Hussars, and fought "alongside" von Blücher against Napoleon at Waterloo. The soprano was not yet 18 at the time of her wedding, and her marriage was a disaster, lasting only five years and producing four children – from whom she was separated by a divorce resulting from her adultery. It's important to remember that Schröder-Devrient was not by training an opera singer. She made her stage debut at the age of 15 as Aricia in Schiller's translation of Racine's *Phèdre*, and for the next two years she performed exclusively in productions of prose theatre, without any specialist training in voice work – beyond what her family was able to transmit within its circle. In 1821, Schröder-Devrient appeared as Pamina in a production of *Die Zauberflöte*, after which she committed to singing. In October, 1829, she appeared as Leonore in Berlin. Writing for the AMZ, Richard Spazier extolled what

> we owe to the actors, who under such circumstances contributed so much to making Fidelio a lasting repertory piece in Dresden, a consideration and the thanks of a special mention. In accordance with the nature of the thing, Mrs Schröder-Devrient, who, through her masterful portrayal of Euryanthe, has become known even elsewhere as one of the foremost German stage actresses in opera, made the biggest contribution here. In the last act her passionate, ardent performance transported us to the point of enchantment.[93]

In the audience was the 16-year-old Richard Wagner. Or, rather, he might have been.[94] Either way, he recalled in Volume 1 of *Mein Leben*:

> If I look back on my life as a whole, I can find no event that produced so profound an impression upon me. Anyone who can remember that

Wilhelmine Schröder-Devrient and German musical discourse in the nineteenth century" in *Geschichte und Repräsentation*. Tel Aviver Jahrbuch für deutsche Geschichte, 46, pp. 33–71.

91 Boyden, Matthew (2021). *The Tenor: a Cultural History*. Ragueneau Press.

92 Sophie Schröder (*née* Bürger) (1 March, 1781 – 25 February, 1868). She outlived her daughter by almost a decade.

93 Senner, Wayne M., Wallace, Robin, Meredith, William (2001). *The Critical Reception of Beethoven's Compositions by his German Contemporaries, Vol. 2*. University of Nebraska Press, No. 240, p. 257.

94 In *Mein Leben*, Wagner claimed to have seen her perform the role in Leipzig, but Schröder-Devrient didn't performance didn't sing in Leipzig in 1829. Wagner either saw her as Leonore in Berlin or as Romeo in Bellini's *I Capuleti e i Montecchi* in March, 1834. In Cosima's *Tagebücher*, Wagner is said to refer to Schröder-Devrient as Romeo on several occasions.

wonderful woman at this period of her life must to some extent have experienced the almost Satanic ardour which the intensely human art of this incomparable actress poured into his veins. After the performance I rushed to a friend's house and wrote a short note to the singer, in which I briefly told her that from that moment my life had acquired its true significance, and that if in days to come she should ever hear my name praised in the world of Art, she must remember that she had that evening made me what I then swore it was my destiny to become.[95]

Whether or not this was true, Wagner was changed by his experience of seeing Schröder-Devrient on stage; more than a decade after her death he memorialised his gratitude when making her the dedicatee of his book *Über Schauspieler und Sänger*.[96] In 1874, he added to the portal of the front door of *Wahnfried*, his house in Bayreuth,[97] the inscription, "*Hier wo mein Wähnen Frieden fand – Wahnfried – sei dieses Haus von mir benannt,*"[98] together with an allegorical sgraffito by the Dresden painter, Robert Krausse, to accompany the property's name.[99] At the centre of the tableau is Wotan/the Wanderer, portrayed with the features of the tenor Ludwig Schnorr von Carolsfeld (the first Tristan). To Wotan's right is Wagner's wife, Cosima, and their son, Siegfried. To the left is Schröder-Devrient – embodied symbolically as Melpomene,[100] the muse of tragedy; her right hand rests on an actor's mask. The classical allusions were characteristic of Wagner, but there was more to the imagery than mere symbolism. Schröder-Devrient was raised in the Greco-German tradition of high theatre,[101] a methodology comparable in its affectation to Japanese Kabuki. A woodcut of the soprano performing the forest scene in *Euryanthe* hints at the stylised, histrionic nature of stage-movement for German performers in the 1820s. She is seen dropped steeply to her left knee, with her arms outstretched in absurdist supplication; her head is thrown back as far as her famously blonde hair will allow, so that she is made to appear like a hare transfixed by the moon.[102] It is an artificial pose

---

95   Dreyfus, Laurence (2010). *Wagner and the Erotic Impulse*. Harvard University Press, p. 55.

96   'On Singers and Actors' (1872).

97   The family moved in on 28 April 1874, while the house was still under construction.

98   'Here where my delusions have found peace, let this place be named Wahnfried.'

99   Cosima was less than pleased with the addition, and shared her sentiments with her diary, writing "I would rather have left our house unadorned…". She agreed to "keep this a secret from R, who is delighted with the decoration." Dreyfus, Laurence (2010). *Wagner and the Erotic Impulse*. Harvard University Press, p. 61.

100   In Greek, 'the one that is melodious.'

101   Wagner's attachment to the pivotal value of classical literature and art was qualified by a healthy loathing for *paedophilia*, which he nonetheless construed, as did most others, with the equally "terrible" sin of "Greek Love". In April, 1873, he wrote, in answer to the question "What is German?": "We must understand a thing in our language if we want to understand it properly […] This is the sense of an *German* culture. What we can never understand in any language about the Greek way, is what wholly separates us from it, e.g., their love – in – pederasty." *Ibid*, pp. 202–203. See also *Die Kunst und Revolution*, in which Wagner wrote "We can make no progress in reflecting on our art without realizing its connection with the art of the Greeks. In truth, our modern art is but a link in the chain of the artistic development of all Europe, and it takes its lead from the Greeks." Wagner, Richard (1897). *Gesammelte Schriften und Dichtungen*, 2nd ed. Siegel, Vol. 3, p. 9.

102   Pagans believed moon-gazing hares to be harbingers of growth, re-birth and abundance. They were

that speaks to a manufactured, romanticised separation from reality, even accounting for the proscenium's suspended disbelief. Her admirer, Ludwig Rellstab, described her performance philosophy as "dialogue, pantomime, gesture, song [...] inform[ing] each other reciprocally,"[103] and in 1843 Berlioz reported from Berlin:[104]

> In Dresden, I had noticed in her very bad singing habits and a scenic action often tainted with exaggeration and affectation.[105]

Schröder-Devrient is often characterised as a modern singer, but many of her notices were critical of what was thought to be an atavistic manner, made worse by the primitivism of her vocal technique. One reviewer in Berlin lamented in 1829:

> Unfortunately, she still adheres to the old ways of singers to the extent that she too often harangues the public through stage tricks, provoking them to express their approval at the close of each number, whereby, particularly in Fidelio, much of the illusion is destroyed.[106]

It is no small irony that, despite becoming a totem for political change, before and following the 1848 revolutions, Schröder-Devrient's work during the 1820s epitomised many of the principles and values which the *Junges Deutschland* movement was determined to excise. The rationalism of young Germans reached further than literary and artistic truth, however. They were exercised by the emancipation of German Jews, the separation of Church and State and, most progressively of all, the political and social liberation of women. The business of promoting female rights was made easier during the *Vormärz* by Schröder-Devrient, whose power, independence and mannish appearance made her the poster-girl for a "new" Germany in which a surprisingly fluid conception of the erotic enjoined male and female characteristics after a fashion that would now be thought androgynous or pan-sexual. The German-ness of her work did not predicate against her performing elsewhere; she was successful in London (famously so with Malibran, in *Otello*) and a favourite in Paris from 1830. Her repertoire was extensive, but unbiased towards native composers, chiefly because there were precious few writing "German" operas that audiences wanted to hear. Even before she worked for Wagner, however, Schröder-Devrient's reputation was indistinguishable from her language and her culture – something that could never have been said of Milder, Sontag, Malibran or Branchu. During the 1830s Schröder-Devrient came to personify the sound and manner of the modern German

---

symbols of hunting, and associated closely with moon-deities.

103   Meyer, Stephen C. (1997). "Das wilde Herz: Interpreting Wilhelmine Schröder-Devrient." *Opera Quarterly*, 14/2, pp. 23–40; p. 26.

104   For the *Journal des Débats*, on 21 October, 1843.

105   *Ibid*. In full, the passage reads, "*Je me souvenais seulement qu'elle me parut admirable à Paris, il y a bien des années, dans le Fidelio de Beethoven, et que tout récemment, au contraire, à Dresde, j'avais remarqué en elle de fort mauvaises habitudes de chant et une action scénique souvent entachée d'exagération et d'afféterie.*"

106   Senner, Wayne M., Wallace, Robin, Meredith, William (2001). *The Critical Reception of Beethoven's Compositions by his German Contemporaries, Vol. 2*. University of Nebraska Press, No.240, p. 257.

soprano. Considering his admiration, and the reach of their collaboration, Wagner nonetheless declared that Schröder-Devrient had

> no voice at all; but she knew how to use her breath so beautifully, and to let a true womanly soul stream forth in such wondrous sounds, that we never thought of either voice or singing![107]

According to Rellstab, she was unable to meet the technical demands of high, florid or legato singing – which doesn't leave a soprano much with which to work.[108] He danced around what qualified precisely as the deficiencies in her technique, and how she compensated for them:

> It will never be the natural power of the tones themselves that enraptures us, indeed, we often even see her struggle with hindrances in her technique that are not inconsequential. And yet she creates a soul for the sound, gives it a heart, so that, flowing out from the innermost recesses of her breast, it irresistibly penetrates into the deepest depths of her heart.

Others observed her avoiding technically difficult passages *come è scritto*, a habit that extended to omitting whole arias if she didn't feel comfortable singing them. These foibles would have been condemned by Mozart, far less Weber and Wagner, so it's fascinating to see how her weaknesses were repositioned as strengths by her admirers at a time when Italian virtuosity was ubiquitous. The contemporary German construction of the foreign as fraudulent (and *vice versa*) justified her speaking passages that were written to be sung – something of which Berlioz complained angrily after seeing her in Berlin as Valentine in *Les Huguenots*:[109]

> I must, however, reproach [Mlle Marx] for two or three spoken monosyllables which was wrong to borrow from the deplorable school of Madame Devrient. I saw the latter in the same role a few days later, and if, by speaking out openly against her way of portraying it, I surprised and even shocked several people of excellent minds who, no doubt out of habit, admire without restriction the famous artist [...].[110]

Luka Nakhutsrishvili has suggested that

---

107 Wagner, Richard (1896). "Actors and Singers," in *Richard Wagner's Prose Works*. Trans. William Ashton Ellis, Vol. 5, p. 219.

108 Nakhutsrishvili, Luka. (2018). "The promising ruins of the German prima donna: Wilhelmine Schröder-Devrient and German musical discourse in the nineteenth century" in *Geschichte und Repräsentation*. Tel Aviver Jahrbuch für deutsche Geschichte, 46, p. 40.

109 For the *Journal des Débats*, on 21 October, 1843.

110 "*Il faut pourtant que je lui reproche deux ou trois monosyllabes parlés qu'elle a eu le tort d'emprunter à l'école déplorable de Mme Devrient. J'ai vu cette dernière dans le même rôle quelques jours après, et si, en me prononçant ouvertement contre sa manière de le rendre, j'ai étonné et même choqué plusieurs personnes d'un excellent esprit qui, par habitude sans doute, admirent sans restriction la célèbre artiste, je dois ici dire pourquoi je diffère si fort de leur opinion. Je n'avais point de parti pris, point de prévention ni pour ni contre Mme Devrient.*"

While she drained the climatic moments of musical fulfillment, she filled the "emptier" sequences, those that are dramatically and musically weaker, such as the recitatives, or that simply do not require participation from the singer, such as the choruses [...]. It was the voiding, shifting and substituting of traditional aesthetic expectations, competences and requirements that from the 1830s earned her the compliment of being a "genius," a "creator."[111]

From a distance, this seems generous – particularly in his use of the appellation "creator." It also admits an argument as between Berlioz, whose loathing of Schröder-Devrient in 1843 was absolute, and Wagner – for whose *Rienzi* she created the role of Adriano in 1842. [112] Two years earlier, during his three-year stay in Paris, Wagner claimed to have attended the Opéra-Comique on only four occasions. In his memoirs he complained of

> the cold productions at the Opera Comique [...] the same lack of enthusiasm displayed by the singers also drove me from Italian opera. The names, often very famous ones, of these artists who sang the same four operas for years could not compensate me for the complete absence of sentiment which characterised their performance, so unlike that of Schröder-Devrient, which I so thoroughly enjoyed.[113]

Wagner's writings are saturated in cultural imperialism. It's unnecessary to rehearse his reputation as a flag-waving racist; indeed, his anti-Semitism gets more air-time than does his equally virulent xenophobia. The thrust and form of most of his prejudice was determined more by what he loved than what he hated, for which Schröder-Devrient became his lode-stone when defining the constituent merits of German cultural, moral and philosophical superiority. He was extremely close to the soprano and her "womanly soul," and uncharacteristically generous in recalling her support, as his more famous elder.[114] Their first collaboration was *Rienzi*, which was first performed in the recently-opened Dresden Opera House (designed by Gottfried Semper) on 20 October, 1842. Despite running for more than six hours, Wagner's Grand Opera was a triumph – even if Schröder-Devrient was unhappy that the (mezzo-soprano) role of Adriano was (like Leonore, at least for some of *Fidelio*) *travesti*, and other than the work's heroine. Wagner acknowledged her unhappiness:

> When we tried the first scene of the second act with the scenery complete, and the messengers of peace entered, there was a general outburst of emotion, and even Schroder-Devrient, who was bitterly prejudiced

---

111   *Ibid.*
112   'The Fairies.' According to Wagner, the soprano had earlier tried (and failed) to persuade the Court Theatre in Dresden to stage the first production of *Die Feen*.
113   '*Mein leben.*'
114   Schröder-Devrient was nine years older than Wagner.

against her part, as it was not the role of the heroine, could only answer my questions in a voice stifled with tears.

His most detailed recollection of Schröder-Devrient records how

her voice, which in point of quality had never been an exceptionally good medium for song, often landed her in difficulties, and in particular she was forced, when singing, to drag the time a little all through. But her achievements were less hampered now by these material hindrances than by the fact that her repertoire consisted of a limited number of leading parts, which she had sung so frequently that a certain monotony in the conscious calculation of effect often developed into a mannerism which, from her tendency to exaggeration, was at times almost painful. Although these defects could not escape me, yet I, more than any one, was especially qualified to overlook such minor weaknesses, and realise with enthusiasm the incomparable greatness of her performances. Indeed, it only needed the stimulus of excitement, which this actress's exceptionally eventful life still procured, fully to restore the creative power of her prime, a fact of which I was subsequently to receive striking demonstrations. But I was seriously troubled and depressed at seeing how strong was the disintegrating effect of theatrical life upon the character of this singer, who had originally been endowed with such great and noble qualities. From the very mouth through which the great actress's inspired musical utterances reached me, I was compelled to hear at other times very similar language to that in which, with but few exceptions, nearly all heroines of the stage indulge. The possession of a naturally fine voice, or even mere physical advantages, which might place her rivals on the same footing as herself in public favour, was more than she could endure; and so far was she from acquiring the dignified resignation worthy of a great artist, that her jealousy increased to a painful extent as years went on. I noticed this all the more because I had reason to suffer from it. A fact which caused me even greater trouble, however, was that she did not grasp music easily, and the study of a new part involved difficulties which meant many a painful hour for the composer who had to make her master his work. Her difficulty in learning new parts, and particularly that of Adriano in Rienzi, entailed disappointments for her which caused me a good deal of trouble [...] I had to handle a great and sensitive nature very tenderly.[115]

It is difficult to reconcile Wagner's judgments of Schröder-Devrient's art when reading what he wrote for her. Act III, Scene 9, for example, begins "*Gerechter Gott, so ist's entschieden schon!*"[116] in which Adriano prays for guidance as he wrestles with his loyalties to the noblemen plotting against Rienzi and his love for Rienzi's daughter,

---

115   '*Mein leben.*'
116   'Righteous God! It is decided.'

Irene. The opening of "*Gerechter*," is strongly redolent of Fidelio's "*Abscheulicher!*" in the force of its opening statement, rhythm and pitching, which veers wildly within the aria's range (C4 to A5). For the phrase "*O Erde, nimm mich Jammervollen auf!*"[117] the singer is required to perform without breathing for six bars, against an orchestra of two flutes, two oboes, a horn, two bassoons, three trombones, and *tremolo* strings, with violins and violas in divisi – all playing fortissimo – as the soprano launches from an F5 to an A flat 5 for "*O Erde*," which is held for a minim and a crotchet before descending F, D flat, A flat, and F an octave lower. From here the singer has to launch back up the stave to an A4 (for the syllable "*Jam* […]") – which resolves *ad libitum* with a *fermata* on a B4 (written as a dotted crotchet) that drops to a C sharp 4 and then, finally, a D4 for the word "*auf*." Over the span of almost two octaves, the soprano is confronted with huge challenges, which are constant over the course of an "episode" that runs for almost seven minutes. Some of the writing is perversely awkward; the section "*der schönsten Liebe Strahl ins Herz*,"[118] is marked *meno mosso*, but sill formed of semi-quavers in triplets, with grace notes, turns and fermatas that would daunt a bel cantante trained to sing Bellini. The writing is asymmetrical, of course, and formed of motivic passages that emerge cyclically throughout the episode; for all the *sturm und drang*, much of the writing is still written as "song" for singing – as Margarete Klose (1942) and Christa Ludwig (1960)[119] demonstrated so memorably on record. While it isn't an aria (analogous to the same work's landmark solo for tenor, "*Allmacht'ger vater*"),[120] it operates as a scene in which a soprano has to sing as well as act Adriano's emotional and psychological turmoil.

All of this suggests that Schröder-Devrient had a *lot* of voice. If she didn't then Wagner was composing under the influence of a woman for whom he was writing in spirit only. The composer's relationship with the singer certainly suggests an uncharacteristic measure of vassalage on his part, redolent of Woody Allen's 1994 comedy, *Bullets Over Broadway*, in which John Cusack's struggling writer, David Shayne, falls under the influence of the fading starlet Helen Sinclair, played by Dianne Wiest.[121] There is more than a little of Sinclair in Schröder-Devrient. In one of the movie's many wonderful scenes (and having repeatedly implored of Shayne "Don't speak! Don't speak!"), the following exchange occurs in the actress' dressing room:

Sinclair:	Make love to me.
David Shayne:	Here? Now?
Helen Sinclair:	I see no reason to wait.
David Shayne:	Jerome Kern is on the other side of the door.
Helen Sinclair:	Yes, he's a wonderful composer. You'll have to meet him. Now hang up your pants.

---

117   'Earth, embrace me in my misery!'
118   'The most beautiful love-beam to the heart.'
119   This complete recording, produced as a radio broadcast by Radio Wien, with Josef Krips conducting the Wiener Rundfunk-Symphonieorchester, is one of the finest of the opera.
120   'Almighty Father.'
121   Allen was not thinking of Schröder-Devrient when writing the screenplay, but there is more than a little of the soprano in Sinclair's fantastic assertion "I am used to playing more overtly heroic women, less tentative, more alluring, certainly not frigid."

Wagner's infatuation was lifelong and platonic, even though she was in and out of marriages and extra-marital relationships throughout her life – a pleasure that brought her an equivalent amount of pain. Wagner's acknowledgement of her circumstances was worded carefully as he recalled how "one main sorrow went through her life: she didn't find the man completely worth her making happy." It never occurred to Wagner to mourn the absence of a man capable of making *her* happy. The miserable men in her life included three husbands, dozens of lovers, and Wagner, whom she humiliated for his lack of sexual experience and his decision to marry at too young an age.[122] The composer told his second wife, Cosima (on separate occasions)

> how Schröder-Devrient once said to him in a passionate agitation, "Oh what do you know, you whom marriage has crippled?" And how strange that made him feel. He was 32 at the time […]. Then he speaks of men who marry early, who are lost; for this reason Frau Schröder-Devrient had complete contempt for him and called him "the marriage cripple."[123]

The soprano's charisma must have been something else, and while it's reasonable to conclude that she "*'sang' with her eyes, her hands, her hair, with everything except maybe her voice,*"[124] the dramatic impact of an actress performing music as difficult as "*Gerechter Gott*" when not being able to sing it in accordance with the pointillist detail of its writing must have been difficult to appreciate midst the ubiquity of singers trained to perform Mozart, Rossini and Meyerbeer. The English critic, Chorley, was among the unpersuaded, writing with discrimination that

> Her tones were delivered without any care, save to give them due force. Her execution was bad and heavy. There was an air of strain and spasm throughout her performances – of that struggle for victory which never conquers.[125]

Conversely, Rellstab traded in *apologia*, most of it couched in the romanticised language of a votary:

> It will never be the natural power of the tones themselves that enraptures us, indeed, we often even see her struggle with hindrances in her technique that are not inconsequential. And yet she creates a soul for the sound, gives it a heart, so that, flowing out from the innermost recesses of her breast, it irresistibly penetrates into the deepest depths of her heart.[126]

---

122 Dreyfus, Laurence (2010). *Wagner and the Erotic Impulse*. Harvard University Press, p. 55.

123 *Ibid.*

124 Nakhutsrishvili, Luka. (2018). "The promising ruins of the German prima donna: Wilhelmine Schröder-Devrient and German musical discourse in the nineteenth century" in *Geschichte und Repräsentation*. Tel Aviver Jahrbuch für deutsche Geschichte, 46, p. 42.

125 Chorley, Henry F. (1862). *Thirty Years' Musical Recollections*, Vol. 1, p. 55.

126 Meyer, Stephen C. (1997). "Das wilde Herz: Interpreting Wilhelmine Schröder-Devrient." *Opera Quarterly*, 14/2, pp. 23–40; p. 26.

The 21st century has become inured to the poverty of music criticism as a genre; most of it traded in platitudes and generalities, particularly in English-speaking countries.[127] Critical banality was rare during the 19th century, however, which causes Rellstab's flowery and meaningless observations to suffer from comparison with Chorley's detail and precision. Having accounted for her flaws, Wagner presented Schröder-Devrient with another role, this time the female lead. The score was more favourably received by the soprano, as Wagner recalled in his memoirs:

> I could count all the more surely on the helpful co-operation of Schröder Devrient, to whom a worthier task was assigned in the leading female part than that which she had had in Rienzi. I was glad to be able thus to rely entirely upon her, as she had grown strangely out of humour with me, owing to her scanty share in the success of Rienzi. The completeness of my faith in her I proved with an exaggeration by no means advantageous to my own work, by simply forcing the leading male part on Wachter, a once capable, but now somewhat delicate baritone. He was in every respect wholly unsuited to the task, and only accepted it with unfeigned hesitation. On submitting my play to my adored prima donna, I was much relieved to find that its poetry made a special appeal to her. Thanks to the genuine personal interest awakened in me under very peculiar circumstances by the character and fate of this exceptional woman, our study of the part of Senta, which often brought us into close contact, became one of the most thrilling and momentously instructive periods of my life.[128]

The composer described Senta, in Der fliegende Holländer,[129] as "completely naïve," which is an understatement when noting how little independence, dignity and agency she has even before she appears on stage. The soprano was uncomplaining of her character's subjugation to a man she has never met, and whose portrait and story haunt her regardless. On meeting the Dutchman, she sacrifices herself to save his soul – a narrative arc that sails close to Wagner's conception of his relationship with Schröder-Devrient, if not all women. Holländer is the composer's first essay in what would prove to be a lifelong obsession with themes of redemption; the parallels between his self-conception as the saviour of German music (and German culture) and the blind service to which Senta (and Schröder-Devrient) submitted without thought of favour conform to his later assertion that his art "began" with Holländer.[130] Schröder-Devrient's submission to Wagner appears in this context to have hinged on her commitment to someone she cannot *truly* have known until he revealed the

---

127 This can be attributed, in part, to the limited amount of copy-space now made available in newspapers, and any publication not given over entirely to music criticism. Even specialist music magazines (as opposed to journals) now make a habit of communicating often very complex issues *reductio ad absurdum*.

128 '*Mein leben.*'

129 'The Flying Dutchman.'

130 *Holländer* is the first of the Wagner canon to be staged regularly at Bayreuth.

origins of the *gesamtkunstwerk*[131] with *Holländer*. Audiences were more interested in Schröder-Devrient's celebrity than Wagner's music. In a letter dated March, 1844, August Röckel reported to Ferdinand Praeger that

> Wagner has returned from Berlin, very morose in temper; the "Flying Dutchman" did not touch the scoffing Berliners, who certainly have less poetical feeling than most Germans; they only saw in Schröder-Devrient a star, and in the touching drama an opera like other operas; yet they pose as profound art critics. Bah! They are simply stupid!"[132]

Almost three years after the first performance of *Holländer* on 2 January, 1843, Wagner presented Schröder-Devrient with the role of her lifetime. Venus in *Tannhäuser* carries a lot of baggage – some of it vocal and dramatic, much of it physical, since the role is, after all, the goddess of love, beauty, desire and sex. In his memoirs, Wagner recalled how, *before* composing *Holländer*:

> As regards her looks, the verdict which, in the following winter, was sent to Paris by Berlioz during his stay in Dresden, was so far correct that her somewhat "maternal" stoutness was unsuited to youthful parts, especially in male attire, which, as in Rienzi, made too great a demand upon the imagination.

For anyone interested in deciding whether Schröder-Devrient was cut out for the role of a goddess, there is a useful point of reference in a painting of the soprano by Joseph Weber, from 1839.[133] The portrait reveals a large woman who is something more than "matronly."[134] She has at least two chins, and neither her hands nor her face have any discernible bone structure. Her eyebrows have been plucked into submission and her hair has been scraped across the top of her scalp into two visible partings, with heavy ringlets hanging either side of the rosiest of apple cheeks. She is looking to her right, away from the viewer, while holding a scroll of music in her left hand.[135] In the lower right hand corner is a laurel bush, to remind the viewer of her plaudits.[136] There is no context in which the woman portrayed by Weber might be thought beautiful. Although she was only 35 at the time, she is a long way from persuading as the ultimate temptress, therefore. Even the fuller-figure "sleeping Venuses" of Girolamo

---

131 'Total work of art.'

132 Praeger, Ferdinand (1892). *Wagner as I Knew Him*. Longmans, Green & Co.

133 Slim, H. Colin (2006). "Joseph Weber's Diva, Pinxit 1839: Visual, Musical, Societal Considerations. Music in Art; Iconography as a Source for Music History, Volume II. *Music in Art*, Vol. 31, No. 1/2, pp. 5–49.

134 Unless the matron was Hattie Jacques (7 February, 1922 – 6 October, 1980) – an English actress and soprano, renowned for her revival of Victorian ballads. Better known for appearing on numerous occasions in films as a hospital matron.

135 On the scroll is written "*Iphigenia,*" beneath which is inscribed music in a soprano clef with the words "*O lasst mich Tiefgebeugte weinen,*" which is the German translation of the first line of "*O malheureuse Iphigénie,*" from Act II of Gluck's opera, *Iphigénie en Tauride*. The incomplete musical quotation conforms to the first, second and fifth bars of the aria.

136 Anecdotally,

da Treviso (1520) and Annibale Carracci (1602), are handsome, though their body shapes are no longer fashionable.[137] Notwithstanding the incongruity of Weber's appearance in 1845, Wagner was thrilled with the performance, although he was critical of Schröder-Devrient in private[138] – as he explained in writing to Wolzogen in a letter dated 5 August, 1846. For her part, the soprano told her third husband, Baron Heinrich von Bock, that for all her admiration of his intellect, she was unsympathetic to Wagner as a composer.

Wagner claimed to have written the role of Elsa in *Lohengrin* for Schröder-Devrient – which she was unable to perform because of the composer's involvement in the Dresden uprising in May, 1849. He later indicated that every subsequent leading soprano role was created with Schröder-Devrient in his mind's ear. In 1878, when talking with Cosima of *Tristan und Isolde*, he asked

> How ever did I create the rapture of the 2nd Act? I know! Through seeing Schröder-Devrient as Romeo, and it isn't so foolish to have a woman in that role, for these little runts of men, mostly tenors, are never any good at those lowly frantic caresses.[139]

During the final rehearsals for *Parsifal*, Cosima reported:

> The big scene between Kundry and Parsifal will surely never be performed in the way he created it. R complains about how oblivious the performers are to all there is in it, and he thinks of Schröder-Devrient, how she would have said "So it was my kiss that made you clairvoyant." Now the music has to take charge of everything.[140]

In her influence over Wagner, Schröder-Devrient was the most consequential woman in the history of German music. It remains to be asked why she held him in such thrall. The common response – that she was the first and foremost *singende Schauspielerin* – is true, to a point. Others have suggested an affair between the singer and the composer, which is a reasonable supposition for a man who sowed more seed than Rehoboam.[141] Typically for Wagner, it was more complicated. In a letter to Verdi's librettist, Arrigo Boito, dated 7 November, 1871, Wagner wrote that, unlike Goethe (who regretted having to return to Germany from Italy), he was pleased to head home because:

> I no longer heard the naive folk song that Goethe had heard in the streets, and in its place I heard the night-time worker indulging in the

---

137 For a vision of Venus more beautiful than Schröder-Devrient when painted by Weber, see also Picasso's *Venus and Cupid* (1949) and *Venus and Cupid, after Lucas the Elder* (1957).
138 Wagner completed his final significant revision for the opera's première in Paris in 1861. He nonetheless remained unhappy with *Tannhäuser* at the time of his death.
139 *Ibid*, p. 56–57.
140 *Ibid*, p. 57.
141 Rehoboam's 18 wives and 60 concubines bore him 28 sons and 60 daughters – only two of whom are identified (*per* I Kings and II Chronicles).

same affected and effeminately cadencing operatic phrases that I can't believe the masculine genius of your nation had produced — and yet, not even the feminine![142]

For all his admiration for Bellini's dramatic structures – and *I Capuleti e i Montecchi* in particular – Wagner dismissed Italian opera as trite and unnatural, failings he discerned in the inability of Italian composers to distinguish between the masculine and the feminine.[143] He may have been influenced in his prejudice by the castrato tradition – which repulsed and intrigued him in equal measure.[144] He decided regardless that Italian music was limited to exploiting the singing voice for its own sake, with neither purpose nor culture to sustain it. Animated by opposition, Wagner threw himself into a nationalist agenda that took its lead from the popular construction of the Germanic tradition as "of the Volk." Wagner was not alone in perceiving folk music as foundational to any meaningful sense of place, culture and prosperity for contemporary nativist art; the same was true of almost every other European composer after 1848.

These convictions were especially important to *Tannhäuser* narrative purpose (subtitled "the Minnesängers' Contest at Wartburg,") and, more obviously, *Die Meistersinger von Nürnberg*. They were fundamental also to his compositional process when translating the "earth" of German folk music into his *Kunstwerk der Zukunft*.[145] Wagner explained "how a folk song evolves" by illustrating for Cosima his transposition of a performance by a village singing society in Hohenschwangau into the Act II fanfares of *Lohengrin*.[146] In *Oper und Drama*, he advocated the replacement of Greek tragedy with folk song as the impetus for creating a new kind of music theatre. Opera for Wagner was no longer a platform for the trinitarian unification of the arts but, rather, a mechanism for the binary synthesis of words and music. The latter ambition was presented by Wagner as possible only in German, by German people united in their cultivation of a uniquely German form of art. Also in *Oper und Drama*, Wagner employed the metaphor of a woman needing the seed of poetry, with a choir serving as the womb from which the orchestra was born; bringing these into alignment through song was the primary burden of the soprano.[147] It's possible the sincerity and conviction of Schröder-Devrient's craft – with its folk-like attachment to an authentically-delivered German language as drama, and an other-than-effeminate cadence when singing it as opera – came closer to *sprechstimme* even than Cosima willed it after she inherited the Bayreuth Festival in 1884. Schröder-Devrient's disregard for "*la chanson pour la chanson*" coincided with Wagner's preternatural obsession with drama as sacrifice, graft and sensuality – but she was never the source of lust for Wagner that she was for so many others, on and off the stage. She appeared remotely

---

142   Anbari, Alan Roy (2007). *Richard Wagner's Concepts of History*. PhD thesis. The University of Texas, p. 112.
143   *Ibid.*
144   At one point, he considered writing the role of Klingsor for a male soprano.
145   'The Artwork of the Future,' the title of a long and important essay by Wagner, first published in 1849 in Leipzig.
146   Diary entry by Cosima, dated 6 November, 1871. *Ibid*, p. 113.
147   Wagner, Richard (1897). *Gesammelte Schriften und Dichtungen*, 2nd ed. Siegel, Vol. 2, p. 232.

as Elsa, Isolde, Sieglinde, Brünnhilde and Kundry, and she was quite properly acknowledged to be Wagner's pre-eminent muse at her death at the age of 53.

Her reputation survived the publication in 1862 of her "memoirs," as *Aus den Memoiren einer Sängerin*.[148] This scandalous epistolary Bildungsroman is now considered a classic of the genre,[149] but Schröder-Devrient had nothing to do with it. Her posthumous celebrity was hijacked by a publisher, August Prinz, who was likely to have been the book's author. A sequel, *Pauline*, appeared in 1875. It is graphic stuff, although the books weren't banned in Germany until 1877.[150] The most striking aspect of *Memoirs of a Singer* is that the protagonist isn't raped, or drugged, or beaten – or subjugated in any way at all. Unlike Hoffmann's *Schwester Monika*, she takes control of her body by deciding what she is going to do with it, and with whom. If Monica's experiences were universal in 1815 then they remained common throughout the 1860s, when the rights of women were increasingly relevant, acknowledged and widespread. Women continued to be treated other than equally, but Schröder-Devrient's example in forging an independent and iconoclastic form of expression resonated for a generation wanting to be heard as something more than wives, mothers and prostitutes.

Of course, the German construction of women as sexualised objects remained in currency, and it's disappointing that Wagner did nothing to defend Schröder-Devrient from the moral-mud being thrown at her corpse. Neither the composer nor his wife referred to Wilhemine's alleged memoirs in their letters and diaries[151] – and it was a wretched finale for a woman who contributed more than anyone else to the mythology of the large-boned soprano crowned by waves of blonde hair, wearing a helmet and carrying a spear. She died sixteen years before the first performance of *Der Ring des Nibelungen*, but it is certain that Schröder-Devrient was as much a *leitmotif* for the composer when writing his epic tetralogy as any that appeared in the scores.

---

148 'From the Memoirs of a Singer.' In another edition, the book was titled *Galante Abenteuer der Sängerin Wilhelmine* ('The Galant Adventures of Wilhelmine the Singer.'). The books appeared for sale in English as "Pauline the Prima Donna, or Memoirs of an Opera Singer," (Locus Elm Press; 2015), as a reprint of an edition first published by the Erotica Biblion Society of London and New York in 1898.
149 Pornography.
150 Schröder-Devrient's spurious memoirs were an inspiration for *Venus im pelz* ("Venus in Furs'), by Leopold von Sacher-Masoch (of masochism fame). The Velvet Underground's 1967 debut album *The Velvet Underground & Nico* included the song "Venus in Furs," which references a number of the book's plot elements.
151 Accepting that they were edited for posterity.

CHAPTER 12

Marianne guidant le peuple

The song, "Blurred Lines," by Robin Thicke, Pharrell Williams, Clifford Harris Jr. and Marvin Gaye,[1] was a *cause célèbre* in 2013, by reason of its lyrics, which speak for themselves:

> Okay, now he was close;
> Tried to domesticate you;
> But you're an animal;
> Baby, it's in your nature (meow);
> Just let me liberate you (hey, hey, hey);
> [...] I know you want it [...];
> You're a good girl (hey, hey);
> [...] When you got them jeans on? (Why?)
> What do we need steam for?
> You the hottest bitch in this place;
> [...] You wanna hug me (hey, hey, hey);
> What rhymes with hug me? (Hey, hey, hey);
> [...] Must wanna get nasty (let go) (I say Rob);
> [...] Let me be the one you back that ass up to;
> [...] Had a bitch, but she ain't bad as you;
> So, hit me up when you pass through;
> I'll give you something big enough to tear your ass in two.

Much of the left-leaning criticism that attacked the song was hysterical and affected – with some denouncing it as a petition to rape. Thicke's verses are anodyne when measured against the majority of American rap music; the accompanying video was another matter entirely. It provoked dismay for many because of the decision taken by a female director, Diane Martel, to subject three female models, Emily Ratajkowski, Elle Evans, and Jessi M'Bengue, to the kind of objectification that would become un-publishable less than a decade later.[2] Some cited the director's gender to validate the video's alarming content; others protested that women were in on the joke. No-one

---

1 Thicke and Williams were sued by Gaye's family for copyright infringement, and found liable by a federal jury in the United States in March, 2015. Gaye died in 1984 but his estate secured a shared-credit for the song's writing and a percentage of royalties.

2 Two videos were produced – one in which the models were "clothed," the other in which the models were naked but for skin-tone g-strings. The latter has had many more views online than the former. It should be noted that Martel's video is vapid when compared with Nelly's "Tip Drill," or Kanye West's "Famous," or Cardi B's "WAP" – all of which are about as offensive as commercial tolerances will allow.

laughed in 2021 after Emily Ratajkowski alleged she was sexually assaulted by Robin Thicke during the filming of the video. The most interesting thing about the whole project is that it was emblematic of what art historians refer to as the "male gaze." Even if women enjoyed "Blurred Lines," nothing in the song or the video was designed with women in mind. As an expression of a male perception of the female, it was definitively exploitative. The video ideated the role of women as stimulants and decoration, purposed to meet the glandular expectations of men preoccupied with thoughts of sex.[3]

The male gaze is an increasingly prevalent issue for anyone working in visual media; writers and academics have begun to consider its effects on pop songs. The same principle has not commonly been applied to art music, or the soprano voice, which is surprising when noting how the best and worst music for women to sing prior to 1945, was composed by men. This is not the forum for debating the status of female composers historically. Much solid work has been done to discover and acknowledge women composers from the 18th and 19th centuries; there's still no getting around the fact that the history of composition until the 20th century is an almost exclusively male narrative. Opera was the ultimate forum for mansplaining.[4] Men *were* better informed and more talented than woman as composers of music theatre. This isn't controversial; it can be gainsaid only with evidence, and there isn't an opera by a woman from before 1900 that warrants production alongside (or in place of) any of the established repertoire. Louise Bertin's *La Esmeralda*,[5] for example, is a curiosity, but it is average and undeserving of prolonged scrutiny. Bertin is more famous for being the daughter of her father, Louis-François, the journalist and newspaper baron who sat for Jean-Auguste-Dominique Ingres in 1832, at the age of 66. The resulting portrait is one of the finest ever; it survives as proof of Bertin's influence after 1830, when he and his family supported the July Monarchy. Bertin was the owner of the *Journal des débats*, whose music critic was Hector Berlioz. The family's intimate circle included Rossini, Delacroix and Victor Hugo – who agreed to allow Louise Bertin to set *Notre Dame de Paris* as an opera, having previously rejected numerous offers after the novel's publication in 1831. Hugo wrote the libretto, based on his own novel; *La Esmeralda* proved to be his only collaboration with a composer.[6]

Bertin's first opera, *Guy Mannering*, after Sir Walter Scott, was first performed privately for the Bertin family in 1825; her second, *Le Loup-garou*[7] was staged at the Opéra-Comique in 1827. Three years later, Bertin turned to Goethe for *Fausto*, which was savaged by the critics and withdrawn after three performances. Six years

---

3 It's a complicated subject. Emily Ratajkowski told *The Guardian* newspaper (4 September, 2015) that the video is "the bane of my existence." It nonetheless made her famous, and she has since succeeded as a model and actress on the basis of her celebrity as one of the "World's Most Beautiful Women." Would Ratajkowski have achieved all that she has but for her appearance in the "Blurred Lines" video?

4 In 2018, Alison Tovey and Ned Dixon wrote an opera / musical, *Mansplaining*, which was produced in Australia.

5 See, generally, Boneau, Denise Lynn (1989). *Louise Bertin and Opera in Paris in the 1820s and 1830s.* Ph.D Thesis, University of Chicago.

6 It is unimportant contextually, but not irrelevant, to note that Louise was born with a condition that prevented her from walking or standing for periods of time. Boyden, Matthew (2018). *Beethoven and the Gothic.* Ragueneau Press, pp. 220–240.

7 'The Werewolf.'

later, Louis-François retained Berlioz to oversee the rehearsals for *Esmeralda* (attended by Rossini, who was seen to "applaud loudly"). In Chapter 48 of his glorious *Mémoires*, the composer praised Bertin as "a writer and a musician of considerable distinction, and one of the most intelligent women of our time." Unfortunately, the *Journal des débats'* politicised the staging, and the premiere resolved in chaos, later recalled by Berlioz:

> one or two people who were particularly hostile to the Bertin family shouted out quite shamelessly, "It's not by Mlle Bertin, it's by Berlioz," and actively fostered the rumour that I had written [Quasimodo's aria] in the style of the rest of the score. It was no more mine than anything else in the work, and I swear on my honour that I did not write a note of it.

Berlioz was telling the truth; there is justifiable suspicion, however, that he had both hands in the orchestration. The piano score was prepared by Liszt,[8] probably in an afternoon, and *La Esmeralda* has been performed and recorded. It is an uninteresting work, strikingly so considering the identity of the librettist. It contains a lot of clichéd, four-square writing for the chorus; the solo parts lack character and melodic distinction. The Act I duet for Phoebus and Esmeralda, "*Daignez me dire*,"[9] is classic light opera, and sweet enough; it is nonetheless the Act's only memorable music. Act IV stands out for Esmeralda's Romance, "*Phoebus, n'est-il sur la terre*,"[10] which is pretty, and singular for its quality. The score wants for confidence and personality. Who might have expected otherwise? It was the composer's fourth opera, and it proved to be her last; she thereafter devoted herself to poetry.

Bertin's experience is important – not for compounding the scarcity of first-rate operas by women, but to emphasise the reasons for their absence, which are obvious and attributable to female deculturation, the scarcity of opportunities and the general burdens attaching to the categorisation of women as secondary to men. Most of the women whose skill and imagination are recognised in this book triumphed in a patriarchal society. Like any other history, the story told by sopranos records the perception of women, in the dramatic-theatrical role of a female character on stage as imagined by a man. In writing for women, male composers and librettists memorialised the male gaze just as surely as did every painter who represented a woman on canvas, wood and paper. The same is true of sculptors and male writers of novels and plays, whose burden when thinking as women occupied the same ontological space that Sartre was seeking to understand with *L'Être et le néant: essai d'ontologie phénoménologique*,[11] his ground-breaking existentialist monograph in which he identified "*le regard*" as a mechanism for the control, exchange and manipulation of power between people and genders.

---

8   Published, and later catalogued, as S.476.
9   'Please tell me.'
10   'Phoebus is no longer on Earth.'
11   'Being and Nothingness: an Essay on Phenomenological Ontology.'

The history of the soprano operates as a protocol for the tracing of female representation by men without validating or requiring critical challenges to the teleological dominion of the male. What was done – and what was composed for women to sing – is *ex post facto*; it cannot be changed by the re-evaluation of unperformed or unpublished music by female composers. The canon is best analysed as a construction of the prevailing dynamic, therefore, in accordance with the cultural, societal and political context in which women's voices were audible only when interpretating the thoughts and feelings of men. The tracing within academia of the male gaze to perennially negative connotations, spanning body image, psychology and behaviour, has lead inevitably to the reduction of women as victims or objects. Where the soprano and the achievements of female singers are concerned, the search for value and meaning among women in their voicing by men is more positive and consequential than the isolation of blame, cause and effect.

Many who study the male gaze focus on the specific attachment of a man's perspective to a woman's thoughts, appearance, personality and identity – as a simulacrum of what a man thinks a woman is, or how she should be. While this has been problematic for painters, many male novelists have also struggled, or failed entirely, to write as women. For every Flaubert (*Madame Bovary*) and William Boyd (Brazzaville Beach) there is a Jeffrey Eugenides (The Marriage Plot) and a Jonathan Franzen (Purity); writing and thinking as women has become increasingly problematic for male authors with so many female writers now in print. The brilliance of Gillian Flynn's *Gone Girl* – with its equivalent male and female perspectives – amplified the challenges for anyone trying to speak for, and as between, the genders. Her novel contained a sophisticated duality that is absent entirely from the history of the soprano until the second half of the 20th century.

Viewed from a distance, it's preposterous but undeniable that every significant female operatic role *ever* written is the invention of a man.[12] That tradition reaches back to the beginning, of course, with Eve eating from a "Tree of Knowledge" according to the men who wrote the Bible. It was difficult for every subsequent male novelist, playwright and composer to avoid the portrayal of women. Shakespeare had a crack at it with *Timon of Athens*,[13] as did David Mamet when writing *Glengarry Glen Ross*; Rachmaninov,[14] Massenet[15] and Britten[16] wrote operas for (named) male voices in isolation, while Puccini,[17] Schoenberg,[18] Poulenc[19] and George Benjamin[20] all wrote operas for women only. The general rule has otherwise provided that composers of operas accommodate men and women in relative equivalence.

---

12   As of 2023, there are more than 500 operas by women composers, according to the database published by the Women's Philharmonic Advocacy.

13   It features *very* briefly two prostitutes, Phrynia and Timandra, who are the only women in the play – aside from the Amazonian at the banquet, who doesn't speak.

14   *Skupój rýtsar* ('The Miserly Knight').

15   *Le jongleur de Notre-Dame.*

16   *Billy Budd.*

17   *Suor Angelica.*

18   *Erwartung.*

19   *La voix humaine.*

20   *Into the Little Hill.*

The male gaze reaches further than the narrative simplicity of the Bechdel Test,[21] which is less useful in its application to abstract or symbolic interpretations of femininity such as "Marianne" – the personification of the French Republic.[22] The best-known portrayal of Marianne is *La Liberté guidant le peuple*,[23] a huge work by Eugène Delacroix, painted to commemorate the July Revolution of 1830.[24] Marianne is shown bare-breasted, carrying the French *Tricolore* in one hand and a bayonetted musket in the other; she wears a Phrygian cap as she leads a group of men over the bodies of the fallen. Marianne's origins are uncertain. The name is an amalgam of Marie and Anne, as the names of Jesus' mother and grandmother, and it appears to have become attached to the Republic through a song, "*La Garisou de Marionno,*"[25] composed in 1792 by Guillaume Lavabre, a village cobbler and minstrel in Puylaurens.[26] The attachment of French identity to the image of a woman was not original. The Polish icon "Polonia" was in currency as early as 1562, and the British first stamped "Britannia" to English farthings in 1672, during the reign of Charles II. The Europe-wide emergence of nationalism during the 1830s was felt acutely in France, where, between the First Empire (1804–1814) and the Paris Commune (1871), the country was in a state of almost constant social, political and cultural flux. The place and presence of women as icons and symbols – all seen with the male gaze – was transformed by Delacroix, Géricault, Chassériau and the great rush of romantic painters who rejected the precision and discipline of their former neoclassical gods, Jacques-Louis David, Antoine-Jean Gros, Pierre-Paul Prud'hon, and the *eminence grisaille*, Ingres. Aggressive brush strokes and vibrant, unmixed colours forged a chromatic intensity that favoured nature, modern history, and contemporary events in place of antiquity. Emotion and the actual displaced the stylised and the mythological. As Delacroix wrote in his journal, "the enemy of all painting is grey."

Romanticism was the language of feeling, red in tooth and claw; its operatic patronage was launched by Italian composers in France – notably Spontini, Cherubini and Rossini, who relocated to Paris in 1824, holding a gold-plated contract from the Opéra. Rossini's arrival was welcomed by the Romantics and spurned by the neo-Classicists. The New York Metropolitan Museum of Art library holds a number of satirical sketches and prints by Delacroix that delineate these tensions. "*Le Grand*

---

21 Named after the American cartoonist Alison Bechdel. The Bechdel test is a measure of the representation of women in fiction. The criteria are that: it must have at least two *named* women in it, who talk to each other about something *other than* a man. When applied to opera, the Bechdel Test is devastating, with almost nothing passing muster. Exceptions include Verdi's *Don Carlos*, because of the exchanges between Eboli and Elisabeth in Acts II and III, and Strauss's *Elektra*.

22 She is an allegory of liberty and reason, and a representation of the Goddess of Liberty; her appearance peppers every corner of French government, including euro coins and postage stamps. There is no one Marianne, so "she" has changed over time, and with circumstance. In 1969 the actress Brigitte Bardot was adopted as her model, followed by Mireille Mathieu in 1978, Catherine Deneuve in 1985, Inès de La Fressange in 1989, Laetitia Casta in 2000, and Évelyne Thomas in 2003 – since when there has been no official successor.

23 'Liberty Leading the People.'

24 Many wrongly continue to think the painting depicts the French Revolution of 1789. Delacroix was born on 26 April, 1798.

25 'The Healing of Marianne.'

26 60 miles north of Toulouse.

Opéra," dated 1821, was published in *Le Miroir*, one of Paris' liberal daily papers, which shows an aging former opera singer in a classical tunic hobbling on crutches; his infirmity pricks the Opéra's decline. On 13 August of the same year, *Le miroir* published another drawing by Delacroix, of Rossini in an heroic pose, his pockets stuffed with music; he holds three of "his" singers/characters aloft: Manuel Garcia as Otello, Joséphine Mainville-Fodor[27] as Rosina, and Felice Pellegrini as Figaro.[28] The editor of *Le miroir* saluted the cartoon's "uncommon boldness," while Stendhal wrote (anonymously) a series of essays in praise of his hero. Delacroix's admiration for Rossini coincided with the Parisian premiere of *Otello*; it proved to be lifelong. On 14 February, 1847 – eighteen months before he began work on *"Othello and Desdemona"* – he wrote in his diary:

> In Rossini, the Italian aspect prevails, i.e., ornament dominates the expression. In many of Mozart's operas it is not otherwise as it is always ornate and elegant, but the expression of the delicate feelings takes a melancholy tone that does not suit all subjects. In the Don Giovanni he does not fall into this problem. The issue, moreover, was wonderfully well chosen, due to the variety of characters. D. Anna, Ottavio, Elvira, are serious characters, especially the first two, in Elvira one can guess a brighter hue and Don Giovanni, alternatively bufo [sic], insolent, insinuating, even tender. There exists an inimitable coquetry in the Peasant; Leporello, perfect from beginning to end. Rossini does not really change both characters. (...) Oh Rossini! Oh Mozart! Oh geniuses inspired by all the arts, who take from things only what the spirit needs to be shown.[29]

On 12 April, 1860, he attended one of Rossini's legendary Saturday *matinées*, after which he wrote:[30]

> With the same human element he adds or removes, modifies his stuff and makes men of his invention, which, however, are true [...] This is one of the strongest traits of the genius. This also happens with Molière,

---

27   Joséphine Fodor (13 October, 1789/1793 – 10 August, 1870); also known by her married name, Fodor-Mainville. She was raised in Saint Petersburg, where her father taught music to the imperial children. She became hugely famous because of her work at the Comédie-Italienne, where she made her debut on 16 November, 1814. Celebrated for her performances from 1819 in Cimarosa's *Il matrimonio segreto*, *Don Giovanni*, *Il barbiere* and *La gazza ladra*. Triumphed in Naples in Otello and Vienna before returning to Paris in 1825. Fodor can be considered the first significant *prima donna* not to have created an important role.

28   The image nonetheless contains a number of classical references, including Rossini as Atlas, Daphne sprouting laurel boughs and Zeus giving birth to Athena from his head. It follows that Delacroix's attack on classicism was not aimed at antiquity (or the pre-Romantic past) but at contemporary practice and the poverty of much contemporary repertoire. See Athanassoglou-Kallmyer, Nina Maria (1991). *Eugène Delacroix, Prints, Politics and Satire, 1814–1822*. Yale University Press, pp. 86–89.

29   Magraner, José Salvador Blasco and Camejo, Francisco Carlos Bueno (2014). "Delacroix, Eugène: The Bridge of Vision, The Image of the Opera in the History of Painting (Delacroix and Rossini´s Otello)." *Global Journal of Human-Social Science*. Vol. 14(2), p. 9.

30   He did not do so with any urgency. The 12th was a Thursday.

and Cervantes, and so it happens with Rossini, with its amalgam. [...]
His fertility is inexhaustible, and he is real and ideal at a time wherever
he decides to be.[31]

Rossini's first new work for Paris was *Il viaggio a Reims*,[32] staged to commemorate
Charles X's coronation; he withdrew it after four performances, and recycled around
half of the music for *Le comte Ory* in 1828. A year later, he produced the last of the
four operas he composed in French, *Guillaume Tell*.[33] Based on Schiller's play from
1804, which drew on the legend of the Swiss revolutionary, William Tell, the score
features three female roles – Hedwige (Tell's wife, scored as a mezzo-soprano), Jemmy
(Tell's son, a *travesti* soprano) and Mathilde (a Habsburg princess, also a soprano). It
nonetheless leads with the infamously taxing tenor role, Arnold, created by Adolphe
Nouritt and made famous by Gilbert Duprez,[34] who sang the first high C from the
chest at the Italian premiere.[35] This would not be the last music Rossini composed
for female voices,[36] but it was to prove his most consequential, insofar as his farewell
to the theatre also marked the maturity of Grand Opera in France, and the first
significant departure by a major composer with the coloratura tradition.

Mathilde's best-known aria, Act II's "*Sombre forêt*,"[37] was characterised by the composer as a "Gallo-Italian hybrid" – a compromise that fused the lyricism for which
Rossini, Bellini and Donizetti were renowned to a more poetic, language-directed
sensibility that purposed virtuosity as a mechanism for the expression of directed sentiment. Rossini employed a huge orchestra[38] with unprecedented care and precision,
not least during "*Sombre forêt*," which is scored for solo clarinet, flute, bassoon, horns
and strings. The recitative, beginning "*Ils s'éloignent enfin; j'ai cru le reconnaître*," is
vibrant and skilfully voiced in its colouring, with a genuine dialogue between the
stage and the pit – which no longer provides mere accompaniment. The soloist has
to tap the emotional and psychological experience of the character, a requirement
that reaches a point of transcendental beauty with the *Andantino*, in which Mathilde
sings:

> *Sombre forêt, désert triste et sauvage,*
> *Je vous préfère aux splendeurs des palais:*
> *C'est sur les monts, au séjour de l'orage,*
> *Que mon cœur peut renaître à la paix.*[39]

---

31 *Ibid*, p. 126.
32 'The Journey to Reims.'
33 'William Tell.'
34 Boyden, Matthew (2021). *The Tenor: A Cultural History*. Ragueneau Press, pp. 48–70.
35 The Italian version of "*Asile héréditare*," ('hereditary asylum').
36 Rossini returned to composition towards the end of his life, memorably with the *Petite messe solennelle*
(1863), at which the sisters Carlotta (8 December, 1835 – 28 June, 1872) and Barbara Marchisio (6
December, 1833 – 19 April, 1919) sang the solo female parts. Barbara outlived her sister by almost fifty
years.
37 'Dark Forest.'
38 It is written for two flutes, two oboes, two clarinets, two bassoons, four horns, two trumpets, two
trombones, a large percussion section and a string orchestra of around 40.
39 'Dark forest, wilderness sad and wild, I prefer you to the splendours of the palace: it is on the

Other than when confessing *"mes secrets,"* (in the repeating phrase *"mais l'écho seulement apprendra [redira] mes secrets,"*[40]) the fully-notated sung line is absent virtuosity or display. It is within the gift of singers to extemporise the aria's coda,[41] but Rossini's intentions were otherwise notated in full. According to Duprez, the composer was happy for singers to add ornaments – and there is good evidence he assisted the first Mathilde, Laure Cinti-Damoreau,[42] with minor amendments; even so, everything written of Rossini's attitude to *canto fiorito* after his retirement suggests he loathed it. According to Duprez's published version of the cadenza to *"Sombre forêt,"* Cinti-Damoreau ended the aria with an elaborate coda; evidence from the first night suggests she sang the music come è scritto.[43] This is believable because the premiere was delayed more than once by the soprano's ill-disposition, brought on by vocal "hoarseness."[44] Cinti-Damoreau was a student of Angelica Catalani (who proposed her stage name) and Rossini, who encouraged Donizetti to cast her in the title role for the Paris premiere of *Elisabetta, regina d'Inghilterra* after taking up the directorship of the Théâtre-Italien. According to Austin Caswell

> [Rossini] tended to rely heavily on the Italian singers of the company, as opposed to the French singers, and he even brought in some new Italian voices. In a few cases, he retained French singers out of political motives or because a particular French singer was trained in the Italian style and familiar with the Italian repertoire. Mlle Cinti was one of the few French members of the Theatre Italien who met these criteria. Moreover, she had already performed in five of Rossini's works alongside native Italian singers. From this point on, she became the French spear-head of Rossini's Italian invasion.[45]

The composer cast her in the role of Countess Folleville in *Il viaggio a Reims*, and she was his first choice for *Moïse et Pharaon*, *Le Siège de Corinthe*, *Le Comte Ory* and, of course, *Guillaume Tell*. In 1830, Cinti-Damoreau sang Elvire at the premiere of Auber's *La Muette de Portici*,[46] and in 1831 she again collaborated with Nourrit for the first staging of *Robert le diable*, a triumph that confirmed Meyerbeer's standing in Paris, and the soprano's status as the Opéra's *prima donna*. Some weeks before the premiere, prints were released of the costumes, designed by François-Gabriel Lépaulle, which did a roaring trade across the city. Cinti-Damoreau is pictured wearing a

---

mountains, the place of the storm / That my heart can regain peace.'
40 'And only the echo will learn [repeat] my secrets.'
41 A good example is Beverly Sills' live-recording from Cleveland in 1968, in which she adds a considerable melisma to the aria's final bars. The prima donna can be forgiven on the basis that the performance is about as perfect as can be imagined.
42 *née* Laure-Cinthie Montalant, 6 February, 1801 – 25 February, 1863.
43 Colas, Damien (2004). "Melody and ornamentation." In *The Cambridge Companion to Rossini*. Ed. by Emanuele Senici. Cambridge University Press, p. 121–122.
44 Caswell, A. (1975). "Mme Cinti-Damoreau and the Embellishment of Italian Opera in Paris: 1820–1845." *Journal of the American Musicological Society*, 28(3), pp. 459–492.
45 *Ibid*, p. 462.
46 Alongside two of her *Guillaume Tell* alumni, Adolphe Nourrit (as Alphonse) and Henri-Bernard Dabadie (as Pietro).

medieval corset, with only her face and hands visible; she forms a compelling silhouette; there is nothing feminine, erotic or sensual in the image, however.[47] In the same
year, and in the same city, Alexandre-Jean Dubois-Drahonet unveiled a libidinous
neo-Classical *odalisque*,[48] seen from the back, while Alexandre-Gabriel Decamps
produced a romantic alternative in which a woman dressed *à la marocain* stands by
a window with a breast exposed, a bird on her hand, and a monkey hanging from
the ceiling. Although not shown in public for many years (and still not viewable at
the Metropolitan in New York), the "private" watercolour by Sarah Goodridge of her
own breasts, now known as *Beauty Revealed*, was completed at around the same time,
in 1828. Goodridge was 40-years-old when painting herself, so the unqualified perfection of the image is, as a female gaze, somewhat idealistic. It can be seen as erotic
because the breasts are isolated in a painted frame of white cloth, which heightens the
anatomical in its separation from the subject's identity. Whatever might have been
said of Goodridge's "courageous" autonomy when representing herself as she did is
undermined by her use of the painting as a calling-card for Daniel Webster, to whom
she sent it either before or during their affair. Whatever Goodridge's intentions, the
gesture proved empty; Webster married another woman.

The sopranos who performed opera in France during the 1830s were constructions of a male gaze that failed to reconcile the lust to which painting and sculpture
alluded and the concomitant risk of scandal whenever a woman opened her mouth
on stage. Considerable efforts were made to ensure a healthy distance between the
soprano and the exotic, therefore – even if a role appeared to require it. Productions
of Cherubini's *Les Abencérages, ou L'étendard de Grenade*,[49] for example, employed
all the hallmarks of Grand Opera, with an amorphous middle-eastern complexion,
large choruses, huge spectacles and extensive ballet music – as well as love-saturated
story-lines in which the female lead personified infatuation unsullied by desire.
The lead role, Noraïme, was created at the premiere on 6 April, 1813, by Caroline
Branchu, a soprano whose respectability out of costume was questionable but who
nonetheless presented on stage as a woman of certain virtue.[50]

---

47 Conversely, Gustave Courbet's painting of the tenor, Louis Guéymard, as Robert (1857) is priapic.
Boyden, Matthew (2021). *The Tenor: A Cultural History*. Ragueneau Press, p. 336.

48 A female slave or concubine, usually in a harem, and commonly nude.

49 'The Abencerrages, or The standard of Granada.' The Abencerrage (from the Arabic for "Saddler's
Son") was a 15th century family in Granada that held great power.

50 Though hard to credit, many women writers across the English-speaking world, and in the United
States in particular, are promulgating in 2023 a neo-Victorian conception of what it is to be "a woman
of virtue." Numerous websites, saturated with allegedly Christian values, advocate a female identity
that predates enfranchisement. "Thegritandgraceproject.org," for example, is written by "a community
of women who have come together to share life lessons learned and wisdom gained, [whose] faith is
paramount to who we are and what we do." The authors of this disturbingly reactionary website ask "Want
to Be a Woman of Virtue?", in answer to which they advocate that all women "Remember These 4 Things;
[a woman of virtue] "is careful not to tear down or destroy. Takes care of her body, is aware of the language
she uses, and makes lifestyle choices that are not selfish or shallow." One can only imagine what the author
of this retrograde nonsense would make of *La Liberté guidant le peuple*, and the many thousands of women
who have acted to fight for female rights, with or without a rifle, when "tearing down and destroying," the
status quo and its imprimaturs. See also, and *inter alia*, Laskarina Bouboulina (1821), Kittur Chennamma
(1824), Countess Emilia Plater (1831), Rani Lakshmibai (1858), Shona (1896), Yaa Asantewaa (1900),
and Rosa Luxemburg (1919).

If illustrating women as women was problematic for men when gazing at them in the theatre, there was no problem portraying them as psychotic. The earliest recorded "Mad Scene"[51] appears in *Orlando Furioso*, Ludovico Ariosto's epic poem from 1532, in which the titular hero's mind collapses after his love for Angelica, a pagan princess, is unrequited. The *commedia dell'arte* relished female psychosis, and it became a dramatic convention across Europe to portray women as delusional – in prose as well as musical theatre. To his credit, Shakespeare's painting of Ophelia's despair and loss of identity as "withered" violets[52] didn't dissuade him from breaking Hamlet's mind also. Composers were uninterested in male insanity; only a handful of the hundreds of "mad scenes" written during the 19th century is ascribed to a male character.[53] Rossini created two minor episodes for women, in *Ermione* ("*Essa corre al trionfo*")[54] and *Semiramide* ("*Deh! Ti ferma*"),[55] as did Bellini, for *Il Pirata* ("*Col sorriso d'innocenza*")[56] and *I puritani* ("*O rendetemi*").[57] The most famous exponent was Donizetti, who made female insanity a stock in trade, ironically given the severity of his own psychotic break in 1846.[58] What qualifies as a "mad scene," as opposed to a momentary loss of reason, continues to be debated;[59] there are clear episodes in *Anna Bolena*,[60] *Torquato Tasso*,[61] *Lucia di Lammermoor*, *Maria Padilla*,[62] and *Linda di Chamounix*.[63] For all their inherent misogyny, the paradoxical value of "mad scenes" is that they were designed for sopranos to show off, with technical opportunities for extremely high voices (to E flat 6 and the occasional F6), monstrous breath-extensions, some floridity (although this is less common than languidity) and dramatic intensity. The women suffering "madness" were insensible because of circumstances, but also because they were women and prone by "nature" to irrationality. The "female brain"[64] was objectified as different to that of the male by doctors as well as philosophers and educationalists; "female" psychosis was (and in some quarters still is) used to account

---

51 The terms "mad" and "madness" are quite properly rejected in the medical and academic communities, globally. They are used here, and in this narrow context, only insofar as they are applied to the convention of "mad scenes" in opera and theatre. This is not political correctness, or "woke" thinking. Only an idiot would consider it appropriate to use language that undermines and demeans individuals suffering from psychosis. The term "idiot" is reasonable in its application to anyone so inclined.

52 Act IV, Scene 5.

53 The one obvious exception is Act III of Mussorgsky's *Boris Godunov*, in which Godunov is tormented by an apparition-hallucination. The finest "mad scene" for a man was written in the 20th century, by Benjamin Britten, when Peter Grimes sings "Steady. There you are, nearly home."

54 'It runs to triumph.'

55 'It stops you.'

56 'With an innocent smile.'

57 'O give me back.'

58 A condition that left him mute for the last two years of his life.

59 On point, it might be argued that if Amina's sleepwalking in *La sonnambula* qualifies (which, in the opinion of the author, it does not), then Nemorino's scene beginning "*Dell'elisir mirabile*" should be considered a "mad scene" also since he is other than sensible at the time – having drunk so much of the magic potion (wine) sold to him by Dulcamara.

60 First performed on 26 December, 1830.

61 First performed on 9 September, 1833.

62 First performed on 26 December, 1841.

63 First performed on 19 May, 1842.

64 See, generally, Malane, Rachel (2005). *Sex in Mind: The Gendered Brain in Nineteenth-Century Literature and Mental Sciences*. Peter Lang.

for everything from the "effects" of menstruation and an unhappy marriage, to independent thought and ambition. "Hysteria" was employed to categorise the fragility of women's minds[65] – until, of course, one of them had to perform "*Il dolce suono*" from Act III of *Lucia di Lammermoor*. Despite making capital of the vulnerability of "the weaker sex," composers were dependent on the strength of women for the success of their work.

Sir Walter Scott's novel, *The Bride of Lammermoor*, was a popular subject for opera before Donizetti picked it up in 1834. Among the many now-forgotten settings are Michele Carafa's *Le Nozze di Lammermoor* (1829), Ivar Bredal's *Brüden fra Lammermoor* (1832), and Alberto Mazzucato's *La Fidanzata di Lammermoor* (1834). Donizetti's opera (which is unique in featuring a "mad scene,")[66] was premiered on 26 September, 1835, at the Teatro di San Carlo in Naples, where Donizetti inherited Rossini's position. He hand-picked and trained the theatre's orchestra and chorus, creating one of the most accomplished companies in the history of music theatre – transforming the stagecraft, the performance diary and the repertoire. In addition to producing and conducting dozens of works by other composers, he staged 18 of his own operas at the San Carlo between July, 1823, and January, 1844. He worked with a large cadre of singers, among whom numbered 30 of the world's best sopranos; the surfeit of talent explains why he chose only rarely to work with any of them more than once. Only three sopranos created more than one role for Donizetti: Luigia Boccabadati[67] (two), Adelaide Tosi[68] (three) and Giuseppina Ronzi de Begnis[69] (three). Most, like Annetta Fischer, were invited to a single premiere[70] before disappearing from the operatic record; others, like Caterina Chiesi,[71] achieved immortality through marriage.[72]

Fanny Tacchinardi Persiani[73] is remembered solely for creating Lucia. Born in Rome, she trained initially with her father, a tenor and eminent vocal coach; after making her debut in Livorno, in 1832, she appeared in Venice, Florence, Milan and Naples in works by Rossini, Bellini and Donizetti. Before originating Lucia, she created the title roles in *Rosmonda d'Inghilterra* in Florence (with Gilbert Duprez, in February, 1834) and *Pia de' Tolomei* in Venice, in 1837. Duprez was the tenor lead for the first performance of Lucia, in which he sang the role of Edgardo. Although the opera was named after its title soprano, Duprez's stellar talent and reputation were sufficient for Donizetti to afford him the rare honour of ending the opera, with "*Tu che a Dio spiegasti l'ali.*"[74] Persiani was less than magnanimous when learning

---

65   See, generally, Fauvel, Aude (2013). "Crazy Brains and the Weaker Sex: The British Case (1860–1900).". In *Clio. Women, Gender, History*. Vol. 37 (1).

66   Which is absent from Scott's novel.

67   *Circa* 1800 – 12 October, 1850.

68   *Circa* 1800 – 27 March, 1859.

69   11 January, 1800 – 7 June, 1853.

70   She created the title role in *Alina, regina di Golconda*.

71   She sang in the first performance of *L'assedio di Calais*, appearing as Eleonora.

72   She became a star as Caterina Barilli (having taken her first husband's name). After his death, she married Salvatore Patti, performing as Caterina Barilli-Patti. She had four children with both husbands. All three of her daughters with Patti achieved success as singers, most famously Adelina.

73   October, 1812 – 3 May, 1867.

74   'You who have spread your wings to God.'

of the composer's decision; so intense was her rage that she provoked a legendary row that cast the mould of the sanguinary, self-obsessed prima donna for succeeding generations. Persiani was the first soprano to "own" a role, which she re-created in Paris in December, 1837 (opposite Giovanni Rubini), and for London in April, 1838. Her celebrity was broadcast through tours with Rubini and the tenor, Mario, in whose company she created the (revised) première of *Linda di Chamounix* in Paris in November, 1842. Persiani spent the majority of her career in Paris and London; she toured widely also, taking advantage of Europe's rapidly-evolving train network. Anton Rubinstein heard her sing in Moscow in 1851, and considered her "one of the very greatest of artists."[75] Persiani's voice was described variously (and inconsistently) as sweet and cold, brittle and elegiac. She is said to have had a powerful chest tone and a brilliant upper register, with easy agility to an F6. Her technique was bullet-proof, and her stamina was such that she could sing comfortably for an hour after the completion of an evening's performance. This mechanical facility enabled her to delay her retirement until 1859, a career spanning almost three decades. Although characterisations of her singing are inconsistent, some commentators suggested it was light, and made special only by her melismatic virtuosity. "*Il dolce suono*" is not typical of the score's exigencies, which begin with an orchestration that prescribes two flutes, a piccolo, two oboes, two clarinets, two bassoons, four horns, two trumpets, three trombones, timpani, triangle, bass drum, cymbals, harp, glass armonica, and a cattery of gut. It is a huge undertaking that prioritises amplitude, line and breath control over coloratura and high notes. It's important to remember also that the first Edgardo, Gilbert Duprez, had a trumpet of a voice, which he employed from the chest and the head for anything above an A4. Domenico Cosselli, Enrico's creator (and the first true baritone in Italo-French opera) was also renowned for his stentorian power.[76] Between them, Duprez and Cosselli must have presented a formidable sonic challenge for a woman with a "light" timbre, particularly one for whom Donizetti wrote no fewer than eight duets in *Lucia*,[77] as well as the most famous sextet in opera, "*Che mi frena in tal momento.*"[78]

"*Il dolce suono mi colpi di sua voce! Ah, quella voce m'e qui nel cor discesa!*"[79] was written originally in F major, although many transpose it to E-flat. Much of the writing is marked piano, and lightly scored, with limited ornaments *come è scritto*. It's accepted that Donizetti was resigned to Persiani and her peers interpolating trills, mordents, turns, runs and cadenzas, as was routine even in productions of operas by Mozart. Lucia's "Mad Scene" continues to represent one of the summits of the bel canto soprano repertoire. Its atmosphere is established during an introduction that makes eerie use of a glass armonica,[80] an instrument invented by Benjamin Franklin

75 Taylor, Philip (2007). *Anton Rubinstein: a Life in Music*. Indiana University Press, p. 30.

76 As distinct from the traditional and then generic catch-all, "bass-baritone."

77 Between Act I's "*Sulla tomba che rinserra*" ('On the grave that he closes') and Act III's "*Dio lo salva in si fiero momento*" ('God spares him at such a proud moment').

78 'Who holds me back at such a moment.'

79 'The sweet sound of his voice hit me! Ah, that voice is here in my descending heart!'

80 This was replaced for the first night, and commonly thereafter, by a flute. In 2006, Sascha Reckert and Philipp Alexander Marguerre revived the armonica for a production at La Scala, starring Mariella Devia.

in 1761. The amonica became associated with mental distress soon after; in 1798, Beethoven's friend,[81] Friedrich Rochlitz, wrote in the AMZ:

> There may be various reasons for the scarcity of armonica players, principally the almost universally shared opinion that playing it is damaging to the health, that it excessively stimulates the nerves, plunges the player into a nagging depression and hence into a dark and melancholy mood, that it is an apt method for slow self-annihilation [...] Many (physicians with whom I have discussed this matter) say the sharp penetrating tone runs like a spark through the entire nervous system, forcibly shaking it up and causing nervous disorders [...] If you are suffering from any nervous disorder you should not play it, If you are not yet ill you should not play it excessively If you are feeling melancholy you should not play it or else play uplifting pieces If tired, avoid playing it late at night.[82]

Marianne Davies was the first to bring the armonica to the concert public's attention. She gave lessons to Marie Antoinette and Anton Mesmer, whose turn as a hypnotist continues to be associated with the instrument's unsettling tone and vibration. The shredding of Davies' nerves was attributed to the armonica, as was the death at the age of 39 of the blind performer, Marianne Kirchgessner.[83] The armonica's eerie, half-lit distortions add to the colouring of Lucia's psychotic break after she murders her husband, Arturo; the "duet" for soprano and armonica is designed to represent a voice that Lucia hears in her mind when committing murder on her wedding night.[84] The spinning vocal line conveys the otherness of her mental collapse. Much of the aria is marked piano, or presumed to be because of the delicacy of the scoring; there are limited ornaments *come è scritto*, but it's accepted that Donizetti was resigned to Persiani's interpolations. The difficulty of the writing helps explain Persiani's status as the leading *bella cantante* of the first half of the 19th century as well as the opera's sudden fall from popularity. There were 19 performances in 1835, four in 1836, 16 in 1837, and two in 1838. Even after the London and Paris premieres it was a "difficult" opera – a reputation that shadowed the first American performance, in New Orleans on 28 May, 1841.

Lucia is a victim of patricidal control and a casualty of her own sexual fantasies – on which she is unable to act by reason of her confinement to an arranged marriage and her equally forced separation from her lover, Edgardo; the music nonetheless

---

81 On 30 April, 1819, in correspondence with Johannes Kreisler, E.T.A. Hoffmann discussed a Beethoven piano trio played on a Streicher four-pedal piano, which required the use of the Armonica or "Una corda" pedal – in combination with the soft and sustaining pedals – to create a sound recalling the "Aeolian harp or armonica." *E. T. A. Hoffmann's Musical Writings: Kreisleriana, The Poet and the Composer, Music Criticism* (1989). Ed. David Charlton. Cambridge University Press, p. 418.

82 Letter sent in 1798.

83 She knew Mozart briefly, inspiring him to write for the instrument.

84 Sadly, a dispute between the theatre and the intended performer of the Armonica meant it was not heard at the first performance, but re-scored instead for flute. See Matsumoto, Naomi (2011). "Manacled Freedom: 19th-Century Vocal Improvisation and the Flute-Accompanied Cadenza in Donizetti's Lucia di Lammermoor." In *Beyond Notes: Improvisation in Western Music of the Eighteenth and Nineteenth Centuries*. Rudolf Rasch, Ed. Brepols, pp. 295–316.

adheres to major keys, and "happy" ones at that. Even Lucia's collapse into uncon-
sciousness and death are painted in tonalities that articulate a positive state of mind
– because, for half the aria's duration, she believes she is being joined in marriage to
Edgardo, an "*armonia celeste*" that she alone is able to hear. The tragedy of the scene
is conveyed as a soliloquy – formed as the experience of Lucia's delusion, rather than
as an incident to be observed. The insight is coincidentally intimate and alienating.
The scene does not speak harmonically to derangement, as would the delusions of
Salome and Elektra; indeed, other than during her entrance in C minor (Beethoven's
favoured key for the "other"), and her A-flat minor vision of a ghost when singing
"*Ohime, sorge il tremendo fantasma,*"[85] there are no minor keys to elicit fear or sadness
because the audience is hearing and seeing what Lucia is experiencing.

The scene is traditional in its architecture, which is formed as a standard
double-aria, with a cavatina and a cabaletta, both prefaced by recitative. The sectional
lengths are unusual, insofar as the 32-bar cavatina is preceded by a recitative 100
bars greater in length. Donizetti employs several modulations and tempo changes, in
addition to broken, interrupted vocal phrases, to illustrate the fragmenting of Lucia's
thoughts. The effect creates a prominent sense of disconnection, corresponding to
the prevailing conception of insanity. Coloratura is used with painterly skill to convey Lucia's psychological decline; melismas are introduced to interrupt the normal
flow of speech and thought with ornaments added to particular words, such as "*da
tuoi nemici,*"[86] and "*a pie dell'ara,*"[87] to magnify the extent to which Lucia's illusions
have altered her memory – which Donizetti characterises through the repetition of
motifs from earlier scenes. Her changed perception collides during the phrase "*Del
ciel clemente un riso la vita a noi sarà,*"[88] with descending melodic lines that depict
joy and forgiveness as gifts from heaven. Lucia's "mad scene" is not the first example
of a composer attempting to convey a woman's thoughts and feelings; Monteverdi,
Handel, Rossini and Mozart all achieved this, to differing degrees, but the articulation of Lucia's psychology and its fragmentation was a water-mark in the history of
opera that would prove of enormous consequence for librettists and composers.

If *Lucia di Lammermoor's* success was slow to mature then Donizetti's influence
in Italy was immediate and ubiquitous – not least for Verdi, who never hesitated to
acknowledge his debt. He composed three mad-scenes for soprano – "*Chi mi to-
glie,*"[89] in *Nabucco,*[90] "*Mentre gonfiarsi l'anima,*"[91] in *Attila,*[92] and "*Una macchia*",[93] in
Macbeth[94] – the last of which he revised for staging in French at the Opéra in 1865,
producing one of his very few failures. "Mad scenes" were otherwise *du jour* in France,

---

85   'Alas, the awful ghost arises.'
86   'From your enemies.'
87   'At the foot of the altar.'
88   'For us life will be a merciful smile from heaven.'
89   'Who takes me away.'
90   First performed on 9 March, 1842.
91   'As the soul swells.'
92   First performed on 17 March, 1846.
93   'A stain.' This fearsomely unsettling aria is by far the best of them.
94   First performed on 14 March, 1847.

with notable examples being produced by Ambroise Thomas (whose *Hamlet*[95] made much of Ophelia's loss of reason with *"Partagez-vous mes fleurs,"*[96]) and Meyerbeer, who added an absurdist moment of derangement to *Dinorah*[97] (*"Ombre légère"*).[98] "Mad women" were popular at the Parisian ballet also, with the title role of Adolphe Adam's *Giselle*[99] losing her mind after falling in love with a nobleman whom she discovers is engaged to another woman. The equivalence of femininity and weakness was extended by the popular attachment of psychosis to the abandonment of women by men. When not seeing women as insane, 19th century composers in France portrayed them as virgins or harlots, or hybrids of the two. It's unclear where the female roles in *La Juive* might be positioned, with the flirtatious and irrelevant Princess Eudoxie (a coloratura), and the virginal, misguided Rachel providing little more than narrative foils for the landmark tenor role of Eléazar.[100] Rachel's hideous experience as 'The Jewess' does not feature a "mad scene," as such; her role can still be considered senseless for what she is forced to endure, and for how her life ends – boiled alive in a cauldron of water.

La Juive was first performed on 23 February, 1835. The production was controversial before it opened because of the opulence of the staging and its enormous cost, with a vast orchestra and chorus, two teams of scene designers (requiring over 20 set-painters and 25 cycloramas), and an on-stage organ for Act I – an idea that Wagner employed without irony for his most anti-Semitic opera, *Die Meistersinger von Nürnberg*. Halévy, the work's conductor, François Habeneck, and Adolphe Nourrit were of a single mind when gifting the role of Rachel to Cornélie Falcon,[101] a 20-year-old soprano who had enrolled at the Conservatoire at the age of fourteen, in 1827. She studied with Adolphe Nourrit, who later became her regular partner at the Opéra. Her city debut on 20 July, 1832, at the age of 18, as Alice, in Meyerbeer's *Robert le diable* was an unexpected triumph because the role held symbolic importance for Parisian audiences, for whom the first production nine months earlier was still a fresh memory. The first Alice was Julie Dorus-Gras,[102] a Belgian soprano admired by Rossini and made famous by her part in the performance of Auber's *La muette de Portici* that triggered the Belgian Revolution on 25 August, 1830. Dorus-Gras was more than ten years older than Falcon, popular and talented – a status recognised by her creation of a number of landmark roles, including Oscar in Auber's *Gustave III*, Pauline in Donizetti's *Les Martyrs*,[103] Princess Eudoxie in *La Juive*, Marguerite de Valois in *Les Huguenots*, and Teresa in Berlioz's *Benvenuto Cellini*. Falcon had enormous shoes to fill, therefore, and it says much of the buzz created by her first rehearsal that the audience for the first night included Rossini, Cherubini, Berlioz,

---

95   First performed on 9 March, 1868.
96   'Do you share my flowers.'
97   Originally *Le pardon de Ploërmel* ('The Pardon of Ploërmel'). First performed on 4 April, 1859.
98   'Lightly shaded.'
99   First performed on 28 June, 1841.
100   Created by Adolphe Nourrit, who also made a valuable contribution to the libretto.
101   28 January, 1814 – 25 February, 1897.
102   7 September, 1805 – 6 February, 1896. Atypically for sopranos born at the beginning of the century, Dorus-Gras lived an incredibly long life, dying at the remarkable age of 90.
103   The French version of *Poliuto*.

Halévy, Auber, Malibran, Branchu, Giulia Grisi and dozens of other musicians, actors, composers, painters, critics and writers, among whom Eugène Scribe, Théophile Gautier, Alexandre Dumas, Victor Hugo, and Alfred de Musset were merely the best known. Falcon was a teenager, so her anxiety must have been acute when meeting the challenge of Alice's first aria. The audience was delirious; Meyerbeer was less satisfied, as he explained in writing to his wife on 18 September, 1832:

> The house was as full as it ever could be, 8700 francs (without subscription) and many people could not find seats. The performance was [...] so fresh [...] like the first performance of the work, not a trace of being played out. About Falcon I dare not reach any definite conclusion [...] only it is evident that she has a strong and beautiful voice, not without agility, at the same time that she is a vividly expressive (but somewhat overcharged) actress. Unfortunately her intonation is not completely pure, and I fear she will never overcome these weaknesses. In sum, I think that she could be an outstanding star, and I will certainly in any case write a principal role for her in my new opera.

Meyerbeer's new opera was *Les Huguenots* and Falcon was duly invited to create the role of Valentine, which has a span of two and half octaves, to D5. Before this epic event, she appeared in a revival of *Don Giovanni* – with Cinti-Damoreau as Zerline, and Nourrit in the title role.[104] Berlioz's judgment of Falcon's performance was reserved:[105]

> Mlle Falcon, so energetic in Robert le Diable, was physically speaking, with her countenance "pale as a beautiful autumn evening," the ideal Donna Anna. She had fine moments in the accompanied recitative sung over her father's body. Why then did she all at once go off the boil in the great aria of the first act [...] Oh! Mlle Falcon, with those black eyes of yours and the incisive voice you possess, there is no need to be afraid. Let your eyes flash and your voice ring out: you will be yourself, and you will be the incarnation of the vengeful Spanish noblewoman whose principal features your timidity veiled from us.

Berlioz's opinion evolved in tandem with Falcon's. By 1835 – at which time the soprano's salary at the Opéra was 50,000 francs[106] – he considered her to be without compare,[107] recalling in his memoirs how her performance of the phrase, "*Il*

---

104   Berlioz was privately extremely critical of Nourrit's vainglorious presumption.

105   In *Rénovateur*, on 6 March, 1834.

106   Somewhere between £250,000 and £300,000 – at a time when a factory worker in Lyon could expect to earn an average of 3 francs a day – or 780 francs a year, approximately 1.5% of what Falcon was paid by the Opéra alone. This made her the highest paid artist at the Opéra. Indeed, she earned almost twice as much as Nourrit and *three times* as much as Dorus-Gras. See Bowring, John, Sir (1835). *Second report on the commercial relations between France and Great Britain. Silks & wine. Presented to both Houses of Parliament by command of His Majesty.* W. Clowes, p. 35.

107   On 23 November, 1834, for example, Berlioz retained Falcon to sing the first performances of his

te tuerant,"[108] from *Les Huguenots*, caused astonishment because of the declamatory power with which she enunciated a line of music formed of repeating notes. Falcon's skill as a dramatist grew into something extraordinary, and Berlioz raised her as the ideal. He did so, in part, because she rose above the political maelstrom that was life at the Opéra. It was predictable that he should have asked Falcon to create the role of Esmeralda for Louise Bertin, on 14 November, 1836.

For all Berlioz's affections, it was Meyerbeer who crowned Falcon's celebrity, alongside Dorus-Gras as Marguerite de Valois and Nourrit as Raoul, with the premiere of *Les Huguenots* on 29 February, 1836. Falcon's achievement was absolute, and acknowledged even by Dorus-Gras. Unusually for the time, she did nothing to invite gossip, so the considerable body of journalism attaching to her work focusses exclusively on her singing, her acting and her appearance. In this sense, she was a modern artist. In the 21st century, nearly everything written about a soprano conforms to whatever a press agent and management company want to read; even criticism is respectful, whether or not a performance warrants it. Falcon's beauty, talent and youth were an aphrodisiac for audiences; composers rushed to hear her produce what must have been a ravishing flood of tone, with a powerful chest voice and a capacity for floated head tones, high above the stave – beyond her natural range as a mezzo-soprano. Having none of the tricks required of a coloratura, she conformed instead to the style and substance of what would become known as a *dramatic soprano* – albeit in the body of a soubrette. The timbre of her voice led to the emergence of the "falcon," a shorthand for a dramatic voice with an effortless, extended upper register. In 1832, Castil-Blaze wrote:

> Her soprano, carrying more than two octaves from B to D, sounded on all points with equal vigour. A silvery voice, with a brilliant timbre, incisive enough that even the weight of the chorus cannot overwhelm it; yet the sound emitted with such force never loses its charm or purity.[109]

The candle that burns brightest burns half as long; Falcon threw hers onto a fire of her own making. During a performance of Louis Niedermeyer's *Stradella* at the Opéra in March, 1837,[110] she failed to sing the words "*Je suis prête,*"[111] in response to Nourrit's question "*Demain nous partirons – voulez-vous?*"[112] Instead, and as Berlioz recalled with unkind eloquence, the soprano produced "raucous sounds like those of a child with croup, guttural, whistling notes that quickly faded like those of a flute filled with water."[113] She fainted and had to be carried from the stage by Nourrit. Despite numerous visits to doctors, and treatments by "specialists," as well as a period

---

new orchestrations of the songs "*La captive*" and "*Le Jeune Pâtre breton*" ('The Young Breton Shepherd,'), a concert at which the premiere of *Harold en Italie* was given also.
108 'He will kill you.'
109 Bouvet, Charles (1927). *Cornélie Falcon.* Alcan, p. 39.
110 Cairns, David (1999). *Berlioz: Servitude and greatness 1832–1869.* University of California Press, p. 151.
111 'I am ready.'
112 'We leave tomorrow – will you.'
113 Bouvet, Charles (1927). *Cornélie Falcon.* Alcan, p. 115.

of recuperation in Italy, Falcon never regained her voice. She gave her final repertoire performance in France on 15 January, 1838, as Valentine – five and a half years after her debut. She returned to the Opéra for a benefit, on 14 March, 1840, to perform selections from *La Juive* and *Les Huguenots*, with Dorus-Gras and Duprez. Writing in the *Débats*, Berlioz described the event, paying particular attention to the Act IV duet with Raoul from *Les Huguenots*, which

> Miss Falcon played superbly throughout. The sentence from the role of Valentine: "Fatal night, night of alarms, I have no future,"[114] was for the singer the subject of a poignant allusion which almost made her lose again what was left of her strength. But the duet completed, the whole room stirred to the very depths of a feeling for which I cannot find a name, called Miss Falcon to applaud her again and cover her with flowers, very weak testimonies of the interest she inspired. Now Miss Falcon must be told that the allusion to Valentine's part, which she so eagerly grasped, lacks accuracy and reality. And yes, no doubt a future remains for her, even if her voice does not return! What prevents her from devoting to drama, to tragedy, the happy faculties with which she is endowed, and which she has hitherto made such an intelligent application to the action of lyrical works? Our first poets will be happy to provide her with the opportunity to conquer on another stage a place equal to that which she abandons at the Opera; and the Théâtre-Français, if it consents, will hasten to imitate their example.[115]

Apart from some performances in Russia, and private concerts for the royal court, Falcon's career was over two months after her 26th birthday. If France's "first poets" wrote anything for her at the Théâtre-Français, she didn't perform it. The British playwright and music critic Bernard Shaw appears never to have met Falcon; even so, he might have been reflecting on her too-long life when observing in Act IV of *Man and Superman* that "there are two tragedies [...] one is not to get your heart's desire. The other is to get it."[116] Falcon lived to the age of 83 – six decades beyond the end of her public life. Never wanting for money, having married a financier, she became a recluse, only rarely leaving her apartment on the Chaussée d'Antin, a short walk from the Opéra.[117] At the end of 1891, she appeared on the stage of the Palais Garnier with the 85-year-old Duprez and the 86-year-old Dorus-Gras to commemorate the centenary of Meyerbeer's birth.[118] She died three years before the 20th century and was

---

114   The words "*Nuit fatal, nuit d'alarmes, je n'ai plus d'avenir,*" feature neither in the published libretto nor Meyerbeer's score. Berlioz was condensing episodes from the long duet to conjure a more-human drama for his readers.

115   *Feuilleton Du Journal des Débats*, 17 March, 1840, pp. 1–2.

116   The line is delivered by Mendoza.

117   The Opéra (or the Théâtre de l'Académie Royale de Musique, as it was at the time), was based at the *Salle Le Peletier* or *Lepeletier* until the opening of Garnier's *Palais* in 1875, on what is now the Place de l'Opéra. The Peletier was a 300-meter walk from Falcon's apartment; the Garnier was a little further, at 800 meters.

118   All three singers died within the space of a year, February, 1896 – February, 1897.

buried in Section 55 of Père Lachaise. No clear reason was isolated for the failure of Falcon's voice; it is hardly a stretch to conclude that performing Grand Opera at the age of 18 in huge theatres with increasingly massive orchestras was to blame. Duprez speculated that a "hard" *passaggio* contributed to her undoing. This is unlikely – at least in isolation; instead, it is more probable that a mixture of under-training and over-work conspired to break what was never fully-formed – a lesson learned more quickly by sopranos than by tenors. In 1844, Chorley wrote of Falcon that she

> was a person to haunt even a passing stranger. Though the seal of her race was upon her beauty, and it wore the expression of a Deborah or a Judith,[119] rather than of a Melpomene, I have never seen any actress, who in look and gesture so well deserved the style and title of the Muse of Modern Tragedy. Large, dark, melancholy eyes, – finely cut features, – a form, though slight, not meagre, – and, above all, an expressiveness of tone rarely to be found in voices of her register, which was a legitimate soprano, – the power of engaging interest by mere glance and step when first she presented herself, and of exciting the strongest emotions of pity, or terror, or suspense, by the passion she could develope [sic] in action – such were her gifts. Add to these the charms of her youth, the love borne to her by all her comrades; – and the loss of her voice, followed by the almost desperate efforts made by her to recover it, and her disastrous final appearance when no force of will could torture destroyed Nature into even a momentary resuscitation, – make up one of those tragedies into which a fearful sum of wrecked hope and despair and anguish enters. Hers is a history, if all tales are true, too dark to be repeated, even with the honest purpose, not of pandering to an evil curiosity, but of pointing out the snares and pitfalls which lie in wait for the artiste, and of inquiring, for the sake of Art as well as of Humanity (the two are inseparable), if there be no protection against them, – no means for their avoidance?[120]

Falcon was the best known victim of Grand Opera; the form was otherwise renowned for chewing through sopranos. Berlioz played his part, as a critic and a composer; he wrote extensively about most of the women who appeared regularly in Paris, and he completed four works for the stage, the first of which, *Benvenuto Cellini*, was first performed at the Opéra on 10 September, 1838 – eight months after Falcon's final

---

119   There is no evidence that Falcon was Jewish; while Chorley was not known to be anti-Semitic, his "casual" observations concerning Falcon's "race" are ignorant rather than malignant. In 1835, Théophile Gautier also commented on Falcon's "Jewishness," writing of the singer that "she is as beautiful as ever. There are still the large, passionately dark eyes, the warm Jewish pallor ['*la chaude pâleur juive*'], the abundant and superb hair [...]." It's worth noting also that Chorley's reference to Melpomene isolated the Levant, and so applied the broadest of brushes, with neither purpose nor success. He may, of course, have been thinking of Ingres' more delicate painting of Cherubini, completed in 1842, in which Melpomene is seen standing behind the composer, with her right-hand extended over his head. From what can be deduced of the surviving paintings, drawings and sketches of Falcon, she shares more than a passing resemblance to Ingres' goddess of tragedy. This may have been more than coincidental.

120   Chorley, Henry (1844). *Music and Manners in France and Germany: A Series of Travelling Sketches of Art and Society*, Vol. 1. Longman, Brown, Green and Longman, pp. 188–189.

performance. The work was a disaster – but not because of his cast, which starred Gilbert Duprez in the title role and Rosine Stoltz[121] as the *travesti* Ascanio. Like Duprez, Stoltz was trained by Alexandre-Étienne Choron, a one-time director of the Opéra, born in 1771; Stoltz died in 1903, at the age of 88. Among the lexicon of sopranos whose biographies reached beyond their work, Stoltz stands out for a number of reasons. She made her debut at the Opéra on 25 August, 1837, in Falcon's creator-role of Rachel, in *La Juive*, partnered with Duprez. It was later claimed she secured her contract at the Opéra because of her recitation of a single line from *La Juive*. There may have been another reason for her instant success. The "Royal Commissioner and Secretary of the Special Commission for the Conservatoire and Royal Theatres" was Léon Pillet, who abused his position despite having no musical training and no experience of life in the theatre. As the Opéra's putative Administrator, he took a keen interest in the casting of female performers; it was common knowledge that Stoltz's elevation was influenced by his own. While this was true, it was also unfair. Stoltz earned her spurs performing in Brussels, where she was admired for her artistry by Auber, Nourrit and the critics; she was also sufficiently capable to enter into proximate rivalry with Dorus-Gras, with whom she competed for roles by Meyerbeer. Her triumph when giving the Belgian premiere of *La Juive* at La Monnaie in December, 1835, ensured an argentate reputation, even if subsequent events threw a shadow over the gamut of her abilities. Stoltz's voice encompassed the contralto and soprano ranges, leading inevitably to comparisons with Falcon; her status as a dramatic mezzo-soprano added definitively to the popularity of this *fach* for composers working in France.

Stoltz's first creation at the Opéra was Ricciarda in Halévy's *Guido et Ginevra* on 5 March, 1838; two years later, Pillet was appointed co-director of the Opéra, alongside Henri Duponchel – who despised Pillet for the political nature of his appointment. After Duponchel resigned in October, 1841, Pillet took to insisting that every new work feature a starring role for Stoltz. The effect of such bias on the life of a woman working in a brutally competitive arena is easy to imagine; it was made harder still by the press, which condemned the scandal and the affair that informed it. *La résistance* was led by Meyerbeer, who refused to allow for the première of *Le prophète* until Pillet agreed to another singer taking the lead;[122] it was undermined by Donizetti, who was happy to accommodate the circumstances, gifting Stoltz the title role in his facetiously christened *La favorite*[123] – in which Stoltz played the part of a mistress.[124] According to an issue of *La france musicale*,[125] she bore Pillet a child, news broadcast by its editors with sledgehammer wit: "Mme Stoltz is suffering from an indisposition for which she will require nine months of recovery."[126] The sensationalism surrounding Stoltz's private life was petty and nasty; it was paid for chiefly by the singer, who developed a reputation for extravagance and unpleasantness. Whether

---

121 *née* Victoire / Victorine Noël, 13 January, 1815 – 30 July, 1903.

122 That singer was Pauline Viardot. See below.

123 'The Favourite,' first performed on 2 December, 1840.

124 Stoltz later created the minor role of Zayda in Donizetti's *Dom Sébastien, roi de Portugal* on 13 November, 1843 – the composer's last opera.

125 In April, 1843.

126 Jordan, Ruth (1994). *Fromental Halévy: His Life & Music, 1799–1862*. Kahn & Averill, p. 122.

she deserved her opprobrium is far from clear, but modern commentary has tended to savage Stoltz *in memoriam*, on the basis that she was a "prize bitch."[127] It is depressing that male writers in the 21st century have promulgated the denigration of 19th century women, given that nearly everything written about them was engineered and authored by men with social, political and personal axes to grind. The vulnerability of women, even those touched by genius, exposed them to exploitation from the first, to which end the male gaze was never more damaging than when steered by public morality, brittle cliché and rooted prejudice.

Pillet's conduct was opposed privately, with Verdi refusing to fulfil his Opéra commission for *Jerusalém* until Pillet had left the building for the last time; Stoltz endured what she did despite being considered one of the finest singing-actors of her generation, revered especially by Halévy, who retained her for three premieres – Catarina in *La reine de Chypre*,[128] Odette in *Charles VI*,[129] and Beppo in *Le lazzarone*.[130] Stoltz's affair condemned her to creating roles in second-rate operas by composers of the third rank, including Marlian's *La xacarilla*,[131] Niedermeyer's *Marie Stuart*,[132] Balfe's *L'étoile de Séville*,[133] and Mermet's *David*.[134]

Berlioz remembered Stoltz without affection; he condemned her in his memoirs as greedy and selfish, and turned thereafter to relatively unknown sopranos for *La Damnation de Faust*,[135] *Les Troyens*, and *Béatrice et Bénédict*.[136] He was equally *pas dérangé* when nominating sopranos for his religious works, only two of which feature prominent parts for female voices – the *Messe solennelle* (1824) and *L'enfance du Christ* (1854).[137] Even for his mélodies and song cycles, Berlioz attached himself to singers whose celebrity fell short of his own. The original piano version of his finest cycle, *Nuit d'etes*, had a single dedicatee – Louise Bertin; the orchestral versions were published by Jakob Rieter-Biedermann with dedications to singers (male and female)

---

127   For example, Steen, Michael (2007). Enchantress of Nations: Pauline Viardot, Soprano, Muse, Lover. Icon Books, p. 36.

128   'The Queen of Cyprus,' first performed on 22 December, 1841.

129   First performed on 15 March, 1843.

130   On 29 March, 1844, Berlioz dismissed the work out of hand, writing that "the orchestration is too grandiose, too pompous, too loud and even too slow for this kind of story." *Ibid*. Stoltz shared the work, and the stage, with Dorus-Gras, whose hatred was inflamed by Stoltz's brassy decision to eat macaroni onstage during Dorus-Gras' tent-pole aria.

131   First performed on 28 October, 1839.

132   First performed on 6 December, 1844.

133   First performed on 17 December, 1845.

134   First performed on 3 June, 1846.

135   First performed at the Opéra-Comique on 6 December, 1846, 'The Damnation of Faust' is not, strictly-speaking, an opera. Berlioz called it a *légende dramatique* ('dramatic legend'). Almost nothing is known of the mezzo-soprano who created the role of Marguerite, Hortense Duflot-Maillard (1808 – 1858).

136   In fairness to Anne Arsène Charton-Demeur (5 March, 1824 – 30 November, 1892), the French mezzo-soprano who created the role of Béatrice in *Béatrice et Bénédict*, first performed on 9 August, 1862, and Didon in *Les Troyens*, first performed 4 November, 1863, she was little known in France when she worked for Berlioz, having spent the majority of her career in England, Italy, Germany and Russia. In his *Mémoires*, Berlioz remembered her beauty and passionate acting, but regretted that she didn't have the voice for Didon. Typically for Berlioz, he was most grateful to Charton-Demeur for her willingness to work for buttons.

137   'The Childhood of Christ.'

known only in Germany: Louise Wolf ("*Villanelle*"), Anna Bockholtz-Falconi[138] ("*Le spectre de la rose*"), Hans von Milde ("*Sur les lagunes*"),[139] Madeleine Nottès ("*Absence*"), Friedrich Caspari ("*Au cimetière*") and Rosa von Milde[140] ("*L'île inconnue*").[141] Berlioz's settings of Gautier's verse were among the earliest examples of the *mélodie* genre. Elegant, atmospheric and at times headily erotic, they are love songs of unusual sophistication. Berlioz is said to have been inspired by his then mistress (and second wife from 1854), the soprano Marie Recio.[142] He used his influence to engineer her debut at the Opéra-Comique on 9 October, 1841, which heralded a single year on the stage, best summarised as calamitous. Her performances as Inès in *La Favorite*, Isolier in *Le Comte Ory* and Alice in *Robert le Diable* generated positive reviews only from Berlioz. If Recio was the cycle's muse then the numerous references to past loves and separation are incongruous and weirdly inappropriate. "*La spectre de la rose*," for example, tells of the ghost of a flower that returns nightly to haunt the dreams of a young woman who wore it to a ball, while "*Sur les lagunes*" is an obsidian lament that begins unambiguously with the words "*Ma belle amie est morte.*"[143] The lowering atmosphere is made more unsettling still by the deathly range of the sung line, which descends as low as most contraltos can sing; he was more generous with "*Absence*" (which he orchestrated especially for Recio), but chose against reason to dedicate the song to Madeleine Nottès when it was published in 1856 – two years after his wedding.

It seems that Berlioz was intolerant of "divas," a term employed with critical zeal by his friend Gautier, who railed at capricious stars regardless of their gender:

> We do not share the dilettanti's terrors in this regard. The king is dead, long live the king! After Pasta, Malibran; after Malibran, Grisi; after Garcia, Rubini; after Rubini, Ronzi; after Taglioni, Elssler; after Elssler, Carlotta. – No one is indispensable, and everyone takes their place![144]

James Q. Davies has reasoned that Gautier's use of the word "diva" owed nothing to modern connotations of ego and celebrity, and that it identified instead a "fantastical creature of multiple overlapping subjectivities,"[145] depicted ironically, and cultivated by the poet as a tribute to the *sognato* rather than in condemnation of the *castigata*. The term "diva" was introduced as early as the fourteenth century, beginning with religious and mythological symbols of women's "divinity" as supernatural. Divas were feminine icons whose voices materialised as the embodiment of training, skill

---

138   11 March, 1815 – 24 December, 1879.
139   'On the lagoons.'
140   The first Elsa in *Lohengrin*. See Chapter 14.
141   'The unknown island.'
142   *née* Marie-Geneviève Martin, 10 June, 1814 – 13 June, 1862.
143   'My dearest love is dead.'
144   Gautier, Théophile (1858). *Histoire de l'art dramatique en France depuis vingt-cinq ans*. Édition Hetzel. Vol. 2. p.165. See also, and generally, Davies, James Q. (2012), "Gautier's 'diva': the first French uses of the word," in *The Art of the Prima Donna in the Long Nineteenth Century*. Eds. Rachel Cowgill and Hilary Poriss. Oxford University Press.
145   *Ibid*, p. 178.

and virtue – at a time when women were still seen prescriptively as instruments for passion and parturition. Gautier took his lead from an episode described by Ernest Legouvé, a friend of Gautier's, involving Maria Malibran, who decided during a walk with friends to climb to the rear of a statuary fountain and sing "*Casta Diva*" *a capella*. The incident was gauche and romantic; it invited everyone present to imprint on Malibran whatever their fantasies allowed – fostering a sense of the Other that made the singer fantastic and unreal as well as untouchable and unattainable. The diva as an archetype collided with the contemporary obsession with the female nude, which was visible in just about every gallery in Paris during the 1840s and '50s; Gautier decried the "*Salon de les Venuses*," not because he didn't like looking at women but because he considered poetry a more capable vehicle for exploring the female form. The extent to which femininity was subjected to irreconcilable paradoxes crystallises in the requirement that women be domesticated and sensual, modest and flamboyant, reserved and romantic – silent and resonant. For the French 19th century, only one soprano managed to meet these disparate expectations, a woman described by Heinrich Heine as

> not merely a nightingale who delights in trilling and sobbing her songs of spring. Nor is she the rose, being ugly, but in a way that is noble. She reminds us more of the terrible magnificence of a jungle rather than the civilized beauty and tame grace of the European world.

Pauline Viardot[146] was baptised Michelle Ferdinande Pauline García – as the younger of Manuel García's two daughters. Her mother was the soprano Joaquina Sitchez; her sister was Maria Malibran, who died when Pauline was 15-years-old. Viardot was born in the year that Beethoven composed his Piano Sonata No.31, Op.110, two months after the death of Napoleon. She died a year after Schoenberg completed his *Fünf Orchesterstücke*,[147] Op. 16 – four years before the outbreak of the First World War. She outlived her sister by 74 years, having cultivated a position in European cultural life with neither precedent nor comparator. In addition to her stellar career as an über-mezzo-soprano, she composed dozens of songs, five chamber operas, and numerous choral and instrumental works. She served as a muse to just about everyone of social, cultural and artistic importance in central Europe between 1840 and 1890; her influence is impossible to convey other than reductively. As a child she toured Europe and the United States with the García company. She watched her parents, her brother and her sister give the American premiere of *Don Giovanni* while seated next to the opera's librettist, Lorenzo Da Ponte. By the age of six she was fluent in Spanish, French, English, and Italian; she would later learn Russian in the company of her lover, Ivan Turgenev. Her father was her first teacher, whose tirelessly brutal method contributed much to her belief in the virtues of discipline and self-denial. After his death, shortly before her tenth birthday, her singing lessons were administered by Malibran and their mother. She was taught counterpoint and harmony by Anton Reicha, a close friend of Beethoven's and a tutor to Berlioz and Liszt; such was her

---

146   18 July, 1821 – 18 May, 1910.
147   'Five Pieces for Orchestra.'

skill as a pianist that Liszt accepted her as a pupil. By the time she entered Parisian society during the 1840s, her talent as a pianist was sufficient for Chopin to join her regularly for duets, in private and in public. Beethoven's friend, Moscheles, and Meyerbeer, Adolphe Adam and Mendelssohn all acknowledged her to be one of the finest pianists of the age,[148] even before she turned her attention to singing.

After giving her first public performance as a 16-year-old, in Brussels, Viardot made her stage debut as Rossini's Desdemona in 1839 – at the age of 19. The questions asked of many of her contemporaries when performing as teenagers can, perhaps, be answered differently where Viardot is concerned because critical opinion was aligned when acknowledging her sensational technique. Noting what has been written previously of teenagers and training, it's reasonable to conclude from everything known of Viardot's freakish ability for learning and application that she was as skilled as most asserted. Her brilliance as a pianist was the product of unblinking focus, routine sacrifice and determined practice, qualities that translated to her mastery of bel canto. Liszt claimed to have formed his legendary *legato* while "sat at the feet of the greatest singers;" and it's easy to see why one of the century's most gifted pianists should also have become its finest singer.

Viardot's appeal as a voice-artist was Gordian. Her rivals were favoured for their dramatic intensity or vocal seduction, or some combination of the two. Viardot was exceptional because she wasn't the greatest actress and her tone and placement were not necessarily the most beautiful. She was possessed of transformative charisma, however, and a voice of exceptional force, amplitude and dramatic incision. Her life-long friend, Camille Saint-Saëns (who made her the dedicatee of *Samson et Dalila*), characterised her voice as being of

> enormous power, with a prodigious range that was equal to every technical difficulty but, marvellous as it was, it did not please everybody. It was not a velvet or crystalline voice, but rather rough, compared by someone to the taste of a bitter orange, and made for tragedy or myth, superhuman rather than human; light music, Spanish songs and the Chopin mazurkas she transcribed for the voice, were transfigured by it and became the triflings of a giant; to the accents of tragedy, to the severities of oratorio, she gave an incomparable grandeur.

Like her sister, Viardot was a source of fevered public scrutiny; unlike Malibran she was thought to be other than beautiful, a commercial metric for artists and a printing industry then making substantial sums of money from the business of celebrity. Heine's nasty comment was unwarranted, as is obvious from Carl von Neff's possibly generous portrait of the soprano in her 21st year. Completed two years earlier, the first of Ary Scheffer's paintings is more accurate, capturing her heavy gaze and the shape of a mouth that would harden with the years, as evidenced by the many photographs taken of Viardot during and after the 1860s. The composition is striking also for the severity of Pauline's dress – which is as black as her hair and lightened only by the meanest of white-lace hems. She wears a small silver cross, and her hair is tied close to

---

148   Her mother forbade her from pursuing a career as a pianist. See Philip Larkin's "This Be The Verse."

her head with puritan zeal, creating an echt impression of conventional morality and bourgeois security at odds with the artistic, philosophical and social freedoms that gained traction across Europe during the 1840s. Viardot was approving of Scheffer's work, for which she paid, in its socially-conservative representation of the artist as a young woman. Given her friendship with many of the defining cultural figures of her time, Viardot might have been thought (or expected) to pick up where her sister had left off; she appears instead to have relished her parents' moral strictures and cultural prejudices, countering her sister's reputation as a woman of negotiable morality. This explains why Viardot became a model *épouse et mère*, whose use of the socially-conditioned moniker "Madame Viardot" for every poster, program, advertisement and publication demonstrated her commitment to the continuity of the threatened social order. Anyone writing about Pauline was careful to use her husband's name since this was known to be her preference.[149]

The oppression of decorum was made brilliant by Scheffer's second painting, completed in 1851, which operated as nothing less than iconography. Viardot is seen to look to the heavens against a backdrop of gold-ground, idealising her status as European music's *Mater Dolorosa*. Her appearance did nothing to stem the flow of suitors – of whom there were many. Unwilling to take any risks, her mother encouraged Pauline to marry young, a prophylactic strategy supported by the soprano's closest friend,[150] George Sand. Pauline was steered towards the independently wealthy, highly educated Louis Viardot, who had known the family as a director of the Théâtre Italien and as an advisor to Malibran. He was trusted, and blessed with Christ-like reserves of patience and understanding. More than twenty years older than his wife at the time of their marriage (when she was 18) their age difference spoke to guardianship more obviously than love, but Louis was devoted to Pauline, and committed himself to the management of her career while accommodating her decades' long relationship with the novelist and playwright Ivan Turgenev.[151] This bizarre *menage a trois* saw them living *en famille*, with the Viardots' children being raised coincidentally by their "two dads."

With nude women commonplace throughout Paris, the shift in prejudice towards middle-class values forced a reaction that abjured idealism for verisimilitude. In 1865, Édouard Manet presented his *Olympia* at the Salon, for which his model was *Titian's Venus of Urbino*. He negated the mythological and the exotic to present a naked French prostitute – a distinction as controversial as wives and daughters being seen and heard to do anything independently of men. This included women composing music and, *pace* Viardot, sopranos accompanying themselves at the piano. In 1853, and after hearing her perform at a concert in Moscow, Vasili Botkin apologised to Turgenev for doubting the reach of Pauline's abilities:

---

149 Fairbank, Rebecca Bennett (2013). *Devastating Diva: Pauline Viardot and Rewriting the Image of Women in Nineteenth-Century French Opera Culture*. Ph.D Thesis, Brigham Young University, pp. 58–59.
150 Until a series of misunderstandings led to a falling out, in 1844. Sand's correspondence with Viardot is sporadically interesting, as the articles she wrote about Pauline in the *Revue des Deux Mondes*. In 1841, Sand began a novel about a prima donna that was modelled on Pauline.
151 It's frequently overlooked that Louis Viardot and Turgenev were extremely close friends *before* he married Pauline. Even so...

> I only now understand your words [...] Those who have not heard
> Madame Viardot at the piano [...] can have no conception of her [...]
> like a naked Venus, radiant with only her own eternal beauty [...] Viardot
> is sure to leave her listeners with an empty place in their hearts.[152]

Her art was attached by Botkin to Venus as an ideal for what it captured of a male fantasy, in terms that would have been inconceivable had women been discussing Mario, whose nakedness might have cropped up in private but never in correspondence or in public. Viardot's gaze as a 19-year-old is unsmiling and superior; she looks down at the viewer as an exemplar of matriarchal probity. She is a clothed, cloistered and accommodating version of Titian's *Venus*, standing in polar opposition to the prostrate Olympia, whose confrontational gaze apostrophises gendered defiance. French society dictated that the most appropriate place for women to display their (always-amateur) training was the drawing room – unless, and only if, they were sopranos paid to perform in concert halls and theatres. Viardot was unusual in being able to straddle public life as a society figure and a performer while remaining morally-upstanding. She was unusual also in being loved and respected by women as well as men, notably Clara Schumann and Fanny Mendelssohn; the only shadow falling on her reputation as a "decent woman" was formed of rumours of an affair with Gounod. Viardot had been a supporter of Gounod during his youth, in a host of ways – some of them musical, some financial, all of them directed towards advancing his career. On 11 April, 1851, she created the title role in *Sapho*, at the Opéra. The work was not a popular success, running for just nine performances; Gounod blamed Viardot, and wrote to a friend that her career was at an end. The work was well-received critically, however, sufficient for a handful of performances to be given at Covent Garden later the same year – with Viardot again in the title role. In April, 1852, Gounod married Anna Zimmerman, the daughter of his former piano professor at the Conservatoire – following which the Zimmermans refused to have anything more to do with Pauline. The reasons for this break remain unclear.[153] Either way, Gounod treated Viardot badly, while she behaved with grace and dignity.

Pauline did not want for company, and the list of works inspired by or dedicated to her include Schumann's *Liederkreis*, Meyerbeer's *Le prophète*; Gounod's *Sapho*; Saint-Saëns' *Samson et Dalila*, "*La brise*," and *Ascanio*; Brahms' *Rhapsodie für eine Altstimme, Männerchor und Orchester*;[154] Massenet's *Marie Magdaleine*; and Fauré's songs, Op. 4 and Op. 7 – the latter including *Après un rêve*. Viardot was an inspiration to writers also, including Turgenev, whose *A Month in the Country* is essentially biographical, and George Sand, whose *Consuelo* tells the life of an opera singer that owes more than a little to Pauline.[155] The most unusual product of Viardot's hero-status was striking for what it manifested of the female gaze, since it was written by George Eliot. Her *Legend of Jubal and Other Poems* was published in 1871, with

---

152 Fitzlyon, April (1964). *The Price of Genius: A Life of Pauline Viardot*. Appleton-Century, p. 294.

153 Apologies were made, and letters written – but Gounod never acted on his promise to meet Pauline for dinner after the dust had settled.

154 Better known as the Alto Rhapsody, Op. 53.

155 *Consuelo* appeared in instalments, between from 1 February, 1842 and 25 March, 1843, in *La Revue indépendante*, a political and literary magazine founded in 1841 by Pierre Leroux, Viardot and Sand.

the touching dedication "To my beloved Husband, George Henry Lewes, whose cherishing tenderness for twenty years has alone made my work possible to me." The collection contains a dramatic poem, *Armgart*, which (like *Middlemarch* and *Daniel Deronda*) confronts the irreconcilability of love and art when created by a woman.[156] She was not the first to explore the issue; Elizabeth Barrett Browning's *Aurora Leigh*[157] features a poet-heroine who is

> Passioned to exalt
> The artist's instinct in me at the cost
> Of putting down the woman's, I forgot
> No perfect artist is developed here
> From any imperfect woman

The actress "Madame Laure" in *Middlemarch* is unable to accommodate her career and her marriage and so murders her husband; the dramatic singer "Alcharisi" in *Daniel Deronda*, encounters a similar conflict, albeit less violently.[158] Armgart is a soprano, modelled on Viardot. Unlike Lewes Eliot, Armgart's husband makes it impossible for his wife to be what she is – as distinct from a man, who is able to define himself by his achievements:

> Men rise the higher as their task is high,
> The task being well achieved. A woman's rank
> Lies in the fullness of her womanhood.

Armgart is "a poor human-hearted song-bird," who "bears Caesar's ambition in her delicate breast." She wrestles with the "unnatural" state of being an artist, whose drive to create sublimates her primal responsibilities as a woman. Graf asks Walpurga:

> Is it most her voice which subdues us, or her instinct exquisite, Informing
> each old strain with some new grace, which takes our sense with any
> natural good?
> Or most her spiritual energy
> That sweeps us in the current or her song?"

Walpurga replies:

> I know not. Losing either, we should lose
> That whole we call our Armgart. For herself,
> She often wonders what her life had been
> Without that voice for channel to her soul.
> She says, it must have leaped through all her

---

156   See, generally, Blake, Kathleen (1980). "'Armgart' – George Eliot on the Woman Artist." *Poetry.* Vol. 18, No. 1, pp. 75–80.
157   Published in 1857.
158   Viardot was clearly an inspiration for this work also.

Limbs – Made her a Maenad – made her snatch a brand
And fire some forest, that her rage might mount
In crashing roaring flames through half a land
Leaving her still and patient for a while.

Eliot was two years older than Viardot and profoundly affected by seeing the soprano perform, either in London or in Germany. Her fascination with the singer's "roaring flames" was informed by the presentiment of independence attaching to the forging of a voice by nature or by God but not, in any circumstances, by a man. Armgart believes herself to be "an artist by my birth – by the same warrant that I am a woman," an origin story against which Graf pushes by requiring Armgart to renounce her art becoming his wife. Armgart comes to believe that Graf's love is formed by what she must sacrifice, as proof of the integrity of her devotion, anticipating Mahler's fateful letter to Alma Werfel, in which he asked:

> If you were to give up your musical ambition to take possession of me and my music […] do you believe you would have to relinquish an indispensable part of your existence?

After losing her voice, Armgart is abandoned by Graf – a hateful denouement that operated as a synecdoche for the millions of women whose existence was tolerated for as long as they presented no threat to the gendered *status quo*. Viardot's achievement was not simply to endure, therefore; it was to triumph as a woman, embracing all that this entailed of her as a singer, a composer, an artist, a muse and a mother – and to attain all that might be achieved without compromise. She was true to herself at a time when the self was sacrificed to men in consequence of their wishes, needs and gaze. Although *Armgart* is not biographical, it speaks to life as it was lived by the majority about every soprano except Viardot.

It's intriguing that Eliot framed Viardot's art as capable of "informing each old strain with some new grace," because she was known for her devotion to contemporary music. Her repertoire nonetheless began and ended with Mozart, whose operas she sang more than any other. Her tastes extended thereafter to most of Rossini's mezzo-heroines, Bellini's *La Sonnambula* and Donizetti's *Lucia di Lammermoor* – roles she premiered in Russia – and the songs of Glinka (of which she gave the first performances in Russia and France). In 1844, she starred in the Russian premiere of *Norma*; two years later she formed a long and productive partnership with Meyerbeer – whose work she sang in Germany for the composer in German. She was a goddess for Berlioz, because she performed for him gratis, and because she supported his arrangement of Gluck's *Orphée et Eurydice*, the title role of which she performed on more than two hundred occasions. Berlioz was a ruthlessly honest critic of everyone but himself, and he wrote in unvarnished tribute that

> Viardot is a great musician […] she unites an irrepressibly impetuous and imperious verve with a profound sensibility and with an almost deplorable faculty for expressing immense grief […] she is one of the greatest artists in the history of music.

Pauline created the role of Fidès at the premiere of *Le prophète*, at the Opéra, on 16 April, 1849 – a role considered by some to qualify as the first for a contralto. She travelled thereafter as Meyerbeer's ambassador, giving dozens of performances as Fidès across Europe and Russia. In January, 1855, Verdi visited her in Paris to invite her to cover for an indisposed Marietta Alboni[159] in a new production of *Il trovatore* at the Opéra; she learned the role of Azucena in less than a week, and gave the opera's British premiere at Covent Garden on 10 May, 1855 – with Jenny Bürde-Ney as Leonora, Enrico Tamberlick as Manrico and Francesco Graziani as the Conte di Luna. In 1859, Verdi transposed the title role of *Lady Macbeth* for Viardot, whose voice had darkened with time. During rehearsals for *Trovatore's* British premiere later the same year, she wrote to a friend:

> Terrible day. I got over-fatigued. I had a concert in the morning and in the evening a rehearsal of Martha from 7pm to midnight. I generally have to assume the part of the stage-manager for the operas which I sing, being the only one who speaks English well, and have to serve as interpreter between all my comrades and the costumiers, machinists, choristers, supers, etc; it is far more fatiguing than singing and after four hours of work on the stage, I am worn out.[160]

On 29 August, 1859, Viardot sang the first public performance of excerpts from *Les Troyens*, on which she collaborated with Berlioz when he worked on the piano reduction. On 18 November, 1859, she gave the premiere of Berlioz's *Orphée et Eurydice* at the Theatre Lyrique; during the run she was saluted by her friend, Charles Dickens, who described

> a most extraordinary performance – pathetic in its highest degree, and full of quite sublime acting [...] I was disfigured with crying.[161]

Pauline performed her official farewell on 24 April, 1863, in Paris, after which she continued to sing in concert and in private into the 1870s. Despite owning a vast apartment in Paris, and the Chateau de Courtavenel, 70 kilometres from the city centre, Viardot and her family left France because of her husband's public opposition to Emperor Napoleon. She settled, with Louis and Turgenev, in Baden-Baden,[162] where

---

159 6 March, 1826 – 23 June 1894. Alboni was frequently referred to as "the Italian Viardot." A true contralto, she studied with Rossini in Bologna as a 13-year-old, and he remained a valuable influence throughout her career. She came to think of him as her second father long before she performed at his funeral in 1868. She was a regular partner to Giulia Grisi, Jenny Lind and Henriette Sontag. Alboni had a range of two and one-half octaves, extending as high as the soprano range; her voice was said to be powerful, sweet, full, and flexible. She made her debut at the Opéra as Fidès, for Meyerbeer, in 1850, a role created the year before by Viardot. She was also admired by Donizetti and Verdi – who praised her as Azucena and Ulric; Verdi also authorised her to appear in the baritone role of Don Carlo in *Ernani* (in London, 1847).

160 Kendall-Davies, Barbara (2003). *The Life and Work of Pauline Viardot Garcia. I: The Years of Fame, 1836–1863.* Cambridge Scholar Press, p. 401.

161 Fitzlyon, April (1964). *The Price of Genius: A Life of Pauline Viardot.* Appleton-Century, p. 355.

162 The enormous house survives in photographs only.

she hosted a salon without rival.[163] A rolodex of Europe's cultural elite would gather weekly to share her company, and to debate the latest in music and literature. Many of her guests[164] would head for the infamous "shrine" she built to display Mozart's autograph score of *Don Giovanni*, which Viardot acquired at a London auction in 1855 while performing in a production of the opera at Drury Lane. She paid only £200 for the score, equivalent to £27,000 at the time of publication.[165] It was a bargain; even so, she had to sell a painting by Rembrandt to meet the cost.[166] One of her regular visitors – initially, at least – was Richard Wagner. Viardot helped him when he was in desperate need of money and struggling to secure a production for *Tannhäuser* in Paris. In February, 1860, she performed part of the recently completed *Tristan und Isolde*, with Wagner performing the other title role, at a private concert in the Parisian home of the society hostess and patron, Maria Kalergis von Nesselrode-Ereshoven. Wagner later wrote "[Isolde] is a very difficult role […] Mme. Viardot surprised me by reading everything from the sheet, so proved it could be sung."[167]

In 1869, he expanded his anti-Semitic essay, *Das Judentum in der Musik*, first published anonymously in 1850. The decision to identify himself as the polemic's author was informed by his self-identification as the guardian of "Holy German Art," a psychological malformation influenced by the success of *Die Meistersinger* in 1867. Viardot attended a performance in 1869, and wrote to congratulate Wagner on his achievement. The following month she read the revised and newly-published *Das Judentum in der Musik*, and was horrified by the essay's content. She wrote to tell him so. Wagner received the letter, as Cosima confirmed in her diary:

> [Richard] brings upstairs with him a letter from Mme Viardot – about the Jewish pamphlet! This nonsense or this profound sense! She is a Jewess, that is now quite clear.

Richard and Cosima concluded in their solipsism that anyone defending Jewish people from racism and hatred must themselves be Jewish, a popular trope among anti-Semites. Viardot was a gentile, and a moralist; her devotion to Meyerbeer – whom Wagner eviscerated in his essay following the commercial success of *Le prophète* – compelled her to speak her mind. The Wagners responded by cutting all ties with the "Jewess" who, with conspicuous timing, gave the first performance on 3 March the following year of Brahms' "Alto Rhapsody."

No other soprano performed such a range of music. She was exceeded in her diversity only by Duprez, with whom she collaborated more than any other of her

---

163   They returned to Paris in 1870, and an apartment on the Boulevard Saint-Germain, where she hosted another much-lauded salon. Turgenev and her husband died within weeks of each other, in 1883.
164   Rossini would genuflect; Tchaikovsky claimed after his first visit to have been in the presence of divinity.
165   This was a tiny sum of money considering the subsequent rise in value of anything written in Mozart's hand – far less one of the Da Ponte operas. In 2019, two short minuets from 1772 were sold at auction for £318,400 / $364,500.
166   Viardot donated the manuscript to the Paris Conservatoire in 1892.
167   Kendall-Davies, Barbara (2003). *The Life and Work of Pauline Viardot Garcia. I: The Years of Fame, 1836–1863*. Cambridge Scholar Press, p. 415.

peers. Her last major role was created in private. Saint-Saens composed *Dalila* for Viardot, but in consequence of censorial opposition to the biblical subject it wasn't staged until 1877 – in Weimar, where Liszt provided the necessary support and funding. Viardot learned the role regardless, and performed the first two acts (including the love scene) with a selection of her students at a salon, with the composer conducting from the piano. Saint-Saëns' acknowledged her "performance of genius [which] made one forget both her age, which was unsuitable for Dalila, and the defects of her voice, and everything else." Dalila was controversial, and it's unlikely the conservative Pauline would have performed the role in public. She lived a long and uniquely productive life as a child of the 18th century – a servant to the gaze, the imagination and will of men. Proof that she outlived her time decades before her death presented itself in 1875 when the first performance of Bizet's *Carmen* announced the birth of the modern.[168]

The search for a mezzo-soprano to create the role of Carmen began in the summer of 1873. The librettists favoured Zulma Bouffar,[169] a French actress and soprano, known for her association with Jacques Offenbach, for whom Bouffar appeared at Bad Ems in *Lischen et Fritzchen* in 1864. For the next 12 years, Bouffar was Offenbach's mistress, and the creator of more than a dozen roles for the composer. Bizet rejected her as unsuitable because she was a comic actress, with a voice conditioned to Offenbach's small-venue operetta style in which articulation was more important than the grand operatic virtue of long-breathed melody. In September, 1873, an approach was made to Marie Roze,[170] who rejected the role because it required her to die on stage.[171] After extensive negotiations, Célestine Galli-Marié[172] agreed to take up the role, to which she committed her all, proving to be as tempestuous as the character she was playing. It was rumoured Gallie-Marié and Bizet were engaged in a love affair during the extensive rehearsals, which began in October, 1874, and ran for so long that the scheduled premiere had to be delayed. The first night on 3 March, 1875, began well and ended in silence. The audience was horrified by the realism of the action and the scandalous autonomy of the opera's anti-heroine. The working-class setting and degenerate morality of all but one of the characters[173] compounded the public's indignation, which echoed throughout the press. Paul de Saint-Victor, writing for *Le moniteur*, condemned

> the excessive struggling of voices against instruments is one of the faults of the modern school. The role of Carmen is not a success for Mme

---

168   Surprisingly, given her popularity and good standing, Viardot appears to have been greatly disliked by the author of Carmen, Prosper Mérimée. On 17 February, 1843, he wrote to "an unknown" correspondent "To-night I have been to the Italian Opera, where, in spite of the constant applause given my enemy, Madame Viardot, I enjoyed myself." Letter 49 in Mérimée, Prosper (1905). "*Letters to an Unknown*." In *Works of Prosper Mérimée*. Ed. George Saintsbury. Brown & Co.

169   *née* Zulma Madeleine Boufflar, 24 May, 1841 – 20 January, 1909.

170   *née* Marie Hippolyte Ponsin, 2 March, 1846 – 2 June, 1926.

171   Dean, Winton (1965). *Georges Bizet: His Life and Work*. J. M. Dent & Sons, p. 110.

172   15 March, 1837 – 22 September, 1905. See, generally, Henson, Karen (2015). "Real mezzo: Célestine Galli-Marié as Carmen." In *Opera Acts: Singers and Performance in the Late Nineteenth Century*. Cambridge University Press, pp. 48–87.

173   Micaëla, created by Marguerite Chapuy, 21 July, 1852 – 23 September, 1936.

Galli-Marié. She is trivial and brutal; she turns this feline girl into a cynical harlot.

In *Le siècle*, Oscar Comettant asserted of Galli-Marié's performance that

> This distinguished artist could have corrected that aspect of the Bohemian character [Carmen], heartless, lawless, devoid of honour, that was portrayed as shocking and repugnant on stage. On the contrary, she exaggerated Carmen's vices by means of a degree of realism that would be barely acceptable in operetta, in a small theatre. In the Opéra-Comique, a subsidised theatre, an honest theatre, Mlle Carmen ought to have restrained her passionate feelings.

The only unqualified praise was delivered by Blaze de Bury (writing in the *Revue des deux mondes* on 15 March, 1875) and the poet Théodore de Banville (writing for *Le National*, on 8 March).[174] The former was overwhelmed by the concluding duet between Don José and Carmen:

> The performance [of the last scene of Carmen] contributes powerfully to its effect [... Galli-Marié] has never seemed so talented as in this dreadful role. You should follow the nuances as a result of which José is only able to see red; watch Galli-Marié's acting, which is skilled, truthful, always simple; no screams, no melodrama, movements that are almost imperceptible but deeply meaningful, fine details of gesture and physiognomy that betray all the ennui and agitation of the character. Carmen is exhausted, overcome, "I cannot lie," she says – those are the words of the character created by Mérimée, whom Galli-Marié has been criticized for interpreting too truthfully, too realistically.

De Banville applauded Bizet as

> The Wagnerian, who violently resists expressing his passions through sung dance tunes [and] Mrs. Galli-Marié, who has adopted a mission to represent poetry, Goëthe and Musset, Mignon and Fantasio, in place of a world wholly rejecting of poetry. She looks like a doe which, by dint of eloquence and intrigue, would have persuaded the fishes from a pond to walk with her on the green grass; they go there, the unfortunates! But she is used to the tranquil waters of *La Dame Blanche* and *Domino Noir* in the prairie where the sun throws its golden javelins; the poor, I mean the characters of the Opéra-Comique, yawn desperately and fall to their final sleep.

---

174 de Banville, Théodore. Le National, 8 March 1875, p. 1. Reprinted in *Carmen: Dossier de presse Parisienne* (2001). Ed. Leslie Wright. Musik-Edition Lucie Galland, pp. 49–54.

De Banville embraced the novelty and bravery of a drama populated with "real" men and women, rather than fantastical "puppets;" he was alone in celebrating Galli-Marié's portrayal of an amoral seductress, which another critic described as "the very incarnation of vice."[175] The role was, of course, shocking for a theatrical audience in 1875 – although it is a long way (and twenty years distant) from *Grand Guignol*. *Réalisme* was new to the musical stage, but it had been a feature of contemporary literature, painting and sculpture for three decades before Bizet tore up the dance floor. Honoré de Balzac's *Le comédie humaine*[176] portrayed men and women across all walks of life objectively, and with an honest eye for the ugly and the vulgar; Flaubert's *Madame Bovary* was so real that its publication in 1856 resulted in a trial for obscenity. Four years earlier, Théophile Gautier published his collection, *Émaux et Camées*,[177] which featured a poem inspired by Prosper Mérimée's novella, *Carmen*.[178] The first verse establishes the seam of danger represented by a woman in control of her sexuality:

> *Carmen est maigre, – un trait de bistre*
> *Cerne son oeil de gitana.*
> *Ses cheveux sont d'un noir sinistre,*
> *Sa peau, le diable la tanna.*[179]

The last verse summarises how Gautier's conception of the modern woman as Venus came closer to Manet's vision than to Titian's:

> *Elle a, dans sa laideur piquante,*
> *Un grain de sel de cette mer*
> *D'où jaillit, nue et provocante,*
> *L'âcre Vénus du gouffre amer.*[180]

The encroaching of reality into fantasy was idealised by the critic and novelist, Champfleury, who published his manifesto, *Le réalisme*, in 1857. He asserted that art should serve as a "daguerreotype" for everyday life – even where the representation of women was concerned. Somewhat ironically, Mérimée was antithetical to the movement, and his faint praise of *Madame Bovary* identified "a talent there, which he wastes under the pretext of realism." His view of Baudelaire's *Fleurs du mal* was harsher still:

---

175 Dean, Winton (1965). *Georges Bizet: His Life and Work*. J. M. Dent & Sons, p. 117.
176 'The Human Comedy.'
177 'Enamels and Cameos.'
178 Published as a periodical in 1856 and in book form the following year, the novella served as the basis for the plot of Bizet's opera. Only the third chapter was utilised by the librettists.
179 'Carmen is lean – a trace of yellow Shadows her gipsy eye. Her hair is a sinister black, Her skin, tanned by the devil.'
180 'She has, in her hot ugliness, A grain of salt of that sea, From where rose, naked and provocative, Acrid Venus with her bitter abyss.'

Simply mediocre, nothing dangerous. There are a few sparks of poetry...
the work of a poor young man who doesn't know life [...] I don't know
the author, but I'll wager that he is naïve and honest. That's why I hope
they don't burn him.

Mérimée's disinterest was scorned by Les frères Goncourt,[181] whose series of novels in
the 1860s examined social milieu in brutal detail, and also Stendhal, Zola, Dickens,
Trollope, Eliot, Dostoyevsky and Turgenev. Champfleury advocated realism to contemporary painters; he heralded Courbet's *The Stone-Breakers* (1849) as emblematic,
with its politicised and unglamorous portrayal of peasant labourers. Jean-François
Millet's *Des glaneuses*[182] (1857), Honoré Daumier's *Le Wagon de troisième classe*[183]
(1864) and Jean-Baptiste-Camille Corot's *Jeune fille lisant*[184] (1868) all added to the
wished-for rejection of artificial and dishonest portrayals of human experience. None
of these paintings dealt overtly with sex; they are studies in working-class dynamics
that anticipated or mirrored Carmen's pursuit of agency as a slave to the factory clock
as well as a miscellany of social, gender and familial politics that allow her control
over little more than her body. That grim and inarguable reality is characterised in
a musical realism that reaches further than Bizet's forced local colour, quasi-Spanish
folk song and still-controversial use of castanets.[185] It is located in the music's development of character – particularly Carmen's paradoxical nature as victim and bully.
She is the first overtly erotic figure in opera – a woman whom many in the first
audience identified as a prostitute. She is intelligent – more so than anyone else in
the drama – but without culture and sophistication. Her resourcefulness equips her
to escape jail, and she is sufficiently capable to manage the smugglers' business trans-
actions. At the same time, she is chained to her embodiment, as a cypher for male
lust and transactional intercourse. Rather than money, Carmen yearns for physical
and emotional closeness. Galli-Marié was believable when breathing vertical life into
Bizet's horizontal writing, which characterises her rolling cigars against her skin, and
calls for her to smoke after the fashion of the female *Commnunards* who contributed
so much to the violent insurrection of 1871. Carmen is throughout a powerful and
threatening caricature; as Susan McClary observed in her landmark study:

> Carmen's powerful sexuality engenders a sense of male inadequacy, and
> it is one of the reasons why the character has to be punished and killed[186]
> at the end of the opera.[187]

---

181   Edmond and Jules.
182   'The Gleaners.'
183   'The Third Class Carriage.'
184   'Corot's Young Girl Reading.'
185   Galli-Marié refused to use them in rehearsals, to Bizet's great irritation. He won the day, however, because Galli-Marié was reported using them at the premiere.
186   A 2018 production at the Teatro Comunale, Florence, changed the ending, with Carmen grabbing a pistol from Don José and shooting him dead. This absurd gesture was welcome by some as a way of breaking with opera's long-standing misogyny. One can only imagine what the Teatro Communale is intending to do with Puccini's canon.
187   McClary, Susan (1992). *Bizet: Carmen*. Cambridge University Press, p. 128.

Carmen pays the ultimate price for her transgressive sexuality; it's believable because of the music she sings, which is among the most expressive for a female voice. In Act III, for example, Carmen turns tarot cards to discover her fate, singing *"Pour tous les deux la mort!"*[188] which Bizet sends so low into the soprano's chest that she joins with the tenor register as it is sung by Don José. In Act II, Carmen sings of *"Les tringles"*[189] – an established euphemism in French for an erection – to music that starts slow and ends in an orgasmic frenzy. The words of the final verse want for subtlety:

> Les Bohémiens, à tour de bras
> de leurs instruments faisaient rage,
> et cet éblouissant tapage
> ensorcelait les zingaras
> Sous le rhythme de la chanson
> ardentes, folles, enfiévrées,
> elles se laissaient, enivrées
> emporter par le tourbillon[190]

In Act I's *Seguidilla* (*"Près des ramparts"*), Carmen offers herself for sex to Don José – *"Oui, mais toute seule on s'ennuie, Et les vrais plaisirs sont à deux."*[191] A few lines later, she adds *"Qui veut m'aimer? Je l'aimerai!"*[192] The music rises and falls with obvious erotic allusion; flutes and a clarinet imitate her vocal line, which adds to the "spinning" quality that echoes shamanic recitations, causing a trance-like state in Don José, who loosens Carmen's ropes and submits to the fallacy that she will love him as he lusts after her. Carmen's most famous aria is her first, the *Habanera* – *"L'amour est un oiseau rebelle."*[193] The opening phrase, which begins *piano*, on a D4, descends chromatically through C sharp, C, B, B flat, A , G sharp, G, and F – passing through an overtly seductive triplet, before resolving on an E3. The sensualised expression of incremental closeness, or penetration, is outrageous taken at face value, even without knowing anything of the "rebellious bird" that cannot be tamed.[194] Achille de Lauzières' review found it to be impossibly offensive; his misogynistic screed for *La Patrie* ended with a summary view of Carmen as:

---

188 'For both it is death!'

189 'The rods.'

190 'Gypsies, with a turn of the arm, their instruments made to rage; and this dazzling din bewitched the zingaras / Under the rhythm of song; burning, insane, fevered, they were left, intoxicated / Carried away by the whirlwind!'

191 'Yes, but all alone, one gets bored, And the real pleasures are for two.'

192 'Who wants to love me? I will love him!'

193 'Love is a rebellious bird.'

194 It was claimed that Galli-Marié contributed much to the writing of the Habanera – which she required Bizet to re-write on 13 ultimately lucky occasions. Henson, Karen (2015). "Real mezzo: Célestine Galli-Marié as Carmen." In *Opera Acts: Singers and Performance in the Late Nineteenth Century*. Cambridge University Press, p. 53.

a savage; half gypsy, half Andalusian; sensual, mocking, shameless; believing neither in God nor the Devil [...] she is the veritable prostitute of the gutter and the crossroads.[195]

Bizet never lived to see *Carmen*'s triumph when staged in Vienna on 23 October, 1875 – five months after his death at the age of 36.[196] He suffered a heart-attack shortly after the work's 31st performance at the Opéra-Comique – during which Galli-Marié collapsed while on stage.[197] The composer Ernest Reyer later alleged that Galli-Marié had similar fortune-telling powers to Carmen:

> One evening, Mme Galli-Marié felt an unfamiliar impression when reading her game of omens of death. Her heart was pounding, and she felt that a great misfortune was in the air. Back in the wings, after intense efforts to get to the end of the piece, she fainted. When she was revived, we tried in vain to calm and reassure her, [but] the same thought constantly haunted her, the same feeling troubled her. But it was not for herself she was afraid; she sang it then, and has since been able to sing [it]. The next day, Mme Galli-Marié learned that, during the night, Bizet had died! I know that sceptics will shrug their shoulders. But we were no less deeply moved by listening the other night to the trio of the cards in the third act of Carmen.[198]

Five months earlier, the Opéra's new home, the Palais Garnier, was inaugurated with a lavish gala, attended by "everyone" from across Europe, Russia and the United States. The program included the overtures to *La muette de Portici* and *Guillaume Tell*, the first two acts of *La Juive* (with Gabrielle Krauss[199] making her Opéra debut as Rachel), and scenes from *Les Huguenots* and Delibes' ballet, *La source*.[200] The new theatre was (and remains) fantastically glamorous; Garnier was nonetheless required to add an underbelly to the design when including a separate entrance for season-ticket holders, the *Abonnés*,[201] to gain access to a lavishly decorated room behind the stage. The *foyer de la danse* was putatively for dancers and singers to warm up before (and during) performances; its surrogate purpose was as a brothel.

---

195 Higgins, Emma (2015). *The mezzo-soprano onstage and offstage: a cultural history of the voice-type, singers and roles in the French Third Republic (1870–1918)*. Ph.D. Dissertation, Maynooth University, p. 122.

196 Brahms was at the first performance, and later attended a further 19 – giving copies of the score to friends as gifts. Brahms may never have married, but he is known to have enjoyed the company of women who would have found much to recognise in Bizet's anti-heroine.

197 There are different views as to the truth of this event. Much was made of it by the Company, however, when marketing subsequent performances of *Carmen*.

198 *Ibid*, p. 204.

199 24 March, 1842 – 6 January, 1906. The Austrian-born Krauss created roles in operas by Anton Rubinstein, Gounod, Saint-Saëns and Antônio Gomes. She also created roles in local premieres for Verdi and Wagner.

200 'The Spring.'

201 'Subscribers.'

Sexual exploitation and social hypocrisy were definitive for artistic and political life in France during the 19th century; the commentary "published" by Édouard Manet in his *Le Déjeuner sur l'herbe*,[202] was merely the most scandalous example of the kind of social criticism rendered in more subtle tones by Degas, who added dark and looming figures to his paintings of ballerinas. Singers and dancers were bought and sold on the floor of the Opéra as products of a value system that vitiated all but a handful of those who managed to forge careers without resorting to prostitution. Few had the connections or the resources to refuse the *Abonnés*, and the power dynamic that prevailed behind the scenes of *Carmen's* rebellion adhered to a culture of manipulation and abuse that framed her eroticised power as suicidal. No-one is expected to care anything about Carmen because she cannot be fully actualised; she is a centre-fold fantasy whose violent death is *her* fault, even to the point of provoking her own stabbing. Tellingly, the opera's last words are performed by her murderer, who pours forth his undying love while covered in her blood. Carmen's transgressive character excuses the audience from empathy and compassion, just as the naked women who appeared in "Blurred Lines" are to blame because they submitted to Robin Thicke and his fraternity. Of course, when compared to the banal and ugly representation of women in modern popular music, *Carmen* can seem like *Pelléas et Mélisande*. Ultimately, the different kinds of male gaze that operated as realism for the late 19th century and as reality for the early 21st were both exploitative. Perhaps the only difference between the eras and the genres is framed by the illusion of choice.

---

202 'Luncheon on the Grass.' The gaze of the painting's naked woman was directed at the men who marched towards, and straight past, the painting when it was first shown at the *Salon des Refusés* in 1863. Each of them is likely to have recognised the setting as the Bois de Boulogne, one of Paris' most popular sites for the business of prostitution.

CHAPTER THIRTEEN

Verdi, and the Death of the Creator

In September, 2022, Italy elected its first female prime minister, Giorgia Meloni. The significance of the election of a woman to high office was lessened by the media's labelling of Meloni and her party, *Fratelli d'Italia*,[1] as fascist. *Fratelli's* ideological platform was conservative[2] and the party's flagship policies were nationalist, nativist, Eurosceptic and hostile to immigration. For all the reactionary populism, however, Italy went to the polls as a member state of the European Union; whatever was feared of the lurch to the right was subject to federal scrutiny and the threat of political and financial consequences.[3] Meloni compared little with Marine Le Pen, whose Renoir-like representation of the *Rassemblement National* as progressive was deceitful, and although her decision to address CPAC[4] in the United States was regrettable,[5] her rhetoric was less inflammatory at home. *Fratelli's* popularity was easy to explain in the light of the humanitarian disaster caused by the flood of immigrants arriving at the country's southern borders, the effects of the Covid pandemic, a cost-of-living crisis (exacerbated by Russia's invasion of Ukraine in 2022), and the prospect of a global recession.

The abridgement of Meloni's achievement by the media eclipsed the significance of her election for a country renowned for the security of its patriarchy. Even with a woman in the Palazzo Chigi,[6] the Catholic Church perpetuates a system of in-stitutionalised misogyny, wherein nuns with advanced degrees are forbidden from representing their religion while being denied a say in who might speak for them in their silence. Italian women were enfranchised only after World War II; the fact that millions of female voters kept returning Silvio Berlusconi, the *sine qua non* of Mediterranean sexism, emphasises the extent to which Meloni's elevation warranted celebration as well as caution. The prevailing dynamic as it was captured by Ibsen's *A Doll's House*[7] remains *au courant* for millions of Italian women, any one of whom *might* yet become President – accepting there is no word in the Italian language for

---

1   'Italian Brothers.'

2   It was not, for example, "*Sorelle d'Italia*".

3   For a clear precedent, the success of Jörg Haider's Freedom Party in 2000 should have led to the extreme right-wing Haider becoming Chancellor. The response from Brussels, and the majority of member states, compelled Haider to step aside in favour of ÖVP leader Wolfgang Schüssel.

4   Conservative Political Action Conference.

5   In February, 2022.

6   In September, 2022, Meloni announced that she and her family would continue to live in their private residence – the first Prime Minister to do so – although official business was to be conducted at the Chigi.

7   A play in which a wife is adored and praised for as long as she remains obedient, and detached from the family's affairs.

her role.[8] Mother Italy was at no time anthropomorphised, in partial consequence of the surfeit of Roman gods; when the country approached unification during the second half of the 19th century, it did so as *la patria*.[9]

The female voice in Italy remains a source of volatile contradictions, with women revered as mothers being desired as sexual objects and idealised as cultural icons. At the same time, the primacy of *Maria di vergine* – even for the irreligious – is an anomaly for a still-Christian nation, with images of the Madonna more frequently seen in public and private than images of Christ. A survey of Italian Catholics in 2007 found that, among those who claimed to pray, only 38.6% invoked Jesus.[10] 42.3% prayed most often to Mary – whose cult was formalised on 8 December, 1854, 20 months after the first performance of "The Fallen Woman,"[11] when Pope Pius IX issued a Papal encyclical defining the dogma of the Immaculate Conception.[12]

For Catholics, Mary was a perpetual virgin, a catechism that originated with the "Protoevangelium of James," a 2nd century apocryphal Gospel. Christians were encouraged to see virginity as a "holy" alternative to marriage and children. Mary was idealised for a time as the personification of "choice,"[13] pursuant to her portrayal in the New Testament as the vibrant, strong-minded and courageous personification of faith. Mary's message was re-positioned during the second millennium as one of social justice, with the impoverished being exalted and the powerful overthrown. Emphasis was placed on her initiation of Jesus' ministry at the wedding of Cana, and her loyalty to her son on his journey to the cross. She was vital to the birth of the Church at Pentecost. With time, Mary was re-cast as submissive, dependent, and unthreatening. Her defining qualities resolved eventually as resignation and acceptance, robbing the mother of Christ of her courage and leadership as well as her sexuality and desire. Long before Simone de Beauvoir dismissed the Marian cult as the "supreme victory of masculinity," Italian culture venerated Mary's purity for what it denied every woman to follow. With Paul's injunction against women speaking at church adopted more widely in the home, the Vatican forbade Mary's depiction in priestly vestments to ensure her status as a virgin-mother occluded her embodiment as someone equipped to lead in her own right.

Riding on the hem of Maria's lapis lazuli robes, the "mamma" became an archetype of easy qualification. Italian woman self-identified as a source of family-directed strength, with mothers doting on their male children, vetoing their choices, and manipulating their emotional and symbolic dependency.[14] This gave rise to *mammismo*,[15] a condition that did much to cause what many perceive to be a crisis for modern

---

8   It would be "*presidentessa*." The Italian language still does not provide for the feminine of numerous professions and representative roles.

9   'The fatherland.'

10   Garelli, Franco (2014). *Religion, Italian Style: Continuities and Change in a Catholic Country*. Ashgate, p. 56.

11   *La traviata*.

12   *Ineffabilis Deus*.

13   It is to state the obvious that Mary never had a say in it.

14   Bravo, Anna (2001). "*Madri fra oppressione ed emancipazione*," in *Storia sociale delle donne nell'Italia contemporanea*, Laterza, p. 78.

15   Loosely, 'mother-ism.'

Italian society, encompassing a collapse in the birth rate, the unequal division of labour within the household between the genders, embarrassing discrepancies in pay, and the nurturing of *bamboccioni*.[16] The construction for Italian society of male and female roles and identities underwent the greatest changes during the second half of the 19th century, a transformation for which the soundtrack was provided by a single composer.

Giuseppe Verdi's status in Italy is unique for being political as well as musical. His emotional attachment to Alessandro Manzoni (whose *Il nome di Maria*[17] amplified the importance of Mary for early 19th century Italians) and his acronymic identification with "Vittorio Emanuele Re d'Italia," and the *Risorgimento* to which he contributed so much, ensured his pivotal status for the unified Italian people. His operas remain important because of the role they played in the crystallising of Italy's national identity, and for how they resonate for audiences spanning language, class and culture. The female voice was central to Verdi's life, privately and professionally; as the first Italian composer to become a figure of national importance, his contribution to the ideation of women and to the evolution of the soprano in particular is impossible to overstate. Like his German rival, Wagner – who was born five months earlier – Verdi was raised in a society saturated with religious, political and cultural semiotics. Also like Wagner, Verdi managed his status and legacy with pointillist care, beginning with the mis-characterisation of his origins.

Verdi was a child of traders and landowners, rather than the poverty and illiteracy to which he laid claim in later life. His mother, Luigia Uttini, was a spinner; his father, Carlo, was an innkeeper. Both were determined to provide their son with a good education, which began at the local church. Verdi was appointed full-time organist at the age of nine; after the family moved to the larger town of Busseto in 1823 he became known as a composer and a performer. When leaving home, Verdi relocated to the home of Antonio Barezzi, a merchant and devoted amateur musician, to whose daughter, Margherita, he gave singing and piano lessons. On 4 May, 1836, Margherita became the composer's first wife. They married at the Oratorio della Santissima Trinità, in Busseto. Though built during the late 14th century, the church contained a number of "modern" features, including a carved door dating from 1794 and a high altar in polychrome marble from 1749.

Nothing is known of the wedding; it can be presumed to have been conducted in accordance with the prevailing liturgy, however. Verdi's convictions are the subject of ongoing research and debate, but religion passes like a seam through his work, framed by the composition of sacred works. Religion is a prominent feature of his operas; some of it is narratised but most of it attaches to death and heresy, with Verdi submitting his sopranos to representations of women in supplication – an aspect of contemporary life that was controversial for suggesting a women might need to pray for something other than her family. The well-trodden political context for Verdi's first theatrical success,[18] the Biblical tale *Nabucco*, was less obvious than the young

---

16   Men who live at home into their thirties.

17   'The name of Mary.'

18   The extent to which his early operas were intended as political and nationalist discourse continues to be debated. See generally Gossett, Philip (2005). "Le 'edizioni distrutte' e il significato dei cori operistici nel Risorgimento." *Il Saggiatore musicale*. 12 (2).

composer's Christian faith, which was typical in being cultural primarily. During the three years preceding *Nabucco*'s first performance at La Scala, on 9 March, 1842, the concept of an omniscient God was tested for Verdi by unimaginable personal circumstances that required him to bury both of his children, Virginia and Icilio,[19] as well as their mother.[20] Verdi persevered and *Nabucco* triumphed, receiving an unprecedented 57 performances at its La Scala revival in 1842. The opera went on to become a totem for national events in Italy, including the composer's funeral – when Toscanini conducted a chorus of 800 in the best known of the work's many prayers, "*Va, pensiero, sull'ali dorate.*"[21] *Nabucco* established two of Verdi's defining tropes – the heroine and the *femme fatale* – personified by the fearless Fenena (who defends her religion and fights for love) and the vengeful, broken Abigaille, whose lust for power resolves in the work's concluding scene, "*Su me; morente; esanime,*"[22] a prayer for forgiveness in which she urges the Jewish people to 'Lift up God,' whom she implores not to curse her in death. It is a thrilling conclusion, conveyed through hesitant, anxious music that resonates with fear, doubt and regret. The conclusion is stygian, and darker still for the soprano, who has to sing music that floats above the stave before dropping into the contralto register.

The role was created by Giuseppina Strepponi,[23] the daughter of a minor-rank composer of operas who enrolled at the Milan Conservatory in 1830. She graduated four years later, having been awarded the bel canto prize for her performance of the cavatina from Bellini's *Beatrice di Tenda*.[24] Strepponi made her debut in December, 1834, in an opera by a family friend, Luigi Ricci; her apprenticeship amounted to little until a performance as Rossini's *Matilde di Shabran* in Trieste prompted bookings in Vienna as Adalgisa in *Norma* and Amina in *La sonnambula*. After returning to Italy in 1836[25] she achieved spectacular notices for appearances in *La gazza ladra, La Cenerentola, I puritani*, and *Lucia di Lammermoor*. After signing a contract with Alessandro Lanari in Florence, Strepponi's talent made her one of the most sought after sopranos in Italy, renowned for her

> limpid, penetrating, smooth voice, seemly action, a lovely figure; and to Nature's liberal endowments she adds an excellent technique.[26]

Her regional status became national after making her debut at La Scala in 1839 as Leonora during the initial run of Verdi's first opera, *Oberto*,[27] in which she replaced

---

19   Neither reached their second birthday.
20   Margherita died of encephalitis, on 19 June, 1840, at the age of 26.
21   'Fly, my thoughts, on wings of gold.' A chorus for enslaved Hebrews, held captive in Babylon – based on Psalm 137.
22   'On me; dying; lifeless.'
23   *née* Clelia Maria Josepha Strepponi, 8 September, 1815 – 14 November, 1897.
24   The composer was, of course, alive at the time – as was Strepponi's father, who died shortly after Bellini, in 1835.
25   Where she remained professionally for the rest of her life.
26   Budden, Julian (1998). "Giuseppina Strepponi," in Stanley Sadie, Ed. *The New Grove Dictionary of Opera*, Vol. 4. Macmillan, pp. 582–583.
27   First performed on 17 November, 1839.

Antonietta Marini-Rainieri,[28] who was taken ill during the premiere. Strepponi worked closely with the composer, who overlooked what was, for many, an untouchably scandalous private life. She became pregnant for the first time, as an unmarried woman, during the spring of 1837; she stopped singing only a few weeks before the birth of her son, Camillo, in January, 1838.[29] The boy's father was unidentified at the time. During the Spring of 1838, she became pregnant again, giving birth on 9 February, 1839, to Giuseppina – hours after completing a performance at the Teatro Alfieri in Florence. She travelled two days later for engagements in Venice. The child's father was thought to be her agent, Camillo Cirelli, whose initial denial of paternity led to the infant being placed in the care of the Ospedale degli Innocenti[30] in Florence, under the name "Sinforosa Cirelli."[31] A month later, on 12 March, Strepponi appeared at La Fenice in a production of Mercadante's *Le due illustri rivali*[32] (appropriately enough, with Carolina Unger), following which Cirelli accepted the child as his own, having been satisfied by Strepponi that he was the father. Strepponi was more fertile than Danaus. In March, 1840, she gave birth to a stillborn girl; twelve months later she became pregnant again, and on 4 November, 1841, her next child was given her mother's surname and passed to the Vianello family, who cared for the baby until its death from dysentery on 4 October, 1842.

The father of each of Strepponi's children was a tenor, Napoleone Moriani.[33] Born into wealth and status, he treated Strepponi as badly as the culture allowed, abusing her as a form of contraception to protect him from having more than the four children he fathered with his wife, Elvira. Moriani's reputation survived intact, while Strepponi's was dragged through the mud of print and gossip. Filtering the strain of public calumny through a Stakhanovian work ethic cost her dearly, and during the early 1840s her doctors warned her she was hastening her death. Strepponi had to drag herself through the first run of *Nabucco's* eight performances, after which she toured the opera throughout the country, with regional premieres in Parma, Bologna and Venice. Despite taking a year's sabbatical, her inability to say no resulted in vocal problems which ossified in 1845 when she was booed by audiences in Palermo. In February, 1846, she was forced to retire, at the age of thirty. Strepponi's diary[34] demonstrates that her final year was given to performances of operas by Verdi, including appearances as Elvira in *Ernani* and Lucrezia Contarini in *I due Foscari*.[35]

---

28 1797 – 1848. She went on to create the role of the Marchesa del Poggio in *Un giorno di regno*, first performed on 5 September, 1840. The role of Imelda in *Oberto* was played by Marietta Sacchi, who was born in 1789 (died 1842), which made her the earliest born soprano to work with Verdi on a premiere. The longest surviving of Verdi's sopranos was Virginia Guerrini – who created the role of Meg Page for *Falstaff* (1893) and died in 1948, at the age of 77. It follows that the lifespan between the first and last of Verdi's sopranos (1789 – 1948) was 159 years.

29 He was baptised as "Sterponi."

30 'Hospital for the Innocents.' The orphans were known unhelpfully as *esposti* ('the exposed'). The building was designed by Brunelleschi, who received the commission in 1419 from the Arte della Seta. It has survived, and now operates as offices, and a gallery.

31 Giuseppina *giovane* died in Florence in 1919.

32 'The two illustrious rivals.'

33 Walker, Frank (1962). *The Man Verdi*. Knopf, p. 88.

34 See Walker, Frank (1962). *The Man Verdi*. Knopf.

35 'The Two Foscari.'

Eight months following her final appearance in Italy, Strepponi relocated to Paris as a singing teacher. Verdi moved to the city the following year, becoming Strepponi's lover soon after. The relationship survived more than half a century, and ended with the singer's death in 1897. There was no issue and Verdi died childless.

The composer's relationship with Strepponi was constant and *mostly* loving; it was creative also, because the soprano contributed to each of his roles for women, from *Macbeth* (1847) to *Falstaff* (1893).[36] She was the first to hear his music for soprano, at home, before it was performed in rehearsal. Having lived together in Paris for two years, the couple returned to Busseto, a small town populated by the unkind and the judgmental. The state of the composer's mind during the first four years of ignominious co-habitation can be discerned, from the operas he completed between 1849 and 1853: *La battaglia di Legnano*,[37] *Luisa Miller*,[38] *Stiffelio*,[39] *Rigoletto*,[40] *Il trovatore*,[41] and *La traviata*.[42] Each hinges on a woman enduring emotional or physical violence, humiliation, social isolation and injustice. Contrary to Catherine Clement's thesis in *Opera, or the Undoing of Women*, the female characters who suffer at Verdi's hands do so because of societal forces, rather than the gender-determined *animus* of men. Strepponi and Verdi stuck it out for ten years in sin, and married only in 1859. The extent to which the moral majority's religiously-infused audit influenced the composer's portrayal of women and Christianity has been the subject of considerable research; the best of it has hinged on the place and function of government, social order and the Catholic Church. No other composer of opera placed such emphasis on religious themes, not even Meyerbeer, but his preoccupation was the product of theatrical and narrative pragmatism rather than personal conviction. On 9 May, 1872, Strepponi wrote to the Countess Clarina Maffei:[43]

> Verdi esteems you too much not to believe your words and to number you, although you are a doctor, among the spiritualists. But, between ourselves, he presents the strangest phenomenon in the world. He is not a doctor, but an artist. Everyone agrees that there fell to his lot the divine gift of genius; he is a shining example of honesty; he understands and feels every delicate and elevated sentiment. And yet this brigand permits himself to be, I won't say an atheist, but certainly very little of a believer, and that with an obstinacy and calm that make one want to beat him. I exhaust myself in speaking to him of the marvels of the heavens, the earth, the sea, *etc.*, *etc.* It's a waste of breath! He laughs in my face and

---

36   See, generally, Mendelsohn, Gerald A. "Verdi the Man and Verdi the Dramatist," *19th-Century Music*, 2, pp. 110–230.

37   'The Battle of Legnano,' first performed on 27 January, 1849.

38   First performed on 8 December, 1849.

39   First performed on 16 November, 1850.

40   First performed on 11 March, 1851.

41   'The Troubadour,' first performed on 19 January, 1853.

42   First performed on 6 March, 1853.

43   An Italian woman of letters, promoter of the Risorgimento, and host of one of the most influential salons in Italy.

freezes me in the midst of my oratorical periods, my divine enthusiasm, by saying: '*You're all mad*,' and unfortunately he says it in good faith.[44]

The first draft of this letter adopted a harsher tone: "this brigand permits himself to be an atheist with an obstinacy and calm that make one want to beat him."[45] Strepponi was a devout Christian, who saw her husband's talent as ordained; she was zealously protective of his reputation and legacy, which was well-established by the time they married. Strepponi recognised how Verdi's "very little" belief was heretical at a time when the power and status of the Catholic Church was under attack. The creeping effect on Italian life[46] of the work of Gianbattista Brocchi[47] and the publication in Italian of Darwin's *Origin of the Species*, in 1864, was a *scandale d'estime* – of interest to a cross-section of the educated, which included Verdi, although he was not, as Strepponi noted, a "scientist." Public debate was stimulated by Filippo De Filippi's inflammatory lecture, *L'uomo e le scimmie*,[48] in which the zoologist attempted to reconcile Darwinism and doctrine by classifying human beings as a fourth natural 'kingdom,' alongside minerals, plants, and animals. Empiricism was subsumed to doctrine. The Church's response to the challenges presented by education materialised with predictable hostility and repression. Verdi saw the primacy of God as antithetical to Man's exponential confidence, attendant to which the Creator found Himself at war with the creative. Principled and anti-clerical, Verdi construed the discourse as good for business; numerous of his operas are coloured by Catholic misogyny and peppered with misogyny, doctrinal exclamations,[49] clerics, incantations, church scenes or overtly Christian plot devices; some are driven by religion in its practice and power – including *Stiffelio*, *La forza del destino*,[50] *Don Carlos*, *Aida* and *Otello*. *Don Carlos* openly condemned the Papacy.[51]

Giovanna d'Arco,[52] and *I Lombardi alla prima crociata*[53] were the first operas of the 19th century to make prominent references to the Madonna. Neither of them was well-received by the censors. As Alberto Rizzuti's critical edition of *Giovanna d'Arco* has demonstrated,[54] the poetry had to be altered to eliminate "the Marian thread

---

44   Walter, Frank (1962). *The Man Verdi*. Alfred A. Knof, p. 280.

45   *Ibid*.

46   See, generally, Crivellaro, F., Sperduti, A. (2014). "Accepting and understanding evolution in Italy: a case study from a selected public attending a Darwin Day celebration." *Evo Edu Outreach*, 7, p. 13.

47   In 1814, Brocchi published *Concchiologia fossile subappenina con osservazioni geologiche sugli Appenini e sul suolo adiacente* ('Sub-Apennine fossil concchiology with geological observations on the Apennines and the adjacent soil'), in which he supported the theory that species can disappear and become extinct, based on his examination of fossilised crustaceans.

48   'Man and the Apes.'

49   Most commonly, "*Dio!*" and "*Gran Dio!*"

50   'The Force of Destiny.'

51   The attainment of national unity in 1861 did not include the Papal State(s). The Italian government was unable to take possession of the city because a garrison, stationed in Rome by Napoleon III, protected Pope Pius IX.

52   'Joan of Arc.'

53   'The Lombards on the First Crusade,' first performed on 11 February, 1843.

54   *Giovanna d'Arco* (2007). Vol. 7 of Works of Giuseppe Verdi. Ed. Alberto Rizzuti. University of Chicago Press.

woven into the original poetry."[55] In Act 1, Temistocle Solera's libretto provided originally "*Ecco mi prostro a te, madre di Dio,*"[56] which became "Ecco mi prostro, riverente e pio,"[57] while "*Sorgi o diletta Vergine, Maria, Maria ti chiama!*"[58] became "*Sorgi! I Celesti accolsero, La generosa brama!*"[59] I Lombardi is striking also for Giselda's prayer to the Virgin – an "*Ave Maria*" that became "*Salve Maria!*" more than forty years before Verdi fulfilled the promise of the earlier scene when composing *Otello*. The role of Giselda in *I Lombardi* and the title role in *Giovanna d'Arco* were created by Erminia Frezzolini,[60] with whom it was rumoured Verdi was having an affair. She was close to the composer, and it's certain he knew enough of her private life to consider her an ideal fit for Giselda, whose traumatic relationship with Arvino was almost as terrible as Frezzolini's relationship with her father, the buffo bass, Giuseppe Frezzolini. He exploited his daughter's success with alarming cruelty when forcing her to sign away her earnings from 1839 until February, 1841 – at which point she was required by contract to pay him 3,000 francs a year for the rest of his life.

Of Verdi's 28 operas, almost half feature a prominent father-daughter theme. It colours three of his first four operas, disappears for five years, and reappears for seven of his next 11 works. The relationships have disastrous consequences in almost every case; indeed, the father (or father figure) causes the death of the daughter on five occasions (*Nabucco, Luisa Miller, Rigoletto, La traviata,* and *Aida*), and on three occasions the daughter is the agent of the father's death (*Oberto, Les vêpres siciliennes*[61]*, and Simon Boccanegra*).[62] In *I Lombardi*, the father fails to kill his daughter, while in *La Forza del Destino*, each is pivotal to the death of the other. Only five of Verdi's operas is named after its female lead; one of them employs a title that was likely to have been used routinely in Busseto when describing Strepponi.[63] All but two are tragic, and many involve women suffering in consequence of their gender or sexuality. As Joseph Kerman noted in his landmark essay "Verdi and the Undoing of Women,"[64] retribution is common to the female experience in most of his operas. On the other hand, even *Rigoletto's* hopelessly naïve Gilda, and *La traviata's* unravelling prostitute, Violetta, are afforded music of unprecedented psychological sophistication, the complexion of which transcends their brutal circumstances.

The Rubicon for the soprano voice in Italian opera, and for Verdi's evolving genius as a composer of character-driven melody, was crossed by the premieres of three operas: *Rigoletto, Il trovatore* and *La traviata*.[65] Each features a landmark soprano role

---

55   Izzo, Francesco (2007). "Verdi, the Virgin, and the Censor: The Politics of the Cult of Mary in *I Lombardi alla prima crociata* and *Giovanna d'Arco.*" *Journal of the American Musicological Society,* Vol. 60, No. 3, pp. 557–597; p. 562.

56   'Here I kneel before you, mother of God.'

57   'Here I kneel, reverent and pious.'

58   'Rise, dear virgin, Mary, Mary is calling you!'

59   'Rise! The heavenly ones welcomed your generous desire!'

60   27 March, 1818 – 5 November, 1884.

61   The Sicilian Vespers;' first performed on 13 June, 1855.

62   12 March, 1857.

63   *La traviata.*

64   Kerman, Joseph (2006). "Verdi and the Undoing of Women." *Cambridge Opera Journal.* Vol. 18, No. 1, pp. 21–31; p. 22.

65   First performed during a period of just two years, between March, 1851 and March, 1853.

that marked the transition from (and eventual break with) coloratura. The first is the least capable of Verdi's objectified women, a self-sacrificing, ill-starred victim of humiliation, rape and murder. Gilda is famous for her high-flying acrobatics, but much of her music is secondary to the parts sung by other characters. Even her celebrated Act I aria, "*Caro nome che il mio cor,*"[66] is unusual for a striking absence of legato phrasing that recalls Lucia's "Mad Scene"; Gilda's stuttering music is analogous to her thinking, insofar as it speaks to near-constant stress, interrupted by the thoughts and deeds of terrible, male-directed hierarchies. For all its acrobatic brilliance, "*Caro nome*" is an atavistic portrait of idealised love; it provides narrative context for Gilda's transformation from ingénue to selfless victim, with coloratura employed as foreshadowing to anticipate a violent, routinely tragic end. Gilda's most intimate scenes are with her father; they culminate in the thrilling Act II duet that concludes, "*Sì, vendetta, tremenda vendetta.*"[67]

The high notes for which Gilda's music is famous do not appear in the score. By the 1850s, the prima donna had become a bane for composers and publishers, most of whom viewed the injunction *com'é scritto* as liturgy; improvisation nonetheless remained a feature of operatic performance into the second half of the 19th century, when it was common for sopranos to indulge themselves at cost to the composer. The most extreme examples involved singers reverting to 18th century practice by ignoring the score entirely. Productions of Rossini's music were rare after 1850, but whenever *Il barbiere* was staged it was common for the "lesson scene" to operate as a platform for the soprano to sing whatever she and the audience deemed appropriate.[68]

Verdi equated such practices with heresy, and his tolerance for the abuses of singers raised in a culture of *ad libitum* expired in 1853 when the first production of *La traviata* was staged in Venice. The history of theatrical singing to the 1850s was characterised by close-working relationships between composers and their creators; while the same was true for Verdi – if only out of necessity – he rarely worked with the same singer more than twice. His collegial sensibilities were coloured by a fanaticism that many read as hostility; he made no allowance for gender, or the Marian capacity of women to create life as well as art. As the decades passed, Verdi's diligence calcified as intransigence; in 1871, he railed to Giulio Ricordi:

> I deny that either singers or conductors can 'create' or work creatively – this, as I have always said, is a conception that leads to the abyss."[69]

In a letter to Verdi from Eugenio Tornaghi (Ricordi's secretary), he employed the word "diva" with contempt when referring to the self-aggrandising Giuseppina Pasqua.[70]

---

66 'Sweet name that made my heart.'

67 'Yes, revenge, terrible revenge.'

68 See, generally, Poriss, Hilary (2009). *Changing the Score: Arias, Prima Donnas, and the Authority of Performance.* Oxford University Press.

69 11 April, 1871. (1942) *Verdi: The Man in His Letters.* Eds. Franz Werfel and Paul Stefan. L. B. Fischer, pp. 301–302.

70 24 October, 1851 – 24 February, 1930. Letter dated 16 August, 1892; in *Verdi's Falstaff in Letters and Contemporary Reviews* (1998). Ed. Hans Busch. Indiana University Press, p. 234. The contralto, Giuseppina Pasqua (24 October, 1851 – 24 February, 1930), was the first Mistress Quickly in *Falstaff.*

During the composition of *Rigoletto*, Verdi was recovering from his long-fomenting dissatisfaction with Marietta Gazzaniga,[71] the creator of *Luisa Miller* at the San Carlo in 1849, and the first Lina, in *Stiffelio*, in 1850. Two years later, after a disastrous performance as Gilda in Bergamo, Verdi claimed never to have liked her work, either as a singer or as an actress. This was peculiar considering her contiguous role-creations (and then at two different theatres), but not improbable when noting the composer's stated preference for Teresa De Giuli Borsi,[72] the first Lidia in *La battaglia di Legnano*. Because *Rigoletto* was commissioned by La Fenice, Verdi had no say in the casting; the invitation extended by the theatre to Teresa Brambilla to create Gilda was sent without reference to the composer.[73] Verdi's refusal to share his (incomplete) score with the cast until rehearsals in Venice left Brambilla days in which to learn, memorise and master Gilda. The first production was hailed by the public and damned by the critics as crude and gaudy.

Brambilla's success as Gilda failed to persuade Verdi or the management of Rome's Teatro Apollo to cast her as Leonora in *Il trovatore*, a role that required a new kind of voice, one capable of force and power as well as line and lyricism. Spinto means "pushed" in Italian,[74] and it's a perfect word for a bel canto voice that needs to be heard at moments of intense drama above a chorus and brass-heavy orchestra. The spinto *fach* has been subjected over the years to a loss of precision, with some applying it lazily to a meaningless range of repertoire. It does not encompass dramatic roles, like Isolde or Elektra, but rather lyric voices that require an additional measure of vibrancy, known as *squillo*.[75] The first Leonora, Rosina Penco,[76] was admired as a singing actress, whose intense stage temperament, virtuoso technique and raw vocal power were prized by Verdi;[77] in her reconciliation of a seamless legato to amplitude she was the model spinto soprano. The composer made similar demands of Manrico (tenor), the Conte di Luna (baritone) and Azucena (mezzo-soprano), roles that threw their singers into competition with an increasingly dense orchestra, complex ensemble writing and prominent choruses. Any first-rate production of *Il trovatore* will include not only "the four best singers on Earth,"[78] but also 30 to 40 strings, a piccolo, a single flute, two oboes, two clarinets, two bassoons, four horns, two trumpets,

---

While she may have been a "diva," it is equally true that he wrote the role specifically for her, and later dedicated the Act 2 aria "*Giunta all' albergo*," ('Arrived at the hotel') to Pasqua.

71   1824 – 2 January, 1884.

72   *née* Maria Teresa Pippeo, 26 October, 1817 – 18 November, 1877.

73   23 October, 1813 – 15 July, 1895. Brambilla was a close friend of Giuseppina Strepponi, with whom she enrolled as a teenager at the Conservatoire in Milan. She was one of five freakishly talented sisters, all of whom became opera singers. Marietta (1807–1875), her elder sister, was a famed contralto who created a number of roles for Donizetti. Her niece, Teresa "Teresina" Brambilla (15 April, 1845 – 1 July, 1921), was renowned for working under Amilcare Ponchielli, whom she married in 1874.

74   As is typical of Italian when translated into English, the verb "*spingere*" can be (and is frequently) translated as to forward, to force, to shove, to run, to jog, to put, to advance, to urge, to propel, and to thrust. It's well to remember that while the Italian dictionary contains approximately 270,000 words, the English dictionary has more than twice that number.

75   '*Ring*.'

76   1823 – 1894.

77   In 1850, Penco appeared in Trieste as Azucena in another *Il trovatore*, by Francesco Cortesi – which was based on the same play as Verdi's opera.

78   Toscanini's answer when asked what was required for *Il trovatore*.

three trombones, a tuba, timpani, triangle, tambourine, castanets, cymbals, anvils, a bass drum and a harp. Azucena, in particular, is an intensely dark mezzo/contralto role, coloured more by *fioritura* than coloratura, although "*Stride la vampa*"[79] features two infamously difficult trills. The ensuing duet with her son, Manrico, is marked by declamatory writing for Azucena, much of it requiring resonance and attack. The role was created by Emilia Goggi,[80] who must have had a formidable technique, considering the low-range of so much of the writing. Her performance was hailed and she played the role in dozens of productions. Goggi died just four years after the premiere, at the age of 39, while preparing to tour England. Verdi was not responsible for her death but he knew he was asking more of his singers than anyone previously; as a notorious taskmaster, he pushed soloists, choruses and orchestras to their limits during rehearsals, generating fabulous results. The composer was nonetheless unable to communicate his wishes to every singer because there were so many singing it. During the three years following its premiere in 1853, there were 229 different productions of *Il trovatore* worldwide.

Verdi's creators were ambassadors and he knew they would be able to translate something of his ambition when travelling. As his model spinto soprano, Penco was his stated preference for the first Violetta and also Amelia in *Un ballo in Maschera*.[81] In 1858, however, he lamented that she had reverted to an "old-fashioned" style of singing – a shorthand for mannered artificiality usurping the "fire" of authenticity. What that meant at the time can be reduced to a reversion to laboured stage-craft, with singers finding a point near the footlights, and sticking to it for the duration. What it means for modern ears can be applied antiphonally to Verdi's wishes and expectations; vibrato was rarely used as colour, while portamento was ubiquitous; declamation was employed solely to highlight word-use and meaning, rather than as a teutonic mechanism for "voice-less" intensity. "Beautiful songs" were fine for Rossini but they were a distraction for Verdi's high-theatre – a value-system memorialised by one of the only soprano creators of a Verdi role to make records, Virginia Guerrini. It's easy to allow the beauty of Verdi's music to obstruct its dramatic power. Lyrical beauty – as a construction of training and cultural tradition – remained a paramount virtue for the composer, but so too was psychological truth. His insights were matched uniquely to a sense of how to speak as, and for, women; Leonora's final aria, in Act IV of *Il trovatore*, "*D'amor sull'ali rosee*,"[82] evidences the reach of the composer's talent and the passing of the age of the coloratura into the spinto:

> *D'amor sull' ali rosee*
> *vanne, sospir dolente:*
> *del prigioniero misero*
> *conforta l'egra mente...*
> *Com' aura di speranza*
> *aleggia in quella stanza:*

---

79 'The flames crackle.'

80 Also known as Emilia Goggi-Marcovaldi, 10 October, 1817 – 29 August, 1857.

81 A role she sang with great success at Covent Garden in London.

82 'On the rosy wings of love.'

lo desta alle memorie,
ai sogni dell'amor!
Ma deh! non dirgli improvvido,
le pene del mio cor!83

To emphasise the anguish experienced by Leonora as she comes to terms with what her love for Manrico is going to cost her, Verdi employs written trills in the soprano's second bar, for the word "*rosee,*" and in bar four, for the word "*dolente,*" This is *fioritura* rather than coloratura – equating to colour more than substance. The rising phrase "*del prigioniero misero,*" resolves on an A flat 4, from which Leonora tumbles through scored demi-semi-quavers to an F3 for the word "*conforta*" – foreshadowing the peace that death alone can bring. Verdi sends light into the darkness of Leonora's cell with the phrase "*Com' aura di Speranza, aleggia in quella stanza,*" only to steer her back to despair when crafting one of the most heart-rending phrases in the soprano repertoire – the wailing "*Ma deh! non dirgli improvvido, le pene del mio cor.*" It's a searing, shocking moment of private grief that takes the soprano to a B flat 4, from which she again tumbles, to a D flat 3 – extended by Verdi through an agonising, breathless line to an A flat 3 that pauses finally on a G3, written as a dotted quaver for the second syllable of "*penne.*" This seemingly-endless phrase continues until it descends to a low F3, in the soprano's chest-voice, and a final, resolving A3 that *should* leave an audience shredded. Beginning "*Ma, deh!*" and concluding "*…del mio cor,*" these three-bars span an octave and a half, and admit few obvious opportunities for breath – even if everyone takes at least two in the theatre. Of course, the majority of sopranos also add *fermatas* to the B flat 4 – D flat 4 – G3 sequence, which can draw the line out considerably, making breath management a function of interpretation more than the composer's notation. The repeat of the final verse takes the soprano to a high C, while some – obviously Callas and Sutherland – vault the written D flat 5. The cadenza is introduced by a trill on the penultimate "*penne,*" and requires as much of a singer as anything by Bellini or Donizetti. Depending on *how* the aria is performed, it can pivot from the regressive to the modern. The performance by Maria Callas in 1951 at the San Carlo[84] bordered on the reactionary;[85] the achingly slow speed and prodigious fermatas amplifed the sensibilities of classic bel canto. Conversely, the performance by Leontyne Price at her Met debut in 1961[86] was driven and defiant, superseding Callas' predilection for resignation and hopelessness. The technical demands created by Verdi's use of extreme intervals fall away when the music is performed with Callas-like deliberation; they generate an entirely different colour if pushed, as is now routine.

---

83 'On the rosy wings of love, go, pained sighs: go to alleviate the sick mind / of the wretch that lies imprisoned… Like a breeze of hope / linger in that room: wake him up to remembrance, to dreams of love! Yet do not imprudently reveal the woes of my heart!'

84 Conducted by Tulio Serafin.

85 This performance is singularly compelling evidence that Callas was as she is remembered, namely one of the relatively few miracles of the age of opera. In matters of tone, articulation and phrasing, the performance is as close to perfection as imagination allows. If Penco was even half as good when singing the aria for Verdi then she must have been sensational.

86 Conducted by Fausto Cleva.

"*D'amor sull' ali rosee,*" was Verdi's swan song to bel canto; the scene that follows,[87] "*Miserere d'un'alma già vicina* [...] *Di te, di te scordarmi!* [...] *Mira di acerbe
lagrime.*"[88] sends Leonora into battle with Manrico, di Luna and Verdi's seething orchestra, throughout which the opera's first audiences would have been acutely aware
that bel canto had transitioned to *con belto*. It was clear also that the days in which
a soprano might distinguish herself through improvisation were over. In his *Style in
Singing*, first published in 1911, W. E. Haslam interviewed singers who had worked
with Verdi – who had died only a decade earlier. When addressing a single feature
of the "*Miserere*," Haslam identified "the well-known change which every soprano
who sings the rôle of Leonora introduces" to the four-times repeated phrase "*di te
scordami*," in her duet with Manrico. That change was the interpolation of a single
high C5 (in place of the B flat 4 written by Verdi),[89] of which Haslam wrote:

> The accepted traditional change certainly conveys the impression of
> Leonora's gradually increasing anguish and terror; not the idea that it is
> introduced merely to exploit a high tone.[90]

Haslam continued that

> this departure from the text must have been sanctioned by Verdi, is,
> I think, proved by the fact that it has always been sung thus, and the
> composer himself must often have heard the substitution. He would
> certainly have forbidden its use, had he not approved of it, for he was
> particularly averse to having changes made in his music.[91]

The soprano's subsequent exchanges with the Count are closer to speech in their
metrical force and febrility; the extreme juxtapositions are vivid and quite different in
tone and character to Verdi's next and most celebrated role for a woman. When planning *La traviata*, Verdi's librettist, Francesco Maria Piave, wrote to the President of La
Fenice to announce that anyone singing the title role had to be "young, have a grace-
ful figure and sing with passion."[92] For his part, Verdi informed the publisher Giulio
Ricordi that "even a mediocrity could possess the right qualities to shine in that opera
and be dreadful in everything else."[93] The first Violetta was required to persuade as a
young and seductive courtesan over whose attentions men were willing to fight and
die, and whose physical degeneration from tuberculosis in Act III had to transcend

---

87 For anyone parsing the end of Act 1 as coloratura, the scene compares better to Richard Strauss'
show-piece for Zerbinetta in *Ariadne aux Naxos* than to the end of *La sonnambula*.
88 'Have mercy on a spirit approaching [...] How could I ever forget you!'
89 The scene, and the interpolation, were promulgated by the Marx Brothers in their glorious *A Night at
the Opera* (1935), in which Kitty Carlisle (as "Rosa Castaldi") sings the duet (more than once) with Allan
Jones (as "Riccardo Barone").
90 Haslam, W. E. (1911). *Style in Singing*. Schirmer, pp. 70–71.
91 *Ibid*, p. 72.
92 Budden, Julian (1978). *The Operas of Verdi, Vol. 2*. Cassell, p. 122.
93 *Ibid*, pp. 343–44.

disbelief. Contrary to Verdi's wishes, the role was given to Fanny Salvini-Donatelli,[94] who was short, well-upholstered and almost 40.[95] Photographs of the soprano from the 1860s attest to come-never features, but she was far from obese.[96] Body shaming was a new construct, born of 18th century colonialism, and formed as much by the corset as by the white supremacy flowing from the Greco-Roman ideals being promulgated through the contemporary mania for museum building.[97] While it was absurd for an audience to look to a proscenium arch for verisimilitude from actors required to speak through song, Verdi's aesthetic was rooted in his sensorial obsession with theatrical realism as it was being cultivated in France. He joined with his public in expecting a soprano to persuade by her appearance as a consumptive in service to an art that traded in fantasy. The composer's priorities were consistent where women were concerned. When casting the premiere of *Macbeth* in 1847, his first choice for Lady Macbeth was Eugenia Tadolini,[98] a soprano admired for her voice, magnetic stage presence and legendary beauty. She was adored by Donizetti, for whom she created the title roles in *Linda di Chamounix* and *Maria di Rohan*, Leonora in *La favorita* and Paolina in *Poliuto*; Giuseppina Strepponi called her "one of the greatest talents we possess."[99] Verdi cast her in 1845 as the title role in *Alzira*, but three years later he denied his preference for Tadolini as Lady Macbeth on the grounds that the singer and her voice were too beautiful. On 23 November, 1848, he wrote to his librettist, Salvadore Cammarano:

> In the interest of the performance, I think it necessary to observe that she has too great qualities for this part. It may seem absurd. Tadolini has a beautiful voice and a beautiful figure and I would like an ugly and wicked Lady. Tadolini sings perfectly and I would like Lady Macbeth not to sing at all. Tadolini has a wonderful voice, clear and powerful; and Lady Macbeth's voice must be diabolical![100]

His demon of choice was Marianna Barbieri-Nini[101] who earlier created the role of Lucrezia Contarini in *I due Foscari*;[102] it's unclear whether she was appreciated by Verdi for being ugly in voice and by appearance but the ramifications of her casting reflected unkindly on both. The audience at the first *La traviata* heckled Salvini-Donatelli during her terminal third Act, despite having cheered her at the

---

94 *née* Francesca Lucchi, *circa* 1815 – June, 1891.

95 The average life expectancy at the time was 32 – in part because of the ravages of TB.

96 She would have been dwarfed by Marietta Alboni, Montserrat Caballé, Alessandra Marc, Debra Voight, Jane Eaglen, Jessye Norman, Angela Meade and Jamie Barton. See Chapter 17.

97 The effect of colonialism on body-shaming is now well-established. See "Fat, Desire and Disgust in the Colonial Imagination." Forth, Christopher E. *History Workshop Journal*, No. 73, pp. 211–239. See Chapter 17.

98 *née* Savorani, 1809 – 11 July, 1872.

99 Ashbrook, William (1983). *Donizetti and His Operas*. Cambridge University Press, p. 641.

100 *I Copialettere di Giuseppe Verdi* (1913). Ed. Cesari, Gaetano and Luzio, Alessandro. Fronti. Letter 67, pp. 61–62.

101 18 February, 1818 – 27 November, 1887.

102 First performed on 3 November, 1844. She went on to create a third role for Verdi, Gulnara, in *Il Corsaro*, first performed on 25 October, 1848.

end of "*Sempre libera*."[103] When the doctor announced that Violetta had only hours to live, the audience responded with laughter, which encouraged a heckler to exclaim, "I see no consumption, only dropsy!"[104] The critic in La Gazzetta di Venezia held the following day that Salvini-Donatelli had sung with "an indescribable skill and perfection. She captivated the theatre."[105] On the other hand, Verdi concluded that "*La traviata ieri sera fiasco. La colpa è mia o dei cantanti?*"[106] His negative perception of the public reaction overstated the opera's failure; he was called out to acknowledge the audience's cheers after the Act I Prelude, and there were ten performances during the inaugural run. Most of the blame was attached to the baritone Felice Varesi (as Germont) and the tenor Lodovico Graziani (as Alfredo), whom Verdi denounced as "marmoreal."[107] Salvini-Donatelli's reputation was retrieved, insofar as she appeared in three further productions of *La Traviata*, in Istanbul (1856), Bologna (1857) and London (1858). The opera's quality was recognised fully in 1854, when Violetta was played by Maria Spezia, who was thirteen years younger and fifty pounds lighter than Salvini-Donatelli.

Violetta's music is remembered chiefly for her Act I showpiece, which is more *fioritura* than coloratura; the genius of Verdi's portrayal is in her transformation from being "*Sempre libera*," to the grim resignation of "*Addio, del passato bei sogni ridenti*."[108] This nostalgic folk-like aria remembers briefly the dramatic soprano of the second act, whose brutal self-sacrifice and rapid decline in health are punctuated by the arrival of a letter from Giorgio, informing her that Alfredo is returning. Knowing she has lost her battle with tuberculosis, Violetta bids farewell to her happiness, and to life. The contrast between the opening act's sparkling confidence and the final scene's blank reflection illustrate Violetta's physical decline and too-late moral dignity, while the symbolic use of a flower echoes the symbolism of sexual availability, signalling the restoration of Violetta's innocence.

During the 11 years to *Traviata*, Verdi composed 16 new operas. Over the ensuing 38 years (spanning *Les vêpres siciliennes* and *Falstaff*), he completed nine.[109] The composer's enormous income supported his aspirations as a gentleman farmer, and helped distract him from the business of being the world's wealthiest, most successful composer. In April, 1856, he wrote to Clarina Maffei:

> I'm not doing anything. I don't read. I don't write. I walk in the fields from morning to evening, trying to recover, so far without success, from the stomach trouble caused me by I vespri siciliani. Cursed operas![110]

---

103 'Always free.'
104 Slang term for oedema, with the primary symptoms being swelling, the build-up of fluid in the body's tissue.
105 *Teatri, arti e letteratura* (1854). Vol. 59, 1853–1854, Gov. della Volpe, p. 22.
106 'La traviata yesterday was a fiasco. Is the blame mine or the singers?'
107 Meaning 'like marble,' to indicate coldness. Warrack, John and West, Ewan (1992). *The Oxford Dictionary of Opera*. Oxford University Press, p. 299.
108 'Farewell, happy dreams of the past.'
109 Not including new editions / versions and revisions of existing works.
110 Walker, Frank (1962). *The Man Verdi*. Knopf, p. 218.

Two years later, Strepponi told the publisher Léon Escudier:

> His love for the country has become a mania, madness, rage, and fury – anything you like that is exaggerated. He gets up almost with the dawn, to go and examine the wheat, the maize, the vines, etc. Fortunately our tastes for this sort of life coincide, except in the matter of sunrise, which he likes to see up and dressed, and I from my bed.[111]

Verdi's commitment to Grand Opera, and the creation of exclusively spinto and dramatic roles coincided with protracted stays in St Petersburg – where *La forza del destino* was first performed on 10 November, 1862 – and Paris, where *Don Carlos* was premiered on 11 March, 1867. The composer chose not to travel to Cairo for the premiere of *Aida* on 24 December, 1871. Verdi was the first truly international composer, and he contributed more than anyone else to the creation of the international singer. His mature operas coincided with the emergence of European and American train networks, and the commercialisation of transatlantic passenger shipping. In 1838, the fastest crossing from Europe to the United States lasted 18 days and necessitated the stacking of coffins;[112] in 1863, the steamship *RMS Scotia* completed the journey in a week.[113] The first soprano to become a global celebrity created only a single role for Verdi, in London in 1847 – three years before she undertook the most extensive and financially successful tour of the USA in the country's history to that time.

Jenny Lind[114] was born in Sweden, where she began singing on stage as a 10-year-old child. She suffered the first of a number of vocal crises at the age of 12; six years later she triumphed as Agathe in a production of *Der Freischütz* at the Royal Swedish Opera. Within three years, her lack of formal training and too many performances caused her voice to fail again. She travelled in consequence to Paris in 1841, and two years' study with Manuel García; Meyerbeer arranged for her to audition (unsuccessfully) at the Opéra. When touring Denmark in 1843 she was wooed (unsuccessfully) by Hans Christian Andersen, who wrote that

> No book or personality whatever has exerted a more ennobling influence on me, as a poet, than Jenny Lind. For me she opened the sanctuary of art.

Meyerbeer arranged for Lind to sing the title role in *Norma* in Berlin in December, 1844, a production that brought her to the attention of Schumann, Berlioz and, most importantly, Mendelssohn, who wrote the soprano solo in *Elijah* for her.[115] It's possible that Lind and Mendelssohn's friendship became something more; shortly

---

111 *Ibid*, p. 219.
112 The paddle steamer SS Sirius, traveling from Cork to New York.
113 At the time of publication, the MS Queen Elizabeth crosses the Atlantic in seven days.
114 *née* Johanna Maria Lind, 6 October, 1820 – 2 November, 1887.
115 Lind was unavailable to sing the Birmingham premiere, for which the part was taken by the French soprano, Maria Caterina Rosalbina Caradori-Allan, who shared the stage with Malibran at her final performance.

before the composer's death in November, 1847,[116] Lind's husband from 1852, Otto Goldschmidt, is said to have destroyed a letter from Felix to Jenny in which he declared his love and threatened suicide if she refused to elope with him to the United States. Lind's perception was that: "he was the only person who brought fulfilment to my spirit, and almost as soon as I found him I lost him again." Mendelssohn later summarised her appeal as a singer when writing that

> Lind has fairly enchanted me [...] her song with two concertante flutes is perhaps the most incredible feat in the way of bravura singing that can possibly be heard."[117]

Lind was a true coloratura, a singer for whom acrobatics mattered more than drama. Her repertoire included the now-established roles in Mozart (in which Henry Chorley considered her without rival) as well as the title roles in *Lucia di Lammermoor, Maria di Rohan, Norma, La sonnambula* and *La vestale*, Adina in *L'elisir d'amore* and Alice in *Robert le diable*. She had a "sparkling" technique, and could tip-toe through any amount of frippery, whether or not it was welcomed by the music. Chorley described her voice as having

> two octaves in compass [from D3 to D5] – a higher possible note or two, available on rare occasions; and that the lower half of the register and the upper one were of two distinct qualities. The former was not strong – veiled, if not husky; and apt to be out of tune. The latter was rich, brilliant and powerful – finest in its highest portions.

Chorley also praised her breath control, her *mezza voce*, her discretion when using ornaments and her absent *passaggio*. He judged her "effects on the stage" to be "over-calculated," and questioned whether her singing in languages she didn't know limited her ability to find appropriate expression. In London, Lind became known as the "Swedish Nightingale," after Hans Christian Andersen's *The Nightingale*, written as a tribute to the soprano in 1843.[118] This affectionate soubriquet was earned as much by her generosity as by her singing, and she gave selflessly of her time and money to a host of charitable enterprises. The British people came to regard her as a saint, and it was Lind's status that persuaded Verdi to present the first staging of *I Masnadieri* in London, at Her Majesty's Theatre. The composer left Italy for rehearsals at the end of May, 1847, arriving in England on 5 June, with the orchestration incomplete. Three weeks earlier, on 4 May, 1847, Lind made her debut at Her Majesty's as Alice, in an Italian-language staging of *Robert le diable*. She gave sixteen performances – each attended by Queen Victoria. Following the first night, *The Times* held:

---

116   Lind was devastated by Mendelssohn's death at the age of 38. When finally she was able to sing the soprano part, she gave a series of performances at Exeter Hall in London in 1848. The £1,000 raised was committed to a scholarship in the composer's name. The first recipient was Arthur Sullivan.

117   From Act III of Meyerbeer's *Ein Feldlager in Schlesien* ('The Camp of Silesia'). The role of Vielka was written for Lind, but first performed by Leopoldine Tuczek.

118   The author fell in love with Lind, but she did not reciprocate his feelings. It is believed he based *The Snow Queen* (1844) on her in consequence.

> We have had frequent experience of the excitement appertaining to "first nights," but we may safely say, and our opinion will be backed by several hundreds of Her Majesty's subjects, that we never witnessed such a scene of enthusiasm as that displayed last night on the occasion of Mademoiselle Jenny Lind's début as Alice.

Verdi had not previously heard Lind perform, and he wanted to modify the score to suit her voice more exactly. When it was rumoured that Lind was unavailable, and disinclined to learn new repertoire, Verdi warned the theatre that he would withdraw his opera if anything was amiss. Everything proceeded to plan, and Verdi conducted the premiere on 22 July, 1847, with Queen Victoria, Prince Albert, the Duke of Wellington and hundreds of London's great and good in attendance. The work was well-received by the audience and the press; Chorley was alone in his lack of judgment when dismissing *I Masnadieri* as "the worst opera that has been given in our time at Her Majesty's Theatre." For good measure, he added "Verdi is finally rejected." Lind's talent for melismatic candy-floss was acknowledged by Verdi, who created "tinsel-like"[119] music for the soprano, some of it with *obligato* flute, after the fashion established by Meyerbeer.[120]

20 months later, Lind announced her permanent retirement from the operatic stage; she was 29-years-old. She gave her last performance, as Alice in *Robert le diable*, on 10 May, 1849. The Queen and numerous other members of the royal family joined in the acclamation. Soon after, and with Victoria's knowledge, Lind travelled incognito to Paris, believing she was to be married to the ailing Frederick Chopin. The letters he wrote in London in May, 1848, prove his admiration for Lind as an artist and his affection for her as a person; they do not declare love. Lind was not given to delusions, so Chopin must have caused her to believe that marriage was a possibility. During the second half of 1848, it emerged that the composer-pianist was unable to meet the cost of life in Paris, so Lind sent him £1,000; in July the following year, as Chopin's health was failing for the last time, she made an anonymous gift of 25,000 francs.[121] After his death three months later, on 17 October, 1849, Lind contributed generously to the creation of his monument at Père-Lachaise.

Neither Lind nor posterity has provided a clear or compelling explanation for why she left the stage when she did. Speculation is pointless; she didn't retire from singing but turned instead to the life of a touring concert artist – the most successful in the history of music to that date. In 1849, P. T. Barnum was looking for an act to tour, having achieved success travelling Europe with Charles Stratton ("General Tom Thumb") in 1845 and 1846. Despite having never heard Lind perform, her reputation for filling even the largest theatres persuaded Barnum to instruct the promoter John Wilton[122] to make Lind an offer. On 9 January, 1850, she agreed to perform 150

---

119 Budden, Julian (1978). *The Operas of Verdi, Vol. 2.* Cassell, p. 318.

120 Act I's "*Venerabile o padre.*" ('Venerable father').

121 Jorgensen, Cecilia and Jorgensen, Jens (2005). "Chopin and Jenny Lind New Research." Fryderyk Chopin Institute and Edinburgh University.

122 The following year, Wilton bought The Albion Saloon and turned it into a 'Magnificent New Music Hall.' This opened in 1859 as Wilton's Music Hall. The venue was at risk for many years, but it has since been restored. It survives as one of the hidden jewels of the British theatre scene (www.wiltons.org.uk).

concerts in the United States for $1,000 a night ($32,000 at the time of publication). Barnum committed $187,500 (approximately $6,107,000 in modern money) to the tour, which included the payment of Lind's fees in advance to Baring's, her bank in London. She left England from Liverpool, where she was cheered by thousands on both sides of the Mersey, with cannon salutes fired from the shore. Barnum engaged a critic to review her final concert, which focussed on the grief caused to the people of Liverpool by Lind's departure. One week before her arrival in New York, Barnum circulated the notice throughout America's newspapers, which helped ensure her celebrity before she arrived. A typical press release promised

> A visit from such a woman who regards her artistic powers as a gift from Heaven and who helps the afflicted and distressed will be a blessing to America.

Barnum couldn't see a button without pushing it, so Lind's abilities as a singer were represented as secondary to her value as a force for religious persuasion. As the embodiment of 1 Corinthians 13,[123] she was presented by Barnum in her programmes on the basis that "It is her intrinsic worth of heart and delicacy of mind that produces Jenny's vocal potency." Just as the United States was "God-given," so too was Jenny Lind. Barnum informed the *New York Herald*:

> If I knew I should not raise a farthing profit I would yet ratify the engagement, so anxious I am that the United States should be visited by a lady whose vocal powers have never been approached by any other human being, and whose character is charity, simplicity and goodness personified.

After her ship docked in New York on 1 September, 1850, the *New York Herald* reported

> the spectacle of some thirty or forty thousand persons congregated on all the adjacent piers. [...] From all quarters, crowds [...] could be seen hurrying down towards the Atlantic's dock [... spectators were] severely bruised, some came off with bloody noses, and two boys, about twelve years of age, appeared to be seriously injured. Had not the rush been checked in time, many lives would have been lost.

Lind was young, but well-versed in pleasing a crowd. As she stepped onto American soil, she kissed her hand to the "Stars and Stripes" and exclaimed, "There is the beautiful standard of freedom, which is worshipped by the oppressed of all nations." Had she sung like a branded pig, her fluffing of American sentimentality would have been sufficient compensation for audiences willing to pay a week's wages to hear her perform. For her part, Lind's discovery of America and the wealth of its richest people prompted her to renegotiate her contract. On 3 September, 1850,

---

123   'And now abideth faith, hope, charity, these three; but the greatest of these is charity.'

Barnum was cornered into giving her the agreed concert fee of $1,000, together with whatever was left of each concert's profits after Barnum had recovered his $5,500 management fee.[124] Whatever might have been achieved by Lind in matters of art was lost to matters of business long before she sang a note. Lind's programmes of arias and songs established the template for popular music as massed-public entertainment.[125] She pushed back only when Barnum's mercantile instincts threatened her brand, as occurred after he began to auction tickets for unhinged prices. Seats for her 13 concerts in New Orleans were in such demand that patrons were charged for admission to the auction.[126] Lind tolerated his auctioneering by persuading him to make a substantial number of tickets available at two dollars for the cheapest seats, and one dollar for the promenade. She was less disturbed by Barnum's pioneering use of merchandising, which extended to the soprano's name being attached to chapels, schools, a steam ship, a "Lind" bed, pies, bonnets, tobacco, alcoholic drinks, recipes and a host of books on singing, none of them authored or authorised by the singer. The February, 1851, edition of New York's *Water-Cure Journal*[127] characterised the Lind phenomenon on the basis that

> We have heard of Jenny Lind Candy, Jenny Lind Steamboats, Jenny Lind horses and cattle, and Jenny Lind Soup, but we never before heard of Jenny Lind Cod-Liver Oil, which we find advertised in the newspapers; said to be good for the tick-dolor-o [sic].[128]

In Joyce's *Ulysses*, Bloom sits in the Ormond bar listening to a tenor sing; his mind wanders to Jenny Lind, whose name was attached to a bland but apparently wholesome soup:

> Glorious tone he has still. Cork air softer also their brogue. Silly man! Could have made oceans of money. Singing wrong words. Wore out his wife: now sings. But hard to tell. Only the two themselves. If he doesn't break down. Keep a trot for the avenue. His hands and feet sing too. Drink. Nerves overstrung. Must be abstemious to sing. Jenny Lind soup:

---

124   In modern money, Barnum earned $176,000 for each concert. When he and Lind parted company, Barnum had earned more than $1m ($32m) for himself.

125   Concerts began at eight o'clock with selections by the orchestra of thirty-five, conducted initially by Julius Benedict and later on by Lind's composer-husband, Otto Goldschmidt. Overtures by Auber and Mendelssohn were especially popular. The baritone, Giovanni Battista Belletti, then appeared as the warm-up; after his two or three numbers, he would leave the stage and return escorting Lind onto stage. There followed between five and seven solos, which ran the gamut from Handel ("I know that my Redeemer liveth" from *Messiah*) to Meyerbeer, by way of Mozart, Rossini and Bellini (famously "*Come per me sereno*," from *La sonnambula* and "Casta diva" from *Norma*). She would finish most concerts with a Swedish folk-tune, the "Herdsman's Song," sung in her mother tongue.

126   One ticket sold for £650 ($21,000).

127   The Journal employed a fantastically ambitious subtitle: "Physiology, Hydropathy, and the Laws of Life," p. 50.

128   A phonetic spelling for "Tic douloureux," a short-hand for trigeminal neuralgia, a severe, stabbing pain to one side of the face, stemming from one or more branches of the nerve that supplies sensation to the face, the trigeminal nerve.

stock, sage, raw eggs, half pint of cream. For creamy dreamy. Tenderness it welled: slow, swelling, full it throbbed. That's the chat. Ha, give! Take! Throb, a throb, a pulsing proud erect. Words? Music? No: it's what's behind. Bloom looped, unlooped, noded, dismoded.

Joyce took his inspiration from *Mrs Beeton's Book of Household Management*, first published in 1861, in which the dish was described as *"Soup à la Cantatrice* (Professional Singer's Soup),"

> the principal ingredients of which, sago and eggs, have always been deemed very beneficial to the chest and throat. In various quantities, and in different proportions, they have been partaken of by the principal singers of the day, including the celebrated Swedish Nightingale, Jenny Lind […] with considerable advantage to the voice, in singing.

Mrs Beeton adapted what had been introduced to England and America as "Mademoiselle Jenny Lind's soup," by Eliza Acton in her 1855 book *Modern Cookery, for Private Families*. The dish and the singer formed the basis of a popular joke at the time: why would Jenny Lind make good soup? Because she's neither Alboni[129] [all bony] nor Grisi [greasy]. The reference to Giulia Grisi was especially topical, being that she toured the United States with her husband, Mario, two years after Lind's return to Europe. They did so as celebrities, adopting many of the tricks and gimmicks coined by Barnum and Lind.

A year in Barnum's company was sufficient for Lind. After 12 months of concerts, she ended her agreement with Barnum and continued to tour using her own team. "Lindomania" made its way to Canada and, even, to Cuba.[130] In 1850, while singing in Boston, she was engaged to perform in the auditorium above the Fitchburg Railroad Depot. The building was topped by two, seventy-foot towers. Because the concert was oversubscribed, fans began to push against the gates, threatening a riot; Lind is reported to have prevented the loss of life by climbing the tower and singing to those without seats. She did nothing of the sort, of course, but the story gained momentum after the tower was bought by "a fan," and relocated to Cape Cod.

Much has been written of Lind's voice; it's clear she must have been something remarkable for the likes of Chopin, Berlioz, Mendelssohn, Meyerbeer and Verdi to agree on anything. She was not a dramatist to accord with Verdi's expectations, and her gift was better aligned with vocal projection and effect, summarised by a critic in Nashville, Tennessee:

> The extreme burst of her voice in the upper portion of its register is far beyond the ordinary range of sopranos, and she has acquired the power of moulding the higher notes entirely at her will. By this she is enabled to produce some of the most astonishing effects upon the listener […].

---

129 A reference to Marietta Alboni.
130 Lind sang at the Teatro Tacón, which opened in Havana, in 1838. The auditorium contained 2,750 seats. So good were the acoustics, that the hall was preserved when the theatre was rebuilt in 1914.

> Another of the more special beauties which particularly mark the voice of Mlle Lind is the unexampled quality and delicacy of its piano [...]. The transition from the high to the low notes is rapidly effected and seems as though it cost her no effort.

Like every great singer, Lind made it look easy; her facility tied her to the contemporary notion of genius being divine when divested of the grit and tar attached by most to the common construction of graft as proletarian. Lind's talents were perceived and promoted in the United States as an ectoplasmic manifestation of the Holy Spirit, with thousands of preachers and Churches identifying her gifts as an expression of God's love. This was because she was generous to everyone except P. T. Barnum. From the 1830s, natural and social scientists had attempted to identify the conditions necessary and appropriate for the cultivation of genius. This required the definition of attributes sufficient to quantify and compare as between individuals across different classes of endeavour. For the United States, this process fed religious belief on the basis that faith promised to bring a subscriber closer to attainment, just as it had protected martyrs from the agonies of burning. Of course, most of those who spoke of Lind's talents as being "of Heaven," were subscribing to superstition or a romantic sentimentality that sought to present women as de-sexualised alternatives to the sophistry of Catholic mother-worship. Lind lived up to her side of her bargain by appearing (and behaving) as a doll; she caused no offence, provoked no unease, and generated no scandal. She was the Everywoman for a society inured to female independence and emancipation. Before genius became a myth and an ideological relic, it was worshipped in secular temples by people standing and cheering rather than bowing and praying; if the setting was different then the circumstances were the same, with Americans unable to divest genius of its deist origins. If He created Eve then He was no less responsible for the nightingale and, by construction, Jenny Lind. Harold Bloom posited geniuses as Kabbalistic representations of God:[131]

> We need genius, however envious or uncomfortable it makes many among us [...] Our desire for the transcendental and the extraordinary seems part of our common heritage, and abandons us slowly, and never completely.[132]

In July, 1851, the 20-year-old American poet, Emily Dickinson, recorded of a Lind concert that the

> bouquets fell in showers, and the roof was rent with applause – how it thundered outside, and inside with the thunder of God and of men – judge ye which was the loudest."[133]

---

131 It's worth stating the obvious. As a literary critic, Bloom's book deals *only* with writers and the craft of writing. The title and subtitle are extremely misleading, therefore, since the individuals on whom he settles his gaze are "exemplary" only insofar as they relate to genius manifested through word-use.

132 Bloom, Harold (2002). *Genius: A Mosaic of One Hundred Exemplary Creative Minds*. Grand Central Publishing, p. 7.

133 Buckingham, Willis J. (1989). Emily Dickinson's Reception in the 1890s: A Documentary History.

Barnum knew more of Man than of God; he is remembered appropriately for his axiom "nobody lost a dollar by underestimating the taste of the American public," a truism that bound Lind to a legacy culture that included Joice Heth ("The 161-year-old Woman"), Myrtle Corbin ("The Four-Legged Girl"), William Henry Johnson ("Zip, The Pinhead"), Prince Randian ("The Living Torso"), and Isaac W. Sprague ("The Human Skeleton"). Lind was a circus "freak" of a new kind and variety, an act that was decent, inoffensive and improving, even, of the moral good. Inside and outside America's infection of churches, Lind personified of all that was right with the world; she set the mould for every subsequent progenitor of saccharine female respectability, including Doris Day, Celine Dion, and Idina Menzel.[134] Lind's actual successor is probably Dolly Parton, a performer whose reputation survived untarnished for more than half a century, and whose philanthropy over the years was of such a scale that the founder of Amazon, Jeff Bezos, honoured her in 2022 with a "Courage and Civility" award, presenting her with $100m to dispense in accordance with her existing programmes and projects.

Lind's status as a moral icon was revived fifty years after her death by *A Lady's Morals*, a vehicle for "*The Tennessee Nightingale*," Grace Moore, who starred as Lind alongside Wallace Beery playing Barnum.[135] The film is fictitious although it trips when passing over a couple of facts, such as Lind losing her voice. The plot is otherwise detached from reality, with Lind falling in love with a composer, "Paul Brandt," who goes blind. Paul's uncle is none other than Manuel Garcia. The greatest of the film's crimes is the representation of Lind as incapable of performing "*Casta Diva*," the strain of which causes her to faint on stage. Produced pre-Code, it was possible for the studio to pitch *A Lady's Morals* as "scandalous," even if the only risky element was the unmarried Jenny and Paul being seen to share a suite (with several rooms) in a fully booked hotel during a snowstorm. A sample of the poster and advertising tag-lines include zingers such as "The heart-hunger, the soul-cravings of a woman in love have never been more powerfully depicted," (24 December, 1930); "The Untold Secrets of a Woman Called 'Too Moral' Exposed For The First Time!" (24 April, 1931); and "It's the romance the world has been waiting for! The immortal story of a celebrated beauty[136] who defied conventions[137] for the man she loved!" (27, January, 1931).

The film was designed by the studio to do for opera in the 1930s what Lind had done for it in the 1850s; to some extent it succeeded, using the same tactics employed by Barnum. Establishing an irritating trope that filtered throughout every subsequent film in which Lind made an appearance, *A Lady's Morals* portrayed the soprano singing music she didn't know, and could never have sung. Other than the "*Rataplan*"

University of Pittsburgh Press, p. 432. Dickinson was all but quoting from Byron's *Child Harolde's Pilgrimage*.

134   30 May, 1971 – . Menzel created the role of Elsa in *Frozen* (2013), Disney's cartoon adaptation of Andersen's *The Snow Queen*.

135   Beery would play Barnum again four years later in *The Mighty Barnum* (1934), with Virginia Bruce playing Jenny Lind.

136   Lind was never a "beauty," celebrated or otherwise. As much is obvious from the many photographs taken of her while she continued to perform.

137   The only convention defied by Lind was being wildly generous with her earnings.

from *La fille du regiment*, and a truncated "*Casta Diva*," Moore's repertoire was written by the operetta composer, Oscar Straus, who did his best when setting Clifford Grey's doggerel verse. More important than authenticity for the studio was the use of lingering shots of a mixed-class theatre audience, which demonstrated how opera was available to everyone, and not merely the wealthy elite.

A decade later, Ilse Werner served a different philosophy as Lind for the Nazi propaganda biography, *The Swedish Nightingale*. Despite being born in Indonesia, to Dutch parents, Werner was adopted by the Nazis as the Third Reich's poster-girl after triumphing in her stage debut in Vienna in 1937.[138] She went on to star in a series of Goebbels-approved movies, embodying the idealised Aryan-German heroine, notably in *Die unruhigen Mädchen*,[139] and *Wunschkonzert*.[140] Lind also proved inspirational for Elvis Costello, whom the Royal Danish Opera commissioned to write *The Secret Songs*, a chamber opera narrating the relationship between Hans Christian Andersen, Lind and Barnum. The project was scaled back, and Costello completed just ten songs, which were premiered in Denmark in October, 2005, with Costello singing the roles of Andersen and Barnum, and Gisela Stille appearing as Lind.

The most recent abuse of Lind was released into the wild in 2017 as *The Greatest Showman*. One of the most awful films of its kind ever made, it paints a grotesquely dishonest portrait of Lind as a glamorous woman infatuated with Barnum – who was, in his actual appearance, the last man to inspire lust.[141] When he doesn't reciprocate her desire she quits his circus, having kissed him on stage to feed rumours of a romance. *The Greatest Showman* is a near-perfect tribute to the gruesome, malformed ethics of Phineas T. Barnum, insofar as it paints him as everything he wasn't – a catalogue of fantastical virtues that encompasses physical beauty, an ethical and emotional concern for the human beings he paraded as "freaks," and an interest in anything other than money. It is no less a work of propaganda than anything overseen by Goebbels in its romanticising of the uniquely American apprehension of "entertainment" as an end worth achieving by any means. The film's original songs includes Lind's presumably ironic "Never Enough," bellowed out by Loren Allred[142] without anyone being expected to question whether a woman introduced by the writers as "Europe's most famous opera singer"[143] should walk onto stage and hammer out a show-tune with all the grace and sophistication of a butcher's bin. The film grossed nearly $500m worldwide. Barnum will not have shifted an inch in his grave.

Lind's international celebrity did no harm to the dissemination of opera as a universal art, and she did more than anyone else to 1852 to cement the status of the soprano as an accessible and relatable icon. Numerous other of Verdi's female singers toured the United States in Lind's commercially temperate wake, including Marietta

---

138   In *Glück* ('Happiness.')

139   'The Restless Girls' (1938).

140   'Request Concert' (1940).

141   In the film, he is portrayed with one-dimensional gusto by Hugh Jackman.

142   Allred sang the music, but the role of Lind was played by the gifted Swedish actress, Rebecca Ferguson, who was alone in surviving the film's assault on taste, judgment and truth.

143   The script was written without reference even to an encyclopedia, as is evidenced by the idiotic comment by one character that Lind had triumphed at the Paris Opéra.

Gazzaniga, who traded heavily on her cachet as the first Gilda.[144] If America was important to the pursuit of prestige and reputation then it wasn't essential; the soprano Marie Constance Sasse, for emaple,[145] never left Europe, but she was one of the first to ride the ubiquity of "Lindomania" during the 1850s. More than any of her peers, she filled the vacuum created by the absent Lind for the Paris Opéra, and she did so by originating important roles from across the geographical operatic world. Her collaborations with the leading French, Italian, German and Brazilian composers of the day did not make her a household name, like Lind, but her contribution to the history of opera was no less important as the creator of Eurydice in Berlioz's rescoring of *Orfeo ed Euridice*, Sélika in Meyerbeer's *L'Africaine*, Elisabeth de Valois in Verdi's *Don Carlos*, Cecilia in Carlos Gomes' *Il Guarany* and Elisabeth at the Paris premiere of Wagner's *Tannhäuser*. Like the Polish tenor Jean de Reszke, Sasse was the first to straddle contemporary Italian, French and German repertoire as a "European" artist. It was fitting, perhaps, that she should have been born and raised in Belgium.

Sasse began her career singing in cafés. During a performance at the *du Géant* in Paris, in her late 20s, she was heard by Delphine Ugalde,[146] one of the city's leading prima donnas. Although just five years older than Sasse, Ugalde offered to teach without charge. In 1858, Ugalde introduced Sasse to Léon Carvalho, director of the Théâtre Lyrique, where Sasse made her debut as "Marie Sax" on 27 September, 1859.[147] She was 30 at the time – a year older than Lind at her retirement. One reviewer acknowledged Sasse's

> magnificent voice, but both as a vocalist and as an actress, she is in the state of raw material – material however of undeniable quality and extraordinary aptitude, and which will undoubtedly reward the discoverer. [...] It is fortunate that Mlle Sax's talents were discovered at an early stage as her voice is still fresh, and she has not been long enough in the exercise of her calling to form any vicious habits. Everything is, therefore, in her favour, and, launched in her present school, time and experience will ere long render her a valuable acquisition to the lyrical stage.

Sasse created her first original role for Berlioz. She was not his preference as Eurydice for his arrangement of *Orphée*,[148] and when he heard that Carvalho wanted "a café chantant [from] the other Champs-Elysées," the composer responded with characteristic wit that the intendant's "good intentions" would "pave the way to hell."[149] Sasse's inexperience collided with the composer's cynicism; Berlioz and his assistant, Camille

---

144   During her first tour, in 1857, her husband died of smallpox on the boat to Havana. The risks attaching to international travel did nothing to dissuade her, and she continued touring the Americas annually until 1870.

145   26 January, 1834 – 8 November, 1907. References to the singer as "Sasse" are constant because she used "Sax" and "Saxe" inconsistently.

146   *née* Élisabeth Gabrielle Pauline Amène Alida Ugalde, 3 December, 1829 – 19 July, 1910.

147   As the Countess in *Le nozze di Figaro*.

148   First performed on 18 November, 1859.

149   Cairns, David (2000). *Berlioz: Servitude and Greatness (1832 – 1869)*. Vol. 2. University of California Press, p. 639.

Saint-Saëns, coached her personally over many weeks, in the company of Pauline Viardot, who was cast as Orphée. During rehearsals Berlioz denounced Sasse as "ignorant as a carp."[150] Viardot was more generous, allowing that she had "a beautiful voice [albeit] without art."[151] The composer's assessment was supported by a popular anecdote. Sasse was standing next to Viardot, watching Berlioz rush around the stage, fussing over every last detail. She leaned towards Viardot and asked "That's Monsieur Gluck, isn't it?" Viardot replied "No, it's one of his friends." Outraged by the presumption, Sasse exclaimed, "Well, he's got a nerve – and in Gluck's absence!"[152]

Sasse's next role placed her in direct competition with Paris' leading prima donna, Marie Caroline Miolan-Carvalho.[153] Having trained at the Conservatoire with Gilbert Duprez, Miolan-Carvalho was Sasse's positive integer – having an iron-clad technique, a world-class education, and the most powerful man in French opera as a husband. Just four years after winning first prize at the Conservatoire, Miolan-Carvalho made her stage debut in Brest, as Isabelle in *Robert le Diable*, a production that led to her being summoned to Paris, where she began a relationship with Carvalho. They married in 1853, at which point she was allowed the pick of each every new role at the Théâtre Lyrique. She created 16 of them, including Marguerite in Gounod's *Faust*,[154] the title role in *Mireille* (1864) and Juliette in *Roméo et Juliette*. She was fundamental to Gounod's perpetuation of the art of coloratura in France, and each of the five roles he wrote for her takes full advantage of her ability to dance without effort on the head of a pin. The most extravagant example of her virtuosity was added by Victor Massé to the title role of *La Reine Topaze*, first staged in 1856, in which Miolan-Carvalho was required to sing a set of variations based on the "Carnival of Venice," a Neapolitan folk song made famous by Niccolò Paganini, whose treatment of the tune was published as his Op.10.[155] On 18 February, 1860, Miolan-Carvalho sang Baucis in the first performance of Gounod's *Philémon et Baucis*. The smaller role of Bacchante was played by Marie Sasse – who had, by this stage, taken to using the name "Sax."[156] The differences between their voices are obvious from Gounod's music; Miolan-Carvalho's brilliantine tone and meticulous coloratura resonate throughout Baucis' Act III recitative and aria "*Ah! pauvre Philémon* [...] *Ô riante nature.*"[157] This rarely heard showpiece for soprano and solo flute is lengthy and demanding; it requires extreme flexibility and access through the clouds to a D6. The waltzing rhythms evoke the coquetry of a young woman relishing the punishment of her husband for having mistaken his wife for someone else. On the other hand, Bacchante's Act II aria "*Debout! Place au choeur de Bacchantes*,"[158] is declamatory

---

150   *Ibid*, p. 638.
151   *Ibid*.
152   Despite the tension, the first night was a famous success, and the house remained packed for each of the initial run of 138 performances. The choreography was designed by Tchaikovsky's ballet master, Lucien Petipa. The timpanist was a 17-year-old student at the Paris Conservatoire called Jules Massenet.
153   *née* Marie Caroline Miolan-Carvalho, 31 December, 1827 – 10 July, 1895.
154   First performed on 19 March, 1859.
155   See, generally, Parr, Sean M. (2012). "Caroline Carvalho and nineteenth-century coloratura." In *Cambridge Opera Journal*, pp. 83–117.
156   She was sued in 1865 by Adolphe Sax, in consequence of which she added the letter 'e' to her name.
157   'Ah! poor Philemon [...] O laughing nature!'
158   'Be upstanding! Your places in the Bacchante choir!'

and written low, with neither coloratura nor bel canto in evidence. The orchestral accompaniment is busy, and the context is noisier still, with a large chorus adding to the need for the soloist to project.

Philémon et Baucis was a failure, and Carvalho pulled it after 13 performances. Sasse relocated shortly after to the Paris Opéra, where she made her debut as Alice, in *Robert le Diable*, on 3 August, 1860. She was chosen by Wagner to create the role of Elisabeth in what would become the notorious "Paris" *Tannhäuser*. Sasse collaborated with Wagner on the production, for which there were 164 rehearsals. The premiere at the Salle Le Peletier on 13 March, 1861, was well-received initially, but the second act provoked whistling and shouting; by the end of Act III the singers were defeated by the chorus of disapproval from the auditorium. The second performance was noisier still, and Wagner chose not to attend the third performance, on 24 March. The uproar as it was reported caused him to withdrew the opera; for all that had gone wrong, he was pleased with Sasse's performance, as evidenced by his gift of a copy of the score inscribed "*A ma courageuse amie, Mademoiselle Marie Saxe. L'Auteur – Richard Wagner.*"[159] Sasse had a trumpet of a voice, and her part in the controversy was subsumed to her success in more popular spinto and dramatic repertoire, which included the first production of *L'Africaine* in 1865.[160] She worked with Meyerbeer for three months during pre-rehearsals, which concluded only shortly before his death on 2 May, 1864. The posthumous premiere on 28 April, 1865, was one of the highlights of Sasse's career. The presence of Emperor Napoleon III and Empress Eugénie, "provided Second Empire society with its most exalted self-presentation in terms of an opera premiere."[161] Sasse sang dozens of performances as Sélika, which received its 100th performance at the Salle Le Peletier on 9 March, 1866 – less than a year after the premiere. She was in demand also as Léonore in Verdi's French version of *Il trovatore* (*Le trouvère*), a role that was created on 12 January, 1857, by another of Sasse's Belgian rivals at the Opéra, Pauline Guéymard-Lauters.[162] In September, 1863, Verdi sought to revive the fortunes of *Les vêpres siciliennes* in Paris. Sasse was his first choice as Helène and, like Wagner, he coached her personally. Sasse's memoirs ("*Souvenir d'une Artiste*"[163]) provide a valuable account of what it was like to work with Verdi:

> I have always loved working with authors and composers listening to their instructions trying to grasp their meaning [...] Ah, but it was not the same as singing to Wagner or Meyerbeer! They were always patient,

---

159   'To my courageous friend, Mademoiselle Marie Saxe. The Author – Richard Wagner.'

160   Meyerbeer composed the role of Sélika for Sasse.

161   Letellier, Robert Ignatius (2008). *An Introduction to the Dramatic Works of Giacomo Meyerbeer: Operas, Ballets, Cantatas, Plays*. Ashgate, p. 172.

162   *née* Pauline Lauters, 1 December, 1834 – 10 May, 1918. Her second marriage was to the tenor Louis Guéymard (in 1858), who sang the first Manrico on 12 January, 1857. They divorced ten years later – 60 years prior to her death shortly before the end of the World War I. *Don Carlos* was performed only months before the premiere of Ambroise Thomas' *Hamlet* – for which Guéymard-Lauters created the role of Gertrude. It would be difficult to imagine more different approaches to writing for the female voice, and for the theatre more generally.

163   Published in 1902.

most careful to in no way hurt the feelings of an artiste. How different Verdi! He was exigeant [sic] hard, at times, I say it, almost cruel. Sharp words escaped him, and many times I have cried at the end of one of these hearings. Then the master, having cooled down would apologize for his roughness, speak kind words of encouragement, and we would begin all over again with enthusiasm. These lessons were of inestimable value to me, and, thanks to Verdi's counsel, my voice, still somewhat rough, became most flexible, and as a result of his teachings I achieved one of the greatest successes of my career.[164]

When interviewed by W. E. Haslam, Sasse recalled Verdi's obduracy where alterations to his music were concerned. She claimed to have petitioned the composer to make some changes to the role of Aida, the tessitura of which was too high for her voice:

As she was compelled by her contract to sing the opera, she asked Verdi to make some slight changes to bring the music within her reach. But he refused absolutely to make the least alteration. The slight modifications, or *pointages*, asked from Verdi, were not, I was assured by Madame Saxe, of a character to alter either the rôle or the opera, and she remarked (I quote her own words): "Why should Verdi have shown himself more unreasonable or less yielding than Meyerbeer or Wagner?" (*plus intransigeant, plus intraitable que* Meyerbeer *ou* Wagner?).

Whatever the limits of Sasse's *tessitura* after 1871, Verdi had Sasse's voice in mind when writing Elisabeth de Valois in *Don Carlos* in 1866; he conceived the role of Princesse Eboli for the contralto Rosine Bloch,[165] but was persuaded to adapt and transpose the part for Pauline Guéymard-Lauters – an older singer, with a higher voice. *Don Carlos* is Verdi's longest opera, at around 4 hours. The two principle female roles are his most thrilling dramatically, and Eboli, in particular, is arduous, occupying as it does a hideously compromised *tessitura*. Elisabeth's music is taxing for a spinto soprano, with extended duets, some of which entail a significant amount of writing in unison with the tenor playing Don Carlos.[166] Considering the complicated nature of Elisabeth's love affair with Carlos (she is married to his father), it is not surprising that much of her music is coloured by melancholy; her Act II aria, "*Oh ma chère compagne*,"[167] is especially bleak. The fifth and final act opens with a terrifying

---

164   Visetti, Albert (1905). *Verdi*. George Bell, pp. 48–49.

165   7 November, 1844 – 1 February, 1891. Bloch played Amneris in the Opéra's first production of *Aida* on 22 March, 1880 – following which she retired from the Opéra, aged only 36. The soprano Teresa Stolz attended the dress rehearsal for *Aida*, in the company of Giuseppina Strepponi. She described Bloch as "a most beautiful Amneris: she may not be an 'eagle,' but in any case, she is much better than our two Milan Amnerises (of this year)." She delayed marriage until 14 May, 1884, when her career was winding down. On 31 October, 1890, she sang Dalila at the Paris premiere of Saint-Saëns' *Samson et Dalila*.

166   For example, Act I's "*De quels transports poignants et doux*" ('What touching and sweet transports.'). This appears in the Italian version as "*Di quale amor, di quanto ardor.*" ('Of what love, of what ardour.').

167   'O my dear companion.' The Italian translation is sung as '*Non pianger, mia compagna.*" ('Don't cry my friend.').

orchestral prelude that makes wildly atmospheric use of themes rehearsed throughout the previous acts; it sets the scene for Elisabeth's appearance on stage alone, although few modern productions adhere to the direction that requires her to be kneeling before the tomb of Charles V. Elisabeth sings "*Toi qui sus le néant,*"[168] a vast, vocally exhausting aria lasting 12 minutes, in which she longs for death ("*Porte en pleurant mes pleurs aux pieds de l'Éternel!* [...] *Pour moi, ma tâche est faite, et mon jour est fini!*"),[169] before entering into another lengthy duet with Carlos. This staggering episode makes unreasonable demands of a soprano, imposing bipolar extremes of register, antipodal dynamics, and a juxtaposition of declamatory and legato singing that has to account for the character's emotional divergences between longing, reverence and resignation, Verdi's preferred emotion for his imagined women. Verdi's invention is ruthless in its adherence to syllabic word-setting and the complete disavowal of coloratura and *fioritura* of any kind. Whoever plays Elisabeth has nothing behind which to hide vocally; singers were now required to act, whether they liked it or not. They had also to be heard, and Verdi's orchestra,[170] and his writing for it, called for something more than a spinto.

It appears that Sasse met the challenge, even if photos of the soprano in costume suggest a mother more than a lover. The critical view was generally approving, with the worst that anyone had to say pivoting on her portrayal being "bored" and "listless." They might have added "exhausted," given that Sasse's long-running divorce was public knowledge at the time. Verdi loathed the speed with which everything moved at the Opéra,[171] and he came to dislike Sasse for reasons unconnected with her art. She was said to be unpleasant to her colleagues, a character flaw abjured by Verdi despite his own reputation for Caesarean irritability. More successful was Pauline Guéymard-Lauters, who scaled the fearsome obstacles presented by Eboli. Of the character's three major scenes, the most important – and one of the highlights in the entire mezzo-soprano canon – occurs in Act IV[172] when Eboli sings her revenge aria, "*O don fatal et détesté,*" in which she curses her pride and beauty,[173] while resolving to save Carlos from the Inquisition. This sensational episode calls for a voice of epic proportions, capable of overcoming a brass and percussion-heavy orchestra, violent accents and a range extending from B3 to B5 (written as a C flat). Verdi's genius was never more transparent than in this astonishing portrait of Eboli's complex of evolving emotions. He characterised her desperation in harsh, angry writing for the orchestra that anticipates Eboli's turmoil. Her first three notes (for "*O don fa*[tal]")

168 'You who know the emptiness.' The Italian translation is almost proximate: "*Tu che le vanità conosce.*" ('You who know only vanity.').

169 'Bear my tears at the feet of eternity [...] For me, my task is done, and my day is done!'

170 The score calls for a piccolo, three flutes, two oboes, a cor anglais, two clarinets, four bassoons, a contrabassoon, four horns, two cornets, two trumpets, three trombones, an ophicleide, timpani, a bass drum, a triangle, bells, cannon, tambourine, castanets, a harp and a harmonium.

171 Rehearsals dragged on for almost a year.

172 Relocated as the finale of Act III in the 1886 Italian edition.

173 It is unfortunate and probably inevitable that many of the mezzos and contraltos to have sung the role of Eboli have struggled to persuade when singing "*O don fatale et détesté present du ciel en sa colère! Tois qui rends la femme si fière, je te maudis, ô ma beauté!*" ('O fatal and detested gift from heaven in its wrath! You who make woman so proud, I curse you, oh my beauty!'). As photos of Guéymard-Lauters in costume demonstrate, she had a head like a cannon ball, and was objectively unattractive.

are written by Verdi in equivalence, as semi-quavers,[174] with the emphasis placed with dramatic purpose on "[fa]*tal*" by the use of crotchets, the second of which is dotted, generating the clearest articulation of spitting rage. The second cluster repeats the rhythm but narrows the intervals for "*et détesté,*" adding navigable malice to the singer's sentiments. For the word "*colère,*" Verdi has Eboli sing a brutal rising ninth from an E flat 3 to an F flat 4, cultivating tensions that are released only with her repetition of "*je te maudis,*" scored as a rising C flat – E flat – A flat motif that plateaus on an unresolved G flat – in anticipation of the motif's reappearance 12 bars later, when it's crowned by a blistering C flat 5 (marked with a fermata) from which Verdi has Eboli descend through two octaves to a C flat 3. The aria's B section is lachrymose, low-written, and heavy with regret; the atmosphere becomes maudlin as Eboli resolves to enter a monastery. Only after her thoughts turn to saving Carlos does she meet her own challenge, for which Verdi provides one of the most exciting conclusions to any aria in the history of opera. Having talked herself into believing she might yet be redeemed, Eboli sings, "*Un jour me reste! Ah! Je me sens renaître, béni soit ce jour, je le sauverai!*"[175] the last three words of which are repeated in an ecstatic cadence, her voice rising in unison with trumpets, that compels a soprano to take on the entire orchestra, punctuated by blaring brass and hammered percussion.[176]

The only composer capable of outdoing this extraordinary climax was Verdi, who achieved something appropriately supernatural when resolving the opera's finale for the 1886 Italian edition. During the meeting between Elisabetta and Carlo at the convent of San Giusto, Filippo II and the Grand Inquisitor arrive, determined to kill them both for treason. A "monk" appears, takes hold of Carlo and drags him into the tomb of Carlo V – Filippo's father. As the King (a bass role) cries out "*Mio padre,*" bursting out 'father' as an F sharp above the stave, Elisabetta exclaims "*O ciel!*"[177] which Verdi scores as an F sharp semi-quaver, rising to a B, scored as a semi-breve. She has to wrestle with the entire orchestra, but only for four beats. On 22 April, 1972, Montserrat Caballé took issue with Verdi and his score during a now legendary performance at the Metropolitan Opera in New York, conducted by Francesco Molinari-Pradelli. Instead of holding the high B for four beats, she opted for 19 – sustaining the note for 15 seconds, until the work's penultimate bar. The audience cracked the plaster when reacting to this lunatic but undeniably entertaining episode.[178]

---

174 This opening phrase is mis-performed (and ruined) by just about everyone – with a fermata (or a dot) being added to the second syllable (a C flat 3, written as a quaver) for the word "*don.*"

175 'I have one day left! Ah! I feel reborn, blessed be this day, I will save him!'

176 Baltsa's performances as Eboli are, perhaps, unrivalled since the invention of recording. Her relationship with Karajan was especially creative; there are various live and studio recordings, all of them worth hearing. The performance recorded at the Vienna State Opera on 6 May, 1979, is among the most sensitive, with Baltsa more water than fire for a change. The cast features Mirella Freni as Elisabetta and Jose Carreras as Carlo, in one of his last appearances before the failure of his voice. Baltsa's "*O don fatale,*" from 1986, with Karajan at the end of his life and career, can be seen on film as well as on disc, and is worth tracking down.

177 'O heaven.'

178 The cast for this performance was legendary by any standards, and at any time: Cesare Siepi (Filippo II), Franco Corelli (Don Carlo), Montserrat Caballé (Elisabetta), Sherill Milnes (Rodrigo), Grace Bumbry (Eboli), John Macurdy (Il Grande Inquisitore), Paul Plishka (Un Frate), Frederica von Stade (Tebaldo), and

Verdi left Paris running for his train; he was slow to return to his desk in Busseto. He would not complete a new opera for another four years. In January and February, 1869, he oversaw the premiere at La Scala of a revised *La forza del destino*, featuring a new overture and a different ending. The role of Leonora was passed to a 34-year-old Bohemian soprano who had made her European debut in Turin just four years earlier. Teresa Stolz[179] was a dramatic soprano – one of the first in Italian opera; from 1865 she was a leading prima donna at La Scala, where her reputation as a Verdi specialist brought her to the professional and personal attentions of Angelo Mariani, a composer better known for his work as a conductor.[180] Mariani recommended Stolz to Verdi, who was seduced by her talent and beauty, although the latter attribute is difficult to judge 160 years later. Stolz was the first important soprano of the 19th century to be photographed more often than she was painted; despite many believing her to be beautiful, her physique bordered on the athletic, her facial features *puissant* to the point of being mannish.[181] Mariani and Verdi both fell in love with her. This created a *ménage à trois*, of which Strepponi was either accepting or ignorant. Verdi invited Stolz to create the role of Elisabetta in the revised version of *Don Carlo* in 1869, in Parma, and she was key to his reasoning when he accepted an offer of 150,000 francs from Isma'il Pasha, the Khedive of Egypt, to write *Aida* for the opening of the Khedivial Opera House. Verdi kept a suite at the Grand Hotel in Milan, minutes by foot from Stolz's home, and for a time the arrangement operated without incident – until Stolz accepted Mariani's proposal of marriage while refusing coincidentally to end her relationship with the composer. Mariani took his frustrations out on Verdi's music, a bourgeois assimilation of the cuckold, of which Verdi complained angrily in writing, "I had only just freed opera from the tyranny of the singer, and his interpretations substituted the tyranny of the conductor." Ever the pragmatist, he continued to rely upon Mariani as a conductor, even after their friendship came to an end.

Stolz was central to the turmoil, becoming a target for private and public censure. She survived her disgrace by focussing on work, which included leading roles in minor operas by Filippo Marchetti and Francesco Malipiero;[182] in 1871, Verdi had to decide on the cast for the premiere of *Aida* in Cairo. In April, Paul Draneht, the general manager of the Cairo Opera, invited Marie Sasse to create the role of Amneris. When this was brought to Verdi's attention, he wrote to the theatrical agent, Battista Lampugnani: "I have no use for her – either as Amneris, who is a mezzo-soprano, or as Aida, for other reasons." He was more direct when writing to Draneht:

Lucine Amara (Voce dal Cielo). The story goes that Corelli had more than once during the performance held onto high notes, in solo and ensemble, and that Caballé was making a point when holding onto her note for as long as she did. The Spanish soprano was known for her wit, so this is entirely plausible.

179   *née* Tereza Stolzová, 2 June, 1834 – 23 August, 1902.

180   Mariani conducted numerous Italian premieres of works by Meyerbeer (*L'Africaine*), Verdi (*Aroldo, the world premiere* on 16 August, 1857, *and Don Carlo, the* Italian premiere, on 27 October, 1867 at the Teatro Comunale di Bologna) and Wagner (*Lohengrin* and *Tannhäuser*).

181   In passing, it is necessary to emphasise the extent to which modern concepts of facial beauty have been transformed by the art and science of make-up. The use of makeup is now so sophisticated that women who would previously have been considered ugly without it, are the subject of television series fixating on their lives and families. Photography in the 19th century may be considered accurate, just as surely as it can now be appreciated as dishonest and misleading.

182   The grandfather of the better-known grandson, Gian Francesco Malipiero.

> I know from experience that it is in the interest of both the management
> and the composer to give her operas in which she is the only soprano,
> or at least an opera which has no other role equal or superior to hers.[183]

Verdi got his way, but none of those who travelled to Egypt for the premiere of *Aida*
on Christmas Eve, 1871, was booked for the first European production at La Scala six
weeks later. The role of Aida was created by Antonietta Pozzoni Anastasi,[184] another
soprano who traded on her consequent reputation when touring Europe and the
United States. Amneris was played by the mezzo-soprano, Eleonora Grossi,[185] who
had resided during the previous two years at the Royal Opera House in London. The
Egyptian premiere was an unqualified success, but Verdi did not attend; after learning
that the audience on the first night had consisted primarily of invited dignitaries,
politicians and critics, he discounted the value and relevance of the Cairo production.
He therefore considered the Italian première, at La Scala, to qualify as the work's first
performance.[186] He was happier also to teach the title role to Teresa Stolz, whose
performance he inevitably considered ideal.

The best evidence for what he was able to achieve when writing for Stolz's voice is
"*Ritorna vincitor*,"[187] from Act I. During the course of this turbulent, seven-minute
aria, Aida soliloquises on the conflicting emotions tearing her between her devotion
to her father, the Ethiopian King, Amonasro, and Radamès, an Egyptian General.
Incapable of deciding who's side she is on, the narrative sails bizarrely close to Verdi's
personal life: Radamès is loved also by Amneris, who tricks Aida into revealing the
truth of her affections by claiming falsely that he is dead. The aria begins with a short,
militaristic prelude using one of the opera's most prominent themes; Aida's opening
words are delivered in music written in the mezzo-soprano register. Beginning on an
A4, the first five syllables of "*Ritorna vinci*[tor]!" are scored as rising quavers, which
climax on "[vinci]*tor*," an F4 minim. The words that follow, "*E dal mio labbro usci
l'empia parola!*"[188] are spat out in a repeating F4, with the final syllable of "*parola*"
settling low in the chest, on an E4. It's a thrilling, wine-dark statement which Verdi
sustains through an ensuing parlando that veers between extremes of head and chest
registers, entailing dramatic octave descents (F sharp 4 to F sharp 3 for the word

---

183 Sasse outlived Verdi by six years, but she died in abject poverty, at the age of 73. She appears not
to have made an application to the *Casa di Risposo per Musicisti* ('Rest Home for Musicians'; also "*Casa
Verdi*"), which opened shortly after the composer's death in 1901. Casa Verdi was conceived, built and
paid for by Verdi as a home for retired opera singers and musicians. The building was designed in the
neo-Gothic style by Camillo Boito – the older brother of Arrigo Boito, the composer of *Mefistofele*, and
the librettist for Verdi's last two operas, *Otello* and *Falstaff*. Verdi and Strepponi are buried in a crypt at the
house. Verdi bequeathed the performing rights for all of his operas to the Casa di Risposo per Musicisti.
Gemma Bosini and Mariano Stabile who appeared in the very first performance of Verdi's final opera,
Falstaff.

184 1847 – 8 April, 1917.

185 1837 – 1879.

186 Led by "Verdi's conductor," Franco Faccio. He was also an early supporter of, and great help to,
Giacomo Puccini.

187 'May he return a victor!'

188 'And from my lips escapes the impious word!'

"*plauso,*"),[189] surging octave ascents (G3 to G4 for "*struggete*"[190]) and a heart-stopping B flat 4 for "*Ah*" that drops another octave to convey her unhappiness ("*sventurata*").[191] The ensuing shifts in dramatic intensity trigger Aida's recollection of her love for Radamès. The ebb and flow of the aria's final section resolves in a hymn-like prayer to the gods, as Aida achieves a hard-won measure of clarity; it ends with a sighing dialogue between the soprano and the orchestra's strings, putatively in A flat minor; as finally she whispers "*soffrir.*"[192] An ethereal major third brings resolution and closure to her emotional convulsion, alluding to the solace that Aida has drawn from her petition to the divine. "*Ritorna vincitor,*" is antithetical to everything for which the Italian bel canto tradition was celebrated, then and now. There are no long or languid melodies, little repetition, and no specialist technical requirements beyond diction, range and amplitude. The fierceness of the aria's opening, and much of what follows, is anything but beautiful; the mood is anxious, dislocating and ugly. Legato is a necessity, as always, but elegant phrasing cannot and is not meant to disguise Aida's turmoil as Verdi painted it. The composer of *Rigoletto* is absent; a soprano equipped to sing Gilda could never have performed Aida.

The nature of Stolz's affair with Verdi remains unclear; it is certain he committed to the staging of the Milanese premiere of *Aida* in 1872,[193] with Stolz in daily attendance; after Mariani's death from cancer in 1873 the Florentine newspaper *Il Pungolo* published the first of five articles revealing intimate details of Stolz's "immoral" relations. A set of leaked letters from Strepponi complicated matters, until they were proven to be forgeries; it all became too much for Strepponi, who presented her husband with an ultimatum:

> Let's get this be over. Be frank and say so, without making me suffer the humiliation of this excessive deference of yours […]. Think sometimes that I, your wife, despising past rumours, am living at the very moment à trois, and that I have the right to ask, if not for your caresses, at least for your consideration. Is that too much?[194]

Having written "Let's get this over," Strepponi added and erased the words "if you find this person so seductive."[195] Verdi clearly found her so, and threatened to commit suicide if Teresa left, but leave she did – while holding a lucrative contract for engagements in St. Petersburg. Conjecture has coloured Verdi's relationship with Stolz as well as Strepponi's attitude to the role played in their lives by the outsider. Conclusions flow naturally from events after Strepponi's died, at which point Stolz became Verdi's companion until his death on 27 January, 1901.[196] It's meaningful also that he retired from opera composition after the first productions in Italy of

---

189 'Applause.'
190 'Struggling.'
191 'Unhappy one.'
192 'Suffering.'
193 The commencement of the affair with Verdi is dated by Frank Walker to 1872.
194 Walker, Frank (1962). *The Man Verdi*. Knopf, p. 432.
195 *Ibid.*
196 Verdi died just five days after Queen Victoria.

Aida. By the time he returned to the theatre in 1887, for *Otello*, Stolz had retired also, having fourteen years earlier crowned her career when performing the soprano solo in the first performance of the Requiem, conducted by Verdi, in the Chiesa di San Marco, Milan.[197] The Requiem was dedicated by Verdi to Stolz, whom he described on the first page of the score as his *"interprete prima."*[198]

When Verdi returned to his desk for what many presumed to be his last opera he did so for Shakespeare. Boito's libretto for *Othello* adheres more closely to its source than di Salsa's text for Rossini while diminishing the play's racial themes in favour of a theological discourse that slid into the slipstream of almost a century's exploitation by opera composers of religion as a metaphor for social division. Religious dissonance is introduced during the opera's opening scene, when Otello identifies himself as the (presumably Christian) usurper of the Turkish navy: *"Esultate! L'orgoglio musulmano sepolto è in mar."*[199] In the words of James Parakilas:

> The authors saw to it that there was hardly anything in their opera to suggest a clash between racial stereotypes in the characters' behavior. Otello's dark skin remains as a visual marker of a difference between him and the other characters- especially between him and the fair Desdemona. But Verdi and Boito together took extraordinary care that their Otello not embody a savagery that would make him seem alien to audiences in Italy or the rest of Europe; rather, he was to embody the savagery that every man in those audiences might imagine himself capable of in Otello's circumstances.[200]

Verdi and Boito portrayed Otello with unprecedented sophistication; conversely, Desdemona and Iago are binary characters, painted in primary colours and reduced to almost satirical extremes of good and evil. Otello's psychological degeneration is driven by his separation from God, whose constant agent throughout the opera is Desdemona, a cipher for Marian female purity, profiled by Verdi in her Act IV *"Canzone di salice,"*[201] and the postliminary *"Ave Maria,"* as antonyms for Iago's malignant *"Credo in un Dio crudel che m'ha creato."*[202] The perfected vulnerability of Desdemona's concluding prayer to Mary, the protector to "wives and virgins,"[203] anticipates *"ora della morte nostra,"*[204] and ends with an *"Amen"* that remembers a shared prayer of thanks from her duet with Otello in Act I.[205] The stripped-down

---

197   She sang in the British premiere also, at the Royal Albert Hall in London, in 1875. She was appeared in the same year as Aida, conducted by Verdi, at the Hofoper in Vienna.

198   He made the dedication only in December, 1897, a matter of days after Strepponi's death.

199   'Rejoice! The Muslim's pride is buried in the sea.'

200   Parakilas, James (1997). "Religion and Difference in Verdi's 'Otello.'" *The Musical Quarterly*, Vol. 81, No. 3, p. 375.

201   'Willow Song,' *"Mia madre aveva una povera ancella."* ('My mother had a poor maid.'), Act IV.

202   'I believe in a cruel God who created me,' Act II.

203   *"Ave Maria, piena di grazia, eletta fra le spose e le vergini sei tu."* ('Hail Mary, full of grace, blessed amongst wives and virgins art thou.').

204   'Hour of our death.'

205   Desdemona: *"Disperda il ciel gli affanni e amor non muti col mutar degli anni."* Otello: *"A questa tua preghiera 'Amen' risponda la celeste schiera."* Desdemona: *"'Amen' risponda."*

simplicity of Desdemona's 16-minute "Willow" scene is heavy with pathos, fear and anxiety, with the surviving impression resolving into acceptance. Rossini and di Salsa had also allowed Desdemona a moment of quiet reflection, but it was secular and brief. Boito and Verdi chose instead to adopt a text whose origins reached back to liturgies from the sixth century; in so doing they gave Desdemona (and the audience) a clear impression of hope and relief, formed of the "knowledge" that Desdemona was part of a community whose faith assured her the protection of God's love, and life eternal – tenuous compensation for her violent murder. The sincerity of the episode is diminished only by a passing reflection on what God had done to Verdi when tolerating the death of his wife and children half a century earlier. Verdi's career was remarkable for a host of reasons, but his transformation of the capacity and dramatic focus of the soprano as an instrument did not extend to his promotion of the voices of women collectively when speaking *as* women. He had toyed initially with the idea of making *Otello* an opera without a chorus, but as James Parakilas notes of Desdemona's reversion to ecclesiastical prayer:

> she now seems to step out of the psychological isolation of dwelling on her own woes and to see herself one again in the community of all who need to Virgin's prayers [...] Her vernacular version even advances the words "for us" to an emphatic first place in the sentence – all the more urgent because it is such a formal construction – from the second place they occupy in the Latin ('*ora pro nobis*') [...] In the hour of her death, however, she has no chorus to lean on or call out to. But Verdi has given her a surrogate chorus, an internalized chorus, in the form of the orchestra of muted strings that sticks faithfully with her, while changing in range and function, all through her Ave Maria. This sound reminds us of the communal nature of Desdemona's identity as a woman just at the moment when her isolation in her marriage is about to cost her not only that identity, but her life. This reminder works most powerfully at the end of the Ave Maria, where the libretto directs that Desdemona lean her forehead against the prie-dieu on which she remains kneeling.[206]

Unlike Otello, which was without precedent for Italian opera in its scale and vocal requirements, Desdemona is a lyrical role, written to be performed by a soprano used to appearing as Violetta. Indeed, by the 1880s the proliferation of opera houses globally was such that the concept of role-attachment, and the routine consignment of sopranos to a particular composer, genre or fach had begun to collapse. Verdi was the first living composer to succeed globally, which meant his operas were performed in countries without traditions to which Verdi and his originators were able to contribute. *Otello* was staged in hundreds of theatres around the world during the five years after its first performance; because many of the venues outside Italy presented operas in their native languages, there were inevitable differences between how the

---

206   Parakilas, James (1997). "Religion and Difference in Verdi's 'Otello.'" *The Musical Quarterly*, Vol. 81, No. 3, pp. 387–388.

"Willow Song" was performed at its premiere by Romilda Pantaleoni,[207] and how it was heard in Vienna, Berlin, Prague, Budapest, Sofia, Stockholm and Madrid. While it is impossible to know anything of what all but a handful of Verdi's singers sounded like, it's clear from the 1906 recording by Lilli Lehmann of "*Ah, fors'è lui* [...] *Sempre libera*," that her approach to style made her incomparable to Nellie Melba, who recorded the same music two years earlier. The dissimilarities are greater still when set against Luisa Tetrazzini's recording of the scene from 1911 – when she was already 40-years of age. Pantaleoni was 53 in 1900; she was only three years older than the first Otello, Francesco Tamagno,[208] so she could have made records. Even in the absence of cylinders and '78s, something can be learned of her voice from her repertoire, which was typical of the growing trend towards a plurality of works, languages and voices. Pantaleoni "specialised" in French and Italian bel canto, French and Italian grand opera, Wagner and verismo.[209] The move towards a one-voice-fits-all sensibility – and the shift towards amplitude as a metric for vocal success – was accelerated by Pantaleoni's rivalry at La Scala with Maddalena Mariani-Masi,[210] who made her Milanese debut as Agathe in *Der Freischütz* in 1874, and later excelled as Lucia, Norma, and Gounod's Juliette, before being cast by Ponchielli in the title role of *La Gioconda* in 1876[211] – supplanting his wife of two years, Teresa Brambilla.[212]

Like Pantaleoni, Mariani-Masi was cast with alacrity across the repertoire; she performed French, German and Italian operas, becoming internationally famous as Marguerite in Boito's *Mefistofele* – a role created by Erminia Borghi-Mamo,[213] a soprano who was quite literally born into the theatre, when her soprano-mother gave birth in a room at the Théâtre Comédie Italienne two hours after a performance as Leonora in *Il Trovatore*. Although best-known for her work for Boito, Borghi-Mamo was acclaimed also as Lucrezia Borgia, Elisabetta and Aida. She was also a renowned Santuzza, in the first verismo opera, Mascagni's *Cavalleria Rusticana* – premiered in 1890. This made her one of the first "transitional" sopranos, reconciling middle and late-century spinto repertoire to the abrasive, theatrical intensity of the modern. Pantaleoni was no less transitional, creating the title role for Ponchielli's *Marion Delorme*[214] and Tigrana for Puccini's second opera, *Edgar*. Her last creation was Santuzza, which she performed at La Scala's first production of *Cavalleria Rusticana*. Pantaleoni retired in 1891, in her thirties, after the death of her long-time lover, Franco Faccio. She was considered to be an exceptional actress, comparable for many to the mother of modern Italian theatre, Eleonora Duse.[215]

---

207 1847 – 20 May, 1917.
208 For an analysis of Tamagno's recordings, see Boyden, Matthew (2021). *The Tenor: A Cultural History*.
209 'Realism.'
210 1850 – 25 September, 1916.
211 First performed on 8 April, 1876.
212 Mariani Masi was again the composer's choice for the premiere of the opera's revised version in 1880.
213 18 November, 1855 – 29 July, 1941. She was named after Verdi's first muse (and possible lover) Erminia Frezzolini, with whom Erminia's parents were close friends.
214 First performed on 17 March, 1885.
215 3 October, 1858 – 21 April, 1924.

Duse's legendary submission to the truth of a character was compounded by an absence of make-up (to allow for changes in skin tone to be appreciated by audiences) and a use of body language and vocal modulation that aligned her with Sarah Bernhardt in technique as well as celebrity. Stanislavski considered her to be the perfect actress – even if her work on silent film proves that she, like Bernhardt, remained attached to a school of gesture-acting that would now be considered mannered and artificial. Dramatic veracity was amplified inevitably by the emergence of verismo and the advances in production design and acting theory emanating from the *Meininger Hoftheatertruppe*[216] (founded in 1866) and Berlin's *Deutsches Theater*,[217] but the premiere in 1893 of Verdi's last opera, *Falstaff*,[218] was untouched by the modern, even if the invention of the through-composed score is a source of infinite wonder. *Falstaff* is an ensemble work, featuring the largest solo cast of all of his operas – with ten significant roles, four of them for female voices: two sopranos (Alice Ford and her daughter Nannetta), a mezzo soprano (Meg Page), and a contralto (Mistress Quickly). Two of the first female cast made '78 recordings:[219] Adelina Stehle[220] (Nannetta), and Virginia Guerrini[221] (Meg).

When listening to their voices, it's worth remembering that Italy was one of the first countries to transmit hydroelectricity to an urban centre,[222] in 1885, just eight years before the premiere of *Falstaff*. Verdi's first opera, *Oberto*, was composed by candle-light and oil lamp; it was premiered a year after Turin introduced gas lighting to a handful of public spaces. Stehle can be heard singing as Mimi in "*Addio dolce svegliare alla mattina!*"[223] from Act IV of *La bohème* (first performed in 1896, five years before Verdi's death), and "*Ma dunque é vero,*" from Cilea's *Adriana Lecouvreur* (first performed in 1902). For both recordings, from 1904, she was joined by Edoardo Garbin,[224] the tenor who created the role of Fenton in *Falstaff*.[225] Both excerpts call for a lyric-dramatic soprano – particularly the scene from *Lecouvreur*. Conversely, Nannetta's music requires a light, floated tone, exemplified by the aria, "*Sul fil d'un soffio etesio.*"[226] Even accepting that voices can harden with time, Stehle's hammering of her duet with Garbin makes it difficult to believe she was ever capable of the child-like lyricism written by Verdi into Nannetta's part; indeed, she was 33-years-old at the time of the first performance, and only 44 when singing into a horn.

For all its harshness of tone, unstable placement and imperfect pitching, it is the voice of a singer chosen – and trained – by Verdi to create a role in his last opera. The same is true of Virginia Guerrini, the mezzo-soprano who created Meg Page,

---

216 'Meiningen Court Theatre Troupe,' founded in 1866.

217 Founded in 1883.

218 First performed on 9 February, 1893.

219 The first Falstaff, Victor Maurel, and the first Fenton, Edoardo Garbin, both made numerous recordings, some of which are of lasting value for more than their historical significance.

220 30 June, 1860 – 24 December, 1945.

221 20 February, 1871 – 26 February, 1948.

222 From Tivoli to Rome, along a 5,000-volt line.

223 'Goodbye, sweet awakening in the morning!'

224 With Maria Camporelli (as Musetta) and Mario Sammarco (as Marcello), the baritone who created the role of Gerard in Giordano's *Andrea Chénier* in 1896.

225 See Boyden, Matthew (2021). *The Tenor: A Cultural History*. Ragueneau Press.

226 'On the edge of an Etesian breath.'

although her recordings are of a different order. Her debut in 1889 was as Ortrud, in *Lohengrin*; she was first heard by Verdi the following year, when appearing as Laura in *La Gioconda* at the Teatro Nuovo in Trieste.[227] She appeared for the first time at La Scala, as Adalgisa, in 1892; so great was her success that she was cast by Catalani as Afra for the premiere of *La Wally*. Guerrini celebrated her 22nd birthday during rehearsals for *Falstaff*; she made her recording of the duet, "*Sola furtiva al tempio*,"[228] from Act I of *Norma*, twenty years later, with Giannina Russ in the title role.[229] With its steel-cut chest register and tight vibrato, her powerful mezzo is eye-widening in its focus and power. The security of Guerrini's placement fosters undeviating service to the poet's words; her pellucid diction embraces a studied ugliness that would cause the majority of modern teachers of singing to lose their minds; her delivery of the phrase "*Dammi, dammi poter baciar*,"[230] delivers a lightning bolt of desire and longing in a tone that sends shivers down more than just the spine. The performance is striking also for the complete absence of sentimentality, with rubato employed as Bellini intended it – as a mechanism for the contained expression of an intense emotional state. Even if the bar-lines are adhered to, with a discipline that borders on the metronomic, the duet unfolds with effortless grace that braves Guerrini's ham-theatrical accents because she makes word-centred use of portamento. The sopranos' voices coalesce as filaments, forming as a singular line of musical and psychological experience that touches the sublime during the exquisitely-painted cadenza. There have been many fine recorded performances of "*Sola furtiva al tempio*"; none is better than this, the first.

The emergence of recording saw the transformation of what had previously been the preserve of memory – and a construction of trust, faith and reputation – into something permanent, as an object capable of analysis and comparison. Many of the recordings issued during the five years after 1900 were heard by men and women who had attended performances by Malibran and Viardot – and yet almost none of the critical commentary published in continental Europe before 1900 indulged the folly of correlation. The first to do so with alacrity was Bernard Shaw, in England; while his criticism remains fascinating, it is difficult to draw much of consequence from his serial reliance on the setting of one singer against another for readers who had heard neither. By 1890, when recording emerged as a viable technology, Verdi's vast influence as the first Italian composer of opera to deny the rights of singers as "creators" fed naturally and effortlessly into the "reality" of recording. With horns capturing voices that would have died previously with the singer, Verd's obsession with his music being performed *com'è scritto* was made empirical by technology. The coincidental emergence of the populist art of verismo with the science of recording coincided with a global expansion in the business of publishing, for amateurs and professionals alike. The effect of absolute commercialisation was seismic, particularly for the soprano.

---

227   Renamed the Teatro Lirico Giuseppe Verdi in the year of the composer's death.
228   'Alone, furtively to the temple.'
229   27 March, 1873 – 28 February, 1951.
230   'Give me, give me the chance to kiss.'

CHAPTER FOURTEEN

Why Wagner?

The 2022 production of *Der Ring des Nibelungen* at Wagner's Festspilehaus in Bayreuth[1] was described in the Festspiel's programme notes by its director, Valentin Schwarz, as "constructively disrespectful." Schwarz was uninterested in "coherence," preferring, like so many before him, a "liberal approach to the plot." The director attributed his priorities to inconsistencies within the work itself. The House of Wahnfried had passed the poisoned grail of directing the *Nibelungen* to a team whose philosophy equated to a rejection of the Theatre of Ideas as it had been memorialised by one of the greatest minds in human history. The *Ring* occupied Wagner for more than a third of a century; the tetralogy is nothing less than the aesthetic encapsulation of Hegel's world view, the sum of which ideated the relationship between self and otherness as the defining characteristics of human impulse and sensibility. The *Ring* speaks to the roots of Mankind's paradoxical desire for objects and the coincidental need for estrangement from them. Notwithstanding the scale of the composer's ambition, Schwarz's dramaturg, Konrad Kuhn, was keen to establish how the new staging "does not make a claim to an overarching world model," because coherence "runs counter to a sense of being in a world characterised by increasing fragmentation." It escaped Kuhn's reading that social and political dissolution were fundamental to Wagner's concerns when he embarked on the cycle's poetry. Of course, the "fragmentation" that so troubled Kuhn and his colleagues was pan-cultural and not, as it was for Wagner, paradigmatically German.

Fashioned by sophistry, the staging was confused and bleak in its callow pretention. The disconnection between the *Ring's* capacity to inspire and provoke, and the carnage vomited onto the stage of the world's most venerated theatre in 2022, was neither unexpected nor unusual. Since the death of Wieland Wagner in 1966, the poverty of imagination among Bayreuth-favoured directors has become as perennial as the starving of the once-Green Hill's lawns of rainfall. So routine is the sound of flailing that a cynical person might think the composer's family desperate to do *anything* to distract audiences from the crushing disassociation between Wagner's intentions as a composer and the singers charged to realise them. During the 1960s and '70s, the word "crisis" was reserved for heldentenors – even with as many as half a dozen singers capable of doing justice to Tristan, Siegmund, Siegfried and Parsifal, the most demanding quartet of roles for tenor voice. The 21st century has seen that crisis extend no less acutely to the heldensoprano, of which there has not been even one exponent to stake a claim to the Bayreuth tradition as it was established

---

1 Delayed from 2020 by the Covid-19 pandemic.

during the previous century. In 2022, Brünnhilde was sung by Iréne Theorin,[2] a fabulous-looking Swedish soprano who was almost 40 at the turn of the millennium. While Theorin was adequate as Isolde at Bayreuth in 2008, her performance as Wotan's daughter 14 years later was little better than noise-pollution. So shot was her voice placement, and so grating the resulting wobble, that members of the audience were seen to do the unthinkable when giving up their seats long before Hagen cried out *"Zurück vom Ring!"*[3] Even in passages marked (and sung) piano, her "vibrato" was so destructive of the written line that only someone with a score in front of them could have hoped to know what she was singing about.

Theorin made her debut, in Copenhagen, as Donna Anna in *Don Giovanni*; she may at that time have been ideal for Mozart, but she was unfit to perform Brünnhilde when subscribing to every prosaism in the big book of Wagner-singing clichés. She was heavy, blonde, and stentorian, with a "cruise-ship" voice: large, ugly, and difficult to manoeuvre. There are dramatic sopranos on the world stage with talent; the American, Christine Goercke,[4] has excelled as Elektra and Brünnhilde – although not yet at Bayreuth. Unlike so many others, she has marshalled her resources, adhering for more than a decade after her debut to lighter repertoire, such as Donna Elvira and the title role of *Iphigénie en Tauride*.[5] When she relocated at the New York Met to singing Strauss (in whose *Die Frau ohne Schatten* she gave a sensational performance as the Dyer's Wife in 2013), Puccini (*Turandot* in 2015), and Wagner (Brünnhilde for the 2018 *Ring*), Goercke proved the virtues of patience and judgment, as well as voice and artistry.[6]

She is not, however, much-recorded, and since she is now in her fifties she will not be entering Valhalla to join even the lesser-known of her predecessors, who made so many records that a Wagner discography spanning live and studios performances would run to an index with thousands of entries. Considering there has never been more technology, or so many people with access to it, it is a biting irony that there is almost no-one worth recording. The current generation of singers will be remembered, if at all, only through their live recordings, absent the benevolence of a studio process capable of affording days of sessions, retakes and editing. Of course, the current state of singing at Bayreuth is unique; very few dramatic sopranos are now capable of meeting the "Wagner challenge" as it has crystallised, from which inarguable fact flows a single leading question: why?

The answer begins with what it is that makes Wagner's operas unique in their challenges. With the sole exception of the first of the *Ring* operas, *Das Rheingold* – which

---

2 *née* Lena Iréne Sofie Theorin, 18 June, 1963 –

3 The last words of *Götterdämmerung*, sung by Hagen, before he is drowned by the Rhinemaidens.

4 1969 –

5 This is her only complete studio operatic role. She can be heard singing the final scene of *Elektra* (with Elza van der Heever) on a Met Opera release of live excerpts (2018), conducted by Yannick Nézet-Séguin, to commemorate his appointment as the House music director. Goercke is very fine indeed, even if her intonation is surprisingly wayward – and some of Nézet-Séguin's gear-changes are incredibly destructive of the scene's natural (and clearly indicated) momentum. If any evidence were needed of the relative death of the recording industry, it can be found in Goercke's negligible recorded legacy, of concert works (spanning Rossini's *Stabat Mater*, Britten's "War Requiem," and Honegger's *Jeanne d'Arc au bûcher*).

6 Goercke is only six years younger than Theorin. She is in her fifties, however, and approaching the gloaming of her career.

is a mere two and a half hours in length – his works are long. The first performance of *Rienzi* ran for more than six hours; the ballet music alone occupies 30 minutes of music. Performed uncut, *Die Meistersinger von Nürnberg*,[7] runs for more than five hours – closer to six depending on the length of the intervals. The first act of *Götterdämmerung*[8] is more than two hours on its own. Of course, no one singer is on stage throughout; even when they are a constant presence, as occurs during *Tristan*, there are longueurs and moments of *relative* restraint. In any event, each performance for *every* singer begins long before the curtain rises. Voices need to be warmed-up – the business of singing for an operatic soprano is akin to running a marathon; even if most don't have to move a great deal on stage, the physical process of vocalising for any leading singer (regardless of their gender) will place massive strain on their body. Most lose pounds during a performance in sweat alone, even with intervals; the majority continue singing to keep their voices "awake." It is not unusual for a lieder recital to require a vocalist to perform for two hours straight, by programme alone. Many are generous with encores, which can take a concert performance into a third hour. Some are even persuaded to sing into the night after decamping with friends and admirers to bars and restaurants.[9]

Wagner knew all of this. He was well-versed in Italian operatic culture – which he admired – but his unsmiling belief in the serious burden facing German music when held captive by Italian aesthetics and composers compelled a number of dramatic departures, many of them attributable to the titanic achievements and influence of Beethoven. These began – and ended – for Wagner with the German word. Text was as important as music, an obsession not shared by his idol, who was as comfortable reading and writing in Italian and French as he was conversing in his mother tongue. Wagner's pre-occupation with the German nation-state, and the greater Reich's potential for moral and artistic superiority, pre-empted the country's unification in 1871, although his nationalism was insufficiently sincere to cause him to re-direct his gruesome manipulation of the tragic Bavarian monarch, Ludwig II, to the first German Emperor.

A uniquely German operatic culture had to feed from its language, which explains Wagner's determination when writing his own libretti. There were many writers to whom he could have turned to create the book for his first opera, *Die Feen*,[10] in 1833; part of his megalomanic charm is rooted, therefore, in his belief that he alone could produce what he needed as a composer when forging German operatic culture. His value system placed the word *at least* in parity with the music, which is where things became more complicated – noting, at all times, the reach of Wagner's vanity to his "genius" as a writer as well as a composer. *Lohengrin*[11] was the last of what can be considered Wagner's "Italian" operas; it was (and remained for many years), his most successful work. The music is Italianate in its adherence to the principles of bel canto.

---

7   'The Master Singers of Nuremberg.'
8   'Twilight of the Gods.'
9   One well-known soprano informed the author of her refusal to attend any restaurant after a performance that was known to have a piano.
10   'The Fairies.' Unperformed during his lifetime, the premiere was given five years after Wagner's death, on 29 June, 1888.
11   First performed on 28 August, 1850.

The writing for voices is lyrical and long-breathed – consistent with what is known of Wagner's self-confessed admiration for the best of Italian singing. For all that he admired in Wilhelmine Schröder-Devrient, her dramatic incision is little evidenced in Elsa's music – which was first performed by a soprano 23 years her junior.

Rosa von Milde,[12] sang at the Weimarer Hoftheater[13] for two years before Liszt recommended her for the role of Elsa. Tellingly, she made her stage debut on 9 June, 1845, in Weimar, as Amina in *La sonnambula*. Her repertoire prior to *Lohengrin* required her to sing with an orchestra formed routinely of around 40 players. The ensemble at the first performance of *Lohengrin*, on 28 August, 1850, had fewer than 50 players – as would now be normal for an opera by Mozart. The symbiosis between stage and pit evolved naturally, with words and music aligning in accordance with technology, acoustics and expectations. After the first performance of *Lohengrin*, Liszt commended von Milde as, "by nature, perfectly suited for the portrayal of Elsa, [who] performed her seraphic singing with the purest understanding of the poetic and musical intention."[14] Von Milde later gave the first German performance of Berlioz's *Benvenuto Cellini*,[15] and the world premiere, in 1858, of Peter Cornelius' *Der Barbier von Bagdad*.[16] She committed her performing life to Weimar, retiring finally in 1867. The first Elsa lived six years into the 20th century – dying only a few months before Emilia Corsi[17] recorded Elsa's "*Einsam in truben Tagen*,"[18] with an orchestra of perhaps 20 players. The performance is fascinating for what it reveals of the contemporary approach to Wagner's music as he was known to admire it. The aria is taken initially at great speed – with a fantastic gear change mid-way through; Corsi enjoys considerable rhythmic largesse, with notation being treated with greater freedom than would have been allowed by Cosima Wagner. There is a gamut of rallentandos, accelerandos and fermatas; none of them does any harm to the music, which is more expressive as a result. She adds accents, turns and generous sides of portamento (shared with the violins); her vibrato is light, her pronunciation is crisp and easy to follow. In short, it is a voice of great beauty and managed drama that adheres to 19th century Italian traditions – with line and lyricism overreaching amplitude and declamation. The composer of *Lohengrin* did not abandon these values for *Tristan und Isolde*, the *Ring* and *Parsifal*. He did, however, take advantage of his celebrity and the money it generated when imagining what his orchestra might sound like.

It's worth dwelling on what that meant for a singer like Corsi, who made her debut in Bologna, in 1886, as Micaëla – a mere 15 years after the city staged the first Italian production of *Lohengrin*. Corsi achieved success as Gilda, Rosina, Amina, Desdemona, Manon Lescaut, and Gioconda – in addition to (rather than in place of) Elsa and Sieglinde. Wagner's appetites as he orchestrated the *Ring* were unprecedented in their extravagance and innovation. Not being satisfied with the

---

12 *née* Rosa Agthe, 25 June, 1827 – 25 January, 1906.
13 'Weimar Court Theatre.'
14 Kutsch, K. J.; Riemens, Leo (2012). Milde, Rosa von. *Großes Sängerlexikon* (4th ed.). De Gruyter, pp. 3126–3127.
15 She created the role of Teresa; her husband sang the role of Fieramosca.
16 'The Barber of Baghdad.'
17 21 January, 1870 – 17 September, 1928.
18 In Italian, and freely translated as "*Sola nei miei prim'anni*." ('Alone in my early days years.').

body of instruments available at the time, he designed and commissioned his own tuba (mid-way in its sonority between the horn and the trombone), and numerous variations of existing instruments, including a bass trumpet, a contrabass-trombone with a double slide, an "alto oboe," (a richer, brighter cor anglais), and what became known as the "Wagner bell," which enabled the bassoon to reach more than an octave below the instrument's natural range. Any faithful production of the *Ring* will need additionally to furnish a piccolo, three flutes (with the third doubling second piccolo), three oboes, a cor anglais (doubling a fourth oboe), three soprano clarinets, a bass clarinet, three bassoons, eight horns (with numbers five through eight doubling as Wagner tubas), three trumpets, a bass trumpet, three tenor trombones, a contrabass trombone (doubling bass trombone), a contrabass tuba, a percussion section with four timpani (and two players), a triangle, cymbals, glockenspiel, and tam-tam. The string section is immense, with 32 violins, 12 violas, 12 cellos, eight double basses and six harps. It's unclear where Wagner thought they would sit in any theatre outside Bayreuth. He also made specific changes for each of the operas. *Das Rheingold* requires a bass drum, an onstage harp and 18 onstage anvils; *Die Walküre* features parts for a snare drum, a D clarinet (played by the third clarinettist), and an on-stage steerhorn; *Siegfried* is presumably unperformable without an onstage cor anglais and an onstage horn. For *Götterdämmerung*, Wagner considered 20 brass voices insufficient, so he added five onstage horns and four onstage steerhorns – one of which to be played by Hagen.

In fairness to Berlioz, Wagner was behind the curve where scale is concerned. The orchestra for the French composer's Requiem (the "Grande Messe des Morts") was (and should be) more than twice the size of what is prescribed for the *Ring*, *Tristan* and *Parsifal*.[19] The key distinction, however, is that Berlioz's Requiem was scored for a vast chorus of between 400 and 700 singers, with only a single movement for a solo voice (a tenor). The Sanctus is accompanied by long held notes from a flute and muted strings, with women's voices singing pianissimo in imitation of the solo line. What Wagner required with his mature works was transformative because a solo voice raised on the "natural" acoustic balance created by the normative works of Mozart, Bellini, Verdi, Gounod and Weber had to adjust overnight to an orchestra that was foreground rather than background, and adversarial rather than accommodating. Wagner's revolution reached further than the numbers suggest; the instruments played at the first performances of *Tristan*, on 10 June, 1865, and the *Ring*, on 13, 14, 16 and 17 August, 1876 (when the cycle was first staged together, at Bayreuth), were different in every case to the instruments of the 20th and 21st centuries. Wagner's brass instruments had narrower bores and smaller bells; wind instruments were made of wood and brighter in tone. Wagner's adoption of valved-horns was purely practical, as he noted during the composition of *Tristan*:

> So much has been gained through the introduction of valves that it is impossible to ignore these improvements, although the horn has undeniably lost some of its beauty of tone and its ability to slur notes delicately.[20]

---

19   Working backwards, Berlioz prescribes 18 double-basses.

20   Brown, Clive (1992). "Performing Practice." In Eds. Millington, Barry and Spencer, Stewart. *Wagner*

His concern for timbre was informed by his travels outside Germany, particularly in France, where wind-instrument manufacturing was a global business. In 1869, he lamented in his essay *Über das Dirigieren*:

> Tone sustained with equal power is the basis of all expression, with the voice as with the orchestra: the manifold modifications of the power of tone, which constitute one of the principal elements of musical expression, rest upon it. Without such basis an orchestra will produce much noise but no power. And this is one of the first symptoms of the weakness of most of our orchestral performances. The conductors of the day care little about a sustained forte, but they are particularly fond of an exaggerated piano. Now the strings produce the latter with ease, but the wind instruments, particularly the wood winds do not. It is almost impossible to get a delicately sustained piano from wind instruments. The players, flautists particularly, have transformed their formerly delicate instruments into formidable tubes.[21]

The E, A and D strings of violins were strung in gut; the G and C strings of violas and cellos were gut also, but they were occasionally wound with silver or silver-plated copper wire – which did nothing to affect the sweetness and warmth of a gut-strung instrument.[22] Metal strings are significantly harsher and more resonant, however, particularly when leaned into. The orchestra gathering at Bayreuth every summer for the past 50 years has been at least 30% "noisier" than the orchestra that played for the composer. Any conductor adhering to Wagner's prescriptions in the 21st century using modern instruments isn't using 60 strings, therefore; with metal-strung instruments, the amplitude is closer to 90. Wagner knew his orchestra would present formidable challenges to singers raised on Italian opera, so he was careful to mark each of his mature scores with dynamic and expressive instructions to allow each voice to be heard. The vocal parts (particularly for Brünnhilde) are littered with "Italian" ornaments, including mordants, trills and appoggiaturas – none of which can be attempted, far less heard, if the pit is drowning the stage. Wagner was a conductor also, so he understood that his works allowed in performance for the achievement of less being more; his understanding of drama as words-formed-of-music was nailed

---

in Performance (1992). Yale University Press, p. 103.

21   "*Gewaltsrohren.*" Wagner, Richard (1897). *On Conducting: A Treatise on Style in the Execution of Classical Music*. William Reeves, pp. 32–33.

22   It's worth noting that the "authentic" performances and recordings of Wagner conducted by Sir Roger Norrington are nothing of the sort, any more than were his idiotic performances of symphonies by Mahler. It's all very well playing on period instruments, but that's not going to make any difference if a conductor actively suppresses the music's capacity to sing – as did Norrington with routine violence. The "phrasing" of the London Classical Players was especially nauseating noting the vast amount of evidence on record, and in print, to confirm that what Norrington was doing with Wagner equated to cultural vandalism. Of course, Norrington's conception of what qualified as "authentic" was revealed as vapid and ignorant when he performed and recorded the "*Liebestod*" with Jane Eaglen – who sang the music like so many other post-war sopranos with a huge, ugly wobble.

to the wings at Bayreuth in his famous prescription: "the big notes will take care of themselves; the little ones and the text are the chief things."[23]

When celebrating the achievements of the Flower Maidens after the premiere of *Parsifal* on 26 July, 1882, he commended the absence of "passionate accent[s]," and the singers' avoidance of any dramatic affectations that risked the "breaking of every melodic line." For Wagner, melody was timbrel as well as structural. As an admirer of Bellini, and bel canto more generally, his concern for lyricism was paramount. This required the preservation of an even line of song, no matter the inelegance of much of Wagner's *stabreim*. There was no trade off because Wagner ensured that Hans von Bülow[24] and Franz Wüllner[25] were fully appraised of the importance of allowing the cast to be audible without having to force their voices. It is a pleasure, regardless, to imagine the reactions of the creators of *Tristan*, and the Munich *Das Rheingold* and *Die Walküre*, after everyone began to appreciate the enormity of the undertaking. Piano rehearsals cannot have prepared Malvina Schnorr von Carolsfeld[26] (the first Isolde) nor Therese Vogl[27] (the creator of Wellgunde in *Das Rheingold*[28] and Sieglinde in *Die Walküre*[29]) for the reach of the composer's ambitions. Neither soprano is likely ever to have seen an orchestra with 60 strings[30] and nearly 100 players, far less performed with one.[31] The prospect of having to engage with so huge an ensemble for hours on end cannot have appealed, and yet Wagner's first nights from 1870 were triumphs. How did everyone adapt so quickly?

The answer is rooted in Wagner's omnipresence throughout the extensive rehearsal process, but also in the singers' prior experience. Malvina Schnorr von Carolsfeld studied in Paris with Manuel García, who trained her in advance of her debut, as Isabelle in *Robert le diable* in 1841. From 1849 she began to move frequently, from Breslau to Coburg, Gotha, Hamburg and, in 1854, Karlsruhe, where she met her future husband, the tenor Ludwig Schnorr von Carolsfeld, who was ten years her junior. They performed together in works by Mozart (*Don Giovanni*), Meyerbeer (*Les Huguenots*), Verdi (*Il trovatore*), and Wagner (*Holländer*, *Tannhäuser* and *Lohengrin*), developing reputations for the richness and power of their voices. Having conducted 70 rehearsals of *Tristan* in Vienna, and being dissatisfied with the tenor Alois Ander, *Tristan* was rumoured to be unperformable. The composer sent copies of the vocal score to the Schnorrs, whose singing for Wagner in his music room made them his first and only choice. The premiere was scheduled for 15 May, 1865, but postponed

---

23   Shawe-Taylor, Desmond (1992). "Wagner and His Singers." In Eds. Millington, Barry and Spencer, Stewart. *Wagner in Performance* (1992). Yale University Press, p. 15.

24   The conductor of the first *Tristan*.

25   The conductor of the first *Die Walküre*.

26   *née* Eugénia Malvina Garrigues, 7 December, 1825 – 8 February, 1904.

27   12 November 1845 – 29 September 1921.

28   First performed on 22 September, 1869, at the National Theatre, Munich.

29   First performed on 26 June, 1870, at the Königliches Court and National Theatre, Munich.

30   Wagner did not prescribe the actual number of strings for *Tristan*. Instead, he wrote "*Die Streichinstrumente sind vorzüglich gut und stark zu besetzen.*" 'The string instruments are to be exquisitely cast in quantity and quality.'

31   When, 60 years later, Flagstad moved into her suite at the Astor Hotel (having arrived a few days earlier for her first season), she wrote to her mother "From the orchestra I heard a lot of nuances, there were more than 100 musicians and the sound was magnificent…"

for three weeks because Malvina was taken unwell. When finally heard by the public, *Tristan* more than lived up to Wagner's expectations as he described them to Mathilde Wesendonck in April, 1859:

> Child! This Tristan is turning into something terrible. This final act!!! – I fear the opera will be banned [...] only mediocre performances can save me! Perfectly good ones will be bound to drive people mad.[32]

He was proven partly right six weeks after the first performance, when the 29-year-old Ludwig died, on 21 July, 1865.[33] Malvina was emotionally and psychologically ruined by her husband's death; she fell into a prolonged depression and never sang again. *Tristan und Isolde* was born into mythology, becoming notorious for its bewildering novelty, sensual extravagance and physical challenges. That the title-role creators performed the opera on only four occasions advanced its reputation as a "voice-killer." Wagner made matters worse by failing to engineer another production for almost a decade. The first stagings of *Die Meistersinger* and the *Ring* – and the building of the Festspielhaus – were understandable distractions, and not until Eduard Lassen staged the opera in Weimar, in 1874, was it heard again. Wagner supervised a production in Berlin, in March, 1876 – just weeks before the premiere of the *Ring*. He thereafter turned to *Parsifal*. *Tristan* was not performed at Bayreuth until 1886, three years after Wagner's death. That production was overseen by his widow, who committed the next four decades to the preservation of a "Wagner sound" that she did more than anyone to ruin.

Wagner appreciated how his operas forged a novel performance culture. In 1865, he submitted a proposal to Ludwig II for a music school devoted to the training of students to perform his works:

> Faced with the prevailing evils of the German theatre, I could see no other way of ensuring decent and correct performances of my more recent dramatic works than by means of model performances, to be given by a specially chosen group of artists trained expressly for the purpose of performing these works in the correct style [...] What has persuaded me to make these demands is certainly not any exaggerated opinion of the individual merits of my works but simply the nature of their style and the resultant requirements with regard to a manner of execution which has nowhere yet been cultivated to the point where it has reached the certainty of a genuine style.[34]

The school was never built, but the issue of style became urgent after Wagner's death, when Cosima inherited his works, his reputation and his Festival. During her two

---

32   Daverio, John (2008). "Tristan und Isolde: Essence and Appearance." In Grey, Thomas S., ed. (2008). *The Cambridge Companion to Wagner*, p. 116.

33   See Boyden, Matthew (2021). *The Tenor: A Cultural History*. Ragueneau Press.

34   Brown, Clive (1992). "Performing Practice." In Eds. Millington, Barry and Spencer, Stewart. *Wagner in Performance* (1992). Yale University Press, p. 99.

decades as Imperatrix of Bayreuth, Cosima oversaw a (localised) transition from the lyrical to the declamatory. She did so in service to what she perceived to be her husband's priorities, originating as they did with the primacy of the word. In 1892, Cosima collaborated with the choral conductor, Julius Kniese, to elevate clarity of text over what Wagner would have characterised with Julius Hey as "German lyricism."[35] Cosima employed bel canto as a "term of abuse,"[36] and with Kniese serving as the "Rottweiler der Herrin," she required every singer performing at Bayreuth to elevate speech above song – a performing style that would become known as *Sprechgesang*.[37]

> Our stage differs from all other operatic stages in Germany in having drama at the centre of all the performances that are given. We look upon as the means, not the end. Drama is the end, and the organ of drama is language [...] and if there must be sacrifice at all [...] sacrifice rather the music (singing) to the poem than the poem (language) to the music.[38]

The primacy for Cosima of diction over line, and the raising of clarity above beauty,[39] led to singers spitting their consonants with such ferocity that "*Konsonanten-Spuckerei*" became the preferred form of expression a decade after Wagner's death.[40] What became known as the "Bayreuth Bark" was embraced as dogma even though the resulting attenuation of lyricism was symptomatic of failure as well as fashion. A singer yielding to age or suffering from fatigue will resort to declamation when compensating for deficiencies of technique; this is commonly manifested commonly as a wobble. It is unfortunate that the briny undulations with which Wagner-sopranos have become synonymous are so frequently confused with vibrato. They are *not* the same thing, and Wagner would have suffered motion-sickness had he been unable to distinguish between a straight-sung note and a trill. There are numerous clues to the composer's conception of vibrato. It is now ubiquitous (at least outside the period performance movement), but it was used sparingly before and during the 19th century. Among wind and brass players it was unheard of.[41] For string players, the prevailing fashion was determined by Joseph Joachim's 1905 *Violinschule*, which provided that

> A violinist who whose taste is refined and healthy will always recognise the steady tone as the ruling one, and will use the vibrato only where the expression seems to demand it.[42]

---

35 Parr, Sean M. (2019). *Wagnerian Singing and the Limits of Vocal Pedagogy*. Current Musicology, p. 105.

36 Fischer, Jens Malte (1992). "Sprechgesang or Bel Canto: Toward a History of Singing Wagner." Trans. Michael Tanner. In *Wagner Handbook*, ed. Ulrich Müller and Peter Wapnewski, trans. John Deathridge. Harvard University Press, pp. 524–546.

37 'Speech-song'.

38 Potter, John (2009). *Tenor: History of a Voice*. Yale University Press, p. 66.

39 Spotts, Frederic (1994). *Bayreuth: A History of the Wagner Festival*. Yale University Press, p. 99.

40 See generally, Parr, Sean M. (2019). "Wagnerian Singing and the Limits of Vocal Pedagogy." *Current Musicology*, 105, p. 58.

41 The French school of wind playing adopted vibrato during the two decades *after* 1900 – at much the same time as French singers.

42 Joachim, Joseph and Moser, Andreas (1905), *Violinschule*, Vol. 2. N. Simrock, p. 96a.

Wagner abjured vibrato for the same reasons everyone else did: it interfered with a singer's palette of expression, disguised as poor intonation, and infected the relationship between voices in ensemble. It was perceived at the time as an effect, to be used only sparingly. During his lifetime, Wagner presumed vibrato's adoption as a colour, after the fashion of Vermeer's reliance on ultramarine, it is now used after the fashion of Yves Klein, with neither context nor variation. *Die Meistersinger's* Act III quintet, "*Selig, wie die Sonne,*"[43] for example, is divine, with each singer's voice differentiated for the purposes of the characters' interaction; it is now normal for the parts to form a jelly-like whole in which line and character are lost to vibrato and wobbling. Anyone in any doubt as to what has been lost over the decades can listen to the sublime recording made on 29 January, 1908, with Johanna Gadski,[44] Marie Mattfeld,[45] Ellison Van Hoose, Marcel Journet, and Albert Reiss. The singers' phrasing is natural, unforced and linear. The words are allowed to unfold, with only the French bass, Journet, interjecting an element of vibrato. Every line and word is clear in its articulation and symmetry; the scene works because the singers' voices co-operate. 103 years later, Glyndebourne staged *Der Meistersinger*, with Anna Gabler as Eva, and Michaela Selinger as Magdalene. During the Quintet, the only audible voice was Gabler's because she over-sang constantly and because she employed an irritating habit of "tugging" at words within phrases, like an ill-trained cellist unable to voice beyond the length of the bow. Gabler duly suffocated the soaring lyricism over which Wagner had obsessed, an outcome made worse by a terrible wobble that infected everything around it, including the male voices, each of whom persevered with laudable patience and musicality.

Wagner's views on vibrato are recorded in his scores. Like Meyerbeer, from whom he learned more than he was willing to admit, Wagner went to the bother of marking vibrato in his scores – from which it can be concluded that, when *not* writing "*vibrirend,*"[46] or "*bebend*"[47] or "*mit schütternder Stimme,*"[48] he presumed it would not be used. He added these words sparingly (as he did in Act III, Scene 3, of *Siegfried*, for a passage played by first and second violins in isolation), and he was careful when adding wavy lines, as he did at certain points in Act I of *Meistersinger*. No such markings, or any instructions at all pertaining to vibrato, were added to the vocal parts. Heinrich Porges' memoirs of the rehearsals for the *Ring* provide further details, such as Wagner requesting the soprano singing the role of Sieglinde to perform the phrase "[*So bleibe hier! Nicht bringst du Unheil dahin*] *wo Unheil im Hause wohnt!*"[49] in such a way that "the initial violence [should give] way to an anguished vibrato."[50]

43 'Blessed, as the sun.'

44 15 June 1870/1872 – 22 February, 1932.

45 1870 — September 18, 1927. Mattfeld made only two recordings, both for the Victor Talking Machine Company. This is shocking when noting her standing and reputation as the creator of roles in the world premieres of *Königskinder* (the Stable girl), *La fanciulla del West* (Wowkle), and *Suor Angelica* (Sister Dolcina).

46 'Vibrating.'

47 'Trembling.'

48 'With a shaking voice.'

49 '[So stay here! You don't bring misery there] where evil dwells in the house.'

50 Brown, Clive (1992). "Performing Practice." In Eds. Millington, Barry and Spencer, Stewart. *Wagner in Performance* (1992). Yale University Press, p. 110.

The principle is self-evident; where requested, or dramatically constructive, vibrato provided a flash of intensity; it was otherwise *verboten*.

As for what Wagner's sopranos sounded like, there are recordings by two of his favoured soloists: Marianne Brandt[51] and Lilli Lehmann. The former was one of three sopranos chosen to create the role of *Kundry* in *Parsifal*. A clue to her range and tone can be found in her repertoire. She made her debut as Rachel, in *La Juive*, in 1867; the following year she moved to the Hofoper in Berlin, where her repertoire was typically diverse, spanning Sesto in *La clemenza di Tito*, Leonore in *Fidelio* (the role in which she made her London debut in 1872), numerous operas by Meyerbeer (famously Selica in *L'Africaine*), and Amneris in the Berlin premiere of *Aida*, in 1874. Brandt first turned to Wagner as Ortrud, in *Lohengrin*, and in 1876 she was engaged by Wagner to create Waltraute in *Götterdämmerung*. In 1882 – the year of *Parsifal's* premiere – she appeared as Amneris, Rachel in *La Juive*, Orfeo in Gluck's *Orphée et Eurydice*, Maffio Orsini in *Lucrezia Borgia* – and as Brangäne in the British premiere of *Tristan und Isolde* (conducted by Richter). In 1883, she sang Brünnhilde in *Die Walküre* for the first time. It follows that Brandt was a contralto, who excelled as Orfeo, Rachel, Kundry *and* Brünnhilde. It is unsurprising that Brandt studied with Pauline Viardot.[52] In 1905, she recorded three sides for Artistikal / Pathé – at the age of 63: Schumann's "*Frühlingsnacht*,"[53] "*Ach! Mein Sohn*,"[54] from Meyerbeer's *Le prophète*, and "*Il segreto per esser felici*,"[55] from *Lucrezia Borgia* (in German as "*Um stets heiter und glücklich zu leben.*"). Unlike the recordings made by her tenor counterpart, Hermann Winkelmann[56] – which are disappointing, at best – Brandt's voice and artistry as they survive on disc are stupendous. If presumably she had access to more of the tone, focus and drama to which her recordings attest, then she must have been sensational on the stage of Bayreuth. The voice in its dotage features a quick, periodic vibrato, and some imperfect intonation, but the dramatic intensity, depth of tone and articulation are of a rare kind and quality. Tellingly, she neither forces her voice nor does she need to; she is resonant, not loud.

Brandt was the second soprano to sing Kundry. The first was Amalie Materna,[57] an Austrian soprano whom Wagner so admired that he turned to her as Brünnhilde for the first *Ring* in 1876, and the Viennese premieres of *Die Walküre*, in 1877, and *Siegfried*, in 1878. Materna was his preference in 1881, when the first Berlin *Ring* was staged at the Victoria Theatre.[58] Materna sang Kundry at every Bayreuth Festival until 1891. She triumphed as Brünnhilde at the first American performance of *Die Walküre*, at the Met, on 30 January, 1885 – which ended at half past midnight. Writing for the *New York Tribune*, Henry Krehbiel praised

---

51   12 September, 1842 – 9 July, 1921.

52   Anyone capable of trilling as Brandt did in her sixties (for the aria from *Lucrezia Borgia*), plainly gave blood, sweat and years to her studies.

53   'Spring Night.'

54   'Ah, my son.'

55   'The secret to being happy.' Also known as the "*Brindisi*" ('Toast.').

56   The creator of the title role of *Parsifal*.

57   *née* Amalia, later Amalie Friedrich-Materna, 10 July, 1844 – 18 January, 1918.

58   Angelo Neumann's staging (which he first produced in Leipzig, in 1878) was, by necessity, modest; the theatre was small, seating only 1,400, and falling apart. It was pulled down in 1891 – only 32 years after it first opened

Frau Materna, whose name is ineradicably associated with it [and] Fräulein Brandt, self-sacrificing and earnest as usual, was the Fricka of the second act, and in the third act did effective service in throwing a deal of energetic life into the scene as one the Wishmaidens [sic]. Her connection with the Bayreuth performances did not begin until three years ago, when she alternated in the impersonation of Kundry in "Parsifal." Nevertheless she, too, stands among the acknowledgedly foremost representations of Wagner characters.

Writing for *The New York Times*, W. J. Henderson hailed what was

In almost all respects [...]as complete a rendering as when it was brought out at Bayreuth, eight years since. [...] Frau Materna's Brünnhilde is a portrayal of world-wide celebrity and her impressive scenes with Siegmund and Wotan last night – scenes in which her deep feeling, expressive tones, and majestic appearance told quite as strongly as the beauty and volume of her voice, were awaited with a confidence that was fully justified by the event. [...] When Fräulein Brandt good-naturedly took upon herself the rather thankless duties of Fricka she did so in the certainty that a finished representation of even so thankless a part would not fail of appreciation. [...] The Walkyries all had comely represent-atives, but in their final interview with Wotan their shrieks were even more out of tune than Wagner intended.

The common view was that these remarkable women were ideal in the roles presented to them by Wagner. Indeed, they were definitive, even if Bernard Shaw couldn't re-strain himself from commenting frequently on Materna's physical size,[59] which he excused on the basis that since "[Kundry] is as old as the hills no complaint need be made on that score;[60] indeed, the part is one which a very young woman would play worse than a mature one."[61] During the 1880s, there emerged inevitably a measure of competition, much of it formed by a generation of sopranos who didn't work with Wagner, including Milka Ternina, Anna von Mildenburg and Emmy Destinn.[62] Less well known, but equally gifted, was Rosa Sucher,[63] who made her debut in Munich in 1871 as Waltraute in *Die Walküre*. She was engaged by Cosima in 1886 and 1888, and committed almost two decades to legendary productions of Wagner's works in Berlin and London. The Hungarian Katharina Klafsky[64] was hailed for her appearances at

---

59   Bayreuth was responsible for establishing most of the originating clichés concerning the size of opera singers specialising in the performance of Wagner's operas. Writing from Bayreuth in 1896, for example, Romain Rolland described "the vast padded bulk" of one Sieglinde as being "from bust to backside [...] as wide as a city wall."

60   It should be noted that Malvina Schnorr von Carolsfeld was a size or two larger than Materna; both of them were dwarfed by Malvina's husband, whose girth was as tremendous as his voice.

61   Shaw, Bernard (1981). *Shaw's Music: The Complete Musical Criticism of Bernard Shaw*. Ed. Dan H. Laurence. The Bodley Head. Vol. I (1876 – 1890); p. 730.

62   Each of whom is considered elsewhere in this book.

63   *née* Rosa Hasselbeck, 23 February, 1849 – 16 April, 1927.

64   19 September, 1855 – 22 September, 1896.

Covent Garden as Isolde and Brünnhilde during the 1880s – and she would have become much better known had she not died of cancer at the age of 41. Gisela Staudigl[65] was a student of Marchesi, who made her stage debut in Hamburg, as Amneris. After relocating to Karlsruhe in 1885, and Berlin from 1887, she specialised as a singer of Wagner's operas. She created the role of Brangäne for the first production in 1886 of *Tristan* at Bayreuth, and during the 1890s she toured the United States, having failed to secure an appointment with Walter Damrosch, the son of Leopold – the founder of an all-German season at the Met in 1884, a year before his death at the age of 52. Damrosch junior oversaw a complement of two mezzo-sopranos (Marie Brandis[66] and Marie Mattfeld)[67] and eleven sopranos: Mathilde Denner, Riza Eibenschutz,[68] Johanna Gadski,[69] Lena Gottich, Lena Hartmann, Marie Hartmann, Mina Schilling, Augusta Vollmar, Georgine von Januschowsky,[70] Lillian Nordica and Lilli Lehmann.

Lehmann and Nordica[71] both made records, although only Lehmann worked with Wagner – having been engaged to create the roles of Woglinde and Helmwige in the 1876 *Ring*. On 2 July, 1908, Lehmann recorded the "*Liebestod*," from the end of *Tristan*. Although the singer was 60-years-old at the time, her singing proves that Wagner neither wanted nor expected his singers to use vibrato, and that "force" – as an excess of amplitude – was unnecessary and unwelcome if it risked doing harm to the words or the singer's voice. Anyone listening to Lehmann perform the "*Liebestod*" should reflect that they are hearing a soprano trained by Wagner, who was still performing Bellini's *Norma* and operas by Mozart. She was considered by her peers to be the finest Isolde of her generation, an achievement made more remarkable when noting the complete absence of vibrato, the perfect intonation, the pronounced portamento, and the relatively modest scale of the voice. The critic Eduard Hanslick wrote of the *young* Lehmann that "nature denied her a voice of penetrating power or luxuriousness," and so "excluded [her] from achieving the strongest and most directly passionate effects." He nonetheless commended her as ideal for "all tragic roles." With time and patience, Lehmann's voice increased in scale, without her needing to over-sing or do damage to her birth-right. Lehmann's performance of the "*Liebestod*" is supported by an orchestra whose small number of string players provides portamento-rich support that binds perfectly to the singer's sensualist aesthetic.

Lillian Nordica also recorded the "*Liebestod*" in 1911; she too sang it *with* portamento and *without* vibrato. She was supported by a much larger orchestra, and her voice was clearly larger (at least in the studio) than Lehmann's. Studios carried no acoustics, which absence lends authenticity to the live recording made by Mapleson of Nordica singing part of the "*Liebestod*" from a complete performance on 9 February, 1903, at the New York Met. Her portamento is even more pronounced in the theatre, and her tone greater still (a function of "living" resonance). What survives as an excerpt is sensational for its intonation, articulation and fluency; there is not the

---

65   *née* Anna Maria Koppmair, 3 September, 1860 – 22 February, 1929.
66   3 October, 1866 – 21 October, 1906.
67   1870 – September 18, 1927.
68   17 February, 1870 – 16 January, 1947.
69   15 June, 1870/1872 – 22 February, 1932.
70   4 October, 1849 – 6 September, 1914.
71   Both sopranos are considered in more detail elsewhere in this book.

slightest hint of effort or force. The lines of song flow from Nordica like a river, more than five hours after she had first begun to warm her voice backstage.

The generation of Wagner sopranos to follow the first did as they were taught by the creators. The Swedish-American, Olive Fremstad,[72] studied with Lehmann, whose shadow falls heavily over Fremstad's recording of the "*Liebestod*," made on 5 November, 1913. Her performance reinforces the traditions established (and maintained) by anyone who worked with Wagner – which *almost* included Richard Strauss, whose father, Franz, was one of Wagner's favourite horn players. Strauss Snr did not reciprocate the composer's admiration; he nonetheless took his son to the rehearsals for *Parsifal* – in which opera Richard later conducted Fremstad as Kundry. Strauss was also admiring of Fremstad's professionalism and artistry as Salome. While preparing for her debut in the role at the Met, she visited a city morgue to spend time in the company of a decapitated head, better to understand how to move on stage when holding one. That she was not given to squeamishness was further evidenced by the large glass jar she kept at her home, in which she stored another human head for students when explaining the physiognomy of singing. The Russian soprano, Félia Litvinne,[73] was another successful student of the redoubtable Viardot. She made her debut in Paris in 1883; two years later, she travelled to New York for the Mapleson Company, only to relocate a year later to the Met, as Valentine in *Les Huguenots*. She left after a single season and returned to Paris, where she was adored for the amplitude and beauty of her voice by the city's leading composers, including Debussy, Fauré and Saint-Saëns, for whom she created the title role in *Déjanire* on 28 August, 1898.[74]

Litvinne was hailed for her performances of works by Gluck, Meyerbeer and Verdi, as well as Wagner. Significantly, Litvinne created the roles of Isolde and Brünnhilde in the French premieres of *Tristan* and *Götterdämmerung* – in 1902. Her conductor on both occasions was Alfred Cortot, now better remembered as a pianist of jejune eccentricity. In the year of *Tristan's* first Parisian production, Litvinne and Cortot recorded the "*Liebestod*" at the piano. Cortot's playing is either hysterical and atrocious or dramatic and thrilling; it is for the listener to decide which they consider more appropriate. Litvinne's singing, on the other hand, is magnificent, and in keeping with contemporary taste – which she helped define throughout France, Russia (where she created numerous roles at the Imperial theatres in Moscow and St Petersburg, from 1890) and London (where she was a favourite at Covent Garden). Her performance of the "*Liebestod*" is wildly overcooked, and all the better for it. The voice is large, but she is in total control of the tone and its placement; her use of a quiver for certain words and phrases is spine-tingling, and even with all the thrashing and crashing from the piano she maintains a magnetic focus of line and expression.

During the 1920s, productions of Wagner's mature works became as ubiquitous globally as Verdi's, but the German school of Wagner-singing remained dominant, particularly after regional productions began to shift to performances in German. The art and intonation of the heldensopran as it was known between the Wars was characterised by two singers, whose recordings set in shellac an ideal that has never

---

72 14 March, 1871 – 21 April, 1951.
73 11 October, 1860 – 12 October, 1936.
74 In the arena at Béziers, for an audience of 8,000.

changed, even with so few living up to the challenge. Frida Leider[75] studied singing while working for a bank in Berlin; it took her many years to establish herself, and she was 35 before a successful performance in Hamburg in 1923 led to her engagement in Berlin as the State Opera's *prima donna drammatica*. Leider's many appearances at Covent Garden (where she shared the leading Wagner roles with the Australian Florence Austral),[76] the Met, La Scala, and the Vienna State Opera turned her into a legend that was made accessible by dozens of fine recordings, the most influential of which was her (heavily edited) performance of the love duet from Act II of *Tristan*, with Lauritz Melchior – conducted with incendiary energy by Albert Coates.[77] In addition, her live and studio recordings of scenes from *Götterdämmerung*, conducted by Beecham and Leo Blech are priceless. Her "Immolation" scene with the latter is a phenomenon of the age of recording; Blech's tempi are very fast, but Leider sails through the performance, creating the linear stability that was written by Wagner into Brünnhilde's music, to serve as a thread against which the spasmodic and dis-associative orchestral score can push and pull without doing damage to the coincidence of beauty and momentum. The scene works only if a soprano is sufficiently resolute to carry the weight of the score's orchestral dynamism; Leider's cantabile is as carbon-fibre – light, strong and flexible, despite the "modernity" of her delicate vibrato; the honey-dew sweetness of tone is more redolent of the Countess and Donna Anna – roles that Leider was able to perform during seasons in which she also appeared as Isolde.

Between 1928 and 1934, Leider was unrivalled at Bayreuth, where Heinz Tietjen and her too-good friend[78] Winifred Wagner considered her to be the "perfect" dramatic soprano. This was probably true, and her performances established a new set of benchmarks which, for good or for bad, changed forever the perception and culture of Wagner singing.[79] Leider's differences were captured in her tone, which is richer and brighter (with the possible exception of Nordica), and more full than that of any soprano to record Wagner before her. Her singing is all the more impressive when noting her technical agility, which is consistent with a bel canto soubrette. Leider's pulsating vibrato was ubiquitous but she used it expressively. It all sounds glorious to ears brutalised since the late 1990s by what has become normal at Bayreuth; for the 1920s, however, it was alien. There is simply nothing to compare between the singing of Frida Leider and Lilli Lehmann. Though born 40 years apart, they were for a couple of years contemporaries, appearing on German stages as exemplars of traditions that were to become as oil and water. There exists a couple of minutes of footage from Bayreuth, in 1934, during a rehearsal of Act I of *Götterdämmerung*, with Franz

---

75   18 April, 1888 – 4 June, 1975.

76   26 April, 1892 – 15 May, 1968.

77   Excerpts from a performance on 3 March, 1933, from the Met, conducted by Bodanzky, are riotously good also.

78   Leider's relationship with the Nazi regime was complicated in consequence of her marriage to a "half-Jew." She remained in Germany throughout the war, but without collaborating. Her divorce from her husband, Rudolf Deman, was forced upon her in 1943, after years of harassment. They remained a couple, however, and remarried after the war. Rieger, Eva (2016). *Frida Leider: Sängerin im Zwiespalt ihrer Zeit*. Olms, p. 124.

79   1928, 1934, 1936, 1937, and 1938.

Volker as Siegfried. The conductor Karl Elmendorff is unseen, but Tietjen, Winifred, the stage designer, Emil Preetorius, and the technical director, Paul Eberhardt, are all captured clearly. It's an amazing document, in which both singers are in typically resonant voice. Leider fluffs her final high C – but only because she is in rehearsal, and saving herself for the performance. The preceding B flats are like laser-beams, however, and the brilliance of her tone, the sensuality of her phrasing and the clarity of her articulation are as close to the modern conception of the perfect Wagnerite as has now to be imagined. This remained true even after the emergence of Kirsten Flagstad,[80] a Norwegian soprano whose career path followed a trajectory that would be trite but for the failure of so many to take heed of it.

Flagstad made her stage debut at the National Theatre, as Nuri in d'Albert's *Tiefland*, in 1913; she was 18-years-old at the time. In the same year, she made her first recordings. To gauge something of the voice in its infancy, her performance from 1914 of the folk song, "*Aa Ola Ola Min Eigen Onge*,"[81] reveals a voice of improbable maturity, sweetness and richness. There is already a pronounced suggestion of the mezzo-warmth and depth of tone that would become her hallmark. After further study, marriage and a child, Flagstad joined the newly created Opera Comique in Oslo, under the direction of Alexander Varnay – the father of the soprano, Astrid.[82] Between 1928 and 1934, she performed with the Stora Teatern in Gothenburg. Her repertoire throughout these formative years was managed carefully, as evidenced by two of her role creations in 1932: Handel's Rodelinda and Wagner's Isolde. She was 37 at the time.

In 1933, having auditioned for Winifred Wagner (who urged her to work on her German), Flagstad sang minor roles at Bayreuth; the following year she was cast as Sieglinde and Gutrune – opposite Frida Leider's Brünnhilde. After the 1934 Festival, Flagstad travelled to St Moritz, to audition for Artur Bodanzky and Giulio Gatti-Casazza – the conductor and general manager of the Met in New York. She was hired instantly, although Bodanzky was clear when requiring her to know the roles of Leonore in *Fidelio*, Isolde, Brünnhilde, and the Marschallin.[83] She had also not to arrive fat. As the singer later remembered it, he spoke bluntly when telling her "Your slender, youthful figure is not the least reason you were engaged."[84] Flagstad's debut at the Met, as Sieglinde on the afternoon of 2 February, 1935, created a sensation – in part because of the reaction to the nationwide broadcast on the Met's syndicated radio program. The intermission was hosted by Geraldine Farrar, who was so affected by what she had seen and heard that she abandoned her notes and announced instead, "I wish you might use my eyes today, for the debut of our newest soprano, Kirsten Flagstad, the eminent young Norwegian of whom we expect great

---

80 12 July, 1895 – 7 December, 1962.

81 'Oh, ola, ola, I lov'd you dearly.'

82 See further below.

83 If she learned the role, she did not sing it. When writing to her mother from the Astor, she wrote "Yesterday we listened to Der Rosenkavalier, it was quite lovely and I merely state the fact that it is beyond any human being to sing the Marschallin without any orchestral rehearsal or a lot of other rehearsals." As things transpired, Flagstad's only notable performance of Strauss' music was the first performance of the "Four Last Songs," in 1950. See also Chapter 16.

84 Vogt, Howard (1987). *Flagstad: Singer of the Century*. Secker and Warburg, p. 46.

things." She followed these remarks with a performance of a section of "*Winterstürme* [*wichen dem Wonnemond*]" – written for the tenor role, Siegmund! – in English, and in still-luxurious voice.[85] Days later, Flagstad sang Isolde, and at the end of the month, Brünnhilde in *Die Walküre* and *Götterdämmerung*. Before the end of her first season, she appeared as Elsa, Elisabeth and Kundry. Thanks to this legendary run of performances, and her subsequent recordings and radio broadcasts, Flagstad was hailed as the world's pre-eminent Wagner soprano. She was also a major asset for the Met, whose coffers she filled at the box office and through nationwide appeals to radio listeners for donations.

Flagstad's career between 1935 and 1941 was stellar, but marred privately by nasty, long-running feuds with Lauritz Melchior and the Met's general manager, Edward Johnson.[86] She suffered also – and unfairly – from ignorance and misrepresentation, in consequence of her decision to remain in Scandinavia during the War. It was especially meaningful that when Flagstad finally recorded *Tristan* in the studio (too late, and in far from ideal circumstances),[87] she did so with Wilhelm Furtwängler,[88] with whom she had collaborated two years earlier for the premiere of Strauss' "Four last Songs." Flagstad bid farewell to the Met on 1 April, 1952 – not in a role by Wagner, but as Alceste, which she had learned during the war in Norway. Her final operatic appearance was as Dido, on 5 June, 1953. As one of the three most revered Wagner sopranos of the 20th century, it is not insignificant that Flagstad should have been *able* to perform works by Gluck and Purcell in her late fifties, after 15 years of singing almost nothing but the heaviest roles in the operatic canon. The root of Flagstad's success was power, primarily; her voice was considered to be enormous, which proved to be a particular aphrodisiac for a country where bigger was synonymous with better. The branches that flowed from amplitude were a burnished, easy tone; exceptional breath control; a seamless legato, and dramatised word-placement. Her art was achieved without palpable effort because she gave more years to training and to patient repertoire-choices than she did to Wagner. Flagstad never pushed or forced her voice because she didn't need to. The lesson that most took from these absolutes was different, and irreversibly destructive.

Leider and Flagstad were not appreciated at the time as anomalies – outliers by the standards of an age when there were many alive who remembered the first *Ring* and the premiere of *Parsifal*. Just as Caruso and Corelli created unmeetable standards for tenors, so too did Leider and Flagstad idealise the heldensopran for their own times, and for everyone who followed. Nine of Flagstad's 70 appearances as Isolde at the Met were broadcast as a Saturday matinee – the effect of which was pivotal to the common mis-conception of what a Wagner soprano was supposed to sound like. That sound was noise. Within 15 years of Leider's debut at Bayreuth, in 1928, the old school had been replaced by a new one, to which a *very* small number of sopranos

---

85   The performance, and Farrar's comments and singing, are widely available online.

86   The rifts were healed, and in honour of Flagstad's 100th appearance as Isolde at the Met, in 1941, she received 100 roses from Melchior and Johnson.

87   Flagstad's top notes during the Act II love duet had to be performed by Elisabeth Schwarzkopf.

88   Made in 1952 (and released the following year), the recording is revered; this status is largely undeserved, however. Furtwängler's conducting is sluggish, and Flagstad is matronly rather than sensual. There are various other problems, mainly Ludwig Suthaus' Tristan.

were capable of adhering without strain. One of the best was Flagstad's successor at the Met,[89] Helen Traubel,[90] an American dramatic soprano with a gleaming voice over which she had absolute control. There were obvious similarities between their voices, as can be heard from Traubel's many broadcasts and live recordings, among the most celebrated of which was a performance on 22 February, 1941, of bleeding chunks from various Wagner operas, conducted by Toscanini, with Melchior. Her performance of *Tristan* from the Teatro Colón in 1943, conducted with Merlin-like skill[91] by Fritz Busch, again with Melchior as Tristan, captures the singers at their best.

The Bayreuth Bark began to yield to yelling during the late '30s and 1940s. A live recording from 1937 of *Götterdämmerung*, with Anny Konetzni[92] singing Brünnhilde, speaks to the change in the Wagner-soprano's timbre, tone and placement (and also that of the Wagner tenor, with Max Lorenz adding considerable vibrato to his Siegfried). They both sing with insight, beauty and drama, but the defining quality – and the lasting message – was volume. Konetzni and Lorenz were *very* loud, as they needed to be, with Hans Knappertsbusch flashing his cufflinks with alacrity during the Act I duet. One of the loudest of them all – and something of a villain of the story, in the light of her longevity and inexplicable popularity – was Astrid Varnay,[93] whose debut at the Met (as Sieglinde, substituting for an indisposed Lotte Lehmann) took place on 6 December, 1941, the day before Japan attacked Pearl Harbour. Her success was broadcast, but otherwise lost to the bigger picture. So too was the scandal of her youth. Varnay was 23 at the time, and because a recording has survived it's possible to consider the circumstances as well as their consequences. The former are that she found herself singing her first Sieglinde next to Lauritz Melchior, the loudest Siegmund of the 20th century. Even by his own Olympian standards, Melchior was in ridiculously stentorian form, and it's impossible not to conclude that the unfortunate neophyte was bullied into forcing her tone to keep pace with his. From the start, Varnay over-sings, with a voice beset by a wide, dislocating vibrato that, even at the age of 23, degenerated into a wobble. This was in 1941 – when the 53-year-old Lotte Lehman (a student of the first Eva in *Die Meistersinger*) was able to perform Sieglinde with a voice that sounded half its age. Varnay had a long and successful career – which transitioned during the early 1970s into mezzo roles – but *that* wobble persevered, bleaching any hope of cantabile or diction. She was loud, but neither the music nor the words gained anything from it. Varnay represented the ultimate, crystallising effect of 200 years of steady causation, after Stendhal first decried the loss of "tender utterances" at the Teatro San Carlo.[94] Even as concerning the music of Wagner, the art shows no sign of recovering what plainly has been lost.

---

89   Traubel performed at the Met between 1937 and 1953.
90   16 June, 1899 – 28 July, 1972.
91   The love duet is ratcheted with fantastic, ruthless precision, unfolding as one gigantic accelerando; Busch achieves something similar with the "*Liebestod,*" cultivating an ultimately frenetic pace with which Traubel copes with Valkyrie-like resolve and focus.
92   12 February, 1902 – 6 September, 1968.
93   *née* Ibolyka Astrid Maria Varnay, 25 April, 1918 – 4 September, 2006.
94   See Chapter 9.

The thrill of volume was levelled in Germany, to an extent, by tradition. Martha Mödl[95] was a fiercely committed dramatic soprano, given to over-singing later in her career, as was true also of Gertrude Grob-Prandl,[96] who cultivated a fast vibrato and laboured portamento to help manage her almost comically-resonant voice. As Elektra, she was sensational, particularly in a theatre with a generous acoustic to absorb the hammering. Most of the live excerpts (and a single complete performance) are from the 1960s, but there are chunks of *Elektra* from the '50s doing the rounds that include a hair-raising, orchestra-killing performance of *"Was bluten muss?"*[97] that is simultaneously thrilling and terrifying. Never has the painting of violent death in music sounded so winningly visceral. As Salome, the Bulgarian Ljuba Welitsch[98] was a phenomenon, and almost certainly the finest interpreter of the role to be recorded in a complete performance.[99] Strauss trained her in the role for six weeks, in advance of her performance in Vienna as part of his 80th birthday celebrations in 1944; he attended every one of her rehearsals as well as the first night. It's easy to appreciate the composer's enthusiasm for her portrayal, which is compelling for its admixture of youth, delirium and bravura. Welitsch's phrasing is as it can be imagined from the score; her serpentine portamento sweetens all that sickens, so it's easy to believe in Herod's seduction long before she takes her clothes off. According to Kenneth Morgan:

> This was truly one of the red-letter days in the history of the Metropolitan Opera, for the performance was greeted with a fifteen-minute standing ovation, which was almost unprecedented in the history of the company. Nothing like such applause had been heard at the Met for a generation, and the impact of this production was talked about for years afterwards.[100]

Welitsch sang little by Wagner, although she could have done so with ease; instead, she preserved her voice over time, rejecting the big-ticket roles of Isolde and Brünnhilde, ensuring a long career and fealty to the composers on whom she doted. At the light-lyric end of the German-voice spectrum, the 1950s was a halcyon time for Wagner sopranos. In particular, six supremely talented singers, born between 1911 and 1921, dominated as Elisabeth, Elsa, Freia, Gutrune, Woglinde and Eva – and also in the operas of Mozart, the light-lyric works of Richard Strauss, and the Vienna-centred culture of the lied. Elisabeth Grümmer,[101] Elizabeth Schwarzkopf,[102]

---

95   22 March, 1912 – 16 December, 2001.

96   11 November, 1917 – 16 May, 1995.

97   'What must bleed?'

98   10 July, 1913 – 1 September, 1996.

99   On both occasions (1949 and 1952), at the Met, conducted by Fritz Reiner.

100   Morgan, Kenneth (2010). *Fritz Reiner, Maestro and Martinet.* University of Illinois Press, p. 128.

101   *née* Elisabeth Schilz, 31 March 1911 – 6 November 1986.

102   *née* Olga Maria Elisabeth Friederike Schwarzkopf, 9 December, 1915 – 3 August, 2006.

Hilde Gueden,[103] Lisa Della Casa,[104] Irmgard Seefried,[105] and Sena Jurinac[106] became the female voices most commonly identified with the revival of Austrian and German musical life immediately after the war.[107] Schwarzkopf, Jurinac, and Seefried were members of the Wiener Mozart-Ensemble, a small-orchestra company created in 1945 by the conductor Josef Krips to assist with the preservation of Viennese performance traditions that focussed on the music of (the largely untainted) Mozart. Because so many Austro-German opera houses and concert venues had been damaged or destroyed by the conflict, the company performed wherever space was available. Many of the venues were small compared to the ruined Vienna State Opera, and this constraint served to emphasise the need for singers and players to account for acoustics as well as each other in performance. Schwarzkopf and company were beautiful,[108] slim, and achingly cosmopolitan. When Della Casa was profiled by BBC television in May, 1963, she appeared on set as if she was being directed by Fellini or Hitchcock; she smoked throughout the interview, and spoke English more beautifully than most of her viewers. In response to the question "what does your husband do?" she replied "he loves me." In 1962, she appeared on US television[109] to perform scenes from *Tosca* with Franco Corelli, in colour; as putative film stars, they were transformative of the pre-war stereotype of opera singers as wobbling in sound and appearance.

The television fed off the lust engendered by the collision of talent and beauty; their perfect vocal techniques were matched to impeccable sensibilities that idealised a German form of bel canto. But for the modernity of their appearance, they were *almost* old-fashioned. As the finest collection of German-voice lyric sopranos to make records – and a great many of them[110] – they drew an inexhaustible abundance of song from everything to which they turned. While their repertoire evolved (with Lisa Della Casa, starting out as Sophie and Zdenka and growing into an unforgettable Marschallin and a peerless Arabella), their style, elegance and lyricism did not. There is almost no significant recording of an opera by Mozart, pre-*Tristan* Wagner or Strauss[111] from the 1950s and early '60s that doesn't feature one or more of Grümmer, Schwarzkopf, Gueden, Della Casa, Seefried, and Jurinac. Their combined catalogue runs to hundreds of recordings, including many of works by Wagner, and while only Della Casa was suited naturally to more dramatic roles (all of which she declined), it is worth reflecting how closely their performing philosophies bound them to Wagner's ambition. They were masters of cantabile and word-use, qualities

---

103   15 September, 1917 – 17 September, 1988.

104   2 February, 1919 – 10 December, 2012.

105   9 October, 1919 – 24 November, 1988.

106   *née* Srebrenka Jurinac, 24 October, 1921 – 22 November, 2011.

107   It should be acknowledged that each of the six had performed before or during the war, even Jurinac. Schwarzkopf was alone in being tainted by her associations (and engagement) with the Nazi regime.

108   It has to be conceded that Grümmer was alone among her colleagues in not being a pin-up – although she sounded like one. She suffered chiefly from what might politely be considered an "English" set of teeth.

109   The Bell Telephone Hour.

110   Jurinac's career on record commenced in 1949 (with *Der Zigeunerbaron*, conducted by Franz Marszalek) and ended in 1981 with *Hänsel und Gretel* (conducted by Solti).

111   Discounting the heavier parts (*i.e.*, Salome, Elektra, Helena *etc.*).

that amplified the idiosyncrasies and characteristics of their singing. None of them had a light voice, such that they could not be heard performing the Wagner roles in which they specialised or, for that matter, when confronted by Strauss' orchestrations in *Der Rosenkavalier* and *Arabella*. The point is not that they should have taken up the challenges of Brünnhilde and Isolde (or Salome and Elektra for that matter), but whether they were better suited to Wagner's music than Astrid Varnay.

With the opening of "New Bayreuth" in 1951, Wieland Wagner did not, of course, engage a lyric soprano to sing the role of Kundry. He turned to Martha Mödl, whose voice tore around the theatre like a pin-ball, even when singing "*Ich sah das Kind an seiner Mutter Brust,*"[112] in Act II, Scene 2. During this aching monologue, Kundry explains to Parsifal how she discovered his name from his mother, who had tried to shield him from his father's fate. She reveals much of Parsifal's history, which leaves him stricken with remorse, both for his mother's death and for having stripped her from his memory. The score for this prolonged episode is among the most intimate in the opera; there is absolutely *no* requirement for a voice of anything like the scale of Mödl's. While she pays attention to many of the expressive and dynamic markings, her singing is nonetheless a blunt weapon compared to what would have been achieved by her more lyric colleagues. Her voice placement is far from stable, and her pitch is frequently uneven; some of her phrasing is lumpen and ugly when noting how much lyricism is hard-written into the sung lines. The shadows of the Bayreuth Bark fall long and hard over her performance, therefore. It would, of course, be absurd to suggest that Elisabeth Grümmer should have been cast as Kundry by Wieland Wagner, but she could have played the role – and achieved a greater approximation of what Wagner *actually* wrote. It is, indeed, certain that she would have made more of the poetry and its emotional substance than did Mödl – a singer who performed neither Mozart nor lieder, two of the most important influences on Wagner's identity as a composer. When comparing voices, it can be asked who came closer in tone, placement and amplitude to Lilli Lehmann: Mödl or Grümmer? Lehmann recorded "*Porgi amor,*"[113] from Act II of *Le nozze di Figaro*, in 1907, so it's possible to compare that performance with any number of the live and studio recordings of the aria by Grümmer. Even allowing for the fact that Grümmer contained herself for the aria, at least as a soffit to taste and discretion, and accepting the incomparability of the recording technologies, Lehmann would have found a great deal to like in the singing of Grümmer. The brightness of her voice on a number of live recordings of the same aria is sublime; even in the studio, conducted in a complete performance of *Figaro* by Ferenc Fricsay in 1951, the elegance of Grümmer's phrasing, effortless breath control, and almost vibrato-free tone allow for every syllable to be heard and understood as clearly as if she was speaking. Mödl's singing of "*Ich sah das Kind,*" on the other hand, would require a native-German speaker to have the score in front of them to understand the words being sung. Grümmer's voice was limpid rather than limp; the power is in its projection, not its weight, which is why she was so successful in *Tannhäuser* and *Lohengrin*; it follows that the issue is not whether Mödl was a superb dramatic

---

112   'I saw the child on its mother's breast.'
113   In German.

soprano, since plainly she was bodice-rippingly dramatic, but rather what, exactly, a dramatic soprano should have sounded like in all the circumstances.

The return to life of the recording industry during the early 1950s was made bacterial by the creation of the LP, which led to an arms race between the competing commercial interests of EMI, Decca, DG and the newly-formed Philips. With complete operas now being made available on manageable (and affordable) small-sets of discs, A&R departments fell over themselves to record the standard repertory with a new generation of talent (*most* of it unconnected with the Third Reich) and a stable of pre-war conductors, a number of whom were lucky to have avoided formal de-Nazification. Time was of the essence, particularly after many of the most celebrated conductors began to die-off in quick succession, starting with Walter Damrosch in 1950, and followed *inter alia* by Willem Mengelberg and Fritz Busch in 1951, Antonio Guarnieri in 1952, Wilhelm Furtwängler and Clemens Krauss in 1954, Guido Cantelli, Erich Kleiber and Hermann Abendroth in 1956, Toscanini in 1957, and Rudolf Moralt in 1958.[114]

As Moralt was leaving, stereo was arriving. With the emergence of a two-channel recording process, thoughts turned to the once-absurd prospect of a *Ring* Cycle on LP. Decca produced the first complete opera at 33 and a 1/3, in 1950 (*Die Entführung aus dem Serail*), but it was assumed across the industry that a studio recording of the *Nibelungen* would be commercially reckless.[115] There had been three productions of *Die Meistersinger* in 1950/51 (conducted by Knappertsbusch (for Decca), Karajan (for EMI), and Kempe (for Urania)), as well as a *Tristan* in 1952 (Furtwängler), but live performances were thought to be the only possible solution to the "*Ring* problem"). Decca taped the 1951 and 1955 cycles at Bayreuth, but chose not to release ether of them.[116] It was proposed instead to engage Knappertsbusch and Flagstad (as Brünnhilde) for a complete set, but the latter was effectively retired while the former's predilection for glacial tempi threatened financially ruinous overruns as well as exhaustion.[117]

Culshaw turned instead to a young pianist and one-time repetiteur for Toscanini at the Salzburg Festival, whose career on the podium had been launched by Decca. Prior to being engaged by Culshaw to oversee the first *Ring* (and then in stereo), Georg Solti's only recording as a conductor (rather than as a pianist) was a benchmark *Arabella*, with Della Casa, in 1957. In September and October, 1958, *Das Rheingold* was recorded with the Vienna Philharmonic, and Kirsten Flagstad as Fricka. Culshaw

---

114 Into the 1960s, Sir Thomas Beecham died in 1961, Bruno Walter in 1962, and Knappertsbusch and Fritz Reiner in 1963.

115 The producer Erik Smith told the author "Mozart pays the mortgage; Wagner and Mahler pay the school fees." Smith knew what he was talking about; he produced (with John Culshaw) the 1958 *Das Rheingold*, conducted by Solti (for Decca), the famously tough sell "Haydn Opera" series, conducted by Antal Dorati (for Philips), and the "Complete Mozart" set of CDs to commemorate the composer's 200th anniversary in 1991 (also for Philips).

116 They were released many years later.

117 "Kna's" habit reached its farcical nadir with his 1961 *Fidelio*, for Westminster, with Sena Jurinac as Leonore. In the same year, Jurinac sang the role for Otto Klemperer at Covent Garden. Klemperer took his time also, particularly in the finale - which barely takes off, only to get faster and faster – with the performers on stage dragging Klemperer towards a suitably climactic momentum. The live recording from that production (with Vickers sensational as Florestan) is very fine indeed.

had been warned by EMI's Walter Legge that a recording of *Das Rheingold* would sell 50 copies; he was proven wrong within a week. The recording was a triumph from the first, competing on the Billboard charts with Elvis Presley and making Decca its money back within a couple of years. It was decided not to record the cycle in order – with *Siegfried* jumping the cue. There was only one singer to whom Decca – or anyone else – could have turned in 1962 for Brünnhilde.

The Swedish Birgit Nilsson made her debut in 1946 – having studied briefly, and unhappily, with Joseph Hislop, the last of Jussi Björling's teachers. Nilsson abjured all tuition in consequence, and declared "the best teacher is the stage."[118] For all that made her wonderful, Nilsson's lack of technique was fundamental to her sound, which wanted for refinement and polish. Her defining quality was power, the like of which has probably never been equalled in the history of singing. Some might wish to read about her career trajectory, or Fritz Busch's tutelage, or her debuts as Glyndebourne in 1951, the Vienna State Opera in 1953, and Bayreuth, as Elsa, in 1954. Others may be interested in her progression as Brünnhilde through productions at the Bavarian State Opera, Bayreuth, Covent Garden and the Met. Ultimately, however, Nilsson's career is reducible to a singular consideration – volume. Her devoted admirers will not allow it, of course, but the fact remains that Nilsson was, in almost everything she did, an entirely artless singer. This will spark hissing fury from her devotees, but there is no getting around the fact that Nilsson lacked technique, and whenever she sang anything requiring it the outcome was either pained or painful. Take, for example, her misguided stabbing of Mozart. In 1959, at the age of 38, she recorded her first Donna Anna, in *Don Giovanni*,[119] for Decca, with Erich Leinsdorf conducting. Her performance of "*Or sai chi l'onore*," in isolation, is a perfect example of what it was that made Nilsson inappropriate for Mozart, and anything else that called on the core elements of art-singing. Her placement is poor, her articulation heavy and her dynamic range flat-lined; what phrasing there is comes across as jagged – thanks to her ill-trained vibrato. Even her intonation is suspect.[120] Worst of all is the tone – which is predictably Wagnerian. Nilsson's singing of "*Crudele? Non Mi Dir,*" is worse still, embarrassing even. As she approaches the skin-tightening moment when Donna Anna sings "*Abbastanza,*"[121] written as a famously awkward rising fifth (E flat to B flat), Nilsson hammers out what Grümmer, Della Casa and Schwarzkopf floated to the heavens and back. Even Ljuba Welitsch, performing the role for Furtwängler at the Salzburg Festival in 1950, managed to phrase the passage beautifully, even if absent the subito-piano / mezza-voce achieved by Grümmer, Della Casa and Schwarzkopf.

A good pair of headphones will reveal the amplitude of Nilsson's voice in its resonance within the studio environment, which is both the part and the sum of her appeal as a soprano. It would be churlish to deny what this meant for anyone privileged to hear her in the theatre; it is less impressive on record, however, because

---

118   Holland, Bernard (12 January 2006). "Birgit Nilsson, Soprano Legend Who Tamed Wagner, Dies at 87." *The New York Times*.

119   She recorded her second in 1967, for DG, with Karl Böhm conducting. It marked no improvement.

120   One need only compare her performance(s) as Donna Anna with *any* by Grümmer, Jurinac or Della Casa. She didn't sing the role, but the studio recording by Schwarzkopf of Donna Anna's "*Crudele ? Non Mi Dir*," is miraculous, and an exemplar for the manner in which Mozart *can* sound.

121   'Enough.'

what made Nilsson so thrilling was the experience of hearing a woman tear through extended fortissimos within a fixed acoustic designed to accommodate the voices of mortals. Anyone who has heard Wagner performed at Bayreuth, or another big theatre, such as the Met, La Scala, the Vienna State Opera and Covent Garden, will understand the thrill of hearing a *truly* large voice, but Nilsson's voice was not "large." In fact, words are useless when characterising the proportions of her voice because it was appreciable only by context. The only singer with whom she worked regularly to keep pace was Franco Corelli, with whom she performed *Tosca* and, more frequently, *Turandot*. Their partnership is remembered – and enjoyed by millions to this day – because of the impossibility of their amplitude. Hearing the two most resonant voices of the 20th century go toe-to-toe in absolute equivalence, even on record, is one of the most thrilling experiences in the history of music. The performances of *Turandot* conducted by Stokowski are especially intoxicating, but *only* because the singers raise each other's stakes to a point where the Met, as a temple of art, was transfigured as a circus tent during their exchanges following "*In questa reggia*,"[122] and the conclusion of Act III, "*Principessa di morte*."[123]

Nilsson's many performances as Brünnhilde and Isolde operated a similar dialectic, with the improbability of her voice's size highlighting the worst aspects of the modern culture of Wagner singing. The elevation of sonority over the primacy of sensibility proved a major dilemma for operas houses casting Tristan. Apart from Jon Vickers, the German repertory had no access to a tenor with the requisite power and stamina to meet Nilsson on a level playing field. She didn't sing *Tristan* with Vickers until the 1970s – late in her career, when even she was beginning to flag[124] – and so all of her recordings, in the studio and from Bayreuth, in the cycles conducted by Solti (which concluded with *Die Walküre* in 1965)[125] and Karl Böhm (1966–67), were alongside a Siegfried who was overtaken routinely by Nilsson. Wolfgang Windgassen was a superb artist, with a very fine tenor voice, but it was recognised by everyone, including Windgassen, that Nilsson was superhuman by *any* standards. Their performance of *Tristan*, taped live at Bayreuth in 1966 is, nonetheless, one of the miracles of the recording age. The success of these performances, and Wieland's now-legendary production, can be attributed to Böhm's stupendous, driven conducting, and also the sound-engineering, which has never been improved upon, for all the technological developments since.

The mezzo-soprano playing Brangäne on Böhm's *Tristan* had one of the longest careers in the history of music, making her debut as Orlovsky in *Die Fledermaus* at the age of 18, in 1946, and giving her last staged performance, as Klytemnestra, at the Vienna State Opera, in December, 1994. Unusually, if not uniquely, however,

---

122 'In this palace.'

123 'Princess of death.'

124 There exists a live recording (in excellent sound) of *Tristan* from 5 December, 1976 (at the Vienna State Opera), conducted by Horst Stein. It is a better testament to Vickers' remarkable talents than to Nilsson's.

125 *Götterdämmerung* was recorded by Decca in 1964, and the complete cycle was finally released in 1968. The cycle conducted by Böhm in 1966–67 was released belatedly by Philips in 1973. The latter is considerably better conducted, and with many of the same cast that worked with Solti in the studio.

Christa Ludwig,[126] sounded at the end of her career almost exactly as she did at the beginning. Her voice was astonishingly beautiful, as sweet, rich and silken in its tone and articulation as any to be recorded. In addition to opera, she was talented as a singer of Bach, oratorio, and lieder, and it was her skill with words that enabled her to attend with undimming success to everything from a legendary recording as Adalgisa, with Maria Callas, in 1960, to performances as the Old Lady in *Candide*, conducted by Bernstein in 1989. The significance of her performance as Brangäne attaches to the richness of the tone, and her flawless cantabile. The "warning" she delivers in Act II of *Tristan* has never been equalled for sheer sumptuousness. Because she developed (and maintained) a flawless technique, which gave her access to a high C, Ludwig was believed by many to be a dramatic soprano, capable of playing Isolde as well as Kundry, which she sang in Vienna for Karajan in 1961,[127] in the studio for Decca in 1972, conducted by Solti, and again with James Levine, at the Met, in 1979. Ludwig declined Isolde and Brünnhilde, but she took all the major mezzo Wagner roles, including Venus, Ortrud, Fricka, Waltraute and, even, Adriano (*Rienzi*). Her artistry and insight as Fricka and Waltraute improved the *Ring* cycles conducted by Solti, Karajan and Levine.

Her importance as a Wagner soprano is captured in recordings, live and in the studio, of the final scene of *Götterdämmerung*, the "Immolation," and the "*Liebestod*." The studio recording of the latter was conducted in 1963, by Otto Klemperer; the former with Heinrich Hollreiser the following year. On 23 March, 1963, she was recorded in concert singing the "Immolation" and the "*Liebestod*" with Knappertsbusch. These performances are unique, for a number of reasons; indeed, they are among the most important ever made. Ludwig's mother, Eugenie Besalla, was herself a mezzo-soprano of great talent; she lost her voice in her late thirties while at Aachen Opera, a tragedy she attributed to Karajan, who was music director at the time, and known to be a task-master. Christa was advised by her mother that if she wanted to continue to sing Bach then she had to tread carefully when singing Wagner. Despite numerous offers, and considerable begging by conductors over more than two decades, Ludwig only sang the "*Liebestod*" and the "Immolation." The performances as recorded are remarkable chiefly for Ludwig's bel canto sensibilities, which introduce more than a little Bellini to music then subject increasingly to yelling and wobbling. Ludwig's presence is made special not by power – although her voice was more than capable of surviving Knappertsbusch's exigencies – but by line, tone and expression. Her voice placement was, for want of a better word, immaculate. She uses her light and variegated vibrato as a paintbrush, to add and remove colour and texture; her portamento and seamless breathing join Wagner's lines of song in a manner that was unique among post-war singers. It's hard to believe that Amalie Materna was as good as this, but if she was then the lessons taught by Ludwig through these precious recordings are available still to teachers and singers in place of the assumptive, absolutist Birgit Nilsson.

For the splenetic reader, it can (and should be) admitted that Nilsson was a force of nature when at full tilt – but Wagner's music is only rarely headlong. There is a

---

126   16 March, 1928 – 24 April, 2021.
127   There is a recording available of this production.

great deal more to be revealed than what can be lost to endless bulb-breaking fortissimos. Even so, the heat and intensity of Nilsson's singing of *Tristan's* second act, and the closing "*Liebestod*," established a sonic ideal to which no other soprano has come close. This makes her Isolde a *very* guilty pleasure because anyone approaching *Tristan* (as a conductor, a singer or a listener) is left commonly concluding that her performance is, and must be, the ideal. The resulting standard is distended and unmeetable, therefore. It forged a praxis that ideates the impractical and the unachievable, compounding the residuum of the school of Varnay on the basis that there was only one Nilsson. There were, however, 100 opera houses staging Wagner's works worldwide at the time – which is where everyone else was left attempting to be something they were not.

Nilsson's influence was equally damaging to Richard Strauss. Her recordings of his evil sisters are revered, but only because they are loud.[128] As Salome, she is distended and unpersuasive, lacking the necessary vocal flexibility, colour and vulnerability; she is a warrior rather than a princess, and entirely uninteresting. The same is true of her Elektra, which resolves as another Brünnhilde – a god-like creature who, by voice alone, should have been able to dig up the axe and kill everyone in the palace without having to wield it. The greatness of Nilsson's voice is inarguable; the manner in which she used it is not – and neither is the value system according to which she remains the ideal. In 1972, she walked alone onto the stage of the New York Met to perform the closing scene from *Salome*, conducted by Karl Böhm, for a televised gala presented in farewell to Rudolf Bing.[129] It is a remarkable feat of singing, to which the audience responds with a suitably volcanic roar as everyone, including the orchestra, stand to their feet. If it isn't Salome then it can be appreciated for what it is, and for what it was – as an outlier of ultimately terrible consequences.

During Nilsson's *long* reign, the best Salome and Elektra after Welitsch was the German Inge Borkh.[130] She played Agamemnon's daughter on nearly 400 occasions, and once in the studio, for DG, in a blistering, never-bettered performance conducted by Böhm. Borkh was the greatest Brünnhilde and Isolde that never was. She sang a magnificent Sieglinde at Bayreuth, conducted by Keilberth, in 1952 – after which Wieland Wagner is said to have begged her to sing Brünnhilde in the following year's *Ring*, conducted by Clemens Krauss. She refused, and the role was again played by Varnay. For reasons that were never made clear, she didn't return to Bayreuth again. In 1953, the role of Sieglinde was played wonderfully by Regina Resnik,[131] a superb Chrysothemis, frequently alongside Borkh and Nilsson. Borkh made only a handful of recordings in the studio[132] – but there are many taped live that attest to the talents of a superb singing actress, during whose nearly 100-year lifespan there emerged no natural (or worthy successor) as Elektra. The depth of her talent was located in her capacity to mine vulnerability as well as power; she was a lyric-dramatic soprano, therefore – and something of an anomaly heading into the

128 The same is largely true of Solti's conducting – for both recordings.
129 The performance is widely available online.
130 *née* Ingeborg Simon, 26 May, 1921 – 26 August, 2018.
131 *née* Regina Resnik, 30 August, 1922 – 8 August, 2013.
132 Apart from Elektra, her only leading performance in the studio was as Turandot, alongside the sheet-metal-working tenor, Mario del Monaco.

1970s. Her career at the Met was brief – with only 22 performances – which many attribute to the pre-eminence for Bing of Leonie Rysanek.[133] This Austrian-born soprano played Chrysothemis at the beginning of her career, in 1953; she gave her last performance, as Klytemnestra, at the Salzburg Festival, in August, 1996. Rysanek never sang Elektra, or Isolde – although she was ideal for both – and even if she continued working beyond the natural lifetime of her voice, she was a sensational actress, stupendous as the Kaiserin, the Marschallin, Helena and Danae. She delayed taking up the role of Salome until 1972, at the age of 46, and past her best. She continued to perform the role of Sieglinde (as whom she made her debut – at Wieland Wagner's invitation – at the 1951 Bayreuth Festival), singing it for the last time in 1988.

The 1970s saw the emergence of four superlative German-repertoire sopranos, each of whom was successful straddling the lyric-dramatic divide. Elisabeth Söderström[134] spent her entire career at her native Royal Swedish Opera, although she travelled widely – with five years at the Met from 1959. She was one of the finest Marschallins of the 1970s, and a committed advocate for Janáček's operas, *Jenůfa*, *Káťa Kabanová*, and *The Makropoulos Affair*. Better known, in consequence of her immensely productive contract with DG, and the shared devotions of Karajan and Böhm, was Gundula Janowitz,[135] a Berlin-born soprano with one of the most recognisable timbres in the history of recorded music. Her voice is also among the most widely disseminated, since it was her recording as the Countess (performing "*sull'aria*," with the Swiss soprano and legendary Mozartian, Edith Mathis),[136] that caused the prison to fall silent during the 1994 film *The Shawshank Redemption*. Like Joan Sutherland, Janowitz was better known for her song than her words, but the beauty of that song was unparalleled. She was a long-surviving and unfailingly elegant throwback to pre-war traditions, particularly when performing Wagner's lighter roles, and even, on occasion, Sieglinde. The 1980s and 1990s where Wagner was concerned was owned by Hildegard Behrens,[137] Helge Dernesch,[138] Brigitte Fassbaender,[139] Anja Silja,[140] Anne Evans,[141] Karita Mattila,[142] and Deborah Polaski.[143] Some of these singers were *much* better than others. It would be churlish not to recognise as special the consistency of Dernesch's beautifully sung Brünnhilde on Karajan's inconsistent *Ring* for DG. Or, for that matter, Silja's incredible early career at Bayreuth, where she made her debut as Senta at the age of 20, followed by seven amazing years as Elsa, Venus, Elisabeth, Eva, Freia, and the Waldvogel.

By the time Barenboim came to perform (and record) the *Ring* at Bayreuth, in 1991–92, the "best heldensopran" in the world was apparently Deborah Polaski, an

---

133   *née* Leopoldine Rysanek, 14 November, 1926 – 7 March, 1998.

134   *née* Anna Elisabeth Söderström, 7 May, 1927 – 20 November, 2009.

135   2 August, 1937 –

136   11 February, 1938 –

137   9 February, 1937 – 18 August, 2009.

138   3 February, 1939 –

139   3 July, 1939 –

140   *née* Anja Silja Regina Langwagen, 17 April, 1940 –

141   20 August, 1941 –

142   5 September, 1960 –

143   26 May, 1949 –

American soprano, whose Brünnhilde, like that of Anne Evans, adhered to the school of Varnay, rather than the Lehmanns and Ludwig. In 2008, Christian Thielemann's live-recorded cycle featured a clutch of wobbling women as the Valkyries, and the sufferable distensions of Eva-Marie Westbroek[144] as Sieglinde and Linda Watson[145] as Brünnhilde. Because no-one has done justice to Wagner's heavier soprano parts since the turn of the millennium, at least who was not established before it, and because Wagner was known to like a happy ending, the final word should go to Waltraud Meier,[146] the only Wagner soprano of modern times to approximate what the composer imagined when writing *Tristan*, the *Ring* and *Parsifal*. Meier made her debut in 1976 – the year of the centenary *Ring*. She didn't relocate to Bayreuth until the 1990s, however, where she sang her first Isolde in Heiner Müller's inexplicably acclaimed staging,[147] conducted by Barenboim, with the tireless Siegfried Jerusalem sharing in the triumph as Tristan. Meier performed Sieglinde in *Die Walküre* in the "Millennium *Ring*," at the 2000 Festival, staged by Jürgen Flimm and conducted by Giuseppe Sinopoli. In the same year, she sang Isolde at the Salzburg Festival, with Lorin Maazel. Meier devoted her entire season, 2003–2004, to concerts (including Bach's *St Matthew Passion*) and lieder recitals; she toured a program of songs by Brahms, Schubert and Hugo Wolf through Europe, Russia and the United States. Meier delayed her return to Isolde until 2005, in a new production by Peter Sellars, at the Opéra Bastille, conducted by Esa-Pekka Salonen. She followed this with performances as Kundry at the Vienna State Opera and the Met – all of them cheered to the gods.

In 2006, Meier was filmed in concert, with Barenboim, at the Philharmonie, Berlin, performing the "*Liebestod;*" she was 50-years-old at the time, and sang magnificently – even though Barenboim dragged everything horribly. In order to appreciate the significance of this performance, as an exemplar for Wagner sopranos now and in the future, it's well to focus on the chronology isolated above. Meier waited 15 years before transferring to dramatic roles – which at no time included Brünnhilde. She paced her career – and her voice – taking a significant sabbatical from opera to allow her to focus on Bach and chamber music. Meier's voice was not huge, but it was focussed – bright and brilliant, never shrill or strained. She phrased Wagner's music like a lieder singer – attending to the words, their shape and their coupling with the music, without sacrificing either to delamination. Her vibrato was light, and her portamento natural; in short, she was as good as anyone since the War, and singular in her achievements. Her art and her longevity were products of intelligence and judgment first, and voice second. Like Ludwig and the Lehmanns before her, Meier considered Wagner an adjunct to Bach – another composer who divined the importance of word-use by dwelling on syllables, and weighting them to ensure their co-operation with the score as it was orchestrated. When *Tannhäuser* was first staged in Dresden, Wagner had the singers' words copied into the parts so that the orchestral

---

144   26 April, 1970 –
145   1956 –
146   9 January, 1956 –
147   The second act was, in particular, indistinguishable from oratorio. That said, the filmed performance is one of the most exciting on record. The love duet is especially thrilling – and superior in *every* respect to Barenboim's torpid studio recording, made a year later – with the Berlin Philharmonic for Teldec.

players might follow the singers' phrasing. Twenty years later, he characterised the orchestra in *Tristan* as "a constituent part of the song." What might he have made of the contortions and distortions forced upon the stage, and from the pit, by progress?

In Act III of *Die Meistersinger*, Hans Sachs teaches Walther von Stolzing how to construct an ideal song. In doing so, he informed everyone else how to do it: the text must be perfectly clear, and the music must express its spirit as well as its meaning. Wagner knew more about singing than anyone, before or since. His genius was formed of practical realities to which he turned as a conductor as well as a composer; it takes a very modern measure of arrogance to think his values misplaced or uninformed. Anyone reading this book can disagree with Wagner. He wasn't right about everything, of course – as is obvious from his repulsive anti-Semitism – but he might have been where the performance of *his* music is concerned.

CHAPTER FIFTEEN

Challenging the Clouds and the Scorching Sun

Human sexuality has been a feature of every significant paradigm shift throughout the history of communication technology. The earliest known bas-relief carvings, the *Kangjiashimenji Petroglyphs* (dating to between 2,000 and 1,000BC), depict a couple engaging in intercourse. 20 years after Gutenberg mastered his "movable type machine" in 1450, an "Allegory of Copulation" employed an inked plate for the first explicit *erotica* in print. On 28 December, 1895, the Lumière brothers showed ten short films in Paris, introducing the world to the wonders of cinema; 11 months later, the first pornographic film, *Le Coucher de la Mariée*,[1] presented Louise Willy stripping.[2] In 1908, six years after narrative cinema was launched by Georges Méliès' *Le Voyage dans la Lune*,[3] the first fully pornographic motion picture was produced, again in France.[4] Many of the earliest movies released onto video cassette in 1976 were pornographic. Photography was not invented in the 1820s by pornographers, but the moment the technology allowed for easy reproduction, distribution became the only hurdle to supply meeting demand. Sexually explicit images were viewed on iPhones the day they were first released in 2007, with the search term "porn" accounting for 37% of incipient usage.[5] A conspicuous number of the earliest web sites created in the United States were solely for the publishing of pornography; many were operated for free by university students. It is estimated that 40% of all global internet traffic in 2023 will be accounted for by pornography of one kind or another.

If visual media is more obviously suited to depictions of *erotica*, then inuendo made its way onto the radio soon after the BBC first broadcast comedy shows in Britain. Fewer than twenty years after Lord Reith established the BBC as a moral vehicle to inform, educate and entertain ("Nation shall speak peace unto Nation"),[6]

---

1 'Bedtime for the Bride.'

2 Louise Willy, also known as "Loulou." (1873 – *circa* 1913). The film was directed by Albert Kirchner, who was credited appropriately enough as "Léar."

3 'Trip to the Moon' (1902).

4 *A L'Ecu d'Or, ou la bonne auberge* ('At The Golden Shield, or the Good Inn').

5 Steve Jobs made it clear that no adult content would ever be sold from Apple's App Store, which made no difference whatsoever to users gaining access to pornographic content when connected to the internet.

6 Significantly, the biblical passage by which this motto was inspired (rather than taken, which is Paul's Epistle to the Philippians 4:8), commends truth rather than peace: "Finally, brethren, whatsoever things are true, whatsoever things are honest, whatsoever things are just, whatsoever things are pure, whatsoever things are lovely, whatsoever things are of good report; if there be any virtue, and if there be any praise, think on these things."

the weekly comedy show, "ITMA,"[7] was engaging in double-entendres with "Mrs Mopp" ("Can I do you now, sir?"),[8] which set the scene for the "degeneration" of the BBC during the 1940s and '50s.[9]

The first recording of a human voice was made on 25 March, 1857, by Édouard-Léon Scott de Martinville, an editor and typographer of manuscripts at a scientific publishing house in Paris. The idea for his invention came to him after he set out to solve "*le problème de la parole s'écrivant elle-même*;"[10] he settled on a design based on the mechanics of the human ear. Having coated a plate of glass with a thin layer of lampblack, he attached a trumpet to a membrane that served as the "eardrum." de Martinville then attached a single boar's hair, approximately a centimetre long, which scarred the lampblack when affected by acoustic vibrations; he called his device a phonautograph, and on 9 April, 1860, a singer[11] was recorded performing the folksong "*Au clair de la lune.*"[12] That recording survived, and can now be heard online, edited by an informal collaborative of American audio historians, engineers, and sound archivists. For many years, the voice was presumed to be that of a woman, because of the speed at which the recording was played after its initial transfer; once the frequencies were adjusted, it became apparent that the singer was a man, almost certainly the inventor himself.

De Martinville well understood that "*Au clair de la lune*" was something other than a folk song for children. Shocking though it may be for those who sang it with a parent or at school, "By the Light of the Moon" is an *echt* example of "ribaldry," littered with sexual references, most of them aimed at Louis XVI, who was rumoured to be other than capable when sharing Marie Antoinette's bed. "*Ma chandelle est morte,*"[13] is a thinly-sheathed reference to the King's "broken arm,"[14] while "*ouvre-moi*

---

7   It's That Man Again.

8   Jean Mann, a Scottish Labour MP, was particularly distressed by Mrs Mopp; during a Parliamentary debate in 1947, she complained "I listen to the wireless whenever I can and I have been very much perturbed for months, nay, for some years past, at the kind of entertainment we are getting at present. With notable exceptions […] the comedians of the B.B.C. seem content with smutty sex jokes. Today, 70 per cent of their wireless programmes are based on jokes of this kind. If families are sitting with us we feel we want to switch off." House of Commons, *Official Report*, 19 February 1947, cols. 1248–9. See, generally, Daniels, Morgan (2011). "The Effects of 'Antiestablishment' BBC Comedy on Politicians, the Public and Broadcasting Values c. 1939–73." PhD Thesis, Queen Mary, University of London.

9   Reith had a low bar for isolating degeneracy. In 1937, while on holiday in Cornwall with his family, he was horrified by the arrival of people "whose advent automatically spreads pestilence of sight and sound." The source of this pestilence was a "jazz gramophone."

10   'The problem of speech writing itself.'

11   As a flight of fancy, it's worth reflecting who else might have been captured for posterity, even in primitive sound, in 1860.

12   'By the light of the moon.'

13   'My candle is dead.'

14   The father of all penis-punners was Shakespeare,who used "arms" more than once to allude to the penis. In Act V of *The Two Gentleman of Verona*, for example, Proteus announces "I'll woo you like a soldier, at arm's end, And love you 'gainst the nature of love: force ye," while in Act V of *Antony and Cleopatra*, Cleopatra says of the dead Antony "His legs bestrid the ocean; his reared arm Crested the world." For the interested, Gordon Williams' magnificent opus, *Shakespeare's Sexual Language: a glossary*, is an infinitely fascinating wildly entertaining work of first-rate scholarship (2006; Continuum). For a different take on profanity and innuendo, *Roger's Profanisaurus* (Dennis Publishing, no longer in print) is one of the funniest books in English, and an essential primer for anyone who wants to understand the

ta porte"[15] is an unambiguous invitation – possibly even to the presumably obliging Pierrot himself. *"On bat le briquet,"* means literally 'We beat the lighter' – which can, of course, be read literally and innocently. More colloquially, it means 'a fire was started,' as a synonym for the onset of love-making, antecedent to The Doors' 1967 song, "Light my fire." For 18th century France, 'lighting the fire' was understood to equate the clashing of flint-stones to the knocking together of a couple's legs; the rest of the song is similarly heavy with satiric allusion. De Martinville was born in 1817; *"Au clair de la lune"* was a popular song during the first ten years of his childhood; it follows that his choice of a *chanson paillarde* for the first recording of a human voice was no accident.

By the time recording matured as a technology, during the last decade of the 19th century, so too had the creative attitude towards sex and women, with writers, painters and composers embracing the "real," codified as *naturalisme* in France, verismo in Italy, and *Naturalismus* in Germany. The movement's putative father was Émile Zola, an author for whom sex was a lifelong obsession, with much of his fiction fixated on themes of desire, pleasure, and perversion. Zola coined the term *Naturalisme* (distinguishing Champfleury's *Réalisme*), which inspired him to increasingly explicit depictions of sexuality, ideations of the body, and digressions on the symbolic, psychological and emotional complications arising. His most ambitious work, *Les Rougon-Macquart* (subtitled, *"Histoire naturelle et sociale d'une famille sous le Second Empire"*)[16] traces the lives of a fictional family across 20 novels; it is remarkable for the manner in which Zola represented sex and women. The ninth book in the cycle, *Nana*, opens with a scene in which the title character, an untrained performer of operetta (who submitted to life as a prostitute at the conclusion of Zola's previous novel in the Rougon-Macquart series),[17] begins to shed her clothing on the stage of the *Théâtre des Variétés*, which the director, Bordenave, characterises synonymically as a brothel. Nana's sexuality reduces the largely male audience to a state of acquiescent lust:

> We were suffocating, the hair was getting heavy on sweaty heads. For three hours that we were there, the breaths had warmed the air with a human odour. In the flaming gas, suspended dust thickened, motionless below the chandelier. The room wobbled, slipped to a dizziness, weary and excited, taken as those sleepy midnight desires that stammer in the depths of the alcoves. And Nana, in front of this swooning audience, these fifteen hundred people huddled together, drowned in the subsidence and nervous collapse at the end of the show, remained victorious with her marble flesh, her sex strong enough to destroy everything in the world and not be touched by it. The play ended. At Vulcan's triumphant

---

language and the people who speak it natively – including the English.

15 'Open your door for me.'

16 'Natural and social history of a family under the Second Empire.'

17 *L'Assommoir.* a colloquialism adapted from the French verb *"assommer,"* meaning to stun or knock out. The term was used commonly during the last ten years of the 19th century in Paris to identity a shop selling cheap liquor distilled on the premises for the working classes.

calls, all Olympus marched past the lovers, with ohs! and ahs! of amazement and jubilation.

Nana's talents are greater in private than in public, which the theatre's manager explains on the basis that that she

> has something else, dammit, and something that takes the place of everything else. I scented it out, and it smells damnably strong in her, or else I lost my sense of smell.

She proceeds to ruin the lives of a succession of lovers, as a force of sexual nature operating as her own agent, literally and metaphorically. Her symbolism of Second Empire excess is at its most incendiary when rounding Paris' increasingly visible preoccupation with lust, an obsession that causes the audience to question her talent as a singer. An engorged patron cries out *"très chic,"* at which point:

> The whole room watched. It was the cherub, the college dropout, his beautiful wide eyes, his blonde face inflamed by the sight of Nana. When he saw the world turn towards him, he became very red for having spoken so loudly, without wanting to. Daguenet, his neighbour, examined him with a smile, the public laughed, as if disarmed and no longer dreamed of whistling; the young gentlemen in white gloves, also gripped by Nana's curves, swooned and applauded.

Nana's corset-straining sexuality eclipsed talent as a metric for success. Zola read the room, and quicker than most; he understood how the world was changing, at least for Parisian society, and particularly for women. He was led to Damascus by Ludovic Halévy, the composer of *La Juive*, who invited Zola backstage to meet the prima donnas of *"le tout Paris,"*[18] Anna Judic.[19] Renowned as a comic actress, Judic's celebrity exploded after she moved to the Eldorado,[20] where she mastered the *avant-garde* art of the *"chansons légères,"* a song form that developed the innuendo-heavy sensibilities consecrated by *"Au clair de la lune"* to an unprecedented measure of sophistication. Her mastery of the double-entendre exceeded her skill as a singer, which made her a perfect fit for Jacques Offenbach, to whose dominion at the Gaîté she made a valuable contribution during the years immediately following the Franco-Prussian War. Most famously, she took the lead in *Le Roi Carotte*,[21] an "opéra-féerie" composed by Offenbach and Victorien Sardou, the author in 1887 of the five-act play, *La Tosca*. After moving briefly to the Bouffes-Parisiens, Judic relocated in 1876 to the Théâtre des Variétés, where she reigned for nearly 20 years. The fast-evolving landscape within ten square miles of Paris manifested naturalist influences from movements across

---

18   Offenbach would send out invitations for first night performances by informing the recipient that "All of Paris" would be in attendance – at theatres with fewer than 1,000 seats.

19   18 July, 1849 – 15 April, 1911.

20   Later the Comédia, and since 2017, Le Théâtre Libre.

21   'The Carrot King.'

Europe, including a group of twenty Belgian painters that formed as "*Les XX*" in 1883 (with Anna Boch invited to join as its only female member), and the circle that collected in Munich around the painter Wilhelm Leibl.[22] In Berlin, the poetic philosophy of Arno Holz and Johannes Schlaf resolved a theory of "consistent naturalism" which they summarised as "Art = Nature – x."[23]

This cosmopolitanism drive towards the real was challenged briefly by Offenbach, whose operetta-satires reconciled the traditions of the Opéra-Comique to the soot-black modernity of the "*chansons légères*," using singing-actors and actresses for whom the word and its subtext mattered more than the mechanics of singing. The power of the conservatoires – spanning all forms and sectors of music, art and design – was attacked from every angle. At the Bouffes-Parisiens, Offenbach was championed by Hortense Schneider ("La Snédèr"),[24] who inspired the composer in his creation of the title roles in *La belle Hélène, La Grande-Duchesse de Gérolstein,* and *La Périchole*, and Boulotte in *Barbe-bleue*. The popularity of Offenbach's works was escalated by the wit, charm and confidence of Schneider and Judic, whose vibrancy informed a measure of celebrity that reached far beyond the theatres. Schneider's sexual liberation, in particular, led to her becoming known as "*Le Passage des Princes*," a reputation accelerated by her affair with King Edward VII. For her part, Judic's appetites served as the model for the relationships of Rose Mignon, her husband, and Steiner in *Nana*.

Zola was inspired most obviously by Émilie-Louise Delabigne, better known as the "Comtesse" Valtesse de La Bigne, a French courtesan and *demi-mondaine* whose rise through the social ranks from prostitute to model, muse, singer, patron of the arts and collector of paintings is one of the most interesting in French history.[25] To reinvent herself, she developed an almost savant-like autodidacticism, reading voraciously, attending studios and salons whenever context allowed, and befriending artists, writers, musicians and politicians. Having changed her name – choosing Valtesse as a soffit to "*Votre Altesse*"[26] – she cultivated a coterie of high society suitors and admirers, surrounding herself with aristocratic luxury, *most* of which she acquired using her own money. One of her clients paid her the modern equivalent of £150,000 a month, while the Prince de Sagan went bankrupt building Valtesse a mansion at 98 Boulevard Malesherbes, in the 17th arrondissement.[27] Before moving in, she commissioned Édouard Lièvre to decorate her bedroom, as well as the bed in which she entertained her guests.[28] It remains functional in its design and dimensions, with "entrances" on each side of the frame's balustrade, which is adorned with two flaming incense burners. The green-painted structure is extraordinary for its detail, and the acres of bronzed gold-leaf. The bedhead features two cupids holding a shield bearing

---

22   Identified in Germany as the "*Leibl-Kreis*."

23   They published their explanatory manifesto in 1891 as *Die Kunst. Ihr Wesen und ihre Gesetze*. ('Art, Its Nature and its Laws.').

24   30 April, 1833 – 5 May, 1920.

25   See, generally, Hewitt, Catherine (2015). *The Mistress of Paris: The 19th-Century Courtesan Who Built an Empire on a Secret*. Icon Books.

26   'Your Highness.'

27   A vast building, on 7 floors, it is, with glorious irony, now occupied by lawyers.

28   The bed is now on display in the Musée des Arts Décoratifs, Paris.

a crowned letter "V," while leering fauns (described by Valtesse as "clever little gods") look down from the top of the canopy, appearing in profile on either side of the shield. It is an outré work of fantasy, and one of the 19th century's most beautiful examples of furniture as art. The walls of Valtesse's apartment were covered with contemporary paintings, and so great was her wealth that she was able to maintain a legendary salon in a city bursting with them. Manet drew her in pastel in 1878,[29] a portrait in which she delighted at its showing in 1880; Henri Gervex painted her more than any other of his muses, even if the full-length portrait he completed in 1879 is ghastly.[30] Photographs of Valtesse taken at the same time prove that she was, indeed, an unusually beautiful woman.

Valtesse was Zola's model for Nana; *La belle Hélène* was his model for *La blonde Vénus*, the work in which Nana achieves her initial success. As a singer, Valtesse first came to public attention performing the small role of Hebe in Offenbach's *Orphée aux Enfers* at the Bouffes-Parisiens. One critic described her as being "red and timid as a virgin by Titian." Despite having no training whatsoever, she continued to play minor parts in a range of Offenbach operettas, including *Le Fifre enchanté*, *La Chanson de Fortunio*, *La Diva*, and *La Princesse de Trébizonde*. Valtesse's first major creation was as Mistress Johnson in the composer's one-act Opéra Bouffe, *La Romance de la Rose*, which proved a failure for all-concerned. Her next role, as Offenbach's mistress, came more easily, at which point she was elevated *almost* to the first rank of impolite society, dining regularly at Louis Bignon's Café de Foy[31] and his Café Riche, as well as other pre-eminent venues in the city, including Noel et Peters, La Maison Dorée, and the Café Tortoni. The only surviving restaurant frequented by Valtesse is Lapérouse,[32] first opened in 1766; it remains one of the city's most fabulous eateries, in part because of the décor and the food, but also because the still-surviving mirrors bear the scars of women testing the authenticity of the diamonds presented to them while dining. Whether in the company of Offenbach, or on her own, restaurants gave Valtesse access to Prudhomme, Flaubert, Maupassant, Daudet, Huysmans, de Goncourt, and Zola – each of whom determined expectations when translating the lives of the city's sopranos into fiction, and then without glamorising the common brutality of the female experience.

Until success was assured and regular, a disturbing number of France's *seconde donne* worked as "*grisettes*"[33] – ladies who sold themselves for sex only if their day-jobs failed to cover the bills. The French tolerance of brothels was state-sanctioned during the Third Republic, which taxed them to the unholy tune of 60 to 70 per cent. The success of houses of ill-repute, such as "*Le Chabanais*" and "*Le Sphinx*," did much to improve the standing of sex workers as well as their patrons, and by the third quarter of the century there were 200 licenced establishments operating under the supervision

---

29   On display at the Metropolitan Museum of Art, New York.

30   On display at the Musée d'Orsay, Paris.

31   Later titled more simply "Bignon's."

32   At 51 Quai des Grands Augustins. The "*Homard entier Victor Hugo, purée Lapérouse,*" is as good as it reads.

33   As distinguished from a "*lorette*," the name given to women who supported themselves exclusively from prostitution. The *lorettes* evolved into "*coquettes*" during the Second Empire and "*grues*" by the end of the First World War.

of the police and with the support of doctors more hypocratic than hypocritical. In the years immediately following the Franco-Prussian war, more than 150,000 women were registered as prostitutes. The police recorded, arrested and prosecuted a further 725,000 workers operating outside the legislative framework. The assault and murder of working women was routine, particularly after the disbandment of the *Brigade des mœurs* in 1881. When "Jack's" murder of (at least) five prostitutes in Whitechapel, London, in 1886 was reported throughout Europe and the United States, the taste for violence against women, whether "guilty" or innocent, crystallised in the popular dramatisation of femicide. On 17 July, 1889, Alice McKenzie, a sex worker, was slaughtered shortly after midnight in Whitechapel. Two months later, the decomposing, headless and de-limbed body of an unidentified woman in her thirties was discovered beneath a railway arch in Pinchin Street, and christened with *aperçu* wit by the British press as the "Pinchin Street Torso." Both were alleged at the time to be victims of the Ripper – although official canon holds them to be "just" run of the mill exemplars of what was fast becoming the routine brutalisation of prostitutes. On 6 October of the same year, the Moulin Rouge opened in Paris – where women unable to succeed as performers in opera and "serious" theatre flocked in their hundreds. The novelty of the female-driven programme was personified by Yvette Guilbert,[34] a diseuse,[35] folk-singer, and actress. She trained neither as an actress nor as a singer; she was nonetheless fiercely intelligent and wildly charismatic, qualities that made her pre-eminent as a performer of *café-concerts*. After successful runs at the Eldorado and the Divan Japonais, she was booked by the Moulin Rouge in 1890, where she became a fixation for the city. Her fan club included Bernhardt, Maeterlinck, Debussy, Proust, Rostand, Gounod and Verdi. She later became friends with Sigmund Freud. Her patter-songs were shamelessly sexual, leaving little but metaphor to the imagination. Among her most devoted admirers was Henri de Toulouse-Lautrec, who was commissioned by the Moulin Rouge to produce a series of posters to help promote the theatre; he was merely the best known of many thousands of painters from around the world for whom Guilbert was something out of the ordinary – both physically, and in consequence of her art. She was tall, unfashionably thin, and dressed habitually in yellow, with arm-length gloves. Her naturally bright red hair added to her aura of otherness. The English painter William Rothenstein described an early performance by Guilbert at the Mill:

> One evening Lautrec came up to the rue Ravignan to tell us about a new singer, a friend of Xanrof, who was to appear at the Moulin Rouge for the first time […]. We went; a young girl appeared, of virginal aspect, slender, pale, without rouge. Her songs were not virginal – on the contrary; but the frequenters of the Moulin were not easily frightened; they stared

---

34 *née* Emma Laure Esther Guilbert, 20 January, 1865 – 3 February, 1944. See, generally, Brécourt-Villars, Claudine (1988). *Yvette Guilbert l'irrespectueuse*. Plon; Guilbert, Yvette (1902). *La vedette*. H. Simonis Empis; and Knapp, Bettina, and Chipman, Myra (1964). *That was Yvette: The biography of the great diseuse*. Holt, Rinehart & Winston.

35 French word meaning "a female entertainer who performs monologues."

bewildered at this novel association of innocence with Xanrof's[36] horrific double entente; stared, stayed and broke into delighted applause.[37]

Although the finest of the many portraits of Guilbert was completed by a now-forgotten symbolist, Joseph Granié,[38] Toulouse-Lautrec remained her best-known and most devoted admirer. The Moulin Rouge reserved him a seat, from where he fed his growing appetites for alcohol and prostitution; his fascination for the "urban underclass," filtered through his paintings, more than 100 of which featured named sex workers. His colleague, Édouard Vuillard, believed that Toulouse-Lautrec's affinity for "outsider" women was a product of *pycnodysostosis*;[39] his fixation with the *interdite* certainly aligned with the Moulin Rouge's conflation of prostitution and inspiration. Weeks before the opening of the Moulin Rouge, four violent attacks against women in Rochechouart (Paris' equivalent of Whitechapel)[40] inspired the press in Britain and France to spread a rumour that Jack the Ripper had relocated to France – where the popular face of prostitution in the opera house belonged to Carmen. The work's initial failure was transformed after the 1889 Exposition Universelle in Paris, which presented Spanish gypsies from Granada performing flamenco.[41] Initially, the reach for atmospheric authenticity did not extend to sopranos playing the title role; the dynamic changed thanks to the sopranos, Emma Calvé[42] and Zélie de Lussan.[43] Calvé was trained in Paris by Manuel García and Mathilde Marchesi,[44] the 19th century's most influential female teacher of bel canto singing.[45] Marchesi's aunt (on her father's side) was Dorothea von Graumann, a pianist and friend of Beethoven, whom Marchesi met as a child.[46] Calvé recalled in her memoirs an occasion when Marchesi took a number of her pupils to meet Liszt:

> He sat silent and unmoved amidst the enthusiastic acclamations of the rest of us. I felt that he did not appreciate my idol, and was almost indignant with him for his indifference. In the course of the afternoon, Madame Marchesi! asked him if he would accompany Madame Krauss, who was about to sing the "Erlkonig." "I do not wish to," he answered

---

36 A reference to Léon Alfred Fourneau, a French humourist, music-hall artist, playwright and songwriter.

37 Rothenstein, William (1934). *Men and Memories, Vol 1. 1872–1900.* Faber & Faber, pp. 65–66.

38 He made much of her features when presenting them against a background of gold leaf.

39 Similar theories suggest that Walter Sickert's *verboten* tastes were informed by the *fistula* that rendered his penis less dynamic than his paintbrush.

40 These were attributed to "a tall, fair-haired man, aged about thirty-five, who spoke French, with a strong German accent." The prejudice extended to Germany and its people in France did not eclipse the country's otherwise insatiable enthusiasm for anti-Semitism, the depths of which were exposed by Zola in 1894 when writing "*J'Accuse*" after the State turned on (the innocent) Alfred Dreyfus.

41 Christoforidis, Michael and Kertesz, Elizabeth (2018). *Carmen and the Staging of Spain: Recasting Bizet's Opera in the Belle Epoque.* Oxford University Press. See, in particular, Ch. 5, "Gypsy Primitivism and the Rise of Emma Calvé."

42 *née* Rosa Emma Calvet, 15 August 1858 – 6 January, 1942.

43 21 December, 1861 – 18 December, 1949.

44 24 March, 1821 – 17 November 1913.

45 Marchesi was a singer also, having made her debut in 1844.

46 Beethoven died two days after Marchesi's sixth birthday.

brutally. "She is too ugly, and she has a tremolo." His hostess, however, quietly insisted. "Very well, then," he conceded grudgingly. [...] Liszt rose and crossed the room, with obvious reluctance. I can see him now, as he sat down at the piano. His lion's mane thrown back, his talons crashing down on the sonorous keyboard, he attacked Schubert's admirable prelude. He, alone, with his incredible force, was as mighty as a whole orchestra. Madame [Marie-Gabrielle] Krauss, who had heard the uncomplimentary remarks of the great man, rose to her feet. Pale but resolute, her eyes fixed on the master's face, she began to sing. Almost immediately he raised his head, attentive, surprised. His eyes met those of the tragedian, and could not leave her face. In a poignant communion, intense, transcendent, their spirits met and mingled. They swept us with them, in their tragic ecstasy. It was tremendous, indescribable! Little by little, Liszt had risen to his feet. As the last notes died away, he held out his arms to the inspired singer. "Forgive me, my sister, my child!" he exclaimed, in a voice broken with emotion. Krauss, completely exhausted by her prodigious effort, could only murmur "Thank you," as she sank into her chair.[47]

Like Calvé, Marie-Gabrielle Krauss[48] lived the best years of her career in the company of composers.[49] She created major roles for Rubinstein, Gounod, Saint-Saëns, and Gomes, as well as a range of local premieres of works by Verdi and Wagner. She spent 13 years at the Opéra, making her debut on 5 January, 1875 – as Rachel, in the first two acts of *La Juive*, at the opening night of the Palais Garnier. On 5 April, 1876, Krauss created the title role in the first premiere to be staged at the Garnier, Auguste Mermet's *Jeanne d'Arc* – a failure on which Tchaikovsky nonetheless relied for his *Maid of Orleans*.[50] Krauss created two roles for Gounod – Pauline in *Polyeucte*,[51] and Hermosa in *Le tribut de Zamora*[52] – and the composer cast her when staging the revised version of *Sapho*, on 2 April, 1884. Calvé's appreciation of Krauss as she wrote it in her memoir is heavily qualified. Having acclaimed her a "great lyric tragedian," she proceeded to recall how

> Her voice was not beautiful, and she had occasionally a marked tremolo.[53] Her appearance ordinarily was unattractive, even ugly; but when she sang, she was transfigured. She became beautiful, inspired! She was able to thrill even the audiences of the Opera, that public of dilettanti so difficult to please or move!

---

47   Calvé, Emma (1922). *My Life*. D Appleton & Company, pp. 38–40.
48   24 March, 1842 – 6 January, 1906.
49   As was true also of her grand-nephew, the conductor Clemens Krauss. His mother, Clementine Krauss, was a dancer in the Vienna Imperial Opera Ballet and later a leading actress and operetta singer.
50   Tchaikovsky's admiration for Krauss' performance as Agathe in Weber's *Der Freischütz* is recorded in a glowing review, published in 1879.
51   7 October, 1878.
52   1 April, 1881.
53   Meaning "vibrato."

It's significant that both Liszt and Calvé commented negatively on Krauss' "tremolo." García's loathing of vibrato is common to all of his books and treatises; Marchesi's pupils were no less aligned as bel canto specialists when avoiding any hint of a shake; as such, it is now a stretch to imagine the voices of Adelina Patti and Nellie Melba singing the roles of Carmen and Michaela.[54] The "big hair" voicing for which Carmen has become synonymous since the 1930s, and the hammered-eroticism of modern performances by Elīna Garanča and Anna Caterina Antonacci, was unthinkable for Galli-Marié and her peers. The "flat phrasing" and bleached tone of many of the final generation of authentic bel canto singers was routine for anyone playing Carmen during the two decades immediately following the premiere. Calvé's disdain for vibrato in 1922 is countered by her own recordings. The 1907 *Habanera* is striking for its richness of tone and indiscriminate (albeit light) vibrato – a colour that generated forced "warmth" while tolerating imperfections and compromises that would have seemed grotesque to García and Marchesi. Intonation was particularly affected by vibrato because pitch adherence compelled a precision that needed to be surgical for any singer relying solely on portamento, dynamics and diction.

The limitations placed by taste and fashion on voice-constructions of character were manifested also by the established approach to acting, which was heavily stylised and largely static. Carmen's emancipation of dance as a feature of expression, independent of actual dancers, added to the palette of expression available to performers who had been limited traditionally to song and the movement of the face and the upper-body in isolation. Calvé was much influenced by the work of Eleonora Duse, on whom the soprano based her use of gesture. The lurch towards real identity (as distinct from local colour) was enhanced through the transformation of Carmen from a "gypsy" caricature into a figure whose cultural and geographical significance made her identifiably Granadan, rather than a *tapas* of "Spanish-Gypsy" clichés. An emergent respect for regional culture was ameliorated by the role of Anita in Jules Massenet's *La Navarraise*,[55] written for Emma Calvé, in which national characteristics collided with the popular taste for realism.[56] Anita's status as a murderer (of Zuccaraga) is unambiguous; Araquil's allegations of prostitution are not. Her consequent suicide attempt and ultimate loss of reason are conveyed in music that favoured dramatic authenticity above lazy stereotypes.

The value of *Carmen's* veracity was increased by the dance performances of Carmencita (*née* Carmen Dauset Moreno) and Carolina Otero,[57] another Spanish dancer and actress whose reputation as a famous beauty was advanced by her appearances at the Folies-Bergère and her work as a courtesan. The transition from bel canto decorum to something more relatable was captured most strikingly in the recordings of Zélie de Lussan, an American soprano of French descent. Even allowing for changes in taste, her performance of the Habanera (from 1903) is more

---

54 Melba sang Micaela often; Patti played Carmen only in London. The former appears to have been a success; the latter was not.

55 First performed on 20 June, 1894.

56 See, generally, Higgins, Emma (2015). *The mezzo-soprano onstage and offstage: a cultural history of the voice-type, singers and roles in the French Third Republic (1870–1918)*. PhD. dissertation, Maynooth University.

57 *née* Agustina del Carmen Otero Iglesias, 4 November, 1868 – 10 April, 1965.

seductive than Calvé's.[58] Her vibrato is similarly light, but the phrasing and rubato are of a different order of expression. The music's implications are fully developed by de Lussan when speaking with saline ambiguity to the navigation of love for sale.

The media and the moral majority were threatened by prostitution's transgression of bourgeois social order, especially if it threatened to infiltrate the corridors of power. The transformation of prostitution into a class war,[59] with sex workers painted as servants in servitude, misrepresented the truth of circumstances in which many courtesans were better educated and more capable as artists than most of those paying for intimacy. The currency of women as *objets d'art et mouvement* was traded by Monet, Manet, Renoir, and Matisse without submitting to the unattractive and the repulsive as it was memorialised by Sickert, Bonnard, Whistler, Vuillard and Toulouse-Lautrec. The spirit of *naturalisme* was captured in Zola's aphorism, "The beautiful is what is ugly," a conviction absent from the music composed by Zola's close friend, Alfred Bruneau,[60] who turned a number of the writer's works into operas. *Naturalisme* did not translate to the French operatic stage as did verismo in Italy, where Zola's gauntlet was picked up with bloody-gusto by Luigi Capuana, Giovanni Verga and Federico De Roberto. Their *giovane scuola*[61] favoured high theatre above psychological and social nuance; plots were rustic and punctuated by brutal acts of violence pre-empted by adultery and betrayal. Theatre was reformed as a social and sexual release for working-class people abjuring the propriety of the bourgeoisie.[62]

Based on a short story by Verga, published in 1880, *Cavalleria rusticana*[63] was the first verismo opera. It was premiered on 17 May, 1890 – a little over six months after the opening of the Moulin Rouge in Paris, and the publication of Zola's violent psychological thriller, *La Bête humaine*,[64] in which Jacques Lantier (Nana's half-brother) explores his psycho-sexual pre-occupation with the murder of women.[65] Although the first of its kind, Mascagni's opera is atypical of the genre, insofar as it concerns a fight to the death between men over women – neither of whom is murdered; it set the tone for every verismo opera that followed. Thousands were written by young composers high on the thrill of the modern; the majority have been lost or forgotten. The best-known subscribers were Alfredo Catalani, Umberto Giordano, Giacomo

---

58   *Carmen* received it 1,000th performance at the Opéra-Comique on 23 December, 1904, with Calvé singing the title role. De Lussan sang the role more often, giving more than 2,000 performances as Carmen – most of them in the United States.

59   See, for example, Zola's *Pot-Bouille* ('Pot Luck'), the tenth novel in the Rougon-Macquart series, published in 1882.

60   Zola and Bruneau collaborated in the creation of *Le Rêve* (1891), *L'attaque du moulin* ('Attack on the Mill.' 1893), *Messidor* (1897) *L'Ouragan* ('The Hurricane,' 1901), *L'Enfant roi* ('The Child King,' 1905), *Naïs Micoulin* (1907), *Les Quatres journées* ('The Four Days,' 1916), and *Lazare* ('Lazarus,' a dramatic-oratorio, produced posthumously in 1954).

61   See Corazzol, Adriana Guarnieri and Parker, Roger (1993). "*Opera and verismo: Regressive points of view and the artifice of alienation,*" Cambridge Opera Journal, Vol. 5, No. 1; pp. 39–53. It's important to note that although the term "*giovane scuola*" was used at the time, it was applied also to the generation of composers who followed Verdi – and before the first performance of *Falstaff*.

62   Abel, Sam (1996). *Opera in the Flesh: Sexuality in Operatic Performance.* Westview press, pp. 118–119.

63   'Rustic Chivalry.'

64   'The human beast.'

65   When Zola visited Italy in the 1890s, he was hailed as the father of Italy's new operatic tradition.

Puccini, Antonio Smareglia, Alberto Franchetti, Franco Alfano, Francesco Cilea, and Riccardo Zandonai; no-one committed to the movement in isolation.

The characteristics of verismo are capricious; the only real constant is the use of a plot concerning episodes from the lives of the ordinary, poor and uneducated, hinging on an illicit sexual act that generates a violent and frequently fatal outcome – routinely for a woman, and occasionally the men without whom their adultery would not have been possible. The simple, well-constructed plots paint characters in primary colours, employing high vocal *tessituras* for male and female voices, irregular rhythms and phrasing, spoken and shouted declamation, heavily charged melodies, tightly-wound harmonies, the contained catch and release of tension, and a routinely thumping orchestra – with whom the soloists are compelled to do battle rather than co-operate. The modernity of verismo was in most cases sensationalist, gaudy, violent and built on the deceit and death of women. As a new kind of music drama, it called for a new kind of singing.

The old kind died with its last exponents, the most famous of whom was Adelina Patti.[66] Her birth culture was defined by composers who were either dead (Mozart and Bellini), about to die (Donizetti), or retired (Rossini). Verdi was an unknown commodity at the time – with his first success, *Nabucco*, being premiered only shortly before Patti's birth. Her father, Salvatore, was a tenor; her mother, Caterina Barilli, was a soprano. Both worked closely with Donizetti. The leading sopranos of Patti's maturity were Thérèse Tietjens[67] and Désirée Artôt.[68] The former sang an extraordinary range of repertoire, spanning Handel's *Semiramide*, Mozart's Da Ponte operas, Gluck's *Armide*, Cherubini's *Médée*, *Fidelio*, *I puritani*, *Lucrezia Borgia*, *Robert le diable*, Otto Nicolai's *Die lustige Weiber von Windsor*,[69] Gounod's *Faust* and *Mireille*, *Der Freischütz*, *Un ballo in maschera*, *Les vêpres siciliennes*, *La forza del destino*, half a dozen Rossini operas, Ortrud in *Lohengrin* and the first performance of Michael Balfe's *Il Talismano*. It is hard to imagine a more vital and diverse range of work – which she performed using a powerful voice spanning three and a half octaves. Tietjens was considered a dramatic soprano, but the diversity of her repertoire renders that label meaningless. Désirée Artôt is remembered also for her diversity,[70] a habit she acquired from her teacher, Pauline Viardot. She made her debut at the Opéra in 1858 as Fidès in *Le prophète*, whereupon she was chosen by Gounod to sing the title role of *Sapho*. Berlioz wrote frequently to praise her in the *Journal des Débats*. In 1859, Artôt appeared in Berlin and London, achieving superb notices for performances in *Il barbiere*, *La Cenerentola*, and *Il trovatore*. She went on to star in European productions of *La fille du régiment*, *La traviata*, and *Norma* (as Adalgisa, with Thérèse Tietjens in the title role) and at Covent Garden, during the 1860s, where she joined a green room of

---

66   *née* Adela Juana Maria Patti, 19 February, 1843 – 27 September, 1919.
67   Thérèse Carolina Johanne Alexandra Tietjens, 17 July, 1831 – 3 October, 1877.
68   21 July, 1835 – 3 April, 1907.
69   'The Merry Wives of Windsor.'
70   The same was true for her daughter, Lola Artôt de Padilla (5 October, 1876 / 1880 – 12 April, 1933), who created the role of Vreli (Juliet) in Frederick Delius' *A Village Romeo and Juliet* on 21 February, 1907. She was also the first in Berlin to sing the title role of Busoni's *Turandot*, Gänsemagd in *Königskinder* (the European premiere, on 14 January, 1911) Strauss' Sophie in *Der Rosenkavalier*, and the Composer in *Ariadne auf Naxos*.

sopranos retained to sing Marguerite in Gounod's *Faust*. In 1868 she visited Russia with a touring company, generating a reputation for a violent temper. Her onstage battles in Moscow during the 1870s with the American dramatic mezzo-soprano, Minnie Hauk,[71] were the stuff of legend while both still lived in Russia. Artôt was famous also for her brief engagement to Tchaikovsky – who composed recitatives for her to sing in a Saint Petersburg production of Auber's *Le domino noir*. She was persuaded not to marry the composer by the ever-insightful Viardot, and five years after the dust had settled, Tchaikovsky and Artôt became friends once more. He composed Six French Songs, Op. 65, for her in 1875 – which he dedicated to the soprano using her now-married name, Désirée Artôt-Padilla. On 29 October, 1875, Tchaikovsky wrote to his muse:

> I have just delivered to my publisher, P. Jurgenson, 6 mélodies which I have written for you, and for which I ask you to consent to accept the dedication. I have tried to please you and I think you could sing all of them – in other words, all six will suit the present range of your voice. I would very much hope that these melodies will please you, but unfortunately, I am not at all sure. I must confess to you that I have been working too much of late, and it is more than probable that my new compositions are rather the product of good intentions than of true inspiration. And then, one is a little intimidated when one is composing for a singer one considers the greatest among the great.[72]

Artôt and Tietjens were the best known among dozens of sopranos born during the middle third of the 19th century to become famous for singing dead repertoire. Patti's instincts and inclinations compounded this tendency. She was born in Madrid, and spoke Spanish, Italian and French natively; after her parents relocated to New York City, before her fourth birthday, Adelina added English to her folio of languages. She trained initially at home, alongside her sisters, Amalia and Carlotta (who became singers), and also their brother Carlo, who became a violinist. Her tuition was passed subsequently to Maurice Strakosch, Amalia's husband, who had studied briefly as a tenor with Giuditta Pasta before turning to piano and composition studies with Bruckner's teacher, Simon Sechter. Strakosch is one of the most important figures in the history of the soprano, a fact much-repeated in his memoirs, *Souvenirs d'un impresario*,[73] published the year before his death in 1887. In addition to his work with Patti, Strakosch and his brother, Maximilian, promoted concerts with the leading sopranos of the second half of the 19th century. His nephew, Carl, married one of them, Clara Louise Kellogg.[74] Patti made her stage debut in the title role of *Lucia di Lammermoor*, at the New York Academy of Music, on 24 November, 1859. She was 16-years-old. Two years later she was invited to Covent Garden to appear as Amina in *La sonnambula*. Such was her success that she was able to buy a house in Clapham,

---

71   *née* Amalia Mignon Hauck "Minnie" Hauk, 16 November, 1851 – 6 February, 1929.
72   Letter 3,700. Published in П. И. Чайковский. С. И. Танеев. Письма (1951), pp. 373–374.
73   'Souvenirs of an Impresario,' first published in Paris by Paul Ollendorff.
74   9 July, 1842 – 13 May, 1916.

south London, mid-way through the season.[75] Patti was triumphant in Paris and Vienna, and in 1862 she toured the United States, riding the coat-tails left behind by Jenny Lind.[76] Like her predecessor, Patti traded in popular song, turning John Howard Payne's "Home! Sweet Home!" into her calling card. In 1862, during the Civil War, she sang it at the end of a concert in the Red Room of the White House,[77] at the invitation of the incumbent President, Abraham Lincoln, and his wife, Mary Todd. They were granted their request for an encore.

In 1869–1870 Patti toured Europe and Russia, forming friendships with Tchaikovsky and Rubinstein. She sang more than once for Verdi, who acclaimed her a

> [...] born artist in every sense of the word. When I heard her for the first time in London [...] I was stunned, not only by the marvellous technique, but by several moments in the drama in which showed that was a great actress. I remember her chaste, modest behaviour when she sits on the soldier's bed in *La sonnambula* and when she, defiled, rushes out of the Libertine's room in Don Giovanni. I remember a certain action in the background during Don Bartolo's aria in *Barbiere*; and more than anything else the rec[itative] before the quartet in *Rigoletto*, when her father shows her lover in the Tavern, saying "And you still love him," and she answers "I love him." No words can express the sublime effect she achieved when she said these words [...]. An exceptional artist.[78]

He later alleged her to be superior to Malibran: "Patti is more complete. A marvellous voice, an extremely pure singing style; a stupendous actress with a charm and naturalness that no one else has." When Giulio Ricordi attempted to persuade Verdi out of retirement, he employed Patti as leverage:[79]

> Knowing Verdi's great admiration for Adelina Patti, he suggested a new opera should be written for her. Meeting with a refusal, [Ricordi] renewed the assault through Giuseppina, to whom he sent a long, reasoned letter to be passed on to Verdi at an opportune moment.[80]

---

75 22 High Street. Incredibly, the property (which survives) doesn't feature a "Blue Plaque."

76 She capitalised also on her own fame as a 9-year-old, when touring the USA in 1852 as "The Singing Doll."

77 The room was used for music by the Lincolns. It is 28 by 22.5 feet (8.5 by 6.9m). Patti was not invited to perform in the East Room – the largest in the house, at 80 by 37 feet (24 by 11m), with a 22-foot (6.7m) high ceiling – since Mary Todd Lincoln had overseen the renovation of the room the previous year. The two possible explanations for the Red Room being preferred are that Patti could not have filled such a space; the other is that the Lincolns could not have managed the emotional strain of hearing "There's No Place Like Home," performed in the same room where the funeral of their 11-year-old son, Willie, was held a few months earlier. Indeed, Mary appears not to have entered the Prince of Wales room, where Willie died, or the Green Room, where he was embalmed.

78 Walker, Frank (1962). *The Man Verdi*. Knopf, p. 471.

79 The strategy proved unsuccessful.

80 *Ibid.*

Verdi's estimation of Patti as "exceptional," and his description of the public's "Indescribable enthusiasm," were written in 1877, following a performance of *Traviata* in Genoa – fifteen years after he heard her for the first time in London. Moreover, Verdi's tributes were countered by one correspondent known to him, who asserted more than once that Patti was other than advertised. The independence of this judgment is questionable, being that it was written by Teresa Stolz. The composer's assessment should not, in any event, be taken at face value, on the basis that he wrote nothing for Patti between 1862 and 1893 – even accounting for the numerous revisions and local premieres over which he assumed personal control. Neither, for that matter, did any composer of note write anything for the soprano.[81] Notwithstanding her parents' enthusiasm for contemporary music, Patti did not, during the course of her substantive career between 1862 and the 1880s perform in a single premiere of note. Indeed, she didn't work with a single important composer. An indication of what was to come emerged during her first full season in the United States, which featured not one contemporary opera: *Lucia di Lammermoor, La sonnambula, Don Giovanni, Il Barbiere di Siviglia, I puritani, Martha, Don Pasquale, and Mosè in Egitto*. When finally she turned to Verdi's music, she appeared only as Violetta, Leonora in *Il trovatore*, and Gilda. By 1870 she was the highest paid singer in the world, commanding $5,000 a night – which had to be paid in gold. Mapleson recalled in his memoirs how Patti's negotiations would be conducted in the company of a parrot trained to shriek, "Cash! Cash!" whenever Mapleson walked into her room. In 1926 – seven years after Patti's death – Jerome K. Jerome recalled:

> We had good opera at Covent Garden and sometimes at Her Majesty's in the Haymarket also. It was the extravagant fees paid to the stars that killed it. I was with a firm of solicitors who acted for Mapleson. Adelina Patti and the others would insist upon sums that were bound to spell loss to the management even when the house was sold out. The argument was that she drew more than she asked. There was no sense in it. Without the orchestra and the chorus and the other performers, the house and all the rest of it, how much would she have drawn night after night?

Patti's fame was world-wide, edespite opting not to sing in Italy. It was carefully engineered also. In fact, she became so famous that her name operated as a short-hand for sung art – even after her death. It has been demonstrated, for example, that when writing "The Adventure of the Retired Colourman" for Sherlock Holmes, in 1926, Sir Arthur Conan Doyle dated the onset of the short-story to Sunday, 17 July, 1898. Bill Mason has traced by date the line "Let us escape from this weary workaday world by the side door of music. Carina sings to-night at the Albert Hall, and we still have time to dress, dine, and enjoy," to a performance by Patti in London that evening, at the Royal Albert Hall – a day after she became a British citizen. Oscar Wilde added Patti to *The Picture of Dorian Gray*,[82] when Lord Henry "Harry" Wotton urges Gray

---

81   In 1893, Patti created the title role of Gabriella in a now-forgotten opera by Emilio Pizzi. Patti had commissioned Pizzi to write the opera for her.

82   Published in 1890.

"You must come and dine with me, and afterwards we will look in at the opera. It is a Patti night, and everybody will be there. You can come to my sister's box. She has got some smart women with her." After the performance, Gray remarks to Basil, "I was at the opera. You should have come on there. I met Lady Gwendolen, Harry's sister, for the first time. We were in her box. She is perfectly charming; and Patti sang divinely."[83]

Jacques Offenbach, Henri Meilhac and Ludovic Halévy identified Patti by name in their 1866 operetta, *La Vie Parisienne*,[84] and she appears in Tolstoy's *Anna Karenina*, Wharton's *The Age of Innocence*, Zola's *Nana*,[85] Jules Verne's *The Village in the Treetops* and, even, "The Deadwood Stage (Whip Crack-Away!)," a song in the musical *Calamity Jane*. At the peak of her celebrity, she was a regular attraction for European monarchy. On 4 July, 1872, Queen Victoria delighted in a private performance at Windsor Castle, of which she wrote:

> I was charmed with Patti, who has a very sweet voice and wonderful facility and execution. She sings very quietly and she is a very pretty ladylike little thing [...] her rendering of "Home Sweet Home," was touching beyond measure, and brought tears to one's eyes.[86]

Like Lind, Patti understood the value of image, and this coloured her sound and sensibility as well as her appearance and character. She was 44 at the time of *Otello*, and two years older when *Cavalleria rusticana* was first performed; from what is known of her voice in its prime, and from what survives on her 27 recordings, she was equipped to sing neither opera. Her voice was light and even in its placement; she applied it to a conception of line and legato that made too pronounced a virtue of portamento for her to attempt anything declamatory. Patti could not have entertained verismo even had she wanted to; as Victoria noted, she sang quietly and was "ladylike." She was, moreover, a diva disinclined to co-operate with a company – an aversion that extended to arrogance when requiring that her name appear larger than any other on a poster. Her disdain for rehearsals was legendary, such that she developed a famously bad habit of sending her secretary to stand in her place – despite earning upwards of £100,000 in modern money for each performance. Patti's approach to verisimilitude was determined without exception by her proximity to the centre of any stage on which she was appearing. In keeping with the bel canto tradition, her priorities were tone and technique rather than narrative and character, a culture that adhered to the rules and rudiments handed down by Manuel García. Legato, diction and effect (evidenced on record by an extraordinary trill) overreached all other considerations, with

---

83 This was most unusual for Wilde, who took little interest in music. His "library," as it has been reconstructed, contained not a single book of note on music or musicians. See among others, Wright, Thomas (2010). *Built of Books: How Reading Defined the Life of Oscar Wilde*. Henry Holt.

84 "*Je veux, moi, dans la capitale, Voir les divas qui font fureur, Voir la Patti dans Don Pasquale* [...]." ("I want, me, in the capital, See the divas that are all the rage, see the Patti in Don Pasquale [...].').

85 "*Le chant, c'est la gaieté, c'est la lumière* [...] *Avez-vous entendu la Patti dans le Barbier?*" ('Singing is gaiety, it is light... Have you heard Patti in the Barber?').

86 *The Letters of Queen Victoria* (1926). Ed Buckle, George. Vol. 2, Part 4. Longmans, Green & Company, p. 221

little or no vibrato, no declamation and a surfeit of rising and falling portamento that must have been intoxicating in duets and trios – assuming her partners joined with her in using it.

If Mark Twain was onto something when holding that "Wagner's music is better than it sounds," then the obverse is true of Patti, who was nothing more than the sound she made. It is miraculous serendipity that her art survived to the age of recording since she was tailored by training and convention for a technology that took no account of acting or movement. Her singing is asexual, and given to making her sound like a young girl, even in her sixties.[87] There is nothing to distinguish between her performances of "*Ah! non credea mirarti*", from *La sonnambula*, and "There's No Place Like Home," both of which are presented within an extremely narrow dynamic range, with barely any articulation and a crystal-like timbre that belies her years. George Bernard Shaw was not a fan. On 18 April, 1890, he wrote:

> It is still possible for a prima donna to bounce on the stage and throw her voice at the heads of the audience with an insolent insistence on her position as a public favourite, and hardly the ghost of a reference to the character she is supposed to impersonate [...]. Madame Patti's offences against artistic propriety are mighty ones and millions. She seldom even pretends to play any other part than that of Adelina, the spoiled child with the adorable voice; and I believe she would be rather hurt than otherwise if you for a moment lost sight of Patti in your preoccupation with Zerlina, or Aida, or Caterina. Nilsson, a far greater dramatic artist, so far stood on her dignity that she never came out before the curtain to bow until there had been applause enough to bring out her rival at least six times (Patti will get up and bow to you in the very agony of stage death if you only drop your stick accidentally.[88]

Shaw proceeded to remember Christina Nilsson slapping a tenor on the back after a performance of "*Ah, si ben mio,*" in *Il trovatore*, and her coincident yelling of "*Bravo!*" He attempted to imagine Ellen Terry doing the same thing for Henry Irving during *The Lady of Lyons*,[89] noting wryly "how far the opera house is behind the theatre in England."[90] Patti was purposefully "old school," as a woman in public life for whom propriety was definitive of contemporary notions of femininity. Patti's cultivation of sound and appearance was designed to preserve her status as a virginal ingénue even if her private life was a mess.[91] Her three marriages were all troubled, and she died childless.[92] Her self-construction as "maidenly" and "ladylike" placed her in

---

87 Patti's recordings included songs, and arias from *Le Nozze di Figaro, Don Giovanni, Faust, Martha, Norma, Mignon* and *La sonnambula*.
88 Shaw, George Bernard (1937). *London Music in 1888–89 as Heard by Corno Di Bassetto (Later Known as Bernard Shaw) with Some Further Autobiographical Particulars*. Constable & Co., p. 354.
89 *The Lady of Lyons; or, Love and Pride* – a five-act romantic melodrama written in 1838 by Edward Bulwer-Lytton.
90 *Ibid.*
91 Freitas, Roger (2018). "Singing Herself: Adelina Patti and the Performance of Femininity." *Journal of the American Musicological Society.* 71 (2), pp. 287–369.
92 The Broadway actress and singer, Patti LuPone (21 April, 1949), is a great-grandniece.

contradistinction with the wild and fantastic Malibran and the dramatic absolutist Viardot. Her subsequent identification as the "Queen of Song," is appropriate, therefore, because she was more obviously a singer of songs than a performer of drama. She continued to sing them well beyond her prime – which some considered to be over while she was in her thirties. In 1878 (at the age of 35), Stolz wrote with prejudice that "her high notes are now forced,"[93] while Hugo Wolf, reviewing her "*adieux à Vienne*" as Rosina in 1883 (when she was 40), considered it was, indeed, time to say goodbye. After an appearance in London's Royal Albert Hall in 1893, Shaw sniped that "time has transposed Patti down a minor third." She made her recordings more than a decade later – still sounding remarkably youthful because of her unwavering aversion to vibrato. Her friend and sometime rival, Clara Kellogg, recalled in her memoirs (published while Patti was alive to read them):

> I have been often asked my opinion of Patti's voice. She had a beautiful voice that, in her early days, was very high, and she is, on the whole, quite the most remarkable singer that I ever heard. But her voice has not been a high one for many years. It has changed, changed in pitch and register. It is no longer a soprano; it is a mezzo and must be judged by quite different standards. I heard her when she sang over here in America thirteen years ago. She gave her old *Cavatina* from *Linda* and sang the whole of it a tone and a half lower than formerly. While the public did not know what the trouble was, they could not help perceiving the lack of brilliancy. Ah, those who have heard her in only the last fifteen years or so know nothing at all about Patti's voice! Yet it was always a light voice, although I doubt if the world realised the fact. She was always desperately afraid of overstraining it, and so was Maurice Strakosch for her. She never could sing more than three times in a week and, of those three, one *role* at least had to be very light. A great deal is heard about the wonderful preservation of Patti's voice. It *was* wonderfully preserved thirteen years ago. How could it have been otherwise, considering the care she has always taken of herself? Such a life! Everything divided off carefully according to *régime*:—so much to eat, so far to walk, so long to sleep, just such and such things to do and no others! And, above all, she has allowed herself few emotions. Every singer knows that emotions are what exhaust and injure the voice. She never acted; and she never, never felt. As Violetta she did express some slight emotion, to be sure. Her *Gran Dio* in the last act was sung with something like passion, at least with more passion than she ever sang anything else. Yes: in *La Traviata*, after she had run away with Nicolini,[94] she did succeed in putting an unusual amount of warmth into the *role* of Violetta.[95]

---

93   Somerset-Ward, Richard (2004). *Angels and Monsters: Male and Female Sopranos in the Story of Opera, 1600–1900*. Yale University Press, p. 214
94   Her lover and, for a time, her husband.
95   Kellogg Strakosch, Clara Louise (1913). *Memoirs of an American Prima Donna*. G. P. Putnam's Sons, pp. 129–130.

Kellogg's insight is considerable. There is nothing in Patti's singing on record touched by feeling or the feminine. Everything is cautious, safe even; she is a singular creature of tone. One can imagine her walking onto stage, assuming a pose and performing the final scene of *La sonnambula*, only to occupy it for a further 20 minutes of ovations. Whatever her heart might have told her never made it onto Patti's sleeve – which is not to suggest she wasn't pleased by what she heard of her voice as it was played back to her. We cannot know what she thought of her first recordings (made in 1890 for Thomas Marshall in New York) since they were lost during her lifetime, but when singing into the horn assembled by the Gramophone & Typewriter Company in December, 1905, and June, 1906, at her Welsh castle, Craig y Nos, her reaction to hearing herself was remembered by her accompanist, Landon Ronald, as

> Ecstasies! She threw kisses into the trumpet and kept on saying, *"Ah! Mon Dieu! Maintenant je comprends pourquoi je suis Patti! Oh oui! Quelle voix! Quelle artiste! Je comprends tout!"*[96] Her enthusiasm was so naïve and genuine that the fact that she was praising her own voice seemed to us all to be right and proper.[97]

Almost everyone – including Tchaikovsky – commented on the assurance of her *fiorituri* and, more than that, the consistency of her intonation. Considering she used little or no vibrato – like the violinists Leopold Auer and Joseph Joachim – her pitching when using so much portamento was no small achievement. Vibrato was increasingly common among singers after 1900 – and Patti's rejection of it bound her to the tradition into which she was born, as it had been nurtured by Rossini. Their friendship has been much commented on, as has his criticism of her interpolations, but Rossini plainly admired Patti's singing, relishing her attentions when his music was all but obsolete. Her recordings are not accurate representations of her prime, or her youth; there is some heavy-handed *marcato*, the placement hardens frequently, and her breathing is laboured. Her 1906 performance of Tosti's *"Serenata,"* is perhaps the best of the discs, with its even tone, beautiful turns, excellent legato and accents, a number of well-judged dynamic shifts, a colouristic use of light vibrato, and *that* portamento. The last note – in diminuendo – wavers dangerously, but this is the sole example of her intonation being less reliable than the tuning of the piano played by Landon Ronald. It is the voice of a girl who happened to be in her sixties, and while some commentators have sought to distinguish it as unique, it is nothing of the kind. One of her (friendly) rivals in the theatre was her near-contemporary, Emma Albani,[98] who also made records late in life. The Canadian-born soprano trained with Gilbert Duprez in Paris, and toured the USA with Maurice Strakosch in 1874, a season that included appearances as Elsa (in Italian) at the Academy of Music – a role she had to learn with two weeks' notice. Apart from *Lohengrin* and *Tannhäuser* (in which she appeared as Elisabeth, at the London premiere, in 1876, during her fifth

---

96   'Ah! My Lord! Now I understand why I am Patti! Oh yes! What a voice! What an artist! I understand everything!'
97   Ronald, Landon (1922). *Variations on a Personal Theme*. Hodder and Stoughton, p. 104.
98   *née* Marie-Louise-Emma-Cécile Lajeunesse, 1 November, 1847 – 3 April, 1930.

season at Covent Garden), Albani's repertoire was similar to that of Patti. So too was her approach to tone and style, which is at its most transparent on her recording of Gounod's *Ave Maria*. In tandem with Patti, there is little or no vibrato, an abundance of portamento (in which she is joined enthusiastically by the solo violinist), and neither declamation nor artifice.

Although she made no recordings, the same qualities were attached by critics to the singing of the "First Great Nilsson,"[99] Christina, the inspiration for Christine Daaé, the heroine of Gaston Leroux's novel *The Phantom of the Opera* – and another point of reference in *The Age of Innocence* and *Anna Karenina*. Born just six months after Patti, Nilsson sang a wider selection of repertoire because of her enthusiasm for contemporary music. In 1864, she accepted an offer from Caroline Miolan-Carvalho and her husband, Léon, to join the Théâtre Lyrique in Paris. She made her debut as Violetta, creating a sensation, and for three years Nilsson and Miolan-Carvalho appeared together in productions of *Die Zauberflöte*, *Don Giovanni*, *Les Huguenot*, and Flotow's *Martha*. Nilsson had the good fortune to hear Miolan-Carvalho as Marguerite in *Faust* – a role she created for Gounod – and they studied the score together before Nilsson performed the opera for the first time at Her Majesty's in 1867. In London, Nilsson appeared as Lucia and Cherubino – roles that were decades old when she played them; not until her transfer to the Opéra in 1868 did she mix with contemporary composers[100] – one of whom, Ambroise Thomas, invited her to create the role of Ophélie in *Hamlet*. The following year she was Gounod's choice to sing Marguerite in the first production of Faust at the Opéra. Since she wasn't Miolan-Carvalho, her performances were "controversial," but her playing of the role in Moscow for her debut at the Bolshoi, in November 1872, moved Tchaikovsky to declare her the embodiment of Goethe's ambition. The Tsar and Tsarina were in agreement, and gifted Nilsson an emerald and diamond necklace and earrings, as was their habit.[101] Her career during the 1870s and '80s was extraordinarily far-reaching. Indeed, she may well have been the world's most travelled soprano prior to the development of international flight. Having toured Scandinavian Houses for 18 months, Nilsson made her debut in January, 1877, at the Hofoper in Vienna as Ophélie (which led to her appointment to the Imperial Austro-Hungarian Court as a *Kammersängerin*. She shuttled back and forth between Budapest, Prague, Hamburg and London before heading back to Russia, where she was appointed an Imperial *kamernyy pevets*.[102] Her Spanish debut was, again, as Marguerite at the Teatro Real in Madrid in 1879. The following year she created Margherita and Helen of Troy for Boito when *Mefistofele* was first produced at Her Majesty's Theatre, London. On 22 October, 1883, Nilsson sang Marguerite for the inauguration of the Metropolitan Opera House, New York. A thorough, if slightly mad review appeared in the following morning's *New York Daily Tribune*, which gave a full column to identifying the

---

99   *née* Christina Jonasdotter, 20 August, 1843 – 22 November, 1921.

100   It's claimed that Meyerbeer, having heard Nilsson for the first time, in 1864, offered her the role of "Ines" in *L'Africaine* – a role that was given after the composer's death, to Marie Battu. He may well have wanted to encourage her, but he would not have considered someone with such limited experience for what was certain to be his last opera.

101   They are now on display at the Kulturparken Smålands museum in Växjö.

102   The Russian equivalent of a Kammersängerin.

"people who were there." Having passed water on the French and German people, and the apparent differences between their cultures, the critic approached Nilsson's part in things, studiously avoiding anything of interest:

> Of Mme. Nilsson's Marguerite there is little to be said that has not been said over and over again. For the transformation which the political character has undergone not she but the authors of the opera are responsible. [...] Nilsson's triumph came in the jewel song, where it was expected, for it is the golden link with which last year she established the connection between her concert room and the memorable night when she first sang her way to the hearts of the people. After she had sung it last night the last film of ice that held the public in decorous check was melted, and an avalanche of plaudits overwhelmed the fair singer. Bouquets rained from the boxes and baskets of flowers were piled over the footlights till it seemed as if there was to be no end. In the midst of the floral gifts there was also handed up a magnificent velvet casket inclosing a wreath of gold bay leaves and berries, ingeniously contrived to be extended into a girdle to be worn in the classic style, and two gold brooch medallions bearing the profiles of Tragedy and Comedy with which to be fastened. The donor was not mentioned, but an inscription told that the gift was in commemoration of the opening of the Metropolitan Opera House.

Nilsson's final appearance in the United States was in June, 1884. Having returned to Sweden, she embarked on another tour of Scandinavia, which took an horrific turn on 23 September, 1885, during a performance from the balcony of the Grand Hotel in Stockholm to a crowd of 50,000. Because of the contained space (which bordered the harbour), push came to shove, causing the deaths and serious injury of dozens of spectators. She tired soon enough of her celebrity, and in March, 1887, she agreed to marry a Spanish aristocrat and diplomatic official; following two farewell performances at the Royal Albert Hall in 1888, Nilsson retired. Her laurels were carried briefly in France by Marie Heilbron,[103] a Belgian coloratura honoured by Massenet with the title role of *Manon* on 19 January, 1884; her repertoire was otherwise dominated by the routine, spanning Gounod, Thomas, and middle-period Verdi. Heilbron died in 1886 at the age of 35.

The best remembered of Patti's contemporaries was Marcella Sembrich.[104] She was born in Wisniewczyk – now a part of Ukraine – and learned both the violin and the piano at a young age. In 1867 she was sent to the Lemberg Conservatory (in what is now Lviv, Poland). Five years later she was invited to play for Liszt, who asked her to sing also; this prompted the composer to advocate dedicated voice training. She relocated to Vienna, where was she tutored by Brahms' friends, Joseph Hellmesberger Sr. and Julius Epstein. Sembrich shared various classes in Vienna with Gustav Mahler,

---

103   1851 – 31 March, 1886.
104   *née* Prakseda Marcelina Kochańska, 15 February, 1858 – 11 January, 1935. She first appeared under the name "Marcella Bosio", because she considered her birthname too difficult for audiences to pronounce. Shortly after, she adopted her mother's maiden name, Sembrich.

with whom she became a correspondent and, eventually, a colleague in New York. On 3 June, 1877, she made her debut as Elvira in *I puritani* – in Athens. She went on to appear in Meyerbeer's *Dinorah, Lucia di Lammermoor, Robert le diable* and *La sonnambula* – operas in which she was adept at the age of 19. Sembrich was more of a polyglot, even, than Patti – speaking and writing in Polish, German, French, English and Italian before the age of 30. In 1880, she achieved international success as Lucia in Dresden and London, and after adding Zerlina, Susanna and Konstanze to her repertoire she established herself as the leading Mozartian of her age.

After joining the New York Met (as Lucia, on 24 October, 1883), Sembrich went on to sing more House debuts than any other performer in the company's history, including the Queen of the Night, Elvira, Violetta, Amina, Gilda, Rosina and Marguerite (*Les Huguenots*). None of these roles was contemporary, of course, and of her more than 450 performances during 11 seasons at the Met none was of a "new" work. The House celebrated her silver jubilee with a farewell gala in 1909. Seven years earlier, she was the first to be recorded by Mapleson on cylinder at the Met – years before she made her first "studio" recordings. The technical limitations are considerable, but it is possible to trace the elements of her singing in her early forties. The excerpts from *Zauberflöte*'s "*Der Hölle Rache kocht in meinem Herzen*" – sung in Italian – reveal an iron-clad coloratura technique, including machine-gun staccato and a suitably fearsome D5. Her passage work is unstable, however, and her vibrato is either non-existent for anything attaching to the stave or rapid above it. The performance is defined by temporal liberties, to which she was presumably entitled by the conductor and because of the power of her voice. Sembrich was a large woman, and her resources as the Queen of the Night are conspicuous even noting the limitations of cylinder technology. Her singing of "*Sempre libera*," recorded the following year by Mapleson, is striking for its resonance and some fantastic changes in pace – which pull the aria in ways that would now be considered vulgar. She sings sharp, indulges some vertiginous swooping that speaks to weaknesses in placement rather than judgment, and her vibrato is, again, very light; there is a keen sense of showmanship and some passing discretion. Sembrich's studio recordings are valuable for what they say of performance practice during the preceding century; her recording on 5 November, 1904, of "*Deh vieni, non tardar*,"[105] from *Figaro* is interesting because Sembrich studied Mozart's music with teachers whose parents co-existed with the composer.[106] It's worth remembering also that these recordings were made only 60 years after Constanze's death, which allows for a reasonable latitude in hindsight. Anyone inclined to know how Mozart's sopranos might have sounded would do well to listen to Sembrich in 1904 before turning to their favourites in stereo. Susanna's "*Deh vieni*," is famous for capturing a lie, as well as Figaro's seduction and Susanna's disguise at the same time. Mozart's genius is concentrated in the skill with which he makes Susanna appear as the Countess, whom he introduces by the use of *accompagnato* recitative, a device reserved traditionally for noble-born characters

---

105   'Oh, come, do not delay.'
106   Two of her teachers, in Milan, were Francesco Lamperti (1811 – 1892), and his son, Giovanni Battista Lamperti (1839 – 1910). Francesco was taught by singers, composers and tutors born during the last quarter of the 18th century.

rather than maids. Mozart adds to the air of misrepresentation by dipping into the soprano's lower register, to imply age as well as lust, particularly when punctuating the words "*foco*" and "*note.*" The 6/8 meter, stately pace and passing notes (such as the F-sharp in "*Vieni ove amore,*") add to the eroticism of the music, which is made less subtle by the extended notes employed for the word "*vieni…,*"[107] accompanied by a suggestively rising run of semi-quavers. Whether Mozart intended to suggest that Susanna was playing at being an aristocrat – further to the essential deception – is unknown, but the challenge for any singer playing Susanna is to seduce, and to persuade as seductive.

Sembrich begins the aria with an enormous rising swoop for the first "*vieni,*" (C4 – F4), which she shadows with the repeating B flat 4 – F sharp 4 for the words "*Vieni ove amore,*"[108] both of which feature prominent portamento. She doesn't repeat the opening slide (again C4 to F4) for the words "*per goder [t'appella]*"[109] which suggests a textual and narrative attachment to the significance of the text and its meaning, rather than a purely musical consideration. During the opening phrase there is not a hint of sensuality; notwithstanding the liberal use of portamento, Sembrich's line is rigid, metrical and dynamically constant. The lilting meter is lost entirely to what becomes cold and static, leaving the listener with nothing but pure tone. Sembrich was acclaimed to be the finest Susanna of her generation; she gave 32 performances as Susanna at the Met, over eight seasons. In 1908 – four years after she recorded "*Deh vieni, non tardar*" – Mahler joined the Met as a conductor for a season. He made his House debut on New Year's Day, 1908, directing the company's 84th performance of *Tristan und Isolde.*[110] Sembrich's final appearances as Susanna were conducted by Mahler; the soprano was 50 years young at the time. Not a single review indicated that she was anything less than the singer she had always been. The following year, Sembrich bade farewell to New York, an event commemorated by the Met with a public gala and a private dinner. Mahler's wife, Alma, attended both:

> […] every artist was eager to take part in the great occasion and so, in-
> stead of a single opera, acts and scenes from several in which she particu-
> larly shone were performed. Caruso, Bonci, Farrar, Eames, Scotti and
> all the conductors, including Mahler, offered their services as a tribute
> to this incomparable singer. Mahler conducted an act from *Figaro.* She
> herself sang all her parts for the last time with a perfection unsurpassed
> even in her best years. At the end, after she had been called before the

---

107 'Come.'
108 'Come where love.'
109 '[calls you] to enjoy.'
110 A week earlier, the Mahlers joined New York's elite for a party a Sembrich's 10th floor apartment in The Kenilworth, at 151 Central Park West – four blocks from the Hotel Majestic, where the Mahlers lived. Alma recalled: "Sembrich invited us to a Christmas party. Caruso was there and others of their circle at the opera. We liked them all, even though intercourse with them was rather superficial. Caruso had genius even as a human being. They all had an instinctive perception of Mahler's importance and treated him with the greatest respect in private life as well as on the stage. Sembrich's Christmas tree caught fire and we were within an ace of being burned to death." Mahler[-Werfel], Alma (1946). *Gustav Mahler: Memories and Letters.* Viking Press, p. 155.

curtain thirty or forty times, the curtain went up and revealed a grove of laurel overhanging the whole stage. The whole company stood in a half-circle round a table, at which the Mayor of New York was seated. He rose immediately and advanced toward Madame Sembrich, who retreated in embarrassment as he presented her with a large rope of magnificent pearls, while the audience stood and clapped. After he had made a speech in praise of her merits as an artist and a woman, all her colleagues came forward with their presents. She had invited us to a ball after the performance, and we all proceeded there laden with the costly tributes of silver and gold which were heaped upon her; there was no other means of transport. The orchestra of the opera surprised her on her arrival at the hotel with a flourish of trumpets and played at the ball throughout the night, to show their gratitude for her generosity after the San Francisco earthquake in which all their instruments had been destroyed and she had given up her salary until they were replaced. She opened the ball by dancing a mazurka with Paderewski. Shortly afterwards the whole opera company gave her a farewell party on her leaving New York. Everyone connected with the opera was present and a few others, including Paderewski. It took place in the Plaza Hotel with the greatest pomp and ceremony, Caruso drew his masterly caricatures and showed them to all save the victim.[111]

Alma's memories are unreliable where they concerned her legacy. Her assessment of Sembrich was consistent with the general critical view, so when writing that she "sang all her parts [...] with a perfection unsurpassed even in her best years," it's likely she based her judgment on more than reputation. Alma was born in 1879, twenty-one years after Sembrich; if she saw the soprano in "her prime," (and, by supposition, as a 19-year-old, in 1898), then Sembrich was 40-years-old when Alma first heard her sing. It can be reasoned that Sembrich was fit for task for Mahler in 1908, therefore, during which season he conducted numerous performances with her as Susanna. At the very least, her singing four years earlier fell within "her best years." Noting all of this, only the charitable would think Sembrich's recording of "*Deh vieni, non tardar*," expressive, characterful or feminine. The cold beauty of her line – enriched by the absence of vibrato and the primacy of portamento – cannot compensate for the occlusive frigidity of the performance.

Patti and her peers were famed for their modesty. Before the 1890s, critics and commentators identified a soprano in performance for her asexuality. Whether she was being raped or suffering mental collapse, committing suicide, or being murdered was defined by the portrayal of women as passive and accommodating on the lyric stage. On 21 February, 1882, for example, the *Cincinnati Enquirer* reported how "Seven Thousand People Again Listen to [Patti]."[112] The paper memorialised "How her Beautiful Singing and Charming Manners Enthused the Immense Audience."[113]

111   *Ibid*, pp. 142–143.
112   The concert (her second at the Music Hall) marked the end of the Opera Festival.
113   At this concert was Oscar Wilde, on his lecture tour of the USA. He was taken backstage to meet

How might a soprano's "charming manners" have manifested themselves in 1882 – as distinct from those of a man? The answer – then and now – was that she needed to sound and appear de-sexualised. Three years after singing in Cincinnati, Patti decided against reason to play the role of Carmen in London; this folly produced the one and only disaster of her career. Neither Patti nor her voice were suited to playing Bizet's sexually-aggressive, manipulative temptress, any more than Patti might have persuaded as Maddalena di Coigny in *Andrea Chénier*. For the last generation of authentic bel canto sopranos with any connection to the genre and its origins, social respectability was as much a priority as *fioriruri*. With the values of the past attaching consciously to a woman's conduct as well as her repertoire, the changes in aesthetics, social mobility and female emancipation that occurred during the decades either side of 1900 were prompted by contemporary music, art, literature, theatre and technology – as it appears in the repertoire and recordings produced after 1890. The soprano voice was wholly changed by those who wrote for it, primarily Wagner. The sound of modernity for everyone else was forged by *naturalisme*, verismo, and the effects of *Plessy v. Ferguson*.[114]

The first soprano to sing a verismo role was Gemma Bellincioni.[115] She made her debut as a 14-year-old, in May, 1879, at the Teatro della Societa Filarmonica in Naples in *Il segreto della Duchessa*, by Giuseppe Dell-Orefice. Eight years later she made her adult debut as Violetta, at La Scala, with the composer in the audience. The soprano was unusually beautiful in her youth, and Verdi preferred her appearance to her singing, which was marked by a weak technique. She was made famous by the second of the *Concorsi* for one-act operas launched by the publisher, Edoardo Sonzogno,[116] first advertised in the July, 1888, edition of *Il Teatro illustrato*. Entry was restricted to composers who had not previously had an opera performed, in public or private. 73 scores were received, of which three were awarded prizes as well as performances. To ensure that each opera was judged as fairly as possible, Sonzogno engaged the same cast for each performance. He chose Bellincioni and her lover, the tenor Roberto Stagno, because her reputation as a "realist" actress distinguished her from the stylised gesturing of Bernhardt and Duse. Bellincioni was one of the first sopranos to make recordings,[117] the earliest in 1903, while still in her vocal prime. It is possible in consequence to hear the creator of Mascagni's Santuzza singing "*Voi lo sapete, o mamma, prima d'andar soldato,*"[118] from *Cavalleria rusticana*, at the age of just 39.

Many of the hallmarks of the verismo style are in evidence; Bellincioni forces her tone throughout, lingering on climaxes, rushing passing phrases, utilising a semi-spoken *parlando* that approximates *sprechstimme*, and indulging aspirates that

---

with Patti, who must have made an impression since he remembered her seven years later, when writing *The Picture of Dorian Gray*.

114   *Plessy v. Ferguson*, 163 U.S. 537, was a disastrous U.S. Supreme Court decision 1896 that established the doctrine that came to be known as "separate but equal."

115   *née* Matilda Cesira Bellincioni, 18 August, 1864 – 23 April, 1950.

116   See, generally, Nannetti Remo (1988). "The Sonzogno Concorsi, 1884–1906," *Renaissance and Other Studies.*

117   For the Gramophone & Typewriter Company in 1903, and for Pathé in 1905.

118   'Mamma, you know that before he went off to be a soldier.'

interrupt and distort the sung line. Even if her diction is sensational, her phrasing is hard, absent portamento and coloured by a ubiquitous bleating vibrato; it's theatrical, for sure, but far from pretty – a compromise that draws the listener's attention to the words (and presumably Bellincioni's gestures) without allowing the music to interrupt the dramatic momentum. Proof that this approach aligned with Mascagni's intentions emerges from Bellincioni's performance – recorded during the same sessions in 1903 – of "*Ah fors'è lui*," which she first performed for Verdi at La Scala 17 years earlier. Her word use is, again, sensational, but her questionable respect for the music leads her to indulge some horrendous fermatas and a number of interpolations, including a tragic cadenza. It is extraordinary that the addition of ornaments and variations to the music of Italy's most revered composer (who died two years earlier) was acceptable whereas Mascagni's music was performed *come è scritto*. Bellincioni's use of dynamic "swelling" is impressive, but an awful "shake" occludes any hope of true legato. She employs little or no portamento, preferring instead to slide down any interval beyond a third; the whole performance is coloured by effort and strain. Her singing is comparable to that of her colleague, the tenor Fernando de Lucia, another transition singer with an ugly vibrato, renowned for verismo and bel canto during the end of the century. For all her vocal imperfections, Bellincioni's talents as an actress seduced Giordano, who choose her to create the title role of *Fedora*, on 17 November, 1898 (when she was partnered by Enrico Caruso as Loris). Eight years later (and three years after she made her first recordings), Bellincioni was trained by Richard Strauss to give the Italian premiere of *Salome* in Turin on 22 December, 1906.[119] It is difficult to reconcile the voice recorded in 1903 to the physical and musical demands of this infamous role, even with the composer's assistance. His steel-cold pragmatism doubtless played a hand in his compromise because Bellincioni's celebrity generated publicity for the most controversial opera ever written. In her autobiography, she recalled:

> after this creation I realized that I had nothing more to give to art and to the public and that the public had nothing more to expect from me [...] and, despite the insistent proposals, I said to myself: enough![120]

Bellincioni can be seen as well as heard. She was the first operatic soprano to transition successfully to cinema – at a time when the vast majority of film actors were relocating from spoken theatre.[121] She worked as a writer, producer, actress and direc-

---

119 The famously messy business of who was to give the first performance involved a war between Turin and Milan, with Toscanini believing he would conduct the premiere at La Scala. As things turned out, Turin secured the official honour on December 22, 1906, but Toscanini's conducting of an open rehearsal the previous night (with the suitably named Solomiya Krushelnytska in the title role) qualified unofficially as the premiere. Strauss later condemned Toscanini for having "slaughtered the singers and the drama" beneath a "piteously raging orchestra," transforming his pointillist opera into "a symphony without singers."

120 Bellincioni, Gemma (1920). *Io e il palcoscenico: trenta e un anno di vita artistica.* Società Anonima Editoriale Dott. R. Quintieri. Bellincioni, Gemma (1943). *Bianca Stagno Bellincioni Intimi.* Arno Press, p. 137.

121 Mosconi, Elena (2013). "Silent Singers: The Legacy of Opera and Female Stars and Early Italian Cinema." In *Researching Women in Silent Cinema: New Findings and Perspectives.* Eds. Dall'Asta, Monica,

tor, forming her own company in Rome in 1917.[122] Only the first of her dozen or so films survived, but it is the most important because it features her playing Santuzza in Ugo Falena's *Cavalleria rusticana*.[123] The extant material is held at the Cinema Nazionale, in Rome; it speaks to a style of melodrama closer to Bernhardt and Duse than is suggested by her reputation for verité. It's possible she was encouraged to adapt to the perceived needs of silent film, since critics praised her performance; the public was less satisfied, however, with many wanting to see a younger actress in the role. When publishing her autobiography in 1920, Bellincioni failed to mention her film work, even in passing. Her career as a film actress ended in 1923 as it had begun as a soprano in 1890, with a violent tale concerning a tormented love affair between a poor, young couple that concludes with a stabbing.[124]

The popular taste for rustic violence was sustained in 1892 by adultery and femicide in Leoncavallo's *Pagliacci*.[125] Though anodyne when compared with *Salome's* extravagant perversion, *Pagliacci* was still shocking for audiences whose most recent experience of seeing a woman murdered on an operatic stage was defined five years earlier by the orientalist romanticism of *Otello*. *Pagliacci's* deep-fried slice of social reality was done in under an hour, and concluded (without consequence for the murderer) in the deaths by stabbing of the lovers. The context for the drama's presentation of Nedda as a harlot, cruelly humiliating the damaged and impotent Canio, was rooted in a social dynamic that equated adultery by women with prostitution. Since adultery affected women as commonly as men, and across every strata of class and education, the construction of a woman's right to be some form of "happy" re-engineered love as a commodity. The ubiquity of violence in Italy was far-reaching, with women in the south exposed to an alarming risk of predation. It became the dominant cliché for foreign conceptions of Italian life. In 1866, for example, Carl Bloch painted *In a Roman Osteria*, a narrative portrait with a pair of well-dressed women sat at a table with their pimp, who stares aggressively at the viewer, with the light dancing off the switchblade in his waistband. The women also look at the viewer; one drinks red wine, the other parts her lips above an unambiguously phallic glass decanter. It's not a subtle painting, but neither was the culture being caricatured by Bloch.

The transition from bel canto to verismo, and the last of the voices to compare with that of Patti, was personified by an Australian soprano, born in a suburb of Melbourne. Nellie Melba[126] was trained in Paris by Mathilde Marchesi, which helps explain why Patti's impresario, Maurice Strakosch, offered her a ten-year contract

---

Duckett, Victoria, and Tralli, Lucia. University of Bologna and University of Melbourne, pp 334–352; p. 340.

122 Gemma Productions. She sold the company in 1920, and started another, with her daughter, in 1921. As the owner of BiancaGemma Film, Bellincioni produced and directed six films starring her daughter, Bianca Stagno Bellincioni, who achieved national fame as an actress after a short career as an opera singer. Bellincioni sold the commercial distribution rights of her films to Aurea Film, who exported them all over the world.

123 1916.

124 *Satanica*.

125 'Clowns,' first performed on 21 May, 1892.

126 *née* Nellie Mitchell, 19 May, 1861 – 23 February, 1931.

for 1,000 francs annually, just 12 months into Melba's studies. Shortly after signing, the Théâtre de la Monnaie, Brussels, offered Melba 3,000 francs a *month*. Strakosch refused Melba's request to be released, and even secured an injunction to bind her to the terms agreed. She was saved by Strakosch's sudden death on 9 October, 1887; three days later, Melba made her debut, in *Rigoletto*, at La Monnaie – having adopted Marchesi's suggestion that she use the name Melba, as a contraction of the city of her birth. She was 26-years-old, and had only seen her first opera a year earlier. With 120 years of recorded hindsight, it is difficult to know how singers from countries without major opera companies were able to learn their craft as well as the culture within which it operated prior to relocating to Europe.[127] Melba succeeded as Gilda despite her inexperience, as she did when playing Violetta for the first time a few days later. In May, 1888, she made her debut at the Royal Opera House, in London, as Lucia. Because of the muted critical reception, Covent Garden's manager, Augustus Harris, limited Melba's forthcoming season to the small role of Oscar, in *Un ballo in Maschera*. Melba took offence and left for Paris. Her subsequent triumph at the Opéra as Ophélie in *Hamlet* was sufficient for Harris to change his mind, and in June, 1889, she was persuaded to return as Juliette, opposite Jean de Reszke's Roméo. Melba would later date the beginning of her career from this performance. Four years later, she appeared as Nedda, with Leoncavallo in the audience; the composer is alleged to have acclaimed her as peerless. If so, he was being polite. In 1901, Melba was recorded by Mapleson on the stage of the New York Met singing the end of Marguerite de Valois's aria *"A ce mot tout s'anime"*[128] from Act II of *Les Huguenots*. It is one of the clearest cylinders in the Mapleson collection and, for that reason, a reliable point of reference for what W. J. Henderson heard when writing for *The New York Times*:

> Those who were present apparently enjoyed the performance extremely, for their applause was frequent and hearty and, at times, had the ring of genuine enthusiasm. The evening's work was well deserving of applause, for the ensemble was excellent, and there were familiar individual merits of a high order: Mme. Melba was made the object of a special demonstration of delight at the end of her florid aria in her [first] scene as Marguerite de Valois. Indeed, she merited it, for she was in fine voice and sang with ravishing beauty of tone and consummate skill. There is a reposeful simplicity about Mme. Melba's cantilena, and there is a freedom from cheap trickery in her *fioriture* which singers of less prominence

---

127   There were "houses," or a variety of theatres, at least, in Melbourne when Patti was a young woman. The Opera House in Bourke Street (also known as the Prince of Wales Opera House and the Melbourne Opera House) opened in August, 1872. An indication of the state of theatre in the city at the time survives in a review of the Bourke Street venue: "The opening of the Prince of Wales Opera-house, the new theatre built by Mr. Henry Hoyt on the site of the old Varieties […] was celebrated on Saturday evening with fitting éclat. It is many years since so interesting an event […] occurred in Melbourne; and there were probably not a dozen persons in the large audience which assembled on Saturday night who witnessed the opening of the Prince's, the only other theatre now standing in this city." From the Argus (Melbourne, Vic.), published on Monday, 26 August, 1872.

128   The cabaletta following *"O Beau Pays."*

would do well to copy. There are many things to praise in Mme. Melba's singing, but nothing is more praiseworthy than the purity of her style.

The curious can judge for themselves whether the singing captured on cylinder more than 120 years ago justified the "special demonstration of delight" heard at the end of her performance. The context for the audience's appreciation presumes Melba's status as among the best sopranos performing at the Met in 1901. The most striking features, which align her absolutely with Patti and the bel canto tradition, are the primacy of portamento and the coincident absence of vibrato. Thereafter, the performance is definitively awful. Melba's tone is "pure," but her intonation is more miss than hit,[129] with some horrendous turns, rushed passage work, snatched articulation, a lumbering trill, and an acidic high D6. The performance is not dated; it is objectively terrible,[130] sufficient to compel the interrogation of taste and expectations in 1901.

On hearing Melba at her best, it's incredible that her performance might have met with Leoncavallo's approval. Quite what the New York Met was thinking when engaging her as Brünnhilde for *Siegfried* in 1896 is impossible to know.[131] Much has been made of the six weeks during which she studied Mimi with Puccini in Italy in 1899, and with good reason considering the differences between her 1907 recording of "*Si, mi chiamano Mimì*,"[132] and the shrieking incarcerated by Mapleson six years earlier. Melba's tone has warmed considerably, with a judicious use of vibrato and some elegant phrasing; whether it qualifies as beautiful is a matter of preference and prejudice. There is a useful comparator in the singing of her American-born rival (and fellow Marchesi pupil), Emma Eames,[133] who was also recorded by Mapleson. The cylinders made during a performance in 1903 of Act II of *Tosca* reveal a vibrato-free line, but Eames' tone is warmer and her articulation better-suited to the kind of drama being represented on stage. Eames' response to the torture of de Marchi's (outstanding) Cavaradossi is stupendously intense, thanks to Luigi Mancinelli's incendiary conducting. Eames was classically trained but capable of finding the vocal form necessary to play characters in narratives that were violent and hysterical. Eight years before Puccini completed *Tosca*, for example, Leoncavallo's characterisation of Nedda's adultery verged on satire; her two-part aria, beginning "*Qual fiamma avea nel guardo!*"[134] conveys the emotional transformation of a character who admits to being "*illanguidita per arcano desio*,"[135] into a woman charged with love and lust, yielding

---

129   For anyone inclined to blame the technology, it's worth noting that the solo flute and clarinet are perfectly in tune.

130   It would be laughable and unkind to compare what survives of Melba's singing with any of Lisette Oropesa's sensational performances of the role at the Paris Opéra in 2018.

131   In fairness to all concerned, except for the delusional Melba. Her performance was not considered a success.

132   The first production of *La bohème* in London was produced by the Royal Opera on 1 July, 1899, with Nellie Melba as Mimì, Zélie de Lussan as Musetta, Fernando De Lucia as Rodolfo, and Mario Ancona as Marcello.

133   13 August, 1865 – 13 June, 1952.

134   'What a flame he had in his gaze!'

135   'Languished by arcane desire.'

to the metaphor of the birds flying above her head, "*Stridono lassù.*"[136] As she envies their freedom when challenging "*le nubi e sol cocente,*"[137] the writing becomes declamatory, bluntly onomatopoeic, and sustained by an otiose orchestral accompaniment that employs 'cellos in unison with the soprano melody. The sung line calls for power and virtuosity, of a kind, with extreme intervals culminating in a rising sequence (to convey the repeating words describing the ascending birds, "*e van*")[138] that climaxes with a B flat 4 of resonant futility. The sense of movement and dramatic energy is constant, and there are few longueurs; the music rewards singers inclined to bark their way through the role – especially during the climactic duet. From what can be heard on record, the first Nedda, Adelina Stehle, was an ideal fit, and her singing is memorable only for its ideation of resonance.

Even when the music was of exceptional quality, the popular appetite for massive orchestras made volume a condition precedent for any woman wanting to be heard as well as murdered on stage. Giordano's most lasting success, *Andrea Chénier*, is a work of full-length verismo that concludes with the ecstatic duet, "*Vicino a te,*"[139] following which the title role and his lover, Maddalena di Coigny, are fed to the guillotine. Nearly every performance since the first has made use of singers with the largest voices; most have engaged with the music without accounting for the absurdity of lovers bellowing their feelings at each other while standing in a tumbril waiting to die. Giordano's score is written for a piccolo, three flutes, two oboes, cor anglais, two clarinets, a bass clarinet, two bassoons, four horns, three trumpets, three trombones, a tuba, four timpani, triangle, bass drum, cymbals, snare drum, tamtam, a harp, and between 40 and 50 strings. The first soprano to play Maddalena, the Spanish-born Avelina Carrera,[140] was used to navigating large orchestras; she made her debut in 1889, as Elsa in *Lohengrin*. Four years later, she appeared at the Teatro de São Carlos, Lisbon, as Brünnhilde in *Die Walküre*, Aida, Rachel in *La Juive* and Alice Ford in *Falstaff*. She was ideal for Maddalena, whose "*La mamma morta*"[141] is one of the finest arias in the verismo canon.[142] Her recollection in Act III of her mother's death by burning is unusual for its transference of a woman's salvation from a man to a heroine (Bersi) who resorts to prostitution when providing for Maddalena. The power necessary for a soprano to take on this stupendous soliloquy is Wagnerian because Giordano, like Leoncavallo, scores much of it in unison with the vocal line. The difference between music theatre in 1896 and 20 years earlier is punctuated during the phrase:

Quando ad un tratto un livido bagliore guizza e rischiara
innanzi a' passi miei La cupa via.[143]

---

136 'Screeching up in the sky.'
137 'The clouds and the scorching sun.'
138 'They go.'
139 'Next to you.'
140 2 January, 1871 – 25 February, 1939.
141 'They killed my mother.'
142 The work is otherwise dominated by its title role, for tenor. See Boyden, Matthew (2021). *The Tenor: A Cultural History*. Ragueneau Press.
143 '[...] when suddenly a bright glow flickers, and lights were ahead of me the dark street!'

This burst of anguish reveals in just three bars of music the horror of Maddalena's memories; the intensity of the imagery is framed in a descending chromatic sequence that crowns on four repeating quavers (an E4 for "[*ba*]*gliore guiza e*") that resolve on a C sharp 4 ("*via*"). The declamatory force of this brief passage is such that many sopranos have attacked it without regard for the rhythm and pitch as notated, with Callas' many recorded performances, creating the most obvious exemplar of theatrical immersion. Most shriek and spit the words, ignoring the notated detail. It would have been impossible for Patti and her peers to sing this music, far less perform it; the bleached and mannered style of the bel cantanti was irreconcilable to the new voicing of verismo. The aria culminates with Maddalena characterising her isolation, fear and despair:

> *Io son divino! Io son l'oblio! Io sono il dio che sovra il*
> *mondo scendo da l'empireo, fa della terra un ciel! Ah!*[144]

As she cries out in anguish, Maddalena drives home a gigantic B4, above the seething orchestra, before collapsing to her chest voice for "[*io son*] *l'amor, l'amor*,"[145] in a rising cadence that bottoms out on an E3, passing through an F sharp 3 before resolving on a sustained G3. Sopranos have taken in recent years to concluding the aria an octave higher – which is to miss Giordano's point entirely.[146] This wretched habit has been formed by questions of technique and voice placement that have gone unanswered by training and discipline; it is a construction of *fach* also – a criterion that fractured at the turn of the century, when changes in repertoire collided with tradition and produced a crisis in casting. Verismo necessitated large voices and acting ability, where the music of previous generations called for what was known increasingly as a "classical" technique. The water mark was Verdi's Desdemona, a role that could be performed by a soprano called on to play Violetta in the same season – but not by a soprano acclimated to Maddalena di Coigny.

This transition was embodied by Celestina Boninsegna,[147] a graduate of the Conservatorio Gioachino Rossini in Pesaro, who made her debut as a 15-year-old in *Don Pasquale*. Her first appearance as an adult was as Marguerite in Gounod's *Faust* in 1889, three decades after the work's first production. Apart from Rosaura in the first Rome performance of Mascagni's *Le maschere*,[148] and two further roles by Mascagni (Maria in *Guglielmo Ratcliff* and Santuzza) and a handful of performances as Puccini's

---

144 'I am divine! I can make you forget! I am the god who descends to earth from the empyrean and makes this world a paradise! Ah!'

145 'I am love, love.'

146 The words immediately following "*L'amor*" are "*E l'angelo si accosta, bacia, e vi bacia la morte! Corpo di moribonda è il corpo mio.*" ('And the angel approaches with a kiss, and he kisses death! a dying body is my body'). The modern tendency has precedent, including (surprisingly) Claudio Muzio, who performed the role in the presence of the composer.

147 26 February, 1877 – 13 February, 1947.

148 'The Masks.' The opera was first performed coincidentally at six opera houses across Italy. The Rome production was conducted by the composer. Boninsegna recorded the "Letter" aria from *Il Maschera* in 1904. Her tone is always magnificent – particularly when measured against her speaking voice, with which the aria begins.

Tosca,[149] Boninsegna's repertoire was dominated by the music of composers who were either dead or retired – primarily Verdi, but also Mozart, Bellini, Donizetti, Berlioz, Meyerbeer, Halévy and Ponchielli. Boninsegna was unwilling to submit to the indignities of verismo, which was producing around 250 new operas a year – many of them adhering doggedly to the now-proven commercial formula. Even if most of these works were staged only rarely, if at all, the culture's turn towards violence and sensationalism was absolute before Puccini began to indulge his femicidal tendencies.

Despite her dramatic inclinations and moral reservation, Boninsegna was modern because she straddled a vast range of repertoire that would not previously have been thought sensible or appropriate for one singer. Notwithstanding the recognised limits of her coloratura, Boninsegna transcended her status as a spinto soprano by singing Brünnhilde (*Siegfried*) as well as Donna Anna, Norma and Aida. She did so in consequence of the near-perfect placement of her voice, which she preserved over a long career, as demonstrated by the consistency of the recordings she made between 1903 and 1917. Audibility was an increasingly pivotal value for conductors, composers and recording engineers, for whom resonance operated as a mechanical and technical pre-requisite; even with volume evolving as prescriptive (encompassing diction, projection, line and articulation). Boninsegna never over-sang, a construction of judgment and discipline that determined her reluctance to submit to verismo's stentorian appetites. Her 1910 recording of "*Visi d'Arte,*" from *Tosca*, is pragmatically artless, employing phrasing that would be dehydrated for anyone versed in performance since the 1950s. Boninsegna's 1905 recording of "*Casta Diva,*" on the other hand, is astonishing for the integrity of the sung line, although a flutter vibrato and an aversion to portamento produce an oppressively rigid theatrical experience. Arthritic phrasing and an absence of charm and seduction cannot detract from the amplitude and richness of her tone, however, which is indulgent, honeyed, and among the most luxurious of any soprano recorded during the first two decades of the century. Few performances compare with Boninsegna's 1904 recording of "*D'amor sull' ali rosee,*" which unfolds as silk, proving how the appetite for volume and declamation did not (at this stage, at least) compel sopranos to bark and shout what was written to be sung.[150] Even at the end of her career, Boninsegna maintained an impressive range and power, above and at the root of the stave;[151] she never abused her resources, as is apparent from the intimacy of her 1917 recording of "*Vicino a te,*" with Luigi Bolis. Some years later, she was visited by the music critic, Max De Schauensee. In 1975, he recalled his experience of meeting the soprano in a public lecture:

> I rang the doorbell and a very large rather untidy woman who I thought must be the cook opened the door. I asked for Signora Boninsegna and she looked at me with very kind eyes and said "I am la Boninsegna." She asked me in and gave me a cup of coffee and we began to talk, sitting in

---

149   At the Teatro Municipale, Santiago, in 1901.

150   The 1917 recording of "*Vicino a te,*" with Luigi Bolis bears no comparison with the sort of caterwauling that would become routine during the 1950s.

151   Her technique was far from perfect. The chest voice is marked by an off-putting break, as evidenced by her 1909 recording of "*Bel raggio lusingher*" from *Semiramide*.

a horribly ornate drawing room … I told her that I sang a little. "I wish you would sing something for me" she said, but I protested that I had been travelling all the summer and had not opened my mouth for two or three months. "No, no, no," she said "that does not matter – I am giving some lessons and my accompanist is here', and she took out the score of *Tosca* and opened it at the first tenor aria. So I embarked on this and when I had got through it I thought that she would say something. But she made no comment except to say "Let's go on," and so she came in, "Mario! Mario! Mario!," and we went on with the duet in the first act. She was not too good a musician, I thought, but her voice was still very remarkable in parts […] The high notes and the low notes were still wonderful – quite marvellous; there was a sort of hole in the middle but that did not make any difference. Her voice was very tremendous in volume, especially on the high notes, and it was all I could do to balance her when we went up to those climaxes. And of course I felt as though I were in a dream. As a child I had had some of Boninsegna's records and here I was singing with this person from another world! When we had finished she said "Let's begin again from the beginning"; so we did and I must say that things went very much better. Then she said "I still have my high C" and she gave me a demonstration, which was marvellous—the whole room rang. Then she plunged down into the low notes and sang the phrase from *Aida*, Amneris's "*Figlia dei faraoni*," and I felt as though Tamagno was in the room—I had never heard such a tremendous sound as this was; then she turned to me with flashing eyes and said "*Questa era la mia glori*" – this was my glory.[152]

The verismo revolution, and the maturation of the soprano voice more generally, was determined by the work of a single composer – Giacomo Puccini. The timing of his international celebrity could not have been more propitious. His first hit, *Manon Lescaut*, was first performed at the Teatro Regio in Turin on 1 February, 1893. Seven days later, and 100 miles distant, Verdi's *Falstaff* received its premiere at La Scala. After *Manon Lescaut's* London premiere, George Bernard Shaw pronounced that "Puccini looks to me more like the heir of Verdi than any of his rivals."[153] The composer's sopranos were all born between 1860 and 1893; most of them became famous because of their work for Puccini, but also because they made recordings – in some cases lots of them. A number appeared on film also. Puccini's choice for the first Manon, and the first Mimi in *La bohème*[154] three years later, was indicative of the changed landscape. Cesira Ferrani[155] started out singing purely lyric repertoire, as Gilda and Gounod's Marguerite. She transitioned to heavier roles in 1892, when appearing at the Teatro Carlo Felice, Genoa, as Amelia in *Simon Boccanegra*, and as the title role in Catalani's *Loreley* – both conducted by Toscanini. Also in 1892,

152 *Recorded Sound*, No. 59, July, 1975.
153 Shaw, George Bernard (1968). *Music in London, 1890–1894*. Vol III, p. 217.
154 First performed on 1 February, 1896.
155 8 May, 1863 – 4 May, 1943.

Ferrani was the sole survivor of the first production of Franchetti's romantic fluff, *Il fior d'Alpe*,[156] and in 1895 she appeared as Suzel in Mascagni's *L'amico Fritz* at the Opéra de Monte-Carlo. The morning after the triumphant premiere of *La bohème* in Turin, Puccini presented Ferrani with his photograph, on which he had written the restrained dedication,[157] "To my true and splendid Mimì, signorina Cesira Ferrani, with gratitude, G. Puccini."

Ferrani made very few recordings. Indeed, it's something of a miracle to be able to hear the first Mimi singing "*Si, mi chiamano Mimi*," just 8 years after the premiere. The recording is revealing of the changes that occurred in taste, training and instinct in the wake of the bel canto-verismo transition. Ferrani's tone is forced, and her phrasing is frequently snatched; the ends of phrases are allowed neither the requisite time, nor their written substance – features of her singing that cannot be attributed to the limitations of phonograph technology. Ferrani's voice-placement is alarmingly uncertain for a singer who was only 41 at the time. It seems improbable that Puccini can have been grateful in 1896 for the strident over-singing that characterises the latter half of the aria in 1904. The spreading vibrato and slackened vowels would have caused the climactic phrase "*ma quando vien lo sgelo il primo sole è mio il primo bacio dell'aprile è mio!*"[158] to send winter chills down the spine of even the most priapic of Rodolfos. Ferrani was attractive, and one can imagine how she might have persuaded as a woman with whom a poet (and a composer) might fall in love – but she wasn't the opera's sexual driver. Puccini added Musetta to the ensemble cast, leaving no doubt that the character was a prostitute, playing a role created to juxtapose Mimi's upstanding integrity by emphasising Musetta's horizontal proclivities – quite literally during her Act II aria, "*Quando me'n vo'*," during which she duets briefly with Mimi. Puccini scored Musetta's scene as a waltz, to emphasise the character's decadence and licentiousness. Musetta arrives at the Café Momus in the company of a client, the elderly Alcindoro; when she sees that Rodolfo is with her former lover, Marcello, she sings:

> *Quando me'n vo' soletta per la via,*
> *la gente sosta e mira e la bellezza mia tutta ricerca in me da capo a piè;*
> *Ed assaporo allor la bramosia sottil, che da gli occhi traspira*
> *e dai palesi vezzi intender sa alle occulte beltà.*
> *Così l'effluvio del desìo tutta m'aggira, felice mi fa!*
> *E tu che sai, che memori e ti struggi da me tanto rifuggi?*
> *So ben: Le angoscie tue non le vuoi dir, ma ti senti morir!*[159]

---

156   'The Alpine Flower.'

157   Restrained because they were sleeping together at the time.

158   '[...] but when the thaw comes, the first sun is mine, the first kiss of April is mine!'

159   When I walk all alone in the street, people stop and stare at me and look for my whole beauty from head to feet; And then I taste the slight yearning which transpires from their eyes and which is able to perceive from manifest charms to most hidden beauties. So the scent of desire is all around me, it makes me happy! And you, while knowing, reminding and longing, you shrink from me? I know it very well: you don't want to express your anguish, but you feel as if you're dying!

Musetta's ill-disguised references to the sexual act (which conclude with "shrinking," after her client has "died,")[160] inspire Marcello to embrace her, leaving Alcindoro wanting a refund. Musetta is not a courtesan. Like Puccini's previous heroine, Manon Lescaut,[161] she walks the streets, mixes with Bohemians, and shares in their poverty; she is willing to humiliate clients, knowing she will not likely see the same one twice. Puccini's writing is erotic and teasing; he colours Musetta's vocal line with sexualised chromaticism and gifts her a sequence of ringing, climactic B4s – the last of which is introduced by an hilarious orchestral *arpeggio* that proves Marcello has returned to the folds. The role of Musetta was created by Camilla Pasini;[162] it could not have been played by any of her predecessors. Indeed, it is inconceivable that Patti, Tietjens, Artôt, Albani, Nilsson or Sembrich – whose "charming" and "ladylike" manners cast them as singing dolls, after the fashion of Offenbach's "Olympia"[163] – could have appeared as (or sung the music written for) Musetta. Not only would they have baulked at playing a character who only ten years previously was demonised as a popular focus for Jack the Ripper's malfeasance, but they would also have been inaudible during the final repeat of the leading theme of "*Quando me'n vo*,'" when Musetta is joined by half a dozen other solo voices, a chorus, and a throbbing romantic orchestra.

Pasini (the sister of Lina Pasini-Vitale,[164] another soprano, better-represented on record) began her career as Norina (*Don Pasquale*), Violetta, and Desdemona, before moving on to verismo roles, including Tosca, Fedora, and Wally, as well as Elsa and Massenet's Grisélidis. The differences between her singing and that of any of her immediate predecessors is obvious from her recordings, the most revealing of which is her 1909 performance of "*Un bel di vedremo*,"[165] from *Madama Butterfly*. The amplitude of the voice is stunning; the tone is rich in its middle register, but anything above an A4 takes on a shrill quality, with a spreading vibrato and too much force.

La bohème made its first cast famous – the pressure of which appears to have been too much for the first Rodolfo, Evan Gorga, who retired from performing three year later, at the age of 34.[166] Ferrani went on to sing in the Genovese "world premiere" of Mascagni's *Le maschere*, in 1904; four years later she was cast by Toscanini for the first performance in Italy, at La Scala, of Debussy's *Pelléas et Mélisande*. Her repertoire in Milan spanned Gounod's Juliette, *Sapho's* Fanny, Charlotte in Massenet's *Werther*, *Simon Boccanegra's* Amelia, Elisabeth in *Tannhäuser*, Elsa in *Lohengrin* and Eva in *Die Meistersinger*. When Puccini completed his next opera, *Tosca*, he relocated from Turin (unified Italy's first capital city) to Rome (the capital after 1870) on the advice of his publisher, Ricordi. The reasoning was written in *le stelle lucenti*, because Sardou's play, *La Tosca*, on which Luigi Illica and Giuseppe Giacosa based their libretto, is set in Rome – on a single day, 17 June, 1800,[167] following the Battle of Marengo. For the

---

160   "*Petite mort*," ('little death,') was a common euphemism for the orgasm.
161   Abbé Prévost's 1731 novel, on which Puccini's opera is based, was banned in 1733 and 1735.
162   6 November, 1875 – 29 November, 1935.
163   Olympia is the singing mechanical doll *in Les Comtes d'Hoffmann*.
164   8 November, 1872 – 23 November, 1959.
165   'One fine day, we shall see.'
166   See Boyden, Matthew (2021). *The Tenor: A Cultural History*. Ragueneau Press.
167   Because the opera season was over in June, it was not possible for *Tosca* to be staged on the centenary of the work's narrative events. The first performance was given "six months early," therefore, on 14 January, 1900.

title role – and the opera's only female voice – Puccini needed an actress as well as singer, because the character is a prima donna, and because of the shadows thrown by Sardou's first Floria Tosca, Sarah Bernhardt. Puccini saw Bernhardt perform the role during her tour of Italy in 1889, and soon after requested Ricordi to negotiate with the author for adaptation rights. Verdi beat them to it, but his interest was dependent on the ending being changed, with Tosca enduring insanity rather than suicide. Illica and Giacosa were of a similar mind, but Sardou was having none of it; neither was Puccini, for whom a woman's violent death was preferable theatrically to derangement. Ricordi made approaches to Enrico Constanzi, the manager (and son of the original builder) of the Costanzi Theatre in Rome.[168] His father, Domenico, had overseen the first performance of *Cavalleria rusticana* in 1890, and the theatre made an ideal venue, particularly considering it was less than four miles from each of the settings of the work's three acts.[169]

Tosca was the second of Puccini's operas to be named after its female lead; six of his ensuing seven operas would follow suit. His first and only choice for the title role was the Romanian Hariclea Darclée[170] – a soprano renowned, like Bernhardt, for her commitment to the contemporary and the modern. She can be considered one of the last generation of Italian-repertoire sopranos to live out her career in the company of living composers. Of her 58 roles (spanning 56 operas), 12 were absolute premières; 16 were regional premières – many of them in Romania, where she was revered as a national heroine. Darclée collaborated directly with 19 composers, including Arrigo Boito (for productions of *Mefistofele*), Alfredo Catalani (for whom she created the title role in *La Wally* at La Scala),[171] Alexis Catargiu (*Enoch Arden*),[172] Isidore De Lara (*Amy Robsart*), Franchetti (*Cristoforo Colombo*),[173] Antônio Carlos Gomes (for whom she created the role of Odalea in *Condor*),[174] Leoncavallo (*I Pagliacci* and *Zaza*), Luigi Mancinelli (*Ero e Leandro*), Mascagni (*Cavalleria rusticana*, *L'amico Fritz*, *I Rantzau*,[175] in which she created the role of Luisa,[176] and *Iris*, in which she created the title role),[177] Massenet (*El Cid*), Ubaldo Pacchierotti (*Eidelberga mia*, in which she created the role of Catina), Ettore Panizza (*Aurora*), Puccini (*La bohème*), Pietro Vallini (*Il Voto*, in which she created the role of Maria),[178] and Richard Strauss (*Der Rosenkavalier*, in which she played the Marschallin at the Italian premiere).[179]

Darclée began her studies at the Iaşi Conservatoire. Having relocated to Paris, and the tutelage of Jean-Baptiste Faure,[180] she made her debut at the Opéra, as Marguerite

168   Later on, and still today, the Teatro dell'Opera di Roma.

169   Act I is set in the Church of Sant'Andrea della Valle, Act II in Scarpia's apartment within the Palazzo Farnese, and Act III at the Castle Sant'Angelo.

170   *née* Haricli, later Hartulari, 10 June, 1860 – 12 January, 1939.

171   On 20 January, 1892.

172   First performed on 19 December, 1904.

173   First performed on 6 October, 1892.

174   First performed on 21 February, 1891.

175   'The Family Rantzau.'

176   First performed on 10 November, 1892.

177   'The Vote,' First performed on 22 November, 1898.

178   On 27 November, 1894.

179   On 14 November, 1911.

180   A uniquely influential French baritone, teacher, art collector and sometime composer of *Chansons*;

in *Faust*, in 1888; the following year she replaced Patti as Gounod's Juliette. Although she toured extensively throughout Spain, Portugal, Russia and South America, Darclée spent most of her career in Italy – where she made a handful of recordings for Fonotipia, in 1904–05. It is frustrating that none of them survived,[181] particularly since one of the sessions included a performance of Tosca's "*Visi d'arte*."[182] 'I lived for art' is the opera's most popular aria, and Puccini's best known music for soprano, after "*Un bel di vedremo*." Puccini was asked to compose the aria by Darclée, who feared the absence of a solo moment midst so much duet and ensemble writing. Puccini did as he was asked since Darclée is likely to have made her request while in bed with the composer. It is an extraordinary soliloquy, a moment of intense, insular grief, in which the singer states her credo while distancing herself from the male-directed political maelstrom for which Cavaradossi has only moments earlier been tortured. "*Visi d'arte*" adheres to Puccini's compositional style for most of his arias, insofar as it begins quietly and builds to a climax that crests on a B flat 4, B4 or a C5; the aria is alarmingly solipsistic and self-justifying – a petition by Tosca to her "*Signor*" rather than "*Dio*" for salvation from an experience that was then unexceptional for the majority of women. Tosca's crisis has become "shocking" for western societies that treat any coercive sexual conduct by a man as an assault.[183] "Marital rape" is now unlawful in every developed society,[184] but in 1900 sexual violence against women, and sex as a commercial and social transaction, rendered Scarpia's proposal less tyrannical than pragmatic. The horror of having to endure sex with a man of wealth and power is as transactional today as it was in 1900; indeed, the episode is tense dramatically only because Tosca is a singer – an artist – who is presumed to be above such grubby entanglements, and because she is being asked to sacrifice herself for the benefit of another. Her predicament crystalises in the wording of her petition to God, in which she expresses the same bafflement at her circumstances as does Christ when lamenting "in a loud voice, '*Eli, Eli, lama sabachthani?* that is to say, 'My God, my God,

---

two of Faure's songs were recorded by Caruso. He was born on 15 January, 1830, and trained as a choirboy by clergy and teachers born in the 18th century. He was picked by Verdi to create the role of Rodrigue, Marquis of Posa, in *Don Carlos* in 1867, and in 1900 he was recorded singing "*Léonor! Viens*" from *La favorite*, in his 70th year. Faure can be considered the earliest-born singer of note to be recorded. He was close friends with Manet, who painted multiple portraits of the singer. At various stages, he owned 67 of Manet's canvases – including *Le déjeuner sur l'herbe* and *Le Fifre*. He was the owner also of *Le pont d'Argenteuil* and 62 other works by Monet, in addition to canvasses by Degas, Sisley, Pissarro, Ingres and Prud'hon. Faure commissioned Monet to paint his villa, "Les Roches" (in Étretat), on 40 occasions.

181   At least one pressing appears to be in private hands, and not (so far) available commercially. In 1992, the auction house, Christie's, listed a 78 by Darclée, which was given an estimate of $1.2 million. The item was withdrawn by the undisclosed owner the day before the auction.

182   There are various alleged recordings, none of them by Darclée. The recordings of Romanian folk songs, made during the 1920s, are likely of her daughter.

183   As of 2021, the following countries have either failed to criminalise, or decriminalised, marital rape: India, Bangladesh, China, Haiti, Laos, Mali, Myanmar, Senegal, Afghanistan, Tajikistan, Lebanon, Malaysia, Singapore, Egypt, Libya, Oman, Yemen and Kuwait.

184   In Italy the law on rape ("*violenza carnale*") accounted for forced sex within a marriage in 1976, pursuant to *Sentenza* n. 12857 del 1976, in which the Supreme Court ruled "*commette il delitto di violenza carnale il coniuge che costringa con violenza o minaccia l'altro coniuge a congiunzione carnale*" ('the spouse who compels the other spouse to carnal knowledge by violence or threats commits the crime of carnal violence').

why hast thou forsaken me?'[185] The pain of abandonment is determined consequently by the status of its victims, just as it was for the characters in Adrian Lyne's 1993 film, *Indecent Proposal*, in which a married couple is offered $1m by a billionaire, played by the still-beautiful Robert Redford, for a single evening's intimacy with the wife, played by Demi Moore. In a mercantile age, and with people doing just about anything *on television* for money, that dilemma now seems guileless. The only source of ethical tension in *Tosca* is the acceptance by Puccini, and the audience, of the soprano's murder of Scarpia for having proposed something that qualified as little more than impertinence. It doesn't happen, of course; the heroine chooses murder in the alternative, not to save Cavaradossi (whom she dooms as she stabs Scarpia) but to protect herself from having to endure a single, non-consensual episode of sexual congress. In deciding not to allow Scarpia inside her, Tosca denies Christ's philosophy of oblation; instead, she enters Scarpia, using a symbol more powerful even than the cross she lays on top of his corpse.

Although delayed – and then restarted[186] – the first performance of *Tosca* was a triumph. The critical reaction was restrained, with the libretto blamed more often than the music. The initial run of twenty-one performances sold-out, regardless, as did the first production at La Scala, launched by Toscanini on 17 March, 1900, with Darclée reprising the title role. The British premiere, at the Royal Opera House, was unveiled on 12 July, 1900, with the Croation soprano Milka Ternina[187] appearing as Tosca. Ternina was a favourite of the Wagner conductor, Anton Seidl, who encouraged her to learn Isolde and the two Brünnhildes. She was among the leading heldensoprans of the 1890s, and when making her North American debut, in Boston in 1896, she appeared as Brünnhilde in *Die Walküre* for the Damrosch Company. Her London debut, in 1898, was as Isolde; on 27 January, 1900, a year after appearing at the Bayreuth Festival as Kundry, Ternina made her debut at the New York Met as Elisabeth in *Tannhäuser*. Twelve months later she was engaged to create the role of Tosca at the American premiere. Mapleson recorded a number of scenes from the initial run, and they are thrilling. Ternina's tone is light for a Wagnerian (compared to the steam-whistle voices of Kirsten Flagstad and Birgit Nilsson), but it is flexible, with a fast, fashionably ubiquitous vibrato. The first act duet is lyrical but loud, and Ternina is well-acquainted with the "modern" taste for verismo declamation, as can be heard when she discovers that Cavaradossi has been executed:

> *Presto! Su, Mario! Mario! Su! Presto! Andiam! Su! Su!*
> *Mario! Mario! Morto! Morto! O Mario, morto? Tu? Cosi?*
> *Finire cosi? Cosi!*[188]

---

185   Matthew 27:46.

186   Latecomers attempting to enter the auditorium caused a disturbance, which disrupted even *Tosca's* brass-heavy five-chord opening. When someone shouted "Bring down the curtain!" the conductor Mugnone stopped the orchestra. The performance was restarted – from the beginning – and proceeded without further interruption, save for the numerous encores.

187   *née* Katarina Milka Trnina, 19 December, 1863 – 18 May, 1941.

188   'Quickly! Up, Mario! Mario! Up! Quickly. Come. Up! Up! Mario! Mario! Dead! Dead!'

Ternina was a sensation as Tosca – giving 18 performances at the Met, Puccini described her as "ideal," an assessment that attests to the popularity of verismo's declamatory vernacular. Equally crowd-pleasing was Puccini's calculated exploitation of the murder and debasement of women. Puccini's misogyny is complicated, of course, notwithstanding the surfeit of evidence. His affairs were legion, but the verismo-origins of his marriage are equally illuminating. During the autumn of 1884, he began an affair with Elvira Gemignani,[189] whose husband, Narciso, was a renowned adulterer. When Elvira became pregnant by Puccini, she left her family home and gave birth to Antonio, an only child, in secret. Elvira then moved with her son, and a daughter by Narciso, (Fosca), to live with Puccini, who decamped everyone to his estate at Torre del Lago in 1889. On 26 February, 1903, Narciso was murdered by the husband of one of his paramours, leaving Puccini and Elvira free to marry in early 1904. The 18-year-old Antonio was legitimised shortly after. There exists a fantastically bleak photo of Puccini with his wife and son, taken in the garden of their home in 1900. An unsmiling mother and child stare at the camera; the composer reads a newspaper, with his chin resting on his left hand. The image speaks to something other than domestic bliss.

The maltreatment of women made for excellent box office receipts, but to suggest that Puccini was feeding as a composer from his personal beliefs and instincts would be facile since his prejudices and psychological impairments were subjugated entirely to commercial prerogatives. His fondness for dramas in which women were tortured and murdered, over and above less sadistic characterisations of the female experience, objectified the *au courant*. In short: misogyny was good for business, even if his next opera failed at first instance. *Madama Butterfly* concerns the quasi-ritual humiliation, debasement and abandonment of the title character, Cio-Cio-San who ends the opera in Seppuku. The score contains some of the most beautiful music written to be sung, with a love duet in Act II, beginning "*Bimba, Bimba dagli occhi pieni di malia,*"[190] that is the most perfect in Italian opera. For all its extravagant beauty, *Butterfly* resists affection because only one of the characters, Sharpless, is likable or relatable.

The original (two-act) version was first staged on 17 February, 1904 – at La Scala – with Rosina Storchio[191] creating the title role. It was an infamous disaster, with the audience united in howling and booing. Puccini described the experience as "a real lynching." When detractors isolated similarities between Butterfly's entrance and the Act III duet of *bohème*, they began to cry out "*Bohème, Bohème!,*" with many others laughing at Storchio's appearance.[192] Despite being trained in coloratura – as can be heard on her 1911 recording of "*Ah! non giunge*" – Storchio's culture was resolutely contemporary. In 1897, she was the first Mimì in Leoncavallo's ill-timed iteration of *La bohème*; three years later she created the title role in Leoncavallo's *Zazà*, an homage to Zola's *Nana* that concerns a French music-hall singer who falls in love with Milio, whom she later discovers is married with children; when she confronts him with the truth of his circumstances, Milio's resulting fury motivates Zazà to

---

189   *née* Bonturi, 13 June, 1860 – 1930
190   'Child, Child with eyes full of enchantment.'
191   19 January, 1872 – 24 July, 1945.
192   She was pregnant with Toscanini's baby.

end their affair. The opera concludes with her emotional and psychological ruin. In 1903, Giordano chose Storchio to sing Stephana in the first production of *Siberia*,[193] a more traditional work of verismo in which Stephana is humiliated and murdered by shooting.

Storchio recorded nothing from *Butterfly*, but she completed numerous sessions in 1904 when recording scenes from *Siberia*, with the opera's original tenor lead, Giovanni Zenatello. Considering the clarity and focus of its tone, the power of Storchio's voice is unusual; it was also increasingly typical of sopranos now expected to commit to repertoire that necessitated amplitude above style. Particularly in New York, the appetite for scale and volume caused the size of a woman's voice to become prescriptive. The first Metropolitan Opera House, inaugurated in 1883, featured a five-balcony auditorium for 3,389 people, with standing room for a further 380. The pit seated as many as 100 players uncomfortably. After revising the score of *Butterfly*, Puccini passed the honour of its next premiere to Solomiya Krushelnytska,[194] a 32-year-old soprano born in Bielawińce,[195] who was much admired in eastern Europe for singing Wagner. Krushelnytska recorded "*Visi d'Arte*" for the Gramophone & Typewriter company, in Warsaw – two years before she first met Puccini, in 1902. The recording served as her calling-card prior to her relocation to Naples for the 1903–1904 season – when Puccini cast her as the second Mrs Butterfly, three months after the first.[196] Krushelnytska recorded "*Un bel di vedremo*," in 1912; it is nothing short of miraculous that a woman renowned for her performances as Isolde and Brünnhilde,[197] and who gave the Italian premiere of *Salome* in 1906 (conducted by her lover, Toscanini), was able to persuade as a fragile teenager. The tone, legato and phrasing are that of an innocent, and incomparable to the tendency among later singers to yell the intimate foreshadowed-reflections of "*Piccina mogliettina, olezzo di verbena.*"[198]

Puccini's next soprano role was written for the United States, and a singer able to persuade as a Western saloon owner – the titular *fanciulla del West*. Rather than cast a natural-born American singer, the composer perpetuated his long-running affection for sopranos from eastern Europe by giving the title role to another of his inamoratas, Emmy Destinn.[199] Six years passed between *Butterfly* and the first performance of *La fanciulla* on 10 December, 1910 – during which time Puccini was able to come to terms with Strauss' modernist sisters, *Salome* and *Elektra*. The musical language is more through-composed than ever, and Toscanini (who conducted the first performance) was onto something when describing the opera as a "great symphonic poem."[200] The more obvious effect of Strauss' impact was manifested in the orchestration, which is technically more advanced and atypically contrapuntal. The score

---

193 First performed on 19 December, 1903.
194 23 September, 1872 – 16 November, 1952.
195 A tiny village, then in Galicia, Austria-Hungary, now Ukraine.
196 First performed on 28 May, 1904.
197 The power of her voice when required is evident from two recordings of excerpts from *Die Walküre*: "*Ho jo to ho!*" and "*War es so schmählich, was ich verbrach.*"
198 'Dear little wife of mine, scented of orange blossom!'
199 *née* Emílie Pavlína Věnceslava Kittlová, 26 February, 1878 – 28 January, 1930.
200 Fisher, Burton D. (2005). *Puccini's The Girl of the Golden West*. Opera Journeys Publishing, p. 22.

prescribes a piccolo, three flutes, three oboes, a cor anglais, three clarinets in B-flat, a bass clarinet in B-flat, three bassoons, a contrabassoon, four horns, three trumpets, three tenor trombones, a bass trombone, a celesta, two harps, a percussion section featuring timpani, cymbals, triangle, snare drum, bass drum, and glockenspiel, at least 50 strings and three onstage *fonicas*.[201] To be audible, especially during the huge Act II duet for Minnie and Johnson, the amplitude of singers was now as important for Puccini as it was for Strauss. The only respite for Destinn was the survival of her character, who is threatened but neither beaten nor murdered. *La fanciulla* is rare in ending happily, and unusual for the only violence against its female lead being coercion by the sheriff, Jack Rance, who accepts Minnie's offer of marriage should he defeat her in a game of cards. The opera concludes with Johnson surviving to the closing curtain, after which he and Minnie are expected to make their way peacefully to California – presumably not as members of the Donner Party.[202]

Destinn changed her name when making her debut at the Dresden Hofoper in 1897, as Santuzza in *Cavalleria rusticana*; she took the name of her teacher in Prague, the mezzo-soprano Marie von Dreger-Loewe, who performed under the pseudonym "Destinn." After moving to the Berlin Hofoper she sang a wide range of old and new roles, including the premiere in 1902 of Eugen d'Albert's *Der Improvisator*, and the first Berlin production of Strauss's *Feuersnot*, in which she performed the role of Diemut. In 1903 she created Elsa in the world première of Bernhard Scholz's *Anno 1757*, the title role in the local première of Charpentier's *Louise*, and Marguerite for the first production of Emil von Reznicek's *Till Eulenspiegel*, on 12 January, 1902. She also sang in the premiere of Leoncavallo's *Roland von Berlin* in 1904, and the first performance of Humperdinck's *Die Heirat wider Willen*[203] in 1905. In 1906, she gave the Berlin premiere of *Salome*; three years later she was Milada in the first German production of Smetana's *Dalibor*. In 1901, she was invited to Bayreuth to play the role of Senta in *Holländer*. Destinn made her London debut at Covent Garden on 2 May, 1904, as Donna Anna, in *Don Giovanni*. *The Times'* critic, Hermann Klein, heralded

> another rich soprano of the Tietjens and Lucca type; Destinn is an ac-
> tress of consummate ability, a splendid Mozart singer, in a word, the
> admirable, very nearly perfect Donna Anna, and with no lack of "fresh-
> ness" in her round and penetrating tones.

In London she sang Nedda and Santuzza (on the same evening) as well as Aida, about which Klein wrote that "the power that she displayed when she rose to the climax of the Nile scene I shall never forget." She gave triumphant performances as Maddalena in *Andrea Chénier*, and the British premieres of the title roles in Frédéric d'Erlanger's *Tess*, and *La fanciulla del West*. Her British and American repertoire included roles in

---

201 The fonica is an electronic instrument, invented by Puccini for *La fanciulla del West*. Puccini's publishers, Ricordi, manufactured the instruments and rented them out for early productions; the results were unsatisfactory, however, leading to the substitution of marimbas.

202 The opera is set in 1849–50, two years after the Donner Party migrated to California, eating each other during the winter of 1846–1847.

203 'The Forced Marriage.'

d'Albert's *Tiefland*, Franchetti's *Germania* and Verdi's *Falstaff*. After creating the role of Minnie, she gave the US premieres of Catalani's *La Wally*,[204] Bedřich Smetana's *Prodaná nevěsta*,[205] and Tchaikovsky's *Pique Dame*.[206] Also in New York, she sang for Gustav Mahler in a revival production of *Don Giovanni*, with an extraordinary cast that included Alessandro Bonci, Adamo Didur, Antonio Scotti, Marcella Sembrich, and Emma Eames. In a review of "a third performance there within six days, and always in the presence of a large audience," Pitts Sanborn wrote for *The New York Globe*:

> In spite of Mr. Mahler, in spite of Mr. Bonci, in spite of Mme. Sembrich, all three of whom might be termed "Mozart specialists," there were too many weak spots in the cast to make the actual performance such as the presence of seven "stars," under the guidance of so distinguished a conductor as Gustav Mahler, might lead the unwary to expect [...]. Nevertheless, the one best guess for Donna Anna remains Bohemian Emmy Destinn. Donna Anna is the most difficult part in the opera, both to cast and perform. To many spectators this distressed lady has been a bore, as she became to Don Giovanni. But, before relegating her to the limbo of troubles to be endured, study her music and consider, too, the dramatic possibilities of the one heroic character in the opera – the woman who has been called "the incarnation of devotion to the male," and who alone is faithful unto death. Jenny Lind and Christine Nilsson were not ashamed to undertake the part, and records do not say they were a bore in it.

In addition to her work as a singer, Destinn was celebrated in Czechoslovakia as an author of novels, essays, plays, poetry and songs – some of which she recorded for the Victor Company.[207] She retired from the theatre in 1926; despite repeated medical advice, on three continents, that she change her diet, Destinn suffered a stroke and died at the age of 52 during the evening of 28 January, 1930. Her many recordings provide a comprehensive overview of her career, spanning French, Italian, German and Czech repertoire. The purity of tone and peerless legato of "*Un bel di vedremo*," and the pathos of Butterfly's farewell "*Tu, tu piccolo iddio*,"[208] are masterly, unsentimental studies in voice-acting. Her performance of "*Vissi d'arte*," just a few months after the first performance of *La fanciulla del West*, is the slowest on record, but it proves how the singer must have been audible to the gods even at the cavernous old Metropolitan. It is fascinating also to hear Destinn's creative use of vibrato, which is absent until the second half of the aria, and her calculated portamento. The climax is fabulous for its resonance, and for the resolving long-held A flat 4, from which Destinn transitions to the resolving G4 by the use of an (unwritten) mordent,

---

204   On 6 January, 1909.

205   'The Bartered Bride,' on 19 February, 1909.

206   On 5 March, 1910.

207   Including, "*Posledny Slzy*" ('Last Tears,'), "Romance," and "*Namluvy*" ('Wooing'), for the Victor Company.

208   'You, you little god.'

all delivered over an expert, affecting diminuendo. Her records have always been controversial; the critical view was consistent in its praise of her technique, intonation and theatricality, but many have recoiled from her indulgence of tone, and a diction so precise that it interferes with the sung line.

After 1910, Puccini worked inevitably with an increasing number of sopranos, despite writing only three more operas – *La Rondine*,[209] *Il trittico*[210] (formed of *Il tabarro*,[211] *Suor Angelica*[212] and *Gianni Schicchi*) and *Turandot*. He was quick to praise and recommend singers, even when he wasn't known to be sleeping with them. In 1921, for example, after seeing Gilda dalla Rizza[213] as Minnie at the Opéra de Monte-Carlo, he remarked, "At last I have seen my true fanciulla."[214] It was no coincidence that he should have proceeded to write two roles for dalla Rizza: the courtesan, Magda de Civry, in *La Rondine*, and the self-slaughtering Liù in *Turandot*.[215] *Il trittico* featured creations by three of the most popular and influential of the composer's ambassadors, Claudia Muzio[216] (Giorgetta in *il tabarro*), Geraldine Farrar[217] (the title role of *Suor Angelica*), and Florence Easton[218] (Lauretta in *Gianni Schicchi*). By 21st century standards, each of them was a modern soprano. Other than in terms of perceived quality – of tone and, to a lesser extent, interpretation – there is nothing to distinguish between Muzio's singing and that of any soprano born after her death in 1936. Her recorded legacy is extensive, and includes an entire first act from *Tosca* from 1932, at which point she was in her forties. Her earliest recordings date from the end of the first decade of the century, and attest to a still-developing physique, technique and style; by 1919, and her recording for Pathé of "*Quando me'n vo'*," and "*Selva opaca*," her art is remarkable for its crystalline, bright timbre, clear articulation, and a notable absence of portamento.

Much nonsense has been written about Muzio's "silent" 1920s; she cut a sizable number of 78s for Edison between 1921 and 1925,[219] the best of them memorable for their dramatic, darkened timbre; her recording of "*Ebben, ne andro lontano*," from *La Wally*, proves how her artistry was becoming something exceptional, if not unprecedented. The phrasing of Catalani's aria is, for its time, what would become routine after 2000 for admirers of Renée Fleming; it is definitively elegant, insightful and expressive. The central section is performed piano, with a touching restraint that creates precisely the context intended by the composer for the aria's emotional resolution. Muzio had by this stage in her career become comfortable in her skin; what survives from the 1930s proves her voice to have been one of the most beautiful to be recorded. It was now rich and even between the registers, and such was her control

---

209 'The Swallow,' first performed on 27 March, 1917.
210 'The Triptych,' first performed on 14 December, 1918.
211 'The Cloak.'
212 'Sister Angelica.'
213 dalla Rizza (12 October, 1892 – 5 July, 1975) was supplanted at the first performance by Toscanini's preference, Maria Zamboni.
214 Kendell, Colin (2012). *The Complete Puccini*. Amberley Publishing.
215 25 July, 1895 – 25 March, 1976.
216 7 February, 1889 – 24 May, 1936.
217 *née* Alice Geraldine Farrar, 28 February, 1882 – 11 March, 1967.
218 25 October, 1882 – 13 August, 1955.
219 It is true that she recorded nothing of note during the late 1920s and very early 1930s.

that her capacity for silken, perfectly-supported pianissimos provoked consternation as well as wonder among critics. Bizarre though it might now seem, her inclination to prefer the colouring of a phrase to the primacy of the theatrical moment was controversial. On the other hand, she was possessed of exceptional diction, a resonant chest voice, a creamy, easily produced top and a musical intelligence that separated her from the majority of her peers. In terms of pure tone, Muzio compares most obviously to Rosa Ponselle, Renata Tebaldi and Fleming; her word-use was superior, however, with every syllable being projected with studied intent and purpose. Muzio was a stupendous musician. By way of an exemplar, her 1935 recording of "*O del mio amato ben*" by Stefano Donaudy is a summary lesson in line, colour and expression. The phrasing is exquisite, with tiny but consequential shifts in weight and enunciation; her dynamic palette is judged perfectly, with swells and diminuendos creating a painterly sense of character and feeling. Muzio's art was proof that the suffering endured by women when being stabbed, strangled, raped and abandoned on stage, in sacrifice to *naturalisme* and verismo, had been worth it. Her singing cannot be compared to that of Patti and Melba *et al.* because it is in every meaningful way superior – more human and relatable than anything recorded by the bel cantanti. Many admired Muzio's attention to the poetry of the words as well as the primacy of the music, including Richard Strauss, whom she impressed in Brazil as the Marschallin. On 5 October, 1920, he wrote to Hugo van Hofmannsthal:

> *Rosenkavalier* has at last been produced here with the greatest possible success – on Saturday, 2nd October – as the final performance of the Stagione Bonetti (during which I have so far conducted six concerts here) under that excellent conductor Serafin, with Claudia Muzio as an exceedingly elegant and charming Marschallin.[220]

Muzio was the first Italian soprano to sing Tosca at the Met. She was young at the time, as *The New York Evening Sun* reported on 5 December, 1916:

> The very stage held pictures of German [*sic*] Temina's great creation of the Roman singer, pictures too of the American beauties, Eames and Farrar. But Muzio really was Tosca. Youth, that gem above rubies, shone like a Kohinoor in her modest crown. The drama, for sheer realism or actuality, had not been so visualized in years before, and the singing of the great song of Tosca's life for art's sake – ever so gently, so tenderly – warmed a social Monday house, the most critical audience in the world, to a demonstration of hand clapping loud and long from all parts of a packed theatre.[221]

---

220   Hammelmann, Hanns, and Osers, Ewald, *Trans.* (1974). *A Working Friendship: the Correspondence Between Richard Strauss and Hugo von Hofmannsthal*. Vienna House, p. 339.

221   Jenkins, Laurence L. (2003). *Claudia Muzio (1889–1936), Her Life and Career*. PhD. Thesis. Massey University Conservatorium of Music College of Fine Arts, Design and Music Wellington, New Zealand, p. 36.

During her thirties, Muzio's voice grew in size and reach, sufficient for her to meet Caruso and Scotti toe-to-toe across the verismo repertoire.[222] As the first Maddalena for the Met's debut production of *Andrea Chénier* she was peerless, even if she remained secondary throughout her career to rivals – real and imagined – including Maria Jeritza,[223] Rosa Ponselle and Geraldine Farrar.

Farrar was seven years older than Muzio; she survived her by 31 years.[224] After initial studies with Emma Thursby, in New York, she relocated to Berlin and studies with one of Verdi's favourite baritones, Francesco Graziani.[225] Her debut at the Hofoper as Marguerite in *Faust* in 1901 caused a sensation, but Lillian Nordica urged that she train further, and recommended her to Lilli Lehmann, with whom she studied for three years in the German capital. Farrar's early career was dominated by French repertoire, including Thomas' *Mignon*, Massenet's *Manon*, and Charlotte in *Werther*. After three years with the Monte Carlo Opera (during which time she created the title role in Pietro Mascagni's *Amica*),[226] Farrar made her debut at the Met in New York on 26 November, 1906, as Gounod's Juliette; she remained with the company until her retirement 16 years later, having given 672 performances of 29 roles. She sang the House premiere of *Madama Butterfly* in 1907 and in 1910 she was able to make good use of her fluent German when creating the role of Gänsemagd in Humperdinck's *Königskinder*,[227] a production for which the soprano trained her own flock of geese. When appearing on stage after the premiere she did so carrying a live bird. In 1915, Farrar created the title role in Umberto Giordano's *Madame Sans-Gêne*, alongside Giovanni Martinelli and Pasquale Amato, conducted by Toscanini; three years later, she was cast by Puccini and Toscanini as the title role in *Suor Angelica*. The Met's General Manager, Giulio Gatti-Casazza,[228] cabled Puccini after the first night that Muzio had been "incomparable" as Giorgetta, that the English soprano, Florence Easton, had secured the biggest hit of the night, with "*O mio babbino caro,*"[229] and that Farrar had been judged a disappointment as Angelica – even with many of her admirers in attendance.[230]

Farrar's reputation was bomb-proof, regardless, thanks to the "Gerry-Flappers," who followed her wherever she sang, and after 1915 because of her work on film. Her first movie was as the lead in Cecille B de Mille's production of Prosper Mérimée's *Carmen* (to music by Hugo Riesenfeld rather than Bizet, because the opera's libretto was under copyright). Among her later films, Farrar's appearance as Jeanne d'Arc in

---

222 Caruso was her most regular tenor partner at the Met, famously so in *Cav* and *Pag*.

223 See Chapter 16.

224 Muzio was dead at 47; Farrar died at the age of 85, two months before The Beatles released their 8th album, *Sgt. Pepper's Lonely Hearts Club Band*, on 26 May, 1967.

225 He created the role of Don Carlos at the first performance of *La forza del destino* in 1862.

226 First performed on 16 March, 1905.

227 'The King's Children,' first performed on 28 December, 1910.

228 He was married (since 1910) to the Antipodean soprano Francis Alda (31 May, 1879 – 18 September, 1952) and some of his views, and judgments, were influenced inevitably by proximity and context.

229 The hit of *Gianni Schicchi*, and the only lasting success from *Il trittico*. Easton recorded the aria in the year of its first performance, and it's reasonable to assert that no-one has sung it better since. See further Chapter 16.

230 Ashbrook. William (1968). *The Operas of Puccini*. Cassell, p. 175.

Joan the Woman (De Mille's first historical epic)[231] was the most successful artistically. The rest of her work on screen, until her last movie, *The Riddle: Woman*, in 1920, spans high romance and bloody violence, adhering broadly to the same theatrical principles determined by *naturalisme* and verismo.[232] Because the aesthetics of early cinema adopted the culture of verismo, there was almost nothing to separate the worlds of opera and film during the first 15 years of the 20th century. Certainly, it is impossible to distinguish between the majority of Farrar's primary stage roles and her work as a film actress. Regardless of the narrative context, she is either a lover, a murderer, or a victim.

On 8 February, 1916, Farrar married the Dutch-born stage and film actor Lou Tellegen, with whom she went on to appear in three movies. Tellegen's fame was established through his work with Sarah Bernhardt – with whom he had an on-off affair during the first decade of the century, notwithstanding the 37-year age gap. Tellegen made his motion picture debut with Bernhardt in 1910, as Armand in *La dame aux camélia* – the source text for Verdi's *La traviata*. The film was directed by André Calmettes, a friend of Camille Saint-Saëns, who provided the music for the director's 1908, *La Mort du duc de Guise*.[233] Music and opera, in particular, were a driver for Calmettes, who went on to direct *Tosca* (1908), *La Tosca* (1908), *Rigoletto* (1909), *Don Carlos* (1910), *Madame Sans-Gêne* (1911) and *Mignon* (1912). Tellegen and Bernhardt made their second film together in 1912, *Les Amours de la reine Élisabeth*,[234] and in 1913, they collaborated for *Adrienne Lecouvreur* – a biopic inspired by Cilea's 1902 opera, itself based on the 1849 play by Scribe and Ernest Legouvé. Tellegen's life with Farrar was fodder for America's increasingly unrestrained gossip columnists since he was already known to be more adulterous, even, than Chaplin. Without irony, he gave his autobiography the title, *Woman Have Been Kind*.[235] Farrar's love affairs were legendary long before her one and only marriage. In 1903, for example, she engaged in a controversial affair with Crown Prince Wilhelm of Germany – the eldest son of the last Kaiser – and in 1908 she began a stormy, seven-year fling with the married Toscanini, who resigned from the Met in New York when she demanded he leave his family to marry her. Farrar was rumoured subsequently to have had affairs with Caruso, Pasquale Amato, and a host of other stage colleagues; many came to consider her the living embodiment of Floria Tosca's iconographic independence. Few were surprised when, after seven years of near-constant scandal, shame and humiliation, Farrar submitted to a miserably public divorce. On 29 October, 1934, while Tellegen was a guest of the society heiress Edna Cudahy, he locked himself in a bathroom and, having shaved and powdered his face, stabbed himself seven times in the heart with a pair of sewing scissors. When doing so, he was standing in front of

---

231 Released in 1917.

232 For example, *The Devil-Stone* (1917), *The Hell Cat* (1918), and *Shadows* (1919), in each of which she is the murderer.

233 'The Assassination of the Duke of Guise.'

234 'The Loves of Queen Elizabeth.'

235 First published in 1931. Farrar's own autobiography, *Such Sweet Compulsion*, was published seven years later. It is a very odd book, with alternating chapters purporting to be in her own words and those of her deceased mother, who recounts her daughter's accomplishments without question or restraint. Farrar did not, of course, sing the title role of *Elektra*.

a full-length mirror, surrounded by newspaper clippings relating to his career. When asked to comment on her former husband's death, Farrar replied "Why should that interest me?"[236]

The growing concurrence of the lurid world portrayed by verismo and the increasingly public lives of the sopranos appearing in theatres and on film was actualised by the death of Puccini on 29 November, 1924, and the first performance two years later of his final, unfinished opera, *Turandot*.[237] This was the last premiere of an Italian opera to be considered newsworthy globally; *Turandot* was also the last opera to be written that "everyone" might be said to know, even if that means nothing more than the Act II tenor aria, "*Nessun dorma*."[238] Opera's decline as a popular and living artform was recognised at the time by many of its most famous performers. Amelita Galli-Curci,[239] for example, was a popular recording artist, but despite being friends with Mascagni and Giordano, her status as a coloratura specialist isolated her from the prevailing appetite for large, dramatic voices.

Galli-Curci was an autodidact who forged her technique by listening to other singers, in theatres and on record, and by reading method books. She made her debut in 1906 as Gilda, and it was as a Verdi and Donizetti coloratura that she became famous throughout Italy – a sweet-voiced rejoinder to the stentorian, blood-and-guts hysterics of the veristi. A few weeks before her American debut on 18 November, 1916, the soprano signed with Victor, with whom she remained until 1930. In 1921, while still under contract with the Chicago Opera, Galli-Curci appeared at the Metropolitan Opera as Violetta, opposite Beniamino Gigli. Nine years later, she retired from staged opera, convinced that the art form was in decline. Her career was emblematic of the growing divergence between singers and composers. Despite becoming one of the first sopranos to be revered internationally through recordings, Galli-Curci created no new repertoire, and she entertained not a single role-directed collaboration. Her only contemporary role of note was Sophie in Strauss' *Der Rosenkavalier*, the South American premiere of which she gave in May, 1915, with the Polish soprano, Rosa Raisa,[240] as the Marschallin and Gilda dalla Rizza as Octavian.

The first staging of *Turandot*, at La Scala, on 25 April, 1926, could not have made use of Galli-Curci in the title role – she would have been inaudible; she might have played the role of Liù, of course. When Gatti-Casazza and the conductor Tulio Serafin were casting the opera in advance of its premiere at the Met,[241] Maria Jeritza was chosen for the title role, while a little-known verismo soprano, Martha Attwood,[242] was invited to make her House debut as Liù – a decision regretted by everyone except Attwood. For all her fame and talent, Galli-Curci played no part in the premieres in Rome (29 April), Buenos Aires (23 June),[243] Dresden (4 July), Venice (9 September),

---

236   His suicide was reminiscent of the death of Richard Gerstl, who killed himself in a similarly dramatic manner in 1908, after the failure of his affair with Schoenberg's wife, Mathilde.

237   First performed on 25 April, 1926.

238   See Boyden, Matthew (2021). *The Tenor: A Cultural History*. Ragueneau Press.

239   18 November, 1882 – 26 November, 1963.

240   30 May, 1893 – 28 September, 1963.

241   On 16 November, 1926.

242   *née* Amelita Galli, October 1886 – 7 April, 1950.

243   With Claudia Muzio as Turandot.

Vienna (14 October), Berlin (8 November), Brussels (17 December), Naples (17 January, 1927), Parma (12 February), Turin (17 March), London (7 June), San Francisco (19 September), Bologna (October 1927), and Paris (29 March 1928). Anyone thinking her voice too light for Liù should reflect that Galli-Curci also sang the music of Leonora (*Il trovatore*), Mimi and Butterfly; it's true her voice was lighter than was then fashionable, but the same was true of later celebrated Liùs, including Mafalda Favero,[244] Helena Arizmendi,[245] Rosanna Carteri,[246] and Anna Moffo.[247] The anomaly of Galli-Curci's isolation as one of the Met's biggest stars was compounded by her fees. For the Met premiere of *Turandot*, Jeritza was paid $2,400 for each performance – making her the highest earner at the Met *but for* Galli-Curci. The tenor, Giacomo Lauri-Volpi, was paid "only" $12,000 a month, while Serafin received $21,000 for a season of eighty-six performances (equating to $244 a night). Martha Attwood's weekly salary was $60 – less than was paid to a member of the orchestra.[248]

Four years before her retirement, Galli-Curci embodied a new era for the soprano, one unconnected with new music. The first Turandot, Rosa Raisa, represented the end of history, at least for Italian opera. She made her North American debut on 14 November, 1913, with Campanini's Chicago-Philadelphia Company as Mimi in *La bohème* – with Giovanni Martinelli as Rodolfo.[249] Her first role in Philadelphia was Isabella of Aragon in the US premiere of Alberto Franchetti's *Cristoforo Colombo*, by which time her voice was thought to be one of the most powerful on the American stage. This equipped her to excel as Santuzza, Klytemnestra in Vittorio Gnecchi's *Cassandra* and as Wagner's Elsa. In November, 1914, Puccini's publisher, Tito Ricordi, helped ensure Raisa's casting in the title role of Riccardo Zandonai's latest opera, *Francesca da Rimini*, which led to engagements in Rome in Romano Romani's *Fedra* and Alberto Nepomuceno's *Abdul*. She made her La Scala debut as Zandonai's Francesca, during which run she was heard for the first time by Puccini who, when asked by Raisa which of his operas he thought best suited to her voice, is said to have replied "there is no opera I have written to which your voice is not suited; they are all the same for you." Toscanini described her as a "female Tamagno," which may or may not have been a compliment. Raisa joined the Chicago Opera in 1916–17, where she shared the green room with Muzio, Galli-Curci and the French soprano, Mary Garden; in addition to standard dramatic fare, like *Aida*, she performed a host of new roles, including Maliella in Wolf-Ferrari's *I gioielli della Madonna*,[250] Maddalena in *Andrea Chénier*, Zina in de Gounzberg's *Le Vieil Aigle*, Basiliola in Montemezzi's *La Nave*, Puccini's *Suor Angelica*, Minnie in *La fanciulla del West*, the title role of Zandonai's *Conchita*, and Toinette in Frank Harling's jazz opera *A Light From Saint Agnes*. Over 17 seasons, she gave almost 500 performances for the Chicago company alone.

---

244 6 January, 1903 – 3 September, 1981.
245 1927 – 2015.
246 14 December, 1930 – 25 October, 2020.
247 27 June, 1932 – 9 March, 2006.
248 Orchestral players was paid $100 for a week of eight performances.
249 Martinelli was again her partner for her final stage appearance, as Rachel in Halévy's *La Juive*, in 1937.
250 'Jewels of the Madonna.'

On 1 May, 1924, Toscanini invited Raisa to Milan to sing the role of Asteria in the posthumous premiere of his completion of Boito's *Nerone*.[251] During rehearsals, Puccini sneaked past Toscanini's famously tight security and was thrilled by the scale of Raisa's voice.[252] After the rehearsal he revealed that he was working on the score of *Turandot*, which he considered suited ideally to her voice. The delighted Raisa claimed to have urged the composer "be sure to put in plenty of high Cs." *Turandot* is the summit of the Italian dramatic soprano repertoire; the opera has killed more voices than any other in the non-German canon, because of the purely musical demands of the role, which compel a soprano to wrestle with a huge orchestra, now armed with wide-bore brass, metal flutes, and instruments bearing metal strings, but also because *Turandot* encourages sopranos to push their voices beyond the natural limits of tone and placement. This has fostered an often ghastly screaming match, with tenors given to shouting their music as Calaf and most Turandots inclined to shout back. This is acute in Act II, long before the final duet (*"Principessa di morte,"*)[253] when Turandot sings *"In questa reggia,"*[254] to explain her reasons for creating the riddle ceremony. The sonic challenge presented by Puccini to anyone taking on the role is not merely contextual (insofar as the Princess has to be heard above a chorus as well as the orchestra), it is cumulative. The aria is long – at more than five minutes – and notable for three huge B4s, which are eclipsed by the interjection of Calaf, who sings (in unison with Turandot) *"Gli enigmi sono tre, la morte è una!"*[255] / *"Gli enigmi sono tre, una è la vita!"*[256] The C5 of *"so[no]"* is marked with a *fermata*, which has since created numerous opportunities for sopranos and tenors to outdo each other.[257]

When the curtain fell on *Turandot*'s French debut, on 29 March, 1928, the soprano landscape was changed irrevocably. So too was the world in which sopranos lived and worked. This was demonstrated most obviously by suffrage, with New Zealand becoming the world's first fully self-governing country in 1893 (a matter of weeks after the premiere of *Manon Lescaut*) and with Britain passing the Representation of the People (Equal Franchise) Act on 2 July, 1928,[258] 12 weeks after the first performance of *Turandot* in France. Less well-publicised, but more revealing, was the

---

251 'Nero.'

252 Raisa's recorded legacy is alarmingly inconsistent. Engineering technology is commonly to blame, as is the size of her voice – which was difficult to capture in the studio. The best of what survives are thrilling performances of *"Suicidio!"* from *La Gioconda*, *"O patria mia"* from *Aida*, and *"L'altra notte,"* from *Mefistofele*.

253 'Princess of Death.' First completed by Franco Alfano (and many others since, including Luciano Berio), but not heard at the premiere. Toscanini stopped the performance at the point where Puccini left the score incomplete, and announced *"Qui finisce l'opera, perché a questo punto il maestro è morto."* ('Here the opera ends, because at this point the maestro died.').

254 'In this Palace.'

255 'The enigmas are three, but death is one!'

256 'The enigmas are three, and life is one!'

257 The most famous pairing since the first (namely, Raisa and Miguel Fleta) was Birgit Nilsson and Franco Corelli, each of whom was recognised to be the loudest and most thrilling singers to play their roles. During one performance, while touring the opera for the Met, Corelli was defeated by Nilsson, which caused the tenor to threaten to abandon the production. The Intendant, Rudolph Bing, advised Corelli to exact his revenge by biting Nilsson during their kiss at the end of Act III. The following morning Bing received a hand-written message from Nilsson: "Cannot continue tour. Have rabies."

258 The Act gave the vote to all women over the age of 21, regardless of property ownership.

opening in 1897 of Le Théâtre du Grand-Guignol,[259] in the Pigalle district of Paris. Founded by Oscar Méténier, and housed in a former church, the theatre traded almost exclusively in *naturaliste* / verismo dramas, featuring "slice-of-life" productions that told working-class and frequently criminal stories, all designed to be as violent and explicit as law and technology would allow. Émile Zola was acknowledged (and name-checked) routinely as the theatre's defining inspiration.[260]

A standard one-hour show typically featured two vicious, brutal tales of horror, involving bloody maiming and murder, and two farcical, sex-based comedies. This alternating pattern was referred to as a *"douche ecossaise."*[261] The theatre's aesthetics evolved to meet the taste for gory spectacle, with designers utilising ever greater amounts of animal blood and tissue.[262] The bizarre and macabre programmes drew audiences from around the world to delight in being spattered with whatever was "pulled" or "cut" from the howling victims. A typical example was Méténier's *Lui!,*[263] which told of a prostitute who slowly realises she has been locked into a room with a deranged killer. It ended badly for the prostitute. In 1898, Méténier sold his interest to Max Maurey, who drove the theatre's repertoire into outright horror; in 1914 – as war was breaking out – the management passed to Camille Choisy. Three years into his tenure, Choisy hired Paula Maxa, a young actress who had recently appeared in the filmed ten-part crime serial, *Les vampires,* directed by Louis Feuillade. Maxa was a sensation, renowned for her unchecked sexuality and her commitment to dying horribly, night after night for more than two decades. She was stabbed, shot, hanged, poisoned, raped, strangled, guillotined, eaten and, even, steamrolled – by men, women, animals, insects and monsters. For one play she was cut into 83 pieces; for another (which ran for 200 performances) she was seen to decompose. Maxa died so often at the Grand Guignol that she earned the title "the world's most murdered woman."[264] She became known also as "the Sarah Bernhardt of the *impasse Chaptal,*"[265] adored by celebrities and royalty, who attended wearing disguises, and by the underclass for whom she so willingly sacrificed herself. Her freedom to act as she did translated only belatedly to enfranchisement, which France failed to enact until 1944; even so, Maxa's defiance of the Napoleonic Code reflected many of the seismic social, economic and cultural changes to which Zola and his followers had so long aspired.

If the dismemberment of women was more palatable than their emancipation, then the Grand Guignol resonated for French society as surely as had verismo for women when earning, owning and exploiting an independence formed by attrition

259   See, generally, Gordon, Mel (2016). *Theater of Fear and Horror: The Grisly Spectacle of the Grand Guignol of Paris, 1897–1962.* Feral House.

260   Gerould, Daniel (1984). "Oscar Méténier and 'Comédie Rosse': From the Théâtre Libre to the Grand Guignol." *The Drama Review.* Vol. 28, No. 1, French Theatre, pp. 15–28.

261   The word means literally "Scottish," and is better understood to refer to a type of dance. As slang, it came to mean "hot and cold shower," which was more probably generous to the Scottish climate than experience warrants.

262   According to her memoirs – some of which might be true – the stage blood was occasionally made from gooseberry jelly, which she would smuggle from the theatre to make tartines.

263   'Him!'

264   It has been estimated that she suffered as many as 10,000 deaths during her time at the theatre.

265   The theatre was (and remains) in a cul-de-sac.

from the appetites of men. The scandal caused in 1922 by Victor Margueritte's novel *La garçonne*, was transcendent because its heroine responded to her fiancé's infidelity by doing whatever she wanted – wearing men's clothes, partying in jazz clubs, and sleeping with women. Maxa's freedom, and the freedom enjoyed by every soprano within the evolution of the *naturalisme* and verismo movements, was the freedom to die three nights a week for often huge amounts of cash. Just as Puccini's misogynistic appetites can be represented metaphorically as a tailor cutting his cloth for his client, so too was the staged-suffering of sopranos and actresses in theatres around the world a means to an end, with the ultimate emancipation of performers operating to liberate their voices as well as their gender to know something better than actual subjugation, cruelty and violence.

CHAPTER SIXTEEN

Dr. S and the Women

Towards the end of August, 1910, Sigmund Freud spent five hours in consultation with Gustav Mahler. It was the composer's fourth appointment, the previous three having been cancelled due to Mahler's illnesses, preparations for the premiere of the 8th Symphony, and the interventions of his wife, Alma. They met in Leiden, the Netherlands, shortly before Freud left for a protracted stay in Sicily. Mahler reached out to the psychoanalyst because he believed he might repair some of the problems affecting his relationship with Alma, whose adultery was near constant. Despite knowing little of psychoanalysis, Mahler was remembered by Freud for having understood its function and purpose more quickly than anyone before him. The details of what was said are not difficult to reconstruct, with Freud's preoccupation with maternal attachments cueing with Mahler's search for a mother figure – something on which Alma commented with questionable accuracy when asserting that her husband had been a forty-year-old virgin at the time of their first meeting.[1] She claimed her husband's alleged celibacy originated with his fear of Die Frau,[2] and his life as "a neurotic."[3] Of the meeting itself, she asserted that Gustav

> gave [Freud] an account of his strange states of mind and his anxieties, and Freud apparently calmed him down. He reproached him with vehemence after hearing his confession. "How dared a man in your state ask a young woman to be tied to him?" he asked. In conclusion, he said: "I know your wife. She loved her father and she can only choose and love a man of his sort. Your age, of which you are so much afraid, is precisely what attracts her. You need not be anxious. You loved your mother, and you look for her in every woman. She was careworn and ailing, and unconsciously you wish your wife to be the same. [...] Freud's diagnosis composed Mahler's mind, although he refused to acknowledge his fixation on his mother. He turned away from notions of that kind.[4]

Alma was silent as concerning Freud's separate, equally valid belief that she was searching perennially for paternal security,[5] a more believable diagnosis when noting

---

1   As Alma was well aware, Mahler had an affair with Anna von Mildenburg – whose son, Roland, he was rumoured to have fathered.
2   'The woman.'
3   Mahler, Alma (1968). *Gustav Mahler: Memories and Letters*. John Murray, p. 159.
4   *Ibid.*
5   Her "Alma Pater.'

the death of her father having died three weeks before her 12th birthday, of which Alma wrote: "I felt I had lost my mentor, the star that guided me, and no-one but him would have understood that. I was used to doing most things for him." Alma's gender presumed her coincident subjugation; she was beautiful and talented, however – advantages that enabled her to resist the *status quo*, using her sexuality and intelligence as irresistible leverage. Her first great love affairs, Gustav Klimt and Alexander von Zemlinsky, were among the most powerful men of their day; both were rendered incapable by Alma. Mahler was literally old enough to be her father;[6] he was alone in being able to demand that she sacrifice her needs to his own. In a now-infamous letter, she yielded: "I am all yours. Apart from your needs and wishes, nothing interests me. My dearest wish is to totally surrender myself to you and to your music."[7] She did not act on this promise; indeed, their relationship was defined by a psychologically-degenerative process of power-dynamics, with each controlling the other through what they were able to give, and what they needed to withhold – a twisted re-fashioning of love as a transactional mechanism that brought a talented woman into a pathologic relationship with a supernaturally gifted man. Neither was able to survive their resulting orbits without fearing the attenuation of a self that mattered more than the other. If love can be defined (at its loosest) as the sacrifice of its source to the needs of its object then Gustav and Alma were separated throughout their marriage by resentments that originated with social, cultural and political causes long before they warranted analysis as psychological effects.

Mahler's earliest female relationships were with his mother, Marie, and his sister, Leopoldine. In 1881, during his 21st year, he was engaged for six months at the Landestheater in Laibach, where, for the first time, he collaborated with professional female musicians when preparing for his debut, conducting *Il trovatore*. After moving briefly to Vienna, and a period as a chorus-master at the Carltheater, Mahler accepted a position in January, 1883, as conductor of the Royal Municipal Theatre in Olmütz. Six months later, he was appointed music director in Kassel, equidistant between Düsseldorf and Leipzig. He arrived with two sopranos, Virginia Naumann-Gungl[8] and Johanna Richter.[9] The former was 12 years older than Mahler, and interesting to the conductor for having studied with Hans von Bülow in Munich;[10] Richter was two years Mahler's senior, and attractive for more traditional reasons. Mahler conducted 26 operas during his tenure at Kassel, many of them with Richter, with whom he fell in love. He wrote a series of poems for the famously beautiful singer, which he later composed as *Lieder eines fahrenden Gesellen*.[11] Mahler's love for Richter is evidenced by his correspondence; the lack of reciprocity is obvious from her only surviving letter, in which she addresses him as "dear good friend," using the formal pronoun, "*Sie*." She manipulated the naïve conductor with skill, as he lamented to his friend, Friedrich Löhr. On 1 January, 1885, Mahler described how he had

---

6   Alma was 19 years younger than her husband.
7   *Gustav Mahler: Letters to His Wife* (2004). Trans. Henry-Louis de la Grange and Günther Weiss. Cornell University Press, p. 84
8   31 December, 1848 – 28 August, 1915.
9   18 August, 1858 – 1943.
10   She gave her last performance, as Isolde, at the Deutsches Nationaltheater in Weimar in 1892.
11   'Songs of a Wayfarer.'

spent yesterday evening alone with her, both of us silently awaiting the arrival of the new year. Her thoughts did not linger over the present, and when the clock struck midnight and tears gushed from her eyes, I felt terrible that I, I was not allowed to dry them. She went into the adjacent room and stood for a moment in silence at the window, and when she returned, silently weeping, a sense of inexpressible anguish had arisen between us like an everlasting partition wall, and there was nothing I could do but press her hand and leave. As I came outside, the bells were ringing and the solemn chorale could be heard from the tower.

Mahler's obvious allusion to *Tannhäuser's* "Rome Narration" speaks to his youth, as does his effusive despair when telling Löhr "I am torn apart, my heart is bleeding, all is lost." Mahler was able to escape his suffering, and Richter's company, after securing a standby contract at the Royal Neues Deutsches Theater in Prague in 1885.[12] 12 months later he began a six-year contract with the Leipzig Opera, from which Mahler resigned in 1888. He headed to Budapest, and critical and popular acclaim conducting Wagner and other now-standard German repertoire. In 1889, both of Mahler's parents, and his sister, Leopoldine, died – compelling him to become a father to his four younger siblings, Alois, Otto, Justine, and Emma. He sent them to live in Vienna. During the spring of 1890, Mahler headed to Italy, in search of new operas. He returned with a copy of *Cavalleria rusticana*, of which he conducted the Budapest premiere on 26 December. The following year, Mahler headed to Hamburg as music director at the Opera. In October, 1897, he was appointed director of the Vienna Hofoper, where he was lionised by audiences and performers alike for his innovation. On 1 November, 1901, Alma was invited to a party, ostensibly to meet the conductor. She declined:

I did not want to meet Mahler. In fact I had purposely and with considerable difficulty avoided meeting him that summer, because of all the stories people told about him. I knew him well by sight; he was a small, fidgety man with a fine head. I was acquainted also with the scandals about him and every young woman who aspired to sing in opera. I had been to the concert that autumn at which he conducted his First Symphony, a work I had thoroughly disliked and even angrily rejected. At the same time, he was of importance to me as a conductor and I was conscious of his mysterious and powerful fascination. But this I now belied.[13]

---

12   He conducted 68 performances of 14 operas over a period of 12 months.
13   Mahler, Alma (1968). *Gustav Mahler: Memories and Letters*. John Murray, pp. 3–5.

Alma and Gustav bonded when debating the merits of Zemlinsky's latest work ("his Hofmannsthal Ballet, *Das Goldene Herz*"),[14] but she was sensible to the power of adolescence and sensuality:[15]

> From the very first moment Mahler observed me closely, not simply because of my face, which might have been called beautiful in those days, but also because of my piquant air.

From the start, Gustav and Alma were a psychoanalytic conference in the making. Neither of them was capable of submitting to the other without recoiling from their vulnerabilities; their sub-conscious, sadomasochistic interactions navigated mutuality only when they served their selfish needs. Alma asserted in her memoir that she "could never have imagined life without [Mahler], even though the feeling that my life was running to waste had often filled me with despair."[16] She opted not to admit to her coincident adultery, while stooping to the worst kind of special pleading, reduced by sophistry to the disingenuous claim that she had "often thought of going away somewhere alone to start life afresh, but never with any thought of another person [because] Mahler was the hub of my existence and so he continued to be."[17] Alma no more understood Freud than she did Mahler; and yet the practical application of psychoanalytic techniques therapeutically was pre-empted by the popularity of the sub-conscious among German-speaking writers, artists and composers – particularly in Vienna. The effect of Freud's dissections crystallised in *The Interpretation of Dreams*, published in 1899, in which he argued that the truth of a suppressed desire and identity could be discovered only through an analysis of the unconscious – a process useful to anyone seeking better to understand the place and function of erotic thoughts and feelings. This repositioning of sex as a mechanism for self-discovery as well as pleasure and procreation was more radical for its effect on women than men, since gender continued throughout the first two decades of the 20th century to determine status as well as capacity. That bias was manifested in the male-dominated conservatoires, galleries, publishing companies, concert halls and opera houses as well as the home. Freud was no feminist;[18] his work nonetheless operated as a construct for feminist theory because the brains of men and women were plainly not so different as to admit as plausible a hierarchy of capabilities. Scientific research necessitated samples – as case studies – but the virtue of any abstract was located in its application to the species as a whole. Freud at no time subscribed to Viola's assertion in *Twelfth Night* that "We men may say more, swear more, but indeed Our shows are more than will; for still we prove Much in our vows, but little in our love."

---

14   Alma and her editor had this wrong. The title of Zemlinsky's ballet was *Der Triumph der Zeit* ('The Triumph of time,'), which was formed of *Das gläserne Herz* ('The Glass Heart,'), *Drei Ballettstücke* ('Three Ballet Pieces,'), and *Ein Tanzpoem* ('A Dance Poem.').

15   For some reason, it has become a cliché that Alma was tall – and significantly taller than Mahler. In fact, she was 5 foot 3 inches (1.52m) – one inch shorter than her husband.

16   *Ibid*, p. 159.

17   *Ibid*.

18   See, for example, Freud's 1933 lecture on "Femininity," in which he addressed the "riddle of femininity" and sexual differentiation; his rhetoric impeached women as "the problem."

His binding of sexuality and subjectivity isolated parity in the binding of ordered symbolic structures to unconscious drivers, all of which exceeded the purview of individual agency. Notwithstanding the dilemmas facing anyone seeking to apply, far less define, psychoanalytic feminism, it is inarguable that Freud's impact on the consideration of difference as a quality contributed substantially to the resolution of tensions between the genders by enabling the unconscious mind to pre-empt and legitimise the place and value of women when audible.

For Austro-German culture approaching the end of the century, the soprano voice reached further than mere entertainment. Isolde, Sieglinde, Brünnhilde, Eva and Kundry coalesced as high-priestesses for a nation state that formalised only in 1871; it was for political as well as cultural reasons that Wagner's procrustean influence proved suffocating, with opera in Germany stagnating creatively during the years immediately following his death in 1883.[19] What emerged looked backwards to folk-song and fairy-tales or, worse still for German nationalists, to the foreign. Heinrich Hofmann, Peter Cornelius, Hermann Goetz, Viktor Nessler, Karl Goldmark and Wilhelm Kienzl all traded in sentimental, imitative vernaculars, while light opera remained popular thanks to the crowd-pleasing *schlagobers* of Johann Strauss II, Carl Millöcker and Carl Zeller. Vienna's biggest staged hit during the early 1890s was by a French composer, Jules Massenet; the premiere of *Werther* was given (in German) at the Hofoper on 16 February, 1892, with the role of Charlotte being created by Marie Renard[20] – the city's most famous Carmen. Renard was admired by Mahler, who retained her to sing in the Vienna premiere of his completion of Weber's *Die drei Pintos*[21] in 1889. In 1890 she played the title role in the Viennese premiere of Massenet's *Manon*, and on 1 January, 1892, she sang Eva in the world premiere of *Ritter Pázmán*, by Johann Strauss II. On 23 December, 1893, Engelbert Humperdinck's *Hänsel und Gretel* was first performed in Weimar.[22] The singers retained by the three female leads were all Bayreuth *alumni* (Luise Tibelti, Ida Schubert and Marie Kayser), and typical of the German soprano insofar as their voices were "suitable" for Mozart, light opera and *Der Ring des Nibelungen*. The emergent school of late romanticism was typified by Hans Pfitzner's *Der arme Heinrich*,[23] and Siegfried Wagner's *Der Bärenhäuter*[24] – both of which called for sopranos raised primarily by the scions of Salzburg and Bayreuth. This movement was especially popular in Weimar, where the second Kapellmeister, from 1889 until 1894, was Richard Strauss – whose solitary contribution to the growing coagulum of Wagneriana was *Guntram*,[25] a knightly-tale with an emotionally and psychologically uninteresting female role, Freihild, created at the premiere by Pauline Maria de Ahna. Strauss first met the soprano in 1887, while she was studying at the School of Music in Munich.

---

19   This does not mean there were not many operas composed and performed. It means only that most of them failed. Gilliam, Bryan (1991). *Richard Strauss' Elektra*. Oxford University Press, p. 3.
20   8 January, 1864 – 19 October, 1939.
21   'The Three Pintos.'
22   The Hamburg premiere, the following year, was conducted by Mahler.
23   'Poor Henry,' first performed on 2 April, 1895.
24   'The Bearskin,' first performed on 22 January 1899.
25   First performed on 10 May, 1894.

Freihild was performed at the premiere by Pauline Maria de Ahna,[26] whom Strauss first met in 1887, as a student at the School of Music in Munich. The budding composer soon became de Ahna's private teacher; when he relocated to Weimar, she travelled with him as his prima donna of choice. During the summer of 1889, Strauss and Pauline were both engaged by the Bayreuth Festival (becoming close friends with Wagner's widow, Cosima) and on 10 September, 1894, they were married. Pauline's instincts were conservative, and she focused on popular German repertoire, spanning Mozart, Beethoven, Weber, Wagner, Humperdinck – and Strauss, who composed his finest early songs for her, including his wedding gift, the four songs, Op. 27:[27] "*Ruhe, meine Seele!,*"[28] "*Cäcilie,*" "*Heimliche Aufforderung,*"[29] and "*Morgen!*"[30] Pauline retired from the stage after the birth of her only child, Franz, on 12 April, 1897. Despite her husband's routine access to the technology as a conductor, Pauline made no recordings; it is fortunate, therefore, that records were made by one of Pauline's colleagues in Weimar, Marie Gutheil-Schoder.[31]

Born in Weimar, Gutheil-Schoder made her debut as the First Lady in *Zauberflöte*, conducted by Strauss, in 1891. Eleven years later, she was recorded by the Gramophone & Typewriter Company, in Vienna, performing a number of excerpts that included a "*Seguidilla,*" in German, from *Carmen*, Frau Fluth's "*Nun eilt herbei,*"[32] from *Die lustige Weiber von Windsor,*[33] and a duet from Boieldieu's *La dame blanche* ("*Ce domaine,*" sung in German as "*Die weisse Dame,*")[34] with the lyric tenor, Franz Naval. The last of these is exquisite, and authentically French in style, colouring and phrasing; Gutheil-Schoder's technique is flawless, and she sings the music with perfect intonation and expression. Excepting a final flubbed high C, the scene from Nicolai's opera is delivered with wonderful clarity, while speaking to considerable reserves of power; the *Seguidilla* supports her contemporary status as a powerful mezzo-soprano. The defining quality throughout is ease; there is not a hint of effort, and her phrasing, while Viennese, is neither as indulgent as it would become for her successors[35] nor as ruthless as it was at the time.[36] Gutheil-Schoder's 1902 recording of the scene from *La dame blanche*[37] is noteworthy because she first performed the role of Anna on the stage of the Vienna Hofoper for Mahler in 1900, shortly after she joined the company – three years into Mahler's appointment as music director.[38] It's possible, therefore, to hear a recording of the voice of a leading soprano, as it

---

26 4 February, 1863 – 13 May, 1950.
27 'Peace, my soul!' 'Cäcilie,' 'Secret Request,' and 'Morning!'
28 'Rest, My Soul.'
29 'The Secret Call.'
30 'Tomorrow.'
31 16 February, 1874 – 4 October, 1935.
32 'Now hurry here.'
33 'The Merry Wives of Windsor,' by Otto Nicolai.
34 'The White Lady.' In the original, the duet performed is the second half of Act II's "*Ce domaine est celui comtes d'Avenel.*"
35 See Elizabeth Rethberg and Maria Reining below.
36 See Chapter 14 above.
37 'The White Lady.'
38 Gutheil-Schoder remained at the Hofoper / Staatsoper for more than a quarter of the century, until 1926.

was known to Mahler. Coincidentally, it is possible to read something of how the changing status of women in Vienna was inspiring to (and being inspired by) writers, poets and researchers.

In 1895, Freud published *Studien über Hysterie*,[39] with Josef Breuer, in which the authors deconstructed five individual studies of women, most famously Bertha Pappenheim – now better known as "Anna O." The essence of Freud's reasoning was to conceive of the mind as stratified, with the innermost and least accessible parts of a personality being rooted in a subliminal mantle that seeped outwards through every other. The work was widely publicised; it divided those for whom it was a masterpiece of original thinking from those who characterized it as "the kind of psychology used by poets."[40] One such poet was Richard Dehmel, whose collection, *Weib und Welt*,[41] was published in 1896, eight months after 'Studies in Hysteria.' The poems were controversial, sufficiently so to warrant the writer's prosecution for obscenity and blasphemy. In a chilling portent for German policy three decades later, the court ordered that any unsold copies of the book be burned. One of the first to read Dehmel's collection was Mahler, whose appointment at the Vienna Hofoper began in October, 1897. 18 months later, on 9 April, 1899, he conducted the first complete performance of his own Second Symphony, at the Musikverein, with Lotte von Barensfeld and Marcella Pregi[42] singing the solo parts for soprano and mezzo-soprano. In the audience was a 25-year-old composer, Arnold, who found much to dislike in the new work;[43] three weeks later, Schoenberg composed a song for soprano voice, "*Erwartung*,"[44] to verses from Dehmel's *Weib und Welt*.[45] The poem describes the anticipation of an encounter between two lovers from the perspective of an observer. It is extraordinarily beautiful, coloured heavily by oil-thick symbolism, mysticism and an early take on psycho analysis, lit as it is by "*der Mond*,"[46] and set "*unter der toten Eiche*."[47] The imagery is formed of juxtaposition – light and dark, day and night, reality and the unconscious; the poem's "painterly aspects"[48] were embraced by Schoenberg, who underscored Dehmel's words with "colour chords," created to blend with "*meergrün*"[49] and "*roten*"[50] to produce a harmonic configuration that resonates as ambiguity. These symbolic triggers were common to *Tristan und Isolde*, an opera admired by Freud; the attachment of the female to antiphonal constructs of the known and the unknown resonated throughout *Weib und Welt* as well as *Studien über Hysterie*.

---

39   'Studies on Hysteria.'
40   Jones, Ernest (1964). *The life and Work of Sigmund Freud*. Basic Books, p. 224
41   'Woman and World.'
42   12 January, 1866 – 28 October, 1958.
43   So much so that Schoenberg refused to attend the Viennese premiere of Mahler's First Symphony in November the following year.
44   'Expectation.' Published as Op. 2, no.1.
45   'Woman and World.'
46   'The Moon.'
47   'Under the dead oak.'
48   Frisch, Walter (1993). *The Early Works of Arnold Schoenberg*. University of California Press, p. 93.
49   'Sea green.'
50   'Red.'

The feminine and the female voice meant something more than gender to German-speaking artists and audiences as something more than gender; Schoenberg's "*Erwartung*" anticipates the neurasthenic sensibilities of *Verklärte Nacht* (another poem from *Weib und Welt*); it was in no way prognostic of his operatic monodrama of the same name, completed a decade later, to a libretto he commissioned from Marie Pappenheim, a relative of the Pappenheim to whom Freud devoted a chapter of *Studien über Hysterie* in 1895. Even so, the final stanza of the song is prescient, with Die Frau stumbling alone through the woods in search of a lover whom she discovers as a corpse. Schoenberg's stated ambition was to present everything that happens psychologically, in a single second of ultimate spiritual animation, stretched to half an hour – a micro-*Ulysses* formed of unprecedented, musically-athematic concentration. The "*Erwartung*" of May, 1899, foreshadows Die Frau's hysteria in 1909, contained by Dehmel as:

> *Aus der roten Villa*
> *Neben der toten Eiche*
> *winkt ihm eine bleiche*
> *Frauenhand.*[51]

The poet's symbolism and the composer's Freudian immersion reached further than opal rings and red mansions. The immediacy of Schoenberg's allusions to sexual consummation and the agony of unconscious hindsight can be attached to the first thrusts of his relationship with the daughter of Alexander von Zemlinsky. Mathilde was the object of his grandest passion, as she would become the source of his greatest pain when she left him during the summer of 1908 for the painter Richard Gerstl – an event that preceded his second *Erwartung*, and Schoenberg's absolute break with tonality. At the beginning of 1909, the composer wrote to Arnold Rosé, leader of the Vienna Philharmonic, and his own legendary string quartet, to ask that he give the premiere of his Second Quartet, Op. 10:

> The third and fourth [movements] are scenes following poems by Stefan George for a high mezzo soprano such as Gutheil (Marie Gutheil Schoder). Both these movements are enormously difficult...

Rosé agreed by return to perform the new work, while noting "Many difficulties, not the least of which will be the honorarium for the singer. Mrs Gutheil will be very happy to take over the singing part..." Schoenberg recalled how

> These songs showed a style quite different from everything I had written before [...] New sounds were produced, a new kind of melody appeared, a new approach to expression of moods and characters was discovered."[52]

---

51 'Out of the red villa, near the dead oak, the pale hand of a woman beckons him.'
52 Simms, Bryan R. (2000). *The Atonal Music of Arnold Schoenberg, 1908–1923*. Oxford University Press, p. 29.

The Second Quartet qualifies as "Freudian," insofar as the music breaks with the linear nature of sung-melody as it had been taught and employed for centuries. The writing for soprano in the second two movements ("*Litanei*"[53] and "*Entrückung*"[54]) is otherworldly and destabilising because it operates outside the conservatoire-principles according to which Schoenberg's contemporaries understood the normative. Strauss and Schoenberg formed their voices as composers of music for women to sing. Many of Strauss' songs were available for men to sing also, but he wrote them either for a specific woman (*i.e.*, Pauline), or as vehicles more generally for women. Conversely, Schoenberg's defining works for soprano are *about* his wife, or they are a product of his marriage – consciously and unconsciously. In navigating his disillusions – as a Jew born into a virulently anti-Semitic culture, as a husband married to an adulterous wife, and as an artist subsumed to Stefan George's credo, "*Ich fühle luft von anderem planeten*,"[55] – Schoenberg settled on what amounted to a teleological detachment from expression as it was known to Mahler and Vienna's cosmopolitana. Even the dedication of the Second Quartet "to my wife" was dislocating considering his living with another man at the time of its writing; moreover, the tone and character of the Quartet were anathematic and obverse to any conventional intonation of love as it had been articulated by George, especially the last movement:

> *In einem meer kristallnen glanzes schwimme*
> *Ich bin ein funke nur vom heiligen feuer*
> *Ich bin ein dröhnen nur der heiligen stimme.*[56]

At the first performance on 21 December, 1908, members of the audience took to hissing when Gutheil-Schoder began to sing; some shouted "stop" and "enough;" others stood up and left the hall. Vienna's newspapers debated what became known as the "Schoenberg affair," without realising the extent to which the music had been cultivated by adultery. The second two movements express its author's private anguish, substantiating atonality as a mechanism for the exploration of psychological states operating below the surface of narrative, feeling and emotion. Schoenberg's disturbed state of mind resonated throughout his settings of George's verses; it was tagged expressly in his contemporaneous "*Testamentsentwurf*,"[57] in which he tore into his wife's deceit using language that bound him to the paradigm shift from conscious cognition to unconscious emotion as it had been described by Freud:

> I am only despairing because I don't believe the facts. I cannot believe. I
> don't regard it as possible that I can have a wife who deceives me. Then
> I never really had one, then she was never really even my wife, and I was
> perhaps never married. The whole thing was only a dream, and only the

---

53 'Litany.'
54 'Rapture.'
55 'I feel the air of other planets,' the first line of "*Entrückung*."
56 *Ibid.* 'In a sea of crystal radiance, I am only a spark of the holy fire; I am only a whisper of the holy voice.'
57 ':draft will [a testament].' 12 pages; unfinished. Written in Gmunden around 26/27 August, 1908. Arnold Schönberg Center; Ref: T06_08.

logical succession of events speaks against this assumption. Because a dream, thank God, is not logical, and that's why disciples and the talented don't dream. Or if they do, then they at least attempt to interpret the dream, to make it more logical in order to bring it at once nearer to their little brains. So if it is no dream, then it is just a fact. And I cannot believe in facts; they do not exist for me.[58]

Schoenberg understood how Freud's characterisation of human psychology had effected a revolution greater, even, than his own as a composer. The voices of women, in particular, were now currency to be explored as more than mere sound – as more, even, than instruments. This radical transcendence of relatable traits compelled sopranos to articulate the unknown and the hidden when performing music that defied normative expressions of feeling. The subversive admission of the right and entitlement of women to think and feel without speaking or being heard qualified as the emancipation of thought and sentiment, framed as it was between Schoenberg's two *Erwartungs*.[59] His Second Quartet is still thematic, with considerable repetition, redolent tonalities and a traditional palette of dramatic expression for the soloist, but these features of the western diatonic canon were absent from his monodrama, completed a few months later.

Gutheil-Schoder's commitment to music that passed over the head of her patriarch, Mahler, was fantastic, even noting her generosity to young composers more generally.[60] She had been privileged to develop her art at the Hofoper, where she was free to balance her intellectual curiosity with Vienna's infamously conservative instincts. Mahler's burden was greater still because he was responsible for navigating the Hofoper's competing interests and a public disdainful of the *avant-garde*. He focused inevitably on establishment works by Mozart, Donizetti, Beethoven, Verdi, Wagner *etc.* while staging and promoting contemporary operas by composers well-known in Vienna – including Kienzl's *Der Evangelimann*,[61] Goetz's *Der Widerspänstigen Zähmung*[62] and Nessler's *Der Rattenfänger von Hameln*.[63] These fell to the gravity of the box office. During a decade as music director, Mahler conducted only three world premieres: Goldmark's *Die Kriegsgefangene*,[64] Zemlinsky's *Es war einmal*,[65] and Josef Forster's *Der Dot Mon*.[66] None of them is a masterpiece. On the other hand, he programmed 300 performances of *Cavalleria rusticana* and *Pagliacci* (in addition

58   *Ibid.*
59   Gutheil-Schoder created *Erwartung* in 1924, in Prague – shortly after giving the premiere of Schoenberg's *Pierrot lunaire*.
60   Mahler had left the Hofoper in 1907, and headed to the United States a year later. He was not able to attend the premiere of the Second Quartet, but of the First he wrote "I have conducted the most difficult scores of Wagner; I have written complicated music myself in scores of up to thirty staves and more; yet here is a score of not more than four staves, and I am unable to read it." Schoenberg, Arnold (1984). *Style and Idea*. University of California Press, p. 42.
61   'The Evangelist.'
62   'The Taming of the Shrew.'
63   'The Pied Piper of Hamelin.'
64   'The Prisoners of War,' first performed on 17 January, 1899.
65   'Once upon a time,' first performed on 22 January, 1900.
66   First performed on 28 February, 1902.

to other works of verismo, by Giordano, Leoncavallo and Puccini). Elsewhere, he scheduled 20 performances of Siegfried Wagner's *Der Bärenhäuter*,[67] 12 of Strauss' second opera, *Feuersnot*,[68] 16 of Pfitzner's *Die Rose vom Liebesgarten*,[69] five of Josef Reiter's *Der Bundschuh*,[70] 24 of Charpentier's *Louise*,[71] seven of Hugo Wolf's *Der Corregidor*,[72] and six of *Lobetanz*,[73] by Strauss' friend, Ludwig Thuille. Each of these operas adhered to some form and formula for which there was ample precedent, and they were suited to the same *fach* as sang everything else. The German-language soprano in 1900 was essentially lyric, with the qualified exceptions being roles by a single composer – Richard Wagner. Although his music would become associated paradigmatically with volume, Wagner's instincts were at all times lyrical, even if his reconstruction of the orchestra compelled uncommon amplitude and projection. Sopranos "specialising" in Wagner at Bayreuth during the summer performed Mozart and Verdi during the autumn and winter. Everything changed with the first performance, in 1905, of *Salome*.

The origins of this world-changing opera date back to 15 November, 1902, when the composer attended the Kleines Theater in Berlin for a private performance of Max Reinhardt's 1901 production of Hedwig Lachmann's translation of Oscar Wilde's *Salomé*. The composer was impressed by the "exquisite" play, which he thought "cried out for music." In Wilde's hands, the biblical story of the girl who danced for Herod in return for the head of John the Baptist (Jochanaan) was transformed into a psychosexual drama in which violence was precipitated by lust – Herod's for Salome, and Salome's for Jochanaan. The opera was jarring for its music as well as its subject, which marked a diabolical transformation in the composer's sound, texture, harmony and invention. When compared to anything antecedent, there is literally no model for *Salome*; the fashionable orientalist atmosphere,[74] incantatory-repetition, savage emotional extremes, and nexus of symbolic discovery and revelation can prostrate audiences even in the 21st century. It is impossible to appreciate the opera's effect in 1905.

Strauss' prescription for the title role was "a 16-year-old princess with the voice of Isolde," a joke that carried within it a kernel of *echt*-Straussian sincerity. He had conducted *Tristan* on numerous occasions and understood how Isolde's relatively static stage persona cannot have prepared or equipped a Wilhelminian-Edwardian soprano

---

67   First staged at the Hofoper on 27 March, 1899.

68   'Fire emergency,' first staged at the Hofoper on 29 January, 1902, with a revised production beginning on 5 June, 1905.

69   'The Rose from the Garden of Love,' first staged at the Hofoper on 6 May, 1905.

70   First staged at the Hofoper on 13 November, 1900.

71   First staged at the Hofoper on 24 March, 1903.

72   First staged at the Hofoper on 18 February, 1904.

73   'Dance of Praise,' first staged at the Hofoper on 18 March, 1901, conducted by Franz Schalk.

74   Orientalism had been popular in visual art for decades (e.g., Ingres's *Odalisque(s)*, the harem paintings of Delacroix and Gustave Moreau's *Salomé dansant devant Hérode*). However, the turn of the century alignment between the feminine, sensuality, hysteria, and the orient was essential not only to Freud, but also the fantastically influential Klimt, whose *Judith and Salome* is far from unique in characterising the painter's misogynistic conception of women as free only when degenerate. See Néret, Gilles (1996). *Gustav Klimt, 1862–1918*. Barnes and Noble Books; also Said, Edward (1979). *Orientalism*. Vintage Books, p. 188.

to seduce, writhe and dance her way around a stage while wrestling with more than 100 instrumentalists, charged collectively with presenting the most complicated and loudest orchestral score ever written. Even before a note was played in rehearsal, it was necessary for the composer (and his conductor at the Semperoper, Dresden, Ernst von Schuch) to persuade his stage-crew, players and singers to accommodate a Christian-biblical theme that presented in Freudian-symbolic musical metaphors an erotic and murderous narrative that concluded with a teenager kissing the mouth of the decapitated head of a prophet. The challenge was made greater still by the consecration fewer than thirty-years earlier of the *Johanneskirche*, the city's first neo-Gothic building.[75] Strauss was careful to accommodate competing tastes and enthusiasms; references to Jesus Christ were scored in suitably reverential terms, while the writing for the "Five Jews"[76] was more anti-Semitic than anything created by Wagner in the *Ring* and *Der Meistersinger*.[77] A number of performers passed up the questionable honour of damnation by association, and when finally[78] Marie Wittich[79] agreed to create the title role she did so on condition that she would not have to perform the "Dance of the Seven Veils."[80]

Wittich made her debut in 1882 as Azucena in *Il trovatore*. She appeared in Basle, Düsseldorf, and Dresden, where she sang the title role in Gluck's *Iphigénie en Aulide* for the inauguration of the Mecklenburgisches Staatstheater in 1886. Three years later she moved to the Semperoper, and triumphant appearances as Leonore in *Fidelio* and Senta in *Der fliegende Holländer*. She was Ernst von Schuch's Brünnhilde of choice (in which role she was seen in 1905 by E. M. Forster, who wrote: "She towered. She soared. Force, weight, majesty! She seemed to make history"),[81] and he cast her for the premieres of *Odysseus' Heimkehr*[82] (the third part of August Bungert's wahn-struck homage to the *Ring* cycle, *Homerische Welt*)[83] and Ignacy Paderewski's *Manru*.[84] On 9 December, 1905, Wittich made history as the first Salome. She was incongruous by reason of her appearance (which was inconsistent with the libretto

---

75   The tall tower and spire of the Church were visible from the Semperoper, just over two miles distant.

76   It has been conjectured that *Salome's* portrayal of Jewish people was a deliberate caricaturing of the musical modernism associated with the music and the personality of Schoenberg. When *Salome* was performed in Dresden the night before the German premiere of Schoenberg's First String Quartet (published as Op. 7) in 1907, the appearance and sounding of the Five Jews "triggered a [...] virulent antisemitism directed against Schoenberg, with allusion to the stereotype of the unassimilated Eastern Jew." Painter, K. (2001). "Contested counterpoint: 'Jewish' appropriation and polyphonic liberation," *Archi Für Musikwissenschaft*, 58(3), p. 202.

77   See Boyden, Matthew (2021). *The Tenor: a Cultural History*. Ragueneau Press; and Boyden, Matthew (1999). *Richard Strauss*. Weidenfeld & Nicolson.

78   Strauss had to tread carefully with Cosima Wagner, who had booked Wittich to sing Isolde at the Bayreuth Festival in 1906 – which meant having to rehearse in November, 1905. Cosima was persuaded.

79   27 May, 1868 – 4 August, 1931.

80   It was danced instead by Sidonie Korb.

81   Forster, E. M. (1963). "My first opera" in *Opera*, Vol. 14, p. 374.

82   'Odysseus' Return,' first performed on 12 December, 1896. The full cycle is Part I: *Kirke* ('Circe') (1898); Part II: *Nausicaa* (1901); Part III: *Odysseus' Heimkehr* (1896); Part IV: *Odysseus' Tod* ('The Death of Odysseus') (1903).

83   'Homeric World.'

84   First performed on 29 May, 1901.

and the narrative),[85] and because she was 21 years older than the character she was playing; Strauss referred to her as "Auntie Wittich." She refused to kiss Jochanaan's severed head, informing the composer: "I won't do it; I'm a decent woman."[86] It made no difference to the opera's success, which prompted 38 curtain calls on the first night, and 50 different productions globally within two years. The audience reaction in Dresden was less scandalised than it would be elsewhere. Anne Seshari has argued that "the Jewish princess Salome [...] transcended her Jewishness and was transfigured [...] some critics further interpreted her transfiguration as a conversion to Christianity."[87] This sense of ecstatic apotheosis was identified overtly by Heinrich Platzbecker in the *Neue Zeitschrift für Musik,* on 13 December, 1905:

> Frau Wittich was more Isolde than Salome, thus the title role achieved the poetic transfiguration that Wagner praises in music [...] When Salome sings at the end to the head of the decapitated one, like Isolde before the body of Tristan, [she sings] in such a manner that she is no longer Salome, she is saved.[88]

Gustav Mahler was unable to persuade the Vienna censor to consent to a production, so the Austrian premiere was given at the Graz Opera in 1906, with Strauss conducting, and Schoenberg, Puccini, Mahler and Alban Berg in attendance. Schoenberg dismissed *Salome* as the work of a *Marzipanmeister*.[89]

> Problems arise for him and are solved by him in the same way: he misunderstands them. But it cannot be disputed that he has dealt with them: he has hidden them under a coating of sugar icing [...] This is not the way of thinking of a man whom God has given a mission.[90]

Had he lived to see *Moses and Aaron*, Strauss would likely have reminded Schoenberg of his version of Liberace's familiar response to criticism: "I shall cry all the way to the bank."[91] The collision of Strauss' genius with unprecedented commercial success warranted jealousy; it did not excuse the sniping of antagonists struggling to pay their

---

85 A vocal coach at the Hofoper, Charles Webber, recalled "her looks of a Viking's daughter, her blond hair and her fine blue eyes." Calico, Joy H. (2012). "Staging Scandal with Salome and Elektra," in *The Arts of the Prima Donna in the Long Nineteenth Century*. Eds. Rachel Cowgill & Hilary Poriss. Oxford University Press, p. 64.

86 Malik, Shireen (2008). "Salome and Her Dance of the Seven Veils" in Jennifer Heath (Ed.), *The Veil: Women Writers on its History, Lore, and Politics*, University of California Press, p. 149.

87 Seshadri, Anne L. (2006). "The Taste of Love: Salome's Transfiguration." In *Women and Music: A Journal of Gender and Culture*. Vol. 10, p. 25.

88 Calico, Joy H. (2012). "Staging Scandal with Salome and Elektra," in *The Arts of the Prima Donna in the Long Nineteenth Century*. Eds. Rachel Cowgill & Hilary Poriss. Oxford University Press, p. 67.

89 'Master of marzipan.'

90 Christensen, Jean (1984). "The Spiritual and the Material in Schoenberg's Thinking." *Music & Letters* Vol. 65, No. 4, p. 339.

91 He is said to have remarked (more than once) that the royalties from *Salome* funded the building of his home in Garmisch-Partenkirchen, Bavaria – where he lived until his death in 1949, and which operates now as a private mausoleum for the now royalty-free family.

rent. *Salome* is an astonishing achievement that managed to reconcile the modernity of Freud's studies in subliminal erotic experience to the increasing freedoms being enjoyed by German-speaking women. It was appropriate that the characterisation of the psychoanalytic method as a "talking cure," by Berta Pappenheim,[92] should have translated so perfectly to singing through the conduit of Wilde's verse. Wilde knew nothing of Freud, and Freud's interest in Wilde reached no further than a solitary reference in his essay on "The Uncanny" to *The Canterville Ghost*. They "met" in Strauss' company because the composer was able to speak where Wilde could not to the extremes of desire at their most authentic. Salome does not touch herself; neither is she touched by anyone else – and yet her release, her psychological orgasm, occurs as she kisses the lips of a dead prophet. Her experience is, by definition, purely emotional. What Wilde was forced to disguise when seeking to write of love as he knew and experienced it, Strauss was able to heave into the mouth of a woman without boundaries, a character of pure feeling incapable of understanding (and uninterested in knowing) what had driven her to seduce her step-father to secure the execution of a man of God, only then to "make love" to his murdered corpse.

What might once have been dreamed in private was now presented in public, with Wilde's perfumed sensibilities subjected to a sound-scape that fused some of the most seductive music ever written for a soprano to an orchestral and ensemble score saturated with contrapuntal dissonance. Thanks primarily to Freud, the Id and the Ego of women were abstracted as "the irrational, the will-less, the uncontrollable, the convulsive, the erratic, the erotic, the ecstatic, the female, the criminal, and a host of collective 'Others.'"[93] The representation of feminine dementia, hysteria and excess in the musical guise of a high and necessarily pressured soprano voice was a perfect fit for a culture defined two years earlier, in June, 1903, by Otto Weininger's *Geschlecht und Charakter: Eine prinzipielle Untersuchung*,[94] a profoundly misogynistic and anti-Semitic monograph in which the author attempted "to place sex relations in a new and decisive light." The substance of the book can be guessed at from just three of its chapter-headings: "The Nature of Woman and her Relation to the Universe" (XII), "Judaism" (XIII), and "Women and Humanity" (XIV).

The juxtaposition of the rapturous and the repellent served additionally to confront the hypocrisies of contemporary society, with Jochanaan's asceticism treated as a metaphor for conservatoire-tradition and gendered decency. That such a bewilderingly inventive and erotic study in psycho-sexuality should have burst from a middle-aged *bourgeois gentilhomme* renowned for his disinterest in sex[95] merely added to the sense of Freudian release that colours Salome's final, monstrous ecstasy and the violence of her demise. Her closing monologue, lasting around 20 minutes, adheres to the

---

92   Breuer, J., & Freud, S. (1895). *Studien über Hysterie*. F. Deuticke, p. 23.

93   Micale, Mark S. (2004). "Discourses of Hysteria in Fin-de-Siècle France," in *The Mind of Modernism*. Stanford University Press, p. 84.

94   Weininger, Otto (2005). *Sex and Character: An Investigation of Fundamental Principles*. Ed. Daniel Steuer and Laura Marcus, trans. Ladislaus Löb. Indiana University Press; and Chandak Sengoopta (2000). *Otto Weininger: Sex, Science, and Self in Imperial Vienna*. University of Chicago Press.

95   He was not unexperienced prior to his marriage to Pauline – but there is no evidence of adultery after they began to court; as Pauline observed more than once, her husband had "managed" only a single child, their son, Paul.

basic structure of an analytic session; she freely associates with Jochanaan's severed head in a therapeutic dialogue that frees her to reveal (and revel in) the truth of her sexuality and her identity more generally. Speech is lost to nonlinguistic symbolism as she places her lips against Jochanaan's; the music reaches a dramatic climax that ends with a chord that has been labelled "the most sickening" in all opera. It captures "the quintessence of decadence: here is ecstasy falling in upon itself, crumbling into the abyss."[96] This polytonal "crunch" articulates Salome's mental collapse, leaving her to express her joy in a final phrase that can, if performed well, survive comparison with Isolde's *Liebestod*: "*Ich habe deinen Mund geküsst, Jochanaan. Ich habe ihn geküsst, deinen Mund.*"[97] Strauss' music affords Salome the satisfaction and release of a *petite mort*, superseded moments later by her actual death.

Marie Wittich delighted Strauss – as she did whenever she appeared in his later works, notably as Elektra, and the Marschallin in *Der Rosenkavalier*. The determinant for Strauss was that Wittich performed his music at all. The composer was infamously mercantile, a reputation to which he contributed more, even, than the jealousy and resentment of the less successful. For example, he dedicated *Salome* to Sir Edgar Speyer,[98] his German-Jewish, London-based banker and financial advisor – a gesture in poor taste when noting the opera's themes and its ill-disguised anti-Semitism. While in Paris the following year to conduct his *Sinfonia Domestica*, Strauss invited Debussy to meet him for lunch. They had not met previously, and neither Debussy nor their host, the publisher Jacques Durand, knew what to expect. In his memoirs, Durand recalled how Strauss spoke only of money and commercial concerns, of the society he had established in Germany to manage royalties and royalty payments. Debussy was embarrassed by the German's vulgarity and said almost nothing. Strauss was unaware that Debussy had spent most of his life in poverty; neither did he realise (or have any reason to know) that Debussy was drowning in debt at the time. Instead of appealing to the self-evident priority of Debussy's interests, Strauss steered the conversation away from art, his own or Debussy's or that of any of the musicians known to them mutually. They might have discussed the work of Mary Garden,[99] a Scottish-born soprano with whom Debussy collaborated four years earlier for the premiere of *Pelléas et Mélisande* at the Opéra-Comique on 30 April, 1902.[100] Garden's association with the role of *Mélisande* was lifelong, but her *succès d'estime* was as Salome – or, rather, Salomé.

The premiere of the French edition (prepared by Strauss's friend, Romain Rolland) was staged at the Théâtre du Châtelet in Paris, and first performed with the composer conducting on 8 May, 1907. Emmy Destinn sang the title role,[101] Natacha Trouhanova[102] danced her veils off, and the German-Jewish financier, Otto H. Kahn,

---

96   Ayrey, Craig. "Salome's final monologue," in Puffett, Derrick, Ed. (1989). *Richard Strauss: Salome.* Cambridge University Press, pp. 123–130.

97   'I kissed your mouth, Jochanaan. I kissed it, your mouth.'

98   It reads to "Meinem Freunde Sir Edgar Speyer."

99   20 February, 1874 – 3 January, 1967.

100   The production was conducted by André Messager, Garden's lover at the time.

101   She had previously sung the first performance in Berlin.

102   She was retained for two further operatic versions of the Salome narrative: Antoine Mariotte's 1910 *Salomé* (when she danced for Lucienne Bréval), and Florent Schmitt's 1912 *La tragédie de Salomé*. She premiered Paul Dukas' *La Péri* and Ravel's *Adelaide*.

paid the bills – having underwritten the staging with yet another massive cheque. The production was profitably controversial, thanks in part to Trouhanova's public confrontation with Strauss after he refused to allow the dancer to take a curtain call beside Destinn – on the basis that he considered "the art of dancing to be inferior" to singing. Trouhanova marched from the production and later described the composer's insult in letters to the press. In the same year, Destinn recorded two short excerpts from Salome's taunting of Jochanaan, beginning with the insult "*Dein Haar ist grässlich!*"[103] which leads into the first ecstatic reference to the prophet's mouth, "*Deinen Mund begehre ich, Jochanaan.*" The recording was conducted by Bruno Seidler-Winkler, a "studio" conductor who knew his place when working for Destinn. It follows that she must, at the very least, have agreed with the frenzied tempo adopted during the recording, snatching at the delirious B4 with which she declaims Jochanaan's name. Instead of slowing down at this point of release, as has every conductor since, Seidler-Winkler drives the music harder still, pushing the soprano in a manner of which Strauss was clearly approving.[104] It should be acknowledged that Destinn's singing is imperfect – marred by slapdash intonation, ill-disciplined word-use and some ashen, over-lit tone. Anyone singing like this in the 21st century would not be invited back. It's all terribly exciting, of course, as it needed to be; the fact remains, however, that Destinn – like many born and raised before the onset of recording – is possessed of a technique that cannot but amplify how great an actress she must have been.

It's not possible to compare Destinn's Salome with Mary Garden's two years later; from what was written of her New York Salomé, however, first heard on 28 January, 1909, it can be reasoned that she reconciled the purity and elegance that characterised what can be gleaned of her singing on record for Debussy and Charpentier (memorably a sublime rendition of Louise's "*Depuis la jour*,") to the intense physicality of Strauss's princess. Like so many others trained prior to the advent of recording, most of her '78s fail to support what was written of her work on stage. One contemporary noted how she

> hardly moved her hands and arms for long stretches of the Shen: her head was usually bowed in submission, but when it moved it had something to contribute to the composition. voice had the pallor of the tomb at times; it was difficult to understand how such misty rose-gray and blue-gray notes could spin from a human throat."[105]

Frances Alda commended Garden's economy of means:

> She was so still. Just that one little phrase, "*il fait froid ici*", as it came from her lips, and you shivered under the chill winds that blow between the worlds of the real and the unreal. Contrasted with it, [Lucrezia]

---

103   'Your hair is hideous!'
104   Strauss' piano roll "recording" of a "fragment" taken from the same section from 1906 is no less urgent.
105   *Ibid.*

Bori's rendering of the line sounded like a schoolgirl who steps out of bed without her slippers."[106]

As Salome, Garden danced in a body-stocking and made out with Jochanaan's severed head with a fervour that outraged the great and the good of Chicago; the new opera company's first-night ticket-holders had no idea what to expect, and the majority left in "silence and in shock." Newspaper editors fell over their Thesauruses when competing to communicate their disgust. *The Tribune* led the way in its characterisation of the departing audience as "oppressed and horrified." This was enough for Arthur Burrage Farwell, President of the Chicago Law and Order League, to demand that the Chief of Police, Roy T. Steward, attend the second performance. His critical assessment would have brought a smile to Strauss' lips:

> It was disgusting. Miss Garden wallowed around like a cat in a bed of catnip. If the same show was produced on Halsted Street, the people would call it cheap, but over at the Auditorium they say it's art.

Despite not attending the production, Farwell issued a statement denouncing Garden as "a great degenerator of public morals." After three sold-out performances, the Chicago Opera's board of directors threw in the towel and cancelled the production. Garden relished the scandal, and built a glittering career on provocation – much of it formed of her apparent disinterest in men, and sex. She is reported to have said that she "never really loved anybody. I had a fondness for men, yes, but very little passion, and no need."[107] Elsewhere, she espoused a radical feminist mantra, holding that

> It is fine that women do no longer love as they did. It will be even finer if they can win absolute freedom. Formerly we were under the man's heel. Now just his little toe is on us. Yet how conscious we are of that little toe.

Her support for contemporary composers was laudable, even if her judgments were eccentric. When performing the title role in *Monna Vanna* (an obscure opera by Henry Février and Maurice Maeterlinck, based on the poet's play of the same name),[108] she appeared on stage naked but for a fur coat. For D'Erlanger, she threw herself into the role of *Aphrodite*, a work featuring lesbianism, a multiracial orgy and the crucifixion of a slave. As Massenet's *Cléopâtre*, she had to visit an Egyptian brothel dressed as a boy making love to another boy of the same age and appearance. Massenet was horrified by Garden's decision (under-written by the impresario Oscar Hammerstein) to perform the title role (written for a tenor) of *Le Jongleur de Notre-Dame*, wearing a jerkin and tights.[109] Her leading role was Mary Garden, to which she committed with self-aggrandising megalomania:

---

106   Alda, Frances (1971). *Men, Women and Tenors*. AMS Press, p. 20.
107   Christiansen, Rupert (1985). *Prima Donna: A History*. Viking Press, p. 277.
108   First performed on 13 January, 1909.
109   She gave the US premiere on 27 November, 1908, at the Manhattan Opera House.

> I believed in myself [...] I have never been nervous in my life and I have no patience with people who are. I never permitted anything or anybody to destroy that belief [...] I wanted liberty and I went my own way.[110]

Her confidence was largely warranted, although it made her a target. During a charity concert at the Chicago Stock Exchange, a man approached her from behind and drew a pistol. A police officer managed to wrestle the would-be assassin to the ground before he could use it. When asked why he wanted to kill the soprano, Garden's antagonist replied, "She talks too much." Anyone keen to test this assessment might listen to any of the various recorded and broadcast interviews with the soprano that survive online.

The favourite of Strauss' early interpreters of Salome was Finnish. Aino Ackté[111] performed the title role at its local premieres in Leipzig, in 1907, and in London, in 1910 (conducted by Sir Thomas Beecham). His affection prompted him to declare Ackté his "one and only Salome" because she was the first to dance the "Seven Veils," and because she was able to persuade as a woman not yet 20. Wittich made no recordings; Ackté did – for Zonophone, the G&T Company, Fonotipa, Odéon and, between 1910 and 1913, Edison. The latter company produced 34 discs – only one of which was released; her scheduled recording of a scene from *Salome* was either lost or destroyed. Ackté's early, such as *"Einsam in Truben Tagen"* from *Lohengrin* ('Elsa's Dream'), are fascinating for the absence of vibrato and the limited use of portamento – which is applied only to descending shifts from above the stave. Her voice has resonance, but it is not especially large – as it didn't need to be considering the use by every orchestra at the time of gut strings, and the ubiquity of narrow-bore brass.[112]

Ackté's letters attest to her dissatisfaction with the recording process, even as late as 1913 – when she was booked to record an excerpt from *Salome*. This was delayed because the orchestral parts (necessary for a greatly reduced ensemble) had not been prepared in time. Across all of her recordings (many of which she introduces in brilliantine French), Ackté's singing is memorable for its stupendous diction and her liberties with tempo and pulse.[113] Less routine is her restrained use of portamento, the appearance of which occurs as she "hears" the orchestra with which she was used to performing. String players during the first decade of the 20th century made common

---

110   *Ibid.*

111   24 April, 1876 – 8 August, 1944.

112   Although she did not perform the role on stage or in the studio, Julia Varady's recording of the final scene for Orfeo, with her husband, Dietrich Fischer-Dieskau conducting, is one of the most perfect because Varady was not a Wagner *heldensopran* but, rather, a near-peerless lyric-soprano; her performance idealises the youth, fragility and erotic distension that makes Strauss' twisted teenager so special. Among complete studio performances, the most sensuous and febrile is by Cheryl Studer, conducted by Giuseppe Sinopoli, for DG. For all its fame, the recording by Birgit Nilsson, conducted by Georg Solti, is impressive, but only after the fashion of the Grand Canyon, or the Shoemaker–Levy 9. Nilsson's voice was too resonant and inflexible in its phrasing to reveal anything of Salome's psychological complexities. As Nilsson's performance ends, one is left with a strong impression that the soldiers commanded by Herod, *"Man töte dieses Weib!"* ('You, kill that woman,') would have dropped their shields, and made a run for it.

113   As evidenced by her multiple takes of the "Jewel Song" from *Faust*. When creating the role of Salome in Italy, she was likely nailed to the score by Strauss, whose 1906 piano roll "recordings" of scenes from *Salome* attest to ruthless urgency.

use of portamento – and then across *all* the desks – which must have caused *Salome* to sound far more erotic and sensuous than in performance *au moderne*. The pollination of voicing, and the blending of instrumental voices capable of portamento,[114] had an obvious effect on every composer's work – although Brahms and his school gained the most from it. From his student works until the end of his life, Strauss's creative identity was the product of a culture formed by a performance tradition for which a pronounced and unbroken legato was routine;[115] he passed no comment on the change in taste and fashion, since to do so would have placed him at the water's edge with King Canute. The difference that portamento made (and would make still) to the performance of music from *any* period (and by just about any composer), can be discerned from two recordings of the same work by the same conductor, separated by a period of 23 years.

In July, 1941, Leopold Stokowski recorded his own arrangement of Bach's Orchestral Suite No.3, BWV 1068 (the 'Air on a G string') with the All-American Youth Orchestra, for Columbia.[116] In April, 1974, he conducted the London Symphony Orchestra in the same work for EMI. The earlier performance will survive as one of the most extraordinary of anything ever recorded; it should probably have been added to the gold disks attached to the Voyager spacecraft in 1977.[117] The phrasing is unique.[118] Stokowski trained the orchestra to sing the music after the fashion of sopranos when performing the *Rosenkavalier* Trio, with the committed use of slow-moving portamento causing Bach's already long phrases to appear endless and breath-defying. Stokowski's counterpoint is made more affecting still by his use of extreme dynamic changes, which create an intensity of expression that borders on the hallucinatory. The interweaving sections and instruments resolve with mounting intensity, such that the lachrymose vocalising takes on the character of wailing. This alarming poignancy can be attributed to the manner in which it is voiced, with the difference in the weighting and length of each player's bowing and sliding[119] portraying

---

114 Excepting the trombone.

115 The blending of singing voices and instrumental voicing is now ancient history, from which the 21st century has nothing to learn, sadly. Strauss, like everyone else, accepted the changes in taste and style, without complaint or, indeed, commentary. This silence had no bearing on his compositional style, which sings even more when it appears not to.

116 Formed by Stokowski the year before.

117 In place, at the very least, of Karl Richter's spiky recording of the Brandenburg Concerto No. 2 in F with the Munich Bach Orchestra.

118 By an orchestra, at least. The Rosé Quartet recorded the same work, arranged by Wilhelmj, employing a similar aesthetic – albeit from nearly half a century earlier, as it was known and cherished by Mahler.

119 His performance during the same sessions of of "*Komm, süsser Tod*" is almost as affecting, and proof of Stokowski's standing as one of the *very* few re-creative geniuses ever to conduct an orchestra. The clouded beat and libertine freedoms he allows his players within the architecture of each phrase, transfigure Bach as Mahler. It is interesting to note also the extent to which Stokowski – having been denied by fashion *any* access to portamento – was compelled in 1974 to rely on *rubato* for expression. This was (and remains) routine for many who viewed (and view still) the use of portamento as "*beklemmt*" as well as *verboten*. On point, and for context, readers should turn to the central section, in C flat, of the fifth movement ("Cavatina") of Beethoven's String Quartet, No. 13, in B flat major, Op.130. When read as Stokowski and the American Youth Orchestra might have voiced it, the composer's agony becomes terrifying and unbearable.

as ecstatic a work that would be merely beautiful in 1974. Within less than a decade, this aesthetic was perceived as atavistic by a period-performance movement for which unchecked sentiment was *verboten*.

Ackté's singing of the "Willow Song" from *Otello* is typical for her time, insofar as the conjoining of string portamento to the singer's linear phrasing generates a potent sense of cohesion as between the stage and the pit; her singing is remarkable also for its tuning-fork intonation, and the ruthless subjugation of vibrato and volume to diction and dynamics. The differences between Ackté's singing as Desdemona (which blooms in amplitude only when the composer requests it, at the aria's close) and that of Leonie Rysanek, by way of a later exemple, is striking, particularly considering the separation of their careers by only two decades.[120] Both sopranos sang Desdemona and Salome, but there is nothing to compare between them.

Salome's vocal range spans more than two octaves. It rises to a B5, the highest note performed typically by a dramatic soprano, and drops to a low G flat 3, in the contralto register – albeit only on two occasions, and then pianissimo.[121] The role otherwise sits high in the voice, and is more demanding in terms of tone and stamina than anything else in the established canon, with the exception of Isolde, Brünnhilde and Elektra. The final scene lasts 20-minutes and, in its dramatic and vocal challenges, is rivalled only by the end of *Götterdämmerung*. The burdens remain as colossal today as they were in 1905, with relatively few being fit for task. *Salome* can be staged successfully only with a soprano blessed with the vocal resources necessary to traduce Strauss' vast orchestra when formed of modern instruments, who is able coincidentally to persuade as young, sexually alluring and bonkers. She has to achieve this while resisting the temptation to force her tone or the placement of her voice.[122] Ljuba Welitsch managed it; Birgit Nilsson did not.

Mental instability was again a prominent feature of Strauss' next work. *Elektra* was the first of the composer's collaborations with the poet Hugo von Hofmannsthal – on whose play of the same name the opera was based; like its predecessor, it adheres to a single-act formula that hinges on a resolving episode of dance by its title role. It was Strauss' fourth work for the stage, and the last of his 16 operas to feature violence against a woman. Elektra dies, in a species of *liebestod*, brought on not by love, but by the consummation of revenge. The suffering meted out to Klytemnestra is off-stage, and heaily implied; the axe blows delivered by Orestes to his mother and her husband, Aegisth, are conveyed through music of graphic, pictorial detail, as are the jewels rattling around Klytemnestra's neck, the neighing of horses, the baying of dogs, and Kytemnestra's blood-soaked dream-sequence. Strauss' implausible genius for "painting" through orchestral music exceeded the semiotic; suggestion is rare, and every subliminal sense, instinct, thought and feeling to which the libretto refers is presented in blazing technicolour. The score is illustrative rather than programmatic (as was true of his catalogue of tone poems); Hofmannsthal's text pre-empts everything to which the score alludes, with implausible detail. The music is neurotic

---

120 Ackté gave her last staged performance in 1920; her final public performances were a the Savonlinna Opera Festival in 1930. Rysanek made her debut in 1949.

121 See, generally, Puffett, Derrick, Ed. (1989). *Richard Strauss: Salome*. Cambridge University Press.

122 The majority of Salomes are better able to play the role than sing it.

and compulsively figurative in its leitmotifs and imagery; Strauss' evocation of the poet's mannered verse is without precedent; not even *Salome* could prepare audiences for *Elektra's* unrelenting imagery and dramatic momentum. Its singular drive is made more intense still by the score's counterpoint and chromaticism, which are bewilderingly complex – albeit never (as is often claimed) atonal. Schoenberg acknowledged the opera as a milestone, and even the miserabilist Stravinsky conceded its importance, distinguishing Strauss' hyper-focussed vertical symbolism with Debussy's horizontal impressionism: "What operas have been written since *Parsifal*? Only two that count – *Elektra* and Debussy's *Pelléas*."[123]

Hofmannsthal's verse was coloured by imagery that can be traced to Nietzsche's *The Birth of Tragedy out of the Spirit of Music*, published in 1871 (which broke with the European romantic tradition by re-casting ancient Greek culture as dark, cruel and chaotic), and Freud's *Studien über Hysterie* (an annotated first edition of which was in Hofmannsthal's library at the time of his death).[124] The poet and the composer drew on a pictorial world in which Dionysian worship and frenzied Maenads served as an authentic psychological tool for the expression of humanity's blood-soaked instincts, and the darkness of Man's soul in its primeval capacity. In this sense only, *Elektra* is a "Freudian" opera; in every other regard it is a work of cinematic story-telling, diagrammatic in its ideation of character, feeling and action. At a time when the limits of verbal communication were cultivating the primitive, sub-conscious and dream-like, Strauss' technical skill as a composer was such that he was able to convey almost anything through music.[125] And so he did; in doing so he memorialised the seen above the hidden. For all that might be read *into* Elektra's psychological turmoil – as the daughter of a murdered father, and as a woman ruined and sterilised by obsession – nothing requires any "reading" at all. Everything is in the score and on the stage, driven by a title role untouched by unconscious experience. Indeed, Elektra is as determined by her words as she is by the actions of everyone around her; she admits no ambiguities, as a one-dimensional totem, painted in pantone brilliance notwithstanding her tattered-outfits and dirt-stained co-existence with the palace dogs. In her self-imposed exile, and asexual, brutalised conception, Elektra was definitively modern. As the most conspicuous character in a drama bearing her own name, she was secondary to no-one, and certainly not a man; even if she depends ultimately on Orestes to dispatch Klytemnestra and Aegisth, she is self-actualising. In a stroke of good timing, a few months after the first performance, on 25 January, 1909, women were allowed to enroll in German universities; a year later, female activists began to hold demonstrations advocating suffrage.[126]

---

123 Taruskin, Richard (1996). *Stravinsky and the Russian Traditions, Volume Two: A Biography of the Works.* University of California Press, p. 982.

124 See, generally, Urban, Bernd (1978). *Hofmannsthal, Freud und die Psychoanalyse : quellenkundliche Untersuchungen.* P. Lang.

125 Strauss once informed a conductor that it was possible to discern how one of the women in his 1888 tone poem, *Don Juan*, had red hair. After composing his *Eine Alpensinfonie*, he boasted that his powers of expression and orchestration were such that he could, if necessary, describe a knife and a fork in music.

126 In 1919, Article 109 of the Weimar Constitution provided that men and women should have the same fundamental rights and duties as citizens, including the right to vote and to hold office.

Anyone taking up the challenge of Elektra is required to invest abnormal resources of stamina and amplitude; the same can be said also of the two other leading female roles, Chrysothemis (written for a lighter, high voice), created by Strauss' favourite soprano at the time, Margarethe Siems,[127] and Klytemnestra, a brutal, disobliging contralto role that Strauss passed with reservations to Ernestine Schumann-Heink.[128] The latter was already 32 years into her career at the time of the premiere – having made her debut in 1877 as a 15-year-old, in a performance of Beethoven's 9th Symphony, alongside Maria Wilt.[129] She achieved great success in Dresden (being made principle contralto at the age of 17) and Vienna (where she became a favourite of Mahler's). She appeared regularly at Bayreuth, between 1896 and 1914, as one of Cosima Wagner's protectors of the Grail. In 1887, Hans von Bülow, the conductor of the premieres of *Tristan* and *Die Meistersinger*, invited her to perform Brahms' *Alto Rhapsody* at a concert in Hamburg, with Brahms in attendance; when, later the same year, the birth of her fourth child prevented her from committing to Bülow's long-planned Mozart series, he refused to work with her again. In 1898, Schumann-Heink relocated to New York, and a contract at the Metropolitan Opera; she took American citizenship ten years later, and became a significant feature of American cultural life, appearing regularly on the radio, record and film.[130] She can be seen and heard in three Vitaphone films, made in 1927 (as a 65-year-old), one of which records a gloriously ham-throated performance of "*Der Erlkönig*." She takes some outrageous liberties, rolls her Rs as well as her eyes, and engages in outright *sprechgesang*.[131] She considered *Elektra*, and the role of Klytemnestra, to be "a fearful din." For his part, Strauss is said to have yelled during rehearsals at von Schuh, "Louder! I can still hear Madame Schumann-Heink!"[132]

The contralto's grievances became legendary, but they were formed at first instance. In an interview with the *Boston Evening Transcript*, published on 30 October, 1909, she complained about the size of the orchestra, which compelled her and her colleagues to abandon their bel canto techniques and inclinations simply to be heard. The paper reported:

> She looks tragic, desperate, proud, solemn, and serio-comic. German and English fail, and she lapses into the dialect of the newspaper cartoonist. "Nefer again! Es war furchtbar! We were a set of madwomen; truly we were. He had written us so, and so we became in very truth."[133]

127 20 December, 1879 – 13 April, 1952.

128 15 June, 1861 – 17 November, 1936 (see further below).

129 30 January, 1833 – 24 September, 1891. Wilt spent many years at the Hofoper in Vienna. In 1877, she moved to Leipzig, where she appeared as Brünnhilde in one of the first complete performances of the *Ring* Cycle outside Bayreuth, conducted by Anton Seidl.

130 Her first appearance on film, in 1915, was as herself in the documentary film *Mabel and Fatty Viewing the World's Fair at San Francisco*, directed by (and also starring) Fatty Arbuckle.

131 *Sprechgesang* ('spoken singing') and *Sprechstimme* ('spoken voice') are expressionist vocal techniques somewhere between singing and speaking. Though used interchangeably, *Sprechgesang* is related directly to operatic performance, and employs pitches that are sung, whereas *Sprechstimme* is closer to speech itself because it does not emphasise any particular pitches.

132 Boyden, Matthew (1999). *Richard Strauss*. Weidenfeld & Nicolson, p. 136.

133 Calico, Joy H. (2012). "Staging Scandal with Salome and Elektra," in *The Arts of the Prima Donna*

Klytemnestra is a difficult role, but it is dwarfed by the vocal and physical demands of Elektra herself, which begins "*Allein*," and ends in an ecstatic duet with Chrysothemis, during which Elektra waltzes herself to death. Contrary to reputation, Strauss' writing is consistently and determinedly lyrical; many big-voice sopranos have nonetheless trampled its beauty beneath admixtures of shrieking and wobbling. The soprano first-favoured by Strauss and von Schuch had a large voice but, as her recordings testify, she used it with restraint. Anny Krull[134] had known Strauss since the beginning of the century, when she created Diemut in the first production of *Feuersnot* – three years after her debut as Agathe in *Der Freischütz*. Krull joined the Dresden State Opera in 1900 and remained with the company for more than a decade. For much of that time she was at war with Marie Wittich, whose animosity was exacerbated by Strauss' decision to pass Elektra's torch to the younger soprano.

Shortly after the premiere of *Elektra*, Krull was recorded in Berlin by Odeon as Elisabeth in a complete performance of Act II of *Tannhäuser*. The singing by all concerned is nothing short of exceptional (unlike the comically terrible "orchestra," which would have given the Portsmouth Sinfonia a run for its money). Krull sounds as she must have done singing Elektra in Dresden and, the following year, in London – when performing in the British premiere for Thomas Beecham. She had a resonant voice, but it was agile also, and she sings with discretion as well as power. Similar qualities were shared by the first sopranos to perform *Elektra* in America and France. Surprisingly, considering the speed with which *Salome* was adopted outside Germany, *Elektra* was slow to make it to New York and Paris. The New York premiere took place on 3 December, 1932, conducted by Artur Bodanzky, with Gertrude Kappel[135] in the title role – 29 years after her debut in *Il trovatore*. There is a recording doing the rounds that is said to have been made at the first night; it is live,[136] and the voice certainly captured sounds analogous to Kappel's live-taped performances as Brünnhilde. Her singing comes closer to that of Gutheil-Schoder in tone and placement than Rose Pauly,[137] the first soprano to record the opera complete;[138] it is a lighter instrument than has become normal since Birgit Nilsson turned everything up to 11. Like Kappel, Germaine Lubin[139] was a famed Isolde before she was chosen by Strauss to create Elektra in Paris. She studied at the Conservatoire with Gabriel Fauré, and privately from 1912 with Félia Litvinne, Lilli Lehmann, Gutheil-Schoder and Jean de Reszke. Her talent and pedigree brought her to the attention of Debussy, Dukas, Massenet, Charpentier, d'Indy and Milhaud – many of whose works she premiered – and Marshal Philippe Pétain. In 1930, she sang her first Isolde at the Opéra

---

in the Long Nineteenth Century. Eds. Rachel Cowgill & Hilary Poriss. Oxford University Press, p. 73.

134   12 January, 1876 – 14 June, 1947.

135   1 September, 1884 – 3 April, 1971.

136   Bodanzky's tempi are whip-driven – and a beat quicker during Elektra's monologue than anyone since.

137   The first "complete" recording of *Elektra* was not made until 21 March, 1937, when Artur Rodzinski was taped conducting a live performance at Carnegie Hall, with the title role played by the Hungarian soprsano, Rose Pauly (15 March, 1894 – 14 December, 1975). Almost 30 years after the premiere, the type and style of voice being presented as "dramatic" was significantly lighter than it would be by the 1950s.

138   The version performed has been heavily cut, although the major scene survive.

139   1 February, 1890 – 27 October, 1979.

– to ecstatic acclaim. She was soon after collaborating with Furtwängler in Berlin, Beecham in London, and De Sabata at Bayreuth, where, in July, 1939, she was the first French citizen to sing Isolde; her recording of the *Liebestod*, with De Sabata conducting, is eye-widening in its animation. Lubin's tone gleams and her phrasing is imperious; as was often the case with French Wagnerians; the diction is poetic rather than declamatory. Her popularity at Bayreuth brought her into close proximity with the Wagner family, who introduced Lubin to the Festival's patron, Adolf Hitler, who told her that "in all my life I have never seen or heard an Isolde such as you."[140] She later protested her innocence, but Lubin committed professionally and emotionally to the Nazi regime, in Germany and in France – where her friendship with Pétain was well-publicised long before they were indicted as collaborators. After the Liberation in 1944, Lubin was arrested, imprisoned and ultimately acquitted – on the basis of testimonials produced by those whom she was alleged to have helped during the oc-cupation. Her sentence to "*dégradation nationale*" for life was reduced to five years on appeal;[141] much of her property, seized as forefeit, including a château in Tours, was returned over time. Lubin complained bitterly of her treatment by "my own people," telling one journalist that the accusations levelled at her "always proved groundless. Except for having eaten the flesh of children, there is nothing I was not accused of."[142] Lubin was emphatic, regardless, that she did "not like to sing the role of victim." In 1953, three years after attempting to re-start her career, her son committed suicide, at which point Lubin retired for good, committing 25 long years to teaching.[143]

Most of the earliest performers of Elektra, during the ten years after its premiere, made increasing use of a variegated vibrato, which distinguished them from Vienna's *prima donna assoluta*, Gutheil-Schoder. In the same year that *Elektra* was first per-formed in Dresden, Schoenberg completed *Erwartung* in Vienna. The premiere was delayed until 6 June, 1924 – in Prague, with Gutheil-Schoder singing the role of Die Frau, conducted by Zemlinsky – by which time German contemporary music had turned away from the late-romantic (characterised by Strauss as "sensual and emotional") and towards the atonal-dodecaphonic (processed by Schoenberg as a mechanism for "yielding [to] our subconscious."). This shift in identity towards a Freudian method was embraced by many inside and outside Germany, including Bartok, whose *Bluebeard's Castle*[144] shares significantly more with Schoenberg's ex-ploration of the unseen and the uncanny than it does with Strauss' predilection for sound and fury. Almost exactly a year to the day after *Elektra's* premiere, the Austrian soprano, Martha Winternitz-Dorda,[145] gave the first performance of Schoenberg's "*Das Buch der hängenden Gärten*,"[146] a fifteen-part cycle of songs set to verses by Stefan George, in which is narrated the failed love affair of adolescents in a garden that ends with the nameless woman's departure, and the garden's disintegration. In

---

140 Christiansen, Rupert (1985). *Prima Donna: A History*. Viking Press, p. 281.
141 Pétain was sentenced to death; Charles de Gaulle intervened, and ordered that he be sent to prison for life.
142 Rasponi, Lanfranco (1984). *The Last Prima Donnas*. Gollancz, p. 92.
143 Of her many students, the best known was Régine Crespin.
144 First performed on 24 May, 1918.
145 28 March, 1880 – 9 December, 1958.
146 'The Book of the Hanging Gardens,' first performed on 14 January, 1910, in Vienna.

tandem with *Erwartung*, the *Gärten* cycle marked the start of Schoenberg's atonal period; in a program note for reading at the premiere he wrote:

> With the George songs I have for the first time succeeded in approaching an ideal of expression and form which has been in my mind for many years. Until now I lacked the strength and confidence to make it a reality. I am being forced in this direction [...] not because my invention or technique is inadequate, but [because] I am obeying an inner compulsion, which is stronger than any upbringing. I am obeying the formative process which, being the one natural to me, is stronger than my artistic education.[147]

Schoenberg was all-but admitting to the influence and effect of unconscious forces. The songs are dreamlike, unsettling and dark. Their obsidian character can, again, be attributed, to his wife's adultery – who was living with Gerstl at the time. The last of the songs is the longest and bleakest:

> *Wir bevölkerten die abend-düstern*
> *Lauben, lichten tempel pfad und beet*
> *Freudig – sie mit lächeln ich mit flüstern –*
> *Nun ist wahr dass sie für immer geht.*
> *Hohe blumen blassen oder brechen*
> *Es erblasst und bricht der weiher glas*
> *Und ich trete fehl im morschen gras*
> *Palmen mit den spitzen fingern stechen.*
> *Mürber blätter zischendes gewühl*
> *Jagen ruckweis unsichtbare hände*
> *Draussen um des edens fahle wände.*
> *Die nacht ist überwölkt und schwül.*[148]

Prominent octaves and step-wise descending fifths herald the end of the cycle, as well as the lovers' relationship. They reappear during the song's final section, two octaves lower and changed in rhythm; the suggestion of collapsing certainties and abandoned hopes mirror the "man's" psychological undoing. It is impossible to read this music other than in performance; even then, no two singers could hope to bring the same or comparable inflection to the isolating and nebulous triadic melody; meaning and subtext are discernible only if looked for. Even when found, they cannot be agreed upon.[149] Like *Erwartung*, the *Gärten* cycle can be heard as a product of the composer's

---

147   Reich, Willi (1971). *Schoenberg: A Critical Biography*, Trans. Leo Black. Longman, p. 48.
148   'We inhabited the evening-dimmed, Arbours, lighted temple, pathway and flowerbed, Joyfully – she with smiles, I with whispering – Now it is true that she is leaving forever. Tall flowers pale or breach, The glassy surface of the ponds pales and breaks, And I miss my step in the boggy grass, Palms stab me with their pointy fingers. The sibilant mass of friable leaves, Is whirled about erratically by unseen hands, Outside about the dull walls of Eden. The night is clouded and sultry.'
149   Schoenberg was thrilled with the "very good and extremely musical" Winternitz-Dorda's creation of the cycle; he evidenced his gratitude three years later when engaging her to sing Tove in the first

broken marriage; Schoenberg could have asked Pappenheim to write *Erwartung* for a male protagonist; he was not obliged to settle on George's poetry. It is probably no coincidence, therefore, that the rage and humiliation experienced by the composer as a husband coincided with his creation of music for women that was alienating and hard to perform and difficult to hear; whether it articulated his emotional and psychological anxiety is less easy to determine, but both works diverged with the lyric tradition as it was known and taught globally to women training as sopranos. That Schoenberg knew this emerges from his correspondence with Winternitz-Dorda; it follows that his reconstitution of the soprano voice qualifies as the contiguous stifling of female representation at a time when women were becoming emancipated, and more vocal in consequence. The probability of Schoenberg's motivation in his rush towards abstraction is evidenced by his response to Winternitz-Dorda's withdrawal from a performance of his music: "as little intelligent as this female may otherwise be [...] she is cunning. Besides: all females lie better than men tell the truth."[150]

With *Elektra* storming the operatic battlements, it was assumed that Strauss would compose a trilogy of mad women. Instead, he created with Hofmannsthal a bourgeois comedy of 18th century manners and sensibilities that established Strauss' reputation as the most talented composer for female voices in the history of opera. *Der Rosenkavalier*[151] was only his fifth stage work; it nonetheless exemplified Strauss' unparalleled genius for writing as, and for, women. *Salome* and *Elektra* are gravid with beautiful music, but any appreciation of their lyricism is hampered inevitably by context. Conversely, the voicing in *Rosenkavalier* – while chromatically avant-garde – is subsumed to neo-classical and Viennese pastiche, a scenic and temporal *locus* that compelled Strauss' alignment to a purposefully quasi-Mozartian melody. Any production of *Rosenkavalier* is a vast undertaking; it has one of the largest casts of any opera[152] – and another massive orchestra, which Strauss prescribed should contain 60 strings (32 violins, 12 violas, ten cellos and eight double-basses). The score is dominated by its female leads: Princess von Werdenberg (the "Marschallin"), her 17-year-old lover, Octavian (a trouser-role for mezzo-soprano), and Sophie von Faninal – the reluctant fiancée of the brutish Baron Ochs, the Marschallin's 'country' cousin. Strauss indulged each role with music of extraordinary opulence, most famously in two scenes: Act II's "Presentation of the Rose," a duet for Octavian and Sophie, and the concluding "*Terzett*," in Act III – a trio for all three sopranos that, within a year of the opera's premiere, had been monumentalised. Indeed, it would not be an overstatement to venerate the *Rosenkavalier* Trio as the supreme testament to the soprano voice. It occupies a space in which the soprano is simultaneously exploited and adulated as the ultimate instrument for the expression of emotion; as

---

performance of "*Gurre-Lieder*" in Vienna. She made a number of recordings for Pathé (in Vienna in 1909) and Parlophon (in Berlin in 1911). A fine example of Winternitz-Dorda in full sail is her sparkling performance of "*Zum Leiden bin ich auserkoren*," from *Die Zauberflöte*.

150 Schoenberg, Arnold (1986). "Attempt at a Diary," Trans. Anita M. Luginbühl, *Journal of the Arnold Schoenberg Institute,* 9 (4), p. 14.

151 'The Knight of the Rose.'

152 There are literally dozens of characters, eight of whom is named. For the first production, the stage director Roller produced designs for every single character's costumes – even "Mohammed," the Marschallin's black page, who appears for seconds only.

an exemplar for humanity's capacity for the joining of creativity and craft in service to the sublime, it warrants a place beside the *Pieta, Hamlet* and *Starry Night*.[153]

As Strauss acknowledged in his long and revealing correspondence with Hofmannsthal, the poet judged to perfection the resolution of the drama's defining love triangle. Gathered together, they address their feelings in soliloquy – each talking only to themselves; Octavian submits to Sophie even though, days earlier, he was besotted with the Princess; Sophie wrestles with her new feelings while the Marschallin struggles with seeing Octavian move on, only to do the same herself, with a maturity befitting her years and social status. By the end of the Trio, everyone has come to terms with their feelings and circumstances. Strauss' use of harmony, key and voicing is predictably articulate, with the direction of each character's music moving in accordance with their outcomes. Strauss uses dissonance and modulation to cue exactly the point at which everyone understands how their lives have now changed – a denouement achieved through phrases of enormous length and interaction. While Octavian and Sophie sing their final word, "*lieb*,"[154] the Marschallin sustains the word "*verstehn*."[155] The music rises to a point of ecstasy, with the trio of voices increasing in pitch and intensity until release is finally achieved; Octavian and Sophie face each other while the Marschallin steps towards Octavian with her arm outstretched; in palpable agony, she sings "*in Gottes Namen*."[156] The Marschallin withdraws, leaving the stage – and love – to the young couple. Only the hardest of hearts can survive this achingly poignant moment;[157] indeed, more than one soprano has yielded to its intensity, even when focused on the performance.[158] There are a number of live recordings available of singers cracking under the emotional strain. The Marschallin was created by Margarethe Siems – a student for a time of Pauline Viardot and Mattia Battistini. Before joining the Dresden Opera, where she was made a Kammersängerin in 1909, Siems was a popular member of the Prague Opera, where she gave the local premieres of *La bohème* and *Madama Butterfly*. It is surprising, perhaps, that the first Marschallin should have been renowned primarily for her work as a coloratura – a facility recognised by Strauss' third role for Siems, the "show-stopping" Zerbinetta in *Ariadne auf Naxos*.[159] Siems' technical skill is apparent from her recording of "*Nun eilt herbei*,"[160] from *Die lustige Weiber von Windsor* (which features one of the longest trills on record); more impressive still is her singing of Heinrich Proch's "Variations," a species of "Carnival of Venice," for which she throws herself to all corners of the wind. Fortunately, she can be heard also as the Marschallin on a recording of the Trio

---

153 Strauss was sufficiently self-aware to recognise the Trio's significance, since he requested that it be played at his funeral. Georg Solti was the conductor.

154 'Love.'

155 'Understand.'

156 'In God's name.'

157 At least one psychologist has investigated the Freudian subtext for the "older woman" as a syndrome for a younger man. See Martin, Peter A., (1964). "A Psychoanalytic Study of the Marschallin Theme from *Der Rosenkavalier*." *Journal of the American Psychoanalytic Association*, Vol. 14 (4).

158 The most affecting performance of the Trio was at Strauss' funeral in 1949, conducted by George Solti. Having broken down at different times, they managed to end together.

159 First performed on 25 October, 1912.

160 'Now hurry up.'

from *Rosenkavalier* – with Eva von der Osten[161] (the original Octavian) and Minnie Nast[162] (the first Sophie). The historical significance of this recording requires no commentary; one can only regret that the composer was not invited to conduct, since whoever was in charge drags the music horribly. What stands out is the vocal tone, which would today be considered bleached. None of the singers uses vibrato, although each employs portamento – as do the string players in the orchestra. In consequence, the voicing is unlike anything that might be considered "normal" today, with excessive vibrato and over-singing suffocating melody, word and legato. Vocal tone and technique are constructions of taste, of course, but the weaving of the voices on the recording from 1911 is significantly more lucid than has become routine since the end of the 20th century. The voices of the original trio are, in effect, instruments, producing a sense of cohesion between the stage and the pit.

When listening to this recording it's well to remember that both Siems and Nast were both celebrated as Isolde before they performed the Marschallin. Within two decades after the premiere of *Ariadne auf Naxos* in 1912 it would have been considered absurd for any singer appearing as Zerbinetta (or Octavian for that matter) to attempt *Tristan*; it presented no difficulty for Strauss, however, who was himself an alumni of Bayreuth – where amplitude mattered less than clarity until the 1950s. A similar latitude prevailed at La Scala,[163] where Tullio Serafin conducted the Italian premiere of *Rosenkavalier* on 1 March, 1911, with Lucrezia Bori[164] in the role of Octavian. Bori made her House debut the year before as Carolina in a production of Cimarosa's *Il matrimonio segreto*.[165] Vienna's first Marschallin was Lucie Weidt,[166] who had three years earlier created the role of Kundry for La Scala. She was renowned also as Brunnhilde, and the first Nurse in *Die Frau ohne Schatten* for Strauss in 1919 – with a large and penetrating voice. Weidt's Octavian was sung by Marie Gutheil-Schoder, using a voice that, but for her portamento, would be considered ideal for performances of 18th century repertoire. Strauss' preferences and priorities were well-established when *Ariadne* was first performed in Stuttgart in 1912; the status quo pivoted with the role of Zerbinetta, the leading artist in a burlesque group, whom Strauss composed as a coloratura, creating in the 13-minute scene, "*Grossmächtige Prinzessin*,"[167] the most entertaining, technically extravagant high-soprano show-piece in all German opera.[168] A recording was made of the first version of the aria in the year following the work's premiere, with Hedwig Francillo-Kauffmann,[169] an Austrian soprano whose performance proves the fallacy of rosy retrospection. Compared to almost all of her

---

161   19 August, 1881 – 5 May, 1936.

162   10 October, 1874 – 20 June, 1956. She went on to direct opera, in which capacity she oversaw the premiere of Strauss's *Arabella* in 1933.

163   Though popular, the performance was booed by purists who considered the waltz suitable only for dance music.

164   24 December, 1887 – 14 May, 1960.

165   'The Secret Marriage,' first performed on 7 February, 1792. Scored for an orchestra formed of strings, eight wind, four brass and timpani.

166   May 11, 1876 – July 28, 1940.

167   'High and mighty princess.'

168   As a role, Zerbinetta was preceded only by that of Adele in Johann Strauss II's *Die Fledermaus* ('The Bat.').

169   30 September, 1878 – 11 April, 1948.

better-known successors, Francillo-Kauffmann's singing is a study in imperfection. For the opera's second iteration, the role of Zerbinetta was passed to Selma Kurz,[170] another Austrian coloratura with a more reliable technique, the backing of Mahler and (after a jubilant appearance in *Mignon* on 3 September, 1899) the adoration of the Viennese public. She remained the Opera's leading coloratura for three decades, restoring a large number of lost and neglected works to the repertoire, including *Il barbiere di Siviglia*, *Les Huguenots*, *Un ballo in maschera*,[171] *Lakmé*, and *Lucia di Lammermoor*. Mahler fell in love with Kurz, and they had a brief affair during the spring of 1900. Her talents extended to contemporary Italian repertoire, particularly *La bohème*, of which she gave 100 performances, and *Madama Butterfly*, of which she gave the Viennese premiere in 1907. Strauss adored her as Sophie in *Rosenkavalier*, and it was a wise commercial move to gift her the second Zerbinetta, which she premiered on 4 October, 1916. She gave 36 performances of the role in Vienna alone. Unusually for a natural coloratura, Kurz's voice had considerable amplitude, which equipped her to perform Elsa and Sieglinde as well as Manon, Frau Fluth in Nicolai's *Die lustige Weiber von Windsor*, the Queen of the Night, Gilda and Violetta. Her many recordings testify to musical intelligence and resolute acrobatic skill, the influence of which was definitive for every subsequent Zerbinetta. Similarly eclectic was the Swiss-soprano Maria Ivogün,[172] whose audition at the Vienna Hofoper in 1913 led to Bruno Walter engaging her at the Hofoper in Munich instead. She made her debut as Mimi in *La bohème*, and three years later she was picked by Strauss to sing the first Zerbinetta in the Viennese premiere of the re-worked *Ariadne*. In the same year, Bruno Walter and the 19-year-old Erich Korngold chose her as the first Laura in the premiere of *Der Ring des Polykrates* – alongside the tenor Karl Erb, whom she married in 1921.[173] In 1917, she created the role of Ighino in the first production of Pfitzner's *Palestrina* – again with Erb, whom she married four years later. Appropriately enough, she was the nominated "*Nachtigall*"[174] in Walter Braunfels's *Die Vögel*[175] – while excelling as a singer of Mozart. On 27 May, 1924, she was Zerbinetta in the London premiere of *Ariadne*, with Lotte Lehmann as Ariadne, Elisabeth Schumann as the Composer, Karl Fischer-Niemann as Bacchus, and Karl Alwin conducting. The work was a failure with British audiences, despite the extraordinary cast; many of the critics were baffled, in particular, by Zerbinetta. Strauss was unfazed; he had enjoyed writing the role and went on to create further coloratura parts.

The role of Aminta in *Die schweigsame Frau*[176] was created by the Romanian-born Maria Cebotari,[177] the first soprano to create a leading role for Strauss to be born in the 20th century. She was only 25 at the time, having made her debut four years earlier,

---

170   15 October, 1874 – 10 May, 1933.

171   Mahler's revivals of *Un ballo in maschera* and Goldmark's *Die Königin von Saba* ('The Queen of Sheba') in 1903 rejuvenated the teaching of coloratura technique in Vienna.

172   *née* Ilse Kempner, 18 November, 1891 – 3 October, 1987.

173   First performed on 28 March, 1916.

174   'Nightingale.'

175   'The Birds,' first performed on 4 December, 1920.

176   'The Silent Woman,' first performed on 24 June, 1935, conducted by Karl Böhm.

177   10 February, 1910 – 9 June, 1949.

as Mimi, at the Dresden Semperoper. Like Kurz, Cebotari was never pigeon-holed as a coloratura. Indeed, when visiting Covent Garden in 1947 with the Vienna State Opera, she performed Salome, Donna Anna in *Don Giovanni* and the Countess Almaviva in *Le nozze di Figaro*. On 27 September, she was Donna Anna to the Ottavio of Richard Tauber,[178] who died the following week from cancer. 18 months later, on 31 March, 1949, Cebotari collapsed during a performance of Millöcker's *Der Bettelstudent* in Vienna. Two weeks later, on 4 April, doctors discovered her liver and pancreas to be riddled with cancer; she died on 9 June, 1949 – at the age of 39. Three months earlier, Strauss described her as "the best all-rounder on the European stage [...] she is never late, and she never cancels."[179]

Cancer also did for Erna Sack, the creator of Isotta, the second coloratura role in *Die schweigsame Frau* – albeit not until after her 80th birthday. Known as the "German Nightingale," Sack was not discovered until the age of 30, when Bruno Walter's wife heard her by chance, and persuaded her husband to invite her to the Berlin State Opera for an audition. Incredibly, she was 36-years-old before she made any progress, and not until 1930 did her ability to place notes almost at the edge of human hearing generate apposite fame. Sack was a phenomenon for whom a high C *above* high C was no obstacle – as evidence for which there are many recordings, some of them filmed – memorably the 1938 costume operetta, *Nanon*, in which she starred alongside Johannes Heesters, one of Hitler's favourite actors, and a personal friend of the dictator.[180] Sack was arguably the first exclusively coloratura soprano of the 20th century because she sang little else. Being able to surmount such stratospheric high notes, to a G7, made her a circus attraction, and her talent for *fiorituri* and extended cadenzas became the only stock in which she was able to trade. Strauss was an instant fan and wrote a new cadenza for Sack to perform as Zerbinetta. By 1916, Strauss' standing allowed him the pick of any singer with the talent to do justice to his music; his works were assigned routinely to the most talented (and expensive) singers available. Frieda Hempel[181] was another coloratura tasked with singing the Marschallin – which she created in Berlin and, later, London. On 9 December, 1913, she played the role in the first American production, at the Met, before taking up the role of Oscar in *Un ballo in Maschera*, opposite Caruso as Riccardo, Emmy Destinn as Amelia and Pasquale Amato as Renato. Hempel's dramatic range enabled her to perform Rosina, the Queen of the Night and Eva in *Der Meistersinger*, and she did so frequently. Like Kurz in Vienna, Hempel was pivotal to the status-restoration of the coloratura in the United States – a *fach* she promoted through a series of popular and much criticised "Jenny Lind" concerts.[182] She nonetheless revived a raft of "archaic" operas by Rossini, Meyerbeer and Donizetti, including *La fille du Regiment*. The career of arguably the most influential coloratura mezzo of her generation, Conchita

---

178 Much of the performance was recorded, and remains widely available.

179 The British pianist, Clifford Curzon and his wife Lucille Wallace adopted her two sons.

180 Goebbels placed Heesters on the *Gottbegnadeten* list, as an artist deemed to be crucial to the preservation and promulgation of Nazi culture. He was the only non-German to be so identified. He died in 2011, at the age of 108.

181 26 June, 1885 – 7 October, 1955.

182 See, generally, Tunbridge, Laura (2013). "Frieda Hempel and the Historical Imagination." *Journal of the American Musicological Society*, Vol. 66, No. 2, pp. 437–474.

Supervía,[183] was also launched by Strauss. The Spanish-born soprano made her debut in 1910, at the age of 15, at the Teatro Colón, Buenos Aires. The following year she was invited – as a 16-year-old – to create the role of Octavian in the first Rome production of *Rosenkavalier*, at the Teatro Costanzi.[184] Supervía is the only singer to have performed the role at an age younger than the character.[185]

Any performer not already a celebrity was made so by Strauss' favour. The most favoured was Maria Jeritza[186] a Czech-born soprano who made her debut in 1910 with Franz Joseph I in the audience; the Emperor was sufficiently impressed to direct that Jeritza receive a contract at the Hofoper[187] where, 12 months later, she created the role of Blanchefleur in Wilhelm Kienzl's *Der Kuhreigen*. Two years into her career, Jeritza was invited by Strauss to create the role of Ariadne / the Composer, in Stuttgart. Her performance was more successful than the work, which Strauss spent four years revising; when the revision was first performed in 1916, in Vienna, Jeritza was the only original cast member to return. On this occasion, the opera prevailed, achieving celebrity for Jeritza and the lifelong gratitude of Strauss. She was similarly revered by Puccini, who attended on her regularly in Vienna. They studied *Tosca* together – in which role she thrilled the composer as the first soprano to sing "*Visi d'arte*" lying down.[188] Hermann Klein, the critic of the London *Times*, reviewed Jeritza's performance of *Tosca* at Covent Garden in 1925, the success of which he attributed as much to her

> winning personality and magnificent acting as to the effect of her ringing, powerful tones and genuinely dramatic singing. Here as I fully expected was an artist who could produce in the opera house a far deeper impression than that created by her gramophone achievements [...]. But what a Tosca! What a combination of all the qualities, human and artistic, that go to the making of that many-sided creature! Jeritza is not exactly like any one of her great predecessors in this role. She unites, though, some of the strongest characteristics that distinguished each, and she brings them into sharp contrast with the adroitness and skill of a

---

183   8 December, 1895 – 30 March, 1936.

184   Hariclea Darclée sang the role of the Marschallin.

185   In 1912, Supervía appeared as Carmen – her most celebrated role – and in 1915 she made her American debut as Charlotte in Werther at the Chicago Opera. At the end of the First World War she returned to Rome, where she launched what would become known as the "Rossini revival" – restoring *La Cenerentola*, *L'italiana in Algeri* and Il barbiere di Siviglia to the repertoire, and then in the original keys. Her astonishing technique (and her youth when achieving her first flush of fame) draw obvious parallels with Cecelia Bartoli – whose voice is strikingly similar, but for the persistent and ruthless vibrato – said by the British critic, Philip Hope-Wallace, to be "as strong as the rattle of ice in a glass."

186   *née* Marie Jedličková, 6 October, 1887 – 10 July, 1982. It is plainly a coincidence, but a curious number of the sopranos who worked closely with Strauss lived enormously long lives, well into the 1980s and, in a couple of cases, the 1990s. Lisa della Casa, who sang for the composer more than once during the 1940s, died in 2012 – 148 years after the composer's birth.

187   She remained a member of the company until 1934, returning for three years in 1950.

188   In consequence of an accident, according to Jeritza. The response to her first night as Tosca was thunderous – unhappily so for the tenor Aureliano Pertile, who had the misfortune to make his debut on the same night.

mistress of her art. Thus by turn she gives you the feline touches of Sarah Bernhardt, the feminine devotion of Ternina, the tempestuous passion of Destinn, the shrinking fear of Emma Eames. Tenderness alternates with jealousy in the church scene; anxiety, alarm and resentment with burning rage, despair, gloating, satisfied vengeance in the terrific duet with Scarpia. Then, after the prolonged physical struggle, whilst she is lying full length on the ground, her face distorted and her wonderful hair all dishevelled, she half murmurs, half weeps the bitter plaint of "Vissi d'arte" with an intensity of emotion such as no Tosca off the stage has ever yet dared to put into a gramophone record. It was not in this air that she "forced" her tone, as has been suggested; but if she did so at all it was at certain moments in the tremendous episode when it was far more pardonable to overstress the fortissimo than do the reverse. At such a climax it seems wonderful how a singer with a temperament like Jeritza's can keep control of her forces as she does; for she makes you feel that the vocalist is not being studied in the least – that all physical power is being reserved to meet the demands of the actress. Altogether, then, her Tosca is an intensely striking and superb performance.[189]

On 16 November, 1926, Jeritza played the title role in the North American premiere of *Turandot* at the Metropolitan. Four years later she was cast by Korngold as the first Hariette/Juliette in *Die tote Stadt*,[190] although she became more famous as Marietta/Marie after the Viennese premiere in January, 1921.[191] In New York, she created leading parts in Janáček's *Jenůfa* (in 1924), Wolf-Ferrari's *I gioielli della Madonna* (in 1925), Korngold's *Violanta* (in 1927), and Suppé's *Boccaccio* (in 1931) and *Donna Juanita* (in 1932). Her most important collaborator was Richard Strauss, who created two further roles for Jeritza, the Kaiserin[192] in *Die Frau ohne Schatten*[193] and Helen of Troy in *Die Ägyptische Helena*.[194] Jeritza proved too expensive for the management of the Dresden Opera when staging the latter, so they passed the honour to Elisabeth Rethberg. The power, warmth and sexuality of Jeritza's art survive in Helen, one of the most thrilling, beautiful and difficult roles in the operatic canon, and Die Kaiserin, another titanic character in a vast opera filled with them. With his nameless *Die Frau*, Strauss again overlooked the inner workings of character-psychology to focus on the symbolic, emotional and sensual fabric of a fairy-tale concerned with the state, condition and acquisition of motherhood. The opera is long, at four hours, and tirelessly inventive in its writing for a large chorus and another bank-breaking

---

189   Klein, Hermann (1990). *Herman Klein and the Gramophone: Being a Series of Essays on the Bel Canto.* Amadeus Press, p. 110.
190   'The Dead City.'
191   This was the role with which she made her Met debut, on 19 November, 1921.
192   'The Empress.'
193   'The Woman Without a Shadow.'
194   'The Egyptian Helen,' first performed on 6 June, 1928.

orchestra.[195] The crowning episode for Jeritza, as The Empress, occurs in Act III, as she sings to her absent father, Keikobad:[196]

> *Vater, bist du's? Drohest du mir aus dem Dunkel her? Hier siehe dein Kind!*
> *Mich hinzugeben, hab' ich gelernt, aber Schatten hab' ich keinen mir erhan-*
> *delt. Nun zeig mir den Platz, der mir gebührt inmitten derer, die Schatten*
> *werfen.*[197]

The scene, in "Strauss' key" of E flat,[198] is introduced by an extended passage for orchestra and solo violin – an instrument used autobiographically by the composer throughout his career.[199] It is ravishing even by the standards of the greatest melodist in the history of music after Mozart. His love for Jeritza (as "his" Empress) resonates in a descending octave (E flat 4 to E flat 3) for her opening word, "*Vater,*" while his professional admiration echoes throughout the ensuing phrase, much of it *a cappella*. Capitalising on the warmth and projection of Jeritza's voice, the setting of the words "*Hier siehe dein Kind*" is extraordinarily moving and the temptation to attribute the passage's sentiment to the composer's feelings for the much younger soprano is overwhelming. The appearance of a solo horn compounds the "love-pairing" between the Empress and her father, just as surely as it speaks to the relationship between the composer and the singer.[200] The scene ends with a remarkable passage during which, with every creeping "*von der wissenschaft*" modulation, the orchestra becomes increasingly frenzied; the Empress has to prevail until the scene rounds with her petition, "*Zeige dich, Vater! Mein Richter, hervor!*"[201] – the final word of which is scored by Strauss as another octave, this time rising (E flat 3 to E flat 4).

Hofmannsthal and Strauss worked closely together; the Empress' refusal to drink from a fountain (the water from which was certain to provide her with happiness at the expense of others) points to Jeritza's rumoured affair with Strauss, whose loyalty to his wife was as legendary as it was improbable. The Empress' transformation, and the source of her magical reward, is engineered masterfully by Strauss; it blooms through music of extravagant, unfolding richness and a dense orchestration over which the soprano singing (and, in the case of the Empress, speaking) has to soar. It is trite that Jeritza soared like no-one else. She made relatively few studio recordings, and none of them bears repetition; some are actively ghastly. They certainly don't align with the substance of her prestige. The disconnect between Jeritza on stage and in the studio was acknowledged at the time by those fortunate to see her perform. In 1925, Hermann Klein wrote for *The Gramophone* magazine that "Experience has

---

195   It requires 112 players.
196   He remains absent throughout the opera.
197   'Father, is it You? Is it You frowning down on me out of this darkness? Look here upon your child! I have learned to surrender myself, but no shadow clings to my heels because of any trade of mine. Now show me the place that is rightly mine among those who cast shadows.'
198   He reserved this key for personally significant episodes and characters. It is also the key of *Die Zauberflöte*.
199   There are too many examples to cite; the best known is the solo in *Ein Heldenleben*.
200   The horn was Strauss' preferred instrument whenever he was referencing his wife, Pauline, in music.
201   'Show yourself father! My judge, come forth!'

now proved that it is the exception rather than the rule for singers to live up to their gramophone reputations."[202] That may have been true for Klein – who attended the Covent Garden premiere of *Aida* in 1876 – but recordings were also becoming dangerous in their influence. By the 1920s, and thanks in no small part to Caruso, records had become reliquaries for the forming of expectations; they served as artefacts for the creation, evidencing, and validating of articles of faith. Their impact on singers was more malignant still. For Jeritza, recordings were symptomatic of a cultural tide that would prove to be more destructive, even, than the airplane,[203] because they created absolutes to which teachers and singers were able to nail their preferences and prejudices in equal measure. Inevitably, perhaps, recordings fostered standardisation, conformity and the forced eradication of difference. After hearing Jeritza, Lehmann and Rethberg, there was no room for Marie Gutheil-Schoder and Aino Ackté. Jeritza was averse to the process as well as the product of recording, which was antithetical to the instincts of a singing-actress for whom the stage and an audience were triggers without which she was able to do nothing more than vocalise. She recalled:

> The records were made in a small room, a room so small that the members of the little orchestra of ten or fourteen men which accompanied me had to sit close together, knee to knee. With the orchestra so close to the singer the sound of the instruments is so overpowering that it drowns the voice and I could not hear myself sing […] I found myself able to overcome this difficulty by holding my hands over my ears […] Then there is the matter of adjusting your position as you stand and sing, so that you are at exactly the right distance from the receiver. For deep register tones one comes closer, for high register tones one moves further away.

Fortunately, the live recordings made of Jeritza at the Vienna Staatsoper demonstrate that she was everything claimed for her by Puccini, Strauss, Korngold and Lehár. The excerpts from her Brünnhilde in *Die Walküre*, recorded in 1933,[204] are sensational, almost disconcertingly so. She hurls herself into the performance, such that some of her singing comes across as undisciplined; the visceral physicality of her appeal to Wotan in Act 3 carries a desperate urgency that must have caused Friedrich Schorr's Wotan to reconsider his decision. So total is her emotional investment that one can forgive the liberties she takes with the score, as well as the missed cues and suspect intonation. None of it matters because her commitment is total. On one occasion, a friend of Strauss complained that Jeritza had sung out of tune, to which he replied "yes, I know, but who cares when everything else is that good!" On another occasion, a repetiteur suggested Strauss intervene after Jeritza deviated from Strauss' score; the composer replied "Leave her alone; she knows what she is doing." The excerpts from her Salome (conducted by Hugo Reichenberger) were recorded in 1936, when she was almost 50-years-old; her singing is, again, incendiary, and no amount of fearful

---

202   Steane, J. B. (1992). *Voices, Singers and Critics*. Duckworth, p. 242.
203   In a 1950s radio interview, alongside her friend and former rival, Lotte Lehmann, both sopranos lamented the damage done to singing and performance practice by the airplane.
204   Conducted by Clemens Krauss.

swooping can tarnish the burnished golden tone and crystalline projection. What survives speaks to an electrifying personality and a talent for which the only comparator is Maria Callas. Klein described her work as "sheer genius," an assessment he applied to no other singer of her generation. Considering the reach of Jeritza's talent, it is surprising she made only a single feature film, *Grossfürstin Alexandra*,[205] produced in 1933, in which she stars as a Czarist-Russian wife who flees Bolshevik-persecution by becoming, an opera singer in Vienna. She performs (live) the song "*Du und Ich*,"[206] composed for her by Franz Lehár, and "*Als Sieger kehre heim*,"[207] – the latter on the stage of the Vienna Staatsoper, with the Philharmonic in the pit.

Jeritza was as beautiful as she was talent; she worked hard to maintain her appearance. In addition to a daily routine of gymnastics, swimming and mountain climbing, she was famous for eating well, abjuring cigarettes and refusing alcohol. It can be assumed that some of the near-constant smoke that followed her around the world during the 1920s, when she replaced Geraldine Farrar at the New York Met, was produced by *actual* fires. She divorced her first husband, Baron Leopold von Popper,[208] in 1934; the following year, she married a Hollywood film executive, Winfield Sheehan. They lived in distended luxury, on a Shangri-La-esque estate in Beverly Hills; the property's dining room could seat 180 guests. After Sheehan died in 1945, Jeritza married Irving Seery, an umbrella-frame manufacturer.[209] He died in 1966, at which point she relocated full-time to her East Coast home[210] and the company of her private secretary of many decades' service.[211] As for her suspected affair with Strauss, there is no evidence it was consummated. It is *extremely* difficult, regardless, not to draw inferences from Strauss' gifting of his *very* last song, "*Malven*,"[212] to the soprano. In March, 1946, he sent Jeritza the original manuscript, inscribed "*Der geliebten Maria, diese letzte Rose*."[213] Strauss did not reveal the song's existence before his death in 1949; it came to light four decades later – two years after Jeritza's passing, at the age of 94. She took the song's secret to her grave.[214]

Jeritza was the best-known of a raft of Medusas created by the Athena-like Strauss. The rivalry he generated between sopranos bordered on the exploitative. It was a feature of 19th century theatrical life that translated badly to the 20th, with its appetites for celebrity and scandal nurtured by a *Tirésean* print media of global proportions.

---

205 'Grand Duchess Alexandra.'

206 'You and I.'

207 A German translation of *Aida's "Ritorna Vincitor."* The actor playing the conductor in this scene is Johannes Riemann (1888–1959), who joined the Nazi party in the year of the film's production. As a committed supporter of Hitler, he was rewarded in 1939 with his appointment as a *Staatsschauspieler*. In May, 1944, he performed at a lavish party for the staff at Auschwitz concentration camp. Not surprisingly, Riemann was out of work for almost a decade after the end of the war.

208 The grandson of Mathilde Marchesi.

209 Jeritza and Seery helped Strauss financially after the war; in 1948, he thanked the "Primadonna of the Century" when writing that she was "the most beautiful woman in the world, noble Empress, all-powerful Princess, Mari-adne, Mari-andl – Maria Jeritza, the gracious […]."

210 200 Elwood Avenue, Newark. Jeritza fitted out the basement as a speakeasy during Prohibition.

211 Jeritza died childless.

212 'Mallow,' a species of *hibiscus*.

213 'To beloved Maria, this last rose.'

214 "*Malven*" was first performed in New York in 1985.

Jeritza's reputation as a *femme fatale* never eclipsed her talent; she nonetheless lived dangerously, causing equal measures of shock and fury when performing bareback on a horse, or dressing as a man, or barely dressing at all. Her flamboyance as an *agent érotiques* fomented hatred from some of her colleagues – most publicly Maria Olszewska,[215] a quick-tempered contralto whose irritation Jeritza delighted in pricking. During a performance of Act II of *Die Walküre* in Vienna, while Olszewska was onstage with her fiancé (appearing as Wotan), Jeritza stood in the wings with another contralto, Hermine Kittel,[216] awaiting their entry. Jeritza's conversation and laughter were audible to Olszewska, who hissed that her colleague should hold her peace. Jeritza's comments intensified in volume and by the substance of their content – which hinged on rumours that Jeritza had been intimate with Olszewska's husband, who was playing Wotan. After Olszewska's patience snapped, she marched to the wings and spat with Olympian force at the soprano – who ducked, leaving the projectile to hit Kittel in the face. The latter's reaction was hysterical, and the performance had almost to be abandoned. Olszewska was fired by the Hofoper the following morning.[217]

Despite employing ambiguous language when referring to Jeritza in her memoirs, Lotte Lehmann[218] acknowledged her genius without qualification[219] – a generous concession considering their decades-long rivalry. Lehmann was a student of Mathilde Mallinger, the creator of Eva in *Die Meistersinger* in 1868; she made her debut in the same year as Jeritza; in 1916 she joined the Vienna Hofoper, where Strauss' revision of *Ariadne* was premiered on 4 October. The role of the Composer was gifted to Marie Gutheil-Schoder, who was taken ill during rehearsals; Lehmann was called upon at the last moment as a replacement. Strauss conveyed his gratitude when inviting her to create the role of Die Färberin[220] in *Die Frau ohne Schatten*. The premiere on 10 October, 1919, was staged in Vienna to commemorate the composer's appointment as the Staatsoper's new music director; Jeritza and Lehmann were acclaimed, as was the work, but the rehearsal process was tense, with the sopranos having to be separated off-stage. In 1924, Strauss completed *Intermezzo*, a *"Bürgerliche Komödie"*[221] in which Lehmann played Christine – a character based on the composer's wife. The opera's failure was attributed to Hofmannsthal's decision not to write the libretto; it can be explained also by the (relatively) prosaic score,[222] the speech-coloured vocal parts (made terse by their syllabic notation), and the palpable smugness emanating from yet another disquisition on the composer's domestic life. *Intermezzo* contains none of the beautiful, sustained melodies (outside of the orchestral interludes) for which

---

215   12 August, 1892 – 17 May, 1969.
216   Creator of the Dryad in the 1916 version of *Ariadne auf Naxos*.
217   She was allowed back after a couple of years, but only to perform on tour, in the regions.
218   27 February, 1888 – 26 August, 1976.
219   Lehmann is generous to Jeritza in her memoirs; Jeritza's memoirs do not contain a single reference to Lehmann.
220   'The Dyer's Wife.'
221   'Bourgeois Comedy.'
222   The five *Sinfonie Zwischenspiele* ('Symphonic Interludes') are the exception; the second, *"Träumerei am Kamin,"* ('Dreaming by the fireside') is especially beautiful.

Strauss was renowned – until the final reconciliation, which reveals the Storches / Strausses at their most loving and sentimental.

Christine was Lehmann's last creation for Strauss; she turned the same year to the role with which she became associated for the rest of her life, the Marschallin. Christine is a problematic role, insofar as she is difficult to like; the need for contrast – and the joyful resolution of marital dissonance – validate the character's sharper edges, but the whole thing feels too real to be believable. Lehmann was able to model her interpretation on prolonged observations of the husband and his wife during a summer-long stay at the family's villa in Garmisch-Partenkirchen. She recalled in her memoirs how Pauline

> derived an almost perverse pleasure from proving to her husband that no amount of fame could alter her personal opinion of him as essentially nothing more but a peasant, a country yokel [...] she explained in great detail, how and why their marriage constituted a shocking *mésalliance* [...] nor was his music, as she readily explained to all who would listen, anywhere near comparable to that of Massenet.[223]

Though born only four months after Jeritza, Lehmann was significantly more "modern" in her temperament, technique and tone. Indeed, by the early 1930s she was the recognised model for the German-repertoire soprano voice, a status achieved because the instrument was almost preternaturally secure and easy in its production. It wanted in consequence for personality, which is not to suggest her singing lacked character – far from it – but her art was conscientiously unidiomatic. On record, as on stage, she is beguiling because the music survives her performance of it; the surfeit of charisma for which Jeritza was celebrated played no part in Lehmann's measured submission to the primacy of the score. Strauss did not need to defend Lehmann's singing of his music; no-one did. This equilibrium made her less exciting, even if the trade-off raised a standard for beauty as a metric in and of itself. Lehmann's tone and inflection are instantly recognisable for their warmth and richness; there is no audible passaggio, and her vibrato is modern in its presence and constancy. Her use of portamento is effortless and natural, a function of judgment and word-use that contributed much to the seamlessness of a near-perfect legato – all of it achieved in the absence of those interruptions, inflections and eccentricities for which Jeritza's wayward style was conspicuous. Her casual reliance on Elisabeth Schumann and others for a ringing B5 at the climax of the *Rosenkavalier* Trio cannot detract from the otherwise palatial splendour of her singing at its best. This can be heard on record, but there is also wonderful footage of Lehmann performing the Marschallin's Act I monologue, "*Da geht er hin*," during a masterclass in Santa Barbara in 1961.[224] It was appropriate that the 73-year-old soprano should consider her reflection, and the lines on her face, when revisiting her portrayal of a character pre-occupied with age. The pathos and dignity with which Lehmann sings "*ist doch der Lauf der Welt*,"[225] reaches

---

223   Lehmann, Lotte (1964). *Singing with Richard Strauss*. Hamish Hamilton, p. 24.
224   She sang the music an octave lower.
225   'it is the course of the world.'

beyond the limits of resignation and towards the self-possession of "*Wie macht denn das der liebe Gott? Wo ich doch immer die gleiche bin,*"[226] which she delivers clutching at her throat in anticipation of the wrinkles to come, only to collapse inwardly into self-amusement after realising that time will only affect her appearance. She will remain forever the Marschallin, whatever her years. It is a masterclass in text and song, notwithstanding the obvious limits of her voice.

Toscanini considered Lehmann to be the most complete singing actress with whom he worked; watching this glorious episode it is easy to appreciate why. In its essence, however, Lehmann's trade was beauty. She may have had a limited upper range, and some have criticised her breath-control, but there is no denying that just about every German-repertoire singer before Lehmann adhered to criteria that defied the reductionism of consensus. There had been "beautiful" voices since women first sang; it would nonetheless have been impossible to persuade any more than a handful of people at any one time, and in more than one place, of what qualified absolutely as ideal. As much is obvious from the vast differences between the singers to whom Strauss turned from 1900 – most of whom were recorded performing roles at the time of their creation. The only quality uniting Strauss' originators prior to the 1920s was discernible by its absence, insofar as none of them was possessed of a "beautiful" voice, and certainly not as it would be ideated by the work of Lotte Lehmann. The voice and performing traditions of Renée Fleming – the most feted German-repertoire lyric soprano of the 21ˢᵗ century – can be traced through Kiri Te Kanawa, Anna Tomowa-Sintow, Lucia Popp, Christa Ludwig, Gundula Janowitz, Evelyn Lear, Elisabeth Grümmer, Sena Jurinac, Lisa della Casa, Elisabeth Schwarzkopf, Eleanor Steber, Rise Stevens, Maria Reining and Viorica Ursuleac to the Rosetta Stone that is Lotte Lehmann. It's a tradition that owes nothing to the voice-culture of Wittich, Ackté, Gutheil-Schoder, or Siems – whose characteristics were formed before the onset of recording. Neither did Lehmann's art – or that of any of her successors – bind to the "extreme" characteristics of *Salome* and *Elektra*, or the works of Schoenberg and the Second Viennese School, excepting the eternal-exception of *Wozzeck.*[227]

It's well-known that singers listened routinely to their peers and rivals on record after 1910, which fostered a culture to which teachers, coaches, repetiteurs, conductors and composers yielded without complaint. They did so only because the mould was formed by a singer whose taste, discretion and voice-placement became definitive. That Lotte Lehmann was the most recorded soprano of her generation merely compounds the gravitational force of her influence between the 1920s and her retirement in 1951.[228] Her hundreds of records include a catalogue of lieder, and collaborations with every major conductor of the time, including Toscanini, de Sabata and Bruno Walter.[229] Lehmann was, of course, closely associated during her lifetime with the music of Strauss (who paid her the tribute carved into her tombstone, "*Sie hat gesungen, dass es Sterne rührte,*"[230]), and she will be forever identified

---

226   'How does the good Lord do that? Because I'm always the same.'

227   Of those named above, Jurinac, Ludwig and Lear each recorded the role of Marie.

228   Although she made her first recordings in 1914, Lehmann's discography did not gather pace until the 1920s.

229   Walter performed as Lehmann's piano accompanist on a number of occasions.

230   'Her singing moved the stars.'

with *Der Rosenkavalier*, as the first soprano to sing all three of the work's female leads. There are four recordings of her Marschallin, each of them worthy of carriage to a desert island. The first was produced as an abridged version by HMV, in September, 1933, conducted by Robert Heger, with Maria Olszewska as Octavian and Elisabeth Schumann as Sophie; the second was recorded live from the Met, on 5 February, 1938, with Kerstin Thorborg as Octavian and Susanne Fisher as Sophie, conducted by Artur Bodanzky; the third is another Met broadcast, with Risë Stevens as Octavian and Marita Farell as Sophie; the last is a recording of Act III only, from the San Francisco Opera House, towards the end of Lehmann's career, on 18 October, 1945, with Risë Stevens as Octavian and Nadine Conner as Sophie, conducted by Georges Sébastian. They are all glorious, notwithstanding some dreadful cuts and the technological limitations; they evidence her trademark nobility of style, and the depth of a portrayal honed over many performances with the composer conducting.

Lehmann was more than the Marschallin, of course; her repertoire included nearly 50 operas. She was a superb Sieglinde – in which a role she made a definitive recording for HMV, with Lauritz Melchior as Siegmund, conducted by Bruno Walter – and there is good evidence for her portrayal of Leonore from a live recording of *Fidelio* on 16 August, 1936, of Act I, conducted by Toscanini. In addition, Lehmann performed the title role in *Turandot*, and leading parts in Julius Bittner's *Die Kohlhaymerin* and *Die Musikant*, Wilhelm Kienzl's *Der Kuhreigen*, and Walter Braunfels' *Don Gil von den grünen Hosen*. She performed in the world or Viennese premieres of Pfitzner's *Palestrina*, Korngold's *Der Ring des Polykrates* and *Das Wunder der Heliane*.

The prominence of Jeritza and Lehmann as "new repertoire" singers is misleading. They were the best-known sopranos to forge reputations for contemporary music written by composers aligned with Strauss rather than Schoenberg; it is equally true that many others were famous for performing music by dead composers only. Frida Leider, for example, was born two months before Lotte Lehmann, but committed little time and enthusiasm to contemporary works. She was one of the most gifted dramatic sopranos of the 20th century, with a voice of exceptional power and sensuality that made her ideal as Salome, Elektra, the Empress, Helena and Daphne. Unusually, however, Leider didn't sing any of these roles. It was an anomaly considering the coincidental force of Leider's celebrity and Strauss' influence during the first two decades of the 20th century.

Almost as famous was Elisabeth Rethberg,[231] whose studies at the Dresden Royal Conservatory led to a contract at the Hofoper, where she made her debut on 16 June, 1915, as Arsena in *Der Zigeunerbaron*,[232] by Johann Strauss II; the title role of Sándor Barinkay was performed by Richard Tauber. Rethberg remained in Dresden until 1922, when she made her Metropolitan debut as Aida; she was loyal to the Met for 20 seasons, singing 30 roles. She achieved huge success at Covent Garden also, where she sang in 1925 and between 1934 and 1939. Rethberg created only a single role of note, Helen of Troy in *Die Ägyptische Helena* – composed by Strauss for Jeritza. It is a grossly underrated work, again in no small part because of Hofmannsthal's libretto, which is more obscurantist than normal. The role of the

---

231 *née* Lisbeth Sättler, 22 September, 1894 – 6 June, 1976.
232 'The Gypsy Baron.'

"Omniscient Seashell" – created by Helene Jung[233] – is a case in point. The end of the first act and the beginning of the second (which opens with Helena's ravishing, *Vocalise*-esque "*Zweite Brautnacht*,")[234] contain some of Strauss' most joyful music. Rethberg's instant association with Strauss did not travel with her, and the rest of her career was determined by Mozart, Verdi and Wagner – whose music forms the greater part of her discography. Rethberg's distinctive voice was coincidentally feminine and penetrating, and she is the infinitely superior artist on live recordings of *Lohengrin*, with Melchior, and *Otello*, with Giovanni Martinelli.

Elisabeth Schumann[235] created no roles for Strauss, but she was revered by the composer as Sophie, and as a performer of his songs; he certainly played for her on many occasions, on tour and in the studio. Schumann spent her first ten years at Hamburg Opera, where she was the first Albertine for the premiere of Busoni's *Die Brautwahl*[236] (a "comic-fantastic"); it was her only role-creation. She performed a number of contemporary works early in her career (Humperdinck's *Königskinder*, Max von Schillings' *Mona Lisa*, Korngold's *Der Ring des Polykrates*, Jan Brandts Buys' *Die Schneider von Schönau*,[237] and Weingartner's *Meister Andrea*), but her only notable concession to novelty during the height of her celebrity was the role of Yvonne in Krenek's *Jonny spielt auf*,[238] of which she was persuaded to give the Viennese premiere in January, 1927, by her erstwhile conductor in Hamburg, Gustav Brecher. The rest of her working life, on the stage and on record, was committed to the music of previous generations – with the exception of Strauss. Her voice was light and focussed; she made creative use of vibrato and portamento, her reliance on which was sufficiently idiosyncratic to allow for her singing to be easily identified. Her projection was exceptional, as was her diction, which made her an exceptional performer of lieder. Schumann and Strauss made a number of recordings together, the first in New York, on New Year's Eve, 1921. They were never released, and are presumed now to be lost. A further 20 minutes of recordings were made during the 1930s, before Schumann emigrated to the United States in 1938; these have been lost also. The only surviving recording is an excerpt from a performance of *Così fan tutte* at the Bavarian State Opera, on 17 August, 1932, conducted by Strauss – with Schumann singing the role of Despina. The excerpts of Schumann performing as Sophie from a 1936 performance of *Der Rosenkavalier* in Vienna (with Lotte Lehmann as the Marschallin and Jarmila Novotná[239] as Octavian) were not, as many assert, conducted by Strauss. They are actually a composite of two different performances, both directed by Hans

---

233 14 June, 1887 – 3 October, 1975. German operatic mezzo-soprano and contralto; she created two further roles for Strauss: the housekeeper in *Die schweigsame Frau*, and Gaea in *Daphne*.

234 'Second bridal night,' first performed on 12 April, 1912.

235 13 June, 1888 – 23 April, 1952.

236 'The Bridal Choice.'

237 'The tailors from Schönau.'

238 'Jonny Strikes Up.'

239 23 September, 1907 – 9 February, 1994. Bohemian soprano and actress, renowned for her work between 1940 to 1956 at the Metropolitan Opera. She was a student of Emmy Destinn, and made her debut in Prague on 28 June, 1925, as Mařenka in Smetana's *The Bartered Bride*. In 1929, she joined Otto Klemperer's Kroll Opera in Berlin, and in January, 1933, she created the female lead in Jaromir Weinberger's *Frühlingsstürme*, opposite Richard Tauber. This was the last new operetta produced in the Weimar Republic; Novotná and Tauber left Germany, and the Nazi regime, shortly after.

Knappertsbusch. Schumann's voice is best described as "pure;" indeed, it is almost weightless in its projection. She is best heard on her recording of Schubert's "*Du bist die Ruh*"[240] (accompanied by her second husband, Karl Alwin), and her 1927 recording of "*Morgen!*" conducted by Lawrance Collingwood. In 1938, she gave up her life in Germany and emigrated to the United States, unlike her colleagues Tiana Lemnitz[241] and the Konetzni sisters (Hilde[242] and Anny[243]). Many others stayed also, of course, giving voice and talent to a regime that Schumann, Lehmann and Jeritza denounced as incompatible with art.

It is often claimed that Strauss' star was in the descendent after *Die Frau ohne Schatten*; there is little evidence for this. It's true that many wanted the composer to adhere to the evolving culture of *modernismus* to which he had made such a potent contribution, but this was to misunderstand the reach of Strauss' lyric-expressive inclinations – which are common to each of his 16 operas. His instincts bound him to a vernacular he had learned at the feet of Brahms and Wagner; indeed, "voice" was no less paradigmatic for Strauss than it had been for Mozart, but pressure from the avant-garde was pulling singers in directions that compelled the taking of sides. The dramatic soprano, Else Gentner-Fischer,[244] spent most of her career at the Frankfurt Opera (1907–1935). Having started out as a soubrette, her voice grew in weight, timbre and projection, which led to her accepting lyric-dramatic roles, including the Marschallin, the Empress, Santuzza, Aida and Tosca; in her vocal maturity, she transitioned to Isolde, Brünnhilde and Kundry. Outside the mainstream, she was a devotee of new music by composers at the cutting edge; in 1912, she created the role of the Gräfin in the premiere of von Waltershausen's *Oberst Chabert*;[245] in 1918, she was the first Carlotta in Franz Schreker's *Die Gezeichneten*,[246] and in 1924 she sang Princess Leonore in Ernst Krenek's *Der Sprung über den Schatten*,[247] a satire on expressionism and psychoanalysis that employed free-atonality, jazz and popular song. In 1929 Gentner-Fischer was Emilia Marty in the German premiere of Janáček's *The Makropoulos Case*, and on 1 February, 1930, she sang the role of the Wife in Herbert Graf's premiere staging of Schoenberg's *Von heute auf morgen*.[248] Though designed as a comedy, Schoenberg's score was dodecaphonic; as the first twelve-tone opera, the music was predictably complex and incomprehensible to many of the performers and most of the audience. It was performed only once more during Schoenberg's lifetime.[249] The vocal score is brutal for any singer fed and raised on the music of Mozart, Wagner and Strauss. The Wife's first phrase, when entering with her husband, is "*Ich bin gar nicht müde. Auch möcht' ich noch nachsehn, ob das Kind schläft.*"[250] It is

240 'You are the rest and peace.'
241 26 October, 1897 – 5 February, 1994.
242 21 March, 1905 – 20 April, 1980.
243 12 February, 1902 – 6 September, 1968.
244 5 September, 1883 – 26 April, 1943.
245 'Colonel Chabert.'
246 'The Branded.'
247 'The Jump over the Shadow.'
248 'From One Day to the Next.'
249 Conducted by the composer – a few months after the premiere, for a radio broadcast in Berlin.
250 'I'm not tired at all. I would also like to see if the child is sleeping.'

scored as 16 quavers (with two quaver rests), spanning a range of less than an octave (E4 to E flat 5). Each of the first 12 notes is necessarily a different pitch; there is no repetition until the 13th note (a B flat 4, first heard as note 11 in the initial row). The challenges presented by this music to a classically-trained soprano are profound; they compel selfless vocal precision, and the coincidental denial of the lyric tradition to which Strauss and his tonally-centred peers were committed. In 1950, a year before his death, Schoenberg claimed "I have proved in my operas *Von heute auf morgen* and *Moses und Aron* that every expression and characterization can be produced with the style of free dissonance."[251] The truth of that assertion has been tested by the elapse of time. The Royal Opera, by way of example, has never staged *Von heute*, and it almost certainly never will. Peter Hall's production of the equally strenuous *Moses und Aaron* received nine performances between June, 1965, and July, 1966; it has not been played since. New York's audiences were more forgiving: Graham Vick's production was also performed on nine occasions, in 1999, but it received three further outings four years later. There have been none since 2003.

It's obvious that anyone singing such jagged, non-normative music has to adapt their training and technique to discern the communicably psychological and expressive in music that is defiantly anti-vocal. Were there any prospect, even, for the *recherché* acceptance of Schoenberg's operas then music colleges and singing contests would encourage graduates and candidates to schedule his music in competition. They don't because the benchmark for quality – and for talent as it is taught universally – isolates the Second Viennese School from those vocal traditions in homage to which the young Schoenberg composed his first *Erwartung* and the glorious *Gurre-Lieder*.[252] It is probably not a coincidence that the 'Songs of Gurre' is the only relatable work by the composer to feature parts for female voices in which any of them is named.[253] *Die glückliche Hand*, his "*Drama mit Musik*,"[254] was written under the influence of his wife's adultery, and also Otto Weininger. None of its chorus of "six women" is identified and the only character with a voice is Ein Mann. *Die glückliche Hand* can be read and heard as extravagantly misogynistic. *Erwartung* also concerns die Frau, while the two female roles in *Von heute auf morgen* are Die Frau and Die Freundin;[255] despite featuring a number of named male characters, *Moses und Aaron's* six female roles are designated only as "Young girl," "Sick woman," and "Naked Virgins" – of whom there are four. This is not the forum for dissecting Schoenberg's views of women; it can nonetheless be asserted with modest confidence that there is a de-humanising, emotionally chilling quality to his writing for nameless female characters whose voices he purposefully stripped of those elements of expressive cognition for which

251   Schoenberg, Arnold (1984). Stein, Leonard (Ed.). *Style and Idea*. Trans. by Leo Black. University of California Press, pp. 244–245.
252   He composed the work between 1900–1903, and 1910–1911; it was first performed on 23 February 1913, at the Musikverein, conducted by Franz Schreker.
253   Tove (a soprano), and the Wood-Dove (contralto). *Gurre-Lieder* was not composed for the stage – and the scoring and instrumentation (which includes 10 horns and six trumpets alone) are prohibitively vast. It is nonetheless wildly theatrical – as the Dutch National Opera set out to demonstrate in 2014 when becoming the first company to stage it, in a production by Pierre Audi.
254   'The Hand of Fate.'
255   'The Friend.'

the soprano was commonly celebrated. For singers and teachers more concerned with producing Toscas and Octavians than "women," Schoenberg's atonality was exceptional as a construction of aesthetics rather than merit.

The anomaly for the Second Viennese School was Alban Berg, whose one completed operatic masterpiece,[256] *Wozzeck*, contains some of the most beautiful and haunting music of the 20th century. The score is mostly-atonal, with hard edges and biting cruelties; as a study in psychological and political isolation it is a titanic achievement – best appreciated as a live experience in a theatre. It does not translate well to recording. The narrative is bleak, and the outcome worse still, with the opera's only soprano role, Marie, being stabbed to death for her adultery by Wozzeck, who then drowns himself in the lake into which he earlier threw the murder weapon – leaving their orphaned son standing by the water's edge. Berg and his conductor in Berlin, Erich Kleiber, knew that Marie could not be performed by a traditional conservatoire-graduate; they turned to a Danish soprano, Sigrid Johanson, of whom almost nothing is known – not even her dates of birth and death. There is no record of her performing elsewhere, and she appears not to have made any recordings. Berg was initially delighted with the premiere[257] and the cast; when Kleiber conducted the first British production at Covent Garden, on 22 January, 1952, he welcomed Johanson as his guest.[258]

Marie was not designated specifically by Berg for a *Sprechgesänger*; by the third scene of Act II, however, the writing is pure *Sprechsgesang*, which requires Marie to ascend a high C sharp, marked triple-*forte*. During the Bible-reading scene at the beginning of Act III, her recitations alternate with her sung expressions of remorse; passages identified by Berg as *Sprechgesang* are further characterised as "*gesprochen*,"[259] "*etwas gesungen*,"[260] and "*ganz gesungen*."[261] One particular phrase, "*Und weil es Niemand mehr hatt' auf der Welt*,"[262] instructs that every note be performed *sprechgesang* – except the last, "*Welt*," which is to be sung in full. As the voice-writing climbs through the *passaggio*, to a high C, Berg marks some of Marie's lines "*mit etwas Gesangstimme*."[263] The purely sung writing extends from an A3 to a C5, which can only allude to the role's technical challenges, which span the affectation of 19th century rhetorical declamation, traditional lyricism, and Wagnerian resonance. The psycho-analytical quality of *Wozzeck's* scratching beneath the surface of socially-engineered suffering represents the only truly Freudian reading of "voice" in German opera; the depths to which the music speaks when sung and performed do nothing more than hint at what is adumbrated by the orchestral score. *Wozzeck* is a harrowing, fearless commentary on

---

256   His second opera, *Lulu*, was incomplete at the time of his death.

257   On 14 December, 1925. Within an hour of the curtain coming down, Berg was in despair – fearing that the work's success indicated artistic failure. Theodor Adorno had to console the desolate composer, who read the shadows of popularity as evidence of failure.

258   The role of Marie was played by Christel Golz (8 July, 1912 – 14 November, 2008).

259   'Spoken.'

260   'Somewhat sung.'

261   'Entirely sung.'

262   'And because no one else in the world has it.'

263   'With some singing voice.'

a society disintegrating in consequence of decisions taken by officers and gentlemen. It was not meant to be "beautiful."

For their part, Strauss and Hofmannsthal were uninterested in social criticism; what proved to be their last collaboration regressed to a 19th century aesthetic, set in the 1860s – *before* the Proclamation of the German Empire on 18 January, 1871. Hofmannsthal described his libretto as being "in the Rosenkavalier style, but lighter still."[264] It was atavistic for some, repulsive for others. Life in Germany had been austere for the majority of its citizens since the early 1920s, and while things improved slightly after 1925, the country's economy collapsed in October, 1929, three months after Hofmannsthal's death at the age of 55. The ensuing world-wide depression bit hard into German manufacturing and trade. By July, 1932, around 20 per cent of the population was unemployed. In January, the following year, Adolf Hitler was appointed Chancellor of Germany by President von Hindenburg. Three months later, the Nazi government passed a swathe of anti-Semitic legislation that either limited or forbade the participation of Jewish people in German public life. On 1 July,1933, *Arabella* was premiered at the Semperoper in Dresden, conducted by Clemens Krauss, with his future wife, Viorica Ursuleac,[265] singing the title role. Born in Chernivtsi (40km inside the border of modern-day Ukraine), Ursuleac made her debut in Zagreb, as Charlotte in *Werther*, in 1922. She moved frequently throughout her career, with short appointments at the Vienna Volksoper, Frankfurt Opera, and the Vienna, Berlin and Bavarian State Operas.[266] Strauss declared her to be "*her die treueste aller Treuen*,"[267] at a time when loyalty was a hard-earned commodity in Germany. In addition to Arabella, Ursuleac created three roles for the composer: Maria in *Friedenstag*[268] (which he dedicated to Ursuleac and Krauss), the Gräfin Madeleine[269] in *Capriccio*,[270] and the title role of *Die Liebe der Danae*.[271]

Arabella is a light comedy populated by caricatures, each of whom would have been recognisable to the privileged, well-born and wealthy in 1933. Almost everyone except for Arabella and Mandryka (a baritone) is drenched in vulgarity, as cyphers

---

264 Strauss, R. and Hofmannsthal, Hugo von (1961). *A Working Friendship: The correspondence between Richard Strauss and Hugo von Hofmannsthal*. Trans. Hanns Hammelmann and Ewald Osers, Random House, p. 442.

265 26 March, 1894 – 22 October, 1985.

266 Her longest appointment (1937–44).

267 'The most faithful of all the faithful.'

268 'Freedom Day,' first performed on 24 July, 1938.

269 'The Countess.'

270 First performed on 28 October, 1942.

271 'The Love of Danae' was to have been premiered in August, 1944. Following the 20 July plot to assassinate Hitler, however, Goebbels declared "*Totaler Krieg*" ('total war') and closed every theatre within the operation of the Third Reich. This prevented any public staging, but a single dress rehearsal was allowed in Salzburg, conducted by Clemens Krauss (on 16 August, 1944), attended by Strauss and an invited audience. Because the work was not played publicly, the first performance is considered to have been given eight years later (three years after the composer's death), on 14 August 1952, at the Salzburg Festival. It was again conducted by Krauss, but the title role was passed to Annelies Kupper (21 July, 1906 – 8 December, 1987) on account of Ursuleac's age rather than her politics. She retired a year later – after recording *Capriccio* with her husband, and Hans Hotter as La Roche rather than Olivier – the role he created at the premiere. The performance has much to recommend it, but Ursuleac was some years past her best in 1953.

for the authors' dim-view of Viennese culture; not without irony, the narrative is populated by a bunch of counts, all crippled by self-delusion. Adelaide holds faith in a fortune teller, her husband Waldner trusts his "investments" in gambling, and the three young aristocrats all mis-read their entitlements, which pivot on the confounding of money as privileges of birth, feeding presumptions most would now consider sexually predatory. For all its symbolic resonance, *Arabella's* primary value is its vocal score, for which the drawn out, sensual melodies are among the most deliriously beautiful in the history of music. As a vessel for pure song, the title role may be considered the most perfect of the 20th century.[272] Strauss was said by Ursuleac to have been embarrassed by some of its melodic and harmonic affluence, the most calculated examples of which are the Act I duet, *"Aber der richtige,"*[273] the Act II duet with Mandryka, *"Sie wollen mich heiraten,"*[274] and the final scene, *"Das war sehr gut."*[275]

With *Arabella*, Strauss exceeded his own exigencies. The last 15 minutes, in particular, are impossibly luxurious, the more so for the constraints to which the drama's characters are subjected by status and gender. Arabella's music is prolonged in its suggestion; having revealed to Mandryka *"Das Glas da habe ich austrinken wollen ganz allein,"*[276] her far from subtle allusion yields to a phrase that requires little interpretation:

> [...] *und still zu Bette gehn, und nicht denken mehr an Sie und mich, und an das Ganze was da zwischen uns gewesen ist bis wieder heller Tag gekommen wäre über uns.*[277]

He set Hofmannsthal's sensual poetry to languorous music that begins leitmotifically with an A3, dropping to an E3 (*"und still"*), marked pianissimo, that falls yet further to a C sharp 3 that rises motivically to an F sharp 3 (*"Bette gehn,"*), from which the composer builds Arabella's yearning, over strings alone, using a breath-squeezing dotted minim–crotchet–semi-breve (written as a D sharp 4 – C4 – F4) for *"Sie und mich."* This becomes tumescent with *"bis wieder,"* which Strauss crowns with a burgeoning A4 for *"heller Tag"* that unfolds as three notes over as many bars, each as flamed by desire as Arabella. Pauline once asked Elisabeth Schumann "What does one do with a man who, when he begins to get sensual, starts composing?"[278] Her loss was music's gain. There is a recording of a 1942 performance of *Arabella* from the Salzburg Festival, conducted by Krauss, with Ursuleac in the title role and Trude Eipperle[279] as her sister, Zdenka. Ursuleac's singing is wondrous; her voice is warm and effortless in

---

272 The author recalls (and celebrates) the joy experienced (and shared) by his then-11-year-old daughter, Lucia, when attending a performance of *Arabella* at the New York Met in April, 2014, with Malin Byström in the title role. On leaving, Lucia exclaimed "I want to be able to sing like that."
273 'But the right one.'
274 'You want to marry me.'
275 'That was very good.'
276 'I wanted to drink that glass all by myself.'
277 '[...] and go to bed quietly and no longer think of you and me, and everything that was between us until daylight came over us again.'
278 Puritz, Gerd (1993). *Elisabeth Schumann: A Biography*. André Deutsch, p. 142.
279 27 January, 1908 – 18 October, 1997.

its production but it is thrilling also above the stave, with a brilliant, silver-metallic resonance. It is easy to appreciate why Strauss rated her so highly. Ursuleac's voice is instantly recognisable for what was then becoming an *echt* Viennese sound – rich, bright and coloured by dialectal phrasing that made ubiquitous use of portamento, even for leading notes. This "scooping" effect would be taken to its extreme by Maria Reining,[280] whose protégé, Lisa Della Casa, tempered the older singer's profligacy in her ideation of the supreme German lyric-soprano voice.

Strauss completed five operas after *Arabella*; two of them feature important roles for women: *Daphne*,[281] and *Capriccio*.[282] Both are ensemble works; indeed, *Daphne* features two of Strauss's finest roles for tenor, Apollo and Leukippos, as well as a furious, wildly inventive orchestral score that asks as much of an orchestra as do *Salome* and *Elektra*. *Daphne* was first staged seven months after the Anschluss – 341 years after the premiere of Jacopo Peri's first opera with the same name. For someone so immersed in history, and aware of his part in it,[283] Strauss' transformation of Daphne from an object of lust into a laurel carried with it a considerable amount of baggage. She sings:

> *Apollo! Bruder! Nimm … mein … Gezweige. Wind. … Wind. Spiele mit mir! Selige Vögel, Wohnet in mir … Menschen … Freunde … Nehmt mich … als Zeichen Unsterblicher Liebe…*[284]

The authors' advocacy for continuity at a time of brutal, violent change exonerated neither Strauss nor Gregor (both of whom acted as propagandists for the Third Reich); Strauss nonetheless poured his heart into Daphne's paean to immortal love, and the great spans of melody resolve in wordless rapture, as if (with rose-tinted spectacles) the world might have been enjoined through art, uncontaminated by the language of prejudice, politics and indoctrination. Strauss and the conductor in Dresden, Karl Böhm, gave the title role to Margarete Teschemacher,[285] as a late-replacement for Meta Seinemeyer,[286] who had recently died of Leukemia, at the age of 35. Teschemacher's repertoire was typically diverse, embracing Pamina (a role she sang at Covent Garden in 1931), Marguerite in *Faust*, Senta, Eva, Sieglinde, Aida, Jenůfa and Minnie in *La fanciulla del West*. The recording made in 1938 of Teschemacher performing Daphne's Transformation, with the conductor and the orchestra that gave the premiere only a few weeks earlier, is a magnificent testament to the quality of the Dresden forces during the 1930s. The timbre and sheen of Teschemacher's voice are light by later "Wagnerian" standards; it is glistening and vibrant above the stave, however, even if she ducks some of the higher notes as written. The instrument

---

280   7 August, 1903 in Vienna – 11 March, 1991

281   First performed on 2 October, 1938, conducted by the opera's dedicatee, Karl Böhm.

282   First performed on 28 October, 1942, conducted by the opera's librettist, Clemens Krauss.

283   Strauss and the librettist Joseph Gregor discussed the symmetry openly in their correspondence.

284   'Apollo! Brothers! Take... my... branches. Wind. ... wind. Play with me blessed birds, dwell in me... people... friends... Take me... as a sign Immortal love...'

285   3 March, 1903 – 19 May, 1959. She joined the Semperoper in 1934 and remained with the company until 1946.

286   5 September, 1895 – 19 August, 1929.

is youthful and feminine, consistent with Daphne's transformation into a symbol for undefiled love; some will want for more personality – after the fashion of Maria Reining, whose 1944 recording as Daphne is loved by many for its creamy tone and flamboyant, eccentric phrasing – but the plunging melodies are better served by a voice that combines with Strauss' meticulously ordered orchestra rather than soaring (and swooping) above it.

Capriccio is another ensemble opera. It is dominated by the Countess' foils, Flamand (a composer) and Olivier (a poet), who embody the philosophical conundrum first dramatized in 1786 by Antonio Salieri in his one-act opera *Prima la Musica e Poi le Parole*.[287] Strauss and Krauss' work is irritatingly clever, and all the more annoying for being genuinely funny and touching, with three-dimensional characters rubbing alongside the absurdist, Feydeauvian "Italian Singers," whose beautiful duet-pastiche "*Addio mia vita, addio,*"[288] satirises the vacuities of 18th century opera. Madeleine is also afforded her own closing scene of extravagant, timeless elegance that operated coincidentally as a personal farewell by Strauss. When asked by Clemens Krauss if he was keen to write another opera after *Capriccio*, the almost 80-year-old Strauss replied, "…it's only possible to leave one will."[289] Strauss' penultimate work for the stage should have been his last. It is a masterpiece of wit, charm and invention. As an intellectual fantasy, it provided much-needed distraction for a composer struggling to process the effects of fascism and war; the questions it asks are cultural rather than emotional or psychological; they are triggered by an allegorical love-triangle in which the players debate or symbolise the problems caused by opera's unavoidable dependence on collaboration. It dances on the metatheatrical head of a pin first pointed in *Ariadne auf Naxos* when challenging the Countess to decide between her suitors, as a metaphor for the impossible choice to be made between words and music. Many at the time regarded the closing scene, "*Wo ist mein bruder,*"[290] to be Strauss' last word for the soprano voice.[291] It is achingly sad music, tailored as a bookend to the life of the most complete master of German-language opera after Mozart and Wagner.[292] The scene is pure emotion, and laced heavily with symbolism; in tearing at the heart-strings, it does exactly what it says in the score – without answering the question asked by the Countess, "*kannst du mir raten, kannst du mir helfen den Schluss zu finden für ihre Oper?*"[293]

No-one expected Strauss to top what he had himself considered definitive. At the time of his death on 8 September, 1949, his last published works as a composer were wordless.[294] In 1950, however, his friend, Ernst Roth, collated his final songs,

---

287 'First the music and then the words.'

288 'Farewell, my life, farewell.'

289 Krause, Ernst (1969). *Richard Strauss: The Man and His Work*. Crescendo Publishing Company, p. 434.

290 'Where is my brother?'

291 *Danae's* closing scene is extraordinarily lovely also, but it has never gained anything like the popularity of *Capriccio*.

292 Strauss liked to repeat von Bülow's gag that he was to be "Richard the Third," since Wagner could have no successor.

293 'Can you advise me, can you help me find the ending for her opera?'

294 Strauss' final works before his "Last" songs primarily instrumental, including the Horn Concerto No. 2, *Metamorphosen*, the Concerto for Oboe, and his Duet Concertino for clarinet and bassoon.

composed in 1948 for soprano and orchestra; they were published as the "*Vier letzte Lieder*,"[295] "*Frühling*"[296], "*September*," "*Beim Schlafengehen*,"[297] and "*Im Abendrot*."[298] It would have surprised Strauss to know that his "last" four compositions would become his most popular, adored around the world for their beauty and relative introversion. The premiere was given at the Royal Albert Hall in London, on 22 May, 1950, by the Philharmonia Orchestra, conducted by Wilhelm Furtwängler. At Strauss' request, the songs were sung by Kirsten Flagstad. The performance was recorded – less than two years after the release of the first long-playing record.[299] Sadly, the acetate discs were damaged before their first transfer; despite a number of restorations, what survives is a disappointing record of one of the last internationally celebrated premieres in the history of art music.

His legacy was well-recognised at the time, and it has become more important with each passing decade. Young women drawn to the idea of singing professionally find more with which to engage in Strauss' music than that of any other composer, with the exception of Mozart; because so much of Strauss' music thrives in repertoire, the odds are good that someone hearing a song or a scene from one of his operas, will be inspired to take up music and formal vocal studies.

Strauss is said to have observed that "the human voice is the most beautiful in-strument of all, but the most difficult to play," and the best of his music will always be difficult for anyone aspiring to do justice to the flood of melody and sentiment that poured out of him for more than seven decades. On the other hand, his writing for the soprano voice is uniquely rewarding of talent, and many have joined with Kiri Te Kanawa when she asserted that "his music fits me like a glove." Strauss was born into an age dominated by Wagner (for whom the music *and* the text were sacrosanct), when sopranos were otherwise encouraged to improvise and extemporise as performers. Strauss' acceptance of Jeritza's extravagance was a compromise, and exceptional for the most part. In every other regard, his freakish pointillism em-braced detail and necessitated discipline, an admixture that precluded the exercise of a singer's free will by actively preventing it. His operatic scores are intransigent in their impulse and momentum, so that anyone thinking to exercise a preference or an idiosyncrasy is doomed to be lost or left behind. This cartographic ruthlessness fos-tered a paradoxical collision between the unstoppable force of female empowerment and the immovable object of Strauss' notation. A free-thinking soprano was better off indulging her instincts with the music of Rossini than Strauss, whose absolute mastery of every function and aspect of a woman's sound, her character and, in many cases, her appearance compelled the subjugation of her own identity to that of the character she was playing.

In 1920, the British music critic, Neville Cardus, wrote a facetious article about Jenny Lind, in which he observed that "in this year of our Richard Strauss," Lind would "strike us rather as a creature much too bright and good for human nature's

295 'Four Last Songs.' There is some debate as to the order in which they should be performed.
296 'Spring.'
297 'When falling asleep.'
298 'At Sunset.'
299 Columbia Records released the first long-playing microgroove record, spinning at 33 1/3 revolutions per minute and holding about 23 minutes each side, in June, 1948.

daily food."[300] He drew an unfavourable comparison between Lind's "sexless purity" and Salome, that "beautiful animal of a woman."[301] He did so not to condemn Strauss, but to bemoan the passing of a time when women were *objects d'art*, required to do little more than be – and sound – pretty. The revelation afforded by the psycho-analytical construction of undiscovered truths no more interested Cardus than it did the sensualist Strauss, for whom women were ultimately instruments on whom he had by necessity to rely. His commitment to a sound-world that apostrophised beauty for its own sake survived the horrors of the Second World War – and flourished after it. Posterity will have ample opportunity to appreciate how the voice of the modern soprano was created by Strauss, and the extent to which he continues to define it.

---

300 Tunbridge, Laura (2013). "Frieda Hempel and the Historical Imagination." *Journal of the American Musicological Society*, Vol. 66, No. 2, p. 460.
301 *Ibid.*

Chapter Seventeen

Corpus Delecti

The phrase "it ain't over till the fat lady sings" is said by the Library of Congress to have been coined in 1978 by a sports writer, Dan Cook,[1] after his town's basketball team managed to secure a slight advantage during a championship game, shortly before the end of the fourth quarter. During one of their worst seasons, in 1988, the Baltimore Orioles placed posters around the city showing an immense soprano wearing a Viking helmet and carrying a spear, with the attendant slogan, "She ain't sung yet." Others claim the words date to propaganda films broadcast in the United States during WWII, in which Americans were portrayed to succeed in the direst of circumstances. At the end of each picture, a statuesque contralto, Kate Smith,[2] would perform Irving Berlin's song "God Bless America." As audiences watched US troops confronting situations from which there appeared no escape, younger viewers would exclaim, "It ain't over till the fat lady sings!" It has been traced also to the use of steam-whistles as a means of communicating a ship's readiness when preparing to leave port; as a boiler (known as a "fat lady") reached its working pressure, a whistle would be sounded to summon a crew for departure.[3] The actual origins of the phrase most likely date back to a Southern US aphorism, "as long as the organ is playing, church isn't out."[4] The allegorical pivot from a congregation to a soloist was brought about by the popularity of opera – in which it was routine from the 1830s for commodious women to perform a work's final scene. That tradition was instituted by Rossini; it reached its apogee with Richard Wagner, whose *Tristan* and *Götterdämmerung* are both rounded by a solo soprano.[5] Anyone leaving either opera ten minutes early is certain to miss their greatest scenes, so the phrase was a point of reference from before the invention of basketball.[6]

As to the identity of "the fat lady," it's likely that whoever first drew upon her as a metaphor was thinking of Brünnhilde, as imagined by Warner Brothers in 1957,

---

1 It is attributed also to the sports commentators, Dan Kirk, Ralph Carpenter, and Lee Arthur, and the coach, Dick Motta – all during the 1970s.
2 1 May, 1907 – 17 June, 1986.
3 This reasoning presupposes a surfeit of perfect pitch among the steam-ship sailing community.
4 17 October, 1872, in *The Daily Picayune*, a New Orleans' paper.
5 At least until the 20th century. The Metropolitan Opera was the first in the USA to admit women (all of them harpists) to the Musicians Union – in 1903. The issue of gender remained problematic into the 1980s. In September, 1982, Herbert von Karajan, hired the clarinettist, Sabine Meyer, to join the Berlin Philharmonic. The rest of the orchestra, all of them male, voted against Meyer's appointment – 73 to 4. The official reason given was the incongruity of Meyer's tone; like everyone else, Karajan knew the real reason to be Meyer's gender.
6 1891. It didn't predate baseball, however – which originated in 1839.

rather than by Johann Füssli in 1807, or Árpád Basch in 1900, or Arthur Rackham in 1910. Cook was 21 in 1957, when "What's Opera, Doc?" was first released in cinemas across the United States. The 7-minute "Merrie Melodies" short, directed by Chuck Jones, was a popular triumph,[7] despite appearing only a decade after the conclusion of the Nuremberg trials. Wagner's revival in the United States was much advanced in January and February, 1951, by Fritz Stiedry's legendary *Ring* cycle at the New York Met (starring Kirsten Flagstad and Helen Traubel in the shared role of Brünnhilde), and in August of the same year, Wagner's grandson, Wieland, re-opened the Bayreuth Festival with a revisionist, de-naturalised *Ring*, conducted by Hans Knappertsbusch and Herbert von Karajan. Jones' overall design of the cartoon is, in many ways, a tribute to Wieland's cleaning of the stables, using lighting, shadow-play and distorted perspectives in place of Bayreuth's pre-war reliance on naturalism. The studio nonetheless adhered to tradition for the best of the cartoon's many gags, when Bugs Bunny enters (as the set-up) wearing the Viking helmet and braided blonde wig worn traditionally by Brünnhilde and her Valkyrie sisters – without undergoing any change in body-shape or proportion. Bugs is drawn *au naturelle*, therefore, in defiance of the Wagnerian trope that sopranos were obese by necessity. The gag's closure is achieved by Brünnhilde's horse, Grane, who appears as the "fat lady," distended and inflated after the fashion of John Boultbee's 1802 painting of The Durham Ox.

"What's Opera, Doc?" drew for its imagery and music on a previous Warner production, Friz Freleng's 1945 cartoon, "Herr Meets Hare"[8] (also starring Buggs Bunny), as well as the *Nibelungen*; the score makes only a single reference to the *Ring*, however.[9] The rest of the cartoon's music is borrowed from the Overture from *Der fliegende Holländer* (the opening storm), the "Bacchanal" from *Tannhäuser* (Elmer and Bugs' ballet scene), and the Overture and "Pilgrims' Chorus" from *Tannhäuser* (for "O Bwünnhilde, you so wuvwy," "Return my love," and the closing scene).

The identification of Brünnhilde as the "fat lady" can be attributed to the stereotypical body-shape of most of the women who sang in the first *Ring* – all of whom were photographed in costume. There isn't a "slim" figure among them. The first sopranos to sing the roles of Isolde and Kundry were generously proportioned also, although Kundry does not, of course, bring the curtain down on *Parsifal*. Of the dozens of sopranos to sing Brünnhilde on the approximately 90 live and studio recordings of *Götterdämmerung* produced between 1928[10] and 2000, only ten were not well-upholstered at the time of recording.[11]

Successive generations of composers and opera producers have navigated the thorny issue of image and representation by treating singers as instruments – a habit for which Kirsten Flagstad was remembered alongside Lauritz Melchior at Covent

---

7   In 1992, the Library of Congress categorised the cartoon as "culturally, historically or aesthetically significant." It has been preserved in consequence at the National Film Registry, the first cartoon short to be so honoured.

8   The debate over Bugs Bunny's actual species (*i.e.*, rabbit or hare) continues to be a focus for a surprising wealth of debate.

9   The horn call from *Siegfried*," for Bugs-Brünnhilde's "O mighty warrior of great fighting stock."

10   The first, conducted by Leo Blech, was recorded at the Berlin Staatsoper.

11   Nanny Larsen-Todsen, Gertrude Kappel, Marta Fuchs, Martha Mödl, Amy Shuard, Helga Dernesch, Ludmilla Dvořáková, Berit Lindholm, Roberta Knie, Jeannine Altmeyer, and Susan Owen.

Garden, where they were expected to do little more than follow "their" spotlight to wherever an "X" was marked on the stage. The size and scale of voices during the 1930s and '40s increased dramatically to account for changes in the sound of orchestras internationally. The standardisation of pitch led to the regulation of instrument design, which necessitated ever-greater resonance from singers.[12] Particularly in the United States, where orchestras leaned predictably towards a preference for volume over texture, manufacturers were encouraged to make instruments that served the needs of youth-driven brass and wind-bands trained to perform in the open, from whose numbers the rank and file drew most of their players. The inclination towards ear-splitting force increased the bore-size of trumpets, trombones and tubas which provoked an arms war with every other instrument – even French horns. Before the end of the 1950s, the back row of an orchestra in Europe, Russia and America began to resemble Le Centre Pompidou. In France, where wooden flutes were essential to the granularity of the "French sound," manufacturers conceded the alleged virtue of amplitude and opted for metal. Anyone interested in knowing how completely different an orchestra sounded in Paris during the 1920s should listen to Stravinsky's 1929 recording of *Le sacre du printemps*.[13] The Introduction, written primarily for wind and brass, is made intense and strange by the instruments' distinctive, peppery voices; textures lost to the ruthless brilliance of a 21st century orchestra, in which a horn can be difficult to distinguish from a bassoon, are revealed through the tumbling, disjointed inflection of voices made remarkable by their divergent personalities. As the rest of the orchestra enters the fray, gut strings and narrow-bore brass add to the pungency of exclusively wooden wind. Even the timpani are small and tight, better suited to a Falabella than a Clydesdale. Equally revelatory is the recording made in Paris four years later of Stravinsky's Octet, performed by a group of players led by the flautist Marcel Moyse. The playing is alien in its bare tone and phrasing; none of the performers uses vibrato, and the voicing would now be considered spartan – or better suited to a period-performance of a Brandenburg Concerto.[14]

The relative calm and cohesion of the French sound (until the 1950s at least) ensured that sung voices did not need to force their tone or breathing. The changes forced by the modern orchestra were consolidated by the LP. Recordings could now be made in concert venues and opera houses, as well as churches, town halls, schools and other buildings benefitting from natural acoustics. The modernised process allowed conductors and performers to hear themselves – and each other – as if in live performance. Tape-technology, and the process of editing, ensured that the recording of a work lasting two and a half hours in a theatre could occupy an orchestra and a company of singers over many days; the scheduling of "sessions" allowed singers to marshal their resources by throwing them to the wind. When Maria Callas recorded

---

12   For a more detailed consideration of the antecedent changes in theatre design and scale, see Boyden, Matthew (2021). *The Tenor: A Cultural History*. Ragueneau Press.

13   'The Rite of Spring.' Recorded with the Orchestre des Concerts Straram. Also revealing is the very fine 1932 recording of Debussy's *La mer* – the first – with the Société des Concerts du Conservatoire, conducted by Piero Coppola.

14   Stravinsky wrote a lot of nonsense about how to perform his music. He claimed to want the Octet to be "played as written" and "not interpreted." His own performances of the work demonstrate the extent to which he was incapable of adhering to his own diktat.

Bellini's *Norma* in 1954, for EMI – in the Cinema Metropol, Milan – the performance was taped over two very long days (23 April and 3 May). The cast was encouraged to sing their solos and ensembles piecemeal; selected passages were isolated and repeated on numerous occasions – to enable the creation of a patchwork of "takes" which a producer would later stitch together, in unspoken homage to Mary Shelley's *Frankenstein*. LPs were, polished fantasies that came as close to representing an ideal as could be achieved, but it came at a cost when transforming opera into oratorio. The sound of a work came to occlude its staging, as well as the appearance of its performers. The millions who could not attend (or afford a ticket to) an opera house could now revel in idealised impressions that rewarded repeated listening. Illusion negated reality as the excitement and danger of a once-exclusively theatrical experience was lost to the sanctity of perceived-perfection. Sonority became a shorthand for talent, of which not everyone was appreciative. Edward W. Said spoke for many in 1991 when criticising the Metropolitan Opera for having "encouraged the idea that opera is about overweight and disturbed people who sing unintelligibly and loudly."[15] The reading of volume as value proved to be a narcotic for singers incapable of the subtleties of expression and articulation that once accounted for the quintessence of sung art. The acoustic coercion did not end with the works of Wagner, Puccini and Strauss, of course. In the absence of a non-proliferation agreement, the music of every composer not requiring sonority was affected by the distribution of roles within companies benefitting from a limited number of voices. Before the stagione system was overtaken by routine international aviation, singers attached to an opera house were expected to perform a wealth of music for which their voices were fundamentally unsuited by definition.

For example, the American mezzo, Edyth Walker,[16] made her debut as a concert singer at the Gewandhaus in 1892; her operatic debut two years later was as Fidès in Meyerbeer's *Le prophète* (in German) at the Berlin Hofoper. In 1895, she moved to Vienna, where she was the company's leading mezzo. Walker created the role of Magdalena in the first Viennese performance of Kienzl's *Der Evangelimann*; she was also acclaimed for her performances as Amneris in *Aida* – in which role she made her British debut in January, 1900. Later the same year she began to take on Wagner, singing Erda, Fricka, Ortrud and Waltraute. On 17 February, 1901, she was chosen by Mahler as one of the soloists for the premiere of *Das klagende Lied*, alongside Elise Elizza[17] and Anna Bahr-von Mildenburg.[18] The former began her professional life as a soubrette, performing operetta at the Carl Theater in Vienna. After receiving lessons from Amalie Materna she was engaged in 1895 in Vienna, where her repertoire included Donna Elvira, Papagena, Agathe, Norma, Inez in *L'Africaine*, Venus, Brünnhilde, Woglinde, Gretel, Aida, Nedda and Tosca. Her recording of "*Libiamo*" from *La Traviata*, and her German-language version of "*Vissi d'arte*,"[19] evidence a

---

15   Said, Edward W. (1991). *Musical Elaborations.* Vintage, p. 59.

16   27 March, 1867 – 19 February, 1950.

17   *née* Elisabeth Lastgroschen, 6 January, 1870 – 3 June, 1926. She joined her husband's name in 1909.

18   29 November, 1872 – 27 January, 1947.

19   Sung as "*Nur der Schönheit weiht' ich mein Leben.*"

large, powerful voice, steered with laudable dynamic control – a talent on which she must have depended frantically when singing Mozart.

Edyth Walker's coincident recording of Handel's "*Ombra mai fu*," reveals no such skill; her plummy, vibrato-less tone speaks to a voice of enormous amplitude and absent expression – Wagnerian in scale, but ghostly and doleful. After falling out with Mahler, Walker returned to the USA and three seasons at the Metropolitan.[20] Having returned to Germany, and a contract at the Hamburg opera, she triumphed as the city's first *Elektra* – which she created in London for Beecham in 1910. In New York, Walker sang roles in *Lucrezia Borgia*, *La favorita*, *Faust* and *Die Fledermaus* – as well as Erda, Ortrud, Fricka, and Brangäne. In Hamburg, she appeared as Isolde, Kundry, Salome – and Donna Anna. Walker's near-exact contemporary, Anna Bahr von Mildenburg, was typical also of the shift towards ubiquity and amplitude. Erwin Stein, a writer on music (and a close friend of Schoenberg's), recalled of Mildenburg's voice that it was

> one of the biggest I have met, but with her this was not the main point, though it gave her an enormous range of expression. Her piano yielded as much variety of tone as her forte, and she could colour or swell the notes at will. Yet whatever her voice was capable of doing, it served the dramatic expression of the music. For she was not only a singer and a fine musician, but – even more important with her – a great tragic actress. Her appearance and movements had the same grandeur of style as her singing. Among the many parts I heard her sing, Isolde was the most outstanding. True, the very top was not her best register and the Cs in the second act caused her discomfort. That was the only flaw. The scope of the part was just the right one for her personality and I have experienced no other singer who could as movingly convey Isolde's tragic figure and the wide range of her conflicting emotions – her love and hate, gloom and rage, tenderness and spite, passion and despair, jubilation and sorrow. Yet the only remaining memento of Mildenburg's voice is a recording two and half minutes long of (of all things) the recitative to the aria "*Ozean, Du Ungeheuer!*" from Weber's *Oberon* made in 1904, and of which only three copies are known to exist.[21]

This solitary recording is a document of immense historical significance.[22] The voice is resplendent, declamatory and redolent of what might be considered the "grand" style. Mildenburg was Mahler's favourite soprano, and his preferred Isolde; it is fascinating, therefore, to hear something of what the conductor considered to be his ideal. The clarity of attack and grandiosity of tone are knowing and artificial; the ill-disposed would dismiss her singing as boiled ham. Others will appreciate the freedom she

---

20   Walker made her House debut on 30 November, 1903, as Amneris – alongside a newly-arrived tenor, Enrico Caruso.

21   Stein, Erwin (1965). "Mahler and the Vienna Opera", in *The Opera Bedside Book*, Ed. Harold Rosenthal. Victor Gollancz, pp. 296.

22   See, generally, Kuner, Christopher (2011). "The recording(s) of Anna Bahr-Mildenburg." *The Record Collector*, Vol. 56 (4), pp. 290–302.

enjoys (and which her pianist allows), as well as the powerful chest registers support-ing the contemporary appreciation of her voice for its thrilling size. The closing B flat 4 that ends the take, for the line "*Stellst Du ein Schreckbild dar*,"[23] is neither appro-priate nor welcome, but it is volcanic – sufficient, in fact, to affect the acoustics of the deadened room in which the recording was made. Having studied with Cosima Wagner and Hans Richter, as well as Mahler, Mildenburg's status as the Brünnhilde of her generation was absolute at Bayreuth, where she reigned without rival until 1914. Her range enabled her to sing Isolde, Elizabeth in *Tannhäuser* at Covent Garden, in 1906; four years later she created the role of Klytemnestra in London's first *Elektra*.[24] In addition, she made frequent appearances in *Fidelio*, *Norma*, *Don Giovanni* and *Die Zauberflöte*. In the shadow of her size and stature, it stretches credulity that Cosima Wagner's favourite Isolde and Brünnhilde was appreciated in equivalence as Pamina. Mildenburg's husband, Hermann Bahr, was not a large man, but the photographs taken of them together during the prime of her career appear always to show her in the foreground. She lost a considerable amount of weight after retiring from singing, but at her best – and most impressive – Mildenburg was at her largest.

With phrasing and voice-placement subsumed to the brutalism of raw power, fat proved to be a feminist issue decades before the publication of Susie Orbach's landmark book in 1978. The challenge presented by Wagner, the *veristi* and Strauss was, of course, fundamental to the re-calibration of a woman's appearance when performing as a soprano. Jenny Lind and Adelina Patti both looked the part, but they were tiny, and neither could have hoped to sing (or be audible as) Isolde. *Salome* and *Elektra* contributed to the debate by encouraging dramatic sopranos to perceive of amplitude as a primary virtue, in pursuit of which physical weight was considered an asset. The correlation between size and volume has enjoined researchers for more than a century; there are hundreds of journal articles and papers addressing the effect (if any) of weight on tone and amplitude. The starting point is mechanical. A soprano needs to be audible across a greater range of notes than any other – spanning three octaves, C3 to C6. This requires a powerful diaphragm to enable projection above an orchestra in an opera house. It doesn't necessitate a large chest cavity, at least not as a condition precedent, but it will assist any singer able to meet the other tests for a so-prano with a "big" voice, namely a "good pair of lungs" and a well-trained diaphragm as mechanisms for managing breath control and voice placement. This is true for men as well as women – but no-one has ever observed "it ain't over till the fat man sings."[25]

The diaphragm is a large muscle that stretches across the base of the rib-cage; it separates the lower organs from the heart and the lungs and, during routine breath-ing, it flexes naturally to pass air into and out of the lungs. Teachers demanding that a student "sings from the diaphragm" are asking that the diaphragm be flattened more

---

23   'Are you panting a picture of horror?'
24   It must have been something to hear Walker as Elektra, Mildenburg as Klytemnestra and an already famous Salome, Frances Rose (21 June, 1875 – 30 April, 1956), as Chrysothemis. All three singers were known for their glass-threatening plangency, and with Beecham at his most energetic the *stucco* must have threatened during the duet to come *unstucco'd*.
25   While many tenors (and a good many baritones and basses), have been obese, the only well-known male opera singer to pack on the pounds and continue working to the best of his abilities was Luciano Pavarotti (known affectionately as "Fat Lucy").

than usual during routine respiration; maintaining that position enables a singer to preserve and control the release of air as it passes through the vocal cords. A flattened diaphragm ensures a measured supply of air, therefore, with which a singer is able to support and conserve its release when placing it properly in the mouth. The finest singers have always made their business seem easy, because they are able to confine the physical process of phonation to the diaphragm, and not (as most assume) the throat and lungs. A well-trained soprano can perform for hours without apparent effort since, like a swan, their grace above the water-line is a construction of their investments below it. That doesn't mean a singer won't suffer as Norma or Isolde – or, for that matter, as Donna Anna or Adina. Rather, the muscles in and around the base of their rib-cage will tire because it is those muscles that support the voice. Sopranos not expected (or required) to perform in a corset have often taken to wearing one regardless because strapping the abdomen provides additional support for anyone needing it.[26] By analogy, an air-filled party balloon will produce a louder noise when it is released slowly (or popped) than will a balloon that has been half-inflated. Air does not create a stentorian sound, in and of itself; it is the pressure behind it that generates tone and amplitude. At its simplest, therefore, a singer with a more than normal amount of fat surrounding her ribs and abdomen will gain, as an operation of physics, a natural (and effortless) layer of additional support. A singer lacking in muscle-tone will have more to gain from assistance – whether from the accumulation of fat or by the use of a corset.

Additional theories suggest that an increase in the amount of fatty tissue surrounding the larynx will increase its capacity to generate resonance. This would be easier to accept if there was any consistency in the effect achieved by particular amounts of tissue; moreover, it's impossible for a singer to produce fatty tissue around the larynx without generating it everywhere else. Another theory holds that the physical act of performing as an opera singer changes the body over time, especially the thoracic wall, and also from the size and capacity of the intercostal musculature extending from the lateral border of the costal grooves to the superior margins of the ribs below.[27] It has been suggested that years of singing can cause a soprano to develop a larger frame, much like longbow-archers in the 15th century, whose physiology was changed by the intense and repeated effort required to string a bow and draw an arrow.

Of course, some women simply eat too much and exercise too little – a habit easily formed and difficult to break for sopranos used to post-theatre dinners at top-end restaurants serving rich food and delicious wine, all of it paid for by devoted friends, admirers, colleagues, managers, patrons, sponsors and promoters. The rush of live performance invariably makes a bad situation worse because singers experience an influx of adrenaline during and immediately after appearing on stage. While body-chemistry enhances the acuity of a performer's abilities, contracting blood

---

26 Many male singers have worn corsets also. There is more than one photograph of Lauritz Melchior being laced up by his dresser.

27 Thorpe, C. William, Cala, Stephen J., Chapman, Janice, and Davis, Pamela J. (2001). "The Voice Foundation Patterns of Breath Support in Projection of the Singing Voice." *Journal of Voice*. Vol. 15, No. 1, pp. 86–104. See also Foulds-Elliott, S. D., Thorpe, C. William, Cala, Stephen J., and Davis, Pamela J. (2000). "Respiratory function in operatic singing: effects of emotional connection." *Logopedics Phoniatrics Vocology*, 25 (4), pp. 151–168.

vessels and directing oxygen to major muscle groups – primarily the heart – the attendant efflux of cortisol causes an increase in appetite. This survives in tandem with the effects of adrenaline for at least an hour after a curtain has fallen – but the same is true for anyone performing on a stage, irrespective of the discipline and context. It is meaningful, therefore, that the inclination to "excuse" or validate weight gain among singers has not translated to other areas of performance. There are, for example *very* few working instrumentalists with a non-normative body shape since weight-gain affects digital dexterity and accuracy. Obvious exceptions among pianists include Arcadi Volodos, Yefim Bronfman, Emanuel Ax, and Grigory Sokolov;[28] there are currently no overweight contemporary conductors and instrumentalists with careers of note, although the past masters Ignaz Schuppanzigh,[29] Eugène Ysaÿe, David Oistrakh, Michael Rabin, Isaac Stern and Itzhak Perlman were all medically obese, at one time or another. The demarcation of singers on account of their size cannot be explained solely by the misconception that fat is a value to assist the mechanics of singing. For the poet, Wayne Koestenbaum, the spectacle of the monstrous body was codified as a form of social contract, entered into because singers

> are hungry creatures – hungry for fame, money, glamour, artistic satisfaction [because] we want to consume the singer; we go to the opera to eat voice, to eat trills and cavatinas and the failed or successful […]. Farrar spoke of the public's cannibalistic urge to see a singer served to it already overcooked by hard work, a talent 'fried brown and curled at the edges.'[30]

With meat as metaphor, the body of a singer has always been constituent to the primacy of appearance as performance. John Waters' muse, Divine[31] – better known to younger audiences through his caricature as Ursula the Sea Witch in Disney's 1989 film, *The Little Mermaid*[32] – ideated the drag-queen-reinvention of fat as formula. It did so because the majority of operatic drag acts have neither the training nor the requirement to excel vocally when on stage. Montserrat Caballé's adoption as a gay-icon after her pairing with the terminally-ill Freddie Mercury in 1987 owed little to her achievements during the 1960s and '70s; by the time of "Barcelona's" release, she was a shadow of her former self – at least vocally. The juxtaposition of the wasting

---

28 Daniel Barenboim has gained weight since 2000, although he was never especially slim to begin with.

29 Schuppanzigh was Beethoven's violin teacher before he led the Quartet that premiered many of his finest works. As was typical of the composer, they fell out often. After arguing in 1801, Beethoven composed a short choral piece entitled "*Lob auf den Dicken.*" ('In Praise of the Fat One,'), WoO 100: "*Schuppanzigh ist ein Lump. Wer kennt ihn nicht, den dicken Sauermagen, den aufgeblasnen Eselskopf? O Lump Schuppanzigh, o Esel Schuppanzigh, wir stimmen alle ein, du bist der größte Esel, o Esel, hi hi ha.*" (Schuppanzigh is a scoundrel. Who doesn't know him, the fat sour-belly, the conceited ass's head? Oh scoundrel Schuppanzigh, Oh donkey Schuppanzigh, We all agree that you are the biggest ass, Oh ass, ha ha.').

30 Koestenbaum, Wayne (1994). *The Queen's Throat: Opera, Homosexuality, and the Mystery of Desire.* Penguin, p. 101.

31 *née* Harris Glenn Milstead, 19 October, 1945 – 7 March, 1988.

32 The role was played in the live remake (2023) by Melissa McCarthy – a loss of a chance to have a drag act irritate Ron DeSantis and his acolytes in the Disney State.

pop-star and the expanded diva made for perfect copy – even if the media's tired reliance on the tread-less duality of the word "consumption"[33] failed to register how few operatic heroines actually die from tuberculosis.[34]

Whatever the cause of (or benefit gained from) fat by a soprano, it would be facile and dishonest to deny the prevalence of larger body-shapes among the general community of sopranos since the first performance of *Tristan* in 1865. Whether that matters is in the eye of the beholder – a truism that extends on reflection to the use of mirrored surfaces; it is also a question of theatrical and dramatic utility. The well-worn detraction that a soprano might have "the perfect voice in the wrong body," has collided in recent years with the monstrous regiment of "wokeness" and inclusivity. The allegedly culture-ending consequences of good manners and sensitivity are trivial, however, where the practical effects of obesity cause to limit or prohibit a singer from doing their job as a composer imagined it. Mildenburg's book on how to act Wagner's operas emphasises the extent to which gesture – and the use of the body by a singing-actor – was valuable for patrons in occupation of the cheaper seats. Whatever might be heard at the back of the Festspielhaus in Bayreuth does not equate to what can reasonably be seen at a distance of 114 feet.[35] That said, the change in the feelings experienced by the lovers during Act II of *Tristan und Isolde* should not be left to the effect of sound alone. The physical movements and facial expressions of the tenor and the soprano playing these roles are, in theory at least, no less expressive than those of any other actor performing without the advantage of music. It is *almost* unheard of for a large actress to perform a major character in a play by Shakespeare; some may consider this to be rank prejudice and body-fascistic; others may conclude that the movie, makeup and fashion industry's un-wavering devotion to imagined body-perfection is a worse violation still. What cannot realistically be argued is the effect and consequence of the movement of a stage actor's facial muscles, and their eyes in particular – all of which are curtailed if the facial musculature is lost to fat.

Another essential feature of an actor's process is eliminated if they are prevented from moving as directed, or in accordance with the essential narrative. The later filmed works of Steven Seagal have been a source of considerable mirth for followers of his oeuvre. As the years have passed, so too have the notches on his belt; Seagal's weight ballooned to a point where he was limited to filming fight scenes sitting down. He took to using body doubles for shots of his characters having to run, or climb, or do anything more strenuous than walking.[36] The loss of the *vérité* that characterised his early work – considered by Seagal to be the finest in the genre – meant that what

---

33 This duality operated in equivalence in French (as "*consommation*"), Italian ("*consumo*") and Spanish (as "*consume*").

34 There are only three of note: Mimi in *La bohème*, Violetta in *La Traviata*, and Antonia in *Les contes d'Hoffmann*.

35 The auditorium of the Festspielhaus is a quadrangle, 35 metres by 35 meters. The fan-shaped seating-arrangement limited the original capacity to 1345 seats in the auditorium proper, with an additional 300 places in two galleries. At its maximum capacity, the Festspielhaus seats 1787 spectators – uncomfortably.

36 Suggestions that his productions – most of which originated in Eastern Europe – are nothing more than vehicles for money laundering are presumably not warranted, and likely to be staunchly denied, regardless.

was once unbelievable cascaded into the preposterous. In the theatre, an actress being cast as Cordelia has to be the "right weight," not because Shakespeare cannot be performed by a larger actress but because the enfeebled Lear has to walk on stage in Act V, Scene 3, carrying her dead body. On an operatic stage, gravity is with Tosca when she jumps to her death from the battlements of the Castel Sant'Angelo; it is less accommodating should a singer be required to climb a scaffold to join her lover Cavaradossi as he paints "her" portrait. Salome asks a lot of a soprano if she wants to seduce an audience as well as Herod; there are otherwise few operas to compare to Samuel Beckett's *Not I*,[37] a monologue, written in 1972, in which a spotlight fixes on an actress' mouth, and nothing more, eight feet above the stage. There are few opportunities for sopranos to do nothing, unless they are singing from the wings as a (wood) bird. While it would be wrong for a performer's size to preclude her from any role falling naturally within her *fach* and ability – at least as a function of policy – the mutation of suspended disbelief as "poetic faith"[38] obliges singers, directors and composers to concede dramatic truth as a composition of lies, each told with sufficient conviction to persuade an audience that whatever is being presented on stage is credible. The voices of the English sopranos Rita Hunter and Jane Eaglen both struck the back of an auditorium like a lightning bolt as Sieglinde, but no-one outside the *adipophiliac*[39] community was likely to subscribe to Siegmund's lust for either of them. That is not to judge them for their weight; it is to hold opera to account for the burden of what is ultimately a narrative-driven art-form – one in which the work, the performers and the staging are expected to compel an audience to relate to the events being presented on stage. Conversely, Suzanne McNaughton's success as Handel's Venus in Covent Garden's 2007 production of *Orlando* was plainly influenced by her appearance, which was broadly consistent with the classical representation of the goddess of love, beauty and desire. Was popular opinion influenced by her willingness to expose her breasts? Yes, it was. Is the judging of McNaughton's breasts controversial? It shouldn't be, since she chose to expose herself as she did; to ignore McNaughton's beauty would risk impoliteness, at the very least. Moreover, her decision to make a virtue of her decolletage *must* have featured in her characterisation as Venus and so warrants commentary in consequence. It would have been a different matter had she done the same as Mimi in Act I of *La bohème*.

The soprano cast as Isolde by Bayreuth in 2022, Katherine Foster, managed to get to the end of *Tristan* – all four hours of it; most of her "*Liebestod*" survived in tune. She is not a "larger lady," but neither is she vocally-suited to the role. In the Festspielhaus, Foster's voice-placement employed more wobble than vibrato, her diction was poor, and she failed to phrase the music as written. Had her appearance brought her into the orbit of Lisa della Casa or Maria Callas – or, for that matter,

---

37 Written for Billie Whitelaw, and first performed by Jessica Tandy.

38 Samuel Taylor Coleridge introduced the term "suspension of disbelief" in 1817; he later refined it as "poetic faith."

39 The medical-psychological term for people attracted sexually to overweight or obese people. The (American) "National Association to Advance Fat Acceptance" (NAAFA) was established to provide advocacy on behalf of fat people in the United States. It has operated also to bring male fat-fetishists (in particular) into contact with what are known affectionately in the community as "tug boats."

Sophia Loren, Monica Bellucci and Rachel Slover[40] – it would have made no difference to anyone listening to the performance on the radio. Birgit Nilsson was never a pin-up – as she conceded – but anyone wanting to hear the "*Liebestod*" as they breath their last is unlikely to reach for a recording by a different soprano. There have been singers whose talents – natural and nurtured – have met every unreasonable expectation, most recently Waltraud Meier, who came closer than anyone else in modern times to ticking the "beauty" box in form and sound as Isolde. In the Italian and French lyric repertoire, Kathleen Battle, Angela Gheorghiu and Anna Netrebko all prevailed as beautiful women with voices to match. Whether they were "better" or "prettier" than Grace Moore, Hilde Güden and Anna Moffo is a percolation of taste and prejudice. What is certain is that none of them was fat when they achieved their greatest successes.

The tension between normative standards of the physical and the sonic are, of course, in constant flux. For western society, there has always existed a general consensus for what qualifies as beautiful; it is hard to imagine anyone arguing against Grace Kelly's idealisation of the feminine, and yet the metric for isolating beauty objectively is more complicated than most will know, or admit. John Singer Sargent's 1884 portrait of Virginie Gautreau[41] was scandalous at the time of its first showing because Sargent painted one strap of her black dress off-the-shoulder. He subsequently held onto the portrait for more than thirty years (turning it into his "Mona Lisa"), and he described it as "the best thing I have done." It is a magnificently erotic painting that hums with sexual energy, but Gautreau is far from classically attractive in her features; her large nose, small mouth and diffident expression when looking away from the viewer cause her to appear haughty rather than unattainable. Compared to the many photographs taken of Gautreau at the time of her sitting, Sargent's towering genius as a portraitist is revealed not in deceit – since the painting was an accurate representation of its subject – but in the process of transformation. The difference between the seen and the perceived is thrilling, therefore – just as it is whenever a soprano is transfigured by her singing. There are infinite examples of this on film – and it can (and should) occur in the theatre more often than it does. A ready exemplar survives in a filmed performance from 1967, in black and white, of *L'elisir d'amore*, conducted by Gianandrea Gavazzeni, with Carlo Bergonzi as Nemorino and Renata Scotto[42] as Adina. Scotto's performance of "*Prendi, per me sei libero,*"[43] from Act II, is inconceivably beautiful – as close, in fact, to perfection as might be imagined. Any proverbial aliens floating above Earth would be able to grasp the essentials of singing, and the human capacity for beauty, from this single performance, which exemplifies the summit of placement, phrasing and phonation. For its duration, Scotto is the incarnation of female perfection; she is the most beautiful woman to have lived – and not only for Nemorino. [44]

---

40 Younger readers may prefer analogously, Eva Green, Kelly Reilly and Gal Gadot.

41 *née* Virginie Amélie Avegno.

42 24 February, 1934 –

43 'Take it, I release you.'

44 She was not, in her appearance, conventionally beautiful – even after her own dramatic process of weight loss. See Chapter 18.

Even so, Scotto's photograph was at no time pinned to the wall of a heterosexual man; her fantastic erotic power was a product of her singing; it was, and remains, appreciable only as a construction of acculturated perception. This is to distinguish Scotto's power as a woman when performing the music of Donizetti from "WAP," a 2020 song by the American rapper Cardi B, featuring guest "vocals" from Megan Thee Stallion. During the first decade of the 20th century, the acclamation of Anna Bahr-von Mildenburg's singing as among the most beautiful in Germany did not displace the actress Erna Morena as a poster-girl for the same community of admirers. Neither was Luisa Tetrazzini[45] expected to look like her stage and screen contemporaries, Alla Nazimova[46] and Mary Pickford.[47] Indeed, Tetrazzini was renowned for her size and the appetite that formed it[48] – in which arena she competed with her close friend and regular collaborator, Enrico Caruso. The incongruity of Tetrazzini's appearance as Lucia, Violetta, Philine (in Thomas' *Mignon*), Oscar, and Gilda did nothing to detract from the qualities that informed her branding as "The Florentine Nightingale." After her debut at Covent Garden on 2 November, 1907, E.A. Baugham wrote in *The Daily News*:

> The quality of tone produced by Tetrazzini ravished the sense. It is soft and golden and yet has none of the impersonal and chilling perfection of the ordinary light soprano […] I have never seen the pathos of Verdi's heroine realized with such grip and sincerity […] I do not think I am exaggerating when I say that Mme Tetrazzini has the voice of the century and stands out from even the great Italian singers we know.[49]

The critic's choice of words was telling. Tetrazzini was "the *voice* of the century," and the thrust of her success and popularity built on her inheritance of Patti's mantel as a "song-bird."[50] No matter where she sang, she occupied a static, anti-theatrical platform on which she had to do little more than perform as she did when standing in front of a recording horn.[51] Such was the nature of her repertoire that little attention was paid to her art beyond its tone, articulation and phrasing. Her use of words – as a function of her expression as an actress conveying the sentiment and

---

45   29 June, 1871 – 28 April, 1940.
46   3 June, 1879 – 13 July, 1945. Russian-American actress, director, producer, screenwriter – and famed beauty. Performed in plays by Ibsen, Chekhov and Turgenev on Broadway, and became a star as *Salome* (1922).
47   *née* Gladys Marie Smith, 8 April, 1892 –29 May, 1979. Legendary screen actress, co-founder of the studio, United Artists, one of the most influential women in film history – and one of its hardest working. In 1909, she appeared in 51 films.
48   Her love of food was legendary – and it survives in a cholesterol-raising recipe that takes her name in the United States, "Chicken / Turkey Tetrazzini." The dish is attributed to Ernest Arbogast, head chef at the Palace Hotel in San Francisco.
The ingredients are spaghetti, shredded chicken, cheese, butter, mushrooms, onion, milk, sour cream, chicken broth and white wine.
49   Gattey, Charles Neilson (1995). *Luisa Tetrazzini: the Florentine Nightingale*. Scolar Press, p. 73.
50   Tetrazzini and Patti became close personal friends.
51   Before 1925, all 78s were recorded acoustically, by means of the artist singing or speaking into a horn; the power of a voice produced vibrations which caused a stylus to cut into the wax of a "master."

experience of a character – contributed little to her work on stage or in the "studio." Insofar as the process of creating a new role was known to compel invention from a singer, and despite co-existing in the United States with Destinn and Jeritza *et al.* – Tetrazzini committed to the still-novel tradition of serving the dead in isolation. Even had she wanted to perform contemporary music, she chose to submit instead to her casting as an instrument *reductio ad absurdum* – circumscribing expectations as an anthropomorphic pipe-organ. This faceless constitution served ironically to mask a huge personality, for which she was loved by many (and loathed ferociously by Nellie Melba). She anatomised as a paradox in which her status as a larger-than-life celebrity survived her objectification as an Olympian automata. As a vocal-mannequin, unable to do more than adhere to an audience's pre-existing conception of what a virtuoso soprano should sound like, Tetrazzini occupied a space analogous to Zelig,[52] a character analysed in the course of Woody Allen's mockumentary by the psychologist Bruno Bettelheim:

> His feelings were really not all that different from the normal, what one would call the well-adjusted, normal person, only carried to an extreme degree, to an extreme extent. I myself felt that one could really think of him as the ultimate conformist.[53]

Tetrazzini's reputation for virtuosity was singular, but she had access to a fine legato (as survives on her recordings of "*Addio, del passato*," from *La Traviata* and "*Ah! non credea mirarti*," from *La sonnambula*), and she was capable of pathos when cornered. Unusually for a coloratura, her voice was also extremely powerful; the aspersion that she suffered from a certain weakness within the stave was a consequence only of the brilliance of everything above it. Her recording of the "Carnival of Venice" – a Neapolitan song made famous by Paganini – lives up to the violinist's archetype; it is astounding for the singer's breathing, runs, trills, *staccati* and vocal ornaments, all of which are topped by eyebrow-raising high notes that might have been performed by a flautist (piccolo doubling). Tetrazzini was comfortable launching high notes in full voice, the bizarre resonance of which survives on most of her recordings from the first decade of the 20th century. Her singing of "*O légère hirondelle*,"[54] from Gounod's *Mireille* is without precedent, and few of her successors have warranted comparison when measured against the absurdist brilliance of "*Io son Titania*,"[55] from *Mignon*.

Tetrazzini did nothing to negate her association with food and the effects of eating too much of it. She was known for announcing, "I am old, I am fat, but I am still Tetrazzini" – a sinecure that bypassed her status and achievements as a singer. Instead, she embodied the transactional nature of the soprano as a mouth for consuming and producing. Would Callas' career have proved metamorphic had she not transformed herself by shedding half her body-weight? Would her death have proved so captivating

---

52 *Zelig* (1983).
53 In Gabbard, Glen O.; Gabbard, Krin (1999). *Psychiatry and the Cinema*. American Psychiatric Publishing, p. 265.
54 'O light swallow.'
55 'I am Titania.'

to her cult had she not withered at the end – mute and empty in the absence of her stage-dependent identity, and so easily diminished *in memoriam*:

> Maria Callas died of a heart attack on September 16, 1977, in her bedroom, a quiet end to a tumultuous life, a life lived in art and for art, art of such intensity that it threatened to consume life, and then, love supplanting art, love of such intensity that it devoured life.[56]

There are numerous routes to interpreting the discourse between the female body and her voice; they are too involved for this (or any single) volume,[57] but there is a clear correlation between the generative capacity of a woman to create life, and the changes and excesses she experiences when committing to the performance of art music. Pregnancy and birth correspond to the sacrifices necessitated by training and life as a soprano. Just as a mother's body evolves during gestation, so too is the shape of a woman altered when delivering music written (for the most part) by men. Inevitably, perhaps, this has been read as another form of societal control and repression – with female singers having to yield their talent and hard-work to the service and benefit of the patriarchy. While this was true for previous generations, it is neither appropriate nor warranted decades into the 21st century – 120 years since the first performance of Ethyl Smyth's *The Wreckers*,[58] starring the celebrated *heldensopran* Paula Doenges[59] as Thirz, and Luise Fladnitzer[60] as Avis.[61] The majority of sopranos would likely consider the neutering of music history to be fruitless and self-destructive; indeed, a woman training to sing will aspire commonly to the performance of works by composers whose gender (and the "war" arising from it) never occurred to them. Presentism, and the interpretation of past events and people according to modern standards, is untenable for anyone submitting to training and tuition as a singer; even so, the liberal trajectory of western society in its accommodation of feminism, and women's rights more generally, has fostered a novel conflict wherein body-positivity has proved to be incompatible with objectivity.

---

56 Dizikes, John (1993). *Opera in America: A Cultural History*. Yale University Press, p. 561.

57 An excellent introduction to the literature can be found in Guaraccino, Serena (2010). "It's not over till the fat lady sings: the weight of the opera diva," in *Historicizing Fat in the Anglo-American West*. Ed. lena Levy-Navarro. Ohio State University Press, pp. 192–212.

58 In Leipzig on 11 November, 1906.

59 17 March, 1874 – 15 June, 1931.

60 1876 – 1918.

61 The conductor of the first production, Richard Hagel, insisted on making serious cuts to the third act. Although the opening night was a success with the audience and critics alike, Smyth's resentment was suffocating. Notwithstanding her good fortune, she removed the parts and the full score, and relocated them to Prague, where she had another offer of a performance. The Czech production was under-rehearsed and failed completely. Mahler was planning in 1907 to stage *The Wreckers* in Vienna – when he left the Hofoper. Smyth later said of Mahler that he was "far and away the finest conductor I ever knew, with the most all-embracing musical instinct, and it is one of the small tragedies of my life that just when he was considering *The Wreckers* at Vienna they drove him from office." (Lebrecht, Norman (1987). *Mahler Remembered*. Faber and Faber, p. 45). In 1909, Beecham agreed to stage *The Wreckers* at Her Majesty's Theatre. Smyth was again dissatisfied, criticising the conductor for forcing rehearsals into "just" 10 days. Beecham nonetheless added the work to his first Covent Garden season in 1910.

Anyone who has attended, or watched a broadcast from, an opera house since 2006[62] will have noticed how so many of the female leads are now attractive, physically if not always vocally. Something similar has determined who gets to make records. Hardly a month passes without a pretty singer producing an album of arias and songs – many of them for small, independent labels. The largest and most influential of them all, Deutsche Grammophon, has been producing records since the 19th century; its opera catalogue is important, and the company continues to drive the business of A&R for theatres and promoters globally. Anyone recording for the "yellow label" can be said to have "made it." During the 1970s, DG's roster of sopranos included Mirella Freni, Teresa Berganza, Agnes Baltsa, Gundula Janowitz, Pilar Lorengar, Anna Tomowa-Sintow and Tatyana Troyanos – all of whom were born within a few years of each other. They will forever remain among the most talented and charismatic singers to make records in stereo; it would be an embellishment, however, to suggest that any of them was classically beautiful, or especially thin. Conversely, during the early 2020s, DG signed contracts with Anna Prohaska, Nadine Sierra, Hera Hyesang Park, Emily D'Angelo, Elsa Dreisig, Isabel Leonard and Jennifer O'Loughlin – all of whom are fit for purpose as models in their adherence to the normative metrics for beauty. To varying degrees, they are all gifted artists, and they may yet be remembered in tandem with their forbears; when considering the huge number of sopranos competing on the world's stages, however, the only quality by which they are united is their appearance. The same can be said of Sonya Yoncheva, Kate Lindsey, Kristine Opolais, Julie Fuchs, Sabine Devieilhe and Lisette Oropesa – all of whom have recorded for rival companies. It would be easy to dismiss as coincidental the commonality of attractiveness. Of course, A&R executives are not alone in capitalising on a singer's looks; each of those named as contemporary maintains a website and a social media presence for which glamourous photography is essential.

The appetite for beauty women is as old as the painted caves of Lascaux, but opera singers didn't become truly exotic until film studios made them so. Between 1913 and 1936, for example, the magazine *Vanity Fair* did much to glamourise sopranos at a time when the defining measure for beauty was projected onto a silver-screen. Edward Steichen's 1928 portrait of Maria Jeritza as Carmen,[63] for example, failed to repeat what the photographer had achieved for Grace Moore[64] five years earlier;[65] he had more with which to work in Lily Pons, for the issue dated 1 March, 1932. Moore and Pons were revered as singers before Hollywood came knocking. Moore was a home-grown talent, whose nickname, the "Tennessee Nightingale," bound her to Luisa Tetrazzini – even if they shared literally nothing else. Moore made her debut at the Met and the Opéra-Comique in Paris, in 1928 – as Mimi; during her 16 seasons in New York she excelled in a limited range of Italian and French operas,

---

62 The Met broadcast the first "live" opera to cinemas – a condensed English-language version of Mozart's *Die Zauberflöte* – on 30 December, 2006.

63 For the issue published 1 February, 1928.

64 5 December, 1898 – 26 January, 1947.

65 "Wearing a tulle dress with flowers." Nickolas Muray's photo of Moore ("wearing an embroidered jacket,") in May, 1922, is superb also.

notably *Louise* – her signature role. For her first film, *A Lady's Morals*,[66] she played Jenny Lind. Moore made a further seven films, until her last, *Louise*, was released in 1939. Abel Gance's film of Charpentier's opera (also starring Georges Thill, as Julien), was produced with the composer on-set throughout; it is the most authentic document of its kind ever made, and near-perfect as a performance. Moore's achievement was astonishing considering her competition. Ninon Vallin[67] was eight years older, French – and an important voice for contemporary composers, including Debussy, who chose her in 1911 to sing the part of the celestial voice in the first performance of *Le martyre de Saint Sébastien*. Three years later, Debussy was her accompanist when she gave the première of his *Trois poèmes de Stéphane Mallarmé* at the Salle Gaveau in Paris. She worked extensively in concert and the studio with Reynaldo Hahn, arguably the finest composer of *chanson* of the first half of the century. She made a handful of films, none of which is memorable, but there is unedited footage from 1936 of her performing Gounod's "*Sérénade*" and Reynaldo Hahn's "*Si mes vers avaient des ailes*,"[68] accompanied by the operetta composer, Georges Van Parys, that provides a summary-lesson in pre-War French vocal style. The light tone, variegated vibrato, delicate phrasing and elegant word-use are astonishing – redolent of a now-extinct school of singing. On record, her performance as Charlotte in *Werther*, conducted by Elie Cohen in 1931, has not been equalled. Vallin's authenticity was pivotal to the popularity of her three successors in French and Italian bel canto and coloratura repertoire: Lily Pons,[69] Bidù Sayão[70] and Mado Robin.[71]

The French-born Lily Pons and the Brazilian Bidù Sayão were two of the brightest stars at the New York Met, where they excelled as Olympia, Philine, Lakmé, Amina, Lucia, and Violetta. The former was a sex-symbol, and marketed as such by her promoters in New York and California, where she was cast in four Hollywood pictures – the first of which, *I Dream Too Much*,[72] was a romantic musical-comedy starring Henry Fonda and Lucille Ball, featuring songs by Jerome Kern and Dorothy Fields. Pons also made a large number of recordings and television appearances, which trace her long career from her debut in 1928 (as Lakmé, conducted by Hahn) to her final concert performance in 1973.[73] Sayão is remembered for unfailing good taste, and an exceptional legato – for which she was adored by her compatriot, Heitor Villa-Lobos; her recording of the *Bachianas Brasileiras* No. 5, conducted by its composer, remains peerless. Equally important are her recordings with her friend and supporter, Toscanini, the first of which captured a sublime performance from Carnegie Hall on 9 April, 1936, of Debussy's *La Damoiselle élue*. The French coloratura, Mado Robin, was famed uniquely for stratospheric high notes – the uppermost of which left Tetrazzini in the dust. Robin was able to fire off C7s without discernible effort,[74]

---

66 Released in the USS in 1930; and as *Jenny Lind* in the United Kingdom and France.
67 *née* Eugénie Vallin 8 September, 1886 – 22 November, 1961.
68 'If my worms had wings.'
69 12 April, 1898 – 13 February, 1976.
70 *neé* Balduína de Oliveira Sayão, 11 May, 1902 – 12 March, 1999.
71 *neé* Madeleine Marie Robin, 29 December, 1918 – 10 December, 1960.
72 1935.
73 Pons gave almost 300 performances at the Met, between 1931 and 1960.
74 That is two octaves *above* high C.

and there are numerous recordings and filmed excerpts that evidence the reach of her technique. She was more than a human-piccolo, however, as can be seen and heard from a television-broadcast performance of the "Mad Scene" from *Lucia*. Her phrasing is coloured by delicate shifts in tone and emphasis – the elegance of which are transformative of music that can sound congested; the resolving B flat 7 is eye-brow lifting because of the security of its placement, but it is less impressive than her shaping of the cadence, which is a model of elegance and refinement.

For all their talents as singers, these women were popular for being everything that Tetrazzini wasn't, namely slim, attractive and feminine; the nexus of their success was to compare favourably in countenance to the women selling love and lust in Hollywood. Opera singers remained famous and glamorous after the War; apart from Maria Callas, however (who made only a single film, *Medea*, for Pasolini),[75] few had the looks to interest Hollywood. Renata Tebaldi, Magda Olivero, Joan Sutherland, Renata Scotto, Katia Ricciarelli, Mirella Freni, Monteserrat Caballé and Jessye Norman were among the most talented sopranos of *any* generation, and they were photographed on thousands of occasions for press, publicity and record covers. Their appearance as professional sopranos mattered little. Until suddenly it did.

In early 2004, the American soprano, Deborah Voigt,[76] was engaged to perform the title role in Christof Loy's Covent Garden production of *Ariadne auf Naxos* – Voigt's breakout role in 1991, in Boston. When the soprano proved too large for one of her costumes, a black cocktail dress, Voigt was sacked. The episode was kept private initially – at Voigt's request; after it came to light, Covent Garden's casting director, Peter Katona, told *The Telegraph* newspaper in London that "Although Ms. Voigt is a wonderful singer, the costume and type of production made it not such a fortunate suggestion that she should be in it."[77] She was replaced by the German soprano, Anne Schwanewilms.[78] Everyone involved at the Royal Opera House was fed to the wood-chipper of public opprobrium – primarily, and bizarrely, on the basis that many of Ms Voigt's predecessors had been morbidly obese also.[79] This was curious reasoning, given that "the past" has routinely advocated and allowed for a great many questionable views and values, but the bottom line was considered to be that "the fat lady" should be entitled to sing, no matter her size. Given the media's talent for hypocrisy, it was unremarkable that just about every newspaper, magazine and online resource that took the Royal Opera to task for its alleged body-fascism was funded by advertising and agency-sourced stories featuring thin and beautiful women. Few were keen to admit additionally to the medical realities of obesity, on the basis, presumably, that wealthy opera singers were less inclined to heart disease

---

75   In 1969. It has nothing to do with Cherubini's opera, and Callas does not sing a note.

76   4 August, 1960 –

77   *The Telegraph*, 7 March, 2004.

78   1967 – . It is, of course, an opinion (to which the author is, perhaps, entitled), but Schwanewilms was, and will remain, a much finer singer and actress than Voigt – which fact should have informed Mr. Katona's casting decision in the first place.

79   Tim Ashley, writing in The Guardian, held that "whatever you think about her weight, Voigt is actually extremely beautiful," a fantastically condescending statement that was missing only the word "despite." Ashley unwittingly emphasised the apparent improbability of any construction of "big" and "beautiful." *The Guardian*, 9 March, 2004.

than the poverty-burdened occupants of sink-estates in Glasgow.[80] It was further asserted that "high" culture should, for some reason, have been immune to the evils of Hollywood codification – even though opera and record companies had been actively distancing themselves as businesses from the clichés embodied by Tetrazzini since the 1920s. For all that Voigt might have said and done, she submitted in June of the year in which she was sacked to gastric bypass surgery, pursuant to which she lost over 100 pounds / 7 stone, dropping from a size 30 to a size 14. After returning to performing, Voigt was booked by the Royal Opera to sing the role from which she had been fired.[81]

It is absurd that Voigt's predicament should have been singled out when prejudice against "large-boned" women dates back centuries. In 1991, the author worked as assistant producer for a recording of Strauss' "Four Last Songs," with the soprano Sharon Sweet,[82] conducted by Rafael Frühbeck de Burgos. Sweet made a splendid noise, as she did over a memorable career that included an unforgettable performance of Tove on the finest recording yet made of Schoenberg's "Gurre-Lieder."[83] Her performance of the songs has lasting merit. It was obvious at the time of the sessions, however, that the soprano was struggling with her weight. Two years later, Sweet was dismissed from a production of *Aida* by Houston Grand Opera for being unable to climb a single flight of stairs. What value inclusion if it accepts the unacceptable? Neither Sweet nor Jessye Norman nor Jane Eaglen would have remained at their largest had a magic elixir existed to enable them to appear as did Callas in 1954. Whether Callas lost her voice when shedding her fat is a question for another chapter; it can, for now, be asserted confidently that Callas would not have become Callas had she remained physically and culturally overweight.

After the dust had settled, Deborah Voigt told one interviewer "I believe that this attitude towards heavy people is the last bastion of open discrimination in our society,"[84] a statement that can have only been made by a white, heterosexual, able-bodied, cis-gendered woman declaring no religious affiliation. In truth, prejudice against the "Rubenesque" is as old as opera and, if anything, it is going to get worse before it gets better, whether or not Lizzo[85] causes a shift in perspective. Opera is no longer a mirror for society since no-one is writing operas that anyone cares about – not even the wildly-gifted Thomas Adès. It is, nonetheless, right and now-hopefully routine for the differently-abled to be encouraged to perform on stage, in live productions. The tenor, Giuseppe Borgatti, was forced to abandon staged performances after his sight failed him, which was a disgrace as well as a tragedy considering his relative youth at

---

80   The author apologises to the fine people of Glasgow. However, according to the most recent "Scottish Health Survey," and at the time of publication, residents of Greater Glasgow and Clyde were almost one-and-a-half times as likely to have <u>had</u> a doctor-diagnosed heart attack (determined statistically as an increased risk of 42%) when compared to the rest of Scotland – a country that prides itself on the battering and deep-frying of "Mars Bars," doner kebabs, and pizza.

81   The author was present, and joined in the audience's *extremely* vocal appreciation of Voigt's loss of weight and her return to the London stage.

82   16 August, 1951 –

83   Conducted by Claudio Abbado, for DG.

84   Guaraccino, Serena (2010). "It's not over till the fat lady sings: the weight of the opera diva," in *Historicizing Fat in the Anglo-American West.* Ed. Iena Levy-Navarro. Ohio State University Press, p. 204.

85   *née* Melissa Viviane Jefferson, 27 April, 1988 –

the time.[86] On the other hand, the exploitation of disability is wretched if it compensates for the absence of talent.[87] The Welsh mezzo-soprano, Katherine Jenkins,[88] is beautiful, and slim, and she has a voice, but she is no more an opera singer than was Vera Lynn, with whom Jenkins can best be compared, at least favourably.

From whichever direction or angle the issue of the "fat lady" is approached, the fact remains that women are expected to be sexually attractive when on stage as figures of desire; that *status quo* is unlikely to change any time soon. It falls to be asked whether equivalent standards have been applied to tenors, baritones and basses. It's a question of taste, of course, but there have been precious few male singers capable of living up to the standards and expectations of the roles to which they have been assigned by composers and directors. Beyond Franco Corelli, the most beautiful male opera singer to be photographed, the number of Hollywood-handsome tenors could be forced into a family sedan; it is in the teeth of this manifest bias that the soprano – and women more generally – can be said to have suffered the most. No matter the reach of society's enlightenment, sopranos will continue to be judged for how they appear as well as how they sound. In Western law, the Latin words "*Corpus delicti*" mean "body of the crime," which requires that an indictment be proved before a person can be convicted. At the time of writing, the greatest crime committed by the soprano is that she is a woman also.

---

86   See Boyden, Matthew (2021). *The Tenor: A Cultural History*. Ragueneau Press.
87   As has been the case on occasion for the tenor, Andrea Bocelli, whose voice would not have equipped him for a regional chorus, but for amplification, and the dark arts of marketing.
88   29 June, 1980 –

CHAPTER EIGHTEEN

The Reluctant Divina

In May, 1879, Sarah Bernhardt[1] and a company of players drawn from the Comédie-Française landed in Folkestone, on the south coast of Britain. They were met by a vast and predominantly British crowd, almost none of whom had seen Bernhardt act, and were never likely to. During her two-month stay in England, she gave 18 performances of semi-improvised productions of *Phèdre*, *L'Étrangère*,[2] *Le Sphinx*, *Zaïre*, *Andromaque*, *Ruy Blas*, and *Hernani* – all of them in French. Tickets were expensive and difficult to acquire; few of the audience spoke French with the fluency necessary to understand Bernhardt's effusive, semi-sung intonation, as it survives on a recording of a scene from Racine's *Phèdre*, made in February, 1910, while Bernhardt was touring the United States.[3] She was 66-years-old at the time and sounded half that age; the vitality of her word-use, projection and breathing are fluid and elastic – sensual in a manner unique to the actress. As a performance, it is overcooked, extravagant and mesmerising – more than sufficient to validate her status as the most adored woman in the history of theatre. That assassin of eminence, Lytton Strachey, wrote of Bernhardt that she could "seize and tear the nerves of her audience, she could touch, she could terrify, to the top of her astonishing bent." D. H. Lawrence, saw the 63-years-old Bernhardt as Marguerite Gauthier in *La Dame aux Camélias* at the Theatre Royal in Nottingham, in 1906, when the actress was 63-years-old. The 23-year-old Lawrence wrote of her performance that she was

> the incarnation of wild emotion [...] She represents the primeval passions of woman [...] I could love such a woman myself, love her to madness; all for the pure wild passion of it. Take care about going to see Bernhardt. Unless you are very sound, do not go. When I think of her now I can still feel the weight hanging in my chest as it hung there for days after I saw her. Her winsome, sweet playful ways; her sad, plaintive little murmurs; her terrible panther cries; and then the awful, inarticulate sounds, the little sobs that fairly sear one, and the despair and death.[4]

---

1   22 October, 1844 – 26 March, 1923.
2   'The Stranger.'
3   For a detailed consideration of Bernhardt's recorded performance, see Boyden, Matthew (2021). *The tenor: A Cultural History*. Ragueneau Press.
4   Mock, Roberta (2007). *Jewish Women on Stage, Film and Television*. Palgrave Macmillan, p. 24.

Three years before Wilde presented Bernhardt with *Salomé* and 16 years before she was immortalised as Berma in *À la recherche du temps perdu*,[5] Bernhardt inspired Victorien Sardou to write *La Tosca*. It was their third collaboration (following *Fédora* and *Théodora*) and like its predecessors it triumph. At the end of the premiere, the actor playing Scarpia, Pierre Berton, appeared on stage for the customary presentation of the author. As Berton began to speak, the audience interrupted repeatedly, yelling the actress' name. He persevered but was overwhelmed time and again. Berton went backstage and implored Bernhardt to join him; she refused until Sardou was introduced to the audience, at which point she walked on stage to thunderous applause and cheering, punctuated by cries of "*Vive Sarah!*" Throughout her career, Bernhardt was renowned for her generosity to colleagues, her talent for extinguishing rivalry and confrontation, and her catchphrase, "*Quand même,*"[6] – which spoke with elegant concision to a philosophy of life that might have been reduced to the equally *aperçu* "just get on with it."

For almost five decades, Bernhardt was the most frequently drawn, painted, photographed and profiled woman on Earth.[7] Alphonse Mucha's posters of her as Hamlet, Gismonda and Tosca sold in their thousands;[8] her autograph was the most valuable during her lifetime – notwithstanding her willingness to sign whatever was put in front of her.[9] She was the "world's greatest actress," more famous than any of her playwrights, with the sole exception of Shakespeare. Sardou was consoled by his royalties, and the crumbs falling from Escoffier's kitchen floor.[10] Not everyone was seduced by Bernhardt's histrionics, of course. George Bernard Shaw despised her "childishly egotistical [mannerisms] she does not enter into the leading character: she substitutes herself for it."[11] He felt he could not "as a theatre critic be fair to Sarah B., because she was exactly like my aunt Georgina,"[12] which revealed more of Shaw's Wodehousean relative than of Bernhardt. The rest of the world obsessed over her beauty regime, her fashion (she liked to dress in Byzantine and Oriental robes), her fees and spending habits, her illegitimate son, Maurice,[13] her lovers, her menagerie of

---

5   Volume One of Proust's five-volume novel, "*Du côté de chez Swann,*" ('Swann's Way,') was published in 1913. The seventh, and final volume, was published four years after Bernhardt's death, in 1927.

6   'So what.'

7   The majority of her biographers agree that Bernhardt was the most photographed woman of the 19th century.

8   At the time of publication, an original lithograph sells for around £35,000 / $50,000 / 39,000 euros.

9   Which distinguished her from Shaw, who signed nothing so that whenever he had to pay for lunch or dinner his cheques were retained, rather than presented, on the basis that a signature was worth considerably more than his money.

10   The chef created various tributes to Bernhardt, including a strawberry dessert, a chocolate-gilded macaroon and, less predictably, a beef broth. His sole tribute at the time of *La Tosca's* premiere was the less than dazzling "*Oeufs Sardou*, the recipe for which is predictably artery-clogging: ham, butter-fried asparagus, poached eggs, artichoke hearts, creamed spinach, hollandaise and minced black truffle. Later versions added anchovies. In 1891, Escoffier created "Lobster Thermidor," in honour of Sardou's play *Thermidor*, for which posterity is in Escoffier's eternal debt. Named for the eleventh month of the French Republican calendar, the play is one of seven by Sardou set during the Revolution.

11   Blom, Philipp (2008). *The Vertigo Years: Change and Culture in the West, 1900–1914*. McClelland & Stewart, p. 315.

12   *Ibid.*

13   Her only child was born on 22 December, 1864; his father was Henri, Prince de Ligne. Bernhardt

exotic animals (including a boa constrictor and an alligator named "Ali-Gaga"), her alleged sleeping arrangements (said to be in a coffin) and, on occasion, her technique and talent as an actress. Bernhardt was the subject of near-constant gossip and anecdotage, some of it true. The oft-repeated story of "society men" filling a bath with 100 bottles of champagne for the actress to bathe in,[14] so that they might drink from it *infusé de Bernhardt*, ended with the punchline (as it did for every woman of whom the story was told) that an extra bottle was necessary when decanting the bathtub.[15]

"The Divine Sarah"[16] was the first actress to become a darling of the media, and the first to be photographed throughout her career after Nadar[17] created his definitive portrait of the (then pregnant) actress to commemorate her 20th birthday. Bernhardt was prescient in directing and managing her reputation and iconography – which she exploited using the vogue for "cabinet cards."[18] She recalled in her memoirs how her "fame had become annoying for my enemies, and a little trying, I confess, for my friends," while admitting how the "stir and noise amused me vastly."[19]

Bernhardt died in Paris on 26 March, 1923, at the age of 78. Eight months later, at the beginning of December, 1923, Maria Callas[20] was born in Manhattan, to Greek immigrant parents. If Bernhardt was the first actress to become famous internationally then Callas was the last soprano to occupy an equivalent status. There have been many sopranos since Callas to warrant fame and fascination, but none have come close by comparison. She was the last *diva* to warrant the positive use of that title, and then for reasons flowing from elements of her biography that gain nothing from repetition. Callas' life and work have been written about more often than any other female singer. Aside from Frank Sinatra, Elvis Presley, Freddie Mercury and Michael Jackson, she is the most studied voice-artist in history. Her fans formed as a cult long before she retired, and every detail of her life has been subjected to scrutiny, analysis and interpretation. Like any other culturally resonant figure, Callas is meaningful for what she reveals of her observers and for how so little of the continuing interest in her life owes more than a passing debt to her art as a singing-actress.

Even before the centenary of her birth, Callas was a source of inspiration for artists outside the worlds of opera and music. There have been dozens of biographies – in which arena she is the only opera singer to have been written about by authors untrained in music.[21] In 2018–2019, she was revived as a hologram for "concerts"

---

never married. Her son died only five years after his mother; they are buried near each other in Père-Lachaise, Paris.

14   Legman, G. (1968). *Rationale of the Dirty Joke: an Analysis of Sexual Humour*. Simon & Schuster, p. 574.

15   Various sources claim (without evidence) that Winston Churchill (a friend of Bernhardt's) was one of those "society men."

16   The sobriquet given to her by Oscar Wilde.

17   Gaspard-Félix Tournachon.

18   In international circulation after 1870, cabinet cards consisted of a thin photograph mounted on card and measuring typically 108mm by 165mm.

19   Bernhardt, Sarah (1907). *My Double Life: Memoirs of Sarah Bernhardt*. William Heinemann, p. 288.

20   *née* Maria Anna Cecilia Sophie Kalogeropoulou, 2 December, 1923 – 16 September, 1977.

21   See, for example, Ariana Stassinopoulos (1981). *Maria Callas: The Woman Behind the Legend*. Simon and Schuster; and Gage, Nicholas (2000). *Greek Fire: The Story of Maria Callas and Aristotle Onassis*. Knopf.

in the USA,[22] Puerto Rico, Mexico, and Europe; in 2019, Monica Bellucci played her in a solo show, "Maria Callas: Letters & Memoirs" – doing something close to justice to the soprano's memory. Conversely, Marina Abramović's grotesque "opera performance," *7 Deaths of Maria Callas*, corresponded to "a boot stamping on [her] face – for ever." At the time of writing, *Maria*, a bio-pic starring Angelina Jolie, is in production, for release at some point before Callas' centenary in December, 2023. Considering the chilling atmosphere of the director's two previous portraits of complex, difficult women,[23] Pablo Larraín's take on Callas is unlikely to call on rose-tinted lenses. According to the thumbnail summary published by the production company, "[the film] follows the life story of the world's greatest opera singer, Maria Callas, during her final days in 1970s Paris." The only prior attempt to dramatise the soprano's life, *Callas Forever*,[24] was preoccupied with her death; Franco Zeffirelli's obscene folly is doubly-revolting having been directed by someone who worked with her. In the title role, Fanny Ardant does little more than anticipate the audience's response to the finished film when alternating between a gamut of pain and disbelief.

In 1982, the American artist and film-maker, Julian Schnabel, produced a frothy quartet of paintings on velvet, the "Maria Callas Series,"[25] that alluded to Margaret Keane's disturbing 1950s kitsch. Schnabel's huge abstracts[26] operate as guarded encomiums to the singer's hard-won grandeur, with splashes of brilliance failing to light an otherwise oppressive atmosphere flushed with vulgarity. Each of these "tributes" fixates on the end of Callas' life in preference to the art that preceded it. The soprano herself was inclined to the morbid, and there is no denying the sickly appeal of her lurid story, which begins with a mother from *Beowulf*,[27] pauses briefly at the apex of triumph, and descends through the alimentary canal of celebrity, peppered by frightful calamities, spanning a decollated love-affair, a ruined voice, a dead child,[28] and a silent, friendless death. As unhappy denouements go, Callas' would have appealed to Thomas Hardy.

The end began in 1960 when Callas opened the La Scala season on 7 December, as Paolina in Donizetti's *Poliuto* – her fifth and final such honour, following her House debut nine years earlier.[29] She had been "*La divina*"[30] for a decade, and it proved

---

22 The Lyric Opera (formerly the Lyric Theater) of Chicago presented the dead Callas with a live orchestra on 7 September, 2019.

23 *Jackie* (2016) and *Spencer* (2021).

24 Released in 2002.

25 Dark purple, black, olive and maroon, respectively.

26 9 x 13 feet.

27 Elmina Evangelia "Litsa" Callas.

28 The issue of her son remains controversial. The boy is said to have died a few hours after his birth, on 30 March, 1960. Her husband stated categorically that she was unable to bear children; Nicholas Gage claimed otherwise. See Gage, Nicholas (2000). *Greek Fire: The Story of Maria Callas and Aristotle Onassis*. Knopf.

29 In *Les vêpres siciliennes*, conducted, somewhat improbably, by Erich Kleiber. Her early career in Greece (from where she headed to Italy on 14 September, 1945) entailed 56 performances in seven operas, and 20 recitals. In 1946, Giovanni Zenatello (the tenor who created *both* Pinkertons for Puccini in *Madama Butterfly* in 1904), engaged her in the title role of *La Gioconda*, at the Arena in Verona – where she met her future husband, Giovanni Meneghini. They married in 1949; two years later, Callas made her debut at La Scala, which marked the beginning of her mature career. She was 28 at the time.

30 'The Divine One.'

to be her final new role[31] and only her third engagement for 1960.[32] The opera was an unusual choice for the soprano, since it belongs to the tenor lead after whom it is named.[33] Allowing someone else to share her spotlight made timeous sense, since she was now exhausted by her celebrity, which reached its peak in November the previous year, when she abandoned her marriage to live with Aristotle Onassis. During the 12 months leading up to *Poliuto's* first night, Callas was the world's most hounded woman. Journalism's appetites were made rapacious by the publication of her mother's book, *My Daughter Maria Callas*, following which the smallest cell of gossip morphed within hours into something idle. Whether or not an opportunity presented itself, her humiliated husband, Giovanni Meneghini, did his best to infect his wife's billionaire lifestyle. The parity between the media-fomented triumvirate of Callas, Meneghini and Onassis, and the central love triangle in *Poliuto*,[34] ensured that the weeks leading up to the opening night were among the most invasive experienced by the soprano. Her nerves were less shredded than Corelli's, but there wasn't much in it and the live recording is one of the most thrilling of anything, ever. As she walked on stage during Act I, the audience applauded loudly, at which point the claques seized their moment and began shouting. Not for the last time, Antonino Votto had to lower his baton and wait for the clamour to fade. Callas' vocal entrance was nervous, and not until the duet with Poliuto, *"Oggetto De'miei Voti,"*[35] did she relax into the performance. Her vocal difficulties were starkly evidenced, regardless, particularly in her spreading vibrato when singing anything above an A4 – which included a truncated D6 at the chaotic end of Act II. She remained *La divina* throughout, but tired and vulnerable.

Ten months earlier, on 5 February, Milan's Capitol Theatre hosted the gala premiere of a film that spoke intimately to Callas.[36] *La Dolce Vita*[37] was the biggest hit of the year in Europe, with 13 million tickets sold in Italy alone. Fellini's Dante-esque journey through the mores and miseries of modern life, and the contemporary obsession with celebrity, is book-marked by scenes involving the pneumatic Anita Ekberg as Sylvia Rank, an impossibly beautiful Swedish actress whose initial command of the tabloid photographers – christened by reference to one of the film's characters, Paparazzo – resolves with Rank being carried away by a police car, the victim of an uncaring media defined by existential cravings. The film's edge is sharpened against a backdrop of dreamlike, romanticised locations, all of which heighten the director's portrayal of the vapid and the vain. Marcello Mastroianni / Rubini's ostensibly perfect life is revealed to be grotesque and vampiric; he is an aging junkie, addicted to

---

31   The opening night was attended by a large number of *glitterati*, including Prince Rainier and Princess Grace of Monaco.

32   The others were a *Norma* at the amphitheatre in Epidaurus, Greece, and her second recording of the opera, again for EMI, conducted again by her mentor, Tullio Serafin, who was now 82 – having been appointed music director at La Scala (for the first time) in 1909.

33   On this occasion, it was Franco Corelli, whose career Callas helped launch in 1954. See Boyden, Matthew (2021). *The tenor: A Cultural History*. Ragueneau Press.

34   Poliuto, his wife Paolina – both ultimately Christians – and the Roman Proconsul Severo.

35   'Subject of my oaths.'

36   Previews were held in Rome on 2 and 3 February, at the Fiamma cinema in Rome.

37   'The Sweet Life.'

emptiness and infected by debauchery. Incapable of giving love, his narcissism brutalises and ruins the only woman of substance in his life, Yvonne Fumeaux's Emma. The film concludes with Marcello's past glories trampled on a beach by a crowd of disinterested youth with an attention span shorter even than his own.

Maria Callas attended the gala opening of *La Dolce Vita* in the company of Antonio Ghiringhelli, La Scala's Intendant. She wore a splendidly vulgar fur coat, with which presumably she was able to disguise her well-advanced pregnancy. On arrival, and when leaving, the soprano navigated banks of photographers as a victim of the brutal, avaricious culture anatomised by the film's writers.[38] Callas and Rank were distinguished by the singer's unusual talent and discipline, but neither quality could dissipate her fame after the media learned of her relationship with Onassis in November, 1959. Within 12 months, and before her first night as Paolina, she had become more famous for *being* Callas – a product of the coincidentally beneficial and destructive phosphorescence that refashioned the elevated as trivial. The collision of art and celebrity crystalised on 19 May, 1962, with Callas' performance of "*L'amour est un oiseau rebelle*," from *Carmen*, for the crowd of more than 15,000 that gathered to honour John F. Kennedy at Madison Square Garden. As Callas walked from the stage, Marilyn Monroe entered wearing a skin-tight, rhinestone-covered dress designed by Bob Mackie.[39] She sang "Happy Birthday, Mr. President;"[40] her sexually-provocative singing embarrassed Kennedy who, when taking the microphone, announced with trenchant wit: "I can now retire from politics after having had Happy Birthday sung to me in such a sweet, wholesome way." Callas attended the after-party and remained for 90-minutes. She was photographed laughing with Monroe; they were the world's two most famous women.[41]

Callas' celebrity was fantastic, rooted as it was in the American-cultivated obsession for the bold and the beautiful. Because so many opera singers transitioned in Europe and the United States to the movies, it was inevitable that opera and the lyric theatre would provide narrative opportunities. The number of films involving characters playing opera singers was staggering, as was the number of actresses working in Hollywood who trained as opera singers. The female star of the Marx Brothers' *A Night at the Opera*,[42] Margaret Dumont,[43] was classically trained during her teens and began performing in the US and Europe as Margaret and then Marguerite Dumont. She made her debut as a teenager in *Sleeping Beauty and the Beast* at the Chestnut Theatre in Philadelphia, and in August, 1902, two months before her 20th birthday, she appeared as a singer and comedian in a vaudeville act in Atlantic City. Almost 40 years later, Dumont appeared in her seventh and last Marx Brothers film – *The Big*

---

38 Federico Fellini, Ennio Flaiano, Tullio Pinelli, Brunello Rondi and Pier Paolo Pasolini.
39 The dress cost $12,000 in 1962. It was sold at auction in November, 2016, for $4.8 million. In a case of life failing catastrophically to imitate art, the dress was worn at the 2020 Met Gala by the reality-TV "personality," Kim Kardashian.
40 Ten days *before* his birthday.
41 Monroe was dead three months later; Kennedy the following year.
42 1935.
43 *née* Daisy Juliette Baker, 20 October, 1882 – 6 March, 1965. In 2016, the director Xavier Giannoli created an homage to Dumont with *Marguerite*, a tragi-comic study of a tone-deaf opera singer (inspired by Florence Foster Jenkins, see Chapter 19), starring Catherine Frot.

Store. Six weeks earlier, RKO released Orson Welles' *Citizen Kane*, in which Kane has an affair with an amateur singer, Susan Alexander,[44] while running for Governor of New York. After Kane and Susan marry she is forced into a career as an opera singer, for which she has neither the talent nor the ambition. Kane builds her a lavish opera house, compounding her humiliation. The film's composer, Bernard Herrmann, created a scene for Susan[45] in a fictional opera, *Salammbo*,[46] that overtly satirises the louder operas of Richard Strauss; during the performance, a member of the audience is heard to declaim "perfectly terrible;" another is seen to be tearing his programme into shreds.

The cruelty of the scene originates with Kane, but its pathos comes from the unsuitability of Susan's voice for a late romantic opera driven by a vast, contrapuntal orchestra. The judgment of ticket-holders is legitimate, of course, but so too is the audience's compassion for Susan after she attacks Kane following the performance. The dynamic of their relationship is diametrical to that of Callas and Onassis, who argued violently over Callas' refusal to perform when still able to do so. Her schedule after 1961 was spartan, and her career was essentially over three years later,[47] a lassitude that caused the unravelling of her personal life in 1968 to be portrayed globally as a modern Greek tragedy rather than the separation of a famous couple.[48]

Between 1971 and 1974, Callas ducked in and out of retirement, giving a series of masterclasses and recitals, the latter in the company of her sometime lover, Giuseppe di Stefano. After she died alone in her apartment, from a heart attack at the age of 53, the world mourned the passing of an opera singer. She was more than that for her legion of devotees, who appropriated her as a golem to which victims of sadness, isolation and persecution could pin their disquiet through fantasies of shared experience. In this sense, she was Wildean – another Janus-like casualty of dissatisfaction and disappointment. Callas compares also to Bernhardt, whose fame she was alone in sharing. They shared little else; where Bernhardt embraced life with impulsive, manic enthusiasm – expressing her elemental creativity through a compass of talents that included painting, sculpture and writing – Callas' forte was solipsism, of a kind and variety that bound her conceptually to Greta Garbo in wanting "to

---

44 Played by Dorothy Comingore.

45 Dubbed by a light-lyric soprano, Jean Forward, from Chicago.

46 Flaubert's *Salammbô* was turned into an opera by Ernest Reyer and Camille du Locle. The title role at the first performance on 10 February, 1890, was created by Rose Caron (17 November,1857 – 9 April, 1930), who six years earlier gave the premiere of Debussy's *L'enfant prodigue* (on 27 July,1884). She sang Marguerite in the stage premiere of Berlioz's *La damnation de Faust*, at Monte Carlo,in 1893. Caron is now better remembered for the amazing portrait painted by Auguste Toulmouche in 1880. She made recordings in 1903 and 1904 – seven years after her retirement. They are worth hearing for the surprising modernity of Caron's phrasing.

47 She made a couple of appearances as Medea at La Scala in 1962 but was largely absent until 1964, when she returned to Covent Garden for Zeffirelli's production of *Tosca* – the second act of which was filmed on 9 February, 1964. She gave two performances in the same role in 1965, at the Met, with Corelli as Cavaradossi. In the studio she made only a recording of *Carmen* (a role she did not play on stage), a second recording of *Tosca* (conducted by Georges Prêtre, with Bergonzi as her lover), and a disc of Verdi arias with Nicola Rescigno.

48 Onassis abandoned Callas for Jacqueline Kennedy, whom he married in the same year, on 20 October, 1968.

be alone." Of course, the media misrepresented Garbo's statement, who clarified for LIFE magazine in 1955 that she had "never said, 'I want to be alone; I only said, 'I want to be *let* alone! There is all the difference.'"[49] Garbo's last film, *Two Faced Woman*, was promoted using a trailer that began with her dancing for a camera that focussed shamelessly on her swaying backside. The graphics shrieked "Who is the screen's RHUMBA QUEEN? Who IS STILL YOUR TOP-RANKING STAR? Who DOESN'T WANT TO BE ALONE ANY MORE." The answer provided was "GARBO. THAT'S WHO...AND HOW." The studio's marketing ignored the talent of its star, and focussed instead on the currency of her celebrity, as an adjunct to the movement of her anatomy.

At the age of 36, and having made 27 movies over 19 years, Garbo retired and moved to Manhattan, where she lived until her death in 1990. Callas was 36 years-old when she began rehearsals for *Poliuto*,[50] and she continued to sing in public after the final performance in the run, even if work was less appealing than her sexually-fulfilling, Champagne-bathed life with Onassis, which allowed her to ignore the premature failure of her voice. It was Onassis who introduced Callas to Garbo, during a dinner on his yacht, *Christina*. The women became fast friends, and on 20 April, 1969, Callas spoke during a TV special in France of her friendship with the actress.[51] It later emerged she had based her characterisation of Violetta on Garbo's *Camille*. The actress' letters and the transcripts of her phone-calls reveal something of her complex personality; for all that has been said and written of her propensity for depression, she lived a fulfilling life in retirement. Conversely, Callas was miserable after 1968; her endurance of loneliness and *ennui* made her fascinating only at a distance. She understood and appreciated the value of her enigmatic status, which explains the care she took to ensure that no-one discovered her continuing relationship with Onassis after his marriage to Kennedy. Assuming she had anything interesting to say, or to write, Callas' cultivated inscrutability precluded her from doing either; her interviews in French and English are dull and predictable. She appears not to have had a sense of humour, which made her more relatable still for those who needed her to be as serious and as sacrificial as her singing of "*Casta diva*."

As a woman more sinned against than sinning, Callas' repertoire of persecuted characters amplified the extent to which she sang for the rejected and the abandoned; the pleasure drawn by her admirers from her suffering explains why the singer's life *after* she left the stage proved more interesting than anything she did when on it. The experiences endured by the characters she played were contiguous to what was known and perceived of her private life, and with the passage of time it's clear that her engagement with extreme states, real and imagined, made her accessible and attainable to audiences and admirers for whom her beauty and glamour served to disguise her stigmata. She was careful never to diminish what her life as the world's most famous singer cost her on each occasion she faced an audience; it was a condition precedent of her contract with the public that they rejoice in her isolation and persecution

---

49 *The Bloomsbury Handbook of Solitude, Silence and Loneliness* (2022). Eds. Julian Stern, Christopher A. Sink, Wong Ping Ho, Malgorzata Walejko. Bloomsbury, p. 200.
50 The first performance was five days after.
51 Booked to coincide with the launch of Pasolini's *Medea*.

whenever she carried her cross to the footlights for their benefit. During her televised French interview in 1969, Callas deliberated at length on the burdens of work, and the misery it caused her; she even characterised success as a wellspring for greater suffering. The frenzied response of the Met's hyper-strung crowd to her entrance as Tosca in 1965[52] didn't resonate as a greeting, therefore, and it wasn't heard as one. Callas and her public were joined in their acclamation of conquest, victory and the subjugation of the self.

There was nothing accommodating in Callas' art or her nature. Her conjunction of the two, in and out of costume, gave a hard edge of truth to her performances – particularly as Tosca. Magnificent though she was when singing "*Vissi d'arte*," Maria Jeritza's triumph as an artist was sustained by her physical engagement with the aria and the character, but it ended with the performance. On the other hand, many of those fortunate to see Callas play the role in the theatre were unable to distinguish fantasy from reality; it was impossible to know where one began and the other ended. She was an amalgam of graft, inspiration and misery, made incandescent by the coexistence in her voice of the definitively expressive and the stridently ugly. She remarked more than once that "it's not enough to have a beautiful voice," and *very* few of her studio recordings qualify for delivery to a desert island. Her first *Tosca*, made in 1953, is stupendous, but the weakness of Di Stefano's Cavaradossi pours water on the otherwise incendiary; her first *Norma* is similarly categorical, and marred only by the Pollione of Mario Filippeschi. Her performance on the opening night of La Scala's 1952 season as Lady Macbeth, conducted by Victor de Sabata, ranks among the most noteworthy of an Italian opera on record. It memorialises Callas' genius as a vocal actress despite the wretched sound engineering. Most of her work after *Un ballo in Maschera* with Antonino Votto in September, 1956, is coloured by a sharpness of tone and an agitated wobble for anything above an A4.[53] Even partnered with the finest among her peers in their prime (most obviously her remake of *Norma*, in 1960, with Corelli as Pollione and Ludwig as Adalgisa), her voice is tattered. Only diehard fans will return home after commuting on London's M25 or Paris' Boulevard Périphérique and play a recording of her singing from the 1960s.

Callas' unorthodoxy as a singing actress draws her into the genus of the technically imperfect Malibran and Pasta; her more immediate antecedent, however, was idolised for having the most perfect Italian-repertoire soprano voice of the early 20th century. Like Callas, Rosa Ponselle[54] was born in the United States to an immigrant family,[55] her parents were joined in supporting and encouraging their daughter's early talent as a pianist and a singer. Rosa was close to her older sister, Carmela,[56] and they sang

---

52   Which survives in a recording that comes close to perfection, thanks in no small part to the balance in the casting, which included the only tenor ever to equal her in voice and charisma, Franco Corelli.

53   Walter Legge dated the decline ("as a patch of vocal difficulties") from 1954, during the recording of *La forza del destino*: "the wobble had become so pronounced that I told her if we dared publish the records Angel and EMI would have to give away a seasickness pill with every side, which we could not afford. She took this to heart and worked hard on steadying down the wide pulse in her voice."

54   *née* Rosa Melba Ponzillo, 22 January, 1897 – 25 May, 1981. The choice by her parents of "Melba" as a middle-name was prescient.

55   Her parents were from Caiazzo, near Caserta, 35 miles from Naples, in the region of Campania.

56   *née* Carmela Ponzillo, 7 June, 1892 – 13 June, 1977.

together in public as children. From 1915, and for three years, "The Ponzillo Sisters"[57] were a headline act on the Keith Vaudeville Circuit, earning large sums of money for their performances of popular arias, duets and songs – one of which, "Comin' thro the rye," they recorded on 12 August, 1919.[58] Callas' childhood was very different. As she recalled, "I was made to sing when I was only five, and I hated it;"[59] her parents argued constantly about how to solve a problem like Maria, with Litsa's vicarious apprehension of parenting causing a stinging rivalry with her older sister, Iakintha ("Jackie"), whom Callas remembered as

> slim and beautiful and friendly, and my mother always preferred her. I was the ugly duckling, fat and clumsy and unpopular. It is a cruel thing to make a child feel ugly and unwanted [...] I'll never forgive her for taking my childhood away. During all the years I should have been playing and growing up, I was singing or making money. Everything I did for them was mostly good and everything they did to me was mostly bad.[60]

Rosa and Carmela's loving relationship survived the death in 1918 of Andrew Keith, whose company cancelled the sisters' act after they demanded a substantial increase in fees. Only a few weeks later, they were invited by the vocal coach, William Thorner, to sing for Victor Maurel and Enrico Caruso;[61] the latter arranged for Rosa to audition for Giulio Gatti-Casazza, the Intendant at the Met in New York, who offered her a contract for the 1918/1919 season. Ponselle made her debut on 15 November, 1918, as Leonora in *La forza del destino*, opposite Caruso and Giuseppe De Luca. She was 21-years-old and largely untrained;[62] it was her first performance in an opera. The New York Times' critic, James Huneker, wrote:

> what a promising debut! Added to her personal attractiveness, she possesses a voice of natural beauty that may prove a gold mine; it is vocal gold, anyhow, with its luscious lower and middle tones, dark, rich and ductile, brilliant in the upper register.

The success of Ponselle's first season is unique in the history of opera. The success of Ponselle's first season is unique in the history of opera, insofar as a woman only recently a teenager triumphed as Leonore, Santuzza, Reiza in *Oberon* and Carmelita in the world premiere of Joseph Breil's *The Legend*. The following two seasons included appearances in *La Juive* (with Caruso in his last new role before his death in

---

57 They were known branded as "Those Tailored Italian Girls."
58 The technical skill of both singers is in clear evidence, particularly during the bel canto cadenza.
59 Petsalis-Diomidis, Nicholas (2001). *The Unknown Callas: The Greek Years*. Amadeus Press, p. 40.
60 "The Prima Donna," *Time*, vol. 68, no. 18, October 29, 1956.
61 Ponselle remembered the tenor's reaction to her audition: "He sat down next to me—I was nervous as a kitten—and said, pointing to his throat, 'You have it here.' Then he pointed to his heart and said, 'And you have it here.' Then he raised his hand to his head and tapped his temple with his finger. 'And whether you have it up here, only time will tell.'"
62 Her sole process of study was with Puccini's protégé, Romano Romani – who coached her in all of her major roles.

1921), *Guglielmo Tell, Ernani, Il trovatore, Aida, La Gioconda, Don Carlos, L'Africaine, L'amore dei Tre re, Andrea Chénier*, and *La vestale*. Her most famous role was *Norma*, in the Met's historic 1927 revival. It was as Norma that she made her tumultuous debut at Covent Garden in 1929, a *success d'estime* unique in the theatre's history. In 1931 she sang her first Violetta, in which role she was broadcast live by the Met on 5 January, 1935, conducted by Ettore Panizza. This is one of the earliest surviving Met broadcasts, and it is one of Ponselle's only live performance to be recorded complete. She was not yet 40-years-old at the time, and she delivers an overwhelming portrayal in which every register is joined perfectly, with seamless phrasing, painterly dynamic variations, and an innate musical understanding. She transposed *"E strano"* down a whole tone (as did Tebaldi), and some of her *fiorituri* are imperfect, but she was a true dramatic coloratura, with an instrument of absurd voluptuousness and resonance. It is the voice of a singer of whom Geraldine Farrar said: "When discussing singers, there are two you must first set aside: Rosa Ponselle and Enrico Caruso. Then you may begin." W. J. Henderson complained of her "assaults" on the vocal line in *Traviata*; others considered her interpretation too forceful and dramatic. The final scene is garment-rending in its emotional intensity, with an indulgent beauty of tone analogous to a *crème brûlée* from Le Petit Châtelet.[63]

Ponselle's career was ended by *Carmen*.[64] Despite achieving popular success in the role, the *New York Times'* Olin Downes tore into her performance, writing a caustic review that cut Ponselle deeply.[65] During her two subsequent and final seasons at the Met she sang only Santuzza and Carmen, roles that presented no difficulties to her weakening upper register. Ponselle's last operatic performance was as Carmen on 22 April, 1937, in Cleveland – three months past her 40th birthday.

According to Walter Legge, Callas' voice began to fail in 1954 (at the age of 31), he suggested she turn to Ponselle for advice. Callas snapped back, "I won't see that woman – she started off with better material than I did."[66] It was almost as if Callas' imperfect technique had become as important to her as the dramatic instincts that compensated for what she lacked – a kind of masochistic self-actualisation that soothed the agony of not being Ponselle. Having retired at the top of her game, Ponselle's vocal perfection intensified the extent to which Callas' choices had undermined and damaged her no less natural, unschooled talent. It's inarguable that her weight loss, and some foolish repertoire decisions, shortened the lifespan of her voice; it's difficult in consequence to classify her *fach* because she roamed widely throughout her career from bel canto to *con belto*. A soprano capable of singing Rosina is not

---

63 Next door to Shakespeare and Company.

64 There is live footage (a screen test) of Ponselle singing the "Habanera" with piano, in 1936, that testifies to the extraordinary range and power of her voice. There is no passaggio, and little sign of breathing. In short, it is a near-perfect illustration of perhaps the most perfect vocal technique of any soprano during the age of recording. As with all the greatest singers, Ponselle makes it look easy. She is able also to act, without resorting to camp or cliché.

65 It can be summarised by the line "We have never heard Miss Ponselle sing so badly, and we have seldom seen the part enacted in such an artificial and generally unconvincing manner."

66 She was revealing insecurity rather than unkindness. Her summary opinion was, "I think we all know that Ponselle is simply the greatest singer of us all." Ponselle, Rosa, and Drake, James A. (1982). *Ponselle: a singer's life*. Doubleday, p.127.

meant also to sing Aida, particularly not after the fashion of her performance in Mexico on 7 March, 1951, when she closed the "Triumphal Scene" with an E flat lasting 18 seconds. Just because she *could* do this – and it is one of the most stupidly thrilling episodes committed to record – doesn't mean she *should* have done it. Serafin was right to claim that Callas could "sing anything written for the female voice," but that was fundamental to her performance-psychology. A singer without a *fach* is presented with unalloyed temptation, the effect of which invites early ruin, which is precisely what happened. Callas was a stupendous dramatic coloratura – unrivalled for the admixture of power and virtuosity that made her a perfect fit for her (mostly) blood-soaked repertoire. She began life as a mezzo-soprano and might have reverted to nature as a *heldensopran* but for Serafin's intervention. Her timbre was always dark, and her chest tones more resonant than those of the majority of her (routinely inferior) tenors. Her friend, John Ardoin, argued that Callas was a soprano *sfogato*[67] – a term used during the 19th century to describe a singer without limits.[68] Prescriptions are healthy, of course, and Callas' huge instrument was in dire need of training before being cast as Isolde, Brünnhilde and Kundry. Henry Chorley's description of Pasta applies equally to Callas:

> She subjected herself to a course of severe and incessant vocal study, to subdue and utilize her voice. To equalize it was impossible. There was a portion of the scale which differed from the rest in quality, and remained to the last "under a veil," to use the Italian term. There were notes always more or less out of tune," especially at the commencement of her performance. Out of these uncouth materials she had to compose her instrument, and then to give it flexibility. Her studies to acquire execution must have been tremendous; but the volubility and brilliance, when acquired, gained a character of their own, from the resisting peculiarities of the organ. There were a breadth, an expressiveness in her roulades, an evenness and solidity in her shake, which imparted to every passage a significance totally beyond the reach of lighter and more spontaneous singers.[69]

Whether or not they are willing to admit it, most of her admirers – then and now – delighted in their idol's personification of the extreme and the concealed.[70] The life of an American-born woman raised by a Greek family in post-war Europe enduring the ministrations of an insanely pushy mother was never going to be easy, and Maria would never be free of her self-conception as an immigrant – whether she was in the USA, mainland Europe or Greece. Regardless of the number of languages she was able to teach herself, the theatre was alone in providing Callas with her identity; it was the one space in which she was able to use a voice that was truly hers. This

---

67 'Vented.'

68 Applicable to Maria Malibran rather than Giuditta Pasta, whose range was comfortable to a high C only.

69 Kimbell, David (1998). *Norma*. Cambridge University Press, p. 109.

70 On the issue of Callas and concealment see Koestenbaum, Wayne (1993). *The Queen's Throat*.

cultivated otherness originated with the duality of Callas' timbre and culminated in a dramatic sensibility that set her apart from competition. Her ability to exceed the still-common reliance on gesture allied her to Stanislavski's dictum that "generality is the enemy of art." She appears not to have studied his Method, but acted in accordance with the advice he was said to have given a singer with whom he was working:

> "No," interrupted Stanislavski, "you are not giving out anything but sounds. You do not as yet need such large sounds for your feelings. Singing is beautiful only when it is natural and expresses something. But singing made up only of pretty sounds is anti-artistic because it is not sparked by inner feelings. You have a voice, a living organ which better than any instrument can express emotion, and you treat it like a trombone. This is unnatural and therefore you cannot speak expressively as in real life.[71]

After slimming, the expressive power of Callas' voice was joined to an intuitive physical elegance and facial plasticity that proved transformative; the coupling of vocal and physical technique was remarkable for the psycho-dramatic capacity it gave her for spontaneous characterisation. This was impressive whenever the soprano occupied a stage in solitude; it was revelatory in collaboration; even the supreme among her peers conceded the wonder of her reach beyond formula and repetition. She was exotic for being able to listen and observe as well as sing and act, a facility that allowed her to improvise from within the structure of a well-rehearsed staging. The alignment of free-thinking and movement, a species of dramatic rubato, compelled everyone else to push themselves to accommodate her natural, unforced spontaneity because she knew every role in a score at least as well as the cast retained to sing it; many believe she would have made a fine conductor. Callas' sway over her colleagues in performance survives in a handful of filmed excerpts – chiefly Act II of Zeffirelli's production of *Tosca* at Covent Garden, in 1964. This mesmerising essay in sung drama traces the effect of single words and phrases as she re-invented them for her colleagues and audiences. It was a superpower that made the improbable natural and believable. Her brilliance as a performer was elevated by her willingness to run with the inspiration of any colleague with a similarly acute flair for the involuntary; it surprised no-one that she did her best work with Tito Gobbi. Equally remarkable was her sensitivity to the continuity of a character's past and future. No scene in which she is present feels singular or isolated; her vocal and physical language reflected the changes to which her character was subjected over time – a form of creative selflessness that prioritised the purpose and value of a scene above the significance of her part in it.

Her otherness was no less a construction of her appearance, and (mostly) effortless sophistication. In becoming a silhouette as well as a sound, she achieved the unusual feat of being taken seriously as an artist while looking like someone for whom talent was inconsequential. It is tempting to wonder whether she would have become "Callas" but for losing half her body weight, just as many have questioned whether

---

71 Stanislavski, Constantin (1975). *Stanislavski on Opera*. Trans. and Ed. Elizabeth Reynolds Hapgood. Theatre Art Books, p. 22.

her transformation killed the thing that made her loved. Gobbi alluded to the debate when writing in his memoirs:

> she was not only supremely gifted both musically and dramatically – she was a beauty too. And her awareness of this invested with fresh magic every role she undertook. What it eventually did to her vocal and nervous stamina I am not prepared to say. I only assert that she blossomed into an artist unique in her generation and outstanding in the whole range of vocal history.[72]

In 1968, Callas told the conductor Edward Downes that she determined to lose weight after realising her size was impeding her instincts:

> I was getting so heavy that even my vocalizing was getting heavy. I was tiring myself, I was perspiring too much, and I was really working too hard. And I wasn't really well, as in health; I couldn't move freely. And then I was tired of playing a game, for instance playing this beautiful young woman, and I was heavy and uncomfortable to move around. In any case, it was uncomfortable and I didn't like it. So I felt now if I'm going to do things right – I've studied all my life to put things right musically, so why don't I diet and put myself into a certain condition where I'm presentable.[73]

There may be some truth to this; Callas liked the movies, and in 1953 seven of the top-ten grossing films of the year starred Deborah Kerr (*From Here to Eternity*), Marilyn Monroe (*How to Marry a Millionaire* and *Gentlemen Prefer Blondes*), Rita Hayworth (*Salome*), Eva Gardner (*Mogambo* and *Knights of the Round Table*), and Jean Simmons (*The Robe*). The last of these legendary women was alone in being British – and sounding like it. Callas was a first generation Greek-American, born and raised in New York City at a time when the local accent was as strong as it would ever be. The stand-up comedian Charlie Callas[74] was born almost exactly one year after Maria, and his accent was typical of Greek-Americans raised in New York. Callas left the US with her mother at the age of 13 to return to Greece; the one accent to which she had no access – at least until 1952, the year in which she made her debut at Covent Garden – was British. By the spring of 1954, she had shed her weight, signed with EMI, made her first recording under her new contract (*Lucia di Lammermoor*), and re-invented herself as a soprano specialising in repertoire for which she was untrained and unsuited.

The most famous coloratura of the 20th century began life as a dramatic soprano. She was engaged by Fausto Cleva to re-open the opera house in Chicago as Turandot

---

72   Gobbi, Tito (1980). *Tito Gobbi: My Life*. Futura Publications, p. 127.
73   Levine, Robert (2003). *Maria Callas: A Musical Biography*. Running Press, p. 125.
74   *née* Charles Callias. He was not related to Maria – although he would claim in routines to have been "named after her."

in 1946,[75] but the company closed before the opening night. Cleva's loss was Serafin's gain; he was looking for a young soprano to play the title role of *La Gioconda* in Verona, and the 22-year-old Callas was:

> Amazing – so strong physically and spiritually; so certain of her future.
> I knew in a big outdoor theatre like Verona's, this girl, with her courage
> and huge voice, would make a tremendous impact.

Serafin's judgment was honed over almost four decades conducting the world's finest Italian-repertoire singers.[76] It was doubly bizarre, therefore, that he should have cast such a young soprano as Isolde. Callas sang the role magnificently ten days after her 26th birthday – a decision that can be defended only on the basis that the conductor was a master of the bel canto tradition and knew what he was asking when presiding over the pit. Callas went on to sing Brünnhilde in *Die Walküre* and Kundry in *Parsifal* (both in early 1949);[77] she recorded the latter for RAI the following year. While singing Wagner at *La fenice*, Serafin asked Callas to learn the role of Elvira in *I puritani* – as cover for the ill-disposed Margherita Carosio.[78] Callas was given six days' notice – mid-way through her run as Brünnhilde. Her faith in Serafin's judgment settled her nerves and she accepted the challenge; on 19 January, 1949, Callas duly achieved what would remain the greatest triumph of her career. No-one could remember hearing Elvira performed by Isolde, particularly with the creeping categorisation of sopranos becoming absolute by the end of WWII, by which time the bel canto repertoire had fallen from fashion in Europe. The frothier end of the spectrum was performed by singers with lighter voices, typified by Carosio.[79] Callas' navigation of Bellinian virtuosity confounded even the sceptical, while her dramatic insights and depth of expression proved the virtue of Serafin's judgment. Notwithstanding a career-repertoire of approximately 40 roles, she reigned without meaningful competition during the 1950s as the world's foremost exponent of a limited range of operas by Rossini, Bellini, Donizetti, middle-period Verdi, and Puccini. Her dramatic reach was unusual for the 1950s; no-one has since has sung Wagner, Donizetti and Puccini, and prevailed across the spectrum.

It's important to remember that Callas was always a "dramatic" soprano; her voice was powerful and resonant when most of the singers specialising in bel canto had lighter voices. Her reigning predecessor as Violetta, Licia Albanese,[80] was modest

---

75   Cleva may have missed out on Callas' US debut, but he conducted her return to the New York Met, as Tosca, almost two decades later, on 19 March, 1965 – with Corelli and Gobbi. Her second performance, with Richard Tucker as Cavaradossi, on 26 March, proved to be her last in the USA. Thereafter, she returned to Paris for *Norma* (having played the role in her city debut a few months earlier), after which she sang one final *Tosca*, in London, in July.

76   Toscanini no longer conducted staged productions, which left Serafin in sole competition with Victor de Sabata, in Italy at least.

77   *Parsifal* in Rome; *Die Walküre* in Venice.

78   7 June, 1908 – 10 January, 2005.

79   Corosio was also expert in more contemporary repertoire, which included the title role of Stravinsky's *Le Rossignol*, Aminta in the first Italian production of Strauss' *Die schweigsame Frau*, and Egloge in the 1935 premiere of Mascagni's *Nerone*.

80   22 July, 1909 – 15 August, 2014. Those dates are correct. Albanese lived 105. She sang more

in tone and emphasis; her approach as it survives on the legendary NBC broadcast conducted by Toscanini is effervescent and hectic, in accordance with the conductor's view that the role should be "like champagne."[81] Callas' portrayal is darker, colder and vulnerable. She mastered the passion of the role, but the best of her performances on record are intimate for the damage they reveal rather than joy they inspire.[82] For all her skill, Callas was never less than a reluctant coloratura; she sang the role of Konstanze in *Die Entführung aus dem Serail*,[83] for example, and there is a live recording of "*Martern aller Arten*" from a 1954 concert in San Remo,[84] performed in Italian as "*Tutte le torture*," that speaks to her virtuosity during the early '50s.[85] Other sopranos (some from the second rank) were superior in their training and discipline; most made a prettier noise. As Armida, Norma, Elvira, Amina, Medea, Lucia, and Anna Bolena she was definitive; the last of this cluster of roles was Callas' statement of case, through which she is best discovered by anyone wanting to know what all the fuss is about. By the time Pasta created the role in 1830, she had gained a considerable amount of weight, a change in diet and body shape that was later blamed for the deterioration in her voice. At her prime, her voice was described in terms that would be employed for Callas after her appearance in La Scala's first 20th century revival,[86] directed by Luchino Visconti[87] In 1824, a critic wrote for the New Monthly Magazine that Pasta's voice was

> a mezzo-soprano, somewhat similar to that of Madame Vestris, but clearer, more powerful, and of greater compass [...]. In point of cultivation and science, she possesses, first of all, the rare merit of a pure intonation. We have not heard her once out of tune. Her voice type was what could be called a soprano *sfogato*. It was described by Stendhal as follows: she can achieve perfect resonance on a note as low as bottom A, and can rise as high as C♯, or even to a slightly sharpened D; and she possesses the rare ability to be able to sing contralto as easily as she can sing soprano. I would suggest [...] that the true designation of her voice is mezzo-soprano, and any composer who writes for her should use the mezzo-soprano range for the thematic material of his music, while still exploiting, as it were incidentally and from time to time, notes which

---

performances as Violetta at the Met and San Francisco Opera than any other soprano in either company's history.

81   Before first performing the role, Albanese visited a hospital to study the behaviour of patients suffering from tuberculosis to understand its psychological effects.

82   The live performance conducted by Giulini at La Scala in 1955 is peerless for many.

83   At La Scala in April, 1952.

84   She shared the programme with Gigli – but they did not sing together.

85   A rehearsal performance from a concert in Dallas three years later, conducted by Rescigno, reveals the extent to which her technique was beginning to fail her – when she was not yet 34-years-old.

86   It is a myth that La Scala's revival for Callas was the first of the 20th century. Sara Scuderi (December 11, 1906 – December 24, 1987) sang the role for a revival at the Liceo in Barcelona in 1947 with Nicola Rossi-Lemeni (who married Callas' supposed successor in the role, Virginia Zeani, in the same year as the Visconti-Callas production at La Scala), Giulia Simionato (who sang the role of Giovanna / Jane in 1957) and Cesare Siepi.

87   Premiered in April, 1957; Callas gave 12 performances.

lie within the more peripheral areas of this remarkably rich voice. Many notes of this last category are not only extremely fine in themselves, but have the ability to produce a kind of resonant and magnetic vibration, which, through some still unexplained combination of physical phenomena, exercises an instantaneous and hypnotic effect upon the soul of the spectator. This leads to the consideration of one of the most uncommon features of Madame Pasta's voice: it is not all moulded from the same *metallo*, as it is said in Italy (which is to say that it possesses more than one timbre); and this fundamental variety of tone produced by a single voice affords one of the richest veins of musical expression which the artistry of a great cantatrice is able to exploit.[88]

In 1829, the critic Carlo Ritorni held that Pasta's voice was directed towards "the most intense passions, accompanying it with expressions of physical action, unknown before her in the lyric theatre."[89] An almost identical vernacular was used to describe Callas 130 years later, when the change in her body-shape was, *contra* Pasta, deemed advantageous. The performance on 14 May, 1957, was recorded. It is one of the most important made of an opera. Callas' Anna is famously regal, but during the concluding scene of the second (and final) act ("*Al dolce guidami castel natio*")[90] her genius is revealed through shocking vulnerability, achieved through hauntingly insular phrasing that turns her vision of Percy, and her wish for "*de' miei primi'anni, un giorno sol del nostro amor...*",[91] into a soliloquy for the broken. Callas shapes the opening bars, descending through joined triplets to convey the tears falling from her eyes. Her grief is punctuated by an F sharp crotchet, for the syllable "*mi*," which Callas binds through a barely perceptible, heart-stopping slide to an E natural crotchet with which the second two-bar phrase begins. She employs portamento to lessen the interruption compelled by her intake of breath – an unteachable moment of eye-widening inspiration that many have attempted to copy since.[92] The graded use of portamento for the words "*castel natio*," is made poignant by a mesmerising *de*crescendo on "*natio*," (scored as a rising sequence, D-F-A) so as to heighten the significance of her remembrance of "Home Sweet Home."[93] Her singing of the phrase when repeated – with doubled triplets and a trill – concludes with an unbroken phrase, formed of eight demi-semi-quavers which, again, she delivers with a decrescendo of impossible tenderness. For the three bars beginning "*Ah*," Callas breathes the falling sequence (E-D-C sharp-B, with semiquaver grace notes attaching), almost

---

88   Pleasants, Henry (1981). *The Great Singers*. Simon & Schuster, p. 374.
89   Ritorni, Carlo (1829). *Annali del teatro della citta di Reggio*. In Rutherford, Susan (2007), "La cantante delle passioni: Giuditta Pasta and the Idea of Operatic Performance," *Cambridge Opera Journal*, Vol. 19 (2), p. 112.
90   'Take me back to the castle of my birth.'
91   'one day of my youth [...] one day of our love.'
92   Most obviously, and least successfully, Anna Netrebko. Angela Gheorghiu copied the effect on a studio recording of the aria for EMI, in which she is greatly assisted by the editor's knife, which allows her to perform the opening four bars without a breath.
93   Donizetti quotes the song's melody.

causing Gavazzenni and the orchestra to stall.[94] She proceeds to swell the line without interrupting the cadence, *tempo primo*. Notwithstanding some overt "conducting" by Callas, her rubato is speech-like, which causes the resulting sense of improvisation to seem intimate even for an audience of more than 3,000.

The soprano's talent can be traced through her sublimation of those expressive tricks on which she was able to rely, so that the wonder of cause is transcended by the power of effect; skill is recalibrated as expression. The range of this part of the scene is essentially D3–D4, low for a bel canto soprano. Of course, neither Pasta nor Callas was typical; indeed, Callas was an anomaly in having confident access for at least five years (and until 1957) to a perfected range of three octaves. She and Pasta were renowned for the power of their lower registers, in which quarter Callas is mesmerising for the unusual richness of her mezzo-chest voice. She was inexact technically; during "*al dolce guidami,*" for example, she fluffs a D3 for the final syllable of "[*primi an*] *ni,*" and the rising run for the first iteration of the words "*del nostro amor,*" is a serried mess. Her upper extension was under terminal strain from 1956, with her vibrato spreading the tone harshly above the stave. She was unfazed because the drama was unaffected; Callas turned every word and note to expressive effect – as the voice of a woman whose emotional state on the eve of her execution would, in all probability, have caused her voice to break when recalling "our love." At the outset of the aria's B section (repeating the words, "*Al dolce guidami,*"), Callas intensifies the quiver in her vibrato to achieve a shift in atmosphere and emphasis – without adding anything to her tone or the amplitude of projection. The change in colour is achieved through texture and timbre, with vibrato used not as a constant but as a tool for the crafting of expression;[95] as the bedrock for all dramatic bel canto, the melodic arc is preserved throughout.

Callas slows the tempo dramatically for "*un giorno rendemi,*"[96] which she delivers in a barely audible, perfectly supported pianissimo; for her repetition of "*giorno sol*"[97] she employs a *subito piano* that is a tour de force of vocal courage and conviction. Others had sung this music before Callas;[98] many have sung it since. From what can be discerned from recordings, no-one has come close to achieving what Callas did in 1957. Sceptics can hear Virginia Zeani[99] charge her way through the music without care or concern for the palette revealed by Callas. Leyla Gencer[100] sang it beautifully, and in obvious submission to Callas' influence, but there is nothing in her recorded performances to compare in the singers' use of line, colour, word placement and rhythmic plasticity. Renato Scotto is the finest among her competition,

---

94   Gianandrea Gavazzeni never received the recognition he deserved. His conducting of this performance is exceptionally expressive, as is the playing of the La Scala orchestra. His attention to Callas is astonishing and, as was typical of many of Callas' finest performances, her collaboration with the conductor is palpably reciprocal.

95   The tenors, Carlo Bergonzi and (the young) José Carreras, did something similar. See Boyden, Matthew (2021). *The Tenor: A Cultural History.* Ragueneau Press.

96   'Make me, one day…"

97   'Sunny day.'

98   Albeit not on record. Callas was the first to be recorded in the scene.

99   *née* Virginia Zehan, 21 October, 1925 –

100   Ayşe Leyla Gencer (*née* Çeyrekgil), 10 October, 1928 – 10 May, 2008.

and better attuned to the aching, dignified beauty of Callas' performance in 1957 performance; even Montserrat Caballé, singing the role at La Scala in 1982, ambles through Donizetti's triplets, communicating little more than the notes as written. Her floated pianissimos are improbably perfect, and she is eternally musical, but the listener's attention is drawn to the singer's technique rather than the character she is playing. A more recent exponent of the role at the Met, Sondra Radvanovsky,[101] recalled Samuel Butler's comment on the music of Robert Schumann: "I should like [it] better than I do."[102]

It didn't matter where Callas was singing for the world to turn up, which included a media more rabid than could have been imagined at the time of her birth. Singers were a source of eternal curiosity, of course, but the reach of enquiry had been contained. In the 1928 edition of *Modern Musicians*,[103] for example, the chapter on Luisa Tetrazzini quoted the singer's summary view of her celebrity in Britain:

> No sooner does a Britisher hear a singer than he wishes to know what she eats and wears and thinks about; whether she is married, and how many children she has. It is most amusing to me.[104]

The attention directed at Callas was never so fluffy. Once fame overreached talent, and consequent to her re-invention as a woman of unconventional beauty, the media's appetite grew by what it fed on, and she was soon enough a celebrity in dozens of countries where she would never appear. Between 1948 and 1965, she sang Norma on 90 occasions – in eight countries. Most of her other roles were confined to Italy. Callas' status was global according to the mechanical and technological limitations of the day, which precluded her from having to travel globally. Her infamous feud with Rudolph Bing at the Met concerned repertoire, not money or contract riders; many remain bitter that Callas gave only 20 performances at the Met during a career lasting two decades – even if most of them were booed. This didn't prevent her from performing in the United States, of course, and her celebrity increased despite her absence from the Metropolitan roster; she was forever in the teeth of tension and controversy, from which she would endeavour always to emerge as victim.

Being the focus of attention in a pre-digital age was problematic for a woman without a stable home speaking four languages – none of them natively. Callas was American because that's what was recorded on her birth certificate; her marriage to an Italian and her near-exclusive commitment to music by Italian composers was sufficient for many in Italy to regard her as one of theirs; her accent and the superiority of her manner made her as English as croquet. It was more complicated in Greece. Shortly after completing her run as Bolena at La Scala in 1957 she made

---

101   11 April, 1969 –

102   He continued "I dare say I could make myself like it better if I tried; but I do not like having to try to make myself like things; I like things that make me like them at once and no trying at all." In Larkin, Philip (1983). "The Pleasure Principle." *Required Writing: Miscellaneous Pieces 1955–1982*. Faber and Faber, p. 82.

103   Cuthbert Hadden, J. (1928). *Modern Musicians: A Book for Players, Singers and Listeners*. Peter Davies.

104   *Ibid*, p. 116.

what was perceived to be her "comeback" at the open-air Theatre of Herod Atticus, at the foot of the Acropolis. She had been invited by the government of Constantine Karamanlis to give two concerts at the Athens Festival, during the first week of August. When arriving at Ellinikon Airport, on 29 July, the country greeted her as Theseus; her experience having landed was closer to that of Odysseus.[105] The Hellenic Parliamentary opposition, led by Georgios Papandreou and Sophocles Venizelos (son of Eleftherios Venizelos, the leader of the national liberation movement), exploited Callas' arrival as a means of sticking it to Karamanlis' administration. Questions were asked in Parliament about the singer's fees, which were sizable, at $9,000 for two appearances.[106] Newspapers loyal to the Liberal coalition whipped the circus into a frenzy – demanding that the performances be boycotted. Despite not being on good terms, Papandreou and Venizelos stayed away. The front page of the Greek paper, *Ta Nea*, featured an article by Dimitris Psathas that hissed:

> This column must honestly confess that it feels ashamed because it has been repeatedly preoccupied with this repulsive prominent lady, who came to grab the dollars of our poverty.

Callas' hotel, the Grande Bretagne (on Syntagma Square),[107] was besieged by angry crowds, formed by warring members of the Greek and foreign press; the site became so dangerous that a large police presence was made necessary; they were joined by the army after a series of bomb threats. Not for the first time in her life, and certainly not for the last, Callas was sequestered out of necessity. When realising that "everyone" was not going to leave her alone – as she is said to have begged – Callas announced she would not be singing. The Festival Committee was unable to change her mind, and a press release was issued in which it was stated that "because of a sudden illness, Mme. Callas' performance has been postponed."[108] The second concert went ahead, not-withstanding the waging of the fourth Trojan war during the intervening weekend by the country's antipathetic newspapers,[109] most of which tore into Callas as a symbol for everything from women's rights and gender equality to cultural imperialism, the death of art, and the corrupting influence of the United States. Writing in *To Vima*, Pavlos Palaiologou declared Callas to be "unworthy" of being considered Greek: "my national pride has been insulted [...] only one road is now available for Callas, and it leads straight to the airport." Palaiologou added that Callas was unfit also for her family, which was a bit much considering what was known of the singer's mother. In an attempt to calm the atmosphere, Greek National Radio invited the soprano to make a statement; she apologised for having missed her first performance, and blamed the "death" of her voice on the climate: "due to Athens' dry weather, which I

---

105   As many noted at the time, Callas took longer to return to Greece (11 years) than did Odysseus after the end of the Trojan War (ten years).

106   Approximately $90,000 in modern money.

107   Even though the hotel has been completely overhauled by the owners, Marriot, the stunning views of the Acropolis from the roof terrace (one of the finest anywhere), have not changed since Callas' residency.

108   It was at no time indicated when the performance might be re-scheduled; and it wasn't.

109   There were three actual wars if one includes Agamemnon's abortive attack on Teuthrania.

am unaccustomed to, being decades abroad, my voice turned hoarse yesterday and I couldn't be there at the Festival launch." She continued:

> I could have sung, perhaps, but with the state of my voice, I wouldn't be any good. I want to be at my best when I sing for you, Athens crowd, because you love me so much and I love you too. In Italy and in the rest of my world I like to give my best, but for you I want to give so much more than my best.

These comments were reported in Italy, where the newspapers wondered why she wasn't willing to give more than her best at La Scala. Callas even drew on recent history, asserting that she "wanted to appeal to the Greek people, with whom we have spent hard times together during the Nazi occupation of 1941 to 1944." She might have left it there; instead, she added:[110]

> I came here just to sing for you, but I was disheartened by the way some people have involved my name with politics. I have nothing to do with politics – all artists shouldn't meddle with politics […] artists belong to the whole world. I belong to [the] Greek people […] I may be married to an Italian man […] but my blood is Greek and nobody can deny that.

Callas' miserable experience was not without precedent. On 12 August, 1891, the *Los Angeles Times* published a sledgehammer parody in which it was asserted that Sarah Bernhardt was "a plain Iowan by birth." As much was said to be obvious from her nature and her manner, which were diagnostically American because of the actress' aversion to "foreign frills." Bernhardt was also exploited as a queen in France's interminable game of political chess; parties and papers failing to secure her support would drag her private life into daylight and subject it to a savage hinting; for all that might actually have been written, the theatre gazettes and newspapers were *relatively* guarded, hampered as they were by contemporary notions of decorum. It was a burden, but no more than dew to grass when compared to the Unreal City of modern times. As Ignacio Ramos-Gay observed in his splendid analysis of the politicisation of Bernhardt's right leg after its amputation in 1915:

> [she] was the first modern celebrity in the current sense of the term, not only due to her popularity but also to her thorough knowledge and mastery of publicity mechanisms, through which she constantly negotiated fact and fiction. Her outrageous scandals were duly transcribed in the media, sweeping audiences into a terrain of volatile, often contradictory, information.[111]

---

110   Callas left as she arrived – pursued by journalists. She refused to return to Greece until August, 1960, when she gave three performances as Norma at the Epidaurus amphitheatre. Before doing so, she donated her $15,000 fee to the creation of a scholarship fund in her name. Hilariously, and with ill-disguised malice, she defined the purpose of the fund as being for the education and training of Greek singers overseas.

111   Ramos-Gay, Ignacio (2018). "Partly American!": Sarah Bernhardt's Transnational Disability in the

The parallels between Callas and Bernhardt's experience of fame are remarkable; their reaction to it was quite different. The actress took to reinventing herself as Baroness Munchausen, telling increasingly tall tales of her life and adventures. As Robert Gottlieb put it: "She was a complete realist when dealing with her life but a relentless fabulist when recounting it."[112] Callas preferred silence, revealing almost nothing during or after her career; her status as a *tabula rasa* for the projection of external narratives and constructions guaranteed her manipulation by forces bent on generating drama where none existed. Her reputation for being in near-constant conflict was undeserved, but her temper made her an easy target for provocation. In November, 1954, for example, she triumphed in Chicago as Cio-Cio-San. Having received nearly half an hour of hysterical acclamation, she headed to her dressing room, where she was greeted by Stanley Pringle, a U.S. Marshall, in the company of a dozen police officers. He handed her a subpoena, arising from a claim filed by a former lover, Richard Bagarozy, whom she had hired as a manager in 1946.[113] Still wearing a kimono, the demure, ritualised Butterfly was photographed with her teeth bared, snarling at Pringle. It was a jarring image for an opera singer, made nefarious by reports that she was shrieking, "they won't sue me! I have the voice of an angel!" The episode featured in a largely negative article attaching to her appearance on the front of *Time* magazine on 29 October, 1956.[114]

Callas' reputation for conflict made her complicated also for her peers and rivals, including Renata Tebaldi,[115] the only soprano to rival Callas in status during the 1950s. Tebaldi was just 22 at the time of her debut as Elena, in *Mefistofele*, in Rovigo. She was cast thereafter in roles for which no-one would today consider so young a singer, including Maddalena di Coigny and, in 1946, Desdemona – the latter for a production of *Otello* starring the tooth-rattling Francesco Merli. Her name and talent came to the attention of Toscanini, for whom she auditioned in 1946. He was smitten, and invited her to join the roster of artists retained to re-open La Scala, on 11 May, when Toscanini conducted her in performances of "*Dal tuo stellato soglio*,"[116] from Rossini's *Mosè in Egitto*, and Verdi's *Te Deum*.[117] Like Callas, Tebaldi was cast also in Wagner (Elsa and Eva) as well as the spinto Italian repertoire; she was not, at the time, a dramatic soprano; neither was she a coloratura. In 1950, however,

American Press (1915–1918)." *Journal of the Spanish Association of Anglo-American Studies*, p. 65.

112   Gottlieb, Robert (2010). *Sarah: The Life of Sarah Bernhardt.* Yale University Press, p. i.

113   Bagarozy blackmailed Callas after she became famous. He threatened to send their love letters to her husband; when she refused to pay, Bagarozy sued for breach of contract as her alleged Manager, seeking $300,000 in damages. In 2007, the letter issued by his lawyers, Wilzin & Halperin (dated 8 February, 1955), and the contract Callas is said to have breached (dated 13 June, 1947) came up for sale at Sotheby's. Bagarozy claimed to have hired Callas for performances in Verona in 1947. On 30 November, 1955, at Callas' request, the Ente Autonomo Spettacoli Lirici Arena di Verona declared that Callas had been engaged by Zenatello and that "it does not appear from the official documents [...] that other people outside the Superintendence have in some way determined Mrs. Meneghini Callas." Bagarozy was a known fraudster, but the contract was nonetheless deemed valid by the court, compelling a settlement.

114   The Prima Donna," *Time*, vol. 68, no. 18, October 29, 1956. The article suggested that Callas' relationship with her mother was more interesting to readers than her art.

115   1 February, 1922 – 19 December, 2004.

116   'From your starry throne.'

117   One of his *Quattro pezzi sacri* ('Four Sacred Pieces'), from 1890.

Toscanini persuaded her to take on Aida, a dramatic role made adversarial by the bug-eyed yelling of her tenor colleague, Mario del Monaco.[118]

Tebaldi made her US debut in 1950, as Aida, at the San Francisco Opera. She appeared for the first time at the Met, as Desdemona, on 31 January, 1955 – two months after Callas made her American debut, as Norma, at the Chicago Opera. Their rivalry was inevitable, even if they shared nothing else. Tebaldi was unattractive and inept as an actress; she adhered in her repertoire to verismo. She had almost no private life, disdained marriage and bore no children. She was committed to the stage, on which she gave 1,262 performances,[119] all but 214 of them in complete works. She retired from opera in 1973, and from recitals three years later – her final US bow being taken at Carnegie Hall in January, and in Italy in May. During her life, and since her death, almost nothing of interest has been said or written by (or about) Tebaldi, despite her being one of the world's most adored singers. It was because of the sound she made – and literally nothing else – that her rivalry with Callas was imagined and invented. In 1952, when Callas was not yet 30, Andrew Porter observed of Callas' debut as Norma at Covent Garden that she was

> the most exciting singer on the stage today. Her virtues? Great range and power, prime necessities. The ability to invest coloratura with dramatic and expressive qualities (needed by all heroines of serious opera so far as the middle Verdi). A great range of vocal colours, allied to an exceptional dramatic understanding. Tones that are affecting, and tones that are thrilling. An imposing presence, gesture and physical expression, command of the stage rarely found today in any actress. In sum, Callas is a star […]. To be sure, there were moments when the tone became less beautiful. They were flecks on a superb assumption.

Critical commentary on Tebaldi focussed on her being the source of the most glorious sound of modern times – an ability that prescribed the span of curiosity. No-one made a major motion picture about her in her centenary year (2022), and neither has her life and work been subjected to anything like the sort of scrutiny for which Callas continues to be remarkable. Only a single biography of "note," was written during the height of Tebaldi's career, a warbling eulogy by Victor Seroff, *The Woman and the Diva,*[120] made interesting only by its nasty references to Callas. No-one has written, or will ever write, "An Intimate Biography."[121] Every book since has focussed on her career and the celebration of her voice as an instrument of sumptuous beauty, rather

---

118   Three years later, she sang the music mimed by Sophia Loren for the film version of *Aida* directed by Clemente Fracassi, later the production manager for the filming of *La dolce vita* and *8 1/2*.
119   Tebaldi was for two decades the Met's leading dramatic Italian soprano, and one of the House's leading box office draws, appearing on 270 occasions as Mimi, Butterfly, Tosca, Manon Lescaut, Mimi, Desdemona, Leonora in *La forza del destino*, Maria Boccanegra, Maddalena di Coigny, Adriana Lecouvreur, and Gioconda.
120   Published in 1961.
121   Edwards, Anne (2001). *Maria Callas: An Intimate Biography*. St. Martin's Press. Ms Edwards previously authored biographies of Judy Garland, Shirley Temple, Katherine Hepburn, Vivien Leigh and Princess Diana.

than the lazy diction and imperfect intonation by which it was impaired. Tebaldi's records continue to sell – as they should, since much of her discography from the 1950s is very fine, even if she was forced too often to share a cell with the murderous Brass Bull of Milan.[122] Her recordings of *La bohème*[123] and *Madama Butterfly*,[124] with Carlo Bergonzi as Rodolfo and Pinkerton, conducted by Serafin, have not been bettered, and they are likely to remain benchmarks for as long as opera continues to matter. In 1963 she withdrew from performances – in her 41st year, when she should have been in her prime. A year of rest, recuperation and study proved unproductive; after she returned to performing her voice was larger and harsher, with an overbright, metallic edge. The richness for which her singing had been notable previously was subjected to extortion, with tension disfiguring what had once been effortless.

Tebaldi's personification of sound for its own sake was set in opposition to Callas' ideation of dramatic expression – a conviction paid for with her voice. *Tono e parola* were cast as rivals, with the singers' fans relishing their entrenchment. Even before either of them was famous internationally, the tabloids relished the presentiment of antagonism. In 1951, Tebaldi and Callas were booked for a recital in Rio de Janeiro; they agreed not to perform encores. When Tebaldi took two of them, Callas was furious – and reported to be. The sopranos were thereafter presented by the media as enemies. In 1956, for example, *Time* magazine printed an alleged comment by Callas, to which Tebaldi responded "the signora says that I have no backbone [...] I have one great thing that she has not – a heart."[125] Elsewhere, *Time* reported Callas as saying that any comparison with Tebaldi was like "comparing Champagne with Cognac. No, with Coca Cola." Witnesses to the interview stated that Callas had employed cognac as a metaphor in isolation, and that someone else in the room had added "Coca-Cola," in fawning obeisance to Callas. If the press was predatory then its columnists were something worse. Tebaldi's champion at the time,[126] Elsa Maxwell, wrote of Callas:

> I confess the great Callas acting in the Mad Scene left me completely unmoved [...] I was intrigued by the red wig she wore through the first two acts but in the Mad Scene she came on as a platinum blonde. Why this change of color? What did it mean to this egocentric extrovert?[127]

This hardly qualified as criticism, and it wasn't meant to. Callas responded in kind:

> Elsa isn't really evil. She never disguises her motives. If she had less girth and more charm she probably could have been as accepted in society as those whose entry she sponsored.[128]

---

122   Mario del Monaco.

123   1959.

124   1958.

125   Stassinopoulos, Ariana (1981). *Maria Callas: The Woman Behind the Legend*. Simon and Schuster, p. 163.

126   She later switched her allegiance to Callas.

127   *Ibid.*

128   Edwards, Anne (2001). *Maria Callas: An Intimate Biography*. St. Martin's Press, p. 144.

During Callas' second New York appearance as Lucia, the baritone singing the role of Ashton, Enzo Sordello, held onto a high note during the second act duet with which Callas was unable to keep pace.[129] She was made to seem short of breath. The audience heard her yell "*Basta,*"[130] which many confused with "bastard." Sordello's contract with the Met was terminated instantly by Bing – at Callas' direction – and the episode was presented as typical of the "temperamental diva." Having been photographed tearing up Callas' photo, Sordello booked a seat on the soprano's return flight to Italy. This was leaked to the press, which turned up in force to capture them standing a few feet apart when boarding the plane. Callas and Tebaldi were eventually reconciled, and each spoke fondly of the other after Callas' retirement from staged performance. The same was not true of her relationship with Renato Scotto.

Despite being eleven years younger than Callas, Scotto was her near contemporary.[131] She performed in public for the first time in her home-town, Savona, on Christmas Eve, 1952 – at the age of 18, as Violetta. The following evening, she made her "official" debut at the Teatro Nuovo in Milan, in the same role. In 1953, Scotto auditioned at La Scala to sing Walter in Catalani's *La Wally* – alongside Tebaldi and del Monaco. After her audition, one of the judges, Victor de Sabata, remarked "Forget about the rest." *La Wally* was the season premiere, on 7 December, 1953; Scotto was summoned for fifteen curtain calls; Tebaldi and Del Monaco each received seven. Four years later, the La Scala company toured their new production of *La Sonnambula* to the Edinburgh Festival, with Callas as Amina. The scheduled performances were so well-received that another was added; Callas had contracted to sing for four performances only and declined to sing any more. She approved of Scotto as her replacement, and Callas' departure from the Festival was explained as a consequence of illness. The fifth performance caused a sensation and made Scotto a star.

Scotto's voice in her prime was unusually expressive, her word-use nothing less than poetic; as a vocal actress she was capable of conjuring moments of ecstasy and introversion, without forcing her distinctive tone. During the 1960s, Scotto was one of a stable of bel canto-coloratura revivalists[132] whose work features on almost every recording of note from the golden age of the LP, between the early 1950s and the late 1970s. The most famous of Callas' "rivals" was the Australian born Joan Sutherland,

---

129   There are no "playful" anecdotes arising from the many occasions when Callas sang alongside Corelli – whose lungs outmatched those of almost anyone else. His "rivalry" with Nilsson resulted in each trying to out-sing the other – but always within the framework of professional respect and friendship. Corelli could almost certainly have held onto a shared note for longer than Callas – notwithstanding the evidence of "that" E flat at the end of the "Triumphal" Scene in *Aida*, in Mexico in 1951.

130   'Enough.'

131   And still working. Having performed for the last time in 2002, she turned thereafter to teaching and directing. She remains active at the time of publication, a year from her 90th birthday.

132   Sopranos: Joan Sutherland, 7 November, 1926 – 10 October, 2010; Beverly Sills 25 May, 1929 – 2 July, 2007; Montserrat Caballé, *née* María de Montserrat Viviana Concepción Caballé i Folch, 2 April, 1933 – 6 October, 2018; Roberta Peters, 4 May, 1930 – 18 January, 2017; Anna Moffo, 27 June, 1932 – 9 March, 2006; Victoria de los Angeles, *née* Victoria de los Angeles López García, 1 November 1923 – 15 January, 2005; Giulietta Simionato, 12 May, 1910 – 5 May, 2010; Shirley Verrett, 31May, 1931 – 5 November, 2010; Teresa Berganza, *née* Teresa Berganza Vargas, 16 March, 1933 – 13 May, 2022; Marylin Horne, 16 January, 1934 – ; Fiorenza Cossotto, 22 April, 1935 – .

who began as a "utility soprano" during the early 1950s at Covent Garden, before accepting engagements as a named soloist in contemporary music, including Lady Rich in Benjamin Britten's *Gloriana* and the first performance of Michael Tippett's *The Midsummer Marriage*, in which she created the role of Jenifer.[133] She was urged by her husband, the conductor Richard Bonynge, to develop her coloratura technique, and in 1959 she was cast as the lead in Zeffirelli's production of *Lucia* at Covent Garden, conducted by Serafin. Sutherland established herself on record the following year with the double LP, *The Art of the Prima Donna*, which secured a Grammy Award in 1962. Sutherland played Lucia in Paris, La Scala and the Met, where her singing of the "Mad" scene received a 12-minute ovation. As "*La Stupenda*,"[134] she was partnered with a young Italian tenor, just four years into his career,[135] called Luciano Pavarotti, with whom she thrilled on stage and in the studio, giving memorable performances[136] of *Beatrice di Tenda, I puritani, la sonnambula, Norma, Lucia di Lammermoor, La fille du régiment, L'elisir d'amore, Maria Stuarda, Rigoletto, La traviata* and *Il trovatore*.[137]

From her first complete studio recordings, as Lucia and Gilda in 1961, until her last full-length staged performance, as Marguerite in *Les Huguenots* in 1990 – at Sydney Opera House (where she sang "Home Sweet Home" as an encore)[138] – Sutherland was the world's most technically accomplished coloratura, with one of the largest, most powerful voices to sing what became "her" repertoire. Her range extended from G3 to F6; she was capable of an F-sharp 6 also, although she never sang it in public. Sutherland compared in consequence to some of her forebears, who shattered the glass wall into the 7th octave, but her range was more than adequate to master the repertoire in which she specialised. The brilliance of her tone was exceptional, and harsh only into the 1970s; the middle register warmed with time and experience, becoming honeyed and cello-like. She had a fine legato also, and a generous dynamic range. What set her apart was the kind of technique for which Tetrazzini was famed. Whatever the challenge, Sutherland could hammer out machine-gun like staccatos, endless runs and leaps that were achievable only by a flautist. No-one – not even Beverley Sills – could rival her in showing off. Unfortunately, Sutherland was boring for anyone interested in what it was that made her repertoire spectacular at first instance. There is a useful parallel in the life and death of the German trapeze artist, Lillian Leitzel,[139] whose act included one-armed planges that required her to dislocate her shoulder momentarily during each turn. She would flip her body on hundreds of occasions during each show for audiences fixated on the possibility that Leitzel's shoulder or her equipment might fail. And fail it did. She died after tumbling during a performance in Copenhagen, which was what everyone had to turned up to see

---

133 First performed on 27 January, 1955.
134 'The Stupendous One.'
135 In Australia in 1965.
136 All of them for Decca, and all of them still available.
137 They also recorded *Turandot* together, although Sutherland never performed the role on stage.
138 Her last public appearance was in a gala performance of *Die Fledermaus* on New Year's Eve, 1990, at Covent Garden, where she was joined by Pavarotti and Marilyn Horne.
139 2 January, 1892 – 15 February, 1931.

even if they didn't care to admit it.[140] A similar danger attaches still to the work of the high-flying soprano, whose tight-rope act is formed of risk and improbability. Even Tetrazzini suffered *"perle nere,"*[141] those operatic disasters for which YouTube has become an abundant oyster bed. Sutherland cracked and split rarely – and certainly not in her prime; as the most reliable soprano of her generation her security rendered safe what was meant to be dangerous. The riveted, steel-lined technique for which she was renowned would not have dissipated dramatic and narrative tension had she presented as vulnerable, or been able to enunciate any word other than "Ah."

In the history of singing since the invention of recording no other soprano has fused such virtuosity to such atrocious diction, especially in Italian – Sutherland's first language as a singer. Rossini's boast, "give me a laundry list and I'll set it to music," was actualised to the point of satire by Sutherland when making a librettist's words too long a sacrifice.

Caballé's diction was better by degree. Like Sutherland, she was a woman of non-conformist appearance, particularly from the middle 1970s, so that her work on stage involved her moving as if on casters. Unlike Sutherland, and uniquely among her peers, Caballé's idiosyncratic tone, granite-hewn technique and aristocratic instincts turned bel canto into *bellisima* canto. The projection of her voice was freakish for its beauty, idiosyncrasy and resonance, just as her instincts were improbable in the security of their judgment. She idealised voice-acting as an admixture of *ton und word*, so that performance transcended the limitations of the score, reaching beyond notation while adhering to a rigorous and disciplined reading of the text. Caballé respected text, tempo, dynamics, phrasing, articulation, form and structure while adorning and enhancing the choreographic aspects of coloratura as a hermeneutic fantasy, sanctifying Mahler's aphorism that "what is best in music is not to be found in the notes." Caballé was deserving of her nickname, *"La Superba."* Her career and repertoire were unusual also for their diversity. She first came to attention during the late 1950s, in Basel, where her repertoire included Mozart (the First Lady in *Die Zauberflöte*) and Strauss (*Salome*) – which she sang in German. After three years in Bremen, she starred in a Lisbon production of *Iphigénie en Tauride*, and in 1962 she made her debut at the Liceu in Barcelona, as Strauss's Arabella. Three years later she replaced a pregnant Marilyn Horne in a concert-performance of *Lucrezia Borgia* at Carnegie Hall, earning a 25-minute ovation. The live recording is shocking for its dramatic intensity when compared to the disappointing studio recording made by Caballé later the same year with the same conductor.[142] Her marshalling of her resources is thrilling not for what she gives to the performance but for what she holds back.[143] The dreamy delicacy of tone emerges as a construction of judgment

---

140 Leitzel was the first performer anywhere to command her own private Pullman train car – which she furnished with a grand piano.

141 'Black pearls.' The term has been used for a while, but it was made popular by the Italian radio (RAI) show *La barcaccia* ('the longboat,').

142 Jonel Perlea, for RCA.

143 She would later forget this when ending *Don Carlo* at the Met on 22 April, 1972 (conducted by Francesco Molinari-Pradelli, and recorded live), with a 16-second B5. She was said to have become irritated by Corelli's tendency that evening to *fermata* high notes during their ensembles; her revenge was to beat him at his own game – knowing he'd be unable to do anything about it.

rather than a function of restraint; the soprano's choices are in absolute service to the music's expressive and dramatic compass despite her indulgence of her legendary talent for mezza voce and silk-spun legatos. She is a phenomenon, but not in real terms a natural coloratura. She had neither the range nor the dexterity of Sutherland or Sills, but her work transcended the increasingly rigid demarcation of *fach* and role. In 1965, Caballé sang her first Marschallin,[144] at Glyndebourne (followed by the Countess in *Le nozze di Figaro*), and three years later she recorded *Salome* for RCA, with Erich Leinsdorf. The performance is far from perfect – Caballé is decorous and matronly rather than dangerous and sensual – but that she was cast at all in a role given traditionally to northern European singers was indicative of unusual versatility. In the three years following *Salome*, she recorded Verdi's Requiem (with Sir John Barbirolli), an album of "Donizetti Rarities," an album of "Puccini Arias" and, in 1970, *Norma*, with Cossotto as Adalgisa. Her work during the 1970s was equally diverse. In 1976 and 1977, she appeared at the Met in *Norma, Aida, Ariadne auf Naxos*, and *La bohème*, and at the San Francisco Opera as Turandot. She returned to San Francisco as Elvira in *Ernani*, La Gioconda, Semiramide, and Tosca. No other soprano straddled the gamut of lyric and dramatic Italian bel canto, Verdi, Puccini, verismo, Strauss and, even, Wagner (Sieglinde and Isolde).[145]

If Caballé's warbling alongside Freddie Mercury in 1987, for "*Barcelona*," did little for opera or for singing then it fed the trope of the "fat opera singer" three years before Pavarotti cemented a cliché[146] to which the unofficial "Three Coloraturas," Beverley Sills, Anna Moffo and Roberta Peters, had contributed nothing. Each was slim, pretty and talented, and they cornered a market opened by Callas through starring roles in many of the finest recordings of the re-established bel canto repertoire. They were also largely uninteresting to the public that bought their records in the millions. Moffo and Peters were central to the Met's programming over hundreds of performances, but Sills was overlooked until 1975 – five years before her retirement. Rudolf Bing admitted to his failure to make use of Sills as the greatest mistake of his career; Sills was unforgiving, observing in 1997 (the year of Bing's death, at the age of 95):

> Mr. Bing is an ass. While everybody said what a great administrator he was and a great this, Mr. Bing was just an improbable, impossible General Manager of the Metropolitan Opera [...]. The arrogance of that man [...].[147]

Sills' repertoire in her youth was varied, featuring a raft of Mozart and Puccini, as well as tentpole French roles, including Louise, Marguerite in *Faust*, Manon, Thaïs, Marie in *La fille du régiment*, and the heroines in *Les contes d'Hoffmann*. Her core Italian repertoire was romantic (Rosina, Elvira, Gilda, Violetta, Maria Stuarda, Lucrezia, and Elisabetta in *Roberto Devereux*) and exceptional for her emotional commitment,

---

144   The recording, conducted by John Pritchard, is readily available, and well worth hearing. Teresa Zylis-Gara and Edith Mathis are very fine indeed, as Otto Edelman is not.

145   She performed the latter role at the end of her career, in 1989, and it is a remarkable testament to her courage and stamina, and little else.

146   The first "Three Tenors" concert was staged in 1990.

147   Morgan, Brian (2006). *Strange Child of Chaos: Norman Treigle*. iUniverse, pp. 176–177.

rhythmic precision, and clean attack. Unlike Sutherland, who was prone to slide around the bar-lines as well as between the notes, Sills' diction in Italian and French opera was outstanding; she also performed in contemporary opera, including Howard Hanson's *Merry Mount*, Douglas Moore's *The Wings of the Dove*, Luigi Nono's *Intolleranza*, Hugo Weisgall's *Six Characters in Search of an Author*, and Gian Carlo Menotti's *La Loca*, which he composed to commemorate Sills' 50th birthday. Her legacy culturally can be traced to her discipline over a long career, spanning 1947 to 1980, rather than her studio recordings, for which she was joined infrequently to singers of equivalent calibre.[148] Live recordings from the early 1970s (including a thrilling final scene from *Anna Bolena*, conducted by Zubin Mehta)[149] attest to the benefits of judgment and discretion for a soprano some years into her sixties; many who could have learned from her example ignored it. Sills, Moffo and Peters were notable for enhancing their celebrity through regular appearances on television; Moffo even hosted her own TV show in Italy during the early 1960s. Dorothy Kirsten[150] was another regularly televised star with a similarly long career that began with popular music in 1937 (as one of the Kate Smith Chorus) and shifted to opera in 1940 with an appearance at the Chicago Grand Opera as Pousette in *Manon*. She retired four decades later in New York, with a performance at the Met of her standout role, Tosca, on 31 December, 1976. Like Sills, Kirsten ascribed her longevity to good decisions:

> I've always believed in the principle of protection, and I never sang a role I felt was not right for my voice. This took courage and drew some criticism along the way, but after 30 years of preserving Puccini's legato and tessitura I don't have to apologize to anyone, do I?[151]

Kirsten's popularity was furthered by film appearances (with a starring role in the lamentable *The Great Caruso*, opposite Mario Lanza) and radio broadcasts with Frank Sinatra, Bing Crosby, Nelson Eddy, Jack Benny, Gordon MacRae, and Perry Como. Her only rivals as Tosca during the early 1950s were Herva Nelli[152] (a favourite of Toscanini), Delia Rigal[153] (an Argentine soprano who joined the Met in the same week as Rudolf Bing), and Zinka Milanov, a student of Milka Ternina.[154] Of all Callas' rivals, the Croatian Milanov's voice was the largest and most penetrating, but it translated badly to the studio. Her recordings with Jussi Björling are loud, angry, artless affairs that do no justice to the soprano's considerable artistry. Her rivalry at the Met with Tebaldi (who arrived on 31 January, 1955) and Callas (who made her debut later the same year) hinged on Tosca – the only role they shared. Milanov's conceit, which many characterised generously as "regal," brought her into conflict with the more famous Callas, and in a 1975 radio interview she observed that "Callas took

148   Her most frequent tenor partner in the studio was Nicolai Gedda. See Boyden, Matthew (2021). *The tenor: A Cultural History*. Ragueneau Press.
149   On 20 April, 1974.
150   6 July, 1910 – 18 November, 1992.
151   *New York Times*, 19 November, 1992.
152   9 January, 1909 – 31 May, 1994.
153   *née* Delia Dominga Mastrarrigo, 6 October, 1920 – 8 May, 2013.
154   17 May, 1906 – 30 May, 1989.

advantage of possibly cheap publicity stunts and major and minor scandals. Those advanced her career." She praised Callas as an actress, but as a singer she reduced her useful life to seven years, between 1949 and 1956: "by the time she debuted at the Met, her voice was already not of the standard expected by audiences."[155] Callas was slow to bite her lip. On hearing that "La Zinka" had received an ovation for merely walking down the aisle during Act I of *Norma* at the Met, she responded "Since she can't get applause for singing Norma, she now gets it by walking."

The only soprano during the 1950s and '60s on whom everyone was able to agree was the African-American Leontyne Price,[156] almost certainly the finest Verdi soprano to make records in stereo. She was born in Mississippi, to a carpenter and a midwife – professions that aligned neatly with the family's deeply religious convictions; as a nine-year-old, she was taken on a school trip to hear the great African-American contralto, Marian Anderson,[157] perform in Jackson.[158] It was Price's first exposure to art music, and it changed her life: "The whole aura of the occasion had a tremendous effect on me, particularly the singer's dignity and, of course, her voice."[159] Anderson was the first African-American to sing with the Met in New York – on 7 January, 1955, at Bing's invitation. She was cast as Ulrica in *Un ballo in maschera* (opposite Milanov and Nelli), a small role which Anderson considered appropriate for "a beginner in opera."[160] As she recalled in her autobiography:

> The curtain rose on the second scene […] and I was there on the stage, mixing the witch's brew. I trembled, and when the audience applauded and applauded before I could sing a note, I felt myself tightening into a knot. I had always assured people I was not nervous about singing, but at that moment I was as nervous as a kitten.[161]

Although she never appeared with the company again (she was almost 60 at the time, and in decline vocally), Anderson was named a permanent member of the Metropolitan company, an achievement she considered valuable because

> It has encouraged other singers of my group to realize that the doors everywhere may open increasingly to those who have prepared themselves well.[162]

As a black singer in a systemically racist country, Anderson was a figure of towering historical importance simply for "being." In 1939, however, the "Daughters of the

---

155   Those expectations had, of course, been formed by Milanov over the preceding four years.

156   *née* Mary Violet Leontyne Price, 10 February, 1927 –

157   27 February, 1897 – 8 April, 1993.

158   See generally Eidsheim, Nina Sun (2011). "Marian Anderson and 'Sonic Blackness' in American Opera." *Sound Clash: Listening to American Studies,* Vol. 63, No. 3, pp. 641–671.

159   *Gramophone*, 6 February, 2017.

160   Anderson, Marion (2002). *My Lord, What a Morning: An Autobiography*. University of Illinois Press, p. 304.

161   *Ibid*, p. 302.

162   *Ibid*. One of the handful of singers she mentions as having "exceptional talent" was Leontyne Price.

American Revolution" objected to her giving a concert on 9 April in Washington DC's Constitution Hall because the city operated a white-performers-only policy; the decision was taken on the basis that the Hall had no segregated bathrooms (required by law at the time), and so precluded black people from attending. The morning after the objection was made public, Charles Edward Russell, co-founder of the NAACP,[163] chaired a meeting for many of the country's leading civil rights leaders. Public demonstrations were held and letters were written – one of them by the First Lady, Eleanor Roosevelt, who explained when resigning from the Daughters of the American Revolution that

> I am in complete disagreement with the attitude taken in refusing Constitution Hall to a great artist [...] You had an opportunity to lead in an enlightened way and it seems to me that your organization has failed.

The established press endorsed Anderson's right to sing, although it was the *Richmond Times-Dispatch* that stated the obvious: "In these days of racial intolerance so crudely expressed in the Third Reich, an action such as the D.A.R.'s ban [...] seems all the more deplorable." Encouraged by his wife, President Roosevelt announced an open-air concert on Easter Sunday, April 9, to be held on the steps of the Lincoln Memorial. Anderson performed to a live audience of 75,000 and a national radio audience running to tens of millions. Two months later, in conjunction with the 30th NAACP conference in Richmond, Virginia, Eleanor Roosevelt presented Anderson with the 1939 Spingarn Medal for distinguished achievement. By the time she was invited to perform at the Met, Anderson had achieved more than anyone could have imagined at the end of the 19th century.[164] Having been raised in the shadows of Jim Crow legislation, and despite giving more than 70 recitals a year across the United States, her life as a touring artist compelled her to accommodate the gruesome realities of a society that entitled racist-owned hotels, restaurants and shops to refuse her service. In 1937 she was denied a hotel room while visiting Princeton University to give a concert; the disgrace was brought to the attention of Albert Einstein, who invited Anderson to stay at his home, at 112 Mercer Street. She was thereafter hosted by Einstein whenever she performed in New York State.[165]

Anderson left many live and studio recordings. Between 1924 and 1966, she was under contract with RCA Victor, for whom she recorded enough music to fill 15 CDs. Among the most important performances are Brahms' "Alto Rhapsody," conducted by Eugene Ormandy in 1945, and Mahler's *Kindertotenlieder*, conducted by Pierre Monteux in 1950. Considering the solemnity of the music it is unfair to judge her work solely from these performances, but she is spellbinding, producing a ravishing tone which she frames with conservatoire-clear diction and instinctive phrasing that speaks to Anderson's experience-generated insights as a woman of colour. Toscanini

---

163   National Association for the Advancement of Colored People.

164   Anderson's mother, Annie Delilah Rucker (1874–1964), was able to see most of them, living almost as long a life as her daughter, who died at the age of 96. Price is the same age at the time of publication, and going strong.

165   Einstein's relationship with Anderson was turned into a play, "My Lord, What a Night," by Deborah Brevoort in 2021.

heard Anderson sing in Salzburg in 1935 and declared her voice to be "of a kind that comes along only once in a hundred years." This is supported by Anderson's performance of the spiritual, "Crucifixion," recorded live at the Lotos Club in New York in 1941. The tempo is slow to the point of stasis, but it works because of Anderson's phrasing, breath-control and word use; her singing of "They pierced him in the side," stops the clocks.[166] It was routine for audiences to respect the atmosphere created by Anderson's performance of the song by refraining from applause.

Leontyne Price was born almost thirty years to the day after Anderson. Her success was attributable to the quality of a *lirico* spinto voice that many consider to be the most beautiful of the century. Her repertoire included everything from *Giulio Cesare*, *Poppea*, and Donna Elvira, to Elvira in *Ernani*, both Leonoras (*Il trovatore* and *La forza del destino*), Amelia in *Un ballo in Maschera*, Aida and Tosca; she was peerless in the title role of *Ariadne auf Naxos*. Her discography is unrepresentative of her talent, and it is fortunate there are as many live recordings as there are. Price was supported early on by Paul Robeson, who performed a benefit concert to help raise funds for her to study at Julliard as one of a small number of African-American students, and the only black member of the cast when making her debut in 1952 as Mistress Ford in a school production of *Falstaff*. Virgil Thomson attended one of the performances and cast her in a revival of his all-black opera, *Four Saints in Three Acts*. The production transferred from Broadway to Paris, from where Price relocated to the Ziegfeld Theatre, Broadway, for a new staging of *Porgy and Bess*. After hearing her in the theatre, Samuel Barber accompanied Price in a recital at the Library of Congress, in 1953, for which the programme included the premiere of the composer's *Hermit Songs*. The following year, the Supreme Court handed down its landmark judgment in *Brown v. Board of Education of Topeka*,[167] that overturned the 1896 decision in *Plessy*. In doing so, it was held that legally mandated public-school segregation was deemed unconstitutional. Months later, Price was cast by NBC as Tosca, the first appearance by an African-American in a leading role in a televised opera. Dozens of syndicating stations across the South refused to take the broadcast.

Rudolf Bing invited Price to the Met in 1958. She declined, because she wanted to gain more experience, and because her conductor at NBC, Peter Herman Adler advised that "When [Leontyne] makes her debut at the Met, she must do it as a lady, not a slave." On 27 January, 1961, Price made a triumphant joint debut, with Corelli, in *Il trovatore*, conducted by Fausto Cleva. The performance concluded with a 40-minute ovation; the surviving recording remains one of the most thrilling of an Italian opera. Not everyone was happy about Price being given top billing in a supporting beam of the repertoire:

> A great diva with a long career behind her was singing Tosca at the Met in 1961. Her dresser asked her whether she had yet heard Leontyne Price, who had just made her unmatched debut as Leonora in Il trovatore. "Ah, yes," purred [the diva]. "Price. A lovely voice. But the poor thing is singing the wrong repertory!" The dresser registered surprise. "What

---

166   There is filmed footage online of Anderson performing the song on stage.
167   347 U.S. 483.

repertory," he asked, "should Price be singing?" The great diva smiled a knowing smile. "Bess," she purred. "Just Bess."[168]

The critical view was less prejudiced; it was typified by the opinion of the New York Times' critic, Harold C. Schonberg, who described Price's voice as

> warm and luscious [with] enough volume to fill the house with ease, and she has a good technique to back up the voice itself. She even took the trills as written, and nothing in the part as Verdi wrote it gave her the least bit of trouble. She moves well and is a competent actress. But no soprano makes a career of acting. Voice is what counts, and voice is what Miss Price has.[169]

The dig at Callas – renowned as the leading singing actress of her generation, despite her voice having been in decline within five years of her debut – reminded readers that the biggest star on Earth had not performed at the Met since 1958; she was hardly a presence for the rest of the country, with most of her few performances after her confrontation with Bing being given in Dallas and Kansas City. Price's rise to dominance in the music of Verdi and, to a lesser extent, Puccini punctuated the extent to which Callas' time had come and gone – even after her (brief) return to the Met as Tosca in 1965. In 1966, the new Metropolitan opened without Callas. Instead, Samuel Barber was commissioned to write an opera, *Antony and Cleopatra*, with the title roles played by Justino Diaz and Leontyne Price. Zeffirelli's production was vulgar and bloated, and the extravagance suffocated the quality of Barber's music; the significance of the occasion nonetheless established Price as America's pre-eminent native-born soprano.

Callas' withdrawal from performance did not diminish her influence. On 13 October 1965, Renato Scotto made her Metropolitan Opera debut, as Butterfly. She went on to sing more than 300 performances in 26 roles at the Met, retiring from the House in 1987. In 1970, Scotto opened the La Scala season as Elena in *I vespri siciliani* – the same role in which Callas made her official La Scala debut 19 years earlier. The sopranos were known to each other, having collaborated famously in 1957 for a production at La Scala of *Medea*, with Scotto appearing as Neris. The recording made live from that production is celebrated, even if it falls in energy behind the performances conducted by Bernstein. The power of Callas' chest register is nowhere better evidenced, and the final ten minutes are a masterclass in timing, momentum and phrasing; she is the embodiment of jealous insanity, and sensational despite the tone and placement of her voice.

Callas attended La Scala for Scotto's performance, sitting in the box reserved traditionally for the theatre's Director; she had not performed in Milan since a final appearance as Medea eight years earlier. When the audience was made aware of Callas' presence they began to shout and applaud, creating a furore that reached the artists' entrance and the green rooms. Callas is said to have done nothing to encourage the

168   Bernheimer, Martin (1985). "But Are We Really Colour-Deaf," *Opera*, pp. 759–60.
169   Schonberg, Harold C. "Opera: Two Debuts in 'Il Trovatore': Franco Corelli and Miss Price Heard." *New York Times*, 28 January, 1961.

scene, but Scotto concluded she had acted to steal her moment. Furious and humiliated, she burst into tears in her dressing room after the performance – even though Callas had sent flowers and was seen to applaud at the end of the performance. In an interview two days later, for a magazine of ill-repute, Scotto was outspoken:

> It certainly wasn't in good taste – Callas didn't behave like a true lady. But what do you expect, when you have nothing left in your life and you've passed your peak [...] you take gratification at whatever cost, even if it means just a few stolen crumbs and so without value [...] I didn't give in to nerves because if I'm a good and sweet person in my day to day life, on stage I'm a tigress. No, I didn't cry, but only because I summoned up all my willpower. I knew that that was what Callas and her zealous fans did as they wanted. They tried to cause me problems with a rude and stupid act, but they failed, I didn't give her or them that satisfaction. I finished the performance without losing control and I think I sang very well. For that matter, the critics too confirmed my success. After the opera, I was invited to attend a party that Callas had organised, but I didn't go. I was very angry, and I still am, because I find it completely unjustifiable and unworthy of a respectable person.

It was reported that the paparazzi had focussed their gaze on Callas, all but ignoring the evening's prima donna. In her interview, Scotto said:

> I don't like high-society, I don't spend time with famous millionaires, I don't do strange things [...] I am a peaceful woman, I love my family and when I lose my voice I will retire without bad feeling, and become a happy housewife.

If Scotto had left it there, she might have walked away unscathed. Unfortunately, she concluded her interview with a roulade of invective:

> Callas was hoping to harm me but she didn't succeed. In fact, I would have loved for her to come on to the stage and sing *I vespri* for me [...] I wonder what she could have done, poor thing! Nowadays she doesn't sing anymore and maybe she believed that it was possible to revive her success in this wrong and rather pathetic way. I'm sure that she would have loved to have been in my place, but not having the means to do so she was content to act out that little show from her box [...] those who were cheering her on were probably the same who several years ago, again at La Scala, he threw vegetables at her. Perhaps Callas needs this 'stolen' applause because she has nothing else left [...] no husband, no man who loves her, no child [...] I am so much richer than she is that I can let her have that applause, if that's all she has left in her decline [...] poor thing!

The interview appeared on the newsstands shortly before the second performance in the production; the *loggionisti* got wind of her comments, and by the third performance the article had been read by everyone with an axe to swing. As Scotto walked on stage, the theatre descended to booing, whistling and jeering; the same thing happened at the fourth performance. The episode haunted Scotto, who never sang again at La Scala in a staged production.[170] For her part, Callas returned only once as a member of the audience, on a single occasion in 1972, to support Giuseppe di Stefano in his delusional turn as Don José.

Callas died in 1977; Scotto continued singing for another quarter of a century – moving into increasingly heavy repertoire, including Elisabetta in *Don Carlo*, Lady Macbeth, Leonora in *Il trovatore*, Fedora, Charlotte in *Werther*, the Marschallin, Kundry (both in 1995) and, even, Klytemnestra (in 2000 and 2002). Unlike Callas, whose judgment of herself was perennially harsh, Scotto sang for two decades beyond the natural lifespan of her voice, performing roles for which she was unsuited in her prime. Her 1980 recording of *Tosca* (conducted by James Levine) is a wretched mess; the wobble that was apparent from 1970 had become grating; it would get worse still over the ensuing two decades, during which time she was encouraged to keep going.

Scotto liked the sound of her own voice;[171] Callas hated listening to herself. Upon first hearing a recording of her singing she is said to have objected: "I don't like the kind of voice I have at all […] I cried like you can't even believe […] I had a horror of myself." Many agree with her – even those who consider her the *prima donna assoluta per sempre*. Terrence McNally's 1995 play about Callas, *Masterclass*, is a love-letter to the exotic sacrifice of the true artist, and a construction of the author's premise that "At almost every performance, Callas paid the price for not being a 'perfect' singer." Based on recordings of her masterclasses at the Juilliard School between October, 1971, and March, 1972, the play is more obviously a response to the series of recitals given by Callas in Europe, in 1973, and the United States, South Korea, and Japan in 1974, with the equally-crippled Di Stefano. These performances were a travesty artistically, even if they made both singers large amounts of money. Callas was a statuary metaphor for the performing artist's need for life after the death of the final curtain. She is McNally's Norma Desmond, a glamorous, caustic, bitter, intolerant cipher for oblation, obsessed with a past that precludes any hope of a future. The play navigates the usual tropes attaching to her body-shape, her rivalries and the scourge of the press, before diving into a monologue triggered by her credo, "*Visi d'arte.*" The lead was created by Zoe Caldwell; it has since been played by a host of fine actresses, notably Patti LuPone, Faye Dunaway, Tyne Daly and Fanny Ardant (the latter directed by Roman Polanski, five years before she was thrown onto the pyre of *Callas Forever*).

As a simulacrum of Dürer's 1515 woodcut of a rhinoceros,[172] *Masterclass* would be better served with Callas played by a drag artist. As a painfully male formulation of a woman's identity and experience, McNally's diva is painted in cliches that

---

170   She returned for a single recital 15 years later.

171   It's a common misconception that singers don't like hearing themselves. Leontyne Price, for example, loved to listen to recordings of herself, while Elizabeth Schwarzkopf chose nine of her own recordings for the BBC radio programme *Desert Island Discs*.

172   The artist drew the animal by reference solely to descriptions, which explains why the woodcut merely resembles the animal as it appears in nature.

apostrophise her status as a long-suffering victim of external forces. The imagined Callas is devoid of personal responsibility, and written as a parody not just of the soprano but of women more generally. Her assaults on students and their egos are representatively more interesting than what might be learned of the art of singing as Callas mastered it. The play ducks the emptiness of the soprano's life after her humiliation by Onassis, and by what *actually* emerged from the masterclasses. When, for example, she attempted to steer Pamela Herbert through "*Casta diva*," the teacher fixated on technical hurdles for which the student was ill-equipped; she ignored the essence of the expressive licence by which Callas' performance as Norma were defined. For ten grinding minutes, she does the least she can to assist Herbert in her serviceable but routine interpretation, communicating little more to the student than that they are working from different editions of the score. McNally wanted presumably to portray the diva as a tigress, made powerful by her taunting of students while demanding coincidentally her genuflection to her greatness. The high camp of the contrivance eluded the bathos of Callas' circumstances. The similarities between the historical misogyny of the drag act[173] – prior to its adoption by members of the LGBTQ community – and the self-hating realities of Callas' life after 1968 align perfectly with the unreality of people appearing in female guise being unable to sing or love as women. With the death in 1975 of the only man with whom she enjoyed sex, Callas' decline was unsurprising. It was fitting also. The adherent-obsession with the emotionally and socially impecunious *regina del dramma* – a down-and-out squatting in a lavish apartment in the XVIe arrondissement[174] – feeds from a macabre predilection for the extinguishing of tortured genius. Fixating on the end of her life, as has every film, play, book and documentary of note, remembers what made her interesting as a marker for her status as "favoured of Heaven so highly, to fall off from their Creator."[175] The greatness of her first few years is made ancillary to everything that followed. In this sense, Callas was self-destructive antiphonally to the triumphant Sarah Bernhardt. It was a fitting coincidence that Callas sang five of Bernhardt's most celebrated roles (Lady Macbeth, Violetta, Tosca and Fedora), as well as arias and duets from seven others: *Le nozze di Figaro*,[176] *Lucrezia Borgia*,[177] *Ernani*,[178] *Otello*,[179]

---

173   There are many, of course, for whom the misogyny is alive and high-kicking. Drag is said to subvert gender norms and stereotypes, but it can also embrace and exploit the pornographic stereotypes it is claimed to dismantle. It is to state the obvious that these stereotypes when attaching to a woman would mark her out as unfit to work with children. On the other hand, Tennessee decided to ban drag acts in public spaces (or near to children) in early 2023, so the issue remains topical as a front for the culture war being waged in the United States between Democrats and Republicans.

174   At 36 avenue Georges-Mandel, a few metres from the location where Diana, Princess of Wales, died on 31 August, 1997. This may explain why there is nothing in situ to commemorate Callas' residency.

175   Milton, John (2005). *Paradise Lost*, Book I. Oxford University Press, lines 30–31, p. 18.

176   "*Porgi, amor*," and "*Sull'aria*."

177   *Lucrèce Borgia*, by Victor Hugo. "*Tranquillo ei posa* [...] *Com'è bello*," ('Calm down and rest [...] How beautiful it is.').

178   *Hernani*, by Victor Hugo. "*Surta è la note* [...] *Ernani ! Ernani, involami*," ('Night has fallen [...] Ernani! Ernani! Fly me away.')

179   'The Willow Song.'

Hamlet,[180] *Le Cid*,[181] and *Adriana Lecouvreur*.[182] Other than as celebrities, however, the artists shared nothing in their approaches to life and art. Whether or not she had carried on performing as she did, Bernhardt's energy and love of life oxygenated every room into which she walked, regardless of what she was doing. Even after turning from the stage to film, she committed to each new project with zeal, not withstanding the amputation of her right leg in 1915. She was pivotal to the creation of Paramount Pictures, when the colourised print of *The Loves of Queen Elizabeth* made so much money in New York after its release on 12 July, 1912, that Adolph Zukor was able to launch the Famous Players Film Company.[183] In 1915, she welcomed cameras into her home for a documentary about her daily life, *Sarah Bernhardt à Belle-Isle*. She continued to paint, sculpt, write and act into her seventies; during the weeks before her death in 1923, she was preparing to make another film from her home, *La Voyante*, directed by Sacha Guitry. As she delighted in telling journalists:

> They're paying me ten thousand francs a day, and plan to film for seven days. Make the calculation. These are American rates, and I don't have to cross the Atlantic! At those rates, I'm ready to appear in any films they make.[184]

Callas suffered neither illness nor amputation, and she experienced nothing of the institutional hatred to which Marian Anderson, Leontyne Price, Shirley Verrett and black people more generally were subject across the United States and Europe. She married an older man whom she left for the richest commoner in the history of the world to that time. What she sang, and when she chose to sing it, was determined on every occasion by Callas, and having appeared in a single film after leaving the stage (and not without success), it was *her* decision to make no others. She rejected every offer of work, wrote no memoirs and left no books; what survives of her writing proves she could have done both with skill. The paradox at the core of Maria Callas is located in what can be observed of her vulnerability as a function of victimhood. As the most influential opera singer of the second half of the 20th century she could have turned her weaknesses into strengths. Sadly, the patina of self-destruction that coloured her voice was revealed no less viscerally through her nature, which transformed integrity into confrontation, passion into rage, privacy into coldness, and art into celebrity. The "Death of Callas" continues a century after her birth to be more

---

180   "*À vos jeux, mes amis* [...] *Partagez-vous mes fleurs* [...] *Et maintenant écoutez ma chanson!*" ('At your games, my friends [...] Will you share my flowers [...] And now listen to my song!). From the setting by Ambroise Thomas.

181   *Le Cid*, by Pierre Corneille. "*De cet affreux combat* [...] *Pleurez! pleurez, mes yeux!*" ('This terrible fight [...] Cry! weep, my eyes!').

182   *Adrienne Lecouvreur*, by Ernest Legouvé and Eugène Scribe. "*Io son l'umile ancella*," ('I am the humble handmaid,') and "*Poveri fiori*" ('Poor flowers'). Cilea's opera (1902) did not appeal to Callas. The music is glorious, as she conceded when singing the title role's best-known arias in concert and on record; she may have recoiled from the subject, Adrienne Lecouvreur (5 April, 1692 – 20 March, 1730), a celebrated actress, considered to be the greatest of her day, who became better remembered for her affair (with Maurice de Saxe) and for her tragic and mysterious death.

183   The name Paramount was adopted formally on 7 November, 1916.

184   Tierchant, Hélène (2009). *Sarah Bernhardt: Madame "quand même."* Éditions Télémaque, p. 350.

interesting to most than the life that preceded it. Her producer at EMI, Walter Legge, recalled that she was

> not a particularly lovable character except to her servants and her dress-maker, and of course to the multitudes of admirers who did not know her personally. She could be vengeful, vindictive, malicious in running down people she was jealous of or had taken a dislike to, often without reason. She was ungrateful: for she refused to work with or even talk to Serafin, who had been her invaluable help and guide since her Italian debut, after he recorded *La Traviata* with Antonietta Stella.[185]

Unlike Bernhardt, who invited journalists to her home for wine and cake, and Ponselle, who enjoyed a stellar career as a teacher, Callas taught only for money and attention; she warred constantly with the press, who were quick to remember it after her death. Bernhardt was "*Quand même*" because of what it conveyed of a woman who did so much with her life. Callas is remembered for having said nothing, and for doing less than she might have done had she been almost anyone else. She failed to live up to "being Callas" because she appears not to have liked her very much. Indeed, Legge doubted that she "really minded" dying young.[186] As a master of tragedy on stage and its dependent when off it, Maria Callas fulfilled in her self-created isolation the duality of the Dark Lady's deceit: "Therefore I lie with her, and she with me, And in our faults by lies we flattered be."[187]

---

185 Schwarzkopf, Elisabeth (1982). *On and Off the Record: A Memoir of Walter Legge*. Faber & Faber, p. 201. It should be added that Legge was, of course, married to Elisabeth Schwarzkopf, a prickly woman in her own right. He also fell out with her after his resignation from EMI.

186 *Ibid*, p.203.

187 Shakespeare, Sonnet 138.

CHAPTER NINETEEN

Waiting for the Berberians

Almost a year to the day after the "Three Tenors" seduced a television audience of 800 million from their Baths in Rome, some enterprising folk identified a passing bandwagon, and threw Renata Scotto, Ileana Cotrubas[1] and Elena Obraztsova[2] on top of it. "The Three Sopranos" was presented from the Amphitheatre in Siracuse, Sardinia, accompanied, for some unspecified reason, by the Czech Symphony Orchestra.[3] The applause as it was captured by the microphones was more enthusiastic than the critics; the obligatory ovation was unwarranted. The "Three Sopranos" concert did nothing for opera, or for the singers, or for music more generally. Five years later, the producer of the "Three Tenors" circus, Tibor Rudas, promoted a version for sopranos at an outdoor concert in Los Angeles. Instead of presenting the three "most famous" female singers of modern times (analogous to Pavarotti, Domingo and Carreras), Rudas engaged a trio of unknown artists: Kathleen Costello, Kallen Esperian and Cynthia Lawrence. 3,000 seats were made available, at a cost of $25, $50 and $100, for a programme of arias, show tunes and popular songs. Another of the producers, Wayne Baruch told the *Los Angeles Times*:

> People love to hear this kind of music, so in this case we think we will create a program, a repertoire, that will captivate people and attract them to these artists who will become better known as time goes by.

The event was not a total failure, but the unknown threesome did not become better known in consequence.[4] Rudas' assertions that there had been a near-constant request for a soprano version of the "Three Tenors" was unpersuasive, as it was for the dozens of subsequent "three soprano" concerts and recordings around the world.[5] When asked about female pretenders to the space occupied by the male triumvirate, José Carreras told *The Washington Post*:

> With all respect to the sopranos we have today, we would not be talking about the same thing. For one thing, the tenor repertory is one sopranos don't have. We can sing not only opera and classical music but the

---

1   9 June, 1939 –

2   7 July, 1939 – 12 January, 2015.

3   The conductor was Armando Krieger.

4   None of them forged successful careers. Lawrence achieved more than her colleagues, in lighter music primarily.

5   For a detailed consideration of the "Three Tenors" see Boyden, Matthew (2021). *The Tenor: A Cultural History*. Ragueneau Press.

> Neapolitan songs that Caruso used to sing, the show tunes and other
> well-known songs like "Grenada" that were designed for the tenor voice.
> The soprano repertory is not that broad, and for mezzos it would be even
> more difficult.[6]

Notwithstanding the absurdity of Carreras' allegations as they concerned the soprano
and mezzo repertoire,[7] his observation that Neapolitan songs and show tunes were in
some way the province of the tenor was countered by volumes of evidence to the contrary. Renata Tebaldi routinely included Neapolitan and Broadway songs in her recitals; she recorded a much-admired album of *Napolitana* in 1957, to which she added
a fine performance of "If I loved you" from *Carousel*. The wider question is not why
there wasn't a "Three Sopranos" event to rival the "Tenors," but who the three might
have been in 1992. Pavarotti and Domingo had long careers, and both remained in
good voice three decades after their debuts. During their peak on the stage, and in the
studio (spanning the middle 1970s to the late '80s), they monopolised the booking
schedules for the world's leading theatres and record labels.[8] It's accepted that Alfredo
Kraus, Franco Bonisolli, Neil Shicoff, among a handful of outliers, were available to
stand in for the Big Three; the fact remains, however, that the decades from 1970 to
1990 were dominated by three singers only. The situation as it concerned sopranos
was *very* different.

For example, 65 live and studio recordings of *Il trovatore* were released between
1969 and 1991; almost half of them feature four tenors: Pavarotti, Domingo,
Carreras and Bonisolli. Conversely, the same recordings make use of 33 different
sopranos as Leonora.[9] The 89 live and studio recordings of *Otello* produced between
1970 and 1991 feature 17 tenors in the title role and 44 sopranos as Desdemona.
This divergence was common across the standard repertory, with many more talented
sopranos than tenors on stage and in the studio during the 1970s and '80s. With so
many to choose from, the concept of "Three Sopranos" made little sense; indeed, it
provoked more questions than it answered – at least until 2000, when there were
three sopranos *nonpareil*.

In 1990, no-one contested the primacy of Pavarotti, Domingo and Carreras;[10]
they had earned their spurs, over many years and thousands of performances and recordings. At the same time, there were at least ten times as many sopranos whose skill
and artistry would have warranted an invitation to join a definitive ternion. When
finally it was attempted, in 1996, the "Three Sopranos" event produced the dampest

---

6   19 May, 1996.

7   When lifted from the operas of Rossini alone, the soprano repertoire exceeds the entirety of the
established tenor catalogue of songs and arias.

8   *Ibid.*

9   Leontyne Price (who sings on half a dozen of the complete sets), Linda Vajna, Montserrat Caballé,
Katia Ricciarelli, Lotte Rysanek, Raina Kabaivanska, Martina Arroyo, Rita Hunter, Gilda Cruz-Romo,
Annabelle Bernard, Elinor Ross, Joan Sutherland, Renata Scotto, Cristina Deutekom, Mizzi van der Lanz,
Katia Ricciarelli, Horiana Branisteanu, Mara Zampieri, Éva Marton, Maria Parazzini, Lou Ann Wyckoff,
Fiorenza Cossotto, Ghena Dimitrova, Adelaide Negri, Teresa Zylis-Gara, Antonella Banaudi, Rosalind
Plowright, Margherita Castro Alberti, Leona Mitchell, Elizabeth Connell, Yasuko Hayashi, Aprile Millo,
Julia Varady.

10   Other than, perhaps, Franco Bonisolli.

of squibs – with two famous singers from the 1970s, Scotto and the Romanian Cotrubas, in fraying form. For her part, form and Obraztsova adopting the singing equivalent of the crash-position. Her especially awful performance of "*Mon cœur s'ouvre à ta voix*," from *Samson et Dalila*, would have caused Samson to pull the Temple on top of himself well before the end of Act II. The applause that greeted this toe-curling performance in Sardinia was typical in its indiscretion and consistent with the landscape as it had been changed by the 1990s, with absent discretion *de jure* at a time when the B4 at the end of "*Nessun dorma*" was doing more harm to opera and the art of singing than anyone realised at the time. The fact that almost every tenor since the 1990 World Cup has had to sing *that* aria and *that* note[11] – whether or not they were equipped for it, or likely to be cast as Calaf – amplified the seriousness of the attachment of operatic culture to the ejaculatory prescriptions of high notes and volume. That unhappy circumstance can be traced through the history of opera, so that critics of Mario del Monaco have first to point their fingers at Martinelli, Gigli, Arámburo, Duprez and Sbigoli before thinking the sin of shouting a uniquely post-war disease. Notwithstanding the malignant effect of larger and louder orchestras, the soprano repertoire is given less obviously to the empty gestures of crowning high notes; indeed, there is a shadow of Mediterranean misogyny in the notion that women should make pleasing sounds only, even after Verdi created Azucena, Eboli and Amneris.

The cult of the "pretty" survived, of course, even though the number of sopranos willing and able to preserve the essence of a voice trained to be beautiful, while remaining distinct and idiosyncratic, declined during and after the 1990s – particularly among singers said to specialise in the increasingly nebulous category of bel canto. Mirella Freni[12] was the last of the pre-war-born generation of sopranos whose careers survived intact to the 2000s. She made her debut at the Teatro Municipale, Modena, on 3 March, 1955, as Micaëla, having been was trained by teachers schooled in 19th century practice and tradition. She left the stage for three years to marry and bear her only child; she returned, at the Teatro Regio, Turin, in what would become her signature role, Mimi.[13] Two years later she secured international acclaim for her performances as Zerlina at Glyndebourne, alongside Joan Sutherland's Donna Anna. Successful appearances followed as Susanna in *Figaro*, Adina in *L'elisir d'amore*, and Nanetta in *Falstaff* – in which role she replaced Renata Scotto at La Scala. Freni's talent and status were confirmed in January, 1963, when La Scala cast her as Mimi for a new production of *La bohème*, directed by Zeffirelli and conducted by Herbert von Karajan. The staging travelled to Vienna the same year, again conducted by Karajan,

---

11   Assuming the singer in question had access to the note as it was anticipated, rather than as written.

12   *née* Mirella Fregni, 27 February, 1935 – 9 February, 2020.

13   There are 29 live and studio recordings with Freni as Mimi, from her first (1963, for EMI), conducted by Thomas Schippers, and her last, 33 years later (a filmed performance from Parma, on 1 February, 1996).

who promoted Freni as one of his favoured sopranos.[14] Reviewing her debut at the Met,[15] also as Mimi, Alan Rich wrote in the *New York Herald Tribune* that Freni was:

> well, "irresistible" will do for a start. Beautiful to look at, an actress of simple naturalness and overwhelming intelligence, she used voice and gesture to create a Mimi of ravishing femininity and grace. The voice itself is pure and fresh, operating without seam from bottom to top, marvelously colored at every point by what seems to be an instinctive response to the urging of the text. There was talk during intermission of a "young Albanese," a young this and a young that. Forget it; the important thing is that she is a young Mirella Freni, a standard unto herself and an artist of the highest qualities [...] The last act eclipsed in musicianship anything, all that had gone on before. Miss Freni spun out a small silvery thread of tone at the end until you felt, rather than heard, the intensity of it all. [...] The audience all but tore the house down and may be at it still.[16]

The soprano's limpid tone and elegant phrasing were protected by uncompromising role-discipline, formed of her refusal to over-sing, or take on repertoire that might have done harm to her voice's elemental purity. She rejected Karajan's invitations to sing Leonora in *Il trovatore* and Turandot, and despite making three recordings as Butterfly – twice in the studio and again for a filmed version in 1974, conducted by Karajan – Freni refused to play the role in the theatre. With time and the settling of her technique, she turned to heavier Verdi roles, including Elisabetta in *Don Carlos*, Desdemona in *Otello* and Leonora in *La forza del destino*. In 1987 she appeared as Aida in Houston, and as Manon Lescaut at the Met in 1990. Her performances as Roméo alongside Corelli are remembered for their chemistry and the powerhouse vocalising, even if the tenor's French, and his approach to style, left much to be desired. Towards the end of her career Freni played a number of verismo roles, including Adriana Lecouvreur, Fedora and Caterina Hubscher in Giordano's *Madame Sans-Gêne*. She gave her final performance, as a teenager in the title role of Tchaikovsky's *Orleanskaja deva*,[17] on 11 April, 2005 – two months after her 70th birthday and 50 years after her debut.

If Freni's example was unusual then so too were her values for a generation addicted to amplitude. Callas, Tebaldi, Nilsson and their peers had gone so far beyond the principles immortalised on record by sopranos during the early 1900s that scale and resonance became fundamental even to the performance of Mozart. Amplitude became normative, and with the replacement of LP by the CD the hunger for large

---

14   She was Mimi and Butterfly for Karajan's Decca recordings of *La bohème and Madama Butterfly*, in 1972 and 1974 – with Pavarotti as Rodolfo and Pinkerton. There is no denying the beauty of the singing, and the playing of the Vienna Philharmonic is predictably gorgeous. Some of Karajan's tempos are very slow, however, and the dramatic energy that characterised his earlier opera recordings were subsumed to an obsession with detail.

15   On 29 September, 1965.

16   *New York Herald Tribune*, 30 September, 1965.

17   'The Maid of Orleans.'

voices choked by what it fed on. Long before Freni's retirement, it became normal for singers to wear out their voices within a decade. Miserable exemplars include Antonella Banaudi,[18] who was typical in having the best of starts – winning the *Concorso Internazionale Voci Verdiane* in Busseto in 1988 before going on to give some fine performances in *Il Corsaro* (in Busseto, in 1988) and *Aida* (in Bari, in March the following year). There is a live recording of the latter, made special by her singing of "*Ritorno Vincitor*" – despite the conductor's glacial tempo. In 1990, Banaudi recorded a concert album of Italian arias in Sweden; the following year, Pavarotti recommended her to Decca when he was invited to make his second (and last) studio recording as Manrico, conducted by Zubin Mehta. Although she sings with expression, and some colour, Banaudi forces her voice throughout – only a few years into her career. Her first studio recording proved to be her last, and her career went nowhere.

Another casualty of poor choices was Cristina Gallardo-Domâs, a Chilean lyric-spinto, born in Santiago, who made her local debut as Cio-Cio San in 1990. She was engaged three years later to sing *La Rondine* at La Scala, for which she achieved excellent notices. Her voice was well-supported, extremely bright – and never shrill. In 1998, Gallardo-Domâs performed the final scene from *Suor Angelica* at the Concertgebouw, with Riccardo Chailly conducting. The concert was televised, and the surviving broadcast attests, initially at least, to her defining qualities – sensitive legato, limpid tone and conservatoire-diction. As the music intensified, however, so too did her effort, with her tone being marred by strain. She was able to rattle the composer-nameplates screwed to the venue's walls, but the aria's atmosphere was lost to what qualified as little more than yelling. In 2001, Teldec chose to record *Aida* with the Vienna Philharmonic conducted by the early-music and period performance specialist, Nikolaus Harnoncourt. The conductor chose Gallardo-Domâs, for the title role. Her most recent successes prior to taking on one of the most demanding dramatic soprano roles in the Italian canon was Liu, not Turandot. The resulting performance was a catastrophe. For all her high-spun legatos, Gallardo-Domâs was woefully mis-cast, as was Vincenzo La Scola, as Radamès, who left the coffin missing only a couple of nails by the time he got to the end of "*Celeste Aida.*" Two years later, Gallardo-Domâs was a disappointing Mimi at La Scala, alongside Marcelo Álvarez as Rodolfo; in 2003, 13 years after her debut, she was televised singing in a gala event, "Live from the Market Square in Leipzig," from *La Wally.* Her performance of "*Ebben? Ne andrò lontana*"[19] began well enough, but by the time she reached the aria's climax, her tone was shrill and her placement undone by a most savage, spreading vibrato. The audience was unsure what to do as the performance ended – the soprano was slim and beautiful, after all; once the applause had begun, however, the rest of large crowd joined in with unschooled cheering and whistling. The performance was deserving of approbation because there was nothing with which the audience was able to compare it – a disconnect that forms a number of attendant, uniquely modern dilemmas.

---

18   Gallardo-Domâs made no further recordings of note; her last and most recent foray in the studio was in 2017, when releasing an album of Spanish-language songs, titled "*Pontes de Amor.*"

19   'Well then! I'll take off far away.'

The common effect for singers who force their voices is the delamination of tone beyond a natural vibrato into what can be described only as a wobble. This is especially gruesome when it befalls the young. A recent case in point is Christianne Stotijn.[20] At the time of writing, she has been a regular collaborator with the British composer, Thomas Adès, Benjamin Britten's natural heir, whose stupendous *The Exterminating Angel*[21] is among the few contemporary operas certain to remain in repertoire. On a 2023 recording of Adès' *Totentanz*, released by the Vienna Philharmonic's self-operated label, Stotijn sang the part for mezzo-soprano. It is impossible to isolate a syllable or a note not undone by the most barbaric ululations; Stotijn was in her middle-forties at the time – her vocal prime.

It is important to appreciate that vibrato is *not* the same thing as wobble, although it was hated with equivalent ferocity before 1900, an aversion informed by something less transient than taste and fashion. Composers, librettists and audiences were unsurprisingly concerned with the clarity of the sung word – particularly when a work was new. This was more important still for anyone singing lieder, with the respective merits of poetry and music aligning in the absence of narrative and stagecraft. Since everything was sung with portamento until it wasn't, it fell to period performance to determine a culture of vocalising that re-conditioned sopranos as wooden flutes. The concept of cantabile as it was understood by Ponselle, Maria Reining, Lisa della Casa, Christa Ludwig and Renée Fleming was rejected, with extreme vibrato, on the basis that wobbling voices are ugly, and consuming of line and text. Only a singer compelled by flawed or unfinished technique, or an enfeebled diaphragm, would submit to Obraztsova's atrocious warbling as one of the "Three Sopranos."

The epitome of bad singing for the majority remains Florence Foster Jenkins,[22] a ridiculous but likable American socialite whose fantasies collided tragically with independent wealth.[23] It would be a delusion worthy of Madame Jenkins to deny the horror of her recordings, which are funny until one scrapes at the surface of their disturbing psychological ramifications. Jenkins was without training or talent; she chose regardless to submit herself to the lion's den of public opinion. Her cult status was encouraged by more deserving celebrities, including Caruso, Cole Porter, Gian Carlo Menotti, Lily Pons, and Sir Thomas Beecham – all of whom were in on a joke of which Jenkins appeared to be ignorant. A joke it was, since Jenkins chose to perform music that was difficult even for trained coloraturas. Her recordings (which she sold only to friends during her lifetime) included The "Queen of the Night's Aria," "*Mein Herr Marquis*" from *Die Fledermaus*, and the "Jewel Song" from *Faust* – all in

---

20   1977 –

21   First performed on 28 July, 2016.

22   *née* Narcissa Florence Foster, 19 July, 1868 – 26 November, 1944. It is nothing more than a tragic coincidence – one recognised presumably by Jenkins – that her given first name originated with Narcissus, the son of the river god Cephissus and the nymph Liriope who, according to Book III of Ovid's *Metamorphoses*, was destined to live a long life, provided he never recognised himself.

23   Stephen Frears' 2016 bio-pic, *Florence Foster Jenkins*, is beautiful, touching and kind; it features an affecting performance in the lead by Meryl Streep, and a Oscar-deserving turn as St Clair Bayfield by Hugh Grant. There is a small amount of archive footage available of Jenkins performing on stage, sadly without sound; she appears to be having a wonderful time, as does the audience. Her movements speak to the chaos and absent discipline of her singing; it must have been riotous fun.

English; she sang the "Bell Song," from *Lakmé*, in something approximating French. It is easy to laugh at Jenkins, and many do. She is far from unique, however. One of the funniest performances ever given, on film at least, is by Natália de Andrade[24] of Leonora's aptly-chosen *"Per esso moriro!"*[25] from Act I of *Il trovatore*. The clip is widely available online,[26] and can be enjoyed initially for the woeful pianism of her accompanist, who appears to have graduated from the Les Dawson Conservatoire. Things do not improve when de Andrade launches into a jaw-dropping performance that bears little relation to music or singing, far less Verdi. If it cannot be described then it can be enjoyed – but only as a guilty pleasure conditioned by the discovery from de Andrade's diaries that she saw herself as a serious artist.[27] Less sincere, but equally diverting, was Leona Anderson,[28] an American silent film actress, retained by Chaplin, who reinvented herself in 1953 as "the world's most horrible singer." The critic, Ned Raggett, wrote of Anderson that

> hearing her crack, strain, burble, and otherwise demonstrate that her singing voice is completely surplus to any requirements might either be seizure-inducing or seizure-removing, depending on how you place your speakers.[29]

For those with a case of wine to hand, Anderson's 1957 album, "Music to Suffer By," is among the greatest treasures of the golden age of recording. A particular highlight is the genius of her self-penned "Rats in My Room," a chokingly funny song featuring the stanza, "Every day I've got more rats in my room; guess I'd better get some cats in my room, so they can handle all those rats in my room." Another candidate for the Hall of Infamy was the bonkers Liberian Congresswoman, Malinda Jackson Parker, whose recordings at the piano from the 1970s include a mesmerising vocal arrangement of Rachmaninov's Prelude in C sharp minor[30] – the second verse of which she announces as "with African drums."[31] A pop-music rival to Jenkins was Elva Ruby Miller,[32] who performed as "Mrs Miller" during the 1960s. From among her various albums, perverts may find something to enjoy in "My Green Tambourine." During the US-Vietnam conflict, the USO sent Miller to distract the troops, all of whom who must have wondered why the Department of War wanted their suffering never to end. Incredibly, Miller's April, 1966, release of "Downtown" – which features some hilarious whistling – reached No. 82 in the Billboard charts, notwithstanding

---

24 1910 – 19 October, 1999.

25 'For this I will die.'

26 As are various recordings – all of which were released as LPs.

27 Incredibly, the television audience (which appears to be made up largely of young people) is delighted by de Andrade's staggeringly awful singing. The singer appears not to be surprised by their appreciation.

28 *née* Leona Aronson, 3 April, 1885 – 25 December, 1973.

29 https://www.allmusic.com/album/music-to-suffer-by-mw0002018305.

30 Albeit not in C sharp minor.

31 Parker's surreal Russian-African synthesis is achieved at the piano, and as "tone poetry." No percussion is introduced at any time; thankfully.

32 *née* Connes; 5 October, 1907 – 5 July, 1997.

Miller's voice being described by one overly generous critic as like "roaches scurrying across a trash can lid."

Bad singing at its most extreme can be entertaining. The audience for the poisoned chalice created by Simon Cowell, wherein the talentless are humiliated by the allegedly famous, has now been embraced in 194 countries,[33] with original versions of the "Got Talent" show being created in 72 of them.[34] There are dozens of rival shows, including American Idol (since 2002) and The Voice (since 2011). In 2019, American audiences were subjected to an especially depressing programme, "The Masked Singer," in which "celebrities" were required to perform covers of popular songs while wearing bloated, lurid costumes to disguise their identities, until one of the judging panel was able to attach a name to a voice. The majority of contestants were no more able to sing than the panel; it was all terrifically entertaining, apparently.

No-one was laughing when Obraztsova cut her own throat as Dalila in Siracuse. Her singing was other than "bad" for the audience that heard her live, and it is troubling that so many sopranos since 1996 have either been allowed or encouraged to develop a vibrato as a wobble while young. At the time of writing,[35] the singing of Erin Morley[36] (as Sophie), Samantha Hankey[37] (as Octavian) and Lise Davidsen[38] (as the Marschallin) in Robert Carson's production of Der Rosenkavalier at the Met made for grim evidence.[39] The voice of the Norwegian Davidsen was, in particular, beset by a frightful wobble, just ten years into her career;[40] that she might to sing like this into her forties is horrifying.[41] The sacrificing of line and cantabile to amplitude and overwork is a crisis that has been too long ignored or accepted as convention – with a few arenas in which exceptions proved to be the rule, chiefly the early music "authentic" movement. Although the origins of "period" performance date back to the 19th century, and the curiosity of Felix Mendelssohn, it didn't gather momentum until the landmark work of Wanda Landowska, Olga Schwind, Carl Dolmetsch and Ralph Kirkpatrick, whose researches, performances and teaching gave credence to recreations of the past when the contemporary was proving to be unpalatable. Sung tone from before the age of recording cannot be guessed at; a huge number of technical guides and primers have been useful for teachers and performers seeking something like the clarity and crispness of instrumental timbre as it is has come to characterise instrumental practice, but historicism can achieve little if Lillian Nordica's voice was

---

33   It can be presumed that North Korea is alone in not broadcasting the programme – which (South) Korea first scheduled in 2011.

34   Singers make up a large number of the early rounds, when the hopeless are allowed their 15 seconds of fame.

35   March, 2023.

36   October 11, 1980 –

37   1994 –

38   8 February, 1987 –

39   Created for Renée Fleming in 2017.

40   One online critic (for the Observer), described Davidsen's voice as "lushly blooming." 30 March, 2023.

41   The same can be said of the even younger Julia Muzychenko-Greenhalgh, a prize-winner at the 2023 Queen Elizabeth Competition, and a worrying number of the soprano entrants in the 2023 Cardiff Singer of the World.

"perfect" for Bach and Handel as well as Verdi and Wagner during the last decade of the 19th century.

Thanks to the asceticism of ensemble and orchestral sound as it was realised during the second half of the 20th century, a new species of soprano had cause to emerge. No-one knows how Baroque singers sounded; even so, the representative characteristics of "authentic" female singers can be defined as a light or non-existent vibrato, the negation of portamento, limited attack, the eradication of anything capable of disturbing the sung line, and the conservation of resources – with amplitude actively discouraged. A characteristically dispiriting example of the modern is Rachel Redmond's performance on a 2023 recording of Mozart's Requiem, conducted by Jordi Savall.[42] She has a beautiful voice, but her tone and phrasing are cold, bleached and analogous to the timbre and line of a wooden flute. A century earlier, the "Handel sound" was memorialised by Clara Butt,[43] a vocally and physically[44] imposing contralto remembered for inspiring Elgar when composing his orchestral song-cycle, *Sea Pictures* – of which Butt gave the premiere on 5 October, 1899. Butt's reputation as a Handelian was secured by the gramophone; her 1917 recording of "*Ombra mai fu*" is typical of her work and her times. She employs little vibrato, but the abundant tone is made luxurious by her cultivated portamento (ancillary to the orchestra). Most importantly of all, she contains her resources so that sound never occludes substance. In matters of style she is old-fashioned; she is *au modern* in her discretion, however, favouring line over colour and character. Butt never took to opera (performing in only two productions, both of *Orfeo ed Euridice*), and her unease with music-theatre is obvious from her 78s, one of which – "*O don fatale*" – is laboured and ineffectual, even if her sung line adheres to Verdi's oft-stated prejudices.[45]

Butt's successor, Kathleen Ferrier,[46] was also trained by 19th century-born teachers; her limited use of vibrato and portamento when performing baroque and classical repertoire nonetheless joined her to post-war practice, as evidenced by her recording of "*Ombra mai fu*," which speaks to obvious changes in taste and discretion reaching further than the British unease with operatic style as it was known through Europe and America. Ferrier's singing of works by Handel with Malcolm Sargent in 1948 is eloquent and unaffected by the romantic vocal palette on which she would rely four years later when recording "*Das Lied von der Erde*" with Bruno Walter. The performance of the work's last movement, *Der Abschied*,[47] is a revelation for its word-centred priorities and absent sentimentality; Ferrier's use of vibrato and portamento is appropriate and cultivated, but her restraint, and the immediacy of her singing, are baroque in effect and impetus. Ferrier sails a great deal closer to what is known of the art of Anna Bahr-von Mildenburg than to any of her successors – including Christa Ludwig.[48]

After the War, the "authentic" movement gained momentum through recordings, with labels formed to exploit the myriad different ways in which the performance

---

[48] An *echt* modern approach to "*Ombra mai fu*," can be found in performances by the French contralto, Nathalie Stutzmann (*née* Dupuy; 6 May, 1965 –), who made use of a strong vibrato as an occasional effulgence to balance her "authentic" training and inclinations. Conversely, the Czech-born Magdalena Kožená (26 May, 1973 –) gave performances of *Das lied von der erde* (including a recording conducted by her husband, Sir Simon Rattle) that featured a prominent amount of straight or almost-straight singing during *Der Abschied*.

of music written during the 17th and 18th centuries might compensate for the near-terminal decline in popular contemporary art music. Singers trained to perform opera in the modern way – loud and with corset-straining resonance – were directed towards a culture in which a singer's voice was preserved by the judgment and discretion of scholarship. That doesn't mean the conclusions drawn were accurate or tenable. Indeed, there is no possibility that the music of Bach and Handel sounded anything like a performance conducted by Karl Richter, John Elliot Gardiner, Frans Brüggen, Philippe Herreweghe, René Jacobs, and Ton Koopman. The skill, precision and professionalism of their collective aesthetic is unlike anything that can have prevailed for what was previously a largely amateur culture. Singers retained by private houses, estates, churches and courts lived short lives, doing with their time than play music – all of it new. There are tens of thousands of musicians in Europe today who have given at least 100 performances of Bach's Mass in B minor; London is home to musicians who have submitted to Vivaldi's *Four Seasons* on more than 1000 occasions. The same composer's *Gloria* was written during his time at the Pio Ospedale della Pietà, where the choir was esteemed for its uncommon skill as well as the enforced sequestration of its members. This was not typical; by the time Mozart began writing for the Church and the theatre it was unheard of.

Group Think produced a consensus to which its subscribers were drawn in opposition to what would now be categorised as the "Furtwängler sound" – huge, romantic and metaphysical. It would be difficult to find a modern audience for an out-dated performance of Mozart's Requiem, a shift in perception and appreciation that purged the shadows as well as the cobwebs. Modern pre-romantic choirs and choruses are commonly small and well-trained; "authentic" orchestras contain fewer than 40 players, and conductors adopt strict and rapid tempi – far quicker than they were during the first half of the 20th century. Conversely, the live-filmed recording of the Requiem conducted by Karl Böhm[49] in 1971, in Vienna's Piaristenkirche, made use of the massed forces of the city's Symphony Orchestra and the Chorus of the State Opera; the venue's acoustics created huge challenges, navigated with superb skill by the conductor and the sound engineers. Böhm's approach to the "*Kyrie*" would now be thought perversely slow; compared to most modern interpretations, it's half speed, and yet the coda – which Böhm directed using gestures that appear unconnected to the resulting wonders – is among the most terrifying episodes in the history of recorded music. The richness of the sound and the concomitant lack of vocal precision are punctuated by hard-headed timpani and a Gothic longueur that eclipses anything done by the ideologically authentic. Mozart's Requiem was written for an occasion, as a commission, which meant a first performance was not presumed to have a second; 230 years later, there are busloads of singers performing fewer than a dozen roles on a regular basis. They know their repertoire from memory because they are required to sing little else. If practice makes perfect then it's equally true that the routine fosters convention. To this end, the "originality" of period performance can be blamed for a concomitant diminution in individuality and character.

---

49   A conductor, born in 1896.

The American soprano, Judith Nelson,[50] for example, followed a traditional route to the opera house, in which forum she was cast in various Mozart roles, including Blonde in *Die Entführung aus dem Serail*, of which there is a live recording from the Schwetzingen Festival on 30 April, 1975. Her singing of "*Durch Zärtlichkeit und Schmeicheln*"[51] is characterful and teasing; she phrases with a quick, pronounced vibrato, which she uses with intelligence. The following year she joined William Christie, Wieland Kuijken and René Jacobs in forming the Concerto Vocale, preceding Christie's Les Arts Florissants by three years. Nelson sang regularly for Christopher Hogwood's Academy of Ancient Music, and Anthony Rooley's Consort of Musicke – routinely in the company of the English soprano, Emma Kirkby.[52] Nelson was the soprano soloist for Hogwood's landmark 1982 recording of Handel's *Messiah*, taped and filmed in Westminster Abbey. Her performance of "I know that my redeemer liveth" might as well be by a different soprano to the one heard performing Mozart in Schwetzingen. Like the Academy's string section, she performs *almost* without vibrato, and with no portamento. Her diction is exceptional, but the only expressive features are changes in dynamics, emphasis and ornament; the tone is beautiful, pure and flavourless – to a point that makes it difficult to learn anything of the singer. Worse still, the performance disconnects the words and the music so that neither convey anything of the sentiments articulated by the composer. "I know that my Redeemer liveth," was drawn from Job and Paul; it represents nothing less than an expression of faith in redemption. The Second Coming of Jesus is announced, with an ascending fourth attaching to the words "I know," which binds the listener to the author's repeated conviction "For now is Christ risen." Anyone not understanding English would be hard-pressed to conclude anything of its meaning from Nelson's performance; certainly no-one would mistake it as a call to the Rapture.[53]

The English contemporaries Emma Kirkby, Evelyn Tubb and Catherine Bott[54] were more ascetic still, and an obvious pill for anyone weary of heaving bosoms and hammered eardrums. Their "repressed" sound as women ideated a crisis-issue formed of women being required to sing like pre-pubescent boys. Trebles do not use vibrato; as a cultural aesthetic, a Tudor choir is unique because boys don't sound like women; it's unclear why so many have wanted female singers to sound like children – who cannot breathe, speak, or think as do their mothers. If music is the articulation of ideas for the expression of feeling then singing is a manifestation of physical processes spanning the nervous, endocrine, cardiovascular, lymphatic, respiratory, and reproductive systems. The psychological-physical interactions experienced by a woman feeling any one of the six essential emotions – sadness, happiness, fear, anger, surprise and disgust – are better revealed as truths for a voice when cueing with a listener's application of the sung word to its meaning as speech. Everyone knows what it is to endure spoken words delivered in a monotone; it is no different for a song when performed without colour.

---

50   *née* Manes, 10 September, 1939 – 28 May, 2012.

51   'With tenderness and pretty words.'

52   26 February, 1949 –

53   A modern example of how things have changed for the better is Céline Scheen, a thrilling performer of 17th and 18th century repertoire.

54   11 September, 1952 –

"Straight-tone" is useful, of course, as a transitory feature of musical voicing, but it should not be its function if it causes music to sound limited or stifled. Prior to her withdrawal for a period of private study and reflection, the violinist Anne-Sophie Mutter played with constant vibrato and without portamento; when making her second recordings of the Beethoven and Brahms Concertos, conducted by Kurt Masur,[55] her playing was unrecognisable. The changes in colour, tone and phrasing, and her embrace of portamento and a variegated vibrato, were shocking in their expressive resonance. Mutter's new sound was rooted in 19th century practice, but it was as unique to Mutter as her fingerprints. The majority of "authentic" recordings of the Beethoven Concerto are impossible to distinguish from one another; they are conformist because of the misconception that denying a player two of the most valuable expressive resources, vibrato and portamento, facilitates originality or individuality. Mutter idealised the articulatory virtues of judgment and discretion, employing less portamento than Mischa Elman (as a teenager) and more vibrato than Joseph Joachim (as an old man); she was revealed as an individual through her rejection of dogma and tradition.

Inveterate vibrato is useful only for a soprano who cannot sing without it. Its prudence as a mask for poor intonation and weak technique rob vocal expression of the power of contrast; a singer choosing between no colour at all or so little of it that a performance becomes anaemic is denying vulnerability as a construct for those fluctuations in articulation that differentiate one singer from another. There is only so much purity one can take before the heart yearns for something more. Kirkby and Bott both recorded "Thy Fair Belinda [...] When I am Laid in Earth" from *Dido and Aeneas*; they did so without addressing the scene's piercing trauma – at least not as the Lament was mortalised during the 1960s by the English mezzo-soprano, Janet Baker.[56] Many have done violence to the integrity of Purcell's music, including Jessye Norman and the French soprano, Patricia Petibon,[57] whose recording of the aria is especially sickly in its affectation and mock sincerity. Because the ideal is easily dismissed as cliché, Baker's shadow was (and remains) suffocating. The intimacy of her filmed performance from Glyndebourne in 1966[58] overreaches her studio recordings of the aria because she was as talented as an actress as a singer. Her dignified translation of Dido's evolving complex of feelings is achieved through a mixture of seamless cantabile and vertiginous dynamic shifts that succeed because the scene embraces hyperbole. "When I am laid in Earth" epitomises the myth of the English "stiff upper lip," which has always buckled under nostalgia; Baker's tracing of the aria's power to extremes of sentiment was measured rather than restrained; her genius was to mine the music's depths without submitting to the histrionics of sentimentality or the frigidity of the "authentic."

---

55   Her earlier recordings were conducted by Karajan.

56   Dame Janet Abbott Baker, 21 August, 1933 –

57   27 February, 1970 –

58   The 13 performances in Glyndebourne's 1966 production (presented as a double bill with Ravel's *L'heure espagnole*), were conducted by Sir John Pritchard, who told the author as a teenager that he had almost to lower his baton when conducting Baker in the aria. He was equally adamant that a number of the London Philharmonic Orchestra's players were seen to weep, although anyone who has ever worked with a London orchestra will attest to the improbability of this recollection.

Among Baker's contemporaries, the American soprano, Arleen Auger,[59] demonstrated rare judgment when performing music from the Baroque and Classical periods without vandalising the lyrical-expressive archetype. Her natural successor, Sylvia McNair,[60] excelled in everything from Bach to Broadway and the American Songbook – to the eternal advantage of both. McNair carried a torch lit by Elly Ameling,[61] a Dutch soprano who began her career singing Bach and Mozart before steering herself towards lieder and, eventually, the music of Gershwin, Porter, Ellington and Sondheim. Ameling's discography dwarfs McNair's, but the latter produced no duds; indeed, it includes near-perfect recordings of *Idomeneo*, *L'incoronazione di Poppea*, and an exceptional turn as Anne Trulove in *The Rake's Progress*. Her performance of the first soprano part in Mozart's C minor Mass, conducted by John Eliot Gardiner, remains unrivalled; her singing, in particular, of "*Et incarnatus est*" sanctifies the radiance of Mozart's imagination, and the profundity of his love for Constanze.

Equally diverse in her repertoire was Dawn Upshaw,[62] whose discography includes Charpentier's *Te deum*; *Figaro*, Massenet's *Chérubin*, Henryk Górecki's Symphony No. 3, two recordings of *The Rake's Progress*, and various albums of American song – including a Grammy Award-winning performance of Barber's wonderful *Knoxville: Summer of 1915*, commissioned and first performed by Eleanor Steber (with Serge Koussevitzky conducting the Boston Symphony Orchestra) on 9 April, 1948. With the "authentic" movement supported by hard-core adherents, notably Barbara Thornton,[63] Mireille Delunsch,[64] Sandrine Piau[65] and Karina Gauvin, the field was made more diverse by Véronique Gens,[66] Diana Montague[67] and Lynne Dawson[68] – sopranos who brought lucid voices and luminous sensibilities to a huge span of music and audiences. Gens was an especially talented interpreter of French *chanson*, producing numerous fine recordings of songs by Berlioz, Debussy, Fauré, Canteloube and Hahn. In this respect, she is the natural heir to France's most important post-war soprano, Régine Crespin.[69]

Neither Crespin nor Gens sang anything by Edgard Varèse, Karlheinz Stockhausen or Nicholas Maw. In fact, none of the sopranos identified above has performed anything by even one of the more contemporary of the composers whose work defined the culture of art-music between the 1950s and the 1980s. The aftershocks of this difficult, anomalous period continue to be felt in conservatoires and universities around the world, where the truly *avant-garde* will never be tonal, approachable or translatable. The roots of abstract modernism date back to the last works by Liszt, but the crystalising moment for the soprano was Schoenberg's *Pierrot Lunaire*, which called

---

59   13 September, 1939 – 10 June, 1993.
60   23 June, 1956 –
61   *née* Elisabeth Sara Ameling, 8 February, 1933 –
62   17 July, 1960 –
63   6 January, 1950 – 8 November, 1998.
64   2 November, 1962 –
65   5 June, 1965 –
66   19 April, 1966 –
67   8 April, 1953 –
68   3 June, 1953 –
69   23 February, 1927 – 5 July, 2007.

for *Sprechstimme*, an expressionist vocal technique somewhere between singing and speaking that originated with Humperdinck's *Königskinder*. Schoenberg's immediate inspiration was Albertine Zehme,[70] who commissioned music for a cycle of poems by the Belgian writer Albert Giraud, to satisfy her obsession with the mystical features of recitation.[71] Zehme was an admirer of Sarah Bernhardt, on whom she modelled her histrionic style of recitation. In a note titled "*Why I must speak these songs*" (provided to the audience at the Berlin premiere in March 1910 of *Pierrot lunaire*) she wrote:

> The words that we speak should not solely lead to mental concepts, but instead their sound should allow us to partake of their inner experience. To make this possible we must have an unconstrained freedom of tone. None of the thousand vibrations should be denied to the expression of feeling. I demand tonal freedom, not thoughts! The singing voice, that supernatural, chastely controlled instrument, ideally beautiful precisely in its ascetic lack of freedom, is not suited to strong eruptions of feeling – since even one strong breath of air can spoil its incomparable beauty. Life cannot be exhausted by the beautiful sound alone. The deepest final happiness, the deepest final sorrow dies away unheard, as a silent scream within our breast, which threatens to fly apart or to erupt like a stream of molten lava from our lips. For the expression of these final things it seems to me almost cruel to expect the singing voice to do such a labour, from which it must go fourth frayed, splintered, and tattered. For our poets and composers to communicate, we need both the tones of song as well as those of speech. My unceasing striving in search of the ultimate expressive capabilities for the "artistic experience of tone" has taught me this fact.[72]

Zehme's concern for the "unconstrained" expressive conception of the voice as an instrument communicating something more than "*beautiful sound alone*" was written the year after Lotte Lehmann created the Dyer's Wife in *Die Frau ohne Schatten*, and a year before the death of Caruso. Her philosophy was adopted in America and France by Varèse, whose *Offrandes*, for soprano and chamber orchestra (1921/1927), required a singer to learn music that was almost impossible to sing. The extreme vocal intervals and quarter-tone pitching necessitate enormous technical skill, as the English soprano, Sarah Leonard,[73] has demonstrated over decades of service to the *idea* of new music by living composers. The splintering after the Second War of musical vernaculars transcended the vocal conventions with which Schoenberg, Stravinsky and Berg never deviated. A soprano trained to sing Mozart could perform

---

70 7 January, 1857 – 11 May, 1946.

71 In 1920, Zehme published a treatise on the subject, *Die Grundlagen des künstlerischen Sprechens und Singens* ('The basics of artistic speaking and singing.').

72 Quoted in Simms, Bryan. *The Atonal Music of Arnold Schoenberg, 1908 – 1923* (2000). Oxford University Press (120–21; 235 note 21). The original German text can be found in *Arnold Schönberg, Sämtliche Werke, Pierrot lunaire*, Josef Rufer (ed.) (Universal Edition AG and Schott Music International (1995), Section 6, series B, 24/1 (307).

73 10 April, 1953 –

anything by any of them, so that the cutting edge of modernity was never so sharp as to make it impracticable. The accessibility of art music for singers without classical techniques ensured it could be taken up by artists uninterested in (or incapable of) the established repertoire. This blurring of sound-worlds was especially impactful in Germany and France, where cabaret allowed actresses to prefer popular songs to through-composed arias. On 31 August, 1928, for example, Kurt Weill and Bertolt Brecht's *Die Dreigroschenoper*[74] – a self-described "play with music" – was premiered at Berlin's Theater am Schiffbauerdamm. The roles of Celia Peachum, Polly Peachum, Lucy Brown and Jenny were created not by sopranos, but by female singers and actors. Rosa Valetti,[75] Roma Bahn,[76] Kate Kühl[77] and Lotte Lenya[78] were all cabaret performers, which did no harm to the success of the work when producers and directors were planning the premiere. Finding singers for *Dreigroschenoper* was easy; selling the work to audiences was easier still. *Offrandes*, on the other hand, was of interest to few, and within the performing capacity of almost no-one.

Among the many who committed to the music of their peers, the Canadian-American mezzo, Ida Gauthier,[79] was renowned for performing almost nothing else. Throughout her long career, she gave the first performances in the United States of hundreds of works by the leading composers of her time, notably Satie, Ravel and Stravinsky; she sang nothing by Varèse or Schoenberg because her voice and sensibilities were attuned to an avowedly 19th century aesthetic. This space was filled most famously by the American sopranos, Jan DeGaetani[80] (a mezzo) and Bethany Beardslee.[81] The latter is remembered for her exceptional performances of works emanating from the Second Viennese School, and for her collaborations with Stravinsky, Milton Babbitt, Boulez, George Perle, and Sir Peter Maxwell Davies. Beardslee was a fearless proponent of the avant-garde faith, telling *Newsweek* in 1961:

> I don't think in terms of the public [...] Music is for the musicians. If the public wants to come along and study it, fine. I don't go and try to tell a scientist his business because I don't know anything about it. Music is just the same way. Music is not entertainment.[82]

---

74 'The Threepenny Opera.' The work was taken from a translation by Elisabeth Hauptmann of John Gay's *The Beggar's Opera*.

75 25 January, 1876 – 10 December, 1937.

76 1896 – 1975.

77 *née* Elfriede Katharina Nehrhaupt, 16 December, 1899 – 29 January, 1970.

78 *née* Karoline Wilhelmine Charlotte Blamauer, 18 October, 1898 – 27 November, 1981.

79 *née* Ida Joséphine Phoebe Éva Gauthier, 20 September, 1885 – 20 / 26 December, 1958.

80 10 July, 1933 – 15 September, 1989.

81 25 December, 1925 –

82 *Newsweek*. Vol. 103, Issue-9. For more of the same, see Beardslee, Bethany (2017). "*I Sang the Unsingable: My Life in Twentieth-Century Music*. University of Rochester Press. Beardslee's analogy was, of course, misplaced. Music is an art form designed (and created) as a means of communication. That it can be enjoyed in isolation, selfishly, does not negate its purposive value as a mechanism for people to speak through *performance* to other people. A scientist's purpose is not performative, even if it can be educational. The analogy was poor in 1961, and no less weak when rehashed by Beardslee for her autobiography.

This self-fulfilling prophesy, told by modernists uninterested in their audience, created the need for a new kind of soprano, for whom there could be no reconciliation between the ancient and the modern. These divided interests are illustrated by singing competitions, of which there are thousands globally, with contests across Europe, the UK, the United States, South Africa, China, Russia, Canada, Australia, New Zealand, Israel, Japan and Singapore. Notwithstanding some exceptions, chiefly the tri-annual Luciano Berio International Composition Competition and the Charleston International Music Competition, the majority of contests open to singers are unlikely to require a singer to perform anything encompassing Beardslee's skill set.

The extreme shifts in expression during the 1950s led to the envelope opened in Darmstadt being shredded by Karlheinz Stockhausen, Luigi Nono, Pierre Boulez, György Ligeti and Elliott Carter. Each of these composers was "challenging" when writing for the female voice; some were more challenging than others. Carter adhered broadly throughout his long career to the notion of the female voice as lyrical. "A mirror on which to dwell," a song cycle based on the poetry of Elizabeth Bishop, for soprano and chamber orchestra, was first performed on 24 February, 1976, by Susan Davenny Wyner[83] – two years after her debut, and only a few months after she was recorded live singing *Erwartung*, conducted by Arthur Weisberg. Wyner went on to work in mainstream repertoire, performing Handel with Sir Colin Davis, Beethoven with Bernstein, and Ravel with André Previn. In 1981, she recorded the title role of *L'Enfant et les Sortileges*, with Arleen Auger as the Princess; in the same year, she made her debut at the Met as Woglinde in *Das Rheingold*, under Erich Leinsdorf. Only a decade into her career, an accident caused irreversible damage to her vocal cords, at which point she turned to conducting. "A mirror on which to dwell" is obtuse and unkind to its singer; Wyner's skill in navigating the music's extreme intervals, expressive monotony and brutalist accompaniments was singular, but it was as nothing compared to the demands placed on Cathy Berberian[84] by Luciano Berio, her husband between 1950 and 1964.

Berberian was one of the first singers to commit to contemporary music from the start of her career, which began in Italy, where she was based for much of her life. She made her formal debut in 1957, at Incontri Musicali, a contemporary music festival in Naples. Her premiere the following year of John Cage's "Aria (with Fontana Mix)" brought her international notoriety. The "score" consists of 20 pages of "notation," formed of 16 black squares denoting "non-musical" vocal sounds, with wavy lines in a range of colours denoting different singing styles for use at will by the soloist. Each page of the score is prescribed to last 30 seconds; the electronic backing track ("Fortuna Mix") is formed of random sounds and noises,[85] none of them music. A performer is at liberty to manipulate page order and time-length, to facilitate alternating programs of changing lengths. The "text" employs random vowels and consonants, as well as words and phrases in Armenian, Russian, Italian, French and

---

83   *née* Susan Davenny, 17 October, 1943 –

84   *née* Catherine Anahid Berberian, 4 July, 1925 – 6 March, 1983.

85   Appropriately enough, one of the only recognisable features of the backing track appears to be a chainsaw.

English. The chaos was shocking at the time; seven decades later it is describably tedious. Berberian's recording of the work survives as a tribute to her magnetic personality and creative impedimenta of voice-generated sounds, now known as an "extended" technique, spanning onomatopoeia, clicks, whistles, squeaking, squawk-ing, out-and-out shrieking and a host of other ululations that must have seemed terrifically exciting at the time.

Berberian was not a one-trick pony; throughout her career she employed classical training (having been taught in Milan to sing music by Monteverdi), cabaret (notably Kurt Weill), and early modernism (Stravinsky and Darius Milhaud). Her rolodex of genres included arrangements of songs by The Beatles and her own compositions, notoriously *Stripsody* (1966), in which she exploits every vocal technique available to grating effect. Berio composed extensively for Berberian (during and after their marriage), most of which she recorded, including *Thema (Omaggio a Joyce)* (1958), *Circles* (1960), *Visage* (1961), *Folk Songs* (1964–73), and *Recital I (for Cathy)* (1972). *Sequenza III* (1965) is especially challenging, and probably impossible to "sing" for anyone not immersed in the avant-garde culture within which it emerged.[86] Part of Berio's notes for the score clarify that

> In *Sequenza III* the emphasis is given to the sound symbolism of vocal and sometimes visual gestures, with their accompanying "shadows of meaning", and the associations and conflicts suggested by them. For this reason *Sequenza III* can also be considered as a dramatic essay whose story, so to speak, is the relationship between the soloist and her own voice.

There are no meaningful time signatures, keys or note lengths; pitch values are vague or non-existent. Berio's expressive markings are precise, however, and include "tense," "urgent," "relieved," "wistful," and "bewildered." The need for specialist sopranos released everyone else from playing dice in service to composers uninterested in tra-ditional voice-techniques. Just as a string-player will refuse any instruction to employ *col legno*[87] against the body of their instrument, so too will most sopranos avoid tackling the once-and-former avant-garde. Among the happy few to commit to the cause was Joan La Barbara,[88] who developed her own vocabulary of sounds, attendant to the originalist Berberian. Her use of whispering, crying, sighing, inhalation, and multiphonics[89] was passé for the Tuvan people of Mongolia; for John Cage, Morton Feldman and Philip Glass, La Barbara was a Titan of the novel and the odd.

Within the orbit of the outsider, there were few odder than Stockhausen, the bogeyman of Modernism, whose *Licht*[90] – a cycle of seven operas, subtitled *Die sieben*

---

86 It may not be appreciated how much "normal" and tonal music Berio composed. His *Folk Songs*, and his ending of *Turandot*, are merely examples of how capable he was when writing other than experimentally.
87 *col legno battuto* ('with the wood [of the bow] beaten.').
88 8 June, 1947 – . See generally the excellent Ripley, Samara (2016). "*Joan La Barbara's Early Explorations of the Voice.*" Masters thesis; Mount Allison University.
89 The production of two or more pitches simultaneously.
90 'Light.'

Tage der Woche[91] – was characterised by the composer as an "eternal spiral" with "neither an end nor a beginning." That is certainly true for anyone who has sat through *Licht's* 29 hours of music. Because the days of the week have been performed so rarely, only a small number of singers can lay claim to legacy. Stockhausen's sopranos of choice were Kathinka Pasveer,[92] Csilla Csövári, Jana Mrazova, Donna Sarley, Anu Komsi, and Annette Meriweather. The difficulty of *Licht's* music for soprano is unfathomable, in part because the notation is impossible to read other than by reference to the (now dead) composer, but also because it involves almost no actual singing. One of the many frustrations presented by Stockhausen's music – particularly the unfinished *Klang* – is that no two performances can adhere to a repeating principle, sufficient to allow for comparisons between realisation and performer. What worked on a Monday neither bound nor liberated anyone singing on a Tuesday, a feature of so much experimental and electronic music that predicated against the evolution of a performance culture capable of iteration and schooling.

Of the very few experimentalists whose music retained a place in concert and opera house schedules, Ligeti is unique in being known to audiences outside the concert hall. His *Requiem*, composed between 1963 and 1965, was made famous by Stanley Kubrick's *2001: A Space Odyssey* (1968), which made powerful use of the "*Kyrie.*" The closing "*Lacrimosa,*" for soloists and orchestra, has gained traction also, thanks to the support and unstinting efforts of Liliana Poli,[93] one of the two female soloists at the Stockholm premiere on 14 March, 1965.[94] Ligeti's 1978 opera, *Le Grand Macabre,*[95] features a number of roles for soprano, the most prominent being Amando/Spermando (created at the premiere by Kerstin Meyer), and Venus, created by Monika Lavén and Kerstin Wiberg. In recent years, "The Mysteries of the Macabre," an arrangement of three coloratura arias sung during the opera, has become a popular concert work, made spectacular by the wildly charismatic Canadian soprano and conductor, Barbara Hannigan.[96] Her 10,000-watt personality is one of the few miracles among sopranos of the 21st century. Unlike the "human sampler" and improviser, Catherine Jauniaux,[97] Hannigan's training is classical, rooted in a discipline that equipped her to give the first performances of Louis Andriessen's *Writing to Vermeer,*[98] Gerald Barry's *The Bitter Tears of Petra von Kant*[99] and *The Importance of Being Earnest,*[100] Jan van de Putte's *Wet Snow,*[101] Kris Defoort's *House of the Sleeping Beauties,*[102] and George Benjamin's *Written on Skin.*[103] Hannigan's appearances as Berg's Lulu (for which she learned to dance *en pointe*), and as Marie in Bernd Alois

---

91   'The Seven Days of the Week.'
92   11 June, 1959 –
93   1 January, 1928 – 14 July, 2015.
94   The other soprano was Barbro Ericson, 2 April, 1930 –
95   First performed on 12 April, 1978.
96   8 May, 1971 –
97   April, 1965 –
98   First performed on 1 December, 1999.
99   First performed on 27 September, 2002.
100 First performed on 17 March, 2013.
101 First performed on 8 June, 2004.
102 First performed on 8 May, 2009.
103 First performed on 7 July, 2012.

Zimmermann's *Die Soldaten*, have been hailed for their invention, emotional conviction and technical bravura. Hannigan is the Pauline Viardot of the 21st century, a woman of astonishing intellect and ability, whose legacy is likely to be perceived as a once-in-a-generation talent wasted on composers lacking the skill and invention to do justice to her incandescent virtuosity.

Hannigan was 44-years-old when she appeared at the Barbican with the LSO and Simon Rattle in 2015 to perform the "Mysteries," dressed as a recherché schoolgirl, chewing gum. Her appearance, energy and vocal confidence would have persuaded anyone that she was half her age, whereas the American soprano, Rachel Willis-Sørensen,[104] who was born in 1984, and is not yet 40 at the time of writing, recorded Strauss' Four Last Songs for Sony,[105] released in March, 2023, as the soprano's second studio album. Her voice is large and wine-dark, with a top that is strikingly redolent of Renée Fleming. She could not be mistaken for Fleming, however, because even in its adolescence Willis-Sørensen's voice is beset by a pestering vibrato that stains the natural beauty of what would otherwise be a glorious sound. The wobbling poisons the line and languor of the songs, so that what might have prevailed as plangency becomes excessively irritating. Willis-Sørensen made her stage debut as the High Priestess in *Aida*, in 2008; over the ensuing decade she developed a reputation as well as her repertoire which, by the 2019/20 season, included Marguerite (*Faust*) in Japan, the Marschallin at the Semperoper, Dresden, Donna Anna in Chicago, Valentine in Genèva, Mozart's Countess in Munich, and a European concert tour with Jonas Kaufmann to support the release of his album, "*Wien*." Willis-Sørensen's 2022/23 season included her role-debut as Elisabeth de Valois in *Don Carlos*, Ellen Orford in *Peter Grimes*, Violetta, Rosalinde, Mimi, Desdemona, Leonora in *Il Trovatore*, Tove in Schoenberg's *Gurrelieder*,

Beethoven's 9th Symphony and an outdoor concert in Berlin with Kaufmann. The range and weight and diversity of Willis-Sørensen's repertoire has been her preference since her first album for Sony, which included arias from *La traviata*, *Il trovatore*, *Otello*, *Rusalka*, *La bohème*, *Die lustige Witwe* and *Don Giovanni*. Again, the tone is refulgent, but her wobble is toxic; whether this is a consequence of training or overwork won't matter within a decade if she continues down the path on which her management has propelled her. That path promises to lead to Bayreuth, with ruinous precipitation; it will at that point be a case of "*und Mutter-Weh, aus Liebestränen eh' und je.*"[106]

If opera is to survive as more than an expensive folly – as something worth saving despite Bethany Beardslee's disdain for entertainment – then it will need to foster art as well as stardom without the latter subverting the former. Careers need to last decades, so that expectation and fan-loyalty can generate the sort of excitement that once accompanied a singer's evolution over time and repertoire. A once-extended apprenticeship with the music of Mozart remains the foundation for any singer seeking to develop the insight and sinew necessary for singing anything more stentorian – an order of process and priority that will always protect young voices against early

---

104   1984 –
105   With the Gewandhaus Orchestra, conducted by Andris Nelsons.
106   'And mother's anguish, from tears of love everlasting...' *Tristan und Isolde*, Act III, Scene 1.

damage. The stagione system that once, trained and refined a company of singers over decades of constancy is over, at least for leading soloists. The freedom afforded by the aeroplane has created more problems than it has solved, with singers travelling by flight enduring air-conditioning,[107] the psychological effects of family separation, and intense rehearsal schedules – the brevity of which, for often complex productions, compounds the strain of life as a professional singer. Previously, singers travelling by boat gained from fresh air, healthy food, enforced exercise and lengthy seasons in prolonged occupation of a single House and an apartment, rather than a hotel with a controlled climate and a ruinous menu. For women, these pressures are made disproportionate by the primacy of beauty and sexuality. It is no coincidence that most of the young women identified in this chapter are, for want of a better word, "hot." Willis-Sørensen is bigger-boned than most, but she is no less beautiful for it – with a Rosetti profile, Nordic blonde hair, and ocean blue eyes, on which her album covers have drawn with forgivable calculation.

If a soprano is to hold her place on the stage for two decades then she will set out in her early twenties and mature in her forties. Well-cared for voices should remain healthy to the age of 60, although many (like Freni and Christa Ludwig) have maintained peak health for considerably longer. Wear and tear is to be expected, of course, but it can be managed – and anticipated. There are obvious case-studies worth highlighting. Magda Olivero,[108] for example, made her debut in 1932, and retired for a decade in 1941, after marrying. She was persuaded to return to the stage by Francesco Cilea, who wanted to hear her sing *Adriana Lecouvreur*.[109] From 1951 until her retirement, Olivero was the most gifted, idiosyncratic Italian-repertoire soprano not to become a household name. She made few records, failed to appear at the Opéra and Covent Garden, and sang only once at the Vienna State Opera. She was heard only rarely at La Scala, and despite making her US debut in 1967 (as Mede, at the Dallas Opera), she wasn't invited to the Met until 1975, in her sixty-fifth year, when she was invited to step in at the last minute for an indisposed Birgit Nilsson. Olivero gave only three performances in the run, but they caused a sensation – to which Rudolf Bing was apparently deaf. She sang for the last time on stage in March 1981, in Poulenc's *La Voix Humaine* – of which she had given the Italian premiere in 1968. Spanning 50 years, her career was exceptional for hundreds of wonderful, intricate, fascinating performances in *Adriana Lecouvreur, Fedora, Tosca, La fanciulla del West, La Wally, Madama Butterfly, Manon Lescaut* and *Mefistofele* – some of which survive on live recordings.[110] Olivero was a model of vocal security, judgment and interpretative refinement; her voice was large but focussed, and it remained fresh to the end. Its longevity was lifelong.[111, 112]

---

107   It is well-known that air-conditioning is the cause of a host of bronchial complications, all of them made worse by jet-lag.

108   *née* born Maria Maddalena Olivero, 25 March, 1910 – 8 September, 2014.

109   She did as she was asked, although Cilea died three months before the performance.

110   Her only "major" studio recording was as Fedora (1970), with Mario del Monaco punching the furniture as Loris.

111   She attributed her long life and robust health to vegetarianism and yoga.

112   She continued to sing privately for small audiences into her nineties, and died at the age of 104.

Unlike Olivero, the British soprano, Josephine Barstow,[113] thrashed her powerful voice early in her career, developing a huge and pernicious wobble that most chose to ignore when she appeared in her signature roles, Amelia in *Un ballo in maschera* (which she recorded with Karajan, shortly before his death in 1989) and Turandot. Barstow did too much, or was pushed too hard; either way, it sounded like one or the other long before it should have done. She was compared in her youth to another big-voiced English soprano, Eva Turner,[114] whose career began during the first decade of the 20th century as a chorus member for the Carl Rosa Opera Company. After taking on larger roles, including Cio-Cio San, Mimi, Santuzza, Elisabeth in *Tannhäuser*, Elsa and, eventually Brünnhilde, she was engaged by Toscanini as Freia and Sieglinde at La Scala in 1924; she attended the premiere of *Turandot* in Milan, and sang the role eight months later in Brescia, and at Covent Garden in 1928, and at La Scala the following year. A performance of *Turandot* at Covent Garden in 1937, with Giovanni Martinelli as Calaf, conducted by John Barbirolli, was recorded; it evidences not only a sensational voice, but the age-defying virtues of patience, discretion and judgment. Martinelli makes an awful noise, as usual, but Turner is incendiary. The Welsh soprano, Margaret Price,[115] was born just six months after Barstow, but managed her resources considerably better, achieving world-wide recognition in Mozart and as a lieder singer before turning to anything more demanding. She made her debut in 1962, as Cherubino, for Welsh National Opera, from where she headed to Covent Garden and a nasty encounter with the hostile, unreceptive George Solti. The conductor did what he could to quash her career, but a last-minute cancellation by Teresa Berganza as Cherubino, gave her the break she needed. In 1967, Britten retained her for the English Opera Group's production of Mozart's *Der Schauspieldirektor*, and as Titania in *A Midsummer Night's Dream*. In the studio, Price's Fiordiligi for Klemperer in 1972 established her international status as a world-class Mozartian. She relocated to Germany in 1971, initially for the Cologne Opera and latterly the Bavarian State Opera, Munich, where she became friends with Carlos Kleiber. After hearing Price sing the Countess in *Le nozze di Figaro*, Harold C. Schonberg wrote in the *New York Times* that:

> San Francisco and Chicago often manage to get great European singers before the Metropolitan opera, and in some quarters music lovers are demanding a Congressional investigation to determine why. Anyway, Miss Price sang the Countess in a melting manner, and with the style that has made her, many believe, the foremost living Mozart soprano. Then, three days later, she sang a ravishing Desdemona in Verdi's "Otello," a role she repeats tomorrow night [...]. The "Otello" audience realized why Miss Price has become one of the most sought-after singers of the day. Being sought after means a heavy schedule, and Miss Price is booked solid in Europe and the United States until 1980. So will she ever be singing at the Metropolitan Opera? [116]

---

113   27 September, 1940 –
114   10 March, 1892 – 16 June, 1990.
115   13 April, 1941 – 28 January, 2011.
116   *The New York Times*, 17 September, 1976, p.51.

She appeared finally at the Met in 1985, as *Aida* – three years after recording *Tristan und Isolde* in the studio with Kleiber. This was controversial casting, as Kleiber understood. Price never sang the role in the theatre, and even with the benefit of recording engineers she is overwhelmed at the beginning of Act II, and briefly during the "*Liebestod*." Her performance is otherwise miraculous because she brings a measure of vulnerability to a role that is all too often played as Brünnhilde. Her Mozartian tone and bel canto legato are revealing of line, character and youth. With access to literally any singer he wanted, Kleiber could have recorded the work with the Swedish soprano, Catarina Ligendza,[117] with whom he collaborated at Bayreuth during the 1970s. Instead, he wanted someone capable of achieving the clarity and beauty on which Wagner had fixated. The opening of Price's "*Liebestod*" is a lesson for everyone; it is as if Mozart's Countess had taken a wrong turn. The opening phrases are delivered as if by a soubrette; the effect is appropriately spine-tingling. Five years after Isolde, Price was recorded live singing Mahler's *Des Knaben Wunderhorn* and lieder by Schubert and Strauss, with Geoffrey Parsons – 25 years after her stage debut.[118] The performances are a testament to the singer's talent as a chamber musician; she sounds decades younger than do many in their twenties. The crispness of her diction, the easy breathing and legatos (especially in the selection of songs by Strauss) are magnificent; everything is easy, for the singer and the listener – which is precisely what the composer wanted.

The same was true throughout Julia Varady's[119] long career (which spanned a vast range of work and genre, but especially Richard Strauss); it didn't apply to the Czech heldensopran, Éva Marton[120] – another loud, hectoring wobbler, the scale of whose voice was misconstrued as dramatic. Similarly overcooked was the Welsh steam-whistle, Gwyneth Jones.[121] Extolled in her youth, during the 1960s, her singing for Wolfgang Wagner's Centenary Ring (a presumably Freudian slip, flowing from his mother's British origins), was tattered, harsh and characterised by a harrowing wobble. By the time she came to record the title role of *Die Ägyptische Helena*[122] with Antal Dorati, in May, 1979, her voice was a torn and bloody affair. If Jones was at least a naturally dramatic soprano then Katia Ricciarelli[123] was typical of the tendency among lyric-sopranos to think themselves capable of shifting gears by will and preference alone. Ricciarelli's hubris was especially destructive given that her voice in 1968, the year of her debut as Mimi, was exceptionally beautiful. Between 1972 and 1975, she made acclaimed debuts in Chicago, La Scala, Covent Garden, and the Met. A pirate recording of her singing "*Chi il bel sogno di Diretta*" from *La Rondine*

---

117   18 October, 1937 –
118   On 8 December, 1987.
119   1 September, 1941 –
120   18 June, 1943 –
121   7 November, 1936 –
122   There is much else to enjoy, despite Jones' wailing, primarily Barbara Hendricks' golden turn as Aithra, and Matti Kastu's ringing Menelaus. For anyone wanting to hear the role at its best, the 2001 recording with Vitalija Blinstrubyte in the title role, Gérard Korsten conducting the Cagliari Teatro Lirico Chorus and Orchestra, is by some way the finest performance of the opera on record. It's worth noting, additionally, the magnificent performance as Menelaus by the tenor Stephen O'Mara.
123   *née* Catiuscia Maria Stella Ricciarelli, 16 January, 1946 –

at Carnegie Hall on 26 October, 1975, proves what was lost within four years. The elegiac tone, seamless legato, and a floated high C for the ages are all miraculous, and enough to cause her work during the 1980s to resolve as tragic – beginning with the surreal folly of a natural Rossini soprano drowning and shrieking as Turandot for Karajan in 1981. Ricciarelli managed, at least, to build a career; Anita Cerquetti[124] and Elena Suliotis[125] were unable to maintain the pressure to which they submitted themselves for more than a handful of seasons; Catherine Malfitano[126] and Carol Vaness[127] qualify as later exemplars of beauty being killed by the beasts of ambition and amplitude.

The Bulgarian soprano, Anna Tomowa-Sintow[128] proved that volume did not require (or compel) admixtures of vulgarity, strain and ugliness. She made her debut at Leipzig Opera in 1967, as Abigaille in Verdi's *Nabucco*; 21 years later, her recording of *Ariadne auf Naxos*, with James Levine and the Vienna Philharmonic, won the 1988 Grammy Award for Best Opera Recording.[129] Her voice was sumptuous throughout a long and stupendous career, much of it lived in close proximity with Karajan, who revered her above any other soprano. Her singing for Levine of Ariadne's "*Sein wir wieder gut*" and, in particular, the opera's closing scene, is no less glorious than was her Marschallin for Karajan five years earlier – or the *Gianni Schicchi* she recorded for Eterna, with Herbert Kegel conducting, in 1973. At a time when there isn't a single young soprano able to lay absolute claim to the lyric Strauss repertoire, the 1970s and '80s were halcyon. Among the most gifted of this remarkable generation were Kiri Te Kanawa,[130] Frederica von Stade,[131] Jessye Norman,[132] and Barbara Hendricks[133] – each of whom proved, like the best of those to precede them, that role-discipline is its own reward. This extraordinary quartet of sopranos sang on many of the finest Strauss recordings of the century, as well as much else to which they were able to turn without risking early ruin. As important as their longevity, and their recorded legacies, was their individuated vocal characteristics. Midst a generation saturated with Strauss sopranos, this quartet of singers (none of whom was German), typified the grandest of the 19th century soprano traditions when developing vocal fingerprints of such distinctiveness that they can be recognised from a single bar of singing. They were able to command in works that had been recorded by many of the sopranos for whom they had been written – subsuming their vocal identities without sacrificing anything of themselves in the process. It was not a simple matter of managing the breath or tuning the muscles, but rather a process of personalising the transition from speech to song so that the singer and the sung co-operated in idealised union.

---

124   13 April, 1931 – 11 October, 2014. She had to leave the stage at the age of 30, having ruined her own voice – and through no fault but her own.

125   28 May, 1943 – 4 December, 2004.

126   18 April, 1948 –

127   27 July, 1952 –

128   22 September, 1941 –

129   But for the poverty of Gary Lakes' paper-and-comb tenor (Bacchus), it would be among the finest made of the opera.

130   6 March, 1944 –

131   1 June, 1945 –

132   15 September, 1945 – 30 September, 2019.

133   20 November, 1948 –

No-one could fail to recognise Pavarotti's voice after hearing it only once; the same was true for the best of the singers whose careers coincided with the golden age of recording as it passed from LP to CD. Noting the tendency of the contemporary towards anonymity, the preciousness of unique vocal characteristics enjoined not only an emotional connection for audiences (and the promoters and record companies feeding from their talent), but also the intimation of shared experience, with the maturation of a voice and a singer's insights forming a connection that would have been impossible prior to the invention of recording. The most extreme of the anomalies fostered by technology was to allow for the tracing by aficionados of changes in their idols' voices that conjured familial, psycho-sexual intimacy and ownership. This presumption caused the admiring and the devotional to cringe and wince whenever a deity bit off more than they could phonate. Enfeebled voices given to wobbling cannot navigate the taxonomy of art music. In this narrow sense, the priority for any woman[134] learning to sing – with freedom and expression – is cantabile and legato. For most of their careers, Gwyneth Jones and Éva Marton could not have performed Bach-Gounod's "*Ave Maria*," other than to feed it to the wood-chipper of imperfect vocal placement and over-singing. It is unlikely that Rachel Willis-Sørensen could sing it now. Conversely, Emma Kirkby would likely have rendered the song passive and genteel. Anyone being introduced for the first time to classical singing techniques will warm more quickly to the contained than the undisciplined.[135]

During the last two decades of the 20th century, there was no shortage of singers capable of singing a tune. Not without irony, many of the most formidable technicians struggled to find one, with the undimming popularity of the coloratura repertoire making a case for the permanence of circus-tent virtuosity. Edita Gruberová,[136] June Anderson,[137] Sumi Jo[138] and Natalie Dessay[139] were a mixed bag, with each meeting the mechanical test, albeit rarely with the requisite personality. It's all subjective, of course, but the increasing tendency among vocal high-wire acts to allow for technique to smother voice is another marker for change being other than healthy. The first album released by DG of the young American, Nadine Sierra,[140] in 2018, contains a performance of "Glitter and Be Gay," from Leonard Bernstein's *Candide*. It is tragically dull. The notes are in the right order, and everything is perfectly in tune, but there isn't the slightest hint of a personality – an absence of glitter made stultifying thanks to Kristin Chenoweth,[141] whose performances on Broadway came closer than any other to meeting the composer's expectations of the aria and the character singing it. Chenoweth had more charisma than 42nd Street on a Saturday night; she

---

134 The principle applies to men as well – of course, but not for the purposes of this book.

135 The reader might wish to engage in the "Teenager Test," which involves subjecting people between the ages of 13 and 18 to a range of recorded voices. It's fascinating to discover what causes interest, and what repels. In nearly every case, the big-voiced wobblers cause the greatest irritation. In the author's experience, the universal levellers, sufficient to cause something other than face-pulling, are Lisa della Casa and Renée Fleming.

136 23 December, 1946 – 18 October, 2021.

137 30 December, 1952 –

138 22 November, 1962 –

139 19 April, 1965 –

140 14 May, 1988 –

141 24 July, 1968 –

was possessed of some fantastic pipes also, but what made her singing of "Glitter and Be Gay" stupendous was her acting of Cunegonde's sentiments and motivations, without the bravura of her coloratura getting in the way. The end was the means, therefore, in which respect Chenoweth spoke to one of the defining problems facing opera and the art of classical singing at the turn of the Millennium.

With no-one able to fill the shoes left empty by Birgit Nilsson and her few successors, the big-voiced repertoire was adopted by efficient, but mostly bland singers like Deborah Voigt[142] and Karita Mattila.[143] The same was true across the board of vocal registers, with resonance and technique occluding expression and temperament. Sopranos trained to sing lighter repertoire made stupendous transitions for single roles – notably Cheryl Studer,[144] whose turn as Salome for DG with Sinopoli is the most perfect performance of the role in the studio. She never sang the opera on stage, but she is alone in conveying the vulnerability, psychological instability and youth that make the filthy Princess so appealing. The vibrancy and nervous energy of Studer's singing is infinitely more dangerous and erotic than the stentorian wailing for which the role has become (wrongly) celebrated. Studer's childlike delivery of the words *Er spricht von meiner Mutter*," when realising that Jochanaan has been referring to her mother, is masterful and chilling in equal measure – a three-hour masterclass captured in a matter of seconds. Equally famous, for different reasons, was Kathleen Battle,[145] whose antics as the Met's leading lyric diva led to her firing, and the wearing of T-shirts by Met staff bearing the legend "I Survived the Battle." In fairness to the pretty and vocally near-perfect singer, she was worth more nonsense than most, and among light-lyric sopranos at the end of the 20th century she had few rivals. For the 1980s the spectrum was framed by Barbara Bonney[146] and Aprile Millo[147] – the former slim, beautiful and habitually classy; the latter, plump, loud and vibrating like the Saturn V.

The landscape changed because of three singers, all born within seven years of each other. They were the "Three Sopranos" for whom a circus might have been built to rival its prototype: Renée Fleming,[148] Angela Gheorghiu[149] and Cecilia Bartoli.[150] They defined their fach and repertoire as the last to be able to achieve what they did, musically and commercially. The context for that certainty is wide-reaching and definitive. Firstly, they were all born at the right time; each began to prosper just as CDs were replacing the LP, which created opportunities for new (and defunct) labels to prosper in competition with the established monoliths. The emergence of Klaus Heymann's Naxos was especially transformative, insofar as it produced thousands[151] of fine recordings of mainstream and forgotten works with talented performers

---

142   4 August, 1960 –
143   5 September, 1960 –
144   24 October, 1955 –
145   13 August, 1948 –
146   14 April, 1956 –
147   14 April, 1958 –
148   14 February, 1959 –
149   7 September, 1965 –
150   4 June, 1966 –
151   The Naxos catalogue contains 9,000 titles.

unable to secure a contract with one of the flagship labels. Naxos' achievement was not reductively commercial, even if it was successful as a business; rather, the label achieved something unexpected in its introduction of audiences to music they would not have listened to but for Naxos making it affordable and accessible. The label's pared-down booklet designs, repertoire-driven marketing and uncompromising negation of celebrity narrowed attention to the repertoire, which included *almost* everything worth hearing. With time, audiences without vast collections of LPs were able to appreciate what qualified as good while coming to understand why. This led to an unprecedented circumstance in which it was possible for unknown singers to be introduced in primary roles to audiences unable to hear them live. Naxos did this on hundreds of occasions. In 2005, for example, they secured a production-recording of *Cenerentola* starring a little-known American mezzo-soprano, Joyce DiDonato.[152] It was a regional staging, with the South West German Radio Symphony Orchestra, conducted by Alberto Zedda, and a supporting cast of equally undiscovered singers.[153] Discretion, rather than a forced diet of "establishment" A&R, allowed audiences to know singers who could be heard far more easily in theatres selling moderately affordable tickets, with seats to spare – as opposed to the relatively small number of opera houses, concert halls and festivals to which the ruling gods were confined. This did no harm to the occupants of Olympus, of course, but it did emphasise how few gods were in occupation after 1990. The deific analogy is warranted where Cecilia Bartoli is concerned. For three decades she has prevailed without rival as the planet's finest coloratura mezzo-soprano. She is also its most famous and the most recorded. Her more than 50 albums for Decca include 20 complete operas – with many more on DVD, a catalogue that traces what will be remembered of the last mezzo-soprano to have a career charted from inception by technology. With the business of recording in near-terminal decline, the era of contracts of the kind to which Bartoli signed with Decca are over. A complete recording of a major work with an A-list cast is now as much of an event as it was in 1903, when Verdi's *Ernani* was the first opera to be recorded complete — on forty discs. For this situation to change, musicians' unions, performers, intendants and agents are going to have to revisit the manner in which the business of music and opera is transacted. As things stand presently, the careers enjoyed by Bartoli, Gheorghiu and Fleming are the last of their kind.

Bartoli's discovery was, appropriately perhaps, on television. In 1985, she appeared on the sixth season of the ambitiously-titled *Fantastico*,[154] a sticky talent show presented by a stickier host, Pippo Baudo, whose constant touching of Bartoli is more ghastly now than it was at the time. She was chaperoned for the show by Katia Ricciarelli, with whom she gives an uninspired performance of the duet from Offenbach's *Les contes d'Hoffmann,* "*Belle nuit, ô nuit d'amour.*" Bartoli's singing of "*Una voce poco fa,*" from *Il barbiere,* is technically imperfect, as might be expected of a 19-year-old – but the voice, and the smile behind it, are astonishing for their

152   13 February, 1969 –

153   DiDonato's only previous recording of note was a disc of Handel duets, with Patrizia Ciofi (7 June, 1967 –), for Virgin Classics.

154   Bartoli appeared in the sixth series. She lost to an unintentionally hilarious pair of ballet dancers, Eugenio Buratti and Francesca Sposi. The winning performances are short, but provide a lifetime's joy.

confidence, maturity and character. It is tempting to imagine that this is as good as were the dozens of singers cited in this book from the 18ᵗʰ and 19ᵗʰ centuries, who began their careers in their late teens. It's unlikely any of them was as accomplished as Bartoli at the same age; it's difficult in consequence not to read malice and loathing into the expression on Katia Ricciarelli's face when she joins in with the applause after Bartoli's beauty, poise and talent have been cheered by the studio audience.

Bartoli studied initially with her parents, both of whom were professional singers, and later, for a short time, at the Santa Cecilia academy in Rome. She made her official debut in 1987, at the Arena in Verona, the success of which brought her to the attention of Daniel Barenboim and Harnoncourt, who encouraged her to concentrate on Mozart. Bartoli's beauty and steel-bending technique made her famous before the majority had heard her sing; from 1990, and ever since, her audiences either drop to their knees or leap to their feet. Triumphs in Paris, Hamburg and Milan (as Isolier in *Le comte Ory*, in 1991), and a ring-binder contract from Decca, made her the hottest property in opera globally. She has maintained that status ever since, with each appearance provoking a frantic rush for tickets, regardless of the repertoire. Initially, this was limited to Mozart and Rossini, but the threat of stagnancy directed her to the lost and the forgotten. In a move loaded with meaning, she chose Haydn's 1791 *L'anima del filosofo* for her 2001 debut at Covent Garden – the delayed premiere of which was given exactly fifty years earlier, in Florence, with Maria Callas as Eurydice, conducted by Erich Kleiber.[155] From 2000, she committed to performing and recording music from the Baroque and early Classical periods, chiefly Gluck, Vivaldi, Haydn and Salieri; in 2012, Bartoli steered a project entitled "*Mission*," to re-discover the music of Agostino Steffani. Untouched by hubris, she completed a study of the life and work of Maria Malibran, the 200th anniversary of whose birth was commemorated in March, 2008.[156] Despite spending much less time in the studio over the past decade, she remains the most recorded singer in history because there is always someone present at each performance with a cell-phone. At the time of writing, she is as busy as ever – and performing as she did almost 40 years ago. Her voice shows little sign of ageing, and neither does Bartoli, who remains paradigmatically vivacious. She is the *sine qua non* of mezzo coloraturas, and certain to remain so in the absence of any real competition.

Bartoli has her critics, inevitably. Many find her exhausting; depending on the repertoire, a two-hour recital is analogous to being trapped in a stalled lift with a cocaine-fuelled Robin Williams. She is capable of glorious, silken legatos, but that's not her choice as often as it should be when considering the luxury of her vocal tone. Her preference for repertoire that calls more obviously on her graphene diaphragm can be attributed (understandably) to vanity, and there is a sense that her value is located in how she does what she does more than her reasons for doing it. In this regard, she occupies a space attendant to the pianist Juja Wang, another artist whose dexterity and agility are comparable to requiring a primate to juggle after having taught it to speak. Ultimately, the better part of Bartoli's talent traces to her charisma and generosity as a performer, she appears never to tire and commits to each

---

155 *L'anima del filosofo, ossia Orfeo ed Euridice.* ('The Soul of the Philosopher, or Orpheus and Euridice.')
156 Notably, Bartoli delayed singing *Norma* until June, 2010 – when she was in her forties.

performance as if it is her last. Based on recent experience, that will happen at some point in the 22nd century.

Similarly ageless and equally beloved is Renée Fleming, another inspired signing by Decca from the 1990s. She is, the perfect German-repertoire lyric soprano – unrivalled in the music of Richard Strauss. She has had many competitors – including Nina Stemme[157] and the extremely talented Anne Schwanewilms[158] – but her status and standing are otherwise unique. Like Bartoli, Fleming is very attractive, an advantage that has contributed much to the obsessive devotion of the "Flemmings," a fan-base that follows their idol around the planet. It is easy to understand why she inspires as she does. *Contra* Bartoli, who is unable to walk past a demi-semi-quaver without wanting to consume it, Fleming's talent is located in her cantabile, and a vocal tone that is the most ravishing and distinctive of any soprano since the 1980s. For many, it is the most opulent since the invention of recording. Sir George Solti – who conducted the music at the funeral of Richard Strauss in 1949 – said of Fleming, "in my long life, I have met maybe two sopranos with this quality of singing; the other was Renata Tebaldi." Unlike Tebaldi, however, Fleming is considerably more than tone. Her most famous role was the Marschallin, which she sang for the first time in 1995, but delayed recording (officially, at least)[159] until 2009, at the age of 50 – five years older than Lotte Lehmann when she recorded the role in 1933, and 18 years older than the character. It is a superb performance, even if the casting of her album of excerpts with the stellar Susan Graham[160] and Barbara Bonney is significantly better in its parts.[161] More impressive still was Fleming's portrayal as Arabella – a role she didn't record in the studio. Fortunately, she was filmed singing the opera in Zürich, in 2009, conducted by Franz Welser-Möst, and again five years later, conducted by Christian Thielemann. The latter performance is better still, in part because of Thomas Hampson's excellent portrayal of Mandryka.

Fleming's voice draws on every conceivable simile for silk, cream and velvet; it is the model of bel canto elegance, managed by pulse-defying breathing, and a technique that includes a robust coloratura and a cantabile of supine eroticism. Her exceptionally well-supported phrasing is coloured by a variegated vibrato and perfectly-judged portamento; she floats high above the stave while utilising a chest voice of biting resonance; she is incapable of making an ugly sound. Uniquely among her peers, Fleming's singing can be characterised as a model of vocal *chiaroscuro*, a throw-back to a Renaissance school that employed super-human techniques to explore extremes of expressive freedom. During Ariadne's monologue, "*Es gibt ein Reich*,"[162] for example, she articulated every vowel and consonant as if she was speaking Hofmannsthal's verse, a talent rare in the history of singing, and dodo-like at the time of writing. Strauss would have loved her for the impression she has always given

---

157   11 May, 1963 –

158   1967 – . On 26 January, 2011, she performed the Marschallin for the jubilee centenary performance of *Der Rosenkavalier* at the Semperoper, Dresden. She made her debut at the Met, on 7 November, 2013, as the Kaiserin in *Die Frau ohne Schatten* – a role she has made her own.

159   Recorded live, with the Munich Philharmonic, conducted by Christian Thielemann.

160   23 July, 1960 –

161   Sophie Koch as Octavian, and Diana Damrau as Sophie both sing with a dreadful wobble.

162   'There is a realm.'

of being unaware that she is singing; such is the ease of production, and the reach of her projection, that she is unique in the 21st century for attending to the poet's words in equivalence with the composer's music. There is little doubt that Fleming has taken to indulging her once-in-a-generation gift. Footage online of a concert performance of Korngold's peerless study in emotional blackmail, "*Glück, das mir verblieb,*"[163] from *Die tote Stadt,*[164] is extravagantly permissive.[165] The tempo is leaden, slower even than for her studio recording of the aria.[166] During the final repeat of the leading melody, Fleming draws out the rising F4 – B flat 5 ("*Neig dein,*"),[167] to which Korngold has added a *tenuto;* she clings to it for considerably longer than is appropriate or probable – until her judgment is validated by the resolving words, "*blass Gesicht,*"[168] which she forms by ducking below the E flat quaver of "*sicht,*" only to lift it as a bridge to the theme of Korngold's submission: "*Sterben trennt uns nicht.*"[169] It's poignant and indulgent – grotesque, even – but that is the key to truly great singing: it is never far from the solipsistic and the vulgar. Fleming's art is caught in the twilight separating good from bad taste; what sets her apart from almost every other soprano to have made records is how effortlessly she has navigated this perilous territory.

Attendant to Bartoli and Fleming in their culminating significance was the Romanian-born Angela Gheorghiu, the last Italian-repertoire lirico-spinto soprano to have a stage career tracked in the studio. She made her debuts at Covent Garden and the Vienna State Opera in 1992, and the Met in 1993, but it was her appearance as Violetta at the Royal Opera House in November, 1994, that launched her to international celebrity.[170] Gheorghiu was almost 30 at the time – geriatric according to the traditions in which she was trained; her performance in Richard Eyre's production of *La traviata,* conducted by Solti, was nonetheless a revelation. The soprano was extravagantly handsome, charismatic and possessed of an absurdly beautiful voice, at the heart of which was a resonance that caused her to sound like Maria Callas or, at least, like Callas had she studied longer and resisted overexertion when young. The similarity between their timbres was frequently unsettling, particularly in the head notes with which Callas struggled two years after her debut. Gheorghiu's voice is instantly recognisable also because she understood how to use vibrato as a colour as opposed to cover. Her phrasing – unlike that of her husband of 17 years, the tenor, Roberto Alagna – is exquisite in its legato; she employs portamento to the most creative effect, joining lines of musical rhetoric that work only because they afford her indulgence of extremes of dynamic, dramatic and musical sense. None of her "effects"

---

163   'Happiness that remained.'

164   'The Dead City.'

165   In the Great Hall of the Moscow Conservatory, on 6 February, 2006.

166   The performance lasts six minutes and 30 seconds. For context, the 1924 recording by Lotte Lehmann and Richard Tauber is *two minutes* quicker. It is interesting *en passant* that Korngold added portamento markings to the vocal score, published in 1920 – proving how, even during the second decade of the century, there was an obvious tendency for singers to ignore *echt* Viennese (and once presumed) expression.

167   'Incline your.'

168   'Pale face.'

169   'Death will not separate us.'

170   The author was present, and it remains one of the most thrilling performances in his experience, partly because it *exceeded* the expectations generated by the considerable hype.

sound like tricks, therefore, because Gheorghiu was one of the most instinctively musical sopranos to make records.

Decca was able to secure her first complete recording, as Violetta (live from Covent Garden); she signed thereafter with EMI, for whom she recorded most of her ground-floor repertoire within a decade.[171] Unfortunately, her husband's attendant contract led to her becoming half of opera's great "power-couple,"[172] and almost all of her best work in the studio was in the company of Alagna, who was routinely dwarfed by her talent. By 2011, and with the recording industry in decline, Gheorghiu's work in the studio was confined to recitals, one of which bore the title "Homage to Maria Callas." It is unclear what this was meant to achieve.[173] Yes, they sound like each other, and each was extremely attractive, but all that emerged, other than further proof of the corrosiveness of celebrity, was the differences between them. Gheorghiu's voice was always more beautiful tonally than Callas', but her word-use was significantly less interesting and expressive. For example, her performance of "*Col sorriso*" (the "Mad" Scene from *Il Pirata*), amplified the bel in her canto, but to the exclusion of everything else that makes Imogene's circumstances (and the aria) interesting dramatically. There is none of the psychological stress for which Callas' 1958 recording is so conspicuous; Gheorghiu plays nice, and pretty, but Imogene is nowhere to be heard. Conversely, Callas' approach to every ornament and detail is calculated to form a sense of dread and unease; the bar-lines are pushed and pulled to generate that profound instability and terror for which the aria *should* be notable. The whole Callas-Homage project, which must have cost a fortune – with lavish CD books, films and video marketing – formed a single question: will anyone create a comparable "Homage to Angela Gheorghiu" in the 22nd century? To what would the future be referring when using a beautiful-sounding singer to honour the achievements of another merely glorious voice?

The terrifying calculation of managed celebrity in the 21st century shows little sign of abating, and any soprano likely to open a La Scala or Met season will now spend at least as much time in the company of agents and social media and PR executives as in rehearsal. The career of the 21st century's "uber" soprano, Anna Netrebko,[174] is a case-study for the ages. Her story had a fairy-tale beginning. She was born in Krasnodar, in the Soviet Union, near the western coast of the Black Sea. While studying at the Saint Petersburg Conservatory, she worked as a janitor at the Mariinsky Theatre. During her audition, the conductor, Valery Gergiev, recognised her and offered to become her mentor. Having achieved local success, she triumphed as Donna Anna at the Salzburg Festival in 2002, in which year she signed an exclusive contract with DG. Her initial repertoire suited her exquisite lyric voice, and she achieved standout successes in Mozart, Bellini, Donizetti and middle-period Verdi (notably

---

171   Between 1994 and 2003: *L'elisir d'amore, Carmen* (in 1995, as Micaëla, with Jennifer Larmore in the title role; and as Carmen in 2002), *Roméo et Juliette, La bohème, Il trittico, Werther, Manon, Messa da Requiem* (Verdi), *Tosca*, and *Il trovatore*.

172   The title of their 2008 album "Angela & Roberto Forever" did, of course, come back to haunt them.

173   Her ex-husband released a far more perverse album in 2019, titled "Caruso 1873: A Personal Tribute," which did nothing more than prove how little Alagna had to give, when adhering to the original meaning of the word "tribute."

174   18 September, 1971 –

as Gilda and Violetta). Her recordings with the superb tenor Rolando Villazón and the Latvian mezzo Elina Garanča[175] are mostly very fine, but after 2010 she did as many do, and turned to heavier repertoire. Within four years, this transition ruined what had been one of the sweetest, most persuasive voices of the century. Beginning in April, 2011, with *Anna Bolena*, at the Vienna State Opera (a role with which she opened the 2011 Met season), Netrebko took on increasingly heavy roles, including Lady Macbeth and Leonora in *Il trovatore*. Overwork and poor choices led to the forcing of her voice and by 2014 her once-silken cantabile was subject to audible stress, as evidenced by her fatuous decision to take up Strauss' Four Last Songs. DG released a live recording of the same, conducted by Barenboim in Berlin, and it is difficult listening. As a natural light-lyric soprano, Netrebko had no place taking on music that, in its range and requirements, calls for a much larger voice, one not corrupted by shrill tone and a abrasive wobble. Netrebko clearly loves the music, and no-one would blame her for doing so, but she was a lightweight boxer in a heavy-weight ring, and the outcome was consistent with the analogy.

Because Netrebko's celebrity entitled her to do whatever she wanted, she was able to take up dramatic and, eventually, verismo roles – including a disastrous Turandot – all of which did more harm to her voice, and the music she sang. Her marriage in December, 2015, to a fifth-rate Azerbaijani tenor, Yusif Eyvazov, resulted in Netrebko pushing his interests as well as his limited voice in ways that have exceeded the embarrassing. Equally toe-curling was Netrebko's refusal to denounce Vladimir Putin following the Russian government's invasion of Ukraine in 2022; after the singer refused to denounce the President, the Met cancelled her diary – provoking litigation. Netrebko was successful, and awarded $200,000 in compensation in March, 2023. The ruling confirmed that there was "no doubt" Netrebko was a supporter of Putin's, but added quite properly that she "had every right to be." Whether or not Netrebko returns to the Met will be decided by politics; if art has a say in the outcome, she should be left on the bench, and replaced by singers better able to exercise judgment and discretion.

The current generation of feted sopranos, all of whom have lighter voices, is most visible through the work of Danielle de Niese,[176] Sonya Yoncheva,[177] Angel Blue,[178] Julie Fuchs,[179] Pretty Yende,[180] Sabine Devieilhe,[181] and Elsa Dreisig.[182] Time, experience and decision-making will determine whether they mature as well as Lisette Oropesa,[183] the finest of the young sopranos on the world stage. Born in New Orleans and raised in Baton Rouge by a family of Cuban *émigrés*, Oropesa's mother was a former singer. She oversaw her daughter's initial training, before enrolling in the voice program at Louisiana State University. She later joined the Lindemann Young

---

175   16 September, 1976 –
176   11 April, 1979 –
177   25 December, 1981 –
178   3 May, 1984 –
179   24 July 1984 –
180   6 March, 1985
181   12 December, 1985 –
182   May 29, 1991 –
183   29 September, 1983 –

Artists Development Program, at the Met, from where she graduated in 2008. After singing a number of smaller parts, she made her official debut, at the Met, as Susanna in Sir Jonathan Miller's production of *Figaro* – scoring considerable success. At the same time, she began to address her weight, which she knew was making it difficult for casting directors who wanted their singers to persuade by appearance as well as voice. The issue was *de jour* because of Deborah Voigt's experience at Covent Garden. Oropesa was very large in her early twenties; she lost almost half her bodyweight through running, and by eating more sensibly. The effect was transformative – and of no consequence to her voice. She now appears as she sounds, which is not to discriminate against larger female singers but simply to recognise her beauty in form as well as function.

The virtue of her judgment was demonstrated in 2014 when she was cast as Sophie alongside Jonas Kaufmann's Werther. Her performance was highly praised, with most acknowledging that she was better able to persuade as a 15-year-old girl, given that she was no longer 15 stone. Oropesa's repertoire expanded, without her taking on roles for which she was ill-equipped vocally, including Marie *in La fille du régiment*, (2014), Violetta (2014), Ophélie in Thomas' *Hamlet* (2017), Humperdinck's Gretel (2017), Rossini's Adina (2018) and Marguerite in *Les Huguenots*. The last of these roles, first performed by Oropesa at the Paris Opéra in 2018, was definitive. Andreas Kreigenburg's sci-fi staging (with glorious set designs by Harald B. Thor) was filmed, and it can be found on DVD.[184] Oropesa's turn as Marguerite is the finest since the Second World War. Her show-stopping performance of "*Ô beau pays de la Touraine*" was even more impressive given that she had been allowed just three weeks in which to learn the role and the production.[185] Her coloratura is dazzling because she makes it seem easy and, even, unremarkable. Like Renée Fleming, she is able to communicate with her audience despite all the high-kicking and wire-walking. Her voice is seamless in its projection, exquisite for its tone, and priceless because she is able to act through song as well as movement. In short, Lisette Oropesa is proof that the future of the soprano is in good hands.

It is to be hoped that her peers are taking notice. Oropesa is exceptional because she has made all the right choices, and because she understands, and feeds off, the primacy of legato and cantabile.[186] Many other sopranos might be as musical intuitively, but it's impossible to know one way or another if they are fighting their own voices to be heard. Amplitude and resonance are necessary, of course, in certain works

---

184 Oropesa has made very few recordings in the studio; her only complete operas (both released in 2022) are a *Traviata* for Pentatone (in which Oropesa is excellent, albeit let down by the tenor singing Alfredo, René Barbera) and a splendid *Theodora* for Erato (with Joyce DiDonato and Michael Spyres in excellent voice). This is either the singer's choice, or the A&R departments within the major labels have run out of money. Numerous of her performances on stage have been filmed, however. Since turning to Bellini's works (in which she is peerless, having triumphed as Giulietta in *I Capuleti e i Montecchi*, at La Scala, and Elvira in *I puritani,* at the San Carlo; both in 2022), there is finally a good reason to start recording these works yet again. Of her recital discs, the album of French arias by Rossini and Donizetti (again for Pentatone) is fine, but nothing more than that when compared to hearing Oropesa live.

185 She was a last-minute stand-in for Diana Damrau.

186 An *echt* example on record of her unusual talent is a live recording from Covent Garden during the Covid-pandemic lock-down of the closing scene(s) from *La sonnambula*, conducted by Antonio Pappano. It is another masterclass in phrasing, placement and expression.

and for certain fachs they are essential; but the loss of so many to the ploughshares of sound and fury can never be a price worth paying for the apparent thrill of hearing someone heave their lungs into a theatre. The flaws of forced tone and imperfect production have done no less damage to tenors, and because this will be self-evident to anyone with ears to hear, listening to a woman's body and acknowledging the limits of nature are duties that fall to teachers, conductors, intendants and directors – each of whom is responsible for protecting talent from the ravages of money and fame. Voice-inflation beyond a singer's natural limits is unforgivable because it is needless and destructive. There is no justification for allowing a soprano to perform a role or music that will harm their instrument. For opera and art singing to survive, it is essential that audiences are able to learn what the best sounds like in the theatre and the concert hall. If a performer cannot be found for a role or a work then it should not be programmed or performed at all. With recording in decline, the need to ensure that an audience knows why they are clapping and standing to their feet has never been greater.

CHAPTER TWENTY

Malignant Melismata

The occasion of Barack Obama's inauguration as President of the United States on 20 January, 2009, was special for many. There were only two musical episodes, because a full concert, titled "We Are One: The Obama Inaugural Celebration," had been held at the Lincoln Memorial two days earlier, for an audience of 400,000, featuring a celestial line-up that included Beyoncé, Mariah Carey, Sheryl Crow, Renée Fleming, Pete Seeger, Shakira, Bruce Springsteen, James Taylor, U2, and Stevie Wonder. For the inauguration itself, the President, his family and their advisors settled on a performance by Yo-Yo Ma, Itzhak Perlman, Gabriela Montero and Anthony McGill of John Williams' "Air and Simple Gifts,"[1] as well as Aretha Franklin[2] singing Samuel Francis Smith's patriotic verse, "My Country, Tis for Thee," to its standard tune, the British national anthem.[3] It was meaningful that Franklin should have been invited to perform on a day she could not have anticipated as a 16-year-old touring with Dr. Martin Luther King Jr., or when singing at his funeral in 1968. Franklin was 66 at the time of Obama's inauguration, and the most celebrated living black female singer to have survived the 20th century. She took the microphone knowing she would be performing before a live audience of almost two million people,[4] and 50 times that number globally.

She was walking in the footsteps of Marian Anderson, who had performed the song as part of her concert at the Lincoln Memorial on 9 April, 1939. Anderson's performance lasted all of 40 seconds. Aretha Franklin took a more circuitous route, one that occupied almost three minutes. Her singing employed ornaments known as melismata, that had become so popular by the time of her performance, particularly in the United States, that anyone not used to it will have wondered what the tune was, and where it had gone. The use of improvised melismata in popular song had, by 2008, become so endemic in the United States that it was a regular focus for ridicule by comedians. Maya Rudolph swung frequently at the worst offenders during her time on Saturday Night Live; in 2006, and without naming anyone, she appeared as a singer invited to perform the National Anthem at the World Series. Bill Hader and Jason Sudeikis played sports-casters, shocked by the horror of it all.[5] The beat within the joke was the realisation that Rudolph's singing was not especially terrible when

---

1   In truth, because of the biting cold, they were compelled to mime.
2   25 March, 1942 – 16 August, 2018.
3   This has always seemed odd for anyone cognisant of the events leading up to the American Revolutionary War.
4   "Period."
5   Season 32.

compared to the atrocities released routinely into the wild by the likes of Mariah Carey and Christina Aguilera.

A bare definition of melisma is the singing of one or two syllables of text while moving between different notes successively; melismatic music can be distinguished from syllabic, which attaches a different note to each syllable of a word.[6] The origins of the melisma are neither contemporary nor western; they date back thousands of years to Greek theatre, and they continue to sustain almost all World Music. Melismatic singing is pivotal to Arabic and Indian culture; it would be impossible to perform the former without being able to sing complex runs and roulades. It forms a major part also of Jewish and Islamic performance cultures, albeit only for male voices.[7] The western adoption of the melisma emerged with church traditions before becoming fundamental to 17th and 18th century opera, and art music more generally. In the majority of cases, coloratura at it was known to Handel, Mozart, Rossini and the bel canto movement entailed a mixture of written and improvised performance. Melismatic singing is *not* the same thing as coloratura, however, which is a creature of surgical precision, requiring years of rigorous training. Coloratura is formed of note-distinct accuracy whereas melisma is looser, messier even, because of its origins and because of the emotional effect it has been designed to achieve. Over time, composers became increasingly hostile to interpolation – wherein singers would cause the mutilation of the written score by adding pretty much whatever they liked, including songs and arias from works by different composers. As the previous chapters in this book demonstrate, sopranos were a singular source of frustration; the temptation to add ever greater numbers (and ranges) of notes was rewarded with plaudits, adulation and money. It was a difficult habit to break. It's important to remember that vocal ornaments as they were heard in opera houses and concert halls have always been disciplined; even when improvised they are easy enough to write down – as occurred frequently during performances by Cuzzoni and Farinelli. Notes were sufficiently clear, crisp and cogent to allow for repetition, a key feature of practice and rehearsal as well as performance.

By the time of the bel canto revival, sopranos were corseted to minor embellishments and cadenzas; the rules have been bent for uber-mezzos, like Cecilia Bartoli, but the general principle where *every* other style of music and performance is concerned adheres to the credo *com'è scritto*. Everything changed with gospel. The origins of what would become a prominently African-American culture reach back to the 17th and 18th centuries, when the form and formula were minimalist and austere. Black gospel grew out of slavery in the United States, with the first book of "Slaves Songs" being published by Northern abolitionists in 1867. Five years later, the Fisk Jubilee Singers, a black a cappella gospel ensemble, was formed to raise funds for

---

6   For an excellent overview of the literature, see Youssef, Mirrae (2017). "Exploring Melisma and the Effects of Emotional Expression In Contemporary Music." Thesis, Macquarie University.

7   Male singers have also made use of the melisma, but many fewer than female. The masculine construction of ornamentation and embellishment is found elsewhere – in the electric guitar solo. There is an interesting book yet to be written connecting the dots between the singing of Farinelli and the David Gilmore's solo in "Comfortably Numb," Mark Knopfler's solo in "Romeo and Juliet," and Stevie Ray Vaughan's "Mary Had a Little Lamb" – among thousands of other compelling exemplars of "lyric vocalising" formed of construct-melodies.

Fisk University in Nashville. The often solemn character of early gospel, typified by "Down in the River to Pray,"[8] provided little opportunity for ornament. After the emergence of ragtime, however, during the 1890s, and Jazz after 1917, the defining feature of black music was improvisation. A definitive exemplar of melisma in jazz singing is the extraordinary 1961 recording by Ella Fitzgerald[9] of "Cry Me a River," which begins with a 16-second, open vowel "instrumental" solo. Typically for Fitzgerald, the melisma serves a purpose; it operates to frame what she does as she begins the song.[10] Many white-European composers, performers and critics, came to embrace Jazz as a positive, creative influence; many others feared it as more African than American. In 1917, the Literary Digest published an article titled "The Appeal of Primitive Jazz," that concluded with a triumphantly racist polemic:

> The groups that play for dancing, when colored, seem infected with the virus that they try to instill as a stimulus in others. They shake and jump and writhe in ways to suggest a return of the medieval jumping mania. The word, according to Walter Kingsley, famous in the ranks of vaudeville, is variously spelled jas, jass, jaz, jazz, and jascz; and is African in origin.[11]

The article attached the word, Jazz, to slavery:

> In old plantation days, when slaves were having one of their rare holidays and the fun languished, some West-Coast African would cry out, "Jaz her up," and this would be the cue for fast and furious fun. No doubt the witch-doctors and medicine-men on the Kongo used the same term at those jungle "parties" when tomtoms throbbed and the sturdy warriors gave their pep an added kick with rich brews of Yohimbin bark.[12]

The perception of Jazz and black music as African and pagan was countered (if never quite distinguished) by the growth of Pentecostalism, through which black Christians in the American South developed a form of sung gospel, made famous by the likes of Blind Willie Johnson and Blind Joe Taggart. The singing-guitarist, Sister Rosetta Tharpe,[13] was the first gospel artist to succeed interracially, but it was Arizona Dranes'[14] fusion of secular influences, including ragtime and blues, that made gospel popular as entertainment. She traded in repeating stanzas – adding increasing levels

---

8   One of the songs published in the first compendium, 1867.
9   25 April, 1917 – 15 June, 1996.
10   It's important to note that one of the limbs of Fitzgerald's genius as a singer was her mastery of scat, which is not the same thing as (and should not be confused with) the melismatic. Scat is vocal improvisation, using word-distinct syllables; it is improvised, and uses the voice as an instrument, rather than as a word-directed medium. Fitzgerald was one of history's greatest singers, but her work is irrelevant to the thrust of this chapter.
11   Anderson, Maureen (2004). "The White Reception of Jazz in America." *African American Review*, Vol. 38, No. 1, p. 136.
12   *Ibid.*
13   *Ibid.*
14   4 May, 1889 or 1891 – 27 July, 1963.

of vocal complication with each consecutive verse to ritualise the repetition. Her recording of "John Said He saw a Number"[15] is typical of the energy and authenticity being introduced to the black sound at a time when white popular music was typified by the likes of Vernon Dalhart's "The Prisoner's Song," an oily, sentimental Country and Western ballad, with obligato violin,[16] that was all the rage during the middle 1920s. The narrative of "The Prisoner's Song" made it impossible for a singer to treat it other than straight. It was a favourite of Johnny Cash, who performed it in concert – and for an episode of his own TV show, on 20 January, 1971. Cash's style and vocal technique would not have allowed for melisma; indeed, his sole purpose as a performer was to convey the narrative and sentiment of a song as a "proper" man at a time when traditional notions of gender were under "targeted attack" from the likes of the Bee Gees. Their first No.1 hit, "How Can You Mend a Broken Heart,"[17] was also released in 1971; it employed an overtly-feminised vocal tone and timbre while banging on about "everything a man could want to do," which included, apparently, "feel[ing] the breeze that rustles through the trees." Cash preferred songs about the male experience of drinking and prison life.

Unlike Jazz, which was primarily syllabic, and concerned generically with social and relationship issues (like Bessie Smith's[18] "Nobody Knows You When You[re'] Down and Out," and "Black Water Blues,"), gospel adhered to scripture; it employed commensurately simple poetic forms, to enable easy and sincere lines of communication. A two or three-verse song was incapable of generating momentum for more than a couple of minutes, other than with the introduction of some kind of variation. Since black culture was no less hostile to the feminised masculine than was the white majority, early gospel made a virtue of the melisma, which equipped women, in particular, with a device for making the routine interesting. Arizona Dranes' recording of "Lamb's Blood Has Washed Me Clean," uses the same austere tune, with the call-and-repeat of the song's title providing a framework for Dranes and her colleagues to dance around the bar-lines, pushing and pulling against a fixed beat and narrow intervallic range. Even if a listener doesn't know the words, or understand their significance for the faithful, it's easy to isolate the sentiments being articulated when hearing them wailed. Conversely, "The Prisoner's Song," could be about almost anything, such is the music's tedium.

The emergence of a uniquely black singing voice was a profound advantage with white supremacy relishing its last generation above the floor boards. The authenticity of black female voices was a function of sound rather than sentiment, however. Given that it was impossible for women to sing about racism or racial persecution – until 1939, at least, when Billie Holiday[19] recorded Abel Meeropol's "Strange Fruit"[20] – the vernacular for African-American women was confined to songs of religion and improvisation. The multi-racial reach of Jazz did not extend to gospel – which is

---

15   Recorded on 17 June, 1926.
16   On one of his recordings, it is plainly a viola.
17   From their ninth album, *Trafalgar*.
18   15 April, 1894 – 26 September, 1937.
19   7 April, 1915 – 17 July, 1959.
20   Under his pseudonym, Lewis Allan.

difficult (but not impossible) for white people to appropriate.[21] During the Great Migration, some six million African-Americans abandoned the poverty and persecution of the South for the urban Northeast, Midwest, and West, taking with them the only musical culture that was inarguably theirs. One of the most powerful voices to arrive in Chicago, and the relative utopia of Bronzeville, was Mahalia Jackson.[22] The grand-daughter of slaves, Jackson moved north in 1928, finding regular opportunities to sing in the many churches abandoned by the city's previous occupants. The black religious experience was relatively subdued at the time; the prevalence of discrimination and the fear of violence were sufficiently real for black pastors to supress anything that risked controversy. With time and confidence, music proved to be a valuable source of release; performances were transformed liturgically as *intermezzi*. It became regular practice among gospel soloists and choirs for a four-minute hymn to be extended through variation, extemporisation and embellishment into an emotional purging lasting upwards of half an hour.

Having been able to pick up work singing at funerals, Jackson collected four dollars to pay an African-American tenor, then training to sing opera, for tuition. During her first lesson he stopped her in her tracks and advised:

> You've got to learn to stop hollering. It will take time to build up your voice. The way you sing is not a credit to the Negro race. You've got to learn to sing songs so that white people can understand them.[23]

Jackson was not persuaded, and her naturally sonorous voice brought her to the attention of Thomas A. Dorsey,[24] a gifted jazz composer, who trained Jackson for two months. The sum of his teaching was to supress her tendency to over-sing, so that she might perform slower songs as well as the quicker-tempo music with which gospel was associated at the time. Everything else was achieved by Jackson as a construction of will and sentiment – all of it without amplification. Dorsey paid his pupil to sing his music on street corners – for sale at ten cents a page. The business venture failed, but their collaboration led to the creation of gospel blues. Dorsey co-founded the Gospel Choral Union of Chicago,[25] which opened chapters across America. There was much resistance within the black evangelical community to Dorsey's up-tempo spirituals – which he branded "Jubilees" – but during the 1930s Jackson's increasing success as one of The Johnson Singers generated momentum for Dorsey's work as a composer. In 1932, Dorsey's wife Nettie died giving birth; their son followed suit

---

21 The unease this can cause anyone who has, for example, had the pleasure and privilege of hearing the choir of the Abyssinian Baptist Church in Harlem, New York, performing live – and then on Palm Sunday – will attest to the power of the cultural connection between gospel and black identity, particularly in the United States. Hearing a white choir performing gospel is reminiscent of Gary Larson's *Far Side* cartoon in which a fat Caucasian woman, wearing pearls and seated in a huge armchair in a palatial living room, asks her equally white husband, sat at a concert-grand piano: "why don't you play some blues, Andrew?"

22 *née* Mahala Jackson, 26 October, 1911 – 27 January, 1972.

23 Jackson, Mahalia, and Wylie, Evan McLeod (1966). *Movin' On Up*. Hawthorn Books, p. 59.

24 Thomas Andrew Dorsey (1899 –1993), an African-American composer, performer and evangelist of great significance to the development of early blues and 20th-century gospel. Not to be confused with the white band leader, Tommy Dorsey (1905 – 1956).

25 Later renamed the National Convention of Gospel Choirs and Choruses.

24 hours later. Overcome by grief, the composer wrote his most famous composition, "Take My Hand, Precious Lord." This became Dr. King's favourite song, and Jackson sang it for him at numerous civil rights campaign events. She did so for the last time at his funeral in April, 1968. The song was first published in 1938, and recorded by Jackson on 27 March, 1956, for the Columbia release, *Bless This House*, with Mildred Falls at the piano and Ralph Jones on the organ. It is a haunting, profoundly moving performance, and probably the finest example of gospel as pop. It is also exemplary of the melisma in its proper form and context. Jackson's approach was to take the tune at its simplest and extemporise melisma at the end of a particular word or phrase – without submitting to formula or repetition. Her expressive range is magnificent, notwithstanding her restrained adherence to a dynamic palette spanning piano – mezzo-forte. Most of the song is quiet and intimate, therefore, which adds to the emotional force of the performance. Jackson never learned to read music, so everything was forged from instinct. As she later observed "All I ever learned was just to sing the way I feel [...] off-beat, on the beat, between beats – however the Lord lets it come out."[26]

Jackson's authenticity was compelling; it is audible in the range of sounds on which she relied in concert and the studio, encompassing moaning, humming, wailing and, even, weeping. Her extensive use of improvised embellishments and her prodigious use of melisma were (and remain) definitive because they are hard-won products of experience. She sold more than 20 million records and performed all over the world – in such previously inaccessible venues as the Concertgebouw, in Amsterdam.[27] During her remarkable career, which did as much to change racial attitudes globally as the work of any musician in history, Jackson broke every rule as it related to singing. She cuts phrases in two, and breathes where she feels like it (and whether or not she needs to); she adopts three or four different vocal tones for a single passage, and some of her pronunciation exceeds the eccentric. Her singing of the word "hush" on her recording of "Summertime," has to be heard to be believed. For all its idiosyncrasy, Jackson's style and sensibility was transformative – for white and black musicians equally.

Not every gospel singer transitioned to the Billboard charts. Sallie Martin,[28] another Dorsey associate, was popular as the founder of the Sallie Martin Singers, and successful as the founder of her own publishing house, Martin and Morris Music, Inc. Shirley Ann Caesar-Williams[29] didn't release her first album until 1977, but almost 30 more followed in quick succession. In 2016, Caesar-Williams found herself back at the top of the Billboard Gospel chart, with "Fill This House." The transition from churches to dance halls, clubs, radio and television was achieved only after gospel singers appreciated the commercial value of secularism. Dinah Washington,[30] another Sallie Martin singer, secured her first top ten US hit in 1959 with a version of "What a Diff'rence a Day Made," followed soon after by her (still-popular) version

---

26   "Two Cities Pay Tribute to Mahalia Jackson" (April, 1972). *Ebony Magazine*, pp. 62–72.
27   In April, 1961.
28   20 November, 1895 – 18 June, 1988.
29   *née* Caesar, born 13 October, 1938 –
30   *née* Ruth Lee Jones, 29 August, 1924 – 14 December, 1963.

of Irving Gordon's "Unforgettable." The relocation of singers from the church was evidenced by Washington's embrace of what became known as "dirty blues." The song "Long John Blues" (putatively a homage to her dentist) contained the words "He took out his trusty drill, told me to open wide. He said he wouldn't hurt me, but he filled my whole [hole] inside." Another song, "Big Long Slidin' Thing," invites no commentary.[31]

The path of gospel music through the '60s and '70s was rocky, with so many other genres in competition, but during the 1970s and early '80s, Emily "Cissy" Drinkard,[32] achieved success as a backing singer for Roy Hamilton, Dionne Warwick, Elvis Presley, and Aretha Franklin. She released her first solo album in 1970, using her married name. *Introducing Cissy Houston* contained not a single track of gospel; in fact, the album was formed entirely of covers, including Burt Bacharach's "I Just Don't Know What to Do with Myself," Bobby Darin's "I'll Be There," The Beatles' "The Long and Winding Road," and Ervin Drake's "I Believe." During the early '80s, Cissy was joined on stage by her daughter, Whitney,[33] a child prodigy who grew up singing gospel at church. Her secular debut at Manhattan's Town Hall on 18 February, 1978, when she was 14-years-old, produced a 10-minute ovation; six months after that performance (of "Tomorrow" from *Annie*), Houston provided background vocals for her mother's solo album, *Think It Over*.

In February, 1983, Clive Davis of Arista Records heard Whitney sing in a New York club; he was sufficiently impressed to offer her a worldwide contract on the spot. Houston was booked soon after to appear on The Merv Griffin Show, performing "Home," from the musical *Wiz*. The episode aired in June, generating massive publicity. While working on her debut album, she recorded a duet with Teddy Pendergrass, "Hold Me," which was released in 1984 and became an instant Top 5 R&B hit. Like her mother's first album, Whitney's debut was self-titled. Released on 14 February, 1985, the album was a phenomenon – selling more than 25 million copies. Her voice was strikingly personal, a quality that made her immediately recognisable, regardless of what she was singing. Although her style was indebted to gospel, each of the songs adhered to the pop-end of the R&B spectrum. It was overproduced, with a range of synth-generated backing-tracks that did more to interfere than to assist, and many of the songs, like "Thinking About You," did little to capitalise on her remarkable voice. Even so, *Whitney Houston* was the first album by a female singer to achieve No. 1 on the Billboard Year End Albums Charts (for 1986). It was recognised to be a "cross-over" album, which meant it appealed to white and black audiences equally – and globally. It was the number one album in the UK, Canada and Australia for months. Forty years later, it remains the best-selling studio album by a black female artist.

Houston's voice had a huge reach and colossal resonance. In this sense, her only precedent was Minnie Riperton,[34] an R&B coloratura with a four octave range, that encompassed a whistle register. Riperton's career was cut short by cancer; her death

---

31   It was said to be about a trombonist. It wasn't.
32   3 September, 1933 –
33   9 August, 1963 – 11 February, 2012.
34   *née* Minnie Julia Riperton Rudolph, 8 November, 1947 – 12 July, 1979.

at the age of 31, in 1979, was a tragedy, of course, but a musical catastrophe also. Houston was plainly aware of Riperton's recordings, an influence that emerges on one of the album's slow-tempo tracks, "Saving All My Love for You." Her approach to the song is especially impressive for a singer in her early twenties. It's all wearily calculated, of course, as might have been expected of a heavily-funded 1980s studio project, but the emotional force of Houston's singing is inarguable. It is unusual also in its adherence to a syllabic structure, with relatively little melismatic singing; in this sense, the album represents a break with the work of her predecessors, Smith, Martin, Jackson and Franklin. For her duet with Jermaine Jackson, "Nobody Loves Me Like You Do," and the chest-thumping theatrics of "The Greatest Love of All," Houston relaxed into what would become her hallmark sound – a gospel-infused seam of mostly-belted, highly-ornamented anthemic pop. "How Will I Know," sounds as if it came easily to the singer, even recorded in a "dead" studio environment. The amplitude of her voice was commanding, as it would prove to be for a generation of imitators.

There are numerous live recordings of Houston doing the rounds, and even some clips of her singing without a microphone. The stunning resonance is, of course, pivotal to her appeal; it's thrilling to hear any voice of such amplitude and discipline, and because of the range of sounds she was able to produce – which encompassed the "classical" placement of certain high notes beyond the chest register – she was at liberty to indulge her formidable technique when engaging in melismata. Houston's most famous use of embellishment was her cover of Dolly Parton's "I will Always Love You," the success of which as a single rocketed past gold after its use for the 1992 film, *The Bodyguard*, in which Houston made her acting debut (alongside Kevin Costner, playing the title role), as a pop singer modelled ostensibly on herself. The film was panned critically, but it churned $411 million at the box office, becoming the tenth highest-grossing film to 1992. The accompanying soundtrack-album, performed by Houston, remains the best-selling *ever*, with almost 50 million copies sold worldwide. 20 million copies alone were purchased of the single "I will Always Love You."[35] Houston's performance of the song is iconic for proving how the right sort of voice can be transformative of mediocre material; her pop-gospel reinvention turns a country ballad into a throbbing masterpiece of emotional blackmail to rival Korngold's "*Gluck das mir verblieb*." The incremental shifts in vocal temperature are enabled by gospel embellishments that add to the performance's soaring, dipping, fluttering and pirouetting tribute to the promise of eternal love. The declamatory "Come to Jesus" climax is all the more powerful because the song begins a capella.

The whole thing is coincidentally overblown and surgical. It does exactly what it was meant to do because Houston was in total control of her voice and her judgment. Anyone doubting the substance of her raw talent should listen to her live performance of "The Star Spangled Banner" at the Superbowl, in Florida, on 27 January, 1991 – ten days after the start of the Persian Gulf War. It remains one of the most impressive performances of the American National Anthem ever recorded. She bounces to the microphone, surrounded by a crowd of almost 80,000, and with a global television audience of 750 million. Wearing what appears to be a tracksuit, and with her hair

---

35   It remains still the best-selling single ever.

tied in a white head-band, she is a study in confident, self-assured beauty. Divine in her appearance before she sings a note, what pours out of her is miraculous; indeed, there is more art in this single performance than on most of her studio albums, for the simple reason that she was at her best when spared the interventions of producers, sound-editors, studio executives and the horror of pre-taped backing tracks. The precision of her few embellishments is jaw-dropping in their expressive variety and colour; the resolving cadence is for the ages.

Many have clearly thought the same thing during the three decades since. Houston's sound, and her melismatic style, were adopted by legions of singers, white and black, who wanted to sound "like Whitney." It would have been better had her imitators listened, instead, to the artists who inspired Houston's mother. The most indelible mark of talent will always be individuality; there has never been a successful voice artist who sounded like anyone but themselves. Florence Welch[36] (of "and the Machine" fame) is about as charismatic as a singer can get before setting herself on fire; her voice is utterly thrilling, but it is also chaotic in its placement and absent finesse. Her intonation is questionable, and her word-use eccentric – which is the point exactly. It is these elements of word-use eccentric *im*perfection that distinguish Welch from everyone else. Anyone who heard her perform with Dizzie Rascal at Glastonbury in 2010 is unlikely to forget the experience. And yet, an aspiring singer in training would be ill-advised to call on an artist who is herself incapable of reaching beyond the advocacy of truth to self. The same applies to every lasting female vocalist – which is not to confuse the business of singing with the art from which it feeds. No-one would class Madonna[37] or Katy Perry[38] as "vocalists," at least not in any technical sense. Yes, they sing for a living, but when doing so live (and before the nightmarish advent of "artificial intonation,")[39] they were prone to achieving less than the Ancient Mariner, who was, at least, able to catch "one in three." Bad or untrained voice-placement caused Nina Simone[40] no difficulty because she wasn't aiming for vocal "perfection," or pop stardom. Young girls wanting to dance around their bedrooms holding a hairbrush were at liberty to do so "Like a Virgin" or when "Wide Awake," but few have wanted to sound like Nina Simone performing "Go to Hell." Her gloomy, hoarse and unstable voice was rarely pretty, and only occasionally true to pitch and timbre; these flaws merely added to her lunging, booming approximation of word and melody, the sum of which was unflinchingly authentic and compelling.

Even if a singer adheres to a more traditional vernacular, it is vocal personality that makes them interesting. Joni Mitchell[41] had a "break" between her registers that was coincidentally irritating and persuasive, but no-one who has ever covered "Big Yellow Taxi" has sounded like Mitchell unless seeking actively to impersonate her.[42] The same can be said of Kate Bush and Tina Turner – each thrillingly original for

---

36   28 August, 1986 –

37   *née* Louise Ciccone, 16 August, 1958 –

38   *née* Katheryn Elizabeth Hudson, 25 October, 1984 –

39   Better known as "auto-tune."

40   *née* Eunice Kathleen Waymon, 21 February, 1933 – 21 April, 2003.

41   November 7, 1943 –

42   This is not to dismiss novel reinventions by singers, or bands, not seeking to imitate Mitchell, like the Counting Crows and Vanessa Carlton, whose version of "Big Yellow Taxi" owes nothing to the original.

caring nothing of whatever anyone else was doing, no matter the consequences for the songs they were singing. Lauryn Hill[43] and Eva Cassidy[44] were both attached to earlier traditions, but no-one is likely to achieve what the former did with The Fugees covering Roberta Flack's[45] "Killing me Softly," or the latter when hurling a gauntlet at Judy Garland with her transcendent version of "Over the Rainbow." Even Amy Winehouse[46] and Adele[47] – both of whom modelled themselves on prior traditions – became iconic because their influences never defined them vocally or expressively. Winehouse was a small-venue artist, a chanteuse, and astonishingly seductive when on form and not on drugs. Adele has a voice that could bring down a cooling tower, and she has taken to stadium gigs with sensational *élan*; this doesn't mean she can't adapt her singing to a 100-seat club, however. The point is that no-one, anywhere, sounds like either of them. Not without irony, there are hundreds of professional impersonators worldwide getting paid for their "homages" to Winehouse and Adele – commonly for weddings and Bar Mitzvahs. No-one is offering to imitate Whitney Houston or Nina Simone because they can't. The technical and creative challenges are simply too great – unless, of course, a singer has access to their own tool-box of vocal resources, and chooses to expend them on copying the elements of what it was that made Houston and Simone special and unique.

The legions that fell into Houston's slipstream were led by Mariah Carey,[48] an essentially talented singer whose flair for notes in the "whistle" register made her famous before she took to ruining every December with the insufferable "All I want for Christmas is You." Arguably the biggest-selling female artist prior to Taylor Swift, Carey's domesticated-diva routine sent her in a different direction to the original girl-next-door, Doris Day,[49] who was able to nail any tune with gratifying sincerity without stooping to Carey's uniquely gruesome flair for the insincere. Carey's hi-jacking of gospel culture resulted in her fouling almost everything she sang with ser-pentine melismas that choked the life out of some potentially wonderful music. The worst example of her grotesque affectation was an assault on "O Holy Night," first released into the atmosphere in 1994. It compares unfavourably to Steve Maudlin's hilarious savaging of Adolphe Adam's carol, which was, at least, meant to inspire sea-sonal joy. The faux-conviction of Carey's performance (ostensibly "live") is noisome, beginning as it does with the singer proving herself incapable of getting through the first four notes without feeding them to a spiralizor. Anyone with a gag reflex is unlikely to survive the ensuing four and a half minutes without reaching for the off-button, or a pistol. The accompanying video makes chillingly cynical use of a black gospel choir, a largely black audience, many of them children, and some fan-tastic lens-filters, for Carey to appear angelic rather than saccharine. She fails to sing the *actual* melody even once. Every line and every word is subsumed to an archetype

---

43   26 May, 1975 –

44   2 February, 1963 – 2 November, 1996.

45   10 February, 1937 –

46   14 September, 1983 – 23 July, 2011.

47   *née* Adele Laurie Blue Adkins, 5 May, 1988 –

48   27 March, 1969 –

49   *née* Doris Mary Kappelhoff, 3 April, 1922 – 13 May, 2019.

of bad taste, creating a mocktail of fish-heads and faeces for consumption only by the fawning and the deaf.

Carey's fame and popularity as a singer metastasised with targeted malignance through American pop, fostering an uneasy culture of black appropriation that encouraged many white singers to darken their skin, wear black hairstyles, and adopt black-stylistic mores, as a construction of linguistics, sound and physical movement. One of the more controversial of Carey's cultural-concubines was Christina Aguilera,[50] who began her performing life as a child on television. In 1991, she auditioned at Disney to become a member of The Mickey Mouse Club; she was rejected because of her youth but was engaged two years later, gaining celebrity and opportunity in equivalence. After a period working in Japan, she made a pitch to Walt Disney Records, sending a cover version of Houston's "Run to You" as her demo. In 1998, Aguilera was booked to perform the song "Reflection," for the film *Mulan*, which reached No. 15 on the Billboard chart. Despite having attained adulthood, at least legally, Aguilera was cast as a teenage sensation for what became known as "bubblegum" pop, an arena dominated at the time by Aguilera's younger colleague at The Mickey Mouse Club, Britney Spears.[51]

The resulting battle between these "pop princesses" was managed and manipulated by dark men in darker corners of an American Psychotic industry in which image and money transcended music or anything redolent of art. The nadir of this parasitic hustle was the release of Spears' debut album, *Baby One More Time*, in January, 1999 – eleven months before Spears' 18th birthday. The album's title song was catchy, after the fashion of plague bacteria, and predicated on the calculation of a video in which Spears dressed as a schoolgirl, presenting herself as paradoxically vulnerable and predatory. In October, 2002, Aguilera released her fourth studio album, *Stripped*, which contained the song "Dirty." The album, her live concerts in support and her portrayal in photographs and videos turned the squeaky clean into something better suited to a petri dish. Spears' camp raised the stakes in 2003 with "Toxic," a dance-techno-bhangra mash-up promoted by another lazy and suggestive video that appealed presumably to the singer's father at least as much as his daughter's money.

The vocal style adopted for much of their music, and their performance of it in concert, was melismatic after the fashion of Carey rather than Houston. There was little sign of any judgment or musical insight, so that the melisma was repositioned not as a mechanism for expression but as a short-cut for feigned emotion. The concomitant transformation of singing into an Olympic sport caused melodies to become unrecognisable; over-singing was increasingly routine. Jeanette Bicknell has characterised the melisma as an element of over-singing, and as "excessive in one or more dimensions: too loud, too ornamented, too melismatic, too expressive or employing too much vibrato."[52] Rather than singing "from the heart," therefore, Aguilera engaged in a manufactured process of essential and debilitating insincerity. In tandem with Spears, she further escalated the sexualisation of a still-teenage market

---

50   18 December, 1980 –
51   2 December, 1981 –
52   Bicknell, Jeanette (2018). "Excess in art: the case of oversinging." *Journal of Aesthetics and Art Criticism*. Vol. 76(1), p. 83.

by making simple and accessible a complex of emotional, psychological and social issues that were incomprehensible to the target audience. Their families and managers focussed with chilling detachment on the wallets of impressionable young girls, who misconstrued sex and voice as co-terminous and liberating. The Conservative media lost what little mind it had to lose when judging the serial abuse and exploitation as evidence for the political, ethical and moral death of the modern world, without fully appreciating (or daring to comment on) the more extreme cultural landscape as it was being terraformed by rap artists.

Aguilera and Spears cast a mould that spread with gruesome perseverance through popular music globally. The scourge of the melisma has for almost two decades been manifesting itself globally through television talent shows, with every second singing sensation being unable to sing a melody without corrupting it. The Norwegian, Angelina Jordan,[53] appeared on the second season of something called "America's Got Talent: The Champions," which aired in January and February 2020. Her first song was "an original arrangement" of Queen's "Bohemian Rhapsody." The judges – including Simon Cowell – were unanimous in considering her performance a revelation, and everyone jumped to their feet. The crowd submitted to frenzy, and viewings of a video of her performance quickly exceeded 10 million.[54] The tens of thousands of comments all adhered to variations of "That's a ONE in A BILLION voice right there." And "What a fantastic performance and arrangement!" Any reader capable of getting through more than 5 seconds of Ms Jordan's performance will neither know nor care for the original song, or for singing. She is unable to manage even the semblance of a melody, diving instead into convulsive warbling – none of it sensible musically. Her melismas are counter-intuitive, disingenuous and, worst of all, destructive of Mercury's composition. There are literally thousands of untelevised talent shows worldwide, which provide a "circuit" for breeding the worst of Jordan's vocal and stylistic habits. Singers are rewarded for shredding 30 notes from a phrase written with five – irrespective of the song or its emotional and expressive context. Legions of screaming adherents confuse warbling with expression, creating armies of fans for whom ornament is substance. The appetite for decoration *in extremis* has fomented a roaring business for singing teachers, most of whom profit from the conspiracy that "more" is always "better." The ability to sing a tune without cramming it with candyfloss has silenced a generation of young voices unwilling or unable to be heard midst all the trilling.

For too long, black artists of talent were sidelined by the commercial preference for white women wearing cornrows and braids and, even, "popcorn hair,"[55] – all prominent, revolving features of Aguilera's chameleon shifts in appearance. Black singers were able to recover some of what had been taken from them in consequence of the achievements of Beyoncé.[56] As one of Destiny's Child[ren], she became a star before becoming an icon, as black music's "Queen Bey." Like so many of her peers born during the early 1980s, she was a child performer, although to Beyoncé's

---

53 *née* Angelina Jordan Astar, 10 January, 2006 –

54 As at the time of writing, it has been viewed on almost 100 millions occasions.

55 A gruesome phrase adopted by the singer to describe her ice-white afro.

56 *née* Beyoncé Giselle Knowles-Carter, 4 September, 1981 –

credit she stuck it out as a member of the choir at St. John's United Methodist Church, Houston, for two years, learning something of her craft and her roots as an African-American. She was "discovered" at the age of eight, and parachuted into a group called Girl's Tyme. As a natural mezzo-soprano, her vocal tone and timbre have always been idiosyncratic, and she has evidenced far more integrity in her choices than Aguilera and Spears. Because of her legitimate access to hip hop and R&B, Beyoncé's gospel routes have remained ever-present, whether or not she is singing a ballad or a stadium anthem. This has not precluded ghastly melismatic outrages, from which she has been able to protect herself only because she knows what she is doing. Later pretenders to the throne, like Leona Lewis[57] and Jennifer Hudson,[58] have been rooted in an authentic black experience, and because they can sing the hinges off a cathedral door they are entitled, to the limits of their ability, to rely on what is ultimately the laziest of vocal sleights of hand.

The most divisive among the melismatics is a French-Canadian singer, Celine Dion.[59] There is no debate that Dion is a virtuoso; she can crack double-glazing when churning out power-ballads, for which she is renowned and still-popular, as she demonstrated during a long residency at Las Vegas. It is because she can sing just about anything, five nights a week, that her judgment can be called into question. There is always a sense with Dion, particularly when performing live, that she might be the most cynical human being since Antisthenes – not because she gives the audience what they want but because she gives them so much of it. The confusion of sentiment with sentimentality, encompassing stagecraft that would have made Liberace wince, extends to an unchecked use of melisma that decimates the substance of a song that doesn't need it. In January, 2023, Rolling Stone Magazine left Dion out of their list of the "200 greatest singers of all time," causing many to be horrified – and rightly so. Dion has sold over 200 million records, and she has one of the most complete female voices to be recorded. What her absence suggested was the magazine's suspicion – *contra* Houston and her predecessors – that she didn't believe in what she was doing. There are so many examples of Dion throwing the kitchen into a song where her apparent emotion – with her eyes closed, her face-pulled,[60] and a hand held aloft in testamentary conviction – looks like an act from a mega-church. In such circumstances, and as is common across the sample, the melismatic is too often ineffectual and aggravating; Dion's representation of the apparent authenticity of *her* feelings doesn't serve the song she is performing; it operates to elevate Dion as its performer.

She is not alone in failing to persuade through technique alone. The American singers Ariana Grande,[61] Kelly Clarkson[62] and Lady Gaga[63] have all leant heavily on

---

57 3 April, 1985 –

58 12 September, 1981 –

59 *née* Céline Marie Claudette Dion, 30 March, 1968 –

60 It is common to nearly every singer indulging ornament that they pull faces when doing so. This is due to a mixture of absent training and theatrical emoting. No operatic coloratura to be photographed or filmed ever pulled a face unless the same was requested by a composer or a director.

61 *née* Ariana Grande-Butera, 26 June, 1993 –

62 *née* Kelly Brianne, 24 April, 1982 –

63 *née* Stefani Joanne Angelina Germanotta, 28 March, 1986. Her Ladyship should know better, having

the melisma, and rarely to the advantage of the music. The disease has spread world-wide, notably to Australia (Jessica Mauboy[64]), the Philippines (Regina Velasquez[65]) and Korea (Sohyang).[66] Britain's Jessie J[67] has a klaxon of a voice, and a steel-riveted technique to support it, but she is given to exploiting both to *her* singular advantage. Alexandra Burke has a fine instrument also, but lousy taste, which has caused the ruin of more than one masterpiece. Her splintering of Leonard Cohen's "Halleluiah," in particular, ignored what it was that made Jeff Buckley's performance of the song so important.

Each of these singers is influential; so too is all the note-spinning The sirens of pop have been dragging their acolytes onto the rocks for decades; even if the appetite for the melismatic has cooled in recent years, it remains a major problem for young singers whose predilection for embellishment is routinely de-culturated, untrained and poorly-employed. Anyone who has had to attend a school concert featuring teenage performers[68] will know that the melisma remains popular among girls, for whom it operates as a mechanism for "authentic" emotion. In his study of especially popular musical vernaculars, Simon Frith wrote that:

> Certain physical experiences, particularly extreme feelings, are given vocal sounds beyond our conscious control – the sounds of pain, lust, ecstasy, fear, what one might call inarticulate articulacy: the sounds made by soul singers around and between their notes, vocal noises that seem expressive of their deepest feelings because we hear them is if they've escaped from a body that the mind – language – can no longer control.[69]

Frith's point is compelling and well-evidenced. In its use by *most* popular singers since the 1980s, the melisma has operated without reference to its social and cultural origins. Young white women raised in middle-class homes with picket fences, tennis club memberships and regular holidays to "the lake house," probably have no place employing a musical device formed within (and still important to) black and gospel cultures. A middle-class African-American woman has a more obvious right to adopt her musical traditions than someone who is ignorant of the routine experience of black people in America. It would, nonetheless, be as difficult to hear one of Barack and Michelle Obama's daughters sing "Strange Fruit" as it is to listen to the English singer, Joss Stone,[70] impersonate her idols.[71] It's reasonable to ask

---

worked closely with one of the most musical singers of the 20th century, Tony Bennett.

64   4 August, 1989 –

65   22 April, 1970 –

66   Kim So-hyang, 5 April, 1978 –

67   *née* Jessica Ellen Cornish, 27 March, 1988 –

68   The author has done so in the UK, France, Italy, Switzerland, Germany and the United States.

69   Frith, Simon (1996). *Performing Rites: On the Value of Popular Music*. Harvard University Press, p. 192.

70   11 April, 1987 –

71   Stone is another alumni of a television talent show (the BBC's Star for a Night in London). Her audition songs were Aretha Franklin's "(You Make Me Feel Like) A Natural Woman," and Whitney Houston's "It's Not Right but It's Okay." Having been passed to the next round, she performed Donna Summer's "On the Radio."

whether the melisma is the vocal equivalent of "black-face," therefore, or a tribute to African-American music? The latter explanation would wash if the status of black and white cultures in those countries where black and white people cohabit was equal. It will disappoint advocates of The Great Replacement theory to know that it isn't, especially in the dis-United States, where half the country opposes the teaching of the place of slavery in its proper context. The writer John Eskow damned Aguilera as part of the "the Hideous Cult of Oversouling"[72] – fundamental to which was "the gratuitous and confected melisma" that "hollows out a song and drains it of meaning." He was adamant that any white performer sounding like a black one presented a kind of "vocal minstrel-show, a theft of real feeling in the service of corny show-biz."[73] He dismissed Aguilera as the 21st century equivalent of Al Jolson singing "Mammy."[74]

Eskow's indignation was righteous, and "essentialist" for presuming the existence of a single "black sound." Indeed, the reduction of black music to "the melisma" might be said to overlook the diversity of African-American practice and the complex ways in which black and white musicians have interacted over time. That counter-argument is absent merit, however, because it doesn't account for the imbalance between white and black experience historically and in modern times. It shouldn't matter whether there is more than one black sound; it should matter *only* that what exists shouldn't be appropriated. The challenges arising from these arguments are not (as some have suggested) analogous to the contemporary dispute as it concerns the rights of actors to perform outside, or contrary to, their sexual orientation. It's nonsense to require a gay character to be played only by a gay actor, since gay actors are perfectly capable of playing heterosexuals; there is, moreover, no damage done to the gay community should a straight actor be cast in a gay role. What harm flows from Jerry Herman and Harvey Fierstein's *La Cage Aux Folles* being performed by actors whose sexual has nothing to do with their ability or their work? Can Shylock be performed only by an actor of Jewish origin or faith? How many of those who have performed Hamlet have been Danish, or a prince? It's reasonable not to invite a white actor to play Othello, but how many black tenors are able currently to do justice to Verdi's operatic translation?[75] Should Aida be performed only by a black singer, or by an African, for that matter? The rhetoric is less stable as it concerns African-American voicing and singing because the cultural origins of the melisma trace specifically to the uncomfortable truth of black-American experience over 350 years of persecution, sequestration and mistreatment.

What makes the melisma so troubling, therefore, is its ubiquity – at least as it relates to music informed by black history and experience. The melisma is an expressive device, using necessarily non-verbal sounds to illustrate the emotional experience of an individual speaking through music. If ornaments can all too easily drain a song of its force and meaning, then musicians, audiences and the wider industry need to consider the harm and hurt caused to artists of black origin when their culture is hijacked by people who have not had to fear for their lives in consequence of the

---

72   Eskow, John (2011). "Christina Aguilera and the Hideous Cult of Oversouling." *The Huffington Post.*
73   *Ibid.*
74   *Ibid.*
75   See Boyden, Matthew (2021). *The Tenor: A Cultural History.* Ragueneau Press.

colour of their skin. The melisma is rarely anything less than awful, but black singers should probably be allowed to retain and make use of a seam of emotional articulacy that served as an engine for a process of emancipation and equality that is a long way from being over.

Acknowledgements

I began researching and writing this book four days after completing *The Tenor*. It too was inspired by people *very* dear to me. Sadly, Jill Watt, Elizabeth Cunningham and Graziella Sciutti are not around to appreciate it, but they are filtered throughout its contents. All three women had strong views on music, singing, women and Maria Callas – whose centenary this book commemorates. Jill and Liz both saw her as Tosca at Covent Garden; Graziella knew her personally, as well as through performance. I was 19-years-old when I first met this wildly eccentric triumvirate; they each changed my life for the better, and in myriad ways; I am proud to have been their friend. I did not appreciate at the time the extent to which the soprano is a female voice – which is why this book is a tribute to these women in particular, among many others I have known through thankfully positive experience.

Additionally, I am profoundly grateful to my editor, Michele McCarty, for her erudition, insight, humour, and patience, and also Lee Haynes, my publisher at Ragueneau Press, for producing another beautiful book. The gifted, infinitely patient Jill Sweet has again been the designer of the manuscript. The writing process has been advantaged by the novelist and reluctant genius, Jonathan Buckley, who twenty-five years ago taught me a *little* of what he knows as a writer. Thereafter, I am indebted, as when writing *The Tenor*, to my friends and colleagues around the world, including the Goethe Institute (London), the National Portrait Gallery (London), the British Library, the New York Public Library, L'Opéra de Paris, La Monnaie (Brussels), the New York Metropolitan Opera, the Teatro Regio Torino, the Gran Teatro La Fenice, the Teatro dell'Opera di Roma, the Komische Oper, Deutsche Oper and Staatsoper, Berlin, and the Staatsoper, Vienna. Special thanks are due to the Chicago Opera for their help with the chapter on Maria Callas. The records and resources to which I have been given access have made the research process an unforgettable pleasure. I look forward to returning for the sequel to this volume, *The Baritone: a Cultural History* (2025). Thereafter, I'd like to extend affection and gratitude to the following associates, assistants, colleagues and friends in the United States and Europe: Angelo Villani, John Pennino, Peter Clark, Maurice Wheeler, Sam Morgan, Bruce Barnard, John Franklyn, Ashley Dawes, Alex Smith, Juliette Smith, James Aveyard, Beth Aveyard, Robert Saville, Geraldine Crofts, Graham Postles, Raffaello Russo and his "piccola" Raffaella, Stefania Sacco, Luisa Rolandi, Grant Nicholson, David Peake, Henry Box, Matthew Taylor, Donal Thorburn-Muirhead, Pietro di Maria, Stefano Monelli, Paola Monelli, Gabriele Monelli, Fabrizio "Basso Profondo" Zanca, Ian Brooks, Lucius Cesare, Cosimo di Giovanni de' Medici III, Tom and Georgina Reed (and the fast-growing Reeds, Henry and Jack), Jay "made by" Hercules, Terrie

Haywood, Rebekah Moore, Luisa Rolandi, Hazel James, Alison Jackson, Miles Slover, Adam Davis, Simon Stanley, Karen Wright, Simon Kendrick, Greg Moor, Matt Riley, Richard Norman and Mark Brain. As before, I could have done nothing without the love, patience and inspiration of my children: Joachim, Lucia, Amelie, Octavia and Atticus.

Finally, I wish to thank Rachel Slover, the book's dedicatee. Having devoted many years of her life to academia, and the experiences and legacies of medieval "women religious," her insight, learning and guidance contributed uniquely to the contents of this book, and far beyond the limits of gratitude. Despite being unable to sing a note, she is the personification of everything to which the composers identified in this book were aspiring when imagining the feminine ideal. It is a thrill to be able to quote Tristan when writing of Rachel, "*Zu ihr, zu ihr!*"

Bibliography

Abdullah, Paul (2020). *"Rossini's Willow Song: Shakespeare Reception and Race in Restoration Paris."* Bollettino del Centro Rossiniano di Studi.

Abel, Sam (1996). *Opera in the Flesh: Sexuality in Operatic Performance*. Westview Press.

Addison, Joseph (1854). *The Works of Joseph Addison*. Ed. by George Washington Greene. G.P. Putnam & Co.

Ademollo, Alessandro (1888). *La bell'Adriana ed altre virtuose del suo tempo alla corte di Mantova*. Citta di Castello.

Alda, Frances (1971). *Men, Women and Tenors*. AMS Press.

Anbari, Alan Roy (2007). *Richard Wagner's Concepts of History*. PhD thesis. The University of Texas.

Anderson, Marion (2002). *My Lord, What a Morning: An Autobiography*. University of Illinois Press.

Anderson, Maureen (2004). "The White Reception of Jazz in America." *African American Review*, Vol. 38, No. 1.

Andrews, Richard (2001). From Beaumarchais to Da Ponte: A New View of the Sexual Politics of "Figaro". *Music & Letters*, Vol. 82, No. 2 (May).

Andrews, Richard (2005). "Isabella Andreini and Others: Women on Stage in the Late Cinquecento." In Women in Italian Renaissance Culture and Society. Ed. Letizia Panizza. Legenda.

Archivio di Stato di Mantova, Archivio Gonzaga, busta 2904, libro 136, fol. 5(iv).

Archivio di Stato, Firenze; Archivio Mediceo, f. 2905, No. 86.

Arnold, Denis (1970). "Monteverdi's Singers." The Musical Times. Vol. 111, No. 1532.

Ashbrook, William (1983). *Donizetti and His Operas*. Cambridge University Press.

Ashbrook. William (1968). *The Operas of Puccini*. Cassell.

Athanassoglou-Kallmyer, Nina Maria (1991). *Eugène Delacroix, Prints, Politics and Satire, 1814–1822*. Yale University Press.

Baldwin, Olive and Wilson, Thelma (1969). "Alfred Deller, John Freeman and Mr. Pate." *Music & Letters*, Vol. 50, No. 1.

Baldwin, Olive and Wilson, Thelma (1982). "Purcell's Sopranos." The Musical Times, Vol. 123, No. 1675.

Baldwin, Olive and Wilson, Thelma (1982). "Purcell's Sopranos." *The Musical Times*, Vol. 123, No. 1675.

Beardslee, Bethany (2017). *"I Sang the Unsingable: My Life in Twentieth-Century Music."* University of Rochester Press.

Beer, Ann (2017). *Sounds and Sweet Airs: The Forgotten Women of Classical Music*. Oneworld Publications.

Belgrano, Elisabeth (2011). *LASCIATEMI MORIRE o faro LA FINTA PAZZA. Embodying Vocal Nothingness on Stage in Italian and French 17th century operatic Laments and Mad Scenes*. University of Gothenburg.

Bellincioni, Gemma (1920). *Io e il palcoscenico: trenta e un anno di vita artistica*. Società Anonima Editoriale Dott. R. Quintieri. Bellincioni, Gemma (1943). Bianca Stagno Bellincioni Intimi. Arno Press.

Bernhardt, Sarah (1907). *My Double Life: Memoirs of Sarah Bernhardt*. William Heinemann.

Bernheimer, Martin (1985). "But Are We Really Colour-Deaf," Opera. 759–60.

Bicknell, Jeanette (2018). "Excess in art: the case of oversinging." Journal of Aesthetics and Art Criticism. Vol. 76(1).

Blake, Kathleen (1980). "'Armgart' – George Eliot on the Woman Artist." *Poetry*. Vol. 18, No. 1

Blom, Philipp (2008). *The Vertigo Years: Change and Culture in the West, 1900–1914*. McClelland & Stewart.

Bloom, Harold (2002). *Genius: A Mosaic of One Hundred Exemplary Creative Minds*. Grand Central Publishing.

Bolt, Rodney (2006). *The Librettist of Venice*. Bloomsbury.

Boneau, Denise Lynn (1989). *Louise Bertin and Opera in Paris in the 1820s and 1830s*. Ph.D Thesis, University of Chicago.

Bouvet, Charles (1927). Cornélie Falcon. Alcan.

Bouvet, Charles (1927). *Cornélie Falcon*. Alcan.

Bowring, John, Sir (1835). *Second report on the commercial relations between France and Great Britain. Silks & wine. Presented to both Houses of Parliament by command of His Majesty*. W. Clowes.

Boyden, Matthew (1999). *Richard Strauss*. Weidenfeld & Nicolson.

Boyden, Matthew (2018). *Beethoven and the Gothic*. Verba et Musica.

Boyden, Matthew (2021). *The Tenor: A Cultural History*. Ragueneau Press.

Bravo, Anna (2001). "Madri fra oppressione ed emancipazione," in *Storia sociale delle donne nell'Italia contemporanea*, Laterza.

Brécourt-Villars, Claudine (1988). *Yvette Guilbert l'irrespectueuse*. Plon; Guilbert, Yvette (1902). La vedette. H. Simonis Empis; and Knapp, Bettina, and Chipman, Myra (1964). "That was Yvette: The biography of the great diseuse." Holt, Rinehart & Winston.

Brett, M.A., Roberts, L.F., Johnson, T.W., Wassersug, R.J. (2007). *Journal of Sexual Medicine*.

Breuer, J., & Freud, S. (1895). *Studien über Hysterie*. F. Deuticke.

Brody, Elaine (1985). All in The Family: Liszt, Daniel and Ary Scheffer. *Nineteenth-Century French Studies*. Vol. 13, No. 4. University of Nebraska Press.

Brown, Clive (1992). "Performing Practice." In Eds. Millington, Barry and Spencer, Stewart. *Wagner in Performance*. Yale University Press.

Brown, Clive (1992). "Performing Practice." In Eds. Millington, Barry and Spencer, Stewart. *Wagner in Performance* (1992). Yale University Press.

Brown, Clive (1992). "Performing Practice." In *Wagner in Performance*. Eds. Millington, Barry, and Spencer, Stewart. Yale University Press.

Brownell, Robert (2013) *Marriage of Inconvenience. Euphemia Chalmers Gray and John Ruskin: the Secret History of the Most Notorious Marital Failure of the Victorian Era*. Pallas Athene.

Buch, Esteban (2021). "Fidelio or the Musical Prison: A Dark Essay on Freedom, Gender, and the State." *Music & Practice*, Vol. 8.

Buckingham, Willis J. (1989). *Emily Dickinson's Reception in the 1890s: A Documentary History*. University of Pittsburgh Press.

Budden, Julian (1978). *The Operas of Verdi, Vol. 2*. Cassell.

Budden, Julian (1998). "Giuseppina Strepponi," in Stanley Sadie, Ed. *The New Grove Dictionary of Opera, Vol. 4*. Macmillan.

Burney, Dr. Charles (1957). *A General History of Music: From the Earliest Ages to the Present Period (1776–89)*. Ed. Frank Mercer. Dover Publications.

Burney, Dr. Charles (1957). *A General History of Music: From the Earliest Ages to the Present Period (1776–89)*. Ed. Frank Mercer. Dover Publications.

Burrows, Donald (2012). *Handel*. Oxford University Press.

Cage, E.C. (2009). "The Sartorial Self: Neoclassical Fashion and Gender Identity in France, 1797–1804." *Eighteenth-Century Studies*. 42, 2.

Cairns, David (1999). *Berlioz: Servitude and greatness 1832–1869*. University of California Press.

Cairns, David (2000). *Berlioz: Servitude and Greatness (1832 – 1869). Vol. 2*. University of California Press.

Calico, Joy H. (2012). "Staging Scandal with Salome and Elektra," in *The Arts of the Prima Donna in the Long Nineteenth Century*. Eds. Rachel Cowgill & Hilary Poriss. Oxford University Press.

Calico, Joy H. (2012). "Staging Scandal with Salome and Elektra," in *The Arts of the Prima Donna in the Long Nineteenth Century*. Eds. Rachel Cowgill & Hilary Poriss. Oxford University Press.

Calvé, Emma (1922). *My Life*. D Appleton & Company.

Carmen: Dossier de presse Parisienne (2001). Ed. Leslie Wright. Musik-Edition Lucie Galland.

Carter, Tim (1980). Jacopo Peri. Music & Letters, Vol. 61, No. 2.

Carter, Tim (1999). "Singing Orfeo: on the performers of Monteverdi's first opera." Recercare. Vol. 11.

Carter, Tim (2002). *Monteverdi's Musical Theatre*. Yale University Press.

Carter, Tim (2003). "Rediscovering Il rapimento di Cefalo." *The Journal of Seventeenth-Century Music*. Vol 9. No.1.

Castiglione, Baldesar (2002). Ed. Javitch, Daniel, *The Book of the Courtier: The Singleton Translation*. Trans. by Charles S. Singleton. W.W. Norton.

Caswell, A. (1975). "Mme Cinti-Damoreau and the Embellishment of Italian Opera in Paris: 1820–1845." *Journal of the American Musicological Society*, 28(3).

Chetwood, W. R. (2018). *A general history of the stage: from its origin in Greece down to the present time*. Forgotten Books.

Chorley, Henry (1844). *Music and Manners in France and Germany: A Series of Travelling Sketches of Art and Society, Vol. 1*. Longman, Brown, Green and Longman.

Chrissochoidis, Ilias (2007). "La Musique du Diable (1711). An obscure specimen of fantastic literature throws light on the elusive opera diva Marie-Louise Desmatins." *Society for Eighteenth Century Music*. Issue No. 11.

Christensen, Jean (1984). "The Spiritual and the Material in Schoenberg's Thinking." *Music & Letters*, Vol. 65, No. 4.

Christiansen, Keith; Weppelmann, Stefan and Rubin, Patricia Lee (2011). *The Renaissance Portrait: From Donatello to Bellini*. Metropolitan Museum of Art.

Christiansen, Rupert (1984). Prima Donna: a History. Viking.

Christoforidis, Michael and Kertesz, Elizabeth (2018). *Carmen and the Staging of Spain: Recasting Bizet's Opera in the Belle Epoque*. Oxford University Press.

Cibber, Colley (1968). *An Apology for the Life of Colley Cibber: With an Historical View of the Stage During His Own Time*. Edited by B.R.S. Fone. University of Michigan Press.

Clément, Catherine (1988). *Opera, or the undoing of Women*. Trans. Betsy Wing. University of Minnesota Press.

Cohen, Albert (1992). *L'Etat de la France: One Hundred Years of Music at the French Court*; Second Series, Vol. 48, No. 3.

Colas, Damien (2004). "Melody and ornamentation." In *The Cambridge Companion to Rossini*. Ed. by Emanuele Senici. Cambridge University Press.

Colbert, F. (2007). Marketing Culture and the Arts, HEC, Montréal.

Cook, Nicholas (1993). *Beethoven: Symphony No. 9*. Cambridge University Press.

Corazzol, Adriana Guarnieri and Parker, Roger (1993). "Opera and verismo: Regressive points of view and the artifice of alienation," *Cambridge Opera Journal*, Vol. 5, No. 1.

Cowart (1994). "Of Women, Sex and Folly: Opera under the Old Regime Georgia Cowart." *Cambridge Opera Journal*.

Craik, Jennifer (1994). *The Face of Fashion: Cultural Studies in Fashion*. Routledge.

Crivellaro, F., Sperduti, A. (2014). "Accepting and understanding evolution in Italy: a case study from a selected public attending a Darwin Day celebration." *Evo Edu Outreach*. 7, 13.

Cruz, Gabriela (2020). *Grand Illusion: Phantasmagoria in Nineteenth-century Opera*. Oxford University Press.

Cunningham, Caroline (1996). *Women Composers: Music Through the Ages*. Eds. Schleifer, Martha Furman; Glickman, Sylvia. G.K. Hill.

Cusick, Suzanne (1994). "'There Was Not a Lady Who Failed to Shed a Tear.' Arianna's Lament and the Construction of Modern Womanhood." *Early Music*. 22(1).

Cusick, Suzanne (1994). "'There Was Not a Lady Who Failed to Shed a Tear.' Arianna's Lament and the Construction of Modern Womanhood." Early Music. 22(1).

Cusick, Suzanne G. (1993) "Thinking from Women's Lives: Francesca Caccini after 1627." *The Musical Quarterly*, Vol. 77, No. 3.

Cuthbert Hadden, J. (1928). *Modern Musicians: A Book for Players, Singers and Listeners*. Peter Davies.

Daniels, Morgan (2011). "*The Effects of 'Antiestablishment' BBC Comedy on Politicians, the Public and Broadcasting Values c. 1939–73*." PhD Thesis, Queen Mary, University of London.

Daverio, John (2008). "Tristan und Isolde: Essence and Appearance." In Grey, Thomas S., ed. (2008). *The Cambridge Companion to Wagner*.

Davies, James Q. (2012), "Gautier's 'diva': the first French uses of the word," in *The Art of the Prima Donna in the Long Nineteenth Century*. Eds. Rachel Cowgill and Hilary Poriss. Oxford University Press.

Davis, Tracy C. (1989). "The Actress in Victorian Pornography." *Theatre Journal*. Vol. 41, No. 3.

Dean, Winton (1965). *Georges Bizet: His Life and Work*. J. M. Dent & Sons.

Dean, Winton (1965). *Georges Bizet: His Life and Work*. J. M. Dent & Sons.

Deutsch, Erich Otto (1965). *Mozart: A Documentary Biography*. Stanford University Press.

Deutsch, Otto (1974). *Handel: A Documentary Biography*. Da Capo Press.

Deutsch, Otto Erich (1965). *Mozart: A Documentary Biography*. Stanford University Press.

Dialeti, Androniki (2004). *The Debate About Women and its Socio-Cultural Background in Early Modern Venice*. PhD thesis. University of Glasgow.

Dialeti, Androniki (2004). The Debate About Women and its Socio-Cultural Background in Early Modern Venice. PhD thesis. University of Glasgow.

Dialeti, Androniki (2011) "Defending Women, Negotiating Masculinity in Early Modern Italy." *The Historical Journal*, Vol. 54, No. 1.

Dialeti, Androniki (2011). "Defending Women, Negotiating Masculinity in Early Modern Italy." *The Historical Journal*. Vol. 54, No. 1 (March).

Dijkstra, Bram (1986). *Idols of Perversity: Fantasies of Feminine Evil in Fin-de-Siecle Culture*. Oxford University Press.

Dizikes, John (1993). *Opera in America: A Cultural History*. Yale University Press.

Donington, Robert (1982). *Baroque Music: Style and performance*. W.W. Norton & Company.

Dorré, Gina M. (2006). "Three Horses and Corsets: Black Beauty, Dress Reform, and the Fashioning of the Victorian Woman," in *Victorian Fiction and the Cult of the Horse.* Routledge.

Dreyfus, Laurence (2010). *Wagner and the Erotic Impulse.* Harvard University Press.

Dreyfus, Laurence (2010). *Wagner and the Erotic Impulse.* Harvard University Press.

Dublin Weekly Herald (15 August, 1840). "Tight Lacing."

E. T. A. Hoffmann's Musical Writings: Kreisleriana, The Poet and the Composer, Music Criticism (1989). Ed. David Charlton. Cambridge University Press.

Edgcumbe, Richard; Earl of Mount Edgcumbe (1834). *Musical Reminiscences, containing an account of the Italian Opera in England, from 1773.* John Andrews & F. H. Wall.

Edwards, Anne (2001). *Maria Callas: An Intimate Biography.* St. Martin's Press.

Eidsheim, Nina Sun (2011). "Marian Anderson and 'Sonic Blackness' in American Opera." *Sound Clash: Listening to American Studies*, Vol. 63, No. 3.

Eisenbeiss, Philip (2013). Bel Canto Bully: The Life of the Legendary Opera Impresario Domenico Barbaja. Haus Publishing.

Emerson, Isabelle Putnam (2005). *Five Centuries of Women Singers.* Greenwood Publishing Group.

Engstrom, Stephen (1992). "The Concept of the Highest Good in Kant's Moral Theory." *Philosophy and Phenomenological Research.* Vol. 52, No.4.

Eschenbach, Wolfram von (1961). *Parzival.* Trans. Helen M. Mustard and Charles E. Passage. Vintage Books.

Eskow, John (2011). "Christina Aguilera and the Hideous Cult of Oversouling." The Huffington Post.

Esse, Melina (2009). "Speaking and Sighing: Bellini's canto declamato and the Poetics of Restraint." *Current Musicology*, No. 87.

Fabbri, Paolo (1994). *Monteverdi.* Trans. by Tim Carter. Cambridge University Press.

Fahy, Conor (2000). "Women and Italian Cinquecento Literary Academies." In Panizza, Letizia (2000). *Women in Italian Renaissance Culture and Society.* Oxford University Press.

Fairbank, Rebecca Bennett (2013). "*Devastating Diva: Pauline Viardot and Rewriting the Image of Women in Nineteenth-Century French Opera Culture.*" Ph.D Thesis, Brigham Young University.

Faust, Veronica T. (2006). "*Music has learn'd the discords of the state': The Cultural Politics of British Opposition to Italian Opera, 1706–1711.*" Masters Thesis. Haverford College.

Fauvel, Aude (2013). "Crazy Brains and the Weaker Sex: The British Case (1860–1900)." In *Clio. Women, Gender, History.* Vol. 37 (1).

Feldman, Martha (1995). *City Culture and the Madrigal at Venice.* University of California Press.

Fenlon, Iain (1980). *Music and Patronage in Sixteenth-Century Mantua, Volume 1.* Cambridge University Press.

Fischer, Jens Malte (1992). "Sprechgesang or Bel Canto: Toward a History of Singing Wagner." Trans. Michael Tanner. In *Wagner Handbook*, ed. Ulrich Müller and Peter Wapnewski, trans. John Deathridge. Harvard University Press.

Fisher, Burton D. (2005). *Puccini's The Girl of the Golden West.* Opera Journeys Publishing.

Fitzlyon, April (1964). The Price of Genius: A Life of Pauline Viardot. Appleton-Century.

Fitzlyon, April (1987). *Maria Malibran.* Souvenir Press.

Ford Madox Ford (1918). "Women and Men". *The Little Review*, 4.

Forster, E. M. (1963). "My first opera" in *Opera*, Vol. 14.

Forth, Christopher E. (2020) "Fat, Desire and Disgust in the Colonial Imagination." History Workshop Journal, No. 73.

Fortune, Nigel (1954). "Italian 17th Century Singing." *Music & Letters.* Vol. 35, No. 3.

Fortune, Nigel (1954). "Italian 17th Century Singing." *Music & Letters*. Vol. 35, No. 3.

Fortune, Nigel (1954). "Italian 17th Century Singing." Music & Letters. Vol. 35, No. 3.

Foulds-Elliott, S. D., Thorpe, C. William, Cala, Stephen J., and Davis, Pamela J. (2000). "Respiratory function in operatic singing: effects of emotional connection." *Logopedics Phoniatrics Vocology*, 25 (4).

Franco, Paola Lunetta (2001). *Francesca Cuzzoni (1696–1778): Lo Stile antico nella musica moderna*. University of Pavia.

Freitas, Roger (2018). "Singing Herself: Adelina Patti and the Performance of Femininity." *Journal of the American Musicological Society*. 71 (2).

Friday, Nancy (1973). *My Secret Garden: Women's Sexual Fantasies*. Simon & Schuster.

Frisch, Walter (1993). *The Early Works of Arnold Schoenberg*. University of California Press.

Gabbard, Glen O.; Gabbard, Krin (1999). *Psychiatry and the Cinema*. American Psychiatric Publishing.

Gage, Nicholas (2000). *Greek Fire: The Story of Maria Callas and Aristotle Onassis*. Knopf.

Gallico, Claudio (1967). *I due pianti d'Arianna di Claudio Monteverdi*. Chigiana XXIV.

Garelli, Franco (2014). *Religion, Italian Style: Continuities and Change in a Catholic Country*. Ashgate.

Garofalo, M., Colella, A., Sadini, P., Bianchi, L., Saraceni, G., Brunocilla, E., Gentile, G., Colombo, F. (2018) *Archivio Italiano di Urologia e Andrologia*, 30:90(3).

Gattey, Charles Neilson (1995). *Luisa Tetrazzini: the Florentine Nightingale*. Scolar Press.

Gautier, Théophile (1858). *Histoire de l'art dramatique en France depuis vingt-cinq ans*. Édition Hetzel.

George Frideric Handel: Collected Documents, Vol. 1, 1609–1725. (2013). Burrows, Donald; Coffey, Helen; Greenacombe, John; and Hicks, Anthony, Eds. Cambridge University Press.

Gerould, Daniel (1984). "Oscar Méténier and 'Comédie Rosse': From the Théâtre Libre to the Grand Guignol." *The Drama Review*. Vol. 28, No. 1, French Theatre.

Gibbons, William James (2006). *Issues of Voice Range and Transposition in Monteverdi's Mantuan Madrigals*. Master' Thesis. Chapel Hill.

Gilbert, Oscar, Paul (1932). *Women In Men's Guise*. John Lane.

Giles, Geoffrey J. (1992). "'The Most Unkindest Cut of All': Castration, Homosexuality and Nazi Justice." *Journal of Contemporary History*, Vol. 27, No. 1.

Gilliam, Bryan (1991). *Richard Strauss' Elektra*. Oxford University Press.

"Giovanna d'Arco" (2007). *Works of Giuseppe Verdi, Vol. 7*. Ed. Alberto Rizzuti. University of Chicago Press.

Glixon, Beth L. (1997). "New light on the life and career of Barbara Strozzi". *The Musical Quarterly*. 81(2)

Glover, Jane (2005). *Mozart's Women*. Harper Collins.

Gobbi, Tito (1980). *Tito Gobbi: My Life*. Futura Publications.

Gonzalez, Erin (2019). "*Mozart's Mezzos*": A Comparative Study Between Castrato and Female Roles in Mozart's Operas. Ph.D thesis, Chapman University.

Gordon, Bonnie (2004). Monteverdi's Unruly Women: The Power of Song in Early Modern Italy. Cambridge University Press.

Gordon, Mel (2016). *Theater of Fear and Horror: The Grisly Spectacle of the Grand Guignol of Paris, 1897–1962*. Feral House.

Gossett, Philip (2005). "Le 'edizioni distrutte' e il significato dei cori operistici nel Risorgimento." *Il Saggiatore musicale*. 12 (2).

Gottlieb, Robert (2010). *Sarah: The Life of Sarah Bernhardt*. Yale University Press.

Grout, Donald Jay (1941). "Some Forerunners of the Lully Opera." Music & Letters, Vol. 22, No. 1.

Guaraccino, Serena (2010). "It's not over till the fat lady sings: the weight of the opera diva," in *Historicizing Fat in the Anglo-American West*. Ed. lena Levy-Navarro. Ohio State University Press.

Gustav Mahler: Letters to His Wife (2004). Trans. Henry-Louis de la Grange and Günther Weiss. Cornell University Press.

Handy, A.B., Jackowich, R.A., Wibowo, E., Johnson, T.W., Wassersug, R.J. (2016). *Sex Medicine*, 4(1).

Hankins, James (2003). *Humanism and Platonism in the Italian Renaissance, Volume 1*, "Humanism." Edizione di Storia e Letteratura.

Harbor, Catherine (2020). "The Marketing of Concerts in London 1672–1749." Journal of Historical Research in Marketing. Vol. 12, Issue 4.

Harrán, Don (1995). "Madama Europa, Jewish Singer in Late Renaissance Mantua." In *Festa Musicologica: Essays in Honour of George J. Buelow*. Thomas J. Mathiesen and Benito V. Rivera, Eds. Pendragon Press.

Harrán, Don (1999). *Salamone Rossi, Jewish Musician in Late Renaissance Mantua*. Oxford University Press.

Haslam, W. E. (1911). *Style in Singing*. Schirmer.

Hawkins, Sir John (2010). *General History of the Science and Practice of Music*. Gale ECCO.

Henson, Karen (2015). "Real mezzo: Célestine Galli-Marié as Carmen." In *Opera Acts: Singers and Performance in the Late Nineteenth Century*. Cambridge University Press.

Henson, Karen (2015). "Real mezzo: Célestine Galli-Marié as Carmen." In *Opera Acts: Singers and Performance in the Late Nineteenth Century*. Cambridge University Press.

Hewitt, Catherine (2015). *The Mistress of Paris: The 19th-Century Courtesan Who Built an Empire on a Secret*. Icon Books.

Higgins, Emma (2015). "The mezzo-soprano onstage and offstage: a cultural history of the voice-type, singers and roles in the French Third Republic (1870–1918)." Ph.D. Dissertation, Maynooth University.

Higgins, Emma (2015). *The mezzo-soprano onstage and offstage: a cultural history of the voice-type, singers and roles in the French Third Republic (1870–1918)*. PhD. dissertation, Maynooth University.

Highfill, Philip H., Burnim, Kalman A., Langhans, Edward A. (1993). *A Biographical Dictionary of Actors, Actresses and Musicians and other stage personnel in London, 1660–1800*, Vol.15. Viking.

Highfill, Philip H., Burnim, Kalman A., Langhans, Edward A. (1993). *A Biographical Dictionary of Actors, Actresses and Musicians and other stage personnel in London, 1660–1800, Vol. 15*. Viking.

Hill, John Walter, (1997). Roman Monody, Cantata and Opera from the Circles Around Cardinal Montalto, 2 vols. Oxford University Press.

Holford-Strevens, Leofranc (1999). "Her eyes became two spouts: Classical Antecedents of Renaissance Laments." *Early Music*, Vol.27.

Holland, Bernard (12 January 2006). "Birgit Nilsson, Soprano Legend Who Tamed Wagner, Dies at 87." *The New York Times*.

Hoxby, Blair (2005). "The doleful airs of Euripides: The origins of opera and the spirit of tragedy reconsidered." *Cambridge Opera Journal*, Vol. 17, 3.

Huebner, Steven (1989). "Opera Audiences in Paris 1830–1870." *Music & Letters*, Vol. 70, No. 2.

Hume, R. D. (2014). "*The Value of Money in Eighteenth-Century England: Incomes, Prices, Buying Power—and Some Problems in Cultural Economics*", Huntington Library Quarterly, Vol. 77 No. 4.

Hunter, Eric J., Švec, Jan G., and Titze, Ingo R. (2006). "Comparison of the Produced and Perceived Voice Range Profiles in Untrained and Trained Classical Singers." *Journal of Voice*. 20(4).

Izzo, Francesco (2007). "Verdi, the Virgin, and the Censor: The Politics of the Cult of Mary in I Lombardi alla prima crociata and Giovanna d'Arco." *Journal of the American Musicological Society*, Vol. 60, No. 3.

Jackowich, R.A., Vale, R., Vale, K., Wassersug, R.J., Johnson, T.W. (2014). *Sex Medicine*. 2(3).

Jackson, Mahalia, and Wylie, Evan McLeod (1966). *Movin' On Up*. Hawthorn Books.

Jacobshagen, Arnold (2022). "Reimagining Rossini" in *Obituaries as Transnational Narratives of Italian Opera*. Eds. by Körner, Axel and Kühl, Paulo M. Cambridge University Press.

Jenkins, Laurence L. (2003). *Claudia Muzio (1889–1936), Her Life and Career*. PhD. Thesis. Massey University Conservatorium of Music College of Fine Arts, Design and Music Wellington, New Zealand.

Jerold, Beverly (2008). "How Composers Viewed Performers' Additions." *Early Music*. Vol. 36, No. 1.

Jerold, Beverly (2008). "How Composers Viewed Performers' Additions." *Early Music*. Vol. 36, No. 1.

Joachim, Joseph and Moser, Andreas (1905), *Violinschule, Vol. 2*. N. Simrock.

Joffe, Natalie F. (1948). "The Vernacular of Menstruation," *WORD (International Linguistic Association)* 4:3.

Johann Burchard, Pope Alexander VI and His Court: Extracts from the Latin Diary of Johannes Burchardus (1921). Ed. F.L. Glaser. N.L. Brown.

Johnson, T.W. and Irwig, Michael S. (2014). *Nature Reviews Urology*. 11(5).

Johnson, T.W., Brett, M.A., Roberts, L.F., Wassersug, R.J. (2007). *Journal of Sexual Medicine*.

Jones, Ernest (1964). The life and Work of Sigmund Freud. Basic Books.

Jordan, Ruth (1994). *Fromental Halévy: His Life & Music, 1799–1862*. Kahn & Averill.

Jorgensen, Cecilia and Jorgensen, Jens (2005). "Chopin and Jenny Lind New Research." *Fryderyk Chopin Institute and Edinburgh University.*

Kellogg Strakosch, Clara Louise (1913). *Memoirs of an American Prima Donna*. G. P. Putnam's Sons.

Kendall-Davies, Barbara (2003). *The Life and Work of Pauline Viardot Garcia. I: The Years of Fame, 1836–1863*. Cambridge Scholar Press.

Kendell, Colin (2012). The Complete Puccini. Amberley Publishing

Kerman, Joseph (2006). "Verdi and the Undoing of Women." *Cambridge Opera Journal*. Vol. 18, No. 1.

Kettledon, Lisabeth M. (2017). *A Lyric Soprano in Handel's London: A Vocal Portrait of Francesca Cuzzoni. Doctoral Thesis*. University of Connecticut.

Kettledon, Lisabeth M. (2017). *A Lyric Soprano in Handel's London: A Vocal Portrait of Francesca Cuzzoni*. Doctoral Thesis. University of Connecticut.

Kimbell, David (1998). *Norma*. Cambridge University Press.

Kinder, Kaylyn (2013). *Eighteenth-century reception of Italian opera in London*. Electronic Theses and Dissertations, 753. University of Louisville.

King, Thomas A. (2006). "The Castrato's Castrian", in *Studies in English Literature, 1500–1900." Restoration and Eighteenth Century*. Vol. 46, No. 3.

Kirkley, Laura (2022). "Mary Wollstonecraft's Translational Afterlife: French and German Rewritings of A Vindication of the Rights of Woman in the Revolutionary Era." *European Romantic Review*, 33:1.

Klein, Hermann (1990). *Herman Klein and the Gramophone: Being a Series of Essays on the Bel Canto*. Amadeus Press.

Koestenbaum, Wayne (1994). *The Queen's Throat: Opera, Homosexuality, and the Mystery of Desire*. Penguin.

Köhler, Joachim (2004). *Richard Wagner: The last of the titans*. Yale University Press.

Kościński, Krzysztof (2014). "Assessment of Waist-to-Hip Ratio Attractiveness in Women: An Anthropometric Analysis of Digital Silhouettes." *Archives of Sexual Behavior*. Vol. 43.

Kramer, Lawrence (1993). "Fin-de-siècle Fantasies: 'Elektra', Degeneration and Sexual Science." *Cambridge Opera Journal*, Vol. 5, No. 2.

Krause, Ernst (1969). *Richard Strauss: The Man and His Work*. Crescendo Publishing Company.

Krister, Konrad (1996). "A Promise Kept? The C Minor Mass, K. 427" in *Mozart: A Musical Biography*, trans. Mary Whittall. Clarendon Press.

Kuner, Christopher (2011). "The recording(s) of Anna Bahr-Mildenburg." *The Record Collector*, Vol. 56 (4).

Kutsch, K. J.; Riemens, Leo (2012). "Milde, Rosa von" in *Großes Sängerlexikon* (4th ed.). De Gruyter.

Lady Morgan, Sydney Owenson (1863). *Lady Morgan's Memoirs: Autobiography, Diaries and Correspondence*, 2 vols. William H. Allen.

Larkin, Philip (1983). *"The Pleasure Principle." Required Writing: Miscellaneous Pieces 1955–1982*. Faber and Faber.

LaRue, C. Steven (1995). *Handel and His Singers: The Creation of the Royal Academy Operas, 1720–1728*. Oxford University Press.

Le Bon, Gustave (2002). *The Crowd: A Study of the Popular Mind*. Dover Publications.

Lee, Junghyun (2020). *An Understanding of Style and of Baroque Ornamentation In Handel's Operatic Arias: A Study of Selected Recordings (1950s – 2010s)*. PhD. Thessis. University of Kenucky.

Legman, G. (1968). Rationale of the Dirty Joke: an Analysis of Sexual Humour. Simon & Schuster.

Lehmann, Lotte (1964). *Singing with Richard Strauss*. Hamish Hamilton.

Leopold, Silke (1993). *Claudio Monteverdi und seine Zeit*. Laaber.

Letellier, Robert Ignatius (2008). *An Introduction to the Dramatic Works of Giacomo Meyerbeer: Operas, Ballets, Cantatas, Plays*. Ashgate.

Levine, Robert (2003). *Maria Callas: A Musical Biography*. Running Press.

Levy, David Benjamin (1979). *Early Performances of Beethoven's Ninth Symphony: A Documentary Study of Five Major Cities*. PhD Thesis. University of Rochester.

Lewalski, Barbara K. (2003). *The Life of John Milton: A Critical Biography*. Blackwell Publishing.

Lewis, Ben (2019). *The Last Leonardo: The Secret Lives of the World's Most Expensive Painting*. Ballantine Books.

Littlejohn, David (1992). *The Ultimate Art: Essays Around and About Opera*. University of California Press.

Lord William Pitt Lennox (1863). *Fifty Years' Biographical Reminiscences*, 2 vols. Hurst and Blackett

Loret, Jean (1857). *La Muze Historique ou Recueil des Lettres en Vers contenent les Nouvelles du Temps, écrits a son Altesse Mademoizelle de Longueville, depuis Duchesse de Nemours, 1650–1665*. Vol. 1–4.

Maffei, Luigi; Iannace, Gino; Ianniello, Carmine; Romano, Rosario (1998). The Acoustics of the Italian Opera House "Teatro di San Carlo" in Naples, Italy. *Acoustical Society of America*.

Magraner, José Salvador Blasco and Camejo, Francisco Carlos Bueno (2014). "Delacroix, Eugène: The Bridge of vision: The Image of the Opera in the History of Painting (Delacroix and Rossini´s Otello)." *Global Journal of Human-Social Science*. Vol. 14(2).

Mahler, Alma (1968). *Gustav Mahler: Memories and Letters*. John Murray.

Malane, Rachel (2005). *Sex in Mind: The Gendered Brain in Nineteenth-Century Literature and Mental Sciences*. Peter Lang.

Malik, Shireen (2008). "Salome and Her Dance of the Seven Veils" in Jennifer Heath (Ed.), *The Veil: Women Writers on its History, Lore, and Politics*. University of California Press.

Mancini, Giambattista (1777). *Pensieri e riflessioni pratiche sopra il canto figurato* [Practical Reflections on Figured Singing]. Trans. and Ed. by Edward Foreman. Masterworks on Singing, Vol. VII. Pro Musica Press.

Manwairing, John (1760). *Memoirs of the Life of the Late George Frederic Handel*. R. & J. Dodsley.

Marek, George (1969). Beethoven: Biography of Genius. William Kimber.

Martens, Lorna (1987). "The Theme of the Repressed Memory in Hofmannsthal's Elektra." *The German Quarterly*, Vol. 60, No. 1.

Martin, Peter A., (1964). "A Psychoanalytic Study of the Marschallin Theme from Der Rosenkavalier." *Journal of the American Psychoanalytic Association*, Vol. 14 (4).

Matsumoto, Naomi (2011). "Manacled Freedom: 19th-Century Vocal Improvisation and the Flute-Accompanied Cadenza in Donizetti's Lucia di Lammermoor." In *Beyond Notes: Improvisation in Western Music of the Eighteenth and Nineteenth Centuries*. Rudolf Rasch, Ed. Brepols.

McClary, Susan (1989). Constructions of Gender in Monteverdi's Dramatic Music. *Cambridge Opera Journal*. Vol. 1, No. 3.

McClary, Susan (1992). *Bizet: Carmen*. Cambridge University Press.

McColley, Diane Kelsey (1984). "Tongues of Men and Angels: Ad Leonoram Romae Canentem." In Milton Studies, Vol. 19, *Urbane Milton: The Latin Poetry, in John Milton Prose: Major Writings on Liberty, Politics, Religion, and Education*, Ed. David Loewenstein. Wiley-Blackwell.

McGeary, Thomas (2000). "Verse Epistles on Italian Opera Singers, 1724–1736." Royal Musical Association Research Chronicle. No. 33.

Mendelsohn, Gerald A. (1978). "Verdi the Man and Verdi the Dramatist," 19th-Century Music, 2.

Mérimée, Prosper (1905). "Letters to an Unknown." In *Works of Prosper Mérimée*. Ed. George Saintsbury. Brown & Co.

Meyer, Stephen C. (1997). "Das wilde Herz: Interpreting Wilhelmine Schröder-Devrient." *Opera Quarterly*, 14/2.

Meyer, Stephen C. (1997). "Das wilde Herz: Interpreting Wilhelmine Schröder-Devrient." *Opera Quarterly*, 14/2.

Micale, Mark S. (2004). "Discourses of Hysteria in Fin-de-Siècle France," in *The Mind of Modernism*. Stanford University Press.

Milton, John (2005). *Paradise Lost, Book I*. Oxford University Press.

Mock, Roberta (2007). *Jewish Women on Stage, Film and Television*. Palgrave Macmillan.

Morgan, Brian (2006). *Strange Child of Chaos: Norman Treigle*. iUniverse.

Morgan, Kenneth (2010). *Fritz Reiner, Maestro and Martinet*. University of Illinois Press.

Mosconi, Elena (2013). "Silent Singers: The Legacy of Opera and Female Stars and Early Italian Cinema." In *Researching Women in Silent Cinema: New Findings and Perspectives*. Eds. Dall'Asta, Monica, Duckett, Victoria, and Tralli, Lucia. University of Bologna and University of Melbourne.

Murata, Margaret (1995). "Why the First Opera Given in Paris Wasn't Roman." Cambridge Opera Journal. Vol. 7, No. 2.

Nakhutsrishvili, Luka. (2018). "The promising ruins of the German prima donna: Wilhelmine Schröder-Devrient and German musical discourse in the nineteenth century" in *Geschichte und Repräsentation*. Tel Aviver Jahrbuch für deutsche Geschichte, 46.

Nakhutsrishvili, Luka. (2018). "The promising ruins of the German prima donna: Wilhelmine Schröder-Devrient and German musical discourse in the nineteenth century" in *Geschichte und Repräsentation*. Tel Aviver Jahrbuch für deutsche Geschichte, 46.

Nannetti Remo (1988). "The Sonzogno Concorsi, 1884–1906," *Renaissance and Other Studies*.

Néret, Gilles (1996). *Gustav Klimt, 1862–1918*. Barnes and Noble Books.

Neumann, F. (1986). Ornamentation and improvisation in Mozart. Princeton University Press.

Newcomb, Anthony (1970). The Musica Secreta of Ferrara in the 1580s. Ph.D. Dissertation; Princeton.

Newcomb, Anthony (1980). *The Madrigal at Ferrara, 1579–1597*, 2 vols. Princeton

Newcomb, Anthony (1980). *The Madrigal at Ferrara, 1579–1597, Vol. 1*. Princeton University Press.

Osborne, Richard (2007). *Rossini*. Oxford University Press.

"Opera, or The Envoicing of Women" in *Musicology and Difference: Gender and Sexuality in Music Scholarship* (1993). Ed. R.A. Solie. Berkeley.

Painter, K. (2001). "*Contested counterpoint: 'Jewish' appropriation and polyphonic liberation,*" Archi Für Musikwissenschaft, 58(3).

Palmer, Fiona M. (1997). *Domenico Dragonetti in England, 1794–1846*. Oxford University Press.

Palmer, R. R. (2014). *The Age of the Democratic Revolution: a Political History of Europe and America, 1760–1800*. Princeton Classics.

Parakilas, James (1997). "Religion and Difference in Verdi's 'Otello.'" *The Musical Quarterly*, Vol. 81, No. 3.

Parr, Sean M. (2012). "Caroline Carvalho and nineteenth-century coloratura." In *Cambridge Opera Journal*.

Parr, Sean M. (2019). "Wagnerian Singing and the Limits of Vocal Pedagogy." *Current Musicology*, 105.

Parr, Sean M. (2019). Wagnerian Singing and the Limits of Vocal Pedagogy. Current Musicology, 105.

Parrott, Andrew (1995). "Performing Purcell," in *The Purcell Companion*. Ed. Michael Burden. Faber & Faber.

Parrott, Andrew (2015). *Composers' Intentions?: Lost Traditions of Musical Performance*. The Boydell Press.

Pasqui, Teresa (2010). *Book of Accounts of the Comedy: the theatrical tailoring of Ferdinando I De 'Medici in 1589*. Nicomp Editorial Laboratory.

Pauline the Prima Donna, or Memoirs of an Opera Singer (2015). Locus Elm Press.

Pauly, Reinhard G. (1948). "Benedetto Marcello's Satire on Early 18th-Century Opera." *The Musical Quarterly*, Vol. 34, No. 2.

Peluso, Pasquale (2013). "The Roots of the Organized Criminal Underworld in Campania. *Sociology and Anthropology*.

Pettegree, Andrew (2014). *The Invention of News: How the World Came to Know About Itself.* Yale University Press.

Phelps, Elizabeth (1873). *What to Wear*. Osgood.

Plato (1961). *The Republic, in The Collected dialogues of Plato*. Eds., Edith Hamilton and Huntington Cairns. Princeton.

Pleasants, Henry (1981). *The Great Singers*. Simon & Schuster.

Poriss, Hilary (2001). "A Madwoman's Choice: Aria Substitution in Lucia di Lammermoor," *Cambridge Opera Journal*, 13.

Poriss, Hilary (2001). "Making Their Way Through the World: Italian One-Hit Wonders." *19th-century Music*, 24

Poriss, Hilary (2009). *Changing the Score: Arias, Prima Donnas, and the Authority of Performance.* Oxford University Press.

Potter, John (1998). *Vocal Authority: Singing Style and Ideology.* Cambridge University Press.

Potter, John (2009). Tenor: History of a Voice. Yale University Press.

Potter, John, and Sorrell, Neil (2012). *A History of Singing.* Cambridge University Press.

Praeger, Ferdinand (1892). *Wagner as I Knew Him.* Longmans, Green & Co.

Prizer, William F. (1985) "Isabella D'Este and Lucrezia Borgia as Patrons of Music: The Frottola at Mantua and Ferrara," *Journal of American Musicology.* XXXVIII.

Prizer, William F. (1999). "Una Virtù Molto Conveniente A Madonne": Isabella D'este as a Musician. *The Journal of Musicology* (Winter, Vol. 17, No. 1).

Prizer, William F. (1999). "Una Virtù Molto Conveniente A Madonne": Isabella D'Este as a Musician. *The Journal of Musicology* (Winter, Vol. 17, No. 1).

Psujek, Jenifer Lauren (2010). *The Intersection Of Gender, Religion, and Culture in Nineteenth-Century Germanic Salons.* Masters thesis. Bowling Green State University.

Puffett, Derrick, Ed. (1989). *Richard Strauss: Salome.* Cambridge University Press.

Radomski, James (2000). *Manuel García: Chronicle of the Life of a bel canto Tenor at the Dawn of Romanticism.* Oxford University Press.

Rajak, Ishwari (2015). "*She Got Her Period: Men's Knowledge and Knowledge and Perspectives on Menstruation.*" PhD thesis. Minnesota State University (Mankato).

Ramos-Gay, Ignacio (2018). "Partly American!": Sarah Bernhardt's Transnational Disability in the American Press (1915–1918)." *Journal of the Spanish Association of Anglo-American Studies.*

Rasponi, Lanfranco (1984). *The Last Prima Donnas.* Gollancz.

Readings in Medieval History, Edited by Patrick J. Geary. University of Toronto Press.

Recorded Sound, No. 59, July, 1975.

Redlich, Hans (1952). *Claudio Monteverdi.* Oxford University Press.

Reich, Willi (1971). *Schoenberg: A Critical Biography,* Trans. Leo Black. Longman.

Rieger, Eva (2016). *Frida Leider: Sängerin im Zwiespalt ihrer Zeit.* Olms.

Ripley, Samara (2016). "*Joan La Barbara's Early Explorations of the Voice.*" Masters thesis; Mount Allison University.

Ritorni, Carlo (1829). Annali del teatro della citta di Reggio. In Rutherford, Susan (2007), "La cantante delle passioni: Giuditta Pasta and the Idea of Operatic Performance," *Cambridge Opera Journal,* Vol. 19 (2).

Riverso, Nicla (2007). La Mirtilla: Shaping a New Role for Women. Modern Language Notes, Vol. 132, 1.

Riverso, Nicla (2016). "Fighting Eve: Women on the Stage in Early Modern Italy." *Quaderni d'Italianistica,* 37, 2.

Roberto Vezzani (2018). "Fascist Indirect Propaganda in 1930s America: The Distribution and Exhibition of Italian Fiction Films," *The Italianist,* Vol. 38.

Ronald, Landon (1922). *Variations on a Personal Theme.* Hodder and Stoughton.

Rosand, David and Rosand, Ellen (1981). "Barbara di Santa Sofia" and "Il Prete Genovese": on the Identity of a Portrait by Bernardo Strozzi. *The Art Bulletin,* Vol. 63, No. 2.

Rosand, Ellen (1978). Barbara Strozzi, "virtuosissima cantatrice": The Composer's Voice. *Journal of the American Musicological Society,* Vol. 31, No. 2.

Rosand, Ellen (1991). *Opera in Seventeenth-Century Venice: The Creation of a Genre.* University of California Press.

Rosand, Ellen (2007). Opera in seventeenth century Venice: the creation of a genre. University of California Press.

Rothenstein, William (1934). *Men and Memories, Vol 1. 1872–1900.* Faber & Faber.

Russo, Paolo (2002). "Giuditta Pasta: cantante pantomimica." Musica e storia, 10.

Rutherford, Susan (2007). "'La cantante delle passioni': Giuditta Pasta and the Idea of Operatic Performance. Cambridge Opera Journal, Vol. 19, No. 2.

Sachs, Harvey (2010). *The Ninth: Beethoven and the World in 1824*. Random House.

Said, Edward (1979). *Orientalism*. Vintage Books.

Said, Edward W. (1991). *Musical Elaborations*. Vintage.

Savage, Roger and Sansone, Matteo (1989). "Il Corago" and the Staging of Early Opera: Four Chapters from an Anonymous Treatise circa 1630." *Early Music*. Vol. 17, No. 4, *The Baroque Stage*.

Schneemann, Carolee (1997). *More Than Meat Joy: Performance Works and Selected Writings*. McPherson

Schneider, Magnus Tessing (2012). Seeing the Empress Again: On Doubling in "L'incoronazione di Poppea." *Cambridge Opera Journal*, Vol. 24, No. 3.

Schoenberg, Arnold (1984). Stein, Leonard (Ed.). *Style and Idea*. Trans. by Leo Black. University of California Press.

Schoenberg, Arnold (1984). *Style and Idea*. University of California Press.

Schoenberg, Arnold (1986). "Attempt at a Diary," Trans. Anita M. Luginbühl, *Journal of the Arnold Schoenberg Institute*, 9 (4).

Schonberg, Harold C. "Opera: Two Debuts in 'Il Trovatore': Franco Corelli and Miss Price Heard." *New York Times*, 28 January, 1961.

Schutz, Alfred (1956). "Mozart and the Philosophers." *Social Research*. Vol. 23, No. 2.

Schwarzkopf, Elisabeth (1982). On and Off the Record: A Memoir of Walter Legge. Faber & Faber.

DeMarco, Laura E. (2002). "The Fact of the Castrato and the Myth of the Countertenor." The Musical Quarterly, Vol. 86, No. 1.

Senner, Wayne M., Wallace, Robin, Meredith, William (2001). The Critical Reception of Beethoven's Compositions by his German Contemporaries, Vol. 2. University of Nebraska Press. No.240.

Seshadri, Anne L. (2006). "The Taste of Love: Salome's Transfiguration." In *Women and Music: A Journal of Gender and Culture*. Vol. 10.

Shaw, Bernard (1981). *Shaw's Music: The Complete Musical Criticism of Bernard Shaw*. Ed. Dan H. Laurence. The Bodley Head. Vol. I (1876 – 1890).

Shaw, George Bernard (1937). *London Music in 1888–89 as Heard by Corno Di Bassetto (Later Known as Bernard Shaw) with Some Further Autobiographical Particulars*. Constable & Co.

Shaw, George Bernard (1968). *Music in London, 1890–1894*. Vol III.

Shawe-Taylor, Desmond (1992). "Wagner and His Singers." In Eds. Millington, Barry and Spencer, Stewart. *Wagner in Performance*. Yale University Press.

Shawe-Taylor, Desmond (1992). "Wagner and His Singers", In Wagner in Performance. Eds. Millington, Barry and Spencer, Stewart. Yale University Press.

Shearman, John (1967). *Mannerism*. Pelican.

Sherr, Richard (1978). "The Publications of Guglielmo Gonzaga." *Journal of the American Musicological Society*, 31.

Sherr, Richard (1980). Gugliemo Gonzaga and the Castrati. *Renaissance Quarterly*, Vol. 33, No. 1.

Silbert, Doris (1946). "Francesca Caccini: La Cecchina." *The Musical Quarterly*, Vol. 32, No.1.

Simkin, Benjamin (1992). "Mozart's Scatological Disorder." *British Medical Journal*, Vol. 305, No. 6868.

Simms, Bryan R. (2000). *The Atonal Music of Arnold Schoenberg, 1908–1923*. Oxford University Press.

Simms, Bryan. (2000). *The Atonal Music of Arnold Schoenberg, 1908 – 1923*. Oxford University Press

Simon, Sherry (1996). *Gender in Translation Cultural identity and the politics of transmission.* Routledge.

Slim, H. Colin (2006). "Joseph Weber's Diva, Pinxit 1839: Visual, Musical, Societal Considerations. Music in Art; Iconography as a Source for Music History, Volume II. *Music in Art*, Vol. 31, No. ½.

Slim, H. Colin (2006). "Joseph Weber's Diva, Pinxit 1839: Visual, Musical, Societal Considerations. Music in Art; Iconography as a Source for Music History, Volume II." *Music in Art*, Vol. 31, No. 1/2.

Solomon, Maynard (1995). *Mozart: A Life*. Harper Perennial.

Somerset-Ward, Richard (2004). *Angels and Monsters: Male and Female Sopranos in the Story of Opera, 1600–1900*. Yale University Press.

Sorba, Carlotta (2006). "To Please the Public: Composers and Audiences in Nineteenth-Century Italy." *The Journal of Interdisciplinary History*, Vol. 36, No. 4, Opera and Society: Part II.

Spotts, Frederic (1994). *Bayreuth: A History of the Wagner Festival*. Yale University Press.

Stanislavski, Constantin (1975). *Stanislavski on Opera*. Trans. and Ed. Elizabeth Reynolds Hapgood. Theatre Art Books.

Stanley Sadie (Ed.). *Wolfgang Amadè Mozart: Essays on His Life and Music*. Clarendon Press.

Stassinopoulos, Ariana (1981). Maria Callas: The Woman Behind the Legend. Simon and Schuster.

Steane, J. B. (1992). *Voices, Singers and Critics*. Duckworth.

Steen, Michael (2007). *Enchantress of Nations: Pauline Viardot, Soprano, Muse, Lover*. Icon Books.

Stein, Erwin (1965). "Mahler and the Vienna Opera", in *The Opera Bedside Book*, Ed. Harold Rosenthal. Victor Gollancz.

Stendhal (1824). *Life of Rossini*. Trans, and Annotated by Coe, Richard N. (1985). John Calder.

Strainchamps, Edmond (1985). "The Life and Death of Caterina Martinelli: New Light on Monteverdi's 'Arianna,'" Early Music History, Vol. 5.

Strauss, R. and Hofmannsthal, Hugo von (1961). *A Working Friendship: The correspondence between Richard Strauss and Hugo von Hofmannsthal*. Trans. Hanns Hammelmann and Ewald Osers, Random House.

Sudai, Maayan (2011). *Sex Ambiguity in Early Modern Common Law (1629–1787)*. Cambridge University Press.

Swafford, Jan (2014). *Beethoven: Anguish and Triumph*. Faber & Faber.

Taruskin, Richard (1996). *Stravinsky and the Russian Traditions, Volume Two: A Biography of the Works*. University of California Press.

Teatri, arti e letteratura (1854). Vol. 59, 1853–1854, Gov. della Volpe.

Thayer's Life of Beethoven (1992). Ed. Forbes, Elliot. Princeton University Press. Vol. 1.

The Art of Dress (1852). Quarterly Review. John Murray.

The Arts of the Prima Donna in the Long Nineteenth Century. Ed. Cowgill, Rachel, and Poriss, Hilary. Oxford University Press.

The Baltimore Sun (11 June, 1860). "Corsets and Consumption."

The Bloomsbury Handbook of Solitude, Silence and Loneliness (2022). Eds. Julian Stern, Christopher A. Sink, Wong Ping Ho, Malgorzata Walejko. Bloomsbury.

The Critical Reception of Beethoven's Compositions by His German Contemporaries, Op. 125. Trans. and Ed. by Wallace, Robin. Boston University.

The Italian Academies 1525–1700: Networks of Culture, Innovation and Dissent (2016). Eds. Jane E. Everson, Denis V. Reidy, Lisa Sampson. Legenda.

The Letters of Queen Victoria (1926). Ed Buckle, George. Vol. 2, Part 4. Longmans, Green & Company.

The Observer (17 March, 1851). "Death from Tight Lacing."

Thorpe, C. William, Cala, Stephen J., Chapman, Janice, and Davis, Pamela J. (2001). "The Voice Foundation Patterns of Breath Support in Projection of the Singing Voice." *Journal of Voice*. Vol. 15, No. 1.

Thulesius, O. (1994). "Nicholas Culpeper, father of English midwifery." *Journal of the Royal Society of Medicine*. 87 (9).

Tierchant, Hélène (2009). Sarah Bernhardt: Madame "quand même." Éditions Télémaque.

Traub, Valerie (2002). *The Renaissance of Lesbianism in Early Modern England*. Cambridge University Press.

Treadwell, Nina (2004). "She Descended on a Cloud 'From the Highest Spheres': Florentine Monody 'alla Romanina'". *Cambridge Opera Journal*, Vol. 16, No.1 (March).

Tunbridge, Laura (2013). "Frieda Hempel and the Historical Imagination." *Journal of the American Musicological Society*, Vol. 66, No. 2.

Tunbridge, Laura (2013). "Frieda Hempel and the Historical Imagination." Journal of the American Musicological Society, Vol. 66, No. 2.

"Two Cities Pay Tribute to Mahalia Jackson" (April, 1972). Ebony Magazine.

Urban, Bernd (1978). *Hofmannsthal*. P, Lang.

Verdi: The Man in His Letters (1942). Eds. Franz Werfel and Paul Stefan. L. B. Fischer.

Verdi's Falstaff in Letters and Contemporary Reviews (1998). Ed . Hans Busch. Indiana University Press.

Visetti, Albert (1905). *Verdi*. George Bell.

Vogt, Howard (1987). *Flagstad: Singer of the Century*. Secker and Warburg.

Wagner, Richard (1896). "Actors and Singers," in *Richard Wagner's Prose Works*. Trans. William Ashton Ellis, Vol. 5.

Wagner, Richard (1897). *On Conducting: A Treatise on Style in the Execution of Classical Music*. William Reeves.

Wagner, Richard (1897). *Gesammelte Schriften und Dichtungen*, 2nd ed. Siegel. Vol. 3.

Wagner, Richard (1897). *Gesammelte Schriften und Dichtungen*, 2nd ed. Siegel. Vol. 2.

Walker, Frank (1962). *The Man Verdi*. Knopf.

Warrack, John and West, Ewan (1992). *The Oxford Dictionary of Opera*. Oxford University Press.

Wassersug, R.J., Zelenietz, S.A., Squire, G.F. (2004). *Archives of Sexual Behaviour*, 33(5).

Webb, J. Barry (1989). *Shakespeare's Erotic Word Usage*. Cornwallis Press.

Weininger, Otto (1903). *Geschlecht und Charakter: Eine prinzipielle Untersuchung*. Wilhelm Braumüller.

Weininger, Otto (2005). *Sex and Character: An Investigation of Fundamental Principles*. Ed. Daniel Steuer and Laura Marcus. Trans. Ladislaus Löb. Indiana University Press.

Weinstock, Herbert (1968). *Rossini*. Oxford University Press.

Weinstock, Herbert (1971). *Bellini: His Life and His Operas*. Knopf.

Wier, Claudia Rene (2020). *Animating Performance: Tracing Venice's Resonant Diva Attraverso Il Palco E La Soglia*. York University.

Wilbourne, Emily (2007). "'Isabella ringiovinita': Virginia Ramponi Andreini before Arianna." Recercare, Vol. 19, No. 1/2.

Winn, James A. (2010). "Confronting Art with Art: The Dryden-Purcell Collaboration in King Arthur." In *Restoration: Studies in English Literary Culture, 1660–1700*, Vol. 34, No. 1/2.

Wolfgang Amadeus Mozart, My Dearest Father (2015). Trans. Stewart Spencer, Penguin Books.

Women Making Music: The Western Art Tradition, 1150–1950, Eds. Jane Bowers and Judith Tick. Urbana and Chicago.

Wong, S.T.S., Wassersug, R.J., Johnson, T.W., Wibowo, E. (2021) *Archives of Sexual Behaviour*, 50(3).

Woodfield, Ian (2003). *Salomon and the Burneys: Private Patronage and a Public Career*. Ashgate Publishing.

Woolf, Virginia (2001). *A Room of One's Own*. Broadview Press.

Woolf, Virginia (2006). *Orlando, a Biography*. Houghton Mifflin Harcourt.

Wright, Thomas (2010). *Built of Books: How Reading Defined the Life of Oscar Wilde*. Henry Holt.

Youssef, Mirrae (2017). "*Exploring Melisma and the Effects of Emotional Expression In Contemporary Music*." Thesis, Macquarie University.

Index

Index

Doegen, Wilhelm   119
Doenges, Paula   455
Dolmetsch, Carl   506
Donizetti, Gaetano   49, 114, 160, 172,
    185–187, 189, 193–194, 199, 201, 204,
    206, 244–245, 247–252, 257, 265–266,
    284, 286, 288, 353, 373, 388, 402, 422,
    453, 464, 475, 477, 479, 488
  Works by:
  Anna Bolena   160, 189, 194, 247, 476,
      479, 489,   529
  elisir d'amore, L'   160, 247, 291, 452, 486,
      501, 528
  Don Pasquale   206, 356–357, 372, 376,
      422
  fille du régiment, La   353, 486, 488, 530
  Roberto Devereux   488
  Linda di Chamounix   247, 249, 288
  Lucia di Lammermoor   32–33, 159, 193,
      199, 247–248, 250–251, 265, 278,
      283, 291, 310, 354, 356, 361, 363,
      367–370, 420–421, 430, 436, 453,
      457–458, 474, 476, 485–486
  Lucrezia Borgia   187, 199, 310, 323, 353,
      446, 487, 496
  Maria di Rohan   288, 291
  Maria Stuarda   204, 486, 488
  Poliuto   252, 288, 464–465, 468
Donzelli, Domenico   201
Dorati, Antal   334, 520
Dowland, John   63
Downes, Edward   474
Downes, Olin   471
Doyle, Sir Arthur Conan   356
Dragonetti, Domenico   141
Draneht, Paul   305
Dranes, Arizona   534–535
Dreisig, Elsa   456
Dreyfus, Alfred   xxi, 226, 349
Drinkard, Emily   538
Dryden, John   83–85, 111, 126
Duflot-Maillard Dukas, Hortense   258
Dumas, Alexandre   xxiii, 66, 154, 253
Dumont, Margaret   466
Dunaway, Faye   495
Duparc, Élisabeth   118, 129
Duponchel, Henri   257
Duport, Louis   212
Duprez, Gilbert   119, 201, 225, 244–245,
    248–249, 255–257,   267, 300, 360, 501
Dupuis, Hylaire   68
Dupuy, Hilaire   73

Durand, Jacques   407
Durastanti, Margherita   101, 104
Dürer, Albrecht   162, 495
Duse, Eleonora   310–311, 351, 366, 368

Eaglen, Jane   288, 318, 451, 459
Eames, Emma   364, 370, 383, 385, 423
Easton, Florence   384, 386
Eberhardt, Paul   328
Edelman, Otto   488
Edgcumbe, Richard   142–143
Edison, Thomas   53, 118, 384, 410
Eibenschutz, Risa   325
Eilish, Billie   xxvii
Einstein, Albert   491
Eipperle, Trude   437
Ekberg, Anita   465
Elgar, Sir Edward   507
Ellington, Duke   511
Eliot, George   51, 263–265, 271, 511
  Works by:
  Armgart   264–265
  Daniel Deronda   264
  Middlemarch   264
Eliot, T. S.   22
Elman, Mischa   510
Elmendorff, Karl   328
Épine, Margherita de l'   96, 102, 115
Erb, Karl   421
Ericson, Barbro   516
Erlanger, Frédéric d'   382, 409
Eschenbach, Wolfram von   8
Escoffier, Auguste   462
Esperian, Kallen   499
Eugenides, Jeffrey   241
Eyre, Richard   527
Eyvazov, Yusif   529

Faccio, Franco   306, 310
Falcon, Cornélie   252–257
Farell, Marita   430
Farrar, Geraldine   328–329, 364, 384–388,
    427, 449, 471
Fassbaender, Brigitte   339
Fauré, Gabriel   263, 326, 415, 511
Faure, Jean-Baptiste   377–378
Feldman, Morton   515
Fellini, Federico   332, 465–466
Feola, Rosa   xxxi
Ferrani, Cesira   374–376
Ferrari, Benedetto   45, 54
Ferrier, Kathleen   xiii, 507

571